READINGS IN
SOCIOLOGY

Joan Schutzman

June 22, 1964

READINGS IN SOCIOLOGY

Second Edition

EDGAR A. SCHULER
Michigan State University

THOMAS F. HOULT
Wayne State University

DUANE L. GIBSON
Michigan State University

MAUDE L. FIERO
Wayne State University

WILBUR B. BROOKOVER
Michigan State University

THOMAS Y. CROWELL COMPANY

New York · Established 1834

First Printing, April, 1960
Second Printing, December, 1960
Third Printing, June, 1961
Fourth Printing, April, 1962
Fifth Printing, January, 1963
Sixth Printing, February, 1964

Library of Congress Catalog Card Number: 60-6065

Designed by Laurel Wagner
Cover design by Herbert S. Stoltz

Manufactured in the United States of America
by Vail-Ballou Press, Inc., Binghamton, N.Y.

PREFACE

to the Second Edition

The editors have sought in this second edition of *Readings in Sociology* to remain faithful to the basic principles which guided the development of the first edition. A book of readings, it is the continuing belief of the editors, should illuminate and promote understanding of the concepts and generalizations of sociology and thus stand as a complement to, not a substitute for, a regular textbook where theories and research findings are treated systematically and analytically. A book of readings, moreover, should be a *balanced* book, incorporating materials from salient areas of sociology, and intended to be of interest and value to the wide audience of students of sociology *generally*, not primarily for students majoring in sociology nor for the even more limited audience of prospective professional sociologists. Such perspectives on the function this volume should perform dictated two major criteria for the choice of articles: (1) sociological relevance and (2) readability. Using these criteria, each of the selections of the first edition was required to compete not only with other significant writings of its own era but also with the many excellent materials that have appeared since 1951. Despite this rugged competition, forty-seven of the selections in the first edition were considered to have a timeless quality of relevance and readability which justified keeping them. A wide search of literally hundreds of sources yielded a fresh roster of possibilities from which sixty-four new selections were finally made. These came from thirty-seven different books, journals, and magazines, all but three of which were published in the last eight years. Careful selection and judicious editing have made it possible to increase the number of readings by about one-sixth without sacrificing the quality and utility of each.

The reactions of teachers and students to the first edition aided greatly not only in the decisions regarding the selections to be used but also with respect to the retention in this edition of such features as the brief introductory paragraphs to highlight the background and purpose

v

of each reading, the biographical notes on each author represented, and the functional index.

The editors responsible for the first edition are happy to include among their number for this revision Thomas Ford Hoult, who brings unique competence to the task because of his special training and his responsibilities in teaching the introductory course at Wayne State University.

In their many hours of deliberating together, the five editors have sought constantly to produce a book that would make a contribution to genuinely *liberal* education; to expand the reader's horizon and human concerns beyond his own immediate place and time; to inculcate a truly scientific humility in the face of diverse peoples, customs and beliefs; and to affirm their own belief in the values of a maturing social science for our own democratic society and for an increasingly rich and humane life for all peoples everywhere.

EDGAR A. SCHULER
THOMAS F. HOULT
DUANE L. GIBSON
MAUDE L. FIERO
WILBUR B. BROOKOVER

ACKNOWLEDGMENTS

The editors wish to thank all authors and publishers who made their work available for incorporation in this volume even though, in a few instances, last-minute exigencies necessitated exclusion of selections of high quality for which permission for inclusion had already been granted. Individual acknowledgment may be found with each selection used.

The consideration and assistance of several library staffs in making publications available were essential to the book's successful completion. Especially helpful were the staffs of Wayne State University Library; Michigan State University Library; Detroit Public Library, particularly the Social Sciences Department; and McGregor Library of Highland Park, Michigan.

The editors wish also to express their deep appreciation for the assistance given by others during this project. Academic colleagues and administrative officials encouraged the undertaking and offered helpful suggestions on selections and organization. Able and conscientious secretarial assistance was provided by Mrs. Viola Banks, Mrs. Almeda Ritter, Mrs. Josephine Wharton, Miss Gwendolyn Gamble, Mrs. Marjorie White and Mr. Christian Ferguson. Mr. Richard Knowles, graduate student at Michigan State University, assembled data on which the biographical notes are based. To all of these the editors extend their thanks.

The editors owe an unmeasurable indebtedness to the students who, by their reactions to the previous work, provided insight into the function of readings in general and the utility of particular selections. And to the members of the editors' respective families, who accommodated to disrupted living patterns for more than a year and rendered substantial assistance at every stage of the effort leading to this book, this final and heartfelt note of gratitude is expressed.

CORRELATION OF THIS BOOK WITH INTRODUCTORY SOCIOLOGY TEXTS

Text Chapters	Bierstedt THE SOCIAL ORDER McGraw-Hill 1957	Bogardus SOCIOLOGY 4th ed. Macmillan 1954	Broom and Selznick SOCIOLOGY 2nd ed. Row-Peterson 1958	Cuber SOCIOLOGY 4th ed. Appleton-Century-Crofts 1959
	Related Articles in *Readings in Sociology*			
1	1–7, 13, 54, Appendix	9, 10, 14, 18, 19, 21, 29–33, 50, 87–90, 95	1–4, 7, 13, 54, Appendix A and B	1, 2, 5, Appendix
2	15–17	10, 11, 16, 22–24, 81–99	10, 12, 18, 22, 23, 27, 28, 30–33, 38, 48, 50, 55, 73, 76, 86–92, 101	3, 4, 7, 13, Appendix B and C
3	7–9, 19, 53	7, 8, 51–54, 95	8, 11, 14, 16, 25, 53, 56, 57, 71, 80, 81, 83, 85, 88, 95, 97, 99, 100, 104–106	6, 100
4	8–14, 19, 20	73–81, 83, 85	8, 9, 19, 20, 22–24, 26, 84, 102	11, 14
5	8–14, 16, 20, 23, 81	26–28, 41, 42, 44, 55–59, 90, 105	29, 30, 33	13, 16, 80
6	12, 14, 18, 20, 22, 28	68–70	12, 21, 41–47, 64	20, 93, 105
7	12, 21–23, 26, 52, 86	37, 62–65	31, 48–50, 66	12, 20, 24, 26, 28, 52
8	29, 30, 33	66, 67, 83	34–37, 39, 40, 98	13, 38, 56, 57, 82, 92, 96, 97, 99
9	18, 20, 32, 73	15, 20, 36, 83, 92–94	15, 17, 74, 75, 79, 80, 83, 98	7–9, 19, 20, 24, 26, 28, 37, 93, 102
10	12, 22, 26, 52	83, 85, 103–107	51–54, 95	7–9, 19, 24, 26
11	51–54, 95	13, 39–43, 45–47, 53, 57, 60, 72, 96–100	40, 61, 76–79	9, 19, 27–29
12	73–80	33, 35, 36, 40, 56, 57, 97, 101–104, 107, Appendix D	20, 36, 45–47, 92, 94	11, 14, 25, 27, 28, 32, 91, 101
13	12, 20, 41–47, 64	14, 39, 48, 49, 60, 61, 71, 76	21, 27, 42, 44, 55–57, 97	7, 18, 19, 25, 46

	Bierstedt THE SOCIAL ORDER (*Continued*)	Bogardus SOCIOLOGY (*Continued*)	Broom and Selznick SOCIOLOGY (*Continued*)	Cuber SOCIOLOGY (*Continued*)
Text Chapters	Related Articles in *Readings in Sociology*			
14	20, 21, 35, 36, 45, 46, 93, 94	38	5, 38, 59–61, 73, 106	3, 4, 20, 37, 84, 93, Appendix B and C
15	1, 5, 18, 31, 48–72, 90	24, 86–90	18, 101	11, 20, 22, 102
16	6, 13, 20, 25, 34–40, 48, 49, 53, 55–57, 82–85, 95, 96–107	1–4, 7, Appendix B and C		21–24, 52
17				10, 18, 29, 30, 32, 33, 48, 73, 86, 87
18				25, 27, 31, 50
19				20, 36, 45, 46, 93, 94
20				15
21				74–76, 79, 80, 82, 83, 85
22				76–79
23				41–47, 64
24				48, 49, 71, 72, 81
25				51–54, 95
26				55–59, 90
27				5, 38, 59–61, 73
28				62–65
29				66, 67
30				18, 22, 32, 33, 55, 77, 83, 85, 97–99, 104, 107
31				86, 89, 90
32				35, 86–88, 95
33				33, 35, 36, 40, 57, 68, 79, 83, 85, 98, 100, 103, 104, 106, 107

	Fichter SOCIOLOGY University of Chicago Press 1957	*Freedman and Associates* PRINCIPLES OF SOCIOLOGY Rev. ed. Holt 1956	*Green* SOCIOLOGY 2nd ed. McGraw-Hill 1956	*Landis* INTRODUCTORY SOCIOLOGY Ronald 1958
Text Chapters	Related Articles in *Readings in Sociology*			
Intro- duction	1–7, Appendix C	——	——	1–8, Appendix
1	8, 9, 19–28, 101, 102	1, 2	1, 2, 5–7, 13, Appendix	1
2	12, 21, 41, 44– 47	1–7, 13, Appen- dix	14, 15	11, 14, 16, 80, 81, 93, 105
3	7, 12, 18, 20, 27, 45, 63, 80, 93	7–10, 12, 18–24, 26–33, 36, 86, 102, 105	10, 21, 22, 29– 33	48, 71
4	34–36, 39, 60, 66, 67, 75, 77, 90, 98	11, 14–17, 83– 85	35, 60, 86–94	53, 56, 57, 68, 72, 96, 98, 99, 103
5	29–33	12, 14, 18, 21, 25, 48	11, 14	13, 79, 82–84, 95– 100, 105
6	5, 73, 80, 81, 84, 103–105	5, 15, 18, 21–23	11, 16, 80, 105	48, 71, 96, 97
7	11, 14, 16, 80– 85	12, 41–47, 64, 93, 94	8, 9, 12, 19, 20, 26	7–9, 19, 23, 26
8	3, 4, 37, 38, 93, 105	73–75, 90–92	12, 24, 27, 28	86
9	5, 12, 21, 26–28, 42, 52, 102	13, 35, 36, 38– 40, 48, 66–68, 71, 72, 95, 96, 98, 99, 103	22, 23, 101, 102	19, 24, 70
10	86–90, 95, 96	15, 73–82	15	18, 29–33
11	48–72	48–59	21, 41, 44–47	73–79
12	9, 11, 16, 53, 56, 57, 63, 68, 80, 81, 96, 97	25, 60, 61, 68– 70, 73, 77, 78, 101	42, 43–46, 63, 64	34–40
13	6, 16, 20, 23, 81	21, 41–47, 64, 67	20, 45, 46, 92– 94	20, 36, 45, 46, 83, 92–94
14	42, 43, 46, 64	48, 71, 72, 103, 104, 106, 107	73–79	86–90, 95
15	13, 48, 49, 53, 56, 57, 63, 67, 68, 71, 79, 82, 83, 85, 94–100		55	10, 86
16	37, 38, 72, 91, 92, 100		56–59, 90	12, 21, 41–47
17	7, 25, 46, 63, 101, 102		5, 33, 38, 59– 61, 106	12, 21, 22, 52

	Fichter SOCIOLOGY (*Continued*)	Freedman and Associates PRINCIPLES OF SOCIOLOGY (*Continued*)	Green SOCIOLOGY (*Continued*)	Landis INTRODUCTORY SOCIOLOGY (*Continued*)
Text Chapters	Related Articles in *Readings in Sociology*			
18	30, 101, 103, 104, 106, 107		23, 53, 95	21
19			51–54	20, 36, 45, 46, 77, 92, 94
20			51, 52	41–44, 64
21				66, 67
22			66, 67	12, 20, 21, 47, 58, 86
23			62–65	42, 43, 46
24			68–70	
25			13, 95–100	24, 29
26			34–40	12, 19, 20, 21, 23, 26–28, 37, 46, 99, 102, 106
27				
28				26–28, 76, 91
29				8, 25, 30, 46, 60, 83
30				13, 23, 35, 40, 56, 57, 77, 79, 82, 83, 85, 96, 97, 99
31				6, 15, 72, 94, 100, 103, 107, Appendix B and D
32				
33				51, 52
34				51–54, 95
35				62–65
36				5, 30, 50, 59–61, 73
37				66, 67
38				55–59, 90
39				68–72
40				97, 99, 103, 106

	Lundberg, Schrag, and Larsen SOCIOLOGY Rev. ed. Harper 1958	Mercer THE STUDY OF SOCIETY Harcourt, Brace 1958	Merrill SOCIETY AND CULTURE Prentice-Hall 1957	Ogburn and Nimkoff SOCIOLOGY 3rd ed. Houghton Mifflin 1958
Text Chapters		Related Articles in *Readings in Sociology*		
1	1, 7	2–5, 7, Appendix	1–7, Appendix	2–4, 7, 54, Appendix A and B
2	2, 5, 6	6, 11, 13, 14, 16, 80, 81, 83	18, 32, 86–92	5, 8, 10, 13
3	3, 4, 7, 54, Appendix C	8, 9, 19, 20, 22–28	86, 87	11, 14, 16, 80, 81, 84
4	15, 17	10, 24, 37, 70	29–33	7–9, 19, 53
5	73–79, 98	18, 29–36, 39, 40, 86	12, 14, 22, 25	15–17
6	24, 31, 38, 70, 105	15, 17	11, 16, 84, 105	21, 30, 33, 35, 55, 83, 87–93, 101
7	7–9, 12, 19, 24, 26–28	18, 32, 40, 73–79	16, 80–85	10, 12, 21, 22, 41–47, 52, 64
8	31, 60, 73–80, 86–92, 94, 95	51–54, 95	7, 9, 19, 24, 26–28	34–40
9	5, 11, 14, 16, 22, 80, 81, 83, 84	66, 67	12, 21, 22, 52	14, 20, 25, 76, 91, 92, 106
10	12, 21, 22, 52	62–65	8, 9, 12, 19, 23	7, 9, 19, 24, 26–28
11	7, 19, 22, 23	5, 38, 59–61, 73	15	8
12	18, 29, 30, 32–40	55–59, 90	9, 83	7, 19, 22, 23
13	37, 70, 71, 91	12, 21, 22, 36, 41–47	20, 36, 45, 47, 77, 92–94	73–79, 98
14	10, 22, 41–47, 64, 93	87–90, 104	41, 44, 63, 64	15, 17
15	5, 31, 48–50, 62–65, 71, 72, 80, 105	14, 20, 36, 71, 72, 76, 92, 94–100	42, 43, 46, 64	15, 17
16	51–54, 95	1, 2, 40, 72, 93, 97, 100–103, Appendix A and D	48, 49, 71	10, 16, 18, 29–32
17	66, 67		51–54, 95	55–59, 90
18	55–59, 90, 96		5, 55–70, 72	5, 38, 59–61, 73
19	5, 38, 50, 59–61, 73, 88, 104		73, 76–78	35, 63, 83–85, 103–107
20	48, 49, 67, 71–85, 95–101, 104, 106		73–75, 79	66, 67
21	1, 6, 100, 106, Appendix		40, 48, 49, 71, 72, 96–100	51–54, 95
22			34–40	5, 8, 59, 63, 67–71, 97

	Lundberg, Schrag, and Larsen SOCIOLOGY (*Continued*)	Mercer THE STUDY OF SOCIETY (*Continued*)	Merrill SOCIETY AND CULTURE (*Continued*)	Ogburn and Nimkoff SOCIOLOGY (*Continued*)
Text Chapters	Related Articles in *Readings in Sociology*			
23			34–40	13, 33, 48, 49, 67, 71, 95, 100
24			44, 66–69, 98	13, 56, 57, 63–65, 68, 71, 72, 82, 83, 85, 94, 96– 100, 103
25			6, 33, 40, 79, 83, 94, 100	31, 34, 35, 40, 44, 99, 101, 104
26				15, 37, 38, 40, 60, 72, 100

	Rose SOCIOLOGY, THE STUDY OF HUMAN RELA- TIONS Knopf 1956	Sutherland, Woodward, and Maxwell INTRODUCTORY SOCI- OLOGY 5th ed. Lippincott 1956	Young and Mack SOCIOLOGY AND SOCIAL LIFE American Book Co. 1959
Text Chapters		Related Articles in *Readings in Sociology*	
1	1–4, 7, Appendix B and C	1–8, 13, 54, Appendix	2–7, Appendix B and C
2	11, 19, 24, 26–33, 93, 105	11, 14, 17, 48, 71	18, 29–36
3	14, 20, 25, 76, 91, 92, 102	13	11, 16, 105
4	7–9, 19–24, 26–28, 64, 84, 101, 102	11, 16, 81, 83, 84, 105	17, 80–85
5	5, 48, 49, 71	11, 16, 80, 81	14, 20, 91–93
6	29, 51–54, 95	7, 9, 19, 24	13, 48, 49, 71, 96–100
7	5, 38, 55–72	8, 9, 19, 23, 24, 26	9, 19, 23, 24, 26–28
8	41–47	8, 9, 12, 19, 21–23	5
9	34–40	9, 20, 22, 7, 31, 32, 42, 102	86–90, 95, 96
10	32, 44, 49, 66, 67, 69, 73, 90, 98	7, 19, 23, 25, 28	12, 21, 22, 52, 55
11	2, 13, 15, 40, 48, 49, 53, 57, 60, 63, 72, 82, 85, 96–100	10, 86, 89, 90	41, 44, 47
12	15, 17	35, 36, 87, 88, 103	20, 36, 45, 46, 92
13	73–80	29, 30, 32, 33	42, 43, 46, 64
14	5, 18, 32, 38, 40, 44, 60, 98	34–40	15, 17
15	40, 56, 57, 62, 68, 79, 93, 97, 104	41–47, 105	———
16	8, 20, 33, 35, 36, 45, 46, 60, 83, 87, 88, 95, 100, 103	45, 46, 77, 83, 92–94	30, 74–79
17	101	15, 18, 73–80	———
18		18, 73–80	79, 80
19		5, 38, 50, 55–61, 73, 83, 90	5, 48, 49, 71
20		1, 62–65	51–54, 95
21		66, 67	62–65
22		49, 68–72	66, 67
23		51–54, 95	55–59, 90
24		13, 15, 17, 32, 41, 48, 85, 95	5, 38, 50, 59–61
25		13, 32, 41, 48, 85, 95–99	

	Rose *SOCIOLOGY, THE STUDY OF HUMAN RELA-TIONS* (*Continued*)	Sutherland, Woodward, *and Maxwell* *INTRODUCTORY SOCI-OLOGY* (*Continued*)	Young and Mack *SOCIOLOGY AND SOCIAL LIFE* (*Continued*)
Text Chapters	Related Articles in *Readings in Sociology*		
26		15, 17, 25, 33, 34–40, 99, 101–104, 107	
27		15, 33, 37, 38, 41, 60, 98	
28		15, 33, 37, 38, 60, 91, 92, 98, 106	

	Biesanz and Biesanz MODERN SOCIETY 2d ed. Prentice-Hall 1959	
	Text Chapters	Related Articles in *Readings in Sociology*
	1	1–4, 7, 8, 54, 87, Appendix A and B
	2	13, 83, 85, 99
	3	11, 15–17, 80, 81
	4	11, 12, 14, 16, 23, 101
	5	16, 18, 30, 32, 33, 48, 71, 85, **96–100**
	6	6, 14, 20, 83, 84, 93, 105
	7	10, 18, 29–40, 73–75, 98
	8	15, 61, 76–79, 101
	9	41–44, 46, 58, 63, 64
	10	35, 45–47, 77, 83, 87, 88, 94
	11	7–9, 19, 21–24, 26, 64, 101, **102**
	12	51–54, 95
	13	62–65
	14	35, 46, 66, 67
	15	15, 16, 82
	16	49, 72, 89, 90, 97, 105, 106
	17	27, 42, 50, 59, 68
	18	41, 42, 44, 55–58, 97
	19	37, 59, 71, 72, 89, 90
	20	16, 17, 32, 82, 90, 100
	21	71, 72, 90
	22	33, 36, 73
	23	5, 8, 38, 98
	24	38
	25	59
	26	60, 61
	27	41, 63, 64, 106
	28	85, 103, 104, 107

CONTENTS

II. ENVIRONMENTAL FACTORS

III. PERSON AND GROUP

IV. SOCIAL ORGANIZATION: TYPES OF GROUP RELATIONSHIPS

V. SOCIAL ORGANIZATION: COLLECTIVE BEHAVIOR

VI. SOCIAL ORGANIZATION: STRATIFICATION AND MOBILITY

VII. SOCIAL ORGANIZATION: INSTITUTIONS AND ASSOCIATIONS

VIII. SOCIAL ORGANIZATION: ECOLOGICAL

IX. SOCIAL PROCESSES

X. SOCIAL AND CULTURAL CHANGE: DISORGANIZATION, PLANNING, AND VALUES

APPENDIX: SOCIOLOGISTS AT WORK

READINGS IN
SOCIOLOGY

PROLOGUE

1. SOCIAL SCIENCE
IN LIBERAL EDUCATION *

STUART CHASE

Some study sociology because they feel it will be useful in earning a living. Many others study it to help them improve the quality of their lives and realize their capabilities as human beings—in other words, it will help them become "liberally educated" adults. Here Stuart Chase sets forth his interpretation of the need for education of this latter type by means of the social sciences. Only when specialists are also broadly educated in order to appreciate the relation between fields of knowledge, says Chase, will they be able to exert critical judgment on their actions as specialists.

. . . . .

To cope with the tough problems ahead of us we should be able to see all the way around them. Experts and specialists are invaluable, but, as specialists, they see only the trees, sometimes only the twigs under the trees. We need power to see the woods. We need generalists who do not get lost in the trees. This does not mean two kinds of people, for everyone is a specialist in some degree, perhaps as a typist, perhaps as a nuclear physicist. It means more room in our minds for the over-all view, especially for relationships and balancing of alternatives.

. . . The competence of the specialist today has overawed the intelligent

* From Stuart Chase, *Some Things Worth Knowing* (New York: Harper & Brothers, 1958), pp. VII–VIII, 6–251, passim. Copyright © 1958 by Stuart Chase. Reprinted by permission of Harper & Brothers.

The author (b. 1888) is a writer of interpretative works of special interest to social scientists. He has held such positions as investigator for the Federal Trade Commission; consultant for the United States Treasury, the Securities and Exchange Commission, UNESCO, and other organizations. His books include *The Proper Study of Mankind; Roads to Agreement; Power of Words.*

1

layman until he says: "It's way over my head; I'll leave it to the experts." How often do we all say or think something like that? Yet it is a dangerous attitude in this day and age. It tends to create an oligarchy of knowledge, which can become a monopoly of power, a series of tight little principalities with no minds left to survey the whole country.

I know a generalist who is also a learned specialist. He has written me that he would like to tell his specialist confreres: "Wake up! Live at the level of your time! Crawl out of that talent-trap which you refer to as your 'field' and look around. You may learn something about the only era you will ever live in, and about the only species you will ever be a member of. You will certainly learn something about yourself!"

To leave learning exclusively to specialists is not only dangerous but weak. It deprives civilized people of an essential part of their life on earth, something that many primitive peoples have naturally exercised —the full expression of curiosity, honestly confronting the mystery of existence, trying to understand their world and themselves. It is pitiful to retreat from this facing of life, especially at a time when so much new knowledge is coming in. Even if the astrophysicists have shown the universe to be far grander and more complex than we used to think, shall we say: "It's all beyond me," and turn our backs and go indoors? Or shall we look up with new wonder and delight, trying to imagine the vast recesses of the whirling sky? Similarly for the marvels unfolding before the electronic microscope, and for new aspects of human behavior now being revealed.

. . . .

. . . What is useful knowledge for this day and age? What should an intelligent citizen have in clear view above the water line? It may be presumptuous to seek an answer, but there the question is, and there it promises to remain for a long time to come.

One should not call the answers to most quiz questions "useless knowledge." Far from it. For some students in some circumstances the answer may be vital, quite apart from passing examinations, or accumulating another eleven thousand dollars on Twenty One. A better distinction is between *general* and *specialized* knowledge. The former is what we should know in our day-by-day living for intelligent judgments and decisions; the latter is what some of us need to know for our livelihood, or our hobbies and pleasure. It is like the distinction between "liberal arts" and vocational or professional education, except that the liberal arts, as often defined, include much that is irrelevant if not useless.

Applying the distinction to the person I know best, namely myself, I have a fair amount of specialized knowledge concerning economics, accounting, semantics, and can lose the intelligent layman rapidly, if I care to, in these subjects. The layman, if he specializes in astrophysics, or the history of the Third Republic, can lose me with equal rapidity. But both of us should possess a body of vital general knowledge where neither becomes lost. . . .

. . . . .

If an expert is somebody who knows more and more about less and less until he knows everything about nothing, and the size of the area in which a person has competence must continually diminish, the logical end would be the collapse of society, where nobody is left with an over‧ all view.

A story that went the rounds of New York's Madison Avenue in 1958 gently mocked the extreme specialist. A copywriter being inter‧ viewed for a job in an advertising agency is asked if he has worked on cigarette accounts.

"Oh, yes."

"On king-size cigarettes?"

"Yes."

"King-size filters?"

"Yes."

"King-size cork-tip filters?"

"Yes."

"King-size cork-tip filters in a flip-top box?"

"Yes."

"Mentholated king-size cork-tip filters in a flip-top box?"

"No. Not mentholated."

"Sorry. We need an expert."

The only way to break this trend toward more and more about less and less is to give specialists enough general knowledge to keep in communication with one another, and to see where their society and their planet are headed. Every intelligent man and woman, for instance, ought to be aware of the world-wide danger of H-bomb fall-out to future generations. Only geneticists, however, are competent to spell out the technical aspects of the danger and the statistical probabilities involved.

Again, everyone should know something about the international agencies in which most civilized nations now cooperate—the United Nations, the World Court, the Postal Union, the weather services, the Red Cross. But only a few fans need to know who won the gold medal for throwing the javelin in the 1936 Olympic Games. Americans should always carry the Bill of Rights in the forefront of their minds, but the fine points of the trial of Alger Hiss can be left to legal specialists.

Forward-looking universities, says John W. Gardner, president of the Carnegie Corporation, want their professional students to have a solid base of general education—"specialists who are capable of functioning as generalists." The narrowly trained specialist, he says, may be in for a nasty jolt as his skills grow out of date. "The only safety for the years ahead lies in a professional training sufficiently broad and flexible so that the individual can survive the ups and downs and adapt himself to changing situations."

President William Stevenson of Oberlin also makes an eloquent plea for generalists: "We must admit quite frankly that we are not as interested in producing skilled people as we are in producing educated people, educated in the sense that they can relate experience and knowledge in one field to problems in others. . . ."

Gilbert W. Chapman, corporation president and friend of good books, says that the problems of an executive become less specialized and more general as he climbs the business ladder. "The specialist cannot function effectively at the top level of management if all he brings to it is his specialty." This agrees with the spreading movement to give top executives in U.S. corporations a sabbatical year in which to study the liberal arts.

A mature mind combines reliable information with good judgment, and one definition of good judgment is appreciation of relationships between fields of information. . . .

The intelligent layman . . . also wants to know what knowledge is available to promote negotiation and accommodation between the great powers. This is a question in the area of the behavioral sciences.

He wants to understand too what can be done to lessen tension between the races, and between worker and employer, and how to improve community relations. He would especially like to understand himself better, and why he often has so much trouble doing what he thinks he ought to do, and how he can get on more happily with his family, and in his personal relations generally.

Aside from these rather practical motives a good generalist possesses a healthy curiosity. . . . How and where [Homo sapiens] originally developed, how he survived as a hunter for many thousands of years, as a farmer and city dweller for a few more thousands; the purpose of his excess brain capacity even beyond what he needs for the intricate skills of language—these are some of the mysteries. The study of various cultures (where indeed the behavioral sciences begin) answers some questions but raises others: for example, which traits are common to man of every age and place, which are unique in a given society or even individual; why can the same complex customs arise independently in widely separate cultures?

.   .   .   .   .

. . . Specialists have distorted the environment of the world today and pulled human behavior out of scale. Generalists are needed in great numbers to offset what the specialists are doing to us. To put it in another way, we need more specialists equipped with wide perspective, to exert critical judgment on what they are doing as specialists. This, I take it, was Robert Oppenheimer's motive when he demurred about working on the hydrogen bomb: his general philosophy came in conflict with his expert knowledge. Almost everyone, as I said earlier, is both specialist and generalist; but the latter function has grown more and more neglected as specialties become more complex and demanding.

In *Fables for Our Time,* James Thurber imagines a conference of ostriches concerned with the loss of their ability to fly. One of them named Oliver complains that men can fly sitting down, while ostriches cannot fly at all. "The old ostrich glared at Oliver severely, first with one eye and then with the other. 'Man is flying too fast for a world that is round,' he said. 'Soon he will catch up with himself, in a great rear-end collision, and man will never know that what hit Man from behind was Man.'"

CHAPTER I

INTRODUCTION

2. THE TRANSITION TO SCIENCE

IN HUMAN RELATIONS *

GEORGE A. LUNDBERG

Sociology consists of the scientific study of human groups. To consider sociology a science means that we stand ready to observe human behavior as scientists would observe any natural phenomena and to look for systematic regularities in this human behavior. In this selection Lundberg, long an exponent of the rigorous application of the natural science approach to the study of human behavior, describes some of the practical results of this approach and presents the future steps which he feels must be taken if the social sciences are to help achieve a more rational "management of social relations."

I

I have expressed the view that the best hope for man in his present social predicament lies in a type of social science strictly comparable to the other natural sciences. We have reviewed some of the objections that have been urged both by physical and social scientists to this proposal. I am not under the illusion that my argument can be established conclusively in so brief a compass. Actually, of course, only time and future scientific development can finally demonstrate the validity of the position which I have outlined.

* George A. Lundberg, *Can Science Save Us?* (New York: Longmans, Green & Co., Inc., 1947) pp. 35–42. Reprinted by permission of the publisher and the author.

The author (b. 1895) is Professor of Sociology and former head of the department, University of Washington. Editor of *Sociometry*, 1941–1945. Research Consultant, United States Air Force, 1952. Recipient of distinguished achievement medal from University of Minnesota. Research Supervisor, Federal Emergency Relief Administration, 1934. Consultant, National Resources Planning Board, Washington, D.C. since 1942. Among his publications are *Foundations of Sociology; Social Research; Sociology;* and many articles in professional journals and periodicals.

In the meantime, we are confronted with the necessity of proceeding on *some* hypothesis as to the way out of our difficulties. It is generally agreed, even by those who differ most radically as to the proper approach, that our first need is a unified, coherent theory on which to proceed. A society cannot achieve its adjustments by mutually incompatible or contradictory behavior, any more than can an individual organism. However we may differ on details and on ends, we must agree on certain broad means, certain principles of action toward whatever ends we do agree upon.

In short, we all apparently agree with Comte's appraisal of the situation as he saw it almost a hundred years ago. Speaking of the theological, the metaphysical, and the positive scientific approaches, he said: "Any one of these might alone secure some sort of social order: but, while the three co-exist, it is impossible for us to understand one another upon any essential point whatever."

Of course there are some who find in our present predicament merely further evidence of the futility of the scientific approach in human affairs. They overlook the fact that, actually, science has as yet not been tried on social problems. Consequently, they advocate a return to theology, or "the" classics, either in their historic forms or in new versions in which the advocates of these approaches personally can play the role of major prophets. If I could see any chance of bringing about a return to theology or "the" classics, I might give it serious consideration, because any one unified approach might be better than two or more contradictory ones. But I see no such possibility in the long run. The commitments we have already made to science, chiefly in our technological culture, are of such character that we can neither go back nor stand still.

Our technological developments and our methods of communication have resulted in a fundamental interdependence which dominates our lives. This state of affairs requires, as we shall see, that we bring our social arrangements into line with this basic technological pattern, rather than vice versa. This basic technological pattern unquestionably rests upon natural science. On this ground, rather than on any assumption of absolute or intrinsic superiority of science as such, I think the following conclusion is inescapable: *In our time and for some centuries to come, for better or for worse, the sciences, physical and social, will be to an increasing degree the accepted point of reference with respect to which the validity (Truth) of all knowledge is gauged.*

If we accept this conclusion, then a number of questions arise. What are some examples of what the social sciences have done or might do in furthering sound and orderly adjustments in human relations? What, if anything, has been achieved in the social sciences to date? . . .

II

What are some examples of types of work by social scientists that are of vast importance in managing human relations?

The work of such agencies as the Census Bureau is known to all and is taken more or less for granted. Without the data and the analyses which it provides, the administration of public affairs would certainly dissolve in chaos and perhaps civil war. It is equally certain that no international organization can function without an elaborate organization of this kind to provide the essential facts regarding people and their characteristics and activities. Perhaps the most permanent contribution of the ill-fated League of Nations was the establishment of an international statistical bureau which still continues to function at Princeton University. The Office of Population Research of the same university is engaged in detailed studies of local population trends in Europe and elsewhere, including predictions of future areas of population pressure. This work would be of the utmost practical importance to the administration of any world organization. The Scripps Foundation, the Milbank Memorial Fund, and many others are engaged in similar or related work of a character that measures up very well to the standards of the physical sciences.

In the meantime anthropologists and sociologists have greatly extended our scientific knowledge of other peoples and cultures. This knowledge has in turn thrown a flood of light on our own civilization and permits the formulation at least of hypotheses regarding human behavior in general. The importance of this kind of knowledge in facilitating our contacts with other cultures during the recent war is too well known to require review. Is it not generally agreed that increasing contacts make the accumulation of such knowledge imperative in peace as well as in war?

We mentioned in the preceding chapter the importance of instruments and methods of observation and measurements in the social as well as in the physical sciences. Hundreds of such instruments have already been invented by means of which vocational aptitudes, success in college and other undertakings, and social behavior of great variety can be accurately measured and predicted. Perhaps the best known, but by no means the only one, of these devices is the public opinion poll. We have in this technique an illustration of how the development of the social sciences may be as significant for the future of social organization as many physical inventions have been in our industrial development.

The degree to which the public will can make itself reliably felt in government and in community action has always been in the foreground of political discussion. With the expansion of the areas within which public opinion must operate, many students of the problem have despaired of the capacity of the town meeting technique adequately to make operative the public will. In the face of this situation, social scientists have developed in recent years an instrument which cheaply and accurately permits us to learn the beliefs, the attitudes, and the wishes of the rank and file of the population. To be sure, the public opinion polls are at present thought of as interesting devices mainly for predicting the outcome of elections. But this is a very minor aspect of their full possible importance. These techniques also have been extensively used in the army and as a guide to the administration of liberated areas in Europe and elsewhere. Under the auspices of Allied Force Headquarters, Stuart C. Dodd developed a polling organization for determining in the invaded areas facts regarding the behavior and conditions of life as well as opinion regarding such subjects as public security, crime and the mores governing its control, the people's satisfaction with governing officials, attitudes toward co-belligerency, status of shelter and clothing, food supply and distribution, etc.

For example, complaints reached Allied authorities in Sicily regarding the malfunctioning of the rationing system. The local officials denied it and pointed to long lines of people ostensibly being served. A survey indicated that very few people had received their sugar ration for five months. Thereupon the local officials were confronted with these facts and were told to get busy. A follow-up survey in a week showed the situation greatly improved, and in two weeks practically corrected. Here we have a public which for the first time in years finds itself consulted on such matters and then observes that its complaints actually bring results. Experience of this kind probably goes farther than any propaganda for democracy that could be invented.

It may well be that in the perspective of history we have here a social invention—a technological device based on social science and on social research—which may rank in importance with gunpowder, telephone, or radio. It may be a device through which can be resolved the principal impasse of our age, namely, the apparent irreconcilability of authoritarian control on one hand and the public will on the other. It may be that through properly administered public opinion polls professionalized public officials can give us all the efficiency now claimed for authoritarian, centralized administration, and yet have that administration at all times subject to the dictates of a more delicate barometer of the people's will than is provided by all the technologically obsolete paraphernalia of traditional democratic processes. In short, it is not impossible that as advancing technology in one department of our lives leads to a threatened breakdown of democracy, so an improved social technology may restore and even increase the dominance of the people's voice in the control of human society.

I envision a time when the science of public opinion will be a science comparable to meteorology; when charts of all kinds of social weather, its movements and trends, whether it be anti-Semitism, anti-Negro sentiment, or mob-mindedness, will be at the disposal of the administrators of the people's will in every land. Dodd formulated and proposed to the United Nations plans for the establishment of a Barometer of International Security designed to detect authoritatively and early the tensions that lead to war. It is true that mere knowledge of these tensions does not automatically operate to alleviate them. But it is also true that a reliable diagnosis of the tension and an understanding of the sentiments that underlie it is essential for an intelligent approach to the problem. Right now it would be helpful to know exactly where are the pressure areas against Negroes and American-born Japanese. Is it not vitally important in postwar Europe to know where high and low pressure areas are in respect to the scores of minorities that must find their places in European society? We shall probably not hear anything more about the Barometer of International Security for the time being. The powers that be are obviously not interested in the wishes of the people who are being mercilessly bartered and moved about like so many pawns. But that does not affect the importance of the instrument as a technological achievement.

It would be easy to continue this recital of how developments in the social sciences already have ameliorated many social problems and have greatly facilitated public administration and policy. But the achievements are not merely in such obvious and practical fields as I have mentioned. The underlying theoretical and scientific knowledge upon which such practical devices rest must also be developed. As only one example of scientific work aiming directly at the construction and verification of scientific theory, I might call attention to Stouffer's study of the mobility habits of an urban population. Stouffer observed the apparently chaotic movements of the people of Cleveland in their frequent change of apartments. But isn't this much too complex for scientific study? Well, he considered various hypotheses which might constitute a generalized description of this behavior. He finally arrived at one hypothesis, which he states in rigorous mathematical terms. He then shows that a comprehensive study of the actual behavior of the people corresponds with remarkable accuracy to this hypothesis. The resulting generalization may be stated as follows: "The number of persons going a given distance is directly proportional to the number of opportunities at that distance and inversely proportional to the number of intervening opportunities." This law has subsequently been tested for other cities and larger areas, and for at least one foreign country. It has already been found to hold with certain modifications and under stated conditions for the movements of the people of the United States as a whole, and for Sweden.

We are not here interested primarily in the possible practical uses of these findings. I cite the case rather as an illustration of the possibility of arriving at scientific generalizations of social behavior essentially of the same sort as those that, in their full development, have proved so valuable in the physical sciences.

To those who constantly have their minds on quick and dramatic solutions to the world's troubles this type of research is likely to seem offensively trivial—a kind of fiddling while Rome burns. "Writers" are fond of referring contemptuously to basic scientific work as an "ivory tower" and as "lecturing on navigation while the ship sinks." Navigation today is what it is because some people were willing to study the *principles* of their subject while their individual ships went down, instead of rushing about with half-baked advice as to how to save ships that could not be saved, or were not worth saving anyway. As A. J. Carlson has recently said: "The failure of bacteria to survive in close proximity to certain moulds looked trivial at first, but few informed people would label the discovery of that initial fact *trivial* today."

So much, then, for a few illustrations, rather than a summary, of the type of work that is being done and that needs to be done in the social sciences. Is there enough of it being done? Clearly not, or we would not need to flounder as we are in national and international affairs, pursuing diametrically opposite courses within the same decade. Can the social sciences ever hope to catch up with the other sciences, the increasingly rapid advance of which constantly creates new social problems? Certainly we can, if we devote ourselves to the business with something like the seriousness, the money, and the equipment that we have devoted to physical research. Consider how the physical scientists are today given vast resources to concentrate on the invention of a new submarine detector or a new bomb, not to mention the peacetime occupations of these scientists with penicillin and sulpha drugs. Obviously, I am not criticizing this action. On the contrary, it is the way to proceed if you want results. Is there anything like that going on regarding the world organization and its numerous subsidiary problems, all of them important to peace and prosperity?

Comparatively speaking, there is almost nothing that could be called fundamental research into the basic nature of human relations. To be sure, there are endless petty projects, surveys, conferences, oratory, and arguments by representatives of pressure groups, as if argument ever settled any scientific questions. Of basic social research there is hardly anything. Why? . . . It is not yet realized that scientific knowledge is relevant to a successful world organization. We still think that common sense, good will, eloquent leaders, and pious hopes are sufficient when it comes to management of social relations.

3. A STUDY OF ATTITUDES *

SAMUEL A. STOUFFER

Significant advances were made in the application of social science research to practical problems in human relations while our country was undergoing one of its most serious crises—World War II. This selection by Samuel A. Stouffer, wartime head of the professional staff of the Research Branch in the War Department's Information and Education Division, describes some of that group's research. The perspective of history may prove, as the author maintains, that the major development of social science research in World War II was in the area of attitudes, just as that of World War I was in the area of "aptitudes." Certainly, the uses of the findings he describes here appear to be manifold.

In July, 1941, the Secretary of War issued an order prohibiting surveys of attitudes of enlisted men. If their attitudes were critical of the Army, the order said, a survey would be "destructive in its effect on a military organization where accepted responsibility on the part of every individual is fundamental."

Five months later, an exception to this rule was permitted. With the personal backing of Chief of Staff George C. Marshall, a group of psychologists and sociologists used anonymous questionnaires to sound out the attitudes of a representative cross section of 1,500 enlisted men in one infantry division in training. The study was made the day after Pearl Harbor. For the first time in any modern army, the new methods of social science research had a chance to show their power in comparison with the reports of visiting officers, who had to get their impressions from haphazard and biased samples of informants.

The report was critical, all right. Straight from the pencils of the men came frank and documented indictments of the training methods,

* *Scientific American*, Vol. 180, No. 5 (May, 1949), 11–15. Copyright, Scientific American, Inc. Reprinted by permission of the publisher and the author.

The author (b. 1900) is Professor of Sociology and Director of the Laboratory of Social Relations at Harvard University. Past President of the American Sociological Association and the American Association of Public Opinion Research. He is the author of *Communism, Conformity, and Civil Liberties;* and coauthor of *The American Soldier: Measurement and Prediction.* His research papers apply quantitative methods in social science.

the leadership system, and other activities of an army which was enmeshed in ancient tradition and only beginning to awake to the needs
of modern mechanized war. The complaints were not just idle gossip
and griping. For example, statistical tables and charts proved that the
men were discriminating in their criticisms: some practices were condemned by nine out of 10; some were approved by almost as large a
proportion.

General Marshall himself read the report on this division. So did
many of the officers on the General Staff. One general started reading
it at midnight and said the next day that it was so exciting and revealing
that he did not put it down until three o'clock in the morning. A considerable number of changes were instituted as a result of that one
study, including a revision of plans for the new Officers' Candidate
Schools. Most important of all, the War Department put such research
on a permament basis. Between Pearl Harbor and the end of the war,
the Research Branch of its Information and Education Division made
more than 200 surveys of representative samples aggregating over half
a million U.S. enlisted men and officers.

The Army had opened up a new channel of communication. The
top command now could replace guesswork about some of the morale
problems with evidence. To be sure, not all officers welcomed it. There
was always opposition, but skepticism diminished as the war progressed.
The standard argument that it would "upset a man's morale" to give
him a chance to say frankly what he thought without fear of reprisal
was easy to refute with evidence.

Moreover, it was possible to show that these surveys, using the best
methods available to social science, got down to some solid realities.
They proved to be of value in predicting the performance of groups
of men in combat. For example, before the Normandy invasion all the
enlisted men in the 108 rifle companies in four divisions were studied
in England. An attitude or morale index was constructed for each company. After two months of fighting in Normandy, each company's record
was compared with its pre-battle attitude index. The criterion of its
behavior under the stress of combat was taken to be its noncombat
casualty rate, because many if not most of the noncombat casualties at
this period were psychiatric in character, and some companies had much
higher noncombat casualty rates than others. Comparing the three rifle
companies with the worst attitude index with the three rifle companies
with the best index in each regiment, we found that on the average the
companies with the worst indexes before combat had 60 per cent more
nonbattle casualties in Normandy than the companies with the best.

The surveys were applied to hundreds of problems, many of which
do not loom large in the perspective of total war, but were important
at the time. Why did men in malarial regions fail to use Atabrine as

regularly as they should? What attitudes and practices were associated with trench foot? Which of two kinds of huts did men in Alaska prefer? What were the favored types of winter clothing among front-line troops in Belgium, Luxemburg and Germany? What radio transcriptions did men want? What did they like most to read in *Yank* magazine? What about needs for athletic equipment? What could be done to improve a difficult laundry situation in Panama? What were the sources of difficulties in soldiers' relations with the French? Such inquiries were routine and were made in increasing numbers.

Some of the larger-scale enterprises were: Studies of soldiers' post-war plans, which provided a factual basis for drawing up the GI Bill of Rights; studies of psychiatric screening which led to the development by the Research Branch, in cooperation with the Surgeon General, of a test that was used routinely in all induction stations in the last year of the war; special surveys of the Air Forces and of other large components of the Army such as the infantry (the idea of the Combat Infantryman's Badge grew out of one of these studies); analyses of problems of occupying troops, which led to changes in occupation policy in Germany.

One of the most useful researches was the one that established the point system for demobilization at the end of the war. The President and the War Department decided that the order of demobilization should be determined in terms of what the soldiers themselves wanted. The idea of a point system was conceived in the Research Branch. Representative samples of men throughout the world were queried, and from their responses the variables of length of service, overseas duty, combat duty and parenthood emerged as most significant. The final weights assigned to these variables yielded point scores which had a close correspondence with the wishes of the maximum number of soldiers, even if they did not exactly reproduce these wishes. Studies of reactions to the point system showed that the response to it was remarkably favorable, except among minorities who felt they were personally most injured by it (for example, combat infantrymen). Even after many men became angered by the alleged slowness of demobilization, the majority, though hostile to many if not most Army policies, continued to approve the point system (which determined the order, not the rate, of demobilization). In view of the explosive tensions in the early demobilization period, historians may find that the establishment of an objective system whose justice was accepted by most men saved the country from what could have been a crisis seriously damaging to American prestige.

Plainly the findings and the experience gained from these many surveys are not limited to the military sphere or to wartime application. While these were all studies of men at war, they have implications of general social importance. For social scientists their chief present interest lies in the question of how the findings and techniques that were developed can be applied to civilian institutions.

One important problem to which they may be applied, for example, is that of increasing job satisfaction. In World War I psychologists first measured *aptitudes* on a large scale, with such crude devices as the Army Alpha test. Out of that work came hundreds of psychological studies in the years between the wars. By World War II psychology was ready with improved techniques of measurement and classification to aid in the selection of airplane pilots, navigators and bombardiers, and to assign soldiers generally on a basis that took account of their abilities. But satisfaction and efficiency on the job depend on more than aptitudes. They depend also on the interests and motivations of men.

In World War II the Research Branch found that aptitudes and attitudes were like the two blades of a pair of scissors. Men who got a chance to volunteer for their specific assignments were much better satisfied than those who never got a chance to choose, even though many of the latter actually were using their civilian skills. It would have been possible for the Army to extend the range of freedom of choice much further. In the future, in civilian industry as well as in the armed forces, it is likely that much more attention will be given to such attitudes. More can be done to glamorize unpopular jobs—the Navy may have shown how to do this with its Seabees.

One of the most important concepts used in the Research Branch was the principle of relative deprivation. This idea reconciled many otherwise paradoxical findings, not only in the field of job satisfaction but elsewhere. For example, two of the most extreme branches of the Army as far as promotion opportunities were concerned were the Air Forces and the Military Police. The Air Forces were full of sergeants and corporals. The MPs were mostly privates. Yet men in the Air Forces complained of lack of promotion opportunities more than did those in the Military Police. Why? The concept of relative deprivation led to an answer. Since most Air Forces men got promotions, those who did not tended to be personally aggrieved. Since few MPs got promotions, those who did not had so much company that they did not take it as a personal injustice. MPs who were promoted were so few that the promotion was a matter of exceptional pride. In other words, one's deprivation was always viewed relative to that of others, and the research problem was to find out who the "others" were.

Almost everyone expected that Northern Negro soldiers stationed in Southern camps would be more dissatisfied than those stationed in Northern camps. It is true that those sent South did complain, often bitterly, of Jim Crow regulations and of treatment by the local police.

But in general their morale was as good as or better than that of Northern Negroes stationed in the North. Why? After elaborate cross-tabulations that eliminated education and other factors as the explanation, it finally appeared, as should have been seen earlier, that relative to civilian Negroes in the South the Negro soldier apparently perceived himself to be well treated. But when a Northern Negro at a Northern camp compared himself with civilian Negroes making big money in the war industries, he apparently felt himself not so fortunate.

In spite of intense eagerness to get home, the job satisfaction of soldiers in the rear areas of active theaters overseas was as high as or higher than that of men doing the same kinds of jobs in the U.S. Why? Part of the explanation, of course, was the sense of the importance of their overseas mission. But another significant aspect appears to be the fact that, relative to the combat troops they knew, the rear-area men had jobs which, though often unpleasant, tended to be safe. Very few were found who had the desire to change places with the combat men.

On the other hand, these rear-area troops and soldiers in overseas noncombat areas such as Panama, Alaska, Iran and most of India-Burma were the most vocal of all in their criticism of officers. Why? Analysis of many studies all over the world indicated that one of the basic factors in enlisted men's antipathy to officers related to the special privileges of rank, which involved many practices alien to American democratic traditions. If the supply of attractive women, liquor or entertainment was severely limited, as was often the case overseas, the problem of equitable distribution became acute. If, as was charged, the officers tended to monopolize such desired objects, the men's resentment is understandable. There was even greater scarcity of these attractions in the front lines, but there the officers and men shared the same deprivations. At camps in the U.S. there was less deprivation; therefore the so-called caste system, though productive of much irritation, was not as heavily criticized there as in places where the relative deprivation of enlisted men as compared with officers was greatest.

All this has significant implications for civilian life. In industry, or in the family, or wherever we are, satisfaction is a relative matter. The key to understanding a given attitude is to learn the context in which the attitude is expressed and the standards of comparison that exist in the given situation.

These studies also made clear the importance of studying what the sociologist calls informal social controls. Perhaps few organizations have more elaborate formal rules than the Army, but in the last analysis, in the Army as elsewhere, the most powerful control is that of one's own fellows. Some searching analyses were made of the process of "goldbricking"—that is, appearing to be busy without really accomplishing much of anything. Goldbricking, an older word for which, significantly, is "soldiering," sometimes was practiced with so hearty a group spirit that it represented high morale from the standpoint of the group—though not from the standpoint of the Army command. Studies showed that there were clear-cut codes about goldbricking. A soldier who refused to conform to the code was a target for scorn from his fellows; on the other hand, when the group felt that a given task was necessary or that the group would be punished if it were not fulfilled, then an individual goldbricker became an object of scorn.

A long series of studies of combat troops, based on thousands of systematic interviews and on personal front-line experiences of Research Branch members, emphasized the central importance of such informal controls, or group opinion, in stress situations. Compared with the feeling that one must not lose face in the eyes of one's fellows or let them down, patriotism, hatred of the enemy and other stereotyped explanations of what keeps a person going in combat seem to have been negligible factors.

One of the greatest weaknesses of social science has been the infrequency of its use of deliberately designed controlled experiments, which are the only sure method of determining whether a change in one variable actually will be followed by a change in another. From the beginning of the war the Research Branch recognized the need for such experiments. But neither the Army nor the U.S. public in general has been in the habit of asking for this kind of evidence from social scientists. Although the Army would not think of adopting a new weapon without exhaustive trials, it was not nearly as ready to try out a new social idea—such as a different personnel policy or a different training method—on a very limited scale, with careful controls to measure exactly what the effects would be.

There were instances in which the Research Branch was able to obtain a kind of experimental proof, even in situations that were not deliberately set up as controlled experiments. For example, the Army tried out in Europe the radical idea of placing an entire platoon of Negro volunteers in a white infantry combat company. This was done in several divisions, most of which saw several months of subsequent battle. At the end of the campaign interviewers polled sample groups of men in several divisions to find out how the attitudes of men who had served with Negroes compared with those of men who had not. In divisions that had no mixed companies, 62 per cent of the soldiers said they would dislike very much to serve in the same companies as Negroes. Of white infantrymen who had fought in the same divisions but not the same companies as Negroes, only 20 per cent said they would dislike it very much. And among white infantrymen who had actually been in the same companies as Negroes, only 7 per cent said they disliked it very much.

There was another very interesting finding. Two thirds of the white men in the mixed companies, when polled after the experience, said that they had been opposed to the scheme beforehand and had thought it would fail. This was almost exactly the same proportion of opponents as was found in divisions that had not experienced the plan; in other words, the retrospective answers about attitudes corresponded closely to those of groups reporting current attitudes, so one finding tended to confirm the other. The findings can therefore be considered, cautiously of course, to approach in reliability the result of a controlled experiment, although it falls far short of the ideal.

Early in the war the Research Branch sought a full-fledged opportunity to demonstrate the value of controlled experiments. This opportunity came in connection with the physical training program.

A committee of physical educators had proposed a new physical conditioning program for the Army, based on modern experience in training football players and other athletes. They believed that the traditional Army regimen of setting-up exercises and hikes was uninteresting to the men, time-consuming and generally inefficient. A Research Branch survey of samples of troops throughout the country, using tests of physical proficiency devised by the committee, confirmed the criticism. It showed that men who had been in the Army six months to a year and had been subjected to the old-fashioned conditioning system made little better scores on tests of strength or of stamina than did new recruits. That the tests were valid measures of physical condition was confirmed by the fact that paratroopers, initially selected for ruggedness and subjected to particularly rigorous physical training, were able to make high scores on them.

A controlled experiment was then set up. Two samples of new recruits, matched on initial proficiency tests, were selected. One sample was put through the conventional Army course of calisthenics and hikes. When retested the group showed only a slight improvement over its initial scores. The other group was given the rigorous new program of training. After six weeks its proficiency scores were far superior, almost as high as those of the paratroopers. Moreover, the men getting this training liked it better than did those in the traditional program. The results persuaded the Army to scrap its traditional procedures and introduce the new program on an Army-wide basis.

While the hopes that this demonstration would induce the Army to try other experiments in handling its human resources were not fully realized, the use of controlled experiments became an important part of the developmental work of the Information and Education Division.

One of the functions of this Division was to make motion picture films to give the soldiers better orientation to the war. The "Why We Fight" series of films, produced under the direction of Colonel Frank Capra, was studied in detail. Analyses were made by the attitude-survey method of the effectiveness of the films in general, the differential effects on different types of soldiers and the impact of specific elements of film content.

Experimental studies also were of use in testing theories on propaganda techniques. For example, is propaganda more effective when it tries to present an opposing point of view and refute it than when it merely reiterates one's own position, *à la* Goebbels? Experimental studies made in the Research Branch suggests that the answer may be yes and no. Presenting both sides seemed to be more effective for winning the better-educated soldiers to the point of view wanted, but less effective among the less educated. The latter tended to get from the two-sided presentation doubts that they might not otherwise have had.

One of the chief obstacles to carrying out controlled experiments is the lack of good criteria of measurement. For example, the Research Branch made extensive studies of fear among soldiers. Thousands of combat men were interviewed. Some experiments were carried out, notably at the school for training paratroopers. But even at the end of the war there was no reliable answer to the following question: Is it better to scare combat soldiers badly from the beginning of their training, to lead them gradually into more and more frightening situations, or not to scare them at all? What complicates the problem is that fear may have either harmful or useful effects: It may freeze a person or cause him to act erratically or run away; on the other hand, it may make him more attentive to danger signals and selective of those to which he must respond in different ways. The trouble is that we have as yet no good criteria for measuring fear and evaluating its adaptive value.

A good case can be made for the hypothesis that this lack of measured criteria is one of the main reasons why experimentation in the social sciences is so rare as compared with the physical sciences, and why the social sciences have moved so slowly. Medical science made similarly slow progress until modern instruments of biological measurement were developed. The Research Branch made some new attacks on the measurement problem in social psychology and sociology, and a considerable part of its report is devoted to a fresh analysis of measurement theory which, it is hoped, will stimulate concerted efforts in this direction. Another decade or two of accumulated experience is likely to see great improvements in social science, particularly as more and more of the newer students get a hardheaded training in mathematics, statistics and the design of experiments.

4. WHAT DO ATTITUDE SURVEYS TELL US? *

PAUL F. LAZARSFELD

The preceding selection summarized some of the findings of wartime attitude surveys. The postwar publication of these surveys in four volumes stimulated much evaluative discussion among social scientists. In a review of two of the volumes, part of which is reproduced here, Paul Lazarsfeld shows us what attitude surveys can do for sociology. In particular he uses striking examples that illustrate the dangers inherent in "common-sense" generalizations about attitudes and behavior.

It will be helpful to consider the special role played by attitude surveys in contemporary social science. Although surveys are only one of the many techniques available, at the moment they undoubtedly constitute the most important and promising step forward that has been made in recent years.

The limitations of survey methods are obvious. They do not use experimental techniques; they rely primarily on what people say, and rarely include objective observations; they deal with aggregates of individuals rather than with integrated communities; they are restricted to contemporary problems—history can be studied only by the use of documents remaining from earlier periods.

In spite of these limitations survey methods provide one of the foundations upon which social science is being built. The finding of regularities is the beginning of any science, and surveys can make an important contribution in this respect. For it is necessary that we know what people usually do under many and different circumstances if we are to develop theories explaining their behavior. Furthermore, before we can devise an experiment we must know what problems are

* From Paul F. Lazarsfeld, "The American Soldier—An Expository Review," *The Public Opinion Quarterly*, Vol. 13, No. 3 (Fall, 1949), 378–380. Reprinted by permission of the publisher and the author.

The author (b. 1901) is chairman of the Department of Sociology and former director of the Bureau of Applied Social Research at Columbia University. Among his books are: *Radio and the Printed Page; Radio Research* (with F. Stanton); *Mathematical Thinking in the Social Sciences; Continuities in Social Research* (with R. K. Merton). An Austrian by birth, Lazarsfeld is widely recognized for his contributions to the social sciences.

worthwhile; which should be investigated in greater detail. Here again surveys can be of service.

Finding regularities and determining criteria of significance are concerns the social sciences have in common with the natural sciences. But there are crucial differences between the two fields of inquiry. The world of social events is much less "visible" than the realm of nature. That bodies fall to the ground, that things are hot or cold, that iron becomes rusty, are all immediately obvious. It is much more difficult to realize that ideas of right and wrong vary in different cultures; that customs may serve a different function from the one which the people practising them believe they are serving; that the same person may show marked contrasts in his behavior as a member of a family and as a member of an occupational group. The mere description of human behavior, of its variation from group to group and of its changes in different situations, is a vast and difficult undertaking. It is this task of describing, sifting and ferreting out interrelationships which surveys perform for us. And yet this very function often leads to serious misunderstandings. For it is hard to find a form of human behavior that has not already been observed somewhere. Consequently, if a study reports a prevailing regularity, many readers respond to it by thinking "of course that is the way things are." Thus, from time to time, the argument is advanced that surveys only put into complicated form observations which are already obvious to everyone.

Understanding the origin of this point of view is of importance far beyond the limits of the present discussion. The reader may be helped in recognizing this attitude if he looks over a few statements which are typical of many survey findings and carefully observes his own reaction. A short list of these, with brief interpretive comments, will be given here in order to bring into sharper focus probable reactions of many readers.

1. Better educated men showed more psycho-neurotic symptoms than those with less education. (The mental instability of the intellectual as compared to the more impassive psychology of the-man-in-the-street has often been commented on.)
2. Men from rural backgrounds were usually in better spirits during their Army life than soldiers from city backgrounds. (After all, they are more accustomed to hardships.)
3. Southern soldiers were better able to stand the climate in the hot South Sea Islands than Northern soldiers. (Of course, Southerners are more accustomed to hot weather.)
4. White privates were more eager to become non-coms than Negroes. (The lack of ambition among Negroes is almost proverbial.)
5. Southern Negroes preferred Southern to Northern white officers. (Isn't it well known that Southern whites have a more fatherly attitude toward their "darkies"?)

6. As long as the fighting continued, men were more eager to be returned to the States than they were after the German surrender. (You cannot blame people for not wanting to be killed.)

We have in these examples a sample list of the simplest type of inter-relationships which provide the "bricks" from which our empirical social science is being built. But why, since they are so obvious, is so much money and energy given to establish such findings? Would it not be wiser to take them for granted and proceed directly to a more sophisticated type of analysis? This might be so except for one interest-ing point about the list. *Every one of these statements is the direct opposite of what actually was found.* Poorly educated soldiers were more neurotic than those with high education; Southerners showed no greater ability than Northerners to adjust to a tropical climate; Negroes were more eager for promotion than whites; and so on.

If we had mentioned the actual results of the investigation first, the reader would have labelled these "obvious" also. Obviously something is wrong with the entire argument of "obviousness." It should really be turned on its head. Since every kind of human reaction is conceivable, it is of great importance to know which reactions actually occur most frequently and under what conditions; only then will a more advanced social science develop.

5. MANIFEST AND LATENT FUNCTIONS *

ROBERT K. MERTON

Most social scientists today are "functionalists." That is, they are more concerned with the functions of various phenomena than with trying to ascertain the "real nature" of the phenomena. Stated another way, modern social science is more concerned with what things do than with what things allegedly are. As

* Reprinted from *Social Theory and Social Structure*, pp. 71–81, by permission of The Free Press, Glencoe, Illinois. Copyright 1949.

The author (b. 1910) is Professor of Sociology, Columbia University. Advisory sociology editor, Harcourt, Brace and Company. Fellow American Academy of Arts and Sciences. International Commission in Study of the Social Relations and History of Science. Author of: *Science, Technology and Society in Seventeenth Century England; Mass Persuasion; Social Theory and Social Structure; The Focussed Inter-view* (coauthor). Coeditor (with Paul F. Lazarsfeld), *Continuities in Social Research: The Scope and Method of "The American Soldier."*

*one investigator has expressed it, the usefulness of electricity
was limited as long as physicists concerned themselves with the
vain attempt to find out what electricity is; progress came
only when men turned to the task of finding what electricity can
do and contented themselves with defining electricity as "that
which does such and such." In this article, Robert K. Merton
applies the same approach to political machines. He is not here
concerned with what political machines may be in any
ultimate sense; he concentrates on what they do, that is, how
they function. In using this approach, Merton illustrates the
basic point that a function may be manifest (that is, obvious
or intended) or latent (that is, hidden or unintended). In
addition, Merton demonstrates that the scientist, as scientist,
aims to describe, not judge; he describes political machines
but he does not blame or praise them.*

SOME FUNCTIONS OF THE POLITICAL MACHINE

Without presuming to enter into the variations of detail marking
different political machines—a Tweed, Vare, Crump, Flynn, Hague are
by no means identical types of bosses—we can briefly examine the functions more or less common to the political machine, as a generic type
of social organization. We neither attempt to itemize all the diverse
functions of the political machine nor imply that all these functions are
similarly fulfilled by each and every machine.

The key structural function of the Boss is to organize, centralize and
maintain in good working condition "the scattered fragments of power"
which are at present dispersed through our political organization. By
this centralized organization of political power, the boss and his apparatus can satisfy the needs of diverse subgroups in the larger community which are not adequately satisfied by legally devised and
culturally approved social structures.

To understand the role of bossism and the machine, therefore, we
must look at two types of sociological variables: (1) the *structural context* which makes it difficult, if not impossible, for morally approved
structures to fulfill essential social functions, thus leaving the door open
for political machines (or their structural equivalents) to fulfill these
functions and (2) the subgroups whose distinctive needs are left unsatisfied, except for the latent functions which the machine in fact fulfills.

STRUCTURAL CONTEXT

The constitutional framework of American political organization
specifically precludes the legal possibility of highly centralized power

and, it has been noted, thus "discourages the growth of effective and responsible leadership. The framers of the Constitution, as Woodrow Wilson observed, set up the check and balance system 'to keep government at a sort of mechanical equipoise by means of a standing amicable contest among its several organic parts.' They distrusted power as dangerous to liberty: and therefore they spread it thin and erected barriers against its concentration." This dispersion of power is found not only at the national level but in local areas as well. "As a consequence," Sait goes on to observe, "when *the people or particular groups* among them demanded positive action, no one had adequate authority to act. The machine provided an antidote."

The constitutional dispersion of power not only makes for difficulty of effective decision and action but when action does occur it is defined and hemmed in by legalistic considerations. In consequence, there develops "a much *more human system* of partisan government, whose chief object soon became the circumvention of government by law. . . . The lawlessness of the extra-official democracy was merely the counterpoise of the legalism of the official democracy. The lawyer having been permitted to subordinate democracy to the Law, the Boss had to be called in to extricate the victim, which he did after a fashion and for a consideration."

Officially, political power is dispersed. Various well-known expedients were devised for this manifest objective. Not only was there the familiar separation of powers among the several branches of the government but, in some measure, tenure in each office was limited, rotation in office approved. And the scope of power inherent in each office was severely circumscribed. Yet, observes Sait in rigorously functional terms, "Leadership is necessary; and *since* it does not develop readily within the constitutional framework, the Boss provides it in a crude and irresponsible form from the outside."

Put in more generalized terms, *the functional deficiencies of the official structure generate an alternative (unofficial) structure to fulfill existing needs somewhat more effectively.* Whatever its specific historical origins, the political machine persists as an apparatus for satisfying otherwise unfulfilled needs of diverse groups in the population. By turning to a few of these subgroups and their characteristic needs, we shall be led at once to a range of latent functions of the political machine.

FUNCTIONS OF THE POLITICAL MACHINE FOR DIVERSE SUBGROUPS

It is well known that one source of strength of the political machine derives from its roots in the local community and the neighborhood.

The political machine does not regard the electorate as a vague, undifferentiated mass of voters. With a keen sociological intuition, the machine recognizes that the voter is primarily a man living in a specific neighborhood, with specific personal problems and personal wants. Public issues are abstract and remote; private problems are extremely concrete and immediate. It is not through the generalized appeal to large public concerns that the machine operates, but through the direct, quasi-feudal relationships between local representatives of the machine and voters in their neighborhood. Elections are won in the precinct.

The machine welds its link with ordinary men and women by elaborate networks of personal relations. Politics is transformed into personal ties. The precinct captain "must be a friend to every man, assuming, if he does not feel, sympathy with the unfortunate, and utilizing in his good works the resources which the boss puts at his disposal." The precinct captain is forever a friend in need. In our prevailingly impersonal society, the machine, through its local agents, fulfills the important social *function of humanizing and personalizing all manner of assistance* to those in need. Food-baskets and jobs, legal and extra-legal advice, setting to rights minor scrapes with the law, helping the bright poor boy to a political scholarship in a local college, looking after the bereaved—the whole range of crises when a feller needs a friend, and, above all, a friend who knows the score and who can do something about it—all these find the ever-helpful precinct captain available in the pinch.

To assess this function of the political machine adequately, it is important to note not only the fact that aid *is* provided but *the manner in which it is provided*. After all, other agencies do exist for dispensing such assistance. Welfare agencies, settlement houses, legal aid clinics, medical aid in free hospitals, public relief departments, immigration authorities—these and a multitude of other organizations are available to provide the most varied types of assistance. But in contrast to the professional techniques of the welfare worker which may typically represent in the mind of the recipient the cold, bureaucratic dispensation of limited aid following upon detailed investigation of *legal* claims to aid of the "client," are the unprofessional techniques of the precinct captain who asks no questions, exacts no compliance with legal rules of eligibility and does not "snoop" into private affairs.

For many, the loss of "self-respect" is too high a price for legalized assistance. In contrast to the gulf between the settlement house workers who so often come from a different social class, educational background and ethnic group, the precinct worker is "just one of us," who understands what it's all about. The condescending lady bountiful can hardly compete with the understanding friend in need. In *this struggle between alternative structures for fulfilling the nominally same function* of providing aid and support to those who need it, it is clearly the machine politician who is better integrated with the groups which he serves than the impersonal, professionalized, socially distant and legally constrained welfare worker. And since the politician can at times influence and manipulate the official organizations for the dispensation of assistance, whereas the welfare worker has practically no influence on the political machine, this only adds to his greater effectiveness. More colloquially and also, perhaps, more incisively, it was the Boston ward-leader, Martin Lomasny, who described this essential function to the curious Lincoln Steffens: "I think," said Lomasny, "that there's got to be in every ward somebody that any bloke can come to—no matter what he's done—and get help. *Help, you understand; none of your law and justice, but help.*"

The "deprived classes," then, constitute one subgroup for whom the political machine clearly satisfies wants not adequately satisfied in the same fashion by the legitimate social structure.

For a second subgroup, that of business (primarily "big" business but also "small") the political boss serves the function of providing those political privileges which entail immediate economic gains. Business corporations, among which the public utilities (railroads, local transportation companies, communications corporations, electric light) are simply the most conspicuous in this regard, seek special political dispensations which will enable them to stabilize their situation and to near their objective of maximizing profits. Interestingly enough, corporations often want to avoid a chaos of uncontrolled competition. They want the greater security of an economic czar who controls, regulates and organizes competition, providing this czar is not a public official with his decisions subject to public scrutiny and public control. (The latter would be "government control," and hence taboo.) The political boss fulfills these requirements admirably.

Examined for a moment apart from any "moral" considerations, the political apparatus of the Boss is effectively designed to perform these functions with a minimum of inefficiency. Holding the strings of diverse governmental divisions, bureaus and agencies in his competent hands, the Boss rationalizes the relations between public and private business. He serves as the business community's ambassador in the otherwise alien (and sometimes unfriendly) realm of government. And, in strict business-like terms, he is well-paid for his economic services to his respectable business clients. In an article entitled, "An Apology to Graft," Steffens suggested that "Our economic system, which held up riches, power and acclaim as prizes to men bold enough and able enough to buy corruptly timber, mines, oil fields and franchises and 'get away with it,' was at fault." And, in a conference with a hundred or so of Los Angeles business leaders, he described a fact well known to all of them: the Boss and his machine were an *integral part* of the organization of the economy. "You cannot build or operate a railroad, or a street railway, gas, water, or power company, develop and operate a mine, or get forests and cut timber on a large scale, or run any privileged business, without corrupting or joining in the corruption of the government. You tell me privately that you must, and here I am telling you semi-publicly that you must. And that is so all over the country. And that means that we have an organization of society in which, *for some reason,* you and your kind, the ablest, most intelligent, most imaginative, daring, and resourceful leaders of society, are and must be against society and its laws and its all-around growth."

Since the demand for the services of special privileges are built into the structure of the society, the Boss fulfills diverse functions for this second subgroup of business-seeking-privilege. These "needs" of business, as presently constituted, are not adequately provided for by "conventional" and "culturally approved" social structures; consequently, the extra-legal but more-or-less efficient organization of the political machine comes to provide these services. To adopt an *exclusively* moral attitude toward the "corrupt political machine" is to lose sight of the very structural conditions which generate the "evil" that is so bitterly attacked. To adopt a functional outlook on the political machine is not to provide an apologia, but a more solid base for modifying or eliminating the machine, *providing* specific structural arrangements are introduced either for eliminating these effective demands of the business community or, if that is the objective, of satisfying these demands through alternative means.

A third set of distinctive functions fulfilled by the political machine for a special subgroup is that of providing alternative channels of social mobility for those otherwise excluded from the more conventional avenues for personal "advancement." Both the sources of this special "need" (for social mobility) and the respect in which the political machine comes to help satisfy this need can be understood by examining the structure of the larger culture and society. As is well known, the American culture lays enormous emphasis on money and power as a "success" goal legitimate for all members of the society. By no means alone in our inventory of cultural goals, it still remains among the most heavily endowed with positive affect and value. However, certain subgroups and certain ecological areas are notable for the relative absence of opportunity for achieving these (monetary and power) types of success. They constitute, in short, sub-populations where "the cultural emphasis upon pecuniary success has been absorbed, but where there is *little access to conventional and legitimate* means for attaining such success. The conventional occupational opportunities of persons in (such areas) are almost completely limited to manual labor. Given our cultural stigmatization of manual labor, and its correlate, the prestige of white-collar work," it is clear that the result is a tendency to achieve these culturally approved objectives *through whatever means are possible.* These people are on the one hand, "asked to orient their conduct toward the prospect of accumulating wealth [and power] and, on the other, they are largely denied effective opportunities to do so institutionally."

It is within this context of social structure that the political machine fulfills the basic function of providing avenues of social mobility for the otherwise disadvantaged. Within this context, even the corrupt political machine and the racket "represent the triumph of amoral intelligence over morally prescribed 'failure' when the channels of vertical mobility are closed or narrowed *in a society which places a high premium on economic affluence, [power] and social ascent for all its members.*" As one sociologist has noted on the basis of several years of close observation in a "slum area":

> The sociologist who dismisses racket and political organizations as deviations from desirable standards thereby neglects some of the major elements of slum life. . . . *He does not discover the functions they perform for the members* [of the groupings in the slum]. The Irish and later immigrant peoples have had the greatest difficulty in finding places for themselves in our urban social and economic structure. Does anyone believe that the immigrants and their children could have achieved their present degree of social mobility without gaining control of the political organization of some of our largest cities? The same is true of the racket organization. *Politics and the rackets have furnished an important means of social mobility for individuals, who, because of ethnic background and low class position,* are blocked from advancement in the "respectable" channels.

This, then, represents a third type of function performed for a distinctive subgroup. This function, it may be noted in passing, is fulfilled by the *sheer* existence and operation of the political machine, for it is in the machine itself that these individuals and sub-groups find their culturally induced needs more or less satisfied. It refers to the services which the political apparatus provides for its own personnel. But seen in the wider social context we have set forth, it no longer appears as *merely* a means of self-aggrandizement for profit-hungry and power-hungry *individuals,* but as an organized provision for *subgroups* otherwise excluded or restricted from the race for "getting ahead."

Just as the political machine performs services for "legitimate" business, so it operates to perform not dissimilar services for "illegitimate" business: vice, crime and rackets. Once again, the basic sociological role of the machine in this respect can be more fully appreciated only if one temporarily abandons attitudes of moral indignation, to examine with all moral innocence the actual workings of the organization. In this light, it at once appears that the subgroup of the professional criminal, racketeer, gambler, has basic similarities of organization, demands and operation to the subgroup of the industrialist, man of business, speculator. If there is a Lumber King or an Oil King, there is also a Vice King or a Racket King. If expansive legitimate business organizes administrative and financial syndicates to "rationalize" and to "integrate" diverse areas of production and business enterprise, so expansive rackets and crime organize syndicates to bring order to the otherwise chaotic areas of production of illicit goods and services. If legitimate business regards the proliferation of small business enterprises as wasteful and inefficient, substituting, for example, the giant chain stores for the hundreds of corner groceries, so illegitimate business adopts the same businesslike attitude, and syndicates crime and vice.

Finally, and in many respects, most important, is the basic similarity, if not near-identity, of the economic role of "legitimate" business and "illegitimate" business. *Both are in some degree concerned with the provision of goods and services for which there is an economic demand.* Morals aside, they are both business, industrial and professional enterprises, dispensing goods and services which some people want, for which there is a market in which goods and services are transformed into commodities. And, in a prevalently market society, we should expect appropriate enterprises to arise whenever there is a market demand for given goods or services.

As is well known, vice, crime and the rackets *are* "big business." Consider only that there have been estimated to be about 500,000 professional prostitutes in the United States, and compare this with the approximately 200,000 physicians and 200,000 nurses. It is difficult to estimate which have the larger clientele: the professional men and women of medicine or the professional men and women of vice. It is, of course, difficult to estimate the economic assets, income, profits and dividends of illicit gambling in this country and to compare it with the economic assets, income, profits and dividends of, say, the shoe industry, but it is altogether possible that the two industries are about on a par. No precise figures exist on the annual expenditures on illicit narcotics, and it is probable that these are less than the expenditures on candy, but it is also probable that they are larger than the expenditure on books.

It takes but a moment's thought to recognize that, *in strictly economic terms*, there is no relevant difference between the provision of licit and illicit goods and services. The liquor traffic illustrates this perfectly. It would be peculiar to argue that prior to 1920 (when the 18th amendment became effective), the provision of liquor constituted an economic service, that from 1920 to 1933, its production and sale no longer constituted an economic service dispensed in a market, and that from 1934 to the present, it once again took on a serviceable aspect. Or, it would be *economically* (not morally) absurd to suggest that the sale of bootlegged liquor in the dry state of Kansas is less a response to a market demand than the sale of publicly manufactured liquor in the neighboring wet state of Missouri. Examples of this sort can of course be multiplied many times over. Can it be held that in European countries, with registered and legalized prostitution, the prostitute contributes an economic service, whereas in this country, lacking legal sanction, the prostitute provides no such service? Or that the professional abortionist is in the economic market where he has approved legal status and that he is out of the economic market where he is legally taboo? Or that gambling satisfies a specific demand for entertainment in Nevada, where it is one of the largest business enterprises of the largest city in the state, but that it differs essentially in this respect from movie houses in the neighboring state of California?

The failure to recognize that these businesses are only *morally* and not *economically* distinguishable from "legitimate" businesses has led to badly scrambled analysis. Once the economic identity of the two is recognized, we may anticipate that if the political machine performs functions for "legitimate big business" it will be all the more likely to perform not dissimilar functions for "illegitimate big business." And, of course, such is often the case.

The distinctive function of the political machine for their criminal, vice and racket clientele is to enable them to operate in satisfying the economic demands of a large market without due interference from the government. Just as big business may contribute funds to the political party war-chest to ensure a minimum of governmental interference, so with big rackets and big crime. In both instances, the political machine can, in varying degrees, provide "protection." In both instances, many features of the structural context are identical: (1) market demands for goods and services; (2) the operators' concern with maximizing gains from their enterprises; (3) the need for partial control of government which might otherwise interfere with these activities of businessmen; (4) the need for an efficient, powerful and centralized agency to provide an effective liaison of "business" with government.

Without assuming that the foregoing pages exhaust either the range of functions or the range of subgroups served by the political machine, we can at least see that *it presently fulfills some functions for these diverse subgroups which are not adequately fulfilled by culturally approved or more conventional structures.*

Several additional implications of the functional analysis of the political machine can be mentioned here only in passing, although they obviously require to be developed at length. First, the foregoing analysis has direct implications for *social engineering*. It helps explain why the periodic efforts at "political reform," "turning the rascals out" and "cleaning political house" are typically short-lived and ineffectual. It exemplifies a basic theorem: *any attempt to eliminate an existing social structure without providing adequate alternative structures for fulfilling the functions previously fulfilled by the abolished organization is doomed to failure.* (Needless to say, this theorem has much wider bearing than the one instance of the political machine.) When "political reform" confines itself to the manifest task of "turning the rascals out," it is engaging in little more than sociological magic. The reform may for a time bring new figures into the political limelight; it may serve the casual social function of re-assuring the electorate that the moral virtues remain intact and will ultimately triumph; it may actually effect a turnover in the personnel of the political machine; it may even, for a time, so curb the activities of the machine as to leave unsatisfied the many needs it has previously fulfilled. But, inevitably, unless the reform also involves a "re-forming" of the social and political structure such that the existing needs are satisfied by alternative structures or unless it involves a change which eliminates these needs altogether, the political machine will return to its integral place in the social scheme of things. *To seek social change, without due recognition of the manifest and latent functions performed by the social organization undergoing change, is to indulge in social ritual rather than social engineering.* The concepts of manifest and latent functions (or their equivalents) are indispensable elements in the theoretic repertoire of the social engineer. In this crucial sense, these concepts are not "merely" theoretical (in the abusive sense of the term), but are eminently practical. In the deliberate enactment of social change, they can be ignored only at the price of considerably heightening the risk of failure.

A second implication of our analysis of the political machine also has a bearing upon areas wider than the one we have considered. The "paradox" has often been noted that the supporters of the political machine include both the "respectable" business class elements who are, of course, opposed to the criminal or racketeer and the distinctly "unrespectable" elements of the underworld. And, at first appearance, this is cited as an instance of very strange bedfellows. The learned judge is not infrequently called upon to sentence the very racketeer beside whom he sat the night before at an informal dinner of the political bigwigs. The district attorney jostles the exonerated convict on his way to the back room where the Boss has called a meeting. The big business man may complain almost as bitterly as the big racketeer about the "extortionate" contributions to the party fund demanded by the Boss. Social opposites meet—in the smoke-filled room of the successful politician.

In the light of a functional analysis all this of course no longer seems paradoxical. Since the machine serves both the businessman and the criminal man, the two seemingly antipodal groups intersect. This points

to a more general theorem: *the social functions of an organization help
determine the structure (including the recruitment of personnel involved in the structure), just as the structure helps determine the effectiveness with which the functions are fulfilled.* In terms of social status,
the business group and the criminal group are indeed poles apart. But
status does not fully determine behavior and the inter-relations between
groups. Functions modify these relations. Given their distinctive needs,
the several subgroups in the large society are "integrated," whatever
their personal desires or intentions, by the centralizing structure which
serves these several needs. In a phrase with many implications which
require further study, *structure affects function and function affects
structure.*

6. A CRITIQUE OF CULTURAL
RELATIVISM *

ROBERT REDFIELD

*In this discussion of the basic theoretical viewpoint known as
"cultural relativity," Robert Redfield does not argue against
the obvious fact that truths may be regarded as relative to
time, place, and a particular culture. But he does assert that
acceptance of relativity does not necessitate rejection of all value
commitments. Redfield's assertion has immense practical
significance because he points to the dangers, as well as to the
logical fallacies, of those who would say, for example, "since
everything is right in terms of its own logic, I cannot condemn
the excesses of totalitarianism." As Redfield shows, science
itself would cease to exist if such an attitude were carried to its
logical extreme.*

In this . . . chapter I will consider some of the questions that arise
when we look at the primitive or the precivilized cultures with a view
to the goodness or the badness of them. . . . My own behavior, as an

* From Robert Redfield, *The Primitive World and Its Transformations* (Ithaca,
N.Y.: Cornell University Press, 1953), pp. 139–164, passim.
     The author (1897–1958) was chairman of the Department of Anthropology
and Distinguished Service Professor at the University of Chicago. His chief interests
lay in ethnological studies. From 1930–1947 he directed ethnological field work in
Yucatan and Guatemala. Among his books are: *The Folk Culture of Yucatan; The
Primitive World and Its Transformations; The Little Community.*

anthropologist, is relevant to the subject now to be discussed, for I am interested here in the way anthropologists do or do not place values on the things they see in prehistoric or in contemporary nonliterate or illiterate societies, and what comes of it if they do. I shall venture to anthropologize the anthropologists, and shall not leave myself out of their number.

. . . Writing of Petalesharoo, the Pawnee Indian who in the face of the customs of his tribe rescued a woman prisoner about to be put to death ceremonially and strove to end human sacrifice among his people, I called him "a hint of human goodness." Plainly I placed a value on his conduct. Looking back twenty-five years, I recall when as a student I first heard the story of Petalesharoo from Professor Fay-Cooper Cole, anthropologist. He told the story with great human warmth, and I know that then I responded sympathetically. Now I begin to wonder if he or I *could* tell the tale barely, neutrally, without implying admiration of the deed.

In the course of these pages, I have not infrequently indicated my admiration for some act, my approval of some turn in human events. The long story of human affairs which I have been sketchily recounting is a story in which I have not pretended to be disinterested. It is the human biography; it is your story and mine; how can we help but care? I have not tried to conceal a certain sense of satisfaction that in the childhood of our race, before there were cities, precivilized men, like the preliterates of today, recognized moral obligations, even if the moral rules were not my rules. I think this better than the unrestrained self-ishness which Hobbes imagined wrongly to characterize the behavior of men before political society developed. So when in the course of these discussions I have encountered in some uncivilized society a custom which I liked or disliked, I think I have in many cases shown how I felt about it. I regret that the Siriono in the Bolivian forest abandon their dying kinsmen without a word, while I come to under-stand the rigors of their life that make such conduct excusable. I am pleased that the Yagua in their big communal houses respect even a child's desire to be alone, and refrain from speaking to him when he turns his face to the wall. . . .

This is, perhaps, a shocking admission. What right have I, who admit to caring about the human career, to speak as an anthropologist? For are not anthropologists enjoined to adopt in their work a rigid objectivity? Professor Kroeber has written that "there is no room in anthropology for a shred of ethnocentricity, of homino-centricity." My ethnocentricity appears in the positive valuations I have placed on the increase and widening of humane standards, for are not such standards a special pride of Euro-American civilization? And my homini-centricity is patent: I have placed myself squarely on the side of mankind, and have not shamed to wish mankind well.

My predicament stimulates an examination of some of the problems of objectivity and value judgment that arise in anthropology. There are a good many of these problems, and I shall try to sort them out and to reach at least the first points of understanding as to what is involved in some of them.

. . . . .

Since Westermarck wrote two books to show that it is not possible to establish one way of thought or action as better than another, if not before that time, anthropologists have taken this position. It has come to have a name: cultural relativism. Most anthropologists would, I think, accept the term as naming their position, or would take the position without perhaps accepting the name. Cultural relativism means that the values expressed in any culture are to be both understood and themselves valued only according to the way the people who carry that culture see things. In looking at a polygamous society and a monogamous society, we have no valid way to assert that the one is better than the other. Both systems provide for human needs; each has values discoverable only when we look at marriage from the point of view of the man who lives under the one system or the other. This is, necessarily then, also to be said in comparing cultures which practice torture, infanticide, in-group sorcery, and homosexuality with those that do not. The gist of cultural relativism as stated by Professor Herskovits, who has discussed the concept at length, is that "judgments are based on experience, and experience is interpreted by each individual in terms of his own enculturation."

With this proposition I do not disagree. I fail to see that having accepted it one finds it necessary to accept everything else that Professor Herskovits says about cultural relativism. . . .

. . . I am persuaded that cultural relativism is in for some difficult times. Anthropologists are likely to find the doctrine a hard one to maintain. The criticisms of philosophers will be directed more sharply against it. Moreover, the experiences of anthropologists are changing, and these changed experiences will work changes in their judgments as to the relativity of values. (It occurs to me that this proposition is itself an application of the principle!) It was easy to look with equal benevolence upon all sorts of value systems so long as the values were those of unimportant little people remote from our own concerns. But the equal benevolence is harder to maintain when one is asked to anthropologize the Nazis, or to help a Point Four administrator decide what to do for those people he is committed to help. The Point Four man is committed to do something to change that people, for he cannot help them without changing them, and what is the anthropologist to say when the Point Four man asks him just what he ought to do? Perhaps the anthropologist can keep on saying: "Do A, and X will result, but

Y will result from doing B—*you* choose which to do." But I doubt that if the anthropologist says only this, he and the administrator will get on very well together. And perhaps the anthropologist, if he continues this neutrality, and yet sees a smash coming, will be just a little restless at night.

At any rate, I should like to point out that the doctrine of cultural relativism does enjoin the benevolence. It is a doctrine of ethical neutralism, but it is not a doctrine of ethical indifference. Ruth Benedict's *Patterns of Culture* is an exemplification of cultural relativism. She wrote in large part to tell us that all cultures are "equally valid." But this meant, for her, not that we are to value none of them, but that we are to value all of them. The book is a call to positive sympathetic valuation of other ways of life than our own. Malinowski has gone so far as to write of "the respect due even to savages." And Herskovits states the positive element in the doctrine very clearly. He is not confused into supposing that cultural relativism is a mere scientific method, a procedure instrumental in reaching statements as to fact. No, he says, "cultural relativism is a *philosophy* which, in recognizing the values set up by every society to guide its own life, lays stress on the dignity inherent in every body of custom, and on the need for tolerance of conventions though they may differ from one's own." And again: "Emphasis on the worth of many ways of life, not one, is an affirmation of the values of each culture."

However, the two parts of this doctrine are not logically or necessarily interdependent. The first part says that people are brought up to see the value in things that their local experience has suggested. The second part says that we should respect all cultures. But there is no true "therefore" between these two parts. It cannot be proved, from the proposition that values are relative, that we ought to respect all systems of values. We might just as well hate them all. . . . It is Professor Herskovits who has intruded upon the objectivity of science a moral judgment, which I personally admire, but for which he can show no demonstration of proof.

The anthropologist is, then, ethically neutral, but unlike him of whom the partisan demanded, "Just who are you neutral for?," the anthropologist is neutral for everybody. This, at least, is the way anthropologists represent their position. It seems to me that their success in living up to their doctrine may be questioned.

The difficulties of doing so were remarked by not a few of the anthropologists themselves when in 1947 the Executive Board of their American professional association submitted a statement to the Commission on Human Rights of the United Nations. The statement urged the Commission to recognize that, not only should the personality of the individual be accorded respect, but that "respect for the cultures of differing human groups is equally important." It declared the principle of cultural relativity and told the UN Commission that therefore any attempt it might make to write something about human rights ("formulate postulates") "that grow out of the beliefs or moral codes of one culture must to that extent detract from the applicability of any declaration of Human Rights to mankind as a whole." So the Commission was advised to incorporate in the Declaration of Human Rights a statement of the right of men to live in terms of their own traditions.

I understand that the UN Commission did not follow this advice. I imagine that some anthropologists are rather relieved that they did not. Such a declaration might seem to authorize the head-hunting peoples to continue head hunting, for would they not, by continuing head hunting, be living in terms of their own traditions? Of course the anthropologists who drafted this statement were not thinking of the head hunters. They knew, as well as you or I, that the head hunters and the cannibals will not be permitted to live in terms of these particular traditions if it is our heads and bodies they go for. They were thinking of the great and influential world civilizations—Indonesian, Indian, Chinese, African, Euro-American. But even here it is not clear just what the writers of the declaration expected to guarantee to these traditional ways of life—the right of a Mississippi human group to maintain its traditional white supremacy, of Russia to maintain a dehumanizing, fear-ridden way of life? At the time the anthropologists wrote their statement it was perhaps nazism that presented to their minds most plainly the difficulties with their statement, for they wrote in the following sentence: "Even where political systems exist that deny citizens the right of participation in their government, or seek to conquer weaker peoples, underlying cultural values may be called on to bring the peoples of such states to a realization of the consequences of the acts of their governments." If we call upon underlying values to save us, it is we, on the outside of the culture, who are making them effective. And what if the underlying approved values are not there? The sentence is, to put it bluntly, a weasel; by including it, the declaration was made self-contradictory. You either respect all values or you do not. If the Nazis had come to have values approving the subjugation of everybody else, we, or the United Nations, would have either to respect this traditional way of life or not respect it. . . .

. . . . .

As soon as the anthropologist puts his attention on the particular human individuals in a primitive society, it becomes difficult to avoid the suggestion if not the fact that he is valuing one culture, or cultural situation, as better than another. It is not uncommon for an anthropologist, now studying a primitive culture disorganized by its contact with civilization, to see that the people he is studying are less comfortable than they were. Some of them, indeed, as those Oceanic natives whom Rivers described, appear now on their way to extinction just because they do not find life worth living any more. The anthropologist can hardly convince us—or himself—that so far as he is concerned a disorganized culture that fails to provide a desire to live is as valid as any other. Equal validity can be safely attributed only to cultures that arrange it so people do what they want to do and are convinced that it is the right thing to do.

But even among such cultures, the well-integrated and the motive-providing, it is not always possible for the anthropologist to avoid at least the suggestion that he is preferring one of them to another. Ruth Benedict was a cultural relativist who told us that cultures are equally valid. Nevertheless, in reading some of her pages, one doubts that she found them equally good. In the seventh chapter of *Patterns of Culture* she introduces the concept of "social waste." Here she leads the reader to see a resemblance between the values of Kwakiutl society and those of his own (Middletown); both emphasize rivalry. But rivalry, wrote Benedict, is "notoriously wasteful. It ranks low in the scale of human values." One asks, Whose scale? Is there a universal scale of values which ranks rivalry low? She goes on to point out not only that "Kwakiutl rivalry produces a waste of material goods," but also that "the social waste is obvious." In Middletown, also, rivalry is "obsessive." Thus she is led to the conclusion that "it is possible to scrutinize different institutions and cast up their cost in terms of social capital, in terms of the less desirable behavior traits they stimulate, and in terms of human suffering and frustration." . . .

　　. . . . .

It is that disturbing fellow, the living human individual, who makes trouble for the scientist's stern principle of perfect objectivity. Whenever the anthropologist looks at him, something human inside the anthropologist stirs and responds. It is easy enough to be objective toward objects; but the human individual refuses to be only an object. When he is there before you, he insists on being judged as human beings are judged in life, if not in science. While the anthropologist is looking at the bones of the dead, at flint implements, or at institutions formally conceived and named—the Omaha kinship system or the tribal ideology —he is not much distracted by these claims upon his own human nature. But when the anthropologist meets and talks with some particular Indian or Oceanic islander, then he is apt to feel for that native while he is trying to describe him objectively. If the society is one that is running along the traditional ways of life, the field ethnologist is apt to respond with sympathy and indeed with favor toward the culture that keeps men's lives going in directions that they find good. If the ethnologist is himself gifted in communicating the human warmth of an exotic scene, as was Malinowski, an account results which communicates not only the humanity of the life described, but something of the enjoyment and satisfactions which the ethnologist himself experienced in coming to know that life. If the culture is one which puts the people who live by it into constant and fearful anxieties, the anthropologist is apt to show the disfavor he feels toward such a life. Reo Fortune's Dobuans are familiar; so I mention here instead the Tzeltal Indians of Chiapas, where Alfonso Villa Rojas found a people often sick, always believing that each sickness was the result of some moral transgression committed by the sufferer or, more terribly, by some one of his near kinsmen, and who are continually ridden by anxiety and compulsions to confess sins. Villa has described this people objectively, in the sense that his report is well documented and obviously trustworthy. But it would be untrue to assert that he has not shown, strongly in conversation and of course much more reservedly in his written description, his own unfavorable view of such a life. Furthermore, if one reads such an account of a people whose traditional ways of life have been disrupted, as, for example, McGregor's account of a reservation community of Sioux Indians, one finds oneself making value judgments that seem to reflect those of the writer, as to the somewhat unhappy predicament in which these people find themselves.

I think that the objectivity claimed by the anthropologist must admit of difficulties and qualifications. Professor Herskovits declares that "a basic necessity of ethnographic research . . . calls for a rigid exclusion of value judgments." This seems a little too strongly put. Rather, I should say, ethnographic research calls for as much objectivity as can be combined with the necessity to come to know the values of the people one is studying. The exception to allow the ethnographer to respect—i.e., value positively—all cultures, has already been noted. Professor R. H. Tawney is then expressing an opinion with which we may suppose that Professor Herskovits would agree when he writes that the student of a society must bring to his study "respect and affection." The necessity to understand the values of the people one is studying requires, I should say, the projection into unfamiliar words and actions of human qualities —sympathy, pride, wish to be appreciated, and so on. Otherwise the ethnologist will not find out what the people he is studying are proud about or what, for them, deserves appreciation. My own opinion is that it is not possible to make use of these human qualities in field work, as I think one must, without also valuing what one sees. In the very necessity to describe the native, one must feel for him—or perhaps against him. The feelings are mixed with valuations. In Indian communities in which I have worked, I have found myself constantly liking and disliking some people as compared with others, some customs as compared with others, and some aspects of the total culture as compared with others. I remember, after having spent a good deal of time in Chan Kom, Yucatan, how I had come to admire a certain quality of decency and dignity about the people, and how bored I had become with their—to me—overemphasis on the prudent and the practical. If they would only once admire a sunset or report a mystic experience, I used to hear myself thinking. I would not know how to find out about a culture without this sort of valuing. Objectivity requires that I hold in suspense each formulation I make about the native life. It requires me to become aware of the values I have that may lead me in one direction rather than another. It demands that I subject my descriptions to the tests of documentation, internal consistency, and if possible the evidence and judgments of other observers. But I do not think that it asks of me that I divest myself of the human qualities, including valuing. I could not do my work without them.

. . . . .

. . . Perhaps we should ask of the field ethnologist, not that he divest himself of values, for that is impossible, nor that he emphasize in every case values predominating in his own times with regard to applied science, increased production, and adjusted personalities, but that he make plain what he does find that is good or bad about the people he reports. And then, also, perhaps he can help to bring it about that he is followed in the same community to be studied by an ethnologist with a contrasting value emphasis! It was the *New Yorker* that suggested that we do not want balanced textbooks; we want balanced libraries. We do not want ethnologists so balanced that they have no humanity. We want a balanced profession, a varied lot of anthropologists.

. . . . .

My praise of Petalesharoo here receives explanation, if not justification. Petalesharoo acted against the customary practice of his people. It is a little easier to do that after civilization than before; in precivilized societies it was harder. So Petalesharoo gets my praise on that count. And when he acted, he acted in conformity with the trend of the human career of which he was ignorant, but which I know about, being some thousands of years older in civilization than was he. So it is not remarkable that I praise him. Perhaps also you, my reader, do too.

If you do, and you are not an anthropologist, no one will scold. But I am an anthropologist, and have taken the oath of objectivity. Somehow the broken pledge—if it is broken—sits lightly on my conscience. In me, man and anthropologist do not separate themselves sharply. I used to think I could bring about that separation in scientific work about humanity. Now I have come to confess that I have not effected it, and indeed to think that it is not possible to do so. All the rules of objectivity I should maintain: the marshaling of evidence that may be confirmed by others, the persistent doubting and testing of all important descriptive formulations that I make, the humility before the facts, and the willingness to confess oneself wrong and begin over. I hope I may always strive to obey these rules. But I think now that what I see men do, and understand as something that human beings do, is seen often with a valuing of it. I like or dislike as I go. This is how I reach understanding of it. The double standard of ethical judgment toward primitive peoples is a part of my version of cultural relativity. It is because I am a product of civilization that I value as I do. It is because I am a product of civilization that I have both a range of experience within which to do my understanding-valuing and the scientific disciplines that help me to describe what I value so that others will accept it, or recognizing it as not near enough the truth, to correct it. And if, in this too I am wrong, those others will correct me here also.

7. THE JUKE MYTH *

SAMUEL HOPKINS ADAMS

In this amusing account, Samuel Hopkins Adams illustrates the importance, to science in general and to social science in particular, of carefully gathered data. Fortunately for the valid development of sociology, our standards of data collection and interpretation today have changed radically from those which prevailed during the time when the Juke study was considered sound research. Another important change that occurred has been in our basic theory of human behavior. Early in this century, as the popularity of the Juke study illustrates, most people were convinced that the behavior of humans is largely inborn. Now, as the following selection and as the selections in Chapter II suggest, the great majority of professional students of human behavior are agreed that the most important factors in human action are learned.

* "The Juke Myth," by Samuel Hopkins Adams. First published in the *Saturday Review*, Vol. 38, No. 14 (April 2, 1955), 13, 48–49. Copyright, 1955, by Saturday Review, Inc.

The author (1871–1958) was a distinguished essayist. Formerly staff member of *McClure's Magazine*. Wrote numerous articles and short stories for leading magazines. Among his works: *The Santa Fe Trail; Erie Canal;* and *Grandfather Stories.*

No other family in American annals is so well and unfavorably known as the Jukes. The name is a synonym for depravity. What the Rothschilds embody in finance the Jukes represent in misdemeanor. If there were an International Hall of Ill Fame they would get top billing.

And they never existed otherwhere than in the brain of an amateur criminologist. Richard L. Dugdale did not precisely invent them; rather, he compiled them from an assortment of human derelicts whom he collected after a method peculiarly his own, for the purpose of bolstering his theory of criminal heredity. He passed on his findings to posterity in his *magnum opus*, "The Jukes: A Study in Crime, Pauperism, Disease, and Insanity."

This classic has permeated the sociology of nations. Geneticists like Giddings, East, and Walter have swallowed it whole. The New York State Prison Association sponsored it. Putnam's brought out three large editions, which were accepted as sociological gospel. Dugdale became the recognized authority on crime. His qualifications as an expert are peculiar. When the Dugdale family came to this country from England in 1851 Richard was ten years old. It was intended that he should go to college. After three years of schooling in New York something went awry in his education. He left school and became assistant to a sculptor. In the evenings he attended classes at Cooper Union, where he won something of a reputation as a debater on social topics.

His career, if such it were, was interrupted by the departure of the family to try farming in the Middle-west. The venture was unsuccessful. The Dugdales returned to New York and Richard turned his hand to manufacturing. He was then twenty-three. The business failed. Richard had a nervous breakdown and withdrew from active endeavor. "For four years I could neither earn nor learn," he records. Such was his technical equipment as a sociologist.

The Jukes came into his life quite by chance. He happened to be in a Kingston, N.Y., police court in 1873, where a youth was on trial for receiving stolen goods. Five relatives were present as witnesses. They came of a breed, to quote the incipient investigator, "so despised that their family name had come to be used generically as a term of reproach." They were alleged to live like haggards of the rock, in the caves of a nearby lake region. "Crime-cradles," our author calls the locality. He was a neat hand at a phrase.

He invented the name Juke for the clan.

The fact that the Juke at the bar of justice was acquitted in no wise discouraged young Dugdale. He made inquiries about the others present. An uncle of the accused is set down as a burglar. No proof is adduced. Two male cousins had been charged with pushing a boy over a cliff, one of whom was convicted. The remaining witnesses, two girls, he lists as harlots. By the Dugdale method "under the heading of harlots are included all women who have made lapses, however seldom." This is fairly indicative of his standards of investigation and attribution.

With this auspicious start he canvassed the neighborhood for further specimens.

With comparatively little inquiry [he writes], it was found that out of twenty-nine male adults, the immediate blood relations of the six, seventeen were criminals and fifteen others convicted of some degree of offense.

Impressed by this suggestive ratio—as who would not be by thirty-two out of a possible twenty-nine?—Dugdale went sleuthing back through the generations until he came upon an old Dutch reprobate who kept a turnpike hostelry in Orange County about the middle of the eighteenth century. Old Max appears to have been a sporting character. Several illegitimate children were imputed to him. He enjoyed a local reputation for drinking, gaming, and wenching, divertissements fairly general in those lusty pioneer days. He became Exhibit A in the Dugdale rogues' gallery, though nothing criminal appears in his record.

Max had two legitimate sons who married into a family of six sisters. With the discovery of the sisterhood Dugdale really hits his stride. The family line of the six is obscure; it "has not been absolutely ascertained," he admits. "One, if not all, of them were illegitimate," he surmises, on what grounds he does not explain. Delia is recorded as a "harlot before marriage," and Bell as a "harlot after marriage." Clara, he notes (presumptively with reluctance), was "reputed chaste." She did, however, marry a man who shot a neighbor. Effie's reputation was unknown to author Dugdale, which was certainly a break for Effie.

Another sister *circa* 1760 is Dugdale's prize specimen. "Margaret, Mother of Criminals," he calls her, although her name was Ada. Apt alliteration's artful aid again! To her goes the credit for "the distinctly criminal line of the family." But, what family? For all that he reveals Margaret-Ada, of unascertained parentage, may have been a Van Rensselaer, a Livingston, a Saltonstall, a Biddle, or the granddaughter of the original Joe Doakes. To be sure, he later characterizes the whole lot as "belonging to the Juke blood." Pure assumption. As their derivation was unknown and they were suspectedly illegitimate anyway, how could Dugdale or anybody else know anything of their ancestry?

As a "Mother of Criminals" Margaret (or Ada) hardly lives up to her name. Her daughter is designated as a harlot, but, by way of palliation perhaps, our author adds, "not industrious." One son was a laborer, "somewhat industrious." The other, a farmer, is stigmatized as having been "indolent" and "licentious in youth." The same might be said of some eminent non-Jukes, including Robert Burns and the Apostle Paul.

Margaret-Ada was married to one of old Max's sons. She had a son of her own, whom Dugdale holds to be co-responsible for the evil

Juke inheritance. But this son was a Juke only in name. He was illegitimate. Dugdale says so.

Thus, the notorious criminal-Juke strain derives on one side from a progenitor who was not criminal (Old Max) and on the other from a line which was not Juke except by Dugdale fiat. (Margaret-Ada through her illegitimate son.)

It sufficed Dugdale. He had his theory; now he set out after supporting facts. He made a year's tour of prisons, almshouses, and asylums, collecting Jukes. The result he published in 1875. It is still regarded by those who have not read it, and even by some who have, as an authoritative document. It established the Jukes as the type-family of degeneration.

Dugdale invented a terminology to go with his Jukes. His thesis is based, so he states, upon "Positive Statistics and Conjectural Statistics . . . Conjectural Statistics consists in Political Arithmetic and the Theory of Probabilities." This recondite process "reduces the method of study to one of historico-biographical synthesis united to statistical analysis," which sounds as if it might have come out of Lewis Carroll.

Applying this yardstick, Dugdale lists 709 alleged Jukes of whom 507 were social detrimentals. Such conventional crimes as murder, arson, rape, and robbery, quite lacking in proof for the most part, are cited. But there were not enough of them to support satisfactorily the Dugdale political arithmetic and theory of probabilities. So he fattens up the record with entries like the following:

Reputed sheep-stealer, but never caught.
Thief, but never caught.
Petty thief, though never convicted.
Guilty of murder, but escapes punishment.
Unpunished and cautious thief.
Bastardy prosecution.
Supposed to have attempted rape.
Cruelty to animals.
Habitual criminal.
Impossible to get any reliable information, but it is evident that at nineteen he was a leader in crime.

And such scattered attributions as "pauper," "harlot," "brothelkeeper," "vagrant," "lazy," "intemperate," "drunkard," "immoral," "lecherous," etc., etc., etc. There was also a "contriver of crime," and a hardened character who, in addition to frequenting a saloon, was accused of breaking a deaf man's ear-trumpet. Like the Juke who started it all, he was acquitted. It did not matter to our investigator; the non-breaker of the ear-trumpet comes down the ages, embalmed in criminal history.

All this might seem rather attenuated evidence on which to indict an entire family. It sufficed Dugdale. He followed the long and proliferating branches of the clan through the generations and worked out a diagram as framework for the composite portrait. This he calls "Leading Facts."

Consanguinity

C	Prostitution	F O R N I C A T I O N	Illegitimacy	P A U P E R I S M
R				
I	Exhaustion		Intemperance	
M				
E	Disease		Extinction	

Not Consanguineous

In other words, *fornication* [the italics are his], either consanguineous or not, is the backbone of their habits, flanked on the one side by *pauperism*, on the other by *crime*. The secondary features are *prostitution*, with its complement of *bastardy*, and its resultant of miseducated childhood; *exhaustion*, with its complement, *intemperance*, and its resultant, unbalanced minds; and *disease*, with its complement, *extinction*.

Dugdale's investigations into hygiene and morality are on a par with his criminological efforts. Insanity, epilepsy, deformity, impotency, and tuberculosis appear to have been as typical Juke phenomena as thievery, bastardy, and general lawlessness. Some of the evidence cited is calculated to astonish students of heredity. For example, it is recorded that the original Max went blind and transmitted the affliction to his posterity. As he lost his sight late in life, after his children were born, it is difficult to see how he can be held responsible for their blindness unless he poked them in the eye with a burnt stick.

Our author's figures on tuberculosis are confident, but where he found them is left a mystery. Nobody bothered to keep statistics in those days. Still more difficult would it have been to gather reliable data on venereal disease. Yet our conjectural statistician specifies, in one branch of the Jukes, forty harlots who contaminated 440 men, presumably eleven per harlot. In another genealogical line he states that 23½ per cent of the females were immoral. That ½ per cent is fairly awe-inspiring.

Not until long after the author's death did anyone rise to challenge his thesis. The late Thomas Mott Osborne, of prison-reform fame and at one time president of that same prison association which certified the Dugdale revelations, studied the Juke records with growing skepticism. Himself a practised investigator, he raised questions about the Dugdale methods which that author might have found awkward to answer.

Whence, Mr. Osborne wished to know, did Dugdale derive those cocksure figures on disease, insanity, and death? Vital statistics at the time of his inquiry were practically non-existent. How did he acquire his data on criminality when court records for the period were notoriously unreliable, if, indeed, they were available at all? What genealogical method did he use in tracing back the Juke line through the mazes of its prevalent bastardy, for a century and a quarter? Legitimate family lines, Mr. Osborne pointed out, were difficult enough to trace; illegitimate were flatly impossible, beyond a generation or two. Further, the objector indicated, a specially trained sociological investigator would have required at least three years to do the work which Dugdale completed in one.

Analyzing the indicated method of investigation, Mr. Osborne suggested that Dugdale based it on a formula of retroactive hypothesis as follows:

That every criminal was a putative Juke.

That every Juke was a presumptive criminal.

By the system which Dugdale employed in tracing down his Jukes, Mr. Osborne concluded, it would be possible to asperse the morality, sanity, and legitimacy of any family in America. As for the Jukes, they were "pure folklore."

Another dissident raised objections in *The Clinical Review* for April 1902. Was it credible, Edmund Andrews asked, that Old Max possessed "such a miraculous energy of vicious propagation that, by his sole vital force, he begat and transmitted the degeneracy of all the Jukes for five generations?" Each descendant in the fifth generation, the critic pointed out, had fifteen other progenitors. Why assign his or her lawless, shiftless, or bawdy habits to Max any more than to any other of the uncharted Jukes or Jakes or Jeeks or Jenkins? A sturdy breeder like Max might well be the ancestor of a couple of thousand great-great-grandchildren, 1,500 of whom, for all that Dugdale knew to the contrary, might have been missionaries.

"It is sheer nonsense," Mr. Andrews contends "to suppose that he (a fifth-generation Juke degenerate) got them all (his vicious proclivities) from that one lazy, but jovial old Rip Van Winkle, the original Juke."

These were but voices crying in a wilderness. To scotch a good, sturdy historical fake, once it has got its growth, is impossible. Nine-tenths of America devoutly believes that Robert Fulton invented the steamboat and that Abner Doubleday was the founder of baseball. So the Jukes will doubtless continue to furnish texts to trusting sociologists, and no great harm done.

But they are in the wrong category. The proper place of a Juke is not in criminology. It is in mythology.

8. A WITNESS AT THE SCOPES TRIAL *

FAY-COOPER COLE

One of the basic ideas learned by serious students of science is that facts never speak for themselves. They "speak" in terms of theoretical assumptions. That is, an individual looks at facts and interprets them in accordance with his basic beliefs. If, for example, one assumes the earth is flat, then data which suggest that the world has a spherical shape may be discounted as optical illusions. Action would also be affected; sailors who believed the world was flat hesitated to sail far from land. Similarly, if one's theory about man is that he was created, full-blown, as he exists today— a theory that was widely accepted for centuries—then one will hardly be motivated to search for data throwing light on the development of man and his ideas through the ages. This is the significance of the Scopes trial discussed by Fay-Cooper Cole. It represented a final and dramatic public test of the long-standing belief about the nature of man. By 1925 at the latest, almost all respected scientists and other learned people had accepted the theory that man and his works were products of evolutionary forces that extended back countless thousands of years. This theory has had a profound effect upon teaching and research in social science and religion. It should be noted, however, that the theory does not and cannot say anything about man's ultimate beginnings and that therefore even traditional religious believers can be, and often are, evolutionists.

"This is Clarence Darrow," said the voice at the other end of the wire, "I suppose you have been reading the papers, so you know Bryan and his outfit are prosecuting that young fellow Scopes. Well, Malone,

* From *Scientific American*, Vol. 200, No. 1 (January, 1959), 121–130.

The author (b. 1881) is Professor Emeritus and past chairman, the Department of Anthropology, University of Chicago. He has done archeological work in the United States and abroad. His chief interest is ethnological research. His books include: *Peoples of Malaysia; Kincaid—A Prehistoric Illinois Metropolis; The Bukidnon of Mindanao.*

Colby and I have put ourselves in a mess by offering to defend. We don't know much about evolution. We don't know whom to call as witnesses. But we do know we are fighting your battle for academic freedom. We need the help of you fellows at the University, so I am asking three of you to come to my office to help lay plans."

That afternoon in Darrow's office three of us from the University of Chicago—Horatio Hackett Newman, professor of biology; Shailer Mathews, dean of the Divinity School; and I—met to outline the strategy for what turned out to be one of the most publicized trials of the century. The Scopes trial proved also to be a historic occasion in the cause of popular understanding of science. A century ago the educated world was shaken by the discoveries of Charles Darwin and Alfred Russel Wallace, and the evidence they presented for the evolution of life on this planet. In 1959, as we celebrate the centenary of the *Origin of Species*, few informed persons, if any, question the theory of evolution. However, the century has witnessed several attempts to stifle investigation and outlaw the teaching of the theory. The best known of these was the Scopes trial, held in Dayton, Tenn., in 1925. The trial resulted in an immense revival of public interest in Darwin and in evolution; there has been no comparable effort since then to suppress this advance in man's understanding of himself and the world he lives in.

To understand the trial and what lay back of it, one must recall the climate of the 1920s. It was a time of uncertainty, unrest and repression. We had just emerged from a world war. Old standards were badly shaken; the young were labeled "the lost generation"; intolerance was rampant. The Ku Klux Klan was on the march, not only in the South but in the North as well. In many towns in Illinois, Indiana and other parts of the Midwest, staid business men—even members of the clergy —put on "white nighties" and burned fiery crosses to put the Negro, the Jew, the Catholic and the immigrant "in their places." The Fundamentalists, under the leadership of William Jennings Bryan, had organized in some 20 states and were putting pressure on all institutions of learning to curb the teaching of science, particularly evolution, which they considered in contradiction to the Bible. Prohibitive bills had been passed in Tennessee and Mississippi and were pending in six other states.

Then came the great opportunity. In the little town of Dayton the high-school science teacher and football coach, 24-year-old John Thomas Scopes, found himself engaged in a discussion of the new law with George W. Rappelyea, a young mining engineer and superintendent of the local coal mines. Scopes expressed bewilderment that the state should supply him with a textbook that presented the theory of evolution, yet make him a lawbreaker if he taught the theory. Rappelyea agreed that it was a crazy law and clearly unconstitutional. Then suddenly he asked: "Why don't I have you arrested for teaching evolution from that text and bring the whole thing to an end?" Scopes replied: "Fair enough."

Scopes was duly arrested. But neither of the principals had any idea of what they were starting. Within a few hours the Chattanooga papers carried the story. Soon it was spread across the nation. The Fundamentalists were quick to realize the opportunity to dramatize their battle against evolution. Bryan and his associates offered their services to the Prosecution. They were accepted. Here was big news.

At this point, it happened, three lawyers met in New York City for a conference on some business matters. They were Clarence Darrow, controversialist and defender of unpopular causes; Bainbridge Colby, an eminent corporation lawyer and, like Bryan, a former Secretary of State; and Dudley Field Malone, a leading Catholic layman and a fashionable barrister. Their conversation turned to the Tennessee situation. One said: "It is a shame. That poor teacher, who probably doesn't know what it is all about, is to be sacrificed by the Fundamentalists." Another said: "Someone ought to do something about it." The third replied: "Why don't we?" Through the American Civil Liberties Union they offered to defend young Scopes. Their offer was accepted.

This was real news! Bryan, three times candidate for the presidency of the U.S., the great Fundamentalist leader and orator, on one side. On the other, three of the nation's most famous lawyers, including Darrow, master jury-pleader. The papers were full of the story.

This was the background of Darrow's call to me and of our meeting at his office in Chicago early in the summer of 1925. By telephone, wire and letter we proceeded to assemble a panel of expert witnesses: scientists to testify on the theory of evolution and theologians to give evidence on the history and interpretation of the Bible. In addition to Newman, Mathews and myself, our panel finally included Kirtley Mather, professor of geology at Harvard; Jacob G. Lipman, director of the New Jersey Agricultural Experiment Station at Rutgers University; W. C. Curtis, professor of zoology at the University of Missouri; Wilbur Nelson, state geologist of Tennessee; Maynard Metcalf, professor of zoology at Johns Hopkins University; Charles Judd, head of the University of Chicago School of Education; and Rabbi Herman Rosenwasser of San Francisco, a noted Hebrew scholar. All of us, along with our counsel, undertook to go to Dayton at our own expense and to serve without fee.

The trial was scheduled for Friday, July 10. But long before that date the town was crowded with newspapermen, Fundamentalist supporters and others who were just curious. No one was willing to house "the heretics," that is, the scientific witnesses and defense attorneys. So an old "haunted house" on a hill overlooking the town was fitted out as a dormitory.

When I reached town, I took care not to associate myself at once with the Defense group, and was able to wander about for a time listening to the talk of the local people. For the most part they were extremely partisan to the Fundamentalist cause. But they were apprehensive of the famous Darrow, and they were not yet aware of his plan to present expert testimony on evolution and the scriptures.

That evening I joined the group at the "haunted house" and there met young Scopes for the first time. He was a fine, clean-cut young man, a little shy and apparently overwhelmed by the controversy he had stirred up. He expressed amazement that famous lawyers like Darrow, Colby, Malone and Arthur Garfield Hays (counsel to the American Civil Liberties Union) should come to his defense, and that a group of well-known scientists should join them.

Little happened on the first day of the trial beyond the selection of the jury. A panel was offered, and Darrow accepted it without change after a casual examination. But he did bring out the fact that 11 jurors were Fundamentalist church members. All admitted that they knew little about science or evolution. One said that the only Darwin he had ever heard about ran a local notion store. One could not read or write.

The events of Sunday provided us with an interesting insight into the local climate of opinion. Charles Francis Potter, a liberal Unitarian minister and writer who had been invited to conduct services at the Methodist-Episcopal church, was barred from the pulpit by the parishioners. Meanwhile Bryan addressed an overflow house at the Southern Methodist church. That afternoon, in an open courtyard in the center of town, Bryan talked to an immense audience. He said he welcomed the opportunity to bring "this slimy thing, evolution, out of the darkness. . . . Now the facts of religion and evolution would meet at last in a duel to the death." It was a fine example of Bryan's oratory, and it swept the crowd.

The court opened on Monday with a prayer in which a local clergyman urged God to preserve his sacred word against attack. It was a scarcely veiled plea to the jury.

The Defense filed a motion to quash the indictment on the ground that the act violated the Constitution of the State of Tennessee and Section 1 of the Fourteenth Amendment of the Constitution of the United States, which extends the Bill of Rights to limit action by the governments of the states. The Defense argued further that the indictment was contrary to a U.S. Supreme Court decision which says: "The law knows no heresy, and is committed to the support of no dogma, nor to the establishment of any sect." In support of this attack on the indictment, the Defense declared that it wished to offer the testimony of scientists and biblical scholars. These expert witnesses, the Defense contended, would show that there was no necessary conflict between evolution and Christianity.

Though the Defense asked that judgment on its motion to dismiss should be reserved until its witnesses had been heard, Judge John T. Raulston ordered the argument to proceed. On motion of the Prosecution, he sent the jury from the courtroom. Apparently the introduction of scientific witnesses had taken Bryan and his associates by surprise. Their ultimate response to our efforts to argue the underlying issues of the case was to lose them the trial in the minds of the American people.

That afternoon Darrow pressed for dismissal with an eloquent attack on ignorance and bigotry. Coatless in the sweltering courtroom, tugging at his suspenders, he paced up and down, firing shot after shot at the Prosecution. He stressed the danger to freedom of press, church and school if men like Bryan could impose their opinions and interpretations on the law of the land. "The fires of bigotry and hate are being lighted," he said. "This is as bold an attempt to destroy learning as was ever made in the Middle Ages. . . . The statute says you cannot teach anything in conflict with the Bible." He argued that in the U.S. there are over 500 churches and sects which differ over certain passages in the Bible. If the law were to prevail, Scopes would have to be familiar with the whole Bible and all its interpretations; among all the warring sects, he would have to know which one was right in order not to commit a crime.

Darrow said: "Your Honor, my client is here because ignorance and bigotry are rampant, and that is a mighty strong combination. . . . If today you can make teaching of evolution in the public schools a crime, tomorrow you can make it a crime to teach it in the private schools. At the next session of the Legislature you can ban books and newspapers. You can set Catholic against Protestant, and Protestant against Protestant, when you try to foist your own religion upon the minds of men. If you can do the one, you can do the other. After a while, Your Honor, we will find ourselves marching backward to the glorious days of the 16th century when bigots lighted the fagots to burn men who dared to bring any intelligence and enlightenment to the human mind."

The speech made a profound impression. Townspeople agreed that anything might happen with that man Darrow around. Judge Raulston adjourned court until Wednesday in order that he might consider the motion to quash.

That night, as we gathered in our haunted house for a conference, a terrific storm swept the town. When a brilliant flash of lightning struck nearby, Darrow said: "Boys, if lightning strikes this house tonight . . . !"

Tuesday was a quiet day. At Rappelyea's office, where he had been invited to take advantage of the secretarial facilities, Potter found that the stenographer would not take dictation from any Unitarian minister. Rappelyea himself was arrested three times for speeding in the course of his service to us as guide and chauffeur. We were besieged by Holy Rollers, who came in from the hills to convert us. We also had to protect ourselves from a supporter. H. L. Mencken had come to town. His vitriolic articles so antagonized the people we wanted most to reach that we had to persuade him to leave the scene.

After the jury was sworn in on Wednesday, the Court ruled against the Defense motion to quash the indictment. The law, said Judge Raulston, did not deprive anyone of speech, thought or opinion, for no one need accept employment in Tennessee. He ruled the law constitutional, saying that the public has the right to say, by legislative act or referendum, whether Latin, chemistry or astronomy might be taught in its schools.

The Prosecution then called the county superintendent of schools, the heads of the school board and seven students. All testified to what Scopes had taught. Darrow limited his cross-examination to establishing simply that the State had furnished the textbook. After offering the King James version of the Bible as an exhibit, the Prosecution rested.

The first witness for the defense was Maynard Metcalf. A recognized scientist, he was also an eminent Congregational layman and teacher of one of the largest Bible classes in the country. Darrow established his competence as a witness, then asked a question on evolution. The Prosecution at once challenged the testimony as irrelevant; according to them the only question was: Did Scopes violate the law?

The judge agreed to hear arguments on this point the next day. Meanwhile he excused the jury, with instructions not to enter the courtroom or to remain within hearing of the loudspeakers. A lot of angry jurors filed out. They had not only lost their reserved seats, but also were barred from the proceedings entirely.

The trial reached its high point on Thursday. After an impassioned plea by the State's Attorney against the admission of expert testimony, Bryan took over for the Prosecution. Instead of making good on his challenge of "a duel to the death," he argued against the presentation of scientific evidence. He said that the jury did not need the help of scientists or Bible experts to decide the facts and to interpret the law: "The law is what the people decided." He then presented an enlargement of the picture of the evolutionary tree from the textbook Scopes had used; it showed man in a circle with other mammals. Bryan shouted: "Talk about putting Daniel in the lions' den. How dare these scientists put man in a little ring with lions and tigers and everything that smells of the jungle. . . . One does not need to be an expert to know what the Bible says. . . . Expert testimony is not needed!"

With that speech Bryan lost the argument with the press and with the radio audience. When Malone had finished his reply, Bryan had also lost the argument, for a time, with most of his Dayton followers.

Malone was a Patrick Henry that day. He asked whether our children are to know nothing of science beyond that permitted by certain sects. "I have never seen greater need for learning," he declared, "than is exhibited by the Prosecution, which refuses information offered by expert witnesses. . . . Why this fear of meeting the issue? Mr. Bryan has said this is to be a duel to the death. I know little about dueling, Your Honor, but does it mean that our only weapon, the witnesses, is to be taken away while the Prosecution alone carries the sword? This is not my idea of a duel. . . . We do not fear all the truth they can present as facts. We are ready. We stand with progress. We stand with science. We stand with intelligence. We feel that we stand with the fundamental freedoms in America. We are not afraid. Where is the fear? We defy it." Then, turning toward Bryan and pointing his finger, he cried: "There is the fear!"

The crowd went out of control—cheering, stamping, pounding on desks—until it was necessary to adjourn court for 15 minutes to restore order.

I was sitting next to the aisle. Beside me was a Chattanooga policeman, one of the squad brought in to protect us from the Ku Klux Klan. As Malone finished, my guard beat the desk in front of me so hard with his club that a corner of the desk broke off. His chief came up and asked: "Why didn't you cheer when Malone made that speech?" My guard replied: "Hell. What did you think I was doing? Rapping for order?"

We had won for the day. Even the hostile crowd was with us.

That night Darrow said: "Today we have won, but by tomorrow the judge will have recovered and will rule against us. I want each one of you to go to the stenographer's room the first thing in the morning and prepare a statement for the press, saying what you would have said if allowed to testify in court."

As we were preparing our statements next morning, Judge Raulston looked in. I was nearest to the door. He asked what we were doing. When I told him, he asked the others in turn. Then he went to Darrow and told him he must not release the testimony: "It might reach the jury." Darrow replied: "Your Honor, you can do what you please with that jury. You can lock it up, but you cannot lock up the American people. The testimony will be released."

When court resumed, the judge ruled against us on all points. Rising and pushing his long hair from his forehead, Darrow spoke slowly and clearly. "The outcome is plain. We expect to protect our rights in some other court. Is that plain?" The judge replied: "I hope, Colonel Darrow, you don't attempt to reflect upon the Court." To which Darrow drawled: "Your Honor has the right to hope." The insult was deliberate. For an instant there was complete silence; then the judge mumbled that he had the right to do something else. A moment later he adjourned court until Monday.

Public reaction to the ruling was emphatic, and Bryan's prestige was shaken. Townspeople admitted to me, one of the "heretics," that they could not understand why Bryan had backed down. They asked: "What can you do now, if you can't talk?"

On Monday Darrow apologized to the Court, momentarily relieving the tension. Then, in order to secure the foundation for appeal, Hays read into the record the prepared statements of the scientific and other scholarly witnesses, and concluded by placing in evidence three versions of the Bible that differed from one another and from the King James version submitted by the Prosecution. Suddenly Hays electrified the crowd with the announcement that the Defense wished to call Bryan to the stand "as a biblical witness."

Darrow submitted Bryan to grueling examination. In reply to Darrow's questions Bryan stated that he accepted the Bible literally as God's revealed word. What he didn't understand he accepted on simple faith. He believed that Eve was the first woman, created from Adam's rib; that God had sent childbirth pains to all women because of her transgression; that the snake must crawl on its belly because it tempted Eve; that everything outside the Ark, except fish, perished in the flood; that all existing animals had descended from the pairs saved by Noah; that all men spoke one language until the Tower of Babel; and that present languages had developed since then. Only once did he falter, when he admitted that the seven days of creation might mean seven epochs. He conceded that he was not familiar with the work of archaeologists, who had uncovered civilizations more than 5,000 years old, but he declared that he had never had much interest in those scientists who disputed the Bible. Repeatedly the State's Attorney tried to stop the questioning, but always Bryan replied: "No. Let it go on. I am not afraid to defend my religion."

Finally Malone intervened, saying he would have asked the same questions, but only to challenge Bryan's literal interpretation of the King James version. As a churchman and a Christian, however, he objected to any effort by counsel for the State to pin Darrow's views of religion on the defense. "I don't want this case to be changed by Mr. Darrow's agnosticism or Mr. Bryan's brand of religion." Malone further observed that this was supposed to be a trial by jury, yet the jury had not been permitted in the court for more than 15 minutes since being sworn in.

On Tuesday Judge Raulston struck the examination of Bryan from the record. The only question remaining, he said, was: What did Scopes teach? To this ruling Darrow replied: "Your Honor, we are wasting time. You should call the jury and instruct it to bring in a verdict of guilty." The Court did so, and Scopes was fined $100.

Scopes had come on to graduate study in geology at the University of Chicago when the Tennessee Supreme Court heard Darrow's appeal and at last handed down its decision in January, 1927. The court narrowly affirmed the anti-evolution statute, but threw out the $100 fine on a technicality. It brought an end to the formal proceedings by advising the State to desist from further prosecution: "We see nothing to be gained by prolonging the life of this bizarre case."

The Defense was also content to accept the Court's advice. No attempt at repression has ever backfired so impressively. Where one person had been interested in evolution before the trial, scores were reading and inquiring at its close. Within a year the prohibitive bills which had been pending in other states were dropped or killed. Tennessee had been made to appear so ridiculous in the eyes of the nation that other states did not care to follow its lead.

At the University of Chicago I had been teaching modest-sized classes. When the University resumed in the autumn my lecture hall was filled. Students were standing along the walls and sitting in the windows. I thought I was in the wrong room. When I asked a boy at the door what class was meeting, he replied: "Anthropology. The prof who teaches it defended that fellow Scopes." From that time on Introductory Anthropology had to be limited to lecture-hall capacity. My mail, mostly hostile, increased until the University gave up trying to put it in my box, but tied it in bundles and sent it to my office.

Some time after the trial I was summoned to the office of Frederick Woodward, acting president of the University. He handed me a long document, a series of resolutions from a Southern Baptist conference. They took the University to task for the part members of its faculty had taken in the trial, taking note of the University's strong Baptist origins. They voiced objections to Professors Judd, Newman and Mathews, but reserved the real condemnation for me—the witness on human evolution. I was "a snake in the grass corrupting the youth of a nation," and so on, concluding with "and we have been investigating Professor Cole still further, and we find that he is not even a Baptist."

I began to laugh, but the president said: "This is no laughing matter. You are a rather new man here, but already we have more demands for your removal than any other man who has been on our faculty.

These resolutions are typical and were considered of such importance that they were read yesterday at the meeting of the Board of Trustees." "Yes," I replied. "And what did they do?" He reached across his desk and handed me a piece of paper. They had raised my salary.

CHAPTER II

ENVIRONMENTAL FACTORS

9. HOW DIFFERENCES IN ENVIRONMENT AFFECTED SEPARATED ONE-EGG TWINS *

HORATIO H. NEWMAN

A long-standing controversy in American social science concerns the relative importance of heredity and environment in the development of human personality: To what extent is human behavior the result of biological inheritance? How do culture, social experience, or learning influence behavior? One way to answer questions of this type is to study the adult personalities of identical twins who were separated early in life. Since such one-egg twins have the same genetic origin, differences that are found in later life presumably result from differences in education, family relationships, and other social experiences. Although this study is based on the relatively few available cases, its findings provide fundamental understanding of the influence of the sociocultural environment on human behavior.

In each of the twenty cases of separated one-egg twins every effort was made to reconstruct the life experiences of the twins and to discover any differences in environment or experience that might have tended to

* From Horatio H. Newman, *Multiple Human Births* (Doubleday and Co., 1940), pp. 189–199. Copyright 1940 by H. H. Newman, reprinted by permission of the author and Doubleday and Co., Inc.

The author (b. 1875) is Professor Emeritus of Zoology at the University of Chicago. He has done extensive research in genetics, embryology, and marine life. Among his books are: *The Physiology of Twinning; Evolution Yesterday and Today; The Phylum Chordata.* Editor and contributor, *The Nature of the World and of Man.*

produce differences in ability, personality or physical condition. We roughly subdivided environment into three categories: educational, social and physical-health.

It was found that whenever the educational experiences of a pair of twins differed to a marked extent the twin with the greater amount of education had a distinctly higher score on all ability and scholastic achievement tests, while in those cases where there was no difference in education, or only a small difference, the scores of the twins of a pair tended to be about as similar as the average of one-egg twins reared together. A few examples of this close correlation between differences in education and those in mental ability will make this important point clear.

THE EFFECTS OF DIFFERENCES IN EDUCATION

In the case of twins *Gladys* and *Helen,* Gladys stopped school after the third grade, while Helen went on through college and became a teacher. There was a difference of about thirteen years of formal schooling in favor of Helen. In the Stanford-Binet Test Helen's I.Q. was one hundred and sixteen (high normal) and Gladys' was ninety-two (low normal), a large difference of twenty-four points. On the Otis S.A.[1] Test Helen had an I.Q. of one hundred and six, Gladys ninety-four, a difference of twelve points. On the International Test Helen scored one hundred and eighty-eight points, Gladys one hundred and forty-three, a difference of forty-five points. On the Stanford Achievement Test Helen had a mental age of eighteen years ten months, Gladys a mental age of thirteen years and one month, a difference of sixty-nine months. It seems certain that in the case of Gladys the great deficiency in education had inhibited the development of the rather high grade of mental ability with which she was endowed by heredity and which was well developed in her twin sister.

In the second case, that of twins *James* and *Reece,* the differences in both education and ability were less striking but quite noteworthy. James completed grade and high school in a town of about two thousand inhabitants, while Reece attended a rural grade school in the mountains which was open only during five months in the year. He attended only when he felt like it and stopped at the eighth grade. On the Stanford-Binet Test James's I.Q. was ninety-six (almost up to average), while Reece's I.Q. was only seventy-seven (commonly regarded as bordering on the "dull and backward" classification), a difference of nineteen points. On the Otis S.A. Test James's I.Q. was one hundred and four (above average) and Reece's was eighty-four, a difference of twenty points. On the International Test James scored one hundred and twenty-

[1] Scholastic Achievement.

four points, Reece eighty-nine, a difference of thirty-five points. On the Stanford Achievement Test James had a mental age of sixteen years, Reece thirteen years, one month, a difference of thirty-five months.

In the third case, that of twins *Eleanore* and *Georgiana,* Eleanore stopped school at the end of the fifth grade, while Georgiana finished grade school and high school and then had three years at normal school, a difference in favor of Georgiana of ten years of schooling. In this case, though both girls were quite efficient as office assistants, their mental rating was considerably below the average. Nevertheless, Georgiana was consistently superior to Eleanore. Georgiana's I.Q. on the Stanford-Binet was seventy-eight, Eleanore's was only sixty-six, a difference of twelve points, but in a part of the scale where a few points are rather significant. On the Otis S.A. Test Georgiana's I.Q. was eighty-four and Eleanore's sixty-nine, a difference of fifteen points. On the International Test Georgiana scored ninety-eight points, Eleanore sixty-nine, a difference of twenty-nine points. On the Stanford Achievement Test Georgiana's mental age was fourteen years, one month, Eleanore's ten years, eleven months, a difference of twenty-eight months. This case shows that with a good education a poorly endowed person can improve his ability to a moderate degree but cannot reach the level of a potentially able but poorly educated person such as the twin Gladys of our first case. Some comment might be made here as to the minimal endowment necessary for successfully completing a course in some normal schools and qualifying as a teacher.

The fourth and last case where there was a considerable difference in education is that of twins *Mabel* and *Mary.* Mary was educated through grade school and three years of high school in a medium-sized city and finished her last year in the high school of a large city. Mabel finished the eighth grade in a small country school near her farm home. As is usually the case in country schools, the terms were short. The difference in years of education was actually about five. On the Stanford-Binet Test Mary had an I.Q. of one hundred and six, Mabel of eighty-nine, a difference of seventeen points. On the Otis S.A. Test Mary's I.Q. was one hundred and eleven and Mabel's ninety-seven, a difference of fourteen points. On the International Test Mary scored one hundred and four points, Mabel ninety-six, a difference of only eight points, but in the same direction as the other differences. On the Stanford Achievement Test Mary had a mental age of seventeen years, three months, Mable fourteen years, five months, a difference of thirty-four months.

Out of the twenty cases studied, these four cases were the only ones in which the differences in schooling between twins of a pair differed more than a year or two. It will be noted that in each of these four cases the better educated twin had a distinctly higher rating on *all* the tests. The consistency of the results on the various tests increases our confidence in the validity of the tests themselves and in the reality of the differences in mental ability of the twins examined. One can hardly question the conclusion that mental ability within certain limits can be improved by education or suffer for the lack of it. In each of these cases we must assume that the twin with the lower I.Q. had an inherited capacity to reach at least the rating of the twin partner with the higher I.Q. If the differences in education had been greater, presumably the differences in I.Q. would have been greater. One's I.Q., then, is not fixed by heredity alone but may be raised or lowered many points according to the type and amount of education the individual experiences.

Remarkably enough, however, the remaining sixteen cases of separated twins, in which differences in education had amounted to no more than a year or two, showed an average difference in I.Q. even slightly less than that of one-egg twins reared together. From this we may draw the conclusion that small differences in education do not appreciably affect ability, but that large differences in education may induce important differences in ability.

EFFECTS OF DIFFERENCES IN SOCIAL ENVIRONMENT

Differences in social environment are difficult to estimate in terms comparable to those in education. The method of estimating these differences was that of rating them by five independent judges and averaging their estimates. When these rated differences in social environment were compared with differences in scores on personality tests there was no reliable correlation of the group as a whole between differences in social environment and differences in personality traits. What is the explanation of this unexpected result? There seem to be two possible answers to this question. Either differences in social environment have no effect on personality traits or else the tests of personality do not bear any direct relation to our rather rough-and-ready estimates of differences in the total social environment. We regard the second answer as more probable than the first.

We find in some cases of separated twins that the chief difference in social environment is one between city life and country life. In other cases the difference is one between relative wealth and relative poverty. In still other cases the difference is mainly one of contacts with cultured as over against relatively uncultured family groups and associates. In one pair of twins one twin had led a respectable life and the other had had a more or less lawless career. In another pair the life of one twin had been full of stimulating social contacts, while the other had led a decidedly sheltered and isolated existence without stimulating contacts of any sort. In another case one twin had a large family of children to whom she had devoted all her energy and affection, while the twin sister, though married, was childless and had followed a professional career. In still another case one twin girl had spent most of her life in London, England, while the other had, since eighteen months of age, lived in a small town in Ontario. These varied types of social environmental difference are so unrelated to each other that one would not expect any summation of such differences to be correlated with differences in scores made on any particular kind of personality test.

If, then, we are to discover any relation between differences in social environment and differences in personality we shall have to find them through the study of individual cases. When this was done we found clear evidence that differences in social experience actually do produce differences in personality.

Perhaps the most striking personality difference of all was that found between twins *Mildred* and *Ruth*. Mildred was the foster child of a banker who was also the mayor of a medium-sized city. He was a well-educated man whose home was a gathering place of interesting and cultured people. Mildred entered into all of these activities. Ruth, on the other hand, was the foster child of a man of little education who was a foreman of laborers. The foster mother disapproved of Ruth's normal associates and kept her at home after school hours, with dolls as her only companions. On all the personality tests Ruth showed an inhibited character, shy, diffident, silent, with lisping speech and an unhappy expression, while Mildred was much more confident, unembarrassed, talkative, happy in facial expression and spoke without a trace of lisping. Although both girls were high school seniors in two different cities and had had equal educational opportunities, Mildred's I.Q. on both the Stanford-Binet and the Otis S.A. tests was fifteen points higher than that of Ruth. From this it might be inferred that the cultured and stimulating home life of Mildred, as contrasted with the barren home life of Ruth, had made a difference in mental ability equal to that of several years of formal schooling in some of the other cases.

Another interesting case was that of *Mary* and *Mabel*. These twins, in addition to the educational differences already described, had lived very different lives. Mary had lived all her life in a town and had devoted herself to her studies and to music and music teaching. Mabel had lived on a large and prosperous farm, participating actively in all the work commonly done by an able-bodied farm woman. On all of the personality tests the scores of these twenty-nine-year-old women were among the most different of the whole twenty pairs. Mabel, the farm woman, was slow and phlegmatic; Mary was far more excitable and responsive, almost neurotic. On the other hand, Mabel was more aggressive and was evidently the leader and manager. She had fewer fears and was less readily shocked by unpleasant words and ideas. She walked about with a firm, almost masculine stride, in contrast with

Mary's ladylike step and manner. The two women seemed totally unlike in overt behavior and gave the impression of having very different personalities.

The case of *Gladys* and *Helen,* who had the greatest difference in schooling, also illustrates the effects of social differences on personality. These social differences are inherent in the fact that Helen had gone through college and was a teacher, while Gladys had been an industrial worker most of her life. In some of the personality tests the scores were very similar; on others very different. It appears that these twins are alike in fundamental personality traits but differ greatly in their reactions to different social situations. The largest contrast was in overt behavior. Helen, the teacher, was much more suave and polished, was much more interested in her personal appearance and made more of an effort to produce a favorable personal impression. Gladys was all business, without social charm or concern about how she impressed others.

In contrast to these cases in which the differences in social environment seemed definitely to have produced appropriate differences in personality, was the case of twins *James* and *Reece.* James had always lived in town with his maternal grandparents. He had had a good high-school education and was engineer for a sand-and-gravel company. He was a steady, respected citizen. Reece, on the contrary, had lived the life of a mountaineer, had never worked steadily, had engaged in illegal pursuits characteristic of his environment and had been caught and punished several times. In spite of this great difference in social experience, these twins, who had never spent a night together since babyhood, were almost indistinguishable as to their behavior when with us. They made highly similar scores on all the personality tests. It appears that the differences in environment and experience have not modified their fundamental personality traits but have merely served to direct the primitive impulses, common to both, into modes of behavior in one case characteristic of a primitive environment and in the other case into those more in accord with the ideals of a higher level of civilized life. Neither of these men is criminalistic in character, but both are rather individualistic, rather stubborn and both tend to resist opposition vigorously. One expressed his strong character by primitive modes of action; the other restrained his primitive impulses in favor of actions which are more socially acceptable in a modern urban community.

EFFECTS OF DIFFERENCES IN PHYSICAL ENVIRONMENT

Under the head of physical environment we include differences in climate, housing, food, physical exercise, hygiene and disease. In no two pairs of separated twins did we find the same combination of these physical environmental differences. In some pairs one of these types of environmental difference was well marked; in others another type. Here again, as in the study of differences in social environment, the case-study method is more likely to reveal the effects of specific differences in the physical environment than is the statistical method.

There were two pairs of twins in which there was a great difference in health. The first of these is the case of twins *Thelma* and *Zelma*, twenty-nine-year-old married women. Thelma was a victim of advanced tuberculosis and was exceedingly frail, weighing only seventy-two pounds; while Zelma was quite healthy and weighed ninety-eight pounds, normal for such a small, delicately formed woman. Apart from this great difference in weight, Thelma was a sort of shrunken replica of Zelma. The second case where the health condition constituted the only marked environmental effect was the case of fifty-eight-year-old twins *Ada* and *Ida*. Ada was a robust and normally healthy woman, while Ida had an enormous goiter and showed very pronounced symptoms of goiter disease (thyroxin deficiency). Ada was vigorous and active, Ida easily fatigued and somewhat sluggish. Ada weighed two hundred and eight pounds, Ida two hundred and twenty-seven, the extra weight due to excess water in the tissues, a condition characteristic of goiter disease.

There were two cases of twins with pronounced difference in muscular development. The first is the case of *Mabel* and *Mary*, twice previously referred to in this chapter. Mable was a muscular farm worker and Mary a sedentary, ladylike music teacher and store clerk. Mabel weighed one hundred and thirty-eight pounds and was hard muscled; Mary weighed only one hundred and ten pounds and her muscles were soft and poorly developed. It is obvious that the great difference in the occupations of these two women was responsible for most of their difference in muscularity and weight. The second of these cases was that of the twins *Paul O.* and *Paul C.* Paul C. had been addicted to gymnastics and Paul O. had led a sedentary life. Paul C. was very well developed, muscularly, while Paul O. was much less so. The difference in weight was over ten pounds in favor of Paul C. and was due entirely to excess muscle.

There was one case of marked differences in the condition of the teeth. The twins *Edith* and *Fay* showed a striking contrast in this respect. Fay, at the age of thirty-eight years, had one of the most perfect sets of teeth I have examined, while Edith's teeth were in extremely bad condition, the incisors discolored and much worn and cheek teeth much decayed. It appears that Edith had had several children in rapid succession while she and her husband were trying to establish claim on a North Dakota farm. During this period food was scarce, especially those foods rich in tooth-building ingredients. It was during this period that Edith's potentially fine teeth deteriorated. Fay, who lived in a city and always had everything a prosperous husband could supply, took care of her teeth and was rewarded by having them in perfect condition.

STATISTICAL COMPARISONS

Comparisons were made between the fifty pairs of one-egg twins reared together and twenty pairs of one-egg twins reared apart. In these two sets of twins the only difference is in the environment. Let us see which characters are least affected and which are most affected by differences in environment.

The twins reared apart were, on the average, no more different than those reared together in measurable physical characters except for one character, body weight, which in twins is largely a measure of differences in food, health and physical exercise. The average difference in weight for twins reared apart was twice as great as that for twins reared together. In all other physical measurements, except those directly dependent on differences in weight, the average differences in the two sets of twins was almost exactly the same.

The situation is quite different when we come to deal with mental differences. The average difference in I.Q. of twins reared together was 5.3 points and for twins reared apart 8.2 points, an excess of nearly three points. This difference was almost entirely accounted for by the four cases in which there was a great difference in education.

The average difference in scholastic achievement for the twins reared apart was more than twice as great as for twins reared together, indicating that achievement tests register more accurately differences in schooling than do ability tests.

Since only one personality test was given to the twins reared together, it was not easy to compare the two sets of twins with respect to differences in personality, but there are many evidences that environmental differences have caused greater differences in personality than in any other traits.

In conclusion, we may fairly say that our researches have done at least two things: 1, they have shown conclusively that the human heredity-environment problem is extremely complex, that it is not one problem but many, that the problem differs with respect to every character studied and that there is therefore no general solution for the problem as a whole; 2, that solutions can be given only for well-defined heredity-environment setups, such as that for children in the same family reared together, and for a limited number of one-egg twins reared under a variety of different environmental conditions.

We realize that while we have helped to solve with some degree of success a few parts of the heredity-environment problem, there remains much to be done. We have at least untangled some of the threads in that very intricate mesh that constitutes the organism we call man.

10. THE SOCIAL ORDER OF CHICKENS *

A. M. GUHL

Over the years several studies of animal populations have indicated that a type of social order exists among nonhumans. For example, some years ago studies of chickens demonstrated the existence of a "pecking order." This term is now commonly used in reference to status differences among humans in various social organizations. Although social scientists recognize that the absence of language and other aspects of culture limit the nature and development of animal societies, an examination of the social organizations among nonhumans provides interesting points of comparison and contrast with human society. In this selection A. M. Guhl makes a detailed analysis of the social order among chickens.

During the past 30 years the social organization and behavior of chickens has interested many investigators, and its study has produced a great deal of fascinating information. The main theme of the investigation has been the trait of dominance, or bossism, but it has also shed important light on other questions of psychology, sociology and biology, and has been helpful in practical poultry husbandry. This article will report recent findings at our zoology laboratory at Kansas State College.

It was T. Schjelderup-Ebbe, a Norwegian psychologist, who discovered the peck-order among chickens. He found that in any flock one hen usually dominated all the others: she could peck any without being pecked in return. Second came a hen which pecked all but the top hen, and the rest were arranged in a descending hierarchy ending in a hapless hen which was pecked by all and could peck no one. Cocks do not normally peck hens, but they have their own peck-order, so a breeding flock usually has two hierarchies, one for each sex.

The late W. C. Allee and his students at the University of Chicago

* From *Scientific American*, Vol. 191, No. 4 (October, 1954), 81–85.
The author (b. 1898) is a professor in the Department of Zoology at Kansas State College. He is past Chairman of the Social Behavior and Socio-biology Section of the Ecological Society of America. For several years prior to his University affiliation he was a high-school teacher in Wisconsin.

found that the male sex hormone increases aggressiveness, so that hens given injections of this hormone fight their way up the social ladder. The female hormone tends to have the opposite effect, making injected individuals more submissive. It is common knowledge that a castrate is more docile than the normal of the species. However, capons will and do form peck-orders and may engage in some harmless fighting.

When grown birds that are strangers to one another are put together in a pen, they engage in a series of single combats, each pairing off against one opponent at a time, until a peck-order has been established for the whole flock. Some individuals submit without a fight, because of lack of aggressiveness, poor health or lack of fighting skill. Once the peck-order has been determined, pecking begins to decline in frequency as members of the hierarchy recognize their superiors; eventually a mere raising or lowering of the head may be enough to signify dominance or submission, respectively. Thus the flock becomes comparatively peaceful and conserves energy.

In flocks of birds reared together from hatching, the dominance order develops gradually. Downy chicks rarely peck; they go no farther than a threatening posture or jump. As they grow older, fighting begins, and it may be repeated frequently before certain individuals learn to give way habitually to others. Peck-orders may be established at 10 weeks of age among pullets and somewhat earlier among cockerels.

A chicken's memory is short. Hens that have been separated for two weeks or more will fight the battle for dominance all over again when they are brought together. If a strange bird enters an organized flock, it has to fight each of the residents to establish its status. Obviously only an exceptionally aggressive outsider can win a respectable rank in the social scale under these circumstances. W. C. Sanctuary at the University of Massachusetts found that when flocks of hens were mixed, there was severe disruption, sometimes causing some birds to stop laying.

Such is the basic social structure of chickens. Now let us examine it more closely. To begin with, what are the advantages of high social status?

Naturally hens that rank high in the peck-order have privileges—first chance at the food trough, the dusting areas, the roost and the nest boxes. The low members of the hierarchy may find themselves driven about ruthlessly in the pen, especially during the earlier phase of peck-order formation. Much of the time they keep out of the way of their superiors in secluded places. They have a cowed, submissive appearance—the head usually lowered, the body feathers ruffled and unpreened. By contrast the high-ranking hens strut proudly like pampered show horses.

We have found that in a flock of young hens the high-ranking birds feed regularly during the day and crowd together on the roosts for warmth at night, whereas the low-ranking birds have to feed at twilight or early in the morning while their superiors are roosting, and at night they hover timidly on the fringes of the roosting group, often singly, even when temperatures drop below freezing. The low-ranking pullets take longer to reach sexual maturity than those of privileged status.

To see how social disorganization affected productivity, we compared two flocks, of which one was allowed to attain a stable peck-order and the other was kept disrupted by frequent shifting of its membership. Birds in the unstable flock fought more, ate less food, gained less weight and suffered many more wounds. The latest comers had the poorest position; the top ranks were occupied by those that had been in the shifting flock longest. In other words, chickens have seniority rights. There are, however, variations of individual aggressiveness: a hen that spends a short time daily with each of several flocks may have different ranks in the different flocks.

How does the peck-order influence sexual behavior? The question of course has considerable practical importance for poultrymen. We investigated it by several rather complex observational experiments.

. . . . . .

We were interested first to find out how hens would respond to courtship by males which lacked the normal male dominance over them. We therefore castrated some cockerels, depriving them of the advantage of masculine aggressiveness, and raised them in a flock of pullets where they were subjected to the peck-order contest. Some of the capons fell in the intermediate ranks, being dominated by some females. We then treated these capons with the hormone estrogen, which restored their sex drive without increasing their aggressiveness. Hens that ranked below these males in the peck-order mated readily with them. But hens that out-ranked them repelled their advances and drove them wildly about the pen. Evidently among chickens dominance by the male is a prerequisite for sexual acceptance by the female. However, we also noted that females fled from males which were too aggressive sexually.

In all-male flocks of young chickens the males often perform sexual treading upon one another, presumably because they have no normal outlet for their sexual drive. Usually the low-ranking males are the objects of these aberrant treadings, and some are driven and trodden so incessantly that they are killed. In flocks of hens, similarly, dominant females may act the male role and tread on hens lower in the peck-order. This behavior is difficult to explain, for the treading hens are not necessarily masculine in any way; they usually respond normally to the advances of a male in the same flock.

Another experiment showed, as was to be expected, that males at the top of the peck-order win out over their inferiors in any competition for mating with hens. When a small group of cocks which had previously shown no significant individual differences in sex drive was placed in a pen with hens, the dominant male was most successful in mating with the hens, while the male ranking lowest in the group's peck-order was least successful. The dominant one suppressed his inferiors' treading to varying degrees. One male was completely suppressed sexually; he failed to react to the hens he knew even when the other males were removed. This condition was called psychological castration.

One would naturally assume that the males most successful in mating would also sire the most offspring, but to make sure we carried out some special experiments with the cooperation of the poultry geneticist D. C. Warren. We used males of different breeds (Rhode Island Red, Barred Rock, White Leghorn), and the distinctively marked offspring demonstrated that the most dominant males do indeed father the most chicks. The lowest-ranking cock in one flock failed to fertilize even one egg.

What of the hens; how does their rank in the peck-order affect their sexual activity? There were already hints that the more dominant females are less likely to submit to coition, and we undertook to investigate this systematically. We raised some large flocks of 30 to 40 pullets each, and after they had established peck-orders, we divided each flock into three groups—the top third, the middle third and the bottom third of the peck-order. The ranking within each group remained the same as before, but each pullet now had fewer birds to dominate or be dominated by. This significantly changed their receptivity to male courtship. The hens in the top third, which had been comparatively unreceptive to males, became more submissive to them (as evidenced by the frequency of crouching), and the middle and bottom thirds became less submissive. In other words, the higher hens stand on the social scale, the less likely they are to mate, whereas the male improves his chances by high social status.

. . . . .

11. THE CONCEPT OF CULTURE *

CLYDE KLUCKHOHN

The beginning student of sociology soon discovers that culture is one of the most significant concepts about which he will learn. At the same time he finds that his previous acquaintance with the variety of meanings popularly attached to the word tends to confuse his grasp of the special meaning given it by social scientists. Since the concept was originally used by anthropologists, its explanation by one of them has particular validity. Clyde Kluckhohn here gives us a clear and readable description of culture. Further comprehension may be achieved by examining some patterns of culture from different societies.

Why do the Chinese dislike milk and milk products? Why would the Japanese die willingly in a Banzai charge that seemed senseless to Americans? Why do some nations trace descent through the father, others through the mother, still others through both parents? Not because different peoples have different instincts, not because they were destined by God or Fate to different habits, not because the weather is different in China and Japan and the United States. Sometimes shrewd common sense has an answer that is close to that of the anthropologist: "because they were brought up that way." By "culture" anthropology means the total life way of a people, the social legacy the individual acquires from his group. Or culture can be regarded as that part of the environment that is the creation of man.

This technical term has a wider meaning than the "culture" of history and literature. A humble cooking pot is as much a cultural product as is a Beethoven sonata. In ordinary speech a man of culture is a man who can speak languages other than his own, who is familiar with his-

---

* Clyde Kluckhohn, *Mirror for Man* (New York: McGraw-Hill Book Co., 1949), pp. 17–36. Reprinted by permission of the publisher and the author.

The author (b. 1905) is Professor of Anthropology and past director of the Russian Research Center at Harvard University. Chairman of the Division of Anthropology and Psychology, National Research Council (1956–1958), and member of the Advisory Committee to Foreign Service Institute, Department of State, since 1956. Author of: *To the Foot of the Rainbow; Beyond the Rainbow; The Navaho* (with Dorothea Leighton, M.D.); *Navaho Means People* (coauthor); *How the Soviet System Works* (with others); coeditor of *Personality in Nature, Society, and Culture.*

tory, literature, philosophy, or the fine arts. In some cliques that definition is still narrower. The cultured person is one who can talk about James Joyce, Scarlatti, and Picasso. To the anthropologist, however, to be human is to be cultured. There is culture in general, and then there are the specific cultures such as Russian, American, British, Hottentot, Inca. The general abstract notion serves to remind us that we cannot explain acts solely in terms of the biological properties of the people concerned, their individual past experience, and the immediate situation. The past experience of other men in the form of culture enters into almost every event. Each specific culture constitutes a kind of blueprint for all of life's activities.

One of the interesting things about human beings is that they try to understand themselves and their own behavior. While this has been particularly true of Europeans in recent times, there is no group which has not developed a scheme or schemes to explain man's actions. To the insistent human query "why?" the most exciting illumination anthropology has to offer is that of the concept of culture. Its explanatory importance is comparable to categories such as evolution in biology, gravity in physics, disease in medicine. A good deal of human behavior can be understood, and indeed predicted, if we know a people's design for living. Many acts are neither accidental nor due to personal peculiarities nor caused by supernatural forces nor simply mysterious. Even those of us who pride ourselves on our individualism follow most of the time a pattern not of our own making. We brush our teeth on arising. We put on pants—not a loincloth or a grass skirt. We eat three meals a day— not four or five or two. We sleep in a bed—not in a hammock or on a sheep pelt. I do not have to know the individual and his life history to be able to predict these and countless other regularities, including many in the thinking process, of all Americans who are not incarcerated in jails or hospitals for the insane.

To the American woman a system of plural wives seems "instinctively" abhorrent. She cannot understand how any woman can fail to be jealous and uncomfortable if she must share her husband with other women. She feels it "unnatural" to accept such a situation. On the other hand, a Koryak woman of Siberia, for example, would find it hard to understand how a woman could be so selfish and so undesirous of feminine companionship in the home as to wish to restrict her husband to one mate.

Some years ago I met in New York City a young man who did not speak a word of English and was obviously bewildered by American ways. By "blood" he was as American as you or I, for his parents had gone from Indiana to China as missionaries. Orphaned in infancy, he was reared by a Chinese family in a remote village. All who met him found him more Chinese than American. The facts of his blue eyes and light hair were less impressive than a Chinese style of gait, Chinese arm and hand movements, Chinese facial expression, and Chinese modes of thought. The biological heritage was American, but the cultural training had been Chinese. He returned to China. Another example of another kind: I once knew a trader's wife in Arizona who took a somewhat devilish interest in producing a cultural reaction. Guests who came her way were often served delicious sandwiches filled with a meat that seemed to be neither chicken nor tuna fish yet was reminiscent of both. To queries she gave no reply until each had eaten his fill. She then explained that what they had eaten was not chicken, not tuna fish, but the rich, white flesh of freshly killed rattlesnakes. The response was instantaneous—vomiting, often violent vomiting. A biological process is caught in a cultural web.

A highly intelligent teacher with long and successful experience in the public schools of Chicago was finishing her first year in an Indian school. When asked how her Navaho pupils compared in intelligence with Chicago youngsters, she replied, "Well, I just don't know. Sometimes the Indians seem just as bright. At other times they just act like dumb animals. The other night we had a dance in the high school. I saw a boy who is one of the best students in my English class standing off by himself. So I took him over to a pretty girl and told them to dance. But they just stood there with their heads down. They wouldn't even say anything." I inquired if she knew whether or not they were members of the same clan. "What difference would that make?"

"How would you feel about getting into bed with your brother?" The teacher walked off in a huff, but, actually, the two cases were quite comparable in principle. To the Indian the type of bodily contact involved in our social dancing has a directly sexual connotation. The incest taboos between members of the same clan are as severe as between true brothers and sisters. The shame of the Indians at the suggestion that a clan brother and sister should dance and the indignation of the white teacher at the idea that she should share a bed with an adult brother represent equally nonrational responses, culturally standardized unreason.

All this does not mean that there is no such thing as raw human nature. The very fact that certain of the same institutions are found in all known societies indicates that at bottom all human beings are very much alike. The files of the Cross-Cultural Survey at Yale University are organized according to categories such as "marriage ceremonies," "life crisis rites," "incest taboos." At least seventy-five of these categories are represented in every single one of the hundreds of cultures analyzed. This is hardly surprising. The members of all human groups have about the same biological equipment. All men undergo the same poignant life experiences such as birth, helplessness, illness, old age, and death. The biological potentialities of the species are the blocks with which cultures are built. Some patterns of every culture crystallize around focuses provided by the inevitables of biology: the difference between the sexes, the presence of persons of different ages, the varying physical strength and skill of individuals. The facts of nature also limit culture forms. No culture provides patterns for jumping over trees or for eating iron ore.

There is thus no "either-or" between nature and that special form of nurture called culture. Culture determinism is as one-sided as biological determinism. The two factors are interdependent. Culture arises out of human nature, and its forms are restricted both by man's biology and by natural laws. It is equally true that culture channels biological processes—vomiting, weeping, fainting, sneezing, the daily habits of food intake and waste elimination. When a man eats, he is reacting to an internal "drive," namely, hunger contractions consequent upon the lowering of blood sugar, but his precise reaction to these internal stimuli cannot be predicted by physiological knowledge alone. Whether a healthy adult feels hungry twice, three times, or four times a day and the hours at which this feeling recurs is a question of culture. *What* he eats is of course limited by availability, but is also partly regulated by culture. It is a biological fact that some types of berries are poisonous; it is a cultural fact that, a few generations ago, most Americans considered tomatoes to be poisonous and refused to eat them. Such selective, discriminative use of the environment is characteristically cultural. In a still more general sense, too, the process of eating is channeled by culture. Whether a man eats to live, lives to eat, or merely eats and lives is only in part an individual matter, for there are also cultural trends. Emotions are physiological events. Certain situations will evoke fear in people from any culture. But sensations of pleasure, anger, and lust may be stimulated by cultural cues that would leave unmoved someone who has been reared in a different social tradition.

Except in the case of newborn babies and of individuals born with clear-cut structural or functional abnormalities we can observe innate endowments only as modified by cultural training. In a hospital in New Mexico where Zuñi Indian, Navaho Indian, and white American babies are born, it is possible to classify the newly arrived infants as unusually active, average, and quiet. Some babies from each "racial" group will fall into each category, though a higher proportion of the white babies will fall into the unusually active class. But if a Navaho baby, a Zuñi baby, and a white baby—all classified as unusually active at birth—are again observed at the age of two years, the Zuñi baby will no longer seem given to quick and restless activity—*as compared with the white child*—though he may seem so as compared with the other Zuñis of the same age. The Navaho child is likely to fall in between as contrasted with the Zuñi and the white, though he will probably still seem more active than the average Navaho youngster.

It was remarked by many observers in the Japanese relocation centers that Japanese who were born and brought up in this country, especially those who were reared apart from any large colony of Japanese, resemble in behavior their white neighbors much more closely than they do their own parents who were educated in Japan.

I have said "culture channels biological processes." It is more accurate to say "the biological functioning of individuals is modified if they have been trained in certain ways and not in others." Culture is not a disembodied force. It is created and transmitted by people. However, culture, like well-known concepts of the physical sciences, is a convenient abstraction. One never sees gravity. One sees bodies falling in regular ways. One never sees an electromagnetic field. Yet certain happenings that can be seen may be given a neat abstract formulation by assuming that the electromagnetic field exists. Similarly, one never sees culture as such. What is seen are regularities in the behavior or artifacts of a group that has adhered to a common tradition. The regularities in style and technique of ancient Inca tapestries or stone axes from Melanesian islands are due to the existence of mental blueprints for the group.

Culture is a way of thinking, feeling, believing. It is the group's knowledge stored up (in memories of men; in books and objects) for future use. We study the products of this "mental" activity: the overt behavior, the speech and gestures and activities of people, and the tangible results of these things such as tools, houses, cornfields, and what not. It has been customary in lists of "culture traits" to include such things as watches or lawbooks. This is a convenient way of thinking about them, but in the solution of any important problem we must remember that they, in themselves, are nothing but metals, paper, and ink. What is important is that some men know how to make them, others set a value on them, are unhappy without them, direct their activities in relation to them, or disregard them.

It is only a helpful shorthand when we say "The cultural patterns of the Zulu were resistant to Christianization." In the directly observable world of course, it was individual Zulus who resisted. Nevertheless, if we do not forget that we are speaking at a high level of abstraction, it is justifiable to speak of culture as a cause. One may compare the practice of saying "syphilis caused the extinction of the native population of the island." Was it "syphilis" or "syphilis germs" or "human beings who were carriers of syphilis"?

"Culture," then, is "a theory." But if a theory is not contradicted by any relevant fact and if it helps us to understand a mass of otherwise chaotic facts, it is useful. Darwin's contribution was much less the accumulation of new knowledge than the creation of a theory which put in order data already known. An accumulation of facts, however large, is no more a science than a pile of bricks is a house. Anthropology's demonstration that the most weird set of customs has a consistency and an order is comparable to modern psychiatry's showing that there is meaning and purpose in the apparently incoherent talk of the insane. In fact, the inability of the older psychologies and philosophies to account for the strange behavior of madmen and heathens was the principal factor that forced psychiatry and anthropology to develop theories of the unconscious and of culture.

Since culture is an abstraction, it is important not to confuse culture with society. A "society" refers to a group of people who interact more with each other than they do with other individuals—who cooperate with each other for the attainment of certain ends. You can see and indeed count the individuals who make up a society. A "culture" refers to the distinctive ways of life of such a group of people. Not all social events are culturally patterned. New types of circumstances arise for which no cultural solutions have as yet been devised.

A culture constitutes a storehouse of the pooled learning of the group. A rabbit starts life with some innate responses. He can learn from his own experience and perhaps from observing other rabbits. A human infant is born with fewer instincts and greater plasticity. His main task is to learn the answers that persons he will never see, persons long dead, have worked out. Once he has learned the formulas supplied by the culture of his group, most of his behavior becomes almost as automatic and unthinking as if it were instinctive. There is a tremendous amount of intelligence behind the making of a radio, but not much is required to learn to turn it on.

The members of all human societies face some of the same unavoidable dilemmas, posed by biology and other facts of the human situation. This is why the basic categories of all cultures are so similar. Human culture without language is unthinkable. No culture fails to provide for aesthetic expression and aesthetic delight. Every culture supplies standardized orientations toward the deeper problems, such as death. Every culture is designed to perpetuate the group and its solidarity, to meet the demands of individuals for an orderly way of life and for satisfaction of biological needs.

However, the variations on these basic themes are numberless. Some languages are built up out of twenty basic sounds, others out of forty. Nose plugs were considered beautiful by the predynastic Egyptians but are not by the modern French. Puberty is a biological fact. But one culture ignores it, another prescribes informal instructions about sex but no ceremony, a third has impressive rites for girls only, a fourth for boys and girls. In this culture, the first menstruation is welcomed as a happy, natural event; in that culture the atmosphere is full of dread and supernatural threat. Each culture dissects nature according to its own system of categories. The Navaho Indians apply the same word to the color of a robin's egg and to that of grass. A psychologist once assumed that this meant a difference in the sense organs, that Navahos didn't have the physiological equipment to distinguish "green" from "blue." However, when he showed them objects of the two colors and asked them if they were exactly the same colors, they looked at him with astonishment. His dream of discovering a new type of color blindness was shattered.

Every culture must deal with the sexual instinct. Some, however, seek to deny all sexual expression before marriage, whereas a Polynesian adolescent who was not promiscuous would be distinctly abnormal. Some cultures enforce lifelong monogamy, others, like our own, tolerate serial monogamy; in still other cultures, two or more women may be joined to one man or several men to a single woman. Homosexuality has been a permitted pattern in the Greco-Roman world, in parts of Islam, and in various primitive tribes. Large portions of the population of Tibet, and of Christendom at some places and periods, have practiced complete celibacy. To us marriage is first and foremost an arrangement between two individuals. In many more societies marriage is merely one facet of a complicated set of reciprocities, economic and otherwise, between two families or two clans.

The essence of the cultural process is selectivity. The selection is only exceptionally conscious and rational. Cultures are like Topsy. They just grew. Once, however, a way of handling a situation becomes institutionalized, there is ordinarily great resistance to change or deviation. When we speak of "our sacred beliefs," we mean of course that they are beyond criticism and that the person who suggests modification or abandonment must be punished. No person is emotionally indifferent to his culture. Certain cultural premises may become totally out of accord with a new factual situation. Leaders may recognize this and reject the old ways in theory. Yet their emotional loyalty continues in the face of reason because of the intimate conditionings of early childhood.

A culture is learned by individuals as the result of belonging to some particular group, and it constitutes that part of learned behavior which is shared with others. It is our social legacy, as contrasted with our organic heredity. It is one of the important factors which permits us to live together in an organized society, giving us ready-made solutions to our problems, helping us to predict the behavior of others, and permitting others to know what to expect of us.

Culture regulates our lives at every turn. From the moment we are born until we die there is, whether we are conscious of it or not, constant pressure upon us to follow certain types of behavior that other men have created for us. Some paths we follow willingly, others we follow because we know no other way, still others we deviate from or go back to most unwillingly. Mothers of small children know how unnaturally most of this comes to us—how little regard we have, until we are "culturalized," for the "proper" place, time, and manner for certain acts such as eating, excreting, sleeping, getting dirty, and making loud noises. But by more or less adhering to a system of related designs for carrying out all the acts of living, a group of men and women feel themselves linked together by a powerful chain of sentiments. Ruth Benedict gave an almost complete definition of the concept when she said, "Culture is that which binds men together."

It is true any culture is a set of techniques for adjusting both to the external environment and to other men. However, cultures create problems as well as solve them. If the lore of a people states that frogs are dangerous creatures, or that it is not safe to go about at night because of witches or ghosts, threats are posed which do not arise out of the inexorable facts of the external world. Cultures produce needs as well as provide a means of fulfilling them. There exist for every group culturally defined, acquired drives that may be more powerful in ordinary daily life than the biologically inborn drives. Many Americans, for example, will work harder for "success" than they will for sexual satisfaction.

Most groups elaborate certain aspects of their culture far beyond maximum utility or survival value. In other words, not all culture promotes physical survival. At times, indeed, it does exactly the opposite. Aspects of culture which once were adaptive may persist long after they have ceased to be useful. An analysis of any culture will disclose many features which cannot possibly be construed as adaptations to the total environment in which the group now finds itself. However, it is altogether likely that these apparently useless features represent survivals, with modifications through time, of cultural forms which were adaptive in one or another previous situation.

Any cultural practice must be functional or it will disappear before long. That is, it must somehow contribute to the survival of the society or to the adjustment of the individual. However, many cultural functions are not manifest but latent. A cowboy will walk three miles to catch a horse which he then rides one mile to the store. From the point of view of manifest function this is positively irrational. But the act has the latent function of maintaining the cowboy's prestige in the terms of his own subculture. One can instance the buttons on the sleeve of a man's coat, our absurd English spelling, the use of capital letters, and a host of other apparently nonfunctional customs. They serve mainly the latent function of assisting individuals to maintain their security by preserving continuity with the past and by making certain sectors of life familiar and predictable.

Every culture is a precipitate of history. In more than one sense history is a sieve. Each culture embraces those aspects of the past, which, usually in altered form and with altered meanings, live on in the present. Discoveries and inventions, both material and ideological, are constantly being made available to a group through its historical contacts with other peoples or being created by its own members. However, only those that fit the total immediate situation in meeting the group's needs for survival or in promoting the psychological adjustment of individuals will become part of the culture. The process of culture building may be regarded as an addition to man's innate biological capacities, an addition providing instruments which enlarge, or may even substitute for, biological functions, and to a degree compensating for biological limitations—as in ensuring that death does not always result in the loss to humanity of what the deceased has learned.

Culture is like a map. Just as a map isn't the territory but an abstract representation of a particular area, so also a culture is an abstract description of trends toward uniformity in the words, deeds, and artifacts of a human group. If a map is accurate and you can read it, you won't get lost; if you know a culture, you will know your way around in the life of a society.

Many educated people have the notion that culture applies only to exotic ways of life or to societies where relative simplicity and relative homogeneity prevail. Some sophisticated missionaries, for example, will use the anthropological conception in discussing the special modes of living of South Sea Islanders, but seem amazed at the idea that it could be applied equally to inhabitants of New York City. And social workers in Boston will talk about the culture of a colorful and well-knit immigrant group but boggle at applying it to the behavior of staff members in the social-service agency itself.

In the primitive society the correspondence between the habits of individuals and the customs of the community is ordinarily greater. There is probably some truth in what an old Indian once said, "In the old days there was no law; everybody did what was right." The primitive tends to find happiness in the fulfillment of intricately involuted cultural patterns; the modern more often tends to feel the pattern as repressive to his individuality. It is also true that in a complex stratified society there are numerous exceptions to generalizations made about the culture as a whole. It is necessary to study regional, class, and occupational subcultures. Primitive cultures have greater stability than modern cultures; they change—but less rapidly.

However, modern men also are creators and carriers of culture. Only in some respects are they influenced differently from primitives by culture. Moreover, there are such wide variations in primitive cultures that any black-and-white contrast between the primitive and the civilized is altogether fictitious. The distinction which is most generally true lies in the field of conscious philosophy.

The publication of Paul Radin's *Primitive Man as a Philosopher* did much toward destroying the myth that an abstract analysis of experience was a peculiarity of literate societies. Speculation and reflection upon the nature of the universe and of man's place in the total scheme of things have been carried out in every known culture. Every people has its characteristic set of "primitive postulates." It remains true that critical examination of basic premises and fully explicit systematization of philosophical concepts are seldom found at the nonliterate level. The written word is an almost essential condition for free and extended discussion of fundamental philosophic issues. Where dependence on memory exists, there seems to be an inevitable tendency to emphasize the correct perpetuation of the precious oral tradition. Similarly, while it is all too easy to underestimate the extent to which ideas spread without books, it is in general true that tribal or folk societies do not possess competing philosophical systems. The major exception to this statement is, of course, the case where part of the tribe becomes converted to one of the great proselytizing religions such as Christianity or Mohammedanism. Before contact with rich and powerful civilizations, primitive peoples seem to have absorbed new ideas piecemeal, slowly integrating them with the previously existing ideology. The abstract thought of nonliterate societies is ordinarily less self-critical, less systematic, nor so intricately elaborated in purely logical dimensions. Primitive thinking is more concrete, more implicit—perhaps more completely coherent than the philosophy of most individuals in larger societies which have been influenced over long periods by disparate intellectual currents.

No participant in any culture knows all the details of the cultural map. The statement frequently heard that St. Thomas Aquinas was the last man to master all the knowledge of his society is intrinsically absurd. St. Thomas would have been hard put to make a pane of cathedral glass or to act as a midwife. In every culture there are what Ralph Linton has called "universals, alternatives, and specialties." Every Christian in the thirteenth century knew that it was necessary to attend mass, to go to confession, to ask the Mother of God to intercede with her Son. There were many other universals in the Christian culture of Western Europe. However, there were also alternative cultural patterns even in the realm of religion. Each individual had his own patron saint, and different towns developed the cults of different saints. The thirteenth-century anthropologist could have discovered the rudiments of Christian practice by questioning and observing whomever he happened to meet in Germany, France, Italy, or England. But to find out the details of the ceremonials honoring St. Hubert or St. Bridget he would have had to seek out certain individuals or special localities where these alternative patterns were practiced. Similarly, he could not learn about weaving from a professional soldier or about canon law from a farmer. Such cultural knowledge belongs in the realm of the specialties, voluntarily chosen by the individual or ascribed to him by birth. Thus, part of a culture must be learned by everyone, part may be selected from alternative patterns, part applies only to those who perform the roles in the society for which these patterns are designed.

Many aspects of a culture are explicit. The explicit culture consists in those regularities in word and deed that may be generalized straight from the evidence of the ear and the eye. The recognition of these is like the recognition of style in the art of a particular place and epoch. If we have examined twenty specimens of the wooden saints' images made in the Taos valley of New Mexico in the late eighteenth century, we can predict that any new images from the same locality and period will in most respects exhibit the same techniques of carving, about the same use of colors and choice of woods, a similar quality of artistic conception. Similarly, if, in a society of 2,000 members, we record 100 marriages at random and find that in 30 cases a man has married the sister of his brother's wife, we can anticipate that an additional sample of 100 marriages will show roughly the same number of cases of this pattern.

The above is an instance of what anthropologists call a behavioral pattern, the practices as opposed to the rules of the culture. There are also, however, regularities in what people say they do or should do. They do tend in fact to prefer to marry into a family already connected with their own by marriage, but this is not necessarily part of the official code of conduct. No disapproval whatsoever is attached to those who make another sort of marriage. On the other hand, it is explicitly forbidden to marry a member of one's own clan even though no biological relationship is traceable. This is a regulatory pattern—a Thou Shalt or a Thou Shalt Not. Such patterns may be violated often, but their existence is nevertheless important. A people's standards for conduct and belief define the socially approved aims and the acceptable means of attaining them. When the discrepancy between the theory and the practice of a culture is exceptionally great, this indicates that the culture is undergoing rapid change. It does not prove that ideals are unimportant, for ideals are but one of a number of factors determining action.

Cultures do not manifest themselves solely in observable customs and artifacts. No amount of questioning of any save the most articulate in the most self-conscious cultures will bring out some of the basic attitudes common to the members of the group. This is because these basic assumptions are taken so for granted that they normally do not enter into consciousness. This part of the cultural map must be inferred by the observer on the basis of consistencies in thought and action. Missionaries in various societies are often disturbed or puzzled because the natives do not regard "morals" and "sex code" as almost synonymous. The natives seem to feel that morals are concerned with sex just about as much as with eating—no less and no more. No society fails to have some restrictions on sexual behavior, but sex activity outside of marriage need not necessarily be furtive or attended with guilt. The Christian tradition has tended to assume that sex is inherently nasty as well as dangerous. Other cultures assume that sex in itself is not only natural but one of the good things of life, even though sex acts with certain persons under certain circumstances are forbidden. This is implicit culture, for the natives do not announce their premises. The missionaries would get further if they said, in effect, "Look, our morality starts from different assumptions. Let's talk about those assumptions," rather than ranting about "immorality."

A factor implicit in a variety of diverse phenomena may be generalized as an underlying cultural principle. For example, the Navaho Indians always leave part of the design in a pot, a basket, or a blanket unfinished. When a medicine man instructs an apprentice he always leaves a little bit of the story untold. This "fear of closure" is a recurrent theme in Navaho culture. Its influence may be detected in many contexts that have no explicit connection.

If the observed cultural behavior is to be correctly understood, the categories and presuppositions constituting the implicit culture must be worked out. The "strain toward consistency" which Sumner noted in the folkways and mores of all groups cannot be accounted for unless one grants a set of systematically interrelated implicit themes. For example, in American culture the themes of "effort and optimism," "the common man," "technology," and "virtuous materialism" have a functional interdependence, the origin of which is historically known. The relationship between themes may be that of conflict. One may instance the competition between Jefferson's theory of democracy and Hamilton's "government by the rich, the wellborn, and the able." In other cases most themes may be integrated under a single dominant theme. In Negro cultures of West Africa the mainspring of social life is religion; in East Africa almost all cultural behavior seems to be oriented toward certain premises and categories centered on the cattle economy. If there be one master principle in the implicit culture, this is often called the "ethos" or *Zeitgeist*.

Every culture has organization as well as content. There is nothing mystical about this statement. One may compare ordinary experience.

If I know that Smith, working alone, can shovel 10 cubic yards of dirt a day, Jones 12, and Brown 14, I would be foolish to predict that the three working together would move 36. The total might well be considerably more; it might be less. A whole is different from the sum of its parts. The same principle is familiar in athletic teams. A brilliant pitcher added to a nine may mean a pennant or may mean the cellar; it depends on how he fits in.

And so it is with cultures. A mere list of the behavioral and regulatory patterns and of the implicit themes and categories would be like a map on which all mountains, lakes, and rivers were included—but not in their actual relationship to one another. Two cultures could have almost identical inventories and still be extremely different. The full significance of any single element in a culture design will be seen only when that element is viewed in the total matrix of its relationship to other elements. Naturally, this includes accent or emphasis, as well as position. Accent is manifested sometimes through frequency, sometimes through intensity. The indispensable importance of these questions of arrangement and emphasis may be driven home by an analogy. Consider a musical sequence made up of three notes. If we are told that the three notes in question are A, B, and G, we receive information which is fundamental. But it will not enable us to predict the type of sensation which the playing of this sequence is likely to evoke. We need many different sorts of relationship data. Are the notes to be played in that or some other order? What duration will each receive? How will the emphasis, if any, be distributed? We also need, of course, to know whether the instrument used is to be a piano or an accordion.

Cultures vary greatly in their degree of integration. Synthesis is achieved partly through the overt statement of the dominant conceptions, assumptions, and aspirations of the group in its religious lore, secular thought, and ethical code; partly through habitual but unconscious ways of looking at the stream of events, ways of begging certain questions. To the naïve participant in the culture these modes of categorizing, of dissecting experience along these planes and not others, are as much "given" as the regular sequence of daylight and darkness or the necessity of air, water, and food for life. Had Americans not thought in terms of money and the market system during the depression they would have distributed unsalable goods rather than destroyed them.

Every group's way of life, then, is a structure—not a haphazard collection of all the different physically possible and functionally effective patterns of belief and action. A culture is an interdependent system based upon linked premises and categories whose influence is greater, rather than less, because they are seldom put in words. Some degree of internal coherence which is felt rather than rationally constructed seems to be demanded by most of the participants in any culture. As

Whitehead has remarked, "Human life is driven forward by its dim apprehension of notions too general for its existing language."

In sum, the distinctive way of life that is handed down as the social heritage of a people does more than supply a set of skills for making a living and a set of blueprints for human relations. Each different way of life makes its own assumptions about the ends and purposes of human existence, about what human beings have a right to expect from each other and the gods, about what constitutes fulfillment or frustration. Some of these assumptions are made explicit in the lore of the folk; others are tacit premises which the observer must infer by finding consistent trends in word and deed.

12. TAKING ONE'S PROPER STATION *

RUTH BENEDICT

One of the most effective ways of learning the meaning of the term "culture" is to compare the conceptions of proper behavior in different societies. In this selection Ruth Benedict describes the codes and values that define many of the relationships between persons in a culture quite different from our own. Sex, age, position in the family, and other factors all serve to define the person's proper relations with others. This article not only helps us to understand traditional Japanese behavior but, by contrast, gives us insight into the way American culture defines our own behavior.

Japan for all its recent Westernization is still an aristocratic society. Every greeting, every contact must indicate the kind and degree of social distance between men. Every time a man says to another "Eat" or "Sit down" he uses different words if he is addressing someone familiarly or is speaking to an inferior or to a superior. There is a different "you" that must be used in each case and the verbs have different stems. The Japanese have, in other words, what is called a "respect language," as

* Ruth Benedict, *The Chrysanthemum and the Sword* (Boston: Houghton Mifflin Co., 1946), pp. 43–75. Reprinted by permission of the publisher.

The author (1887–1948) was an anthropologist, educator, poet (under the name Ann Singleton). Member of staff, Department of Anthropology, Columbia University. Her researches guided Allied propaganda in World War II. Studied Mission, Blackfoot, Apache, Pueblo, and Pima Indians on location. Special studies of mythology, folklore, and primitive religions. Among her books are *Patterns of Culture* and *Race, Science and Politics*.

many other peoples do in the Pacific, and they accompany it with proper bows and kneelings. All such behavior is governed by meticulous rules and conventions; it is not merely necessary to know to whom one bows but it is necessary to know how much one bows. A bow that is right and proper to one host would be resented as an insult by another who stood in a slightly different relationship to the bower. And bows range all the way from kneeling with forehead lowered to the hands placed flat upon the floor, to the mere inclination of head and shoulders. One must learn, and learn early, how to suit the obeisance to each particular case.

It is not merely class differences which must be constantly recognized by appropriate behavior, though these are important. Sex and age, family ties and previous dealings between two persons all enter into the necessary calculations. Even between the same two persons different degrees of respect will be called for on different occasions: a civilian may be on familiar terms with another and not bow to him at all, but when he wears a military uniform his friend in civilian clothes bows to him. Observance of hierarchy is an art which requires the balancing of innumerable factors, some of which in any particular case may cancel each other out and some of which may be additive.

There are of course persons between whom there is relatively little ceremony. In the United States these people are one's own family circle. We shed even the slight formalities of our etiquette when we come home to the bosom of our family. In Japan it is precisely in the family where respect rules are learned and meticulously observed. While the mother still carries the baby strapped to her back she will push his head down with her hand, and his first lessons as a toddler are to observe respect behavior to his father or older brother. The wife bows to her husband, the child bows to his father, younger brothers bow to elder brothers, the sister bows to all her brothers of whatever age. It is no empty gesture. It means that the one who bows acknowledges the right of the other to have his way in things he might well prefer to manage himself, and the one who receives the bow acknowledges in his turn certain responsibilities incumbent upon his station. Hierarchy based on sex and generation and primogeniture are part and parcel of family life.

Filial piety is, of course, a high ethical law which Japan shares with China, and Chinese formulations of it were early adopted in Japan along with Chinese Buddhism, Confucian ethics and secular Chinese culture in the sixth and seventh centuries A.D. The character of filial piety, however, was inevitably modified to suit the different structure of the family in Japan. In China, even today, one owes loyalty to one's vast extended clan. It may number tens of thousands of people over whom it has jurisdiction and from whom it receives support. Conditions differ in different parts of that vast country but in large parts of China all people in any village are members of the same clan. Among all of China's 450,000,000 inhabitants there are only 470 surnames and all people with the same surname count themselves in some degree clan-brothers. Over a whole area all people may be exclusively of one clan and, in addition, families living in far-away cities are their clan fellows. In populous areas like Kwangtung all the clan members unite in keeping up great clan-halls and on stated days they venerate as many as a thousand ancestral tablets of dead clan members stemming from a common forebear. Each clan owns property, lands and temples and has clan funds which are used to pay for the education of any promising clan son. It keeps track of dispersed members and publishes elaborate genealogies which are brought up to date every decade or so to show the names of those who have a right to share in its privileges. It has ancestral laws which might even forbid them to surrender family criminals to the State if the clan was not in agreement with the authorities. In Imperial times these great communities of semi-autonomous clans were governed in the name of the larger State as casually as possible by easy-going mandarinates headed by rotating State appointees who were foreigners in the area.

All this was different in Japan. Until the middle of the nineteenth century only noble families and warrior (*samurai*) families were allowed to use surnames. Surnames were fundamental in the Chinese clan system and without these, or some equivalent, clan organization cannot develop. One of these equivalents in some tribes is keeping a genealogy. But in Japan only the upper classes kept genealogies and even in these they kept the record, as Daughters of the American Revolution do in the United States, backward in time from the present living person, not downward in time to include every contemporary who stemmed from an original ancestor. It is a very different matter. Besides, Japan was a feudal country. Loyalty was due, not to a great group of relatives, but to a feudal lord. He was resident overlord, and the contrast with the temporary bureaucratic mandarins of China, who were always strangers in their districts, could not have been greater. What was important in Japan was that one was of the fief of Satsuma or the fief of Hizen. A man's ties were to his fief.

Another way of institutionalizing clans is through the worship of remote ancestors or of clan gods at shrines or holy places. This would have been possible for the Japanese "common people" even without surnames and genealogies. But in Japan there is no cult of veneration of remote ancestors and at the shrines where "common people" worship all villagers join together without having to prove their common ancestry. They are called the "children" of their shrine-god, but they are "children" because they live in his territory. Such village worshipers are of course related to each other as villagers in any part of the world are after generations of fixed residence but they are not a tight clan group descended from a common ancestor.

The reverence due to ancestors is paid at a quite different shrine in the family living room where only six or seven recent dead are honored. Among all classes in Japan obeisance is done daily before this shrine and food set out for parents and grandparents and close relatives remembered in the flesh, who are represented in the shrine by little miniature gravestones. Even in the cemetery the markers on the graves of great-grandparents are no longer relettered and the identity even of the third ancestral generation sinks rapidly into oblivion. Family ties in Japan are whittled down almost to Occidental proportions and the French family is perhaps the nearest equivalent.

"Filial piety" in Japan, therefore, is a matter within a limited face-to-face family. It means taking one's proper station according to generation, sex, and age within a group which includes hardly more than one's father and father's father, their brothers and their descendants. Even in important houses, where larger groups may be included, the family splits up into separate lines and younger sons establish branch families. Within this narrow face-to-face group the rules that regulate "proper station" are meticulous. There is strict subservience to elders until they elect to go into formal retirement (*inkyo*). Even today a father of grown sons, if his own father has not retired, puts through no transaction without having it approved by the old grandfather. Parents make and break their children's marriages even when the children are thirty and forty years old. The father as male head of the household is served first at meals, goes first to the family bath, and receives with a nod the deep bows of his family. There is a popular riddle in Japan which might be translated into our conundrum form: "Why is a son who wants to offer advice to his parents like a Buddhist priest who wants to have hair on the top of his head?" (Buddhist priests had a tonsure.) The answer is, "However much he wants to do it, he can't."

Proper station means not only differences of generation but differences of age. When the Japanese want to express utter confusion, they say that something is "neither elder brother nor young brother." It is like our saying that something is neither fish nor fowl, for to the Japanese a man should keep his character as elder brother as drastically as a fish should stay in water. The eldest son is the heir. Travelers speak of "that air of responsibility which the eldest son so early acquires in Japan." The eldest son shares to a high degree in the prerogatives of the father. In the old days his younger brother would have been inevitably dependent upon him in time; nowadays, especially in towns and villages, it is he who will stay at home in the old rut while his younger brothers will perhaps press forward and get more education and a better income. But old habits of hierarchy are strong.

Even in political commentary today the traditional prerogatives of elder brothers are vividly stated in discussions of Greater East Asia policy. In the spring of 1942 a Lieutenant Colonel, speaking for the War Office, said on the subject of the Co-prosperity Sphere: "Japan is their elder brother and they are Japan's younger brothers. This fact must be brought home to the inhabitants of the occupied territories. Too much consideration shown for the inhabitants might engender in their minds the tendency to presume on Japan's kindness with pernicious effects on Japanese rule." The elder brother, in other words, decides what is good for his younger brother and should not show "too much consideration" in enforcing it.

Whatever one's age, one's position in the hierarchy depends on whether one is male or female. The Japanese woman walks behind her husband and has a lower status. Even women who on occasions when they wear American clothes walk alongside and precede him through a door, again fall to the rear when they have donned their kimonos. The Japanese daughter of the family must get along as best she can while the presents, the attentions, and the money for education go to her brothers. Even when higher schools were established for young women the prescribed courses were heavily loaded with instruction in etiquette and bodily movement. Serious intellectual training was not on a par with boys', and one principal of such a school, advocating for his upper middle class students some instruction in European languages, based his recommendation on the desirability of their being able to put their husband's books back in the bookcase right side up after they had dusted them.

Nevertheless, the Japanese women have great freedom as compared to most other Asiatic countries and this is not just a phase of Westernization. There never was female foot-binding as in the Chinese upper classes, and Indian women today exclaim over Japanese women going in and out of shops, up and down the streets and never secreting themselves. Japanese wives do the family shopping and carry the family purse. If money fails, it is they who must select something from the household and carry it to the pawnshop. A woman runs her servants, has great say in her children's marriages, and when she is a mother-in-law commonly runs her household realm with as firm a hand as if she had never been, for half her life, a nodding violet.

The prerogatives of generation, sex, and age in Japan are great. But those who exercise these privileges act as trustees rather than as arbitrary autocrats. The father or the elder brother is responsible for the household, whether its members are living, dead, or yet unborn. He must make weighty decisions and see that they are carried out. He does not, however, have unconditional authority. He is expected to act responsibly for the honor of the house. He recalls to his son and younger brother the legacy of the family, both in material and in spiritual things, and he challenges them to be worthy. Even if he is a peasant he invokes *noblesse oblige* to the family forebears, and if he belongs to more exalted classes the weight of responsibility to the house becomes heavier and heavier. The claims of the family come before the claims of the individual.

In any affair of importance the head of a family of any standing calls a family council at which the matter is debated. For a conference on a betrothal, for instance, members of the family may come from distant parts of Japan. The process of coming to a decision involves all the imponderables of personality. A younger brother or a wife may sway the verdict. The master of the house saddles himself with great difficulties if he acts without regard for group opinion. Decisions, of course, may be desperately unwelcome to the individual whose fate is being settled. His elders, however, who have themselves submitted in their lifetimes to decisions of family councils, are impregnable in demanding of their juniors what they have bowed to in their day. The sanction behind their demand is very different from that which, both in law and in custom, gives the Prussian father arbitrary rights over his wife and children. What is demanded is not for this reason less exacting in Japan, but the effects are different. The Japanese do not learn in their home life to value arbitrary authority, and the habit of submitting to it easily is not fostered. Submission to the will of the family is demanded in the name of a supreme value in which, however onerous its requirements, all of them have a stake. It is demanded in the name of a common loyalty.

Every Japanese learns the habit of hierarchy first in the bosom of his family and what he learns there he applies in wider fields of economic life and of government. He learns that a person gives all deference to those who outrank him in assigned "proper place," no matter whether or not they are the really dominant persons in the group. Even a husband who is dominated by his wife, or an elder brother who is dominated by a younger brother, receives no less formal deference. Formal boundaries between prerogatives are not broken down just because some other person is operating behind the scenes. The façade is not changed to suit the facts of dominance. It remains inviolable. There is even a certain tactical advantage in operating without the trappings of formal status; one is in that case less vulnerable. The Japanese learn, too, in their family experience that the greatest weight that can be given to a decision comes from the family conviction that it maintains the family honor. The decision is not a decree enforced by an iron fist at the whim of a tyrant who happens to be head of the family. He is more nearly a trustee of a material and spiritual estate which is important to them all and which demands of them all that they subordinate their personal wills to its requirements. The Japanese repudiate the use of the mailed fist, but they do not for that reason subordinate themselves any the less to the demands of the family, nor do they for that reason give to those with assigned status any less extreme deference. Hierarchy in the family is maintained even though the family elders have little opportunity to be strong-armed autocrats.

Such a bald statement of hierarchy in the Japanese family does not, when Americans read it with their different standards of interpersonal behavior, do justice to the acceptance of strong and sanctioned emotional ties in Japanese families. There is very considerable solidarity in the household. . . . It is important in trying to understand their demand for hierarchy in the wider fields of government and economic life to recognize how thoroughly the habit is learned in the bosom of the family.

13. VANISHING CULTURES *

ROBERT HEINE-GELDERN

We commonly think of learning about nonliterate (commonly termed "primitive") cultures through a careful reconstruction of evidence obtained by archeological excavation of long-extinct societies. As Heine-Geldern makes clear in this selection, however, there still exist a few opportunities to study isolated communities relatively untouched by the complexities of the mid-twentieth century mechanized world. In fact, the author urges that these studies be made at once, pointing to a number of golden opportunities to learn about certain simple cultures, now lost because we failed to study them before they were subjected to the influences of industrialization.

Imagine that, on an island in some remote corner of the earth, an explorer were to discover a tribe of people still living in the Old Stone Age more or less as man lived 50,000 years ago. One might suppose that scientists would be eager to rush off to that anthropological paradise to study the miraculously preserved living remnant of man's long-lost past. Well, precisely such a discovery was made not too long ago, and men allowed the opportunity to slip from their fingers. Toward the end

* From *Scientific American*, Vol. 196, No. 5 (May, 1957), 39–45.
  The author (b. 1885), a native of Austria, is Professor, Asia Institute, and Research Associate, American Museum of Natural History. Onetime lecturer New York University, Columbia University and University of California.

of the 18th century French and British explorers came to the island of Tasmania, off the southern coast of Australia. They found a dark, woolly-haired people with an incredibly primitive culture—more primitive even than that of the Australian aborigines. The Tasmanians lived by hunting and food-gathering; they had no domesticated animals, not even dogs; their only weapons were clubs, stones and pointed sticks shaped like early Stone Age spears; their chipped-stone implements were as crude as those of Neanderthal man. These people would have been looked down upon as savages even by men of the latter part of the Old Stone Age, who had advanced to specialized flint and bone tools and cave painting. The Tasmanians offered, or, rather, could have offered, to modern science the closest surviving approach to the sort of culture that our human ancestors may have had before the last Ice Age.

Yet no anthropologist ever visited the Tasmanian aborigines. Instead they were hunted like wild animals by the white settlers who followed the explorers to the island. By 1830 no more than 200 of the thousands of natives who had inhabited the island were left, and the last Tasmanian died in 1876. An invaluable opportunity was lost forever.

In 1890 the great British anthropologist Sir Edward Tylor wrote of the Tasmanians: "Looking at the vestiges of a people so representative of the rudest type of man, anthropologists must join with philanthropists in regretting their unhappy fate. We are now beginning to see what scientific value there would have been in a minute careful portraiture of their thoughts and customs." And H. Ling Roth, who collected the all too meager scraps of knowledge we possess about the Tasmanians and published them in a book, woefully observed: "The sad and untimely destruction of this interesting primitive race is one of the greatest losses anthropology has suffered."

Of course there are understandable reasons for the failure to appreciate and exploit this opportunity at the time. Anthropology was then still in an embryonic stage. But what should concern us now is whether or not we have learned the lesson. I am afraid we have not, or at least not sufficiently.

It is true that in recent years anthropologists have carried out many investigations of still-extant hunting and food-gathering tribes, notably among the Eskimos, the Australian aborigines, the Pygmies of central Africa and the Negritos of the Malay Peninsula. But many others have been completely neglected, and disease and changed conditions of life are destroying them, or at least their cultures, with appalling rapidity. The urgency of time is particularly well illustrated by the case of the primitive Indian tribe known as the Yamana, on the island of Tierra del Fuego off the tip of South America. In the 1920's the anthropologists Martin Gusinde and Wilhelm Koppers, then working in Chile, found these people in the nick of time. Their magnificent reports on the

Yamana tribe show how much we would have lost had they come a few years later. The tribe has now disappeared. . . .

In 1890 Sir George Scott Robertson encountered in the Hindu Kush Mountains, between Afghanistan and what now is Pakistan, the fierce tribes called the Kafirs. They were an isolated people who spoke Indo-European languages, had an ancient pagan religion, hunted with bows and arrows and erected stone monuments and wooden statues in honor of their dead. The whole country must have been a living museum of cultural remnants dating back to various periods of antiquity. Here was a living culture still reflecting the social institutions and religious beliefs of some group of ancient Aryans. But Robertson's book on the Kafirs, with its all too scanty details, is practically our only source of information on their ancient culture, for it has now vanished. A few years after Robertson's visit the Afghans conquered the Kafirs and converted them forcibly to Islam.

One of the great lost opportunities was Easter Island, about which probably more nonsense has been written than about any other spot on the earth. When it was discovered by Europeans in the 18th century, its enormous stone statues at once excited the imagination, and later the island's interest was enhanced for anthropologists by the surprising discovery that its inhabitants possessed a script and written documents. But no one thought of sending competent scholars to investigate its culture. In the second half of the 19th century a curious notion seems to have prevailed, according to which navy paymasters were particularly qualified to carry out field research on Easter Island. In 1882 the paymaster of a German warship was given such an assignment and was allowed three and a half days for the task. In 1886 W. J. Thomson, paymaster of the U.S.S. *Mohican,* was given 11 days on the island for investigation of its mysteries. Fortunately Thomson was a person of unusual ability and zeal, and he accomplished a remarkable amount of valuable work. But Easter Island was a task for extended research by trained scholars. When at last the first scientific expedition arrived on the island in 1914, it was too late. The old culture had disintegrated.

Mrs. Scoresby Routledge, the head of the expedition, came just in time to discover that there had been two different kinds of script on Easter Island. The first, preserved in about two dozen tablets in museums, was no longer known to any living native on the island. Mrs. Routledge found an old man who knew how to write the second script, but he died within a few weeks, leaving her only a single sheet of paper with a few undeciphered lines.

Mrs. Routledge and the few anthropologists who visited the island in later expeditions collected every scrap of knowledge and tradition that was still to be found, but despite all their endeavors our knowledge of the island's old culture remains fragmentary. It is exasperating to realize that we might easily have learned a great deal about this fascinating culture had our predecessors had more vision and recognized in time the importance and urgency of research. The full scope of our loss became apparent recently when Thomas S. Barthel of the University of Hamburg succeeded in deciphering some of the tablets and showed that they throw light on the cultural history not only of Easter Island but also of a large part of Polynesia.

It would be easy to list similar instances of lost opportunities by the dozen and from every part of the world. Ever since the great era of world exploration began in the 15th century, the extermination of non-European cultures and ancient tribes has been going on in wholesale fashion. Now the Second World War and its aftermath have greatly accelerated this process. All over the world ancient cultures are being broken up and annihilated at unprecedented speed. Tribes are being absorbed by the larger neighboring populations. Cultures and languages which have never been properly recorded are disappearing. Modern technology and economic developments are proving more efficient in erasing traditional cultures than were the firearms of the conquerors of former centuries.

Anthropologists have speeded up their field research and accomplished an impressive amount of work since the war. But we must face the hard fact that we are racing against time. Within 10 or 15 years many of the ancient cultures and languages still surviving will be gone.

. . . . .

A complete list of the obscure tribes of our world would easily fill a whole volume. Large areas of India, Burma and Indochina, some islands of Indonesia, parts of Africa, great tracts in South America—these and other places remain practically unexplored from the anthropological point of view.

Why are we so interested in the cultures and languages of these small eccentric tribes of a few hundred or a few thousand people? Is it justified to spend a great deal of labor and money to search them out? The president of an important international organization remarked not long ago: "If these languages will disappear anyway, why should we study them?"

Any anthropologist or linguist can give many important reasons. An almost dead language spoken by only a few dozen people may occasionally hold the key to the solution of problems of enormous scope. For instance, there is in central India a small tribe, the Nahal, whose language is said to be very unlike the major languages now spoken in India. Could this possibly be a remnant of the languages spoken by the aboriginal inhabitants of India (the "Veddoids") before the invasions by the Aryans and Dravidians from the west and the Mundarians from the east? If so, its importance can hardly be overestimated. Not only would it tell us about the original tongues of the "Veddoids" (whose descendants now number 20 million) but it might well show influences on the Aryan, Dravidian and Mundarian languages. Therefore the language of the small Nahal tribe might help us understand certain aspects of the languages of the hundreds of millions who today inhabit India.

Looking at the situation from another point of view, suppose that the Negrito tribes on the Andaman Islands had died many thousands of years ago and an archaeologist suddenly discovered some of their artifacts. The *Illustrated London News* might publish a sensational article on this new discovery of a surprisingly primitive Stone Age culture, and the diggers would get busy excavating the remains. Why must peoples and cultures be dead and gone in order to stimulate the imagination of the general public? From excavations of the dead past we can get only the bones of a culture, but in the living tribes we have its flesh. To be sure, it would be wrong to assume that any of the present primitive cultures correspond exactly to those of the distant past, but they do give us the only certain guide to what man's economy, society and religion may have been like in prehistoric antiquity.

We have been spending comparatively enormous sums to conquer Mount Everest and other mountain peaks—sums which could finance anthropological expeditions beyond our wildest dreams. Let us reflect that the mountains will still be there hundreds or thousands of years from now, but many of the vanishing cultures will not last another generation. The critical situation in anthropology, all the world over, should call for a supreme effort on the part of scientific workers and for support by those who are able to provide the means for research. Otherwise a vast part of the human heritage will be lost forever.

14. FUNDAMENTAL NOTIONS OF THE FOLKWAYS AND OF THE MORES *

WILLIAM GRAHAM SUMNER

The manners, usages, folkways, mores, and institutions of every society tend to be regarded by the members of that society as the only right and proper ones. Perhaps Sumner's famous book, Folkways, published in 1906, did more than any other to demonstrate the great variety of human behavior patterns thus regarded. As a result, it has induced many people to pause before they say—or even to refrain from thinking—"My ways —our ways—are the only civilized ways of behaving." The terms "folkways" and "mores," first given currency as sociological terms in Sumner's book, are now a part of our everyday language.

DEFINITION AND MODE OF ORIGIN OF THE FOLKWAYS

If we put together all that we have learned from anthropology and ethnography about primitive men and primitive society, we perceive that the first task of life is to live. Men begin with acts, not with thoughts. Every moment brings necessities which must be satisfied at once. Need was the first experience, and it was followed at once by a blundering effort to satisfy it. It is generally taken for granted that men inherited some guiding instincts from their beast ancestry, and it may be true, although it has never been proved. If there were such inheritances, they controlled and aided the first efforts to satisfy needs. Analogy makes it easy to assume that the ways of beasts had produced channels of habit and predisposition along which dexterities and other psychophysical activities would run easily. Experiments with newborn animals show that in the absence of any experience of the relation of means to

---

* William Graham Sumner, *Folkways* (Ginn and Company, 1940, Centennial Edition), sections 1–3, 28–29, 31–32, 34–35, 66–68. Reprinted by permission of the publisher.

The author (1840–1910) was an economist, sociologist, rector. One of the pioneer American sociologists with Ward, Giddings, and Small. Became Professor of Political and Social Science at Yale in 1872. Studied in Universities of Göttingen and Oxford. Among his books are *A History of American Currency; What Social Classes Owe to Each Other; Earth Hunger and Other Essays; The Science of Society* (with A. G. Keller).

ends, efforts to satisfy needs are clumsy and blundering. The method is that of trial and failure, which produces repeated pain, loss, and disappointments. Nevertheless, it is a method of rude experiment and selection. The earliest efforts of men were of this kind. Need was the impelling force. Pleasure and pain, on the one side and the other, were the rude constraints which defined the line on which efforts must proceed. The ability to distinguish between pleasure and pain is the only psychical power which is to be assumed. Thus ways of doing things were selected, which were expedient. They answered the purpose better than other ways, or with less toil and pain. Along the course on which efforts were compelled to go, habit, routine, and skill were developed. The struggle to maintain existence was carried on, not individually, but in groups. Each profited by the other's experience; hence there was concurrence towards that which proved to be most expedient. All at last adopted the same way for the same purpose; hence the ways turned into customs and became mass phenomena. Instincts were developed in connection with them. In this way folkways arise. The young learn them by tradition, imitation, and authority. The folkways, at a time, provide for all the needs of life then and there. They are uniform, universal in the group, imperative, and invariable. As time goes on, the folkways become more and more arbitrary, positive, and imperative. If asked why they act in a certain way in certain cases, primitive people always answer that it is because they and their ancestors always have done so. A sanction also arises from ghost fear. The ghosts of ancestors would be angry if the living should change the ancient folkways.

THE FOLKWAYS ARE A SOCIETAL FORCE

The operation by which folkways are produced consists in the frequent repetition of petty acts, often by great numbers acting in concert or, at least, acting in the same way when face to face with the same need. The immediate motive is interest. It produces habit in the individual and custom in the group. It is, therefore, in the highest degree original and primitive. By habit and custom it exerts a strain on every individual within its range; therefore it rises to a societal force to which great classes of societal phenomena are due. Its earliest stages, its course, and laws may be studied; also its influence on individuals and their reaction on it. It is our present purpose so to study it. We have to recognize it as one of the chief forces by which a society is made to be what it is. Out of the unconscious experiment which every repetition of the ways includes, there issues pleasure or pain, and then, so far as the men are capable of reflection, convictions that the ways are conducive to societal welfare. These two experiences are not the same. The most uncivilized men, both in the food quest and in war, do things which are painful, but which have been found to be expedient. Perhaps these cases teach the sense of social welfare better than those which are pleasurable and favorable to welfare. The former cases call for some intelligent reflection on experience. When this conviction as to the relation to welfare is added to the folkways they are converted into mores, and, by virtue of the philosophical and ethical element added to them, they win utility and importance and become the source of the science and the art of living.

FOLKWAYS ARE MADE UNCONSCIOUSLY

It is of the first importance to notice that, from the first acts by which men try to satisfy needs, each act stands by itself, and looks no further than the immediate satisfaction. From recurrent needs arise habits for the individual and customs for the group, but these results are consequences which were never conscious, and never foreseen or intended. They are not noticed until they have long existed, and it is still longer before they are appreciated. Another long time must pass, and a higher stage of mental development must be reached, before they can be used as a basis from which to deduce rules for meeting, in the future, problems whose pressure can be foreseen. The folkways, therefore, are not creations of human purpose and wit. They are like products of natural forces which men unconsciously set in operation, or they are like the instinctive ways of animals, which are developed out of experience, which reach a final form of maximum adaptation to an interest, which are handed down by tradition and admit of no exception or variation, yet change to meet new conditions, still within the same limited methods, and without rational reflection or purpose. From this it results that all the life of human beings, in all ages and stages of culture, is primarily controlled by a vast mass of folkways handed down from the earliest existence of the race, having the nature of the ways of other animals, only the topmost layers of which are subject to change and control, and have been somewhat modified by human philosophy, ethics, and religion, or by other acts of intelligent reflection. We are told of savages that "It is difficult to exhaust the customs and small ceremonial usages of a savage people. Custom regulates the whole of a man's actions,—his bathing, washing, cutting his hair, eating, drinking, and fasting. From his cradle to his grave he is the slave of ancient usage. In his life there is nothing free, nothing original, nothing spontaneous, no progress towards a higher and better life, and no attempt to improve his condition, mentally, morally, or spiritually." All men act in this way with only a little wider margin of voluntary variation.

FOLKWAYS DUE TO FALSE INFERENCE

Folkways have been formed by accident, that is, by irrational and incongruous action, based on pseudo-knowledge. In Molembo a pestilence broke out soon after a Portuguese had died there. After that the natives took all possible measures not to allow any white man to die in their country. On the Nicobar islands some natives who had just begun to make pottery died. The art was given up and never again attempted. White men gave to one Bushman in a kraal a stick ornamented with buttons as a symbol of authority. The recipient died leaving the stick to his son. The son soon died. Then the Bushmen brought back the stick lest all should die. Until recently no building of incombustible materials could be built in any big town of the central province of Madagascar, on account of some ancient prejudice. A party of Eskimos met with no game. One of them returned to their sledges and got the ham of a dog to eat. As he returned with the ham bone in his hand he met and killed a seal. Ever afterwards he carried a ham bone in his hand when hunting. The Belenda women (peninsula of Malacca) stay as near to the house as possible during the period. Many keep the door closed. They know no reason for this custom. "It must be due to some now forgotten superstition." Soon after the Yakuts saw a camel for the first time smallpox broke out amongst them. They thought the camel to be the agent of the disease. A woman amongst the same people contracted an endogamous marriage. She soon afterwards became blind. This was thought to be on account of the violation of ancient customs. A very great number of such cases could be collected. In fact they represent the current mode of reasoning of nature people. It is their custom to reason that, if one thing follows another, it is due to it. A great number of customs are traceable to the notion of the evil eye, many more to ritual notions of uncleanness. No scientific investigation could discover the origin of the folkways mentioned, if the origin had not chanced to become known to civilized men. We must believe that the known cases illustrate the irrational and incongruous origin of many folkways. In civilized history also we know that customs have owed their origin to "historical accident,"—the vanity of a princess, the deformity of a king, the whim of a democracy, the love intrigue of a statesman or prelate. By the institutions of another age it may be provided that no one of these things can affect decisions, acts, or interests, but then the power to decide the ways may have passed to clubs, trades unions, trusts, commercial rivals, wire-pullers, politicians, and political fanatics. In these cases also the causes and origins may escape investigation.

HARMFUL FOLKWAYS

There are folkways which are positively harmful. Very often these are just the ones for which a definite reason can be given. The destruction of a man's goods at his death is a direct deduction from other-worldliness; the dead man is supposed to want in the other world just what he wanted here. The destruction of a man's goods at his death was a great waste of capital, and it must have had a disastrous effect on the interests of the living, and must have very seriously hindered the development of civilization. With this custom we must class all the expenditure of labor and capital on graves, temples, pyramids, rites, sacrifices, and support of priests, so far as these were supposed to benefit the dead. The faith in goblinism produced other-worldly interests which overruled ordinary worldly interests. Foods have often been forbidden which were plentiful, the prohibition of which injuriously lessened the food supply. There is a tribe of Bushmen who will eat no goat's flesh, although goats are the most numerous domestic animals in the district. Where totemism exists it is regularly accompanied by a taboo on eating the totem animal. Whatever may be the real principle in totemism, it overrules the interest in an abundant food supply. "The origin of the sacred regard paid to the cow must be sought in the primitive nomadic life of the Indo-European race," because it is common to Iranians and Indians of Hindostan. The Libyans ate oxen but not cows. The same was true of the Phœnicians and Egyptians. In some cases the sense of a food taboo is not to be learned. It may have been entirely capricious. Mohammed would not eat lizards, because he thought them the offspring of a metamorphosed clan of Israelites. On the other hand, the protective taboo which forbade killing crocodiles, pythons, cobras, and other animals enemies of man was harmful to his interests, whatever the motive. "It seems to be a fixed article of belief throughout southern India, that all who have willfully or accidentally killed a snake, especially a cobra, will certainly be punished, either in this life or the next, in one of three ways: either by childlessness, or by leprosy, or by ophthalmia." Where this faith exists man has a greater interest to spare a cobra than to kill it. India furnishes a great number of cases of harmful mores. "In India every tendency of humanity seems intensified and exaggerated. No country in the world is so conservative in its traditions, yet no country has undergone so many religious changes and vicissitudes." "Every year thousands perish of disease that might recover if they would take proper nourishment, and drink the medicine that science prescribes, but which they imagine that their religion forbids them to touch." "Men who can scarcely count beyond twenty, and know not the letters of the alphabet, would rather die than eat food which had been prepared by men of lower caste, unless it had been sanctified by being offered to an idol; and would kill their daughters rather than endure the disgrace of having unmarried girls at home beyond twelve or thirteen years of age." In the last case the rule of obligation and duty is set by the mores. The interest comes under vanity. The sanction of the caste rules is in a boycott by all members of the caste. The rules are often very harmful. "The authority of caste rests partly on written laws, partly on legendary fables or narratives, partly on the injunctions of instructors and priests, partly on custom and usage, and partly on the caprice and convenience of its votaries." The harm of caste rules is so great that of late they have been broken in some cases, especially in regard to travel over sea, which is a great advantage to Hindoos. The Hindoo folkways in regard to widows and child marriages must also be recognized as socially harmful.

. . . . . .

THE FOLKWAYS ARE "RIGHT"

The folkways are the "right" ways to satisfy all interests, because they are traditional, and exist in fact. They extend over the whole of life. There is a right way to catch game, to win a wife, to make one's self appear, to cure disease, to honor ghosts, to treat comrades or strangers, to behave when a child is born, on the warpath, in council, and so on in all cases which can arise. The ways are defined on the negative side, that is, by taboos. The "right" way is the way which the ancestors used and which has been handed down. The tradition is its own warrant. It is not held subject to verification by experience. The notion of right is in the folkways. It is not outside of them, of independent origin, and brought to them to test them. In the folkways, whatever is, is right. This is because they are traditional, and therefore contain in themselves the authority of the ancestral ghosts. When we come to the folkways we are at the end of our analysis. The notion of right and ought is the same in regard to all the folkways, but the degree of it varies with the importance of the interest at stake. The obligation of conformable and coöperative action is far greater under ghost fear and war than in other matters, and the social sanctions are severer, because group interests are supposed to be at stake. Some usages contain only a slight element of right and ought. It may well be believed that notions of right and duty, and of social welfare, were first developed in connection with ghost fear and other-worldliness, and therefore that, in that field also, folkways were first raised to mores. "Rights" are the rules of mutual give and take in the competition of life which are imposed on comrades in the in-group, in order that the peace may prevail there which is essential to the group strength. Therefore rights can never be "natural" or "God-given," or absolute in any sense. The morality of a group at a time is the sum of the taboos and prescriptions in the folkways by which right conduct is defined. Therefore morals can never be intuitive. They are historical, institutional, and empirical.

World philosophy, life policy, right, rights, and morality are all products of the folkways. They are reflections on, and generalizations from, the experience of pleasure and pain which is won in efforts to carry on the struggle for existence under actual life conditions. The generalizations are very crude and vague in their germinal forms. They are all embodied in folklore, and all our philosophy and science have been developed out of them.

THE FOLKWAYS ARE "TRUE"

The folkways are necessarily "true" with respect to some world philosophy. Pain forced men to think. The ills of life imposed reflection and taught forethought. Mental processes were irksome and were not undertaken until painful experience made them unavoidable. With great unanimity all over the globe primitive men followed the same line of thought. The dead were believed to live on as ghosts in another world just like this one. The ghosts had just the same needs, tastes, passions, etc., as the living men had had. These transcendental notions were the beginning of the mental outfit of mankind. They are articles of faith, not rational convictions. The living had duties to the ghosts, and the ghosts had rights; they also had power to enforce their rights. It behooved the living therefore to learn how to deal with ghosts. Here we have a complete world philosophy and a life policy deduced from it. When pain, loss, and ill were experienced and the question was provoked, Who did this to us? the world philosophy furnished the answer. When the painful experience forced the question, Why are the ghosts angry and what must we do to appease them? the "right" answer was the one which fitted into the philosophy of ghost fear. All acts were therefore constrained and trained into the forms of the world philosophy by ghost fear, ancestral authority, taboos, and habit. The habits and customs created a practical philosophy of welfare, and they confirmed and developed the religious theories of goblinism.

. . . . .

DEFINITION OF THE MORES

When the elements of truth and right are developed into doctrines of welfare, the folkways are raised to another plane. They then become capable of producing inferences, developing into new forms, and extending their constructive influence over men and society. Then we call them the mores. The mores are the folkways, including the philosophical and ethical generalizations as to societal welfare which are suggested by them, and inherent in them, as they grow.

TABOOS

The mores necessarily consist, in a large part, of taboos, which indicate the things which must not be done. In part these are dictated by mystic dread of ghosts who might be offended by certain acts, but they also include such acts as have been found by experience to produce unwelcome results, especially in the food quest, in war, in health, or in increase or decrease of population. These taboos always contain a greater element of philosophy than the positive rules, because the taboos contain reference to a reason, as, for instance, that the act would displease the ghosts. The primitive taboos correspond to the fact that the life of man is environed by perils. His food quest must be limited by shunning poisonous plants. His appetite must be restrained from excess. His physical strength and health must be guarded from dangers. The taboos carry on the accumulated wisdom of generations, which has almost always been purchased by pain, loss, disease, and death. Other taboos contain inhibitions of what will be injurious to the group. The laws about the sexes, about property, about war, and about ghosts, have this character. They always include some social philosophy. They are both mystic and utilitarian, or compounded of the two.

Taboos may be divided into two classes, (1) protective and (2) destructive. Some of them aim to protect and secure, while others aim to repress or exterminate. Women are subject to some taboos which are directed against them as sources of possible harm or danger to men, and they are subject to other taboos which put them outside of the duties or risks of men. On account of this difference in taboos, taboos act selectively, and thus affect the course of civilization. They contain judgments as to societal welfare.

. . . . . .

MORE EXACT DEFINITION OF THE MORES

We may now formulate a more complete definition of the mores. They are the ways of doing things which are current in a society to satisfy human needs and desires, together with the faiths, notions, codes, and standards of well living which inhere in those ways, having a genetic connection with them. By virtue of the latter element the mores are traits in the specific character (ethos) of a society or a period. They pervade and control the ways of thinking in all the exigencies of life, returning from the world of abstractions to the world of action, to give guidance and to win revivification. "The mores [*Sitten*] are, before any beginning of reflection, the regulators of the political, social, and religious behavior of the individual. Conscious reflection is the worst enemy of the mores, because mores begin unconsciously and pursue unconscious purposes, which are recognized by reflection often only after long and circuitous processes, and because their expediency often depends on the assumption that they will have general acceptance and currency, uninterfered with by reflection." "The mores are usage in any group, in so far as it, on the one hand, is not the expression or fulfillment of an absolute natural necessity [e.g. eating or sleeping], and, on the other hand, is independent of the arbitrary will of the individual, and is generally accepted as good and proper, appropriate and worthy."

RITUAL

The process by which mores are developed and established is ritual. Ritual is so foreign to our mores that we do not recognize its power. In primitive society it is the prevailing method of activity, and primitive religion is entirely a matter of ritual. Ritual is the perfect form of drill and of the regulated habit which comes from drill. Acts which are ordained by authority and are repeated mechanically without intelligence run into ritual. If infants and children are subjected to ritual they never escape from its effects through life. Galton says that he was, in early youth, in contact with the Mohammedan ritual idea that the left hand is less worthy than the right, and that he never overcame it. We see the effect of ritual in breeding, courtesy, politeness, and all forms of prescribed behavior. Etiquette is social ritual. Ritual is not easy compliance with usage; it is strict compliance with detailed and punctilious rule. It admits of no exception or deviation. The stricter the discipline, the greater the power of ritual over action and character. In the training of animals and the education of children it is the perfection, inevitableness, invariableness, and relentlessness of routine which tells. They should never experience any exception or irregularity. Ritual is connected with words, gestures, symbols, and signs. Associations result, and, upon a repetition of the signal, the act is repeated, whether the will assents or not. Association and habit account for the phenomena. Ritual gains further strength when it is rhythmical, and is connected with music, verse, or other rhythmical arts. Acts are ritually repeated at the recurrence of the rhythmical points. The alternation of night and day produces rhythms of waking and sleeping, of labor and rest, for great numbers at the same time, in their struggle for existence.

The seasons also produce rhythms in work. Ritual may embody an idea of utility, expediency, or welfare, but it always tends to become perfunctory, and the idea is only subconscious. There is ritual in primitive therapeutics, and it was not eliminated until very recent times. The patient was directed, not only to apply remedies, but also to perform rites. The rites introduced mystic elements. This illustrates the connection of ritual with notions of magical effects produced by rites. All ritual is ceremonious and solemn. It tends to become sacred, or to make sacred the subject-matter with which it is connected. Therefore, in primitive society, it is by ritual that sentiments of awe, deference to authority, submission to tradition, and disciplinary coöperation are inculcated. Ritual operates a constant suggestion, and the suggestion is at once put in operation in acts. Ritual, therefore, suggests sentiments, but it never inculcates doctrines. Ritual is strongest when it is most perfunctory and excites no thought. By familiarity with ritual any doctrinal reference which it once had is lost by familiarity, but the habits persist. Primitive religion is ritualistic, not because religion makes ritual, but because ritual makes religion. Ritual is something to be done, not something to be thought or felt. Men can always perform the prescribed act, although they cannot always think or feel prescribed thoughts or emotions. The acts may bring up again, by association, states of the mind and sentiments which have been connected with them, especially in childhood, when the fantasy was easily affected by rites, music, singing, dramas, etc. No creed, no moral code, and no scientific demonstration can ever win the same hold upon men and women as habits of action, with associated sentiments and states of mind, drilled in from childhood. Mohammedanism shows the power of ritual. Any occupation is interrupted for the prayers and prescribed genuflections. The Brahmins also observe an elaborate daily ritual. They devote to it two hours in the morning, two in the evening, and one at midday. Monks and nuns have won the extreme satisfaction of religious sentiment from the unbroken habit of repeated ritual, with undisturbed opportunity to develop the emotional effects of it.

THE RITUAL OF THE MORES

The mores are social ritual in which we all participate unconsciously. The current habits as to hours of labor, meal hours, family life, the social intercourse of the sexes, propriety, amusements, travel, holidays, education, the use of periodicals and libraries, and innumerable other details of life fall under this ritual. Each does as everybody does. For the great mass of mankind as to all things, and for all of us for a great many things, the rule to do as all do suffices. We are led by suggestion and association to believe that there must be wisdom and utility in what all do. The great mass of the folkways give us discipline and the support of routine and habit. If we had to form judgments as to all these cases before we could act in them, and were forced always to act rationally, the burden would be unendurable. Beneficent use and wont save us this trouble.

15. MAN'S CHALLENGE: THE USE OF THE EARTH *

JULIAN HUXLEY

Social scientists often devote their attention rather exclusively to the immediate and local environment simply because it impinges so directly on their senses. For example, the population problems and the use of natural resources in their own communities and state right now may occupy their attention to the exclusion of long-run considerations on a wider front which are even more important to us all. Here in this selection the distinguished biologist Sir Julian Huxley counters this provincialism by an examination of the consequences of present trends in world-wide population growth and the ill-considered use of our natural resources.

At the dawn of civilization, say 5,000 years ago, the total population of the world cannot have numbered much more than 20 million. Today the mere yearly increase in world population is nearly twice this amount. Apart from occasional temporary setbacks, world population has steadily increased. It reached the billion mark in the 1850's and the two-billion mark in the 1920's.

Population is, of course, self-multiplying, like money at compound interest; and what is even more alarming than its absolute growth is that its compound interest rate of increase has also been steadily increasing. Before the discovery of agriculture the rate cannot have exceeded one-tenth of 1 per cent; 300 years ago it was less than half of 1 per cent, and it only reached 1 per cent well on in the present century.

* From "Man's Challenge: The Use of the Earth," *Horizon* (published by American Heritage, New York), Vol. 1, No. 1 (September, 1958), 49–55.

The author (b. 1887) is a writer and biologist. Onetime Professor of Zoology, King's College, London. Director General UNESCO, 1947–1948. Among his works are: *Essays of a Biologist; The Stream of Life; Man in the Modern World;* and *Evolution and Ethics.*

It is now about 1⅓ per cent and is still increasing. Even with the aid of the industrial and technological revolution, whose beginnings we can date around 1650, it took nearly two centuries from that date to double world population; but unless some cataclysm occurs, today's population will double itself in less than fifty years from now. (One projection made by the United Nations Population Branch envisages an even faster increase and estimates that by the year 2000, world population may exceed 6¼ billion.)

As a result, some of the more thoughtful men and women alive today are beginning to ask new questions about humanity. They are trying to consider the present situation of the world *sub specie evolutionis*. From the point of view of the continuing process of evolution, what are the functions for which the surface of our planet is needed, and how satisfactorily are they now being carried out? When we begin thinking along such lines, we find ourselves coming up against many facts, principles, and ideas which earlier generations did not bother their heads about.

There is first the obvious fact that the surface of the globe is limited. Man cannot envisage an indefinite increase in numbers (or in any human activity) but must begin thinking in terms of equilibria; the immensely rapid changes of the last few thousand years are symptoms of human youth and, indeed, immaturity. Whether we succeed in manufacturing synthetic nutriment or not, it is safe to prophesy that a large proportion of man's food will continue to be grown naturally, under cultivation, as it is today. In countries at a high technological level and with a high density of population, like Britain, there is already serious competition between the use of land for food production and for purposes such as housing, roads, and airfields. It is worth remembering that the area of London just about doubled between 1900 and 1950.

The absolute growth in size of cities is another result of general population growth. Cities like New York, Tokyo, or London have now reached a size at which they are defeating their own aims. Large numbers of their inhabitants have to spend two or three hours every day in great discomfort getting to and from their work, and the problems of traffic and parking seem to be approaching insolubility.

Besides food production, there is the problem of moisture conservation and the prevention of erosion. Large areas once covered by forest— for instance in China and in the Middle East—have been denuded of trees, the climate has been altered, and the fertile topsoil has been partly or wholly eroded away. A scientific survey could establish what area of the world's surface requires to be reafforested or otherwise devoted to antierosion measures.

But before pursuing the subject from the positive point of view, of the optimum use that man might make of his terrestrial home, let us look at it from the gloomiest possible angle. Hamlet apostrophized man as "the paragon of animals," and this is a fair description of our species as the latest dominant type in evolution—so long as he does not over-reach himself. But if he allows himself to multiply unchecked, he is in danger of becoming the planet's cancer.

After all, what is a cancer? It is a monstrous, or pathological, growth whose cells have ceased to be controlled in their proliferation, have embarked on a course of unlimited multiplication, and have lost some or all of their organization. The cancer becomes a parasite on the organized body; its cells start invading and destroying normal tissues, and groups of them may get carried off in the blood stream to form the destructive secondary growths called metastases. Eventually the normal healthy body is killed by the cancer—either starved to death, or its healthy tissues eaten away or simply crowded out by the abnormal, overactive cancerous tissues.

Our planet is not an organism, but it is an organic system with inter-related parts. Water, soil, mineral resources, air, green plants and animals, bacteria and men—up until recently they have been held together in a web of balanced interdependence; and the whole system has evolved, slowly and majestically, through a series of self-transformations which have realized new and marvelous possibilities for the whole, especially for animal life. Until recently there has never been overmultiplication or overexploitation, by man any more than by any other organism. Human increase has been subjected to various checks and limitations—partly the same checks of disease and starvation and ruthless competition that apply to other animals, but also partly self-generated checks like war, or self-imposed limitations like infanticide or abstention from sexual intercourse.

But now unchecked multiplication is bringing about a state of affairs that can properly be called cancerous. Deforestation and bad methods of cultivation have caused aridity and erosion and have removed much of the soil that is the basis of food production. In the last century, man has started to live increasingly on capital resources—of coal, oil, and other minerals; he is using up in a few generations or centuries what it took tens of millions of years to accumulate. His per capita consumption of resources has steadily mounted, sometimes to a fantastic extent. Thus the consumption of metals and mineral fuels by the United States since 1918 exceeds the total consumed by the whole of mankind in all preceding history. No other species has ever shown this unbridled increase both in proliferation and in consumption. Nor did man himself during his early history.

And as the balance between resources and human numbers is up-set, the quality of the population will, without question, go down. The earth will be bled white, all to maintain an excess of frustrated, underdeveloped, and essentially parasitic creatures. The conversion of the lord of creation into a cancer of earth will, it can be calculated, happen within a century unless something is done to prevent it. In biological evolution, successful animal types eventually become stabilized through automatic checks and balances. Modern man has emancipated himself from these; he needs to aim consciously at stabilization with the aid of deliberate checks and balances. We have reached a phase where the only alternative to man's becoming a pathological phenomenon is to practice a conscious population policy. The spectacular spread of death control has made necessary a world-wide diffusion of birth control.

This brings me back to the positive aspect of the problem. As I suggested earlier, we have to get down to first principles and ask ourselves, What are the functions for which the surface of our planet is needed? What are those which its human population can most desirably perform? How can they best be carried out? If we like to put the question in a still more general way, What should be the aim of man? How should he, as the dominant organic type on earth, direct the future evolution of himself and his planet?

The most general answer is that he should aim at the maximum realization of possibilities. The mere quantitative increase in number of human beings is not itself a desirable aim: improvement of life and health, and quality and variety of experience and activity must be our goal.

One function of the earth whose importance we have only just begun to recognize is that of *wilderness,* the function of allowing men and women to get away from the complications of industrial civilization and make contact with fine scenery and unspoilt nature. Of course, it is not everyone who likes wilderness; perhaps luckily, a considerable number of people enjoy crowds and prefer their vacations to be organized. But wilderness-lovers constitute a sizable minority—and also include a sizable proportion of interesting characters and original thinkers. Wilderness is, in the long run, one of the major functions humanity demands from the surface of the globe. National parks and similar areas where the enjoyment of nature is paramount are attempts to meet this need. But, of course, wilderness is compatible only with a very low population density.

Then there is the function of scientific and natural conservation. Thus there must be areas in which the interests of wild life, or at least the interests of humanity in enjoying wild life, are paramount over those of agriculture, urbanization, or anything else. No one who has seen large animals in natural surroundings can forget the thrilling spectacle: it makes one realize the beauty and wonder, the interest and strangeness, of the achievements of evolving life. It has value in and for itself, and also for the conscious experiences which it can bring to us human beings

Vast quantities of big game and other large animals have been exterminated in the past hundred years—indeed, in the quarter-century since I saw swarms of wild antelopes and zebras and hippos, game has been wiped out over large areas of Africa—and it is now clear that we must set aside areas in which their preservation, and not human cultivation or habitation, shall be paramount.

The same holds for smaller mammals, for birds both rare and common, for interesting and beautiful insects and plants. In addition to the enjoyment that wild creatures can provide, there is the scientific duty of preventing the extinction of species and of preserving at least samples of the world's various ecological habitats and communities. In the most general terms, the function of conserving nature is one to which we must assign a not inconsiderable area of the globe's surface.

Elsewhere, the function of watershed control and of preventing erosion will be paramount, and the job of growing trees will be the most important aim. In other words, over very considerable areas the production of forests, not of human beings or their food, will be the essential function. In various parts of the world, for instance in India, these two aims are already coming into conflict.

It is thus clear that we need a careful plan for the best exploitation of our planet's resources. Large sectors of its surface must never be allowed to develop a high population density; on them, other functions must prevail.

This would be so even if the human species were adequately nourished. Within the trifling time of three or four generations, unchecked human multiplication would bring human numbers and human density to a point of diminishing returns, after which the level of human fulfillment would start to go down instead of up. But the fact is far different. Actually about two-thirds of the more than 2½ billion people in the world today are inadequately nourished, either through sheer lack of calories or through lack of some vitamin or other dietary factor needed for full health, growth and energy.

Thus what we need above all is an agreed world population policy, enabling us to reverse the present disastrous trend while at the same time remedying the plight of the malnourished majority. The present course is leading toward overexploitation of resources and overproduction of increasingly frustrated, overcrowded and inadequately developed human specimens. So far, human history has been on the whole a record of progress: more human beings enjoying a higher degree of fulfilment have come into existence, and the upper level of human achievement has been progressively raised. But, as an evolutionist, I would definitely forecast that a doubling of present human numbers will mean a reversal of this progressive trend of human evolution. It will mean that the world's population will be overly dense, less well nourished and developed physically, and with reduced opportunities for enjoyment and fulfillment. Man will still be the biologically dominant type, but he will have embarked on a degenerative trend, a downward slope.

There is a gleam of hope on the horizon. Three powerful countries —India, Japan, and China—now have official policies of population control, and official birth-control schemes have been set in train in a few dependent territories. The adoption of a population-control policy by China is of extreme importance, not only because China contains over 600 million people, but because it is a Communist country, and the Russian Communists have so far officially maintained a bitter ideological opposition to the whole notion. They have even gone so far as to assert that overpopulation is impossible because scientific and technical advance will always be adequate, and indeed to charge that the very idea of over-population is the invention of the economists and sociologists who are the henchmen of Western capitalism and imperialism. The fact of the matter, of course, is that the U.S.S.R. is at the moment underpopulated; but it will be suffering from population pressure in a matter of three or four generations at the outside.

It is one of the most curious phenomena of the modern world that the Russian Communists and the Roman Catholics agree that birth control is wicked—about the only subject on which they are in agreement. We may hope that the Russians will be influenced by the policy of their powerful partner, China, as well as by the facts. And fortunately the Roman Catholic Church is not in principle opposed to all ideas of keeping down human numbers. On the occasion of the United Nations Conference on World Population in Rome, the Pope himself declared that excess population could be a very serious matter and lead to great distress, and he commended the study of the population problem to all thoughtful Catholics.

. . . . . .

Humanity needs to make up its mind as to the ultimate, or at least the dominant, purpose of human existence. Is it physical enjoyment in this world? Is it salvation in a world after death? Is it national power? Is it obedience to some superindividual code of morality? Is it knowledge? Is it wealth?

Personally, I can see no escape from the conclusion that man's dominant aim must be to continue the billion-year dominant trend of evolution toward greater fulfillment and the realization of more and better possibilities. Man is now the sole agent by which the evolutionary process can continue that trend; but that is no reason why this should happen automatically—it would be just as possible for his future history to be degenerative as for it to be progressive. In any case, the only way in which he can make sure that he is moving in the right direction is by utilizing to the full two of his unique properties—his capacity for conscious planning on the basis of scientific survey and comprehension and deliberate accumulation of knowledge, and his capacity for operating on a world-wide scale.

Once such a point of view is adopted and it is recognized that the existence both of too few and of too many people will interfere with human fulfillment, the way is open for a rational world policy.

The assumption that anything which makes it possible to keep more human beings alive—like new sources of food from the sea, or the manufacture of synthetic food in the laboratory—must be good and right, is at once seen to be fallacious. There must be an optimum magnitude for human numbers and human density. Below that general level, men will not have the opportunity to develop the sciences and the arts and their applications adequately, to produce noble architecture or efficient means of transport. Above that level, man will be, as it were, cutting off his nose to spite his face—he will be making life more inconvenient and less beautiful; will be making certain things, like the enjoyment of solitude and wild nature, impossible; will be destroying other living species; and will finally be condemning later generations to undernourishment, shortened life span, and general frustration.

One new symptomatic phenomenon of our epoch, brought about by the combination of increased human numbers and greater facility of transportation, has been the incipient vulgarization of the outstandingly beautiful cities created by man. To take one example, Venice is unique and is now becoming so overcrowded with tourists that enjoyment of its beauty is beginning to be interfered with. And we cannot very well produce duplicate Venices to meet the demand! The same sort of thing is beginning to happen to overly publicized places of natural beauty.

. . . . .

To sum up the problem, there are only two alternatives. One is to let population increase continue in the same fashion as it has in the past. This will, without question, bring about a condition of world overpopulation and overutilization of resources from which it will be hard to recover. The other alternative is to extend the method of science to human reproduction, and to study the entire problem thoroughly, with a view to a world population policy that shall be at one and the same time inspiring and practical.

As a preliminary, we need an authoritative study of what may be called "earth use," in which all the different factors involved in the future evolution of the earth as the home of man should be taken into account, from efficiency to beauty, from food production to speedy communication, from industrial development to the enjoyment of wild nature. . . .

The matter is urgent. The earth is already being badly misused today by its more than 2½ billion human inhabitants. Unless we do something about it, it will be worse misused by our grandchildren, who are pretty certain to number 5 billion. What is more, man is misusing himself by his unbridled multiplication. If we do nothing to prevent our grandchildren's grandchildren (less than a century and a half in the future) from numbering 10 or more billion, we shall deserve the obloquy of many generations to come.

16. A STUDY OF VALUES *

EVON Z. VOGT AND JOHN M. ROBERTS

If it can be shown that the inborn characteristics of groups of people do not differ significantly, yet it is observed that particular groups solve similar problems quite differently, then the differences must be ascribed to the learned factors which sociologists and anthropologists call "culture." This point is illustrated by Evon Z. Vogt and John M. Roberts as they demonstrate that persons basically similar biologically, but having different cultures, may settle in the same general geographical area and yet develop markedly different modes of life.

"No tenet of intellectual folklore has been so damaging to our life and times as the cliché that 'science has nothing to do with values.' If the consideration of values is to be the exclusive property of religion and the humanities, a scientific understanding of human experience is impossible."

In these words the anthropologist Clyde Kluckhohn recently defined a major challenge and frontier of social research. The forming and choosing of values is a central concern of all men and societies. Conceptions of the desirable, the fitting and the good vary widely among the world's 3,000 or so cultures. They strongly influence the selection of the modes, the means and the ends of human behavior. The social scientist cannot view "man in culture" as conditioned only by economic forces and biological impulses. People see the world through cultural lenses compounded of particular combinations of values; they respond in

* From *Scientific American*, Vol. 195, No. 1 (July, 1956), 25–30.

Evon Z. Vogt (b. 1918) is Associate Professor of Anthropology at Harvard University. Books include: *Modern Homesteaders, The Life of a Twentieth-Century Frontier Family; Navaho Means People* (coauthor).

John M. Roberts (b. 1916) is Professor of Anthropology at the University of Nebraska. He has written *Three Navaho Households* and *Zuñi Law*.

different ways in accordance with their differing values. We must recognize that people are not just "driven" by situational pressures: they are also "pulled" by the ideals and goals of their cultures.

As we advance the frontiers of the social sciences it becomes increasingly clear that values must be studied as a part of our actual subject matter and not left entirely to the humanists and philosophers. Values are, in fact, the subject of an increasing number of investigations today. But how can values be brought under the same kind of objective study as linguistic systems and the techniques of salmon fishing?

The apparent difficulty is reduced if we recall that the object of such study is not to make an ethical judgment of goodness or badness. We want to know, rather, how values function in organizing behavior. Since it is virtually impossible to experiment with human cultures, the social scientist must find his laboratory situation ready-made. Preferably he should be able to observe and compare the role of values in one or two cultures other than his own. Ideally he will find a situation where he can observe variations in values against a background in which other variables are relatively constant.

This article is concerned with . . . the region south of Gallup, N.M., where communities of five different cultural traditions—Zuñi and Navaho Indians, Mormons, Catholic Spanish-Americans and Protestant-American homesteaders from Texas—all contend with the same high-altitude semi-arid environment. Since our research has not yet reached the phase of synthesis and final theory construction, it is still too early to summarize the project's over-all results. At this stage, however, we are able to report that the Gallup region has given us a practically ideal laboratory for investigation of the manifold questions presented by the role of values in human life.

The value study . . . has engaged the collaboration of 30 investigators from the disciplines of anthropology, sociology, psychology, philosophy, history, government and law. They have approached their common concern with values through a wide variety of topical interests, such as religion, cultural change, politics, land use, child rearing, adult personality, mythology, music and graphic arts. The full battery of research techniques—direct observation, participant observation, personal interviews, group discussions, interaction analysis, psychological tests and questionnaires—is represented in the immense documentation now assembled. Since the populations of the five communities are small (3,000 Zuñis, 650 Navahos, 700 Spanish-Americans, 250 Mormons, 250 Texans) it has been possible to emphasize intensive methods and reduce the problems of sampling and statistical analysis which attend so much social research. The extensive existing literatures on some of the cultures have helped to give the study historical depth.

In all its undertakings the values study has been faced with the delicate problem of rapport and public relations in the five communities. No research could be conducted that might endanger future investigations. Among the Zuñi, for example, it has so far not been politic to study prayers, ceremonials and other religious matters at close range. Because we have had to be careful to protect individuals and groups in every way, this is the first over-all account of the project to be published outside a few specialized professional journals and monographs.

The geography of the Gallup region establishes some much-needed constants for a study that is otherwise bedeviled by a multiplicity of uncontrolled variables. Each of the peoples of the five cultures see the same plateau and mesa country, sparsely covered with gramagrass, sagebrush, pinyon and juniper and with stands of ponderosa pines at the higher elevations. All of the people must contend with the same fluctuation in rainfall, averaging only 12 to 15 inches per year, and with the short, changeable growing season typical of the American Southwest at this 7,000-foot altitude. There are permanent springs in the region, but the small Zuñi River, a tributary of the Little Colorado, is the only year-round stream. Soils, however, are fertile and productive when watered.

To meet the problems of making a living in this landscape, each of the five communities has essentially the same technology available to it. In face-to-face contact with one another for a generation or more, all have been subjected to markedly similar historical pressures. These pressures have mounted during the last 10 years, as hard-surface roads, telephone lines and public power have spread through their country. The five communities remain distinct, however, and present significant contrasts.

Each of the cultures, for example, has worked out its own solution for the problem of physical survival. The Zuñis, oldest of the peoples in the region, conduct a long-established irrigation agriculture supplemented by stock-raising and by crafts, notably the making of silver jewelry. The Navahos were originally roving hunters and gatherers and came into the region only a century ago; they have become dry farmers and sheepherders with wage work providing an increasing percentage of their income as contact with our American culture becomes more extensive. Livestock ranching and wage work provide the principal income for the three Spanish-American villages, which were settled about 75 years ago. The Mormons, also established in this region since the 1880's, have been conspicuously successful at irrigation farming; they also engage in livestock ranching and wage work. The Texans staked out the last Homestead Act lands in the region during the 1930's, as refugees from the dust bowl to the east; they raise cattle and carry on a commercial and largely mechanized dry-land farming, with pinto beans as their principal crop.

The five cultures present corresponding contrasts in their community organization and family life. The sedentary Zuñis spend their winters in the stone houses of their large central pueblo, moving in the agricultural season to three farming villages. Their social structure is based on the matrilocal household (with the husband living with his wife's kinfolk), matrilineal clans, and various priesthoods and other religious groupings. The Navahos also have matrilocal extended families and matrilineal clans. They are less tightly organized, however, and families dwell in widely scattered hogans: hexagonal log houses with dirt roofs. As compared to the other two non-Indian cultures, the Mormons resemble the Zuñis in having a strong sense of identity with their community. Their life centers around the single village of Ramah, where the values study maintains its field headquarters. For the Spanish-Americans the family and the Catholic church are paramount institutions. The Texan homesteads are scattered over several townships; their identity is loosely maintained by competing Protestant churches and cliques.

The values study seeks answers to a number of questions that are suggested by the differences among these five cultures. It has set out to define, first of all, the value system of each of them and to establish the role that values play in making these cultures different from one another. The changes in values that are occurring in each culture represent another important line of inquiry. Of equal challenge is the question of why their different value systems persist, despite their contact with each other and their exposure to the same environmental pressures.

One of the most promising areas of investigation is the connection between the values and the social structures of the various communities. For example, the Spanish-Americans lay strong emphasis upon "lineality" —the view that social relations are desirable when they are consistent with the hierarchy of their society. In their communities younger relatives are subordinate to older kinsmen, females to males, and the *peón* to his *patrón*. The secular structure gears into the hierarchically arranged Catholic church with its offices extending from the parish priest through the bishops, archbishops, cardinals and on up to the Pope. Much the same type of hierarchy is found in the sacred world of the Spanish-Americans, from the local images of the saints up to the Deity.

The Texan homesteaders, in marked contrast, place a strong American-frontier stress upon individualistic social relations in which each man is expected to be self-reliant and to be "his own boss." The social order of the community is composed of relatively isolated families, each living on its own farm and competing with other families for position and prestige. Instead of the single, hierarchically arranged church, the homesteaders subscribe to no less than 10 competing Christian denominations, each distinguished by a slightly different doctrine and type of service.

The Texan homesteaders fail to understand why "anybody wants to live all bunched up in a little village and take orders from the big land-holders and the priests." The Spanish-Americans say of the Texans that "everybody tries to be his own *patrón*."

The Mormons present still another picture. The formal structure of the Mormon church has hierarchical aspects with lines of authority running upward from the local ward bishops through the state presidents to the 12 apostles and church president in Salt Lake City, Utah. But within this framework the local community enjoys much autonomy to work out its own affairs, and great value is placed upon collateral, cooperative economic and social relationships. Around the village and the large cohesive family system there is a proliferation of cooperatives in economic affairs. The little village of Ramah boasts a mutual irrigation company, a cooperative land and cattle company and a cooperative dairy. The spirit of individualistic competition which pervades the Texan community is consciously suppressed in favor of the values of cooperation in the Mormon village.

These values have deep roots in Mormon history. Joseph Smith, the founder of the church, proposed the "law of consecration" which required that all who had surplus wealth must impart it through the church to the poor. Although this "law" was abandoned as early as 1838, the values it expressed lent a strong cooperative bias to much of later Mormon activity. The compact village settlement was a social invention of the Mormons, motivated by a sense of urgent need to prepare a dwelling place for the "Savior" at "His second coming." Through the years cooperation became a strong defense against "persecution" by the "gentiles," first in the Middle West and later in the Far West, when the political and legal movements to stamp out Mormon polygamy came to a head. The cooperative spirit was also strongly reinforced in the arid West by the requirements of irrigation agriculture—the construction of storage reservoirs, the building and maintaining of networks of ditches, and the necessity of organized arrangements for the distribution of scarce water supplies among the various farms within a village.

The Spanish-Americans, Texans and Mormons, different as they are, belong to a single major historical tradition which contrasts with that of the Zuñis and Navahos. In former times Zuñi was ruled by a theocracy. Today personal relationships among the Zuñis are organized in a complicated series of interlocking religious, kinship and secular units, in which the individual strikes a delicate balance with external authority. No true Zuñi wishes to live away from Zuñi, particularly in the wintertime. The Zuñis have been characterized as having a kind of "middle of the road," "avoidance of excess" approach to life, in the manner of the ancient Greeks. Although this characterization must be qualified, it still symbolizes the Zuñi ideal.

While both Mormons and Zuñis can be characterized as "cooperative" and both societies manifest important linkages between their cooperative value systems and the requirements of irrigation agriculture, there are some interesting differences between them. In the Mormon community the values of cooperation are propounded by a single organized church which embraces the entire community. The Zuñi spirit of cooperation is expressed and institutionalized in the activities of a whole series of priesthoods, dancing groups and curing societies, in which the individual Zuñi may hold two or more memberships. Cooperation is stressed also as a matter of Zuñi kinship obligation. Kinship is important to the Mormons, but sustained kinship-based activity seldom goes beyond the closest relatives. In Zuñi there are large groups of near and distant relatives to whom one owes duties and from whom one derives benefits and position.

The Navahos, with their scattered hogans are more like the Texans in their settlement pattern. Except near agencies and railroad towns, they have no villages. From the core of the extended matrilineal family the Navaho views his relationships as reaching outward to include an ever-widening circle of kinsmen, some of whom he may rarely, if ever, see during the course of a year or more. Until recent times the Navahos have had no organized political leadership, the "tribe" consisting merely of a series of local bands which shared the same language and customs.

Although the Texans and Navahos can be characterized as being less communally inclined and more "individualistic" than the Mormons and Zuñis, there are, again, interesting differences in pattern and emphasis. The Texan focus is upon the individual farmer and his immediate family engaged in a competitive struggle with others for economic wealth and social prestige within the community. The Navaho sense of kinship involves no idea of striving and competing. Navahos cooperate easily with kinsmen and neighbors when the occasion arises, such as the work of putting on the larger ceremonials. But there are no organized and regular cooperative activities on a community-wide basis, unless these are actively promoted by Indian Service officials or other whites.

Differences in culture can thus be related to differences in values. The relationship comes into sharper focus when we consider the varying cultures in the context of their adjustment to their relatively unvarying natural environment, the constant in our laboratory situation. First we shall describe the general orientations of the five groups toward nature and time. Then we shall see how the values thus expressed relate to the way each of the groups reacts to the environmental problem of drought.

The Spanish-Americans have what might be called a "normal curve" view of the workings of nature. Out of so many children born, so many die before maturity; from every row of seeds, only so many plants come up; and out of every 10 or so summers, two or three are bound to be without rain. One can do little but accept what comes. Corresponding to this view of nature is an orientation in time that lays stress upon the present, as opposed to the past, which slowly recedes into obscurity, or to the even more elusive future. Life flows secure in the traditional familial mold; the important thing is the present, with its immediate drama, color and spontaneity. It is foolish to work too hard, and to worry about the future is even more ridiculous. About the mysteries of the world neither curiosity nor knowledge extend much beyond a shrug of the shoulders and a *"Quién sabe?"* These Spanish-American values find concrete expression in the traditional fiesta, a combined religious and recreational affair which is conducted each year in honor of the patron saint of the village. Catholic Masses and processions, combined with drinking, dancing, singing and visiting, express at once the solemn traditionalism and the love of present excitement and drama in the life of the small Spanish-American village.

By contrast the Texan frontier homesteaders manifest a drive for mastery over the workings of nature. Nature is defined as something to be controlled and exploited by man for his own ends and material comfort. The homesteader therefore equips himself with the most modern type of tractor, practices modern farming methods and attempts to extend even further his control over nature in the face of great odds in this semi-arid environment. The past can be forgotten, even rejected, and the present is merely a step along the road to the future. If the crops fail, there is always the hope that "next year we'll make it." There is strong perennial optimism that "progress" will continue and that their crossroads will eventually grow into a modern city. While the homesteaders feel that their Spanish-American neighbors are lazy and "not getting any place," the latter feel just as strongly that the homesteaders are senselessly working themselves to death in a life in which one should live fully in the present.

The Mormon villagers share with the Texan homesteaders the view that mastery over nature is desirable. Indeed, in some respects they carry this idea much further, for they hold the theological view that the Mormon people have "put on the uniform of the flesh" and live out this earthly life in order to learn about and attain mastery over gross matter. "The Latter-Day Saints," as the Mormons call themselves, have developed a work-health-education-recreation value complex to guide their activities: work to gain mastery over the world; health to keep man effective in the struggle for continuing progress; education to accelerate his progress; and recreation to strengthen both man's body and the community he lives in. Like the Texans, they emphasize the future, but not so much for the purpose of economic development as for participation in the eternal progress of the universe in which man himself progresses toward godhood.

To the Zuñi the universe looks very different. He neither feels that he is a master of nature nor that he is its victim. In his colorful and beautiful religion he has developed techniques of cooperating with nature. This attitude is of course sustained by a body of realistic information on ways to make a living in a difficult environment. The Zuñi equivalent of the Spanish-American fiesta has an important place in his life, but he is less taken with its recreational aspects. He lives in the present, but in many things, much more than any of his neighbors, he looks back to the past. It is a glorious past, an ancient mythological time when Zuñis came up from the "wombs" of the earth, wandered around, and finally settled at "the middle place," where their descendants to this day still maintain a shrine to mark the center of the universe.

The Navahos resemble the Spanish-Americans and the Zuñis in their orientation to nature and time. Like the Zuñis, the Navahos view man as having an integral part to play in a general cosmic scheme. But they see the universe as more powerful than man and profoundly threatening. In dealing with nature circumspection is the best guide to action, and fear is the dominant emotional theme. Yet the Navaho is not completely fatalistic. There are small things one can do to maintain and restore harmony in the scheme. Thus individual curing ceremonials, performed with care, can keep matters from becoming worse. The present is the important time-dimension, but the Navahos also recall a "holy people" who came up from the underworld, created four sacred mountains and the "earth surface people" and then departed for their permanent homes in the six directions: east, south, west, north, zenith and nadir.

For all five cultures the annual drought is a serious common concern. Each group responds differently to this problem in terms of its distinctive value-orientation. The Zuñis increase the intensity and tempo of their ceremonial activity; they give more attention to the planting of prayer feathers and to the fasting and prayers of the rain priests. This is in line with their view of the ultimate harmony of nature; man need only do his part and the gods will do the rest. With centuries of summer rains to testify to the soundness of this view, Zuñi is deeply opposed to rainmaking with airplanes and silver iodide.

The Navahos also tend to respond to drought by increasing ceremonial activity. But they are not so certain of the efficacy of their rainmaking ceremonies. They direct less ritual to that purpose and are more humble in the face of a more threatening universe.

The Spanish-Americans, on the other hand, seem to do little or nothing about drought beyond collecting in small groups on the plaza to talk about it. In their view, to attempt to alter the course of natural events by ceremonial is as useless as trying to alter it by rainmaking.

Against the ceremonial response of the Zuñis and Navahos and the fatalistic response of the Spanish-Americans, the behavior of the Mormons and Texans draws a dramatic contrast. They actively support the artificial rainmaking projects; they reduce their livestock herds and crop acreages, and they organize to enlist government aid in meeting the drought conditions. The Navahos and Zuñis, in contrast, have to be forced by the government to practice acreage restriction in bad years.

Ceremonial and ritual responses are not entirely lacking, however, in the Mormon and Texan communities. Mormons occasionally say prayers in church for rain. The Texans have held special prayer meetings during droughts; indeed, the governor of Texas set aside a special day for such meetings during the recent severe southwestern drought. A minority within each community also feels that seeding the clouds is "interfering with the work of the Lord." But the majority responds in the vein expressed by one of the more articulate farmers in the Texan community, who declared: "The Lord will look down and say, 'Look at those poor ignorant people. I gave them the clouds, the airplanes and the silver iodide, and they didn't have the sense to put them together.'"

Thus systems of values may promote and justify radically different modes of behavior among people confronted with the same objective problem. Why do such different values persist in the same tiny region among peoples living so close to one another? There appear to be at least two basic aspects to this question. First, we know that the values are intricately related to the total structure of each culture. Accordingly, unless the structure breaks down completely, values will tend to persist as functional parts of the whole. Second, we have also discovered that face-to-face contacts between the five cultural groups have not always encouraged the easy communication and interaction which might eventually level the differences between them. In fact, some of the inter-cultural contacts appear to have reinforced, rather than changed, the original value systems. There is, for example, good evidence that Navahos and Zuñis cling tenaciously to certain of their aboriginal values precisely because missionaries and other agents of white culture bring strong pressure upon them to change.

17. THE WIND THAT MEANS
LIFE TO INDIA *

SANTHA RAMA RAU

*This selection describes the struggles of an entire society with the
persistent question of how to relate to a dominant feature of its
geographical environment—the wind. Note that man's behavior is
not simply being determined by the geographical phenomenon but,
rather, the society is systematically seeking ways to cope with it,
to modify it to serve man's ends. As W. D. Wallis has said,
"Geographical environment is the cradle in which man's genius
awaits the promptings of motives which give him mastery over his
fate."*

Sometime at the end of every April winds spring up off the west
coast of South America and these, so the meterologists tentatively suggest, travel westward across more than half the world to produce one of
the world's most spectacular climatic phenomena. In the early part of
their annual journey they are not particularly dramatic winds. They
move easily at about fifteen or twenty miles an hour as part of the
trade winds of the southern hemisphere, blow across the Marquesas
Islands, include Tahiti in their scope and carry with them, for the most
part, clear days and warm nights.

By the middle of May the winds have reached the Samoan Islands
and continue along the course determined for them by the turning earth.
They move across the Ellice Islands, the Solomons and New Guinea, and
the long island chain of Indonesia.

In June the winds reach the Indian Ocean, and it is only then that
their whole character changes. They sweep entirely out of their course,
slacken their speed, acquire a special name and such enormous importance
that without them the 500 million people who live in India, Pakistan, Ceylon, Burma, Indo-China and Siam would not be able to survive in their
homelands. By the time the first rain clouds burst over the Malabar coast

* From *The New York Times Magazine* (June 8, 1952), 12, 24, 26–27. Copyright
© 1952 by Santha Rama Rau.
    The author (b. 1923) was educated at Wellesley and now lives in India. Author
of best-seller *Home to India*.

those winds have become the great southwest monsoon, India's most valued—and most capricious—blessing.

From the time of the spring equinox onward, as the sun's rays strike the earth more and more directly, the huge land mass of continental Asia begins to heat up. With growing intensity through the weeks that follow, the heat continues unrelieved. In late May and early June temperatures recorded in North India have reached as high as 126 degrees F. The capital city, Delhi, has an average daytime temperature for May of 104 degrees. Then the Government offices and the foreign embassies switch to summer hours—the working day begins at 7:30 A.M. and finishes at 1:30 P.M. A large part of every day becomes devoted simply to avoiding the heat. Chiks (the slatted, bamboo screens) are lowered all day over windows and verandas to keep the interiors of homes and offices cool and shaded from the sun and glare. Only after sunset are windows and houses opened up to the slightly cooler air of evening. Only in the late short twilight do people sit in their gardens or walk in the parks.

The sea's moderating influence does not spread very far inland and only the cities immediately on the coast benefit by reasonably temperate weather. But in the plains of the north and east of the great plateaus of the center of India the heat is a strong and a curiously personal enemy. The earth bakes into a hard cracked surface, rivers dry up entirely or shrink to thin opaque trickles, and all farming comes to a standstill. This is also the season of the Loo, a dreaded, searingly hot wind that blows in from the Rajasthan desert, raises the temperature by 15 or 20 degrees and sweeps the surface soil into dust storms. All kinds of illnesses and nervous ailments are attributed to it, heat-stroke, hysteria and uncertain tempers, and, at the first hint of the rising Loo, doors and windows are shut and bolted against its dust, heat and evil influence.

At the end of May the prolonged and acute heat has formed an enormous low pressure area in the atmosphere over India, and something like a huge whirlwind begins to circulate around its edges. As the heat increases, the speed of the air circulation grows until at last it has acquired suction strong enough to reach below the equator and pull the southeastern trade winds into India. Here, as the monsoon, for three months they move east and north across the country pouring out the water accumulated over 10,000 miles of ocean. Eventually they are checked by the great mountain barriers of the Himalayas which serve to contain the monsoon and conserve the major force of the rains for India. This mountain wall makes it possible for parts of Assam to have a rainfall of 450 inches in one summer while beyond the Himalayas Tibet gets between five and ten inches a year.

As the sun enters its autumnal phase, the earth, already cooled by the rains, is further cooled by the sun's declining intensity, and gradually the monsoon retreats from India to rejoin its old route south of the equator. If anything were to interfere with the process—if, for instance, a string of large volcanic islands were to spring up between the African Coast and Cape Gormorin, the southern tip of India, to deflect the monsoon, or if the heat in Central Asia should, by the cooling of the earth, be reduced and the force to pull in the monsoon should vanish—then India would become a desert. Only a thin coastal strip and the banks of the Ganges might remain green and habitable.

It is not surprising, then, that the chief of the Vedic gods, the oldest of all India's deities and the father of the whole pantheon of gods is Indra, the god of rain. A child born under his auspices is certain to be fortunate and prosperous, and the monsoon, his season, is traditionally connected with fertility, production and richness.

For weeks before the rains begin priests in the temples of the west coast compute from ancient scriptures and old astronomical charts the exact date the monsoon will arrive. With equal seriousness (and, according to the priests, hardly more reliable results) scientists and Government meteorologists collect data from their many coastal stations, study advance reports of weather conditions from island outposts in the Indian Ocean and attempt to predict when the rains will come. For days beforehand, prayers and chanting in the temples urge Indra not to withhold his gift. In some parts of India raindances and drumbeats are performed to call the rain. In Delhi, Government officials more prosaically get on with the job of seeing that plans for water storage, more and deeper wells and bigger irrigation schemes are completed in case this year, again, the monsoon should fail.

Some years ago, one of India's former Ministers of Finance, in presenting his budget to the Indian Parliament, opened his speech with the remark, "The Indian budget is a gamble in rain." Just as Indian agriculture depends entirely on the monsoon to provide its water to fill the country's rivers and reservoirs, and to make irrigation possible, so Indian industry relies to a great extent on the same sources for its power. The electric light and power supply in all the major cities depends on the water reserves which, in turn, are replenished only by the monsoon. Without question, the greatest single factor in maintaining the functioning economy of India is the rain of high summer.

Although the monsoon has never entirely failed to appear, there has never been a recorded year in which the rains have been satisfactory in every part of the country. The day the rains break there is an extraordinary relaxing of tension everywhere. Strangers in city streets smile at each other in relief that the heat has broken. Children rush out yelling in excitement to stand in the first downpour and adults touch the damp ground in gratitude. Every newspaper carries the news on the front page, and compares the arrival of this year's rain with previous monsoons. But after a night of singing and exhilaration and thanksgiving, the anxiety begins again.

So many things can go wrong. There can be too much rain all at once and this will cause floods. Lives will be lost, property damaged, and yet more of India's thin, infinitely precious top soil will get washed away. There may be too little rain and that will result in droughts and famine. There may be long breaks in the monsoon which can mean that the seeds which are sown immediately the rains begin don't germinate, or that later, seedlings wither.

The rains may begin too early or too late, and continue too long or end too abruptly. Then crops will rot in the fields before they are ripe for harvesting, or they may dry up before they are fully grown. In fact, one of the most important of the monsoon festivals, Bombay's Coconut Day, comes at the end of the heavy rains. At that time the gods of the ocean are appeased and offerings of food and flowers and fruit are taken down to all the beaches so that the monsoon seas will abate and allow the fishing craft to leave the harbors again. In all the aspects of the arrival, distribution, timing and departure of the monsoon the Indian farmer most of all, the industrialist and the Indian Government must gamble on the rains.

Just how uncertain a gamble it is and how disastrous the results of losing it, the last five years have shown more clearly than any other period since 1876. The monsoon, which has been known to give some places thirty inches of rain in one day, can equally give other parts of India only five inches for the whole year. Normally, over two or three seasons things even themselves out, but recently the monsoon shortcomings have been so widespread and so consistent as to produce in some areas what is described by the meteorologists as "a chronic condition of the failure of the rains."

. . . . .

In the countryside around Delhi . . . things are getting serious. Wells are drying up and the new program for sinking tube wells in many of the drought areas cannot move fast enough to alleviate the immediate crisis—there is too much survey work and experimentation to be done first. In a desperate attempt to find short cuts to the findings of the geological surveys, the Government of India has even hired a waterdiviner. . . .

The Point Four technicians who are arriving now in India . . . deal first with the water problem. Tube well experts have arrived to work with Indian geologists, and the plans go ahead. But however such schemes may insure the prosperity of the future, and to whatever extent they may remove the country's reliance on the uncertainties of the monsoon rains, at the moment nothing can keep the country from widespread drought and famine except a good, or better still, a series of good and well-distributed monsoons. Meanwhile, Indians have three months in which to watch with anxious speculation the fluctuations of the monsoon, and finally a winter of either rejoicing or of tragedy. In September, they will know which.

18. THE PRISONER COMMUNITY AS A SOCIAL GROUP *

NORMAN S. HAYNER AND ELLIS ASH

Wherever there is autocratic control—that is, rigorous rules established and enforced from above—the development of "communities within a community" is common. Such subcommunities have their own distinct set of "mores, attitudes, activities and gradations of status" entirely separate from those established by the official order. This is illustrated by the "prisoner community" described by N. S. Hayner and Ellis Ash. If the reader considers this a unique and atypical situation, let him consider objectively the comparable patterns of behavior in a school. Obviously, much less autocratic control appears in a school than in a prison, but the same community-within-a-community tends to develop.

A clear distinction should be made between the prison community and the prisoner community. To the casual visitor, the only community at a prison is the one maintained by the administration. Closer acquaintance with any American prison reveals a sub-rosa organization composed entirely of inmates. The major common interest in this prisoner group is release, but there are also, as in a normal community, distinctive mores, attitudes, activities, and gradations of status. It is to the prisoner community that attention is directed in this paper.

* *American Sociological Review*, Vol. 4 (June, 1939), 362–369. Reprinted by permission of the publisher and the authors.

Norman S. Hayner (b. 1896) is Professor of Sociology, University of Washington. He was a member of the State Board Prison Terms and Paroles, State of Washington (1951–1955), and Chairman (1955–1956). His major interest is in criminology. Author: *New Patterns in Old Mexico; Hotel Life;* and numerous articles and monographs on penology and correctional administration.

Ellis Ash has been Director of Public Housing for the city of Baltimore.

Most convicts identify the research man with the administration and are dishonest in dealing with him because they consider him a "screw" (guard). Ordinary statistical or case methods are obviously inadequate to reveal the customs of the prisoner community. The more informal technique of the participant observer seems to be required.

The basic method employed in gathering the data for this study was that of recording at the earliest opportune moment significant social situations in the daily lives of the inmates during a four months' residence at the Washington State Reformatory at Monroe. Frequent short visits over a period of one year supplemented the original observations. Pertinent overt behavior, enlightening casual conversations, and subsequent contact with men released from the institution contributed to the fund of information accumulated. This study is in no sense an exposé of conditions at Monroe. As a matter of fact, the administration is progressive and an objective rating would probably place this institution in a better than average position among the reformatories of the United States. It is the typical characteristics of the prisoner community at Monroe that are being emphasized, rather than what is unique or peculiar.

To secure accurate information, it was necessary for the junior author to be accepted by both inmates and officers. To begin with, both groups were suspicious and both resented the investigator's presence. To obtain the information desired from the prisoners, it was necessary to convince them of his honorable intentions. He had to go through a "proving process" at the hands of the inmate body. This consisted of being placed in situations of their choosing so that they could observe his reactions. He was subjected to cat calls, boos, and hisses; he dodged missiles propelled from unknown and unseen experimenters; he was present during an evident infraction of minor regulations to get his "ratting" (reporting to authorities) response.

After a stay of some two weeks in the institution, the leaders of the inmate body became evident and their acquaintance was definitely cultivated. Acceptance by them meant acceptance by all the inmates. These key men were partially informed of the investigator's purpose in the Reformatory. It was necessary to indicate to the prisoners that, while he was their friend and would perform little services for them not in violation of regulations, still it was impossible to maintain a neutral position in the institution and at the same time flagrantly connive with them. In the beginning, there was no effort to explain the kind of information sought. Interviews were not staged or created artificially. Upon becoming accepted by the inmate body through their leaders, it was possible to mingle with the men without creating an unnatural situation. Many topics were discussed with little restraint. In the prisoner community, as in any other, men enjoy talking shop. Their prejudices for or against particular features of prison life became apparent during the course of these conversations.

Meanwhile, the fact that the field worker had become accepted by the administration was a distinct advantage. The officers as a group did not have leaders whose word was sufficient evidence that a person was acceptable. The confidence of each officer on the staff had to be won individually. By aiding in the organization of a classification clinic, the investigator was able to pay his way with the administration. By offering to relieve various officers on duty in case of emergency, or otherwise, his possible utility was recognized. He was allowed the complete run of the Reformatory at all hours and permission to see anything that went on. Personal bits of information were shared by each officer with him.

Each contact with a man, whether inmate or officer, meant establishing a closer rapport and freer discussion. It was some months, however, before a pattern of community life in the inmate body began to appear. Although this pattern is not yet entirely clear, some of its outlines are presented here.

In the normal community, contacts are to a considerable extent determined by the type of occupation and the neighborhood of residence. This is also true in a prison. At Monroe, for example, work is divided on the basis of crews, each of which is responsible for specific lines of endeavor. The laundry, power house, tailor shop, office, education, and farm crews are examples. The place of residence, or cell, is usually determined by the crew on which the inmate works. Cells are arranged in two large blocks which are further divided into sides and tiers. In the "old block," the men are under rigid supervision. Immediately after supper, they are locked in their "drum" (cell) for the night. In the "new block" are located most of the trusties, the men with better jobs. Since the work of many trusties requires freedom of movement in both blocks, these selected inmates are allowed to leave their cells in the evening. Each tier in a block becomes a street with its characteristic occupational types. The tierman, who is the middleman between the officers and the inmates for each tier, becomes the runner for his street. If a man settles down in one particular cell for any length of time he tends to develop his closest associations with his neighbors.

The men who have social diseases are segregated on one tier; the "fish" (newcomers) are quarantined on another tier; on still another is the town jail, better known as "deadlock," where incorrigibles are placed. The "hole," or "solitary," is out in the wilderness, so to speak; its occupants are cut off from any communication with their fellow prisoners. In this community, however, prisoners in deadlock or solitary do not lose the respect of the inmate group as a whole; their isolation is physical rather than social.

"Conniving" is a basic process in the interaction between prisoners. It embodies a distinct code of behavior, a set of rules and regulations and a guiding principle for the maintenance of status within the prisoner community. It is responsible for the development of those sub-rosa institutional forms which are an essential part of the community organization. It is a reaction to the dull routine of reformatory life. It is a way of adjusting to the situation, of "making the best of the circumstances." It is not limited to inmate life, but may be identified in any group which operates under coercion.

Each inmate is forced to passive participation in conniving by virtue of his role as a convict. Even though he may wish, as an individual, to adhere rigidly to the rules and regulations of the administration, he must at the same time live up to the "con" (convict) rule—"You must not squeal." This is one of the most important elements in the mores of the prisoner community. A "stool" (spy) for the administration runs constant danger of bodily harm from his fellows if discovered. In most cases, the stool is the scum of the inmate body, the one that possesses no allegiance to the inmate group.

Frequently an inmate will hesitate to engage himself actively in conniving for fear of endangering his opportunities for early parole. This attitude is common to the first-timer from a conventional social background. He soon discovers, however, that he endangers his position more by maintaining this attitude than by relaxing and joining the inmate group. To maintain it means that he becomes an outcast from his fellow cons. The naive first-timer from a normal social environment finds this role much less desirable than that of active participation with other inmates. Under ordinary circumstances, as he becomes "conwise," he discovers that he desires certain things denied him by the prison administration. In the prison environment, these things assume an importance out of all proportion to their actual value. They are available if he supports the conniving activities. Whole-hearted support will, he finds, mean less danger of discovery and increased benefits.

Variety in the prisoner community, even more than in the outside world, is the "spice of life." It serves to bridge the days on end which would be a constant repetition of formalized responses if each regulation were obeyed to the letter. It is impossible for the officers continually to observe each inmate and many activities contrary to the rules may be enjoyed.

Gambling in the Reformatory is especially popular. It is in violation of regulations; it furnishes a certain spice and thrill; and if one is lucky, he "stands to gain." The excessive interest in this "fighting play" is a commentary on the drab routine of reformatory life. Inmates will gamble on any pretext: the state of the weather many days hence, or the outcome of some local or national situation concerning which there is no scientific evidence cn which to base a prediction. Frequently they will bet on whether they can accomplish some other conniving activity and this is an added incentive to the successful completion of that activity. The competitive element is present, the spirit of the game. The medium of exchange for this betting may be any service or commodity capable of transfer from one inmate to another. A cell partner will often pay off a gambling debt by performing the necessary cleaning of the cell for a stipulated period.

Since the loser of a bet in the prisoner community cannot hide, the winner has a distinct advantage. This probably accounts for the fact that there are relatively few inmates who owe large sums to individual prisoners. An inmate might owe small sums to several of his fellows, however, and still maintain his credit. If it becomes apparent that a prisoner is unable to "pay off," the group concerned may take collective action and proceed to rough up the debtor in true pound-of-flesh fashion. In one instance at Monroe, an inmate with a large number of debts endeavored to escape in an effort to avoid group disapproval. He preferred the danger of being shot, of serving time in deadlock, and of being given a longer sentence, to the probable treatment he would receive from the inmate group if he did not pay up. The dramatic nature of the incident was intensified by the fact that the boy had one of the most desirable trusty jobs and was thought of by the administration as an ideal inmate. He decided to leave on the spur of the moment. It was the only release he could think of from the obligations to his fellow inmates. He was captured by the officers within a very short time. The case demonstrates the pressure which an inmate group can exert upon a social deviate.

Let us take another example of conniving. Coffee, or any other beverage with the exception of water, is to be had only in limited quantity at stipulated times. It becomes greatly desired during periods of inactivity, such as "cell time." Once the men are locked in their cells, supervision is relaxed. Unless it becomes obvious that "peace is being disturbed," they are allowed to "go about their business" within the confines of their cells. With due caution, they may smoke "tailor-mades" or roll "skins" (cigarettes), both of which are taboo. Coffee and other delicacies, likewise taboo, are available in the kitchen. An organization must be set up to secure them for distribution. The cost element is always present. In this case, it is the risk involved in bringing the coffee from the kitchen to the consumer rather than the cost of production. Contact must be made with a con who is working on the kitchen crew and has access to the supplies. If this con can procure the coffee, but has no opportunity to smuggle it into the cell block, a middleman is necessary. The one who smuggles it into the block may be unable to hand it over to the consumer. Each participant in the process must have his cut.

Then there is the problem of cooking utensils. Any discarded can will do as a coffee pot. If it is impossible for the cook to obtain this can directly, the proper men must be contacted and paid off. Next, there is the question of a heater. This requires another can or bottle, a wick and fuel. The wick is simple to prepare, but kerosene or some other fuel is precious. Possible sources of supply are the boys working on crews where kerosene is used for cleaning purposes. Again the proper individuals must be approached and paid off. Inmates who are too poor to pay the high price for kerosene use bits of cardboard for fuel. Finally, there is the actual problem of preparation. Some individual in a position to give warning of a screw's approach must be willing to give instant and reliable service. The heater is suspended in the toilet bowl where it is out of sight and where the makings may be easily discarded in case of emergency. Talcum powder is blown into the air at intervals to remove the coffee odor. At last the "jo" (coffee) is ready, together with a skin, and what promised to be a dull evening is transformed into a thrill-packed experience. The successful evasion of a rule is even more satisfying than the finished product. With apologies to Robert W. Service we might conclude: "It isn't the jo that I'm wanting so much as just making the jo."

Occasionally, an extremely successful "brewer" with convenient access to the ingredients will become a wholesaler. He will prepare sufficient amounts of jo to provide for a number of customers and specified quantities will be delivered to the consumers by runners. This may involve a contract for so much coffee over a definite period of time, the brewer assuming all responsibility for delivery.

Although one must pay for services received, barter plays a more important part than in other communities. The man who desires coffee, for instance, may pay for it by providing extra clothes or contacts with the outside. Tobacco is a favorite medium of exchange, but "white" money, i.e., legal currency, is preferred. The men are only allowed to draw two dollars per week from their account and this is in "hickeys" (tokens) rather than in real money. Visitors occasionally succeed in passing money to inmates, but this is dangerous. Generally, it is received through contacts with the farm crew which works at some distance from the Reformatory stockade. The farm crew is an essential feature of the conniving process. This is especially true of the small group that remains overnight on the farm. Men in this group have an opportunity to pick up articles from the side of the road—articles left by motorists during the night. The location of the cache is determined in advance during a visit with a prisoner at the Reformatory. A member of the permanent farm crew may pick up the money and pass it on to a member of the crew that works at the farm only during the day. Each participant must receive some service in return.

The multiplicity of commodities and services available through such means as these requires organization. How is this achieved?

Within the prisoner community there is clear-cut evidence of class divisions. These divisions are based on the relative influence and authority of each class. Since the primary function of the inmate organization is to provide commodities and services denied them by the administration, status is achieved not by "conspicuous consumption" as in the outside world, but by ability as promoters or contact men. Division of labor arises out of unequal opportunities to engage in specific types of conniving. The formal "uppercrust" is popularly known as "politicians' row." This group may or may not include the "right guys," that relatively small select group of natural con-wise leaders. It does include many of the key men in the conniving process.

Politicians' row often takes a hand in gambling activities and sponsors a game on a grandiose scale. A pool may be formed to which many inmates can contribute. The winner makes a substantial sum, but the promoter also profits. Boys who are members of the education crew may easily act as promoters. Since they must make the round of all the tiers each evening to deliver "home study papers" or to give aid on school problems, they are in a position to see every inmate and to find out if he desires to participate in the pool. Payments to winners may be made in a similar fashion.

Entrance to this "community council," i.e., politicians' row, seems to vary with the type of administration. If control is lax and violations of regulations are openly permitted, the hardened racketeers or "rangatangs" become the politicians. If, on the other hand, the administration is relatively strong in its control (the present situation at Monroe), politicians' row takes on an entirely different character. The rangatangs, or trouble makers, are under close supervision and do not have an opportunity to work themselves into the key jobs within the institution. This means that they do not have the freedom of movement and association that goes with these jobs. The better-adjusted boys with the best records receive the favored jobs. By virtue of these positions, they become the "town fathers" of the prisoner community and the leading connivers. The importance of membership in politicians' row is, however, largely a matter of tradition. Although members tend to play the role ascribed to them, their actual significance may be more superficial than real. Either a right guy or a rangatang may exploit this situation to advantage. He will endeavor to use willing members of the row as a front for his activities, and will utilize their privileged positions for his individual enhancement.

Another significant fact about the prisoner community is that it is a world of men without women. In a reformatory, the population is primarily composed of young adult males in the virile years of life. The average age of men at the Washington State Reformatory is twenty-two. About four per cent of the 500 inmates (1937) were incarcerated because of their divergent sexual or marital behavior. Sexual starvation is a serious problem in this community. The common trend toward sex topics in male conversations is accentuated. As in other one-sex groups, homosexual behavior is to be expected.

The average warden of a penal institution looks upon sexual perversion as an evil that upsets the routine essential to a well-disciplined group of men. It is antagonistic to the mores of the outside world. It is sometimes regarded as an index to natural criminal tendencies. We find, therefore, that men are committed to penal institutions for sexual perversions, expected to reform in an atmosphere more highly conducive to their practice, and are punished for behavior which is in some cases an integral part of the total personality without being aided in any other way than by being told that it is "wrong."

Normal impulses are many times turned to perversions upon being transplanted to an abnormal situation. In a prison, "smut" stories are told that would cause a "professional" dirty story teller in a college "bull-session" to cry with envy. Faithfulness to one woman is ridiculed. "Get what you can, when you can, from whom you can," is the motto. Men are occasionally "railroaded" into prison to protect the name of some girl who was jointly responsible for the situation. Such an occurrence embitters these men against the entire feminine sex. Status in the prisoner community can be raised by tales of sexual exploits. Many of the young men in a reformatory have never before been confronted with abnormal sex behavior, yet they are suggestible to the point where they may become willing "punks" for a "smoothie" at the game. It is essential to realize that deviations from the conventional sex code within prison walls become acceptable to many merely because they represent an opportunity to defy the forces of law and order. There are also additional incentives in the form of money, candy, and protection. First-timers come in contact with young men no older than themselves who have had a wide variety of sexual experiences. The adventures are told with lurid details; a "proposition" is made; and a convert is won for the cause.

"Love for your fellow man" gets a new definition in the prisoner community. Deviations from the conventional sex code are tolerated by the convicts, for perversions are regarded as inevitable. Even if the sex drive is not satisfied in an abnormal manner, the mental conflicts produced in the individual may be more disturbing than the actual consummation of perversions. Not only may the sex attitudes of inmates be distorted by the prison experience, but the lives of sweethearts and wives may be made miserable after the men graduate from this type of "reformation."

It has long been recognized that our reformatories do not actually reform. Contrary to popular belief, however, old timers have no definite educational policy for the youngsters. Inmates learn new and improved techniques in our prisons, to be sure, but this is more or less an incidental feature of the prisoner community. Conversations in the reformatory are primarily with fellow convicts. As in groups on the outside, talk commonly turns to shop. Each type of con describes those varieties of technique with which he is best acquainted. The forger talks of forgery; the embezzler, of stock manipulation; the burglar, of methods for entering homes and stores; the stick-up man, of ways to overcome resistance. Thus many an inmate with a sincere desire to go straight on re-entering society is continually confronted with this kind of conversation. Whether he wishes to or not, he assimilates new crime techniques.

The prisoner community is a social group developed by the outcasts of the larger society. The organization of this community is primarily an economic arrangement devoted to obtaining goods and services denied by the administration. Its entrepreneurs, middlemen, class structure, politicians, and social deviates are comprehensible in terms of the social situation in which the convicts find themselves. The development of conniving, with its code of deception, means that inmates have daily training in traits that make reformation difficult. The prisoner community with its connivings, its perversions, and its exchange of crime techniques re-enforces those behavior tendencies which society wishes to prevent. One cannot expect to break down anti-social habits in an atmosphere that is definitely anti-social.

CHAPTER III

PERSON AND GROUP

19. FINAL NOTE ON A CASE OF EXTREME ISOLATION *

KINGSLEY DAVIS

For centuries there have been reports of children who were raised by animals or in some other way managed to live in complete isolation from human beings. If such feral men could be found, they would have great significance for social science, since they would provide crucial means of determining the nature and extent of sociocultural influence on human behavior. Investigation of all reported cases has, however, shown them to have little validity and to be heavily laden with myth and rumor. It is highly doubtful if any child ever lived without at least some human association. In recent years a few verified instances have been found in which extremely limited association occurred. Kingsley Davis gives here his final report on such a case and makes some comparisons between the child, Anna, and another child, Isabelle, who lived under similar circumstances. One cannot be sure to what extent Anna's failure to achieve the level of socialization of a normal 10-year-old was due to organic deficiency. Clearly, however, a tremendous change

* *The American Journal of Sociology*, Vol. 52, No. 5 (March, 1947), 432–437. Reprinted by permission of the University of Chicago Press and the author.

The author (b. 1908) is Professor of Sociology at the University of California, formerly Director, Bureau of Applied Social Research, Columbia University. Past president of the American Sociological Society. Author: *Youth in Depression; Human Society; Modern American Society* (with others); *The Population of India and Pakistan* (with Hilda Hertz); *The Pattern of World Urbanization*. Editor: *Current Sociology*.

*took place in her behavior after the isolation was ended. It
seems certain that many typically human behavior patterns were
not achieved until Anna was able to associate with other
humans from whom she could learn such behavior.*

Early in 1940 there appeared . . . an account of a girl called Anna.[1]
She had been deprived of normal contact and had received a minimum
of human care for almost the whole of her first six years of life. At that
time observations were not complete and the report had a tentative
character. Now, however, the girl is dead, and, with more information
available, it is possible to give a fuller and more definitive description
of the case from a sociological point of view.

Anna's death, caused by hemorrhagic jaundice, occurred on August
6, 1942. Having been born on March 1 or 6, 1932, she was approximately
ten and a half years of age when she died. The previous report covered
her development up to the age of almost eight years; the present one
recapitulates the earlier period on the basis of new evidence and then
covers the last two and a half years of her life.

EARLY HISTORY

The first few days and weeks of Anna's life were complicated by frequent changes of domicile. It will be recalled that she was an illegitimate child, the second such child born to her mother, and that her
grandfather, a widowed farmer in whose house her mother lived, strongly
disapproved of this new evidence of the mother's indiscretion. This
fact led to the baby's being shifted about.

Two weeks after being born in a nurse's private home, Anna was
brought to the family farm, but the grandfather's antagonism was so
great that she was shortly taken to the house of one of her mother's
friends. At this time a local minister became interested in her and
took her to his house with an idea of possible adoption. He decided
against adoption, however, when he discovered that she had vaginitis.
The infant was then taken to a children's home in the nearest large
city. This agency found that at the age of only three weeks she was
already in a miserable condition, being "terribly galled and otherwise in
very bad shape." It did not regard her as a likely subject for adoption
but took her in for a while anyway, hoping to benefit her. After Anna
had spent nearly eight weeks in this place, the agency notified her
mother to come to get her. The mother responded by sending a man
and his wife to the children's home with a view to their adopting Anna,
but they made such a poor impression on the agency that permission

[1] Kingsley Davis, "Extreme Social Isolation of a Child," *American Journal of
Sociology,* XLV (January, 1940), 554–65.

was refused. Later the mother came herself and took the child out of the home and then gave her to this couple. It was in the home of this pair that a social worker found the girl a short time thereafter. The social worker went to the mother's home and pleaded with Anna's grandfather to allow the mother to bring the child home. In spite of threats, he refused. The child, by then more than four months old, was next taken to another children's home in a near-by town. A medical examination at this time revealed that she had impetigo, vaginitis, umbilical hernia, and a skin rash.

Anna remained in this second children's home for nearly three weeks, at the end of which time she was transferred to a private foster-home. Since, however, the grandfather would not, and the mother could not, pay for the child's care, she was finally taken back as a last resort to the grandfather's house (at the age of five and a half months). There she remained, kept on the second floor in an attic-like room because her mother hesitated to incur the grandfather's wrath by bringing her downstairs.

The mother, a sturdy woman weighing about 180 pounds, did a man's work on the farm. She engaged in heavy work such as milking cows and tending hogs and had little time for her children. Sometimes she went out at night, in which case Anna was left entirely without attention. Ordinarily, it seems, Anna received only enough care to keep her barely alive. She appears to have been seldom moved from one position to another. Her clothing and bedding were filthy. She apparently had no instruction, no friendly attention.

It is little wonder that, when finally found and removed from the room in the grandfather's house at the age of nearly six years, the child could not talk, walk, or do anything that showed intelligence. She was in an extremely emaciated and undernourished condition, with skeleton-like legs and a bloated abdomen. She had been fed on virtually nothing except cow's milk during the years under her mother's care.

Anna's condition when found, and her subsequent improvement, have been described in the previous report. It now remains to say what happened to her after that.

LATER HISTORY

In 1939, nearly two years after being discovered, Anna had progressed, as previously reported, to the point where she could walk, understand simple commands, feed herself, achieve some neatness, remember people, etc. But she still did not speak, and, though she was much more like a normal infant of something over one year of age in mentality, she was far from normal for her age.

On August 30, 1939, she was taken to a private home for retarded children, leaving the county home where she had been for more than a year and a half. In her new setting she made some further progress, but not a great deal. In a report of an examination made November 6 of the same year, the head of the institution pictured the child as follows:

Anna walks about aimlessly, makes periodic rhythmic motions of her hands, and, at intervals, makes guttural and sucking noises. She regards her hands as if she had seen them for the first time. It was impossible to hold her attention for more than a few seconds at a time—not because of distraction due to external stimuli but because of her inability to concentrate. She ignored the task in hand to gaze vacantly about the room. Speech is entirely lacking. Numerous unsuccessful attempts have been made with her in the hope of developing initial sounds. I do not believe that this failure is due to negativism or deafness but that she is not sufficiently developed to accept speech at this time. . . . The prognosis is not favorable. . . .

More than five months later, on April 25, 1940, a clinical psychologist, the late Professor Francis N. Maxfield, examined Anna and reported the following: large for her age; hearing "entirely normal"; vision apparently normal; able to climb stairs; speech in the "babbling stage" and "promise for developing intelligible speech later seems to be good." He said further that "on the Merrill-Palmer scale she made a mental score of 19 months. On the Vineland social maturity scale she made a score of 23 months."

Professor Maxfield very sensibly pointed out that prognosis is difficult in such cases of isolation. "It is very difficult to take scores on tests standardized under average conditions of environment and experience," he wrote, "and interpret them in a case where environment and experience have been so unusual." With this warning he gave it as his opinion at that time that Anna would eventually "attain an adult mental level of six or seven years."

The school for retarded children, on July 1, 1941, reported that Anna had reached 46 inches in height and weighed 60 pounds. She could bounce and catch a ball and was said to conform to group socialization, though as a follower rather than a leader. Toilet habits were firmly established. Food habits were normal, except that she still used a spoon as her sole implement. She could dress herself except for fastening her clothes. Most remarkable of all, she had finally begun to develop speech. She was characterized as being at about the two-year level in this regard. She could call attendants by name and bring in one when she was asked to. She had a few complete sentences to express her wants. The report concluded that there was nothing peculiar about her, except that she was feeble-minded—"probably congenital in type."

A final report from the school, made on June 22, 1942, and evidently the last report before the girl's death, pictured only a slight advance over that given above. It said that Anna could follow directions, string beads, identify a few colors, build with blocks, and differentiate between attractive and unattractive pictures. She had a good sense of rhythm and loved a doll. She talked mainly in phrases but would repeat words and try to carry on a conversation. She was clean about clothing. She habitually washed her hands and brushed her teeth. She would try to help other children. She walked well and could run fairly well, though clumsily. Although easily excited, she had a pleasant disposition.

INTERPRETATION

Such was Anna's condition just before her death. It may seem as if she had not made much progress, but one must remember the condition in which she had been found. One must recall that she had no glimmering of speech, absolutely no ability to walk, no sense of gesture, not the least capacity to feed herself even when the food was put in front of her, and no comprehension of cleanliness. She was so apathetic that it was hard to tell whether or not she could hear. And all this at the age of nearly six years. Compared with this condition, her capacities at the time of her death seem striking indeed, though they do not amount to much more than a two-and-a-half-year mental level. One conclusion therefore seems safe, namely, that her isolation prevented a considerable amount of mental development that was undoubtedly part of her capacity. Just what her original capacity was, of course, is hard to say; but her development after her period of confinement (including the ability to walk and run, to play, dress, fit into a social situation, and, above all, to speak) shows that she had at least this much capacity—capacity that never could have been realized in her original condition of isolation.

A further question is this: What would she have been like if she had received a normal upbringing from the moment of birth? A definitive answer would have been impossible in any case, but even an approximate answer is made difficult by her early death. If one assumes, as was tentatively surmised in the previous report, that it is "almost impossible for any child to learn to speak, think, and act like a normal person after a long period of early isolation," it seems likely that Anna might have had a normal or near-normal capacity, genetically speaking. On the other hand, it was pointed out that Anna represented "a marginal case, [because] she was discovered before she had reached six years of age," an age "young enough to allow for some plasticity." While admitting, then, that Anna's isolation *may* have been the major cause (and was certainly a minor cause) of her lack of rapid mental progress during the four and a half years following her rescue from neglect, it is necessary to entertain the hypothesis that she was congenitally deficient.

In connection with this hypothesis, one suggestive though by no means conclusive circumstance needs consideration, namely, the mentality of Anna's forebears. Information on this subject is easier to obtain, as one might guess, on the mother's than on the father's side. Anna's maternal grandmother, for example, is said to have been college educated and wished to have her children receive a good education, but her husband, Anna's stern grandfather, apparently a shrewd, hard-driving, calculating farmowner, was so penurious that her ambitions in this direction were thwarted. Under the circumstances her daughter (Anna's mother) managed, despite having to do hard work on the farm, to complete the eighth grade in a country school. Even so, however, the daughter was evidently not very smart. "A schoolmate of [Anna's mother] stated that she was retarded in school work; was very gullible at this age; and that her morals even at this time were discussed by other students." Two tests administered to her on March 4, 1938, when she was thirty-two years of age, showed that she was mentally deficient. On the Stanford Revision of the Binet-Simon Scale her performance was equivalent to that of a child of eight years, giving her an I.Q. of 50 and indicating mental deficiency of "middle-grade moron type."

As to the identity of Anna's father, the most persistent theory holds that he was an old man about seventy-four years of age at the time of the girl's birth. If he was the one, there is no indication of mental or other biological deficiency, whatever one may think of his morals. However, someone else may actually have been the father.

To sum up: Anna's heredity is the kind that *might* have given rise to innate mental deficiency, though not necessarily.

COMPARISON WITH ANOTHER CASE

Perhaps more to the point than speculations about Anna's ancestry would be a case for comparison. If a child could be discovered who had been isolated about the same length of time as Anna but had achieved a much quicker recovery and a greater mental development, it would be a stronger indication that Anna was deficient to start with.

Such a case does exist. It is the case of a girl found at about the same time as Anna and under strikingly similar circumstances. A full description of the details of this case has not been published, but, in addition to newspaper reports, an excellent preliminary account by a speech specialist, Dr. Marie K. Mason, who played an important role in the handling of the child, has appeared. Also the late Dr. Francis N. Maxfield, clinical psychologist at Ohio State University, as was Dr. Mason, has written an as yet unpublished but penetrating analysis of the case. Some of his observations have been included in Professor Zingg's book on feral man. The following discussion is drawn mainly from these enlightening materials. The writer, through the kindness of Professors Mason and Maxfield, did have a chance to observe the girl in April, 1940, and to discuss the features of her case with them.

Born apparently one month later than Anna, the girl in question, who has been given the pseudonym Isabelle, was discovered in November, 1938, nine months after the discovery of Anna. At the time she was found she was approximately six and a half years of age. Like Anna, she was an illegitimate child and had been kept in seclusion for that reason. Her mother was a deaf-mute, having become so at the age of two, and it appears that she and Isabelle had spent most of their time together in a dark room shut off from the rest of the mother's family. As a result Isabelle had no chance to develop speech; when she communicated with her mother, it was by means of gestures. Lack of sunshine and inadequacy of diet had caused Isabelle to become rachitic. Her legs in particular were affected; they "were so bowed that as she stood erect the soles of her shoes came nearly flat together, and she got about with a skittering gait." Her behavior toward strangers, especially men, was almost that of a wild animal, manifesting much fear and hostility. In lieu of speech she made only a strange croaking sound. In many ways she acted like an infant. "She was apparently utterly unaware of relationships of any kind. When presented with a ball for the first time, she held it in the palm of her hand, then reached out and stroked my face with it. Such behavior is comparable to that of a child of six months." At first it was even hard to tell whether or not she could hear, so unused were her senses. Many of her actions resembled those of deaf children.

It is small wonder that, once it was established that she could hear, specialists working with her believed her to be feeble-minded. Even on nonverbal tests her performance was so low as to promise little for the future. Her first score on the Stanford-Binet was 19 months, practically at the zero point of the scale. On the Vineland social maturity scale her first score was 39, representing an age level of two and a half years. "The general impression was that she was wholly uneducable and that any attempt to teach her to speak, after so long a period of silence, would meet with failure."

In spite of this interpretation, the individuals in charge of Isabelle launched a systematic and skilful program of training. It seemed hopeless at first. The approach had to be through pantomime and dramatization, suitable to an infant. It required one week of intensive effort before she even made her first attempt at vocalization. Gradually she began to respond, however, and, after the first hurdles had at last been overcome, a curious thing happened. She went through the usual stages of learning characteristic of the years from one to six not only in proper succession but far more rapidly than normal. In a little over two months after her first vocalization she was putting sentences together. Nine months after that she could identify words and sentences on the printed page, could write well, could add to ten, and could retell a story after hearing it. Seven months beyond this point she had a vocabulary of 1,500-2,000 words and was asking complicated questions. Starting from an educational level of between one and three years (depending on what aspect one considers), she had reached a normal level by the time she was eight and a half years old. In short, she covered in two years the stages of learning that ordinarily require six. Or, to put it another way, her I.Q. trebled in a year and a half. The speed with which she reached the normal level of mental development seems analogous to the recovery of body weight in a growing child after an illness, the recovery being achieved by an extra fast rate of growth for a period after the illness until normal weight for the given age is again attained.

When the writer saw Isabelle a year and a half after her discovery, she gave him the impression of being a very bright, cheerful, energetic little girl. She spoke well, walked and ran without trouble, and sang with gusto and accuracy. Today she is over fourteen years old and has passed the sixth grade in a public school. Her teachers say that she participates in all school activities as normally as other children. Though older than her classmates, she has fortunately not physically matured too far beyond their level.

Clearly the history of Isabelle's development is different from that of Anna's. In both cases there was an exceedingly low, or rather blank, intellectual level to begin with. In both cases it seemed that the girl might be congenitally feeble-minded. In both a considerably higher level was reached later on. But the Ohio girl achieved a normal mentality within two years, whereas Anna was still markedly inadequate at the end of four and a half years. This difference in achievement may suggest that Anna had less initial capacity. But an alternative hypothesis is possible.

One should remember that Anna never received the prolonged and expert attention that Isabelle received. The result of such attention, in the case of the Ohio girl, was to give her speech at an early stage, and her subsequent rapid development seems to have been a consequence of that. "Until Isabelle's speech and language development, she had all the characteristics of a feeble-minded child." Had Anna, who, from the standpoint of psychometric tests and early history, closely resembled this girl at the start, been given a mastery of speech at an earlier point by intensive training, her subsequent development might have been much more rapid.

The hypothesis that Anna began with a sharply inferior mental capacity is therefore not established. Even if she were deficient to start with, we have no way of knowing how much so. Under ordinary conditions she might have been a dull normal or, like her mother, a moron. Even after the blight of her isolation, if she had lived to maturity, she might have finally reached virtually the full level of her capacity, whatever it may have been. That her isolation did have a profound effect upon her mentality, there can be no doubt. This is proved by the substantial degree of change during the four and a half years following her rescue.

Consideration of Isabelle's case serves to show, as Anna's case does not clearly show, that isolation up to the age of six, with failure to acquire any form of speech and hence failure to grasp nearly the whole world of cultural meaning, does not preclude the subsequent acquisition of these. Indeed, there seems to be a process of accelerated recovery in which the child goes through the mental stages at a more rapid rate than would be the case in normal development. Just what would be the maximum age at which a person could remain isolated and still retain the capacity for full cultural acquisition is hard to say. Almost certainly it would not be as high as age fifteen; it might possibly be as low as age ten. Undoubtedly various individuals would differ considerably as to the exact age.

Anna's is not an ideal case for showing the effects of extreme isolation, partly because she was possibly deficient to begin with, partly because she did not receive the best training available, and partly because she did not live long enough. Nevertheless, her case is instructive when placed in the record with numerous other cases of extreme isolation. This and the previous article about her are meant to place her in the record. It is to be hoped that other cases will be described in the scientific literature as they are discovered (as unfortunately they will be), for only in these rare cases of extreme isolation is it possible "to observe *concretely separated* two factors in the development of human personality which are always otherwise only analytically separated, the biogenic and the sociogenic factors."

20. THE TRANSMISSION OF RACIAL ATTITUDES AMONG WHITE SOUTHERNERS *

OLIVE WESTBROOKE QUINN

The previous selection illustrates the importance of association with with other human beings in the development of human personality. Since the transmission of human habits, attitudes, and beliefs to children goes on constantly in every family and school and in other groups, our sensitivity to this pervasive social process is commonly dulled. In this selection Olive Quinn shows how a particular set of attitudes, which is condemned by many people, is acquired by the children in a large segment of American society.

We are not concerned in this paper with the content of racial attitudes which find expression in the behavior of southern white people toward Negroes, nor with an appraisal of these attitudes; rather, we are interested in discovering, as far as may be, the mechanisms of transmission of racial attitudes among white southerners. An historical consideration of the problems of the cultural education of the southern white person would examine those influences which have built up through time the accepted white philosophy of race; another approach is through a study of the forces which transmit that philosophy to the individual born into the society. The latter approach is used here in an effort to find how the white child finds his place in relation to the Negro.

Because racial learning is but one aspect of social learning and not a thing apart from it, an understanding of the ways in which the child learns his racial role necessarily involves or presupposes knowledge of the mechanisms of social learning itself. Learning that one is white is part of the process of learning the identity of the self and the symbols and expectations appropriate to the position of that self. The racial role is but one of many which the individual must learn, and behavior proper

* From *Social Forces*, Vol. 33, No. 1 (October, 1954), 41–47.

The author (b. 1914) is a sociologist with the Laboratory of Socio-Environmental Studies at the National Institute of Mental Health, working chiefly in the area of mental health, race relations, and in related areas of social psychology. Has written numerous articles for professional journals.

to these roles is socially defined. Davis points out that "socialization is not simply the process of learning the specific skills of tool-using, language, and social organization, but implies as well the learning of these cultural behaviors as they are defined by a particular society." The society in which a child is reared has ready for him the answer to his question, "Who am I?" The answer is different in different contexts and relationships, and the child must discover in a variety of ways the answer appropriate to his immediate situation.

We have asserted that racial learning is but one aspect of social learning, and we have indicated that in learning his racial role a child finds part of the answer to the question of his identity. A major task for the developing child is the definition of his relationship to people about him. In answering the question, "Who am I?" he must necessarily answer its corollary, "And who are all of those?" He does not make these definitions alone, of course; most of them are made for him by his society through the medium of his parents, his peers, and others with whom he comes into contact. To say, though, that the child does not make his own definitions does not explain how he learns them, and this is the problem with which we are immediately concerned. We must approach the acquisition of racial attitudes as an aspect of the emergence of a sense of self.

That racial attitudes are involved in a sense of self is demonstrated in the following excerpts from interviews with southern white young people.

People who say "nigger" say it, I think, to make themselves feel superior. I don't feel superior, but I don't feel inferior, either, and I don't have to belittle other people to make myself big.

I feel a protective attitude toward the Negro; I always have. But I'll have to admit that I enjoy being of the Old South, too. I know it is a pose, or at least I think it is; yet it has glamour, and I am afraid I am duped by it.

I can remember in Junior High School being so disgusted with the kind of kid who blustered about, saying, "Why, if a nigger gets fresh with me, I'll break his neck!" Perhaps I am a little more kindly toward them because I so dislike that kind of behavior. I look on it as lower class behavior and lower class attitude. . . . I don't like it.

Perhaps my attitude has been altered by the fact that I expect to be a singer. There is no denying that in the field of music there are some great artists who are Negroes. It would be tragic to deny them their rightful place, and so deny all of us the pleasure of their talent. Then, I think that if they are to be allowed to have positions of prominence in my field, there is no reason why they should not be recognized in other fields. I guess everyone starts his thinking from himself.

A young woman who attended a summer school session at a northern university had this to say about an experience in the classroom:

We were seated in alphabetical order, and a friend of mine and I were in seats next to Negroes. After class we went to the professor and asked to be moved. He wanted to know why. I said, "We are from the South, and we aren't used to sitting by Negroes." He was so mad at us! He said we were prejudiced and ignorant, and he said all kinds of things to us. My friend said, "Yes, I know we are all you say; but that is the way we are, and we aren't used to sitting by Negroes." Well, he raved some more, and finally I said, "I'm sorry that I feel this way, but I do feel this way, and if I can't have a different seat, I'll have to take a different course." He talked to us a long time about how wrong we were, but he moved us, and after that he was real nice to me.

Each of the statements above is an individual's attempt to define his attitude toward race, but it is something more than that; it is a public announcement of the kind of person the speaker thinks of himself as being, a projection of the picture which he has of himself. Racial attitudes, then, seem to be acquired as a part of the individual's attitude toward himself, as one of the areas of definition of his relationships with other people. It is important that we should try to understand how the sense of self arises, and it is to this question that we now turn our attention.

One of the most rewarding approaches to the problem of the emergence of self is that of George Herbert Mead, and it is his concepts and his framework of analysis which we shall use in an effort to understand how the racial role becomes incorporated into the individual's sense of self. Mead points out that we learn who we are (i.e., what kind of person we are) from the reactions of other people toward us. And it is in this way that in any given situation we learn to assess our own behavior. Other individuals indicate to us by their reactions the meaning of our behavior; and by taking the role of the other, we are able to make indications to ourselves which serve as guides for future behavior. Sometimes these indications are made in the form of direct verbal responses; often they are but behavioral responses to our own behavior.

Where racial attitudes are concerned, direct instruction seems to play a relatively unimportant part. The most perceptive and self-analytical of the young people interviewed often are unable to produce any memories of direct teaching with respect to racial attitude. For the most part, verbal instruction is avoided, even when it is given, it is usually justified in other than racial terms. The one exception to this seems to occur with respect to the term "lady." Over and over again the young people interviewed told of quite explicit instruction in the use of this word.

Once when I was a little girl a Negro woman came to the door. I told my aunt a lady wanted to see her. She went to the door, and when she came back she told me that I should have said a woman was there to see her. I wondered about it a little, but I think I didn't question it.

Once when we were in the car, I said, "Oh, Mother, look! That colored lady has on a dress just like yours." Well, Mother was a little upset about the dress, but she didn't say so. She said, "Agnes, call them colored women. There are no colored ladies."

I remember when I learned that lesson. I told Mother the washlady was here. She said to say "woman," and I asked why. Mother explained that you never say "Negro lady." She said "lady" was a term of respect applied to few white ladies and to no Negroes at all.

About five years ago we were riding through Memphis one day, and I saw a Negro standing on the street corner. She was all dressed up, and she looked very pretty. I said to Mother, "Isn't that a pretty Negro lady?" Mother called me down for it. She told me to say "woman." I wanted to know why, and she didn't answer me. I said, "I don't believe there is any reason. I think you just don't like them—like Grandmother." Golly, was I sorry I'd said that! Mother lectured me about respect for my elders, and she said if I ever spoke to her like that again she'd punish me severely.

It is interesting to note that instruction was given only after a child had erred in his racial behavior. In the majority of cases reported, no explanation was given except in general terms, that these are accepted usages. If a child was not satisfied but sought further reasons, he was told that ladies are always white; and if he questioned this judgment, he was punished for disrespectful behavior toward his elders. The rationale for the punishment was given in terms of the younger-older person relationship, but the association of the punishment with a transgression of racial patterns did not fail. In the last instance reported above, this association was strong enough to stop further questioning:

Not long after that I came in late to lunch one day. Everyone had eaten except the cook, and I started to sit at the table with her and eat. Mother asked her to move. I didn't understand it, and I was just about to ask why when I remembered the Memphis incident and decided not to. So I did not protest. But I was embarrassed; I didn't think Mother should have done that. She might have told me later not to do it again.

In general, it seems that verbal indications that Negroes are different from whites are used only when the child has violated the racial folkways. Every instance of explicit verbal instruction, as reported by these young people, was preceded by some such incident.

One time when I was leaving to go to kindergarten, I kissed my nurse. Father waited until I was in the car with him, and then he told me not to. I asked why, but Father is very domineering, and he told me I was too young to understand and that I'd just have to do as he said.

I don't dare open my mouth on the subject at home. I did once, but I was already in disgrace. Daddy wasn't speaking to me at the time, but when I said I thought Negroes should have the vote, he spoke. And he told me never to discuss the subject in his house again. He thinks the professors and student body at college are all Communists.

While it is generally true that direct verbal instruction is seldom used as a method for teaching racial attitudes, it is not true that verbal indications of an indirect kind are avoided. Indeed, indirect verbal instruction, given by the simple expedient of letting the child "overhear" adult conversation, accounts for most of the stereotyped verbalizations in terms of which young people express their feelings about Negroes. The importance of the kind of adult talk a child is allowed to hear cannot be overemphasized. Certainly, it is not accident, except in a few cases, that determines what the child hears. Ordinarily parents are very careful to see to it that their children hear from them only those things considered appropriate to their years. Perhaps these decisions are not always made at a conscious level, but when adults talk freely about sexual looseness and immorality among Negroes, while maintaining a strict silence before their children on the subject of sexual irregularities among white people, it is difficult to escape the judgment that they make this difference because they want their children to believe the one and to disbelieve the other. Reconstruction stories are kept vividly alive not because of historical interest but because they provide the emotional set which any good southerner is supposed to have. Shortcomings and deficiencies of Negro servants are paraded, stereotyped and exaggerated because such a picture of the Negro is appropriate to the treatment accorded him, and this treatment is deemed necessary to "keep the Negro in his place." When a Negro who obviously does not fit the stereotype comes upon the scene, he is explained away as an exception, but for the most part white children simply do not see these exceptional Negroes. Judgments are given the child not in any direct way, but by allowing him to listen to adult talk without participating in it.

I knew Alma lived with men. It's funny, I never heard much talk about the morals of white people; it came to me as a decided shock that white people are often sexually immoral, but I have always known—or nearly always—that colored people are not hampered by morals. I never heard any tales of sexual immorality involving white people until I was considered grown.

I have heard lots of stories about their criminality, about how they cut each other up and cut white people up. I've heard about that lynching a hundred times. What did I hear? Well, they told me that a nigger shot a policeman and they found him and shot him and hanged him on a telephone pole down there by Link's Cafe. They say the Negroes behaved for a long time after that and they were scared to come out for a week or two. Every time the men at the store start talking about how uppity niggers are now, someone tells about that lynching.

I have very vivid recollections of Reconstruction stories. The Negroes were hateful and cruel to white people then. There is much unrest in Memphis at the present time. The Negroes think they can do just anything. They are forming clubs: there is the Bump Club, you know about that, and then all these Eleanor Clubs.

The following excerpt from a diary kept during the collecting of the interviews is revealing on this point:

Tonight I went to Bea's for the evening. She and her mother were very much elated that at last they had found a Negro woman who had agreed to come to the house and do the laundry. All of us were sitting on the front porch, Bea, her mother, Sue and I. Mrs. White was laying plans for the morrow. "Bea," she said, "remind me to lock up the silver tomorrow. We don't know a thing about this nigger." Then she turned to me, "You know, you just can't trust any of them. I always lock up my good silver."

None of Mrs. White's remarks was addressed to her granddaughter, Sue, yet none escaped her. Listening to the casual conversation of adults, she had been told once again that Negroes are untrustworthy. This lesson was driven home every time a strange Negro entered the house. She, like other children, mimicked her mother and her grandmother, even in behavior and attitudes of which she was critical. When children seek to identify themselves with others, a common manifestation of this identification is found in imitative behavior. It is not surprising that a young person who has observed that a certain kind of behavior in an adult brings approval from his associates should "try on" this behavior, for this is the way a child grows up—by practicing grown-up behavior, seeking to call out in others the desired responses. Such imitation is often the occasion for direct instruction against it, as when children begin to give orders to the servants. Then the parents make it quite clear that giving orders is the special prerogative of adult members of the household. In this case, however, the child's behavior is socially incorrect only in that he has overstepped the boundaries of his age-grade, and he is made to understand that such behavior must wait upon maturity.

Another kind of indirect indication is seen in instructions given to children that they are not to make disparaging remarks about Negroes; rather, they must not let the Negro know that he is considered inferior. Such instruction cannot but make the inferiority an unquestioned fact to the white child.

Servants should be well cared-for, and they should be treated with consideration. We should always be considerate of their feelings; they are human beings. I was always expected to obey my nurse, and I was not allowed to abuse her.

You know, I think from the fact that I was told so often that I must treat colored people with consideration, I got the idea that I could mistreat them if I wanted to.

Here is a very telling clue to the way in which race attitudes are instilled. The first quotation suggests respect for the Negro's feelings and rights, yet the overtone points unmistakably to the essential helplessness, servility, and inferiority which are supposed to characterize the Negro servant. There is a great difference in the respect required of young people for elders of their own family and social rank and the consideration invoked in behalf of serving people. It is one thing to respect the rights of those who hold unquestioned authority; it is another to respect the rights of those who owe those rights to the protection of an authoritative group which claims the child as its own. The white child becomes "Miss" or "Mister" very early to the servant in the home, and while this is not purely a racial phenomenon, it probably occurs earlier when the servants are Negroes than when they are members of the dominant racial group.

It should be pointed out that the servant himself, having accepted his role in relation to the various members of the family, becomes a teacher to the child. A maid, nurse, cook, or yardman may give very direct training with regard to the expected behavior of the young white person. This is especially true when the Negro undertakes to train the child in "manners."

I had a Negro nurse, Aunt Jennie; she nursed both my brother and me. When the doorbell rang, we wanted to answer the door. She said we were not supposed to. She told me I had to be a lady, and if I wasn't one, she would use the hairbrush on me.

Rosie is scornful of the lack of manners of young Negroes. She calls me "Elsie," and that is all right, but she thinks it is disgraceful when younger colored girls call white girls by their first names.

We have reviewed at some length examples of verbal indications, both direct and indirect, as they relate to the problem of the transmission of racial attitudes. As important as these methods are in teaching the southern white child his racial role, they account for a very limited proportion of the total racial learning of the white southerner. It has been pointed out earlier that the occasion for most direct verbal instruction is some kind of infraction of the rules governing the behavior of white people in their relationships with Negroes. It is the behavior itself which is most carefully taught. The prevailing norms of behavior provide a frame of reference within which the child makes his judgments, and the surer he is in the practice of these norms, the more likely he is to find a rationale which defends them.

For the most part the South does not teach attitudes to its white children. Such teaching is not necessary; in establishing practices, by precept, by example, and by law, which separate the races and make distinctions between interracial and intraracial behavior, the South has established a way of life which can have but one meaning for those who diligently practice it. And to escape such practice has, until very recent times, been extremely difficult, for racial etiquette has been woven into the entire institutional fabric of southern culture.

A child who is constantly treated with deference by members of a group visibly distinguishable from himself on physical grounds can hardly escape the conclusion that he is superior to members of that group. If, in addition, in learning his various roles he is able to evoke deference by imitating the dominant example of his elders, this conception of himself is reinforced.

If in public transportation his accommodations are separate from and superior to those of the other racial group, he is likely to take this difference as a matter of course and to accept it as his due. Once the expected behavior is established, the individual can be counted on to defend it, for he must do so if any question arises which threatens his ego, and this will certainly occur if his behavior is called into question. An individual's ego consists of his conception of himself in relation to others, and this relationship is a behavioral relationship. It happens that in the South great importance is attached to "manners"; but manners are, of course, simply the rules which define the relationship of the individual to others and which call for certain specific behaviors as indicating this relationship.

I guess the thing that is stressed most in a southern girl's training is manners, etiquette. I think it is very important to be sure that your behavior is correct.

You know, where you are makes a lot of difference about how you behave. It's all very well to say I'm for this and against that, but actually, all of us—or I should say most of us—fear criticism from the people we must live with. I sat down by a Negro here in Memphis one time. He was in a funny place; you wouldn't expect to find a Negro there. There were white men across the aisle, and I didn't notice that he was a Negro. I felt very strange, and when a seat opened up across the aisle, I moved. In the North or West it wouldn't have bothered me at all. But many people here were looking at me curiously, some with disgust. I wouldn't have got up if there had been no place to move to, but I'll tell you, it was hard to know what to do.

A ministerial student, who at a church conference can declare for equal treatment for Negroes on the conference grounds, does not pursue the point in the college dining room where he is a student waiter and works with an elderly Negro man.

There is an old Negro who works with us and who has been here for years. We call him "Jones," and he calls me "Mr. Peter." I would not object to calling him Mr. Jones, but it would serve no good purpose to do so. I am sure he would be embarrassed if I did, and all the white people who were not antagonized would certainly be surprised. I'd be set down as a nut.

A militant minister who appeals to the F.B.I. for justice for Negro citizens and who insists upon preaching what he believes, thereby alienating some members of his congregation, nevertheless submits to the social dictum which requires visits with his Negro friends to be at his instigation and in their homes.

Dr. Sales, the president of the Negro college here, is my personal friend. I like him very much, and he and his wife and my wife and I have many good visits together. I often go to his home to visit, but that is the way the visits must be. He wouldn't dare come to my home to visit.

The parent who would really rather not teach her child the prevailing attitudes with respect to race, still feels that she must see to it that her child's behavior is correct as judged by the existing norms.

A few weeks ago something came up that was really hard for me to handle. The people next door to us had a little Negro girl come in to wash dinner dishes. They gave her dinner and a little bit of money—I don't know how much, but it was really very little. Well, they decided they didn't need her any longer. She lives in one of those little shacks down near the railroad. Sue came in one night and wanted to know if we couldn't give Janie some dinner. I had noticed that very often the little darkie would call to Sue over the fence. One afternoon she came over and asked for Sue. Fortunately, she was not at home. Well, as I said, Sue came to me and said, "Mother, she is hungry. Can't we give her something to eat?" So I fixed a plate, and the little girl sat on the back steps and ate, and Sue sat and talked with her while she ate. It disturbed me a little. The next day Sue wanted to know if Janie couldn't eat with us and wash our dishes. I told her I was afraid not. She couldn't understand why not. I told her we couldn't do it because we didn't need Janie, that she could get a job somewhere else. I guess actually we could have taken her on and used her very well, but we could also get along without her, and I didn't want her around because it would be so hard to explain to Sue why she must not have a little colored girl for a friend. You know, you hate to bring your child up to be a snob; but you know I couldn't have that. I didn't want the colored child to get any ideas, and I didn't want Sue doing something that other people would question and think queer. It was just an impossible situation.

Attitudes, then, seem to be transmitted not so much by verbal instruction as by the provision of the kinds of experiences in which the child learns behavior appropriate to his racial role, and by a shielding of the child from those experiences in which he might learn behavior inappropriate to his position.

An adequate explanation of the means by which racial attitudes are transmitted must take into account and explain failures of transmission. Many observers assert that racial attitudes are changing, that young people today hold attitudes considerably more favorable toward the Negro than those of their parents. If this is so, and it may well be, the change is understandable in terms of our analytical framework.

We have asserted that racial attitudes reflect the behavior of individuals in interracial relationships, that the attitude is in a sense the rationale of the act. The racial behavior of earlier generations grew out of a social order that no longer exists. The young white southerner is no longer brought up in the care of a "mammy"; it is a rare white family that has even one full-time Negro servant, and the behavior appropriate to the "master" class is not an ever-present example in the home. Opportunities for parents to teach racial behavior are fewer than they used to be, and the lessons cannot be so thoroughly learned. Since the master-servant relationship and all the practices appropriate to it are so little in evidence, the old verbalizations and stereotypes are losing some of their authority. Perhaps some unconscious awareness of weaknesses inherent in verbal indications of racial attitudes has accounted for the apparent reluctance of the bearers of the culture to attempt to transmit the attitudes through direct verbal insruction; certainly, without the reinforcement of carefully trained racial behavior, these attitudes are beginning to be altered.

It is customary in the sociological field to talk about relationships between and among different racial groups in terms of social distance. Robert E. Park pointed out that social distance might be either vertical or horizontal, and he thought of the former—with the Negro in the subordinate position—as characterizing racial relationships in the South, as opposed to horizontal social distance—with the Negro relegated to a different sphere of activity—which was characteristic of northern racial relationships. Economic changes in the South are bringing increased social distance of a horizontal type; it may well be that when this distance is great enough the vertical distance will be negligible. Perhaps this change is an important one for a change in racial attitudes, for it will certainly bring a change in definition of behavioral relationships of Negroes and whites. As more white people find themselves in jobs in which Negroes are their clients and their customers, it is inevitable that the behavior defining these relationships should give rise to new attitudes. A sixteen-year-old white girl who lives in a southern town of about 16,000 population reports:

> You know, I've been working at Wilkie's Shoe Store. A lot of Negroes come in there, and I wait on them. Once I was so startled to hear myself saying "ma'am" to one.

And a seventeen-year-old boy from the same town tells:

> Last summer I worked at the ice plant. There was a Negro there I liked. He really was a swell fellow. He was a grown man. Everyone liked him. . . . I wouldn't mind working with them. A year ago I might have said I wouldn't like it, but this Negro down at the ice plant did a lot to make me see things differently. I wouldn't particularly like to work under one—no, I shouldn't say that, 'cause I know I wouldn't mind working under the one at the ice plant.

Racial definitions are an inevitable part of the southerner's point of view because social forces dictate a racial etiquette which cannot be ignored. In many instances these social definitions of racial roles are legal definitions as well. Jim Crow is not only a folkway but also a law, and this fact puts a heavy drag on the rate of social change. The white person inclined to protest segregation can be hauled into court if he attempts to make an issue of the principles. Myrdal has observed that liberalism in the South holds an anomalous position in that it runs counter to law. Conservative forces have not only custom but legal right on their side. Thus it is extremely difficult for the southern white person to act against custom, and the social pressures are bulwarked by police and courts. The legal aspects of race relations lag behind economic and social changes brought about by industrial development and the urgencies of war.

But laws, like attitudes, may be thought of as reflections of already established patterns of behavior, and it seems reasonable to expect that changing racial behavior will be reflected in a new rationale and an accompanying rewriting of legal definitions of racial relationships.

21. STATUS AND ROLE *

RALPH LINTON

As members of various groups, people acquire statuses and perform certain roles. Ralph Linton's discussion of these two concepts has become a classic in sociological and anthropological literature. He examines the theory of status and role with illustrations from both nonliterate and complex societies.

The term *status*, like the term *culture*, has come to be used with a double significance. A *status*, in the abstract, is a position in a particular pattern. It is thus quite correct to speak of each individual as having many statuses, since each individual participates in the expression of a number of patterns. However, unless the term is qualified in some way, *the status* of any individual means the sum total of all the statuses which he occupies. It represents his position with relation to the total society. Thus the status of Mr. Jones as a member of his community derives from a combination of all the statuses which he holds as a citizen, as an attorney, as a Mason, as a Methodist, as Mrs. Jones's husband, and so on.

A status, as distinct from the individual who may occupy it, is simply a collection of rights and duties. Since these rights and duties can find expression only through the medium of individuals, it is extremely hard for us to maintain a distinction in our thinking between statuses and the people who hold them and exercise the rights and duties which constitute them. The relation between any individual and any status he holds is somewhat like that between the driver of an automobile and the driver's place in the machine. The driver's seat with its steering wheel, accelerator, and other controls is a constant with ever-present potentialities for action and control, while the driver may be any member of the family and may exercise these potentialities very well or very badly.

* From *The Study of Man*, by Ralph Linton, pp. 113–121. Copyright, 1936, D. Appleton-Century Co., Inc. By permission of Appleton-Century-Crofts, Inc.

The author (1893–1953) was Sterling Professor of Anthropology at Yale University. Formerly Chairman of Anthropology at Columbia University (1938–1945). He was Assistant Curator of North American Ethnology, Field Museum of Natural History. He has been described as one of the two or three greatest anthropologists of the present era. Among his works are: *Acculturation in Seven American Indian Tribes; The Cultural Background of Personality; Most of the World: The Peoples of Africa, Latin America, and the East Today; The Tree of Culture.*

A *rôle* represents the dynamic aspect of a status. The individual is socially assigned to a status and occupies it with relation to other statuses. When he puts the rights and duties which constitute the status into effect, he is performing a rôle. Rôle and status are quite inseparable, and the distinction between them is of only academic interest. There are no rôles without statuses or statuses without rôles. Just as in the case of *status,* the term *rôle* is used with a double significance. Every individual has a series of rôles deriving from the various patterns in which he participates and at the same time a *rôle,* general, which represents the sum total of these rôles and determines what he does for his society and what he can expect from it.

Although all statuses and rôles derive from social patterns and are integral parts of patterns, they have an independent function with relation to the individuals who occupy particular statuses and exercise their rôles. To such individuals the combined status and rôle represent the minimum of attitudes and behavior which he must assume if he is to participate in the overt expression of the pattern. Status and rôle serve to reduce the ideal patterns for social life to individual terms. They become models for organizing the attitudes and behavior of the individual so that these will be congruous with those of the other individuals participating in the expression of the pattern. Thus if we are studying football teams in the abstract, the position of quarterback is meaningless except in relation to the other positions. From the point of view of the quarterback himself it is a distinct and important entity. It determines where he shall take his place in the line-up and what he shall do in various plays. His assignment to this position at once limits and defines his activities and establishes a minimum of things which he must learn. Similarly, in a social pattern such as that for the employer-employee relationship the statuses of employer and employee define what each has to know and do to put the pattern into operation. The employer does not need to know the techniques involved in the employee's labor, and the employee does not need to know the techniques for marketing or accounting.

It is obvious that, as long as there is no interference from external sources, the more perfectly the members of any society are adjusted to their statuses and rôles the more smoothly the society will function. In its attempts to bring about such adjustments every society finds itself caught on the horns of a dilemma. The individual's formation of habits and attitudes begins at birth, and, other things being equal, the earlier his training for a status can begin the more successful it is likely to be. At the same time, no two individuals are alike, and a status which will be congenial to one may be quite uncongenial to another. Also, there are in all social systems certain rôles which require more than training for their successful performance. Perfect technique does not make a great violinist, nor a thorough book knowledge of tactics an efficient general. The utilization of the special gifts of individuals may be highly important to society, as in the case of the general, yet these gifts usually show themselves rather late, and to wait upon their manifestation for the assignment of statuses would be to forfeit the advantages to be derived from commencing training early.

Fortunately, human beings are so mutable that almost any normal individual can be trained to the adequate performance of almost any rôle. Most of the business of living can be conducted on a basis of habit, with little need for intelligence and none for special gifts. Societies have met the dilemma by developing two types of statuses, the *ascribed* and the *achieved*. Ascribed statuses are those which are assigned to individuals without reference to their innate differences or abilities. They can be predicted and trained for from the moment of birth. The *achieved* statuses are, as a minimum, those requiring special qualities, although they are not necessarily limited to these. They are not assigned to individuals from birth but are left open to be filled through competition and individual effort. The majority of the statuses in all social systems are of the ascribed type and those which take care of the ordinary day-to-day business of living are practically always of this type.

In all societies certain things are selected as reference points for the ascription of status. The things chosen for this purpose are always of such a nature that they are ascertainable at birth, making it possible to begin the training of the individual for his potential statuses and rôles at once. The simplest and most universally used of these reference points is sex. Age is used with nearly equal frequency, since all individuals pass through the same cycle of growth, maturity, and decline, and the statuses whose occupation will be determined by age can be forecast and trained for with accuracy. Family relationships, the simplest and most obvious being that of the child to its mother, are also used in all societies as reference points for the establishment of a whole series of statuses. Lastly, there is the matter of birth into a particular socially established group, such as a class or caste. The use of this type of reference is common but not universal. In all societies the actual ascription of statuses to the individual is controlled by a series of these reference points which together serve to delimit the field of his future participation in the life of the group.

The division and ascription of statuses with relation to sex seems to be basic in all social systems. All societies prescribe different attitudes and activities to men and to women. Most of them try to rationalize these prescriptions in terms of the physiological differences between the sexes or their different rôles in reproduction. However, a comparative study of the statuses ascribed to women and men in different cultures seems to show that while such factors may have served as a starting point for the development of a division the actual ascriptions are almost entirely determined by culture. Even the psychological characteristics ascribed to men and women in different societies vary so much that they can have little physiological basis. Our own idea of women as ministering angels contrasts sharply with the ingenuity of women as torturers among the Iroquois and the sadistic delight they took in the process. Even the last two generations have seen a sharp change in the psychological patterns for women in our own society. The delicate, fainting lady of the middle eighteen-hundreds is as extinct as the dodo.

When it comes to the ascription of occupations, which is after all an integral part of status, we find the differences in various societies even more marked. Arapesh women regularly carry heavier loads than men "because their heads are so much harder and stronger." In some societies women do most of the manual labor; in others, as in the Marquesas, even cooking, housekeeping, and baby-tending are proper male occupations, and women spend most of their time primping. Even the general rule that women's handicap through pregnancy and nursing indicates the more active occupations as male and the less active ones as female has many exceptions. Thus among the Tasmanians seal-hunting was women's work. They swam out to the seal rocks, stalked the animals, and clubbed them. Tasmanian women also hunted opossums, which required the climbing of large trees.

Although the actual ascription of occupations along sex lines is highly variable, the pattern of sex division is constant. There are very few societies in which every important activity has not been definitely assigned to men or to women. Even when the two sexes coöperate in a particular occupation, the field of each is usually clearly delimited. Thus in Madagascar rice culture the men make the seed beds and terraces and prepare the fields for transplanting. The women do the work of transplanting, which is hard and back-breaking. The women weed the crop, but the men harvest it. The women then carry it to the threshing floors, where the men thresh it while the women winnow it. Lastly, the women pound the grain in mortars and cook it.

When a society takes over a new industry, there is often a period of uncertainty during which the work may be done by either sex, but it soon falls into the province of one or the other. In Madagascar, pottery is made by men in some tribes and by women in others. The only tribe in which it is made by both men and women is one into which the art has been introduced within the last sixty years. I was told that during the fifteen years preceding my visit there had been a marked decrease in the number of male potters, many men who had once practised the art having given it up. The factor of lowered wages, usually advanced as the reason for men leaving one of our own occupations when women enter it in force, certainly was not operative here. The field was not overcrowded, and the prices for men's and women's products were the same. Most of the men who had given up the trade were vague as to their reasons, but a few said frankly that they did not like to compete with women. Apparently the entry of women into the occupation had robbed it of a certain amount of prestige. It was no longer quite the thing for a man to be a potter, even though he was a very good one.

The use of age as a reference point for establishing status is as universal as the use of sex. All societies recognize three age groupings as a minimum: child, adult, and old. Certain societies have emphasized age as a basis for assigning status and have greatly amplified the divisions. Thus in certain African tribes the whole male population is divided into units composed of those born in the same years or within two- or three-year intervals. However, such extreme attention to age is unusual, and we need not discuss it here.

The physical differences between child and adult are easily recognizable, and the passage from childhood to maturity is marked by physiological events which make it possible to date it exactly for girls and within a few weeks or months for boys. However, the physical passage from childhood to maturity does not necessarily coincide with the social transfer of the individual from one category to the other. Thus in our own society both men and women remain legally children until long after they are physically adult. In most societies this difference between the physical and social transfer is more clearly marked than in our own. The child becomes a man not when he is physically mature but when he is formally recognized as a man by his society. This recognition is almost always given ceremonial expression in what are technically known as puberty rites. The most important element in these rites is not the determination of physical maturity but that of social maturity. Whether a boy is able to breed is less vital to his society than whether he is able to do a man's work and has a man's knowledge. Actually, most puberty ceremonies include tests of the boy's learning and fortitude, and if the aspirants are unable to pass these they are left in the child status until they can. For those who pass the tests, the ceremonies usually culminate in the transfer to them of certain secrets which the men guard from women and children.

The passage of individuals from adult to aged is harder to perceive. There is no clear physiological line for men, while even women may retain their full physical vigor and their ability to carry on all the activities of the adult status for several years after the menopause. The social transfer of men from the adult to the aged group is given ceremonial recognition in a few cultures, as when a father formally surrenders his official position and titles to his son, but such recognition is rare. As for women, there appears to be no society in which the menopause is given ceremonial recognition, although there are a few societies in which it does alter the individual's status. Thus Comanche women, after the menopause, were released from their disabilities with regard to the supernatural. They could handle sacred objects, obtain power through dreams and practise as shamans, all things forbidden to women of bearing age.

The general tendency for societies to emphasize the individual's first change in age status and largely ignore the second is no doubt due in part to the difficulty of determining the onset of old age. However, there are also psychological factors involved. The boy or girl is usually anxious to grow up, and this eagerness is heightened by the exclusion of children from certain activities and knowledge. Also, society welcomes new additions to the most active division of the group, that which contributes most to its perpetuation and well-being. Conversely, the individual who enjoys the thought of growing old is atypical in all societies. Even when age brings respect and a new measure of influence, it means the relinquishment of much that is pleasant. We can see among ourselves that the aging usually refuse to recognize the change until long after it has happened.

In the case of age, as in that of sex, the biological factors involved appear to be secondary to the cultural ones in determining the content of status. There are certain activities which cannot be ascribed to children because children either lack the necessary strength or have not had time to acquire the necessary technical skills. However, the attitudes between parent and child and the importance given to the child in the family structure vary enormously from one culture to another. The status of the child among our Puritan ancestors, where he was seen and not heard and ate at the second table, represents one extreme. At the other might be placed the status of the eldest son of a Polynesian chief. All the *mana* (supernatural power) of the royal line converged upon such a child. He was socially superior to his own father and mother, and any attempt to discipline him would have been little short of sacrilege. I once visited the hereditary chief of a Marquesan tribe and found the whole family camping uncomfortably in their own front yard, although they had a good house built on European lines. Their eldest son, aged nine, had had a dispute with his father a few days before and had tabooed the house by naming it after his head. The family had thus been compelled to move out and could not use it again until he relented and lifted the taboo. As he could use the house himself and eat anywhere in the village, he was getting along quite well and seemed to enjoy the situation thoroughly.

The statuses ascribed to the old in various societies vary even more than those ascribed to children. In some cases they are relieved of all heavy labor and can settle back comfortably to live off their children. In others they perform most of the hard and monotonous tasks which do not require great physical strength, such as the gathering of firewood. In many societies the old women, in particular, take over most of the care of the younger children, leaving the younger women free to enjoy themselves. In some places the old are treated with consideration and respect; in others they are considered a useless incumbrance and removed as soon as they are incapable of heavy labor. In most societies their advice is sought even when little attention is paid to their wishes. This custom has a sound practical basis, for the individual who contrives to live to old age in an uncivilized group has usually been a person of ability and his memory constitutes a sort of reference library to which one can turn for help under all sorts of circumstances.

In certain societies the change from the adult to the old status is made more difficult for the individual by the fact that the patterns for these statuses ascribe different types of personality to each. This was the case among the Comanche, as it seems to have been among most of the Plains tribes. The adult male was a warrior, vigorous, self-reliant, and pushing. Most of his social relationships were phrased in terms of competition. He took what he could get and held what he had without regard to any abstract rights of those weaker than himself. Any willingness to arbitrate differences or to ignore slights was a sign of weakness resulting in loss of prestige. The old man, on the other hand, was expected to be wise and gentle, willing to overlook slights and, if need be, to endure abuse. It was his task to work for the welfare of the tribe, giving sound advice, settling feuds between the warriors, and even preventing his tribe from making new enemies. Young men strove for war and honor, old men strove for peace and tranquillity. There is abundant evidence that among the Comanche the transition was often a difficult one for the individual. Warriors did not prepare for old age, thinking it a better fate to be killed in action. When waning physical powers forced them to assume the new rôle, many of them did so grudgingly, and those who had strong magic would go on trying to enforce the rights which belonged to the younger status. Such bad old men were a peril to young ones beginning their careers, for they were jealous of them simply because they were young and strong and admired by the women. The medicine power of these young men was still weak, and the old men could and did kill them by malevolent magic. It is significant that although benevolent medicine men might be of any age in Comanche folklore, malevolent ones were always old.

22. CULTURAL CONTRADICTIONS
AND SEX ROLES °

MIRRA KOMAROVSKY

As is implied by the preceding article, difficulties arise for those who have conflicting statuses. In our own society, such contradictory statuses may be particularly serious for college women. Many college coeds who read this article will recognize some of the problems reported by Mirra Komarovsky. They are dilemmas that confront the individual in our changing contemporary society when the norms associated with her various statuses and roles are incompatible.

Profound changes in the roles of women during the past century have been accompanied by innumerable contradictions and inconsistencies. With our rapidly changing and highly differentiated culture, with migrations and multiplied social contacts, the stage is set for myriads of combinations of incongruous elements. Cultural norms are often functionally unsuited to the social situations to which they apply. Thus they may deter an individual from a course of action which would serve his own, and society's, interests best. Or, if behavior contrary to the norm is engaged in, the individual may suffer from guilt over violating mores which no longer serve any socially useful end. Sometimes culturally defined roles are adhered to in the face of new conditions without a conscious realization of the discrepancies involved. The reciprocal actions dictated by the roles may be at variance with those demanded by the actual situation. This may result in an imbalance of privileges and obligations or in some frustration of basic interests.

Again, problems arise because changes in the mode of life have created new situations which have not as yet been defined by culture. Individuals left thus without social guidance tend to act in terms of egotistic or "short-run hedonistic" motives which at times defeat their

° *American Journal of Sociology*, Vol. 52, No. 3 (November, 1946), 184–189. Reprinted by permission of the University of Chicago Press and the author.

The author (b. 1906) is Professor of Sociology and Chairman, the Department of Sociology, Barnard College. Author of: *The Unemployed Man and His Family; Women in the Modern World: Their Education and Their Dilemmas.*

own long-term interests or create conflict with others. The precise obligation of a gainfully employed wife toward the support of the family is one such undefined situation.

Finally, a third mode of discrepancy arises in the existence of incompatible cultural definitions of the same social situation, such as the clash of "old-fashioned" and "radical" mores, of religion and law, of norms of economic and familial institutions.

The problems raised by these discrepancies are social problems in the sense that they engender mental conflict or social conflict or otherwise frustrate some basic interest of large segments of the population.

This article sets forth in detail the nature of certain incompatible sex roles imposed by our society upon the college woman. It is based on data collected in 1942 and 1943. Members of an undergraduate course on the family were asked for two successive years to submit autobiographical documents focused on the topic; 73 were collected. In addition, 80 interviews, lasting about an hour each, were conducted with every member of a course in social psychology of the same institution— making a total of 153 documents ranging from a minimum of five to a maximum of thirty typewritten pages.

The generalization emerging from these documents is the existence of serious contradictions between two roles present in the social environment of the college woman. The goals set by each role are mutually exclusive, and the fundamental personality traits each evokes are at points diametrically opposed, so that what are assets for one become liabilities for the other, and the full realization of one role threatens defeat in the other.

One of these roles may be termed the "feminine" role. While there are a number of permissive variants of the feminine role for women of college age (the "good sport," the "glamour girl," the "young lady," the domestic "home girl," etc.), they have a common core of attributes defining the proper attitudes to men, family, work, love, etc., and a set of personality traits often described with reference to the male sex role as "not as dominant, or aggressive as men" or "more emotional, sympathetic."

The other and more recent role is, in a sense, no sex role at all, because it partly obliterates the differentiation in sex. It demands of the women much the same virtues, patterns of behavior, and attitude that it does of the men of a corresponding age. We shall refer to this as the "modern" role.

Both roles are present in the social environment of these women throughout their lives, though, as the precise content of each sex role varies with age, so does the nature of their clashes change from one stage to another. In the period under discussion the conflict between the two roles apparently centers about academic work, social life, vocational plans, excellence in specific fields of endeavor, and a number of personality traits.

One manifestation of the problem is in the inconsistency of the goals set for the girl by her family.

Forty, or 26 per cent, of the respondents expressed some grievance against their families for failure to confront them with clearcut and consistent goals. The majority, 74 per cent, denied having had such experiences. One student writes:

> How am I to pursue any course single-mindedly when some way along the line a person I respect is sure to say, "You are on the wrong track and are wasting your time." Uncle John telephones every Sunday morning. His first question is: "Did you go out last night?" He would think me a "grind" if I were to stay home Saturday night to finish a term paper. My father expects me to get an "A" in every subject and is disappointed by a "B." He says I have plenty of time for social life. Mother says, "That 'A' in Philosophy is very nice dear. But please don't become so deep that no man will be good enough for you." And, finally, Aunt Mary's line is careers for women. "Prepare yourself for some profession. This is the only way to insure yourself independence and an interesting life. You have plenty of time to marry."

A Senior writes:

> I get a letter from my mother at least three times a week. One week her letters will say, "Remember that this is your last year at college. Subordinate everything to your studies. You must have a good record to secure a job." The next week her letters are full of wedding news. This friend of mine got married; that one is engaged; my young cousin's wedding is only a week off. When, my mother wonders, will I make up my mind? Surely, I wouldn't want to be the only unmarried one in my group. It is high time, she feels, that I give some thought to it.

A student reminisces:

> All through high school my family urged me to work hard because they wished me to enter a first-rate college. At the same time they were always raving about a girl schoolmate who lived next door to us. How pretty and sweet she was, how popular, and what taste in clothes! Couldn't I also pay more attention to my appearance and to social life? They were overlooking the fact that this carefree friend of mine had little time left for school work and had failed several subjects. It seemed that my family had expected me to become Eve Curie and Hedy Lamarr wrapped up in one.

Another comments:

> My mother thinks that it is very nice to be smart in college but only if it doesn't take too much effort. She always tells me not to be too intellectual on dates, to be clever in a light sort of way. My father, on the other hand, wants me to study law. He thinks that if I applied myself I could make an excellent

lawyer and keeps telling me that I am better fitted for this profession than my brother.

Another writes:

> One of my two brothers writes: "Cover up that high forehead and act a little dumb once in a while"; while the other always urges upon me the importance of rigorous scholarship.

The students testified to a certain bewilderment and confusion caused by the failure on the part of the family to smooth the passage from one role to another, especially when the roles involved were contradictory. It seemed to some of them that they had awakened one morning to find their world upside down: what had hitherto evoked praise and rewards from relatives, now suddenly aroused censure. A student recollects:

> I could match my older brother in skating, sledding, riflery, ball, and many of the other games we played. He enjoyed teaching me and took great pride in my accomplishments. Then one day it all changed. He must have suddenly become conscious of the fact that girls ought to be feminine. I was walking with him, proud to be able to make long strides and keep up with his long-legged steps when he turned to me in annoyance, "Can't you walk like a lady?" I still remember feeling hurt and bewildered by his scorn, when I had been led to expect approval.

Once during her freshman year in college, after a delightful date, a student wrote her brother with great elation:

> "What a wonderful evening at————fraternity house! You would be proud of me, Johnny! I won all ping-pong games but one!"
> "For heaven's sake," came the reply, "when will you grow up? Don't you know that a boy likes to think he is better than a girl? Give him a little competition, sure, but miss a few serves in the end. Should you join the Debate Club? By all means, but don't practice too much on the boys." Believe me I was stunned by this letter but then I saw that he was right. To be a success in the dorms one must date, to date one must not win too many ping-pong games. At first I resented this bitterly. But now I am more or less used to it and live in hope of one day meeting a man who is my superior so that I may be my natural self.

It is the parents and not the older sibling who reversed their expectations in the following excerpt:

> All through grammar school and high school my parents led me to feel that to do well in school was my chief responsibility. A good report card, an election to student office, these were the news Mother bragged about in telephone conversations with her friends. But recently they suddenly got worried about me: I don't pay enough attention to social life, a woman needs *some* education but not that much. They are disturbed by my determination to go

to the School of Social Work. Why my ambitions should surprise them after they have exposed me for four years to some of the most inspired and stimulating social scientists in the country, I can't imagine. They have some mighty strong arguments on their side. What is the use, they say, of investing years in training for a profession, only to drop it in a few years? Chances of meeting men are slim in this profession. Besides, I may become so preoccupied with it as to sacrifice social life. The next few years are, after all, the proper time to find a mate. But the urge to apply what I have learned, and the challenge of this profession is so strong that I shall go on despite the family opposition.

The final excerpt illustrates both the sudden transition of roles and the ambiguity of standards:

I major in English composition. This is not a completely "approved" field for girls so I usually just say "English." An English Literature major is quite liked and approved by boys. Somehow it is lumped with all the other arts and even has a little glamour. But a composition major is a girl to beware of because she supposedly will notice all your grammar mistakes, look at your letters too critically, and consider your ordinary speech and conversation as too crude.

I also work for a big metropolitan daily as a correspondent in the city room. I am well liked there and may possibly stay as a reporter after graduation in February. I have had several spreads [stories running to more than eight or ten inches of space], and this is considered pretty good for a college correspondent. Naturally, I was elated and pleased at such breaks, and as far as the city room is concerned I'm off to a very good start on a career that is hard for a man to achieve and even harder for a woman. General reporting is still a man's work in the opinion of most people. I have a lot of acclaim but also criticism, and I find it confusing and difficult to be praised for being clever and working hard and then, when my efforts promise to be successful, to be condemned and criticized for being unfeminine and ambitious.

Here are a few of these reactions:

My father: "I don't like this newspaper set-up at all. The people you meet are making you less interested in marriage than ever. You're getting too educated and intellectual to be attractive to men."

My mother: "I don't like your attitude toward people. The paper is making you too analytical and calculating. Above all, you shouldn't sacrifice your education and career for marriage."

A lieutenant with two years of college: "It pleased me greatly to hear about your news assignment—good girl."

A Navy pilot with one year of college: "Undoubtedly, I'm old-fashioned, but I could never expect or feel right about a girl giving up a very promising or interesting future to hang around waiting for me to finish college. Nevertheless, congratulations on your job on the paper. Where in the world do you get that wonderful energy? Anyway I know you were thrilled at getting it and feel very glad for you. I've an idea that it means the same to you as that letter saying 'report for active duty' meant to me."

A graduate metallurgist now a private in the Army: "It was good to hear that you got that break with the paper. I am sure that talent will prove itself and that you will go far. But not too far, as I don't think you should become a career woman. You'll get repressed and not be interested enough in having fun if you keep after that career."

A lieutenant with a year and a half of college: "All this career business is nonsense. A woman belongs in the home and absolutely no place else. My wife will have to stay home. That should keep her happy. Men are just superior in everything, and women have no right to expect to compete with them. They should do just what will keep their husbands happy."

A graduate engineer—my fiancé: "Go right ahead and get as far as you can in your field. I am glad you are ambitious and clever, and I'm as anxious to see you happily successful as I am myself. It is a shame to let all those brains go to waste over just dusting and washing dishes. I think the usual home life and children are small sacrifices to make if a career will keep you happy. But I'd rather see you in radio because I am a bit wary of the effect upon our marriage of the way of life you will have around the newspaper."

Sixty-one, or 40 per cent, of the students indicated that they have occasionally "played dumb" on dates, that is, concealed some academic honor, pretended ignorance of some subject, or allowed the man the last word in an intellectual discussion. Among these were women who "threw games" and in general played down certain skills in obedience to the unwritten law that men must possess these skills to a superior degree. At the same time, in other areas of life, social pressures were being exerted upon these women to "play to win," to compete to the utmost of their abilities for intellectual distinction and academic honors. One student writes:

I was glad to transfer to a women's college. The two years at the co-ed university produced a constant strain. I am a good student; my family expects me to get good marks. At the same time I am normal enough to want to be invited to the Saturday night dance. Well, everyone knew that on that campus a reputation of a "brain" killed a girl socially. I was always fearful lest I say too much in class or answer a question which the boys I dated couldn't answer.

Here are some significant remarks made from the interviews:

When a girl asks me what marks I got last semester I answer, "Not so good—only one 'A.' " When a boy asks the same question, I say very brightly with a note of surprise, "Imagine, I got an 'A!' "

I am engaged to a southern boy who doesn't think too much of the woman's intellect. In spite of myself, I play up to his theories because the less one knows and does, the more he does for you and thinks you "cute" into the bargain. . . . I allow him to explain things to me in great detail and to treat me as a child in financial matters.

One of the nicest techniques is to spell long words incorrectly once in a while. My boy-friend seems to get a great kick out of it and writes back, "Honey, you certainly don't know how to spell."

When my date said that he considers Ravel's *Bolero* the greatest piece of music ever written, I changed the subject because I knew I would talk down to him.

A boy advised me not to tell of my proficiency in math and not to talk of my plans to study medicine unless I knew my date well.

My fiancé didn't go to college. I intend to finish college and work hard at it, but in talking to him I make college appear a kind of a game.

Once I went sailing with a man who so obviously enjoyed the role of a protector that I told him I didn't know how to sail. As it turned out he didn't either. We got into a tough spot, and I was torn between a desire to get a hold of the boat and a fear to reveal that I had lied to him.

It embarrassed me that my "steady" in high school got worse marks than I. A boy should naturally do better in school. I would never tell him my marks and would often ask him to help me with my homework.

I am better in math than my fiancé. But while I let him explain politics to me, we never talk about math even though, being a math major, I could tell him some interesting things.

Mother used to tell me to lay off the brains on dates because glasses make me look too intellectual anyhow.

I was once at a work camp. The girls did the same work as the boys. If some girls worked better, the boys resented it fiercely. The director told one capable girl to slow down to keep peace in the group.

How to do the job and remain popular was a tough task. If you worked your best, the boys resented the competition; if you acted feminine, they complained that you were clumsy.

On dates I always go through the "I-don't-care-anything-you-want-to-do" routine. It gets monotonous but boys fear girls who make decisions. They think such girls would make nagging wives.

I am a natural leader and, when in the company of girls, usually take the lead. That is why I am so active in college activities. But I know that men fear bossy women, and I always have to watch myself on dates not to assume the "executive" role. Once a boy walking to the theater with me took the wrong street. I knew a short cut but kept quiet.

I let my fiancé make most of the decisions when we are out. It annoys me, but he prefers it.

I sometimes "play dumb" on dates, but it leaves a bad taste. The emotions are complicated. Part of me enjoys "putting something over" on the unsuspecting male. But this sense of superiority over him is mixed with feeling of guilt for my hypocrisy. Toward the "date" I feel some contempt because he is "taken in" by my technique, or if I like the boy, a kind of a maternal condescension. At times I resent him! Why isn't he my superior in all ways in which a man should excel so that I could be my natural self? What am I doing here with him, anyhow? Slumming?

And the funny part of it is that the man, I think, is not always so unsuspecting. He may sense the truth and become uneasy in the relation. "Where do I stand? Is she laughing up her sleeve or did she mean this praise? Was she really impressed with that little speech of mine or did she only pretend to know nothing about politics?" And once or twice I felt that the joke was on me: the boy saw through my wiles and felt contempt for me for stooping to such tricks.

Another aspect of the problem is the conflict between the psychogenetic personality of the girl and the cultural role foisted upon her by the milieu. At times it is the girl with "masculine" interests and personality traits who chafes under the pressure to conform to the "feminine" pattern. At other times it is the family and the college who thrust upon the reluctant girl the "modern" role.

While, historically, the "modern" role is the most recent one, ontogenetically it is the one emphasized earlier in the education of the college girl, if these 153 documents are representative. Society confronts the girl with powerful challenges and strong pressure to excel in certain competitive lines of endeavor and to develop certain techniques of adaptation very similar to those expected of her brothers. But, then, quite suddenly as it appears to these girls, the very success in meeting these challenges begins to cause anxiety. It is precisely those most successful in the earlier role who are now penalized.

It is not only the passage from age to age but the moving to another region or type of campus which may create for the girl similar problems. The precise content of sex roles, or, to put it in another way, the degree of their differentiation, varies with regional class, nativity, and other subcultures.

Whenever individuals show differences in response to some social situation, as have our 153 respondents, the question naturally arises as to the causes. It will be remembered that 40 per cent admitted some difficulties in personal relations with men due to conflicting sex roles but that 60 per cent said that they had no such problems. Inconsistency of parental expectations troubled 26 per cent of the students.

To account for individual differences would require another study, involving a classification of personalities in relation to the peculiar social environments of each. Generally speaking, it would seem that it is the girl with a "middle-of-the-road personality" who is most happily adjusted to the present historical moment. She is not a perfect incarnation of either role but is flexible enough to play both. She is a girl who is intelligent enough to do well in school but not so brilliant as to "get all 'A's"; informed and alert but not consumed by an intellectual passion; capable but not talented in areas relatively new to women; able to stand on her own feet and to earn a living but not so good a living as to compete with men; capable of doing some job well (in case she does not marry or, otherwise, has to work) but not so identified with a profession as to need it for her happiness.

A search for less immediate causes of individual reactions would lead us further back to the study of genesis of the personality differences found relevant to the problem. One of the clues will certainly be provided by the relation of the child to the parent of the same and of the opposite sex. This relation affects the conception of self and the inclination for a particular sex role.

The problems set forth in this article will persist, in the opinion of the writer, until the adult sex roles of women are redefined in greater harmony with the socioeconomic and ideological character of modern society. Until then neither the formal education nor the unverbalized sex roles of the adolescent woman can be cleared of intrinsic contradictions.

23. CONTINUITIES AND DISCONTINUITIES IN CULTURAL CONDITIONING *

RUTH BENEDICT

This article by the late Ruth Benedict has been widely reprinted because it so effectively demonstrates how a particular aspect of culture, namely "continuities and discontinuities," affects personality development. As used by Dr. Benedict, the term "continuity" refers primarily to types of child-rearing which gradually prepare a child for his adult roles and thus help to prevent maladjustment. An example of a cultural discontinuity is the fact that in our society unmarried young adults are expected to have no sexual experience, yet are supposed to become, "overnight" so-to-speak, adequate husbands or wives as soon as they marry.

All cultures must deal in one way or another with the cycle of growth from infancy to adulthood. Nature has posed the situation dramatically: on the one hand, the newborn baby, physiologically vulnerable, unable to fend for itself, or to participate of its own initiative in the life of the group, and, on the other, the adult man or woman. Every man who rounds out his human potentialities must have been a son first and a father later, and the two roles are physiologically in great contrast; he must first have been dependent upon others for his very existence, and later he must provide such security for others. This discontinuity in the life cycle is a fact of nature and is inescapable. Facts of nature, however, in any discussion of human problems, are ordinarily read off not at their bare minimal but surrounded by all the local accretions of behavior to which the student of human affairs has become accustomed in his own culture. For that reason, it is illuminating to examine comparative material from other societies in order to get a wider perspective on our own special accretions. The anthropologist's role is not to question the facts of nature, but to insist upon the interposition of a middle term between "nature" and "human behavior"; his role is to analyse that term, to document local man-made doctorings of nature, and to insist that these doctorings should not be read off in any one culture as nature itself. Although it is a fact of nature that the child becomes a man, the way in which this transition is effected varies from one society to another, and no one of these particular cultural bridges should be regarded as the "natural" path to maturity.

From a comparative point of view, our culture goes to great extremes in emphasizing contrasts between the child and the adult. The child is sexless, the adult estimates his virility by his sexual activities; the child must be protected from the ugly facts of life, the adult must meet them without psychic catastrophe; the child must obey, the adult must command this obedience. These are all dogmas of our culture, dogmas which, in spite of the facts of nature, other cultures commonly do not share. In spite of the physiological contrasts between child and adult, these are cultural accretions.

It will make the point clearer if we consider one habit in our own culture in regard to which there is not this discontinuity of conditioning. With the greatest clarity of purpose and economy of training, we achieve our goal of conditioning everyone to eat three meals a day. The baby's training in regular food periods begins at birth, and no crying of the child and no inconvenience to the mother is allowed to interfere. We gauge the child's physiological make-up and at first allow it food oftener than adults, but, because our goal is firmly set and our training consistent, before the child is two years old it has achieved the adult schedule. From the point of view of other cultures, this is as startling as the fact of three-year-old babies perfectly at home in deep water is to us. Modesty is another sphere in which our child training is consistent and economical; we waste no time in clothing the baby, and, in contrast to many societies where the child runs naked till it is ceremonially given its skirt or its pubic sheath at adolescence, the child's training fits it precisely for adult conventions.

In neither of these aspects of behavior is there need for an individual in our culture to embark before puberty, at puberty, or at some later date upon a course of action which all his previous training has tabooed. He is spared the unsureness inevitable in such a transition.

The illustration I have chosen may appear trivial, but, in larger and more important aspects of behavior, our methods are obviously different. Because of the great variety of child training in different families in our society, I might illustrate continuity of conditioning from individual life histories in our culture, but even these, from a comparative point of view, stop far short of consistency; and I shall, therefore, confine myself to describing arrangements in other cultures in which training, which with us is idiosyncratic is accepted and traditional and does not, therefore, involve the same possibility of conflict. I shall choose childhood rather than infant and nursing situations, not because the latter do not vary strikingly in different cultures but because they are nevertheless more circumscribed by the baby's physiological needs than is its later training. Childhood situations provide an excellent field in which to illustrate the range of cultural adjustments which are possible within a universally given, but not so drastic, set of physiological facts.

The major discontinuity in the life cycle is of course that the child who is at one point a son must later be a father. These roles in our society are strongly differentiated; a good son is tractable, and does not assume adult responsibilities; a good father provides for his children and should not allow his authority to be flouted. In addition the child must be sexless so far as his family is concerned, whereas the father's sexual role is primary in the family. The individual in one role must revise his behavior from almost all points of view when he assumes the second role.

I shall select for discussion three such contrasts that occur in our culture between the individual's role as child and as father: (1) responsible-nonresponsible status role; (2) dominance-submission; (3) contrasted sexual role. It is largely upon our cultural commitments to these three contrasts that the discontinuity in the life cycle of an individual in our culture depends.

1.   RESPONSIBLE-NONRESPONSIBLE STATUS ROLE

The techniques adopted by societies which achieve continuity during the life cycle in this sphere in no way differ from those we employ in our uniform conditioning to three meals a day. They are merely applied to other areas of life. We think of the child as wanting to play and the adult as having to work, but in many societies the mother takes the baby daily in her shawl or carrying net to the garden or to gather roots, and adult labor is seen even in infancy from the pleasant security of its position in close contact with its mother. When the child can run about, it accompanies its parents still, doing tasks which are essential and yet suited to its powers, and its dichotomy between work and play is not different from that [which] its parents recognize, namely, the distinction between the busy day and the free evening. The tasks it is asked to perform are graded to its powers, and its elders wait quietly by, not offering to do the task in the child's place. Everyone who is familiar with such societies has been struck by the contrast with our child training. Dr. Ruth Underhill tells me of sitting with a group of Papago elders in Arizona when the man of the house turned to his little three-year-old granddaughter and asked her to close the door. The door was heavy and hard to shut. The child tried, but it did not move. Several times the grandfather repeated: "Yes, close the door." No one jumped to the child's assistance. No one took the responsibility away from her. On the other hand there was no impatience, for after all the child was small. They sat gravely waiting till the child succeeded and her grandfather gravely thanked her. It was assumed that the task would not be asked of her unless she could perform it, and, having been asked, the responsibility was hers alone just as if she were a grown woman.

The essential point of such child training is that the child is from infancy continuously conditioned to responsible social participation, while at the same time the tasks that are expected of it are adapted to its capacity. The contrast with our society is very great. A child does not make any labor contribution to our industrial society except as it competes with an adult; its work is not measured against its own strength and skill but against high-geared industrial requirements. Even when we praise a child's achievement in the home, we are outraged if such praise is interpreted as being of the same order as praise of adults. The child is praised because the parent feels well disposed, regardless of whether the task is well done by adult standards, and the child acquires no sensible standard by which to measure its achievement. The gravity of a Cheyenne Indian family ceremoniously making a feast out of the little boy's first snowbird is at the furthest remove from our behavior. At birth the little boy was presented with a toy bow, and from the time he could run about serviceable bows suited to his stature were specially made for him by the man of the family. Animals and birds were taught him in a graded series beginning with those most easily taken, and as he brought in his first of each species his family duly made a feast of it, accepting his contribution as gravely as the buffalo his father brought. When he finally killed a buffalo, it was only the final step of his childhood conditioning, not a new adult role with which his childhood experience had been at variance.

The Canadian Ojibwa show clearly what results can be achieved. This tribe gains its livelihood by winter trapping, and the small family of father, mother, and children live during the long winter alone on their great frozen hunting grounds. The boy accompanies his father and brings in his catch to his sister as his father does to his mother; the girl prepares the meat and skins for him just as his mother does for her husband. By the time the boy is 12, he may have set his own line of traps on a hunting territory of his own and return to his parent's house only once in several months—still bringing the meat and skins to his sister. The young child is taught consistently that it has only itself to rely upon in life, and this is as true in the dealings it will have with the supernatural as in the business of getting a livelihood. This attitude he will accept as a successful adult just as he accepted it as a child.

2. DOMINANCE-SUBMISSION

Dominance-submission is the most striking of those categories of behavior where like does not respond to like, but where one type of behavior stimulates the opposite response. It is one of the most prominent ways in which behavior is patterned in our culture. When it obtains between classes, it may be nourished by continuous experience; the difficulty in its use between children and adults lies in the fact that an individual conditioned to one set of behavior in childhood must adopt the opposite as an adult. Its opposite is a pattern of approximately identical reciprocal behavior; the societies which rely upon continuous conditioning characteristically invoke this pattern. In some primitive cultures the very terminology of address between father and son, and, more commonly, between grandfather and grandson or uncle and nephew, reflects this attitude. In such kinship terminologies, one reciprocal expresses each of these relationships so that son and father, for instance, exchange the same term with one another, just as we exchange the same term with a cousin. The child later will exchange it with his son. "Father-son," therefore, is a continuous relationship he enjoys throughout life. The same continuity, backed up by verbal reciprocity, occurs far oftener in the grandfather-grandson relationship or that of mother's brother-sister's son. When these are "joking" relationships, as they often are, travellers report wonderingly upon the liberties and pretensions of tiny toddlers in their dealing with these family elders. In place of our dogma of respect to elders, such societies employ in these cases a reciprocity as nearly identical as may be. The teasing and practical joking the grandfather visits upon his grandchild, the grandchild returns in like coin; he would be led to believe that he failed in propriety if he did not give like for like. If the sister's son has right of access without leave to his mother's brother's possessions, the mother's brother has such rights also to the child's possessions. They share reciprocal privileges and obligations which in our society can develop only between age mates.

From the point of view of our present discussion, such kinship conventions allow the child to put in practice from infancy the same forms of behavior which it will rely upon as an adult; behavior is not polarized into a general requirement of submission for the child and dominance for the adult.

It is clear from the techniques described above, by which the child is conditioned to a responsible status role, that these depend chiefly upon arousing in the child the desire to share responsibility in adult life. To achieve this, little stress is laid upon obedience but much stress upon approval and praise. Punishment is very commonly regarded as quite outside the realm of possibility, and natives in many parts of the world have drawn the conclusion from our usual disciplinary methods that white parents do not love their children. If the child is not required to be submissive, however, many occasions for punishment melt away; a variety of situations which call for it do not occur. Many American Indian tribes are especially explicit in rejecting the ideal of a child's submissive or obedient behavior. Prince Maximilian von Wied, who visited the Crow Indians over a hundred years ago, describes a father's boasting about his young son's intractability even when it was the father himself who was flouted; "He will be a man," his father said. He would have been baffled at the idea that his child should show behavior which would obviously make him appear a poor creature in the eyes of his fellows if he used it as an adult. Dr. George Devereux tells me of a special case of such an attitude among the Mohave at the present time. The child's mother was white and protested to its father that he must take action when the child disobeyed and struck him. "But why?" the father said, "he is little. He cannot possibly injure me." He did not know of any dichotomy according to which an adult expects obedience and a child must accord it. If his child had been docile he would simply have judged that it would become a docile adult—an eventuality of which he would not have approved.

Child training which brings about the same result is common also in other areas of life than that of reciprocal kinship obligations between child and adult. There is a tendency in our culture to regard every situation as having in it the seeds of a dominance-submission relationship. Even where dominance-submission is patently irrelevant we read in the dichotomy, assuming that in every situation there must be one person dominating another. On the other hand some cultures, even when the situation calls for leadership do not see it in terms of dominance-submission. To do justice to this attitude, it would be necessary to describe their political and especially their economic arrangements, for such an attitude to persist must certainly be supported by economic mechanisms that are congruent with it. But it must also be supported by—or what comes to the same thing, express itself in—child training and familial situations.

3. CONTRASTED SEXUAL ROLE

Continuity of conditioning in training the child to assume responsibility and to behave no more submissively than adults is quite possible in terms of the child's physiological endowment if his participation is suited to his strength. Because of the late development of the child's reproductive organs, continuity of conditioning in sex experience presents a difficult problem. So far as their belief that the child is anything but a sexless being is concerned, they are probably more nearly right than we are with an opposite dogma. But the great break is presented by the universally sterile unions before puberty and the presumably fertile ones after maturation. This physiological fact no amount of cultural manipulation can minimize or alter, and societies, therefore, which stress continuous conditioning most strongly sometimes do not expect children to be interested in sex experience until they have matured physically. This is striking among American Indian tribes like the Dakota; adults observe great privacy in sex acts and in no way stimulate children's sexual activity. There need be no discontinuity, in the sense in which I have used the term, in such a program if the child is taught nothing it does not have to unlearn later. In such cultures, adults view children's experimentation as in no way wicked or dangerous, but merely as innocuous play which can have no serious consequences. In some societies such play is minimal and the children manifest little interest in it. But the same attitude may be taken by adults in societies where such play is encouraged and forms a major activity among small children. This is true among most of the Melanesian cultures of Southeast New Guinea; adults go as far as to laugh off sexual affairs within the prohibited class, if the children are not mature, saying that since they cannot marry there can be no harm done.

It is this physiological fact of the difference between children's sterile unions and adults' presumably fertile sex relations which must be kept in mind in order to understand the different mores which almost always govern sex expression in children and in adults in the same culture. A great many cultures with preadolescent sexual license require marital fidelity, and a great many which value premarital virginity in either male or female arrange their marital life with great license. Continuity in sex experience is complicated by factors which it was unnecessary to consider in the problems previously discussed. The essential problem is not whether or not the child's sexuality is consistently exploited—for even where such exploitation is favored, in the majority of cases the child must seriously modify his behavior at puberty or at marriage. Continuity in sex expression means rather that the child is taught nothing it must unlearn later. If the cultural emphasis is upon sexual pleasure, the child who is continuously conditioned will be encouraged to experiment freely and pleasurably, as among the Marquesans; if emphasis is upon reproduction, as among the Zuni of New Mexico, childish sex proclivities will not be exploited, for the only important use which sex is thought to serve in his culture is not yet possible to him. The important contrast with our child training is that, although a Zuni child is impressed with the wickedness of premature sex experimentation, he does not run the risk as in our culture of associating this wickedness with sex itself rather than with sex at his age. The adult in our culture has often failed to unlearn the wickedness or the dangerousness of sex, a lesson which was impressed upon him strongly in his most formative years.

4. DISCONTINUITY IN CONDITIONING

Even from this very summary statement of continuous conditioning, the economy of such mores is evident. In spite of the obvious advantages, however, there are difficulties in its way. Many primitive societies expect as different behavior from an individual as child and as adult as we do, and such discontinuity involves a presumption of strain.

Many societies of this type, however, minimize strain by the techniques they employ; and some techniques are more successful than others in ensuring the individual's functioning without conflict. It is from this point of view that age-grade societies reveal their fundamental significance. Age-graded cultures characteristically demand different behavior of the individual at different times of his life and persons of a like age-grade are grouped into a society whose activities are all oriented toward the behavior desired at that age. Individuals "graduate" publicly and with honor from one of these groups to another. Where age society members are enjoined to loyalty and mutual support, and are drawn not only from the local group but from the whole tribe, as among the Arapaho, or even from other tribes as among the Wagawaga of Southeast New Guinea, such an institution has many advantages in eliminating conflicts among local groups and fostering intratribal peace. This seems to be also a factor in the tribal military solidarity of the similarly organized Masai of East Africa. The point that is of chief interest for our present discussion, however, is that by this means an individual who at any time takes on a new set of duties and virtues is supported not only by a solid phalanx of age mates but by the traditional prestige of the organized "secret" society into which he has now graduated. Fortified in this way, individuals in such cultures often swing between remarkable extremes of opposite behavior without apparent psychic threat. For example, the great majority exhibit prideful and non-conflicted behavior at each stage in the life cycle, even when a prime of life devoted to passionate and aggressive head hunting must be followed by a later life dedicated to ritual and to mild and peaceable civic virtues.

Our chief interest here, however, is in discontinuity which primarily affects the child. In many primitive societies, such discontinuity has been fostered not because of economic or political necessity or because such discontinuity provides for a socially valuable division of labor, but because of some conceptual dogma. The most striking of these are the Australian and Papuan cultures where the ceremony of the "Making of Man" flourishes. In such societies it is believed that men and women have opposite and conflicting powers, and male children, who are of undefined status, must be initiated into the male role. In Central Australia the boy child is of the woman's side, and women are taboo in the final adult stages of tribal ritual. The elaborate and protracted initiation ceremonies of the Arunta, therefore, snatch the boy from the mother, dramatize his gradual repudiation of her. In a final ceremony he is reborn as a man out of the men's ceremonial "baby pouch." The men's ceremonies are ritual statements of a masculine solidarity, carried out by fondling one another's *churingas,* the material symbol of each man's life, and by letting out over one another blood drawn from their veins. After this warm bond among men has been established through the ceremonies, the boy joins the men in the men's house and participates in tribal rites. The enjoined discontinuity has been tribally bridged.

West of the Fly River in southern New Guinea, there is a striking development of this Making of Men cult which involves a childhood period of passive homosexuality. Among the Keraki it is thought that no boy can grow to full stature without playing the role for some years. Men slightly older take the active role, and the older man is a jealous partner. The life cycle of the Keraki Indians includes, therefore, in succession, passive homosexuality, active homosexuality, and heterosexuality. The Keraki believe that pregnancy will result from post-pubertal passive homosexuality and see evidences of such practices in any fat man, whom, even as an old man, they may kill or drive out of the tribe because of their fear. The ceremony that is of interest in connection with the present discussion takes place at the end of the period of passive homosexuality. This ceremony consists in burning out the possibility of pregnancy from the boy by pouring lye down his throat, after which he has no further protection if he gives way to the practice. There is no technique for ending active homosexuality, but this is not explicitly taboo for older men; heterosexuality and children, however, are highly valued. Unlike the neighboring Marindanim, who share their homosexual practices, Keraki husband and wife share the same house and work together in the gardens.

I have chosen illustrations of discontinuous conditioning where it is not too much to say that the cultural institutions furnish adequate support to the individual as he progresses from role to role or interdicts the previous behavior in a summary fashion. The contrast with arrangements in our culture is very striking, and against this background of social arrangements in other cultures the adolescent period of *Sturm und Drang* with which we are so familiar becomes intelligible in terms of our discontinuous cultural institutions and dogmas rather than in terms of physiological necessity. It is even more pertinent to consider these comparative facts in relation to maladjusted persons in our culture who are said to be fixated at one or another pre-adult level. It is clear that if we were to look at our social arrangements as an outsider, we should infer directly from our family institutions and habits of child training that many individuals would not "put off childish things"; we should have to say that our adult activity demands traits that are interdicted in children, and that, far from redoubling efforts to help children bridge this gap, adults in our culture put all the blame on the child when he fails to manifest spontaneously the new behavior or, overstepping the mark, manifests it with untoward belligerence. It is not surprising that in such a society many individuals fear to use behavior which has up to that time been under a ban and trust instead, though at great psychic cost, to attitudes that have been exercised with approval during their formative years. Insofar as we invoke a physiological scheme to account for these neurotic adjustments we are led to overlook the possibility of developing social institutions which would lessen the social cost we now pay; instead, we elaborate a set of dogmas which prove inapplicable under other social conditions.

24. G. H. MEAD'S THEORY OF
INDIVIDUAL AND SOCIETY *

CHARLES W. MORRIS

G. H. Mead's great contribution was his theoretical analysis of the relationship between the person and the group. His

* George Herbert Mead, *Mind, Self, and Society, from the Standpoint of a Social Behaviorist* (Chicago: The University of Chicago Press, 1934), pp. xx–xxvi. Edited, with introduction, by Charles W. Morris. Reprinted by permission of the publisher.

George Herbert Mead (1863–1931) was an American philosopher and social

"social behaviorism" emphasized the role of language in the development of human behavior and stressed that the human mind is a social phenomenon. The present selection, taken from Charles Morris' introduction to a compilation of Mead's lectures entitled Mind, Self, and Society, *presents some of the concepts that have had major impact on sociology.*

The transformation of the biologic individual to the minded organism or self takes place, on Mead's account, through the agency of language, while language in turn presupposes the existence of a certain kind of society and certain physiological capacities in the individual organisms.

The minimal society must be composed of biologic individuals participating in a social act and using the early stages of each other's actions as gestures, that is, as guides to the completion of the act. In the "conversation of gestures" of the dog fight each dog determines his behavior in terms of what the other dog is beginning to do; and the same holds for the boxer, the fencer, and the chick which runs to the hen at the hen's cluck. Such action is a type of communication; in one sense the gestures are symbols, since they indicate, stand for, and cause action appropriate to the later stages of the act of which they are early fragments, and secondarily to the objects implicated in such acts. In the same sense, the gestures may be said to have meaning, namely, they mean the later stages of the oncoming act and, secondarily, the objects implicated: the clenched fist means the blow, the outstretched hand means the object being reached for. Such meanings are not subjective, not private, not mental, but are objectively there in the social situation.

Nevertheless, this type of communication is not language proper; the meanings are not yet "in mind"; the biologic individuals are not yet consciously communicating selves. For these results to transpire the symbols or gestures must become significant symbols or gestures. The individual must know what he is about; he himself, and not merely those who respond to him, must be able to interpret the meaning of his own gesture. Behavioristically, this is to say that the biologic individual must be able to call out in himself the response his gesture calls out in the other, and then utilize this response of the other for the

psychologist. Career spent almost exclusively at University of Chicago as professor of philosophy. Essays appeared in *International Journal of Ethics* and *Journal of Philosophy.* Writings, unpublished manuscripts, classnotes, edited under the following titles: *The Philosophy of the Act; Mind, Self, and Society; Movements of Thought in the Nineteenth Century.*

Charles W. Morris (b. 1901) is Lecturer in Philosophy, University of Chicago; Guest Lecturer, Institute of Design, Chicago, and New School for Social Research, New York. Author, *Six Theories of Mind; Logical Positivism, Pragmatism and Scientific Empiricism; The Open Self; Foundation of the Theory of Signs; Signs, Language and Behavior.*

control of his own further conduct. Such gestures are significant symbols. Through their use the individual is "taking the rôle of the other" in the regulation of his own conduct. Man is essentially the rôle-taking animal. The calling out of the same response in both the self and the other gives the common content necessary for community of meaning.

As an example of the significant symbol Mead uses the tendency to call out "Fire!" when smoke is seen in a crowded theater. The immediate utterance of the sound would simply be part of the initiated act, and would be at the best a non-significant symbol. But when the tendency to call out "Fire!" affects the individual as it affects others, and is itself controlled in terms of these effects, the vocal gesture has become a significant symbol; the individual is conscious of what he is about; he has reached the stage of genuine language instead of unconscious communication; he may now be said to use symbols and not merely respond to signs; he has now acquired a mind.

In looking for gestures capable of becoming significant symbols, and so of transforming the biologic individual into a minded organism, Mead comes upon the vocal gesture. No other gesture affects the individual himself so similarly as it affects others. We hear ourselves talk as others do, but we do not see our facial expressions, nor normally watch our own actions. For Mead, the vocal gesture is the actual fountainhead of language proper and all derivative forms of symbolism; and so of mind.

Mind is the presence in behavior of significant symbols. It is the internalization within the individual of the social process of communication in which meaning emerges. It is the ability to indicate to one's self the response (and implicated objects) that one's gesture indicates to others, and to control the response itself in these terms. The significant gesture, itself a part of a social process, internalizes and makes available to the component biologic individuals the meanings which have themselves emerged in the earlier, non-significant, stages of gestural communication. Instead of beginning with individual minds and working out to society, Mead starts with an objective social process and works inward through the importation of the social process of communication into the individual by the medium of the vocal gesture. The individual has then taken the social act into himself. Mind remains social; even in the inner forum so developed thought goes on by one's assuming the rôles of others and controlling one's behavior in terms of such rôle-taking. Since the isolation of the physical thing is for Mead dependent upon the ability to take the rôle of the other, and since thought about such objects involves taking their rôles, even the scientist's reflection about physical nature is a social process, though the objects thought about are no longer social.

. . . . .

It is the same agency of language which on this theory makes possible the appearance of the self. Indeed, the self, mind, "consciousness of," and the significant symbol are in a sense precipitated together. Mead finds the distinguishing trait of selfhood to reside in the capacity of the minded organism to be an object to itself. The mechanism by which this is possible on a behavioristic approach is found in the rôle-taking which is involved in the language symbol. In so far as one can take the rôle of the other, he can, as it were, look back at himself from (respond to himself from) that perspective, and so become an object to himself. Thus again, it is only in a social process that selves, as distinct from biological organisms, can arise—selves as beings that have become conscious of themselves.

Nor is it merely the process of being aware of one's self that is social: the self that one becomes conscious of in this manner is itself social in form, though not always in content. Mead stresses two stages in the development of the self: the stages of play and the game. In play the child simply assumes one rôle after another of persons and animals that have in some way or other entered into its life. One here sees, writ large as it were, the assumption of the attitudes of others through the self-stimulation of the vocal gesture, whereas later in life such attitudes are more abbreviated and harder to detect. In the game, however, one has become, as it were, all of the others implicated in the common activity—must have within one's self the whole organized activity in order to successfully play one's own part. The person here has not merely assumed the rôle of a specific other, but of any other participating in the common activity; he has generalized the attitude of rôle-taking. In one of Mead's happiest terms and most fertile concepts he has taken the attitude or rôle of the "generalized other."

Through a social process, then, the biologic individual of proper organic stuff gets a mind and a self. Through society the impulsive animal becomes a rational animal, a man. In virtue of the internalization or importation of the social process of communication, the individual gains the mechanism of reflective thought (the ability to direct his action in terms of the foreseen consequences of alternative courses of action); acquires the ability to make himself an object to himself and to live in a common moral and scientific world; becomes a moral individual with impulsive ends transformed into the conscious pursuit of ends-in-view.

Because of the emergence of such an individual, society is in turn transformed. It receives through the reflective social self the organization distinctive of human society; instead of playing his social part through physiological differentiation (as in the case of the insect) or through the bare influence of gestures upon others, the human individual regulates his part in the social act through having within himself the rôles of the others implicated in the common activity. In attaining a new principle of social organization, society has gained a new technique of control, since it has now implanted itself within its component parts, and so regulates, to the degree that this is successfully done, the behavior of the individual in terms of the effect on others of his contemplated action.

25. THE DANGERS OF NONCONFORMISM *

MORRIS FREEDMAN

No society can continue to exist unless its members manifest at least minimum agreement with prevailing standards. All societies face the problem of dealing with the nonconformist; how much and what type of nonconformity will be permitted? This is a question that is answered very differently depending upon the time and circumstances involved. The nonconformist himself faces a different problem; he who wishes to be against one standard is necessarily placing himself in league with another. Hence the so-called nonconformist does not really exist. It is with ideas of this sort that Morris Freedman is concerned in this very brief but insightful article.

Not long ago I heard one of this country's professional intellectuals —a former university president, a present foundation president—address a university gathering of several hundred persons. The gentlemen attacked the blight of conformism in the United States; he deplored the fact that men in gray flannel suits had become "interchangeable"; he lamented the loss of true individualism. What struck me while listening to his urbane talk was his own "interchangeable" appearance: neat, three-button blue suit, plain tie, precisely coiffured graying hair, erect

* Reprinted from *The American Scholar*, Volume 28, Number 1 (Winter, 1958–1959), 25–32, passim, by permission of the publisher, The United Chapters of Phi Beta Kappa.

The author (b. 1920) is a member of the department of English at the University of New Mexico. Onetime Associate Editor of *Commentary*, he has published studies of Milton, Dryden, and contemporary literature.

carriage: the very model of a model executive, not only interchangeable with dozens of men in similar positions and in "gentlemen of distinction" ads, but ready to be played in the movies by a dozen or so actors— Walter Pidgeon, Cary Grant, Gregory Peck, Ray Milland. It struck me as somewhat odd, too, that several hundred persons should applaud in unison a speech urging nonconformity, and that during the question period one of the questions that did not "conform" with the speaker's views should be greeted with derision.

Of course one man's conformism may be another man's heresy. But what seems to have taken place in American intellectual life in recent years is the rising of just about any nonconformity to the status of respectable orthodoxy. . . .

. . . . .

It has been well-established that nonconformists, instead of responding to the values of tabloid newspaper, subway car, or television advertisements, respond to a no less specific and no less rigid set, particularly those in the advertisements of *The New York Times, The New Yorker,* the *Saturday Review* and the like, or of the commercials of FM stations that broadcast classical music all day. Although the nonconformist may refuse with a shudder to engage in the barbaric practice of drinking instant coffee, he will no less eagerly sip *espresso*. If you can construct a stereotype of the man in the street, you can build an equally plausible one of the man out of the street. . . .

. . . . .

It was not so long ago that a position taken by a Luce publication would have been instinctively opposed by large numbers of nonconformists; but *Life* in recent years has so well caught the importance of being fashionably nonconformist that it is now a leader in establishing accepted nonconformist thought, which, of course, some while ago spilled over from the highbrow crest onto the extensive middle-brow plateaus. On the matter of education, for example, *Life* and other media shaping mass nonconformist ideology have now laid down the party line, making it intellectually suicidal to suggest that possibly the educators have their own peculiar problems to solve before they can reshape their curricula to respond to the present pressures. On most campuses, I venture, a professor in liberal arts would be read out of the ranks if he said a good word about colleges of education, let alone about educational television, which combines two bogeys. . . .

. . . . .

. . . Let me catalogue from my own recent experience a number of other positions, attitudes, and habits of behavior and thought no nonconformist in good standing can hold these days. These are, of course, subject to rapid change, like fashions in ladies' dress. Also, I should say, it is not essential to reject *all* to remain a respectable nonconformist— only most of them.

It is impossible, then, for the nonconformist to say a good word about Dulles, Nixon, Lyndon Johnson, or (since Dwight MacDonald's critique in *Commentary*) James Gould Cozzens, or a bad one about Henry James, Adlai Stevenson, Lionel Trilling, or Freud; to express approval of any television show (except *Omnibus*, Ed Murrow, or Sid Caesar), or of any American movie (except the inexpensive and badly lighted ones, or the solemn westerns, like *High Noon*); to dislike any foreign films (except those imitating American ones); to believe that you can buy ready-made a good hi-fi set; to wear a non-Ivy-league suit or long hair if a man, or to wear or not wear a sack dress if a woman (I am not sure what feminine nonconformism calls for at the moment); to prefer American cars to European; to believe that there may be any justice in the official position on Oppenheimer; to defend Western diplomacy on any basis; to invite company to dinner without candles on the table and chamber music in the background; to criticize Arthur Miller or Tennessee Williams as playwrights or otherwise; to like Tchaikovsky or Irving Berlin, or to dislike Leonard Bernstein or Mozart; to express admiration for Marilyn Monroe or any other American movie star; to disparage Alec Guinness; and so on. . . .

There is no more self-righteously, high-mindedly closed a mind than that of a nonconformist. He will begin every conversation with some such gambit as "I know this isn't a popular position, but. . . ." He will insist that no one since Galileo or Joan of Arc has had as much courage as he. Challenge him, and he will dismiss you as a peasant not worth his attention. "If you don't know what's wrong with American culture," I heard one champion nonconformist say down his nose to someone who mildly demurred on the subject, "then there's no point even talking with you."

26. RIESMAN ON SOCIETY AND CHARACTER *

DAVID RIESMAN, WITH NATHAN GLAZER AND
REUEL DENNEY

The book titled The Lonely Crowd *by David Riesman and
his co-workers has created a sensation outside as well as inside
what might be termed "the sociological fraternity." The reason
appears to be the provocative analysis that the authors have
made of certain significant trends in modern Western society.
Our society, they contend, has gradually become one in which
people are decreasingly "inner-directed" and increasingly
"other-directed." To Riesman* et al. *the inner-directed person
is one who makes decisions with little regard to their current
social acceptability; the other-directed individual is one who
tends to commit himself to values or programs only after he has
assessed their general social acceptability. These definitions
are developed more fully in the following extracts from* The
Lonely Crowd. *It should be noted parenthetically (in the
selection by Bell, for example) that many writers have expressed
criticism of the Riesman thesis that the trend from inner-
to other-direction (if there is such a trend) means that ours
is becoming a "mass" society.*

A DEFINITION OF INNER-DIRECTION

In western history the society that emerged with the Renaissance
and Reformation and that is only now vanishing serves to illustrate the
type of society in which inner-direction is the principal mode of securing
conformity. Such a society is characterized by increased personal mobility, by a rapid accumulation of capital (teamed with devastating technological shifts), and by an almost constant *expansion:* intensive ex-

---

* From *The Lonely Crowd* (1953) by David Riesman, pp. 29–40, passim, permission granted by Yale University Press.
    The author (b. 1909) is University Professor at Harvard University. Trained in
law he devoted several years to legal and government work before turning to teaching, research, and writing in the social sciences. In addition to *The Lonely Crowd* he
has written *Faces in the Crowd; Thorstein Veblen; Individualism Reconsidered and
Other Essays.*

pansion in the production of goods and people, and extensive expansion in exploration, colonization, and imperialism. The greater choices this society gives—and the greater initiatives it demands in order to cope with its novel problems—are handled by character types who can manage to live socially without strict and self-evident tradition-direction. These are the inner-directed types.

The concept of inner-direction is intended to cover a very wide range of types. Thus, while it is essential for the study of certain problems to differentiate between Protestant and Catholic countries and their character types, between the effects of the Reformation and the effects of the Renaissance, between the puritan ethic of the European north and west and the somewhat more hedonistic ethic of the European east and south, while all these are valid and, for certain purposes, important distinctions, the concentration of this study on the development of modes of conformity permits their neglect. It allows the grouping together of these otherwise distinct developments because they have one thing in common: *the source of direction for the individual is "inner" in the sense that it is implanted early in life by the elders and directed toward generalized but nonetheless inescapably destined goals.*

We can see what this means when we realize that, in societies in which tradition-direction is the dominant mode of insuring conformity, attention is focused on securing external *behavioral* conformity. While behavior is minutely prescribed, individuality of character need not be highly developed to meet prescriptions that are objectified in ritual and etiquette—though to be sure, a social character *capable* of such behavioral attention and obedience is requisite. By contrast, societies in which inner-direction becomes important, though they also are concerned with behavioral conformity, cannot be satisfied with behavioral conformity alone. Too many novel situations are presented, situations which a code cannot encompass in advance. Consequently the problem of personal choice, solved in . . . [a tradition-directed period] by channeling choice through rigid social organization, in the period of . . . [inner-direction] is solved by channeling choice through a rigid though highly individualized character.

This rigidity is a complex matter. While any society dependent on inner-direction seems to present people with a wide choice of aims —such as money, possessions, power, knowledge, fame, goodness—these aims are ideologically interrelated, and the selection made by any one individual remains relatively unalterable throughout his life. Moreover, the means to those ends, though not fitted into as tight a social frame of reference as in the society dependent on tradition-direction, are nevertheless limited by the new voluntary associations—for instance, the Quakers, the Masons, the Mechanics' Associations—to which people tie themselves. Indeed, the term "tradition-direction" could be misleading if the reader were to conclude that the force of tradition has no weight for the inner-directed character. On the contrary, he is very considerably bound by traditions: they limit his ends and inhibit his choice of means. The point is rather that a splintering of tradition takes place, connected in part with the increasing division of labor and stratification of society. Even if the individual's choice of tradition is largely determined for him by his family, as it is in most cases, he cannot help becoming aware of the existence of competing traditions—hence of tradition as such. As a result he possesses a somewhat greater degree of flexibility in adapting himself to ever changing requirements and in return requires more from his environment.

• • • • •

A DEFINITION OF OTHER-DIRECTION

The type of character I shall describe as other-directed seems to be emerging in very recent years in the upper middle class of our larger cities: more prominently in New York than in Boston, in Los Angeles than in Spokane, in Cincinnati than in Chillicothe. Yet in some respects this type is strikingly similar to *the* American, whom Tocqueville and other curious and astonished visitors from Europe, even before the Revolution, thought to be a new kind of man. Indeed, travelers' reports on America impress us with their unanimity. The American is said to be shallower, freer with his money, friendlier, more uncertain of himself and his values, more demanding of approval than the European. It all adds up to a pattern which, without stretching matters too far, resembles the kind of character that a number of social scientists have seen as developing in contemporary, highly industrialized, and bureaucratic America: Fromm's "marketer," Mills's "fixer," Arnold Green's "middle class male child."

It is my impression that the middle-class American of today is decisively different from those Americans of Tocqueville's writings who nevertheless strike us as so contemporary, and much of this book will be devoted to discussing these differences. It is also my impression that the conditions I believe to be responsible for other-direction are affecting increasing numbers of people in the metropolitan centers of the advanced industrial countries. My analysis of the other-directed character is thus at once an analysis of the American and of contemporary man. Much of the time I find it hard or impossible to say where one ends and the other begins. Tentatively, I am inclined to think that the other-directed type does find itself most at home in America, due to certain unique elements in American society, such as its recruitment from Europe and its lack of any feudal past. As against this, I am also inclined to put more weight on capitalism, industrialism, and urbanization—these being international tendencies—than on any character-forming peculiarities of the American scene.

Bearing these qualifications in mind, it seems appropriate to treat contemporary metropolitan America as our illustration of a society—so far, perhaps, the only illustration—in which other-direction is the dominant mode of insuring conformity. It would be premature, however, to say that it is already the dominant mode in America as a whole. But since the other-directed types are to be found among the young, in the larger cities, and among the upper income groups, we may assume that, unless present trends are reversed, the hegemony of other-direction lies not far off.

If we wanted to cast our social character types into social class molds, we could say that inner-direction is the typical character of the "old" middle class—the banker, the tradesman, the small entrepreneur, the technically oriented engineer, etc.—while other-direction is becoming the typical character of the "new" middle class—the bureaucrat, the salaried employee in business, etc. Many of the economic factors associated with the recent growth of the "new" middle class are well known. They have been discussed by James Burnham, Colin Clark, Peter Drucker, and others. There is a decline in the numbers and in the proportion of the working population engaged in production and extraction—agriculture, heavy industry, heavy transport—and an increase in the numbers and the proportion engaged in white-collar work and the service trades. People who are literate, educated, and provided with the necessities of life by an ever more efficient machine industry and agriculture, turn increasingly to the "tertiary" economic realm. The service industries prosper among the people as a whole and no longer only in court circles.

. . . . .

These developments lead, for large numbers of people, to changes in paths to success and to the requirement of more "socialized" behavior both for success and for marital and personal adaptation. Connected with such changes are changes in the family and in child-rearing practices. In the smaller families of urban life, and with the spread of "permissive" child care to ever wider strata of the population, there is a relaxation of older patterns of discipline. Under these newer patterns the peer-group (the group of one's associates of the same age and class) becomes much more important to the child, while the parents make him feel guilty not so much about violation of inner standards as about failure to be popular or otherwise to manage his relations with these other children. Moreover, the pressures of the school and the peer-group are reinforced and continued—in a manner whose inner paradoxes I shall discuss later—by the mass media: movies, radio, comics, and

popular culture media generally. Under these conditions types of character emerge that we shall here term other-directed. . . . *What is common
to all the other-directed people is that their contemporaries are the source
of direction for the individual—either those known to him or those with
whom he is indirectly acquainted, through friends and through the mass
media. This source is of course "internalized" in the sense that dependence on it for guidance in life is implanted early. The goals toward which
the other-directed person strives shift with that guidance: it is only the
process of striving itself and the process of paying close attention to the
signals from others that remain unaltered throughout life.* This mode of
keeping in touch with others permits a close behavioral conformity, not
through drill in behavior itself, as in the tradition-directed character,
but rather through an exceptional sensitivity to the actions and wishes
of others.

Of course, it matters very much who these "others" are: whether
they are the individual's immediate circle or a "higher" circle or the
anonymous voices of the mass media; whether the individual fears the
hostility of chance acquaintances or only of those who "count." But his
need for approval and direction from others—and contemporary others
rather than ancestors—goes beyond the reasons that lead most people
in any era to care very much what others think of them. While all people want and need to be liked by some of the people some of the time,
it is only the modern other-directed types who make this their chief
source of direction and chief area of sensitivity.

. . . . .

. . . We must differentiate the nineteenth-century American—
gregarious and subservient to public opinion though he was found to be
by Tocqueville, Bryce, and others—from the other-directed American as
he emerges today, an American who in his character is more capable
of and more interested in maintaining responsive contact with others
both at work and at play. This point needs to be emphasized, since the
distinction is easily misunderstood. The inner-directed person, though
he often sought and sometimes achieved a relative independence of
public opinion and of what the neighbors thought of him, was in most
cases very much concerned with his good repute and, at least in America,
with "keeping up with the Joneses." These conformities, however, were
primarily external, typified in such details as clothes, curtains, and bank
credit. For, indeed, the conformities were to a standard, evidence of
which was provided by the "best people" in one's milieu. In contrast
with this pattern, the other-directed person, though he has his eye very
much on the Joneses, aims to keep up with them not so much in external
details as in the quality of his inner experience. That is, his great sen-

sitivity keeps him in touch with others on many more levels than the externals of appearance and propriety. Nor does any ideal of independence or of reliance on God alone modify his desire to look to the others —and the "good guys" as well as the best people—for guidance in what experiences to seek and in how to interpret them.

27. THE ORGANIZATION MAN *

WILLIAM H. WHYTE, JR.

Like the previous selection, this one is taken from a recent publication that has attracted a wide audience. The author, William H. Whyte, Jr., has written numerous articles interpreting business and related segments of society. This excerpt from The Organization Man *briefly analyzes several typical aspects of human behavior in American bureaucratic organizations. It shows how the changing structure of American society, particularly in business, has produced dramatic changes in human behavior and ideology.*

This . . . is about the organization man. If the term is vague, it is because I can think of no other way to describe the people I am talking about. They are not the workers, nor are they the white-collar people in the usual, clerk sense of the word. These people only work for The Organization. The ones I am talking about *belong* to it as well. They are the ones of our middle class who have left home, spiritually as well as physically, to take the vows of organization life, and it is they who are the mind and soul of our great self-perpetuating institutions. Only a few are top managers or ever will be. In a system that makes such hazy terminology as "junior executive" psychologically necessary, they are of the staff as much as the line, and most are destined to live poised in a middle area that still awaits a satisfactory euphemism. But they are the dominant members of our society nonetheless. They have not joined together into a recognizable elite—our country does not stand still long

* From William H. Whyte, Jr., *The Organization Man,* pp. 3–15. Copyright © 1956 by William H. Whyte, Jr. Reprinted by permission of Simon and Schuster, Inc.

The author (b. 1917) has been an editor of *Fortune.* In 1953, he received the Benjamin Franklin Magazine writing award and the Liberty and Justice book award. In addition to *The Organization Man,* his works include *Is Anybody Listening?* and numerous articles.

enough for that—but it is from their ranks that are coming most of the first and second echelons of our leadership, and it is their values which will set the American temper.

The corporation man is the most conspicuous example, but he is only one, for the collectivization so visible in the corporation has affected almost every field of work. Blood brother to the business trainee off to join Du Pont is the seminary student who will end up in the church hierarchy, the doctor headed for the corporate clinic, the physics Ph.D. in a government laboratory, the intellectual on the foundation-sponsored team project, the engineering graduate in the huge drafting room at Lockheed, the young apprentice in a Wall Street law factory.

They are all, as they so often put it, in the same boat. Listen to them talk to each other over the front lawns of their suburbia and you cannot help but be struck by how well they grasp the common denominators which bind them. Whatever the differences in their organization ties, it is the common problems of collective work that dominate their attentions, and when the Du Pont man talks to the research chemist or the chemist to the army man, it is these problems that are uppermost. The word *collective* most of them can't bring themselves to use— except to describe foreign countries or organizations they don't work for —but they are keenly aware of how much more deeply beholden they are to organization than were their elders. They are wry about it, to be sure; they talk of the "treadmill," the "rat race," of the inability to control one's direction. But they have no great sense of plight; between themselves and organization they believe they see an ultimate harmony and, more than most elders recognize, they are building an ideology that will vouchsafe this trust.

. . . America has paid much attention to the economic and political consequences of big organization—the concentration of power in large corporations, for example, the political power of the civil-service bureaucracies, the possible emergence of a managerial hierarchy that might dominate the rest of us. These are proper concerns, but no less important is the personal impact that organization life has had on the individuals within it. A collision has been taking place—indeed, hundreds of thousands of them, and in the aggregate they have been producing what I believe is a major shift in American ideology.

Officially, we are a people who hold to the Protestant Ethic. Because of the denominational implications of the term many would deny its relevance to them, but let them eulogize the American Dream, however, and they virtually define the Protestant Ethic. Whatever the embroidery, there is almost always the thought that pursuit of individual salvation through hard work, thrift, and competitive struggle is the heart of the American achievement.

But the harsh facts of organization life simply do not jibe with these precepts. This conflict is certainly not a peculiarly American development. In their own countries such Europeans as Max Weber and Durkheim many years ago foretold the change, and though Europeans now like to see their troubles as an American export, the problems they speak of stem from a bureaucratization of society that has affected every Western country.

It is in America, however, that the contrast between the old ethic and current reality has been most apparent—and most poignant. Of all peoples it is we who have led in the public worship of individualism. One hundred years ago De Tocqueville was noting that though our special genius—and failing—lay in co-operative action, we talked more than others of personal independence and freedom. We kept on, and as late as the twenties, when big organization was long since a fact, affirmed the old faith as if nothing had really changed at all.

Today many still try, and it is the members of the kind of organization most responsible for the change, the corporation, who try the hardest. It is the corporation man whose institutional ads protest so much that Americans speak up in town meeting, that Americans are the best inventors because Americans don't care that other people scoff, that Americans are the best soldiers because they have so much initiative and native ingenuity, that the boy selling papers on the street corner is the prototype of our business society. Collectivism? He abhors it, and when he makes his ritualistic attack on Welfare Statism, it is in terms of a Protestant Ethic undefiled by change—the sacredness of property, the enervating effect of security, the virtues of thrift, of hard work and independence. Thanks be, he says, that there are some people left—e.g., businessmen—to defend the American Dream.

He is not being hypocritical, only compulsive. He honestly wants to believe he follows the tenets he extols, and if he extols them so frequently it is, perhaps, to shut out a nagging suspicion that he, too, the last defender of the faith, is no longer pure. Only by using the language of individualism to describe the collective can he stave off the thought that he himself is in a collective as pervading as any ever dreamed of by the reformers, the intellectuals, and the utopian visionaries he so regularly warns against.

The older generation may still convince themselves; the younger generation does not. When a young man says that to make a living these days you must do what somebody else wants you to do, he states it not only as a fact of life that must be accepted but as an inherently good proposition. If the American Dream deprecates this for him, it is the American Dream that is going to have to give, whatever its more elderly guardians may think. People grow restive with a mythology that is too distant from the way things actually are, and as more and more lives have been encompassed by the organization way of life, the pressures for an accompanying ideological shift have been mounting. The pressures of the group, the frustrations of individual creativity, the anonymity of achievement: are these defects to struggle against—or are they virtues in disguise? The organization man seeks a redefinition of his place on earth—a faith that will satisfy him that what he must endure has a deeper meaning than appears on the surface. He needs, in short, something that will do for him what the Protestant Ethic did once. And slowly, almost imperceptibly, a body of thought has been coalescing that does that.

I am going to call it a Social Ethic. With reason it could be called an organization ethic, or a bureaucratic ethic; more than anything else it rationalizes the organization's demands for fealty and gives those who offer it wholeheartedly a sense of dedication in doing so—*in extremis,* you might say, it converts what would seem in other times a bill of no rights into a restatement of individualism.

But there is a real moral imperative behind it, and whether one inclines to its beliefs or not he must acknowledge that this moral basis, not mere expediency, is the source of its power. Nor is it simply an opiate for those who must work in big organizations. The search for a secular faith that it represents can be found throughout our society— and among those who swear they would never set foot in a corporation or a government bureau. Though it has its greatest applicability to the organization man, its ideological underpinnings have been provided not by the organization man but by intellectuals he knows little of and to- ward whom, indeed, he tends to be rather suspicious.

Any groove of abstraction, Whitehead once remarked, is bound to be an inadequate way of describing reality, and so with the concept of the Social Ethic. It is an attempt to illustrate an underlying con- sistency in what in actuality is by no means an orderly system of thought. No one says, "I believe in the social ethic," and though many would subscribe wholeheartedly to the separate ideas that make it up, these ideas have yet to be put together in the final, harmonious synthesis. But the unity is there.

In looking at what might seem dissimilar aspects of organization society, it is this unity I wish to underscore. The "professionalization" of the manager, for example, and the drive for a more practical educa- tion are parts of the same phenomenon; just as the student now feels technique more vital than content, so the trainee believes managing an end in itself, an *expertise* relatively independent of the content of what is being managed. And the reasons are the same. So too in other sectors of our society; for all the differences in particulars, dominant is a grow- ing accommodation to the needs of society—and a growing urge to justify it.

Let me now define my terms. By social ethic I mean that contemporary body of thought which makes morally legitimate the pressures of society against the individual. Its major propositions are three: a belief in the group as the source of creativity; a belief in "belongingness" as the ultimate need of the individual; and a belief in the application of science to achieve the belongingness.

. . . The gist can be paraphrased thus: Man exists as a unit of society. Of himself, he is isolated, meaningless; only as he collaborates with others does he become worth while, for by sublimating himself in the group, he helps produce a whole that is greater than the sum of its parts. There should be, then, no conflict between man and society. What we think are conflicts are misunderstandings, breakdowns in communication. By applying the methods of science to human relations we can eliminate these obstacles to consensus and create an equilibrium in which society's needs and the needs of the individual are one and the same.

Essentially, it is a utopian faith. Superficially, it seems dedicated to the practical problems of organization life, and its proponents often use the word *hard* (versus *soft*) to describe their approach. But it is the long-range promise that animates its followers, for it relates techniques to the vision of a finite, achievable harmony. . . .

Like the utopian communities, it interprets society in a fairly narrow, immediate sense. One can believe man has a social obligation and that the individual must ultimately contribute to the community without believing that group harmony is the test of it. In the Social Ethic I am describing, however, man's obligation is in the here and now; his duty is not so much to the community in a broad sense but to the actual, physical one about him, and the idea that in isolation from it—or active rebellion against it—he might eventually discharge the greater service is little considered. In practice, those who most eagerly subscribe to the Social Ethic worry very little over the long-range problems of society. It is not that they don't care but rather that they tend to assume that the ends of organization and morality coincide, and on such matters as social welfare they give their proxy to the organization.

It is possible that I am attaching too much weight to what, after all, is something of a mythology. Those more sanguine than I have argued that this faith is betrayed by reality in some key respects and that because it cannot long hide from organization man that life is still essentially competitive the faith must fall of its own weight. They also maintain that the Social Ethic is only one trend in a society which is a prolific breeder of counter-trends. The farther the pendulum swings, they believe, the more it must eventually swing back.

I am not persuaded. We are indeed a flexible people, but society is not a clock and to stake so much on counter-trends is to put a rather heavy burden on providence. . . .

. . . No one can say whether these trends will continue to outpace the counter-trends, but neither can we trust that an equilibrium-minded providence will see to it that excesses will cancel each other out. Counter-trends there are. There always have been, and in the sweep of ideas ineffectual many have proved to be.

It is also true that the Social Ethic is something of a mythology, and there is a great difference between mythology and practice. An individualism as stringent, as selfish as that often preached in the name of the Protestant Ethic would never have been tolerated, and in reality our predecessors co-operated with one another far more skillfully than nineteenth-century oratory would suggest. Something of the obverse is true of the Social Ethic; so complete a denial of individual will won't work either, and even the most willing believers in the group harbor some secret misgivings, some latent antagonism toward the pressures they seek to deify.

But the Social Ethic is no less powerful for that, and though it can never produce the peace of mind it seems to offer, it will help shape the nature of the quest in the years to come. The old dogma of individualism betrayed reality too, yet few would argue, I dare say, that it was not an immensely powerful influence in the time of its dominance. So I argue of the Social Ethic; call it mythology, if you will, but it is becoming the dominant one.

. . . . .

This . . . is not a plea for nonconformity. Such pleas have an occasional therapeutic value, but as an abstraction, nonconformity is an empty goal, and rebellion against prevailing opinion merely because it is prevailing should no more be praised than acquiescence to it. Indeed, it is often a mask for cowardice, and few are more pathetic than those who flaunt outer differences to expiate their inner surrender.

I am not, accordingly, addressing myself to the surface uniformities of U.S. life. There will be no strictures . . . against "Mass Man"—a person the author has never met—nor will there be any strictures against ranch wagons, or television sets, or gray flannel suits. They are irrelevant to the main problem, and, furthermore, there's no harm in them. I would not wish to go to the other extreme and suggest that these uniformities per se are good, but the spectacle of people following current custom for lack of will or imagination to do anything else is hardly a new failing, and I am not convinced that there has been any significant change in this respect except in the nature of the things we conform to. Unless one believes poverty enobling, it is difficult to see the three-button suit as more of a strait jacket than overalls, or the ranch-type house than old law tenements.

And how important, really, are these uniformities to the central issue of individualism? We must not let the outward forms deceive us. If individualism involves following one's destiny as one's own conscience directs, it must for most of us be a realizable destiny, and a sensible awareness of the rules of the game can be a condition of individualism as well as a constraint upon it. The man who drives a Buick Special and lives in a ranch-type house just like hundreds of other ranch-type houses can assert himself as effectively and courageously against his particular society as the bohemian against his particular society. He usually does not, it is true, but if he does, the surface uniformities can serve quite well as protective coloration. The organization people who are best able to control their environment rather than be controlled by it are well aware that they are not too easily distinguishable from the others in the outward obeisances paid to the good opinions of others. And that is one of the reasons they do control. They disarm society.

I do not equate the Social Ethic with conformity, nor do I believe those who urge it wish it to be, for most of them believe deeply that their work will help, rather than harm, the individual. I think their ideas are out of joint with the needs of the times they invoke, but it is their ideas, and not their good will, I wish to question. As for the lackeys of organization and the charlatans, they are not worth talking about.

Neither do I intend . . . a censure of the fact of organization society. We have quite enough problems today without muddying the issue with misplaced nostalgia, and in contrasting the old ideology with the new I mean no contrast of paradise with paradise lost, an idyllic eighteenth century with a dehumanized twentieth. Whether or not our own era is worse than former ones in the climate of freedom is a matter that can be left to later historians, but . . . I write with the optimistic promise that individualism is as possible in our times as in others.

I speak of individualism *within* organization life. This is not the only kind, and someday it may be that the mystics and philosophers more distant from it may prove the crucial figures. But they are affected too by the center of society, and they can be of no help unless they grasp the nature of the main stream. Intellectual scoldings based on an impossibly lofty ideal may be of some service in upbraiding organization man with his failures, but they can give him no guidance. The organization man may agree that industrialism has destroyed the moral fabric of society and that we need to return to the agrarian virtues, or that business needs to be broken up into a series of smaller organizations, or that it's government that needs to be broken up, and so on. But he will go his way with his own dilemmas left untouched.

I . . . argue that he should fight the organization. But not self-destructively. He may tell the boss to go to hell, but he is going to have another boss, and, unlike the heroes of popular fiction, he cannot find surcease by leaving the arena to be a husbandman. If he chafes at the pressures of his particular organization, either he must succumb, resist them, try to change them, or move to yet another organization.

Every decision he faces on the problem of the individual versus authority is something of a dilemma. It is not a case of whether he should fight against black tyranny or blaze a new trail against patent stupidity. That would be easy—intellectually, at least. The real issue is far more subtle. For it is not the evils of organization life that puzzle him, *but its very beneficence.* He is imprisoned in brotherhood. Because his area of maneuver seems so small and because the trapping so mundane, his fight lacks the heroic cast, but it is for all this as tough a fight as ever his predecessors had to fight.

Thus to my thesis, I believe the emphasis of the Social Ethic is wrong for him. People do have to work with others, yes; the well-functioning team is a whole greater than the sum of its parts, yes—all this is indeed true. But is it the truth that now needs belaboring? Precisely because it *is* an age of organization, it is the other side of the coin that needs emphasis. We do need to know how to co-operate with The Organization but, more than ever, so do we need to know how to resist it. Out of context this would be an irresponsible statement. Time and place are critical, and history has taught us that a philosophical individualism can venerate conflict too much and co-operation too little. But what is the context today? The tide has swung far enough the other way, I submit, that we need not worry that a counteremphasis will stimulate people to an excess of individualism.

The energies Americans have devoted to the co-operative, to the social, are not to be demeaned; we would not, after all, have such a problem to discuss unless we had learned to adapt ourselves to an increasingly collective society as well as we have. An ideal of individualism which denies the obligations of man to others is manifestly impossible in a society such as ours, and it is a credit to our wisdom that while we preached it, we never fully practiced it.

But in searching for that elusive middle of the road, we have gone very far afield, and in our attention to making organization work we have come close to deifying it. We are describing its defects as virtues and denying that there is—or should be—a conflict between the individual and organization. This denial is bad for the organization. It is worse for the individual. What it does, in soothing him, is to rob him of the intellectual armor he so badly needs. For the more power organization has over him, the more he needs to recognize the area where he must assert himself against it. And this, almost because we have made organization life so equable, has become excruciatingly difficult.

To say that we must recognize the dilemmas of organization society is not to be inconsistent with the hopeful premise that organization society can be as compatible for the individual as any previous society. We are not hapless beings caught in the grip of forces we can do little about, and wholesale damnations of our society only lend a further mystique to organization. Organization has been made by man; it can be changed by man. It has not been the immutable course of history that has produced such constrictions on the individual as personality tests. It is organization man who has brought them to pass and it is he who can stop them.

The fault is not in organization, in short; it is in our worship of it. It is in our vain quest for a utopian equilibrium, which would be horrible if it ever did come to pass; it is in the soft-minded denial that there is a conflict between the individual and society. There must always be, and it is the price of being an individual that he must face these conflicts. He cannot evade them, and in seeking an ethic that offers a spurious peace of mind, thus does he tyrannize himself.

There are only a few times in organization life when he can wrench his destiny into his own hands—and if he does not fight then, he will make a surrender that will later mock him. But when is that time? Will he know the time when he sees it? By what standards is he to judge? He does feel an obligation to the group; he does sense moral constraints on his free will. If he goes against the group, is he being courageous—or just stubborn? Helpful—or selfish? Is he, as he so often wonders, right after all? It is in the resolution of a multitude of such dilemmas, I submit, that the real issue of individualism lies today.

28. THE THEORY OF MASS SOCIETY °

DANIEL BELL

This article by Daniel Bell should provide a broader perspective for judging and dealing with the ideas expressed in the two preceding articles. In discussing his conviction that there is no really substantial evidence for the theory that Western society is increasingly a "mass" society—blanketing and preventing the

° Reprinted from *Commentary*, Vol. 22, No. 1 (July, 1956), 75–83. Copyright by the American Jewish Committee. The essay also appears, in revised form, in Daniel Bell, *The End of Ideology* (Glencoe, Ill.: The Free Press, 1960).

The author (b. 1919) is Labor Editor of *Fortune*, an Associate Professor, Sociology, Columbia University. His chief interests are in industrial relations and industrial sociology. His books include: *American Marxist Parties; Work in the Life of an American; The New American Right* (editor).

expression of individual interest—Bell stands relatively alone, since the mass society thesis is a basic assumption of most current social science texts.

The sense of a radical dehumanization of life which has accompanied events of the past several decades has given rise to the theory of "mass society." One can say that, Marxism apart, it is probably the most influential social theory in the Western world today. While no single individual has stamped his name on it—to the extent that Marx is associated with the transformation of personal relations under capitalism into commodity values, or Freud with the role of the irrational and unconscious in behavior—the theory is central to the thinking of the principal aristocratic, Catholic, or Existentialist critics of bourgeois society today. These critics—Ortega y Gasset, Karl Mannheim, Karl Jaspers, Paul Tillich, Gabriel Marcel, Emil Lederer, and others—have been concerned, less with the general conditions of freedom, than with the freedom of the *person,* and with the possibility for some *few* persons of achieving a sense of individual self in our mechanized society.

The conception of "mass society" can be summarized as follows: The revolutions in transport and communications have brought men into closer contact with each other and bound them in new ways; the division of labor has made them more interdependent; tremors in one part of society affect all others. Despite this greater interdependence, however, individuals have grown more estranged from one another. The old primary group ties of family and local community have been shattered; ancient parochial faiths are questioned; few unifying values have taken their place. Most important, the critical standards of an educated elite no longer shape opinion or taste. As a result, mores and morals are in constant flux, relations between individuals are tangential or compartmentalized rather than organic. At the same time greater mobility, spatial and social, intensifies concern over status. Instead of a fixed or known status symbolized by dress or title, each person assumes a multiplicity of roles and constantly has to prove himself in a succession of new situations. Because of all this, the individual loses a coherent sense of self. His anxieties increase. There ensues a search for new faiths. The stage is thus set for the charismatic leader, the secular messiah, who, by bestowing upon each person the semblance of necessary grace, and of fullness of personality, supplies a substitute for the older unifying belief that the mass society has destroyed.

In a world of lonely crowds seeking individual distinction, where values are constantly translated into economic calculabilities, where in extreme situations shame and conscience can no longer restrain the most dreadful excesses of terror, the theory of the mass society seems a forceful, realistic description of contemporary society, an accurate reflection of the *quality* and *feeling* of modern life. But when one seeks to apply the theory of mass society analytically, it becomes very slippery. Ideal types, like the shadows in Plato's cave, generally never give us more than a silhouette. So, too, with the theory of "mass society." Each of the statements making up the theory, as set forth in the second paragraph above, might be true, but they do not follow necessarily from one another. Nor can we say that all the conditions described are present at any one time or place. More than that, there is no organizing principle— other than the general concept of a "breakdown of values"—which puts the individual elements of theory together in a logical, meaningful—let alone historical—manner. And when we examine the way the "theory" is used by those who employ it, we find ourselves even more at a loss.

As commonly used in the term "mass media," "mass" implies that standardized material is transmitted to "all groups of the population uniformly." As understood generally by sociologists, a *mass* is a heterogeneous and undifferentiated audience as opposed to a *class*, or any parochial and relatively homogeneous segment. Some sociologists have been tempted to go further and make "mass" a rather pejorative term. Because the mass media subject a diverse audience to a common set of cultural materials, it is argued that these experiences must necessarily lie outside the personal—and therefore meaningful—experiences to which the individual responds directly. A movie audience, for example, is a "mass" because the individuals looking at the screen are, in the words of the American sociologist Herbert Blumer, "separate, detached, and anonymous." The "mass" divorces—or "alienates"—the individual from himself.

. . . . .

Presumably a large number of individuals, because they have been subjected to similar experiences, now share some common psychological reality in which the differences between individual and individual become blurred; and accordingly we get the sociological assumption that each person is now of "equal weight," and therefore a sampling of what such disparate individuals say they think constitutes "*mass* opinion." But is this so? Individuals are not *tabulae rasae*. They bring varying social conceptions to the same experience, and go away with dissimilar responses. They may be silent, separate, detached, and anonymous while watching the movie, but afterward they talk about it with friends and exchange opinions and judgments. They are once again members of particular social groups. Would one say that several hundred or a thousand individuals home alone at night, but all reading the same book, constitutes a "mass"?

One could argue, of course, that reading a book is a qualitatively

different experience from going to a movie. But this leads precisely to the
first damaging ambiguity in the theory of the mass society. Two things
are mixed up in that theory: a judgment as to the *quality* of modern
experience—with much of which any sensitive individual would agree—
and a presumed scientific statement concerning the disorganization of
society created by industrialization and by the demand of the masses for
equality. It is the second of these statements with which this essay
quarrels, not the first.

Behind the theory of social disorganization lies a romantic notion of
the past that sees society as having once been made up of small "organic,"
close-knit communities (called *Gemeinschaften* in the terminology of
the sociologists) that were shattered by industrialism and modern life,
and replaced by a large impersonal "atomistic" society (called *Gesellschaft*) which is unable to provide the basic gratifications and call forth
the loyalties that the older communities knew.

. . . . .

It is asserted that the United States is an "atomized" society composed of lonely, isolated individuals. One forgets the truism, expressed
sometimes as a jeer, that Americans are a nation of joiners. There are in
the United States today at least 200,000 voluntary organizations, associations, clubs, societies, lodges, and fraternities with an aggregate
(but obviously overlapping) membership of close to eighty million men
and women. In no other country in the world, probably, is there such
a high degree of voluntary communal activity, expressed sometimes in
absurd rituals, yet often providing real satisfactions for real needs.

"It is natural for the ordinary American," wrote Gunnar Myrdal,
"when he sees something that is wrong to feel not only that there should
be a law against it, but also that an organization should be formed to
combat it." Some of these voluntary organizations are pressure groups—
business, farm, labor, veterans, trade associations, the aged, etc., etc.—
but thousands more are like the National Association for the Advancement of Colored People, the American Civil Liberties Union, the League
of Women Voters, the American Jewish Committee, the Parent-Teachers
Associations, local community-improvement groups, and so on, each
of which affords hundreds of individuals concrete, emotionally shared
activities.

Equally astonishing are the number of ethnic group organizations
in this country carrying on varied cultural, social, and political activities.
The number of Irish, Italian, Jewish, Polish, Czech, Finnish, Bulgarian,
Bessarabian, and other national groups, their hundreds of fraternal,
communal, and political groups, each playing a role in the life of America, is staggering. In December 1954, for example, when the issue of
Cyprus was first placed before the United Nations, the Justice for Cyprus

Committee, "an organization of American citizens," according to its statement, took a full-page advertisement in the New York *Times* to plead the right of that small island to self-determination. Among the groups listed in the Justice for Cyprus Committee were: the Order of Ahepa, the Daughters of Penelope, the Pan-Laconian Federation, the Cretan Federation, the Pan-Messian Federation, the Pan-Icarian Federation, the Pan-Epirotic Federation of America, the Pan-Thracian Association, the Pan-Elian Federation of America, the Dodecanesian League of America, the Pan-Macedonian Association of America, the Pan-Samian Association, the Federation of Sterea Ellas, the Cyprus Federation of America, the Pan-Arcadian Federation, the GAPA, and the Federation of Hellenic Organizations.

We can be sure that if, in a free world, the question of the territorial affiliation of Ruthenia were to come up before the United Nations, dozens of Hungarian, Rumanian, Ukrainian, Slovakian, and Czech "organizations of American citizens" would rush eagerly into print to plead the justice of the claims of their respective homelands to Ruthenia.

Even in urban neighborhoods, where anonymity is presumed to flourish, the extent of local ties is astounding. Within the city limits of Chicago, for example, there are eighty-two community newspapers with a total weekly circulation of almost 1,000,000; within Chicago's larger metropolitan area, there are 181. According to standard sociological theory, these local papers providing news and gossip about neighbors should slowly decline under the pressure of the national media. Yet the reverse is true. In Chicago, the number of such newspapers has increased 165 per cent since 1910; in those forty years circulation has jumped 770 per cent. As sociologist Morris Janowitz, who studied these community newspapers, observed: "If society were as impersonal, as self-centered and barren as described by some who are preoccupied with the one-way trend from '*Gemeinschaft*' to '*Gesellschaft*' seem to believe, the levels of criminality, social disorganization and psychopathology which social science seeks to account for would have to be viewed as very low rather than (as viewed now) alarmingly high."

It may be argued that the existence of such a large network of voluntary associations says little about the cultural level of the country concerned. It may well be, as Ortega maintains, that cultural standards throughout the world have declined (in everything—architecture, dress, design?), but nonetheless a greater proportion of the population today participates in worth-while cultural activities. This has been almost an inevitable concomitant of the doubling—*literally*—of the American standard of living over the last fifty years. The rising levels of education have meant rising appreciation of culture. In the United States more dollars are spent on concerts of classical music than on baseball. Sales of books have doubled in a decade. There are over a thousand symphony

orchestras, and several hundred museums, institutes, and colleges purchasing art in the United States today. Various other indices can be
cited to show the growth of a vast middlebrow society. And in coming
years, with steadily increasing productivity and leisure, the United States
will become even more actively a "consumer" of culture. . . .

It has been argued that the American mass society imposes an excessive conformity upon its members. But it is hard to discern who is
conforming to what. The *New Republic* cries that "hucksters are sugar-
coating the culture." The *National Review,* organ of the "radical right,"
raises the banner of iconoclasm against the liberal domination of opinion-
formation in our society. *Fortune* decries the growth of "organization
man." Each of these tendencies exists, yet in historical perspective,
there is probably less conformity to an over-all mode of conduct today
than at any time within the last half-century in America. True, there
is less bohemianism than in the twenties (though increased sexual
tolerance), and less political radicalism than in the thirties (though the
New Deal enacted sweeping reforms). But does the arrival at a political dead-center mean the establishment, too, of a dead norm? I do not
think so. One would be hard put to it to find today the "conformity"
Main Street exacted of Carol Kennicott thirty years ago. With rising
educational levels, more individuals are able to indulge a wider variety
of interests. ("Twenty years ago you couldn't sell Beethoven out of
New York," reports a record salesman. "Today we sell Palestrina, Mon-
teverdi, Gabrielli, and Renaissance and Baroque music in large quantities.")

One hears, too, the complaint that divorce, crime, and violence
demonstrate a widespread social disorganization in the country. But the
rising number of divorces . . . indicates not the disruption of the family,
but a freer, more individualistic basis of choice, and the emergence of
the "companionship" marriage. And as regards crime . . . , there is actually much *less* crime and violence (though more vicarious violence
through movies and TV, and more "windows" onto crime, through the
press) than was the case twenty-five and fifty years ago. Certainly, Chicago, San Francisco, and New York were much rougher and tougher
cities in those years. But violent crime, which is usually a lower-class
phenomenon, was then contained within the ecological boundaries of
the slum; hence one can recall quiet, tree-lined, crime-free areas and
feel that the tenor of life was more even in the past. But a cursory look
at the accounts of those days—the descriptions of the gang wars, bor-
dellos, and street-fighting in San Francisco's Barbary Coast, New York's
Five Points, or Chicago's First Ward—would show how much more
violent in the past the actual life of those cities was.

At this point it becomes quite apparent that such large-scale abstractions as "the mass society," with the implicit diagnoses of social

disorganization and decay that derive from them, are rather meaningless without standards of comparison. Social and cultural change is probably greater and more rapid today in the United States than in any other country, but the assumption that social disorder and *anomie* inevitably attend such change is not borne out in this case.

This may be owing to the singular fact that the United States is probably the first large society in history to have change and innovation "built into" its culture. Almost all human societies, traditionalist and habit-ridden as they have been and still are, tend to resist change. The great efforts to industrialize under-developed countries, increase worker mobility in Europe, and broaden markets—so necessary to the raising of productivity and standards of living—are again and again frustrated by ingrained resistence to change. Thus in the Soviet Union change has been introduced only by dint of wholesale coercion. In the United States—a culture with no feudal tradition; with a pragmatic ethos, as expressed by Jefferson, that regards God as a "workman"; with a boundless optimism and a restless eagerness for the new that has been bred out of the original conditions of a huge, richly endowed land—change, and the readiness to change, have become the norm. This indeed may be why those consequences of change predicted by theorists basing themselves on European precedent find small confirmation.

The mass society is the product of change—and is itself change. But the *theory* of the mass society affords us no view of the relations of the parts of the society to each other that would enable us to locate the sources of change. We may not have enough data on which to sketch an alternative theory, but I would argue that certain key factors, in this country at least, deserve to be much more closely examined than they have been.

The change from a society once geared to frugal saving and now impelled to spend dizzily; the break-up of family capitalism, with the consequent impact on corporate structure and political power; the centralization of decision-making, politically, in the state and, economically, in a group of large corporate bodies; the rise of status and symbol groups replacing specific interest groups—indicate that new social forms are in the making, and with them still greater changes in the complexion of life under mass society. With these may well come new status anxieties —aggravated by the threats of war—changed character structures, and new moral tempers.

The moralist may have his reservations or give approval—as some see in the break-up of the family the loss of a source of essential values, while others see in the new, freer marriages a healthier form of companionship—but the singular fact is that these changes emerge in a society that is now providing one answer to the great challenge posed to Western—and now world—society over the last two hundred years:

how, within the framework of freedom, to increase the living standards of the majority of people, and at the same time maintain or raise cultural levels. American society, for all its shortcomings, its speed, its commercialism, its corruption, still, I believe, shows us the most humane way.

The theory of the mass society no longer serves as a description of Western society, but as an ideology of romantic protest against contemporary society. This is a time when other areas of the globe are beginning to follow in the paths of the West, which may be all to the good as far as material things are concerned; but many of the economically underdeveloped countries, especially in Asia, have caught up the shopworn self-critical Western ideologies of the 19th century and are using them against the West, to whose "materialism" they oppose their "spirituality." What these Asian and our own intellectuals fail to realize, perhaps, is that one may be a thorough going critic of one's own society without being an enemy of its promises.

CHAPTER IV

SOCIAL
ORGANIZATION

Types of Group Relationships

29. PRIMARY GROUPS *

CHARLES HORTON COOLEY

*Professor Cooley, the author of this selection, is recognized as a
pioneer in the field of social psychology. One of his very fruitful
contributions to sociology is the concept of primary groups as the
"nursery of human nature." Here he explains the universality of
primary groups and contrasts their characteristics with what we
now designate as secondary groups. He carefully defines "human
nature," which he declares to be fundamentally the same the world
over. Although more recent discoveries have revealed certain
limitations in his data, such as his statement in this selection about
differences in racial capacities, in most essentials his thinking is
sound and illuminating. Since 1909, when the book in which this
selection appears was published, much progress has been made in
developing the scientific research methods of both psychology and
sociology; but many of Cooley's ideas, of which the primary-group
concept is one, have a timeless quality.*

By primary groups I mean those characterized by intimate face-to-
face association and coöperation. They are primary in several senses,

* From *Social Organization*, 23–31. Reprinted with permission of Charles Scribner's Sons, copyright 1909 Charles Scribner's Sons; renewal copyright 1937 Elsie
Jones Cooley.

The author (1864–1929), an American social philosopher, was Professor of
Sociology, University of Michigan, at the time of his death. Made contributions of
great range and depth to the field of sociology. His important works include *Personal Competition; Human Nature and the Social Order; Social Organization; Social
Process; Life and the Student; Sociological Theory and Social Research.*

but chiefly in that they are fundamental in forming the social nature and ideals of the individual. The result of intimate association, psychologically, is a certain fusion of individualities in a common whole, so that one's very self, for many purposes at least, is the common life and purpose of the group. Perhaps the simplest way of describing this wholeness is by saying that it is a "we"; it involves the sort of sympathy and mutual identification for which "we" is the natural expression. One lives in the feeling of the whole and finds the chief aims of his will in that feeling.

It is not to be supposed that the unity of the primary group is one of mere harmony and love. It is always a differentiated and usually a competitive unity, admitting of self-assertion and various appropriative passions; but these passions are socialized by sympathy, and come, or tend to come, under the discipline of a common spirit. The individual will be ambitious, but the chief object of his ambition will be some desired place in the thought of the others, and he will feel allegiance to common standards of service and fair play. So the boy will dispute with his fellows a place on the team, but above such disputes will place the common glory of his class and school.

The most important spheres of this intimate association and coöperation—though by no means the only ones—are the family, the playgroup of children, and the neighborhood or community group of elders. These are practically universal, belonging to all times and all stages of development; and are accordingly a chief basis of what is universal in human nature and human ideals. The best comparative studies of the family, such as those of Westermarck or Howard, show it to us as not only a universal institution, but as more alike the world over than the exaggeration of exceptional customs by an earlier school had led us to suppose. Nor can any one doubt the general prevalence of playgroups among children or of informal assemblies of various kinds among their elders. Such association is clearly the nursery of human nature in the world about us, and there is no apparent reason to suppose that the case has anywhere or at any time been essentially different.

As regards play, I might, were it not a matter of common observation, multiply illustrations of the universality and spontaneity of the group discussion and coöperation to which it gives rise. The general fact is that children, especially boys after about their twelfth year, live in fellowships in which their sympathy, ambition and honor are engaged even more, often, than they are in the family. Most of us can recall examples of the endurance by boys of injustice and even cruelty, rather than appeal from their fellows to parents or teachers—as, for instance, in the hazing so prevalent at schools, and so difficult, for this very reason, to repress. And how elaborate the discussion, how cogent the public opinion, how hot the ambitions in these fellowships.

Nor is this facility of juvenile association, as is sometimes supposed, a trait peculiar to English and American boys; since experience among our immigrant population seems to show that the offspring of the more restrictive civilizations of the continent of Europe form self-governing play-groups with almost equal readiness. Thus Miss Jane Addams, after pointing out that the "gang" is almost universal, speaks of the interminable discussion which every detail of the gang's activity receives, remarking that "in these social folk-motes, so to speak, the young citizen learns to act upon his own determination."

Of the neighborhood group it may be said, in general, that from the time men formed permanent settlements upon the land, down, at least, to the rise of modern industrial cities, it has played a main part in the primary, heart-to-heart life of the people. Among our Teutonic forefathers the village community was apparently the chief sphere of sympathy and mutual aid for the commons all through the "dark" and middle ages, and for many purposes it remains so in rural districts at the present day. In some countries we still find it with all its ancient vitality, notably in Russia, where the mir, or self-governing village group, is the main theatre of life, along with the family, for perhaps fifty millions of peasants.

In our own life the intimacy of the neighborhood has been broken up by the growth of an intricate mesh of wider contacts which leaves us strangers to people who live in the same house. And even in the country the same principle is at work, though less obviously, diminishing our economic and spiritual community with our neighbors. How far this change is a healthy development, and how far a disease, is perhaps still uncertain.

Besides these almost universal kinds of primary association, there are many others whose form depends upon the particular state of civilization; the only essential thing, as I have said, being a certain intimacy and fusion of personalities. In our own society, being little bound by place, people easily form clubs, fraternal societies and the like, based on congeniality, which may give rise to real intimacy. Many such relations are formed at school and college, and among men and women brought together in the first instance by their occupations—as workmen in the same trade, or the like. Where there is a little common interest and activity, kindness grows like weeds by the roadside.

But the fact that the family and neighborhood groups are ascendant in the open and plastic time of childhood makes them even now incomparably more influential than all the rest.

Primary groups are primary in the sense that they give the individual his earliest and completest experience of social unity, and also in the sense that they do not change in the same degree as more elaborate relations, but form a comparatively permanent source out of which the latter are ever springing. Of course they are not independent of the larger society, but to some extent reflect its spirit; as the German family and the German school bear somewhat distinctly the print of German militarism. But this, after all, is like the tide setting back into creeks, and does not commonly go very far. Among the German, and still more among the Russian, peasantry are found habits of free coöperation and discussion almost uninfluenced by the character of the state; and it is a familiar and well-supported view that the village commune, self-governing as regards local affairs and habituated to discussion, is a very widespread institution in settled communities, and the continuator of a similar autonomy previously existing in the clan. "It is man who makes monarchies and establishes republics, but the commune seems to come directly from the hand of God."

In our own cities the crowded tenements and the general economic and social confusion have sorely wounded the family and the neighborhood, but it is remarkable, in view of these conditions, what vitality they show; and there is nothing upon which the conscience of the time is more determined than upon restoring them to health.

These groups, then, are springs of life, not only for the individual but for social institutions. They are only in part moulded by special traditions, and, in larger degree, express a universal nature. The religion or government of other civilizations may seem alien to us, but the children or the family group wear the common life, and with them we can always make ourselves at home.

By human nature, I suppose, we may understand those sentiments and impulses that are human in being superior to those of lower animals, and also in the sense that they belong to mankind at large, and not to any particular race or time. It means, particularly, sympathy and the innumerable sentiments into which sympathy enters, such as love, resentment, ambition, vanity, hero-worship, and the feeling of social right and wrong.

Human nature in this sense is justly regarded as a comparatively permanent element in society. Always and everywhere men seek honor and dread ridicule, defer to public opinion, cherish their goods and their children, and admire courage, generosity, and success. It is always safe to assume that people are and have been human.

It is true, no doubt, that there are differences of race capacity, so great that a large part of mankind are possibly incapable of any high kind of social organization. But these differences, like those among individuals of the same race, are subtle, depending upon some obscure intellectual deficiency, some want of vigor, or slackness of moral fibre, and do not involve unlikeness in the generic impulses of human nature. In these all races are very much alike. The more insight one gets into the life of savages, even those that are reckoned the lowest, the more human, the more like ourselves, they appear. Take for instance the natives of Central Australia, as described by Spencer and Gillen, tribes having no definite government or worship and scarcely able to count to five. They are generous to one another, emulous of virtue as they understand it, kind to their children and to the aged, and by no means harsh to women. Their faces as shown in the photographs are wholly human and many of them attractive.

And when we come to a comparison between different stages in the development of the same race, between ourselves, for instance, and the Teutonic tribes of the time of Cæsar, the difference is neither in human nature nor in capacity, but in organization, in the range and complexity of relations, in the diverse expression of powers and passions essentially much the same.

There is no better proof of this generic likeness of human nature than in the ease and joy with which the modern man makes himself at home in literature depicting the most remote and varied phases of life— in Homer, in the Nibelung tales, in the Hebrew Scriptures, in the legends of the American Indians, in stories of frontier life, of soldiers and sailors, of criminals and tramps, and so on. The more penetratingly any phase of human life is studied the more an essential likeness to ourselves is revealed.

To return to primary groups: the view here maintained is that human nature is not someting existing separately in the individual, but a *group-nature or primary phase of society,* a relatively simple and general condition of the social mind. It is something more, on the one hand, than the mere instinct that is born in us—though that enters into it—and something less, on the other, than the more elaborate development of ideas and sentiments that makes up institutions. It is the nature which is developed and expressed in those simple, face-to-face groups that are somewhat alike in all societies; groups of the family, the playground, and the neighborhood. In the essential similarity of these is to be found the basis, in experience, for similar ideas and sentiments in the human mind. In these, everywhere, human nature comes into existence. Man does not have it at birth; he cannot acquire it except through fellowship, and it decays in isolation.

If this view does not recommend itself to common-sense I do not know that elaboration will be of much avail. It simply means the application at this point of the idea that society and individuals are inseparable phases of a common whole, so that wherever we find an individual fact we may look for a social fact to go with it. If there is a universal nature in persons there must be something universal in association to correspond to it.

What else can human nature be than a trait of primary groups? Surely not an attribute of the separate individual—supposing there were any such thing—since its typical characteristics, such as affection, ambition, vanity, and resentment, are inconceivable apart from society. If it belongs, then, to man in association, what kind or degree of association is required to develop it? Evidently nothing elaborate, because elaborate phases of society are transient and diverse, while human nature is comparatively stable and universal. In short the family and neighborhood life is essential to its genesis and nothing more is.

Here as everywhere in the study of society we must learn to see mankind in psychical wholes, rather than in artificial separation. We must see and feel the communal life of family and local groups as immediate facts, not as combinations of something else. And perhaps we shall do this best by recalling our own experience and extending it through sympathetic observation. What, in our life, is the family and the fellowship; what do we know of the we-feeling? Thought of this kind may help us to get a concrete perception of that primary group-nature of which everything social is the outgrowth.

30. CONTRASTING TYPES OF
GROUP RELATIONSHIPS *

JOHN B. HOLLAND

Sociologists have introduced a number of terms to characterize "types" of social relationships. The primary-group concept described in the previous selection, the contrasting secondary-group concept developed later, and the Gemeinschaft *and* Gesellschaft *concepts developed by Ferdinand Tönnies are probably most widely used to identify differing patterns of social interaction. In the following selection John Holland defines "Gemeinschaft" and "Gesellschaft" and illustrates their usefulness in social analysis.*

The individual lives in a world made up of many groups of people. While we think of ourselves as individuals, separate and distinct from all other individuals, we do not, nor can we live without others. We

* From *Source Book for Effective Living*, 196–199, reprinted by permission of the Michigan State University Press.

The author (1910–1953) was Associate Professor in the Department of Sociology and Anthropology and the Social Science Department at Michigan State University. Coauthor of *Community Involvement* and articles on the nature of attitudes.

are not only individuals, we are at the same time group members. We participate in many kinds of social groups. More than that we find ourselves at times, both as individuals and as group members, in conflict with other groups. And in a complex modern world we find ourselves affected by still other groups about whom we may be unaware.

The nature of these many associations that we as individuals have with other people is complex, varied, and often difficult to determine. Some progress may be made toward clarifying these relations, however, if we will distinguish between two quite different kinds of human relations. We shall use the classification of Tönnies, a German sociologist, and explore the meaning of the terms Gemeinschaft and Gesellschaft.

Before doing so it is necessary to be critical of any attempt to classify all human relations into only two general categories. Further, rather than thinking of Gemeinschaft and Gesellschaft as two separate and distinct kinds of human relations, it would seem more nearly correct to think of them as occupying the extreme ends of a straight line.

The extreme ends of such a scale represent pure types or polar extremes. Our own concrete and real experiences with other people usually fall somewhere along this scale rather than at one end or the other. Our relations with others are generally in terms of more or less rather than all or none, for usually these relations involve both Gemeinschaft and Gesellschaft. Nevertheless, by clearly defining the polar extremes we may classify many of our relations as an individual in the group, for generally one or the other kind of relationship is predominant. The scale furnishes us with a convenient device to measure many of the kinds of associations we have as group members, though we need not assume that all human relations can be made to fit into one or the other of these categories.

This way of classifying our relations with others is not new. The ideas we are to explore here have been most explicitly developed by Tönnies, but they are really a refinement of the thinking of many others who have gone before. Confucius and Plato, Aristotle and Cicero, St. Augustine and Thomas Aquinas, to mention only a few, have attempted to understand and account for the different kinds of human relationships which they observed. Their classifications are similar to that of Tönnies. This way of looking at people, therefore, is not new, it has been useful to many of the great thinkers of the ages, and it is useful to us because it gives us a new pair of glasses with which we may look at facts which are familiar to all of us.

GESELLSCHAFT RELATIONS

First, let us define Gesellschaft, not because it comes first, but because it is the easiest to explain. A brief definition may be given as "Rational relations based on calculation of individual self-interest." Like all brief statements there are many points covered in that definition. What are some of them?

. . . . .

First of all, our Gesellschaft relations with others are based upon reason and not feeling. Second, we are concerned with our individual self-interest. Third, our obligations are limited to whatever specific contract is stated or implied. Fourth, our relationship with others covers only a specific and clearly-defined area of interest. Fifth, it is not necessary, in fact it is entirely irrelevant whether or not we have any interests in common other than these specific, individual interests which we hope to further by our relationship.

In terms of concrete, flesh and blood people what does this mean? What kind of relations do we have with other people which serve our immediate interests and are largely Gesellschaft in character?

Take an inventory of your daily activities. Whom do you see and what do you do when you are with other people? When you buy a loaf of bread is it primarily an intimate and friendly exchange, or is it a contract between buyer and seller? If you get a check from Veterans Administration do you have a warm personal feeling for the man who signed the check, or do you look to see if it is made out correctly and delivered on time? If you have a part-time job, do you usually prop your feet upon the boss's desk for an hour of friendly conversation, or do you have specific, well-defined duties which you are expected to perform? When you registered at this college, although the cashier may have been very friendly, was this principally Gesellschaft or otherwise? The illustrations could be multiplied indefinitely in terms of your own experiences, but these serve to point out the fact that you and I, living as we do in a complex society, spend a great deal of time busily engaged with the pursuit of our own self-interests. And we have many contacts with other human beings who are likewise concerned with their own interests. In this pursuit of self-interest people have little reality for us as human beings, as personalities who think, feel, and act, and have personal problems even as we. Because so many of our relations with others are largely Gesellschaft in character it is not surprising that we sometimes fail to recognize the reality of groups and the effect on us and our personalities of our many associations with others.

GEMEINSCHAFT RELATIONS

Just as Gesellschaft is a polar type which characterizes one kind of human relations, so Gemeinschaft is the other. Broadly stated Gemeinschaft is everything that Gesselschaft is not. Gemeinschaft comes logically first in human relations.

Gemeinschaft is easier to define but harder to explain. A brief definition is: "Intimate relations based on sentiment." That is, Gemeinschaft relations are based on the way we feel about people. They are intimate relations. In such contacts with others people are real. Our concern is not with rational calculations and limited obligations but with flesh and blood people and our felt obligations to them.

We may make further contrasts. Whereas in Gesellschaft we enter into a relationship because of rational consideration of individual self-interest, in Gemeinschaft our motives are general and indefinite in character. This is so because they are not carefully calculated but are a part of our feelings. Gemeinschaft relations cover a multitude of interests not well defined at all. For example, if you are married why did you marry? There are many answers, not one or two single, specific reasons. You married for love, to have a home, to raise children, to obtain what we may call psychic security—that is, emotional security and approval. If I ask you why you entered the college bookstore you can tell me exactly. But if I ask you why you married this particular person, why you like certain friends, why you have a friendly feeling for the old home town, it is difficult to explain. This is natural since sentiments and feelings, being nonrational, are hard to explain by rational means. Frequently, however, we feel called upon to justify our feelings and in so doing we depend upon rationalizations which we offer as "good reasons" to explain our behavior.

A second contrast with Gesellschaft relations is that in Gemeinschaft obligations are unspecified and unlimited. There is no specific contract. The burden of proof is on him who would evade an obligation arising out of a Gemeinschaft relation. Let us examine the obligations in marriage. In a general sense a marriage between two people involves a ceremony in which certain obligations are stated. But these are blanket obligations which in the final analysis mean an obligation on each of the marriage partners to help in whatever contingencies arise in their common life together. A married veteran is going to school. There is nothing in the marriage contract which says that his wife will take a full or part-time job to help him in that process. And yet many veterans' wives are doing just that. If a friend of yours is down and out and needs ten dollars there is no written obligation on your part to meet his need. But if you've got the money and if he is a real friend of yours, one for whom you have an intimate and deep-seated liking, you loan him the money, even though you do not expect to get it back.

A third point that may be made about Gemeinschaft relations is that not only are obligations unlimited but they can be ignored only because of the prior obligations of another Gemeinschaft relationship. To illustrate, if you are a doctor you would not, as a husband, ordinarily leave your wife's bridge party. But if it were necessary for you to make an emergency call you would do so. Or again if you were about to meet with a friend who was in a tough spot and needed you to help him regain his bearings, you would cancel the engagement if your child were to be injured or suddenly taken ill. But it should be noted that you are relieved of one Gemeinschaft obligation only because another and higher Gemeinschaft obligation supersedes. You do not customarily ignore Gemeinschaft obligations for Gesellschaft obligations, or if you do we may safely say that there was no deep Gemeinschaft feeling on your part in the first place.

Finally, Gemeinschaft obligations are both moral and ethical in character. I mean by that that individuals in a Gemeinschaft relationship have individual interests but these interests are integrated and a part of the ultimate values of the group. It is safe to say that as a member of a family, insofar as you have intimate feelings for that family, you share in common certain beliefs and ideals. There are certain moral responsibilities that you feel and these moral responsibilities are a part of your individual codes of ethics, your standards, your values. Gemeinschaft relations are shared relations. They extend beyond individual self-interest. In Gemeinschaft relations your individual purposes and ends are integrated and a part of the purposes and ends of the group.

These are the principal characteristics of Gemeinschaft. Relations are intimate and based on feelings or sentiment, not upon reason or calculation. In Gemeinschaft there is what we might call a bond or feeling of belonging. Thus we speak of the bond that unites man and wife or friends or a group of neighbors who are intimately acquainted with each other.

We can illustrate Gemeinschaft concretely for ourselves again in terms of the groups of people with whom we associate in a day. Whom did you see today? How intimately are you concerned with their welfare? Not abstract persons, but real people about whose welfare you are genuinely and personally concerned? What bonds do you have with others and what would it take to break them?

In summary, then, Gemeinschaft relations are intimate relations based on sentiment; Gesellschaft relations are rational relations based on calculation of individual interest. These two types of relations are polar extremes and our actual relations with others vary from extreme, intimate, personal relations with others to extreme, rational calculation of people as means to serve our own immediate ends. It is useful to make this classification because it enables us to analyze more clearly our relations with others and to see in proper perspective our actions as they affect and are affected by others. But even beyond that we need to appraise what is involved in gaining and losing Gemeinschaft relations because we live in a world which is based increasingly upon Gesellschaft. How well each of us personally can survive by rational concern with limited and specific interests alone is a problem which confronts us both as individuals and as group members.

31. INTERPERSONAL RELATIONS
IN A BUREAUCRACY *

RALPH H. TURNER

To the uninitiated a bureaucracy, with its many rules of operation and its highly organized and formalized structure, might not seem subject to personal influences. Actually this impersonality seldom exists, as Ralph H. Turner here shows. The bureaucrat's personal relations with his superiors, subordinates, and equals in the hierarchy constantly affect the operation of bureaucracy. Although Turner has described this process in terms of the Navy disbursing officer, every bureaucratic structure produces strikingly similar sociological phenomena.

Every administrative structure exists in order to achieve certain goals, which goals normally originate outside the structure and are imposed on it from the top. A bureaucratic administrative system is supposed to function as a nearly impersonal machine, individual discretion entering only when alternate procedures are compatible with the system. The ordinary official is expected to apply procedures with blind precision, irrespective of the degree to which they achieve or subvert the general goals.

Needless to say, actual administration often fails to adhere closely to the goals of the organization. Reasons for the divergence may be inadequacies of the procedural pattern and conflicting procedures, conflicting goals within the organization, inadequacies of the bureaucrats

* "The Navy Disbursing Officer as a Bureaucrat," *American Sociological Review*, Vol. 12, No. 3 (June, 1947), 342–348. Reprinted by permission of the publisher and the author.

The author (b. 1919) is Professor of Sociology and Social Psychology, University of California at Los Angeles. His interests include stratification, role theory, and race relations. Author of "The Relative Position of the Negro Male in the Labor Force of Large American Cities" and other articles in professional journals.

themselves, and, most important, the position of each functionary as not only a square on the organization chart but also as a focus of pressures applied by a number of informal structures not envisaged in the formal pattern.

The purpose of this paper is to describe a few of the sociologically relevant influences which bear on a certain type of bureaucratic official, namely, the Navy disbursing officer. Bureaucracy is conceived as defined by Max Weber. Though certain types of influence are more clearly displayed in the position of the disbursing officer, most of what is said will also apply to any Supply Corps officer and, to a lesser degree, to all naval officers. The findings are the result of participant observation by the writer, both as a disbursing officer during the war and as an observer of other officers in a similar position.

From the standpoint of the present analysis there are three characteristics which distinguish the disbursing officer in degree from the remainder of the naval organization. First, disbursing officers handle matters of immediate personal importance to their clients. Navigation, gunnery, etc., may be more vital to the lives of the men, but their problems are vague to those not directly concerned. An error in a pay account or a delay in pay day is more quickly recognized and more loudly protested by the rank and file than deficiencies in most other departments aboard ship. Consequently the disbursing officer and his staff are under constant bombardment for favors and incessant criticism for their mistakes—real or imagined—or failures to grant favors.

Second, the disbursing officer is a bureaucrat serving a larger bureaucracy of which he is an integral part. Robert Merton has noted the important fact that a government servant is usually superordinate to his clients, not in any formal sense, but because the client has no direct authority over him and no effective access to anyone of superior authority. Superordination and subordination are clearly defined in the Navy by the label which each man carries on his uniform. Though most of the disbursing officer's clients are enlisted men and hence subordinate, a good many will be officers of senior rank who are thereby empowered to reward or punish him in various ways. Thus in adhering to the formal patterns relating to disbursing the officer must often act counter to the larger formal pattern by defying a senior officer.

Finally, the disbursing officer, unlike most other bureaucrats, is personally accountable and financially liable for any deviation from regulations in the expenditure of government funds in spite of any contrary order from a superior officer.

Three characteristics of the social structure in which the disbursing officer finds himself which make it difficult for him to behave as the ideal bureaucrat will be discussed. First is the frequent conflict between regulations (as interpreted by the disbursing officer) and orders from superiors, both of which are supposed to be obeyed. Second is the subordination of the disbursing officer through rank to many of his clients. Third is the network of informal structures, which exert particular pressure on the disbursing officer because of the crucial services which he dispenses. The facilitating conditions for the operation of these influences include the following: the disbursing officer's incomplete command of voluminous and rapidly changing regulations; the ambiguousness or incompleteness of regulations with respect to many situations; acceptance of properly signed vouchers as proof of fact by the General Accounting Office in auditing disbursing accounts, so that certain documents can be falsified with impunity; those personality traits of the officer which resist strictly impersonal behavior.

Within the formal structure the distinctive problem of the disbursing officer is that of reconciling orders from superiors with regulations when they seem to conflict. Orders may be issued by senior officers in the supply department (of which disbursing is a part) or by the commanding and executive officers of the activity. Conflicts with superior officers in the supply department are usually reconciled fairly smoothly because the supply officer understands the problem of disbursing accountability, often from earlier experience as a disbursing officer, and because of fairly close relationships between them. Conflicts stemming from orders by the commanding and executive officers, who have little knowledge of and little patience with disbursing regulations, and who are generally not accustomed to being asked by a subordinate to discuss the advisability of an order they have issued, present a ticklish problem. If the order seems to be at all important to the officer in question, the senior supply officer can usually be expected to add his pressure, through threats and suggested devices for "getting around" the law. The subsequent careers of disbursing and supply officers can be materially affected by notations which the commanding officer may enter in "fitness reports" submitted periodically to the Bureau of Naval Personnel.

The conflict between regulations (as interpreted) and orders from superiors is not limited to the disbursing function or even to military organizations. The conflict is incipient in every bureaucratic structure because the rational type of authority, as Weber has indicated, involves recognition both of rules and the right of officials to issue orders. Though the hierarchy of officials exists only to administer the rules, which in turn express the purposes of the organization, it is patent that official behavior and commands may often counter the rules. In the small informal organization of a business hiring only a handful of employees, rules may be largely unformulated and procedures passed verbally down the hierarchy as required, thereby eliminating the conflict by making orders supreme. Or the opposite extreme in which authority is expressed solely through a code of rules, each functionary being left to apply the rules without supervision, might be imagined but hardly realized in an actual situation. Because of the inadequacy of either rules or hierarchical authority alone to serve the purposes of bureaucratic administration, both must be present. Thus the ideal type, bureaucracy, is itself a compromise between two ideal extremes, utilizing and compromising two channels of authority which may be in conflict.

Bureaucracies differ, however, in the degree to which they emphasize chain of command or rules. Business organizations tend to vest greater authority in the chain of command, minimizing numbers of rules and winking at violations if the official achieves results. "Cutting through red tape," is the popular phrase for de-emphasizing rules. Government bureaucracies stress rules more strongly because of their different aims and because of fear of abuse of authority by officials, and through civil service regulations functionaries are given more authority to defy superiors in the application and interpretation of rules. Many a former business executive serving as a naval officer in charge of civilian employees in navy yards has been startled to find his orders called into question by subordinates, and to find himself powerless to enforce his orders. As businesses get larger the emphasis on rules to insure uniform practice reduces the contrast with government bureaucracy. Custodians of funds in business or government are more tighly bound by rules and less subject to arbitrary orders from superiors.

In the Navy, and probably in other bureaucratic structures, the intensity of the conflict varies with different levels in the hierarchy. For the lower ranks of enlisted men the conflict hardly exists because they are explicitly denied the right to make decisions on their own. At the higher levels the official is confronted with fewer and broader orders so that in the top ranks the conflict arises less frequently. Thus the conflict between orders and regulations is most acute at the intermediate levels, from ensign to lieutenant in particular.

In business and in most naval positions, this conflict is resolved in favor of the order, the functionary not being held responsible for violating a rule in compliance with an order from a superior official. As indicated previously, the personal accountability of the disbursing officer denies this way out. Consequently, the Navy, recognizing the possibility of conflict, has provided two procedures for its resolution. The disbursing officer is to point out the apparent discrepancy to the superior and, if no understanding is reached, an inquiry may be sent to the Bureau of Supplies and Accounts. Or, the matter may be referred to the commanding officer who may order the disbursing officer to make the expenditure "under protest," the commanding officer thereby assuming full financial liability. The former procedure was used often during the war for minor issues, but senior officers are often unwilling to wait several months for answers and a disbursing officer who frequently resorts to this tactic is soon in poor standing. A disbursing officer considering the second method invariably pictures himself being transferred to "amphibs" and suffering various awful fates at the hands of a wrathful commanding officer, so the method is seldom employed. However, the occasional disbursing officer who has courage enough to threaten its use usually finds the commanding officer unwilling to assume the personal risk involved in defying him.

The very training given the disbursing officer in the supply corps school teaches him that the above methods are not approved ways of handling such difficulties. The young officer is taught that he must be a "Can do paymaster," in contradistinction to the type of officer who is always ready to cite the paragraph in the *Manual* which prevents any particular action being taken. The "Can do" officer can almost always find a way to do anything he is ordered to do. This emphasis, of course, partly reflects a general de-emphasis of rules fostered by the war. But it further reinforces the tendency for the disbursing officer to find "informal" ways of dealing with matters and to deviate from the ideal pattern of a bureaucrat.

The second obstacle to impersonal functioning by the disbursing officer is the system of rank. As indicated by Weber, military officers are marked off by class distinction. And Talcott Parsons has observed that, "there is no legitimate order without a charismatic element." It is the union of class distinctions with a strong element of "charisma of office" which gives the rank structure its peculiar and powerful nature. Senior officers are expected to be treated with deference irrespective of their actions. Because of "class" levels, senior officers are usually able to punish or reward a lesser officer indirectly. However, through their charisma officers are generally held in far greater awe than their actual powers or inclinations warrant, and a lesser officer is often afraid even to suggest to a superior that his request is not in keeping with regulations. One of the problems of military organization lies in the rather widespread fear of superiors which creates extra labor and ill-feeling on the part of men who feel that they must find some way to conform to an erroneous or careless order. Rank has been too widely discussed to need further elaboration here except to note that the disbursing officer, who is at once both a functionary with specified duties and a position in a system of levels, sometimes finds that he cannot act without violating one of these roles.

A third obstacle to bureaucratic impartiality is the system of informal social groupings. Philip Selznick's three characteristics of the informal structure as found in business and labor union bureaucracies, namely, spontaneity, network of personal relations, and orientation toward control, apply equally to naval situations.

These informal structures are of three sorts. Relatively enduring *friendship patterns* weigh heavily where the disbursing officer belongs to the same primary associations as do many of his clients. Particularly aboard ship where a relatively small number of officers live, eat and play poker together in a small space is this true. "Say, 'Pay,' I sure could use about twenty dollars before payday," or, "Isn't there some way I can get flight pay this month?" is the sort of appeal which comes constantly from friends. As a human being the disbursing officer wants to help his friends, and the penalty for brusque disposal of such requests is social ostracism.

A second type of *simulated friendship* or, in Navy jargon, "earbanging" relationships includes less enduring and more uncertain influences. Nevertheless, these are in many cases sufficiently persistent and organized relations among persons to justify the term "structure." They take a multitude of well-known forms: an officer treats one of lesser rank as an equal, he compliments the disbursing officer on the good reputation of his office, he jokes and attempts to appear as an old friend. The aim is always, first, to be defined as a person rather than an applicant in the disbursing officer's eyes, and second, to be defined favorably.

The third and most extensive sort of informal structure is that which may be called an *exchange system*. The officer who assigns staterooms aboard ship finds it easy to get extra food from the galley. The ship's photographer who makes some personal pictures of the supply officer gets first choice when the next shipment of fountain pens reaches "ship's store." Such exchanges are not usually verbalized as such among officers, but the officer who does another a favor has no doubt that there will be a return. However, there also exist extensive and well-verbalized systems for distribution of favors and certain types of supplies, especially at shore stations. The exchange structures extend so far that it is often difficult for a man to secure those services and equipment which are essential to his job unless he can promise some return. Aboard a large ship one attempt was made in the ship's store to sell the limited stock of watches and cigarette lighters on the basis of impartial drawings. Complaints were so many and vigorous from persons who claimed they had been promised a watch or were owed one that thereafter the "spoils" system was used, with much less complaint. Even some enlisted men in key positions, such as the mail clerk and carpenter's mates, are able to exercise influence over officers because of the services at their disposal. Needless to remark, any resort to strictly formal procedure impairs the disbursing officer's potentially exceptionally good position in the system of mutual benefits. Denunciations of these exchange structures are periodically issued by some commands, but such pronouncements are read by only a few and are seldom implemented by more than one or two courts-martial for petty thievery. Furthermore, commanding officers are frequently among the beneficiaries of such systems.

To the participants these exchange systems are widely different from bribery. Bribery is impersonal and is recognized as contrary to law and morals. Favor exchange systems are eminently personal. As long as the system functions smoothly it is just one man doing a favor for a "buddy," and only when a return favor is not forthcoming will the idea of exchange be stressed. And secondly, the exchange system incorporates its own code of behavior. The individual who puts legal technicality ahead of reciprocity is reprehensible, is spoken of with almost moral indignation. The system is not "wrong" or "crooked"; it is a moral system of its own and anyone who puts legality first is a hypocrite. However, there is an ambivalence of attitude toward the system. The official who follows it deliberately and impersonally in order to acquire too great a quantity of goods is disliked, though with a mixture of envy. The system is supposed to operate in leisurely fashion, maintaining the appearance that the goods acquired are secondary to the friendships involved.

The three sorts of systems described operate not only to grant favors to some but to withhold fair consideration from others. Since disbursing officers generally are stereotyped as acting slowly, being tied up in red tape and giving unsatisfactory assistance, prompt careful attention to the business of a client is often defined as a favor. Persons not favorably placed in the informal structures may be deprived of pay because of inadequate attention to their accounts or may suffer undue delay in the handling of their business.

The influence of these systems is felt not only directly by the disbursing officer but also through the enlisted men in his office. Because of their lack of official status, enlisted men develop especially elaborate and powerful informal structures. A new disbursing officer, in the interest of fairness, stopped the dispensing of favors by his enlisted men. A serious morale problem ensued because the disbursing office personnel, no longer able to contribute services, were simply dropped from the status-producing structures, or, as they complained, they had lost their "drag."

Under the combined impact of the informal structures and his formal office, what solutions does the disbursing officer reach? Four types of disbursing officer will be suggested on the basis of their divergent resolutions of the conflicting forces at work. These will be ideal constructs, but have sufficient empirical validity that any disbursing officer should be able to recognize them as applying to other officers he has known and also to tendencies within himself.

The *Regulation* type approximates the true bureaucrat in that he remains impervious to rank, informal structures, and orders of his superiors, but goes further in employing the narrowest possible interpretation of every regulation. For fear of the General Accounting Office his rule is, "When in doubt, don't." He is the stereotyped disbursing officer and the stereotyped bureaucrat. This type is not in a majority during wartime, and consists chiefly of "green" officers who have not yet felt the full pressure of the contrary influences or have not yet learned how easily regulations may be manipulated, and of "mustangs," former enlisted men who have secured commissions.

Opposite is the type who doubts the potency of the General Accounting Office and feels that, "They can't hold me," if money is expended loosely. He will do anything for a friend or superior without debate. This type is limited to a very few reserve officers who seldom last very long, though many officers have sought escape from the anxieties of their position in the assurance that after the war Congress will pass a "relieving act."

On a different axis, and also fairly infrequent, is the *Sincere* type. He fails to recognize conflicts between regulations and orders from superiors and is unaware of the importance of the informal systems. Apparent conflicts he attributes to his own incomplete understanding of regulations, and rules are seen less as controls than as tools for the execution of orders. He is 100 per cent "sold" on the Navy, is well liked by his superiors and will be assigned positions of favor and responsibility so long as he is a junior officer. His naivete places him in less favor when he reaches higher levels.

The commonest type is the *Realist*. Regulations are seen as illogical concatenations of procedures, restrictions and interpretations, frequently ambiguous, sometimes contradictory, and often, when strictly applied, defeating the purpose for which they were constructed. Rules specify chiefly the papers which must be filed in support of expenditures, and these may be correct without the payment being correct. The most successful career men of the supply corps include many of this type. They assume the regulation façade when the client is not fortunately placed in the informal or rank structure, but know how any payment may be made "legally" if the request comes from an important enough source.

Many conscientious officials join this type when they come to recognize that strict interpretation of rules often works injustice in terms of the rules' obvious intent and that efforts at strict enforcement are frequently nullified because other people know how to prepare papers in "correct form." Such an official begins by helping a client whose claim is payable within the intent of the law but is invalidated by a technicality to give the "right" information to insure payment. Differential treatment of clients on this basis is hard to maintain, so the officer soon finds himself giving such aid without reference to justification, or more frequently, under varying pressures and moods, wavering between a regulation attitude and an opportunistic attitude.

Two general tendencies emerge among disbursing officers as the consequence of orders conflicting with regulations and the pressures of rank and informal structure. One is differential treatment of clientele. Because of the time consumed in extra-routine treatment of persons on the "in," others get summary treatment. The second tendency is for loopholes in regulations to become tools in the hand of the disbursing officer to elevate his own status. Thus he may become more concerned with his own bargaining power than with correct application of rules.

In sum, what has been shown is that during this last war powerful influences were at work on the Navy disbursing officer, diverting him from functioning as an ideal-typical bureaucrat. These influences move him, not in the direction of ultra-formalism so frequently observed for bureaucrats in other contexts, but toward personal functioning within systems of power and status in which rules become of secondary importance.

32. THE SOCIAL "WORLD" OF THE TRANSIENTS' CAMP *

JOHN STEINBECK

The talented writer of fiction sometimes presents social reality in a clear and vivid fashion, and more interestingly than the prosaic social scientist. The Grapes of Wrath, *Steinbeck's classic novel of the migrant farm family, "tractored out" of Oklahoma and hopeful of a better life in California, contains many such insights into social reality. The selection from that book given here shows how quickly human relationships develop regularities, become "organized," even in so transitory a situation as the overnight camp of the westward-moving migrant farm families.*

* From *The Grapes of Wrath* by John Steinbeck, pp. 264–269. Copyright 1939 by John Steinbeck. Reprinted by permission of The Viking Press, Inc.

The author (b. 1902) is a Pulitzer-Prize-winning American novelist. His well-known works include: *Tortilla Flat; Of Mice and Men; The Moon Is Down; East of Eden.*

The cars of the migrant people crawled out of the side roads onto the great cross-country highway, and they took the migrant way to the West. In the daylight they scuttled like bugs to the westward; and as the dark caught them, they clustered like bugs near to shelter and to water. And because they were lonely and perplexed, because they had all come from a place of sadness and worry and defeat, and because they were all going to a new mysterious place, they huddled together; they talked together; they shared their lives, their food, and the things they hoped for in the new country. Thus it might be that one family camped near a spring, and another camped for the spring and for company, and a third because two families had pioneered the place and found it good. And when the sun went down, perhaps twenty families and twenty cars were there.

In the evening a strange thing happened: the twenty families became one family, the children were the children of all. The loss of home became one loss, and the golden time in the West was one dream. And it might be that a sick child threw despair into the hearts of twenty families, of a hundred people; that a birth there in a tent kept a hundred people quiet and awestruck through the night and filled a hundred people with the birth-joy in the morning. A family which the night before had been lost and fearful might search its goods to find a present for a new baby. In the evening, sitting about the fires, the twenty were one. They grew to be units of the camps, units of the evenings and the nights. A guitar unwrapped from a blanket and tuned—and the songs, which were all of the people, were sung in the nights. Men sang the words, and women hummed the tunes.

Every night a world created, complete with furniture—friends made and enemies established; a world complete with braggarts and with cowards, with quiet men, with humble men, with kindly men. Every night relationships that make a world, established; and every morning the world torn down like a circus.

At first the families were timid in the building and tumbling worlds, but gradually the technique of building worlds became their technique. Then leaders emerged, then laws were made, then codes came into being. And as the worlds moved westward they were more complete and better furnished, for their builders were more experienced in building them.

The families learned what rights must be observed—the right of privacy in the tent; the right to keep the past black hidden in the heart; the right to talk and to listen; the right to refuse help or to accept, to offer help or to decline it; the right of son to court and daughter to be courted; the right of the hungry to be fed; the rights of the pregnant and the sick to transcend all other rights.

And the families learned, although no one told them, what rights are monstrous and must be destroyed: the right to intrude upon privacy, the right to be noisy while the camp slept, the right of seduction or rape, the right of adultery and theft and murder. These rights were crushed, because the little worlds could not exist for even a night with such rights alive.

And as the worlds moved westward, rules became laws, although no one told the families. It is unlawful to foul near the camp; it is unlawful in any way to foul the drinking water; it is unlawful to eat good rich food near one who is hungry, unless he is asked to share.

And with the laws, the punishments—and there were only two—a quick and murderous fight or ostracism; and ostracism was the worst. For if one broke the laws his name and face went with him, and he had no place in any world, no matter where created.

In the worlds, social conduct became fixed and rigid, so that a man must say "Good morning" when asked for it, so that a man might have a willing girl if he stayed with her, if he fathered her children and protected them. But a man might not have one girl one night and another the next, for this would endanger the worlds.

The families moved westward, and the technique of building the worlds improved so that the people could be safe in their worlds; and the form was so fixed that a family acting in the rules knew it was safe in the rules.

There grew up government in the worlds, with leaders, with elders. A man who was wise found that his wisdom was needed in every camp; a man who was a fool could not change his folly with his world. And a kind of insurance developed in these nights. A man with food fed a hungry man, and thus insured himself against hunger. And when a baby died a pile of silver coins grew at the door flap, for a baby must be well buried, since it has had nothing else of life. An old man may be left in a potter's field, but not a baby.

A certain physical pattern is needed for the building of a world— water, a river bank, a stream, a spring, or even a faucet unguarded. And there is needed enough flat land to pitch the tents, a little brush or wood to build the fires. If there is a garbage dump not too far off, all the better; for there can be found equipment—stove tops, a curved fender to shelter the fire, and cans to cook in and to eat from.

And the worlds were built in the evening. The people, moving in from the highways, made them with their tents and their hearts and their brains.

In the morning the tents came down, the canvas was folded, the tent poles tied along the running board, the beds put in place on the cars, the pots in their places. And as the families moved westward, the technique of building up a home in the evening and tearing it down with the morning light became fixed; so that the folded tent was packed in one place, the cooking pots counted in their box. And as the cars moved westward, each member of the family grew into his proper place, grew into his duties; so that each member, old and young, had his place in the car; so that in the weary, hot evenings, when the cars pulled into the camping places, each member had his duty and went to it without instruction: children to gather wood, to carry water; men to pitch the tents and bring down the beds; women to cook the supper and to watch while the family fed. And this was done without command. The families, which had been units of which the boundaries were a house at night, a farm by day, changed their boundaries. In the long hot light, they were silent in the cars moving slowly westward; but at night they integrated with any group they found.

Thus they changed their social life—changed as in the whole universe only man can change. They were not farm men any more, but migrant men. And the thought, the planning, the long staring silence that had gone out to the fields, went now to the roads, to the distance, to the West. That man whose mind had been bound with acres lived with narrow concrete miles. And his thought and his worry were not any more with rainfall, with wind and dust, with the thrust of the crops. Eyes watched the tires, ears listened to the clattering motors, and minds struggled with oil, with gasoline, with the thinning rubber between air and road. Then a broken gear was tragedy. Then water in the evening was the yearning, and food over the fire. Then health to go on was the need and strength to go on, and spirit to go on. The wills thrust westward ahead of them, and fears that had once apprehended drought or flood now lingered with anything that might stop the westward crawling.

The camps became fixed—each a short day's journey from the last.

And on the road the panic overcame some of the families, so that they drove night and day, stopped to sleep in the cars, and drove on to the West, flying from the road, flying from movement. And these lusted so greatly to be settled that they set their faces into the West and drove toward it, forcing the clashing engines over the roads.

But most of the families changed and grew quickly into the new life. And when the sun went down——

Time to look out for a place to stop.

And—there's some tents ahead.

The car pulled off the road and stopped, and because others were there first, certain courtesies were necessary. And the man, the leader of the family, leaned from the car.

Can we pull up here an' sleep?

Why, sure, be proud to have you. What State you from?

Come all the way from Arkansas.

They's Arkansas people down that fourth tent.

That *so?*

And the great question, How's the water?

Well, she don't taste so good, but they's plenty.

Well, thank ya.

No thanks to me.

But the courtesies had to be. The car lumbered over the ground to the end tent, and stopped. Then down from the car the weary people climbed, and stretched stiff bodies. Then the new tent sprang up; the children went for water and the older boys cut brush or wood. The fires started and supper was put on to boil or to fry. Early comers moved over, and States were exchanged, and friends and sometimes relatives discovered.

Oklahoma, huh? What county?

Cherokee.

Why, I got folks there. Know the Allens? They's Allens all over Cherokee. Know the Willises?

Why, sure.

And a new unit was formed. The dusk came, but before the dark was down the new family was of the camp. A word had been passed with every family. They were known people—good people.

33. GROUPS AND CIVILIZATION *

GEORGE C. HOMANS

*The preceding readings in this chapter emphasize the roles
of primary and secondary groups in the socialization process
and in community life. In this article Homans examines an
even wider horizon: the relation of the small human group to a
whole civilization. He maintains that the problems of interpersonal
relations are always dealt with successfully at the level of small,
informal groups. The basic question facing us all, he says, is
this: How can these relationships be equally well handled
at the level of large, complex, centralized societies, such as our
own, and finally of world civilization itself?*

* From *The Human Group* by George C. Homans, pp. 454–468, copyright, 1950, by Harcourt, Brace and Company, Inc.

The author (b. 1910) is Professor of Sociology at Harvard University. Sometime Visiting Professor of social theory at Cambridge University, England. His major interests include industrial relations and sociological theory. In addition to *The Human Group* his writings include: *An Introduction to Pareto; English Villagers of the Thirteenth Century;* and numerous articles in professional journals.

THE GROUP AND SOCIAL COHESION

At the level of the tribe, the village, the small group, at the level, that is, of a social unit (no matter what name we call it by) each of whose members can have some firsthand knowledge of each of the others, human society, for many millenia longer than written history, has been able to cohere. To be sure, the cohesion has been achieved at a price. Intelligent men have always found small-town life dull, and the internal solidarity of the group has implied a distrust and hatred of outsiders. But society has at least been able to cohere. This is not to deny that groups have succumbed to the severity of the environment and the violence of enemies, but they have had at the same time few problems of internal social organization. They have even tended, as we have seen, to produce a surplus of the goods that make organization successful: morale, leadership, and co-operation between increasingly large numbers of people.

THE BIRTH OF CIVILIZATION

Throughout human history, groups have used this surplus in the attempt to grow. For most of them, the environment, physical and social, has put an end to the process before it went very far. A few have been more successful. Given an environment neither too severe nor too luxurious, groups have grown and multiplied, and social units larger than the group have begun to appear. The challenge of the environment, to use Toynbee's phrase, posed an internal challenge: If large-scale co-operation could be achieved, it would pay for itself in an increased control over a bountiful nature. In the beginning, the challenge was met most successfully in broad river valleys. There the surplus of co-operativeness, applied to clearing, draining, damming, and irrigating, brought enormous returns and encouraged further co-operation. Finally, one of the groups, much like the others but possessing some of their qualities in a higher degree, consolidated the gains, and a civilization was born. Again and again this has happened. Now a little Chinese principality at the Great Bend of the Yellow River acts as the catalyst, now a city-state in central Italy, and now a tribe, called the Franks, settled on the south shore of the English Channel. The tribes have multiplied; one, more tribal than the rest, has brought the others together.

In our view, and here we are following Toynbee again, ancient Egypt and Mesopotamia were civilizations. So were classical India and China; so was the Greco-Roman civilization, and so is our own Western civilization that grew out of medieval Christendom. These societies on the grand scale have had many characteristics in common. At its height, each has been inventive: it has devised and used a more powerful technology than any at the command of the tribes coming before and after it. Each has been coterminous geographically with a communications network. In fact the existence of such a network has been the necessary precondition allowing one tribe to unite the others. Thus the Mediterranean Sea, with its satellite roads, made possible the Roman Empire. Since the organization of a tribe is incapable of controlling an empire, each civilization has also developed new formal organizations, in law, government, warfare, and religion, linking the tribes to the new center. And almost every one of the civilizations has worked out and adopted a single body of values and beliefs, shared in some degree by all the citizens. Such until recently was Christianity for the Western world.

DECLINE AND FALL

The appalling fact is that, after flourishing for a span of time, every civilization but one has collapsed. The ruling class, if there was one, has lost its capacity to lead; the formal organizations that articulated the whole have fallen to pieces; the faith has no longer commanded the allegiance of the citizens; much of the technology has even been forgotten for lack of the large-scale co-operation that could put it in effect; and after a last and inevitably futile effort to hold society together by force, the civilization has slowly sunk back to a Dark Age, a situation, much like the one from which it started out on its upward path, in which the mutual hostility of small groups is the condition of the internal cohesion of each one. At the end of the cycle the names of the tribes are different from what they were in the beginning—the Saxons are not the Sabines—but tribal behavior is much the same. Society can fall this far, but apparently no farther, and having fallen this far, it may start all over again. In some parts of the world, the cycle of civilization and decay has been repeated at least twice. One can read the dismal story, eloquently told, in the historians of civilization from Gibbon to Toynbee. The one civilization that has not entirely gone to pieces is our own Western civilization, and we are desperately anxious about it. Can it get out of the rut into which the others have fallen?

To account for the decay, the historians have developed many explanations, each more adequate than the last, but the sociologists may still be able to contribute something. Our own theory, in its main lines, would run as follows. At the level of the tribe or group, society has always found itself able to cohere. We infer, therefore, that a civilization, if it is in turn to maintain itself, must preserve at least a few of the characteristics of the group, though necessarily on a much expanded scale. Civilizations have failed in failing to solve this problem. In fact the very process by which civilization emerges has, up to now, made failure inevitable. But let us look more closely.

THE DISSOLUTION OF THE GROUP

The development of civilization has meant technical change, economic expansion, and warfare, usually all three. All have the effect of breaking up old social units without putting anything in their place. One characteristic result was the great cities of the Roman Empire, especially those of the Near East, filled with traders, artisans, and slaves, uprooted from their former homes, whether in Egypt, Canaan, Greece, Gaul, or Spain, and huddled into slums with other people of many different traditions. Another such result is our own great cities, like Detroit and Los Angeles, where, save for some difference in physical surroundings, the same conditions hold. Our study of Hilltown is typical of the reverse of the coin: the decaying society from which the uprooted come. In the old society, man was linked to man; in the new agglomeration —it cannot be called a society—he is alone. He has not had time to be anything else.

Now all the evidence of psychiatry, and it has not been our purpose to include it here, shows that membership in a group sustains a man, enables him to maintain his equilibrium under the ordinary shocks of life, and helps him to bring up children who will in turn be happy and resilient. If his group is shattered around him, if he leaves a group in which he was a valued member, and if, above all, he finds no new group to which he can relate himself, he will, under stress, develop disorders of thought, feeling, and behavior. His thinking will be obsessive, elaborated without sufficient reference to reality; he will be anxious or angry, destructive to himself or to others; his behavior will be compulsive, not controlled; and, if the process of education that makes a man easily able to relate himself to others is itself social, he will, as a lonely man, bring up children who have a lowered social capacity. The cycle is vicious; loss of group membership in one generation may make men less capable of group membership in the next. The civilization that, by its very process of growth, shatters small group life will leave men and women lonely and unhappy.

No harm would be done if new groups appeared to take the place of the old ones, new groups with some of the characteristics of the old. And we know that in fact such groups are always forming. The seed of society is always fertile. Yet it may be that at times the new growth does not keep pace with the rot, and that there is a net increase in the number of isolated individuals, superficially attached to the bare skeleton of formal organization but lacking the old feeling of belongingness.

Each of the sociologists—Durkheim, LeBon, Figgis, Brooks Adams—who began, just before World War I, to point out the signs of decay in our society, used the same metaphor. They said that society was becoming a dust heap of individuals without links to one another.

THE NEW GROUPS

The process cannot go on unchecked indefinitely. Society does not dissolve without a struggle, but produces antibodies to check the rot. The reaction often takes a religious form. Among the uprooted of the big cities—Antioch, Alexandria, Ephesus, Rome, Detroit, Los Angeles— all sorts of religions spring up. They are seldom the religions of the tribes from which the uprooted come, and never the religion of the civilization itself. If men have not found a society satisfying, they will not find its beliefs satisfying either. Whatever spiritual unity the civilization may once have had is broken. The new religions are highly emotional: they cater to the exaggerated emotionality of the isolate. Their elaborate theology is a tribute to his obsessions. But they have something more important to offer than a release for the emotions and a subject for metaphysics. Each new religion is also a new society. Each is made up of cells or congregations, which offer to the isolate some of the feeling of full belongingness that he has lost. This was true of early Christianity, as the Acts of the Apostles and the Epistles of St. Paul bear witness. It was probably true of the mystery cults of the Roman Empire. Who shall say it is not true of the sects that fester in the social wilderness of our own cities, from Jehovah's Witnesses to Communism? Not all the cults survive. In the Roman Empire, Christianity was the only one that survived in strength, and some hope for mankind lies in the fact that Christianity set high ethical standards and addressed itself to man's spiritual, not just his physical, needs. If our civilization goes the way of the others, it may, like the Europe of the Dark Ages, be stimulated to recovery by some new synthesis of moral norms. But whatever the influence of its doctrines may have been, Christianity at least spread its network of new and tough groups, which finally set a term to the decay of the Empire, and, together with the Germanic tribes, formed the matrix out of which a new society could be carved.

In the end, the new groups provided a basis for the reconstruction of civilization, but we must notice that in the beginning they were irreconcilably hostile to the reigning order. Rome was the whore of Babylon, whose destruction St. John confidently predicted. A frustrated person, we are often told, turns to aggression. One is not loyal to a society in which one has been lonely and anxious. The decay of civilization would be much less rapid than history shows it to be if the new groups that absorb the isolated individuals did not have opposition to existing society as their very principle of organization and did not therefore, in the beginning, accelerate the decay.

In the history of Western civilization, the successor of the classical, the problem can be stated in much the same way. Erich Fromm, in his *Escape from Freedom,* says that in the last four hundred years men have been gradually set free from the restraints of traditional society. But in losing these restraints, they have also lost the sense of belonging to a group whose members co-operate in securing the deepest interests of each. If freedom is to mean no more than emotional isolation, it will not survive. Men will do any mad thing, even merge in a mass under the sword of a tyrant, to escape from a freedom of this kind. Every religion, every revolutionary movement claims it will restore the brotherhood of man, and sometimes has really done so in the form of the congregation or cell. Brotherhood, of the kind they get in a small and successful group, men must have. But at the level of civilization, the search for the lost brotherhood of man, by creating antagonisms that can only be resolved by force, may end in the worst of tyrannies. Our best instincts hurt us most. Although society, like the human body, has immense restorative powers, they are blind. Left to itself, a broken leg may knit again, but it will certainly knit crooked, and in the same way the forces of equilibrium in society will restore some kind of integration, though the new level may well be lower than the last. To achieve an advancing adaptation, the maintenance of a civilization rather than a relapse before a new start, intelligence must direct the restorative powers.

GROUP CONFLICT

The problem of emotional isolation, or psychosocial isolation as the social scientists call it, is not the only one that civilization raises, and it may not be the most important. We have already seen that this problem is inextricably intermixed with the problem of group conflict. As civilization advances, a process often takes place on a large scale that much resembles what took place on a small scale in the Electrical Equipment Company. An advancing civilization means, among other things, that the technical and economic adaptation of society to its environment changes. Since the internal system is continuous with the external, this change disturbs the relations between groups within society and exacerbates their mutual antagonisms. The antagonisms find expression in ideological differences, and civil war may break out. Something very much like this occurred in the sixteenth century, in the last great crisis of Western civilization before the present one. With economic expansion and organizational changes in industry and agriculture, the middle class rose rapidly in importance. The members of this class were apt to be isolates; they also came, as a group, into conflict with the other classes in society. The former balance between the classes was destroyed, and antagonisms once kept under control awoke. In the ideological controversies, which were then religious and political as they are now economic and political, the middle class took one side; the upper and lower classes together took the other. The issues were not considered on their merits; they became the mere flags of parties whose real energy was drawn from class antagonisms. The result was the civil wars in France and England, and the Thirty Years' War in Germany. Civilization escaped wreck, but only just escaped. England suffered least and even gained by the conflict, which was less severe there than elsewhere; France survived at the price of adopting absolute monarchy, and the development of Germany was so retarded that she has suffered from a national feeling of inferiority ever since. Perhaps we are going through a similar conflict today, but our capacities for wrecking are much greater.

CIRCULATION, COMMUNICATION, AND CONTROL

Other problems raised by an advancing civilization, and closely related both to emotional isolation and to group conflict, are the problems of circulation, communication, and control. Let us take them up in this order. By *circulation* we shall mean the process by which able persons are brought to positions of responsibility in a society. In the small group, the choice of a leader is an obvious and natural thing. The leader is the man who most fully lives up to the ideals of the group. He expresses the aspirations of the group, and it is this, more than anything else, that allows him to carry the group with him. In a civilization at its best, the leaders are of the same kind. Scipio Africanus, William of Orange, Elizabeth, and Washington not only possessed great intellectual capacity but were also felt by their followers to represent the best in society. Their strength lay in this double fact. Yet as civilization advances, as the channels of advancement become more complex, and as conflict widens, the choice of leaders who have the twofold qualification for their job becomes more difficult. Able men may be available, but their skill lies in making money, in intrigue, in using force, or in exploiting the increasing antagonisms between groups. A split grows up between leaders and led, until the latter are no longer led but driven or bribed.

The problem of *communication* is close to that of circulation. We have seen that, in the small group, communication flows naturally toward the leader, and that he cannot do his job unless he is well informed in this way. Now civilization, which is, in one of its aspects, centralization, implies a lengthening of the channels of communication between followers and top leaders in the great formal organizations that articulate the whole. Even in the small group, the seeds of breakdown are latent in the emotional relation between leader and follower, and with every lengthening of the channels of communication, the difficulties increase. The subordinate, dependent on his superior for advancement, may tell the latter only what he wants to hear and only so much as will protect the subordinate's position. It is not enough that good communication should exist between most neighboring positions in the communication lines. If only one link is weak, the flow of information from bottom to top will be impaired. The separate channels of communication from bottom to top may multiply, as the rise of staff departments in every large organization shows, and yet this very multiplication may impede communication. Each channel transmits only part of the story; no one is responsible for paying attention to the whole. And every new channel may increase the insecurity of men located on the other channel, for it by-passes these men and transmits information that, in the hands of a leader inadequately skilled, may bring criticism back down upon them. Finally, adequate communication depends to a great degree on the leader's awareness of the items that ought to be communicated. He hears what he wants to hear, and he wants to hear only what he has been trained to hear. In American industry, for instance, communication is excellent on questions of sales and engineering, but tends to be poor on questions of internal social organization. This kind of information may be inherently hard to communicate, but it is also true that the American administrator is not taught to think it important.

For the ordinary follower in an organization, communication is not a matter of transmitting abstract understanding of a situation. It is a matter of transmitting to the leader an awareness of those problems on which, in the follower's view, action needs to be taken, and of the fact that the follower feels as he does. If action is not then taken by the leader, communication, for the follower, has failed. In the big organizations of modern society, communication in this sense is all too liable to failure. Trade and industrial unions may arise in an unconscious attempt to repair some of the damage, but they are big organizations too, and may fall into the old difficulties. We are in danger of producing a body of men wholly lacking confidence in leadership and organization of any kind whatever. Such a group would much resemble the "internal proletariat," demoralized, without opportunity for spontaneous group action of its own, and sullenly resistant toward its leaders, so characteristic of the later Roman Empire. For the problem is not just that of communication from follower to leader. The leader must also explain, in such a way that the followers will accept it, the plan of action that the society needs to adopt. If communication fails in one direction, it will fail in the other.

We have seen that in the small group, *control* over persons that threaten to depart from the norms of the group is often exceedingly effective but is not imposed from without. Instead it is implicit in the system of relations in the group. We have also seen that the leader, in close communication with his followers, does not ask them to take action that will not receive their spontaneous obedience. As civilization develops, as groups dissolve, as society divides into warring groups, and as the difficulties of communication between leader and follower increase, this spontaneous control tends to dissolve in favor of a control imposed by force and by the central power. Of course it is true that a certain amount of force must always be used in controlling society. What we are talking about now is a civilization that has reached the stage at which, in the view of its leaders, it can be held together only by force. Their diagnosis may be correct, if the dissolution of groups and the increase of conflict have gone far enough. But as for force as a long-run remedy, the evidence of history is that this stage marks the beginning of the downward path of civilization. Forced co-operation only hastens the decay that would have taken place in any event. In the words of Durkheim, "A society made up of a boundless dust-heap of unrelated individuals, whom an overdeveloped state tries to hem and hold in, is a true sociological monstrosity." And yet all dictators, from Napoleon onward, have tried to create something like this monstrosity. Just as Napoleon broke up the ancient provinces of France and divided them into departments, fearing that the provinces with their local loyalties and traditions of self-government would provide centers of resistance to his regime, so all dictators since his time have tried to break up or bring under central domination all social units independent of the state. Rousseau provided them with a rationale for their actions. He argued that the individual should be set free from the trammels of society, but when he faced the question how this should be done, he went on to say that "every citizen should be wholly independent of all the others and excessively dependent on the state . . . , for only the force of the state makes the liberty of its members." In short, man must be compelled to be free.

Let us repeat: all of these problems—psychosocial isolation, conflict, circulation, communication, and control—are handled more or less well at the level of the group. Therefore human society never dissolves beyond this level. What is true of the group must also be true of the civilization if the latter is to maintain itself. Civilization fails when it cannot solve these problems on its own vast scale, and when it even prevents its constituent groups from solving them.

DEMOCRACY

Our own civilization has not wholly failed. It has made some institutional inventions that have turned out, in certain times and circumstances, to be valuable in solving the problems of the group at the level of the civilization. One complex of such inventions is democracy. We do not use the word here in its literal sense of "rule of the people." That gets us into the question of the location of sovereignty in a nation. Sovereignty, which is another word for authority, does not lie in any one element or organ of a nation but in the social system as a whole. Nor do we use it in the sense of "democratic way of life." That, as we have said, gives aid and comfort to the dictators by letting them say that they are as "democratic" as anyone else. So loose is the meaning of democracy in this sense that no one can prove they are not. We use the word here to mean the complex of governmental and legal institutions common to such nations as the United Kingdom and the United States: representative and parliamentary government, universal suffrage, the secret ballot, the habeas corpus, trial by jury, and the various freedoms named in the Bill of Rights.

Note how all these devices are addressed to the problem of maintaining, at the level of a nation if not of a civilization, the values of the small group. The election of executive officers and representatives aims at maintaining for the nation the method of choosing leaders that is characteristic of the small group. Together with the freedoms of speech and press, it also aims at effective communication between the led and the leaders. Trial by jury and the various freedoms are so many admissions that the spontaneous self-control of a society may be much more effective than any imposed control. Finally, representative government is an effort to establish that kind of relationship between leaders and followers on which a spontaneous obedience, rather than a forced one, can be based. A further pursuit of this main idea might lead to many important insights.

But democratic institutions do not exist in a vacuum; they exist in a society, and they cannot live long unless the society is of a certain kind. This is a field in which political science, in co-operation with sociology, must do much more work than it has so far. Democracy cannot be successful unless the nation is well educated and enjoys a standard of living so high that men do not have to worry about sheer survival. Just how high the standard of education and the standard of living need to be we cannot say, but we recognize that at least some minimum level must be achieved. How few countries in which we Americans blithely ask that democratic government be established meet these conditions! How unrealistic we are, and what frustration our unrealism leads us to!

These are only the minimum conditions. There are others. If democratic institutions do something to create the conditions in which they can survive, they do not do everything. Democracy cannot solve the problem of psychosocial isolation, and it cannot help greatly to solve the problem of conflict. No one believes that, even in the most flourishing circumstances, conflict disappears in a society. Conflict is built deeply into any social order, which would be uninteresting without it. As usual, the question is: How much conflict and in what areas? If social conflict does not go too deep, representative government provides a method for deciding the issues, with much salutary release of emotion. We are all ready to accept a large amount of verbal violence in our politics. Our tolerance for it is high, and we admire a man that gives and takes hard knocks. But if conflict goes deep enough, as the United States once learned, and as the communist propagandists know well, democratic methods do not lead to the peaceful resolution of conflict but to civil war. For democracy to survive, the members of society must enjoy some area of consensus, supported by the informal contacts of daily life, by formal communication networks, and by common ideals. We know little of the nature of this consensus, but we are aware that in some countries of Europe, which were formerly, or now are, democracies in the technical sense, this consensus never existed. Moreover, as we have seen, some characteristics of a developing civilization tend to put the consensus in danger.

Democracy does something to solve the problems of circulation, communication, and control, but its machinery is not applied, and probably cannot be applied, in vast areas of our national life. No one has seriously suggested that production schedules in a factory should be determined by popular vote or even that the factory manager should be elected. And yet in these vast areas the tensions of modern civilization are being generated. We can resolve them not by blindly applying existing democratic methods but by addressing ourselves to the problem to which democracy itself was addressed: How can the values of the small group be maintained on the scale of the civilization?

THE SOLUTIONS OF THE PROBLEM

We have seen some of the problems that an advancing civilization makes for itself. Apparently its rise creates the conditions that lead to its fall. How shall we escape from this dreary cycle? The usual conservative has nothing more to offer than the advice: "Stop change. Any change will be for the worse." But from beginning to end civilization means change. Stop change and, we infer, civilization also stops. And while the conservative is giving his advice, the business firms he admires are making his words idle by stimulating enormous social change. The real problem is this: How can a social order change without either dissolution into a dust heap or cleavage into hostile camps? How can we, to use Elton Mayo's phrase, create an "adaptive society"? Another kind of conservative—he is usually called an "old-fashioned liberal"—growls about "the curse of bigness" and argues that social groups of all kinds should be more independent of state control. He has some idea of the nature of the problem, but his solution is mistaken. Civilization means centralization. It means that men and women will be related to one another in increasingly large organizations, and that these organizations will be brought more and more under the influence of the central directing body of the society, the government. Whether or not modern society requires large-scale organization if it is to maintain its complex adaptation to the natural environment, the fact certainly is that the process of centralization is still going on both in business and in government. If government did not centralize, business would; neither one is in a position to blame the other. The real problem is not how to keep social groups wholly independent and autonomous but how to organize their relation to central control in such a way that they can maintain their own life while contributing to the life of organized society. In the social organism, how can we keep the center strong without destroying the life of the periphery? How can we centralize without stagnating?

As for the modern liberal, not the old-fashioned one, all he has to offer to solve the problems of large-scale organization is more of the same. For big private business he would substitute bigger government business. He rushes into the leviathan state without having the faintest notion how to deal with some of its important human problems. He assumes our present methods are adequate. Take, for instance, the problem of restriction of output, which is a typical problem of the relation between the central direction of an organization and the small working groups of which the organization is made up. The liberal may not know about restriction in American industry, but if he does, he will say that it is specifically a result of business organization and not of modern big organization in general, including the kind he advocates, and that restriction will wither away when the government becomes socialist and the labor leaders are in power. But the difficulties are stubborn and their roots run deeper than we thought. Society is made up, among other elements, of countless small groups of the kind we have described in this book. If advancing civilization, which means an increasingly centralized control, does not destroy them altogether, which hardly seems likely, it will have to deal with them, and yet, as we have seen, advancing civilization tends to weaken the kind of relation between leader and follower in which the leader can carry the group wholeheartedly with him and the follower can accept leadership without fear that his views will be disregarded. Suppose we organize the welfare state and still find thousands of small groups sullenly resisting the advice of their official leaders? That the problem is not academic, the industrial experience of Socialist government shows. If social control is increasingly centralized, the reason must be that such control is necessary, but a central control that cannot be exercised would seem to mean stagnation and not progress. Shall we then use force to bring the recalcitrant into line?

History seems to show that this does not solve the problem but rather starts civilization on its downward path. The decline of the Roman Empire began with its birth—the dictatorship of Augustus. This is not an argument against the welfare state; it is a plea that we study more carefully than we have so far the conditions that must be realized if the centralized state is not to stagnate. Let us put our case for the last time: At the level of the small group, society has always been able to cohere. We infer, therefore, that if civilization is to stand, it must maintain, in the relation between the groups that make up society and the central direction of society, some of the features of the small group itself. If we do not solve this problem, the effort to achieve our most high-minded purposes may lead us not to Utopia but to Byzantium. The problem will not be easily solved, but one step we can take in the beginning is to learn the characteristics of the human group.

CHAPTER V

SOCIAL
ORGANIZATION

Collective Behavior

34. THE MEN FROM MARS *

JOHN HOUSEMAN

Collective behavior depends upon some form of communication. Any expansion in the means of communication, such as radio or television, increases the areas for possible stimulation, direction, and control of behavior. In this entertaining and significant article John Houseman gives a graphic account of a startling and rather disquieting episode precipitated by a radio program designed only for entertainment. Realism was necessary to ensure the full dramatic effect in its presentation. So skillful was the technique used that thousands believed an actual invasion from Mars was taking place. The panic, the irrational behavior of many people who chanced to tune in, is an interesting example of the propaganda potentials of radio and television. Houseman rejects the idea that the incident can be dismissed as an example of the "incredible stupidity and gullibility of the American public." Instead, he indicates many other important factors that must be considered in any explanation of the effects stimulated by the broadcast.

RADIO WAR TERRORIZES U.S.—*N.Y. Daily News*, October 31, 1938

Everybody was excited I felt as if I was going crazy and kept on saying what can we do what difference does it make whether we die sooner or later? We

* *Harper's Magazine*, Vol. 197, No. 1183 (December, 1948), 74–82. Reprinted by permission of the author.
    The author was cofounder of Mercury Theater, New York, in the 1930's. Supervised Voice of America programs during World War II for the Radio Program Bureau, O.W.I.

were holding each other. Everything seemed unimportant in the face of death. I was afraid to die, just kept on listening.—*A listener*

Nothing about the broadcast was in the least credible.—*Dorothy Thompson*

The show came off. There is no doubt about that. It set out to dramatize, in terms of popular apprehension, an attempted invasion of our world by hostile forces from the planet Mars. It succeeded. Of the several million American citizens who, on the evening of October 30, 1938, milled about the streets, clung sobbing to one another or drove wildly in all directions to avoid asphyxiation and flaming death, approximately one-half were in terror of Martians—not of Germans, Japanese, or unknown enemies—but, specifically, of Martians. Later, when the excitement was over and the shadow of the gallows had lifted, some of us were inclined to take credit for more deliberate and premeditated villainy than we deserved. The truth is that at the time, nobody was more surprised than we were. In fact, one of the most remarkable things about the broadcast was the quite haphazard nature of its birth.

In October 1938, the Mercury Theater, of which Orson Welles and I were the founding partners, had been in existence for less than a year. Our first Broadway season had been shatteringly successful— "Julius Caesar," "The Cradle Will Rock," "Shoemaker's Holiday," and "Heartbreak House" in the order of their appearance. In April, Orson, in a straggly white beard, made the cover of *Time* Magazine. In June, the Columbia Broadcasting System offered him a radio show—"The Mercury Theater on the Air," a series of classic dramatizations in the first person singular with Orson as master of ceremonies, star, narrator, writer, director, and producer. He accepted. So, now, in addition to an empty theater, a movie in progress, two plays in rehearsal, and all seven of the chronicle plays of William Shakespeare in preparation, we had a radio show.

We opened on July 11. Among our first thirteen shows were "Treasure Island," "39 Steps," "Abraham Lincoln," "Three Short Stories" (by Saki, Sherwood Anderson, and Carl Ewald), "Jane Eyre," "Julius Caesar" (with running commentary by Kaltenborn out of Plutarch), and "The Man Who Was Thursday." Our second series, in the fall, began with Booth Tarkington's "Seventeen," "Around the World in Eighty Days," and "Oliver Twist." Our fifth show was to be "Life with Father." Our fourth was "The War of the Worlds."

No one, as I remember, was very enthusiastic about it. But it seemed good programming, between the terrors of Dickens' London slums, and the charm of Clarence Day's New York in the nineties, to throw in something of a contrasting and pseudo-scientific nature. We thought of Shiel's *Purple Cloud*, Conan Doyle's *Lost World*, and several others before we settled on H. G. Wells' twenty-year-old novel, which neither of us, as it turned out later, remembered at all clearly. It is just possible that neither of us had ever read it.

II

Those were our golden days of unsponsored radio. We had no advertising agency to harass us, no client to cut our withers. Partly because we were perpetually overworked and partly because that was the way we did things at the Mercury, we never seemed to get more than a single jump ahead of ourselves. Shows were created week after week under conditions of soul- and health-destroying pressure. On the whole they were good shows. And we *did* develop a system—of sorts.

It worked as follows: I was editor of the series. With Welles, I chose the shows and then laid them out. The writing, most of it, was done by Howard Koch—earnest, spindly, six-foot-two—a Westchester lawyer turned playwright. To write the first draft of an hour's radio script took him about five days, working about fifteen hours a day. Our associate producer was Paul Stewart, a Broadway actor turned director. His function was to put the broadcast through its first paces and preliminary rehearsals. Every Thursday, musicless and with rudimentary sound effects, a wax record of the show was cut. From this record, played back later that night, Orson would give us his reactions and revisions. In the next thirty-six hours the script would be reshaped and rewritten, sometimes drastically. Saturday afternoon there was another rehearsal, with sound—with or without Welles. It was not until the last day that Orson really took over.

Sundays, at eight, we went on the air. Beginning in the early afternoon—when Bernard Herrmann arrived with his orchestra of twenty-seven high-grade symphony players—two simultaneous dramas were regularly unfolded in the stale, tense air of Studio Number One: the minor drama of the current show and the major drama of Orson's gargantuan struggle to get it on. Sweating, howling, disheveled, and single-handed he wrestled with Chaos and Time—always conveying an effect of being alone, traduced by his collaborators, surrounded by treachery, ignorance, sloth, indifference, incompetence and—more often than not—downright sabotage! Every Sunday it was touch and go. As the hands of the clock moved relentlessly toward air time the crisis grew more extreme, the peril more desperate. Often violence broke out. Scripts flew through the air, doors were slammed, batons smashed. Scheduled for six—but usually nearer seven—there was a dress rehearsal, a thing of wild improvisations and irrevocable disaster. (One show was found to be twenty-one minutes overlength, another fourteen and one-half minutes short.) After that, with only a few minutes to go, there was a final frenzy of correction and reparation, of utter confusion and absolute horror, aggravated by the gobbling of sandwiches and the bolting of oversized milk-shakes. By now it was less than a minute to air time. . . .

At that instant, quite regularly week after week—with not one second to spare . . . the titanic buffoonery stopped. Suddenly out of chaos, the show emerged—delicately poised, meticulously executed, precise as clockwork, and smooth as satin. And above us all, like a rainbow over storm clouds, stood Orson on his podium, sonorous and heroic, a leader of men surrounded by his band of loyal followers; a giant in action, serene and radiant with the joy of a hard battle bravely fought—a great victory snatched from the jaws of disaster.

In later years, when the Men from Mars had passed into history, there was some bickering among members of the Mercury as to who, exactly, had contributed precisely what, to that particular evening's entertainment. The truth is that a number of us made a number of essential and incalculable contributions to the broadcast. (Who can accurately assess, for instance, the part played by Johnny Dietz's perfect engineering, in keeping unbroken the shifting illusion of imperfect reality? How much did the original old H. G. Wells, who noisily repudiated us, have to do with it? Or the second assistant sound man? Or individual actors? Or Dr. Goebbels? Or Charlie McCarthy?) Orson Wells had virtually nothing to do with the writing of the script and less than usual to do with its preliminary rehearsals. Yet first and last it was his creation. If there had been a lynching that night, it is Welles the outraged populace would have strung up—and rightly so. Orson was the Mercury. "The War of the Worlds," like everything we did, was his show.

Actually, it was a narrow squeak. Those Men from Mars barely escaped being stillborn. Tuesday afternoon—five days before the show —Howard Koch telephoned. He was in deep distress. After three days of slaving on H. G. Wells' scientific fantasy he was ready to give up. Under no circumstances, he declared, could it be made interesting or in any way credible to modern American ears. Koch was not given to habitual alarmism. To confirm his fears, Annie, our secretary, came to the phone. She was an acid and emphatic girl from Smith College with fine blond hair, who smelled of fading spring flowers. "You can't do it!" she whined. "Those old Martians are just a lot of nonsense. It's all too silly! We're going to make fools of ourselves! Absolute fools!"

For some reason which I do not clearly remember our only possible alternative for that week was a dreary one—"Lorna Doone." I tried to reach Welles. He was at the theater and wouldn't come to the phone.

The reason he wouldn't come to the phone was that he was in his thirty-sixth successive hour of dress-rehearsing "Danton's Death," a beautiful, fragmentary play by Georg Buechner out of which Max Reinhardt, in an augmented form, had made a successful mass-spectacle in the twenties. Not to be outdone, Orson had glued seventeen hundred masks on to the back wall of the Mercury Theater, and ripped out the entire stage. Day after day actors fell headlong into the rat-ridden basement, leaped on and off erratically moving elevators, and chanted the "Carmagnole" in chorus under the supervision of Marc Blitzstein.

Unable to reach Welles, I called Koch back. I was severe. I taxed him with defeatism. I gave him false comfort. I promised to come up and help. When I finally got there—around two the next morning—things were better. He was beginning to have fun laying waste the State of New Jersey. Annie had stopped grinding her teeth. We worked all night and through the next day. Wednesday at sunset the script was finished.

Thursday, as usual, Paul Stewart rehearsed the show, then made a record. We listened to it rather gloomily, long after midnight in Orson's room at the St. Regis, sitting on the floor because all the chairs were covered with coils of unrolled and unedited film. We agreed it was a dull show. We all felt its only chance of coming off lay in emphasizing its newscast style—its simultaneous, eyewitness quality.

All night we sat up, spicing the script with circumstantial allusions and authentic detail. Friday afternoon it went over to CBS to be passed by the network censor. Certain name alterations were requested. Under protest and with a deep sense of grievance we changed the Hotel Biltmore to a non-existent Park Plaza, Trans-America to Intercontinent, the Columbia Broadcasting Building to Broadcasting Building. Then the script went over to mimeograph and we went to bed. We had done our best and, after all, a show is just a show. . . .

Saturday afternoon Paul Stewart rehearsed with sound effects but without Welles. He worked for a long time on the crowd scenes, the roar of cannon echoing in the Watchung Hills and the sound of New York Harbor as the ships with the last remaining survivors put out to sea.

Around six we left the studio. Orson, phoning from the theater a few minutes later to find out how things were going, was told by one of the CBS sound men, who had stayed behind to pack up his equipment, that it was not one of our better shows. Confidentially, the man opined, it just didn't come off. Twenty-seven hours later, quite a few of his employers would have found themselves a good deal happier if he had turned out to be right.

III

On Sunday, October 30, at 8:00 P.M., E.S.T., in a studio littered with coffee cartons and sandwich paper, Orson swallowed a second container of pineapple juice, put on his earphones, raised his long white fingers and threw the cue for the Mercury theme—the Tchaikovsky

Piano Concerto in B Flat Minor ♯ 1. After the music dipped, there were routine introductions—then the announcement that a dramatization of H. G. Wells' famous novel, *The War of the Worlds*, was about to be performed. Around 8:01 Orson began to speak, as follows:

WELLES

We know now that in the early years of the twentieth century this world was being watched closely by intelligences greater than man's and yet as mortal as his own. We know now that as human beings busied themselves about their various concerns they were scrutinized and studied, perhaps almost as narrowly as a man with a microscope might scrutinize the transient creatures that swarm and multiply in a drop of water. With infinite complacence people went to and fro over the earth about their little affairs, serene in the assurance of their dominion over this small spinning fragment of solar driftwood which by chance or design man has inherited out of the dark mystery of Time and Space. Yet across an immense ethereal gulf minds that are to our minds as ours are to the beasts in the jungle, intellects vast, cool, and unsympathetic regarded this earth with envious eyes and slowly and surely drew their plans against us. In the thirty-ninth year of the twentieth century came the great disillusionment.

It was near the end of October. Business was better. The war scare was over. More men were back at work. Sales were picking up. On this particular evening, October 30, the Crossley service estimated that thirty-two million people were listening in on their radios. . . .

Neatly, without perceptible transition, he was followed on the air by an anonymous announcer caught in a routine bulletin:

ANNOUNCER

. . . for the next twenty-four hours not much change in temperature. A slight atmospheric disturbance of undetermined origin is reported over Nova Scotia, causing a low pressure area to move down rather rapidly over the northeastern states, bringing a forecast of rain, accompanied by winds of light gale force. Maximum temperature 66; minimum 48. This weather report comes to you from the Government Weather Bureau. . . . We now take you to the Meridian Room in the Hotel Park Plaza in downtown New York, where you will be entertained by the music of Ramon Raquello and his orchestra.

At which cue, Bernard Herrmann led the massed men of the CBS house orchestra in a thunderous rendition of "La Cumparsita." The entire hoax might well have exploded there and then—but for the fact that hardly anyone was listening. They were being entertained by Charlie McCarthy—then at the height of his success.

The Crossley census, taken about a week before the broadcast, had given us 3.6 per cent of the listening audience to Edgar Bergen's 34.7 per cent. What the Crossley Institute (that hireling of the advertising agencies) deliberately ignored, was the healthy American habit of dial-twisting. On that particular evening, Edgar Bergen in the person of Charlie McCarthy temporarily left the air about 8:12 P.M., E.S.T., yielding place to a new and not very popular singer. At that point, and during the following minutes, a large number of listeners started twisting their dials in search of other entertainment. Many of them turned to us—and when they did, they stayed put! For by this time the mysterious meteorite had fallen at Grovers Mill in New Jersey, the Martians had begun to show their foul leathery heads above the ground, and the New Jersey State Police were racing to the spot. Within a few minutes people all over the United States were praying, crying, fleeing frantically to escape death from the Martians. Some remembered to rescue loved ones, others telephoned farewells or warnings, hurried to inform neighbors, sought information from newspapers or radio stations, summoned ambulances and police cars.

The reaction was strongest at points nearest the tragedy—in Newark, New Jersey, in a single block, more than twenty families rushed out of their houses with wet handkerchiefs and towels over their faces. Some began moving household furniture. Police switchboards were flooded with calls inquiring, "Shall I close my windows?" "Have the police any extra gas masks?" Police found one family waiting in the yard with wet cloths on faces contorted with hysteria. As one woman reported later:

I was terribly frightened. I wanted to pack and take my child in my arms, gather up my friend and get in the car and just go north as far as we could. But what I did was just sit by one window, praying, listening, and scared stiff, and my husband by the other sniffling and looking out to see if people were running. . . .

In New York hundreds of people on Riverside Drive left their homes ready for flight. Bus terminals were crowded. A woman calling up the Dixie Bus Terminal for information said impatiently, "Hurry please, the world is coming to an end and I have a lot to do."

In the parlor churches of Harlem evening service became "end of the world" prayer meetings. Many turned to God in that moment:

I held a crucifix in my hand and prayed while looking out of my open window for falling meteors. . . . When the monsters were wading across the Hudson River and coming into New York, I wanted to run up on my roof to see what they looked like, but I couldn't leave my radio while it was telling me of their whereabouts.

Aunt Grace began to pray with Uncle Henry. Lily got sick to her stomach. I don't know what I did exactly but I know I prayed harder and more earnestly than ever before. Just as soon as we were convinced that this thing was real, how petty all things on this earth seemed; how soon we put our trust in God!

The panic moved upstate. One man called up the Mt. Vernon Police Headquarters to find out "where the forty policemen were killed." Another took time out to philosophize:

I thought the whole human race was going to be wiped out—that seemed more important than the fact that we were going to die. It seemed awful that everything that had been worked on for years was going to be lost forever.

In Rhode Island weeping and hysterical women swamped the switchboard of the Providence *Journal* for details of the massacre, and officials of the electric light company received a score of calls urging them to turn off all lights so that the city would be safe from the enemy. The Boston *Globe* received a call from one woman "who could see the fire." A man in Pittsburgh hurried home in the midst of the broadcast and found his wife in the bathroom, a bottle of poison in her hand, screaming, "I'd rather die this way than that." In Minneapolis a woman ran into church screaming, "New York destroyed this is the end of the world. You might as well go home to die I just heard it on the radio."

The Kansas City Bureau of the AP received inquiries about the "meteors" from Los Angeles; Salt Lake City; Beaumont, Texas; and St. Joseph, Missouri. In San Francisco the general impression of listeners seemed to be that an overwhelming force had invaded the United States from the air—was in process of destroying New York and threatening to move westward. "My God," roared an inquirer into a telephone, "where can I volunteer my services, we've got to stop this awful thing!"

As far south as Birmingham, Alabama, people gathered in churches and prayed. On the campus of a Southeastern college——

The girls in the sorority houses and dormitories huddled around their radios trembling and weeping in each other's arms. They separated themselves from their friends only to take their turn at the telephones to make long distance calls to their parents, saying goodbye for what they thought might be the last time. . . .

There are hundreds of such bits of testimony, gathered from coast to coast.

IV

At least one book [1] and quite a pile of sociological literature has appeared on the subject of "The Invasion from Mars." Many theories have been put forward to explain the "tidal wave" of panic that swept the nation. I know of two factors that largely contributed to the broad-

[1] *The Invasion from Mars* by Hadley Cantril, Princeton University Press, from which many of the above quotations were taken.

cast's extraordinarily violent effect. First, its historical timing. It came within thirty-five days of the Munich crisis. For weeks, the American people had been hanging on their radios, getting most of their news no longer from the press, but over the air. A new technique of "on-the-spot" reporting had been developed and eagerly accepted by an anxious and news-hungry world. The Mercury Theater on the Air by faithfully copying every detail of the new technique—including its imperfections—found an already enervated audience ready to accept its wildest fantasies. The second factor was the show's sheer technical brilliance. To this day it is impossible to sit in a room and hear the scratched, worn, off-the-air recording of the broadcast, without feeling in the back of your neck some slight draft left over from that great wind of terror that swept the nation. Even with the element of credibility totally removed it remains a surprisingly frightening show.

Radio drama was taken seriously in the thirties—before the Quiz and the Giveaway became the lords of the air. In the work of such directors as Reis, Corwin, Fickett, Welles, Robson, Spier, and Oboler there was an eager, excited drive to get the most out of this new, all too rapidly freezing medium. But what happened that Sunday, up on the twentieth floor of the CBS building was something quite special. Beginning around two, when the show started to take shape under Orson's hands, a strange fever seemed to invade the studio—part childish mischief, part professional zeal.

First to feel it were the actors. I remember Frank Readick (who played the part of Carl Phillips, the network's special reporter) going down to the record library and digging up the Morrison recording of the explosion of the Hindenburg at Lakehurst. This is a classic reportage —one of those wonderful, unpredictable accidents of eyewitness description. The broadcaster is casually describing a routine landing of the giant gasbag. Suddenly he sees something. A flash of flame! An instant later the whole thing explodes. It takes him time—a full second —to react at all. Then seconds more of sputtering ejaculations before he can make the adjustment between brain and tongue. He starts to describe the terrible things he sees—the writhing human figures twisting and squirming as they fall from the white burning wreckage. He stops, fumbles, vomits, then quickly continues. Readick played the record to himself, over and over. Then, recreating the emotion in his own terms, he described the Martian meteorite as he saw it lying inert and harmless in a field at Grovers Mill, lit up by the headlights of a hundred cars— the coppery cylinder suddenly opening, revealing the leathery tentacles and the terrible pale-eyed faces of the Martians within. As they begin to emerge he freezes, unable to translate his vision into words; he fumbles, retches—and then after a second continues.

A few moments later Carl Phillips lay dead, tumbling over the microphone in his fall—one of the first victims of the Martian Ray. There followed a moment of absolute silence—an eternity of waiting. Then, without warning, the network's emergency fill-in was heard—somewhere in a quiet studio, a piano, close on mike, playing "Clair de Lune," soft and sweet as honey, for many seconds, while the fate of the universe hung in the balance. Finally it was interrupted by the manly reassuring voice of Brigadier General Montgomery Smith, Commander of the New Jersey State Militia, speaking from Trenton, and placing "the counties of Mercer and Middlesex as far west as Princeton and east to Jamesburg" under Martial Law! Tension—release—then renewed tension. For soon after that came an eyewitness account of the fatal battle of the Watchung Hills; and then, once again, that lone piano was heard—now a symbol of terror, shattering the dead air with its ominous tinkle. As it played, on and on, its effect became increasingly sinister—a thin band of suspense stretched almost beyond endurance.

That piano was the neatest trick of the show—a fine specimen of the theatrical "retard," boldly conceived and exploited to the full. It was one of the many devices with which Welles succeeded in compelling, not merely the attention, but also the belief of his invisible audience. "The War of the Worlds" was a magic act, one of the world's greatest, and Orson was just the man to bring it off.

For Welles is at heart a magician whose particular talent lies not so much in his creative imagination (which is considerable) as in his proven ability to stretch the familiar elements of theatrical effect far beyond their normal point of tension. For this reason his productions require more elaborate preparation and more perfect execution than most. At that—like all complicated magic tricks—they remain, till the last moment, in a state of precarious balance. When they come off, they give—by virtue of their unusually high intensity—an impression of great brilliance and power; when they fail—when something in their balance goes wrong or the original structure proves to have been unsound—they provoke, among their audience, a particularly violent reaction of unease and revulsion. Welles' flops are louder than other men's. The Mars broadcast was one of his unqualified successes.

Among the columnists and public figures who discussed the affair during the next few days (some praising us for the public service we had rendered, some condemning us as sinister scoundrels) the most general reaction was one of amazement at the "incredible stupidity" and "gullibility" of the American public, who had accepted as real, in this single broadcast, incidents which in actual fact would have taken days or even weeks to occur. "Nothing about the broadcast," wrote Dorothy Thompson with her usual aplomb, "was in the least credible." She was wrong. The first few minutes of our broadcast were, in point of fact, strictly realistic in time and perfectly credible, though somewhat boring, in content. Herein lay the great tensile strength of the show; it was the structural device that made the whole illusion possible. And it could have been carried off in no other medium than radio.

Our actual broadcasting time, from the first mention of the meteorites to the fall of New York City, was less than forty minutes. During that time men traveled long distances, large bodies of troops were mobilized, cabinet meetings were held, savage battles fought on land and in the air. And millions of people accepted it—emotionally if not logically.

There is nothing so very strange about that. Most of us do the same thing, to some degree, most days of our lives—every time we look at a movie or listen to a broadcast. Not even the realistic theater observes the literal unities; motion pictures and, particularly, radio (where neither place nor time exists save in the imagination of the listener) have no difficulty in getting their audiences to accept the telescoped reality of dramatic time. Our special hazard lay in the fact that we purported to be, not a play, but reality. In order to take advantage of the accepted convention, we had to slide swiftly and imperceptibly out of the "real" time of a news report into the "dramatic" time of a fictional broadcast. Once that was achieved—without losing the audience's attention or arousing their skepticism, if they could be sufficiently absorbed and bewitched not to notice the transition—then, we felt, there was no extreme of fantasy through which they would not follow us. We were keenly aware of our problem; we found what we believed was the key to its solution. And if, that night, the American public proved "gullible," it was because enormous pains and a great deal of thought had been spent to make it so.

In the script, "The War of the Worlds" started extremely slowly—dull meteorological and astronomical bulletins alternating with musical interludes. These were followed by a colorless scientific interview and still another stretch of dance music. These first few minutes of routine broadcasting "within the existing standards of judgment of the listener" were intended to lull (or maybe bore) the audience into a false security and to furnish a solid base of realistic time from which to accelerate later. Orson, in making over the show, extended this slow movement far beyond our original conception. "La Cumparsita," rendered by "Ramon Raquello, from the Meridian Room of the Hotel Park Plaza in downtown New York," had been thought of as running only a few seconds; "Bobby Millette playing 'Stardust' from the Hotel Martinet in Brooklyn," even less. At rehearsal Orson stretched both these numbers to what seemed to us, in the control room, an almost unbearable length. We objected. The interview in the Princeton Observatory—the clock-work ticking monotonously overhead, the woolly-minded professor mumbling vague replies to the reporters' uninformed questions—this, too, he dragged

out to a point of tedium. Over our protests, lines were restored that
had been cut at earlier rehearsals. We cried there would not be a
listener left. Welles stretched them out even longer.

He was right. His sense of tempo, that night, was infallible. When
the flashed news of the cylinder's landing finally came—almost fifteen
minutes after the beginning of a fairly dull show—he was able suddenly
to spiral his action to a speed as wild and reckless as its base was solid.
The appearance of the Martians; their first treacherous act; the death
of Carl Phillips; the arrival of the militia; the battle of the Watchung
Hills; the destruction of New Jersey—all these were telescoped into a
space of twelve minutes without overstretching the listeners' emotional
credulity. The broadcast, by then, had its own reality, the reality of
emotionally felt time and space.

v

At the height of the crisis, around 8:31, the Secretary of the Interior
came on the air with an exhortation to the American people. His words,
as you read them now, ten years later, have a Voltairean ring. (They
were admirably spoken—in a voice just faintly reminiscent of the President's—by a young man named Kenneth Delmar, who has since grown
rich and famous as Senator Claghorn.)

THE SECRETARY

Citizens of the nation: I shall not try to conceal the gravity of the situation
that confronts the country, nor the concern of your Government in protecting
the lives and property of its people. However, I wish to impress upon you—
private citizens and public officials, all of you—the urgent need of calm and
resourceful action. Fortunately, this formidable enemy is still confined to a
comparatively small area, and we may place our faith in the military forces
to keep them there. In the meantime placing our trust in God, we must continue the performance of our duties, each and every one of us, so that we
may confront this destructive adversary with a nation united, courageous, and
consecrated to the preservation of human supremacy on this earth. I thank you.

Toward the end of this speech (*circa* 8:22 E.S.T.), Davidson Taylor,
supervisor of the broadcast for the Columbia Broadcasting System, received a phone call in the control room, creased his lips, and hurriedly
left the studio. By the time he returned, a few moments later—pale
as death—clouds of heavy smoke were rising from Newark, New Jersey,
and the Martians, tall as skyscrapers, were astride the Pulaski Highway
preparatory to wading the Hudson River. To us in the studio the show
seemed to be progressing splendidly—how splendidly Davidson Taylor
had just learned outside. For several minutes now, a kind of madness

had seemed to be sweeping the continent—somehow connected with our show. The CBS switchboards had been swamped into uselessness but from outside sources vague rumors were coming in of deaths and suicides and panic injuries.

Taylor had requests to interrupt the show immediately with an explanatory station-announcement. By now the Martians were across the Hudson and gas was blanketing the city. The end was near. We were less than a minute from the Station Break. The organ was allowed to swirl out under the slackening fingers of its failing organist and Ray Collins, superb as the "last announcer," choked heroically to death on the roof of Broadcasting Building. The boats were all whistling for a while as the last of the refugees perished in New York Harbor. Finally, as they died away, an amateur shortwave operator was heard from heaven knows where, weakly reaching out for human companionship across the empty world:

> 2X2L Calling CQ
> 2X2L Calling CQ
> 2X2L Calling CQ
> Isn't there anyone on the air?
> Isn't there anyone?

Five seconds of absolute silence. Then, shattering the reality of World's End—the Announcer's voice was heard, suave and bright:

ANNOUNCER
    You are listening to the CBS presentation of Orson Welles and the Mercury Theater on the Air in an original dramatization of *The War of the Worlds,* by H. G. Wells. The performance will continue after a brief intermission.

The second part of the show was extremely well written and most sensitively played—but nobody heard it. It recounted the adventures of a lone survivor, with interesting observations on the nature of human society; it described the eventual death of the Martian Invaders, slain— "after all man's defenses had failed by the humblest thing that God in his wisdom had put upon this earth"—by bacteriological action; it told of the rebuilding of a brave new world. After a stirring musical finale, Welles, in his own person, delivered a charming informal little speech about Halloween, which it happened to be.

I remember, during the playing of the final theme, the phone starting to ring in the control room and a shrill voice through the receiver announcing itself as belonging to the mayor of some Midwestern city, one of the big ones. He is screaming for Welles. Choking with fury, he reports mobs in the streets of his city, women and children huddled in the churches, violence and looting. If, as he now learns, the whole thing is nothing but a crummy joke—then he, personally, is coming up to New York to punch the author of it on the nose! Orson hangs up quickly. For we are off the air now and the studio door bursts open. The following hours are a nightmare. The building is suddenly full of people and dark blue uniforms. We are hurried out of the studio, downstairs, into a back office. Here we sit incommunicado while network employees are busily collecting, destroying, or locking up all scripts and records of the broadcast. Then the press is let loose upon us, ravening for horror. How many deaths have we heard of? (Implying they know of thousands.) What do we know of the fatal stampede in a Jersey hall? (Implying it is one of many.) What traffic deaths? (The ditches must be choked with corpses.) The suicides? (Haven't you heard about the one on Riverside Drive?) It is all quite vague in my memory and quite terrible.

Hours later, instead of arresting us, they let us out a back way. We scurry down to the theater like hunted animals to their hole. It is surprising to see life going on as usual in the midnight streets, cars stopping for traffic, people walking. At the Mercury the company is still stoically rehearsing—falling downstairs and singing the "Carmagnole." Welles goes up on stage, where photographers, lying in wait, catch him with his eyes raised up to heaven, his arms outstretched in an attitude of crucifixion. Thus he appeared in a tabloid that morning over the caption, "I Didn't Know What I Was Doing!" The *New York Times* quoted him as saying, "I don't think we will choose anything like this again."

We were on the front page for two days. Having had to bow to radio as a news source during the Munich crisis, the press was now only too eager to expose the perilous irresponsibilities of the new medium. Orson was their whipping boy. They quizzed and badgered him Condemnatory editorials were delivered by our press-clipping bureau in bushel baskets. There was talk, for a while, of criminal action.

Then gradually, after about two weeks, the excitement subsided. By then it had been discovered that the casualties were not as numerous or as serious as had at first been supposed. One young woman had fallen and broken her arm running downstairs. Later the Federal Communications Commission held some hearings and passed some regulations. The Columbia Broadcasting System made a public apology. With that the official aspects of the incident were closed.

As to the Mercury—our new play, "Danton's Death," finally opened after five postponements. Not even our fantastic publicity was able to offset its generally unfavorable notices. On the other hand, that same week the Mercury Theater on the Air was signed up by Campbell Soups at a most lavish figure.

Of the suits that were brought against us—amounting to over three quarters of a million dollars for damages, injuries, miscarriages, and distresses of various kinds—none was substantiated or legally proved.

We did settle one claim however, against the advice of our lawyers. It was the particularly affecting case of a man in Massachusetts, who wrote:

"I thought the best thing to do was to go away. So I took three dollars twenty-five cents out of my savings and bought a ticket. After I had gone sixty miles I knew it was a play. Now I don't have money left for the shoes I was saving up for. Will you please have someone send me a pair of black shoes size 9B!"

We did.

35. WHERE VIOLENCE BEGINS *

NORMAN COUSINS

The development of distrust and hostility between people who have long lived together in harmony is sometimes hard to understand. This selection by Norman Cousins, however, demonstrates how close friends may be caught up in mass suspicion and resort to violence against each other. The function of fear and rumor in breaking down the mutual confidence developed through long association is clearly evident.

This is about Kamilal Deridas of India, who killed his friend. The killing occurred about seven years ago. All his life Deridas had followed the non-violence teachings of Mahatma Gandhi. He kept his thoughts free of fear and hate. And then one day, suddenly, he reached for a knife and slew his friend. Up until now that killing has had no direct connection with the American people; but it now becomes important for us to think about it as hard and carefully as we have thought about anything in our lives.

I met Deridas at a refugee camp on the outskirts of Delhi in February 1951. When I returned to India recently I tried to find him and learned that he had made himself a new home somewhere to the north of Delhi; no one knew exactly where. But, though I was unable to locate him, I shall never forget the things he told me about his ex-

* From *Saturday Review,* Vol. 37, No. 3 (January 16, 1954), 22–24, 33.

The author (b. 1912) is editor of the *Saturday Review.* Sometime exchange lecturer India, Pakistan, Ceylon and Japan. He has been chairman of the Connecticut Fact Finding Commission on education, recipient of Thomas Jefferson Award for Advancement of Democracy in Journalism (1948); Wayne University award for national service to education (1956). Author: *The Good Inheritance; The Democratic Chance; Who Speaks for Man?*

periences during India's ordeal in the summer of 1947, when the country was partitioned into three units—India proper, Pakistan West, and Pakistan East. The two sections of the new Pakistan were united politically, but they were separated by the geographical expanse of India at its widest. If you can imagine that Mexico, instead of being situated south of the United States, were to be split in half, with one part in Southern California and the other in New England, then you may have a fair idea of the geographic relationship of Pakistan to India, as well as the difficulties surmounted so heroically by the Pakistani leaders in operating a unified and free government.

The background of partition is long and involved. It was the culmination of more than a century of dual struggle—the struggle for national independence against England, and the struggle for power inside India between Hindu and Moslem. Centuries ago the Moslems ruled the northern part of India. When the British quit India in 1947 there were perhaps 100,000,000 Moslems in all of India, as against more than 325,000,000 Hindus. With partition some sixty-five million Moslems formed the population of the new Pakistan, the balance remaining in India. Today the population of Pakistan is more than seventy-five million, with close to forty million Moslems still in India proper.

Partition and national independence were part of the same historical event. Neither was then possible without the other. But the sudden rupture of a great nation caused it to bleed hideously. The struggle for national independence had been waged for centuries but it came virtually overnight and no one was prepared for it. The new Free India had only a bare governmental skeleton with which to administer the affairs of the second most populous nation in the world. Pakistan started absolutely from scratch, having to use empty crates for government desks.

And in those early days of uncertainty and confusion people became panicky. Whatever the animosity had been between Hindu and Moslem before Independence, the people had managed to live side by side. There had been recurrent violent flare-ups, to be sure, but they were not too serious. With partition, however, millions of people suddenly became jittery and insecure. A Hindu who lived in a city near the border like Lahore wondered what was to happen to him now that Lahore was to become part of Pakistan. A Moslem who lived on the outskirts of Calcutta wondered what was to happen now that there would be a separate Moslem Government in Pakistan that did not include him. The insecurity and confusion became multiplied as millions of people decided to move in order to be governed by their own group.

Then came violence. At first there were only sporadic incidents. A Moslem in Dacca, for example, would smash the shopwindows of a clothing store owned by a Hindu, claiming he had heard that Hindus were looting Moslem shops in Calcutta or Delhi. A Hindu in Calcutta would set fire to a Moslem home, in open view of a crowd, yelling that he had heard that Moslems were burning homes of Hindus who remained behind in Dacca or Karachi. Some Hindus or Moslems would try to take advantage of the national turmoil by seizing business properties or homes.

Each incident, of course, fed on rumors and begat even greater rumors. Outrages were carried out in the name of retaliation. Soon a civil war without battle-lines or armies raged throughout the subcontinent. People rushed through the streets with sticks or torches or whatever could be used to kill a man.

Kamilal Deridas was one of those who used a knife. When he spoke to me about it, four years later, he found it difficult to believe that it was his own arm that swung the knife over the shoulder and into the chest of a man who had been his friend.

Like millions of others who lived through the dark days of 1947, Deridas doesn't like to talk about what happened or his own part in it. It was only after we had spent many hours together, discussing the event in a general way, that he began to speak in terms of his individual experiences. I had told him that I found it difficult to understand how people who achieved so much through their belief in non-violence could suddenly abandon that belief at the very moment of its fulfilment. It was inexplicable that a non-violent victory should produce such volcanic violence within the nation itself. And what about the people, I asked. How could they allow themselves to become something they had never been? The Hindus and Moslems I knew were gentle people, peaceable people. I couldn't imagine them as killers. And Deridas's reply to my question was simple and vivid.

"I can answer you because I know how it was. I was part of it. From the very beginning I was part of it. I was twenty-six at the time. My wife, my two little boys, and I lived with my parents in a nice house on the edge of Lahore. My father operated an arts-and-crafts shop. Lahore was something of a world convention city. The weather is clear and good almost the entire year and there were generally meetings that brought many people to the city.

"I had gone to college, studying law, but had deferred setting up an office of my own because my father was ailing and it was necessary for me to look after the business, which had prospered over the years. I had many friends in Lahore—among both Hindus and Moslems. Those of us who had gone to college thought all the old antagonisms were foolish, and we were bored by the traditional hostilities of the older people. Two of my closest friends were Moslems and they were as indifferent to the old religious and cultural rivalries as I was. The name of one was Faiz; the other Ahmed.

"After plans for the partition were made in 1947 Faiz came to me and said that he was worried about talk he had heard in town. He had heard that certain Hindu homes would be requisitioned after Pakistan came into being in order to make room for the many Moslems who could be coming to the city. And our home was on one of the lists.

"My father dismissed this talk as nonsense. He said that the new Pakistan would not tolerate such outrages because there were more Moslems in India than Hindus in what was to be the new Pakistan. He said the new Government would know only too well how much worse it would fare than India in any contest of seizure of private property. He told me to forget about it.

"But as the time for partition neared, and as reports reached Lahore of local riots in sections where there were mixed populations, I became very alarmed. One night Faiz came to my home through the back door and begged me to get my belongings together as quickly as I could, take my family, and flee Lahore.

"He said that there had been a secret meeting a few hours earlier in town and that reports were read which told of Hindu looting of Moslem shops in Delhi and Bombay and also that in several places Moslem women had been violated by Hindus and put on public exhibition. He said there were also reports that many, many thousands of Moslem homes had been seized by Hindu crowds throughout India. The men at the meeting were hysterical with rage and called for immediate retaliatory action.

"There were some at the meeting who cautioned against anything that might start a riot. They pointed out that they had lived side by side with their Hindu neighbors for many years and that these people were not responsible for the outrages that happened to Moslems many hundreds of miles away. But most of the others turned on these cautious few and shouted them down, saying they were traitors, and then the cautious few spoke no more. My friend said he knew terrible things were going to happen, and that the police would be powerless to do anything.

"I made up my mind that we would have to leave within a week at most and began to plan a way out and also to plan some way of getting the most valuable items in our store to a place of safety. I sought the help of Ahmed, who agreed to keep the most valuable items in the cellar of his home. That night and the next night, between one A.M. and four A.M., we transported the valuables in Ahmed's car from our store to his home. It was a courageous thing for him to do. It would have meant his death if he had been discovered.

"Then Ahmed and Faiz and I met in order to make plans for us to get out of Lahore until some measure of stability returned to the city. My father was difficult to persuade about this but something terrible that happened to us two days after Faiz came to warn me changed his mind. Our store was located in the resort section, which is the far side of the city. Early in the morning, shortly after I had opened the shop, I heard the sounds of a great commotion coming from afar. I locked the store, then rushed towards the center of the town. As I approached I saw that the looting and the burning had already begun. There was smashed glass all over the streets. Not far away I could see smoke rising from the heart of the city.

"I ran back to the store. My father and my brother-in-law were waiting when I got there. They were very agitated. My twenty-one-year-old sister had been missing since eight A.M. It was now ten A.M. We barricaded the store to the best of our ability, then rushed home. We never saw my sister again. That night my brother-in-law learned that she had been abducted, along with sixty or seventy young Hindu wives. We could only pray for her life and her integrity of physical self, but I feared the worst.

"That night, in accordance with our plan, we left the house one by one, dressed in Moslem style, and were picked up by Faiz and Ahmed in their cars and brought to Ahmed's house, where we were to stay secretly until we completed arrangements for getting out of Lahore. It was lucky we had left our house when we did. Part of it was wrecked the very next day and the part that remained was occupied.

"Our plan for leaving Lahore was a simple one. We would travel in three pony carts. My wife, my two sons, and I would be in one cart. My father and mother would be in another. My brother-in-law and his little boy in the third. After a day's travel from Lahore we would slip over the border at night and then get a train to Delhi, 250 or 300 miles distance. At Delhi, we would try to find a place to live.

"But much was to happen to us before we left Lahore. In no time at all the riots had swept all through the city. We heard incredible stories of what was happening not only in Lahore but throughout India and Pakistan. Thousands of women and young girls on both sides were being abducted and violated. Mobs were rushing through streets, seizing people and tearing them apart. It was unbelievable—but it was happening.

"Then one night—it was after mid-night—Ahmed came to the small room in his house where we were all hiding. I could see that there was something wrong. He was almost hysterical. He had just been told that his parents had been burned to death the night before in their beds. They lived in Batala, just over the border. My father tried to calm him by saying it could not be so, that Hindus would not do such a thing; and Ahmed said that there was no doubt about it. He said he knew that there were outrages on both sides; he had wanted to stay free of them, and had risked his life and the lives of his immediate family to help Hindus, and that this was now his reward—a mother and father burned in their beds by Hindus.

"My father again insisted that it was not so, and that someone had lied to Ahmed, and before I knew what was happening my father and Ahmed were quarreling and shouting at each other. I begged them to be quiet, for they were certain to rouse the entire neighborhood. But those were no days of calm tempers; we had all been without sleep and were on edge and had been infected by the ugly passions that were sweeping over the two countries. My father and Ahmed continued to shout at each other, accusing each other; then my father in a moment of rage said that he was certain that all Ahmed was after was our valuables which we had stored with him. And Ahmed, insane with grief over the killing of his parents, went into a blind fury, reached for a knife, and started after my father.

"Right then something happened to me. I don't remember it clearly; in fact, I don't remember it at all, but my wife told me about it later. The sight of the knife after everything that had happened in the past few days—the burning and the lootings and the killings and the attacks on women and having to be huddled together secretly wondering what would happen to us—all this made me lose my senses when I saw Ahmed going at my father with a knife. I took a knife that Ahmed had given me earlier for my own safety. I killed him. I reached over his shoulder with my knife and I killed him.

"Right after that we left the house, taking Ahmed's car, even though it had been decided earlier, that we would not use an automobile because cars on the road going to the border attracted too much suspicion. We knew the pony carts were small enough for the back roads. But now we had no choice. How we finally made the border is almost too incredible to tell. But we made it. Anyway, that is not what you wanted to know about. You wanted to know how peaceable men could forget all their convictions, forget everything, and kill. I have tried to tell you.

"There are many, many thousands of people like me. No one knows how many people became killers during those dark days. What we know is that maybe 300,000 were killed; maybe half a million; maybe a million. No one stopped to count. But we do know that twelve million people lost their homes and fled in terror. Seven or eight million Hindus. Four or five million Moslems. Maybe more.

"I have talked about my part in the dark days to very few people. But one man to whom I spoke had known Gandhiji, and you know that Gandhi himself was killed in that terrible period during partition. And this man, who would know what Gandhiji would say if he knew what I had done, told me that what had happened was not my sin alone but the sin of all the people of India and Pakistan. Gandhiji made no distinction in his life between Hindu and Moslem; he loved us all. And his friend told me that Gandhi would have said that I had temporarily lost my sanity with all the others but that I should work for friendship between Hindu and Moslem as the only way of paying for my crime.

"What he said helps. It also helps to remember that when men are soldiers they kill because they are caught up in something larger than themselves. I hope I have answered your question."

I said that he had; but I could see there was something more he had to say.

"Perhaps you are wondering," he resumed after a minute or two, "whether these terrible things happened here in India and Pakistan only because—well, because there is something perhaps primitive or un-civilized about these people; and that this could never happen to people like yourselves who are educated and refined. One thing I surely learned during that time was that everything is swept aside in panic. I was a college man; Ahmed was a college man. College men were in the crowds that set fire to the shops and the homes. And in the Western world a high literacy rate didn't keep the German people from going in for mass murder. And there were many outrages in your own Civil War. I'm afraid I would have to say that what happened to us could happen to anyone when suddenly the structure of law and order is re-moved and the people are governed only by their fears. It is then that the worst elements in the society can set the pattern for society itself.

"At a time like that is when the very great men in a society show themselves. And it was then that the world really knew that Jawaharlal Nehru was fit to wear the mantle of Gandhiji. For it was Nehru who risked his life to save Moslems during the Delhi riots. It was Nehru who rushed out into Connaught Circle late at night and thrust himself be-tween a Hindu looter and his intended victim. And it was Nehru who while on the spot ordered Hindu police to shoot at Hindu looters. And the rioting and the killing receded faster in Delhi than anywhere else —because of Nehru.

"And it is Nehru's presence in the Government that has caused many millions of Moslems to stay behind in India. By working for Moslem-Hindu friendship in India he is fulfilling the debt we must all pay to our consciences for what happened during those awful days. Both Hindus and Moslems have sinned deeply. Only in friendship can they clear those miserable stains. And Nehru is trusted by the Moslems in India. They shudder—and I shudder with them—when we think of what would happen in India if anything happened to him.

"For there is still great uneasiness in the two countries. And I trem-ble with my entire being lest something might happen that would throw things out of balance and bring on again even more bloodier and darker days.

"There are many issues which are unsettled between Hindus and Moslems as the result of partition. And the people are pressing for settlement. I have had to live with my family in tents or shacks, without proper sanitary facilities, since 1947. What about our property in Lahore? Shouldn't there be some payment for our store and our home? And what about the abducted women? Pakistani have many of the same claims against India. Then, to top everything, of course, is the Kashmir dispute.

"The situation between the two countries is far from ideal. Zealots on both sides are trying to inflame the people. Moslem religious fanatics think Pakistan ought to wage a holy war against India and unite the entire country on the basis of Moslem rule. And we have our own Hindu fanatics who want to sweep into Pakistan and bring about reunification through force and then set up a theocratic Hindu state.

"That is why I pray that these two countries may have peace."

I began this account by saying that Deridas's story about the dark days of 1947 in India has a special meaning today for the American people. America is in a position today to exercise a profound influence on the affairs of India and Pakistan. If we are wise we can contribute to the peace and well-being of both countries. If we are foolish or insensitive we can upset a precarious equilibrium and help to touch off a subcontinental civil war.

Of all the issues outstanding between India and Pakistan today none is more difficult or more combustible than the Kashmir dispute. There is no clear-cut question of right and wrong here between India and Pakistan. Anyone who has attempted to study the problem on the spot knows the difficulty of striking a balance between the claims of both parties. Similarly, anyone who has made a sensitive appraisal of the situation knows that the present Prime Ministers of both countries are far more moderate in their approaches, far more convinced of the necessity for and possibility of a peaceful settlement, than large segments of public opinion in their respective countries. Both Mohammed Ali and Jawaharlal Nehru have demonstrated a sense of total responsibility in opposing the growing extremist factions.

In the midst of this touch-and-go situation comes the report that America is preparing to send arms to Pakistan. The effect has been exactly what was to be expected. In India it has already strengthened the hands of the extremists who want to press for a forcible seizure of the Kashmir. It gives the Communists the most powerful weapon they have had since India became independent. It puts them in a position where they could claim leadership against what they denounce as the vacillating policies of Nehru. It enables them to exploit the passions of the militant Hindus, playing upon their fears that the religious fanatics in Pakistan would seize the upper hand and use American arms against India. It makes the entire nation fearful that Pakistan would be in a stronger position in the event of a showdown over the Kashmir.

There are forty million Moslems in India. If Nehru's policies of moderation are to be swept aside by an alliance of Communists and militant Hindus then the last barrier will have been removed to a resumption of the dark days of 1947.

America says it is against Communism. Nothing that organized Communism has done in Asia—whether in China or India—can compare with the impetus we will give Communism in Asia as the result of the chaos resulting from a Hindu-Moslem explosion. Russia does not want peace in Asia. Russia has no way of coping with peace in Asia. Russia wants chaos in Asia. We are proposing to make her that gift.

It is one of history's most stupendous paradoxes that step by step, day by day, in the name of anti-Communism we seem to be doing the very things that will give Communism control over the majority of the world's peoples.

Our business in the world is the business of peace. If we are to do anything for Asia let us do the things that are in keeping with the American character. If we want to help Pakistan build real defenses against Communism let us put up giant dams and power installations. Let us help her develop her farms and her industries. If we are concerned about Communism in India let us fight the threat where it exists today—in the farms and villages and factories—by helping to prove to the Indian people that Communism is the false answer to famine, poverty, illiteracy. We can prove that democracy is the right answer by putting democracy to work. But if we can do none of these things let us not set the stage for mass murder.

We have yet to develop our knowledge of the world to match our power in the world. For we will survive not through power alone but through a deep sensitivity to the wants and the hurts of others, and through the appeal of great ideas. This is the test of the American moral fiber if there ever was one.

36. LYNCHERS DON'T LIKE LEAD *

JOE JORDAN

Joe Jordan has here described in a vivid manner an extremely violent type of collective behavior—that of the mob—and shows how it was handled. In sharp contrast with "The Men from Mars" (article 34), in which mass panic was quickly

* The Atlantic Monthly, Vol. 177, No. 2 (February, 1946), 103–108. Reprinted by permission of the publisher and the author.
    The author has been City Editor of Lexington Herald-Leader, Lexington, Kentucky. The Atlantic Monthly refers to him as a "Kentuckian from 'way back."

*halted by prompt dissemination of the actual facts, the situation
in this case was one in which the facts could not get an
audience. Appeals to reason proved useless. It has been said
that "a mob acts as one man but as no one man would act
alone." All inhibitions are cast off, while the sense of power
is greatly increased. Violence, irresponsibility, and destructiveness
characterize this type of collective behavior. Sometimes, under
powerful personal appeal, reason does prevail over the mob.
But at other times, as on the occasion described here by
Jordan, a display of physical force becomes necessary to
re-establish order.*

. . . On February 9, 1920, a mob at Lexington, Kentucky, bent
upon lynching a Negro who was on trial for murdering a white child,
charged the Fayette County courthouse. The members of the mob,
all white men, were fired upon and repulsed by white soldiers
and white civil officers. Six men were killed and fifty or more were
wounded. Of the hundreds of newspapers throughout the United
States which hastened to praise Fayette County officials for their somewhat astonishing stand against mob violence, many pointed out, as
did the *Brooklyn Eagle* in a typical comment, that the Lexington
incident marked "the first time south of Mason and Dixon's Line that
any mob of this sort had actually met the volley fire of soldiers."

At the time, a number of the writers of editorials indicated a
cautious belief and hope that the "Second Battle of Lexington" might
mark a turning point in the method of dealing with mobs. It now appears
that they were right. In 1919, mobs had lynched eighty-three persons
in the United States. That figure has not been approached since the
Lexington mob was dealt with so vigorously. In 1944, there were only
two lynchings in the entire country. To avoid the danger of selecting
by chance two unusual years, it is safer to consider five-year averages.
In the five years preceding 1920, mobs had lynched an average of sixty-
one victims a year; in the five years preceding 1945, lynchings averaged
fewer than four a year.

A decisive encounter between determined officers and a determined
mob was bound to occur sometime. It occurred at Lexington, that
February day in 1920, because the mob picked the wrong town for a
lynching party. Fayette County had not seen a lynching in fifty years.
It didn't see one then, and it hasn't seen one since. Thousands of
outsiders flocked to Lexington on the day of the trial, and some Ala-
bamians who arrived the day before, disclosed to reporters that they
had made the long trip to have a part in the expected lynching. They
misjudged the temper and underestimated the courage of the county

officials, who had issued plain warnings that anyone attempting to take the prisoner from them would be killed.

Will Lockett, the Negro who was to be tried, had killed a ten-year-old white girl at South Elkhorn, in the southern section of Fayette County. It was a revolting crime. The child had been seized when she was walking to a country school less than 400 yards from her home. She had been dragged into a cornfield and there her skull had been crushed by repeated savage blows with a large rock. Her body, half hidden under a fodder shock, had been found after she failed to appear at school.

Lockett, a World War I veteran who still was wearing his Army uniform, had left a country store in the neighborhood shortly before the crime was committed, and was suspected immediately. He was found six hours later, six miles away. A doctor and two other civilians who captured him took him to Lexington hurriedly, for they feared a mob would form and they wanted to get him into the hands of the law.

At Lexington police headquarters, Lockett confessed promptly. He was removed to the county jail, but almost at once the officers decided it would be safer to take him to the state penitentiary at Frankfort. When he was led out of the jail, a crowd already was beginning to form in the street, but it was not large enough to menace the officers who had him in charge, and within an hour he was behind the walls of the Frankfort prison.

As news of the crime spread, the crowd in front of the jail increased, and by dark it numbered several hundred. Its members refused to accept the jailer's statement that Lockett had been taken to Frankfort. There is a traditional procedure in such cases, and it was followed. The jailer consented to admit a committee to search the jail and inspect the prisoners. The committee, which included a farmer by whom Lockett had been employed, looked into the faces of all the frightened Negroes in the jail and went out to assure the crowd that Lockett was not there.

Of course, there have been similar cases in which the wrong man has been identified and dragged out, but the Negroes in the Lexington jail were lucky that night. The mob then went to police headquarters, where a similar search was permitted. Convinced that Lockett had been taken to Frankfort, the mob's leaders attempted to charter inter-urban electric cars for the trip to the state capital, but traction-company officials refused to accommodate them, and approximately three hundred men set out in automobiles.

The late Edwin P. Morrow, then Governor of Kentucky, was informed by telephone that the mob was on its way to Frankfort. He acted with characteristic vigor. One hundred special deputies, armed with shotguns and rifles, were sent to the penitentiary to reinforce the regular guards there. Governor Morrow took charge at the prison gate.

Meanwhile Sheriff Bain Moore of Franklin County had taken a force of men to the outskirts of Frankfort, on the Lexington Pike. He stopped the first cars in the caravan from Lexington, had them turned crosswise of the road to establish a blockade, and warned the mob members that they would meet certain death if they attempted to remove the prisoner from the penitentiary. Most of the men turned back. A few who got past the sheriff's barricade were arrested on Governor Morrow's order when they appeared at the prison gate.

The crime was committed and Lockett was arrested on Wednesday, February 4. A Fayette County grand jury indicted Lockett the next day on a murder charge, and his trial was set for the following Monday, only five days after the slaying.

Everybody realized that a serious situation could develop when Lockett was returned to Lexington for the trial. Circuit Judge Charles Kerr and County Judge Frank A. Bullock—in Kentucky the county judge is the administrative head of the county government—conferred with other county officials, with Mayor Thomas C. Bradley of Lexington, and with Governor Morrow. It was decided that there would be no running away from the issue by postponing the trial to a secret date or ordering a change of venue. Governor Morrow promised a company of state troops from Campbell County, in northern Kentucky.

It was admitted that the public did not have so much respect for "Home Guards" as for Regular Army soldiers, and the officials looked longingly toward Camp Taylor, less than a hundred miles away, where the crack First Division Regulars, veterans of World War I, were stationed. The Governor could not obtain Federal troops, however, without certifying that a state of lawlessness existed with which the state authority was unable to cope.

In the interval between Lockett's arrest and his trial, the Lexington newspapers pleaded for peace and order. Negro organizations adopted resolutions "condemning the horrible outrage" and demanding that the guilty member of their race "be punished promptly and adequately." A group of South Elkhorn residents met Saturday afternoon at the courthouse and issued an appeal by T. L. Hardman, brother of the slain girl, which was carried in both Lexington newspapers Sunday morning.

"As a brother of Geneva Hardman, who was murdered by Will Lockett, and as a representative of her family," he said, "I request all of our friends and all those who sympathize with us not to indulge in any violence or create any disturbance when he is brought here for trial. The authorities have acted promptly, the man is under arrest, he has been indicted promptly, and his trial fixed for Monday. I feel sure that a prompt and speedy trial will take place and that any jury impaneled will find him guilty and punish him adequately for the horrible crime he has committed. . . . I would hate to see the life of any other person endangered as the result of violence by reason of conflict over a brute like this, and I therefore urge all citizens, for the good name of the county and in the interest of law and order, to do nothing to interfere with the orderly processes of the law."

In an editorial headed, "Let the Law Take Its Course," the *Lexington Leader* commented: "If this bereaved brother can assume such an attitude at this time, certainly those who sympathize so deeply with him can afford to await calmly the verdict of the jury. . . . The people of Fayette County can afford to let the law take its course in this case. They cannot afford to incur the just criticism of the people of the nation which would follow a resort to mob rule." The *Lexington Herald* advanced similar arguments. Sunday morning the congregation of the South Elkhorn Christian Church, composed entirely of neighbors of the murdered child, adopted a resolution calling for orderly administration of the law. Every effort was being made to prepare the public for the crisis expected on Monday.

These appeals appeared to have had the desired effect in Fayette County itself. In a news story the day before the trial, the *Herald* reported: "Indignation on the part of the citizens last night turned into determination that the law should take its course." The *Leader* found that "the mob spirit, which was prevalent immediately after the atrocity was committed, has died down and has been replaced by a willingness to let the law take its course." The *Leader* added, however, that there had been "reports that other counties would send delegations here to 'get' Lockett."

Both newspapers repeatedly assured the public that there could be but one outcome of the trial—speedy conviction and a death sentence. Said a *Leader* news story: "It is anticipated that if Lockett is sentenced to be electrocuted, as it is generally believed he will be, the same military protection will be given him while he is on his way to the penitentiary where the electrocution will take place. . . . It is thought the trial will be a speedy one. After the jury is chosen, the actual trial ought to be over in a very short time." Thus it was hoped to make clear to the public that the issue was not whether Lockett would be punished, but whether the punishment would be carried out lawfully or by a mob.

Adjutant General J. M. Deweese, who was to be in charge of the state troops, issued a brief, forceful warning: "The responsibility for any bloodshed at this trial will rest on those who disregard their duty as citizens and attempt to take the law out of the hands of the constituted authorities." Fayette County Sheriff J. Waller Rodes, who had hurried home from a business trip to Texas to take charge of the county's defense measures, said, "Under no circumstances will the prisoner be taken away from the guards."

At one o'clock Monday morning, the day of the trial, police began stretching steel cables in the empty streets, to keep spectators at a distance from the courthouse. The lines were no more than boundary markers, since it would be easy enough to slip through them. At 3.45 A.M., a special train arrived from Frankfort, bringing Sheriff Rodes, General Deweese, the prisoner, and the state troops. The train stopped before it reached Union Station, and the soldiers marched two blocks with their prisoner and entered the courthouse without incident.

By seven o'clock, a crowd had begun to form on Main Street, in front of the courthouse. It grew rapidly. The trial had been set for nine o'clock. When that hour approached, there were immense crowds on the Main Street and Short Street sides of the building, but officers kept everyone outside the cables except officials, prospective jurors, newsmen, and just enough spectators to fill the courtroom.

The approach to the main entrance of the courthouse is by broad flights of stone steps which lead to the second floor. All ground-floor entrances had been barred. The first flight of front steps ends at a level landing which runs off to the right and left to connect with walks from Upper Street and Cheapside, at an elevation higher than the Main Street sidewalk and the front lawn. Soldiers were stationed behind the stone parapet around the front of this landing. A machine gun had been set up on the landing. At the top of the highest flight of steps, just inside the wide front doors, were more soldiers with rifles and deputies with shotguns. Soldiers also had been stationed in various offices in the building, at open windows commanding the steps.

The defense setup appeared to be adequate. Men attempting to reach the front doors would have to get through the cable barrier (which would not be difficult, but would separate them from the crowd), then cross a bare, level space approaching the steps, and mount the steps in the face of fire from the protected soldiers, who had been posted in positions that would enable them to sweep the steps with rifle and machine-gun fire. That it would be the height of folly to attempt to storm such a position, any man of judgment could see—but mobs are not made up of men of judgment.

The crowd that surrounded the courthouse square was estimated by some observers to number 8,000 to 10,000. Such guesses usually are high. A conservative estimate would be 5,000 to 6,000. Of these, comparatively few were there with any serious idea of attempting to take the prisoner out of the courthouse. Most of them had come out of curiosity, half hoping, perhaps, that they would see fighting. University of Kentucky students (I was one of them) had left the campus in droves, flocking to the downtown district to share in the excitement, in spite of repeated warnings for all peaceful citizens to stay out of the danger zone. The authorities had pointed out that spectators would be in as much danger as participants if a battle developed. Many lookers-on were in a nervously jovial mood, exchanging jokes about how fast they would run if shooting started.

Presently people began to point out a man with a coil of rope over his left shoulder. He pushed his way forward to the cable, at a point directly in front of the steps. In addition to the ones who appeared to be in his party, other grim-faced men began sifting through the crowd and gathering around him. The merely curious spectators who happened to be in that vicinity dropped back and were replaced by additional angry, cursing men who "meant business."

Thus the nucleus of the mob was formed. It appeared to be unplanned, this concentration. Naturally, the ones who actually considered rushing the courthouse would gather at the spot from which the charge would have to start, and as they got together and bolstered one another's courage, perhaps no one of them wanted to appear cowardly before his fellows and so they all persuaded themselves that the thing could be done, that the civil officers and soldiers would not dare shoot white men to protect a Negro murderer.

The courthouse clock struck nine times. Everybody realized that if anything was to be done, it would have to be done soon. The threats and cursing became louder up near the barrier, while those in the background ceased their joking, suddenly aware that the situation might turn dangerous after all.

Inside the courthouse, as we were to learn later from the newspapers, the trial started promptly. Judge Kerr was on the bench. Every seat in the courtroom was filled, but no one was allowed to stand in the spectators' section, behind the rail. In front of the rail, in the space reserved for jurors, attorneys, and court officials, a few men were standing, among them County Judge Bullock. Lockett sat at the defense table, surrounded by four deputies. The bailiff rapped for order, pounding his gavel on a desk across which he had laid an automatic shotgun.

As had been predicted, the trial proceeded with a minimum of delay. A jury was selected quickly. The only question asked each prospective juror was whether he had any conscientious scruples against the death penalty. The court had appointed two leading members of the bar as defense counsel, George R. Hunt and Colonel Samuel M. Wilson. Mr. Hunt filed a demurrer to the indictment, explaining that he was doing it "as a matter of form," but that the indictment appeared to be properly drawn.

Asked whether he wished to plead guilty or not guilty, Lockett mumbled a reply inaudible to the spectators. "Defendant pleads guilty, your Honor," the clerk announced.

Only one witness testified, a man who established the fact of the child's death and told of finding her with a heavy stone on her face. The defendant did not take the stand. Colonel Wilson read Lockett's

honorable discharge from the Army, which stated that his character was
"very good," and then read a statement in which the defendant asked
for a life sentence. "I know I do not deserve mercy," it said, "but I
am sorry I committed the crime and I would give anything if the little
girl could be brought back to life."

Colonel John R. Allen, Commonwealth's Attorney, made a brief
prosecution argument to the jury. "In all the history of crime in the
United States," he said, "there has been none to equal this in cruelty.
In the name of the law, and of the little girl who was murdered, I ask
you to act quickly, and suggest that you return a verdict without leaving
the jury box."

While this was taking place in the courtroom, the crowd in the street
became more restive. A deputy sheriff engaged in a brief fist fight with
a man who had crawled under the cable barrier, and the man was
dragged away by two policemen. A newsreel cameraman had been
admitted to a cleared space on the lawn and had set up his camera near
the equestrian statue of Confederate General John Hunt Morgan. He
had taken pictures of the soldiers and the crowd, but apparently he
wanted something showing action or emotion. "Shake your fists and
yell!" he called out to the nearest spectators. They obligingly did so.

The people who shook their fists and yelled to please the cameraman
were just outside the cable barrier, but they were a hundred feet or so
east of the nucleus of the real mob. Their action, however, was like a
spark in the highly charged atmosphere. It was answered by a roar
from the mob—a savage, bestial roar. I was not to hear anything like
it again until the radio carried to America the roars with which a Nazi
mob responded to an impassioned harangue by Hitler on the eve of
Munich.

Men in the forefront of the mob hoisted the cables and went under
them quickly, as if the shouts had been a signal. The man with the
rope was among the leaders.

General Deweese had taken a stand in an open space at the approach to the first flight of steps. His men had orders not to shoot unless
he fired his revolver twice into the air. As the leaders of the charge approached the General, he backed about twenty steps, pistol in hand.
When they reached him, he grappled with two of them, and struck one
over the head with the pistol. The others surged around him and in a
moment had mounted the first flight of steps and reached the landing.
They bowled over a machine gunner and kicked his gun aside.

Deweese fired the two signal shots, and a withering volley was discharged. Men piled up on the steps, some wounded, others dropping
to escape the bullets. A dozen or more who had passed the landing
before the firing began rushed on up the remaining steps to the front
doors, but turned back and ran when the soldiers and deputies who had

been stationed inside the doors surged out with rifles and shotguns pointed at them.

The one burst of firing, which lasted only a few seconds, had halted the mob, and the soldiers held their fire. Some witnesses estimated that as many as fifty shots had been fired by members of the mob at the defenders of the courthouse; others denied it. That there was some firing from the mob was certain, for three policemen and one soldier were wounded, and today there are still chipped places where bullets struck the stone front of the courthouse.

All the merely curious spectators—except the ones who had been hit —broke and ran as soon as the firing started. The action-seeking cameraman, lugging his camera, tripod and all, sped past many of them before they reached Limestone Street, a block east. (For some strange reason, almost everyone ran east, even those who had been standing west of the steps.) The number of spectators hit never was determined accurately. Some of the soldiers said later that they had fired over the heads of the mob leaders who were mounting the steps. Their bullets went into the crowd or shattered store windows across the street. At least one man was fatally injured, who had been standing backed up against a store front on the opposite side of Main Street. A woman clerk inside a store was struck in the ankle by a bullet.

Of those who had fallen on the steps, the uninjured and slightly injured crawled away, and the others were carried away. One man was taken to a doctor's office near-by and died there within a few minutes. Four others died at hospitals before midnight. The sixth victim died several days later.

Twenty-one wounded persons were treated at hospitals. The newspapers said "scores" were treated at drugstores for less serious injuries, such as being peppered by nearly spent buckshot or being knocked down and trampled. Fearing prosecution, several members of the mob who were shot were reported to have been taken home by friends. Avoiding hospitals, they were treated by their physicians, and no reports were made. That as many as fifty were wounded appears to be a conservative estimate.

In the courtroom, Colonel Allen was making the closing statement to the jury when the crowd's roar was heard, followed by firing. "It's started!" several spectators shouted, leaping to their feet. Deputies pointed pistols and commanded them to sit down. The trial proceeded.

The jurors quickly reached the expected verdict—death. Lockett was called around and Judge Kerr stood to pronounce sentence. At that moment an excited man ran into the courtroom and shouted, "Judge, you better let 'em have the nigger! They're going to tear the courthouse down if you don't!"

Again the deputies pointed their pistols and Colonel Allen—not an honorary but a military colonel, to whom it would be no new experience to be under fire—calmly counseled the crowd in the courtroom to remain seated. Judge Kerr as calmly proceeded with the sentencing, specifying that Lockett should die March 11 in the electric chair at Eddyville Penitentiary and concluding, "May the God of All Mercy have mercy on your soul."

Down in the street, as soon as the first shock was over and the mob members grasped the unbelievable fact that the officers and soldiers actually had fired upon them, had wounded many, and probably had killed a number of them, a cry for vengeance went up. Now they wanted not the prisoner alone, but the men who had stood up against them. Crowds broke for the pawnshops, seeking weapons. Several farsighted pawnbrokers had had their places locked all day, the doors barred and the windows shuttered.

Two shops were open. Joe Rosenberg later reported to police that "forty or fifty" pistols had been taken from his shop; Harry Skuller said he had been robbed of "fifty or sixty" weapons. Boxes of cartridges were picked up along with the pistols. (Later, the two pawnbrokers wasted money on newspaper advertisements appealing for the return of their property. Not a single one of the "borrowed" weapons ever was recovered.)

The shooting had cleared out all the idlers, and the surly crowd that milled around in front of the courthouse was now composed exclusively of those who "meant business." As the news spread, more and more armed men arrived and the situation, to all appearances, was worse than it had been before the shooting. There were reports that dynamite had been sent for, that the courthouse would be blown up, that a special train loaded with mountaineers from eastern Kentucky was on the way to Lexington.

Unknown to the mob was the fact that Governor Morrow had decided he now could certify truthfully to Federal authorities that there existed a state of lawlessness with which the state authority was unable to cope. The First Division Regulars had entrained at Camp Taylor and were on their way to Lexington.

The shooting had begun at 9:28 A.M. Then came the raids on pawnshops and the arrival of reinforcements for the mob. During the succeeding hours, one of the *Leader's* numerous extra editions related, "The courthouse was besieged by increasing numbers of armed men, who displayed an increasingly threatening attitude." By General Deweese's order, Judge Kerr, Judge Bullock, and other county officials remained inside the building, for by that time they were as much the objects of the mob's wrath as the prisoner himself. Lockett sat in a prisoners' lockup adjacent to the courtroom, handcuffed, with his head bowed. He had taken little apparent interest in the trial, and barely had raised his head when he heard the firing outside the building.

As the day wore on, tension increased minute by minute and the besieging force steadily grew larger, but the leaders of the mob bided their time. There were reports that they were waiting for dynamite, that they were waiting for reinforcements, that they were waiting for darkness so they could shoot out the street lights and overwhelm the defenders of the building. The strain was beginning to tell on the "Home Guards," many of whom were teen-age boys whose previous military experience had been confined to drilling one night a week in a National Guard armory. They looked frightened.

Finally, at 3.20 P.M., the special train from Camp Taylor steamed through the yards and stopped at Mill and Water Streets, only two blocks from the courthouse, but out of sight of the mob. Out of the coaches poured streams of battle-hardened veterans, who quickly fell in and marched north on Mill Street with bayonets fixed. Leading them was a color guard bearing the United States flag, a banner which in the sixties often had been carried into Lexington to the accompaniment of despairing groans from the town's leading citizens.

Lexington during the War Between the States had been a Confederate stronghold in a border state. It had been captured and recaptured, and had lived alternately under the United States and Confederate States flags. Now it was being occupied again, but there were no groans that day from the leading citizens as the Regulars executed a smart turn into Main Street and bore down upon the mob, with the Stars and Stripes at the head of the column. Indeed, one of the beleaguered county officials peering out of the courthouse windows—a man who, like most of us Kentuckians, had been taught from childhood to take pride in being an Unreconstructed Rebel—laughingly admitted later that he had been somewhat astonished to hear himself shouting, "That's the prettiest flag I ever saw!"

The soldiers moved steadily east on Main Street and swept the mob before them. No shots were fired from either side. Here and there an occasional inflamed individual attempted to put up an argument and was cracked over the head with a rifle butt; now and then a sullen straggler was hurried along by a light prick with a bayonet point. But for the most part the men who had been so bloodthirsty instantly lost interest in fighting and took to their heels. Magically, within five minutes, all streets approaching the courthouse had been cleared. Khaki-clad sharpshooters looked over the eaves of all structures in sight of the county building.

Never did a city submit more happily to invading forces than Lexington surrendered that day to the United States troops. Martial law was declared, and the citizens marveled at the efficiency with which the soldiers took charge. Twelve patrols were organized and assigned head-quarters. As darkness approached, soldiers began patrolling Negro districts, the tobacco-warehouse district,—which had been threatened because the sheriff and several other county office-holders were interested financially in the warehouses,—and the Union Station, to guard against the expected arrival of the mountaineers, which never came to pass.

Another place that needed guarding was the ROTC Armory at the University of Kentucky, which contained hundreds of rifles and thousands of rounds of ammunition. Twice during the day, members of the mob had made unsuccessful attempts to enter it. Directly across Limestone Street from the campus was a fire-department station, which an Army captain selected as convenient headquarters for his patrol. To his request that the station be kept open all night, a surly fire-department captain replied that he intended to lock up the lower floor and retire with his men to the dormitory above. The fireman was arrested and hustled off to jail. The military was in charge, and before long that fact was impressed upon all citizens, whether or not they sympathized with the mob.

The next day Brigadier General Francis C. Marshall, commanding the U.S. troops, summarized Monday's events in a terse statement: "This community has set a fine example against Bolshevism and lawlessness and has killed several of its own citizens in upholding law and order."

"Folly's Harvest of Sorrow" was the heading over a *Leader* editorial the day after the riot. It said in part: "The folly of a few men, maddened for the moment by a spirit of revenge, seeking the life of a miserable creature at the very instant condemned to die for his crime, compelled the servants of the law to fire upon a mob in Lexington Monday morning. The majesty of the law was upheld, but at frightful cost."

The *Herald* expressed sympathy for the families of the victims, but added that "there is pride that the law was protected, that the officers of the law observed their solemn oath both to execute and to defend the law." It said the affair proved two facts: that the guilty would be punished surely and swiftly, and that "he who attempts to violate the law goes to meet death."

Jere Reagan, Chief of Police, commented: "There can be no question as to the absolute necessity of firing. Those who forced their way through the lines meant business. I am sorry innocent persons have been killed, but enough warning had been given."

Further evidence that General Marshall was the law in Fayette County was given Thursday, when he directed Judge Kerr to summon a special grand jury to investigate the law violations that had occurred Monday, and to indict the guilty persons. The jury commissioners selected what was recognized immediately as a "hand-picked" grand jury, composed of citizens who would not hesitate to indict the mob members. A week later, this jury was discharged, since it appeared that any indictments the body voted probably would be thrown out of court because the names of the jurors had not been drawn by chance from the jury wheel in the usual manner.

A new jury was drawn from the wheel. It heard witnesses and reported that the members of the mob were "mostly from other counties than Fayette, who were there for the avowed purpose of rescuing the prisoner from the authorities." It called the bloody riot "an unfortunate affair," and concluded that it would be unwise to return indictments, since the subsequent trials "would only tend to aggravate an already tense situation."

"Here we find a new principle injected into the processes of the law," the *Leader* declared in a bitter editorial. "Officers of the law, instead of seeking to punish the guilty and acquit the innocent, must first determine whether the trials of men presumably guilty of serious crimes and misdemeanors would disturb the public mind and 'tend to aggravate bitter feelings in the state.'" There the matter rested.

Lockett had been taken out of Lexington Tuesday night, under the protection of 400 soldiers. No attempt was made to sneak the prisoner out of town. The soldiers openly marched through the streets with him to the Union Station. Thirty-two officers and 472 soldiers remained in Lexington to maintain order. This force was reduced gradually until, on February 22, thirteen days after the riot, General Marshall proclaimed an end to martial rule, "law and order having been restored."

Lockett died in the electric chair at Eddyville Penitentiary on March 11, in the presence of nineteen Fayette County witnesses, including two brothers of his victim. Three days before the execution, he confessed the slaying of four women, one in Indiana, one in Illinois, and two in Kentucky, all by choking. Thus the child he killed in Fayette County had been his fifth victim.

The Kentucky General Assembly, which was in session at Frankfort when the Lexington riot occurred, enacted a law changing the penalty for rape from death in the electric chair to public hanging in the county in which the crime had been committed. Presumably the theory was that the mob lust for vengeance would be appeased by a convenient outdoor hanging which all could witness. A number of revolting exhibitions were staged under this law. The type of persons attracted to such events enjoyed themselves so thoroughly and behaved so atrociously that the law was repealed. Any effort to appease the mob spirit probably was unnecessary, anyway; the Second Battle of Lexington appeared to have dampened Kentuckians' ardor for lynching parties.

37. PUBLIC RELATIONS—
THE INVISIBLE SELL *

ROBERT L. HEILBRONER

The art of making men act collectively (that is, do the same things in response to given stimuli) has been developed almost to a professional level in recent years. Advertising is a general example; "public relations" is a more specific instance. The public relations expert, often using data collected under the rigidly controlled conditions specified for scientific observation, aims to create—on a mass basis if possible—favorable attitudes toward particular individuals, groups, or products in an attempt to control some of our relevant behaviors. His success in doing so, often without our being aware of what motivates us in an immediate sense, is described by Robert L. Heilbroner in his article on "The Invisible Sell."

Mixed up in the affairs of the Atomic Energy Commission, the Institute of Boiler and Radiator Manufacturers, Elvis Presley, and United States Steel; welcomed into the inner sanctum of church, corporation, and cabaret alike; as indispensable to a modern hospital as a surgeon and to a big labor union as an organizer, you will find the representatives of one of the newest, fastest growing, and certainly most significant professions of our times. These are the members of the public relations fraternity—a brotherhood of some 100,000 whose common bond is its profession, and whose common woe is that no two of the practitioners can ever quite agree on what that profession is.

Whatever it is, public relations is the wonder child of our age. Turn back to the Manhattan classified telephone directory for 1935 and look up the listing for public relations: you will find ten names. Go through the catalogues of the universities twenty years back, and you search for a course on public relations in vain. Investigate the public relations staff of General Motors for 1931, and you will discover one man, Paul Garrett, who had just been hired.

* *Harper's Magazine*, Vol. 214, No. 1285 (June, 1957), 23–31. Copyright © 1957 by Robert L. Heilbroner. Reprinted by permission of the author.

The author is a writer of technical and interpretative materials on economic subjects. President of Magazine Writers of America, 1955. Author of *The Worldly Philosophers* and *The Quest for Wealth*.

Today the listing in the telephone directory runs on for seven columns and over seven hundred names—in Manhattan alone. Last year 653 colleges taught something called "public relations"; eleven (including such pillars of respectability as Columbia and New York University) offered it as an undergraduate major; and one, Boston University, had a School of Public Relations which gave an M.S. degree. And last December when Paul Garrett retired from General Motors as a full vice president (to set up his own public relations firm), his staff numbered some two hundred people, exclusive of clerical help, and cost well over $1,000,000 a year.

That is, however, only evidence of public relations' meteoric rise. Even more impressive is its present extent. According to *Fortune* magazine, nearly five thousand corporations now support public relations departments or engage public relations counsel. An already outdated report by the Bureau of the Budget lists 5,211 full-time "information officers" for the federal government. Add in the labor unions, the private welfare organizations, the charities, causes, and not least, the celebrities who also buy what public relations men sell, and you arrive at the not unimpressive figure of at least half a billion dollars spent for PR hired help alone. How much is spent not for the hired hands, but on public relations itself, nobody even hazards a guess.

And what is this thing called "public relations" on which all this money is expended? It is not one thing, but many, for the practice in which the brotherhood engages is indeed a motley one. In the name of public relations you will find the boys "institutionalizing" a TV comic, "personalizing" an institution, or just plain peddling a product or an idea. Public relations includes such virtuous aims as making the public "aware" of muscular dystrophy and such dubious ones as putting pressure on a legislature through phony consumer fronts. It runs the gamut from philosophizing on social trends before a board of directors, to advising that same board on how best to pulverize the opposition in a proxy fight. It takes in the planted item in the gossip column and the artfully contrived mention of a client's product in a magazine article ostensibly about something else. It embraces the cozy corporate brochure "About Us Folks," and the hard-breathing advertisement of the "facts" concerning a strike. In a word, public relations covers a lot of acreage—blurring out into advertising, slopping over into selling, dipping down into publicity, and touching—or at least aspiring to—the "making" of public opinion itself.

And what, one may ask, after reading this ill-assorted catalogue, *is* public relations? Perhaps we can sum it up by calling it the business of the Invisible Sell. . . . In the arresting, if chilling, phrase of Edward L. Bernays, a pioneer in the field, public relations is "the engineering of public consent."

And this makes the brotherhood somewhat more interesting than just another bunch of guys out to make a buck. For we are all of us to some extent hooked by the Invisible Sell—enthusiastic about people we have never met, persuaded of the virtues of products and institutions with which we have no direct contact, contented captives of ideas we are scarcely aware of having picked up. If the public relations men are capable of *manufacturing* these enthusiasms, persuasions, and ideas, it would not be too much to claim that they practice the most important occupation of our day. Or perhaps one should say the most portentous. Or perhaps merely the most pretentious. Whatever the final verdict, it would certainly seem worth while to meet the fraternity members themselves.

UP FROM BROADWAY

. . . . .

Of the 700-odd public relations firms in New York and the 2,000-odd in the nation, a very considerable number—perhaps as many as two-thirds—represent the ventures of bright young men, who start with a general background in publicity, a client or two, and a few hundred dollars in cash. This is where enterprising youth goes these days, instead of West. A career in point is that of an ex-publicity man named Alan Brandt. Good-looking, voluble, and an absolute garden sprinkler of ideas, Brandt took the plunge sixteen months ago from a well-paid position as publicity director of station WNEW in New York. . . .

"I just got tired of working for someone else," says Brandt, "so I went out and got myself a room with one window, one desk, one phone, one size of stationery, one girl—and one client. I was in business."

The client was the producer of Captain Kangaroo, a TV kiddies' show, and Brandt publicized it as the children's show that *parents* would like. It was a good pitch and made several magazine breaks, and thereupon the phone began to ring. A hair-products firm wanted to know if Brandt could think of some way of publicizing buns and chignons: Brandt got a TV hair styles contest started. A Boston radio station showed up looking for a publicity idea: Brandt printed records which fitted the new Chrysler car-phonograph and which interrupted their music with, "Are you missing the news? Tune in on station WHDH." A TV morning show wanted to be talked about: Brandt put Salvador Dali on to explain that the cauliflower was the basis of all art, and had an art dealer choose between six masterpieces worth over $100,000 and six fake copies worth less than $100, by slashing the fakes—while Brandt quietly perspired behind the camera. A book publisher wondered if something could be done about a novel set in a small New England town. Brandt got an item in the Associated Press about a book that would blow up Gilman-ton, New Hampshire, and *Peyton Place* was a best seller before it even reached the bookstores.

. . . . .

HOW TO CATCH A WHALE

. . . . .

Now since there are very few magazines or newspapers which would be interested in running a story about typewriters, wool, or dog food, and still fewer which would give free advertising to Underwood, the Wool Institute, or the Gaines Dog Food Company, the public relations man must disguise his hook with fancy feathers. The Underwood people therefore prepare "5 Sprightly Stories" on such themes as *How To Keep Your Boss Happy,* or *The Girl With The Halo* (your secretary); the Wool Institute offers *How's Your AQ?* (Appearance Quotient) and *Wool in History and Legend*—"the fascinating story of the thousands-of-years-old romance of the use of wool"; and the dog food people establish the Gaines Dog Research Center—"a research and educational institution created as a public service." These are offered free to editors.

Needless to say, the mortality rate of such PR productions reaches epidemic proportions, but since the birth rate is high, a certain number of brain-children survive. A considerable number as a matter of fact, No PR firm of any stature cannot boast of having "placed" stories in *Life, Look, Saturday Evening Post,* or *Reader's Digest,* not to mention the *New York Times. . . .*

One of the most successful product promoters is the firm of Ruder and Finn, which began like Brandt Public Relations, on a shoestring. Not quite ten years ago Bill Ruder, a young publicity man for Sam Goldwyn, and David Finn, a hopeful painter, decided to put their curi-ously diverse talents together in public relations. They took a room in the Hotel Lombardy—the size of which can be judged by the fact that it is now the hotel linen closet—and landed that essential First Account. It was a promotion job for Perry Como's records, and they performed it so artfully that Como thanked them publicly in an ad in *Billboard.* Then *their* phone began to ring. And they began to think.

"We didn't want to be just publicity boys all our lives," says Finn. "And while we were beating our brains to think of a way not to be, Bill remembered the nation-wide publicity network that Goldwyn used. We decided to try the same deal for product promotion." By writing to independent PRs around the country, Ruder and Finn established a gossamer-thin tie-up with small out-of-town public relations firms, and this they then hawked as the Ruder & Finn Field Network. Into its flimsy meshes promptly swam a whale. A major soap company was about to launch a new soap and it wanted just such point-of-sale promotion. The soap brass descended from its glassy heights to the brownstone basement into which Ruder and Finn had moved their operation (and where they had spent the previous twenty-four hours frantically adding twenty-seven men to their "network"), and—perhaps with suds in its eyes—approved of what it saw.

After that it was easy. Today, with seventy employees, a Field Network of over 190, and a gross take in excess of $1,200,000, Bill Ruder and Dave Finn run one of the six biggest PR firms in the country.

   . . . . .

What is public relations at the R & F level? Of course it includes product promotion via the Invisible Sell, as witness a technique used to push Skotch Koolers, a picnic carrier. R & F sent samples of the Koolers to professional photographers and TV studios, merely suggesting that they might be used as studio props. They were. You may have noticed the Kooler alongside the man with the beard in a Schweppes ad, or next to a bathing beauty extolling skin cream. Without spending a nickel on advertising, R & F dangled its product before the eyes of several million people, a pleasing number of whom swallowed the bait.

But the public relations bait does not consist of products only. Indeed, the publics to which R & F professionally relates its clients tend to include fewer and fewer customers, and more and more groups such as stockholders, employees, or even bankers. For these publics Ruder and Finn will design a client's annual report and compose dignified but warm letters to his shareholders, will edit his employee newspaper, or make his name known among the Wall Street community. Or, in the jargon of the trade, they will create and sell his "image."

   . . . . .

. . . At the powerhouse of public relations maintained by General Motors, only a fraction of the PR effort is aimed at making people like GM *cars*. . . . Sales Promotion does *that*. What public relations must do is the far more difficult job of selling General Motors itself—as a community asset, a helpful company, a corporation with solid ideas, a big business with its heart in the right place—in a word, as a great institution, and by implication, one which should not be meddled with.

When Paul Garrett arrived in Detroit twenty-five years ago to begin General Motors' public relations program, the first question fired at him was: "How do you make a billion dollars look small?" Garrett said damned if he knew, and furthermore damned if he thought that was his job. Public relations, he argued, was not an "act," but a continuing effort on the part of management to win the confidence of the people with whom it came into contact. Hence you will find General Motors engaged in a host of activities in which altruism and self-interest come together in a creamy blend. Plant, City and Field Relations, for example, stimulates local GM participation in the community affairs of the sixty-eight cities where it has factories, thereby helping both the community and itself. Educational Relations works with the schools, providing them with such useful educational material as films on safe driving, and providing itself with a flow of applicants for jobs. The Speakers Bureau is glad to send a company-sponsored lecturer to your club or association to edify it with an inspirational talk—or to educate it with a "sound" economic one. Institutional Advertising tells the story of GM's role in supporting some twenty thousand suppliers, and leaves you with the pleasant impression that what's good for General Motors is good for small business, too. The billion dollars may not look any smaller as a result of these efforts. But it looks much, much nicer.

THE IMAGE-MAKERS

This same kind of quiet winning of friends and influencing of people is practiced by the biggest public relations firms. At Hill & Knowlton, for instance, which runs neck and neck with Carl Byoir & Associates as the largest PR outfit in the country (H & K's minimum fee $36,000; Byoir's, $50,000, but H & K has more accounts), only 6 or 7 per cent of the firm's effort is spent on publicity. The rest is largely concentrated on showing corporations how to do Good Works and how to present their side of the story—which is always known as The Facts.

Thus for its biggest account, the American Iron and Steel Institute (which is incidentally the biggest PR account in the country), H & K provides a whole panoply of services, none of which is calculated to sell a single ton of steel, but all of which are calculated to sell the steel industry and its point of view. It publishes *Steelways,* a magazine which is sent to 100,000 key people, such as editors and educators, who pass along interesting bits of information to an audience estimated at 12,-000,000. It puts out booklets on "timely topics of importance" such as the industry's lagging profit rate. It runs a field service which counsels individual companies on such matters as how to conduct plant tours, or how to work with the local school board, or who should go on the Institute's mailing list.

And it runs such interesting services as the Community Resources Workshop. This is a project to acquaint teachers with industry and its potential helpfulness in providing educational material. It also aims at giving teachers an insight into the problems of steel—not on a "propagandistic" basis, but just the way steel executives honestly see them. Dr. Albert L. Ayars, the educator who heads the Workshop, has stated that he would resign if his project were ever used for the propagation of distorted facts. "I suppose you could say," he admits, "that as a result of these experiences the teachers will be more receptive to some legislation which would be of benefit to industry and the public. But again, not because they have been coerced into it. All that we would have done from the standpoint of our client, American Iron and Steel Industry, is to have exposed them to the facts."

For those who picture public relations at the summit as the cunning manipulation of minds, or the subtle exercise of devious techniques, the actual practice of Big PR must look tame indeed. That it is often transparently self-serving, under the guise of serving the public, is perfectly true; and that the motives which prompt it are not entirely spiritual, needs hardly to be pointed out. It is the Invisible Sell on a huge scale, but whereas one may not always particularly like what is being sold, it is hard to get much worked up over the salesmanship.

That goes for nine-tenths of Big PR. Of course there is also the tenth tenth. Witness, for example, the public-relations tactics in the Pennsylvania railroad-truckers fight in 1952. The client here was the Eastern Railroads Presidents Conference; the PR firm was that of Carl Byoir & Associates (Hill & Knowlton's big competitor); and the issue at stake was a bill increasing the size and weight limits for trucks on the state roads. It was not by accident that Byoir was chosen for the task of beating the bill. As the company explained in a letter to one of the railroad vice presidents (in charge of public relations), it was good at that sort of thing, modestly mentioning a chain-store bill it had licked in New York State for the A & P, and a tax reduction it had secured in Louisiana for the Freeport Sulphur company. And so, for a fee of $150,000 it got the job.

And brought home the bacon. In due course the bill was vetoed by the Governor.

Not that the Governor acted out of any but the best interest. He had before him, for example, an early report of the Maryland State Roads Commission containing very unfavorable data on road damage. He was faced at every turn by newspaper and magazine articles on the evils of trucking, and across his desk passed a succession of interesting studies by institutions such as the New Jersey Citizens Tax Study Foundation. Certainly not absent from the Governor's mind was the opposition of the State Association of Township Supervisors, which had mailed out thousands of postcards protesting the truck bill, and of the State Grange, a politically powerful organization.

When Governor Fine vetoed the bill, it must have seemed to him that he was only expressing the will of the people; but how much of this will of the people was the result of the activities of the Byoir agency who spent several hundred thousand dollars in their campaign?

. . . . .

All this, however, is aside from the crucial point. It is not the excesses, but the run of the mill of big PR, not its faults but its very virtues which need examination. The basic question is not the power which resides in bad public relations, but that inherent in *good* public relations; not the ability of public relations to subvert, but its capacity to convince. The really important question about the power of public relations is whether it can influence what men *think*.

WHERE THE DOUBT BEGINS

This brings us to an impressive demonstration concerning the making of public opinion that took place in Cincinnati in 1947.

For six months Cincinnati became the focus for an unprecedented crusade—a powerful, well-planned, and well-financed attempt to teach it what to think. Specifically, Cincinnati was the target of an all-out effort to make a typical American city "United Nations conscious."

The crusade was a thorough and intelligent one. It was launched at every level of city life. On blotters, matchbooks, streetcar signs, and billboards. Cincinnatians read "Peace Begins with the United Nations—the United Nations Begins with You." Local radio stations broadcast UN facts and news daily—one of them on 150 spots a week. The newspapers played up the theme. Every schoolchild in the city was given literature about the United Nations to take home; the PTA, the Council of Churches, and the Catholic Church all climbed enthusiastically aboard the bandwagon. Club women rallied round with letters and telegrams pledging their support to the American delegation to the UN. In the last three months as the campaign reached a crescendo, 225 meetings were held; hundreds of documentary films shown, 59,588 pieces of literature distributed.

Then they took a poll of the results.

At the end of six months only *half* as many people considered the United Nations a means of preventing war as thought so at the beginning.

There was almost no change in the number who thought the United States should take an active part in world affairs.

There was a drop in the number of those who were in favor of having the United States join an international police to keep peace.

Fewer people thought there should be some sort of international control of atom bombs.

There was almost no change in the numbers who knew what the main purpose of the United Nations was, or who had heard of the veto power, or who knew how the UN worked.

In a word, the campaign was a gigantic frost.

Why? The answer may be shocking, but it is simplicity itself: people in Cincinnati just didn't give a damn about the United Nations one way or another. For all the matchbooks and the meetings, the UN was something far off, vague, abstract, unconnected with daily life. Hence the propaganda went in one ear and out the other, and save for the pleasant friction stimulated in transit, it left no imprint at all.

And the moral, for public relations, seems to be that most people don't give a damn about most things, unless those things are part and parcel of their concrete lives. They just don't listen. For many years, Hill & Knowlton has sought to put across such simple (and true) messages as that the steel industry is not a dangerous place to work, or that steel's profit margins, by comparison with other industries, have been low. The results: slightly *more* people thought steel was dangerous in 1955 than in 1946 or 1943, and there continues to be "considerable belief" (in Hill & Knowlton's own words) that steel's profits are too high.

Or take the case of General Motors. For nearly twenty years, along with seven other large corporations, GM has tested its popularity by means of a continuing opinion poll called the Link Audit. On the face of it, results were excellent: the proportion of people who "liked" General Motors (and all the other companies) rose from less than 60 per cent in the late 'thirties to over 80 per cent today. The only trouble is, no one quite knows what "like" means. Every time there is a strike in any *one* of the eight companies, the popularity of *all* them goes down. For some unfathomable reason all the corporations are more popular in fall than spring. And every time there is something to get mad about, the Link Audit "liking" doesn't seem to prevent people from boiling up: when Harlow Curtice, GM's president, testily denied to a Senate Committee last year that there was anything wrong with General Motors' dealer relations, something akin to a whirlwind of angry protests materialized out of the blue. Chastened, Mr. Curtice appeared again in a more conciliatory mood. The whirlwind disappeared. And the Link Audit once again showed that everybody "liked" General Motors.

Hence the public-opinion researchers are, to put it mildly, skeptical about the ability of public relations to engineer the public's consent and dubious about the depth of the affections it arouses. "Give the PR something real and specific—a personality, a product, or even a precise enough idea—and he can usually make an impact," says one professional public-opinion measurer. "But ask him to sell a big fuzzy thing like a 'nice' company or a 'sound' doctrine, and the result is usually an absolutely monumental indifference."

Or worse, skepticism. One opinion researcher, Douglas Williams, measuring the effect of a company's effort to "sell" its employees on Free Private Enterprise, found the net outcome to be an increase in hostility and suspicion. "Those people knew about free enterprise in terms of their own jobs and incomes," he explains. "They didn't like having those realities 'justified' with fancy abstractions. Instead they asked, 'What's really the matter, that they have to sell this thing to me?'"

The wiser public relations men are well aware of these facts. "Make no mistake about it," says Earl Newsom, who counsels, among others, Ford and Standard Oil of New Jersey, "a corporation does not win the confidence of the American people by trying to 'educate' them to its point of view." A case in point is Newsom's client, "Jersey," which has long ago wearily resigned itself to living with the popular opinion that it is still part of the oil trust which broke up some forty years ago. It just doesn't bother to argue any more—because it realizes that it probably wouldn't do any good if it did.

But whereas the public relations men themselves have salutary doubts about the efficacy of their efforts to sell those nice big ideas, their clients share no such hesitations with them. For if there is one part of the public which is really a patsy for the power of public relations, it is that hard-headed pragmatic character, the American big businessman himself. Not content with using public relations to publicize or promote his wares, or to cement his relationships with his employees or stockholders—all of which it can do very well—he is convinced that it can serve to get his "message" across to an eagerly attentive public, and to enshrine his corporation, as well as its products, in their hearts. Nor does he, curiously enough, demand proof of this conviction, for he has swallowed the Invisible Sell hook, line, and sinker.

WHAT IS IT WORTH?

If the public relations brotherhood is not quite so powerful as its enthusiastic clients think, neither can it be shrugged off as just a collection of publicists, pitchmen, and commercial philosophers. Public relations is more than just an occupation or a bunch of occupations: it is a social force—and as such it has left two indelible marks on our world.

The first mark is its part in the general debasement of communications from which we suffer. It is only a banality to point out the need for effective public communication in today's complex society, but communication has become more of a fetish than a function. Science has a technical term which describes the result of forcing more messages along a carrier than it can accommodate: it calls the result *noise*. We live in a noisy society: one in which everyone talks and few say anything; one in which the spurious, the insincere, the meretricious, and most of all the *empty*, crowd out the meaningful, the useful, the important. People who live in such a society learn not to listen—or worse, when they do listen, they learn to disbelieve what they hear.

In this process of the debasement of communication, public relations must bear its share of the blame. No one can quarrel with the essential function that public relations fills as the purveyor of genuine ideas and information. No one denies that many public relations men, working for corporations as well as for colleges or causes, honestly communicate things which are worth communicating. Nor can anyone absolve public relations for loading the communications channels with noise. We read the news and suspect that behind it lies the "news release." We encounter reputation and ascribe it to publicity. Worst of all, we no longer credit good behavior to good motives, but cheapen it to the level of "good public relations."

It is not *that* bad, of course. But if we step back to view that whole big thing called Public Relations and then attempt to weigh what it has meant to our values and beliefs, it is hard to avoid the conclusion that the net effect of the Invisible Sell has been to further a cynical judgment of the motives behind human behavior.

That is one side of the coin, but there is another, and shinier. If public relations has cheapened the face value of good conduct, at the same time it has enormously increased the prevalence of good conduct. For regardless of its motive or its incessant self-advertisement, good conduct *is* more prevalent on the business scene, and public relations can rightly take much of the credit. The reason is a curious one. It is that something called Good Public Relations has come to be regarded as an indispensable attribute of business—as much a sign that a business is "modern and progressive" as a shiny new glass office building (which is also, of course, a good public relations move). Quite simply, business has sold itself the bill of goods it originally intended to sell the public.

"If you ask me," said one shrewd public relations man, "the aim of a big corporation should be invisibility. But no. It insists on being as visible as possible. Its directors get nervous unless people say what wonderful public relations the company has. So it has to *have* wonderful public relations. It has to *act* lovable. It has to *be* progressive. It has to *become* socially responsible—not because the management necessarily thinks that way, but because that's what Good Public Relations is."

Hence by an unexpected twist, public relations has become a weapon whose recoil is greater than its muzzle blast. Good Public Relations has come to be something very much like the corporate conscience —a commercial conscience, no doubt, but a conscience none the less. If the public relations profession can bolster this role, if it can become the corporate conscience openly, fearlessly, and wisely, speaking not only *for* business but *to* business, then it will have more than redeemed its name.

38. THE NATURE OF PERSONAL
INFLUENCE *

PAUL F. LAZARSFELD, BERNARD BERELSON, AND
HAZEL GAUDET

Collective behavior, like any other form of social behavior, operates within a framework of communication. Sometimes this framework is an indirect one involving the use of mass media, but very often it is a system of face-to-face relationships. In this selection Lazarsfeld and his associates systematically examine the nature of personal influence in determining the actual vote in a presidential election. Although this is a study of "decision making" in politics, the principles described have broad general application to many kinds of collective behavior involving personal relationships.

The political homogeneity of social groups is promoted by personal relationships among the same kinds of people. But for a detailed and systematic study of the influence of such relationships—the political role of personal influence—a systematic inventory would be needed of the various personal contacts and political discussions that people had over a sample number of days. . . . Such complete data are not available in the present study, but enough information has been collected to indicate the importance of personal relationships so far as their direct political influence is concerned. Our findings and impressions will be summarized

* Paul F. Lazarsfeld, Bernard Berelson, and Hazel Gaudet, *The People's Choice: How the Voter Makes Up His Mind in a Presidential Campaign* (2nd ed., New York: Columbia University Press, 1948), 150–158. Reprinted by permission of the publisher and the senior author.

For a biographical sketch of Paul Lazarsfeld, see selection 4.

Bernard Berelson is Director, Behavioral Science Program, Ford Foundation, and Professor, Graduate School of Business, University of Chicago. Sometime Chairman, Committee on Communication, and Professor of Library Science and Social Sciences, University of Chicago; Dean, Graduate Library School, University of Chicago. Past President American Association of Public Opinion Research. Author: *The Library Public; Reader in Communication and Public Opinion* (with Morris Janowitz); *Content Analysis.*

Hazel Gaudet was associated with the Bureau of Applied Social Research, Columbia University.

without much formal statistical data. The significance of this area of political behavior was highlighted by the study but further investigation is necessary to establish it more firmly.

In comparison with the formal media of communication, personal relationships are potentially more influential for two reasons: their coverage is greater and they have certain psychological advantages over the formal media.

PERSONAL CONTACTS REACH THE UNDECIDED

Whenever the respondents were asked to report on their recent exposure to campaign communications of all kinds, political discussions were mentioned more frequently than exposure to radio or print. On any average day, at least 10% more people participated in discussions about the election—either actively or passively—than listened to a major speech or read about campaign items in a newspaper. And this coverage "bonus" came from just those people who had not yet made a final decision as to how they would vote. Political conversations, then, were more likely to reach those people who were still open to influence.

For example, people who made up their minds later in the campaign were more likely to mention personal influences in explaining how they formed their final vote decision. Similarly, we found that the less interested people relied more on conversations and less on the formal media as sources of information. Three-fourths of the respondents who at one time had not expected to vote but were then finally "dragged in" mentioned personal influence. After the election, the voters were given a check list of "sources from which they got most of the information or impressions that caused them to form their judgment on how to vote." Those who had made some change during the campaign mentioned friends or members of their family relatively more frequently than did the respondents who kept a constant vote intention all through the campaign.

THE TWO-STEP FLOW OF COMMUNICATIONS

A special role in the network of personal relationships is played by the "opinion leaders.". . . We noted that they engaged in political discussion much more than the rest of the respondents. But they reported that the formal media were more effective as sources of influence than personal relationships. This suggests that ideas often flow *from* radio and print *to* the opinion leaders and *from* them to the less active sections of the population.

Occasionally, the more articulate people even pass on an article or point out the importance of a radio speech. Repeatedly, changers referred to reading or listening done under some personal influence. Take the case of a retired school teacher who decided for the Republicans: "The country is ripe for a change . . . Willkie is a religious man. A *friend read and highly recommended* Dr. Poling's article in the October issue of the *Christian Herald* called 'The Religion of Wendell Willkie.'"

So much for the "coverage of personal contacts." The person-to-person influence reaches the ones who are more susceptible to change, and serves as a bridge over which formal media of communications extend their influence. But in addition, personal relationships have certain psychological advantages which make them especially effective in the exercise of the "molecular pressures" finally leading to the political homogeneity of social groups. We turn now to a discussion of five such characteristics.

NON-PURPOSIVENESS OF PERSONAL CONTACTS

The weight of personal contacts upon opinion lies, paradoxically, in their greater casualness and non-purposiveness in political matters. If we read or tune in a speech, we usually do so purposefully, and in doing so we have a definite mental set which tinges our receptiveness. Such purposive behavior is part of the broad area of our political experiences, to which we bring our convictions with a desire to test them and strengthen them by what is said. This mental set is armor against influence. The extent to which people, and particularly those with strong partisan views, listen to speakers and read articles with which they agree in advance is evidence on this point.

On the other hand, people we meet for reasons other than political discussion are more likely to catch us unprepared, so to speak, if they make politics the topic. One can avoid newspaper stories and radio speeches simply by making a slight effort, but as the campaign mounts and discussion intensifies, it is hard to avoid some talk of politics. Personal influence is more pervasive and less self-selective than the formal media. In short, politics gets through, especially to the indifferent, much more easily through personal contacts than in any other way, simply because it comes up unexpectedly as a sideline or marginal topic in a casual conversation. For example, there was the restaurant waitress who decided that Willkie would make a poor president after first thinking he would be good. Said she: "I had done a little newspaper reading against Willkie, but the real reason I changed my mind was from *hearsay*. So many people don't like Willkie. Many customers in the restaurant said Willkie would be no good." Notice that she was in a position to overhear bits of conversation that were not intended for her. There are many such instances. Talk that is "forbidden fruit" is particularly effective because one need not be suspicious as to the persuasive intentions of the speakers; as a result one's defenses are down. Furthermore, one may feel that he is getting the viewpoint of "people generally," that he is learning how "different people" think about the election.

Such passive participation in conversation is paralleled in the case of the formal media by accidental exposure, e.g., when a political speech is heard because it follows a favorite program. In both conversation and the formal media, such chance communication is particularly effective. And the testimony to such influence is much more frequent in the case of personal contacts. The respondents mentioned it time and again: "I've heard fellows talk at the plant . . . I hear men talk at the shop . . . My husband heard that talked about at work. . . ."

FLEXIBILITY WHEN COUNTERING RESISTANCE

But suppose we do meet people who want to influence us and suppose they arouse our resistance. Then personal contact still has one great advantage compared with other media: the face-to-face contact can counter and dislodge such resistance, for it is much more flexible. The clever campaign worker, professional or amateur, can make use of a large number of cues to achieve his end. He can choose the occasion at which to speak to the other fellow. He can adapt his story to what he presumes to be the other's interest and his ability to understand. If he notices the other is bored, he can change the subject. If he sees that he has aroused resistance, he can retreat, giving the other the satisfaction of a victory, and come back to his point later. If in the course of the discussion he discovers some pet convictions, he can try to tie up his argument with them. He can spot the moments when the other is yielding, and so time his best punches.

Neither radio nor the printed page can do anything of the kind. They must aim their propaganda shots at the whole target instead of just at the center, which represents any particular individual. In propaganda as much as in other things, one man's meat is another man's poison. This may lead to boomerang effects, when arguments aimed at "average" audiences with "average" reactions fail with Mr. X. The formal media produced several boomerangs upon people who resented what they read or heard and moved in the opposite direction from that intended. But among 58 respondents who mentioned personal contacts as concretely influential, there was only one boomerang. The flexibility of the face-to-face situation undoubtedly accounted for their absence.

REWARDS OF COMPLIANCE

When someone yields to a personal influence in making a vote decision, the reward is immediate and personal. This is not the case in yielding to an argument via print or radio. If a pamphlet argues that voting for the opposite party would be un-American or will jeopardize the future, its warning may sound too remote or improbable. But if a neighbor says the same things, he can "punish" one immediately for being unimpressed or unyielding: he can look angry or sad, he can leave the room and make his fellow feel isolated. The pamphlet can only intimate or describe future deprivations; the living person can create them at once.

Of course all this makes personal contacts a powerful influence only for people who do not like to be out of line. There are certainly some people who gain pleasure from being nonconformists, but under normal circumstances they are probably very much in the minority. Whenever propaganda by another person is experienced as an expression of the prevailing group tendencies, it has greater chances of being successful than the formal media because of social rewards. For example, here is a woman who was for Roosevelt until the middle of the campaign: "I have always been a Democrat and I think Roosevelt has been all right. But my family are all for Willkie. They think he would make the best president and they have been putting the pressure on me." She finally voted for Willkie. This aspect of personal contact was especially important for women.

The rewards of compliance to other people are learned in early childhood. The easiest way for most children to avoid discomfort is to do what others tell them to do. Someone who holds no strong opinions on politics and hence makes up his mind late in the campaign may very well be susceptible to personal influences because he has learned as a child to take them as useful guides in unknown territory. The young man who was going to vote for Roosevelt because "my grandfather will skin me if I don't" is a case in point.

TRUST IN AN INTIMATE SOURCE

More people put reliance upon their personal contacts to help them pick out the arguments which are relevant for their own good in political affairs than they do in the more remote and impersonal newspaper and radio. The doubtful voter may feel that the evaluations he reads or hears in a broadcast are plausible, for the expert writer can probably spell out the consequences of voting more clearly than the average citizen. But the voter still wonders whether these are the issues which are really going to affect *his own* future welfare. Perhaps these sources see the problem from a viewpoint entirely different from his own. But he can trust the judgment and evaluation of the respected people among his associates. Most of them are people with the same status and interests as himself. Their attitudes are more relevant for him than the judgments of an unknown editorial writer. In a formal communication the content can be at its best; but in a face-to-face contact the transference is most readily achieved. For example, here is the case of a young laborer who professed little or no interest in the campaign and who did not even expect to vote until late October: "I've been discussing the election with the *fellows at the shop* and I believe I'll vote, but I haven't decided yet who for." His constant exposure to the views of his fellow-workers not only brought him to the ballot booth but also brought out his final Democratic vote in line with his colleagues.

A middle-aged woman who showed great interest in the campaign was undecided until late October and then voted for Willkie: "*I was talking politics just this morning with a friend, a businessman.* He says business will improve if Willkie is elected and that Willkie promises to keep us out of the war. FDR is getting too much power. He shouldn't have a third term." Her friend had apparently run out for her what amounted to a small catalogue of Republican arguments and he was impressive enough to clinch her vote, which had been in the balance throughout the campaign. Her trust in his judgment settled her mind.

Trust in another person's point of view may be due to his prestige as well as to the plausibility of what he has to say or its relevancy to one's interests. It is obvious that in all influences prestige plays a considerable role. The degree of conformity is greater the higher the prestige of the person in our group who seeks to influence us. The plausibility of the consequences he presents will seem greater if he is important. (Of course, the formal media are also important in this respect.) The heightening of trust through the prestige of certain personal contacts was clear in the case of the driver of a bread truck who changed to Willkie because the prominent president of a business firm had done him the honor of persuading him in that direction. Then, too, there is the case of a middle-aged housewife with little education who was for Willkie from May through September, became undecided in October, and finally voted for Roosevelt. She left Willkie because of the statements of people whom she considered authorities: "I talked with *a college student* from Case, in Cleveland, and students are for Roosevelt because he has helped recreation. I talked, too, with a *man from Chicago who is very interested in politics,* and he doesn't seem to think that Willkie is a big enough man to handle international affairs."

PERSUASION WITHOUT CONVICTION

Finally, personal contacts can get a voter to the polls without affecting at all his comprehension of the issues of the election—something the formal media can rarely do. The newspaper or magazine or radio must first be effective in changing attitudes related to the action. There were several clear cases of votes cast not on the issues or even the personalities of the candidates. In fact, they were not really cast for the candidates at all. They were cast, so to speak, for the voters' friends.

"I was taken to the polls by a worker who insisted that I go."

"The lady where I work wanted me to vote. She took me to the polls and *they all voted Republican so I did too."*

In short, personal influence, with all its overtones of personal affection and loyalty, can bring to the polls votes that would otherwise not be cast or would be cast for the opposing party just as readily if some other friend had insisted. They differ from the formal media by persuading uninterested people to vote in a certain way without giving them a substantive reason for their vote. Fully 25% of those who mentioned a personal contact in connection with change of mind failed to give a real issue of the campaign as a reason for the change, but only 5% of those who mentioned the formal media omitted such a reason. When personal influence is paramount in this way, the voter is voting mainly for the personal friend, not the candidate.

PRACTICAL IMPLICATIONS

In a way the outcome of the election in Erie County is the best evidence for the success of face-to-face contacts. It so happened that for some time the Republican machine in that area worked much more vigorously than its Democratic opponent. When asked whether they knew people who had good ideas about politics, our respondents mentioned considerably more Republican than Democratic local politicians. A few people who did not expect to vote but finally went to the polls mentioned Republican canvassers as the main influence, but we could not trace a similar success for the Democratic machine.

However, one should not identify the personal contacts discussed in this chapter with the efforts of the *professional* political machines. These personal contacts are what one might call *amateur machines* which spring up during elections—individuals who become quite enthusiastic or special groups that try to activate people within their reach. One might almost say that the most successful form of propaganda—especially last-minute propaganda—is to "surround" the people whose vote decision is still dubious so that the only path left to them is the way to the polling booth. We do not know how the budget of the political parties is distributed among different channels of propaganda but we suspect that the largest part of any propaganda budget is spent on pamphlets, radio time, etc. But our findings suggest the task of finding the best ratio between money spent on formal media and money spent on organizing the face-to-face influences, the local "molecular pressures" which vitalize the formal media by more personal interpretation and the full richness of personal relationships into the promotion of the causes which are decided upon in the course of an election.

In the last analysis, more than anything else people can move other people. From an ethical point of view this is a hopeful aspect in the serious social problem of propaganda. The side which has the more enthusiastic supporters and which can mobilize grass-root support in an expert way has great chances of success.

39. NOTES ON A NATURAL HISTORY OF FADS *

ROLF MEYERSOHN AND ELIHU KATZ

Fads, which are sometimes defined as short-lived or very particularized fashions, are dramatic and often highly visible evidences of the tendency of human beings with similar backgrounds to react similarly to the same stimuli. Fads such as the hula hoop and the Davy Crockett hat may sweep across a whole nation or they may be limited to a single community. In either case, they demonstrate the general phenomenon of human collective behavior. Such collective behavior does not, however, occur simply at random but has what might be termed a "natural history." This is illustrated in the article by Rolf Meyersohn and Elihu Katz.

The study of fads and fashions may serve the student of social change much as the study of fruit flies has served geneticists: neither the sociol-

* Reprinted from "Notes on a Natural History of Fads," *The American Journal of Sociology*, Vol. 62, No. 6 (May, 1957), 594–601, by Rolf Meyersohn and Elihu Katz, by permission of The University of Chicago Press. Copyright 1957 by The University of Chicago.

Rolf Meyersohn (b. 1926) is Research Director, Center for the Study of Leisure, at the University of Chicago. He has also written in the areas of public opinion and communication.

Dr. Elihu Katz (b. 1926) is Assistant Professor of Sociology at the University of Chicago. His major fields of interest include public opinion and communication within small groups. Coauthor of *Personal Influence.*

ogist nor the geneticist has to wait long for a new generation to arrive.

Fads provide an extraordinary opportunity to study processes of influence or contagion, of innovative and cyclical behavior, and of leadership; this has been long recognized by social thinkers, most of whom tended, however, to regard fads and fashions as one form of permanent social change.

To regard change in fads exclusively as a prototype of social change is to overlook several fundamental distinctions. In the first place, the process by which fads operate is typically confined to particular subgroups in society, and, although fads may change violently and swiftly, the subgroup remains the same; the network of fad communication usually remains stable. On the other hand, patterns of communication that create new social movements—for example, a new religious sect—also create a new social structure; here both the content and the network of communication are new. This distinction is well made by Blumer, who points out that social movements, unlike fads, usually leave stable organizations in their wake:

> Not only is the fashion movement unique in terms of its character, but it differs from other movements in that it does not develop into a society. It does not build up a social organization; it does not develop a division of labor among its participants with each being assigned a given status: it does not construct a new set of symbols, myths, values, philosophy, or set of practices, and in this sense does not form a culture; and finally, it does not develop a set of loyalties or form a we-consciousness.

Popular music illustrates this distinction. Every few months a new "content" in the form of new hits flows through the same "network" of distributors (disk jockeys, etc.) and consumers (primarily teen-agers and other radio audiences). While an occasional song may attract some distributors or consumers who are not regularly a part of the system—for example, the recently popular song "Morität" from Brecht and Weill's *Threepenny Opera* found high-brow listeners outside the regular music audience—these stray elements usually get out as quickly as they came in. The popular-music world as a whole remains unchanged and goes on as before to produce its continuous cycle of discontinuous hits.

Each new fad is a *functional alternative* for its predecessor: this hit for that hit, this parlor game for that one. On the other hand, the processes involved in broader social changes, such as religious conversions, an increase in the birth rate, or a movement toward suburban living, are too complex to permit simple substitution. Following Merton, who, in arguing against the functional indispensability of a social structure, points out that the range of possible variation is more relevant, one may say that in fashion the range of functional alternatives is far greater than in other domains of social change.

Perhaps this is so because fashions are found in relatively super-ficial areas of human conduct—in the trivial or ornamental. Many more changes have occurred in the styling of automobiles (e.g., in the length of tail lights) than in their engines. In a brilliant essay on fashion Simmel discusses the selective process whereby some cultural items are subject to fashion and others not, and he points out that the former must be "independent of the vital motives of human action."

Fashion occasionally will accept objectively determined subjects such as religious faith, scientific interests, even socialism and individualism; but it does not become operative as fashion until these subjects can be considered inde-pendent of the deeper human motives from which they have risen. For this reason the rule of fashion becomes in such fields unendurable. We therefore see that there is good reason why externals—clothing, social conduct, amuse-ments—constitute the specific field of fashion, for here no dependence is placed on really vital motives of human action.

Triviality, of course, does not refer to the amount of emotion, affect, and functional significance surrounding an object but rather to its life-expectancy, its susceptibility to being *outmoded*. Every object has a finite and estimable life-span; a pair of nylon stockings may last a few weeks, a dress a few years, an automobile a decade or two, a house much longer. It is one of the characteristics of fashion that replacement is made before the life-span ends. Such objects are acquired without regard for their durability. This is one definition of "conspicuous consumption."

Hence we arrive at one possible indication whether an item is a carrier of fashion. Simmel has illustrated this point very well:

When we furnish a house these days, intending the articles to last a quarter of a century, we invariably invest in furniture designed according to the very latest patterns and do not even consider articles in vogue two years before. Yet it is obvious that the attraction of fashion will desert the present article just as it left the earlier one, and satisfaction or dissatisfaction with both forms is determined by other material criteria. A peculiar psychological process seems to be at work here in addition to the mere bias of the moment. Some fashion always exists and fashion per se is indeed immortal, which fact seems to affect in some manner or other each of its manifestations, although the very nature of each individual fashion stamps it as being transitory. The fact that change itself does not change, in this instance endows each of the objects which it affects with a psychological appearance of duration.

Since most fads are of a minority or subculture, they may of course exhibit contradictory or countervailing trends all at once. While the fashion system as a whole may rely on an incompleted life-span for a part of its *élan*, certain subsystems of fashions operate in the opposite way. Thus, the trend today may be to trade in perfectly usable automobiles; yet there are those who drive nothing but antique automobiles. Such people attempt to *exceed* the structural limits of this particular item, and their possessions are as much a part of the fashion system as the latest, newest, the "most unique."

Several approaches to the study of fads can be distinguished. One is concerned with the function of fashion generally for society, groups, and individuals. . . .

Fashions have also been examined in terms of their specific content, and many attempts have been made to relate a particular trend, style, or motif to a *Zeitgeist*, a "climate of opinion," or an ideology. . . .

A third approach to fashion deals not with the content of fashions but with the network of people involved. A fashion "system" may be seen in the interaction among producers, distributors, and consumers, which works as a spiral-like closed circuit. . . .

A fourth approach to the study of fashions, one which differs from the three cited above, though it operates within their orbits, seeks to determine the origin of a given item, the conditions of acceptance by the first participants (the "innovators"), the characteristics of those whom the innovators influence, the shifts from minority to majority acceptance, its waning, and where it goes to die. This is its natural history. The natural history of any phenomenon which is ephemeral and which comprises a specific content (e.g., popular music) with its particular network (e.g., the flow from song writers to publishing companies to record companies to disk jockeys to teen-agers, to juke-box listeners, etc.) can obviously be studied. It is based on the premise that different *stages* of a fad can be isolated and studied. In the past this premise has been used in studies of crowds, race riots, lynching mobs, and even political movements, all of which have been described in terms of discrete evolutionary steps, isolated according to their patterns of person-to-person interaction. Each stage, furthermore, has been described as paving the way for the next stage.

Fads and fashions, too, have been subjected to such analysis. Almost every textbook in social psychology points out how aspirants to social mobility continually try to pre-empt the symbols of higher status, thereby forcing their former holders to search ever for replacements. This is how the story of fashions, and sometimes of all consumer purchasing, is usually told. While it is certainly likely that one function of fashion is in the display of social ascent and that one network for its transmission is from the upper classes downward, the extent to which this traditional view of fashion remains valid cannot be told without refined empirical study—without tracing the diffusion of particular fads and fashions in time and through their relevant social structures.

In the continuing absence of such refined empirical data, this paper presents on the basis of crude observations some notes on the stages in the natural history of any fad; beginning at the point where some change has just begun to occur, it traces very roughly the fad's probable course.

Fads are not born but rediscovered. Where do new fads come from? In many instances they have existed all along but not as fads. For example, in the past several years a large number of songs that went under the collective title of "Rhythm and Blues" rose to the top of the "hit parade." Now these songs and this type of music were not new. The music industry had known about them for many years, largely under the title "race records." They had been produced for consumption by a Negro audience, a number of small record companies and publishers devoting themselves almost exclusively to this market. Trade journals carried separate ratings for such music, ranking each new song according to its popularity within this special category.

Then, all of a sudden, "rhythm and blues" songs invaded the general market, and "feedback points" (including the disk jockeys, fan clubs, listings of sheet-music sales, record sales, juke-box sales, etc.) all began to indicate a new trend. This particular new trend had existed for a good long time but in a different audience. It had been a little pocket in the music world as a whole which sustained it not as a fashion but as a "custom." What happened was that minority music was becoming majority music.

These minority social systems seem to feed many kinds of fashions to the majority. This is true not only of racial groups; the word "minority" is here used in the sense of engaging only a small segment of the population. Some "minorities" are more likely to be fashion-feeders, of course; the classic view of fashion assumes that a minority either in the upper classes or tangential to them engages in certain choices, and these are then "discovered" and made fashionable by lower strata.

. . . . .

In areas of life where "new" products are in demand or vital to the continuation of the industry, such "discoveries" are clearly more frequent. Since fashions serve a symbolic function and must be recognized in order to be transmitted, their greatest motility is likely to be found in those areas which are most visible. Thus, changes in dress are likely to be more frequent than in underclothes. Furthermore, the search for something new—what Simmel has called "exceptional, bizarre, or conspicuous"—will be greater there.

In the popular-music industry, where such a search is conducted on a monthly basis, the life-span of a "hit" being approximately that long, new discoveries are essential. Hence, every pocket of the musical world is sooner or later "discovered." "Rhythm and blues" is one of many such pockets, if more successful than some of the others; for a time African songs were hits; South American music has followed this pattern; hillbilly music shows the same trend; even classical music was "discovered" when suddenly the first movement of a Tchaikovsky piano concerto exploded all over America.

Minorities not only provide material to majorities but are also an integral part of the total system. Not only do they offer a pretest—"If it goes well in Tangiers, maybe it has a chance here!"—but they are also a shelf and shelter for dangerous or threatening ideas. Mark Benney suggests that bohemias serve this function. For urban societies their bohemias are a kind of social laboratory. Here something new can be tried out—because it is expected—without threatening either the bohemian minority or the urban population as a whole. The city watches, Benney suggests, and confers respectability on what it likes. Wrought-iron furniture, Japanese scrolls, charcoal-gray flannel suits, not to mention new literary forms and ideological movements, have indeed been bred in these quarters.

The tastemakers. While the community, the music industry, or the clothing world as a whole may watch and wait for new ideas in many places, the task of scouting seems to fall to one particular set of people. By the nature of their tasks, they must be intimately acquainted with two worlds, the majority and the minority. . . .

A good example in the popular-music industry is the success of the current artist and repertoire director (the "A&R Man") at Columbia Records, Mitch Miller. A concert oboist himself, he was thoroughly trained as a serious musician. With an established reputation and a semi-bohemian personality which manifests itself in harmless ways, such as the wearing of a beard and keeping odd hours, he has been able to utilize good judgment in the popular-music world not only by being better educated but by having a far broader range of minorities to draw on for inspiration. Thus he is familiar with the attributes of French horns and harpsichords, with echo chambers and goat bells, and has been able to use all to full advantage. One reason for his using esoteric "effects" is that in the music industry any popular hit is immediately copied, but his arrangements have been made so complex by the use of such "gimmicks" —as the music industry calls them—that imitation is very difficult. In addition of course, the gimmicks have given Columbia Records a unique reputation.

In any case, certain individuals in society are equipped to scout for new ideas and products to feed the various fashion systems. What is perhaps more important is to examine the fate of the original producer of the particular minority "custom" once it has been "exported" and translated into a fashion.

The exporter becomes self-conscious. At some time in the past Parisian clothes were "discovered" and made fashionable throughout "society" in other countries. Before that, undoubtedly, a stable relationship existed between the Paris *couturières* and their customers, and designs were made with a very particular "audience" in mind. In the course of "discovering" these designs, one element which probably attracted the early innovators was precisely the product which emerged from this relationship. But, once discovered, what happened? As Simmel said, "Paris modes are frequently created with the sole intention of setting a fashion elsewhere." The exporter becomes self-conscious, tries to appeal to his wider circle of customers, and *changes* the product. Another well-known example is found in oriental porcelain. In the nineteenth century, European art collectors "discovered" Chinese and Japanese pottery, and in a very short time the potters began manufacturing "export ware," creating an industry quite separate from the production of domestic "china." Another example is the shift from the 1954 to the 1955 MG car; the most popular British car in this country, the MG had been designed in a somewhat old-fashioned way, with a square hood; but recently the British Motor Company decided to build it more along the lines of the latest American styles.

There are, of course, some occasions when the exporter does not become self-conscious. This would be most true where there is no return for more: composers who work folk songs into concert music, like Mozart, Beethoven, and Béla Bartók, do not affect the folk "producers."

What happens to the original consumers is not clear. Those who find their own customs—pizza or Yiddish melodies or canasta—becoming widely popular undoubtedly enjoy some sense of pride as well as mixed feelings about the inevitable distortions and perhaps yield to the temptation to make some accommodation from then on in the hope of being "picked up" once again.

Statistical versus real fashions: a case of pluralistic ignorance. Who can say that something is a fashion? Who knows about it? It may happen that a number of people in various parts of this country, for a variety of reasons, will all buy a certain item. They may all "go in" for "rhythm and blues" music or good musical sound reproduction or raccoon-skin caps, all unaware that others are doing the same thing.

Such situations, in which no one realizes that others are doing the same thing, probably occur all the time. They are similar to what social psychologists have called "pluralistic ignorance," a state in which nobody knows that others maintain an attitude or belief identical with their own. If this coincidence persists long enough, however, the point will be reached at which one cannot help noticing the unself-conscious, "inner-directed" activity of large numbers of people in making identical choices. At this point the phenomenon which had been statistical becomes a real fad; here another important stage is reached—the labeling of a fad.

The label and the coattail. The birth of a fad is really accompanied by two labels; the phenomenon is given a name, and it is named as a fad. The fad is defined as real and in consequence becomes so.

Such a definition, however, must be made not only real but public. It must be translated from the specialized professional, business, or trade vocabulary into more popular terms—in short, into a label or a slogan.

While there are certainly plenty of labels which do not represent fads, there are no unlabeled fads or fashions. It is usually through the label that the fashion acquires fame—even beyond its consumer audience. Thus the "New Look," "hi-fi," "motivation research," "automation," and "charcoal gray."

The ground swell immediately after the labeling is caused partly by the activities of indirectly related enterprises. Machines that yesterday were ordinary phonographs and radios are suddenly called "hi-fi"; coonskin headgear becomes Davy Crockett caps; a lever makes of an industrial machine "automation"; an ordinary open-ended question converts a public opinion survey into "motivation research."

Thus the coattails which dress the fashion. Although the original minorities—whether devotees of recordings of high quality and accurate sound reproduction or Negroes who have been hearing certain kinds of "pop" music for years—may not recognize the $29.95 portable radio as "hi-fi" or the ordinary hit of the week as "rhythm and blues," the respective producers have found something that "works," and every commodity within labeling distance has a chance to be included.

The flow. Where the various fashions find their victims depends on their specific nature. Beginning in the minority, the fad is "discovered," then is labeled, and ultimately reaches the mass audiences. In the case of clothing, there is sometimes a stage, mentioned by Simmel and later by contemporary social psychologists and sociologists, which precedes or accompanies the labeling process, when the fashion is adopted by a group of acknowledged respectability. The fashion is perhaps borrowed from a fringe group within the society, or even outside it, and touted as an "esoteric" discovery. But in a society such as ours very little can be kept private, and providing clues to "better living," tips on the stock market, and advice on clothing, furniture, and virtually every other artifact is the professional job of all the media of communication. Thus, a product associated with a respected group or class is likely to spread, through being publicized, to other groups as well. From here it moves to groups which aspire to be like the advocates. These are not necessarily lower in status, although often so described. It may be that the lower group innovates— as in the "do-it-yourself" fad, a phenomenon which all farmers and lower-income groups have been aware of all their lives—but it is more likely to be a somewhat esoteric group, as the bohemians who flocked to New

York's Greenwich Village after World War I, followed by the middle-class New Yorkers after World War II.

Regardless of the direction of the flow, for a time the original possessors of a fashion-to-be will maintain the fashion for themselves and their kind, for people of the same social status are more likely to hear about people of their own level, especially in the upper classes. But after a time the innovation will cross the boundary line of the groups who adopted it and pass into other groups, in the process losing some of its distinguishing characteristics.

The old drives in the new. The story of fads is, then, one of constant change. And the changes themselves do not change, or at least not so much that they cannot be followed.

The process of change occurs necessarily at every point, leaving, as it were, a vacuum when the fashion departs for its next point. Eventually, the vacuum is filled, even to overflowing, by its successor. When a fad has reached full bloom, its distinguishing features become so blurred that some are totally lost. If everything is called "hi-fi," nothing is high-fidelity. Furthermore, if more than just certain classes are *aficionados*, the self-conscious among the class-conscious will want something new for themselves.

Thus, at some point before a dress design hits the Sears-Roebuck catalogue, a sports car the secondhand automobile dealer, and a modern chair the suburban rummage sale, once again it is time for a change.

The feedback. Producers notoriously see an undifferentiated audience before their eyes. They tend so often just to count that they miscalculate demand.

William McPhee and James Coleman have suggested that, while one group may be oversaturated with a fad, another may be very receptive—and only accurate reporting (feedback) about each group can tell the whole story. For example, since teen-agers are the major purchasers of records and sheet music and the major investors in juke boxes, and since these three commodities are the major tests of demand consulted by the producers, teen-agers can make or break a song. Disk jockeys also play a role in feedback, but it is primarily the "top" jockeys with the large teen-age followings who are the key informants. Yet there is another audience for popular music to whom the producers have almost no access—the daytime radio listeners: the housewives, traveling salesmen, commuters. Their tastes are thus inferred—of all places—from teen-agers!

In other words, the skewed feedback of the music industry is responsible in part for the volatility of its fads; exaggerating as it does the tastes of an already erratic group considered as its primary audience, its fads fluctuate beyond all expectation. With perfect information, a normal distribution of tastes can be expected at most times and for most things.

In certain industries, and among certain subgroups, the distribution is less likely to be normal, in part due to the pressures for new commodities, to the superficiality of the appeals themselves, to the publicity accompanying every product, and in the case of teen-agers, to their unstable moods. When information comes only or largely from teen-agers, who are at the fringes of the distribution curve, so to speak, then the music industry is rendered excessively phrenetic. Kurt and Gladys Lang, in studying the Chicago MacArthur Day parade of 1951, found that the television reporting of this rather slow-moving and dull event was systematically distorted to give the impression of a vast crowd, a glorious spectacle, and an unremitting enthusiasm. Here, as in the case of the popular-music industry, the requirements to hold an audience from switching to another station or channel or losing interest in popular music or a given song force such emphasis on the manic.

Hence, while the feedback from consumer to producer makes, at first, for a frenzied increase in a fashionable product, it may also make for a more rapid saturation than is warranted or, if the gauge is placed somewhere else in society, for an oversupply.

40. COMMUNITY IN DISASTER *

WILLIAM H. FORM AND SIGMUND NOSOW

Perhaps the most dramatic form of collective behavior is that occasioned by a widespread community disaster. This selection represents case studies of response to a tornado which swept a suburb near Flint, Michigan in June 1954. The data seems to cast some doubt on the assumption that victims of such a disaster normally go through an extended period of shock, accompanied by random and disorganized behavior. In fact, volunteer rescue teams from within the stricken area played a large part in bringing order to the devastated community.

After the impact of the tornado, the community was turned into chaos, but rescue behavior was immediately instituted. This postimpact stage (the *emergency stage* of community relations) was marked by three

* From William H. Form and Sigmund Nosow, with Gregory P. Stone and Charles M. Westie, *Community in Disaster* (New York: Harper & Brothers, 1958), pp. 33–46. Copyright © 1958 by William H. Form and Sigmund Nosow. Reprinted by permission of Harper & Brothers.

Dr. Form (b. 1917) is Professor of Sociology and Anthropology and Research Director, Labor and Industrial Relations Center, Michigan State University. His chief different periods: the first, during which rescue was performed by the victims and persons from the impact and contiguous areas; the second, during which help was supplemented by local organizations; and the third, during which help was supplemented by external agencies. Those periods provide an overall structural view of the disaster process, the relationships among the victims, rescuers, and organizations.

However, from the point of view of the victims and rescuers, the postimpact period was one during which their own patterns of behavior followed given forms, some activities persisting and others changing. It is possible to discern patterns of *personal behavior* and to classify these in terms of different phases. . . .

The *first phase* for an individual was concerned with action immediately after the impact. During this phase dominant activities were checking on the safety of one's family and oneself, appraising the immediate damage, and making decisions as to the appropriate ensuing behavior. This was followed by *phase two,* which reflected a change in the patterns of activity, or a change in the site of such activity, or a change in the social orientation of the activities. *Phase three* was also characterized by a shift in activities and social orientations. This was reflected in increased mobility, sporadic activity, and finally, a general withdrawal from the scene of rescue.

The meaningfulness of this classification is best illustrated by . . . contrasting cases of personal behavior in the Flint-Beecher disaster. These case studies are of groups that were more or less enduring, more or less effective, and more or less "spontaneous."

Of the two cases presented, the first dealing with the "Rudenko" family is perhaps the most representative of the types of activities that occurred during the emergency stage. This family is described because most of its members were interviewed and because their case histories contain detailed descriptions of their activities. The second case study of adolescents provides some insights into the types of behavior that might be expected from such a group during an emergency. . . .

I. A CASE STUDY OF A FAMILY'S RESCUE ACTIVITIES

The family may be considered the basic rescue group within neighborhoods or communities in cases of disaster. Its internal integration is such that the obligations of the members to one another are clearly de-

interests are industrial and occupational sociological research. In addition to *Community in Disaster* he is coauthor of *Industrial Sociology* and author of numerous articles in professional journals.

Sigmund Nosow (b. 1920) is Associate Professor of Social Science, Michigan State University. His major interests are in areas involving both economics and sociology. In addition to *Community in Disaster* he is the author of several articles in his fields of interest.

fined. Its integration into the neighborhood makes it an ideal rescue unit because its members are usually identified with the neighborhood and because they know the physical layout of the homes and the area. This case study of the Rudenko family describes a group consisting of six functioning adult members. The Rudenko house was the only house in its immediate vicinity that survived the tornado.

The active members of the Rudenko family included a 63-year-old grandfather and his 58-year-old wife. Living with them in the same household were their youngest son (25) and his wife (22) and a child. When the tornado struck (8:29 P.M.), the son was at work (did not return until 11 P.M.), but his wife and daughter were at home. Visiting their parents at this time were the oldest son (35), his wife (32), and their three sons (the oldest being 9). The family group, then, was composed of six adults and four children.

The father and son were working in the garden. When it started to rain the father said to his son, "You'd better put that tractor back in the garage—I don't like the looks of that cloud." In the basement of the house, the two daughters were ironing clothes. With them were the two older children, while the grandmother was upstairs with the two babies.

After the rain began, the two men went down to the basement to look at the water pump. The grandmother, upstairs, saw the tornado coming and began to pray. Describing the situation, she said, "I couldn't decide whether to run to the cellar with one baby or go in the dining room for the other baby. People yelled, 'Get the baby and come down here.' I finally went down with one baby."

Fortunately, the house escaped major damage and the second baby was found unharmed upstairs after the tornado had struck.

Not so fortunate was the nearest neighbor, living across the street, whose immediate plight mobilized this rescue group. His account of what happened to him is among the most lucid and complete obtained.

I ran for the house. As I ran, I saw the tornado pick up a car on Clio Road. As I put my foot on the front door steps, it came down the driveway and took me. It didn't seem to come from the west because it carried me north. It threw me into a tree first, then slid me along the grass. . . . I was conscious all the time. It threw me against the basement wall of my house on my head. I just laid there, then looked up and saw the house raising on the foundation. I got up on my hands, raising up; the wind grabbed me again and took me up in the air. While I was going up, something swatted me on top of my head, and I landed right in my basement (the house was gone by then). Incidentally, while I was laying against the basement wall the porch fell on my leg.

Members of the Rudenko family emerged from their house and saw that three of the immediate neighbors' houses were gone or partially destroyed. The father ran to one house and his son to another. The father found his best friend's wife (Mrs. Able) badly injured, but was unable to locate his friend. He ran for aid and located the State Police, who were trying to get into the area. With their aid and that of others, Mrs. Able was placed in a private car and taken to the hospital.

Meanwhile, the son went to Mr. Corn's house, found him and his injured children, and helped them into an automobile, which took them to the hospital. They were careful to withhold from Mr. Corn the information that his wife was dead. Her body had been found by the son 800 feet away from their home. The Rudenko father and son then searched the area and found the body of Mr. Able, who was Rudenko Sr.'s good friend and neighbor. After this, they went to the aid of other victims. Those who were not badly injured were taken to the Rudenko home to be cared for, or given first aid.

The women in the family group remained at home, and for the most part cared for the injured and homeless members of the two families whose other members had been taken to the hospital. In the words of one of the daughters:

"We just tried to calm the Riveras. The Riveras were crying and carrying on. We tried to calm them. . . . We then bandaged them up and took a piece of wood from the Rivera woman's leg."

The above description covers the first phase of activities for most members of this rescue group. This family appears to have followed a rather strict division of labor along sex lines. The women stayed at home, and cared for the children and the injured people whom the men sent to the house. The men remained in the field, performing immediate rescue functions, especially looking for those who they knew were in the area and whose homes were destroyed or damaged.

After the immediate emergency, the father appears to have stayed near the house, while his son worked with others. When the son was asked who helped him, he replied, "I guess I worked with 25 or 30 fellows—Dad, my brother, Mr. Pennel, Fred at the gas station, the man in the white house at the corner of Clio and Coldwater, and Mr. Harris the dairyman. Those are all I knew."

The influx of volunteers from the surrounding area appears to have swelled the membership of rescue groups that started out with a few people in the area working together. Almost no respondent could identify by name more than a half-dozen people with whom he worked during the course of the night.

The Rudenko family rescue group changed its character when most of the rescue work in the immediate neighborhood was finished about 11:00 P.M. After this, the father stayed close to home, while the two sons (one having just returned from work) ranged farther from home. This marked the end of the second phase for most of the Rudenko family.

Later, the eldest son went to inspect his own home some distance away. The parents of the older daughter-in-law arrived about 3:00 A.M. to take their daughter and grandchild to their home.

To summarize, this family rescued, gave first aid to and generally cared for three families of neighbors involving some fifteen to eighteen persons. They located other dead and injured, and looked for and ascertained the welfare and whereabouts of other neighbors who might have been trapped in their homes. They rapidly worked out an effective division of labor according to age and sex role patterns. It was possible for them to devote full energy to the rescue task because all members were aware of the facts that none of the family was injured, that the house was not severely damaged, and that the children were being adequately cared for. Their knowledge of the neighborhood and the family composition of victim groups enabled them to find or account for all potential or actual victims.

When asked whether their group could have done a better job, the oldest son reported: "There wasn't anything else we could do. I did wish I knew how to stop the Rivera kids from crying—you can't stop kids from crying." And the father's reply was, "There wasn't anything else we could do."

Although the Rudenko family constituted perhaps a most highly integrated and most enduring rescue unit, it cannot be conceived of as a team having a high amount of internal cohesion, permanence, and leadership. Rather, these family members set for themselves certain tasks (search, rescue, transportation, calming, first aid, care of children, and checking property). At times they worked with each other, at times with neighbors or friends, and at times with strangers, State Police, ambulance drivers, or others. There was no leadership or authority in the field or in the home. Verbal communication among members apparently was slight, because they were unable to report what functions other members of the family had performed.

The emergent division of labor enabled the Rudenkos to function effectively as individuals because they played appropriate and complementary social roles. Despite the fact that they lived in a marginal area of Beecher that was socially and economically heterogeneous, they had sufficient information about the neighbors to enable an efficient and effective rescue effort to be launched.

II. A CASE STUDY OF ADOLESCENT BEHAVIOR IN DISASTER

It is commonly observed that adolescents in contemporary society are denied adult prerogatives that they feel capable of assuming. Some sociologists and anthropologists have challenged the alleged discontinuity between adolescent and adult roles. Disaster conditions, with concomitant relaxation of social controls, initially create a situation that may permit adolescents to assume adult responsibilities. In order to test whether the adolescents in fact can assume adult roles under disaster conditions a sample of 12 boys and girls, ages 15 to 19, were interviewed intensively.

The following case presents materials gathered on the behavior of a group of adolescent boys, ages 14 to 17 years, during the postimpact period. None of the boys resided in the stricken area; all lived in the periphery. However, initially, two of them did not know whether or not their families had been injured. While the activities of five adolescents are described, at no time were there more than three boys in continuous interaction. Two of them very soon dropped out of the group and either went home or worked with adults. The nucleus of this group consisted of Jim Wilson, Lou Olesky, and Ted Braden.

8:25 P.M.

Marty Johnson (age 14) was helping his father and a neighbor (Mr. Blake) repair the door on their house when the siren from the Beecher fire station sounded. Mr. Johnson immediately left for the fire station, since he was a volunteer. As the wind and noise increased in severity, the boy, his mother, and Mr. Blake went into the basement for protection.

Meanwhile Jim Wilson and Ted Braden were driving around Flint just south of Beecher.

Lou Olesky (age 16) was puttering around the drug store where he worked part time. There were no customers in the store. As he looked outside, he saw the trees waving, and thought there was a bad storm brewing.

Hal McNaughton (age 16) was at his next-door neighbor's house when the wind started to blow. He didn't think much about it. About five minutes later, Hal went home. His father, also a volunteer with the Beecher Fire Department, was getting his gear together to join other volunteers at the station. Hal decided to go to the station with his father.

8:32 P.M. (PHASE ONE)

Marty Johnson's father returned from the station to check on his family, and then took Mr. Blake back with him to assist in the rescue activities. Marty remained at home with his mother.

Ted and Jim had driven to an auto parts store and heard over the radio that a tornado had struck the Beecher area. They got into the car and drove toward the stricken area.

Lou was still in the drug store. The lights had gone out, and he saw and heard ambulances going by. He also saw obviously injured people in cars.

8:55 P.M. (PHASE TWO)

Marty was still at home with his mother. Jim and Ted drove their car to where they lived and assured their mothers that they were all right. They then picked up a flashlight at Jim's house and went toward the impact area. On the way they picked up Marty and all three then went toward the fire station.

Lou, who had been joined by his younger brother, was still at the drug store. They saw some injured people being transported in cars toward Flint, and decided to go to the stricken area. They took a flashlight and started off. They wanted to see what had happened and did not particularly anticipate participating in any rescue activity.

9:00 P.M.

While the three boys—Marty, Jim, and Ted—were working their way through the debris toward the fire station Marty became separated from the other two. He was shocked and nearly overcome with nausea at the sight of the dead, the injured, and the damage. He wandered around in this state until he finally went home. He maintained that he went to various parts of the stricken area and its periphery looking for relatives.

Jim and Ted worked their way closer to the fire station. Ted became separated from Jim and never did get to the fire station. He said he worked alone and with different individuals. Meanwhile, Lou Olesky, on his way from the drug store, became separated from his younger brother. When Lou arrived at the fire station he saw Jim and Hal there. From this point on, these three boys—Jim, Hal, and Lou—constituted a group and were together until about 2:00 A.M.

The following is a log of their activities:

The fire station, although partially damaged, was overrun with activity. Not only were there firemen coming and going, but other persons (victims, volunteers, and residents) crowded the station. The boys were asked whether they had or could locate any flashlights and batteries. Since they could not find either in the storeroom of the fire station, they thought they should try to find some at nearby hardware stores.

As they left the fire station they noticed a panel truck belonging to one of the local hardware dealers. Finding the keys in it, Hal decided that they should take the truck and see what they could do to help in the rescue activities. So they loaded some old stretchers, sheets, and blankets in the back of the truck. They then got in and drove off. Later on, the boys revealed that they had had no specific plan in mind, but they had all agreed on the idea of taking the truck anyway. Two of them claimed that they had obtained permission from Mr. Cumberland, the owner, but the other boy denied this.

They drove the truck around the area and into the heart of the damaged sections where a bulldozer had cleared the way. They stopped where they saw a group of firemen digging out bodies, and they let the firemen load the bodies into the truck.

After picking up the first load of victims, they proceeded through the area and stopped at the baseball diamond of the school where some men were working. The workers piled two more victims into the truck. The boys still did not know what to do with the victims. Someone suggested they go to the State Police post. They did, and were told to take the victims to Hurley Hospital.

When they arrived at the hospital, the workers there told them to leave. When the boys informed them that there were victims in the truck, they were let in and the truck was unloaded. The boys then asked if anyone wanted to go back to Beecher with them. They gave one man a ride part of the way back. Then they drove to the area but had to wait in line to get in because the roads were blocked. Since they saw they could not get into the heart of the damaged area, they drove the truck back to the fire department. At the fire station, Jim and Lou got out of the truck.

Hal decided to take the truck to see if he could get water from the dairy back to the fire department. He did not succeed. When he came back he picked up Lou and took him home so that Lou could tell his mother that he was all right. They then went back to the fire station, where Hal dropped Lou off.

At this point, the group of three adolescents had broken up. Jim left the area and could not get back in because the police denied him access. Lou met his father, and went with him to check on some relatives. Hal kept the truck and drove it around performing errands, such as driving a fireman to City Hall to get batteries. He drove the truck around, visited here and there, went back home at 7:00 A.M., and then returned to the area with the truck. He did not return the truck to the owner until noon.

Unlike many of the others involved in rescue the adolescent group did not have injured or threatened family members to hamper their operations. How they would have performed under this kind of stress is, of course, unknown. However, it is clear that they did not behave like adult males. In general, their activity was regulated by others, and they showed only little initiative. At no time did they handle any of the injured, nor did they indicate any desire to do so. The three members of the group did not work out a plan for a division of labor. Any opportunity to utilize their skills was largely dissipated, because they remained together and did essentially what was a one-person job, namely, driving a truck. The fact that they remained together all this time suggests that they needed one another for moral support. Apparently they shunned the opportunities to do different tasks. Thus they neither loaded nor unloaded bodies, searched for victims in any systematic way, nor assumed any systematic liaison function. The implication gained from this case study is that adolescents may perform useful functions in an emergency if they are given task direction by adult members of the community.

The lack of a social definition of useful, responsible roles for adolescents in modern American society is strikingly documented by the behavior of these boys and by the adult attitudes expressed toward them. However, the ability of adolescents to imitate adult activity, assume responsibility, and make decisions was evident in other situations where there was serious doubt about the safety of their own families. At such times they seemed adequate to meet some of the needs of the disaster situation. Without such specific types of social definitions of behavior for *family members* guiding them, the adolescents described in the case study devolved into either errand boys, random wanderers, or emotionally dependent children who could not cope with the terror of the aftermath of the tornado.

This analysis of adolescent behavior underscores the general point that the knowledge, skills, and creativity of any group may just as well not exist if no social definition allows them to be brought into play. . . .

CHAPTER VI

SOCIAL
ORGANIZATION

Stratification and Mobility

41. THE NEW MAJORITY *

PETER F. DRUCKER

*One of the basic articles of faith in the Marxian creed has been that
industrialized societies inevitably produce increasingly large
numbers of exploited "blue-collar" workers. Recent research,
however, indicates that, in the United States at least, the number
of blue-collar workers is declining sharply. As Peter Drucker here
indicates, the largest single American socioeconomic grouping
today is the salaried middle class. This suggests that soon it will be
realistic, statistically as well as ideologically, to speak of the United
States as a mass middle-class society. The consequences of this
development, Drucker shows, are profound. But one should not
conclude from Drucker's analysis that America will become a
one-class (or "classless") society. Status and other differences
among members of the middle class will continue to be nucleii for
the development of new groupings having varied power and
prestige. These new groupings will be the social classes of the
future.*

During the past two or three years, professional, technical, and
managerial people have become the largest group in the American work-

---

* From *The Listener* (British Broadcasting Corporation publication), October
23 and October 30, 1958. Two lectures broadcast on the Third Programme of the
BBC. Copyright, 1958, by Peter F. Drucker; reprinted by permission of BBC and
the author.

The author (b. 1909) is Professor of Management, Graduate School of Business
Administration, New York University. Born in Austria, educated in Germany. Author:
Concept of the Corporation; The New Society; The Practice of Management.

ing population. "Professional, technical, and managerial" is a statistical term. But it is not just a pompous circumlocution for "white-collar employees." "Professional, technical, and managerial" does not include clerical people, or the sales-girl in the shop. It does not even include foremen in the factories. "Professional, technical and managerial" people, according to our definition in the United States, either determine the work of other people, or apply specialized knowledge in their own work. I know only one short term for these groups: it would be the "salaried middle class."

It is this salaried middle class that has now become our largest working group, larger in fact than the blue-collar people, the machine operators. This signals drastic changes in social structure, in the American economy, and in American politics. Thirteen years ago, when we came out of the second world war, the industrial workers were clearly still the largest single group in the American working population—almost one out of every four belonged to it. This was the end of a long historical process that went back to the early years of the 19th century when manufacturing industries were first started on American soil, a process that began to gather momentum in the early years of our century, and that brought about the great changes within the last generation: the change in domestic politics that expressed itself in the New Deal, and the change internationally that led to the emergence of the United States as the greatest industrial and military power in the West. At the end of the war, the professional, technical, and managerial group was already a sizeable group; and it had been growing fast for some time. But it was still one of the smaller groups in the working population, not much more than half the size of the blue-collar workers, that is of industrial labor, and smaller even than office and service employees or farmers. In those thirteen years industrial production in the United States has almost doubled. Both total and working population have been growing fast. But the manual labor needed for this output of goods has remained the same. The number of salaried middle-class people, however, which the economy now requires and which now are employed has almost doubled: it has grown by two-thirds and is growing much faster than either total or working population. By now, one out of every five people at work in the United States works as a professional man, as a technician, or in some managerial capacity—some 13 million of them altogether.

More important than numbers is the direction of the development. All signs point to a further growth of this group, perhaps even a faster growth. By 1975—only seventeen years away—we expect our total production in the United States to be about twice what it is now. Our working population should be one-third larger than it is today. But the only group of employees which will have to grow much faster—a great deal faster than either total population or working population—will again be the salaried middle class. Seventeen years from now, when the boys and girls who are starting their first years in school will have finished their education, in 1975, we should have twice as many people in the salaried middle class as we have today. By then they should be almost two-fifths of the total working force. While there will be a real and continuing need for more highly skilled manual workers, we shall not be needing many more of the "typical" industrial workers, the semi-skilled machine operators, the men who work on the assembly lines or in the steel mills. Indeed, the three industries in the American economy where employment is likely to grow the fastest are education, electronics, and chemistry—and all three employ primarily highly educated middle-class people rather than machine operators.

Already the machine operators represent the past rather than the future. Twenty-five years ago they were by and large the youngest group in our working population. Perhaps the only exception were office personnel where there are so many young unmarried women. Shop stewards in the plants, for instance, in those days, during the great wave of unionization in the 'thirties, tended to be ten or fifteen years younger on average than the management people they dealt with. Today the industrial worker in the United States tends to be older than the population in general. Union leaders today are almost without exception older by ten years or so than their negotiating partners in management. The typical industrial worker, the machine operator, belongs to what is both a stagnant and an ageing group. Growth and youth are in the professional, technical, and managerial ranks.

. . . . .

An important question is what this shift in the structure of our work population might do to the direction in which the economy in the United States will develop. The large expansion since the end of the war has been in goods for the consumer—such things as houses, washing machines, television or furniture. As people's jobs and income improved, they bought things, that is, material objects. Is this likely to continue as the salaried middle class becomes the biggest group, and the one that is growing the most rapidly? Certainly, these salaried, middle-class people will not go without these consumer goods, without houses or without appliances. But our manufacturers are finding out that it is the industrial worker who is more likely to buy a second television set or to trade in an old but still serviceable washing machine for a new one. The status symbols of the salaried middle class are much more likely to be different. For instance, more education both for themselves and for their children. Travel is another high priority of this group. Also, its members—for whatever reason—use the telephone much more, especially for toll calls.

Already there are signs of such a shift. The real "growth" industry in the United States in the last ten years was, for instance, not television, though it was certainly the most visible one. It was probably the publishing of paper-back books; and there has been a great shift in their public and their market and their content: history, foreign affairs, art, and religion are rapidly becoming paper-back staples. In other words, a paper-back is becoming one of the chief consumer goods of the new middle classes. Schools, travel, paper-backs, or telephone service, require other things. A shift in economic preferences would not necessarily lessen the demand for material production. But in requiring different things, the shift in the structure of our working population raises real questions regarding the direction of American economic growth.

It is not only the American economy which is being transformed; the emergence of the salaried middle class is also affecting our social life—our politics, culture, values, our society as a whole. The new salaried middle class is already the leading group in our society. Take, for instance, the pleasant suburb outside New York City where I live. The people who were the "big men" in the town then, the people who headed the community activities—the hospital board, the vestries of the churches, or the school board, the golf club committee, and the Boy Scouts, and all the thousand-and-one activities for civic and personal improvement which are the real living body of American social life—these people, only thirty years ago, were either respected professional men such as a leading lawyer or owners of businesses. Today, almost all these activities are headed by managerial or professional employees, the chief engineer of this company, the sales manager of another, or the personnel director of a third.

In politics these people are much less likely to form permanent party affiliations than either the industrial worker or the business owner. They tend to be independent in their vote, or, to the pained surprise of the politician, to split their vote. But they also tend increasingly to be impatient with traditional party organization, traditional party slogans, traditional issues.

Both our chief parties, the Republicans and the Democrats, are trying desperately to restore and to maintain their traditional alliances and allegiances, the allegiances of Theodore Roosevelt's or of Franklin Roosevelt's times respectively. Both attempts seem doomed to failure. But the new alignments, which will draw the new salaried middle classes into active politics, are still obscure, the new issues still hidden.

The greatest question, however, may be what the shift in structure of our working population means for our society. There have been many studies of the new salaried middle class of professional, technical, and managerial employees—in England as much as in our country. But we still know little about them. We know even less about a society in which this group predominates and in which it leads. They are "professional people," at least in their own eyes; but they are employed. They are subordinates, as a rule; but they consider themselves part of "management." They are managers or hope to become managers; but they are not "capitalists" any more than they are "proletarians."

The last great theory of society in the Western world was that of Karl Marx: it is now a century old. It was based on the vision—then extremely bold—of the emergence of the industrial worker or the machine operator, as the dynamic, growing class in society. For seventy-five years the machine operators were indeed the most rapidly growing group. Though they never became the majority in any industrial country, they became in every one of these countries the largest single group. This made Marxism such a powerful creed and philosophy despite its many obvious weaknesses. Today—and not only in the United States—an entirely new class is growing and is rapidly becoming the largest single group: the professional, technical, and managerial employees who are neither "capitalists" nor "proletarians," neither "exploiter" nor "exploited." But as yet we have no social theory, no social philosophy, not even adequate facts and knowledge, about the new middle-class society and the new pace-setters within it.

. . . . .

The United States has become, within a short thirty years, an educated society; that is, a society in which almost everybody is expected to have the advanced, long, formal schooling which a generation ago was still confined to a small élite group. It is worth noting that there is only one other country in which something comparable has happened during the same period: the Soviet Union. . . .

Our word "school," and all its synonyms in other European tongues, comes from a Greek word meaning "leisure." Thus language still testifies to mankind's old conviction and experience that education unfits man for productive work. Only too obviously the man of education, however limited it may be, will shun the heavy toil, will forsake plough and potter's wheel. Throughout history, therefore, society has never been able to afford more than a small minority of educated people. In fact, ever since systematic education first began, educators themselves have always been haunted by the spectre of the "educated proletariat," by the danger of an unemployable and decaying surplus of educated parasites, too numerous for the few available job-opportunities for educated people, and too highly educated for honest work.

Today, however, we cannot get enough educated people. The job market in the United States last summer [1958] is a good example. With a recession, and with unemployment of six to seven per cent of the total labor force, one would have expected that jobs would be scarce for the newcomers leaving school. So it was indeed for those who had no more education than secondary school—that is no more than twelve years or so of formal schooling. College graduates, who had four more additional years of schooling, usually with some degree of specialization in a major area, all got jobs, though for the first time in five years they had to hunt for them unless they were trained in such highly specialized and still scarce areas as engineering or teaching. But there was no recession for the holders of advanced degrees: indeed, the starting salaries offered them were considerably higher last summer than they had been in 1957 or even in the over-employment of 1956.

Today, in other words, we realize that our economic progress, our defense strength and our political position in the world depend more and more on constantly increasing the supply of highly educated people both in quantity and in quality. This has long been a slogan; Jefferson preached it in the late seventeen-hundreds; Macaulay in the early years of the last century. But now, for the first time, it is fast becoming social reality. Knowledge—rather than "labor" or "capital"—is fast becoming the central and the most productive resource of our society.

In the past the question has always been: How many educated people can a society afford? Today it is increasingly: How many people who are *not* highly schooled can a society afford? For anyone, we are now beginning to realize, who is not educated to the limit of his abilities (and some of us—I belong to them—would greatly prefer to say: who is not educated quite a bit beyond the limit of his abilities) is a social weakness and a productive loss. The knowledge which the educated person brings to work is also a very different resource from either "labor" or "capital." It demands different jobs, different ways of organizing the work, different opportunities, and different rewards. This is true not just for those who hold, or will hold, jobs in management or research or who work in a profession. It is true for the great majority—for they all increasingly have the background and expectations of the highly schooled person.

"Automation" is largely a first impact of this shift in the educational status of the population. Automation is not the replacement of human work by machine. The essence of automation is the replacement of manual labor, whether skilled or unskilled, by knowledge. It is not "saving of labor": automation usually does not mean fewer people at work; often it means more people at work. But it means different people doing different work. It requires such knowledge as is brought to work by the logician, the mathematician, the psychologist, the chemist, the engineer, the economist—a whole host of highly educated people where formerly we employed manual workers.

That we are moving fast to automation in the United States, much

faster than anyone thought possible only a few years ago, is precisely because of the changed educational structure of the country. The young
people who became available for work today have been sitting on school
benches for twelve to sixteen years or more. They may not have learned
much—I am not trying to judge the quality of the education they have
received, and having four of my own children in school I am sceptical—
but they certainly do not look forward to manual work, even to highly
skilled manual work, and even to very well paid manual work. They are
not looking for jobs, in other words, in the pre-automated factories or the
pre-automated office. They expect jobs in which they will put knowledge
and theory to work, jobs in which they apply what they have learned
rather than jobs in which they apply skill gained through experience. It
is no exaggeration to say that the assembly line which only a short time
ago was considered really advanced productive technology is, in the
United States, already obsolete, socially at least, if not yet technically.

But this raises a big question: just what do these people with their
advanced formal schooling expect from work and jobs, from incentives
and opportunities, from careers and working conditions? Most of them
will stay in modest jobs all their lives. Yet these jobs, too, will be knowledge jobs requiring high-grade theoretical training and considerable
judgment. All these people will have received an education which, in their
fathers' time, was reserved for small, essentially upper and upper-middle
class groups.

We have perhaps no idea how one really manages this kind of
people. Our personnel management ideas, our personnel management
policies, are based largely on experience with rank-and-file manual labor,
especially in metal-working industries: essentially this is experience of the
first world war. We all know that our ideas were never really effective or
successful even for manual workers with a limited degree of formal education and with limited expectations in respect of opportunities. It is
unlikely that they have even much relevance to these highly educated
people who now come to work in industry and government and the armed
forces. It is likely that we face brand-new problems which we do not even
understand at all yet.

. . . . .

The greatest impact, however, which the educational revolution in
the United States is likely to have is on social values and social structures.
It is at one and the same time the fulfilment of the American dream of
social equality, and a threat of a new class-structure, of a system of
privilege based not on money or birth but on education. As higher education becomes general, access to opportunities becomes increasingly
open to all. But at the same time—and the process is going on at high
speed—opportunities are increasingly being restricted to the highly edu-

cated. It is no longer uncommon for employers to demand a college degree even for sales-girls or secretaries; and without a secondary-school
degree even an unskilled factory job may today be hard to get. This is not
necessarily absurd. In hiring a sales-girl the employer may hire a future
department-head; in hiring a machine operator he may hire a future
foreman or works-manager. But the fact remains that the higher degree
is rapidly becoming what it never was before in the United States: the
passport to opportunities.

I have tried to present two basic changes in American social structure: the emergence of the salaried middle class of professional, technical,
and managerial people as the largest and fastest growing group in the
United States; and the rapid, almost sudden conversion of the majority
of the American people into people of higher, if not of advanced, education. I have tried to report rather than to appraise, and I certainly have
not tried to judge.

But, in conclusion, I would like to raise the question whether these
two developments have not fundamentally changed the character of
American society. For almost 100 years it has been fashionable on both
sides of the Atlantic to believe that American social developments follow,
with a time-lag, those of Europe; Marx was the first to assert this, and it
became almost an article of the faith for people on the left, Americans
and Europeans, especially in the 'twenties and 'thirties.

This was always a debatable proposition. But there was some merit
to it. It did, in some measure, explain to Europeans what was happening
in this complicated, confused, complex country that is America. Thirty
years ago, for instance, we in the United States were still much more of
an agricultural society than Britain or Germany; and it made sense then
to expect that the continuing shift to an industrial economy would produce in the United States such results as the growth of labor unions, of
social welfare and state control; in other words, things that paralleled
earlier developments in Europe. Thirty years ago we ourselves thought
that it was our job to catch up educationally with Europe: the development of the modern American university was one result of this belief.

Today, however, it is the professional, technical, and managerial
group that is our leading group; and in education, certainly in respect of
quantity and length of schooling, ours is rapidly becoming a society of
universal advanced education. These developments may be good or they
may be bad. They may be specifically American or they may indicate the
roads which Britain and western Europe will travel too. But what is
certain is that, for better or worse, we are developing something distinct.
What is certain is that to understand this society of ours one will increasingly have to understand these developments. What is certain, finally,

is that increasingly the success or failure of this American society of tomorrow will depend on its success or failure as an industrial economy, in which knowledge is the truly scarce and truly productive resource, and as a middle-class society of managerial and professional highly educated people.

42. PORTRAIT OF A STRIVER *

JOHN P. MARQUAND

Here in the colorful prose of J. P. Marquand, one of America's most popular present-day fiction writers, is a picture of an upward-striving young man. The interpersonal relations and the private feelings of an upwardly mobile middle-class man are sharply portrayed—the tensions, the insecurities, the need for watching every step, and the satisfactions. Vividly illustrated, if one is to achieve social-financial success in this type of setting, is the importance of skills in many areas other than that of accurate and rapid performance of one's assigned work.

Shortly before the outbreak of the European war, Charles had begun taking the eight-thirty. This was a privilege that had raised him above the ruck of younger men and of shopworn older ones who had to take the eight-two. It indicated to everyone that his business life had finally permitted him a certain margin of leisure. It meant that he was no longer one of the salaried class who had to be at his desk at nine.

The eight-thirty train was designed for the executive aristocracy, and once Mr. Guthrie Mayhew, not one of the Mayhews who lived on South Street, not George Mayhew, but Guthrie Mayhew, who was president of the Hawthorn Hill Club and also president of Mayhew Brothers at 86 Broadway, had even spoken of getting an eight-thirty crowd together who would agree to occupy one of those club cars with wicker chairs and card tables and a porter, to be attached to the eight-thirty in the morning and again to the five-thirty in the afternoon.

* From *Point of No Return*, by John P. Marquand, by permission of Little, Brown & Company. Copyright 1947, 1948, 1949, by John P. Marquand.

The author (b. 1893) is an American novelist and short-story and detective-fiction writer. Overseer of Harvard University; member of editorial board, Book-of-the-Month Club, Inc. His books include *The Late George Apley* (Pulitzer Prize Winner); *So Little Time; Stopover Tokyo; Thank You Mr. Moto; Sincerely Willis Wade.*

Charles remembered Mr. Mayhew's idea vividly, if only because it had come up at the same time that Mr. Burton had suggested that Charles call him Tony.

Charles could still recall the glow he had felt on this occasion and the sudden moment of elation. Mr. Burton had been shy about it in a very nice way, as an older man is sometimes shy. Charles remembered that Mr. Burton had fidgeted with his onyx pen stand and that first Mr. Burton had called him "feller." It had all happened one evening when they had stayed late talking over the Catlin estate, which was one of the largest accounts in the trust department.

.   .   .   .   .

"Now you may remember," Mr. Burton had said, "that Mrs. Burton and I took a little trip in 1933. You hadn't been with us long then, but I don't believe that you or anyone else will forget how tense things were in 1933, and now and then I found I was getting a little taut, so when things eased up I decided to go away somewhere to get a sense of perspective. That was when Mrs. Burton and I went to Bagdad. You ought to go there sometime."

.   .   .   .   .

The first morning he and Mrs. Burton had gone to the museum to see the treasure from Ur, parts of which looked like something in a case at Cartier's. You got a lot out of travel if you kept your eyes open. There had been a man in the museum, a queer sort of British archaeologist, who showed him some mud bricks that were actually parts of an account book. When you got used to them, you could see how they balanced their figures; and on one brick, believe it or not, there was even an error in addition, preserved there through the centuries. This had meant a great deal to Mr. Burton.

That clerical error in mud had given him an idea for one of the best speeches he had ever written, his speech before the American Bankers' Association in 1936 at the Waldorf-Astoria. Mr. Burton had opened a drawer and had pulled out a deckle-edged pamphlet.

"Take it home and read it if you have the time," he said, "I dashed it off rather hurriedly but it has a few ideas. It starts with that mistake in addition."

The pamphlet was entitled *The Ancient Art of Banking, by Anthony Burton, President, the Stuyvesant Bank, Delivered before the American Bankers' Association, May 1936.*

"Why, thanks very much, sir," Charles had said, "I certainly will read it." It was not the time to say that he had read the speech already or that for years he had made a point of reading all Mr. Burton's speeches.

"Look here, feller," Mr. Burton said, and he had blushed when he said "feller," "why not cut out this sir business? Why not just call me Tony?"

That was in 1941 but Charles still remembered his great joy and relief, with the relief uppermost, and that he could hardly wait to hear what Nancy would say.

"You know, Charles," Mr. Burton had continued, "Guthrie Mayhew and I have quite an idea. We're going to get hold of Tommy Mapes on the New Haven and see if he can't get us a special car on the eight-thirty. How about getting aboard? My idea is to call it the Cracker-barrel."

"Why, thanks," Charles had said. "I'd like to very much, Tony."

He had worked late that night and he could not remember what train he had taken home, but Nancy had been asleep when he got there.

"Nance," he said, "wake up. I've got something to tell you. Burton's asked me to call him Tony." And Nancy had sat bolt upright in her twin bed.

"Start at the beginning," Nancy had said. "Exactly how did it happen, and don't leave out anything."

They must have talked for a long while, there in the middle of the night. Nancy had known what it meant because she had worked downtown herself.

"Now wait," she had said. "Let's not get too excited. Who else calls him Tony?"

"I don't think anyone else does," Charles had told her, "except the officers, and old Jake when he speaks of him."

"Who's old Jake?" Nancy asked.

It surprised him that Nancy did not know, for she usually kept everything straight, but when he told her that old Jake was a day watchman in the vault who had been there when Mr. Burton had first started at the bank, Nancy had remembered.

"Darling, we ought to have a drink of something, shouldn't we?" she said, but it was pretty late for a drink. "Darling, I knew it would happen sometime. I'm pretty proud of you, Charley."

It was only a week later that they found out that Mr. Burton had also asked Roger Blakesley to call him Tony and they never could find out whom Mr. Burton had asked first.

.   .   .   .

Though you seldom talked of salaries at the Stuyvesant, your social status was obvious from the position of your desk. Charles occupied one of the two flat mahogany desks that stood in a sort of no man's land between the roll-top desks of the officers and the smaller flat-tops of lesser executives and secretaries crowding the floor of the bank outside the cages. A green rug extended from the officers' desks, forming a neat and restricted zone that just included Charles's desk and the one beside it which was occupied by Roger Blakesley. Charles could see both their names, Mr. Blakesley and Mr. Gray, in silver letters, and he was pleased to see that he had got there first from the eight-thirty, a minute or two ahead of Roger and Mr. Burton and ahead of everyone else near the windows.

Mr. Burton's desk, which had the best light, was opened already and so was that of Mr. Stephen Merry, the oldest vice-president, and so were all the others except one. This was the desk of Arthur Slade, the youngest vice-president of the Stuyvesant, who had died in a plane accident when returning from the West Coast six months before. The closed desk still gave Charles a curious feeling of incompleteness and a mixed sense of personal gain and loss because he had been more friendly with Arthur Slade than with anyone else in the Stuyvesant—but then you had to die sometime. Once Arthur Slade had sat at Charles's own place but that was before Mr. Walter Harry, who had been president when Charles had first come to the bank, had died of an embolism and everyone had moved like players on bases—Burton to Harry, Merry to Burton, Slade to the vacant roll-top—and so on down to Charles himself. The Stuyvesant was decorously accustomed to accident and death and now it was moving time again and it was so plain where one of two persons might be moving next that it was embarrassing. Any observing depositor and certainly everyone employed in the bank, right up to the third floor, must have known that either Mr. Blakesley or Mr. Gray would move to Arthur Slade's desk by the window. Undoubtedly they were making side bets out in back as Charles used to himself when he had first come there from Boston. Undoubtedly the clerks and the secretaries and the watchmen had started some sort of pool.

. . . . .

Tony Burton looked very fit, in spite of his white hair and his roll-top desk which both conspired to place him in another generation. For years Charles had accepted him as a model willingly, even though he realized that everyone else above a certain salary rating also used Tony Burton as a perfect sartorial example, and he was pretty sure that Tony himself was conscious of it. Charles never rebelled against this convention because Tony had everything one should expect to find in a president of a first-rate bank. It was amusing but not ridiculous to observe that all the minor executives in the Stuyvesant, as well as the more ambitious clerks, wore conservative double-breasted suits like Tony Burton's at the same time allowing undue rigidity to break out into pin stripes and herringbones, just like Tony Burton's. They all visited the barber once a week. They all had taken up golf, whether they liked it or not, and most of them wore the same square type of wrist watch and the same stainless steel strap. They had adopted Tony Burton's posture and his brisk, quick step and even the gently vibrant inflection of his voice. In fact once at one of those annual dinners for officers and junior executives when everyone said a few words and got off a few local jokes about the bank, Charles had brought the matter up when he had been called upon to speak. Speaking was always an unpleasant ordeal with which he had finally learned to cope successfully largely from imitating Tony. He remembered standing up and waiting for silence, just as Tony waited, with the same faint smile and the same deliberate gaze.

"I should like to drink a toast," he had said, "not to our president but to everyone who tries to look like him. When I walk, I always walk like Tony, because Tony knows just how to walk; and when I talk, I always talk like Tony, because Tony knows just how to talk; and when I dress, I always dress like Tony, in a double-breasted suit. But no matter how I try, I cannot be like Tony. I can never make myself sufficiently astute."

It was the one time in the year, at that annual dinner, when you could let yourself go, within certain limits, and Tony Burton had loved it. He had stood up and waited for the laughter to die down and then he had spoken easily, with just the right pause and cadence. He had said that there were always little surprises at these dinners. He had never realized, for instance, that there could be a poet in the trust department, but poetry had its place. Poetry could teach lessons that transcended pedestrian prose.

"And I'm not too old to learn," Tony Burton had said, "and I'm humbly glad to learn. Sometimes on a starlit night I've wondered what my function was in the Stuyvesant. I'm very glad to know it is that of a clothing dummy. It's a patriotic duty. It's what they want us to be, in Washington."

That was back in 1941, but Tony Burton still had the same spring to his step, the same unlined, almost youthful face, and the same florid complexion; and he had the same three pictures on his desk, the first of Mrs. Burton in their garden, the second of their three girls standing in profile, like a flight of stairs, and the third of his sixty-foot schooner, the *Wanderlust* (the boat you were invited on once every summer), with Tony Burton in his yachting cap standing at the wheel. Time had marched on. All of the girls had come out and all were married, and the *Wanderlust* had been returned by the navy in deplorable condition, but Tony Burton had no superficial scars.

No matter how well Charles might know him, in that half-intimate, half-formal business relationship, he still had a slight feeling of diffidence and constraint. It was the same feeling that one had toward generals in wartime or perhaps toward anyone with power over one. There was always a vestige of a subservient desire to please and to be careful. You had to know how far to go, how long to laugh, and how to measure every speech.

. . . . .

Sycamore Park had been developed in 1938 on the forty-acre grounds of an old estate and the subdivision had been excellently managed by the local real estate firm of Merton and Pease. As Mr. Merton had said, it was a natural, and he had never understood why someone had not dreamed it up long ago—not too far from the shopping center and the trains, and yet in the neighborhood of other larger places. Every place had its own acre, and no house was to be constructed for a cost of less than thirty thousand dollars. It would have been wiser, perhaps, never to have gone there but to have bought a smaller place.

It would have been wiser, easier, and much safer. He had not at that time been moved up in the trust department and in 1939 all he had was twenty thousand dollars in savings, part of which was in paid-up life insurance. He could never analyze all the urges that made him lay everything on the line in order to live on a scale he could not immediately afford, discounting the possibilities of illness or accident and relying on possibilities of promotion. He only remembered having had an irrational idea that time was of the essence, that he would always stay on a certain business level if he did not take some sort of action, and Nancy too, had shared that feeling.

. . . . .

Not since he had left Clyde had Charles ever felt as identified with any community as he had since he had been asked to join the Oak Knoll Country Club. They were in a brave new world involving all sorts of things, of which he had scarcely dreamed after they had moved to Sycamore Park. This cleavage between past and present, Charles realized, was a part of a chain reaction that started, of course, with one of those shake-ups in the bank. Charles had known that he had been doing well. He had known for a year or so, from the way Mr. Merry and Mr. Burton and particularly Mr. Slade had been giving him little jobs to do, that something was moving him out of the crowd of nonentities around him. He was aware also that Walter Gibbs in the trust department was growing restless. There had been a premonition of impending change, just like the present tension. One day Walter Gibbs had asked him out to lunch and had told him, confidentially, that he was going to move to the Bankers' Trust and that he was recommending Charles for his place.

Charles was not surprised, because he had been a good assistant to Walter Gibbs, and he was glad to remember that he had been loyal to his chief, ever since the old days in the statistical department.

"Charley," Walter Gibbs had said, "a lot of people around here have been out to knife me. You could have and you never did, and I appreciate it, Charley."

He had known, of course, for some time that Walter Gibbs was not infallible, that he was fumbling more and more over his decisions and depending more and more on Charles's support, but Walter had taught him a lot.

"Slade keeps butting in," Walter had said, and then he went on to tell the old story which Charles had often heard of conflicting personalities and suspicions. Walter had felt that frankly he was more eligible for a vice-presidency than Slade, and the truth was he had never been the same after Arthur Slade had been selected. "If they don't like you enough to move you up," Walter had said, "it's time to get out, Charley."

God only knew where Walter Gibbs was now. He was gone like others with whom you worked closely once and from whom you were separated. Walter Gibbs was gone with his little jokes and his bifocal glasses and the stooping shoulders that had given him a deceptively sloppy appearance. He was gone with his personality that would never have permitted him to be a vice-president of anything.

Charles was ready, not surprised, when Tony Burton, though of course he did not call him Tony then, had called him downstairs and had asked him if he knew what was coming, that he had been with them for quite a while and that they had all had an eye on him ever since he had done that analysis on chain stores. Even if you were prepared for such a change there was still an unforgettable afterglow, and an illuminating sense of unrealized potentiality. It was a time to be more careful than ever, to measure the new balance of power, and not to antagonize the crowd that you were leaving. One day, it seemed to Charles, though of course it was not one day, he was living in a two-family house in Larchmont that smelled of cauliflower in the evenings, stumbling over the children's roller-skates and tricycles, taking the eight-three in the morning, keeping the budget on a salary of six thousand a year. Then in a day, though of course it was not a day, they were building at Sycamore Park. The children were going to the Country Day School. They were seeing their old friends, but not so often. Instead they were spending Sundays with Arthur Slade. There was a maid to do the work. He was earning eleven thousand instead of six, and he was an executive with a future. New people were coming to call; all sorts of men he had hardly known were calling him Charley. It was a great crowd in Sycamore Park and he was asked to join the Oak Knoll Country Club. They were a great crowd in Sycamore Park.

It would have made quite a story—if it could have been written down—how all those families had come to Sycamore Park. They had all risen from a ferment of unidentifiable individuals whom you might see in any office. They had all once been clerks or salesmen or assistants, digits of what was known as the white-collar class. They had come from different parts of the country and yet they all had the same intellectual reactions because they had all been through much the same sorts of adventures on their way to Sycamore Park. They all bore the same calluses from the competitive struggle, and it was still too early for most of them to look back on that struggle with complacency. They were all in the position of being insecurely poised in Sycamore Park—high enough above the average to have gained the envy of those below them, and yet not high enough so that those above them might not easily push them down. It was still necessary to balance and sometimes even to push a little in Sycamore Park, and there was always the possibility that something might go wrong—for example, in the recession that everyone was saying was due to crop up in the next six or eight months. It was consoling to think that they were no longer in the group that would catch it first, or they would not have been at Sycamore Park—but then they were not so far above it. They were not quite indispensable. Their own turn might come if the recession were too deep. Then no more Sycamore Park, and no more dreams of leaving it for something bigger—only memories of having been there once. It was something to think about as you went over your checkbook on clear, cold winter nights, but it was nothing ever to discuss. It was never wise or lucky to envisage failure. It was better to turn on the phonograph—and someday you would get one that would change the records automatically. It was better to get out the ice cubes and have some friends in and to talk broad-mindedly about the misfortunes of others. It was better to go to the club on Tuesday evenings and to talk about something else—and that was where Charles Gray was going.

43. SNOBBERY *

ERNEST VAN DEN HAAG

The "snob," as Ernest van den Haag indicates, is particularly concerned with climbing the ladder of social success. But, according to Van den Haag, the snob tries to achieve social success by utilizing various types of shortcuts; instead of doing something significant himself, he attempts to reach his goals by clothing himself in the reflected glory of those who have accomplished something. Whether or not one agrees with this particular thesis, it is clear that snobbery is a significant sociological topic because the snob is, among other things, involved in the phenomenon of status striving (which, in turn, is one aspect of vertical mobility).

Status is a rank on the prestige scale maintained by taking an appropriate role. To raise it is to increase the respect of others. Ordinarily status is changed by means of winning or losing the things which form the status base: in Melanesia, enemy heads; in Western society, offices, titles, occupations, etc. The yearning for higher status, for more fame, honour, respect and deference inspires accomplishments of varying social usefulness as does the craving for higher income. All societies approve some way of raising one's status, punish others and finally ridicule some.

When there is a genuine concern also for the achievement which changes the status base, status ambition can be of great social benefit. "Fame is the spur that the clear spirit doth raise/ To scorn delights and live laborious days." The wish for the lasting esteem of our fellowmen— status ambition—has motivated many a deed of war and peace. "*Exegi monumentum aere perennius*" (I built a monument more lasting than bronze), Horace exclaims. His poems shall assure his fame—his status— through the ages. Thus, he comforts himself, "*non omnis moriar*" (I shall not wholly die). A Japanese samurai committing *hara-kiri*—ritual suicide —and an American white-collar employee working hard to make expen-

* From *The Fabric of Society* by Ralph Ross and Ernest van den Haag, pp. 157– 160, © 1957 by Harcourt, Brace and Company, Inc. Originally published in *British Journal of Sociology*, Vol. 7 (September, 1956), 212–216.
The author (b. 1914) is Adjunct Associate Professor, Division of General Education, New York University; Lecturer in the New School for Social Research. Special areas of interest include both economic and social theory. Author: *Education as an Industry; The Fabric of Society.*

sive Christmas gifts are both motivated by status concern. Competitive gift-giving or sometimes destruction of one's own property—often referred to by the Chinook (American Indian) word *potlatch*—is an ancient custom known in most primitive tribes. It survives in manifold ways today and always includes attempts to raise, demonstrate or maintain one's status. Thorstein Veblen regarded it as an element of the "conspicuous waste" which he dourly satirized in his *Theory of the Leisure Class.*

Prestige, the esteem of others, can be gained and lost in countless ways. To acquire "the bubble reputation," people may go quite literally to the length, the height and the depth Shakespeare suggests.

The savage by wearing a lion's mane hopes to impress on others that he slew a lion; in a sense he hopes to add to his status that of the lion. That is also the aim of the cannibal who eats the slain enemy: he hopes to acquire his qualities by incorporation; mainly, he hopes to appropriate the enemy's fame; sometimes literally to appropriate his name, too.

Likewise, a hostess may bag a famous "lionized" man to get some of his reputation and enhance her status, in short, to partake of the deference paid him. She reverses the cannibal's procedure—she feeds her victim—but she hopes for the same result. Hostess and cannibal have discovered that by association, such as eating or feeding each other, one can take over some of the fame, the *mana* of one's victims or guests. This is also the belief of many faithful who incorporate the religious hero through ritual eating—direct or symbolic—of his body. Totemic feasts and communal meals are part of many religious observances.

Hostesses discovered something primitives did not know: a reputation can be built without achievements or deeds of valor simply by being associated in the public eye with those who have high status. One can manipulate one's status without changes in the status base. With this discovery, snobbery was born. And it must have been snobbery that was in Milton's mind when he called fame "that last infirmity of noble mind."

Snobbery is an attempt to vest oneself with an undeserved prestige by striking an attitude sheerly for the sake of the prestige it is to bring and therefore spurious, or by presuming on an association entirely because of the prestige it carries. Snobbery may involve more than this but never less. Purely "social" snobbery is perhaps least harmful. The craving is sated by misusing one's personal relationships without misusing much else. Few of us do anything without an occasional sidelong glance at the effect it will have on our status. From there to doing things—ever so little—for the sake of that effect is a brief step. An element of snobbery inheres in many social actions of non-snobs. In the snob, that element becomes dominant, and in the pure snob, it excludes all others.

Snobbery proliferates in untold ways. The array of occasions is bewildering. There is literary, intellectual, aesthetic, political, sexual snobbery—a baffling multiplicity of forms. Any activity or endeavour can be misused to slake the snob's thirst for unearned glory. He pretends to countless attitudes, feelings, beliefs or achievements to enhance his status.

To raise one's status, one may seek to associate with famous people or status groups above one's own; one can claim to have succeeded by "dropping" names or indicating participation (even mere presence) at status-conferring events such as exclusive parties or premières. Other "firsts," attendance and achievements, or "mosts" serve too. One may try to be the first man through the newly-dug tunnel; or to set foot on the Jungfrau; or eat the most pancakes; or sit longest on a flagpole. The quality of the achievement is less important than the renown it brings. The bizarre competes with the great and defeats the unspectacularly good without trying. "Firsts" enhance status perhaps because to be first (*princeps, primus:* whence prince, principal, primary, primate, etc.) originally meant to lead. And to be presented with something first meant a recognition of leadership status. However, to go to premières or to race through the new tunnel first is neither assumption nor recognition of leadership, nor even actual presumption any longer. It expresses at most a yearning (possibly unconscious) to be thought to belong to a high status group. One does if enough others think so.

A pining to be publicized above all, or to associate with those who are, is the outstanding peculiarity which marks the democratization of snobbery in our time. To crave the limelight of publicity is to want prestige and acceptance not in a specific highly regarded group but among the broadest mass of people. The inchoate longing for "popularity" expresses the same craving for indiscriminate acceptance, a wish to be reputed in the largest rather than the highest group; or it reveals identification of these two. Whereas the ambition to belong to a high status group, the original ambition of the old-time snob, presumes a stable and acknowledged hierarchy, the contemporary egalitarian snob measures his prestige by the number of people who defer to it.

A negative form of democratized snobbery ought not to go unrecorded. The anxiety generated by the prospect of losing prestige and popularity may lead people to act so as not to distinguish themselves. If the action or inhibition occurs for the sake of avoiding loss of prestige and not as an end in itself, we are faced with negative democratized snobbery. (It must be clear now that some snobbery is indispensable as normative cement in the fabric of society.)

Whether democratic or aristocratic, snobbery is a degenerate offspring of status ambition. The snob does not try to achieve a high status by doing what is required—by leading in slaying enemies, making money or writing poems. He tries to sneak into the high status by associating with those who have it. But even the association is not genuine. The snob does not hope, as the cannibal does, to acquire the famed person's qualities, nor is he moved by admiration for the achievement of the high status group. He does not wish to emulate it for any intrinsic merit he finds in it. The snob craves fame, deference or reputation, not the qualities that won it. He is not interested in anything he does but for the effect it may have on his status. The object of his ambition is the effect achieving it will have on others, nothing else. Though his ambition be true, any ostensive objects are spurious. Snobbery is based on judgment of one social fact: reputation. All other matters are disregarded; in respect to them the snob at most rationalizes his disregard into prejudice. The pure snob—a limiting case—is interested in objects, achievements and persons only in terms of their social existence, the prestige they command or may procure him.

Snobbery is in a sense the most purely social of relationships. Snobbish association is independent of the personalities of the people, or of the qualities of the things, or of the meaning of actions sought after or snubbed. Free of any taint of economic, intellectual, sexual or political motivation and of personal preference, it is association for the sake of sheer social effect. Only to that extent is it snobbery.

. . . . .

Snobbery may seem a trifling matter; but it is anything but that to those concerned and to the student of behaviour. The belief—actually a moral judgment—that snobs are interested in petty matters does not make matters petty to them. And the consequences to persons and groups "snubbed" can be far-reaching. Finally, none of us is entirely free from snobbery, a motivation difficult to disengage from other more legitimate forms of status ambition. A man may like a girl; or date her because she is liked. One may read Jean Paul Sartre because one is interested in his ideas, or because one wishes to appear to be for prestige reasons, or, finally, one may wish to become interested for prestige reasons. One seldom is interested in the actual qualities of anything, without being impressed by its reputed qualities. We think we perceive and admire aesthetic qualities in a famous painting; but our change of attitude once we are told that the painter was not Leonardo—that the signature was faked—should give food for thought, for the aesthetic qualities of the painting we just admired have not changed—only its reputation. And we do look differently at our neighbour once we learn about his fame—even though he has not changed. Not that this makes us pure snobs. Our judgment is not entirely based on reputation nor do we look at the painting or associate with the neighbour only for the sake of our status. Rather, our motives are mixed.

Often, something connected with a famed action, or person, serves to make tangible both the fame and that which brought it. Perhaps we do think that some of it rubs off on that which was connected with it. Thus, the autographed book and the desk used by the great man or the flag that flew in the decisive battle, or the shirt worn by the saint have prestige in our eyes from having been there and perhaps having absorbed some of the *mana* of the event or person. (So it is also with personal keepsakes.) The flag is glorious, the shirt a holy relic, etc. None of these are prized for their material or symbolic value. (Any other flag would do as symbol.) Though our interest in something because of its fame is akin to snobbery, it need not be entirely snobbish. We may prize the flag or the saint's shirt because of our reverence for the events they witnessed. Our interest in the *fame* of these events or in the effect of our association with them on our fellowmen need not be primary. Once more, snobbery is exclusive concern with repute and unconcern or spurious concern with the cause or merit of it—desire for prestige and unwillingness or inability to earn it on one's own merits. Few people want to be president because of sheer snobbery. But many snobs want to have lunch with whoever becomes president. . . .

44. WHY WHITE COLLAR WORKERS CAN'T BE ORGANIZED *

ANONYMOUS

Relatively few white-collar workers belong to unions. Only a small percentage of teachers, for example, are members of the American Federation of Teachers, A.F.L.-C.I.O. Because it is so highly "respectable" in middle-class terms, because it is stable and secure (however poorly paid), teaching as a profession, like similar white-collar occupations, seems to draw those who epitomize middle-class living patterns. These patterns include that particularly important middle-class article of faith that if one is only virtuous enough and works hard enough he can rise to the top on the basis of his own individual efforts. Whether or not this faith is justified in the modern world may be a debatable point, but the consequences of the faith are objectively ascertainable and are discussed in part by the anonymous author of this article.

Except for a few highly specialized professions—like musicians, teachers, actors, and newspapermen—white collar workers are largely virgin territory for unionization. Take a look at your own community. Is there a big insurance company? A big department store? A big indus-

---

* *Harper's Magazine*, Vol. 215. No. 1287 (August, 1957), 44–50. Copyright © 1957, by Harper & Brothers. Reprinted from *Harper's Magazine* by special permission.

trial plant with a substantial office force? Any one of these groups might mean 1,000 or more members in a single local unit—the best kind of target for an organizing campaign.

Workers in small shops are harder to round up than their brothers who share anonymity with hundreds or thousands in a big plant or office. Besides, a large group offers another asset that any businessman understands: the larger the group, the smaller the service cost per member.

"Our job," Industrial Union Department Director Al Whitehouse told the unions' white collar conference, "is to make the white collar worker understand that his interests and ours are one and the same."

If this is true, it seems strange that white collar workers aren't clamoring to be let into unions, as industrial workers did in the 1930s when the Congress of Industrial Organizations first declared that it would "organize the unorganized."

A man who was an organizer for several different CIO unions told me how relatively easy his work was in those depression days of despair, hope, cynicism, and optimism.

"An organizer could just walk down the street," he said, "and the workers seemed to come out of the plants to him, begging to be organized. It didn't make any difference what industry you were supposed to be organizing in. Workers from all industries would hear you were around and would come to you. All you had to do was sign them up."

WHITE COLLAR WORKERS ARE DIFFERENT

Today, there is no movement among white collar workers that even remotely parallels that surge of the 1930s. The reason, simply, is that white collar workers *are* different.

It might be appropriate to ask, Why *do* people join unions? One reason overshadows all others: the need for dignified treatment. For members of unions, it has found expression in the seniority system rather than promotion based on friendship, and in the grievance procedure which has replaced arbitrary discharges. Wage increases, company-paid insurance plans, pension rights, and all other fringe benefits—including the guaranteed annual wage—are secondary to this goal that the bargaining table itself symbolizes.

When this scale of union values is applied to the white collar worker it goes topsy-turvy. White collar workers are different because they do have a kind of will-o'-the-wisp dignity as part of their occupations. It is manifested in many ways but is most dramatic when contrasted with the plight of industrial workers in the early days of the CIO.

A man who worked in a meat-packing plant in the days before the union once told me what it was like at that time. It was largely seasonal employment and when the "hog rush" was on the hours were unbearably

long. Men would stagger to work at four in the morning and work straight
through till midnight. My friend told me of men doing the sweaty job of
guiding freshly killed hogs through the scalding vat, with steam soaking
their clothing so thoroughly that they looked as if they had just climbed
out of the vat. A man would ask a foreman to allow him to go to the toilet
and would be told to urinate in his clothes since they were all wet
anyway.

"In those days," my friend told me, "a man would have joined anything to get help, even if it cost him his job. Things couldn't get any
worse for him."

Office workers and department store clerks have suffered indignities
too, but they seem to prefer to swallow them in silence.

Even today, when most of the degradation and human misery to
which the packing house worker referred have gone out of industrial
work, the man or woman who works in a factory has no real attachment
to his particular job, unless he is quite highly skilled. To a factory
worker, "it's a job," and he shrugs his shoulders when he says it to you.
He's interested in what he gets from it in terms of money and other
concrete benefits. He can transfer from job to job and feel no emotional
loss. Thus, it's not suprising that the names of industrial unions—names
like *United Automobile Workers, Amalgamated Clothing Workers,* or
United Steelworkers of America—contain no reference to the hundreds
of specific occupations and trades within the jurisdiction of these unions.
Industrial workers invariably refer to their industry rather than their
particular job when asked about their occupation.

Listen to a lawyer examining a jury panel:

"Mr. Jones," the lawyer says, "what is your occupation?"

"I work at Minneapolis-Moline," Mr. Jones answers.

"And what is your capacity there, Mr. Jones?"

"I'm a molder in the foundry."

The lawyer turns to a smartly dressed young woman in the second
row. "Miss Smith," he says, "what is your occupation?"

"I'm a stenographer," she answers.

"Where are you employed?"

"In the Minnesota Mining and Manufacturing office."

JOB-HOPPING

The white collar worker thinks in terms of her skill, which she can
carry with her from employer to employer. She didn't fall into her job
haphazardly as the result of lining up before a personnel supervisor. She
has some training, perhaps some talent, invested in it. She is likely to
be just as concerned about what she contributes to the job as she is about
how well the job pays.

I talked with a time-study man about joining an office union. His first objection was that he was concerned about his own integrity (he sets job standards for production workers). Beyond that, he felt that the union offered him no security that he didn't already have.

"I'm a *good* time-study man," he said. "I can go anywhere in this town and get just as good a salary or better than what I'm getting now."

Moving to another job, incidentally, is the way he and most other white collar workers solve their working problems. Their skill gives them a certain independence and enables them to talk to the boss person to person.

In turn, the clerk or secretary or accountant comes to think that his employer has a right to expect a certain standard of work from him. He asks himself how his demands for better pay or different working conditions will affect that standard. As one sociologist put it, the white collar worker is more *means* conscious while the blue collar worker is more *ends* conscious.

"Sure, I think we need a union in here, but I want to be fair to the company."

Unless he has had some pretty rough treatment from his employer, the average white collar worker with whom I have talked will begin the discussion with words like these: "I think unions have done a good job for some people, but . . ." Or, "I'm not against unions, now, but . . ."

It is these "buts" that loom large when the organizer is trying to get a majority vote for the union in a bargaining election.

There is a tendency among white collar workers to want to look at both sides of the argument about unions—the union's side *and* the company's side. Many of their complaints, moreover, about working conditions are focused against a particular supervisor rather than against a basic company policy. This makes it difficult for an organizer to find a common denominator which he can exploit in an organizing campaign.

Unions which have been successful in the field of white collar organization have encouraged this pride in skill. The *Guild Reporter*, official journal of the American Newspaper Guild, devotes almost as much space to discussion of professional standards and newsy items about members' promotions as it does to bread-and-butter issues. Membership in the Guild, Actors Equity, the musicians' and—in some cities—teachers' unions is considered to be evidence of professional standing.

However, the same "professional" approach cannot be used to appeal to office workers and department store clerks in a town-wide or industry-wide organizing drive. It doesn't work with an office staff which includes stenographers, file clerks, accountants, bookkeepers, dispatchers, receptionists, and a host of other occupational groups, each with its own notion of professional standards.

THE AMERICAN DREAM

The Great American Dream still has a firmer hold on white collar workers than on blue collar workers. While a man working in a mine or factory is likely to accept his job as his ultimate lot in life, the white collar worker—except for the young woman who thinks of her job as a transition between school and marriage—is likely to aspire to something above and beyond his present occupation. A union may interfere with the promotions of a young man on the make.

I have talked with white collar workers who hesitate to sign membership cards because they have been promised promotions by their employers. In many cases, these turn out to be just promises. However, there are enough examples of ambitious office workers rising to the top to put them in a dilemma about where their future lies. If the labor organizer tries to shatter this dream of upward mobility—as the sociologists call it— he finds himself in the position of apparently blocking a person's advancement, or of talking defeat.

Another problem for the organizer is the average white collar worker's misunderstanding of a union's seniority provisions. Literally dozens of times I have had to explain patiently that such a system does not mean that an incompetent with seniority gets an available promotion. To any honest union, the seniority system means that a *qualified* person with the most seniority gets first chance at an available promotion.

Frankly, however, I doubt if I have changed the feelings of one tenth of the white collar workers I have approached with this argument.

In thinking about personal goals, white collar workers are more inclined to follow the lead of professionals with whom they identify themselves than to respect a union organizer's logic. A teacher, who should have known better explained to me why she decided against joining the teachers' union in her community. "My brother's a chemist and he told me other professionals would look down their noses at me if I joined the union," she said.

White collar workers, in many instances, feel that the status they obtain from their jobs is worth the sacrifice in income. Once, when I explained to a $57-a-week secretary in a factory office that her income was substantially below that of a woman on a common labor rate in the plant, she shot back, "I don't care what they make in the plant. My job is ten times better. I wouldn't work in that plant if they paid me twice what she's making."

Labor leaders feel that white collar workers' attitudes toward union organization have been deliberately shaped by business and industrial leaders. AFL-CIO President George Meany told the union white collar conference:

"The white collar worker has been the victim of propaganda for many years. The boss has always said, 'Well, the union is not for you people. It is all right for the fellow who works in a factory or drives a truck, but a union is not for office workers. You people are above that sort of thing.'"

Actually, Mr. Meany gives management more credit than it deserves. The reasons for a white collar worker's resistance to unions are much deeper than an employer's pep talk. There is a difference in basic attitudes.

Before I went to work for a union I was a newspaper reporter who had covered his share of Rotary lunch speakers and Junior Chamber of Commerce rallies. The first time I went to a local union meeting I was astonished at the candor I found there. It is the same at most local union meetings, I have discovered. If a member thinks another member's motives are questionable, he stands up on the floor of the union hall and says so. There is no beating about the bush, no fear of offense, no hesitation about attacking the other man's integrity. Conflicts are settled right here and now.

The average union member has been largely uncontaminated by the etiquette of "human relations" that has become a way of life for many other groups in our society. Instead, he speaks his mind frankly—with his boss (if he has a strong union), with the officers of his union, with his fellow workers, and probably with the members of his family. There is no good reason why he shouldn't be candid. He earns his living at a job that requires no skill at "getting along" (is there any point to smiling at a lathe or a blast furnace?). Since his contribution to our economy is measured according to his production of things the rest of us can eat, drive, wear, and live in, he can be downright surly if he wants to and fear no reprisal.

Not so with the salesman who lives by the motto, "sell yourself," nor with most of the 26,000,000 persons in our economy who are "meeting the public" through their occupations in wholesale and retail trade, finance, insurance, real estate, government, and service. These are the job-holders who make up the big salesroom that C. Wright Mills wrote about in *White Collar*. David Riesman pointed out in *The Lonely Crowd* that the character of a society depends a good deal on the kind of work it does. So too with the individual. If a production worker were to become a salesman, his personality would change and so would his attitude toward unions and employers.

Thus, it is an oversimplification to say that a white collar worker's resistance to joining a union is a consequence of his being a "victim of propaganda for many years." On the contrary, as one organizer put it, "The white collar worker is just a different breed."

HE WANTS TO BE LOVED

Not only does the average office worker look to management for personal models and advancement—he is also often repelled, even frightened, by the idea of getting involved in union activities, chiefly strikes.

"I never saw a group of people so afraid of the idea of a strike," the same organizer said. "They keep asking me if they have to go out on strike if some auto plant across the country walks out. Their ignorance is really something. At first I laughed at some of the things they said, but then I began to realize that this was serious business with them. I leveled with them. I told them it was up to them whether or not they would ever have to strike. I explained how they would have to take a strike vote and all that. Well, finally they understood it, I think, but they sure didn't like the idea."

No one likes strikes. However, a factory worker's life is not so closely tied to a regular weekly income as the white collar worker's. When an Auto Workers representative was trying to explain the guaranteed annual wage to an audience of union members' wives, he asked the question, "How many of you women here can go into a store and buy something and tell the man that you'll be able to make a regular weekly payment for the next fifty-two weeks?" Not a single woman in the audience raised her hand. Certain periods of unemployment—whether through lay-offs or strikes—are an accepted part of a blue collar worker's life. However, to a white collar worker—who mortgages his regular paycheck months in advance and has to meet installments due on his house and refrigerator —a period of unemployment is catastrophic.

Catastrophe, crisis, and militancy are scare words to white collar workers. They want to be dignified, professional, and loved. They want to be promoted; they want to be secure; and they don't want to have to fight. . . .

45. THE WHITE MAN'S THEORY OF COLOR CASTE *

GUNNAR MYRDAL

Americans tend to pride themselves on the conviction that this country permits social and economic advancement by able and energetic persons. A society which provides for such mobility is said to have an "open-class" system: one in which persons may move freely up, or down, within the socioeconomic hierarchy. At the other extreme is a "closed-class," or "caste," system. The essence of the caste system is that a person's status is completely determined by biological inheritance, and that he is prevented from crossing caste lines through marriage. In his famous study of the Negro in America, Myrdal shows some aspects of caste are characteristic of our society, despite popular beliefs to the contrary. In this excerpt Myrdal presents the white man's attitudes concerning antiamalgamation, which maintains the separate strata in America.

Every widening of the writer's experience of white Americans has only driven home to him more strongly that the opinion that the Negro is unassimilable, or, rather, that his amalgamation into the American nation is undesirable, is held more commonly, absolutely, and intensely than would be assumed from a general knowledge of American thought-ways. Except for a handful of rational intellectual liberals—who also, in many cases, add to their acceptance in principle of amalgamation an admission that they personally feel an irrational emotional inhibition against it—it is a rare case to meet a white American who will confess that, if it were not for public opinion and social sanctions not removable by private choice, he would have no strong objection to intermarriage.

The intensity of the attitude seems to be markedly stronger in the South than in the North. Its strength seems generally to be inversely

* From Gunnar Myrdal, *An American Dilemma* (New York: Harper & Brothers, 1944), pp. 57–67.

The author (b. 1898) is Professor, the Lars Hierta chair of political economics and public finance, at Stockholm University, Sweden. Former member of the Swedish senate. Since 1947, the Executive Secretary of the United Nations Economic Commission in Europe. Author: *Population; A Problem for Democracy; Economic Theory and Under-Developed Regions.*

related to the economic and social status of the informant and his educational level. It is usually strong even in most of the non-colored minority groups, if they are above the lowest plane of indifference. To the poor and socially insecure, but struggling, white individual, a fixed opinion on this point seems an important matter of prestige and distinction.

But even a liberal-minded Northerner of cosmopolitan culture and with a minimum of conventional blinds will, in nine cases out of ten, express a definite feeling against amalagamation. He will not be willing usually to hinder intermarriage by law. Individual liberty is to him a higher principle and, what is more important, he actually invokes it. But he will regret the exceptional cases that occur. He may sometimes hold a philosophical view that in centuries to come amalagamation is bound to happen and might become the solution. But he will be inclined to look on it as an inevitable deterioration.[1]

This attitude of refusing to consider amalgamation—felt and expressed in the entire country—constitutes the center in the complex of attitudes which can be described as the "common denominator" in the problem. It defines the Negro group in contradistinction to all the non-colored minority groups in America and all other lower class groups. The boundary between Negro and white is not simply a class line which can be successfully crossed by education, integration into the national culture, and individual economic advancement. The boundary is fixed. It is not a temporary expediency during an apprenticeship in the national culture. It is a bar erected with the intention of permanency. It is directed against the whole group. Actually, however, "passing" as a white person is possible when a Negro is white enough to conceal his Negro heritage. But the difference between "passing" and ordinary social climbing reveals the distinction between a class line, in the ordinary sense, and a caste line.

This brings us to the point where we shall attempt to sketch, only in an abstract and preliminary form, the social mechanism by which the anti-amalgamation maxim determines race relations. This mechanism is perceived by nearly everybody in America, but most clearly in

---

[1] The response is likely to be anything but pleasant if one jestingly argues that possibly a small fraction of Negro blood in the American people, if it were blended well with all the other good stuff brought over to the new continent, might create a race of unsurpassed excellence: a people with just a little sunburn without extra trouble and even through the winter; with some curl in the hair without the cost of a permanent wave; with, perhaps, a little more emotional warmth in their souls; and a little more religion, music, laughter, and carefreeness in their lives. Amalgamation is, to the ordinary American, not a proper subject for jokes at all, unless it can be pulled down to the level of dirty stories, where, however, it enjoys a favored place. Referred to society as a whole and viewed as a principle, the anti-amalgamation maxim is held holy; it is a consecrated taboo. The maxim might, indeed, be a remnant of something really in the "mores." It is kept unproblematic, which is certainly not the case with all the rest of etiquette and segregation and discrimination patterns, for which this quality is sometimes erroneously claimed.

the South. Almost unanimously white Americans have communicated to the author the following logic of the caste situation which we shall call the *"white man's theory of color caste."*

1. The concern for "race purity" is basic in the whole issue; the primary and essential command is to prevent amalgamation; the whites are determined to utilize every means to this end.

2. Rejection of "social equality" is to be understood as a precaution to hinder miscegenation and particularly intermarriage.

3. The danger of miscegenation is so tremendous that the segregation and discrimination inherent in the refusal of "social equality" must be extended to nearly all spheres of life. There must be segregation and discrimination in recreation, in religious service, in education, before the law, in politics, in housing, in stores and in breadwinning.

This popular theory of the American caste mechanism is, of course, open to criticism. It can be criticized from a valuational point of view by maintaining that hindering miscegenation is not a worthwhile end, or that as an end it is not sufficiently worthwhile to counterbalance the sufferings inflicted upon the suppressed caste and the general depression of productive efficiency, standards of living and human culture in the American society at large—costs appreciated by all parties concerned. This criticism does not, however, endanger the theory which assumes that white people actually are following another valuation of means and ends and are prepared to pay the costs for attaining the ends. A second criticism would point out that, assuming the desirability of the end, this end could be reached without the complicated and, in all respects, socially expensive caste apparatus now employed. This criticism, however adequate though it be on the practical or political plane of discussion, does not disprove that people believe otherwise, and that the popular theory is a true representation of their beliefs and actions.

To undermine the popular theory of the caste mechanism, as based on the anti-amalgamation maxim, it would, of course, be necessary to prove that people really are influenced by other motives than the ones pronounced. Much material has, as we shall find, been brought together indicating that, among other things, competitive economic interests, which do not figure at all in the popular rationalization referred to, play a decisive role. The announced concern about racial purity is, when this economic motive is taken into account, no longer awarded the exclusive role as the *basic* cause in the psychology of the race problem.

Though the popular theory of color caste turns out to be a rationalization, this does not destroy it. For among the forces in the minds of the white people are certainly not only economic interests (if these were the only ones, the popular theory would be utterly demolished), but also sexual urges, inhibitions, and jealousies, and social fears and cravings for prestige and security. When they come under the scrutiny of scientific research, both the sexual and the social complexes take on unexpected designs. We shall then also get a clue to understanding the remarkable tendency of this presumably biological doctrine, that it refers only to legal marriage and to relations between Negro men and white women, but not to extra-marital sex relations between white men and Negro women.

However these sexual and social complexes might turn out when analyzed, they will reveal the psychological nature of the anti-amalaga-mation doctrine and show its "meaning." They will also explain the com-pressed emotion attached to the Negro problem. It is inherent in our type of modern Western civilization that sex and social status are for most individuals the danger points, the directions whence he fears the sinister onslaughts on his personal security. These two factors are more likely than anything else to push a life problem deep down into the sub-conscious and load it with emotions. There is some probability that in America both complexes are particularly laden with emotions. The Amer-ican puritan tradition gives everything connected with sex a higher emo-tional charge. The roads for social climbing have been kept more open in America than perhaps anywhere else in the world, but in this upward struggle the competition for social status has also become more absorb-ing. In a manner and to a degree most uncomfortable for the Negro people in America, both the sexual and the social complexes have become related to the Negro problem.

These complexes are most of the time kept concealed. In occasional groups of persons and situations they break into the open. Even when not consciously perceived or expressed, they ordinarily determine inter-racial behavior on the white side.

. . . . .

It has . . . always been a primary requirement upon every Negro leader—who aspires to get any hearing at all from the white majority group, and who does not want to appear dangerously radical to the Negro group and at the same time hurt the "race pride" it has built up as a defense—that he shall explicitly condone the anti-amalgamation maxim, which is the keystone in the white man's structure of race prej-udice, and forbear to express any desire on the part of the Negro people to aspire to intermarriage with the whites. The request for intermarriage is easy for the Negro leader to give up. Intermarriage cannot possibly be a practical object of Negro public policy. Independent of the Negroes' wishes, the opportunity for intermarriage is not favorable as long as the great majority of the white population dislikes the very idea. As a defense reaction a strong attitude against intermarriage has developed in the Negro people itself. And the Negro people have no interest in defending the exploitative illicit relations between white men and Negro women. This race mingling is, on the contrary, commonly felt among Negroes to be disgraceful. And it often arouses the jealousy of Negro men.

The required soothing gesture toward the anti-amalgamation doctrine is, therefore, readily delivered. It is iterated at every convenient opportunity and belongs to the established routine of Negro leadership. For example, Robert R. Moton writes:

> As for amalgamation, very few expect it; still fewer want it; no one advocates it; and only a constantly diminishing minority practise it, and that surreptitiously. It is generally accepted on both sides of the colour line that it is best for the two races to remain ethnologically distinct.

There seems thus to be unanimity among Negro leaders on the point deemed crucial by white Americans. If we attend carefully, we shall, however, detect some important differences in formulation. The Negro spokesman will never, to begin with, accept the common white premise of racial inferiority of the Negro stock. To quote Moton again:

> . . . even in the matter of the mingling of racial strains, however undesirable it might seem to be from a social point of view, he [the Negro] would never admit that his blood carries any taint of physiological, mental, or spiritual inferiority.

A doctrine of equal natural endowments—a doctrine contrary to the white man's assumption of Negro inferiority, which is at the basis of the anti-amalgamation theory—has been consistently upheld. If a Negro leader publicly even hinted at the possibility of inherent racial inferiority, he would immediately lose his following. The entire Negro press watches the Negro leaders on this point.

Even Booker T. Washington, the supreme diplomat of the Negro people through a generation filled with severe trials, who was able by studied unobtrusiveness to wring so many favors from the white majority, never dared to allude to such a possibility, though he sometimes criticized most severely his own people for lack of thrift, skill, perseverance and general culture. In fact, there is no reason to think that he did not firmly believe in the fundamental equality of inherent capacities. Privately, local Negro leaders might find it advisable to admit Negro inferiority and, particularly earlier, many individual Negroes might have shared the white man's view. But it will not be expressed by national leaders and, in fact, never when they are under public scrutiny. An emphatic assertion of equal endowments is article number one in the growing Negro "race pride."

Another deviation of the Negro faith in the anti-amalgamation doctrine is the stress that they, for natural reasons, lay on condemning exploitative illicit amalgamation. They turn the tables and accuse white men of debasing Negro womanhood, and the entire white culture for not rising up against this practice as their expressed antagonism against miscegenation should demand. Here they have a strong point, and they know how to press it.

A third qualification in the Negro's acceptance of the anti-amalgamation doctrine, expressed not only by the more "radical" and outspoken Negro leaders, is the assertion that intermarriage should not be barred by law. The respect for individual liberty is invoked as an argument. But, in addition, it is pointed out that this barrier, by releasing the white man from the consequences of intimacy with a Negro woman, actually has the effect of inducing such intimacy and thus tends to increase miscegenation. Moton makes this point:

> The Negro woman suffers not only from the handicap of economic and social discriminations imposed upon the race as a whole, but is in addition the victim of unfavourable legislation incorporated in the marriage laws of twenty-nine states, which forbid the intermarriage of black and white. The disadvantage of these statutes lies, not as is generally represented, in the legal obstacle they present to social equality, but rather in the fact that such laws specifically deny to the Negro woman and her offspring that safeguard from abuse and exploitation with which the women of the white race are abundantly surrounded. On the other side, the effect of such legislation leaves the white man, who is so inclined, free of any responsibility attending his amatory excursions across the colour line and leaves the coloured woman without redress for any of the consequences of her defencelessness; whereas white women have every protection, from fine and imprisonment under the law to enforced marriage and lynching outside the law.

But even with all these qualifications, the anti-amalgamation doctrine, the necessity of assenting to which is understood by nearly everybody, obviously encounters some difficulties in the minds of intellectual Negroes. They can hardly be expected to accept it as a just rule of conduct. They tend to accept it merely as a temporary expedient necessitated by human weakness. Kelly Miller thus wrote:

> . . . you would hardly expect the Negro, in derogation of his common human qualities, to proclaim that he is so diverse from God's other human creatures as to make the blending of the races contrary to the law of nature. The Negro refuses to become excited or share in your frenzy on this subject. The amalgamation of the races is an ultimate possibility, though not an immediate probability. But what have you and I to do with ultimate questions, anyway?

And a few years later, he said:

> It must be taken for granted in the final outcome of things that the colour line will be wholly obliterated. While blood may be thicker than water, it does not possess the spissitude or inherency of everlasting principle. The brotherhood of man is more fundamental than the fellowship of race. A physical and

spiritual identity of all peoples occupying common territory is a logical necessity of thought. The clear seeing mind refuses to yield or give its assent to any other ultimate conclusion. This consummation, however, is far too removed from the sphere of present probability to have decisive influence upon practical procedure.

This problem is, of course, tied up with the freedom of the individual. "Theoretically Negroes would all subscribe to the right of freedom of choice in marriage even between the two races," wrote Moton. And Du Bois formulates it in stronger terms:

. . . a woman may say, I do not want to marry this black man, or this red man, or this white man. . . . But the impudent and vicious demand that all colored folk shall write themselves down as brutes by a general assertion of their unfitness to marry other decent folk is a nightmare.

Negroes have always pointed out that the white man must not be very certain of his woman's lack of interest when he rises to such frenzy on behalf of the danger to her and feels compelled to build up such formidable fences to prevent her from marrying a Negro.

With these reservations both Negro leadership and the Negro masses acquiesce in the white anti-amalgamation doctrine. This attitude is noted with satisfaction in the white camp. The writer has observed, however, that the average white man, particularly in the South, does not feel quite convinced of the Negro's acquiescence. In several conversations, the same white person, in the same breath, has assured me, on the one hand, that the Negroes are perfectly satisfied in their position and would not like to be treated as equals, and on the other hand, that the only thing these Negroes long for is to be like white people and to marry their daughters.

Whereas the Negro spokesman finds it possible to assent to the first rank of discrimination, namely, that involving miscegenation, it is more difficult for him to give his approval to the second rank of discrimination, namely, that involving "etiquette" and consisting in the white man's refusal to extend the ordinary courtesies to Negroes in daily life and his expectation of receiving certain symbolic signs of submissiveness from the Negro. The Negro leader could not do so without serious risk of censorship by his own people and rebuke by the Negro press. In all articulate groups of Negroes there is a demand to have white men call them by their titles of Mr., Mrs., and Miss; to have white men take off their hats on entering a Negro's house; to be able to enter a white man's house through the front door rather than the back door, and so on. But on the whole, and in spite of the rule that they stand up for "social equality" in this sense, most Negroes in the South obey the white man's rules.

Booker T. Washington went a long way, it is true, in his Atlanta speech in 1895 where he explained that: "In all things that are purely social we [the two races] can be as separate as the fingers, yet one as the hand in all things essential to mutual progress." He there seemed to condone not only these rules of "etiquette" but also the denial of "social equality" in a broader sense, including some of the further categories in the white man's rank order of discrimination. He himself was always most eager to observe the rules. But Washington was bitterly rebuked for this capitulation, particularly by Negroes in the North. And a long time has passed since then; the whole spirit in the Negro world has changed considerably in three decades.

The modern Negro leader will try to solve this dilemma by iterating that no Negroes want to intrude upon white people's private lives. But this is not what Southern white opinion asks for. It is not satisfied with the natural rules of polite conduct that no individual, of whatever race, shall push his presence on a society where he is not wanted. It asks for a general order according to which *all* Negroes are placed under *all* white people and excluded from not only the white man's society but also from the ordinary symbols of respect. No Negro shall ever aspire to them, and no white shall be allowed to offer them.

Thus, on this second rank of discrimination there is a wide gap between the ideologies of the two groups. As we then continue downward in our rank order and arrive at the ordinary Jim Crow practices, the segregation in schools, the disfranchisement, and the discrimination in employment, we find, on the one hand, that increasingly larger groups of white people are prepared to take a stand against these discriminations. Many a liberal white professor in the South who, for his own welfare, would not dare to entertain a Negro in his home and perhaps not even speak to him in a friendly manner on the street, will be found prepared publicly to condemn disfranchisement, lynching, and the forcing of the Negro out of employment. Also, on the other hand, Negro spokesmen are becoming increasingly firm in their opposition to discrimination on these lower levels. It is principally on these lower levels of the white man's rank order of discrimination that the race struggle goes on. The struggle will widen to embrace all the thousand problems of education, politics, economic standards, and so forth, and the frontier will shift from day to day according to varying events.

Even a superficial view of discrimination in America will reveal to the observer: first, that there are great differences, not only between larger regions, but between neighboring communities; and, second, that even in the same community, changes occur from one time to another. There is also, contrary to the rule that all Negroes are to be treated alike, a certain amount of discretion depending upon the class and social status of the Negro in question. A white person, especially if he has high status in the community, is, furthermore, supposed to be free, within limits, to overstep the rules. The rules are primarily to govern the Negro's behavior.

Some of these differences and changes can be explained. But the need for their interpretation is perhaps less than has sometimes been assumed. The variations in discrimination between local communities or from one time to another are often not of primary consequence. All of these thousand and one precepts, etiquettes, taboos, and disabilities inflicted upon the Negro have a common purpose: to express the subordinate status of the Negro people and the exalted position of the whites. They have their meaning and chief function as symbols. As symbols they are, however, interchangeable to an extent: one can serve in place of another without causing material difference in the essential social relations in the community.

The differences in patterns of discrimination between the larger regions of the country and the temporal changes of patterns within one region, which reveal a definite trend, have, on the contrary, more material import. These differences and changes imply, in fact, a considerable margin of variation within the very notion of American caste, which is not true of all the other minor differences between the changes in localities within a single region—hence the reason for a clear distinction. For exemplification it may suffice here to refer only to the differentials in space. As one moves from the Deep South through the Upper South and the Border states to the North, the manifestations of discrimination decrease in extent and intensity; at the same time the rules become more uncertain and capricious. The "color line" becomes a broad ribbon of arbitrariness. The old New England states stand, on the whole, as the antipode to the Deep South. This generalization requires important qualifications, and the relations are in process of change.

The decreasing discrimination as we go from South to North in the United States is apparently related to a weaker basic prejudice. In the North the Negroes have fair justice and are not disfranchised; they are not Jim-Crowed in public means of conveyance; educational institutions are less segregated. The interesting thing is that the decrease of discrimination does *not* regularly follow the white man's rank order. Thus intermarriage, placed on the top of the rank order, is legally permitted in all but one of the Northern states east of the Mississippi. The racial etiquette, being the most conspicuous element in the second rank, is, practically speaking, absent from the North. On the other hand, employment discriminations, placed at the bottom of the rank order, at times are equally severe, or more so, in some Northern communities than in the South, even if it is true that Negroes have been able to press themselves into many more new avenues of employment during the last generation in the North than in the South.

There is plenty of discrimination in the North. But it is—or rather its rationalization is—kept hidden. We can, in the North, witness the legislators' obedience to the American Creed when they solemnly pass laws and regulations to condemn and punish such acts of discrimination which, as a matter of routine, are committed daily by the great majority of the white citizens and by the legislators themselves. In the North, as indeed often in the South, public speakers frequently pronounce principles of human and civic equality. We see here revealed in relief the Negro problem as an American Dilemma.

46. CROSSING THE COLOR-LINE *

ST. CLAIR DRAKE AND HORACE R. CAYTON

If the reader has ever observed the members of a large audience of Negroes, he has doubtless noted the wide range of shades of skin color. Probably he reflected on how this color variation came about in a society which has such a strong taboo on interracial marriage. If he noted that some of the "Negroes" present were of fairer complexion than many "white" persons, he may also have speculated on what is known as "passing": crossing the color line. Richard Wright, famous Negro writer, describes the book from which this selection is taken as a "definitive study of Negro urbanization." One phase of urbanization for the Negro is that very special type of social mobility—"passing." Here is a fascinating treatment of "passing" by two Negro social scientists.

A ROSE BY ANY OTHER NAME

"Passing" is one of the most prevalent practices that has arisen out of the American pattern of race relations. It grows from the fact that one known drop of "colored" blood is sufficient to make an otherwise completely white person a Negro. As there are thousands of Negroes whom neither colored nor white people can distinguish from full-blooded whites, it is understandable that in the anonymity of the city many Negroes "pass for white" daily, both intentionally and unintentionally.

* From *Black Metropolis* by St. Clair Drake and Horace R. Cayton, pp. 159–173, copyright, 1945, by Harcourt, Brace and Company, Inc.

St. Clair Drake (b. 1911) is Professor of Sociology and Anthropology, Roosevelt College, Chicago. Consultant for the Twentieth Century Fund Survey in tropical Africa, 1954. *Black Metropolis* received the Anisfeld-Wolf Award in 1945 for its contributions to race relations. Author of *Churches and Voluntary Associations in the Chicago Negro Community*.

Horace R. Cayton (b. 1903) is a writer, lecturer, sociologist. Formerly Director of Chicago's Parkway Community House. Author: *Black Workers and the New Unions* (with George S. Mitchell) and *We Have Tomorrow*.

But, should white people become aware of their remote colored ancestors they would, in all probability, treat them as Negroes.[1]

There are few figures on the amount of passing which takes place in the United States. Estimates of the number of people who permanently leave the Negro group and are assimilated into white society each year vary from 25,000 to 300,000. These are only estimates, and no conclusive body of statistical data is or ever could be available, especially on those who pass only temporarily or occasionally. There is not, however, a single Negro family known to the authors that has not been aware of instances, sometimes of scores of instances, in which friends, acquaintances, or relatives have crossed the color-line and become white —"gone over to the other side," as Negroes phrase it.

There are various degrees of passing, accompanied by different degrees of estrangement from the Negro group and emotional identification with the white community. Thousands of Negroes pass unintentionally daily. In a large city such as Midwest Metropolis, light-skinned Negroes who go into restaurants, who seek choice seats at a theater, or who are hired in certain jobs are mistaken for white without their being aware of it. A very light woman recently went to an exclusive photographer to have her picture taken. She returned at a later date with her daughter, who was obviously a Negro. The photographer refused to take the daughter's picture and told the mother that he did not care for colored patronage. Only then did she realize that she had been unconsciously passing for white.

Often, when caught in a situation in which he or she is taken for white, a Negro will carry through the bluff even when challenged, in order to avoid embarrassment. A young lady who did not approve of passing related the following incident:

"Speaking of passing—a strange thing happened to me this summer. When I went down to visit my father in Kentucky, I had to change trains at a station on the other side of the Mason-Dixon line. The porter took my bags and escorted me to the coach. I wasn't paying any attention to him. I just took it for granted that he was taking me to the correct coach. When I stepped into the coach, I immediately knew that he had made a mistake. All of these white people were seated and there I was! I said, 'Listen, porter—' and that's all the further I got. He said, 'That's all right, miss, the conductor will call your stop.' He passed my bags overhead and tipped his hat and walked away. So I sat down and was so ill at ease.

[1] The authors have interviews which suggest that some white people in the North are willing to overlook a small infusion of Negro blood provided the person who is passing has no social ties with Negroes. Several persons when questioned on this matter said that they knew of white people who were suspected of having Negro blood and that it was a joking matter. In one case everybody, including the suspect, saved face by saying it was perhaps *Indian* blood.

"I noticed several of the white people glancing at me and then after the second look, they looked off. I had had my hair freshly done, and when it is fresh it looks dark brown and wavy, and I did look decent because I was wearing my best. I took a magazine and began reading. After a bit, the conductor came up and after removing his hat and apologetically clearing his throat said, 'I know this is highly irregular, miss, but—uh—pardon me—may I ask you what nationality you are? Uh—are you Jewish?' I could have kissed the conductor for giving me that lead, because as soon as he started talking, I knew what he was going to say. I knew that if I said I was a Negro and tried to explain that I wasn't trying to pass, he wouldn't believe it. Also, to have to go back into the Negro coach with the conductor leading the way would be quite embarrassing to me. The Negroes would think I was trying to pass and got caught. So I decided to play up the situation. 'After all,' I said, 'this is highly ridiculous. Yes, I am a Jewess, and I consider this a grand insult.' I wore my haughtiest expression, and I was scared to death. By this time several of the white people had turned around and were listening to us.

"The conductor flushed and was very much embarrassed. I just know how he must have felt. He apologized again and then walked away. I was scared. I didn't enjoy the ride at all, and but for the company of a little eight-year-old white child, I talked to no one. It was lucky for me that I hadn't told Father I was coming. Suppose he had been at the station to meet me—then I would have been in a mess. I told Daddy about it and he just laughed. He thought it was a joke! And that's why I couldn't be bothered with trying to pass. I'd rather be colored and not be bothered. That's why I hate the South."

As the above incident suggests, passing in the South can often lead to serious trouble—it violates both custom and law. There are numerous stories about the dashing young man who comes to a southern town, cuts quite a figure, perhaps becomes engaged to a socially prominent local girl, and then suddenly and mysteriously disappears, never to be spoken of again. It is discovered by accident in such instances, so the tales go, that the man, though he appeared to be white, had Negro blood. In the North, however, where the population is not so sensitized, and in the crowded and impersonal atmosphere of the big cities, little thought is given to the possibility that someone might be passing, and no punitive action is taken by the society even when a person who is passing is discovered. In Midwest Metropolis, many Negroes pass merely for convenience. A light-complexioned girl remarked to one of the authors, "Whenever I am downtown alone I always go to one of the better restaurants. They think I am white, I guess; I never ask them. I wouldn't think of going with my husband, who is dark, for they might refuse us and we would be humiliated. Of course I never speak about this to him, as he is so sensitive about his color." It is common practice for very light women to patronize white beauty parlors where, according to them, they can get better service cheaper and without waiting. Often, too, a light person will purchase theater tickets for darker persons so that the latter will not be Jim-Crowed with other Negroes in the theater, or refused seats on the main floor.

From the initial state of passing unintentionally or passing for convenience, there often develops, in more adventurous persons, a practice of passing for fun. This behavior, too, can be engaged in without any feeling of guilt or disloyalty to the race; it is looked upon as having fun at the white folks' expense. Couples, and sometimes parties, will go to white cabarets and exclusive dancing places just to see what they are like and to get a thrill. Even in these cases, however, the persons involved are rather careful about relating these escapades to their friends for fear of censure from the darker persons. "I wouldn't tell everyone this, but you get around and would understand," said a light complexioned girl. "The other night I was out with Harry—you know he can pass for white—and after we had seen a show in the Loop he said, 'Let's go over to the Pump Room.' We did and had a glorious time and it wasn't any more expensive than the Rhumboogie. No, I wasn't in the least nervous. How could they tell we were colored? There were no colored waiters who might have recognized us. After this I am going to places like that any time I am out with him." Light-complexioned people who go out with white persons of the opposite sex frequently prefer to go to white places, for there is less fear of detection on the part of the Negro community, which in the case of a woman is a matter of some concern.

A fourth type of passing arises out of economic necessity or advantage. Negro girls have had difficulty in obtaining employment in white-collar jobs. Positions as stenographers, telephone operators, receptionists, and clerks are usually closed to anyone who is known to be colored. As there are many Negro girls of superior ability and training who wish such jobs, it is not unusual for some of them to pass, if they can, in order to obtain such work. There is no way of knowing how frequently such passing occurs, but there are few upper- or middle-class Negroes who do not claim knowledge of persons who have passed for economic reasons. Men in this category usually pass to obtain technical positions, and there are verifiable instances where eminent positions as scientists, physicians, and public administrators are held by these "white Negroes."

Usually the individual returns to the Negro community for all of his social contacts and uses his light skin color simply as a method of circumventing economic discrimination. Friendships with whites are generally avoided, as they would lead to complications. One girl reported:

"My mother is very fair and passes for white on most of the jobs she has had, but she doesn't like to do it. It always brings about so much trouble. She makes friends and soon they want her to come to see them and they want to come to see her. One friend that she had had for over a year used to invite Mother to her apartment. This woman knew Mother had two children, and she would say, 'You'll just have to bring those children over so I can see them.' We would have fun talking about it. Well, she finally had to quit; the girl was becoming too chummy."

The final stage of passing—crossing over completely to the other side of the color-line—involves passing in order to associate socially with white people. For a Negro to pass socially means sociological death and rebirth. It is extremely difficult, as one loses in the process his educational standing (if he has gone to a Negro school), intimate friends, family, and work references. People well established in the Negro world and older people seldom pass socially and completely. There is too much to lose and too little to be gained.

WHO CAN PASS?

Scholars have speculated about the amount of Negro blood which a person must have to pass. One concludes that persons with an eighth or less of Negro blood are frequently able to pass as white in a society that is not highly discriminating. Another believes that individuals with one-sixteenth colored ancestry are always able to pass as white. In Midwest Metropolis, a person with still a greater amount of Negro blood can no doubt pass. In other parts of the country, where there are many Mexicans, Puerto Ricans, and South Americans, it is even more difficult to detect persons with considerable Negro blood.

Passing is dependent on many factors other than skin color. Many fairly dark persons with sharp features are taken for Indians, East Indians, Egyptions, or members of other dark groups. The texture of the hair in many borderline cases plays an important role. But no single factor is so important as the general configuration of skin coloring, texture of hair, and facial characteristics in determining whether a person may be "taken for white." Because of the large admixture of Indian blood among Negroes, many have a Mongolian cast to their features. These individuals, if they have straight hair, can pass for non-Negro, even if quite dark. Then there are many subtle characteristics such as dress, general deportment, mannerisms, and degree of self-assurance which all play their parts.

Quite apart from all these factors and from any objective analysis of the individual's physical make-up is the factor of the social situation. In instances where Negroes are out of the conventional role, whites who have stereotyped notions of what Negroes should do, where they might be found, and how they should act are led to mistake obvious Negroes for white or other racial stock. A young Negro student entered a cab at the railroad station and asked to be taken to the University of

Chicago. Although he was brown-skinned and had woolly hair, the cab driver asked if he was not Argentinian. A prominent Negro went to an exclusive night club with a white party, and even though he was introduced to the manager as a Negro, the manager refused to believe his eyes or the statement of the white members of the party. This sort of mistake is also sometimes made by Negroes. At a high school where all the students were colored, but it was the custom to have a white speaker for the commencement exercises, a light brown-skinned Negro addressed the audience and was thought by the majority of the student body to be white. Americans, white and black, see with their emotions as well as with their eyes, and actualities are colored by stereotyped expectations.

On the other hand, any white person—including the lightest blond can, if he wishes, pass for colored. Dr. Robert Park, the eminent sociologist, on two occasions passed for a Negro in order to obtain a room in a Negro hotel. A white girl who worked at a social agency in the Black Belt found out to her amazement, after working with Negro people for a year, that almost all of them not only thought she was a Negro, but refused to believe that she wasn't joking when she said she was white. Some white persons married to Negroes habitually pass for Negro in order to gain some advantage or to avoid embarrassment. The white wife of a Negro railroad waiter related the following incident:

"I have an annual pass with the railroad company my husband is with. I used it a couple of times. Yes, I was questioned when I used the pass and I said that although you might not think so, I have colored blood. I was telling the truth because I have red blood in my veins, and that's colored. The man who questioned me was a southerner and I told him that if he doubted my identity he could wire my husband at my expense."

Many persons, especially white southerners and Negroes, believe that they are so sensitized to Negro racial characteristics that they can detect persons who are attempting to pass for either white or Negro. The following incident illustrates a belief in this special ability. Speaking of her mother, who was passing for white for economic reasons, an informant said:

"She used to hold a nice position at a hotel here. One day a man called her name and said, 'You remind me of a little colored girl.' She thought the most suitable answer was, 'You remind me of a little colored boy.' He said, 'Maybe I am.' It turned out that he was colored and lived on the South Side. It is kind of funny how colored people know one another almost ten times out of ten."

The authors found, however, that among the staff of the Cayton-Warner research, one dark-complexioned white girl was constantly mistaken for colored and one very light Negro girl was identified by most visitors, both white and Negro, as not being colored. Mixed parties have been held in the Negro community where white girls have passed for

Negro and Negro girls for white, to the utter confusion of all of the guests. Although persons particularly sensitized to racial differences may be a bit more astute in identifying racial characteristics, a point is reached where it is impossible with even the most refined anthropological measurements to distinguish Negroes from whites. The racial identification of such marginal persons is sociological rather than biological; and what really determines their "race" is how much the public knows about their ancestry

PASSING AS A PROCESS

Few people, regardless of how light they may be, grow up as Negroes and then suddenly make an intellectual decision to pass for white. Those who pass over the color-line do so step by step until the emotional ties which bind them to Negroes are severed, on the one hand, and new relationships with members of the white community achieved, on the other hand. The first step, as has been indicated, is usually unintentional passing, where a Negro with a light skin suddenly realizes that in going about the city, outside of the Negro community, he is taken for white. Later the individual becomes more adventurous and begins to pass for some minor convenience, such as obtaining a Pullman when traveling in the South. The individual then may find a subtle pleasure in fooling white people and going places where he knows he would not be welcomed as a Negro. Still later he may seek employment in the white community with every intention of keeping all social relations among Negroes. But as intimate friendships are established with white fellow-workers, in many cases the individual is gradually drawn farther and farther away from his emotional attachment to members of the black community. For such an individual the final break comes when the irritations of trying to remain colored and the attractiveness of the white world outweigh his trepidation.

For one who is not firmly anchored in the Negro community emotionally, there is much temptation to take such a step. At first he finds that the color-line in Midwest Metropolis seems to disappear for him. There is no close scrutiny by his new-found white working companions and friends. There is no fear of any more reprisal than being fired from a job or losing some new acquaintances. Then more and more difficulties begin to arise. He begins to dread meeting old Negro friends while out with the new white ones. There are cases where daughters have refused to speak to their mothers on the street and sons have looked the other way, when accompanied by whites, upon encountering their Negro fathers. As the new job and the new friends become of more emotional importance, the individual has a constant, haunting fear of being discovered. There is the possibility that an old Negro enemy may turn him in, or that some white person may accidentally discover him and work vengeance on him.

Then there arises a moral crisis. On the one hand, it is hard to continue to live in two worlds; but on the other hand, there is a sense of guilt over being unfaithful to the Negro world with which he and his family have been identified. Then it is that many an individual either announces to a startled office manager, foreman, or fiancée that he is a Negro and would prefer to be known as such, or commits sociological suicide, to be reborn on the white side of the color-line.

An individual who makes the latter choice is not operating in a vacuum. There is the constant and disturbing pressure of the Negro community which both pushes and pulls him. Many very light men, especially, feel uncomfortable in the Negro community. They are very conspicuous when out with Negro groups except when all are as light as they. This is the push which exerts itself on them from birth. They are always suspect—the community feels that in most cases they are only looking for a chance to escape the confines of color. Passing episodes are carefully concealed from most of their Negro friends, for the community would in most cases censure them; and even when they pass solely for economic reasons, only a partial and begrudging sanction is given them. Finally, the condemnation of the Negro group itself operates in the same way as the attractiveness of moving freely in white society, to allow them to make a moral decision to cross over the line. Although there is far from unanimity on the subject, many Negroes would agree with a young woman who said:

"Well, I don't see anything wrong with it, if the person can get something out of it. But personally, I don't like it. I think if for commercial reasons it is done as Mary Malone is doing [she named a well-known Negro girl who passes for white on the stage], that's not so bad; but I wouldn't want to deny my race otherwise. And then I would associate with colored people after I was finished work. What I mean is that I would pass only for business purposes and not because I didn't want to be colored."

There is a widespread belief in the community that Negroes protect other Negroes who are passing. One white woman married to a Negro stated:

"Some people would try to prevent a person from holding a job if they knew he wasn't entitled to it because of color. My husband knows a man who is colored and who is working as a white man, but my husband never recognizes him. There is a sort of code of honor among colored people not to reveal the identity of a person who is working as white."

Although there are occasional instances of Negroes exposing others who are passing, in general there is great tolerance on the part of Negroes if they know they are not being slighted or are being slighted for economic reasons only. The difference in attitude of two colored girls who worked in a downtown department store illustrates this point:

"Mary and I got a job working at Field's one Christmas. Mary had

had much more practice at passing than I. But she was scared to death that someone—some colored person—would see her and recognize her. They put her in the costume jewelry section right on the first floor. Negroes would come in and she would try to avoid them and turn her back. Then they made a point of trying to speak to her. Finally she became a nervous wreck and had to quit. They put me in the handkerchief section on State Street, and people were coming in all the time that I knew; but I always spoke to them and would wait on them if they came to my counter. So I got along all right. Lots of people who sensed that I was going to speak to them would just nod and move away quickly. They weren't resentful. I really needed the money; but it wasn't a life-and-death matter, so I couldn't think of not speaking to someone that I knew."

The practice of passing for economic reasons is so frequent and the Negro's economic position is so desperate that some years ago the Chicago *Defender* gave partial sanction to this behavior in an editorial mainly slanted toward poking fun at the attitude of whites:

In our big department stores in the Loop can be found many sons and daughters who come back "home" at the close of the day, and by the same token would come back home to stay if their identity was found out. They are not as fair as lilies but the fact that most of the stores are "manned" by Jewish girls whose complexion and hair is swarthy helps the situation out materially. It is a shame and a disgrace that we must be forced in order to make a livelihood, to live this life each day, but there is not another way. We pour thousands of dollars, hard earned, into the coffers of the storekeepers and yet we are denied recognition or a chance to earn some of it back except we apply for some menial position like running an elevator or janitorship, and in many places we are even denied this class of employment. That our men and women are superior in every way to the average wage-earner found in these stories is without question, but worth doesn't count when prejudice creeps in, so we must fight fire with fire, and those that are able to "get by" peace be with them and it is our duty not to hinder them in any way. Last Monday was the Jewish New Year and all of that faith were given a holiday—without pay—by the store managers. This, of course, made a number of our young ladies who were Jewish pro tem take two days off. "There are tricks to all trades," said one of them laughingly, "and we had it to do to allay suspicion." So even with the serious side of it there comes something in the lighter vein. But it does seem with a concerted effort this situation could in a measure be changed for the better, patronize the store that offers the most to you and yours and you will be aiding materially in the movement.

A ROSE IS A ROSE IS A ROSE

Although thousands of Negroes are lost to the Negro race each year by passing, scores of thousands have passed for a while only to return to the—for them—warmer and more comfortable milieu of the Negro community.

A prominent colored physician reported that for some years after he left college he passed for white in practicing medicine. He could never feel quite comfortable and was particularly concerned about his relationships with his family. After having established a successful practice, he suddenly decided to return to the Negro group and there achieved a position of prominence which he could never have attained in the larger society. Another well-known Negro businessman for a number of years lived on the North Shore, but he too returned to the Black Belt and, with the capital he had accumulated and the insight into white business practices he had obtained, was able to establish one of the most successful enterprises in the community.

In both of these instances, as in many others, passing was profitable at one period of the individual's life, when he had no money and little experience, but it was equally profitable later on to return to the Negro community. Usually the fact that he has passed is a guarded secret, for it would indicate that at one time he had severed his emotional identification with the community and he would be suspected of demonstrating a similar disloyalty again. Men pass for noneconomic reasons more frequently than women; it is also more common for men to return to the Negro group. Once a light girl has passed, she would be considered disloyal—sullied, and not to be trusted—and would not be able to make such an advantageous marriage were she to return to the Negro group. While it is common knowledge that thousands of Negroes pass, cases of those who return are relatively infrequent. In the lives of many prominent Negroes, however, are gaps which can be explained only in terms of a temporary passing over the color-line.

Passing has been described as a process where one gradually relinquishes his social relationships and emotional identification with the Negro community. It should not be thought, however, that every person who passes completely goes through each step of this process; it is merely the pattern generally followed. Many people are never successful in breaking their ties completely with either group, and severe maladjustment often results.

Passing is one way of crossing the color-line. It does not challenge the mores of the society, for it is surreptitious. It does, however, bring with it miscegenation, introducing a constant stream of Negro blood into the white population. In fact, as Louis Wirth and Herbert Goldhamer state, "One southern state legislator, in speaking against an especially severe bill restricting Negro-white intermarriage, is reported as saying that if the definition of Negro incorporated in the bill were accepted there would not be enough white people in the state to pass it."

Midwest Metropolis is not aware of the volume of passing nor disturbed enough about it to take punitive action. Nevertheless anyone discovered is usually considered a Negro. If such an individual has attained a position of great importance, however, the episode is often hushed up. Negroes claim to be aware of many cases of this kind, and numerous stories on the subject circulate throughout the community.[2] It is even widely believed that there has been at least one "Negro" president of the United States.

A TWO-WAY PASSAGE

In Chicago people do occasionally cross the color-line. And when they do, they may encounter difficulties. But hundreds of Negroes have lived and are living as white, and a small group of whites have become sociological Negroes. It can and does happen here—but not with the frequency which would warrant the irrational fear of "amalgamation" held by many white people.

What does this race crossing mean? More Negro blood than most suspect finds its way into the white population—not enough, however, to change the physical characteristics of that group at all. Passing is of much more serious import to Negroes. Yearly a number of "white Negroes" pass over the line. This perhaps robs the Negro group of possible leaders and well-trained persons who could add immeasurably to the welfare of the group. But it should be noted that a relatively small proportion of those who can pass really do cross over completely, and there are some who have passed completely but who "return to their race" with capital and experience which allows them to become leaders. It's a two-way passage in many instances.

Intermarriage, on the other hand, operates to introduce more white blood into the Negro group, modifying to an extent that physical type. The study of the "American Negro" is not merely the study of Negroes so designated because they are culturally distinct from the Negroes of Africa, but is also the study of the formation of a relatively distinct physical type. Intermarriage (though nonlegal miscegenation is much more important in this connection) is one of the means by which this new type—the brown American—has come into existence.

THE "BLACK BABY" BUGABOO

Mixed couples usually express a desire for either light brown-skinned children or children who can pass for white. People who oppose passing often cite the "danger" of a "black baby"—a "throwback"—sometime cropping up should the Negro who has passed, or his descendants, marry a white person. Negroes who are passing occasionally hesitate to

[2] Such stories are hard to verify. Occasionally, however, an incident becomes a matter of public record. Just before the First World War, for instance, a wealthy Chicago publisher, always considered white, was found to be a "Negro" when his darker relatives showed up at his funeral. A similar case appeared in the neighboring state of Indiana in 1940 when a leading businessman and philanthropist was revealed as colored at his funeral.

get married or to have children for fear that "Negro blood will out." This emphasis upon the "black baby" arriving to embarrass its parents has a dual significance. On one hand it reflects the general attitude of the dominant white American culture toward "typical" Negro physical traits —the definition of black skin, thick lips, and kinky hair as "ugly." On the other hand, it expresses a desire that children shall not look so different from the parents as to excite embarrassing stares or malicious gossip.[3]

The "black baby" bugaboo is often cited as the primary objection to passing. Edward M. East, the geneticist, has discussed the probable origin of such black babies as do appear in the following passage:

"A favorite short-story plot with which melodramatic artists seek to harrow the feelings of their readers is one where the distinguished scion of an aristocratic family marries the beautiful girl with telltale shadows on the half-moons of her nails, and in due time is presented with a coal-black son. It is a good framework, and carries a thrill. One waits shiveringly, even breathlessly, for the first squeal of the dingy infant. There is only this slight imperfection—or is it an advantage?—it could not possibly happen on the stage as set by the author. The most casual examination of the genetic formulae given above demonstrates its absurdity. If there ever was a basis for the plot in real life, the explanation lies in a fracture of the seventh commandment, or in a tinge of negro [*sic*] blood in the aristocrat as dark as that in his wife."

The genetic formulae referred to by East, and generally accepted by geneticists and anthropologists, support the following conclusions: [4]

1. In the case of two persons both theoretically white but having, whether they know it or not, some Negro blood, an accentuation of some Negro characteristics may occur in their offspring, but in all probability the offspring of such unions will be able to pass for white.

2. It is impossible for the offspring of a recognizable Negro and a pure white person to be any darker than the Negro partner, and in all probability it will be lighter.

3. The offspring of two mixed-bloods (e.g., mulattoes or quadroons) may be darker than either, but in all probability would not be black.

---

[3] Esthetic standards vary from culture to culture. Many Central African groups think that thin lips, white skin and straight hair are ugly. And among white people there are many who can recognize "black" beauty or "yellow" beauty as well as white. There are people, too, who in choosing a mate do not put such standards in the primary place. Students of Latin American countries have frequently called attention to the fact that the marriage of whites to very Negroid types is not unusual, and that the white partners feel no shame in such cases. Yet, often, very devoted couples of this type want children who are blends and consider a dark child unfortunate.

[4] In detailing these conclusions we have used the expression "Negro blood" instead of the more precise formulation in terms of genes that govern characteristics such as skin-color, hair form, shape of nose, etc. Obviously, however, blood has nothing to do with heredity, but it is probable that the colloquial use of the term

Even a widespread knowledge of these facts will not dispel the "black baby" bugaboo, for what white person can be sure that he has no Negro blood, or what Negro who is passing that he will not marry a "white" person who has a few drops from way back? The chances of such marriages producing a "black baby" are extremely remote—but it could happen. "In all probability" is not a very reassuring phrase. So long as "blackness" of skin is considered a misfortune, the bugaboo will remain. Even if the habit of stigmatizing people because of their skin-color were to disappear, a "black baby" would still be considered a misfortune until everyone knew that an occasional dark child born to lighter parents did not constitute *prima facie* evidence of interracial adultery.

47. THE ETA:

A MARGINAL JAPANESE CASTE *

HUGH H. SMYTHE

It is impossible to describe a complex caste system, such as may be found among Hindus in India, in a brief article. The two previous selections have described some aspects of a caste-like system in our society. This selection by Hugh Smythe describes a sharply defined caste stratum in Japan. It is well to bear in mind that a pure caste system in which there is no mobility is actually unknown in contemporary society.

Today in Japan there exist some three million persons, ethnically Japanese, who are virtually social outcasts living largely on the margins of Japanese society. These are the Eta. Their racial similarity with other Japanese, coupled with caste status and economic overtones in a society in which Western political patterns have been overlaid on a centuries-old feudalistic foundation, hold out rich promise for those interested in new aspects of the general problem of caste and class.

"Negro blood" will remain long after the general public is aware that it really refers to "genes for Negro traits."

* Reprinted from "The Eta: A Marginal Japanese Caste," by Hugh H. Smythe, *The American Journal of Sociology*, Vol. 58, No. 2 (September, 1952), 194–196, by permission of The University of Chicago Press, Copyright 1952 by The University of Chicago.

The author (b. 1913) is Research Director, W. B. Graham and Associates, New York. Lecturer, Graduate Division, Brooklyn College. An anthropologist, his major interest is in the area of race and culture contact.

FOUNDATIONS OF CASTE

Historically, the Eta developed out of the feudalistic economy of the Middle Ages, their identity as a special group arising near the close of the fourteenth century. Although work with leather was their major occupation, they performed services as executioners, butchers, handlers of the dead, and disposers of offal and did other jobs avoided by people in general as being unclean. Because of their association with occupations considered degrading they were even refused work as domestics in the homes of farmers and merchants. Thus in the feudal social system their status was at the bottom, and they became social outcasts on the basis of occupation. During the long period of internecine warfare in the fifteenth and sixteenth centuries, when the demand for leather goods was great, the Eta occupied a preferred economic position, although their social status remained low. The embattled warlords competed with one another to gain their services and to attract them to their castle towns, and they were given special protection, since their help was indispensable. However, when the long period of isolation and relative peace set in with the inception of the Tokugawa regime at the beginning of the seventeenth century, the demand for leather goods declined, the Eta lost their favored status, and they were segregated in special villages or special sections of towns and villages.

In 1871, soon after the beginning of the modern period in Japanese history in 1868, the identity of the Eta as a special caste was officially abolished by imperial decree, and they were legally absorbed into the category of commoners, being permitted to follow any occupation they wished. But in reality their caste status remained intact, and by 1873 the general population had set them apart as the "new commoners." Socially they were shunned; marriage with them was abhorred, and they were excluded from social functions. They were forced to continue in their traditional occupations and were limited to such others as day laborer, peddler, tenant farmer, and handicraft worker. Their segregated living quarters, although no longer recognized, persist even today: the Eta are referred to as the "special *buraku* people."

The limited and fragmentary work done on the Eta by Japanese scholars has been almost wholly historical; thus there are no substantial sociological or anthropological data available. This limitation of detailed research materials frustrates attempts at even a partial interpretation of their present role and function in Japanese society. Their current situation is, therefore, here empirically discussed for the purpose of pointing the way for detailed and comprehensive study.

GENERAL PROBLEM

Economic role and mobility. The historical development of the Eta accounts for their concentration today mainly in central and southern Japan, with their population about equally divided between rural and urban areas. There is very little internal migration in Japan, and many Eta, especially those in villages and rural areas, continue to live in localities which they have inhabited for generations. In prewar times the more enterprising sons of Eta sometimes were able to escape their inferior status by emigrating to Japanese-held Dairen, Port Arthur, and Korea. Some attended the Japanese-established imperial universities— Keijo in Korea and Taihoku in Formosa—secured training, returned to Japan, and entered other occupations, losing their identity in new occupations and in the general population of cities. Since their names and physical appearance are in general indistinguishable from those of the general population, their potential mobility is relatively great.

Although the position of the Eta in the post-surrender period was improved somewhat (under the Occupation all forms of social, religious, racial, and political discrimination were made illegal), today the Eta continue to function largely within their traditional occupations as slaughterers of animals; proprietors of butcher shops, shoe stores, and repair shops; leather-workers; basket-weavers; and clog- and sandal-makers. In the villages they usually occupy the bottom rung of the economic ladder and cultivate the smallest farms.

Cultural isolation and coalescence. Like the Classic Black Belt, Jewish ghetto, and immigrant slums of American and European cities, the Eta neighborhoods are set apart. But unlike the former, which are customarily large continuous concentrations, the Eta settlements are small and spotty, although there are a few villages populated almost entirely by them. When villages and towns have merged into cities, their settlements have remained as peripheral enclaves and the Eta continue to live in isolation as a marginal neighborhood group.

The period since the surrender has afforded them greater political participation, yet in their villages as well as in the towns and cities they share in political life, as a rule, as Eta. Part of this is due to the fact that in most villages assembly men, in practice, are elected by their own *buraku* rather than by the village-at-large; and because he is segregated in special *burakus* or confined to a certain part of a *buraku* in very small places, an Eta customarily represents his community only when such representation is on a *buraku* basis.

Being Japanese and indistinguishable physically and linguistically from the general population, the Eta are able to participate inside the larger Japanese society. Their problem here appears to be one fundamentally sociopsychological, arising from their occupational caste status and the inhibitions which this promotes. The sociopsychological effect of the term "Eta" is undoubtedly a restraint, since it has a derogatory connotation similar to that of "nigger," "kike," "wop," "greaser," "chink," "monkey chaser," and other terms applied in America to minority groups. Their economic status also isolates them from full cultural participation: generally the poorest group in the population and segregated in special areas, they live a ghetto life, a limited and growth-retarding existence.

Integration and assimilation. Considering their physical oneness with the general Japanese population, the constricted status of the Eta makes a vivid impression upon the observer. Superficially they appear to occupy an apparently undifferentiated position, but further examination reveals that they are socially excluded, economically depressed, and politically powerless. The Eta still experience segregation and discrimination, despite Occupation reforms, and their occupational-caste status continues to be accompanied by social restrictions, particularly in personal relations and in religion.

Even where the Eta have achieved economic success and political acceptance, marriage into the majority group is still rigidly taboo. Since the Japanese place great stress upon the "stock" of a family, non-Eta families never consider the marriage of their son or daughter to an Eta, for they feel that, no matter how much worldly success an Eta might achieve, he can never overcome the taint of his lineage.

The Eta have attempted on a mass scale to escape their proscriptive position. In the early 1920's they formed a nation-wide organization, *Suiheisha* (Levellers Association) to effect their emancipation, and in a national convention in Kyoto on March 3, 1922, they set forth a declaration of equality. In several instances they were forced to resort to force to resist those interested in keeping them in their subordinate status.

The postwar period has helped some of them individually to escape their ethnic enclaves, especially the young women. The Eta women are reputedly among the most attractive in Japan. During the Occupation some of them became *pen-pans* (street prostitutes); others went to the large cities and became taxi dancers in the night clubs, dance halls, and restaurants; still others entered the employment of Occupation dependents. In this way they met Allied soldiers and sometimes married them, while in others they remained in the cities and continued in their newly found pursuits, thus escaping their caste-ridden traditional occupations and conditions.

SUMMARY

In the light of the foregoing and because of their size and dynamic character it is apparent that the Eta merit wide, detailed, and comprehensive study. Research on aspects of the Eta phenomenon can make significant contributions to the study of problems of caste, class, social distance, minority groups, social differentiation, intergroup and race relations, social mobility, and occupation-status relationships. Findings from such research should provide materials useful for comparative treatment with other status and ethnic groups. Among possible research projects are the following: (1) their geographic origin and prior occupational and status characteristics; (2) differences in degrees of social, economic, religious, and political acceptance and nonacceptance, in urban and rural settlements; (3) factors encouraging or mitigating their cultural coalescence and how far they have operated in either direction since the war; (4) studies of their ethnic enclaves, the reduction of their isolation, and possibility of their incorporation into the larger society; (5) the effect of the term "Eta" as a concept of derogation on the stigmatized group and its social function in the larger society; (6) intercaste and intra-caste behavior; (7) majority stereotypes of Eta characteristics; (8) the extent to which caste restrictions operate upon Eta who have obtained a high level of education and wealth; (9) intermarriage between the Eta and other Japanese.

CHAPTER VII

SOCIAL
ORGANIZATION

Institutions and Associations

48. PARKINSON'S LAW *

C. NORTHCOTE PARKINSON

Although written with tongue in cheek, C. Northcote Parkinson's "Law" clearly illustrates one of the most fundamental facts about human society. Human groups, he says, tend to devise increasingly complicated organized ways of doing things (a process that is often termed "institutionalization") and then to keep on doing them in the established way even when it doesn't make sense. Vested interests might suffer if some change were introduced. The consequences of this tendency are legion: social change is impeded, taxation and business costs increase, people become concerned with techniques more than with goals, bureaucrats multiply like rabbits. Such consequences are specifically illustrated in one sense or another in the articles by Marion K. Sanders (49), John Williams Andrews (59), Theodore H. White (60), Anton T. Boisen (66), and Shirley Basch (71).

I. PARKINSON'S LAW OR THE RISING PYRAMID

Work expands so as to fill the time available for its completion. General recognition of this fact is shown in the proverbial phrase "It is the

---

* This selection from C. Northcote Parkinson, *Parkinson's Law and Other Studies in Administration*, 1957, pp. 2–12, 59–69 passim, is reprinted by permission of and arrangement with Houghton Mifflin Company, the authorized publishers.

The author (b. 1909) was Raffles Professor of History, University of Malaya, Singapore, is now at the University of Illinois. Lecturer and visiting professor, University of Liverpool and Harvard. Author: *Trade in the Eastern Seas; Britain in the Far East; Evaluation of Political Thought.*

busiest man who has time to spare." Thus, an elderly lady of leisure can spend the entire day in writing and dispatching a postcard to her niece at Bognor Regis. An hour will be spent in finding the postcard, another in hunting for spectacles, half an hour in a search for the address, an hour and a quarter in composition, and twenty minutes in deciding whether or not to take an umbrella when going to the mailbox in the next street. The total effort that would occupy a busy man for three minutes all told may in this fashion leave another person prostrate after a day of doubt, anxiety, and toil.

Granted that work (and especially paperwork) is thus elastic in its demands on time, it is manifest that there need be little or no relationship between the work to be done and the size of the staff to which it may be assigned. A lack of real activity does not, of necessity, result in leisure. A lack of occupation is not necessarily revealed by a manifest idleness. The thing to be done swells in importance and complexity in a direct ratio with the time to be spent. This fact is widely recognized, but less attention has been paid to its wider implications, more especially in the field of public administration. Politicians and taxpayers have assumed (with occasional phases of doubt) that a rising total in the number of civil servants must reflect a growing volume of work to be done. Cynics, in questioning this belief, have imagined that the multiplication of officials must have left some of them idle or all of them able to work for shorter hours. But this is a matter in which faith and doubt seem equally misplaced. The fact is that the number of the officials and the quantity of the work are not related to each other at all. The rise in the total of those employed is governed by Parkinson's Law and would be much the same whether the volume of the work were to increase, diminish, or even disappear. The importance of Parkinson's Law lies in the fact that it is a law of growth based upon an analysis of the factors by which that growth is controlled.

The validity of this recently discovered law must rest mainly on statistical proofs, which will follow. Of more interest to the general reader is the explanation of the factors underlying the general tendency to which this law gives definition. Omitting technicalities (which are numerous) we may distinguish at the outset two motive forces. They can be represented for the present purpose by two almost axiomatic statements, thus: (1) "An official wants to multiply subordinates, not rivals" and (2) "Officials make work for each other."

To comprehend Factor 1, we must picture a civil servant, called A, who finds himself overworked. Whether this overwork is real or imaginary is immaterial, but we should observe, in passing, that A's sensation (or illusion) might easily result from his own decreasing energy: a normal symptom of middle age. For this real or imagined overwork there are, broadly speaking, three possible remedies. He may resign; he may ask to halve the work with a colleague called B; he may demand the assistance of two subordinates, to be called C and D. There is probably no instance in history, however, of A choosing any but the third alternative. By resignation he would lose his pension rights. By having B appointed, on his own level in the hierarchy, he would merely bring in a rival for promotion to W's vacancy when W (at long last) retires. So A would rather have C and D, junior men, below him. They will add to his consequence and, by dividing the work into two categories, as between C and D, he will have the merit of being the only man who comprehends them both. It is essential to realize at this point that C and D are, as it were, inseparable. To appoint C alone would have been impossible. Why? Because C, if by himself, would divide the work with A and so assume almost the equal status that has been refused in the first instance to B; a status the more emphasized if C is A's only possible successor. Subordinates must thus number two or more, each being thus kept in order by fear of the other's promotion. When C complains in turn of being overworked (as he certainly will) A will, with the concurrence of C, advise the appointment of two assistants to help C. But he can then avert internal friction only by advising the appointment of two more assistants to help D, whose position is much the same. With this recruitment of E, F, G, and H the promotion of A is now practically certain.

Seven officials are now doing what one did before. This is where Factor 2 comes into operation. For these seven make so much work for each other that all are fully occupied and A is actually working harder than ever. An incoming document may well come before each of them in turn. Official E decides that it falls within the province of F, who places a draft reply before C, who amends it drastically before consulting D, who asks G to deal with it. But G goes on leave at this point, handing the file over to H, who drafts a minute that is signed by D and returned to C, who revises his draft accordingly and lays the new version before A.

What does A do? He would have every excuse for signing the thing unread, for he has many other matters on his mind. Knowing now that he is to succeed W next year, he has to decide whether C or D should succeed to his own office. He had to agree to G's going on leave even if not yet strictly entitled to it. He is worried whether H should not have gone instead, for reasons of health. He has looked pale recently—partly but not solely because of his domestic troubles. Then there is the business of F's special increment of salary for the period of the conference and E's application for transfer to the Ministry of Pensions. A has heard that D is in love with a married typist and that G and F are no longer on speaking terms—no one seems to know why. So A might be tempted to sign C's draft and have done with it. But A is a conscientious man. Beset as he is with problems created by his colleagues for themselves and for him—created by the mere fact of these officials' existence—he is not the man to shirk his duty. He reads through the draft with care, deletes the fussy paragraphs added by C and H, and restores the thing back to the form preferred in the first instance by the able (if quarrelsome) F. He corrects the English—none of these young men can write grammatically —and finally produces the same reply he would have written if officials C to H had never been born. Far more people have taken far longer to produce the same result. No one has been idle. All have done their best. And it is late in the evening before A finally quits his office and begins the return journey to Ealing. The last of the office lights are being turned off in the gathering dusk that marks the end of another day's administrative toil. Among the last to leave, A reflects with bowed shoulders and a wry smile that late hours, like gray hairs, are among the penalties of success.

. . . . .

Further and detailed . . . analysis of departmental staffs would be inappropriate in such a work as this. It is hoped, however, to reach a tentative conclusion regarding the time likely to elapse between a given official's first appointment and the later appointment of his two or more assistants.

Dealing with the problem of pure staff accumulation, all our researches so far completed point to an average increase of 5.75 per cent per year. This fact established, it now becomes possible to state Parkinson's Law in mathematical form: In any public administrative department not actually at war, the staff increase may be expected to follow this formula—

$$x = \frac{2k^m + 1}{n}$$

k is the number of staff seeking promotion through the appointment of subordinates; l represents the difference between the ages of appointment and retirement; m is the number of man-hours devoted to answering minutes within the department; and n is the number of effective units being administered. x will be the number of new staff required each year. Mathematicians will realize, of course, that to find the percentage increase they must multiply x by 100 and divide by the total of the previous year, thus:

$$\frac{100\ (2k^m + 1)}{yn} \cdot \%$$

where y represents the total original staff. This figure will invariably prove to be between 5.17 per cent and 6.56 per cent, irrespective of any variation in the amount of work (if any) to be done.

. . . . . .

II. PLANS AND PLANTS OR THE ADMINISTRATIVE BLOCK

Every student of human institutions is familiar with the standard test by which the importance of the individual may be assessed. The number of doors to be passed, the number of his personal assistants, the number of his telephone receivers—these three figures, taken with the depth of his carpet in centimeters, have given us a simple formula that is reliable for most parts of the world. It is less widely known that the same sort of measurement is applicable, *but in reverse,* to the institution itself.

Take, for example, a publishing organization. Publishers have a strong tendency, as we know, to live in a state of chaotic squalor. The visitor who applies at the obvious entrance is led outside and around the block, down an alley and up three flights of stairs. A research establishment is similarly housed, as a rule, on the ground floor of what was once a private house, a crazy wooden corridor leading thence to a corrugated iron hut in what was once the garden. Are we not all familiar, moreover, with the layout of an international airport? As we emerge from the aircraft, we see (over to our right or left) a lofty structure wrapped in scaffolding. Then the air hostess leads us into a hut with an asbestos roof. Nor do we suppose for a moment that it will ever be otherwise. By the time the permanent building is complete the airfield will have been moved to another site.

The institutions already mentioned—lively and productive as they may be—flourish in such shabby and makeshift surroundings that we might turn with relief to an institution clothed from the outset with convenience and dignity. The outer door, in bronze and glass, is placed centrally in a symmetrical façade. Polished shoes glide quietly over shining rubber to the glittering and silent elevator. The overpoweringly cultured receptionist will murmur with carmine lips into an ice-blue receiver. She will wave you into a chromium armchair, consoling you with a dazzling smile for any slight but inevitable delay. Looking up from a glossy magazine, you will observe how the wide corridors radiate toward departments A, B, and C. From behind closed doors will come the subdued noise of an ordered activity. A minute later and you are ankle deep in the director's carpet, plodding sturdily toward his distant, tidy desk. Hypnotized by the chief's unwavering stare, cowed by the Matisse hung upon his wall, you will feel that you have found real efficiency at last.

In point of fact you will have discovered nothing of the kind. It is now known that a perfection of planned layout is achieved only by

institutions on the point of collapse. This apparently paradoxical conclusion is based upon a wealth of archaeological and historical research,
with the more esoteric details of which we need not concern ourselves.
In general principle, however, the method pursued has been to select
and date the buildings which appear to have been perfectly designed
for their purpose. A study and comparison of these has tended to prove
that perfection of planning is a symptom of decay. During a period of
exciting discovery or progress there is no time to plan the perfect headquarters. The time for that comes later, when all the important work
has been done. Perfection, we know, is finality; and finality is death.

. . . . . .

Just such a sequence can be found in the history of the League of
Nations. Great hopes centered on the League from its inception in 1920
until about 1930. By 1933, at the latest, the experiment was seen to have
failed. Its physical embodiment, however, the Palace of the Nations, was
not opened until 1937. It was a structure no doubt justly admired. Deep
thought had gone into the design of secretariat and council chambers,
committee rooms and cafeteria. Everything was there which ingenuity
could devise—except, indeed, the League itself. By the year when its
Palace was formally opened the League had practically ceased to exist.

. . . . .

It is natural . . . to ask at this point whether the Palace of Westminster, where the House of Commons meets, is itself a true expression
of parliamentary rule. It represents beyond question a magnificent piece
of planning, aptly designed for debate and yet provided with ample
space for everything else—for committee meetings, for quiet study, for
refreshment, and (on its terrace) for tea. It has everything a legislator
could possibly desire, all incorporated in a building of immense dignity
and comfort. It should date—but this we now hardly dare assume—from
a period when parliamentary rule was at its height. But once again the
dates refuse to fit into this pattern. The original House, where Pitt and
Fox were matched in oratory, was accidentally destroyed by fire in 1834.
It would appear to have been as famed for its inconvenience as for its
lofty standard of debate. The present structure was begun in 1840, partly
occupied in 1852, but incomplete when its architect died in 1860. It
finally assumed its present appearance in about 1868. Now, by what we
can no longer regard as coincidence, the decline of Parliament can be
traced, without much dispute, to the Reform Act of 1867. It was in the
following year that all initiative in legislation passed from Parliament to
be vested in the Cabinet. The prestige attached to the letters "M.P."
began sharply to decline and thenceforward the most that could be said

is that "a role, though a humble one, was left for private members." The great days were over.

The same could not be said of the various Ministries, which were to gain importance in proportion to Parliament's decline. Investigation may yet serve to reveal that the India Office reached its peak of efficiency when accommodated in the Westminster Palace Hotel. What is more significant, however, is the recent development of the Colonial Office. For while the British Empire was mostly acquired at a period when the Colonial Office (in so far as there was one) occupied haphazard premises in Downing Street, a new phase of colonial policy began when the department moved into buildings actually designed for the purpose. This was in 1875 and the structure was well designed as a background for the disasters of the Boer War. But the Colonial Office gained a new lease of life during World War II. With its move to temporary and highly inconvenient premises in Great Smith Street—premises leased from the Church of England and intended for an entirely different purpose— British colonial policy entered that phase of enlightened activity which will end no doubt with the completion of the new building planned on the site of the old Westminster Hospital. It is reassuring to know that work on this site has not even begun.

But no other British example can now match in significance the story of New Delhi. Nowhere else have British architects been given the task of planning so great a capital city as the seat of government for so vast a population. The intention to found New Delhi was announced at the Imperial Durbar of 1911, King George V being at that time the Mogul's successor on what had been the Peacock Throne. Sir Edwin Lutyens then proceeded to draw up plans for a British Versailles, splendid in conception, comprehensive in detail, masterly in design, and overpowering in scale. But the stages of its progress toward completion correspond with so many steps in political collapse. The Government of India Act of 1909 had been the prelude to all that followed—the attempt on the Viceroy's life in 1912, the Declaration of 1917, the Montagu-Chelmsford Report of 1918 and its implementation in 1920. Lord Irwin actually moved into his new palace in 1929, the year in which the Indian Congress demanded independence, the year in which the Round Table Conference opened, the year before the Civil Disobedience campaign began. It would be possible, though tedious, to trace the whole story down to the day when the British finally withdrew, showing how each phase of the retreat was exactly paralleled with the completion of another triumph in civic design. What was finally achieved was no more and no less than a mausoleum. . . .

The elaborate layout of the Pentagon at Arlington, Virginia, provides another significant lesson for planners. It was not completed until the later stages of World War II and, of course, the architecture of the great victory was not constructed here, but in the crowded and untidy Munitions Building on Constitution Avenue.

Even today, as the least observant visitor to Washington can see, the most monumental edifices are found to house such derelict organizations as the Departments of Commerce and Labor, while the more active agencies occupy half-completed quarters. Indeed, much of the more urgent business of government goes forward in "temporary" structures erected during World War I, and shrewdly preserved for their stimulating effect on administration. Hard by the Capitol, the visitor will also observe the imposing marble-and-glass headquarters of the Teamsters' Union, completed not a moment too soon before the heavy hand of Congressional investigation descended on its occupants.

It is by no means certain that an influential reader of this chapter could prolong the life of a dying institution merely by depriving it of its streamlined headquarters. What he can do, however, with more confidence, is to prevent any organization strangling itself at birth. Examples abound of new institutions coming into existence with a full establishment of deputy directors, consultants and executives; all these coming together in a building specially designed for their purpose. And experience proves that such an institution will die. It is choked by its own perfection. It cannot take root for lack of soil. It cannot grow naturally for it is already grown. Fruitless by its very nature, it cannot even flower. When we see an example of such planning—when we are confronted for example by the building designed for the United Nations— the experts among us shake their heads sadly, draw a sheet over the corpse, and tiptoe quietly into the open air.

49. MUTINY OF THE BOUNTIFUL *

MARION K. SANDERS

This selection by Marion K. Sanders illustrates, in a serious vein, the phenomenon that Parkinson spoofs in his "Law" described in the previous article. Sanders deals with health organizations but the same behavior can be observed in some educational institutions, religious groups, government departments, and business establishments.

* *Harper's Magazine*, Vol. 217, No. 1303 (December, 1958), 23–31. Copyright © 1958, by Harper & Brothers. Reprinted by permission of the author.
    The author (b. 1905) has been assistant Director of Public Relations, Port of New York Authority; Editor, Magazine *America;* candidate for Congress. Author: *The Lady and the Vote.*

A truly appealing picture of a child with a runny nose has yet to be produced. As a result we are denied the privilege of joining in an annual Sniffle Crusade, and the Common Cold Foundation wheezes along on a mere fifty thousand a year, collected mainly from a few industries. This is a puny war chest to fight a public health menace which is said to cost the nation around five billion dollars a year in lost production, wages, and medical bills. But the sniffles, alas, do not tug at the heart strings; and though murderous ills may follow, no one ever died of sneezing. Crusades are built on pity and terror, not statistics.

We contribute, for example, about the same sum in behalf of 150,000 victims of muscular dystrophy as for the nine million who are mentally ill. Arthritis and rheumatism—of which there are said to be more than ten million cases—get less.

No one knows just how many different groups are soliciting funds across the country for how many different diseases. Last spring in a spot check of Chatham County, Georgia, the Savannah *Morning Herald* tallied up nineteen organizations passing the hat for the blind; seven for disabled veterans; six for the crippled; four for mental illness; five for cancer; two each for muscular dystrophy, polio, leprosy, brain injury, and alcoholism; and one apiece for heart disease, retarded children, cerebral palsy, deafness, tuberculosis, multiple sclerosis, arthritis, myastheni gravis; nephrosis, facial disfigurement, tropical diseases, diabetes, epilepsy, allergic diseases, hemophilia, and paraplegia.

Most American communities of any size are equally lavishly endowed. John A. Lincoln, President of the Stamford, Connecticut, Chamber of Commerce spoke with the voice of many when he remarked recently,

"We are punch drunk trying to keep up with all these appeals."

To be sure, not all of these outfits blanket the nation or conduct house-to-house campaigns. Those that do, have tried to carve up the calendar into non-overlapping segments. It is not, in fact, considered cricket among fund-raisers to muscle in on someone else's day, week, or month. But with some fifty nationwide campaigns competing with thousands of lesser causes and local appeals it is often impossible to clear the tracks even between major drives. Thus, for instance, a Shellsburg, Iowa, farmer, Glenn McClintock, who was dunning his neighbors for the cancer crusade had the awkward but not unusual experience of being forced to lurk in his car waiting for Mrs. Jim Peacock to finish her pitch for the heart drive. Both of them turned in their campaign kits shortly thereafter.

There are signs of resistance too among the kind-hearted givers. This summer, for instance, I talked with a young matron in Grosse Ile, Michigan, who announced to me firmly that she would no longer part with a dollar for a disease drive even if the solicitor was a personal friend.

"This morning," she said dramatically, "I actually turned down the mother of a retarded child!"

Such protests are, at present, about money and ways of raising it. They are being followed, however, with lively interest by experts in public health and philanthropy who have long held that splintering up the human body into competing sovereignties is a poor way to fight disease or to promote habits of health. For years, no one but other experts paid much attention to them. But of late a number of people have begun to listen and to wonder how such a noble idea as a citizens' war against disease managed to get so far out of hand.

. . . . .

The result is a growing tug of war between local and national interests. Even more sharply in conflict are two opposing philanthropic concepts: the one aims at balancing services with human needs, the other at developing whatever programs the public can be persuaded to support. Both sides have ardent and forceful supporters, who are currently locked in combat. The issues have been obscured by a blinding public-relations barrage from both sides. In essence, however, this is the same struggle which gave birth to the Community Chest movement of the 1920s.

The businessmen in Cleveland, Rochester and other cities who introduced federated fund-raising to the health and welfare scene after World War I did not have clear sailing. There were anguished wails from orphanage boards, scout leaders, hospital superintendents, and other free-wheeling philanthropic types, particularly at the prospect of a budget committee peering over their shoulders. There was trouble too with parochial-minded natives who objected to sharing the local charity pot with national outfits like the Y's and the Salvation Army. These differences were eventually ironed out, and all concerned found it a great relief to devote one strenuous week a year to the Red Feather-Community Chest campaign and the other fifty-one to their own affairs.

DIVIDED THEY STAND

In the 1930s and 1940s the health appeals began moving into town. As they multiplied, the Red Feather campaign became just another drive, competing with many others for time, newspaper space, and man- and woman-power. When the fund-raisers swarmed not only into homes but into offices and factories their managers began to reckon the cost. The Ford company, for example, calculated that every plant solicitation meant, apart from contributions, a $40,000 loss in executive time and production. Union men, for once, were in hearty agreement with management.

"The results just didn't justify the amount of effort we were putting into all those appeals," said Andy Brown of the United Auto Workers in Detroit. "We had to find a more efficient way to get the job done."

The plan pioneered in Detroit in 1949 was an all-encompassing campaign known as the Torch Drive, which would raise funds for the Community Chest and the national health agencies in a single annual appeal. The auto magnates spearheaded a massive push for substantial gifts from corporations and their executives. The union backed a payroll deduction plan for employee contributions. The Torch Drive was a spectacular financial success and has steadily grown in subsequent years. Variations of the same plan known as United Funds or United Community Chests have since been set up in more than a thousand cities. They have been particularly successful in industrial centers where union members and management, dunned once a year, have become the chief supporters of voluntary philanthropy.

Inside the factories, multiple health drives are vanishing, for industry has shut the door on them. The federal government has also clamped down and now permits (in addition to the Red Cross roll call) just two solicitations a year of its employees on the job—one for community chests, the other for a combined health drive.

Though temporarily routed on these fronts, the health campaigners are regrouping their forces. They assail payroll deductions and plant quotas for charity as "stark unbridled materialism in action." They attribute sinister imperialist aims to the United Funders who are, in truth, all autonomous groups.

"Divided we stand, united we fall!" was the rather odd battle cry sounded last May by Dr. Robert W. Wilkins of the Heart Association. Under such banners the health agencies are currently presenting themselves to the nation as champions of the American Way, freedom of choice, and true charity. In the privacy of their New York offices, however, more practical questions are discussed. Many doubt, with good reason, that people who give a dollar apiece to six drives will kick in six dollars for one campaign however well sold. What will happen to The Organization if it loses its constituents—the door-to-door brigades? For a money-raising outfit without an annual drive is like a political party without an annual election. . . .

From the outset, the TB Association turned thumbs down on joint drives. This caused relatively little fuss since it is generally felt that the Christmas Seals don't compete with anyone but Santa Claus. March of Dimes also declined with great firmness—which surprised no one since its generalissimo, Basil O'Connor, is a celebrated lone wolf who successfully kept the Red Cross out of Community Chests during his tenure as President from 1944 to 1949. In the current controversy, however, the Red Cross has taken a neutral position, leaving the matter up to its local chapters; more than 900 have now joined United Funds.

It has taken the other agencies some time to rally for defense. A number of them were stuck with state and local chapters headed by men who were members of the same bridge games and foursomes as the chiefs of the new United Fund. As a result, it was natural for many local chapters to join up with the united drives despite the dismay of their national offices. Within the past two years resistance has stiffened. The Heart Association will not permit any more chapters to join United Funds. Last June the Cancer Society went a step further by ordering all those now in to get out by 1960.

This edict precipitated a minor civil war. Outraged protests were made in New Orleans and San Francisco. Chapters in Danville, Virginia, Detroit, and Rochester, New York, voted to secede from the parent body. The sounds of this internecine strife reverberated noisily in the local press.

"If the Cancer Society can do it, the Baldheaded League can do it and we'll have a different drive every day of the year," said Msgr. Thomas J. Tobin, one of the founders of the United Fund in Portland, Oregon.

Faced with this prospect, some of the United Funders have resorted to strong counter-measures. In Pittsburgh, for example, when the Heart and Cancer Societies declined to join, the united drive directors none the less included "heart and cancer research, education, and services" in their fund-raising package and in effect incited a boycott of the independent drives. This stratagem was denounced by the Pittsburgh Heart Association as "sheer trickery which shows an amazing lack of integrity by our leading citizens." Even more irate was Dr. John W. Cline, a former AMA President who charged that money raised in this way is "tainted with the spurious claims under which it was raised, the broken promises of professional promoters . . . and the certainty that freedom in research will disappear. . . ."

Despite this dire forecast, the tainted dollars have been happily accepted by local research foundations in more than a dozen cities and states. In the future, contributions for research may go to a new foundation for the support of basic research set up within the past year by the National Fund for Medical Education, with the blessing of the United Community Funds and Councils of America.

CUYAHOGA COUNTY UPRISING

Meanwhile, the Heart and Cancer Societies along with the March of Dimes have spurned funds collected for their disease rather than their organizations. The million dollars or more that has thus been kept out of their collective treasuries has not, in their view, been too high a price to pay in the defense of autonomy. More costly in the long run may be the loss in popular esteem, for the fury of a contributor scorned can pack quite a wallop. This was lately demonstrated by some 10,000 Ohio housewives.

Two years ago the women of Gates Mills, a prosperous Cleveland suburb, decided to save time by staging a one-shot combined drive for all the health agencies. Their modest experiment became a *cause célèbre* when the National Foundation ordered its Cleveland chapter to give back $1,322 which the ladies had collected for polio. This was not only a snub to womankind; it was an affront to a native hero, for the local March of Dimes is headed by baseball star Bob Feller. The press was aroused.

"Arrogant blindness," wrote Sidney Andorn in a sizzling column in the Cleveland *News*. "The women who went from house to house collecting gifts are not slaves to the bidding of emperors perched on a national throne in New York. . . . The Health Drives have done and are doing a service for humanity. They couldn't do it at all if it were not for more fortunate humanity at the grass-roots level. On this level they face a strike of the women volunteer workers."

Thus incited, the ladies of Cuyahoga County reacted like an oppressed nation. From the well-nourished grass roots of Gates Mills the revolt spread to humbler back yards and garden apartments. The Gates Mills affair became a prime discussion topic in a dozen towns. Action committees sprang up headed usually by the wives of public officials, officers of women's clubs, and past chairmen of the assorted health drives. Everywhere the motif was the same: the volunteers had stopped volunteering. One weary chairman reported that it had taken 200 phone calls to recruit a captain for her last campaign.

"The situation has deteriorated," said Mrs. Warren North of Middleburg Heights, "to a point where a woman agrees to work only if contacted by a very dear friend. And dear friends are getting fewer by the week."

To all the rebels a combined drive in the Gates Mills style seemed the right solution. Village councils, Rotary Clubs, and Chambers of Commerce seconded the plan enthusiastically. The point was clinched when the ladies circulated a questionnaire and found their neighbors overwhelmingly in favor of having the doorbell ring just once a year in the name of health.

The scattered groups kept in touch with each other by telephone. Sixteen towns to the east of Cleveland set up a joint command post in the home of Mrs. George J. Urban, wife of the Mayor of South Euclid. Here they worked out details, such as a separate listing of the participating agencies on one envelope, allowing the contributor free choice among them. They agreed also to synchronize their drives which were all staged in May.

Last summer, in the course of a cross-country trip, I stopped off in Cleveland to ask Mrs. Urban how they had made out. A forthright, orderly person, she produced neatly-typed tally sheets with the returns tabulated by towns and causes. The total looked impressive—more than $200,000.

"We should have done better than that," Mrs. Urban acknowledged. "The business slump hurt us, I think, and some of the towns got started too late to be well organized."

She was disappointed too because the allocation to cancer was less than the yield of the Society's independent drive the year before.

"I don't say we've found the perfect answer," she said. "We have a lot to learn about how you educate people for this kind of appeal. But I do know we can't handle all those drives. It's always the busiest woman who gets stuck with these jobs—the one who's willing to take on one more task. We can never get help from the ones with time on their hands."

The national health agencies see the matter differently.

"Sure the old pros are tired," I was told by Willis Nichols, an able young Cincinnati businessman who is an ardent Heart Association partisan. "But there are thousands of women who have never been asked to do anything. All we have to do is find them."

Some of the agencies are doing this by hiring professional solicitors who pick names at random from the reverse (or geographic) telephone directory and keep calling until they recruit enough hands to blanket a neighborhood with campaign literature. This may be a practical way to raise money. But it seems doubtful that the casual labor so assembled can permanently replace the kind of women who are on strike in Cuyahoga County.

Their tribe is the chief treasure of voluntary philanthropy—the dedicated few who choose to give their leisure to service. Since they believe in the purposes of the health drives why, one may ask, are they unwilling to make the rounds for them? An evening's stroll through the neighborhood is not an arduous task compared to the labor many of these citizens happily give to the cub scouts, the League of Women

Voters, the ambulance corps or, according to their persuasion, to Hadassah or the Society for the Propagation of the Faith.

The trouble may well be that the health agencies are asking not too much but too little of them. The protest is, in large part, against a form of philanthropy which downgrades the volunteer to a mere messenger and coin-collecting machine manipulated by professionals. The health agencies have not, of course, done this deliberately. If they could dream up worthy projects, most of them would like to keep their volunteers happily employed as the Cancer Society proposes to do in its current mammoth statistical research venture. In general, however, since they do not operate community institutions they are in much the same position as the national committees of political parties which can offer their constituents nothing to do between campaigns.

Resentment against their lowly role in the philanthropic scheme of things appears widespread among women. Although there are few organized resistance movements outside of Cuyahoga County, I have yet to find a housewife who regards door-to-door fund-raising as "a satisfying outlet for creative energy," a claim made by Dr. Lowell T. Coggeshall of the Cancer Society.

"It's like falling into a bottomless well," said an energetic young mother of four who is a pillar of civic and charitable causes in Minneapolis. "Every year there are new drives and all the old ones keep right on going. You would think a couple of them might quit or get together."

Reasonable as this notion sounds, it is like asking Oklahoma to merge with Texas. Causes can multiply like rabbits, but old agencies never die. . . .

50. BUREAUCRACY °

MAX WEBER

Contemporary American and other Western societies are
characterized by highly bureaucratic organization. This structure
is typical of business and private social institutions as well as

° From *Max Weber: Essays in Sociology,* edited and translated by H. H. Gerth and C. Wright Mills, 196–244. Copyright 1946 by Oxford University Press, Inc. Reprinted by permission.

The author (1864–1920) was a German sociologist and political economist. Held chair of political economy at Freiburg. Weber's sociology is based on his extensive knowledge in economic, political, social, legal, military, and religious fields. He is especially well known for his typological studies of charismatic authority, feudalism, and bureaucracy. A pioneer in sociology of religion. Among his translated works are *General Economic History; The Protestant Ethic and the Spirit of Capital-*

governmental agencies. Here Max Weber has systematically analyzed the nature and technical advantages of bureaucratic organization. Although this analysis was written four decades or more ago and is based largely upon German and other European data, there has appeared no statement on the subject that is more thorough or significant sociologically.

CHARACTERISTICS OF BUREAUCRACY

Modern officialdom functions in the following specific manner:

I. There is the principle of fixed and official jurisdictional areas, which are generally ordered by rules, that is, by laws or administrative regulations.

1. The regular activities required for the purposes of the bureaucratically governed structure are distributed in a fixed way as official duties.

2. The authority to give the commands required for the discharge of these duties is distributed in a stable way and is strictly delimited by rules concerning the coercive means, physical, sacerdotal, or otherwise, which may be placed at the disposal of officials.

3. Methodical provision is made for the regular and continuous fulfilment of these duties and for the execution of the corresponding rights; only persons who have the generally regulated qualifications to serve are employed.

In public and lawful government these three elements constitute "bureaucratic authority." In private economic domination, they constitute bureaucratic "management." Bureaucracy, thus understood, is fully developed in political and ecclesiastical communities only in the modern state, and, in the private economy, only in the most advanced institutions of capitalism. Permanent and public office authority, with fixed jurisdiction, is not the historical rule but rather the exception. This is so even in large political structures such as those of the ancient Orient, the Germanic and Mongolian empires of conquest, or of many feudal structures of state. In all these cases, the ruler executes the most important measures through personal trustees, table-companions, or court-servants. Their commissions and authority are not precisely delimited and are temporarily called into being for each case.

II. The principles of office hierarchy and of levels of graded authority mean a firmly ordered system of super- and subordination in which there is a supervision of the lower offices by the higher ones. Such a system offers the governed the possibility of appealing the decision of a lower

ism; On the Methodology of the Social Science; The Theory of Economic and Social Organization.

office to its higher authority, in a definitely regulated manner. With the full development of the bureaucratic type, the office hierarchy is mono-cratically organized. The principle of hierarchical office authority is found in all bureaucratic structures: in state and ecclesiastical structures as well as in large party organizations and private enterprises. It does not matter for the character of bureaucracy whether its authority is called "private" or "public."

When the principle of jurisdictional "competency" is fully carried through, hierarchical subordination—at least in public office—does not mean that the "higher" authority is simply authorized to take over the business of the "lower." Indeed, the opposite is the rule. Once estab-lished and having fulfilled its task, an office tends to continue in existence and be held by another incumbent.

III. The management of the modern office is based upon written documents ("the files"), which are preserved in their original or draught form. There is, therefore, a staff of subaltern officials and scribes of all sorts. The body of officials actively engaged in a "public" office, along with the respective apparatus of material implements and the files, make up a "bureau." In private enterprise, "the bureau" is often called "the office."

In principle, the modern organization of the civil service separates the bureau from the private domicile of the official, and, in general, bureaucracy segregates official activity as something distinct from the sphere of private life. Public monies and equipment are divorced from the private property of the official. This condition is everywhere the product of a long development. Nowadays, it is found in public as well as in private enterprises; in the latter, the principle extends even to the leading entrepreneur. In principle, the executive office is separated from the household, business from private correspondence, and business assets from private fortunes. The more consistently the modern type of busi-ness management has been carried through the more are these separations the case. The beginnings of this process are to be found as early as the Middle Ages.

It is the peculiarity of the modern entrepreneur that he conducts himself as the "first official" of his enterprise, in the very same way in which the ruler of a specifically modern bureaucratic state spoke of himself as "the first servant" of the state. The idea that the bureau activities of the state are intrinsically different in character from the management of private economic offices is a continental European no-tion and, by way of contrast, is totally foreign to the American way.

IV. Office management, at least all specialized office management—and such management is distinctly modern—usually presupposes thor-ough and expert training. This increasingly holds for the modern executive and employee of private enterprises, in the same manner as it holds for the state official.

V. When the office is fully developed, official activity demands the full working capacity of the official, irrespective of the fact that his obligatory time in the bureau may be firmly delimited. In the normal case, this is only the product of a long development, in the public as well as in the private office. Formerly, in all cases, the normal state of affairs was reversed: official business was discharged as a secondary activity.

VI. The management of the office follows general rules, which are more or less stable, more or less exhaustive, and which can be learned. Knowledge of these rules represents a special technical learning which the officials possess. It involves jurisprudence, or administrative or business management.

The reduction of modern office management to rules is deeply embedded in its very nature. The theory of modern public administration, for instance, assumes that the authority to order certain matters by decree —which has been legally granted to public authorities—does not entitle the bureau to regulate the matter by commands given for each case, but only to regulate the matter abstractly. This stands in extreme contrast to the regulation of all relationships through individual privileges and bestowals of favor, which is absolutely dominant in patrimonialism, at least in so far as such relationships are not fixed by sacred tradition.

THE POSITION OF THE OFFICIAL

All this results in the following for the internal and external position of the official:

I. Office holding is a "vocation." This is shown, first, in the requirement of a firmly prescribed course of training, which demands the entire capacity for work for a long period of time, and in the generally prescribed and special examinations which are prerequisites of employment. Furthermore, the position of the official is in the nature of a duty. This determines the internal structure of his relations, in the following manner: Legally and actually, office holding is not considered a source to be exploited for rents or emoluments, as was normally the case during the Middle Ages and frequently up to the threshold of recent times. Nor is office holding considered a usual exchange of services for equivalents, as is the case with free labor contracts. Entrance into an office, including one in the private economy, is considered an acceptance of a specific obligation of faithful management in return for a secure existence. It is decisive for the specific nature of modern loyalty to an office that, in the pure type, it does not establish a relationship to a *person*, like the vassal's or disciple's faith in feudal or in patrimonial relations of authority.

Modern loyalty is devoted to impersonal and functional purposes. Behind the functional purposes, of course, "ideas of culture-values" usually stand. These are *ersatz* for the earthly or supra-mundane personal master: ideas such as "state," "church," "community," "party," or "enterprise" are thought of as being realized in a community; they provide an ideological halo for the master.

The political official—at least in the fully developed modern state— is not considered the personal servant of a ruler. Today, the bishop, the priest, and the preacher are in fact no longer, as in early Christian times, holders of purely personal charisma. The supra-mundane and sacred values which they offer are given to everybody who seems to be worthy of them and who asks for them. In former times, such leaders acted upon the personal command of their master; in principle, they were responsible only to him. Nowadays, in spite of the partial survival of the old theory, such religious leaders are officials in the service of a functional purpose, which in the present-day "church" has become routinized and, in turn, ideologically hallowed.

II. The personal position of the official is patterned in the following way:

1. Whether he is in a private office or a public bureau, the modern official always strives and usually enjoys a distinct *social esteem* as compared with the governed. His social position is guaranteed by the prescriptive rules of rank order and, for the political official, by special definitions of the criminal code against "insults of officials" and "contempt" of state and church authorities.

The actual social position of the official is normally highest where, as in old civilized countries, the following conditions prevail: a strong demand for administration by trained experts; a strong and stable social differentiation, where the official predominantly derives from socially and economically privileged strata because of the social distribution of power; or where the costliness of the required training and status conventions are binding upon him. The possession of educational certificates —to be discussed elsewhere—are usually linked with qualification for office. Naturally, such certificates or patents enhance the "status element" in the social position of the official. For the rest this status factor in individual cases is explicitly and impassively acknowledged; for example, in the prescription that the acceptance or rejection of an aspirant to an official career depends upon the consent ("election") of the members of the official body. This is the case in the German army with the officer corps. Similar phenomena, which promote this guild-like closure of officialdom, are typically found in patrimonial and, particularly, in prebendal officialdoms of the past. The desire to resurrect such phenomena in changed forms is by no means infrequent among modern bureaucrats. For instance, they have played a role among the demands of the quite proletarian and expert officials (the *tretyj* element) during the Russian revolution.

Usually the social esteem of the officials as such is especially low where the demand for expert administration and the dominance of status conventions are weak. This is especially the case in the United States; it is often the case in new settlements by virtue of their wide fields for profit-making and the great instability of their social stratification.

2. The pure type of bureaucratic official is *appointed* by a superior authority. An official elected by the governed is not a purely bureaucratic figure. Of course, the formal existence of an election does not by itself mean that no appointment hides behind the election—in the state, especially, appointment by party chiefs. Whether or not this is the case does not depend upon legal statutes but upon the way in which the party mechanism functions. Once firmly organized, the parties can turn a formally free election into the mere acclamation of a candidate designated by the party chief. As a rule, however, a formally free election is turned into a fight, conducted according to definite rules, for votes in favor of one of two designated candidates.

In all circumstances, the designation of officials by means of an election among the governed modifies the strictness of hierarchical subordination. In principle, an official who is so elected has an autonomous position opposite the superordinate official. The elected official does not derive his position "from above" but "from below," or at least not from a superior authority of the official hierarchy but from powerful party men ("bosses"), who also determine his further career. The career of the elected official is not, or at least not primarily, dependent upon his chief in the administration. The official who is not elected but appointed by a chief normally functions more exactly, from a technical point of view, because, all other circumstances being equal, it is more likely that purely functional points of consideration and qualities will determine his selection and career. As laymen, the governed can become acquainted with the extent to which a candidate is expertly qualified for office only in terms of experience, and hence only after his service. Moreover, in every sort of selection of officials by election, parties quite naturally give decisive weight not to expert considerations but to the services a follower renders to the party boss. This holds for all kinds of procurement of officials by elections, for the designation of formally free, elected officials by party bosses when they determine the slate of candidates, or the free appointment by a chief who has himself been elected. The contrast, however, is relative: substantially similar conditions hold where legitimate monarchs and their subordinates appoint officials, except that the influence of the followings are then less controllable.

Where the demand for administration by trained experts is considerable, and the party followings have to recognize an intellectually developed, educated, and freely moving "public opinion," the use of un-qualified officials falls back upon the party in power at the next election. Naturally, this is more likely to happen when the officials are appointed by the chief. The demand for a trained administration now exists in the United States, but in the large cities, where immigrant votes are "cor-raled," there is, of course, no educated public opinion. Therefore, popular elections of the administrative chief and also of his subordinate officials usually endanger the expert qualification of the official as well as the precise functioning of the bureaucratic mechanism. It also weakens the dependence of the officials upon the hierarchy. This holds at least for the large administrative bodies that are difficult to supervise. The su-perior qualification and integrity of federal judges, appointed by the President, as over against elected judges in the United States is well known, although both types of officials have been selected primarily in terms of party considerations. The great changes in American metro-politan administrations demanded by reformers have proceeded essen-tially from elected mayors working with an apparatus of officials who were appointed by them. These reforms have thus come about in a "Caesarist" fashion. Viewed technically, as an organized form of authority, the efficiency of "Caesarism," which often grows out of democracy, rests in general upon the position of the "Caesar" as a free trustee of the masses (of the army or of the citizenry), who is unfettered by tradition. The "Caesar" is thus the unrestrained master of a body of highly qualified military officers and officials whom he selects freely and personally with-out regard to tradition or to any other considerations. This "rule of the personal genius," however, stands in contradiction to the formally "dem-ocratic" principle of a universally elected officialdom.

3. Normally, the position of the official is held for life, at least in public bureaucracies; and this is increasingly the case for all similar structures. As a factual rule, *tenure for life* is presupposed, even where the giving of notice or periodic reappointment occurs. In contrast to the worker in a private enterprise, the official normally holds tenure. Legal or actual life-tenure, however, is not recognized as the official's right to the possession of office, as was the case with many structures of authority in the past. Where legal guarantees against arbitrary dis-missal or transfer are developed, they merely serve to guarantee a strictly objective discharge of specific office duties free from all personal con-siderations. In Germany, this is the case for all juridical and, increas-ingly, for all administrative officials.

Within the bureaucracy, therefore, the measure of "independence," legally guaranteed by tenure, is not always a source of increased status for the official whose position is thus secured. Indeed, often the reverse holds, especially in old cultures and communities that are highly differ-entiated. In such communities, the stricter the subordination under the arbitrary rule of the master, the more it guarantees the maintenance of the conventional seigneurial style of living for the official. Because of the very absence of these legal guarantees of tenure, the conventional esteem for the official may rise in the same way as, during the Middle Ages, the esteem of the nobility of office rose at the expense of esteem for the freemen, and as the king's judge surpassed that of the people's judge. In Germany, the military officer or the administrative official can be removed from office at any time, or at least far more readily than the "independent judge," who never pays with loss of his office for even the grossest offense against the "code of honor" or against social conventions of the salon. For this very reason, if other things are equal, in the eyes of the master stratum the judge is considered less qualified for social intercourse than are officers and administrative officials, whose greater dependence on the master is a greater guarantee of their conformity with status conventions. Of course, the average official strives for a civil-service law, which would materially secure his old age and provide increased guarantees against his arbitrary removal from office. This striving, however, has its limits. A very strong development of the "right to the office" naturally makes it more difficult to staff them with regard to technical efficiency, for such a development decreases the career-opportunities of ambitious candidates for office. This makes for the fact that officials, on the whole, do not feel their dependency upon those at the top. This lack of a feeling of dependency, however, rests primarily upon the inclination to depend upon one's equals rather than upon the socially inferior and governed strata. The present conservative movement among the Badenia clergy, occasioned by the anxiety of a presumably threatening separation of church and state, has been expressly determined by the desire not to be turned "from a master into a servant of the parish."

4. The official receives the regular *pecuniary* compensation of a normally fixed *salary* and the old age security provided by a pension. The salary is not measured like a wage in terms of work done, but according to "status," that is, according to the kind of function (the "rank") and, in addition, possibly, according to the length of service. The relatively great security of the official's income, as well as the rewards of social esteem, make the office a sought-after position, especially in countries which no longer provide opportunities for colonial profits. In such countries, this situation permits relatively low salaries for officials.

5. The official is set for a *"career"* within the hierarchical order of the public service. He moves from the lower, less important, and lower paid to the higher positions. The average official naturally desires a mechanical fixing of the conditions of promotion: if not of the offices, at least of the salary levels. He wants these conditions fixed in terms of "seniority," or possibly according to grades achieved in a developed system of expert examinations. Here and there, such examinations actu-

ally form a character *indelebilis* of the official and have lifelong effects on his career. To this is joined the desire to qualify the right to office and the increasing tendency toward status group closure and economic security. All of this makes for a tendency to consider the offices as "prebends" of those who are qualified by educational certificates. The necessity of taking general personal and intellectual qualifications into consideration, irrespective of the often subaltern character of the educational certificate, has led to a condition in which the highest political offices, especially the positions of "ministers," are principally filled without reference to such certificates.

. . . . .

TECHNICAL ADVANTAGES OF BUREAUCRATIC ORGANIZATION

The decisive reason for the advance of bureaucratic organization has always been its purely technical superiority over any other form of organization. The fully developed bureaucratic mechanism compares with other organizations exactly as does the machine with the non-mechanical modes of production.

Precision, speed, unambiguity, knowledge of the files, continuity, discretion, unity, strict subordination, reduction of friction and of material and personal costs—these are raised to the optimum point in the strictly bureaucratic administration, and especially in its monocratic form. As compared with all collegiate, honorific, and avocational forms of administration, trained bureaucracy is superior on all these points. And as far as complicated tasks are concerned, paid bureaucratic work is not only more precise but, in the last analysis, it is often cheaper than even formally unremunerated honorific service.

Honorific arrangements make administrative work an avocation and, for this reason alone, honorific service normally functions more slowly; being less bound to schemata and being more formless. Hence it is less precise and less unified than bureaucratic work because it is less dependent upon superiors and because the establishment and exploitation of the apparatus of subordinate officials and filing services are almost unavoidably less economical. Honorific service is less continuous than bureaucratic and frequently quite expensive. This is especially the case if one thinks not only of the money costs to the public treasury—costs which bureaucratic administration, in comparison with administration by notables, usually substantially increases—but also of the frequent economic losses of the governed caused by delays and lack of precision. The possibility of administration by notables normally and permanently exists only where official management can be satisfactorily discharged as an avocation. With the qualitative increase of tasks the administration has to face, administration by notables reaches its limits—today, even in England. Work organized by collegiate bodies causes friction and delay and requires compromises between colliding interests and views. The administration, therefore, runs less precisely and is more independent of superiors; hence, it is less unified and slower. All advances of the Prussian administrative organization have been and will in the future be advances of the bureaucratic, and especially of the monocratic, principle.

Today, it is primarily the capitalist market economy which demands that the official business of the administration be discharged precisely, unambiguously, continuously, and with as much speed as possible. Normally, the very large, modern capitalist enterprises are themselves unequalled models of strict bureaucratic organization. Business management throughout rests on increasing precision, steadiness, and, above all, the speed of operations. This, in turn, is determined by the peculiar nature of the modern means of communication, including, among other things, the news service of the press. The extraordinary increase in the speed by which public announcements, as well as economic and political facts, are transmitted exerts a steady and sharp pressure in the direction of speeding up the tempo of administrative reaction towards various situations. The optimum of such reaction time is normally attained only by a strictly bureaucratic organization.[1]

Bureaucratization offers above all the optimum possibility for carrying through the principle of specializing administrative functions according to purely objective considerations. Individual performances are allocated to functionaries who have specialized training and who by constant practice learn more and more. The "objective" discharge of business primarily means a discharge of business according to *calculable rules* and "without regard for persons."

"Without regard for persons" is also the watchword of the "market" and, in general, of all pursuits of naked economic interests. A consistent execution of bureaucratic domination means the leveling of status "honor." Hence, if the principle of the free-market is not at the same time restricted, it means the universal domination of the "class situation." That this consequence of bureaucratic domination has not set in everywhere, parallel to the extent of bureaucratization, is due to the differences among possible principles by which polities may meet their demands.

The second element mentioned, "calculable rules," also is of paramount importance for modern bureaucracy. The peculiarity of modern culture, and specifically of its technical and economic basis, demands this very "calculability" of results. When fully developed, bureaucracy also

---

[1] Here we cannot discuss in detail how the bureaucratic apparatus may, and actually does, produce definite obstacles to the discharge of business in a manner suitable for the single case.

stands, in a specific sense, under the principle of *sine ira ac studio*. Its specific nature, which is welcomed by capitalism, develops the more perfectly the more the bureaucracy is "dehumanized," the more completely it succeeds in eliminating from official business love, hatred, and all purely personal, irrational, and emotional elements which escape calculation. This is the specific nature of bureaucracy and it is appraised as its special virtue.

The more complicated and specialized modern culture becomes, the more its external supporting apparatus demands the personally detached and strictly "objective" *expert*, in lieu of the master of older social structures, who was moved by personal sympathy and favor, by grace and gratitude. Bureaucracy offers the attitudes demanded by the external apparatus of modern culture in the most favorable combination.

51. THE AMERICAN FAMILY:

WHAT IT IS—AND ISN'T *

KINGSLEY DAVIS

A social institution is an organized and stable procedure for achieving given social goals. The family as an institution is a procedure for regulating sex relationships and rearing children. But these universal functions of the family have different structural manifestations in various societies; that is, the form of the family differs according to time and circumstance even while its basic functions remain the same. The form of the American family is only one of the many possibilities. Since this particular form is important to us it is, therefore, vital that we have a clear picture of what the American family is—and isn't. It is this topic that concerns Kingsley Davis here.

Nearly all social commentaries on America, foreign and domestic, tend to touch upon the American family as if it were a universally understood and somewhat disreputable institution. Bewildered foreigners especially, reading our popular novels and magazines, picture the American family circle as an assemblage of delinquents and neurotics—flying apart at the seams under the influence of TV, Kinsey Reports and divorce-court scandals. Considering the distortions about our family life circulated at

* From *The New York Times Magazine*, September 30, 1951, pp. 18, 41–42. For a biographical sketch of the author, see selection 19.

home, it is not surprising that few Americans are equipped to deal with the opinions that are held abroad—that the American family consists exclusively of wild adolescents, domineering wives and henpecked business men, escapists all from solid home ties. This hardly speaks well for our side of the world debate over democracy's future.

Perhaps, therefore, it is wise to give Americans some factual ammunition with which to counter such unflattering and damaging misconceptions. In doing so, I shall have to speak of the average American family, although of course no such family actually exists. All our families are average in some respects, but none is average in all respects. The picture given here is accordingly synthetic, but is drawn from the best information available and should modify some false notions that even Americans entertain about themselves.

First of all, let us note that the American family is extremely "marriage-centered." Except in certain classes such as the ultra-élite or the immigrants from peasant countries, it is built around the married pair, the other kin not counting for much. The newly married couple strives to live apart from the in-laws, not because Dorothy Dix advises it but because certain conditions, such as our extraordinary geographical mobility and our perpetual social climbing, favor it. The Census Bureau finds that one-fifth of the native population lives in a state different from that of its birth, and that one out of every five adults changes his residence each year.

Since it is usually only the immediate family that moves, this migratory tendency drives a wedge between the young couples and their respective parental families. An additional wedge is driven by the fact that the young pair often occupy a class position different from their parents. One community study found, for example, that less than 10 per cent of the professional men had fathers who were in professional pursuits, and that only 39 per cent of the skilled workers had fathers in skilled trades. The expansion of the professional and commercial occupations in our economy, plus a higher birth rate in the lower occupations, has produced a current of upward social movement never before equaled. As a result the young couple often find themselves differing from their parents not only in age but also in class position, culture and standard of living.

The segregation of the immediate family from other relatives, though characteristic of all industrial societies, has gone further in America than anywhere else, and affects every aspect of our family life. For instance, our ideal, in contrast to that still prevailing in Asia and to some extent in European and Latin-American countries, is that young people should have the privilege of picking their own mates without parental interference. The founding of the new household is thus put squarely in the hands of the potential marriage partners themselves, though they are young and often incapable of making an intelligent choice.

This freedom of choice accounts for the strong interest we take in courtship, in the trials and tribulations of "winning" a mate. In fact, the process of mate selection is part and parcel of our competitive social order, with individual initiative getting a free hand. Our movies, short stories and novels deal incessantly with this adolescent competition—so much so that the foreigner justifiably reaches the superficial conclusion that we are a nation of mental adolescents.

We even have college courses designed to help young people choose a satisfactory mate. Indeed, the sociologists and psychologists of America, always anxious to be practical, have devised tests which prospective couples can take and from which their "marriage and prediction score" can be computed. But, let us hasten to add, America is still ruggedly individualistic; if a young couple have a low score, no governmental or parental edict can prevent them from going ahead and marrying anyway. All they need is a strong attraction for each other, however temporary and misguided it may be.

This brings us to another trait which often astonishes foreigners— namely, our firm belief that the purpose of marriage is happiness. We have ponderous tomes on how to achieve happiness in marriage, as well as tests designed to measure our "marital happiness score" and to determine what it is about mates that proves annoying. Marriage partners are sometimes asked to rate themselves on a seven or five point scale: "Extraordinarily happy, decidedly more happy than average, somewhat more happy than average, about average happy," etc. Other traits of the couples are then studied to determine what factors lead to happiness or unhappiness in marriage.

All of this, you will say (especially if you are a good American), is innocent enough. Why shouldn't young people choose their own mates, and why shouldn't they be concerned with happiness? Well, I certainly have no objection. I am simply describing some salient features of our family system. But one should realize that the salient features are all connected. The preoccupation with courtship and the cult of marital happiness not only reflect the degree to which our family is "marriage-centered," but they are also integrally related to other features which some groups at least find objectionable, such as our low birth rate, our young age at marriage and our high divorce rate.

If marriage exists for the purpose of individual happiness, if it is entered into and maintained because of personal attraction, the decision to have or not to have children will be made by the couple themselves in terms of their own wishes. They may be so happy together that children would seem an interference.

Most couples, however, decide that children—though not many—

will be an adjunct to their happiness. Consequently, the great reduction in the birth rate has come, not from childlessness, but from the desire to have only one, two or three offspring. In America the large brood has become virtually extinct. The rate for births of seventh and higher orders has dropped 60 per cent in the last three decades, and even during the recent war and post-war baby boom, the rates for the higher orders continued downward. The average wife in the United States has, during her lifetime, about three offspring, barely enough to replace the population.

Although this statement may seem questionable in view of the recent baby boom, the truth is that the spectacular increase in births during the Nineteen Forties was a result of temporary causes and must itself therefore be temporary. The Nineteen Thirties represented a depression decade during which people postponed getting married or having children. In the four years 1930 through 1933, for example, approximately 800,000 marriages did not occur which normally would have occurred. After that, except for 1937, the number of marriages continued to be below normal until rearmament got under way in 1940. Then the concurrence of both business improvement and the military draft not only brought about many marriages that had been postponed but also induced many to marry earlier than they normally would have done.

The result was the mightiest wave of marriages the country had ever witnessed. During the 1940 decade the number was approximately 3,670,000 above normal. Since these were in part marriages "borrowed" from the future, we must necessarily expect a marriage rate below normal in the Nineteen Fifties, even if times are good.

The number of new marriages affects the number of births, especially first births. But in addition, independently of fluctuations in marriages, the birth rate changes with war and prosperity. During the depression, for instance, many married couples postponed having children. In the Nineteen Forties these couples not only had a sizable portion of the children they had postponed but also the new couples resulting from the extremely high marriage rate had offspring earlier than they would ordinarily have done. The net result was a temporary but impressive rise in the birth rate, made up principally of first, second and third births.

Such a temporary rise does not mean that couples have suddenly changed the number of children they want ultimately to have, but simply the time when they want to have them. Having had two or three children in the Nineteen Forties, they will tend to have few in the Nineteen Fifties. The birth rate must inevitably decline again; in fact, in 1950 it was one-tenth lower than in the peak year of 1947.[1]

[1] Editors' note: The foregoing paragraphs, written in 1951, indicate the difficult nature of population forecasting. Although the author's analysis is valid in most respects, his implied forecast of a continued decline in the birth rate during the Nineteen Fifties did not materialize. In fact the rate was higher in the latter half of the decade than at the time of Davis's writing.

With the small number of children and the tendency to live apart from in-laws, the American household has been getting steadily smaller. Most old people, whether still married or widowed, like to maintain a separate place of their own, a feat made possible by high real income in America. Thus in 1940 the median number of family members living together per household was 3.15, and by 1947, despite the rise in the birth rate, the number dropped slightly to 3.07.

In some countries a low birth rate is achieved partly by the postponement of marriage. In our country, despite popular belief to the contrary, people are tending to marry younger. In 1890 the average male first married at the age of 26.1, but in 1947 he married at the age of 23.7. The average female married at the age of 22.0 in 1890, but by 1947 she did so at the tender age of 20.5.

The gradual lowering of the age at marriage since 1890 apparently reflects the changing character of wedlock among us. With increased employment of women, the old notion that a man must be economically established before marrying has been abandoned. Even college students claim the right to matrimony. With scientific birth control and growing social benefits for children, a young marriage does not necessarily mean a burden of more children than can be supported. Finally, marriage is not nearly so irrevocable as it once was. If the initial venture turns out to be irksome, divorce is easy to obtain.

The divorce rate has risen to the point where, on the average, one out of every four marriages is ending in legal dissoluton. Indeed, the rate has risen so high that, with the extension of average life-expectancy, divorce has temporarily replaced death as the main way in which marriages end.

The rising divorce rate is not exclusively an American phenomenon. All other urban-industrial countries are experiencing a rise also. During the last forty years the rate has climbed more rapidly in Great Britain, Sweden, the Netherlands, Denmark, France and several other countries than it has in the United States, although, to be sure, the rate was lower in these countries to start with and the United States still leads them.

If we still lead most of the world in divorce, it is because our conception of the family has changed more radically. To the extent that we base marriage on personal attraction and value it for the happiness it brings, we feel that it has no excuse for being, once such attraction is gone and the two parties are unhappy together. To the extent that we view it as a companionship to be experienced by the young, we cannot regard it as a fixed status, for companionship cannot be forced. To the extent that we have taken the economic functions from the family and have absorbed women into the labor force, the dissolution of marriage brings no overpowering financial loss to either party and no disruption to the production of goods. Only the children suffer; but as already mentioned, there are fewer children now.

Our rising frequency of divorce has not meant, as is commonly assumed, a corresponding increase in the number of broken families. The proportion of broken families depends not only on legal divorce but also on separation, desertion and death. Although figures on separations and desertions are impossible to get, there is reason to believe that they have been somewhat displaced by divorce.

Something else which also served to reduce the number of broken families is the increasing popularity of remarriage. Census figures show that in 1940 the proportion of remarried women among those previously widowed or divorced was about one-sixth greater than in 1910. Approximately 75 per cent of those procuring divorces during the five years from 1943 to 1948 were already remarried in 1948; and of those divorced earlier (between 1934 and 1943) approximately 86 per cent had remarried by 1948.

In view of these facts, the hue and cry about the children orphaned by divorce is rather louder than it should be. Not only are few children involved in relation to the total number of divorces, but most of them soon become parts of a complete family again (one that is often better adjusted) when one or the other parent remarries. Divorce is certainly not easy on children, nor is it easy on the adults.

By way of summing up, suppose we see what happens to the average American couple in the successive stages of marriage, parenthood, and old age. We have already noted that couples marry earlier than they did sixty years ago, and we can add that the average gap between the husband's and the wife's age, three years, is about one year less than it was then. Despite the use of contraception, the average parents wait only about one year to have their first child and they have their subsequent children rather close together—about two years apart. The average couple who bear any children at all have as a rule only three, because they prevent the birth of more children.

This means that the parents have generally finished their reproduction within five or six years after their wedding. Due to an early marriage and rather rapid childbearing, they reach this point at a very young age —an age much earlier than people ended reproducton in any previous civilization. In fact, the typical mother in America bears her final child at about the age of 27 years.

Since women in the United States now live seventy years on the average, and men sixty-five years, the normal mother has completed her childbearing long before the midpoint of her life. Because her children tend to marry early, the average parent today has a long period of life remaining after her last child has left home. Whereas in 1890 the average parent did not even survive to that point, both parents today tend to live eleven years after their last child has married, and the mother, in case she survives her husband, on the average lives about twenty-four years after that event.

These changes are revolutionary in their importance. The modern couple, for instance, face a situation in their declining years which few couples had to face in past times. They must somehow adjust to life without their children, a life often lonely and pointless. Frequently they sell their house and move to an apartment; sometimes they feel unwanted. Finding the adjustment hard to make, the breadwinner often faces still another painful change—retirement. The problem of the empty household thus merges with and makes more difficult the other trials of old age.

The modern American family is thus a new model, radically different in many ways from the old. Like any other variation of this ancient social institution, it has its stresses and strains, its human problems. At the same time it has solved some of the old problems. Though exposed to a high risk of divorce, it suffers less from dissolution by death and desertion. Though often provided with too few children for satisfaction, it gives its young a better and less restrictive upbringing. Though frequently characterized by a bleak old age, it achieves more companionship and democracy than its predecessor.

On the whole it is far better than the patriarchal mode of peasant-agricultural countries, far better than the *mariage de convenance* of the European upper classes, and far better than the concubinous polygyny of Latin America. Foreign misconceptions of our family life are based on superficialities which the American who knows the facts can repudiate.

52. ROLES AND MARITAL ADJUSTMENT*

LEONARD S. COTTRELL, JR.

Institutions develop to fulfill persistent basic social needs. Sometimes institutional experience is unsatisfying, however, because persons have learned to play roles unsuited to the

* Publication of the American Sociological Society, Vol. XXVII, No. 2, *Papers*, May, 1933, University of Chicago Press, 1933. Reprinted by permission of the author and the publisher.

The author (b. 1899) is Social Psychologist, Russell Sage Foundation. Chief Sociologist and Director of Survey Analysis, Research Branch, Information and Edu-

*institutional situation in which they find themselves. Or their
expectations regarding the behavior of others in the institution
are unfulfilled. In this selection L. S. Cottrell, Jr. discusses the
importance of an understanding of role-behavior and role-
expectation in studying the adjustment of husbands and wives
to the institutions of marriage and the family.*

There are certain points concerning the concept of the rôle which,
though recognized by those who developed and refined the concept, need
for our purposes added emphasis.

First, in our use of the concept rôle we are prone to think of certain
characteristic responses or tendencies to respond which the person makes
or tends to make to persons or situations. Frequently we fail to recognize
clearly enough what might be called expectations entertained by the
subject as to actions or responses which to come from other persons.
The writer recognizes that it is impossible to separate these two things
since in reality they are aspects of the same thing. There is no conception
of one's rôle, conscious or unconscious, without reference to what action
is expected of the situation of which the rôle is a part. It is well, however,
to emphasize the expectancy aspect, particularly in using the notion in
the study of marriage situations. A number of our cases of marital difficulty seem capable of analysis in terms of the inability of one mate to fit
into the expected response pattern called for by the other.

A second point to be called to mind is that in marriage the partners
do not play single rôles with respect to one another, although a single
rôle may be most characteristic of a given person in his marriage relations. Cases seem to indicate a multiplicity of rôles. For example, a wife
may play a much depended upon mother-rôle, a hated sister-rôle, and a
loved brother-rôle at different times for her husband. The husband may
in turn be for his wife her distantly respected father, her hated younger
brother, and her loved older sister. The startling ambivalence frequently
displayed by married persons for one another may not be true ambivalence in the strict Freudian sense. It may actually be the result of
corresponding attitudes for different rôle patterns derived from early
family relations. Thus a husband may call out affectionate as well as
hostile responses from his wife by playing rôles of members of her family
who earlier called out the different responses. Of course it is not at all
necessary nor even likely that either husband or wife will be aware that
he is playing such rôles.

A third point to be mentioned is that rôles may be stereotyped and

cation, War Department, 1942–1945. Coauthor, *Part Time Farming and Industrial
Employment in the Southeast; Delinquency Areas; Predicting Success or Failure in
Marriage; Developments in Social Psychology; American Opinion on World Affairs
in the Atomic Age; Identity and Interpersonal Competence: New Directions in
Family Research.*

unique. The stereotyped rôles, for example, of husband and father, wife and mother, are defined in the folkways and mores of society. But within these definitions by a given culture there are individual patterns or rôles that are determined by the peculiar social experience of the individual. Thus an adult may continue to play an infantile rôle as a result, let us say, of his having been the youngest child in a family that has coddled him a great deal.

A fourth point which needs emphasis is that, frequently, we might say usually, many of the rôles that persons play are unconscious. If all of the rôles a married pair play for one another are not unconscious, the most significant ones are frequently so.

We shall not here attempt an exegesis of the conception of the unconscious. It is sufficient for our purposes to realize that, if we analyze any act or series of actions, we find that there are phases of the act which can be said to be unknown to the actor, and are, moreover, not subject to his unaided conscious scrutiny and reflection. The conscious phase of the act in which the individual has defined for himself or has defined for him his objects and purposes and motives is one phase only. There are preliminary to and concomitant with his acts, goals, motives, etc., of which he is unconscious. Examples might be taken from the cases cited by Mr. H. D. Lasswell in his *Psychopathology and Politics* in which the conscious political activity directed against a present order turns out to be a displacement of drives and hostilities of the child with respect to its parent or sibling. Of these more primary and elementary motives the person is not aware and accepts his own definitions of goals and reasons as the only ones present in the action. Our contention here is that the same kind of unconscious character can be attributed to much of marital activity.

There may be some objection to thinking of rôles as unconscious. We do not hold that all rôles are unconscious. Some seem to be completely unconscious; some only partially so. We are not wedded to a word. If the term "rôle" is to be used only for conscious action patterns and relationships, then we must give another name to these unconscious patterns and relationships that exist in fact.

The narrowed angle of approach represented in this paper, namely, the study of marriage as an adjustment of rôles, may be indicated by laying down certain propositions.

First, marriage adjustment may be regarded as a process in which marriage partners attempt to re-enact certain relational systems or situations which obtained in their own earlier family groups. Or, in other words, marriage partners tend to play the habitual rôles they evolved in their childhood and adolescence.

Second, the kinds of rôles that marriage partners bring to the marriage will determine the nature of their marriage relationship and the degree of adjustment that they will achieve.

Third, that maladjusted marriages may be regarded as results of the failure of the marriage situation to provide the system of relationships called for by the rôles which the marriage partners bring to the marriage.

Now the writer is quite aware that these propositions leave out of account a great many important factors—cultural, economic, etc.—and there is no effort to deny that such factors are of importance. Let it be emphatically affirmed that these propositions are laid down in an effort to make a logical delimitation of the problem. However, there is considerable justification for the opinion that the unique rôle patterns are the chief determinants of the success or failure of marriages in which the persons come from similar cultural backgrounds. And it should not be forgotten that the greater number of marriages are contracted by persons of reasonably similar cultural backgrounds.

Let us consider the case of Mr. and Mrs. A. who have been married about a year.

Mr. A. (aged 24) is the youngest of a family of seven. When asked to tell about his childhood, he launches into a rather enthusiastic account of his happy and satisfactory family life. From his story one gathers that his mother was a powerful and aggressive personality, the chief center, drive, and control factor in the family. She ran the father's affairs, planned the children's vocational and social activities, maneuvered the daughters' marriages, and tried to maneuver the sons' marriages. Mr. A. boasts of her iron will. He is proud of her determined look, and tells how her spirit never sagged. He tells how she faced death with the same unshaken will and determination never to admit defeat.

The father is described as a pleasant, reliable, steady, quiet, and meek person who seemed to figure merely as an unimportant though kindly fixture in the household. He worked steadily, turned his earnings over to his wife, never seriously opposed her, and after her death, agreeably allowed his daughters to place him in an old people's home.

The three sisters are described as being very much like the mother, particularly the two older ones. These two have married husbands to whom they play pretty much the same rôle which their mother played toward her husband. The youngest sister, whom we shall call Martha, is two years older than Mr. A. Although not quite so Amazonian as her sisters, she is fairly aggressive, active, and adequate in meeting situations. She has played a decidedly mothering rôle to Mr. A., especially since the death of their mother when Mr. A. was about fifteen years old. He says of Martha in an interview, "We have always been very close together. She has comforted me and consoled me in my troubles. I have confided in her and she has shielded me. She used to advise me and tell me what to do." He used to sleep with his sister, and he tells of his surprise on discovering recently that people thought such an arrangement strange. He says: "Even after I was 16 or 17 if I was blue or worried about my future she would take me to bed with her and comfort me."

This occurred more frequently after the mother's death. Soon after his marriage he felt he *had* to leave his wife, to get away and think things out. He went home for a visit. The first few days he was very worried and upset. He couldn't sleep at night and one night fell to weeping. Martha took him to bed with her and consoled him. He says: "I felt a motherly warmth and felt released from my troubles and went to sleep. After that I slept in her room every night and felt much better." Mr. A. denies ever having sexual impulses or ideas about Martha at any time, although they have discussed sex quite freely.

In speaking of all the sisters he says: "I was always proud to go places with my sisters. They were lively and popular and I was proud of them. I could walk around and enjoy myself and they could take care of themselves." (This was said in comparing his sisters with his wife, who depends too much on him, he says, for pleasant times at social gatherings.)

Mr. A. does not feel that there was much conflict in his home. Things seemed to be secure and to run smoothly under the orderly supervision of the mother. He feels that the home life was happy. He says: "There was always something going on at my home. My mother and sisters were always doing interesting things, having people over and having jolly times that I like to remember. They didn't sit around like she does (alluding to his wife) and wait for something to happen. My father is quiet and never participated much in what was going on, but he enjoyed watching and listening to other people. I am like my father. I liked to watch and listen, and, if I felt like it, put in a word or do something. I hate to feel I *have* to talk or take the initiative." (This remark also was made with reference to his wife's irritating dependence upon him.)

Mr. A.'s two brothers are interesting. The older brother, who is also the oldest child, is called the black sheep. His relations with the mother and with the sister next to him were particularly hostile. He rebelled and left home early. The next brother is the middle child. He was the mother's favorite. He was and still is a dependable, quiet, kindly, non-aggressive person. The children say he is the mainstay of the family. Mr. A describes him as a kind of parent to the younger children.

Mr. A. says that his parents and siblings were always kind to him. "They always took care of me, and my brother told me he would send me to school. My sisters like to have me come to their homes, and they enjoy giving me the comforts of a home. They say, 'You need the comforts of a home'; and I believe they are right, because I often wish I could feel that I had a father and mother and a home I could go back to."

He was punished very little. A typical instance is revealing. His mother and brother scolded him and threatened to punish him for not practicing his music. They told him he should be willing to practice for them if they paid for his lessons. Mr. A.'s comment is interesting: "I remember I was very angry that they should expect anything from me just because they paid for the lessons. I hated to feel obligated." (This represents an attitude characteristic of Mr. A.—that of expecting the environment to minister unto him with no obligation or responsibilities on his part.)

One gets the impression from Mr. A.'s conversation that he was an extremely dependent, much indulged, and coddled child; that he resented any responsibility or expectation or demand from him on the part of the environment; and that he felt insecure in situations where he was thrown on his own initiative. He tended to assume a passive rôle, expecting the environment to furnish aggressive support, backing, and leadership. On several occasions he made what he describes as attempts to win his independence by leaving home. He usually went under the tutelage of a decisive and aggressive boy friend who told him he ought to learn to stand on his own feet. On each occasion when he faced a shortage of jobs or money he felt forced to retreat home. After a few attempts he was ashamed to go home and would retreat to the family of the girl he finally married. He said: "I just can't bear feeling all alone in a strange place with no money and no home I can go to."

Mr. A. met his wife shortly before his mother's death. He says: "I was timid and bashful, but she was pleasant and talked to me and I felt comfortable with her." Soon after Mr. A.'s mother died the girl's family moved to another city. A. wept the night before her departure and said: "First I lose my mother; then I lose you." (The girl had the same first name as Mr. A.'s mother.) He told her he loved her at that time, but felt that he had said more than he meant; and the next day he contrived to arrive at the railroad station too late to see her off. Largely through the girl's efforts, a correspondence was kept up between the two. Later, after some of his unsuccessful forays into the world of affairs, he would seek the shelter of the girl's home. She would be very sympathetic about his trials and tribulations and she readily accepted his alibis for failure and excused him to himself. When she consoled him on his retreats from unsuccessful attempts to make good in the world (which, by the way, he expected to do in short order) he would tell her that she was just like his sister. As he was forced to repeat his returns to the girl's family, he became more and more uncomfortable; for he felt himself more and more obligated to assume responsibilities with respect to the girl. He seemed unable to do without a good deal of sympathetic reassurance; but he became increasingly panicky as it grew more evident that marriage was expected of him.

Before we discuss further the relations between Mr. A. and his wife, it is necessary to describe briefly Mrs. A.'s family. The families of both

Mr. and Mrs. A. represent the same cultural and economic levels; if there is any difference, it is slight and in favor of Mr. A.'s family.

Mrs. A. (aged 23) describes her father as a successful merchant until a few years ago, when he developed an interest in gambling and taking extended vacations. He had never saved money but his business kept the family in good circumstances. For some time now, however, he had been very improvident and irresponsible. He has obtained good positions, but has given them up for very trivial reasons. Mrs. A. says she used to admire and respect her father, but since he has allowed the family to come upon evil days she has lost respect for him and feels very resentful toward him. The father accuses the mother of being responsible for the condition of the family. He says: "You should have taken the money from me and not allowed me to gamble." And "You should have made me attend to our business." Mrs. A. feels her father has acted as something of a spoiled child toward his wife.

The mother is described as patient, long suffering, submissive. Mrs. A. feels that she is close to her mother because, as she says, "I am very much like my mother and can understand her." She has always taken sides with her mother in family arguments, which seems to align the father and older brother against the mother and Mrs. A. These arguments turn out to be tongue lashings from the father and older brother, with the mother and daughter passively resisting.

The oldest brother is very harsh toward the mother, but she submits to his dominating and overbearing treatment. She appears to resent it somewhat, but she excuses him. When he flies into rages and leaves home to avoid paying room and board, the mother will feel sorry for him and will cook up cakes and other dainties, which she carries to his abode and lays at his feet. She treats the father in much the same way, patiently accepting his occasional beratings. When some of the children complain of their father's incompetence the mother will make excuses for him. She will say, "Your father has worked hard all his life and now just look at him. It isn't fair."

There are three children in the family, an oldest son, Mrs. A., and her younger brother. Mrs. A. speaks bitterly of the intense hatred she bears her older brother, who appears from her description to be a very domineering, overbearing, egocentric person. But she follows her statements of hostility toward him with the admission that she secretly admires his aggressiveness and capabilities and envies his assertiveness. She has wished all her life that he would love her. When on rare occasions he would be kind to her or give her a birthday gift, she would feel much encouraged and hope for better relations. She would experience great disappointment when he would resume his usual tactics.

The son's hostilities toward his mother and sister seem to date from early childhood. Mrs. A. has fought back somewhat, but she usually cries, feels blue, and suffers inwardly. She still dreams of having bitter fights with him, but in these dreams her rôle is one of defending herself against his attacks. Occasionally she will dream of a more aggressive rôle in which she vehemently commands her brother to get out of the house. She says that one reason she liked Mr. A. was that he seemed to be the opposite of her brother in every way.

Mrs. A. is fond of her younger brother and feels that they were quite close as children, though their relationship is not so close now.

Mrs. A.'s conversation gives one the impression of a person with some hostile drives, who, nevertheless, tends to assume a passive rôle in all situations. She tends to wait for something to happen, for others to make suggestions and to take the initiative. Her lack of decisive self-assertion is a characteristic which drives her husband, so he says, to distraction.

With this all too meager account of the backgrounds of our subjects, let us turn again to their relationship with one another.

Mr. A. became more and more frightened and restless as it became clearer to him that the natural and expected result of his relationship to Mrs. A. was marriage. He made some attempts to extricate himself by protesting to her that they were in no position to marry and by leaving her home. Quoting from an interview with him: "I wanted to be away to be free to work out my problems alone, but I felt myself dragged deeper and deeper." Early attempts to leave and get a job resulted in failure and an inevitable return to the girl, who was always ready with her sympathy and mothering solicitude. Her family was hospitable; but what worried Mr. A. was that they assumed his frequent returnings for prolonged visits to mean that he was intent on marriage. The father finally became more urgent and tried to encourage the diffident young man by letting him know that what he needed to settle him down was marriage.

These urgings and expectations on the part of the family plus the pleadings of the girl, plus his own inability to do without some sympathetic reassuring, proved too much for him. Finally, he says, he shut his eyes and jumped. We do not have time to give his description of his mental anguish as he walked the streets for two days trying to make up his mind. "Then," he says, "with super-human effort I forced myself to go to the courthouse and say 'I want a marriage licence.' "

After the marriage Mr. A. began to have many fears and forebodings. He was afraid Mrs. A.'s mother or father would die and he would have to help take care of Mrs. A.'s younger brother. He feared that he had wrecked his chances to realize his best self and should get out of the marriage. He began to find Mrs. A. ugly; and this, he said, outraged his aesthetic sensibilities. But the main theme throughout his interviews is: "My wife is a drag on me. She depends too much on me. Instead of feeling myself being pulled forward, I feel like she is pulling me backward. Why can't she be like my sisters? She is weak and casts a gloom over my spirit that I can't shake off. I must go away so I can feel free again and be on my own."

He did break away once to go to his sister for comfort and solace. He said: "While I was there I was happy again unless I thought of my plight. My sister said 'all you need is the comfort of your home' and she was right. While I was with her I felt all right."

The wife complained that she didn't feel secure with her husband. She wished that he could be like other men who seem to know what they want to do and how to go about it, who seem to take charge of things and forge ahead and not appear so helpless. She resented the fact that, although her husband was out of work and she was supporting him, he seemed to take that for granted as his due. Moreover, he showed great irritation toward her if she came home tired and, as he puts it, "sagging and weak looking." He says: "I simply can't stand that sagging, droopy look."

Their sexual adjustment is interesting when seen on this background. Neither knew how to proceed and their first attempts at intercourse were clumsy and unsuccessful. The husband's history shows considerable curiosity during childhood, and avoidance and fear in adolescent encounters. Even after receiving coaching from a physician and becoming somewhat adept in sexual technique, he is still described by his wife as clumsy and diffident in his approaches. He himself reveals a certain resentment and resistance to assuming the rôle of aggressor in relation with his wife. He has to assume a rôle in the sexual situation that runs contrary to his desires.

In both husband and wife there are evidences of strong repressions of sexual drives. These specifically sexual attitudes are undoubtedly a part of the situation, but they may also be thought of as parts of the basic rôle patterns, particularly in the case of the husband.

This represents the barest outline of some of the high spots in the case, but if we could present all of our materials they would hardly do more than amplify the picture which must be evident from even such a scant description.

The central problem in this case is a problem of basic rôles, which are apparently the result of the early family relationships.

The husband is looking for a solicitous, protecting, aggressive, decisive, parent environment which the wife, who expects something of the same sort of environment, cannot supply. She was able to furnish sympathy and to that extent supplied the rôle of mother and sister in the husband's family. But she is not equipped to supply the more positive and aggressive part of the rôles that these people represented in Mr. A.'s personality development.

Neither of them is quite fully aware of what the basis for their trouble is. The husband thinks his marriage is a mistake, that he is not cut out for marriage, that his artistic temperament needs complete freedom to realize itself. The wife thinks the husband is sulky, inconsiderate, selfish, and jealous of her interest in her family. They both think that relief of the financial tension would be a partial solution.

Those who take the psychoanalytic approach would probably classify the man as a homosexual type, and interpret the difficulties on that basis. If we recognize that for the male the category "homosexual" applies to general psycho-sexual traits of passivity rather than to certain specific sexual attitudes merely, then the classification is probably valid. But it should be pointed out that the classification is not fully descriptive of the rôle pattern Mr. A. represents. He is not only passive but has an infantile dependent attitude or rôle which is not necessarily characteristic of the homosexual.

The case might also be interpreted as a result of guilt feelings which arise when Mr. A. engages in sexual activity with a person who stands as a substitute for his sister Martha. Sexual impulses with reference to his sister must have been heavily repressed and, when they are allowed expression on a love object that stands for her, they give rise to strong guilt feelings from which Mr. A. seeks to escape by terminating the marriage. Even here, however, we get into a usage of the notion of rôles. But it is apparent that this specifically sexual explanation leaves out of account too much of Mr. A.'s general pattern of response to all types of situations.

The writer would suggest that, at the present stage of the game, it seems preferable to use concretely descriptive categories of rôle types. It may turn out later that some such set of master categories as those now used in the psychoanalytic field will apply. But their application should be made when empirical evidence justifies such usage.

Turning to a different approach, it should be pointed out that analysis of marital problems in terms of the usual categories of economic, cultural, response, temperamental, health, and other tensions is rather sterile unless such analysis is done with the insight that rôle analysis supplies. Any and all of the usual tensions may and do appear in a given case, but frequently they are meaningless unless seen in reference to the basic problem of rôles.

53. TECHNOLOGY, BIOLOGY AND
THE CHANGING FAMILY *

M. F. NIMKOFF

Even though social institutions tend to be stable, nevertheless they do sometimes change in form and function. According to this article by M. F. Nimkoff, our technological information and devices are developing so rapidly that even the child-bearing function of the family, assumed to be so permanent and fundamental, might someday be altered beyond recognition.

. . . We may experience in the near future a revolution in the biological functions of the family comparable to the revolution which has occurred in the economic functions during the last two hundred years. This new impact on the family derives from discoveries in the rapidly developing field of the biology of sex and reproduction. . . . As a first example, consider the progress that has been made in determining the sex of the child before conception. This is not to be confused with the prediction of the child's sex before birth, which can now be made in certain cases on the basis of various tests, although with less than 100 per cent accuracy.

For some time we have known that the child's sex is determined by the type of sperm cell contributed by the father. There are two types of sperm cell, the male-producing Y-sperm and the female-producing X-sperm, whereas in the ova there is only one type of sex cell, the X-type. Each parent contributes one sex chromosome to the child; if two X's combine, the child is female; an X and a Y produce a male. So it is the father, or at least his sex chromosomes, that determines the sex of his children, and the mother has nothing to do with it. Yet many a wife in ignorance of this fact has felt guilty because *she* did not present her husband with a son. King Farouk of Egypt divorced his queen, according to press accounts because she bore him no son.

* Reprinted from "Technology, Biology, and the Changing Family," by M. F. Nimkoff, *The American Journal of Sociology*, Vol. 57, No. 1 (July, 1951), 20–26, by permission of The University of Chicago Press. Copyright 1951 by The University of Chicago.

The author (b. 1904) is Professor and Chairman of the Department of Sociology, Florida State University. Author: *The Child; Marriage and the Family;* coauthor: *Technology and the Changing Family; Sociology.*

The X-chromosome is slightly larger than the Y-chromosome, and the female-producing sperm contains slightly more chromosomal material, making it slightly more dense. Harvey has calculated that the Y-sperm should have a density of 1.07132 and the X-sperm a density of 1.1705. By means of a special centrifuge apparatus (the vacuum type turbine centrifuge) and the use of a proper medium for the density gradient (a 20 per cent dextrin in Ringer's solution), Harvey thinks it possible to separate these two kinds of cells. The refinement of technique required for success is comparable, Harvey points out, to that which separated Uranium 235 and 238. For this reason, says Harvey, "we may designate any process of sorting the two kinds of sperm for control of sex as essentially a separation of biological isotopes."

It should be emphasized that the separation of male-producing and female-producing sperm has not yet been accomplished, but one would be bold indeed who would argue that it will not be done in the future. If and when the two cells are separated, use of them for purposes of reproduction would involve artificial insemination. There is, however, at the present time no important objection to this procedure when the donor is the woman's husband.

. . . . . .

Even if scientific research should give us the knowledge of how to control the sex of the child, the question remains: Would we use the knowledge? And, if so, how? Do we have a preference for boys or girls? It may be observed at once that, even if there is no general preference for one sex over the other in a society, individual parents may still prefer one sex to the other, or a certain ordering of their families according to sex, in which case the ability to achieve this end may be deemed to contribute to the happiness of the couple. Margaret Mead in *Male and Female* has stated that there are no social reasons why parents in the United States should prefer boys to girls or vice versa, but there is at least the reason that boys preserve the family name, in which there may be pride. Mead thinks most American parents would like to have a balanced family of boys and girls, but the preference is probably that the firstborn be a boy, which means that a son would be the more common choice of one-child families, if there were control.

This discussion assumes that the mores would be favorable to the new knowledge and that prospective parents would be permitted to utilize it. But we have no assurance that the control, if achieved, would be socially sanctioned, especially if it resulted in an appreciable imbalance in the sex ratio. There seems to be no great demand for control of the sex of the child at the present time. At least such a demand, if it exists, is not evident in any considerable application by scientists to the task of solving the technical problems involved. But if a differential in the size of the male population establishes the superiority of one nation over another in war, then it is conceivable that sex control may be encouraged in the future even as a high birth rate, without reference to the sex of the children, is now encouraged in nearly every Western nation by means of subsidies for babies. Dictatorial governments in particular may find sex control appealing and may derive an advantage from the reluctance of democratic states to adopt the practice and/or to favor male births.

We may consider briefly the implications of an unbalanced sex ratio as it relates to the marriage system. The evidence from primitive peoples indicates that an appreciable surplus of women in a society, resulting mainly from the high mortality of male hunters in late adolescence and early manhood, is a condition disposing to polygyny, whereas a surplus of men, usually resulting from female infanticide and/or religious cloistering, disposes toward polyandry. War in modern times in many Western nations has led to a large surplus of women of marriageable ages, but, barring another war, the imbalance in the sex ratio has been temporary, correcting itself in the next generation. If the sex of the child were controlled by science, and a continuing preference for males were to be expressed by a society, it would seem that the bases would exist for a trend toward polyandry. Considerable changes might be expected in the status of the sexes, their social roles, and their attitudes toward each other.

We may speculate further on what effect, if any, controlling the sex of the child would have on the relations of husbands and wives. If sex control is utilized, then procreation must occur by artificial insemination. During the past century or so, the trend has been to emphasize the psychological rather than the procreative function of coitus, as the reduction in the size of the family bears witness. Sex control would presumably further this trend; indeed, procreation and coitus might be rendered entirely separate functions. The fertile period would be emphasized more, and there would be more birth control. In the latter connection we may note in passing another probable biological development in the near future, namely, a long-term contraceptive. Knowledge of how to inhibit ovulation already exists, but such regulation disturbs the balance of the endocrine system.

A further significant discovery in the biology of sex has to do with the preservation of human germ plasm. Success has been reported in preserving human sperm 125 days in dry ice after vitrification in liquid nitrogen, with no appreciable decline in motility in this period beyond the decline of the first two hours. As much as 60 per cent of the human sperm survived the treatment so far as motility is concerned. The limit was 125 days, because an assistant failed to resupply the dry ice after that time, and the sperm warmed up. The experiment was not resumed, but the experimenter believes that vitrified sperm will keep indefinitely at the temperature of dry ice. But whether they would be able to fertilize, he, of course, does not know. He reports that he was unable to get an adequate yield of sperm other than human to survive at very low temperatures and was therefore unable to perform fertilization experiments.

The doctors object to using preserved semen in human subjects, since they do not know how it will work. Experience with animal insemination has been limited to using semen that has been kept only a relatively short time, a maximum of about 168 hours. If it could be demonstrated that no harmful effects result from the use of vitrified human sperm, the opposition might disappear. The objection would persist if donor semen were used, but where the male is the woman's husband there probably would be no organized religious objection, to judge by the present position of the churches on artificial insemination. If there is no objection, many new possibilities are opened up. For instance, a woman who is married a short time before a war and who bears no children before being separated from her husband may still bear her husband's child even if the husband is killed in action, if his semen is preserved beforehand. Widowhood under the circumstances may become a somewhat different experience from what it now is. Semen banks are a possibility in such a situation.

. . . . .

. . . Reference has been made to the use of the sex hormones. This is another brilliant chapter in the book of recent advances in the biochemistry of reproduction, to which we can here refer only briefly. The literature deals mainly with the lower animals, with whom experimentation is permissible. In one experiment a prepubertal castrated chimpanzee was paired with an intact male. The administration of male sex hormones led to the social dominance by the castrated animal, whereas female sex therapy resulted in its subordination. Following injection of a female rat with estrogen and progesterone, mating responses were induced despite the congenital absence of gonadal tissue. Hormone therapy has also succeeded in reversing sex roles. Thus a single-comb Brown Leghorn hen displayed male mating behavior following successive implants of testosterone propionate pellets, in contrast with the earlier negative findings following single daily injections of the hormone. Some experiments on human subjects have also been made. When 101 women under treatment for endocrine disorders were given androgen administered intramuscularly, subcutaneously, or orally, all but 13 reported some increase in libido. In another experiment progesterone depressed excessive libido and androgen decidedly increased both libido and general well-being, with best results obtained by implantations of pellets of testosterone propionate. On the basis of such experiments, it has been conjectured that the amount of androgens greatly affects the vigor of the sex drive and that the absolute or proportionate amount of estrogens affects its direction. It is, of course, not implied that learning and experience are not also important factors affecting the sex drive but only that constitutional factors are important, especially the hormones of the glands of internal secretion.

The foregoing are only a few of the remarkable developments in the biology and chemistry of reproduction, sufficient perhaps to indicate to us what promise for the future this infant science holds. Time does not permit more than the briefest mention of important developments in other areas, notably the biochemistry of nutrition. For instance, aging in rats has been greatly postponed by heavy doses of vitamin A in the early years. If a comparable result were to be achieved in man, this one fact alone could have a significant effect on the relationship between the sexes and on the relations of parents and children.

Confronting these discoveries, sociologists must consider what social implications they may have. An important consideration is the mores: if they are hostile, the new knowledge will not be widely utilized. Hostile mores are also an obstacle to scientific discovery itself. But, as we have seen, many of the changes which would be effected by the new discoveries are possible within the limits of the existing sex mores. There seems to be no objection to new scientific procedures if they are employed exclusively within marriage. For instance, the Roman Catholic church sanctions artificial insemination if the husband is the donor and if insemination by the physician follows normal coitus. Some of the innovations mentioned above can be confined to the marital pair, and presumably on this account there would be no objection. Such would be the case as regards the control of the sex of the child. But this would involve art'ficial means in separating the two types of sperm, and to this there might be objection from certain groups, though not all, just as there is objection at present to obtaining the husband's semen by methods other than normal marital coitus, for purposes of assisting in the insemination of the wife. So we conclude that certain of the procedures will meet with acceptance and that other procedures may meet with opposition.

We cannot be certain as to what the public practice will be with regard to many of the biological innovations, since they create new situations for which the old definitions are not adequate. Such is the case, for instance, with artificial insemination at the present time. Artificial insemination has been introduced into our culture by the doctors, and thousands of inseminations have been performed. There is as yet no body of law or clearly defined public opinion regarding the practice. Certain church bodies have taken a stand against it when the donor is not the woman's husband, and there are a few contradictory court decisions. In due course public policy may be formulated on the issue, but it may not be the same in all societies, just as public policy on abortion and birth control varies in different cultures at the present time. Moreover, even if at first there is opposition to the practice, the opposition may eventually moderate, for the mores change.

It may also be observed that the systematic opposition of the group to a practice does not necessarily mean that the practice will not exist. There are many thousands of abortions each year despite the taboo against them. Where a need exists, and the knowledge of how to fill it, it is difficult to suppress the practice in a complex, heterogeneous, rapidly changing society. What the doctors and their patients do in our complex society is not generally known: the statement that thousands of persons have been artificially inseminated is probably news to most citizens.

So we conclude that, even if there is opposition to new biological practices and knowledge, there may still be not a little diffusion of the innovations, with considerable effects on family practices. But it is too soon yet to say whether there will be opposition to many of the discoveries that are in process of being made in the field of biology and chemistry of reproduction. It may, furthermore, be noted that not all scientific discoveries are put to use. For one reason and another, the death rate of inventions and discoveries is high. But if the innovation has great human significance and there is a demand for it, there is considerable probability that it will be developed and diffused.

To sum up, the family in the past has been shaped by changes in the social system of which it is a part, and particularly by changes in technology and economic organization, which are among the most dynamic elements of the social system. These changes in technology have during the past century and a half been revolutionary and have forced radical readjustments in the correlated parts of culture, including the family. These technological changes have been exterior to man the animal and have required changes in adaptation without any radical change in the constitution of man. But now the revolution in science has extended to the sciences of man, and the probabilities are great that discoveries in human biology will revolutionize the constitutional bases of human behavior. There are great discoveries also in the psychological realm of which this paper has taken no account; family behavior may be greatly affected in the years ahead by new knowledge regarding the learning process and the way personality is shaped by group and culture. Sociologists seem to be more mindful of the possibilities in the psychological realm, and they have given some attention to the correlations of technology and the rest of the social order. But there does not seem as yet to be much awareness of the social influences that the biological discoveries may exert. . . .

54. NEW DIRECTIONS FOR RESEARCH
ON THE AMERICAN FAMILY *

LEONARD S. COTTRELL, JR.

*A historical look at the research done on any institution will show
interesting shifts in the aspects deemed important in the institution,
the approaches thought useful, the conclusions considered valid.
Here Cottrell reviews the trends in research dealing with one
institution—the family. He then proceeds to demonstrate the new
paths which family research might appropriately take. In doing so,
he introduces the concept of interpersonal competence—skill in
controlling the outcome of episodes of interaction—and describes
the components or dimensions of that concept. Cottrell believes
that family research should now concern itself with what that
institution is able to do toward socializing the individual in this
special respect.*

In general, we can say that in any given period the stimulation and
orientation of research on the family have come from the particular
complex of problems or crises on which people have focused their attention. Thus, in the 1920's the widespread manifestations of the weakening of the traditional codes of sexual morality claimed a large share of
concern. . . . During the thirties, the threat to the economic security
of the family and the problems of stable adjustment of partners in
marriage occupied the center of the stage in public concern. . . . World
War II forced attention on the problems caused by the separation of
husband and wife and of parents from children. . . .

The situation of the current decade, both as to identification of major
problems requiring attention and as to specification of the kinds of
research which need to be done, is the subject of this discussion. The
task is not easy, partly because it is always harder to get perspective on
contemporary situations than it is on the past; partly because the problems are actually more complex today; and partly because we are confronted with a situation that requires us to be clearer now than ever
before, both about the values and goals to which we are committed and

* From *Social Casework*, Vol. 34, No. 2 (February, 1953), 54–60.
For biographical sketch of the author see selection 52.

about the means by which we seek to implement these values and goals.

Let me comment briefly on these three sources of our difficulty in structuring our problem. First, it is hard to maintain proper perspective in the midst of the press of the current situation. In this the present decade is not unique. The same was true in the twenties, thirties, and forties, but at this distance we see only what finally emerged as the dominant centers of attention. Ten or twenty years hence we shall make the same oversimplified characterization of the fifties. This does not mean that we should refrain either from making such simple characterizations of past periods or from seeking to identify major features of the current scene. We merely take note here that life and human history are like this. Second, I think it fair to say that our present problems are actually more complex, or at least we are more keenly aware of the necessity for attending to their complex ramifications than in previous decades. The critical dilemmas of morality and sex adjustment, of family loyalty and personal success, of economic insecurity and family stability, of national emergency and needs and concerns of the family have not by any means been resolved; they have overlapped and accumulated and remained with us as we add new crises and new problems, with the deepening of what some have called "the permanent emergency."

This sense of continuing crisis—of an unremitting state of impending threat and tension—has become so much a part of our present experience and of our anticipations of the future of our generation that we are almost ready to stop wishful thinking and look at our age for what it is—a chronic headache, a time of mortal peril to everything we hold dear, and a magnificent opportunity for human progress beyond imagination. Every great period of crisis presents these discomforts, threats, and opportunities, but if we are to maximize our chances of capitalizing on the opportunities at hand we must have a correct diagnosis of our current problems and crises, a clear conception of values and goals that are to guide our action, and a will and capacity to implement them in action. And let me point out here that the American family and the agencies concerned with its welfare have a profoundly critical role to play in determining how the American people will meet this challenge. I shall try a little later to indicate more specifically what I think this role should be.

Various commentators identify different aspects of the current situation as the source of threats to our welfare: the menace of Communism, the threat of war, uncontrolled inflation, the continued weakening of ties of the individual to stable communities and groups, an increasing prosperity coupled with a loss of a sense of any but the most transient and immediate meanings in life, and so forth. I shall make no attempt to exhaust the list or to add to it. However, for the purpose of providing a context for research on the family and criteria for action programs to strengthen the family, I wish to make the following observations:

1. Running through most of the efforts to identify the basic forces that threaten our society and its values is the recognition, explicit or implicit, that the increasing size and complex interdependence of the community bring with it corresponding increase in the need for co-ordination and a tendency to centralized direction and control. This is true both of government and of private enterprises, national and international.

2. This trend has been accompanied by the development of mass organizations that seek to influence or control the agencies of central co-ordination and direction.

3. Both these trends have produced and depended upon the development of the technology of mass control by which the individual becomes less and less a participant and more and more the object of manipulation.

4. The end result is the totalitarian society manifested in the modern Communist and Fascist dictatorships, with their rejection of the values of preserving the integrity of the individual.

5. The values to which we are committed require that we maintain an effectively integrated complex social system not only along with, but in the interest of maximizing, the worth and integrity of the individual.

There are some people in this country who have given up the search for an answer to this riddle. Most of us are, as most Americans always have been, unwilling to admit the existence of any problem that we cannot solve if we but try. To some this may appear idle boast and bluster. I believe that in this instance, however, there is substance to such a claim. There are certain powerful assets deeply imbedded in our beliefs and practices: the idea that, by and large, if people are given the necessary information on a problem they will come to a reasonable and workable solution; the idea that the individual has a responsibility to participate intelligently in the achievement of common goals; and, moreover, we have a strong tradition of pragmatic experimentalism in our approach to social problems. To be sure, these values frequently get overlaid and lost sight of, but they exist and they are remarkably vigorous.

Now let me state the proposition that a society composed of individuals possessing the motives, qualities, capacities, and skills that are needed for competent participation in the processes of defining goals and development of means for their implementation will develop maximum capacity to solve its problems and realize its goals without resort to the totalitarian forms of social organization. With this proposition, we can return to the subject of our discussion and consider some new lines of research on the family and on agencies concerned with the family.

NEW LINES OF RESEARCH

First, let me point out that the proposition confronts us with the necessity for specifying the kinds of personal qualities, capacities, and skills required for competent participation in a democratic social system. It is both surprising and extremely embarrassing that social psychologists have never given systematic attention to the problem of specifying those characteristics that make for competent functioning of the individual in a democratic context.

My first recommendation for a new line of research, then, would be a thorough and systematic attempt to identify what we may call the components of personal competence for functioning in a democratic social system. This is no easy task, as anyone finds who tries it himself. Professor Foote and I made some efforts along this line which he has continued with his associates in the Family Study Center at Chicago. Results thus far, while none too satisfactory, have pointed to some clusters of personal qualities, capacities, and skills that seem likely to prove highly important for personal competence and about the development of which little is known. Here only a brief mention will be made of this tentative list of five components of competence.

1. Empathic capacity. This is sometimes referred to as social perceptiveness or social sensitivity. People appear to differ rather widely in their ability to interpret correctly the attitudes and intentions of others; in the accuracy with which they can perceive situations from the perspectives of others in the situation; in their ability to anticipate and predict the behavior of others with whom they interact. This type of social sensitivity and related ability rests on what we call the empathic responses. Empathic responses are basic to the ability to "take the role of the other" and hence are basic to social interaction and the communicative processes upon which rests social integration. They are central in the development of the social self and the capacity for self-conscious behavior. No human society is possible without the processes indicated by this term, and least of all democratic society. For this reason we must include empathic capacity as one of the essential components of personal competence.

2. Social inventiveness. This cluster is sometimes referred to as creativity. What we have in mind here are those skills and qualities that pertain to the capacity of the individual to invent and try new ways of dealing with others when previous patterns of relationships appear to defeat the values of the situation. This component is perhaps the least amenable to precise definition and measurement. It is interesting that the so-called tough-minded scientists and hard-headed people are inclined to look askance at this category as a proper object of scientific study, and yet all these practical people demand appraisals of this quality in anyone they may be considering for positions entailing heavy responsibilities and calling for leadership and imagination. The idea of creativity is commonly associated with artistic and intellectual activities. We conceive of it broadly as any demonstrated capacity for innovations in behavior or real reconstruction of any aspect of the material for social environment. It involves the ability to develop fresh perspectives on all traditional and established routines and to make novel combinations of ideas and objects in defining new goals, endowing old ones with fresh meaning and inventing instrumentalities for their realization. Important factors entering behavior that we regard as creative are probably curiosity, self-confidence, something of the venturesomeness and risk-taking tendencies of the explorer, a flexible mind with the kind of psychological freedom that permits the psychological orientation of spontaneous play. We realize this is none too satisfactory as a delineation of creativity, but let us begin here and invite participation in the search for a more adequate conception.

3. *Self-other balance.* By this somewhat awkward term we mean those attitudes and qualities that enable the person to be self-respecting, self-directing, self-reliant, self-confident, and to maintain his own integrity while at the same time he can balance these self-regarding attitudes with respect, confidence, and trust in others, all of which lead him to act as a responsible and co-operative member of society. In our judgment it would be hard indeed to imagine competent functioning in a democratic society without a high degree of self-respect, self-reliance, and a capacity for self-direction, properly balanced by the appropriate other-regarding tendencies of respect, confidence, and trust.

4. *Intelligence.* Since this component has been studied widely for about two generations, there is no necessity for us to elaborate upon it here. The kinds of capacity we have in mind are: scope of perception of relationships among events; the capacity to abstract and symbolize experience and to manipulate the symbols into meaningful generalizations; the capacity to be articulate in communication; skill in mobilizing the resources of the environment; and experience in the service of a variety of goals. There is probably little cause for debate about including this as an essential component of competence. There are, however, new directions that research could take in this respect, the most important of which would be experimentation with conditions of the family and other relevant institutions which could maximize the development of latent intellectual capacities and of skill in their utilization.

5. *Health.* Here again we have a component of competence about which there will be little debate. We include it, not only because it is an obvious essential to competent functioning but to call attention to the fact that as a component of competence it signifies much more than mere absence of disease. Rather it must represent the progressive maximization

of the ability of the organism to exercise all its physiological functions, and to achieve its maximum of sensory acuity, strength, energy, co-ordination, dexterity, endurance, and immunity. While the relation of the family to the problem of cure and prevention of disease must always be an object of research attention, we must without delay increase our knowledge of the actual and potential contributions of family living to this positive maximization of the biological potentialities of its members.

There is no inclination on my part to defend this as the final or best formulation of the essential components of personal competence for functioning in democratic society, but I am prepared to contend that it represents worthy effort and that it points to new problems of great importance both to theoretical social science and to the present problem of democracy's answer to the challenge of those who would abandon or destroy it.

"All well and good," one may say, "but what about fortifying families in troubled times? And what about new research on the family?" The latter question I answer with a second recommendation for new directions of research on the family—that a major part of family research for the next decade be devoted to the experimental testing of hypotheses on the conditions of family life which enhance or inhibit the development of the essential components of competence. Whether our list is correct or not, it is fairly certain that whatever the basic components may be, the family will be found to have a critical role in their development. Thus, the development of the components of competence in the human personality presents problems that provide a major program of research on the family. I include in this recommendation research designed to test the impact of conditions outside the family which may influence its effectiveness in developing in parents, marriage partners, and children those qualities and capacities we have been considering. A special field of research in this connection should be on the direct and indirect impact of family service agencies in influencing the degree of effectiveness families will possess for the performance of this function.

My answer to the question concerning what this has to do with fortifying families in troubled times can be stated as follows: Institutions are strong when they have vital functions to perform and when their participants are aware of these functions and are convinced that they are important. Our task at this time in our history is not to go back to some pattern of the past or to shore up particular ideologies, beliefs, and institutional forms. Rather it is to clarify for ourselves and for all Americans the real values that the family serves: old enduring values, old values redefined in terms more appropriate to our age, and new values and goals that are emerging; and to contribute all our knowledge, wisdom, and skill to the development of those capacities and instrumentalities necessary for the implementation of these values. In so doing we shall be fortifying the family in a truly fundamental way. It is just this kind of strengthening I had in mind when pointing to some of our basic American values, the kinds of personal qualities needed for implementing those values, and the basic role of the family in the production of these qualities as the foundation for a meaningful program for research on the family.

SHIFTS IN RESEARCH ORIENTATION

The kinds of research I suggest will be greatly facilitated by an increased ability of research workers to shift their orientation to their problems and the way they study them. In the first place, there is need for them to shift from the more conventional orientation of a relatively passive descriptive approach in which they merely seek to describe what is and stop there, to a more active experimental orientation in which they seek to determine what processes can be designed and tested which will yield the products needed for competent behavior. There are many studies that describe, for example, the practices and personality resultants of families of different social classes, but few that can show what happens when changes are made in familial situations in order to enhance certain skills in dealing with certain problems. We constantly try to do this in good clinical treatment and casework but we need to develop a more systematic design for research if our knowledge is to provide useful generalizations in addition to useful wisdom which the worker and clinician accumulate. This means, of course, that research workers cannot avoid the responsibility of participating in making value judgments as to what products are desirable. Social scientists have contended that they should avoid value judgments like poison. Actually, they constantly make value judgments, although they frequently make themselves believe that they do not. In my opinion it is very important to recognize the value judgments we make and thus avoid the errors of hidden and uncontrolled unconscious bias.

A shift from the detached contemplative orientation to one that is active and judgmental requires also a shift from the conception of the scientist as an outsider who manipulates and who does things to people without revealing his objectives, to a conception of the scientist as one whose pattern of work is what we are beginning to call participant experimentation, whereby the subject participates actively and knowingly in the design and conduct of the experiment. This orientation and pattern of operation places scientific experimentation on human behavior squarely within the American tradition of respect for the integrity of the individual. And, equally important, it is far more likely to yield valid and usable knowledge than is the conventional orientation.

A third shift in orientation is indicated by the fact that in this paper

I have spoken of competence rather than adjustment even though nearly all research on the modern family has been centered around the concept of adjustment. It is obvious to persons who work in this field that adjustment is not only a passive term but a very ambiguous one. It is appropriate to speak of adjustment to society when that society is relatively static. But in a changing world we have to do more than passively adjust to change if we are to have any part in determining our own destiny. To have this part we must be competent to meet the problems of changing conditions and actively shape them to our own ends. The concept of adjustment implies a static world and static personal attributes adapted to that world. Competence denotes capacities and skills that enable a person to operate positively on his world. Again, this is in the American tradition.

So that my position will be entirely clear, let me emphasize that I do not decry research done with the orientation of contemplative description from the standpoint of the detached scientist, or research aimed at the phenomena of adjustment wherever that research is appropriate. There are problems and conditions in which these orientations are proper. My objection is to making a fetish of the conventional orientations, with the result that we find ourselves unable to shift our perspectives and patterns of research when a shift is necessary. The problems of our day, the practical ones as well as those of theoretical social science, call for a substantial amount of research in the orientations that I have recommended. . . .

55. THE DIVISION OF LABOR
IN SOCIETY °

EMILE DURKHEIM

One of the recurring basic criticisms of modern society is that the "whole man"—the personality—has been weakened because of specialization, or "division of labor." Said one philosopher, "It is a sad commentary that we have come to the state where we never do

° Reprinted from *The Division of Labor in Society*, pp. 396–409, by permission of The Free Press, Glencoe, Illinois. Copyright 1947.

The author (1858–1917) was a French sociologist and philosopher. Taught at University of Bordeaux and at the Sorbonne. Successor to Auguste Comte. Particular interest: moral sociology; central theory: collective representation. Besides doctoral dissertation from which this selection is taken, Durkheim's main works are *The Rules of Sociological Method; The Elementary Forms of the Religious Life; Suicide: A Study in Sociology.*

*anything more than make the eighteenth part of a pin." Said
another, "In so far as the principle of the division of labor receives
a more complete application, the art progresses, the artisan
retrogresses." Many, comparing the life of the modern workman
with the "free, bold life of the 'noble' savage," have found the
second much preferable to the first. Adoption of such a philosophy,
carried to its logical conclusion, would lead to drastic changes
in all of social life. This idea, perhaps most popular in the
nineteenth century, still flourishes today. Consequently, in
vocational planning, we may be given contradictory advice:
Specialize. Do not specialize. The result of specialization, in the
thinking of Rousseau and others, is the "splintering" of personalities
and societies. Emile Durkheim, however, in this conclusion to his
The Division of Labor in Society argues that specialization is the
chief source of social solidarity and is becoming the foundation of
our present moral order.*

I

If there is one rule of conduct which is incontestable, it is that which
orders us to realize in ourselves the essential traits of the collective type.
Among lower peoples, this reaches its greatest rigor. There, one's first
duty is to resemble everybody else, not to have anything personal about
one's beliefs or actions. In more advanced societies, required likenesses
are less numerous; the absence of some likenesses, however, is still a sign
of moral failure. Of course, crime falls into fewer different categories;
but today, as heretofore, if a criminal is the object of reprobation, it is
because he is unlike us. Likewise, in lesser degree, acts simply immoral
and prohibited as such are those which evince dissemblances less profound but nevertheless considered serious. Is this not the case with
the rule which common morality expresses when it orders a man to be
a man in every sense of the word, which is to say, to have all the ideas
and sentiments which go to make up a human conscience? No doubt, if
this formula is taken literally, the man prescribed would be man in
general and not one of some particular social species. But, in reality, this
human conscience that we must integrally realize is nothing else than
the collective conscience of the group of which we are a part. For what
can it be composed of, if not the ideas and sentiments to which we
are most attached? Where can we find the traits of our model, if not
within us and around us? If we believe that this collective ideal is that
of all humanity, that is because it has become so abstract and general
that it appears fitting for all men indiscriminately. But, really, every
people makes for itself some particular conception of this type which
pertains to its personal temperament. Each represents it in its own image.

Even the moralist who thinks he can, through thought, overcome the influence of transient ideas, cannot do so, for he is impregnated with them, and no matter what he does, he finds these precepts in the body of his deductions. That is why each nation has its own school of moral philosophy conforming to its character.

On the other hand, we have shown that this rule had as its function the prevention of all agitation of the common conscience, and, consequently, of social solidarity, and that it could accomplish this role only by having a moral character. It is impossible for offenses against the most fundamental collective sentiments to be tolerated without the disintegration of society, and it is necessary to combat them with the aid of the particularly energetic reaction which attaches to moral rules.

But the contrary rule, which orders us to specialize, has exactly the same function. It also is necessary for the cohesion of societies, at least at a certain period in their evolution. Of course, its solidarity is different from the preceding, but though it is different, it is no less indispensable. Higher societies can maintain themselves in equilibrium only if labor is divided; the attraction of like for like less and less suffices to produce this result. If, then, the moral character of the first of these rules is necessary to the playing of its role, it is no less necessary to the second. They both correspond to the same social need, but satisfy the need differently, because the conditions of existence in the societies themselves differ. Consequently, without speculating concerning the first principle of ethics, we can induce the moral value of one from the moral value of the other. If, from certain points of view, there is a real antagonism between them, that is not because they serve different ends. On the contrary, it is because they lead to the same end, but through opposed means. Accordingly, there is no necessity for choosing between them once for all nor of condemning one in the name of the other. What is necessary is to give each, at each moment in history, the place that is fitting to it.

Perhaps we can even generalize further in this matter.

The requirements of our subject have obliged us to classify moral rules and to review the principal types. We are thus in a better position than we were in the beginning to see, or at least to conjecture, not only upon the external sign, but also upon the internal character which is common to all of them and which can serve to define them. We have put them into two groups: rules with repressive sanctions, which may be diffuse or organized, and rules with restitutive sanctions. We have seen that the first of these express the conditions of the solidarity, *sui generis,* which comes from resemblances, and to which we have given the name mechanical; the second, the conditions of negative solidarity and organic solidarity. We can thus say that, in general, the characteristic of moral rules is that they enunciate the fundamental conditions of social solidarity. Law and morality are the totality of ties which bind each of us to society, which make a unitary, coherent aggregate of the mass of individuals. Everything which is a source of solidarity is moral, everything which forces man to take account of other men is moral, everything which forces him to regulate his conduct through something other than the striving of his ego is moral, and morality is as solid as these ties are numerous and strong. We can see how inexact it is to define it, as is often done, through liberty. It rather consists in a state of dependence. Far from serving to emancipate the individual, or disengaging him from the environment which surrounds him, it has, on the contrary, the function of making him an integral part of a whole, and, consequently, of depriving him of some liberty of movement. We sometimes, it is true, come across people not without nobility who find the idea of such dependence intolerable. But that is because they do not perceive the source from which their own morality flows, since these sources are very deep. Conscience is a bad judge of what goes on in the depths of a person, because it does not penetrate to them.

Society is not, then, as has often been thought, a stranger to the moral world, or something which has only secondary repercussions upon it. It is, on the contrary, the necessary condition of its existence. It is not a simple juxtaposition of individuals who bring an intrinsic morality with them, but rather man is a moral being only because he lives in society, since morality consists in being solidary with a group and varying with this solidarity. Let all social life disappear, and moral life will disappear with it, since it would no longer have any objective. The state of nature of the philosophers of the eighteenth century, if not immoral, is, at least, *amoral*. Rousseau himself recognized this. Through this, however, we do not come upon the formula which expresses morality as a function of social interest. To be sure, society cannot exist if its parts are not solidary, but solidarity is only one of its conditions of existence. There are many others which are no less necessary and which are not moral. Moreover, it can happen that, in the system of ties which make up morality, there are some which are not useful in themselves or which have power without any relation to their degree of utility. The idea of utility does not enter as an essential element in our definition.

As for what is called individual morality, if we understand by that a totality of duties of which the individual would, at the same time, be subject and object, and which would link him only to himself, and which would, consequently, exist even if he were solitary,—that is an abstract conception which has no relation to reality. Morality, in all its forms, is never met with except in society. It never varies except in relation to social conditions. To ask what it would be if societies did not exist is thus to depart from facts and enter the domain of gratuitous hypotheses and unverifiable flights of the imagination. The duties of the individual towards himself are, in reality, duties towards society. They correspond to certain collective sentiments which he cannot offend, whether the offended and the offender are one and the same person, or whether they are distinct. Today, for example, there is in all healthy consciences a very lively sense of respect for human dignity, to which we are supposed to conform as much in our relations with ourselves as in our relations with others, and this constitutes the essential quality of what is called individual morality. Every act which contravenes this is censured, even when the agent and the sufferer are the same person. That is why, according to the Kantian formula, we ought to respect human personality wherever we find it, which is to say, in ourselves as in those like us. The sentiment of which it is the object is not less offended in one case than in the other.

But not only does the division of labor present the character by which we have defined morality; it more and more tends to become the essential condition of social solidarity. As we advance in the evolutionary scale, the ties which bind the individual to his family, to his native soil, to traditions which the past has given to him, to collective group usages, become loose. More mobile, he changes his environment more easily, leaves his people to go elsewhere to live a more autonomous existence, to a greater extent forms his own ideas and sentiments. Of course, the whole common conscience does not, on this account, pass out of existence. At least there will always remain this cult of personality, of individual dignity of which we have just been speaking, and which, today, is the rallying-point of so many people. But how little a thing it is when one contemplates the ever increasing extent of social life, and, consequently, of individual consciences! For, as they become more voluminous, as intelligence becomes richer, activity more varied, in order for morality to remain constant, that is to say, in order for the individual to remain attached to the group with a force equal to that of yesterday, the ties which bind him to it must become stronger and more numerous. If, then, he formed no others than those which come from resemblances, the effacement of the segmental type would be accompanied by a systematic debasement of morality. Man would no longer be sufficiently obligated; he would no longer feel about and above him this salutary pressure of society which moderates his egoism and makes him a moral being. This is what gives moral value to the division of labor. Through it, the individual becomes cognizant of his dependence upon society; from it come the forces which keep him in check and restrain him. In short, since the division of labor becomes the chief source of social solidarity, it becomes, at the same time, the foundation of the moral order.

We can then say that, in higher societies, our duty is not to spread our activity over a large surface, but to concentrate and specialize it. We must contract our horizon, choose a definite task and immerse ourselves in it completely, instead of trying to make ourselves a sort of creative masterpiece, quite complete, which contains its worth in itself and not in the services that it renders. Finally, this specialization ought to be pushed as far as the elevation of the social type, without assigning any other limit to it. No doubt, we ought so to work as to realize in ourselves the collective type as it exists. There are common sentiments, common ideas, without which, as has been said, one is not a man. The rule which orders us to specialize remains limited by the contrary rule. Our conclusion is not that it is good to press specialization as far as possible, but as far as necessary. As for the part that is to be played by these two opposing necessities, that is determined by experience and cannot be calculated *a priori.* It is enough for us to have shown that the second is not of a different nature from the first, but that it also is moral, and that, moreover, this duty becomes ever more important and pressing, because the general qualities which are in question suffice less and less to socialize the individual.

It is not without reason that public sentiment reproves an ever more pronounced tendency on the part of dilettantes and even others to be taken up with an exclusively general culture and refuse to take any part in occupational organization. That is because they are not sufficiently attached to society, or, if one wishes, society is not sufficiently attached to them, and they escape it. Precisely because they feel its effect neither with vivacity nor with the continuity that is necessary, they have no cognizance of all the obligations their positions as social beings demand of them. The general ideal to which they are attached being, for the reasons we have spoken of, formal and shifting, it cannot take them out of themselves. We do not cling to very much when we have no very determined objective, and, consequently, we cannot very well elevate ourselves beyond a more or less refined egotism. On the contrary, he who gives himself over to a definite task is, at every moment, struck by the sentiment of common solidarity in the thousand duties of occupational morality.

II

But does not the division of labor by making each of us an incomplete being bring on a diminution of individual personality? That is a reproach which has often been levelled at it.

Let us first of all remark that it is difficult to see why it would be more in keeping with the logic of human nature to develop superficially rather than profoundly. Why would a more extensive activity, but more dispersed, be superior to a more concentrated, but circumscribed, activity? Why would there be more dignity in being complete and mediocre, rather than in living a more specialized, but more intense life, particularly if it is thus possible for us to find what we have lost in this specialization, through our association with other beings who have what we lack and who complete us? We take off from the principle that man ought to realize his nature as man, to accomplish his ὀικεῖον ἔργον, as Aristotle said. But this nature does not remain constant throughout history; it is modified with societies. Among lower peoples, the proper duty of man is to resemble his companions, to realize in himself all the traits of the collective type which are then confounded, much more than today, with the human type. But, in more advanced societies, his nature is, in large part, to be an organ of society, and his proper duty, consequently, is to play his role as an organ.

Moreover, far from being trammelled by the progress of specialization, individual personality develops with the division of labor.

To be a person is to be an autonomous source of action. Man acquires this quality only in so far as there is something in him which is his alone and which individualizes him, as he is something more than a simple incarnation of the generic type of his race and his group. It will be said that he is endowed with free will and that is enough to establish his personality. But although there may be some of this liberty in him, an object of so many discussions, it is not this metaphysical, impersonal, invariable attribute which can serve as the unique basis for concrete personality, which is empirical and variable with individuals. That could not be constituted by the wholly abstract power of choice between two opposites, but it is still necessary for this faculty to be exercised towards ends and aims which are proper to the agent. In other words, the very materials of conscience must have a personal character. But we have seen that this result is progressively produced as the division of labor progresses. The effacement of the segmental type, at the same time that it necessitates a very great specialization, partially lifts the individual conscience from the organic environment which supports it, as from the social environment which envelops it, and, accordingly because of this double emancipation, the individual becomes more of an independent factor in his own conduct. The division of labor itself contributes to this enfranchisement, for individual natures, while specializing, become more complex, and by that are in part freed from collective action and hereditary influences which can only enforce themselves upon simple, general things.

It is, accordingly, a real illusion which makes us believe that personality was so much more complete when the division of labor had penetrated less. No doubt, in looking from without at the diversity of occupations which the individual then embraces, it may seem that he is developing in a very free and complete manner. But, in reality, this activity which he manifests is not really his. It is society, it is the race acting in and through him; he is only the intermediary through which they realize themselves. His liberty is only apparent and his personality borrowed. Because the life of these societies is, in certain respects, less regular, we imagine that original talents have more opportunity for free play, that it is easier for each one to pursue his own tastes, that a very large place is left to free fantasy. But this is to forget that personal sentiments are then very rare. If the motives which govern conduct do not appear as periodically as they do today, they do not leave off being collective, and, consequently, impersonal, and it is the same with the actions that they inspire. Moreover, we have shown above how activity becomes richer and more intense as it becomes more specialized.

Thus, the progress of individual personality and that of the division of labor depend upon one and the same cause. It is thus impossible to desire one without desiring the other. But no one today contests the obligatory character of the rule which orders us to be more and more of a person.

One last consideration will make us see to what extent the division of labor is linked with our whole moral life.

Men have long dreamt of finally realizing in fact the ideal of human fraternity. People pray for a state where war will no longer be the law of international relations, where relations between societies will be pacifically regulated, as those between individuals already are, where all men will collaborate in the same work and live the same life. Although these aspirations are in part neutralized by those which have as their object the particular society of which we are a part, they have not left off being active and are even gaining in force. But they can be satisfied only if all men form one society, subject to the same laws. For, just as private conflicts can be regulated only by the action of the society in which the individuals live, so intersocial conflicts can be regulated only by a society which comprises in its scope all others. The only power which can serve to moderate individual egotism is the power of the group; the only power which can serve to moderate the egotism of groups is that of some other group which embraces them.

Truly, when the problem has been posed in these terms, we must recognize that this ideal is not on the verge of being integrally realized, for there are too many intellectual and moral diversities between different social types existing together on the earth to admit of fraternalization in the same society. But what is possible is that societies of the same type may come together, and it is, indeed, in this direction that evolution appears to move. We have already seen that among European peoples there is a tendency to form, by spontaneous movement, a European society which has, at present, some idea of itself and the beginning of organization. If the formation of a single human society is forever impossible, a fact which has not been proved, at least the formation of continually larger societies brings us vaguely near the goal. These facts, moreover, in no wise contradict the definition of morality that we have given, for if we cling to humanity and if we ought to cling to it, it is because it is a society which is in process of realizing itself in this way, and with which we are solidary.

But we know that greater societies cannot be formed except through the development of the division of labor, for not only could they not maintain themselves in equilibrium without a greater specialization of functions, but even the increase in the number of those competing would suffice to produce this result mechanically; and that, so much the more, since the growth of volume is generally accompanied by a growth in density. We can then formulate the following proposition: the ideal of human fraternity can be realized only in proportion to the progress of the division of labor. We must choose: either to renounce our dream, if we refuse further to circumscribe our activity, or else to push forward its accomplishment under the condition we have just set forth.

III

But if the division of labor produces solidarity, it is not only because it makes each individual an *exchangist*, as the economists say; it is because it creates among men an entire system of rights and duties which link them together in a durable way. Just as social similitudes give rise to a law and a morality which protect them, so the division of labor gives rise to rules which assure pacific and regular concourse of divided functions. If economists have believed that it would bring forth an abiding solidarity, in some manner of its own making, and if, accordingly, they have held that human societies could and would resolve themselves into purely economic associations, that is because they believed that it affected only individual, temporary interests. Consequently, to estimate the interests in conflict and the way in which they ought to equilibrate, that is to say, to determine the conditions under which exchange ought to take place, is solely a matter of individual competence; and, since these interests are in a perpetual state of becoming, there is no place for any permanent regulation. But such a conception is, in all ways, inadequate for the facts. The division of labor does not present individuals to one another, but social functions. And society is interested in the play of the latter; in so far as they regularly concur, or do not concur, it will be healthy or ill. Its existence thus depends upon them, and the more they are divided the greater its dependence. That is why it cannot leave them in a state of indetermination. In addition to this, they are determined by themselves. Thus are formed those rules whose number grows as labor is divided, and whose absence makes organic solidarity either impossible or imperfect.

But it is not enough that there be rules; they must be just, and for that it is necessary for the external conditions of competition to be equal. If, moreover, we remember that the collective conscience is becoming more and more a cult of the individual, we shall see that what characterizes the morality of organized societies, compared to that of segmental societies, is that there is something more human, therefore more rational, about them. It does not direct our activities to ends which do not immediately concern us; it does not make us servants of ideal powers of a nature other than our own, which follow their directions without occupying themselves with the interests of men. It only asks that we be thoughtful of our fellows and that we be just, that we fulfill our duty, that we work at the function we can best execute, and receive the just reward for our services. The rules which constitute it do not have a constraining force which snuffs out free thought; but, because they are rather made for us and, in a certain sense, by us, we are free. We wish to understand them; we do not fear to change them. We must, however, guard against finding such an ideal inadequate on the pretext that it is too earthly and too much to our liking. An ideal is not more elevated because more transcendent, but because it leads us to vaster perspectives. What is important is not that it tower high above us, until it becomes a stranger to our lives, but that it open to our activity a large enough field. This is far from being on the verge of realization. We know only too well what a laborious work it is to erect this society where each individual will have the place he merits, will be rewarded as he deserves, where everybody, accordingly, will spontaneously work for the good of all and of each. Indeed, a moral code is not above another because it commands in a drier and more authoritarian manner, or because it is more sheltered from reflection. Of course, it must attach us to something besides ourselves but it is not necessary for it to chain us to it with impregnable bonds.

It has been said with justice that morality—and by that must be understood, not only moral doctrines, but customs—is going through a real crisis. What precedes can help us to understand the nature and causes of this sick condition. Profound changes have been produced in the structure of our societies in a very short time; they have been freed from the segmental type with a rapidity and in proportions such as have never before been seen in history. Accordingly, the morality which corresponds to this social type has regressed, but without another developing quickly enough to fill the ground that the first left vacant in our consciences. Our faith has been troubled; tradition has lost its sway; individual judgment has been freed from collective judgment. But, on the other hand, the functions which have been disrupted in the course of the upheaval have not had the time to adjust themselves to one another; the new life which has emerged so suddenly has not been able to be completely organized, and above all, it has not been organized in a way to satisfy the need for justice which has grown more ardent in our hearts. If this be so, the remedy for the evil is not to seek to resuscitate traditions and practices which, no longer responding to present conditions of society, can only live an artificial, false existence. What we must do to relieve this anomy is to discover the means for making the organs which are still wasting themselves in discordant movements harmoniously concur by introducing into their relations more justice by more and more extenuating the external inequalities which are the source of the evil. Our illness is not, then, as has often been believed, of an intellectual sort; it has more profound causes. We shall not suffer because we no longer know on what theoretical notion to base the morality we have been practicing, but because, in certain of its parts, this morality is irremediably shattered, and that which is necessary to us is only in process of formation. Our anxiety does not arise because the criticism of scholars has broken down the traditional explanation we used to give to our duties; consequently, it is not a new philosophical system which will relieve the situation. Because certain of our duties are no longer founded in the reality of things, a breakdown has resulted which will be repaired only in so far as a new discipline is established and consolidated. In short, our first duty is to make a moral code for ourselves. Such a work cannot be improvised in the silence of the study; it can arise only through itself, little by little, under the pressure of internal causes which make it necessary. But the service that thought can and must render is in fixing the goal that we must attain. That is what we have tried to do.

56. THE MONSTROUS MACHINE
AND THE WORRIED WORKERS *

WARNER BLOOMBERG, JR.

The rapid increase in mechanization of production, exemplified in the extreme by "automation," has tremendous consequences for those who man the machines. These consequences, both good and bad, we are only beginning to realize. Here in this brief selection are dramatically illustrated some of the concerns and insecurities aroused in workers by the new industrial developments.

* From *The Reporter*, Vol. 9, No. 5 (September 29, 1953), 28–32. Copyright 1953 by The Fortnightly Publishing Co., Inc.

The author is Assistant Professor of Sociology, Syracuse University. As a graduate student at the University of Chicago, he did social-psychological research on political influence in an industrial community. He also worked in a Gary, Indiana steel mill.

I first became acquainted with the technology of the future, which is rapidly becoming established in our present factories, while I was still on production in a Gary, Indiana, mill. It was part way through an evening shift's long lunchtime that a friend and fellow worker, Walt, suddenly closed his lunchbox and said: "Hurry up and finish feeding your face. I'll show you a machine that can make six-hour days." He got to his feet.

Now what? I wondered as I hurried after him. We walked quickly through several departments I had already visited and then, as we moved through a large passageway into what looked like a new shed and a very big one, I heard a loud roaring. We turned the corner and Walt made a wide-swinging gesture with his big hands: "There's the greatest hunk of machinery you ever saw!"

I could hardly hear him above the noise of this, the mill's newest supermachine. Although I had worked in eight different factories and had been through a score of plants, I was unprepared for the fantastic yet obviously real engine of production we faced. Like the perennial time traveler of science fiction, I gaped in awe at this sample of a new technology.

Tremendous towers of steel, showing here and there tiny brilliant flashes from fires within, rose fifty feet above us, as high as many city apartment buildings. Walt led me beside the giant and pointed down. I leaned over and looked into a shaft extending deeper below the vibrating floor where we stood than the double basements of some department stores. A speeding ribbon of steel about a yard wide flashed down from the heights of the superstructure into the depths of the pit and up again. It was part of some three thousand feet of continuous sheet steel, ranging in thickness from one fifteen-thousandth of an inch to half that, which rushed endlessly through the various processes, disappearing into one roaring chamber after another, reappearing as a taut silver gleam here and there between the machine's titanic parts.

Just opposite us huge electric motors, a small part of the supermachine's many muscles, were winding the fast-flowing steel ribbon into a giant coil that might weigh ten or twelve tons when completed and ready to be hauled away by one of the factory's mechanical beasts of burden, the big fork-lift tractors. It was difficult to see the details at the other end, over three hundred feet away, where similar but untreated coils were being unwound to feed the machine.

"Some setup!" Walt shouted to me above the din. "They call it the continuous annealer. Only a couple like it in existence. That's the factory of the future, boy!"

A good steady worker, this continuous annealer has just enough brains to do its job—heating steel and then cooling it again. Its nervous system comprises a large basement full of panelboards of electronic equipment—meters, vacuum tubes, relays, resistors, condensers, and transformers.

Miles of wiring and special measuring devices such as electric eyes co-ordinate its gigantic yet delicate efforts and report to the human beings concerned what goes on within its awesome guts.

The monster's boss, the man supervising the operations on that turn, watched its work on a master control panel which stretched along the opposite wall. He walked about checking the recording charts and instrument dials, occasionally giving instructions to the various men attending the machine by means of a booming public-address system.

"It's still pretty much of an experiment," Walt continued, "Lot of bugs to get ironed out. It's still on the company's restricted list. They don't let out much information on what it can do or what it'll be doing when they get it perfected."

. . . . .

THE "FEEL" OF STEEL

Marshall, a giant Negro with whom I worked, epitomizes the old way and the old skills. He began work in the mill on jobs that demanded great physical strength. He stacked sheets of steel and tinplate, lifting a pile weighing three hundred pounds and slamming it down with such force that the compression of the air pounded the eardrums of a bystander. (It also prevented friction between the plates from binding them for that bare instant he needed to jiggle them into a neat pile.)

Today few men handle heavy materials directly. Marshall drives a big fork-lift tractor, but that mechanical handler of materials is essentially an extension and enlargement of his own powerful body as he hurries about picking up and setting down four and five thousand pounds of steel with the same deft competence with which he once handled three hundred pounds with his own hands. Indeed, he calls the tractor his horse, and when its batteries are low he reports that it is tired. Like Marshall, the operator of a lathe or plane or press "feels" through and with his machine the material with which he works. The finest and most refined products of our familiar conventional technology are but large, powerful, and complicated extensions of the operator's body and the skills he has acquired. Like the good ditchdigger who uses the simplest of tools, the industrial craftsman has needed experience more than theory and accumulated his technique through years of practice. Under such a system, promotion by seniority works well.

SERVING THE GIANT

. . . "Of course, they'll always need *me*," a thin, wiry mechanic with over twenty years' service told me during a long conversation on a slow night turn. "All this new machinery just means more work for maintenance. But I know guys with more know-how in one hand than you'll ever have, guys who started on production when I hired in, and they're back hooking with the cranes. 'Cause what they know isn't worth a damn any more and they're too old to start studyin' the books. Listen, this thing's just getting started! Some day the only people in this damn mill will be us mechanics, you electricians, the bright boys who push the buttons, and the fellows who sweep the floors. And the bosses. Don't forget the bosses! They don't seem to be able to invent a machine that can sit in an office all day with its feet on a desk."

He spat and got up from the bench where we were sitting to go back to his job. "Hell!" he added reflectively before he walked away, "even the sweepers ride around on machines now." . . .

57. AUTOMATION AND THE FUTURE SOCIETY *

ARNOLD M. ROSE

The preceding selection attempted to give the reader some feeling for the worker's perspective on automation. This selection approaches the subject from the point of view of its meaning for all *segments of society. It should be read not solely for its portrayal of change in a single important social institution but also as an illustration of a* method *for examining the impact of major changes which can occur in any social institution.*

* Excerpts from Arnold M. Rose, "Automation and the Future Society," reprinted from *Commentary*, Vol. 21, No. 3 (March, 1956), 274–280. Copyright American Jewish Committee. This is a condensation of a longer unpublished paper, "The Coming Industrial Revolution and Future Social Change."

The author (b. 1918) is Professor of Sociology, University of Minnesota. During World War II he served as a statistician with the War Department. Major field of interest: social psychology. Author: *The Negro in America; Union Solidarity; Theory and Method in the Social Sciences;* coauthor: *Mental Health and Mental Disorders.*

A number of technologists and economists have predicted that we are on the verge of a series of radical changes in industrial technology which will revolutionize productive processes. The consequences, in terms of human relations and social institutions, of such a revolution are certain to be enormous. But it is not so easy to foresee these consequences. Predictions in this area have to be tentative and subject to constant modification, since they are not based on careful measurement of experimentally controlled observations, but (1) on analysis of social changes following *previous* technological innovations, and (2) on our general knowledge of the structure and dynamics of contemporary society.

. . . . .

The technological elements of the new revolution look to be, first, energy derived from fissionable materials that are easily transportable; and second, the introduction of those processes of machine production known as "automation." A new source of energy involves no basic change in the *manner* of production, but will profoundly affect cost, location, speed, and other factors.

Automation will have at least three generalized types of effect on the manner of production, according to George B. Baldwin and George P. Schultz . . . :

1. The linking together of conventionally separate manufacturing operations into lines of continuous production, along which the product will move "untouched by human hands." This development, which depends primarily on mechanical engineering for its adoption, we shall refer to simply as "integration," a term already in wide use in the metal-working industries.

2. The use of "feed-back" control devices, or servo-mechanisms, which will allow individual operations to be performed without human control. "Feed-back" refers to a built-in automatic device that will compare the way in which work is actually being done with the way in which it is supposed to be done, and then automatically make any adjustments necessary. "Feed-back" technology is primarily dependent not on mechanical but on electrical engineering and techniques.

3. The development of general- and special-purpose computing machines capable of recording and storing data (usually in the form of numbers) and of performing both simple and complex mathematical operations with such data. This, too, depends primarily on new developments in electrical engineering.

Automation will not affect all industries; and even those in which it can be used are not likely to rely upon it completely. Some industries are more amenable to automation than others—notably those engaged in the production and assembling of parts, those engaged in processing (e.g. of chemicals, flour, oil), and those relying heavily on bookkeeping (e.g. insurance, banking, public utilities). Industries already largely automatic (e.g. canning, oil processing), those in which production requires constant judgment or irregular variation (e.g. slaughtering, construction), and those producing goods the demands for which are continually subject to changes in taste and fashion (e.g. the garment industry) will be least affected by the trends toward geographic decentralization and the concentration of ownership. Agriculture, mining, transportation, service industries, and retailing will be little affected directly by automation.

Most factories that automatize will not do so, as I have said, completely. The engineers think it is often feasible to automatize 80 per cent, say, of a plant's equipment, but the remaining 20 per cent tends to be too expensive to automatize. Hence automation will not come immediately or completely in the near future. . . .

On the assumption that automation and nuclear power will be introduced to a significant extent during the next twenty or thirty years, what effects are they likely to have on the structure of industry, the labor market, the lives of workers, education, government, international relations, and even on what might be called the "mental life" of society?

Industry should become less dependent on heavy fuels that are expensive to transport, like coal, oil, and water power, and on unskilled manpower in large supply; hence it should become more mobile and easier to decentralize. The present need to be close to markets and sources of raw materials will remain, however, so that decentralization will probably not be radical. Existing investments in real estate and plain inertia will probably serve further to slow down the rate of decentralization. But gradual decentralization there will be—to avoid high land costs, high taxes, congestion, and other undesirable aspects of our present large urban industrial concentrations. Another effect of automation will be to diminish the benefits to industry of moving into areas that offer a large supply of cheap, unskilled labor—the South, for instance. The skilled workers required for automation, and the schools for training skilled workers, are more readily available in the North and Midwest, and the wages for skilled workers show little regional differential. Given the advantage of the proximity of the large Northern markets, it is likely that industries that automatize will tend to locate in the North.

An economist, Wassily Leontief, has made a careful study of the costs of automation and finds it relatively inexpensive, hence capable of being introduced rapidly. . . .

. . . . . .

But larger firms will be readier to spare both the time, however short, and the capital for the change-over; they will also be in a better position to take advantage of the possibilities of decentralization. Thus automation may encourage concentration of ownership unless the government steps in to assist small firms with loans, information, etc., etc.

There will be a need for new kinds of skills, and a sharp drop in the demand for unskilled labor. To keep employed, many unskilled or semi-skilled workers will require schooling, and some categories of skilled workers will have to be retrained. It seems nonsense to expect wide-spread permanent unemployment as a consequence of machines taking the place of workers. Workers released from one job or industry will be required in another. But they will be needed with different skills and perhaps in different places, so that temporary unemployment and dis-location are likely.

Older workers will suffer greater hardship. Since the expense of their retraining will net a smaller total return to employers, they are less likely to be given the opportunity for re-education. Untrained older workers will either be downgraded, or—if pensions become available at a lower age—retired earlier. On the other hand, the retirement age for the worker retrained to operate automatic machinery may be raised be-cause of the ensuing shortage of skilled labor—one that will last for many decades—and because work itself will become easier physically than it is now.

Some categories of female labor will find it harder to obtain the kind of unskilled employment now available to them because unskilled and incidental clerical and factory jobs will be greatly reduced in number. (Waitresses and saleswomen, however, will be unaffected by automation.) Women are also less likely to be offered training as machinists and maintenance workers, which are the jobs that will be most plentiful in automatized factories.

The general upgrading of the average skill levels of workers may be expected to have some effect on unions. Skilled workers have traditionally favored strong unions and, given the need of labor in general for security amid the dislocations brought on by automation, they will probably be-come unionized in increasing number. Unions will probably also be strengthened by an increase in their functions. At the same time, some of their traditional *bêtes noires* will be eliminated: piecework pay, incen-tive systems, the speedup, and other features associated with individual production. Also, as part of the long-term trend associated with increasing productivity, the service industries will (as Colin Clark foresees) pre-empt a steadily increasing proportion of the labor force; service workers have been the hardest to unionize, but may become less so as more and more of them are recruited from previously unionized labor.

The great rise in productivity may be expected to raise real incomes and the general standard of living sharply, while further reducing hours of work. Such a change will, of course, have innumerable secondary effects which can only be guessed at. Two are particularly worth speculating about.

The continuing rise in the standard of living will reduce still further the consumption differentials between classes, especially as automatically produced goods are expected to be of higher quality. The lower-income groups will be able to afford more of the things now available only to the wealthy. And there will be a greater flowering of leisure-time activities. Present trends suggest a considerable variation in this development: not only will there be more recreation and social participation of the kinds already familiar to us, but small "side-line" businesses will multiply, along with "do-it-yourself" work around the home, gardening, "creative art," etc., etc. Since many people are not yet prepared to cope with an abundance of leisure, its sudden increase will probably provoke a great deal of boredom and dissatisfaction at first. New small industries and occupations purely exploitative in purpose may arise.

Education, too, will of necessity be greatly affected by automation. Industries that automatize will in most cases be compelled to train employees themselves, probably under the joint supervision of management and unions, while the training of young people for their future careers will probably remain in the hands of the kinds of schools now in existence. Pressure is already being exerted to change these schools to meet the needs of the new industrialization. At the secondary school level, the need for technical training will be greater than ever before. Since teachers adequately trained in technological disciplines are in increasingly short supply because of the relatively low salaries in their field, not only will teachers' salaries be raised (by Federal or industry-aid plans), but differential salaries by subjects may be expected to appear.

At the university level, the rise of engineering, natural science, and social science may be expected to continue at the expense of the humanities and "education." The humanities will be able to retain their importance in general education by subordinating themselves to science as *the* major subject. But managers and engineers will more than ever need the breadth that only the humanities can provide. Higher education will continue to be increasingly important for social mobility. Leadership in industry, government, and civic life generally will depend more than ever on the ability at least to understand, if not guide or manage, the newer technology and the social readjustments it will entail.

The effects on government of the changes in technology will be secondary insofar as they will derive from the effects on industry and labor. If industry and population are decentralized, the many material and cultural services now provided by municipalities will have to be assumed by state and Federal government, or by new metropolitan and/or regional authorities not yet in existence. The exodus to the suburbs is already straining the cities' capacity to collect taxes to provide the services which suburbanites still use. If industrial ownership becomes concentrated among a decreasing number of firms, government controls in industry may be expected to multiply. Since the new "monopolies" will, presumably, not be inefficient or try to restrict production—in fact, they can be expected to do the contrary—the new government controls will move in the direction set by the Federal Communications Commission and the Securities and Exchange Commission, rather than in that of the old-fashioned "trust-busting" of the Sherman and Clayton acts.

A broadened social security program—as safeguard against unemployment, interruptions of income during retraining periods, and in old age—is already being recognized as essential to personal and social stability. Social security will become even more necessary with increasing technological unemployment and the loss of incidental privileges such as pension rights, vacation rights, seniority, etc., etc. Probably not all of the different kinds of security benefits will be provided by the government—some unions have already moved to require industry to provide severance pay and a "guaranteed annual wage."

Government will play a new role in education, under the pressure of industry and labor alike. Federal aid to education is about to become a reality, and in the coming years it may have to provide a major part of school revenue. It is even likely that the Federal government will grant increasing funds to private colleges; it has already begun to do so in the form of research subsidies and agricultural extension work.

Internal migration policies, and agencies to implement them, will probably become necessary in all industrialized countries. Information about job opportunities, job requirements, and wage levels can parallel the crop-reporting service the Federal government has long provided. Small loans to pay for transportation of families and household goods cannot be provided by the usual lending agencies, limited as they are by their collection facilities and by state law; a Federal agency will probably have to be set up for this purpose. Social services to provide aid in finding housing and in helping migrants adjust to new communities will be greatly in demand. These and other related innovations can be handled by a "Division of Migration Service" in one of the existing departments of the Federal government.

A major factor in world politics today is the difference in productive capacity between the industrialized and the so-called "underdeveloped" countries. The new technology will only increase the difference. The first effect of the newer technology will be to make it even more difficult for the underdeveloped countries to "catch up" with the West. The abundance of capital and of workers with specialized skills required for automation are lacking in backward countries. But if capital and training are provided for them by more advanced countries like our own, they may be able to modernize, and even ultra-modernize, their economies with relative swiftness.

* * * * *

Automation will also be helped in underdeveloped countries by the fact that most of their towns and cities are small and scattered. Automatic production does not need the large urban agglomerations developed in the West under industrialism over the past one hundred and fifty years. Introduced into hitherto unindustrialized countries, automation can avoid the dislocations caused by extreme and rapid urbanization.

* * * * *

We have heard much of the ruinous effects of over-specialization and the meaninglessness of work on the assembly line. The fourth industrial revolution may be expected to check and even reverse this tendency. The typical new worker will be skilled and technically educated, not the unskilled or semi-skilled hand that the earlier industrial revolutions called for. In an automatized factory he will be able to "see" a given productive process from beginning to end. His main job will be to control, tend, and repair machines, and this active role will not permit the machines to set the rhythm of his work.

There is a dangerous tendency current to treat automation and the technological changes it will entail as things mysterious and superhuman. Scientists, engineers, and some businessmen are among those who most frequently conjure up such spectres. Labor leaders have tended on the whole to avoid Sunday-supplement language in dealing with the subject. Economists and other social scientists seem the most restrained.

The mathematician Norbert Wiener (of "cybernetics" fame) has perhaps been the one most guilty of using scare language in speaking of automatic machinery and its effects. A typical and widely quoted book *The Human Use of Human Beings* (Houghton Mifflin, 1950) says: "It is perfectly clear that this [automation] will produce an unemployment situation in comparison with which . . . the depression of the 30's will seem a pleasant joke." Another mathematician, John Von Neumann, has "proved mathematically" that a machine can be constructed which will "reproduce itself" and that its offspring will likewise be capable of "reproduction," but by this he only means that a machine could be constructed and programmed so that, when the proper parts are inserted in it, the machine would assemble them into another machine just like itself.

A tendency to personify automatic machines by lending them the attributes of human beings likewise serves to make them seem more frightening. Edmund Callis Berkeley has entitled his book on the new computing machines *Giant Brains*. The machines themselves—which, after all, do nothing but add and subtract at a tremendous speed—have been given such names as "Mark" and "Edna," which are not frightening in themselves but do imply that such machines have human powers. At least two electronic processes have been described by their inventors as "learning." Out of the Bell Telephone Laboratories has come a mechanical "mouse" that can "learn" to find a piece of cheese in a maze with increasing speed. (The first time this little mobile electronic gadget bumps into the walls of the maze almost at random, but because it records these "errors" it is able the second time around to thread the maze without a false move.) At the Cambridge Mathematical Laboratory in England, Dr. Maurice V. Wilks has invented an electronic device that can be "conditioned" gradually to respond to only one out of all the digits; this is also described as "learning." Without disparaging such devices, an eminent neurologist, Professor Warren McCulloch of the University of Illinois, has estimated (New York *Times*, August 8, 1954) that to build a gadget with as much "intelligence" as an earthworm, it would take all the electronic power that could be generated by Niagara Falls, and would require all that cataract's water to cool the electronic tubes.

. . . . .

There will probably be fewer heavy, dirty, and boring jobs in automatized factories than in the equivalent contemporary plants, and factory work generally will be cleaner and safer. Many workers will be able to wear white collars instead of overalls. John Diebold goes so far as to say:

In an odd and entirely unexpected way, automation may bring us back to the human and psychological values of the self-respecting craftsman. Electrical and mechanical repair work, instrument adjustment, and general mechanical tinkering can provide challenges, pleasures, and satisfactions very much like those enjoyed by the swordsmith or cabinetmaker of old.

. . . . .

. . . such downright unpleasant jobs as those in the mining and slaughtering industries will probably not be susceptible to automatization in the next few decades. But hours of work will go down in all industries, and this will make even the most unpleasant of occupations more bearable. The mental life of the worker of the future will be much more determined by what he does during his leisure time than what he does during his working hours. As his job ceases to dominate his life, political, family, religious, and "cultural" activities may take on greater significance. It is difficult to see how a democratic state can channel leisure-time activities, except by making the facilities for them, whatever their nature, more freely available. But it is likely that the things that fill the leisure time of the average citizen will shape the future to a greater extent than any other set of factors.

All in all, the net prognosis for the coming industrial revolution under automation seems to be for a happier, more vital people, not a Huxleyan "brave new world" of mechanical monstrousness. Planning, foresight, and a modicum of intelligent action on the part of the public and private organizations should see to that.

58. VEBLEN *

ANONYMOUS

Some of Veblen's colorful phrases are probably much more widely known than his name. Here the reader has an opportunity to become more completely acquainted both with the man and with the broad range of his ideas. Staff writers from Fortune, *after systematically examining the writings of Veblen and of those who have written about him, present in a popular vein his theories about business as a social institution.*

Thorstein Veblen, the Wisconsin-born social philosopher who died obscurely in California in 1929, did what every thinking man would like to do if he had the time, the tenacity, and the mental endowment. Hungry for knowledge and understanding, but absorbed in the problems of their own lives and generations, most men never acquire more than scattered fragments of mankind's immense and constantly growing store of learning. Even the scholars for the most part are forced to live out their lives in the valleys, tending some single one of the narrow gardens into which academic specialists have marked off man's study of himself and his world. Veblen was the one man in a million—or in a thousand million—with courage and capacity to do more. Taking all knowledge for his province, he climbed a mountaintop and surveyed the whole life of mankind.

Because, in his sweeping view, men's beliefs and conduct are shaped primarily by the ways in which they earn a living and acquire wealth, Veblen is often classified as an economist. But his powerful, searching, original mind ranged far beyond the conventional limits of economics.

* Reprinted from the December, 1947, issue of *Fortune*, 133–202, by Special Permission of the Editors; Copyright 1947 Time, Inc.

He investigated art and religion and education, fashions and social customs, government and war and peace. He delved deep in history, literature, anthropology, psychology, biology, technology, the physical sciences. He has been called "the last man who knew everything."

But he was no scholarly magpie. Discovering new relationships of cause and effect, he wove everything he learned into a critical, coherent account of the development of Western civilization. His purpose was to understand the society he lived in, to explain the goals men strive for and the reasons for their striving, and to point out the goals they might attain.

What he saw and reported from his lonely peak was disturbing and unwelcome to his contemporaries. Most of them simply ignored it, and tried to ignore him. Most people still do. To Americans in general, he is only a name, vaguely identified as a Gilded Age satirist of business and the rich, a radical and an eccentric whose reputation for polysyllabic profundity frightens most readers away from even his famous first book, *The Theory of the Leisure Class. . . .*

Yet Veblen has already won the philosopher's reward defined by the late Justice Holmes: "men who never heard of him" are "moving to the measure of his thought." Every American who is skeptical of business glories, suspicious of great enrichment, contemptuous of social climbing and wealthy ostentation, dubious of the merits of keeping up with the Joneses, probably owes something to Thorstein Veblen's intellectual adventuring. More than any other single thinker except Karl Marx, he inspired and shaped the modern intellectual attack on business and the values of a business-dominated civilization.

That attack, currently still at a relative war-prosperity ebb after its latest depression flood, stems from many intellectual springs. Even before the New Deal, the streams of pre-Marxian socialism, Populism, Progressivism, Marxism, and Brandeisian antagonism to bigness and monopoly were so intermingled that it was difficult to determine each one's precise influence. But it seems clear that Thorstein Veblen's attitude and vocabulary were major contributions to the common cause.

Veblen, though a blaster of economic complacency, was not first in the field. Marx and his predecessors, who strongly influenced Veblen but never converted him to full acceptance of any socialist system, had touched off their charges long before *The Theory of the Leisure Class* appeared. But conventional U.S. economists at the turn of the century still regarded business-as-usual with uncritical calm. Accepting the prevailing attitudes and practices of businessmen as the working out of immutable natural laws, they held that all goods and services (except frankly criminal ones) are socially valuable simply because they are in demand. Almost their sole concerns were to describe the workings of the system, and to figure out the precise balance of painful acquisition and pleasurable consumption that gave each article or service its market value.

Like Marx, Veblen declared that economics must be an evolutionary science. Following the trail blazed by Darwin and Huxley and Sumner, he insisted that economists, too, should study the origins of institutions; they should examine the social as well as the market value not only of goods and services but also of business practices. They should, for example, not stop with asking how a stock exchange or a holding company works, but should go on to ask what human needs and notions shaped its birth and development, and whether it is still in fact necessary or useful to the common welfare.

That such an approach to economic problems is now a matter of course is in no small measure a result of the fact that Thorstein Veblen spent his life asking and answering just such questions. ". . . As for the professional economists of the present generation and the fundamental aspirations of current economics," wrote Horace M. Kallen in his obituary of Veblen in *The Forward*, "they owe to Veblen more than to any single mind of his own time." Economist Paul T. Homan wrote shortly before Veblen's death: "It falls little beyond the truth to say that almost all the new leads in economic thinking which have been fruitfully followed during the past twenty years are in some degree directly traceable to him."

But Veblen's questions and answers, brilliant and stimulating as they are, have probably had less popular influence than the manner of his asking and his answering. Marx had already put much the same questions, and returned answers very different in kind but basically similar in substance. But Marx's attack was ferocious, and his conclusions openly revolutionary. The verbal blunderbuss of an avowed enemy and would-be destroyer of the capitalist system could—until his disciples seized control of the world's largest country—be safely ignored by capitalist professors and businessmen.

Veblen's approach, on the other hand, was one of aloof and urbane irony. Some vitriol crept into his later books, but in his earlier writing, and especially in *The Theory of the Leisure Class*, he seems to be examining the rich and powerful of the earth, and their envious imitators, with the detachment of a worldly zoologist explaining the antics of a cageful of monkeys. The revolutionary implications are there, but they are masked in a wondrously involved and thoroughly delightful style, deadpan, sesquipedalian, mock-pedantic, and sometimes uproariously funny, that has won Veblen some acclaim as a literary craftsman. With it he made "leisure-class" credos and conduct seem not only antisocial but more than slightly ridiculous.

The professors might try to ignore him, or dismiss him with curt contempt, but neither they nor the world at large could long ignore the insidious sting of such great phrases as "conspicuous leisure," "conspicuous consumption," "conspicuous waste," "invidious distinction," "the kept classes." It was these phrases and this attitude that captured the imaginations of youthful intellectuals rebelling against the materialism of American life at the century's turn. Gleefully they hurled Veblen's barbs at the rich and mighty and pretentious through Teddy Roosevelt's Square Deal and Woodrow Wilson's New Freedom. By the 1920's a knowledge of Veblen had become standard intellectual equipment for U.S. social rebels. The Veblen influence shone clear and strong in the writings of such critics as Stuart Chase, Lewis Mumford, Max Lerner, John Chamberlain, and Sinclair Lewis, such future New Dealers as Henry Wallace, Isador Lubin, Rex Tugwell, and Adolph Berle.

Writers of the *Nation—New Republic* school might be inspired by Marx's militant program, but Veblen was the man to quote. Whether they aimed at revolution or reform, the intellectuals knew that, in that era of prosperity, sophisticated skepticism and urbane ridicule were far more effective weapons than savage denunciation. Through journalists and fiction writers, the Veblen attitude spread in ever widening circles. Then, with the coming of depression, it burst its intellectual bounds entirely and suspicion of big business became a national fashion.

While the Battle of Business raged in the thirties, it was impossible for any business partisan to read Veblen with judicious calm. During the present lull, it may be profitable to investigate the man and the philosophy that produced the satire.

ODD MAN

Even his admirers, calling the man "strange," "aloof," "remote," "complex," have never pretended to understand Veblen fully. But his bias, at least, seems readily explained by the facts of his unhappy life. The definitive biography, a distinguished work of intellectual history, is *Thorstein Veblen and His America*, by Joseph Dorfman. It makes plain that he was always an alien spirit in the U.S., never at home in it, never at ease.

Born on a raw Wisconsin farm in 1857 and reared on another in Minnesota, Veblen was one of nine children of poor Norwegian immigrants. From the first he was set apart from the native community. The frontier "Norskie" settlers of his youth dwelt in clannish isolation, preserving their language and customs, distrusting their Yankee neighbors and in turn despised by them.

Veblen's sharp, curious mind made him an alien, too, among his parents' stolid countrymen. Even to them he was an "odd" youth— irreverent, jeering, sarcastic, unpopular. But he was enough a part of the midwestern community to share deeply in the late-nineteenth-century agrarian unrest that, mixed with the yeast of pre-Marxian socialism brought by the immigrants of 1848, produced the Populist revolt and the continuing radicalism of Wisconsin and Minnesota. Veblen's temperament made him uncommonly receptive to the bitter resentment of the railroads, and the deep suspicion of what he was to call the "massive vested interests that move obscurely in the background" in Wall Street, which dominated that time and place.

Poverty and lack of English helped bar him from a normal social life at Carleton College. Lonely, shy, and debt-ridden, but still as contentious and acid-tongued as ever, he went on to Johns Hopkins and Yale for a Ph.D., hoping to become a teacher of philosophy. His rustic manners and skeptical beliefs, plus the fact that divinity students were then preferred as philosophy professors, closed academic doors to him. Pleading ill health, he went back to Minnesota in defeat, to live off his family (and later his wife's family) for seven miserable years.

In 1891, aged thirty-four, he determined to make a fresh start and went off to Cornell to study the social sciences. Wearing a coonskin cap and corduroy trousers, with long hair, weak drawl, anemic looks, and shambling gait, he was still a bizarre figure in the campus world. But the years of "reading and loafing" had not been so idle as they seemed to his long-suffering kinsmen. Ranging from Icelandic mythology to Cretan history and beyond, he had stored up an impressive knowledge of man's habits and beliefs from earliest times, and thought deeply and originally about them. The quality of his mind and the sweep of his learning at last won him recognition and a $520-a-year academic foothold at the new University of Chicago.

Veblen became a brilliant teacher, but never a popular one. To a few receptive students he gave the incomparable exhilaration that comes of glimpsing a new pattern in the swirling complexities of human life. But he was irked by classroom routine and impatient of dullness and ignorance; he mumbled through most of his lectures. Equally irked by the proprieties, he was the kind of defiant campus eccentric who keeps tongues clacking happily in faculty clubs and parlors. All his life he had trouble getting and holding a job. Embroilment with two wives and a succession of mistresses ("But what is one to do if the woman moves in on you?" he asked) forced him to move on from Chicago to Stanford to Missouri, and finally to the metropolitan haven of New York City, where in the years of World War I and after he helped edit *The Dial* and lectured at the New School for Social Research. Everywhere he left behind him legends of his unconventional ménages, his ill-fitting clothes and monogrammed cigarettes, his unmade beds and primitive dishwashing machine (barrel plus garden hose).

Veblen never earned more than $2,400 a year by his teaching, and the royalties from his books added only $500 a year at their peak. When the New School fell into financial straits, he was able to stay on only because a former student anonymously paid his salary. Finally, in 1926, he went back to his mountain cabin in California, "a deserted and lonely man," as Lewis Mumford recalls, "feeble, ill, pale, wistful, demonic, proud." He died less than three months before the Great Crash came to fulfill his prophecies of capitalistic disaster.

IS HUMAN NATURE NATURAL?

Veblen's writings revolve around his contrast between the predatory and the productive traits and activities of mankind. Developing this theme, he insisted on a sharp distinction between "business" and "industry." Industry, he said, is the productive process of making goods; business is the predatory process of making profits.

Veblen hailed technologists and engineers, devoted to efficient production, as the real industrialists. Businessmen—in which category he lumped absentee owners, major executives, financiers, salesmen, advertising men, stockbrokers, promoters, and all others not directly concerned with production and essential distribution—he called "parasites" and worse than useless. Intent on "getting something for nothing," they impede the flow of goods by killing off competitors and "sabotaging" the industry they control through a "conscious withdrawal of efficiency" to keep goods scarce and prices high.

The Veblen critique of business would be indisputably true—if it were applied to a world wholly composed of unselfish, non-competitive, cooperative human beings with plenty of everything for everybody. Confronted with the simple facts of existing human nature and material production, his whole argument seems to collapse. But it is precisely at this point that Veblen really begins to argue.

Human nature, he declares, is not foreordained and unchangeable. Seen in the perspective of man's whole life on the planet, what we regard as fixed characteristics of human nature are simply traits that men have developed in the process of adapting themselves to their environment. Since environment constantly changes as men evolve new ways of providing themselves with life's necessities and luxuries, it might be expected that human nature would change with it.

The flowering of the machine process in the Industrial Revolution, for example, has made it possible for the first time in history to produce enough goods so that every human being can have all the material things he needs for a comfortable, healthful life. Hence there is no longer any material reason why men should not stop their quarrelling and settle down to peaceable production and sharing of that possible abundance.

But, said Veblen, the adaptation of human nature to this new environment has been and is still being grievously impeded by the "leisure class"—the rich and powerful of the earth. Over the centuries they have developed and still vigorously defend a massive fabric of codes and institutions. These are designed, consciously or unconsciously, to perpetuate the selfishness, pride, greed, competitiveness, ruthlessness, clannishness, and other traits that human beings developed when there was not enough to go around, when men did not know how to produce enough for everybody and the strong took from the weak. Only men's loyalty to these outworn codes and institutions keeps them from entering at last into a world of peace and abundance.

This is the thesis that emerges when one has penetrated the thickets of Veblen's prose; this is the vision of past and future he saw from his lonely mountaintop. To those who understand it, his satirical bitterness becomes in turn understandable. It is the bitterness of the prophet against a world that refused to listen to him, and failed to understand him; against codes of social standing, business success, luxurious living, dress, etiquette, sport, patriotism, and institutions of business, government, education, religion, and all others that, in their existing forms and inspirations, he saw as stumbling blocks on the road to a new life for mankind. This is why, beginning in *The Theory of the Leisure Class*, he devoted all of his immense learning and penetrating imagination to "destructive" explanations of how and why these codes and institutions have developed.

THE BIRTH OF PRIDE

Far back in the beginnings of time, he wrote, before the dawn of history, primitive men actually did live together in sluggish good will. They were peaceful, indolent, non-competitive, mutually helpful. There was no urgent reason why they should not be; their needs and tastes were few and simple. A man might keep a club or trinket or piece of clothing for his personal use, but that was the extent of individual ownership. Everything else belonged to the group and was shared in common.

Then, as humans multiplied and ranging hunters clashed with members of strange groups, the predatory era dawned. Fighting men began capturing and bringing home enemy women. At first the captives were simply trophies of victory, and their capture brought glory not to the captor but to his group.

But, as the centuries passed, the beginning of handicraft and agriculture brought more and more work into human life. Women, the weaker sex, had always done whatever drudgery was involved in preparing primitive food and clothing, so it was only natural that the captives should be put to use at these new tasks. The trophies acquired productive value.

There was some point, now, in the captor's wanting to keep them for himself. The institution of marriage began to take shape, as households with a male head were established. Since strength and wiliness were required to capture women from enemy men, the possession of a number of them came to be a mark of their captor's prowess. He enjoyed not only their personal service and the products of their work, but also the esteem and envy of his fellows.

This, says Veblen, was probably the origin of individual ownership "as a conventional right or equitable claim." With it, because all useful work except hunting was assigned to women and other inferiors (later including captive men as well as women), came the beginning of men's feeling that productive work is inherently shameful, a thing with which no superior man will soil his fingers or his dignity. Thus began what Veblen calls "conspicuous leisure," i.e., leisure enjoyed not for its own sake but as a visible mark of the idler's superiority. And thus arose an "invidious distinction" [1] between the leisure class and persons forced to work for a living.

With the establishment of this difference between persons, the "regime of status" was born. Social emulation—the desire to equal or excel another in social standing—entered the world as a major motive in human conduct.

But man, says Veblen, is by nature an agent. He is impelled by a sense of purpose and so "possessed of a taste for effective work, and a distaste for futile effort . . . a sense of the merit of serviceability or efficiency and of the demerit of futility, waste, or incapacity." This "instinct of workmanship," developed in the peaceful ages before the predatory era began, is forever at war with man's acquired sense of the dignity of leisure. He cannot rest content with mere idleness.

The leisure class hence needed something to do, some occupation with a sense of purpose and accomplishment about it that offered rewards for efficient performance, yet carried no slavish stain of productive industry. Hunting and warfare were naturals for the purpose. While it remained primarily a source of food, hunting of course dangerously resembled useful industry. But, Veblen hastens to point out, it was not really industry; like war, it was exploit, seizure by force. Other occupations found to meet the leisure-class requirements of purposeful, nonproductive employment were government, priestly service, sports.

Because these were the activities of superior men, they came to be regarded as "honorable"—a concept that in primitive societies "seems to to connote nothing else than assertion of superior force." For thousands of years, while productive labor remained the despised (and therefore

---

[1] *Invidious*, adj. 1. *Tending to excite odium, ill will, or envy; likely to give offense; esp., unjustly and irritatingly discriminating;* as, invidious *distinctions . . .* 2. *Worthy of envy; enviable;* as, an invidious *income*—Webster.

irksome) province of women and slaves, efficiency in these leisure-class pursuits filled the performer with pride and the beholders with admiration and envy. Human beings naturally grew to admire also the "manly virtues" required for success in these pursuits: ferocity, ruthlessness, selfishness, clannishness, shrewdness, trickery.

Hand in hand with conspicuous leisure and the regime of status came "conspicuous consumption"—the accumulation and consumption of goods not solely for their utility but in part, or wholly, to impress the neighbors. Here simple expensiveness is the touchstone. But as chiefs and kings and nobles vied with each other to display more and better-trained and richer-liveried servants, greater houses and castles, more resplendent clothes and jewels, rarer and more abundant food, conspicuous leisure and consumption combined to produce "conspicuous waste" as a ruling canon of leisure-class life.

Veblen defined economic waste as any expenditure of time or effort or material that does not contribute to "the physical comfort and fullness of life" of the community or mankind. The resulting article or activity may, he concedes, give the individual genuine pleasure, and so not be wasteful in the conventional sense. But the pleasure, he argues, derives less from the thing itself than from the prestige attached to it. According to the code of conspicuous waste, the more wasteful any visible activity or service or article is, the more it redounds to the prestige of the consumer, as a display not only of his wealth but also of his contempt for productive effort. Thus fox hunting bestows more social prestige than deer hunting (the deer can be eaten), a butler or footman more than a cook, handmade shoes or lace more than machine-made.

These are the notions whose history Veblen examines in *The Theory of the Leisure Class.* He is far less concerned with conscious "social climbing" or with the rich themselves than with the way their standards have burrowed into the human subconscious and shaped conventional ideas of what is right and good and beautiful.

WOMEN AND SERVANTS

For a long time after captive women began to be put to use, the wife (or chief wife) of the leisure-class household remained little more than its chief servant. But as the honorific value of conspicuous leisure rose, it began to seem more and more essential to the prestige of the head of the house that his wife should not demean him by stooping to any form of useful labor.

This feeling grew even more widespread when the social value of male conspicuous leisure—or rather the social disgrace of male industry—began to diminish. Two historic developments made it socially permissible for a gentleman to go to work (though still not to actual production). The spread of law was one; it grew increasingly difficult and dangerous for predatory men simply to grab what they wanted. And the Industrial Revolution, changing the world's economy, made it possible for forceful men of the lower classes to rise to wealth by methods other than armed conquest. The older aristocracy, whose ancestors had secured their wealth by the "honorable" means of armed force, might continue indefinitely to look down on people "in trade," but the power of wealth could not be denied.

The self-made man, however, continued to respect the older aristocracy's codes. He made his obeisance to that of conspicuous leisure increasingly at second hand, through his wife and daughters and servants. Among both old and new rich, the woman's conspicuous leisure remained a very different thing from that of the man. Like the leisure of the superfluous servant, it was designed to enhance not her own prestige but that of her master. It was, in Veblen's phrase, "vicarious leisure." Her costume, like that of the liveried butler or footman, was designed to display her master's wealth and contempt for industry not only by its obvious costliness but also by its obvious evidence that the wearer could engage in no productive activity while so clothed. Hence the corset, the long skirt, the bustle, the hoop skirt, the high heel, the towering coiffure of the eighteenth century. Hence also the artificially deformed feet of the Chinese—and the New Look. That these things are uncomfortable is of no more moment than the fact that a woman may be bored by her enforced idleness. The possessor of vicarious leisure is not intended to enjoy it.

BEAUTY AND FASHION

How does it happen that such obviously grotesque devices as the corset, the bustle, the high heel can in themselves, or in their effect, actually seem beautiful?

The "underlying norms of taste," says Veblen, were probably formed before men began trying to outdo each other in displays of wealth. According to these norms, "the requirements of beauty, simply, are for the most part best satisfied by inexpensive contrivances and structures which in a straightforward manner suggest both the office which they are to perform and the method of serving their end."

But the standards of pecuniary display have all but obliterated this "untutored" sense of beauty. Consciously or unconsciously, we admire and buy things according to their expensiveness and waste. This accounts for the vogue of dresses, houses, furniture, automobiles, etc., that are large, intricate, and ornate, obviously involving waste of labor and materials.

These things, however, are offensive to underlying tastes, to the "instinct of workmanship" that admires efficiency and dislikes futility. Hence changing fashions. "The process of developing an aesthetic nausea takes more or less time," but eventually one set of grotesqueries is swept away in favor of a new and different set.

But temporary admiration of fashionable things is not usually hypocritical. "A fancy bonnet of this year's model unquestionably appeals to our sensibilities today much more forcibly than an equally fancy bonnet of the model of last year; although when viewed in the perspective of a quarter of a century, it would, I apprehend, be a matter of the utmost difficulty to award the palm for intrinsic beauty to the one rather than to the other of these structures. So, again, it may be remarked that, considered simply in their physical juxtaposition with the human form, the high gloss of a gentleman's hat or of a patent-leather shoe has no more of intrinsic beauty than a similarly high gloss on a threadbare sleeve; and yet there is no question but that all well-bred people (in the Occidental civilized communities) instinctively and unaffectedly cleave to the one as a phenomenon of great beauty, and eschew the other as offensive to every sense to which it can appeal. It is extremely doubtful if anyone could be induced to wear such a contrivance as the high hat of civilized society, except for some urgent reason based on other than aesthetic grounds."

KEEPING UP WITH THE JONESES

So Veblen goes on through the range of human institutions, everywhere finding evidences of the way human adaptation to the new industrial environment is slowed by conspicuous leisure, conspicuous consumption, conspicuous waste. College sports, he asserts for example, glorify and perpetuate the "archaic virtues" of ferocity, trickery, and clannishness. In so doing, sports may be extremely helpful to the individual preparing for life in a predatory world. But as for their pretended benefit to general student health, he drily notes: "It has been said, not inaptly, that the relation of football to physical culture is much the same as that of the bullfight to agriculture."

Religious observances, he further declares, perpetuate the regime of status even in spiritual matters. Men act as if their God were a worldly prince. They seek to glorify Him by building conspicuously wasteful churches like castles: large, costly, richly decorated. They pay Him the servitor's tribute of vicarious leisure by refraining from work on Sunday, going to church in clothes unsuited for work, sitting in uncomfortable pews.

Veblen sums up the ruling motive of modern life as "pecuniary emulation." Men work primarily, he says, to earn a living. But the things a family really needs for comfortable, healthful living can normally be bought with a relatively small income. Beyond that, most men try to earn more money and accumulate more goods primarily to prove their prowess. In a pecuniary civilization like that of the U.S., the success of all but a few such men as scientists, poets, and college presidents is measured in terms of money. Unless a man is so notoriously rich that he can afford to dress in shabby comfort and have bad manners, he normally feels that he must provide continuous evidence that he is at least as successful as, and preferably a little more successful than, most of the people in his community or social class. He can normally do this only by visibly maintaining or excelling their standards of leisure, consumption, and waste in house, furnishings, grounds, dress, automobile, manners, entertainment, sports, clubs, schools. Americans call it "keeping up with the Joneses," "having what other people have," "giving our children the advantages the other children have," or, when purchasing power dwindles, just "keeping up appearances."

Any failure to maintain these standards brings instant social opprobrium. If a man does not spend sufficient money on these things, the obvious conclusion is that he lacks the money, and is therefore less successful than his neighbors. For the ordinary man, this is more than a matter of winning or keeping his community's respect and envy. Just as he feeds his pride by getting and spending, so he loses his self-respect if he is a failure in the eyes of his community and family.

In this race there is no rest. The anxiety about "security," which the ordinary man suffers, is less a fear of losing the means of his family's subsistence (now guaranteed in the U.S.) than of being forced to a drastic lowering of its standard of living. No man can ever be guaranteed against that.

Says Veblen with worldly wisdom: "It is much more difficult to recede from a scale of expenditure once adopted than it is to extend the accustomed scale in response to an accession of wealth. Many items of customary expenditure prove on analysis to be almost purely wasteful, and they are therefore honorific only, but after they have once been incorporated into the scale of decent consumption, and so have become an integral part of one's scheme of life, it is quite as hard to give up these as it is to give up many items that conduce directly to one's physical comfort, or even that may be necessary to life and health . . .

"But as fast as a person makes new acquisitions, and becomes accustomed to the resulting new standards of wealth, the new standard forthwith ceases to afford appreciably greater satisfaction than the earlier standard did . . . The end sought by accumulation is to rank high in comparison with the rest of the community in point of pecuniary strength. So long as the comparison is distinctly unfavorable to himself, the normal, average individual will live in chronic dissatisfaction with his present lot; and when he has reached what may be called the normal pecuniary standard of the community, this chronic dissatisfaction will give place to restless straining to place a wider and ever-widening pecuniary interval between himself and this average standard . . .

"In the nature of the case, the desire for wealth can scarcely be satiated in any individual instance, and evidently a satiation of the average or general desire for wealth is out of the question. However widely, or equally, or 'fairly,' it may be distributed, no general increase of the community's wealth can make an approach to satiating this need, the ground of which is the desire of everyone to excell everyone else in the accumulation of goods."

EMANCIPATOR OF THE MIND

Reminiscent as it is of Christ's admonitions that happiness cannot be found by laying up "treasures upon earth," *The Theory of the Leisure Class* suggests a plausible explanation of Thoreau's made-in-America observation: "The mass of men lead lives of quiet desperation." Even after discounting Veblen's satirical exaggerations, many a reader of this American classic has probably resolved to sweep pecuniary pride out of his own heart and life.

Veblen himself had no hope that the world can ever be righted by such individual changes of heart. His later books are increasingly permeated by a sense of impending doom. Like Marx, he concluded that the inner contradictions of capitalistic society, including the conflict between production and profit seeking, and the impossibility of satiating "the average or general desire for wealth," must inevitably lead to increasingly severe depressions, wars, revolution, and general collapse.

"What can be done," he asked in *The Theory of Business Enterprise* (1904), "to save civilized mankind from the vulgarization and disintegration wrought by the machine industry?" Not until *The Engineers and the Price System* (1921) did he supply an affirmative answer. Parting company with Marx, he denied that the proletariat might bring salvation. Workingmen, he declared, understand the necessities of modern industry no better than businessmen do; the labor unions' "sole and self-seeking interest converges on the full dinner pail." The world can have peace and abundance, Veblen suggested, only if production-minded engineers somehow unite in a "soviet of technicians" and take over the world.

Fortunately for himself, Veblen died too soon to see his fascist-minded proposal flare and fizzle during the early thirties in Howard Scott's Technocracy. Velben's reputation remains that of a great diagnostician, not a healer, of social ills. But no one who has really explored Veblen's thought—the breadth and subtlety of which are barely suggested in this brief account—is likely to dispute the tribute paid him by a disciple and former student, Columbia University's distinguished economist Wesley C. Mitchell, in a reminiscent speech at the University of Chicago:

"There was the disturbing genius of Thorstein Veblen—that visitor from another world, who dissected the current commonplaces which the student had unconsciously acquired, as if the most familiar of his daily thoughts were curious products wrought in him by outside forces. No other such emancipator of the mind from the subtle tyranny of circumstance has been known in social science, and no other such enlarger of the realm of inquiry."

59. U.S. VS. A&P: BATTLE OF TITANS *

JOHN WILLIAMS ANDREWS

Two basic institutional systems in American society are business and government. Both are powerful institutions vested with extensive systems of social control. At numerous points these two areas of power and control have come into conflict. John W. Andrews describes the Great Atlantic and Pacific Tea Company and analyzes its attempt to prevent the federal government from regulating this corporation's power to eliminate competition. The article illustrates the corporate organization of American economic institutions and the struggle between these corporations and the agencies of government.

The Great Atlantic & Pacific Tea Company—the name brings up an image of global enterprise, trade winds and oceans of discovery, the romance of the East. Actually, the enterprise was purely American; two young business men from Maine, expanding, in the middle of the last century, their modest hide-and-leather business into tea, sold at cut-rates in a gaudy little store in Vesey Street, New York. It was not until the nineteen-thirties that it became truly global. It was not until the nineteen-forties that it began seriously to tangle with a companion Titan, the United States government. Today, the continuation of A&P, as America has known it for ninety years, depends on the outcome of a great new anti-trust action, United States *versus* A&P.

* *Harper's Magazine*, Vol. 201, No. 1204 (September, 1950), 64–73. Reprinted by permission of the author.

The author (b. 1898) is a lawyer and writer. He is president of Andrews Associates, Inc., Cleveland, Ohio. Formerly served with the United States Department of Justice. Has written on biological and historical subjects. His articles and poems have appeared in numerous publications.

A&P began, back in 1859, as the Great American Tea Company, selling teas for thirty cents that had been selling for a dollar, advertising the elimination of the middleman, and accumulating the anguished squawks of the harried competition. A band played on Saturdays in the store; red, white, and blue globes shone in the windows; and a huge gaslight "T" swayed over the sidewalk. As new stores were opened, they were in the Vesey Street pattern. A Baltimore newspaper of the seventies reported the new Baltimore store as "more resembling the fairy palaces . . . in the Arabian Nights than the business establishments one generally sees in this section." "Tea Clubs" were formed by mail to stimulate the country business, and premiums were given away to the tune of "This is the day / They give babies away / With half-a-pound of tea."

By 1869 the Great Atlantic & Pacific Tea Company had been formed, embodying, it has been suggested, the Founders' ambition to emulate the Union Pacific Railroad in linking the two oceans. By 1880 there were a hundred stores, scattered up and down the Eastern seaboard, and the older founder, George F. Gilman, had retired to a life of splendor in Bridgeport, Connecticut. By the early nineties, George Huntington Hartford, the younger founder, and his sons, George and John, still expanding the chain, had begun the manufacture of A&P products—baking powder made by a chemist behind a screen in Vesey Street. By 1900, there were two hundred stores; by 1912, there were four hundred. A&P wagons—with teas, coffees, and groceries—moved over some five thousand peddlers' routes. By 1916, sales were running close to the forty-five million level.

The true spurt into vastness, however, came just before America's entry into World War I. John Hartford, the younger son, had discovered the magic of "economy stores"—one-man, standardized affairs, operating without deliveries, credit, or premiums, and putting all savings into lower prices. Seven thousand five hundred of these stores were opened in some nine hundred working days; they revolutionized the food merchandising business in America. By the end of 1924, A&P could boast no less than 11,413 stores across America. By June 1926, it had 14,220 stores, sales were close to the half billion mark, earnings before taxes were over $13 million. By 1932, about the time that A&P's competitors, ahead of A&P, were launching into the Super-market, A&P had over 15,000 stores. It was a Titan, vaster than Henry Ford at his peak; vaster than James Cash Penney, Sears Roebuck, and Montgomery Ward together; approximately equal to the entire automobile business of 1932. It was the Great American Food Romance. By 1942, its sales were almost a billion and a half, its profits close to thirty millions.

Today, with sales still climbing and the Atlantic and Pacific truly linked, A&P faces what the management calls the "destruction" of A&P, and the government calls "divestiture in the public interest." If the government is successful, A&P will be split into seven competing retail chains; the manufacturing phases of the business will be divorced from the retail phases and from each other; and the great Atlantic Commission Company, the vast A&P purchaser of fresh fruits and vegetables, will be wholly dissolved.

It is a curious case. We have had other divestitures—the Pullman case, which broke up the old empire of the Pullman cars; the Paramount Motion Picture case, in which, after years of trial and error, the courts decreed the separation of the production phase from the exhibition phase; the still undetermined cases against American Telephone & Telegraph and Western Electric, against du Pont, U. S. Rubber, and General Motors, against the Big Four Meat Packers. These cases have made their flurries in professional circles, but the man-and-woman-in-the-street have paid little heed. The A&P case is different. It has reached down into the homes. Husbands and wives discuss it over the breakfast table. You can pick up an argument in any train or street car. Opinion is passionate, personal—even violent.

It is largely on the side of A&P. The Gallup poll of November 20, 1949, showed almost twice as many people for A&P as for the government. Editorial opinion is even more weighted, if the forty-eight-page reprint of 728 editorials and commentaries, issued by A&P, is an accurate reflection. Each of our 150,000,000 people must eat; a wife or husband in each of our 38,000,000 families must buy its daily bread; the A&P case, in its basic issue of consumer prices, involves not only those who buy from A&P, but all who buy. It is not extraordinary that the case should be occupying the attention of such a large proportion of the public. It is not even extraordinary that opinion should be one-sided, considering the fashion in which the story has thus far been presented to the American people.

II

The A&P divestiture action was filed by the United States Department of Justice on September 15, 1949, and, for a day or so, created little or no stir. The Sherman anti-trust laws are part of the folklore of the American people, but the legal and economic implications are, at best, only generally understood; the dry reading matter of an anti-trust action cannot compete with the comics or the morning's murder.

On September 20, 1949, however, the situation began to change. On that day, in some two thousand newspapers across the country—big dailies and little country weeklies—the first of the great A&P advertisements appeared. Under the generalship of Carl Byoir, A&P's public-relations counsel, tall headlines rode across full pages in the finest tradition of expert advertising. "DO YOU WANT YOUR A&P PUT OUT OF BUSINESS?" "Do You Want Higher Prices?" "This would mean higher food prices for you . . . less food on every dinner table. . . . Do they [the American people] want to continue to enjoy low prices and better living? Or do they want to break up A&P and pay higher prices, and have lower living standards? What do you want? . . . If A&P is big, it is because the American people, by their patronage, have made it big."

On Thursday, September 29, 1949 (regular chain-store "ad" day) the second A&P ad appeared—a full page again. "WHY DO THEY WANT TO PUT A&P OUT OF BUSINESS? They say . . . *and these are the anti-trust lawyers' own words* . . . that we 'have regularly undersold competing retailers.' TO THIS CHARGE WE PLEAD GUILTY: we confess that for the past ninety years we have constantly stepped up the efficiency of our operations in order to give our customers more and more good food for their money." The sub-heads shouted, "Do You Want Higher Prices?" The text painted a picture of America mobilized behind A&P—customers, farmers, suppliers, "our 110,000 employees," the labor leaders. "The entire American system of efficient, low-cost, low-profit distribution which we pioneered will face destruction and the public will suffer."

On October 18, 1949, Attorney-General McGrath, speaking to the Connecticut Bar Association, quickly struck back on behalf of the government. "The successful prosecution of the pending civil suit," he said, "will not increase, but should decrease, grocery prices. . . . The existence of monopoly power and its ruthless use in disregard of the public interest threaten economic freedom, retard efficiency, and curtail progress. Our system of free enterprise cannot survive unless the advantages of competition accrue to all of us."

On the same day, Assistant Attorney-General Bergson, in charge of the Anti-trust Division, spoke in Chicago, "A&P," he said, "has over-looked a very significant fact in its advertisements. The filing of the recent civil suit did not mark the beginning of the Department's anti-trust litigation against A&P. In 1942, the Department instituted a criminal anti-trust case, involving the same conduct that is the subject matter of the civil suit. . . . After six months of careful consideration . . . the Court found A&P guilty. . . . A&P appealed to the Court of Appeals. . . . In February of 1949 that court unanimously held that A&P had been properly convicted. A&P could have asked the Supreme Court of the United States to review this conviction. . . . They chose not to do so. Instead, they paid maximum fines totaling $175,000. . . .

"Suppression of the truth is equivalent to the suggestion of what is false. In a mild way, that sums up A&P's advertising. . . . A typical deception is found in the advertisement which reads, quote: 'They say . . . and these are the anti-trust lawyers' own words . . . that "we have regularly undersold competing retailers," ' end quote. This advertisement asserts that this is the charge against A&P. And to this charge A&P in headline type pleads guilty. . . . These words were deliberately lifted out of context. I'll read you the paragraph of the complaint in which they are found:

Defendants, by coercing and receiving unlawful buying preferences, have become enabled to and *have regularly undersold,* regularly taken patronage away from, and sometimes eliminated *competing retailers. . . .*

"The Court did not convict A&P of being big. . . . A&P was convicted . . . because, and I quote the Court, of the 'predatory application of its mass purchasing power' and the abuse of that power through boycotts, blacklisting, preferential rebates, price wars, and below-cost retailing in strategic areas in order to eliminate local competition. . . . The aim of this case is to restore active and vigorous competition to the food industry."

It was not to be expected that these speeches would reach many ears. A curious story developed at this time, of how certain sections of the press excluded or attenuated coverage of the government's side of the case. Don Hollenbeck treated the matter in some detail in broadcasts over WCBS on October 22 and November 26, and some historian, in years to come, may include a footnote on a possible relationship between newspaper advertising and editorial policy. But even with comprehensive coverage, it would not have been possible for a few inches of a speech by a government official, couched in legal terminology, to make much headway against broadsides which multiplied, week after week, themes designed to dismay and alarm the food-and-price conscious American householder. The scareheads—"Higher Prices," "Less Food," "Less Money in the Pay Envelope" were sandwiched with glowing references to America the Wonderful, American Sportsmanship, and A&P's beneficent mission.

On January 5, 1950, a new theme began to develop—the "THEY HAVE BEEN WRONG BEFORE" theme—"they" being, as usual, the Washington anti-trust lawyers, pictured as engaged in a personal vendetta against A&P. The new ads took up the "Washington Bread Case" and the "North Carolina Potato Case," in each of which A&P was acquitted by directed verdict, and the "Dallas Case," where an indictment against A&P was abandoned by the government in favor of an identical criminal complaint in the Federal District Court at Danville, Illinois. No mention, naturally, was made of the Cease and Desist Order of the Federal Trade Commission in 1938, calling upon A&P to conform to the provisions of the Robinson-Patman Act; nor of the two indictments in 1941, which resulted in fines to A&P; nor of the four civil actions in 1941, in which A&P, with other defendants, consented to decrees prohibiting price-fixing and the coercion of price-cutting grocers.

The "Danville Case" was mentioned, with a promise to tell the public all about it. This promise was fulfilled on May 12, 1950. The super-head ran: "THIS TIME THE ANTI-TRUST LAWYERS WON A CASE AGAINST A&P. . . . They say that this suit [the divestiture suit] is based on the fact that they won a suit against us at Danville, Illinois, in 1946. They did. . . . Immediately thereafter, in a letter explaining his decision, Judge Lindley wrote: 'I HAVE NOT CONDEMNED THE A&P SYSTEM. I HAVE NOT MADE A FINDING WHICH COULD BE THE BASIS FOR A SUIT OF DISSOLUTION.' So, now we have the anti-trust lawyers saying that their suit to dissolve A&P is based on Judge Lindley's decision; while Judge Lindley himself says his decision could not be the basis for a suit of dissolution."

On the day on which this statement appeared, Judge Lindley gave the *Chicago Daily News* a somewhat different version of his decision.

"I decided," said Judge Lindley, "that they violated the law. I did not attempt to make a finding to be the basis of a suit for dissolution. I was not asked to do this. This was beyond my province in the case before me. Whether the conduct of A&P since my decision has been such as to correct the abuses I found or of such character as to justify a decree of dissolution is a question for the court in which the suit is pending."

Judge Lindley told the *Daily News* that the letter mentioned by A&P was "a casual answer to criticism" following his decision. "He did not remember," said the *News*, "to whom he had written."

III

The Danville case was a remarkable affair, not because of the legal issues involved (there was little or no new law), nor because of the length of the trial (twenty-five weeks), nor the length of the record (some 60,000 pages). It was extraordinary because, for the first time in its eighty-five years of existence, the A&P was revealed in its full stature and inner workings. *Business Week*, when the Dallas indictment was handed up in 1942, remarked: "The Department of Justice did contrive, of legal necessity, to work in a few Winchellisms, which will give the trade a peek through A&P's hitherto blacked-out keyhole." With the Danville trial, the full curtain went up.

A&P was shown to be a completely integrated empire, fourteen corporations piled one on top of the other, pyramiding upward, through two great holding corporations, to the George Huntington Hartford Trust, of which the two brothers, Mr. John and Mr. George Hartford, were the sole trustees. The Trust held 99.97 per cent of the voting stock of the Great Atlantic & Pacific Tea Company of New York; A&P New York held all of the stock of A&P Maryland, which in turn owned outright the three great manufacturing companies—Quaker Maid Company, which made for A&P stores two hundred and more products, from baking powder to vinegar; White House Milk Company, with milk-processing plants in Wisconsin; and Nakat Packing Corporation, America's largest canner of Alaskan salmon and operator of great Alaskan fishing fleets. A&P Maryland owned outright the enormous American Coffee Corporation, buyer of green coffees from Columbia and Brazil; A&P New Jersey, which roasted and packed the coffees and also operated retail stores in twenty-four states; A&P Nevada and A&P Arizona, which operated stores in sixteen additional states; and the super-colossal fruit and vegetable purchaser, Atlantic Commission Company. There was not even a shade of a minority interest anywhere from A&P New York on down.

The retail stores were an empire in themselves, scattered from coast to coast, operating in forty states and the District of Columbia, with A&P Delaware holding A&P rights to do business in the states not yet invaded. Thirty-seven wholesale warehouses supplied the stores, receiving the A&P-manufactured products and the products purchased by the A&P divided into seven great divisions—New England, Atlantic, Eastern, Southern, Central, Central Western, and Middle Western. No division was a separate corporation, but each was fully equipped with a president, vice-presidents, a board of directors, and operating officers. Each division was divided into units, each unit being also an operating segment in itself.

An elaborate system of bookkeeping kept the financial relationships between the parts of the empire in order—bookkeeping "profits" for the companies and for each business phase, goods "sold" from level to level, rebates, discounts, allowances. But the whole was monolithic. "It is all the A&P Tea Company to me," an official testified at Danville, and this concept carried down to the littlest clerk. All of A&P's "real" profits, with the exception of certain profits of Atlantic Commission Company (Acco), were made from the over-the-counter sales to the American housewife.

A&P might spread huge across the United States; it might reveal, in its slightest gesture, the presence of a colossus; its titanic sales (835 million pounds of meat in 1946, 2 million *tons* of fresh fruit and vegetables, 300 million loaves of bread, 74 million pounds of butter, 100 million dozen eggs, 100 million pounds of poultry, 17,500 tons of cheese, 245 million pounds of coffee, 50 million dozen doughnuts—to mention but a few items) might involve it in activities the world over. But A&P's basic operation was utterly simple, cutting through all its corporate lines. It was just a blown-up grocery store, buying or manufacturing the supplies it sold to the housewife over the counter.

Its basic operating policy was equally simple: to buy at the lowest possible price, and, except where the strategies of empire dictated otherwise, to sell at the lowest possible price. A&P officials referred to this policy as the "two-price level" policy—the lower price (both buying and selling) for A&P and the higher price (both buying and selling) for A&P's competitors. It was excesses in pursuit of this policy that first brought A&P in conflict with laws against restraints of trade.

IV

The A&P's side of the dispute with the government has been so widely heard, and the government's side so little heard, that it seems essential for understanding to set forth the story of the A&P's methods as the courts found them (Judge Lindley in the District Court and Judges Minton and Kerner and Chief Judge Major in the Circuit Court). According to their version of the story, A&P entered a new phase as early as 1925.

At that time, in the various produce centers of the country, A&P maintained "brokerage" offices, ostensibly independent of A&P and often run under the names of the managers, but actually under the strict control of headquarters in the Graybar Building in New York, where the Hartfords had their offices. These brokerage offices bought merchandise for A&P, exacting, through the weight of A&P's vast purchasing power, large reductions in cost, and receiving also, on top of these discounts, a brokerage commission which went into A&P's coffers as a further reduction in cost—a differential not available to A&P's competitors. (This unequal device, in the early days of the Depression, had been one of the causes for the outcry against chain stores, which resulted in the passage of the Robinson-Patman Act.) "In 1935," said the Circuit Court, "gross revenues from this source amounted to $2,500,000."

After the Robinson-Patman Act had outlawed this device, A&P made the first of its shifts of method. The "brokerage" offices were rechristened "field buying offices" and, as the Circuit Court put it, "buyers, instead of getting credit for alleged brokerage, induced their suppliers to reduce their price further to A&P by the amount of the brokerage fee." This was called "net buying." The "inducement," the Court found, included "blacklisting" of recalcitrant suppliers. An A&P official had written: "Any canner who declines to work on a net basis . . . we feel should then be placed on the Unsatisfactory List." Lists of manufacturers were prepared, with appropriate symbols:

N—Have agreed to a NET basis. (Be sure it's really net when trading.)

G—Have definitely agreed to hold the brokerage for us until our Headquarters officials figure out a practical method for this to be paid legally. . . .

R—Refused either plan and under no circumstances is any business to be given except with the writer's OK.

P—Have been approached but no definite agreement and should be aggressively followed, therefore, until agree to either net or gross . . . no business should be done without the writer's approval.

Blacklisting has, for years, been held by the courts to be an unfair method of competition.

Promptly, A&P ran afoul of the Federal Trade Commission. The A&P attorneys argued mightily for the legality of "net buying"; but a Cease and Desist Order was issued against A&P, requiring it to cease accepting allowances and discounts in lieu of brokerage. A&P appealed to the Third Circuit, which upheld the order, and to the Supreme Court, which refused review.

A&P then made its second shift of method. In a national release to the trade, it announced that it would no longer buy from any supplier who offered to sell to it through a broker or who so sold to others. The new device was called "direct buying," and it did not bother A&P that its action "clearly affected the business of brokers." The District and Circuit Courts both quoted the remark of an A&P official: "The brokers are dying hard." Nor did it bother A&P that their action affected that part of the trade which could not buy direct. But the device boomeranged when the Danville case came to trial.

An A&P official had written in connection with "net" buying: "If net prices are not agreeable to a seller, a quantity discount or advertising contract should be essayed, effective the date brokerage payments stop and payable to Headquarters." The same devices were being used in connection with "direct buying." But such discounts and allowances, under the Robinson-Patman Act, could be paid preferentially only where the seller could make savings in his costs of manufacture or shipment because of the quantities purchased, or where true services were rendered.

The trouble was that A&P's discounts did not seem to bear any direct relationship to the economics inherent in large-scale manufacture for a large buyer. A&P's contracts with suppliers were "rigged," as the Circuit Court put it; they were designed to give a "semblance of compliance with the Robinson-Patman Act"; but the primary consideration with A&P seemed to be "to get the discounts, lawfully, if possible, but to get them at all events."

"Whatever the system used," said the Circuit Court of this pattern of A&P's buying, "or by whatever name designated, A&P always wound up with a buying price advantage. . . . Only A&P was blessed, and the supplier had to make his profit out of his other customers at higher prices, which were passed on to the competition A&P met in the retail field."

The device of advertising allowances effected the same result. Newspaper space advertising allowances "were contracted for, not alone at the cost of the advertising, but at cost plus one hundred per cent to A&P." A&P would also contract with its suppliers for a percentage allowance, agreeing in the vaguest terms that it would display the goods of the supplier in just such a fashion as it would ordinarily be expected to display them. In other words, it would get paid for what the Court refers to as "pretended services," which no supplier would pay for who was not under pressure to do so. It was A&P's policy, "and a usually successful one," to get "a larger allowance of this kind than its competitors. If it did not get the allowance it sought, the threats to take away the business of A&P were used and brought the supplier into line."

These practices, illegal under the Robinson-Patman Act, and outlawed by Congress to give the small fry a chance to compete with the great chains, did not make for the kind of fair competition which must exist if the little fellows are to survive in the jungles of Big Business.

Atlantic Commission Company, wholly-owned buying arm of A&P, engaged in these same practices—and others. In the early days, Acco had exacted the highest possible discounts, piling on top of them a buyer's brokerage, shifting with A&P to net buying, shifting again with A&P to direct buying. "Its practices over the years," said Judge Lindley, "leave a bad odor."

Acco's other activities still further cut away the chances of the smaller concerns. Acco acted as broker-*seller* for the surplus produce of suppliers, collecting brokerage which went into A&P's pocket, selling at prices which made the goods expensive to A&P's competitors, and also getting first choice of the supplier's produce and selling the balance, which "might be and often was an inferior grade." Acco acted as broker-*buyer* for jobbers who sold to A&P's competitors, collecting brokerage which went to A&P, while the higher price was passed on to the competition. Acco used its huge buying power to buy on cash terms, but refused to accept the "risks-in-transit" burden which less favored competitors had to assume. Acco bought on a "sales arrival" basis, forcing the shipper to assume the risks of any price-change. Acco took merchandise on consignment—it could buy for A&P at A&P's large discount, or it could sell and pocket a commission. Each of these devices still further increased the two-price differential in favor of A&P.

Acco sold produce to jobbers in carload lots, with simultaneous agreements to buy back less than carload lots—but at the lower or carload rate—and it gave its less-than-carload-lot business to jobbers who bought through Acco, price and quality being the same.

Acco even exacted *double* brokerage. "Vetter at Louisville," said Judge Lindley, "bought the same merchandise through Macaluso and Acco, although the purchases had been completed through Macaluso. . . . Other dealers paying unearned brokerages to Acco were the Gordon Fruit & Produce of New Haven, and DeCarlo of Buffalo, and the Mercurio Company of Providence. These odorous unjustified transactions cannot be excused in any manner."

Acco "made a determined and persistent effort to establish a close relationship with and influence over growers' co-operatives." Judge Lindley mentions the Northwest Apple Growers, Sowega Products, Farmers' Co-operative Exchange of North Carolina, and Florida Citrus Exchange, the transactions with the latter coming, as the Court put it, "dangerously near being an agreement in restraint of trade in itself."

Acco promoted the famous Super-Coop, which caused the food trade, in 1940, to cry out, "monopoly!" Super-Coop was designed to "secure a larger and more effective control of the shippers by Acco. . . . Acco was to benefit in the form of a lower expense rate"—the usual A&P purpose—"resulting from the larger volume handled, a greater availability in quantity and selection of supplies for A&P, and an organization readily useful as a propaganda agency to fight A&P's enemies." Super-Coop "was camouflaged to make it appear as though the shippers were the moving force in the organization." John Hartford was doubtful as to Super-Coop's legality, and it was finally dropped by A&P, but not until it had become notorious.

The trouble with Super-Coop was the same old trouble. A&P, "by the use of its integrated power and control," could buy merchandise at prices it "would not otherwise have obtained, at prices less than those of competitors, with a resulting handicap to competitors."

A&P even turned its manufacturing potential to the same use. When it could not get the discounts or allowances it thought were its due, it would threaten to go "into the manufacturing and processing business itself, since it already possessed a considerable establishment and experience that would enable it to get quickly and successfully into such business if a recalcitrant supplier, processor, or manufacturer did not yield." The prime illustration in the record is the case of the Ralston Purina Company, which raised its discount rate to A&P from 7½ cents a case to 17½ cents a case. The government, at Danville, introduced a letter from Ralston which read in part: "The discounts allowed in this contract are not made in lieu of brokerage, but represent an arbitrary reduction from our list prices which it was necessary to make to hold the flake cereal business of the Great Atlantic & Pacific Tea Company and to secure from them an agreement not to enter into the business of manufacturing flakes for five years."

Counsel for A&P, in their appeal brief, dismissed this letter as "no more than the extravagant words of a supplier trying to defend prices that he knew were too high." On this and kindred evidence, however, the Circuit Court was convinced that this type of threat, designed still further to decrease the chances of the competition, represented a general A&P practice.

According to the findings of the Court, A&P seems not to have left even the smallest stone unturned. It forced suppliers to discontinue store deliveries. because. with its warehouse system, it could reap no advantage and was unwilling for its competitors to do so. It forced suppliers to abandon premiums, not wanting itself to bother with them. On "bag and label allowances" it realized a "substantial difference between the cost to it and what it realized out of the transaction from other suppliers." "Everything," said the Circuit Court, "was grist to the mill that was grinding down prices to A&P to enable it to maintain the two-price level to its advantage."

But it was at the retail level—down at the grass-roots where Mr. and Mrs. America buy their daily bread—that the effects of this policy had their clearest impact. The two-price level, so carefully cultivated at the buying level, could, at the selling level, be translated into an overwhelming power to harry or eliminate competition. "Profit margins are slight," said Judge Lindley. "The difference between profitable operation and loss is fractional. . . . When the net profit is in the neighborhood of 2 per cent, an advantage of 5 per cent in buying in one dealer immediately places him in an overpowering position so far as his competitors are concerned."

A&P's practices had created this advantage. With the funds realized from savings on buying prices—whether by discriminatory preferences, discriminatory allowances, or whatever—the A&P policy makers could manipulate the retail policies of their empire pretty much at will. A&P's retail operating policy, it clearly appears, was to capture volume—25 per cent of the available business, said the government, and Judge Lindley said: "I think it clear that the amount of available business in any given area was the starting point on which A&P's activity in that territory was planned, and that, in many instances, it was A&P's definite program that its supermarket merchandising should eventually enjoy 25 per cent of the available business. . . . To reach this goal, reduction of gross profit rates was continuously made in various places. . . ."

He gave examples of below-cost operations: "Boston," he said, "operated at a loss from 1934 to 1941; Providence from 1934 to 1940. . . . Toledo operated at a loss from 1932 to 1938 inclusive; Indianapolis in all the same years except 1936; Detroit in the years from 1932 to 1937 inclusive; Cincinnati from 1932 to 1937 inclusive. . . . For two years after 1938 the Atlantic Division was operated at a loss, resulting in an increase in volume from $108,000,000 to $151,000,000." In 1941, in the Albany unit, the sales activity resulted "in the astonishing actual retail operation of the entire unit at a net loss of $28,999." And there were many other illustrations in the record; for example, in 1939 the New England Division and Atlantic Division both lost money—$252,665 for the first, $288,752 for the second.

Judge Lindley discussed the government's deduction from the record —that, in 1925–1926, of A&P's thirty-three units, only one had more than 15 per cent of the total available business in its territory, eleven had from

10 to 15 per cent, twelve from 5 to 10 per cent, and nine had less than 5 per cent; whereas in 1941, of A&P's thirty-nine units, eight had from 15 to 20 per cent, eighteen from 10 to 15 per cent, ten 5 to 10 per cent and three less than 5 per cent. He referred to the board of directors' meeting of the Central Division in May 1941, when a program of supermarkets and special development stores was outlined, "aiming at obtaining 20 per cent of the available food business in cities where there was an available volume of $20,000 or more per week." "There were in the Division," he said, "eight cities where A&P had over 50 per cent of the available business, fifteen cities from 40 to 50 per cent, fifty-one from 30 to 40 per cent, fifty-one from 20 to 30 per cent, fifty-five from 10 to 20 per cent, seven with less than 10 per cent."

The Circuit Court drew a sharply outlined picture of the relationship between low-price or below-cost sales and the capture of volume. "If Area X is having a tough experience competitionwise," it said, "or the area looks prospective in which to increase the volume of business, the gross profit percentage in this area is lowered. This lowers the price at which goods may be sold and the volume increases at the expense of somebody. Sometimes the gross-profit rate is fixed so low that the store runs below the cost of operation, even with all the advantage derived by the store in reduction of the cost of its merchandise occasioned by the headquarters' allocation of its predatory profits and accumulations."

The Circuit Court noted the general formula by which A&P operated. "When the gross profit rate is reduced in Area X," it said, "it is an almost irresistible conclusion that A&P had the power to compensate for any possible decline in net profits by raising the gross profit rate and retail prices in Area Y . . . . Thus Area Y, at the desire of the policy makers of A&P, can be brought to aid in the struggle in Area X, which in numerous instances, as the record shows, sustained heavy net losses for periods extending over a substantial number of consecutive years. There must inevitably be a compensation somewhere in the system for a loss somewhere else, as the over-all policy of the company is to earn $7 per share per annum on its stock."

The Circuit Court summed up the entire A&P enterprise—the immense food empire, sprawled across the United States, engaged in processing and manufacturing, wholesaling and retailing, and pressing its advantages at every point. "The inevitable consequence of this whole business pattern," said the Court, "is to create a chain reaction of ever-increasing selling volume and ever-increasing requirements and hence purchasing power for A&P, and for its competitors hardships not produced by competitive forces, and, conceivably, ultimate extinction."

The Court, obviously, had two major elements in mind, though in the long run they would come to one and the same thing. "There is evidence in this record," it said, "of how some local grocers were quickly eliminated under the lethal competition put upon them by A&P when armed with its monopoly power." The evidence in the record, cited by Judge Lindley, included, among others, the plight of one Culwell, of Dallas, Texas, who "testified that . . . A&P conducted every day sales at retail prices below his cost. His sales in 1937 were $73,000, profit, $4,000; his sales in 1938, $65,000, his profit, $3,000; 1939, sales were $62,000, net profit $2,000; 1940, $60,000, net profit $2,000; 1941, $59,000, net profit $1,100. In June 1942, A&P moved its neighboring store fourteen blocks away. Culwell's business jumped from $59,000 in 1941 to $80,000 in 1942, net profit to $3,000. The Court also included the boast of an A&P executive of "past achievement of financial ruin to other competitors," and a letter from an A&P official to the manager of the Richmond warehouse, "I certainly don't think that the Sanitary next door to you at Carey Avenue is a competitor and the hotter we can make our program the quicker this outfit will realize that they have no place in the supermarket business in Richmond."

The second aspect was not less important—affecting, as it does, the ultimate consumer, the housewife. Already, on the facts found, the housewife who did *not* buy at A&P was paying higher prices in her particular food store, because of the deliberately executed two-price-level buying policy of A&P. But the housewife who purchased "good foods at lower prices" in the A&P itself was also subject to A&P's strategical manipulations. Where volume was being captured through below-cost selling, she might benefit; but in areas supporting the below-cost areas, her prices would be higher—at the whim of A&P.

And, potentially, there might be nothing except A&P's own self-imposed restraint to keep prices down. Already A&P could balance division against division, unit against unit, store against store. Already, because of its size, backed by the practices cited above, it could undersell at will. In plain language, the Court could forsee a time when A&P's low-buying, low-selling, volume-capturing practices would have eliminated competition. Then prices could be raised at will. It seems a correct analysis of the Court's view that A&P already possessed the power to slay or let live, and that this was a situation the Sherman Act had been expressly designed to prevent.

v

So much for the charges against the A&P as the courts have found the facts. What are we to say about them? That is a difficult question to answer. In the first place, the housewife—or her husband—who reads this article should bear one point in mind: It is impossible to evaluate the activities of the A&P empire from the worm's-eye-view one gets from trading with one particular A&P market. It requires the over-all view—

that which a court obtains after six months of trial, or which attorneys get, on either side, after months and years of preparation for trial.

Beyond this, there is the matter of the anti-trust laws themselves. They are "good laws"—even A&P makes that statement in one of its ads, though protesting their application to itself. Whatever their faults of vagueness and occasional ineptitudes, they have contributed as much to the greatness of America as the businesses, big and small, that they were designed to control and protect. Not long ago, there appeared a magazine article entitled, "Competition Is So Vulgar," dealing with the accepted system of restraints of trade which has been Great Britain's way of doing business for generations. Competition, as we know it, is a comparative rarity in Britain. Prices have long been set and policed to protect the weakest links in the production and distribution chains. We are paying a lot of money these days for Britain's inability to compete effectively in world markets, a situation due, at least in part, to her non-competitive system. And it is interesting to note that many people in Great Britain, and also in the nations on the Continent which have promoted the doctrines of nationalization, are now looking with increasing interest at the American anti-trust laws, which they once thought were only "window dressing," as a possible alternative to government control. Whenever these laws are stiffly enforced in the United States, there is always an outcry; yet even those who join in it recognize the value of competition to American industry.

One may add that it is unfortunate that the A&P advertising campaign to date should have been couched in such terms that if divestiture of A&P should be ordered by the courts, important segments of the American public will doubt the soundness of the judicial process. Not long ago I received a letter from a woman of profound understanding in many matters; she wrote: "Whether the A&P combination is legal or illegal, honest or dishonest, the low A&P prices have been a boon to all housekeepers, rich and poor alike." Such opinion is very general, but it misses the point. The Sherman Act does not directly concern itself with prices, whether high or low. It concerns itself with the full play of competition, on the theory that competition, given full play, will further the American principle of "freedom to compete" and will, in the long run, keep prices down. Even a distinguished judge missed the point. "What does it matter," he asked, "what will happen fifteen years from now?"

The issue is deep and far-reaching. Monopoly and high prices come when competition dies. When competition is dead, it can scarcely be revived, yet control must be exercised—and the only control presently available is governmental control. This is another way of saying that business monopoly leads to governmental monopoly, which is another way of saying socialism.

The question of whether or not the courts will order dissolution of

A&P will be long in doubt. The government will argue that "A&P has made it clear that it is incapable of abandoning its predatory activities merely because a court orders it to do so"; hence, that divestiture is necessary. A&P will argue, at a minimum, that it has put its house in order. Whatever may be the decision in the District Court, appeals seem certain—to the Circuit Court, and, thereafter, to the Supreme Court. It will be several years before divestiture, if ordered, becomes an accomplished fact.

In the meantime, it is important that no propaganda campaigns should be permitted to obscure the true issue at the root of the A&P case. Anti-trust experts have a phrase: "Show me the power and I will show you its abuse." Or, as that American oracle, a taxi-driver, remarked to me recently, "What's the use of power if you don't abuse it?" There is no such thing as a permanently benevolent tyranny.

60. THE BATTLE OF ATHENS, TENNESSEE *

THEODORE H. WHITE

The social-control function of government, because of the accompanying power necessary for efficiency, often encourages particular individuals or groups to use government for the attainment of goals that are not generally regarded as in the public interest. A typical example of the social factors involved in a fight to displace an entrenched group that was misusing the power of government is described by Theodore H. White in this article.

The Sweetwater River, a pleasant mountain stream that falls into the basin of the Tennessee, cuts through McMinn County beneath a canopy of high tension wires. The people of McMinn County, like the taut, coppery wires, hum with subdued peaceful activity until they are disturbed; and then, like the wires, they snap in a shower of sparks and violence. It took several killings, ten years of extortion and thuggery, a world war and an official invasion by legal gunmen to bring on the

* *Harper's Magazine*, Vol. 194, No. 1160 (January, 1947), 54–61. Reprinted by permission of the author.

The author (b. 1915) is a journalist. Formerly a war correspondent in both the Pacific and European Theaters and Editor of *New Republic*. Recipient of numerous journalistic awards. Author, *Thunder Out of China* (with Annalee Jacoby). Editor, *The Stillwell Papers; Fire in the Ashes*. Contributor to national magazines.

violence of August 1, 1946, and the bloody siege of the Athens jail. But when it was over, democracy was firmly established and authority once again rested with the citizenry.

The people of McMinn County are God-fearing men and women. When the Robert E. Lee highway climbs out of the Shenandoah Valley, which can take its religion or leave it, into east Tennessee on the road to McMinn the highway is sprinkled with signboards telling the godless wayfarers that "Jesus is coming soon" or warning them "Prepare to Meet God." McMinn itself is relatively free of such shrieking witnesses to faith; McMinn's religion is Methodist and Baptist, quiet, bone-deep, and sober. On Saturday afternoon when farmers throng the town, preachers are allowed to call sinners to repentance in the shade of the courthouse at the county seat. But most of McMinn meets God in the serenity of Sunday morning at the red brick or white board house of worship in peace and devotion. The church-goers have made liquor illegal, and Sunday movies are unlawful, too.

Next to religion, politics is the most important thing. But until 1946, religion absorbed so much of the spirit of right-thinking people that politics fell automatically to the bad. First, it was the Republicans. They had McMinn County for years and years. The Republicans would let a Democrat get elected now and then, but the sheriff was theirs and they held tight to the county trustee who disbursed funds and issued poll-tax certificates. Then, from 1936, when Paul Cantrell won the election and established an eastern outpost of the Crump machine, it was ten years of Democrats.

Paul Cantrell, state senator from the McMinn area and boss of the county, was a medium-sized, bespectacled man of sallow complexion, a big head, and little neck. Cantrell loved two things: money and power. He had a nervous, fidgety way about him; he rarely looked directly at a man when he talked to him; towards the end, an armed deputy accompanied Cantrell as guard when he strolled through Athens, the county seat. Pat Mansfield, his sheriff, was a tall, handsome man from Georgia. Pat was kind to his family and gave money to his church. He might have been popular but many people resented the sour troop of plug-uglies he had recruited to be his deputy sheriffs. Pat did Cantrell's bidding.

The Cantrell forces were hard, well-connected people. Cantrell was allied with Burch Biggs in neighboring Polk County; the pair were tied tight to the Crump machine, and Crump ran all of Tennessee. They were so close to the Crump machine that George Woods, who represented McMinn in the state legislature, was speaker of the house in the legislature of the State of Tennessee.

The machine bossed the county with a rough hand. The sheriff had sixteen regular deputies and about twenty or thirty other men he would deputize in "emergencies." Three of the deputies had served penitentiary terms. One of them had been convicted of taking a little girl out and violating the age of consent. It wasn't rape, but then it wasn't good, either; and God-fearing people like those who farmed and worked in McMinn didn't like it. When the deputies arrested a man they often slugged him until he was sensible. Nobody talked back much in public because it wasn't safe. The deputies threatened to kill people they didn't like. They were brutal men, ready to beat, blackjack, or bully anyone. One GI who was home on leave during the war was shot and killed by a deputy at a public entertainment house near Athens; a sailor home on leave was killed at the other end of the county.

The gambling joints and bootleggers were all tied to the machine. They paid off the proper people and operated punchboards and slot machines, sold liquor, did as they pleased. As a matter of fact, if someone was in the pen the best way to get him out was to work through the small-time racketeers to get the machine to go easy.

The take from the bootleggers and gamblers wasn't the only source of revenue for the machine. The county was directed by fee-grabbers. A tourist comes riding down the highway; maybe he has a bottle of beer. The deputies arrest him and take him to court. In the court is a little man, called "the informer," who says he is a lawyer. He advises the tourist to plead guilty, pay his fine, and go his way. Sixteen dollars and a nickel. No one will ever know how many people paid their sixteen dollars and a nickel, over and over again, to support the sheriff and his deputies. The sheriff was paid five thousand dollars a year and expenses, but he got seventy-five cents a day for every man in jail that had to be fed. When a drunk was arrested, he was put back on the street next day with a clear head and an empty stomach, but the charge to the county was two days' food at seventy-five cents each. In ten years, county expenses for the sheriff's office had run to over three hundred thousand dollars. McMinn has an audit committee working on the books now.

There was nothing that could be done about it, because you couldn't vote the machine out of office. The machine had taken the county from the Republicans by a famous vote-grab in 1936; some people still tell how the last ballot box from a normally Republican precinct was fixed to show just enough lead to carry the county.

From then on, no matter how people voted, the machine counted the votes. In the key districts when the polls closed the deputies took the ballot boxes to jail, or another safe place, and counted them without any opposition watchers present. Then they would announce the results and always the Cantrell men won. There was nothing that could be done about that either. Appeal to the courts was useless; the Republicans tried that but no suit-at-law was ever won by the opposition.

Things had been that way for a long time when the war came, taking thirty-five hundred boys from McMinn homes and flinging them across the face of the earth. Folks kept writing to their sons about affairs in McMinn County; sometimes the boys would visit on furlough and then write to their friends in camps all around the world. There were four years to think about McMinn County, and Ralph Duggan, who was a lieutenant in the Navy, says he thought a lot more about McMinn County than he did about the Japs. Many were thinking as Ralph did—that if democracy was good enough to put on the Germans and Japs, it was good enough for McMinn County, too. It got to be a saying in Athens: "Wait till the GI boys come home."

By spring of 1946, the GI boys were trickling back to McMinn from France and Germany and Italy and the Pacific. The people of McMinn say there is nothing but what some good doesn't come of it, and what happened afterwards in McMinn came from the war. The boys learned a lot about fighting and more about patriotism in the Army; when they came home they were ready to do something about democracy in Tennessee.

In February they set to planning. They met secretly because the Cantrell forces had the guns, the blackjacks, and the law; and the deputies could make life hell for anyone they could catch. Once in the summer campaign, they seized one boy, locked him up, took his poll-tax receipt from him, and then, threatening his life, made him sign a statement that no such incident had ever taken place. There were five GI's and one civilian in on the first secret meetings. They decided that in the summer election for sheriff and county officials the GI's would put up a complete slate of their own. Mansfield, Cantrell's sheriff, was going out of office and Cantrell was running for sheriff himself.

The veterans sounded out general feeling and in May they called a mass meeting. To get into the GI meeting you had to show your discharge papers, or your membership card in the American Legion or VFW. The veterans picked a non-partisan slate: three Democrats, two Republicans. Knox Henry, a tall handsome boy who had been hurt in North Africa and ran a filling station, was the man for sheriff. He was Republican, but the county trustee was to be Frank Carmichael, a farmer and a Democrat. Carmichael had been a major in the war and was badly wounded at Saint Lô. The other candidates were GI boys, too, except Charlie Pickel who had been in the first World War and had returned with his wounds to be a carpenter. Jim Buttram, a sturdy, solid chunk of combat infantryman, was to be campaign manager. Jim's family had a grocery store in Athens and Jim was new to politics.

With the slate chosen, the campaign picked up speed. Ralph Duggan, who had come back from the Navy to his law practice, was legal adviser and they pored over the Tennessee Code to see what the laws allowed them. The business men who feared the Cantrell forces con-

tributed money secretly. They were afraid to give openly because the
machine could raise the taxes, or arrest them, or generally make life
hard. But eight thousand dollars came into the campaign fund and
soon loudspeaker trucks were rolling over the hill roads, the *Daily Post-
Athenian* was carrying campaign ads, and the local radio station was
putting out fifteen minutes of talk a day. Up and down the pockets and
roads went GI's calling meetings in evenings at schoolhouses or homes,
begging, urging, pleading with everyone to get out and vote. It wasn't
hard to pin scandal on the Cantrell forces; McMinn County had lived
with the scandal for almost ten years. Nothing had been done about it
for two reasons: first, the only alternative was the old Republicans; and
second, it did no good to vote because the Cantrells always counted
themselves to victory anyway. So over and over, like the beating of a
drum in the darkness, the GI campaign chanted its theme: "Your vote
will be counted as cast, your vote will be counted as cast."

"Everybody knew we were trying to do the right thing," said Jim
Buttram. "We had twelve public meetings and we knew they were
damned good. About three weeks before elections we knew we had won
the votes and the hearts of the people of McMinn County. But the hardest thing to do was to build an organization to help us see we got a fair
count on election day."

The GI's asked the governor for help; but the governor was elected
with Crump backing and was silent. They asked the Attorney General
in Washington for help; he did nothing. They made contact with the
FBI office in Knoxville; the FBI agent said he couldn't do anything unless
Washington told him to, and Washington wasn't telling. The GI's were
on their own.

II

Election day dawned sweet and clear over McMinn County. Mc-
Minn numbers twelve voting precincts but the decisive vote is cast in
two townships, Etowah and Athens. Etowah is some ten miles in the
hills from the main highway, but Athens, the county seat, is dead center.
Athens sprawls fragrant and green about the old white courthouse; the
Robert E. Lee hotel sits on one side, Woolworth's and a movie house on
another, stores and offices on the other two sides. One block up from
the courthouse lies the red brick county jail. Maple trees and green lawn
surround the courthouse; old people sun themselves on the benches,
children romp on the grass, blue-denimed farmers stroll casually about
buying supplies for home and land.

Election day saw Athens an armed camp. As the voters came to the
polls, they found the Cantrell machine in ominous demonstration of
force. Almost two hundred armed deputies strutted about, pistols and

blackjacks dangling from their belts, badges gleaming. The deputies were strangers. Mansfield claims he asked the governor for National Guardsmen to help him, and the governor authorized him to get deputies where he could. The machine had turned up a sodden gang of plug-uglies, most of them from foreign counties, some from as far as Georgia. Fred Puett, the Chamber of Commerce secretary, said that they looked as though they were drugged; their eyes seemed as cold and arrogant and hard as those of a band of Nazis.

By the Tennessee Code of Law, each polling place must be staffed with watchers from both parties, and the GI's had chosen boys of the best families, with the best war records, to stand as their representatives at each place. As the polls opened in Etowah, one of the GI watchers asked to see the ballot box opened and demonstrated empty as required by law. "Hell, no," said one of the deputies; an argument sputtered, a highway patrolman was summoned and Evans, the GI poll watcher, was hauled off to jail.

At 9:30 trouble flickered in Athens; the machine charged Walter Ellis, a GI watcher, with an unspecified federal offense, took him from his appointed place at the polls and put him in jail, too. At three in the afternoon Tom Gillespie, a colored man, appeared at the eleventh precinct complete with poll-tax receipt. "You can't vote here," said the machine watchers.

"He can too," contradicted the GI spokesman.

"Get him," yelled one of the deputies and someone slugged Gillespie. Gillespie broke for the door and ran down the street. As he ran, a deputy at the door drew his pistol and shot him in the back. Gillespie was taken to the hospital. Fifteen minutes later, Bob Hairell, another GI watcher at the twelfth precinct, was in trouble. The machine wanted to vote a nineteen-year-old girl; Hairell objected. One of the deputies settled the argument by pulling his blackjack and laying Hairell's head open. Hairell was off to the hospital. The *Daily Post-Athenian* sent a reporter to get the story on Hairell. He, too, was slugged and told not to ask questions.

At four, the polls closed. In the eleventh precinct, the two GI watchers, Charles Scott, Jr. and Ed Vestal, were thrust to one side as the machine prepared to count the vote. Through the plate glass door of the polling place, the people could see the two boys penned in their corner of the large room. By this time, Jim Buttram, the campaign manager, had decided that the vote of the eleventh precinct wasn't worth trading off against the lives of two of his men. Twelve armed deputies had cleared the sidewalk in front of the eleventh precinct polling place, but hundreds of people stood on the opposite side. They watched Jim and Mr. Scott, father of Charles Scott, cross the street to speak to Mansfield, the sheriff.

Mansfield was sitting in a red 1946 Dodge. There were six men in the car. Buttram offered to give him the precinct in return for the release of the watchers.

"Are you trying to tell me how to run this election?" asked Mansfield. "You go over and get them yourself if you want them."

"You wouldn't want me to get shot, would you?" said Jim. A deputy sitting beside Mansfield lifted his thirty-eight from his lap and said: "Buttram, I ought to shoot you right now, you're the son-of-a-bitch who started the whole thing."

Mansfield knocked Moses' gun down and told him to shut up, he was doing the talking.

Mr. Scott leaned over and said: "If you won't let my boy out of there and anything happens to him, you'll have to pay for it."

Pat grabbed his gun, snarled, "Let's settle this right now," and started to open the door of the car. Buttram slammed the door on him, and he and Scott hastily made their way back to the cover of the crowd.

A few minutes later Neal Ensminger, the editor of the local paper, strode over to the precinct door to see if he could get a tabulated count. As he asked one of the deputies a question, the two GI's in the polling place broke for safety. With his shoulder down, young Scott burst the door and pounded out, followed in a moment by Vestal. Bleeding, they ran across the street to the crowd as the deputies trained their guns on the boys. By this time women were screaming, children were crying, and the veterans—still unarmed—stood cursing and shouting from the opposing pavement. The deputies held their fire as the two boys slipped among the people.

It was five now, and following their practice the Cantrell forces removed the ballot boxes of the eleventh and twelfth precincts to the security of the jail for counting.

III

The GI's had promised to get the vote counted as cast, and they gathered at their campaign headquarters around the corner to confer. As they stood in the street, two Mansfield deputies approached to break up the group. Otto Kennedy was watching from his tire store as the deputies walked up the street. With Otto was his brother Oley Kennedy, just out of the Navy, and his brother J. P. "Bull" Kennedy, just out of the Army.

"Pat Mansfield said he was going to give us a fair and square election," said Kennedy, "and then we saw those sons-of-bitches from Georgia, walking around with their guns and badges, telling us to kiss their neck. They'd put our boys in jail, they were running all over us. I stepped up to the door. I saw them coming. I just couldn't take it. I said to my brother: 'Bull, let's get them.' "

As the deputies stepped into the crowd, the GI's closed about them. They hit hard and high and low. The guns were taken and distributed among the GI's. Three more deputies, then two more walked into the crowd. All were disarmed and the guns handed out. The deputies were loaded on cars, taken to the woods, stripped of their clothes, and left to walk their way out.

The GI's were still indecisive and the Kennedys became cautious. They had struck the first blow; they were vulnerable. Otto decided to go home, telling the veterans that if they decided to do anything the Kennedys were ready to come back; otherwise they were staying away. Dusk was settling and the vets talked. A city policeman walked by to say that Mansfield was coming with tommy-guns and tear gas. Then something happened.

From dusk to dawn, the story of the siege of Athens dissolves into anonymity. The people had voted the GI ticket, trusting the GI guarantee of a fair count. Five districts which had been fairly tabulated by evening had already given the GI's almost a three-to-one lead. But the ballot boxes of the eleventh and twelfth precincts were being counted in the jail. Tomorrow the Cantrell forces would have victory and no one would be safe. On the one hand, the Common Law says that every citizen has the right to prevent a crime or felony from taking place; on the other hand, to take the jail by storm against the lawfully deputized thugs seemed perilously close to insurrection. A very fine point of law is involved and Crump still runs Tennessee. Therefore, no man knows or tells who played precisely what role in Athens on the night of Thursday, August 1, 1946.

Down the highway from Athens is one of the armories of the National Guard. By eight o'clock rifles and machine guns were held by dozens of the veterans. It was a quiet movement. There was no raving or shouting. They collected at their headquarters and gravely, under cover of darkness, walked the two blocks to the jail where the sheriffs had taken the ballot boxes. Behind the jail is a barbed wire enclosure. Facing it, across the street, is a low hill covered with vines and several houses and buildings. The deputies had made a mistake that the battle-wise GI's recognized immediately: they had concentrated forty or fifty of their number in jail and left no reserves in town. The GI's deployed in the darkness in a semicircle above the jail, on the hill behind the cover of vines, on rooftops. A veteran strode into the street and yelled at the silent jail a demand for the ballot boxes and the release of the GI prisoners.

A voice answered, "Are you the law?"

The GI yelled back, "There isn't any law in McMinn County."

A lone shot went off from within the jail. The man that answered from the hill answered with a tommy-gun.

There were several hundred veterans in the semicircle and hundreds of boys and civilians. Some had rifles, a few had tommy-guns, others had bird guns and hunting pieces. The fusillade rose and fell above the night, echoing into the suburbs and hills. Bullets spattered the Chamber of Commerce and the newspaper office a block away. A block down the road, a man standing on the corner of the courthouse square was nicked in the arm.

The local radio station had sent a reporter with a microphone to cover the action; up and down the county farmers tuned in to the running account. Some of them put their clothes on, got their guns, came to join in the shoot. Boys too young to cock a rifle came down to see the fun and remained to learn how to shoot in the night.

The deputies were safe behind the thick brick wall of the jail, and the bullets of the GI's could do no more than cut out chunks of the wall. As the sporadic shooting dragged on hour after hour, the veterans realized with a sick feeling that night was wearing away and, with daylight, state patrolmen—perhaps even the National Guard—might be called in to reinforce the garrison of deputies. Defeat would mean that McMinn County would never be safe again for any man who had taken part in the night's firing. It was go through with it, or get out of town.

At midnight a detachment went over to the county farm where a case of dynamite was located. During a lull, the veterans yelled that unless the ballot boxes and prisoners were released in twenty minutes they would blast the jail. An hour went by and the jail made no answer. Somebody fitted a cap to a stick of dynamite and tossed it into the street. A second stick followed. On the third throw two sticks were tied together and thrown across to the sidewalk of the jail. The fourth throw of two sticks landed on the porch of the jail and tore it wide apart. Somebody had learned about demolition in the war; for the last try they decided to prepare a homemade satchel charge of the rest of the case and place it under the jail wall. But before the charge could be placed, the jail was yelling surrender. It was 3:30 in the morning.

"We're dying in here," came a call. "Don't use any more dynamite, we're giving up."

No one was dying. Four of the deputies were pretty badly hurt and required hospitalization; ten of the GI's were wounded in the day's action but the war was over.

The vets ordered the deputies to march into the courtyard with their hands up, leaving their guns behind. As they marched out, the crowd gathered round, yelling, cursing, and booing. Someone in the crowd reached out with a razor and slashed at one of the deputies, laying his throat open. Duggan tried to stop the man; the man explained that the deputy had arrested him before, taken him to jail and kicked in four of his ribs. Duggan tried to reason with him, but he made another razor pass. Then Duggan slugged him into obedience and led the deputy off to the hospital. Behind them a file of deputies, guarded by GI's, paraded through the street to the courthouse and back so that the people might see and taunt their unthroned impotence.

By this time dawn was lighting the county and the radio station, broadcasting the victory, was bringing farmers in from all the hills to see what was happening. The state capital had been alerted and the State Commissioner of Public Safety, Lynn Bomar, called up to locate a GI to negotiate. Ralph Duggan answered the phone and spoke to George Woods at the state capital. Woods, who was Election Commissioner of the county, promised—if given a safe conduct—to return to Athens on Monday and certify the election of the entire GI slate. Duggan announced the victory to the crowd at six in the morning and then went home.

Violence flickered on for several more hours. The GI's had had their fill, but the civilians and boys were carrying on. They smashed in windows of the deputies' automobiles, turned them over, burned cars indiscriminately. It was the GI's now who had to restrain the civilians and protect their prisoners. By ten o'clock, however, the fury had spent itself and the GI's were carefully escorting their prisoners out of town. At three, a giant mass meeting was held in the courthouse, men jamming the assembly hall, overflowing onto the steps and the lawn. The Reverend Bernie Hampton read the twenty-third psalm and asked the body of citizens what their will was. Someone suggested the appointment of a three-man committee to administer the county till things settled down. The three-man committee was elected immediately and from Friday to Monday it conducted the county's affairs on a volunteer basis.

It summoned the county court—the local legislative body—to a meeting on Monday morning. The county court declared vacant the offices held by machine contestants in the elections and declared the GI slate duly elected. Six of the twelve precincts' votes were thrown out entirely, for no fair count had been given there. When the GI's broke into jail they found that some of the tally sheets marked by the machine had been scored fifteen to one for the Cantrell forces. Where the GI's witnessed the count, the margin was three to one GI. Thus it was decided that only in those precincts where both parties had watched should the count be accepted. By Monday afternoon, Knox Henry was sheriff of McMinn County and the law was safe.

IV

McMinn is quiet and peaceful again. The courthouse has been painted for the first time in years, and the big clock has been fixed so that it strikes the hours loud, clear, and free over the entire town. The jail has been repaired but it is curiously empty. Within a month Henry was running McMinn County with eight youthful GI deputies. Saturday night no longer filled the cells with fifty or sixty men waiting to be fined; by the end of the month, Saturday night found only three men in jail. The four city policemen had been fired and replaced by veterans. Pat Mansfield was back in Georgia, working as a fireman on a railway. Paul Cantrell was in Nashville and didn't want to come back.

The gambling joints have been closed down, the bootlegging ring has been smashed, fee-grabbing ended. There are no more slot machines or punchboards. Henry has pledged the new regime that the sheriff will live on his lawful salary.

The GI party, too, has been disbanded, but a Good Government League has succeeded it. The Good Government League has branches in fifteen different communities of the county and is the public whip. The county court still has a majority of old Cantrell men, but they don't come up for election till next summer. Meanwhile the Good Government League suggests various actions to it, and the court pays heed.

The first thing the county court was persuaded to do was to establish an audit committee. The Good Government League wants to see what resources are available for the two most pressing local problems: schools and roads. Schools are pretty bad in McMinn. Pay for teachers is so poor that all the best teachers are leaving. In some places in McMinn, teachers get eighty-five dollars a month for the eight months they work; that averages less than fifteen dollars a week, year-round, as take-home pay. Even a waitress at the hotel makes more than that. Highest pay is at the high school and that comes to only thirty dollars a week for a teacher with a master's degree. The Good Government League wants to divert money from the sheriff's heavy budget to the education budget. When the schools and school buses are fixed, they want to do something about the roads. Maybe after that the League will move on to such long-range plans as a permanent county-manager system and a new structure of government.

The GI's like McMinn and they think they can keep it healthy. There will always be bootlegging unless the church people let the county make liquor legal. But now the government will be master of the bootleggers instead of the bootleggers masters of the government. The GI's say they aren't interested in "issues"; they aren't interested in unions or poll-tax laws or running the country. This was a McMinn matter, strictly a battle to give McMinn fair and square elections and force Boss Crump back to Shelby County.

It is true, of course, that Crump still runs the rest of Tennessee and that Crump helped send back to Washington a man named Kenneth McKellar. And until November 1946, McKellar was president of the

Senate of the United States of America, called the greatest deliberative body in the world.

61. THE "DISFRANCHISED" URBANITES *

RICHARD LEE STROUT

The way in which a particular social institution functions is integrally and continuously related to other institutions and social forces. The current shifting of American population from rural to metropolitan areas is a major force affecting many aspects of society. In this selection Richard Lee Strout describes how the system of representative government based on a rural ecology is no longer representative in states with large metropolitan populations.

Consider, my friends, the case of Louis Cahoon. He represents the town of Victory in the Vermont legislature. He also is the father of eight —four sons, four daugthers—and a solid citizen. Formerly he was selectman and justice of the peace. Now he is a lister—the Vermont term for "appraiser"—tax collector, and constable. If you live in Victory, he can set your tax, send you the bill, and arrest you if you don't pay it.

If you are driving through Vermont, you may have a little trouble finding Victory. Before you get there, the power line stops and the telephone stops and the macadam gives out. Mr. and Mrs. Cahoon read by kerosene lamps. So do the forty-seven other inhabitants of Victory. But they have their own representative in the state legislature becaus« Vermont gave each town a seat in the lower house in 1793—and hasn't changed the rules since.

When Mr. Cahoon is serving as a legislator, he sits not far from Joseph Moore, who represents the thriving city of Burlington. Its population is 33,000. Since Vermont is still operating under a system of apportionment set up 166 years ago, Victory and Burlington have equal representation. That means that one rural vote is equal to some 670 city

* Originally published as "The Next Election Is Already Rigged," in *Harper's Magazine* (November, 1959). Reprinted by permission of the author.

The author has been a Washington correspondent for the *Christian Science Monitor* since 1924, except for a period spent serving as war correspondent during World War II. Coauthor, with E. B. White, of *Farewell to Model T.*

votes. The people of Burlington are not merely second-class citizens; politically speaking, they are the poor relations of Mr. Cahoon and his Victorian neighbors. As everybody knows, the farmers run Vermont— and under this setup, it is easy to see how.

But Vermont, after all, is a notoriously conservative state. All over the country Americans are leaving the farms for the cities, taking with them their fond folk memories of country life. How fortunate for all of us, they are probably thinking, that Vermont, at least, keeps alive the quaint old custom of equating a tiny village with a thriving city.

So, by way of contrast, let's see how they do things in progressive, up-to-date California. A fairly typical California politician is Charles Brown. He runs the general store at Shoshone and serves as the representative in the state senate of the 14,014 residents of three cow counties —Inyo, Mono, and Alpine.

And there is Dick Richards, a prominent young lawyer with political aspirations. He sits in the senate too, representing the 38th district. The 38th—oh, that's the county of Los Angeles. It has a population of 5,970,000. It gets one senator, just like Inyo, Mono, and Alpine. One rural vote here is worth 425 city votes—not quite as bad as Vermont, but hardly what we think of as "democracy" where every man's vote is supposed to be as good as any other's.

This kind of political deck-stacking is not confined to the Coasts. It is common all through the country, and it is distorting the whole political process. It is growing worse, as more and more people move to the cities. It has given the farmers vastly more than their fair share of political power. (A fact which helps explain why our ridiculous and costly scheme of farm subsidies can persist so long.) It has spread to the national House of Representatives, where farm areas now have from twenty to thirty more seats than their population entitles them to.

So long as we permit it to go uncured, this warping of our political system throws the fairness of every election in doubt. It rigs the results of the voting far more effectively than all the ballot-stuffing and bribery which went on in the bad old days of machine politics.

The most astonishing thing about it is that the cities do not revolt. What prevents them?—that is the mystery. Maybe the answer is that most city people simply don't know how badly they are being cheated.

[At present there are approximately] seven out of every ten Americans living in urban areas—but the balance of political power still rests with the country districts and the small towns. In Kansas, for example, one-third of the population—the most rural part—can elect a majority of the state senate. In Maryland it is 16 per cent. In Rhode Island is it 14 per cent. Indiana has six counties which contain almost half of its population—yet get only a third of the seats in both houses. Michigan's voters are concentrated largely in Detroit and its suburbs, which means that two-fifths of them live in Wayne county; but they can elect only one-fifth of the state senate. This fact underlies most of the state's recent financial troubles. The upstate farmers with their bagful of representatives simply aren't willing to vote the tax money which the urban majority thinks it needs to run a modern community.

A similar situation is building up in Florida as it becomes increasingly urbanized. Two-thirds of its people live in nine counties; they can elect less than a quarter of the legislature.

Nearly every state constitution begins with a sonorous statement of the basic rule of democracy—one man equals one vote—and goes on to direct regular reapportionment of the legislative seats at stated intervals. But the record shows a disgraceful disregard of these constitutional directives. Only sixteen states actually carried out their reallocation of seats and legislative redistricting on the last two occasions when they were required to do so by their own constitutions. And in some of these cases the adjustments were minor. For example, the Illinois legislature simply ignored the reapportionment clause in its constitution from 1901 to 1954—thus setting its people a bland example of lawlessness for half a century. Finally, in 1955, after suffering outrageous under-representation in both houses of the legislature for years, Chicago agreed to have this injustice frozen permanently in the senate in exchange for a fair allotment of seats in the lower house.

In much the same way New York City is hobbled in Albany. Eight million city people elect only 90 members of the legislature, while seven million upstaters have 118. The hostility that has resulted is one of the deep-seated aspects of Empire State politics. The city's budget is half a billion dollars larger than New York State's (and larger than any state's in the union) but its officials must make annual trips to Albany hat-in-hand. There the metropolis is treated like a feckless stepchild which can be trusted to levy only certain taxes and only on a short-term basis, and is seldom, if ever, allocated its proportionate share of state revenues.

In Colorado, in the same fashion, the legislature doles out to Denver only $2.3 million a year school aid for 90,000 children. But adjacent, semi-rural Jefferson County gets a generous $2.4 million for 18,000 pupils. In Pennsylvania the legislature pays $8 a day for the care of indigent patients to every non-sectarian hospital in the state—except Philadelphia's city-owned General Hospital. The exception costs the city $2.5 million a year.

"I think Philadelphia is even more disliked by our state legislature than New York City by the New York State legislature," Mayor Richardson Dilworth blurted out at a recent Congressional hearing. "Every mayor of a city over half a million has reported the same condition."

Only a political innocent could miss the meaning of this nation-wide feud. Outside of the South, the cities are generally Democratic while

Republican strength tends to be concentrated in the rural areas. The latter, of course, gain from the imbalance in representation. In New York, Illinois, Michigan, and other important states, the upper chamber of the legislature has been given, virtually in perpetuity, to the Republicans. It has become a rural conservative fortress, a kind of petty House of Lords almost above the swings of majority rule.

What has happened to the normal process of democracy when Governor Mennen Williams wins popular majorities for six successive terms in Michigan but has never yet won control of the legislature? When New Jersey shifts regularly between the parties in national and gubernatorial elections, but the state senate remains forever Republican? When Adlai Stevenson won the governorship of Illinois by 570,000 in 1948 but faced a Republican senate throughout his term of office? When there has been a Democratic governor in Albany during twenty-five years since 1920, but the Republicans have held a majority of the senate in all but eight of those years and lost control of both chambers in only one?

Our curious system of misrepresentation has its roots down in the counties which are the home bases of most state lawgivers. (In New England it is the township.) County government is in widespread decay; most counties are headless and disintegrating. This obsolete unit of government supports a variety of strange elective offices such as the sheriff (descended from the English shire-reeve who preserved the shire's peace) and the coroner (a Crown officer around 1194 who kept his eye on the shire-reeve). Today when the proud voter parades to the polling place in a county election, he takes his choice between a couple of seedy undertakers to determine whether there shall be Democratic or Republican autopsies in the next biennium. There are over 3,000 counties and they are the dark continent of American government.

However, jobs on the county payroll and county construction contracts and purchases are an important source of nourishment to the rural grassroots of our political parties. State lawgivers are usually picked by the county organization and have a parochial outlook. State legislatures generally meet for only a few months and some convene only every other year. Many of the state assemblymen and senators are first-rate men. But inevitably they look askance at the teeming problems of the exigent cities.

This does not prevent them, however, from being inveterate backseat drivers. A stop light at the corner of Main and Elm? Let the city fathers first consult state officials. A city tax on cigarettes? St. Paul and Minneapolis won permission for such a levy in 1949 from the state legislature, which then appropriated the money for the state budget.

But these are mosquito bites compared to the real problem. In the United States, great super-cities are forming, not metropolises but megalopolises. Already, one vast urban region stretching six hundred miles from New Hampshire to Washington, D.C. holds a fifth of the country's population. Similar agglomerations will run from Los Angeles to San Diego, from Cleveland to Pittsburgh, and among the cities along the St. Lawrence Seaway—Detroit and Toledo, Chicago and Milwaukee. How can rural lawmakers—men who never rode a subway—deal with the super-cities' staggering transportation, industrial, housing, and other social problems? In fact, they don't.

Back in 1953 President Eisenhower was determined to scale down centralized government by returning more functions to the states. So he set up a Commission on Intergovernment Relations headed by one of his Special Assistants, Meyer Kestnbaum, a much respected business magnate. The Kestnbaum report proclaimed facts which college professors had vainly tried to tell the nation for years; cities are bringing problems to Washington because state legislatures won't handle them.

"In a majority of the states," said the report, "city-dwellers outnumber the citizens of rural areas. Yet in most states the rural voters are overwhelmingly in control of one legislative house and overweighted if not dominant in the other. . . . If the states do not give the cities their rightful allocation of seats in the legislature, the tendency will be toward direct federal-municipal dealings."

This is why Senator Joseph S. Clark of Pennsylvania last summer introduced a bill to set up a special federal commission on metropolitan problems. Such a device might conceivably help the city voter to get a better shake in Washington, but the odds are heavily against him.

As we know, Nevada with 160,000 people has two U.S. Senators, just like New York with its 14.8 million. But the House was to be the "grand depository of the democratic principle" with membership determined proportionately by population. It has not worked out that way. Rurally biased state legislators draw the boundaries of Congressional districts and have been most obliging in giving Representatives from the hinterland safe, sparsely populated fiefs. In Texas, for instance, Sam Rayburn's district has a population of around 200,000 while the state's lone Republican, Bruce Alger of Dallas, has nearly three times as many constituents. Republican-dominated South Dakota, on the other hand, splits its two Congressional seats so that the Democrat has 494,000 constituents, the Republican 159,000.

Some of the worst inequities result, not from positive acts of injustice but from no action whatever. The controlling faction in the state legislature simply does nothing while population within the states gravitates toward the cities. This is the "silent gerrymander" which has done much to devalue the city-dweller's vote. Partisanship is not always a factor. Thus in Ohio the 3rd and 15th Districts are both Republican, but the 3rd, which includes Dayton, has nearly double the population of the semi-rural 15th. This follows the political rule that Republicans where possible shortchange Democrats and Democrats where possible short-change Republicans, and both shortchange city-dwellers.

The irony of our present situation is that the Senate has become more urban-minded than the House, for in most states Senators can't win without city votes. Many Representatives, on the other hand, come from districts that don't even have a large town. After World War II the Senate passed public-housing bills three times before one got through the rural-minded House and became law. Since then the House has repeatedly voted to reduce or eliminate public housing and similar appropriations needed by the cities. Slum clearance, urban renewal, city-health benefits all tend to fare better in the Senate than the House. In both houses, the seniority system of picking committee chairmen also handicaps city-dwellers; Congressmen from one-party districts are bound to outlast urban Representatives who often face fierce competition and must battle every two years for the votes of a huge, constantly changing constituency.

Rural over-representation involves one more thing—the Constitution. After Congress passes an amendment, it goes for ratification to the state legislatures. How representative is this jury? The fate of the 18th Amendment might have been very different if it had been voted on by the people rather than by state legislatures fearful of Wayne B. Wheeler. The 22nd Amendment limiting the President to two terms (which has lost its glitter for some of its original backers) also had a peculiar charm for conservative rural legislators who chronically mistrust executive power, whether the governor's or the President's.

. . . . .

Most state legislatures go about redistricting as though they had "some sort of popular mandate directing the victor to monopolize the spoils," writes Dr. Gordon E. Baker of the University of California in his pamphlet *Rural versus Urban Political Power*. In fact, the dominant party can draw any boundaries it thinks the public will stand for without gagging. Few courts will interfere and there are few laws to restrain it.

Until 1929 a federal statute did require state legislatures to make Congressional districts compact, contiguous, and reasonably equal in population. After the 1920 Census, the House and Senate couldn't agree on a new apportionment act. When one finally passed in 1929 it omitted the old fair-apportionment clause, although Congress lacked the effrontery to repeal it expressly. When the matter was brought to the Supreme Court by a Mississippi citizen in 1932, the Court drily declined to intervene on the grounds that Congress deliberately intended to drop the voters' safeguard. President Truman asked Congress to restore it in a special message in January 1951. Almost certainly our next President,

Republican or Democrat, will make the same appeal. . . . Will Congress heed? Not if the public reaction is no greater than that given to hearings called by Chairman Emanuel Celler of the House Judiciary Committee. He has been trying to rouse interest in a reform bill but has stirred hardly a ripple.

Even if Congress fails to act, the oppressed city-dweller could—if he chose to do so—bring about some changes. The chief weapons at his disposal are these:

The courts. Until very recently the Supreme Court and state courts generally declined to intervene in redistricting questions. However, a three-judge federal court in Minnesota, July 10, 1958, required the legislature to obey the state constitution and undertake reapportionment. An encouraging precedent has thus been set.

Pressure by civic groups. The League of Women Voters, long an active proponent of reform in several states, is now compiling a nation-wide record from data collected by local chapters. Municipal organizations are also awakening to the problem. Many "greenbelt" suburbs (often Republican) are now growing faster than parent cities (usually Democratic). This gives a new, refreshingly bi-partisan impetus to the drive for reform.

Initiative. The constitutions of twenty states make it possible to force legislative reforms by circulating petitions among the electorate. Initiative has been used, in recent years, to increase urban representation in four states: Washington, Colorado, Oregon, and Arkansas.

None of these remedies is easy to apply or certain of success. Attempts at reform have been known to backfire, for there is a powerful vested interest in preserving malapportionment. Strong groups within the cities themselves which are content with the status quo, make common cause with conservative rural lawgivers—they are, perhaps, easier to manipulate than city types.

Consider what happened in California in 1948. A bi-partisan group with labor support initated a petition for reapportionment. There was little doubt as to the need: the four million residents of Los Angeles then —as now—had only a single senator in Sacramento.

But the reform was fought tooth and nail by—of all people—the Los Angeles Chamber of Commerce (which had backed reapportionment a few years earlier). Other business groups denounced it and so did the metropolitan press almost without exception. (Less surprisingly, the Farm Bureau and the Grange were opposed.) In a frenzied attack, the petition was called "a labor plot," "a Communist plot," "un-American," an effort by "crackpots" to impose ruinous taxation on "city home-owners and wealth-producing farm areas." The project was over-whelmed; it didn't carry a single county. Even the under-represented cities voted against it.

All of which brings us back to our original question: How long will 115 million city suckers stay under the green thumb of 57 million country slickers?

Maybe the urban voter needs a psychiatrist. Floating before his inner eye is the image of a trim white farmhouse—a purity symbol. Next door, in his subconscious, is the guilty, haunting memory of ancient American municipal corruption labeled Tammany Hall. The psychiatrist might try to explain why the obsession lingers on, even though the reform of so many city governments is one of the inspiring developments of the past twenty-five years.

Yet the buttercup myth of rural superiority survives. It sprouts in every American when he goes to school and reads "The Village Blacksmith" and "Snowbound." Along with Jefferson he learns to mistrust men who don't till the soil. And he cherishes the lost simplicity of a Vermont farmhouse with pump, and flakes floating down that are either apple petals or snow. Here is the true America of Longfellow, Whittier, and Robert Frost. A lovely image. The only trouble with it is that it stands between the city-dweller and the city's new sewage disposal plant.

62. HAVE OUR SCHOOLS FAILED? *

SPENCER BROWN

Americans value education highly as a means, on the one hand, to maintain cultural continuity and, on the other, to promote rational social change. The increasing average number of years our youth spend in school attests to the importance we attach to formal education. Although nearly all Americans consider the schools an important social force, they are not all in agreement as to just what it is the schools are supposed to do. Many have recently criticized the schools for failure to produce a higher academic achievement among graduates. Some have contended that only drastic changes in the schools will meet society's present and future needs. In this selection proposals for differentiated curricula for several strata of children are suggested as one means to meet more adequately the needs of society. The subsequent selection,

* Reprinted from *Commentary*, Vol. 25, No. 6 (June, 1958), 461–471. Copyright American Jewish Committee.

The author teaches at the Fieldston School in Riverdale, New York. Author: *They See for Themselves; My Father's Business and Other Poems.*

by Bettelheim, analyzes the consequences of such differentiated
educational programs for a democratic society.

Within the teaching profession as well as outside it, the reaction of
each person to Sputnik has been predictable from his previous utterances.
Those who belabored the schools before do so now; those who were
generally happy about the schools are no less happy now—except that,
they say, Sputnik shows we must appropriate more money for everything. Many teachers and administrators feel that we should not be
"stampeded by Sputnik" into "rash innovations." Some of them feel, in
fact, resentful of the increased pressure put on them; they do not want
to become "a part of the war hysteria"—a defense of the status quo that
seems as much political as educational. It may be no exaggeration to say
that the profession views Sputnik just as it did World War II—everybody
should do what he has been doing, but do it better; do more things for
more people; pay more attention to gifted children, but be more understanding of the others; teach more mathematics and science, without
neglecting the humanities. The program of the Sputnik-centered school
is to be a slight emendation of Sam Gompers—*more*, except for driver
training.

Amid such confusion a few clear and sensible voices are heard. One
of these is Paul Woodring, whose *Let's Talk Sense About Our Schools*
was notable, a few years ago, for intelligence and balance. . . .

Now in *A Fourth of a Nation* Dr. Woodring has provided a masterly
summary of the educational controversy of our times and has made two
revolutionary proposals on curriculum reform and the training of teachers. His account of the "classical thesis" and the "progressive antithesis,"
together with his proposed synthesis, deserves the attention of any reader
more interested in being informed than in merely choosing sides and
rushing into battle. Unfortunately there is space here only to commend
his lucidity of thought and style and to touch on some of his concrete
suggestions.

The fate of the "upper third" of American students is of particular
concern to Dr. Woodring. . . . Dr. Woodring ridicules comparison of
European and American schools. Of course the European student is
ahead of the American student of like age—the European student represents a selected third, or tenth; the American student represents everybody. Dr. Woodring agrees with the American ideal of educating all
students through high school, but he is emphatic in his recommendation
that they be grouped by ability and the ablest be pushed ahead farther
and faster. The social arguments often adduced against such selection he
discounts, since accelerated students in large schools will always have

the company of their peers. The selection should be made, however, by the schools; "at present the choice (of an academic rather than a vocational program) is made much more often on the basis of parental expectation or of family income than upon learning capacity." As to the apprehension that such grouping is undemocratic, "Such a fear," he says, "borders on hypochondria. . . . If we ever have an elite, it is not likely to be an intellectual one."

Dr. Woodring's proposed reorganization of the curriculum is based on a two-speed system: at the age of seven, or seven and a half, the faster students would proceed from an ungraded primary school, roughly the equivalent of our kindergarten and the first two grades, into the four grades of an elementary school. At eleven or twelve they would go into a three-year high school and thence to a four-year college. They would be ready for graduate or professional schools at nineteen.

Slower students, who would be grouped with the faster ones of their age and social maturity in home rooms and extracurricular activities, would proceed generally two years behind, ending their two or three years of high school at sixteen or seventeen. They would then go to work or to junior college or trade school. Dr. Woodring envisages this system as flexible enough to take care of the student who is, for example, good in mathematics and weak in literature. Such a student would take part of his work in one sequence and part in another. The program obviously is suitable only to large schools with competent guidance, but these— consolidated schools or school systems—are becoming more and more the rule in America.

As an equally important corollary, Dr. Woodring would reorganize teacher-training, requiring all teachers to go through his reconstituted liberal arts colleges and then a two-year course leading to a teaching degree. Until such organization has come about, however, he is willing to settle for the five-year program (college plus one year of graduate work and apprentice teaching) now being experimentally tried in a number of colleges, with subsidies from the Fund for the Advancement of Education.

Dr. Woodring's plan, even if wholly sound, is sure to encounter the objection that it would involve enormous change and expense. A somewhat similar plan, however, to which this objection is less valid, has been offered by James Bryant Conant, former president of Harvard, who has been conducting a survey of American high schools for the Carnegie Corporation.

Dr. Conant's proposal, sketchily pictured in *Life,* has the merit of being a composite of actual practices. He suggests three main sequences, for the bright, the average, and the slow student. The bright student is not accelerated, but by the time he has finished high school his work is wholly on the college level in mathematics, science, and language; his destination is obviously college. The average student follows a solid but less advanced academic course with considerable vocational training, leading perhaps to business or highly skilled labor ("building contractor" is *Life's* example). The slow student pursues simplified general studies and basic shop courses and is headed for semi-skilled or skilled labor. All three groups come together for home room, extracurricular activities, typing, mechanical drawing, music, and twelfth-grade social studies. The plan is most appropriate for large, comprehensive high schools, many of which already exist and more of which are being consolidated from small and inadequate schools—a policy Dr. Conant recommends. No provision seems to be made for driver training, even for the boy who is graduating to "Joe's Garage." Presumably his fellow garage attendants will teach him the requisite ruthlessness toward man and machine.

However attractive such proposals as Dr. Woodring's and Dr. Conant's may be, it will be hard to adopt them widely in the near future. Education is one of America's largest industries, with a tremendous investment in a plant whose function cannot be quickly changed; we cannot close down the industry for re-tooling; it suffers from a chronic labor shortage; its labor is highly skilled and relatively inflexible in skill; and training new workers is slow and costly. The most serious shortage is in the college—the final assembly line from which roll the Sputnik-builders—for here labor is most departmentalized and takes longest to train. You can build a college in a year, amass a library for it in five, and get a good faculty in ten—but only assuming that you have more money than your competitors. At that, you will not have alleviated the college shortage, since you will have raided other colleges for your professors.

. . . . .

The question of numbers is not peripheral but central. For more students must go to college to become the teachers to staff colleges and schools—not to mention the scientists and engineers and executives to run society, launch moons, and otherwise compete with the Russians.

To meet the situation, both school and college will have to institute numerous piecemeal reforms, and extensions of current practices, rather than a single sweeping revolution. To increase opportunities in higher education, we may be forced to keep colleges open the year round (Oberlin College has proposed two quarters of teaching, one of study, and one of vacation, enabling the same number of teachers to carry twice as many students); to increase college size and enrollment; to set up more junior colleges and local colleges; to make existing junior colleges more demanding intellectually; to make some use of television and (the forgotten medium) radio; to use increased competition for admission to a favored few colleges as a means of elevating standards in all; to make better use of the oldest "visual aid"—books—as an alternative to the lecture system, which was the medieval substitute for books; and somehow to find money to pay professors well and so keep able men from drifting into business and industry.

With the aid of both major and minor reforms, the American colleges may be able to turn out a sufficiently large number of well-trained young people. Yet it would be a pity if we did not use the emergency also as an opportunity to examine and improve the colleges. The hand of vocationalism, as has been observed by critics as far apart as William H. Whyte, Jr., and Robert M. Hutchins, is far too heavy on the curriculum. The best engineering schools are now, perhaps too late, becoming concerned with the literacy and cultural sophistication of their students. And professors of the humanities are desperately striving to keep their few islands of culture in the liberal-arts colleges from being washed away by the rising tide of "business majors" and other quasi-vocational courses, most of which are of very dubious value even in training for any known vocation.

Perhaps as important as curricular reform, however, is the attitude of administrators and admissions officers toward eccentric and original students and applicants. Colleges today are entirely too successful in molding boys into organization men. College presidents orate publicly on the need for brains and original thought; but their colleges officially foster all kinds of activities, innocent but inconsequential campus affairs as well as the insanity of big-time "amateur" athletics and the barbarous snobbery of fraternities, that have nothing to do with this need except perhaps to make it worse.

Waste is another matter. Some waste is inevitable. All leisure classes throughout history are prodigally wasteful of time and energy; culture is a by-product of waste. And our college students are our leisure class. They will waste their time and energy having fun, and some of the fun will be cultural; but they are capable of their own waste without the help of the administration.

To attack the American undergraduate for this waste is futile. Other notably successful educational systems have paralleled the waste, and not to recognize the parallel is mere literal-mindedness. Nineteenth-century Oxford and Cambridge performed miracles of elegant indolence. For every Arnold or Clerk-Maxwell or Housman there were a hundred passmen who rode to hounds or otherwise went to the dogs. Modern Russia also has its leisure class, but its waste is organized—in meetings, agitation, ritual speeches and applause, ideological tightrope-walking, heresy-sniffing, and state-directed murder. This kind of leisure activity the Russian student, with humorless intensity, learns by doing. Our students prefer athletics, college radio stations and newspapers, beer, music, and bull-sessions.

Contrary to public belief, there is as yet no real college shortage. There is enormously increased competition for admission to some thirty or fifty well-known colleges and universities, but there are many times that number of intellectually respectable colleges still in need of capable students. Within a few years all good colleges *may* be full of good students, and it will then be necessary to improve the colleges that are not good. This is really what the shouting is about. But in the meantime the problem is being artificially aggravated by the insistence of many well-to-do non-students (or of their parents) on college, the willingness of many admissions officers to take them, and the irrelevance of some of the criteria for admission. Admissions officers have become—like the rest of us—highly sophisticated in amateur psychiatry. They (and we) are quick to spot and reject the deviant, to reward the well-adjusted, to confuse a knowing eye for the main chance with emotional maturity.

. . . . . .

The scientific, technological, military, and political crisis demands trained minds. I think it is possible to secure them without sacrificing the advantage of universal education—but not with a single blueprint for every school and a single solution for all teaching problems. Some sort of Conant-Woodring plan, involving two, three, or more paths through school, is in the long run unavoidable. Nevertheless these programs will bring more problems with them.

For instance, we have never solved the difficulty of providing a decent "terminal education" in the high school for the student unable or unwilling to go on. Dr. Hutchins would teach him the Great Books. I'd like to see him do it; college teachers in general and Dr. Hutchins in particular have no conception of how to teach a really low IQ; they have never had to try. Yet the Conant-Woodring plans, it seems to me, contemplate far too calmly a vocationally oriented, culturally stunted curriculum. And neither Dr. Conant nor Dr. Woodring has considered the cruel pressures that would be put on average or below-average children by middle-class parents ambitious for them to undertake an accelerated program. In schools abroad, the evils of early discrimination among children's abilities, the crucial examinations at the age of eleven, the intolerable strain on moderately able adolescents, have led England, France, and even Russia to question results achieved at such cost. There is no point in importing diseases: we have enough of our own without infecting every tot with a fevered ambition for a career to which high marks are the only path.

Good schools demand good teachers. More college graduates—in both absolute and relative numbers—are going into teaching than ever before. But what are these among so many? The numbers do not come near matching the need. We might get more teachers if teachers enjoyed enhanced prestige and encountered less overwork. But in these matters the best schools are as guilty as the worst. True, a good teacher must be a guide and friend; he is too often encouraged to be nursemaid and probation officer and family counselor; and he is rarely encouraged to be (within the limits of his subject, the age of his pupils, and his own intellect) a philosopher and scholar. Endless meetings with parents and educators, bales of paper work and reports and surveys, each purporting to streamline the educational system and achieving only more plastic tailfins and chromium grillwork, busy-work to feed the administrative ego, and chaperonage of student activities better abolished or allowed to run themselves—these hardly promote any philosophy but cynicism, or any scholarship but Parkinson's Law.

Scholarship, however, will carry little prestige in America unless it is well paid. And recruiting partly trained housewives for stop-gap "teachers' aides" to do the paper- and busy-work has been proved unnecessary in school systems where salaries are raised enough to attract teachers. The average American teacher (salary $4,055) must work on other jobs evenings, week ends, or vacations, or all three, to make ends meet. The Federal government, including the President, has stood on the safe side of the line talking. Any other industry as large and vital as education would have enjoyed a major strike long ago. But despite the efforts of the American Federation of Teachers the industry remains unorganized; and even the AFT does not favor strikes, since the children suffer (a most unlaborlike sentimentalism: the consumer suffers in every strike). Thus teachers have been striking in the only way open to them— by leaving the profession if they get the chance. A widely advocated lure, merit pay, or extra salary for special competence, is anathema to teachers' organizations, since it can be used administratively to cow independence, originality, or intelligence. But good administration will not use it so, and bad administration can be fired. The shortage is of teachers, not administrators. . . .

The time has come to state a few simple educational laws: (1) Education costs money. Though expense does not guarantee success, more and better education always costs more. (2) American education has not so much progressed as yawed wildly from one extreme to another. Let us tack, if necessary, but not yaw. Many of our schools, in David Riesman's phrase, are still "correcting for deficiencies of an earlier day." The conservative critics may charitably be said to be over-compensating for an over-correction. But the real axe-grinders are venting their religious or philosophical rage at Dewey's destruction of their pet absolutes. Hence they try to behead the schools under the pretext of giving them a haircut. (3) All schools make mistakes. The bitterness of almost every debate on education attests nearly universal ignorance of this truth. (4) American education has grown by crazy accretion. We always add and never purposefully discard. The schools are already trying to do too much. Therefore let us never add anything without inspecting and discarding at least two other things.

Should we then acquiesce in the loud campaign to drop alleged trivia, beginning with driver training? Not without more sober examination than any axe-grinder condescends to make. To strip the curriculum of "frills" is plausible economy. If they really are frills, it is wisdom. But it is both costly and stupid if in so doing we destroy opportunities for aesthetic experience, for originality, for the amassing of apparently useless information, for experiment and vitality through recreation, for independence of judgment. These are necessary to all children, especially the ablest, if we are to have trained, resourceful minds and sturdy personalities to meet the scientific and political crisis. Those who shout, "Down with Dewey and driver training," besides demonstrating incompetence through inability to make distinctions, are unwittingly making a colossal task impossible.

63. SPUTNIK AND SEGREGATION *

Should the Gifted Be Educated Separately?

BRUNO BETTELHEIM

The preceding selection presented proposals for differentiated school curricula for children having presumed differences in levels of learning ability. This movement, which is being increasingly promoted, to separate school children on such a basis, says Bettelheim in this selection, has been stimulated as much by unreasoned fear of Russia and the desire to have the schools provide differential status symbols as by the rational conviction that such schooling will more efficiently meet society's needs. Bettelheim raises some searching questions about the impact of such education programs on the present and the future of our democratic society. The author makes a striking point of the possibility that current

* Reprinted from *Commentary*, Vol. 26, No. 4 (October, 1958), 332–339. Copyright American Jewish Committee.

The author (b. 1903) is Professor of Educational Psychology, University of Chicago. Special areas of interest are child development and child psychoanalysis. Born in Austria; Ph.D., Vienna. Author: *Love Is Not Enough; Symbolic Wounds; Truants from Life.*

educational trends toward special classes and groupings in our schools may simply result in new and more intensive patterns of social stratification.

First there was Little Rock; then came Sputnik. First there was excitement about equal schooling for all children irrespective of race, and then about the need for special schooling for the gifted child. One might think that the two are totally unrelated, that there exists no connection between desegregation and the education of the gifted. Persistent headlines on both issues seem just pure chance, or one of the vagaries of history.

Yet with Sputnik in the sky, the Russian advances in science and technology—long known to all experts—suddenly aroused vast anxiety among wide circles of the population. There was a strong emotional reaction to the realization that we are not always the biggest and the best, that we were not, in fact, the first to send a dog into orbit. And suddenly the education of the gifted became everybody's concern. We must have more and better scientists, and our educational system must immediately be reformed so as to supply this need—if not by today, then certainly by tomorrow.

It hardly seems necessary to mention the powerful emotions which the issue of desegregation in the schools arouses both in the North and the South; the liberal North excitedly telling the South what ought to be done, and when and how, and the South just as vehemently insisting that the North mind its own business, and consider what is going on in its big cities and genteel suburbs. Both sections of the country point at each other and cry, "Look who's calling the kettle black!" It is difficult to say with much conviction who in this controversy is kettle and who is pot. The South—ever so reluctantly and not just occasionally in bad faith —seems to be moving from "separate but equal" toward integration; while the white, liberal, middle-class North seems to be aiming (not in principle, not according to doctrine, but in actual practice) at school arrangements which can best be described as separate and unequal. It is no accident that public interest was shown in both issues—desegregation and education of the gifted—at the same time.

Behind the shouting and the newspaper demands that we stop the inequities of Southern school segregation, there is often hidden the fact of Northern segregation. Here, the separation of the "nice" white children from the poor white and Negro children is accomplished both by the enlargement of private and parochial school systems, and by the move to the suburbs—a move for which the family's main reasons are usually the better suburban schools and the fact that the children will associate with more desirable playmates than would be the case in the city. In the white suburbs the children are supposed to enjoy better cultural opportunities. These opportunities, strangely enough, are no longer equated with being close to the cultural facilities that an urban center offers, but rather with lawns and trees, though historically cultural advances have been tied to urban and not to rural life. That the chief reason for moving to the suburbs is the wish to keep the middle-class child from having to go to school with children from "undesirable" homes, is further suggested by the fact that suburban real estate developers usually make the good school system their main selling point. And sure enough, once the children are no longer of school age, many of the suburban families move back into the cities, precisely because commuting is a bother and the cultural advantages of the city are more available.

But moving to the suburbs is not the only way in which middle-class parents avoid having their children go to integrated schools. They also send their children to private schools, which has led to increased enrollment in the existing ones and the creation of new private schools. Yet the very expensive private schools can hardly begin to meet the demand and so we see an even more remarkable growth of segregated religious school systems, Protestant, Catholic, and Jewish, even as the segregated public schools are abolished by law.

Now what has all this to do with Sputnik? The connection between integration in the schools and education for the gifted is indeed intricate. School integration—not as a social obligation or a question of moral justice, but as adjudged by the Supreme Court—is required because in states where the schools are segregated the educational facilities for Negro children are inadequate. The public demand for better provision for the gifted child is based on exactly the same premise; i.e., that educational facilities are inadequate, in this case for the gifted child. Thus both have for their common denominator the lack of adequate educational facilities.

If we try viewing the great excitement over Little Rock and Sputnik as a case of post hoc, ergo propter hoc, the sequence of events may be as follows: we wish to see our schools integrated—so much so that we try to enforce this aim by law. Our reason is that we desire to promote literacy and academic achievement, and secure equal educational opportunities for all children. As a result, large numbers of children will enter our schools who are less well educated than the rest of the population, because they have never before enjoyed equal educational opportunities and because the educational background of their parents is inferior. The process will improve the educational opportunities of the new arrivals, but at the same time it will lower the over-all average for academic achievement. This result, it is hoped, will not be permanent, but only a temporary consequence of integration. But at the moment we face the paradox that what was meant to raise academic achievement tends temporarily (and perhaps permanently) to lower the educational level of one part of the population while, hopefully, raising the average of the population as a whole. All this is going on while the "not-so-cold" war leads to demands for an acceleration of scientific achievements. The solution to the problem of risking a drop in the top levels of intellectual achievement (through equality in education designed to bring up all levels of achievement) while trying to step up intellectual efforts, seems to be to create special educational opportunities for the gifted. Thus the argument runs both ways: higher average achievement by means of equal educational opportunities for everybody (Little Rock); and organization of special educational facilities for gifted children (Sputnik). By now the discussion begins to echo the Orwellian principle that all animals are equal, but some more equal than others. All too often the same people who insist that all men are equal (and hence fight against segregation according to race) claim just as heatedly that some are more equal— and hence demand a different type of schooling for the gifted.

In the vanguard of the fight for desegregation is a section of the liberal intelligentsia. The argument thus acquires the ominous character of a fight for equal opportunities for the rest of the population, plus special opportunities for our own group, the intelligentsia. Or, closer to fact, the special educational privileges of white over Negro should be eliminated, but special educational opportunities should be created for the intellectual elite.

But perhaps all this is exaggeration. It may be that the plans for the education of the gifted do not imply the creation of a new, separate, and unequal education system. Let us see what in fact is being proposed for the education of the gifted. Since last fall, to take only one example, the ideas of Professor Paul Woodring have obtained wide public attention. First *Life* magazine (September 2, 1957) devoted a big spread to his plan for revising the school system; then his book, *A Fourth of a Nation*, was widely discussed; and more recently an editorial in *Science* (February 21, 1958), the official organ of the American Association for the Advancement of Science, the largest scientists' group in this country, notes the "widespread attention" accorded to his plan for a new education system. In the *Life* article, entitled "Reform Plan for Schools," he suggested a school population that would eventually separate into three large groups: bright, average, and below-average students. The latter group would prepare for unskilled occupations only, their schooling to end at sixteen or seventeen. The education of the average group would permit them to engage in skilled trades or clerical work; they would remain in school until about eighteen. The bright students would be expected to enter the universities and the professional graduate schools. Professor Woodring says nothing to indicate that students would not receive a common schooling in the primary grades (first and second). But already in the third grade they could be taught differently, while at the high school level they would definitively be separated, by subject, into bright, average, and below-average.

· · · · ·

Perhaps I am unfair in suggesting that the purpose of such a school system would be at least as much to separate an elite from the rest of the population as to secure more scientific talent—something, after all, no known school system has so far succeeded in suppressing.

· · · · ·

A case could be made for the proposition that the more democratic nature of our government and social system came about because, in theory, all children are subject to identical educational experiences during their first twelve years in school, while the radical separation of those who are to benefit from higher education takes place only at about the age of eighteen, when the personality is nearly fully formed. True, there are drop-outs from about ninth grade on, but the great division is still that between the college and non-college population, separating fully grown persons from each other. The younger the child, the more his attitude to school and learning, and with it his school achievement, reflects his home background and parental attitudes. It is usually only in high school, often only in the senior years, that the young adult can free himself sufficiently from the handicaps his home background may contain so as to develop mainly in terms of his own native talents. If differentiation is begun at an earlier level, instead of the school's equalizing differences in home background it only adds to them the agony of intellectual differences.

Such early division would discriminate in favor of all those children who come from "nice" homes. It would in fact discriminate even more against Negro (and Mexican, Puerto Rican, etc.) than against "poor white" children, as may be seen, for example, from a preliminary study by the Education Testing Service of Princeton . . . to determine the relative academic achievement of school children in Atlanta. Surveying the fourth, sixth, and twelfth grade students, it found that the average fourth grade Negro student was scholastically 1.6 years behind the average white fourth-grader, while the Negro twelfth-grader was four years behind. If differentiation were to begin at about second grade level, the average white student would have an incomparably better chance of a superior education than the average Negro student. Not, I should add, because of superior native endowment, but because of the difference in home background.

If we are to be serious about providing a child with a fair chance to succeed academically, even when he comes from a home that does not support his educational efforts, we would have to provide him with teachers who, because of their excellence, could counterbalance the deficiencies of the home background. In many of our present city school systems lip service is at least given to the notion that the best teachers should teach those most difficult to teach, i.e. those who are falling behind. Yet Professor Woodring makes the special point that in high school, "It will be essential that the teacher of Group A (the gifted) be selected for their superior scholarship and intelligence." Thus the best teachers will attend to those who are easiest to teach. And while it is not stated outright, it seems to follow that the poorest teachers will attend to those who are most difficult to teach. Discriminatory as it is, Professor Woodring's proposal on this score is not as revolutionary as it may seem, since quite a few of our large high school systems already have an A, B, and even C grouping, the first being "accelerated" or college preparatory for the gifted, the last based on preparing for the trades. Among some of our most famous high schools we find establishments that have not only three different curricula, but five, sometimes numbered A, B, C, X, and XX. Some large cities have solved the problem in still another way: New York with its high schools for children showing special talents, such as the High School of Music and Art, or Bronx Science High School; Philadelphia with its Central High School; Boston with its Latin High Schools. But most of these at least give all children the same chance up to grades seven or nine, enough time for the children from deprived homes to benefit for at least seven years from equal educational opportunities, however uneven the equipment with which they enter school.

But again, why all this fuss about the gifted child? Have these so-called gifted children been winding up in the coal mines, have so few of them managed to enter Harvard, Yale, City College, or the University of Chicago? Has the present system suddenly stopped working? Do gifted children find there is no longer place for them in the universities; are there fewer scholarships available for them? Are our colleges unwilling to accept them before the age of eighteen? Having for years been connected with the University of Chicago, where strenuous efforts were made to attract not only the gifted but to have them enter college early, I recall only too well that this plan of early entrance had to be modified, simply because not enough students were interested in moving ahead fast academically, and this for good reasons. Gifted youngsters still go to college and graduate school; scholarships and fellowships go begging each year for want of takers; several great universities are ready to accept youngsters at an early age if they show sufficient promise.

All this again leads us back to the question of why the educated classes in this country (particularly the liberals) have become interested in the two problems of desegregation and the gifted at precisely the same time? It appears that the cause is an unconscious desire to create a segregation based on the intellect, and that only by trying to secure this aim for their children can the intelligentsia continue to fight publicly for desegregation on the racial level. Large numbers of the intelligentsia can advocate desegregation of the public schools all the more freely as their own children (the "gifted" children) are already segregated, either by placement in special classes for the gifted, or in private schools, or in the suburbs. It is not that these groups who fight against segregation, and for special facilities for the gifted, wish to establish a new color line. On the contrary, they want to do away with the old-fashioned color line, to replace the "white color" elite, by a more up-to-date "white collar" elite, composed of all highly educated persons of all colors. Their education and language will be so different from the rest that they will live and think, act and interact, on a different plane from the rest of the population.

That the system of separating the groups works, indeed works only too well, and would work even more perniciously the younger the age level at which children are separated, can be seen from what happens when the groups part at the high school level. In those public high schools where special programs for the gifted are set up ("accelerated," "pre-collegiate," etc.) the system certainly works effectively for mutual alienation. Those who attend the special programs, though willing to study hard to remain in the category of "gifted" child, try even harder to make sure they will keep out of the "desegregated" classrooms. It is interesting to see what a strong incentive the latter is to hard work. On the other hand, children placed in the non-collegiate programs, finding themselves marked as a lower breed and now surrounded by all too many who are not interested in acquiring any education, acquire even less of it than they would if there were some good students around with whom they could identify. Some Negro children are in the classes forming these special programs, but they are usually those who have a "better" social background. Thus the lower class whites and Negroes who need very much to be challenged and motivated by being surrounded with examples of intellectual achievement are deprived of just such stimulation to learn. On the other hand, when left behind as second-class citizens (educationally speaking), and with the little support they are apt to derive from home, they find themselves in a predicament which they are poorly equipped to overcome. Dimly realizing this, with few exceptions, they soon feel hopeless. Should spontaneous leadership arise, or outstanding ability develop among some of the children in the non-gifted group, such individuals are drawn away by being encouraged to join their intellectual peers, the gifted group. All this is happening already, and is kept within bounds only by the eight preceding years all children share in school, and because this separation is still viewed as basically undesirable. The underlying ideal is still a common curriculum for all. But all this would cease if the separation were made early, and came to be viewed as desirable.

Besides the wish to beat Russia in the cold war race for superior technology, there is a general concern that our curricula do not do justice to the gifted, that they are held back and possibly thwarted in their growth by learning situations designed for the average child. This is true, but there is another side to the problem: by giving premiums to the gifted child because of his achievement, he may be pushed beyond what is good for him, encouraged to overstrain his abilities in order to remain at the top, and in consequence find himself at the end of his education intellectually exhausted, if not more seriously damaged. Moreover, while there can be little doubt that, academically speaking, special classes for gifted children may help them to graduate and take their place in life sooner, problems are created by taking them out of the regular schoolroom situation.

Thus, among the arguments for special classes for the gifted is that quite a few of the children who are at the top of their classes state that they are bored in class during the school year. But it could be argued that tasks already learned by the gifted child were repeated by him because they were reassigned for the benefit of the slower learner; in this way a great deal of overlearning characterizes the school experience of most gifted children. In the absence of controlled studies of this problem, it seems quite possible that it was just such overlearning, and with it the much greater recall and ease in meeting intellectual tasks which are typical results of overlearning, that helped these children later on to do better than their age mates.

I have observed closely what has happened when a gifted child is taken out of a very accelerated and highly competitive school situation, and placed in one where the course content is so easy for him as to be "boring," according to adults and his own statements. No longer having to worry about keeping up, this student, who in the special school for gifted children lacked time to develop his own (rather than a teacher-induced) critical judgment, began to reflect spontaneously on many problems, some of which were outside of what was taught in the new school. He acquired, again on his own, a much deeper appreciation of life, art, literature, and other human beings.

Another question that could be raised is whether the feeling of security which the gifted child acquires because of the ease with which he learns, does not later make it possible for him to tackle difficult intellectual problems. If, on the other hand, such a child is put into a special class where learning is not so easy for him, he himself might come to feel that he had only average abilities, and hence might lack the courage to work on difficult problems later on. Again, while it is argued that to place a gifted child in an average group creates boredom in the gifted child, it has also been held that to mix children of different abilities in a learning situation creates anxiety in the slower learners. This may be so, but how do anxieties become manageable? Only through socialization, through working together, through a friendly relationship with those whom we feel to be superior—in this case the faster-learning children in the classroom.

Because it is so difficult to agree on what is the "best" education for the child, the argument is often switched from what is best for the child to what is supposedly best for society. We are told that we need more scientists or more engineers to "survive" and therefore we must swiftly move ahead those who have talents in such fields. But should this be done at the price of their personal happiness? Also, do we really know what we will need thirty years hence to survive? Might we not for survival need new ideas about how to organize a world-wide society, new ideas to fire the imagination, rather than technicians or physicists? And since ideas mature slowly, maybe what we need is not a speeding up but a slowing down of our all-too-rapid pace, with long vacations for reading and thinking, free time to play and grow, rather than the busyness of competitive sports or camp activities?

By now our educational system seems to have neglected the slow learner, the gifted, and the average child, a situation that is probably due to the fact that our schools were supposed to bring about the millennium, and naturally failed. Maybe the answer, without assuring the millennium and without being able to do equal justice to all children, is one that helps the average and the gifted child by helping the slow learners. I have stressed the importance of a common school experience for all until at least the high school level, preferably later. Here I would like to go further. At present we collect all children at the ripe age of five and drop them into one and the same school situation, although their preparation in home background is so different as to skew the actual school experience; then we hope that the socially handicapped will catch up with the others by the time they get to high school. Let us, instead, for a period of a year or two, help prepare these "underprivileged" in home background to make better use of their future classroom learning. Let us try to speed up these slow learners, and use the first two years of their education to persuade those who have come doubting them. Let us slowly educate these five-year-olds in the manners, attitudes, and will to learn, in the ability to sit still and concentrate, and all the rest, which are the prerequisites of being able to make best use of the teacher and the school. We would have to employ our very best teachers for this difficult task, and make the preparatory classes very small. But we could and would help our slow learners (with the exception of those whose mental equipment is considerably below par) turn into at least average learners.

Then, at about seven, they could all start school together with a better chance for all. Along the same line of reasoning it would follow that our newcomers to the big cities—whether from Puerto Rico, the Ozarks, or the deep South—should be given the benefit of two years of the very best teaching at whatever age they arrive, before they are introduced into the mainstream of our educational system.

Despite these comments on the gifted child, I am not suggesting that we should leave well enough alone. On the contrary, much can be improved in our present school system. The point I am trying to make is simply that arguments for the special education of the gifted do not yet rest on solid ground, any more than do arguments to the contrary, only some of which have been mentioned.

If we, the educated group, feel that—with an end to racial segregation and with the pressure of the cold war—we have to create a new elite through an educational caste system by creating a new class of schoolmen, a new scholasticism (only this time not based on Aristotle, but on relativity, quantum theory, or what not) then we should at least not betray the essence of our calling, which is intellectual honesty. Let us be honest about our intentions and state them openly. In doing so, it will at least be easier to recognize the similarity of a caste system based on intellectual gifts and educational achievement with that of Mandarin China, a comparison which suggests the thought whether such a society is likely to do well in competition with other social systems. Such thoughts may lead to some second reflections about the desirability of the recently proposed special school systems for gifted children, while there is still time.

64. THE SOCIAL ORIGINS OF NATIONAL MERIT SCHOLARS *

HORACE MANN BOND

The National Merit Scholarship program was initiated to help meet the need for increasing numbers of highly educated people,

* Reprinted from "The Productivity of National Merit Scholars by Occupational Class," *School and Society*, Vol. 85, No. 2116 (September 28, 1957), 267–268, with the permission of Stanley Lehrer, Managing Editor.

The author (b. 1904) is President of Lincoln University, Pennsylvania. Formerly Head, Department of Education, Fisk University. Awarded the Susan Colver Rosenberger prize for outstanding social science thesis, University of Chicago, 1936. Author: *The Education of the Negro in the American Social Order; Education in Alabama* (Educational Research Association Award); *A Study in Cotton and Steel.*

especially by providing educational opportunities for able youth from lower socioeconomic strata of the society. The data presented in this brief selection, however, indicate that most of the merit scholarships do not go to persons in these strata. The data tend to support Bettelheim's hypothesis in the preceding article that selection of the academically elite for higher education is essentially only a slight modification of the present basis of social stratification and may actually reinforce it.

The 1956 *Report* of the National Merit Scholarship Corporation includes a table (p. 18) that gives the "Occupations of fathers as reported by scholars." When the occupations listed by scholars are grouped according to the major occupational categories of the United States Census, it is possible to work out a ratio between scholars and numbers of workers, called here an "Index of Productivity of National Merit Scholars by Occupational Class." The following table is the result.

A further breakdown of sub-occupational groups yields even more striking suggestions as to the factors involved in the productivity by occupational classes of National Merit Scholars. The five highest subgroups in productivity were:

Librarians	6,390 producing 2 scholars (index of 3,195)
College Presidents, Professors and Instructors	96,030 producing 28 scholars (index of 3,429)
Architects	22,830 producing 5 scholars (index of 4,566)
Lawyers and Judges	165,300 producing 34 scholars (index of 4,861)
Clergymen	112,679 * producing 13 scholars (index of 8,667)

* Corrected by subtracting Catholic Clergy from U.S. Census totals.

Thus, an American child, whose father is a librarian, has 1,120 times the chance to win a National Merit Scholarship as a child whose parent is a laborer. The odds against a child, whose father is in one of the farming occupations, to win a National Merit Scholarship in competition with a child of one of the professional occupations is 30–1. While 168,000 physicians produced 26 scholars, 972,300 carpenters produced seven, 516,360 machinists produced three, 289,140 plumbers produced two, and 1,376,910 truckers produced three.

Some will argue, of course, that the spread of "aptitude" represented by these distributions is a fairly accurate index to the distribution of "native intelligence" in occupational classes. The author prefers a contrary explanation.

The National Merit Scholarships were awarded—as, indeed, they

Table 1. The Productivity of National Merit Scholars by Various Basic Occupational Classes, 1956

Major U.S. Census Occupational Groups, ranked in order of their proportionate productivity of National Merit Scholars	The Number of Male Workers in these classes, 1950 Census	The Number of Scholars who reported this group for father's occupation, 1956	The Index of Productivity of Scholars by occupational class (how many workers required to produce one scholar)
I. Professional, Technical, and Kindred Workers	2,955,350	234	12,672
II. Managers, Officials, and Proprietors	4,272,510	115	37,153
III. Sales Workers	2,639,490	34	77,632
IV. Clerical and Kindred Workers	2,670,870	28	95,380
V. Craftsmen, Foremen, and Kindred Workers	7,846,290	56	140,112
VI. Operatives and Kindred Workers	8,470,740	27	313,731
VII. Service Workers	2,563,890 *	7	366,270
VIII. Farmers and Farm Managers, Farm Laborers and Foremen	6,234,300 *	16	389,643
IX. Laborers, Except Farm and Mine	3,581,370	1	3,581,370
TOTAL, Male Workers, 1950	42,068,820	510	81,213

* Lack of specification in the reports of occupation of scholars' fathers has led us here to combine, in "Service Workers," the two separate classifications used by the census, "Private Household Workers" and "Service Workers except Private," and the two census categories for farm workers, "Farmers and Farm Managers," and "Farm Laborers and Foremen."

had to be awarded—on the basis of competitive tests (after state quotas had been established). These "aptitude" tests accurately measure the degree of facility in the manipulation of verbal and mathematical symbols by the student. Children in whose homes such symbols are now a part of the occupational stock-in-trade of parents (homes where such facility probably has characterized family operations for several generations) almost invariably will surpass children—testwise—from homes not so privileged.

．　．　．　．　．

65. TALK TO UNDERGRADUATES *

ROBERT OPPENHEIMER

The eminent scientist Dr. J. Robert Oppenheimer said America's so-called "eggheads" would have to share the blame for the fact our youth often idolize an athlete or a singer more than a man of thought. He believes that something must be done to make "smartness smart" in a nation whose future depends on brainpower. This selection is a transcript of an informal lecture Dr. Oppenheimer gave to students at the California Institute of Technology in March 1957. In it he examines the importance of education and the difficult issues educators and students face in the contemporary world. His feelings about the frustration, the challenge, the fellowship of scholarly endeavor is reflected here.

One of the features of this time is that we live under a palpable threat of an apocalypse. I have talked with you enough so that you know that I don't regard this as inevitable; on the contrary, I think that for anyone who has an opportunity of working to avert it, that is a valid full-time job. It isn't like the apocalypse that was expected in the year 1000, but it is very much at the back of our minds in everything we do.

It is a strange time, too, in that never in the history of the world

* From an address to students at the California Institute of Technology, March 4, 1957. Printed in *Engineering and Science Magazine* (published at the California Institute of Technology), March, 1957; in Edward Hutchings, Jr. (ed.), *Frontiers in Science* (New York: Basic Books, Inc., 1958); and in the *Kansas Teacher*, February, 1959.

The author (b. 1904) is Professor and Director of Physics, Institute for Advanced Study, Princeton, New Jersey. Director of the Los Alamos Scientific Laboratory, Los Alamos, New Mexico, 1943–1945. Member of the Board of Overseers, Harvard University.

has there been as rapid a growth of knowledge, as rapid a growth in understanding, or as great changes. I suppose that, in the 18th century, men talked about how knowledge doubled every 50 years. I think we could make a case for saying that it doubles every 10 years now.

This creates problems. But it also creates problems of the use of that knowledge, of the vast powers that it seems to make available, of the choices. It creates a world of incredibly rapid change. Almost nobody can look back to a schooling with a feeling that it is entirely relevant to the problems that he is now dealing with. Almost everyone has to have the sense that he goes to school all his life.

In some ways, this situation, which I think is a natural continuation of the fluidity and openness of American society—an openness now not with regard to the physical frontier, but with regard to the frontier of knowledge—has given this country a strange destiny. I cannot believe that other parts of the world will not also very rapidly be caught up in changes comparable to those in which we live. They are not prepared for it; they have remained in relatively steady, relatively quiet, relatively enduring forms. And how we deal with this, certainly will not be an example that other peoples will inevitably or rightly follow. But how we deal with it cannot be irrelevant to the future of the whole world.

A CHARACTERISTIC IRONY

This is also a time when the very rapidity of change seems to me to underline the irony that is so characteristic of history—the irony which makes the event, the outcome, so different from the human purpose.

Think of the communist movement; it began in compassion, and now it is probably the least compassionate of any major political force the world has seen for a long, long time. Think of China, with its pattern of respect and love for the family and the past, its addiction to reflection, and almost private beauty. Think what the Chinese have embraced in the way of forced, quick, violent, brilliant change—and how little they are prepared for it. Think of India, if you will, and a government in India which is a direct consequence of Cambridge, of Oxford and of London—these symbols of two centuries of oppression. And think of us, who founded ourselves in independence, and who are inextricably stuck in the most monstrous kind of interdependence—both here, where the vastness of all our affairs makes the individual's wink invisible, and even interdependent with very remote parts of the globe. Think of the irony of the great weapons, which, developed to give a military answer to the problem of security, have assumed such proportions that they almost cannot be used, and have produced for the general staffs that evoked them a nightmare of almost total insecurity.

All these things—and there are many more—could easily, it seems to me, make in the times a kind of bitterness and a kind of feeling that the individual had better see to his own delight and to heck with society and to heck with virtue. That is not so different from the way it was in the decade when I grew up, after the first World War, where a kind of revolt was characteristic in the colleges, and in the arts. It was a revolt which said that what we have had from the past was not much of a guide for the future, a revolt where there was a hope of improvising something gay and new, where the bitter fruit of that terrible war seemed to call for a kind of new, fresh departure.

It isn't really quite like that now. I think that today, if I know you and your friends through the country, you hold very close to the ancient imperatives—the imperatives of Christianity, of our traditions, of our country. I think you are not after novelty and improvisation in art or politics or philosophy, or manners. I think that, even if the end of our time should come, you are quite content that we live out these days faithful to the gospels, faithful to the sense of responsibility, which we have from times past.

These are some of the things that are in the background. Of course, the present problem of young people at college is the same everywhere. They are finding their way into an enormous cognitive jungle, the jungle of everything there is to know. They are finding their way into it with very little guide, either from synoptic kinds of knowledge, like philosophy, which say: This is important; this is unimportant; this fits in here; this fits in there—or from the state of the world, which doesn't, in any very clear or loud voice, say: Learn this; ignore that; learn this well; skip over that lightly.

IMPOSSIBLE CHOICES

There is, in most places, the vast trouble of impossible choices. I have talked with and been among undergraduates—and school boys and graduate students as well—in some places around the country, and a typical agony is: "What do I do? Where am I headed?" The complement of that, of course, is to be told what to do, and in a measure, that is what goes on here at Caltech. I think it varies from place to place, and there is no doubt that Caltech is far on one side of the spectrum—of the spectrum between openness and permissiveness on the one hand, and rather strict and specific guidance on the other; between knowledge as an end in itself, something to study because of the joy of it and the beauty of it— and knowledge as an instrument, as a way of getting on in the future. I think Caltech is very much on the instrumental side and very much on the predetermined side.

But the sense of loss which I hear in you—I don't know whether it is exaggerated in our talk but I'm sure it's there—of the things which you are not studying; the sense of loss at all that you might be learning, and aren't; the slight fear that this might not be easy to make up at a later time; this is a much larger thing, a quite general part of human life. There is much more that one might know than any of us are ever going to know. There is much more to know than any of us are ever going to catch up with; and this is not just the trivial fact that we don't work hard enough; it is not the trivial fact that things are difficult to learn. *It is that any form of knowledge really precludes other forms; that any serious study of one thing cuts out some other part of your life. Narrowness is not an accident of one place, but it is a condition of knowledge.*

CHOICE IS BUILT IN

I think myself that, with the growth of knowledge—the immense perplexity, the pervasive mutual relevance of different things to each other—all we can do is to accept the state of affairs, to affirm it and to accept it deeply. It is not that some courses are not better than others and some worse, some even good and some evil; it is that, in the balance between ignorance and loss on the one hand, and knowledge and richness of experience on the other, we have to keep the affirmative love of the knowledge and the richness very close and never deny that most of what men can know, we don't know; that much of what man can know, nobody knows.

Of course, in a certain sense, this is trivial and people have always known it. When it comes to the will, the element of choice has always been clear. The fact that you had one course which precluded another; you could take a job, or you could continue to study; you could marry, or you could say goodbye; everybody knows that. But I think it has not been quite as clear how, in the very conditions of knowledge, *choice is built in and exclusion is part of depth.*

I don't want to try to derive this from anything in science because it seems to me quite deep and quite commonsensical, and very much a part of all our experience. But I do want to give three examples from three different areas in science which illustrate it rather sharply. One is from the physiology of perception, one is from the psychology of learning, and one is from physics.

The philosophers like to talk about sense data as though they were something that came to all men who were properly constituted, a replica, a picture, a sign of something outside; and all philosophers have always been very confident that the sense datum was something very solid to build on. But, in being able to perceive, we take a far more active part, and not necessarily a conscious one.

There is, for instance, an experiment of great simplicity having to do with hearing. The nerves running from the hair cells in a dog's ear toward the cortex can be tapped, and one can see what kind of electrical impulses travel along them. And if you take a dog so "hooked up," you will soon learn to recognize the electrical pattern of the signal that comes along when the dog hears a bell ring. If you put a piece of meat in front of the dog, that signal disappears. The way this happens is that, along with the afferent nerve fibers, there are finer nerve fibers which, so to speak, tell the nerves what to do, what to hear and what signals to send. This is not understood in detail. But the coding which we always assume characterizes the human brain—the organization of material, the focusing of attention, animadversion, concentration, memory—this coding pervades the most primitive parts of the cognitive system, and the dog may or may not hear the bell. It isn't something that he fixes up inside himself; it is a question of what he is attuned to.

There are very similar experiments, having to do, for instance, with language—a whole series of them reported from the Harvard Cognition Project. It is astonishing what people will notice and what they will ignore. For instance, if you take some sounds that have some variations in them and say them, then an American who is attuned only to our language will hear differences—but only those differences which correspond to the way we spell and write, to our phonetic elements. Of course, we don't spell and write very accurately, but we recognize *a* as distinct from *e*, and *r* as distinct from *n* and so on. If you take a Navaho who doesn't know English, he will hear quite different things. He won't distinguish our vowels, but he will distinguish by the length of the vowel. You can teach the Navaho to notice the English differences and the American to notice the Navaho differences, but he doesn't normally do it. The possibility of communicating, of course, rests on the fact that we don't hear too much. You are hearing my talk, but only that part of it which really has meaning in English. All the rest of it—the rumble and roar that goes with it—you don't hear. It isn't that you hear it and ignore it.

Of the incredibly many examples, one of the most striking comes to anyone who tries to translate the words for colors from one language to another, even two languages that are Indo-Germanic. The English words for color distinguish spectrally what we call color, by the hue. The Greek words have to do almost entirely with depth and brightness, and you can't find a Greek word for blue. You can find one that sometimes means blue. All these questions of animadversion are extremely primitive.

AN EXAMPLE FROM PHYSICS

And what is the example from physics? It is the one that I talk about much too much. Of course, if one is learning about atomic theory, one learns Schroedinger's equation in quantum mechanics, and it all seems very unphilosophical and practical. It is a wonderful way of describing atomic phenomena, and one tries to get the techniques and get it over with. But to anyone who lived with the development of this, it was quite a different story, because what one had to get through his head was something quite odd.

We are used to a world in which we can find out anything of interest about a large physical system without in any way questioning the means by which we can find it out. The classical examples are that we can tell where a planet is, and, by observing it successively, we can tell how fast it is moving. The question where this observation could have any paradoxical features in it never arises. But in atomic mechanics, we had to learn that, although experiments in some ways like finding where a planet is, and in some ways like finding out its velocity, are indeed possible, and are indeed a part of describing what is going on, the kind of arrangement that is suitable for doing one of these experiments not only makes it impossible to do the other, but makes it logically contradictory to assume that the other quantity has a value, or has one of a number of values. In other words, we came to realize that, in the atomic scale, one can realize, by the way one goes about it in the laboratory, that there is some free choice. This is not free in the sense of an ethical problem, but just free for the physicist to decide what he is interested in or what he wants to study. Having made that choice, one has closed out the chance of doing the other thing, so that both are valid measurements, or so that he can even imagine that he has done both and that each has had a given result. If he imagines thus, and starts to draw the consequences, he will get a prediction for the future of that atom that has no relation to what he will find in the laboratory.

These are just three examples of the pervasiveness with which, in all scientific things, one meets again the fact that knowledge, by the very techniques, powers, and facts of its acquisition, by its organizing the chaos that is the world around us, precludes other knowledge.

A NEW PICTURE OF THE COGNITIVE WORLD

This makes a picture of the cognitive world which, in many ways, is not the one we have inherited. It isn't as though we were in a room just looking at it, then, if we wanted to know some more, looking some more, exhausting all the properties of it, being able to talk about it all— as though we were in a temple and could go back over and over again, studying the peculiarities of the temple until there was nothing more to know, and then making a description of this room or this temple which was total and global.

It is much more as though we had deep, not always connected

parts of knowledge—knowledge of physics, knowledge of life, knowledge of man, knowledge of history. *Between these things that are known to any one of us, there is always potential relevance,* so that one can never say, even of the most implausibly abstract kind of mathematics: this will not be relevant to psychology or physics. But the image that comes to my mind is not that of the chamber that can be exhausted, but of an essentially infinite world, knowable in many different ways; and all these paths of knowledge are interconnectable, and some are interconnected, like a great network—a great network between people, between ideas, between systems of knowledge—a reticulated kind of structure which is human culture and human society.

This means that I am very suspicious of statements that refer to totality or completeness; that I am very suspicious of our ability to have more than partial knowledge, in the very real sense that it can be supplemented and that it doesn't close. It means that I am very suspicious also of order which is hierarchical in the sense that it says that some things are more important than others—that some things are so important that you can derive everything else from them. These were great hopes of man, and philosophical systems are their monuments. I don't think that the prospects of their being realized look very good.

THE COLLAR

Now, one could take an attitude of real horror toward this and say that one can't live with it—that this is to offer man not knowledge, but chaos. I don't think that is right. We have all had the experience of seeing the relevance of something that we hadn't known before, of learning at all times in our lives something deep and new and wonderful that had been hidden before. We have all had the experience of what companionship and intercourse and an open mind can do; and I don't think the absence of global traits to our knowledge is a cause for despair. But I'd like to read you a poem that seems to me to fit a little, not only with this general situation, but perhaps even with the local situation. It is not a new poem; it is three centuries old and the language is archaic, and I can't be sure you'll like it—but I can say I like it. It is called "The Collar," and it is by a devout Anglican named George Herbert. Some of you may know it; it goes like this:

> I struck the board, and cry'd No more;
> I will abroad.
> What? Shall I ever sigh and pine?
> My lines and life are free; free as the road.
> Loose as the wind, as large as store.
> Shall I be still in suit?
> Have I no harvest but a thorn

To let me blood, and not restore
What I have lost with cordial fruit?
    Sure there was wind,
Before my sighs did dry it: there was corn,
    Before my tears did drown it.
Is the year only lost to me?
    Have I no bays to crown it?
No flowers, no garlands gay? all blasted?
    All wasted?
Not so, my heart: but there is fruit,
    And thou hast hands.
Recover all thy sigh-blown age
On double pleasures: leave thy cold dispute
Of what is fit, and not forsake thy cage,
    Thy rope of sands,
Which petty thoughts have made, and made to thee
Good cable, to enforce and draw,
    And be thy law.
While thou didst wink and wouldst not see.
    Away: take heed:
    I will abroad.
Call in thy deaths head there: tie up thy fears.
    He that forebears
    To suit and serve his need,
        Deserves his load.
But as I raved and grew more fierce and wild,
    At every word,
Methought I heard one calling, Child;
    and I reply'd, My Lord.

Having spoken so, and tried to measure what the flowering, changing, rich, but only partially ordered world of the mind means for us, it may not be inappropriate to stress what seem to me a few of the things that will be useful in living with it. They are certainly not new things; they have always been useful.

The first is to have a kind of deep reverence, not, certainly, for the learned man or the stuffed shirt, but for learning, for knowledge and skill; and to hold tight to it, and not to be talked out of it by any superficial parody of what it is, the kind of thing we learn in school where we learn to do and create and understand, and where we learn really to act with the knowledge we get.

This is something that isn't easy to come by. It hasn't been easy for man; it isn't being easy now, and it is incredibly precious; and the world is full of it. Accounts of this—stories (whether in general education or in *Life* Magazine), short cuts, and synopses—miss most of the point. It is just the technique and the wonder of one's own ability to do it that is part of the value of it. And in ourselves and in other people this is, I think, to be held on to very tight. If you have learned how to be something, how to be a competent professional, you will know a great deal about what is good in this world. You will have a bond in common with every other man who is a scholar or a scientist.

The greatest of all protections against narrowness, and the greatest relief and opening, is comradeship, and that ability to learn from others of what their world is like. Learn from books for sure; learn from people, but learn with a kind of sense that every man enriches you and enlarges you if you only have the strength, the wit, the openness, the fortitude to learn what he is all about and what he knows.

THE OTHERNESS OF PEOPLE

And very much we need tolerance. We are all incredibly different. I think sometimes that one of the unexpected fruits of biological research may be that we can, on occasion, be made to feel more like somebody else than we normally do, and so get some impression of the immense diversity in human experience. But, of course, as it is, we don't have that. Through art, through affection, we have some sense of a global kind of what other people are like, of what life means to them, of what makes them tick, and of what their learning and their understanding is. But an immense sense of the otherness of people, and the otherness of possible worlds and ideas is, I guess, the basis of tolerance. I don't mean, in any simple way, tolerance of evil in one's self, but rather a recognition that even two people, hearing the same words, living together, seeing the same things, have some measure of gulf between them; and a recognition that when we are dealing with remote peoples, remote traditions, we need to bring an overpowering humility to our estimate of what they are, and our measure of them.

I have the impression that if we, in this time and this age, manage properly to live with the wealth of knowledge, the wealth of change, the responsibility and the traits of impotence, which these times dish up, we will really be quite something, and that maybe there will be places and peoples and times that come after who will have reason to be grateful to us.

66. DIVIDED PROTESTANTISM

IN A MIDWEST COUNTY °

A Study in the Natural History

of Organized Religion

ANTON T. BOISEN

*Sociologists study religion—its structure and function—as another
of the institutions basic to the lives of people everywhere. As an
institution, Protestant religion (in America, at least) exhibits some
interesting phenomena. Protestant churches, when they grow in
size and power, tend to become more complex and formal; whenever
segments within a church disagree with the main body of belief,
they often break away and form a separate denomination, resulting
in a proliferation of competing sects; the larger and more powerful
a church becomes, the more likely it is to become concerned with
organization and the less likely it is to be concerned with its
particular theological reason for being. In this selection, A. T.
Boisen, writing from the standpoint of a participant observer,
illustrates these generalizations as they were found in an Indiana
town.*

Sociology and history are commonly distinguished one from the
other on the basis that history is the record of temporal sequences which
are not likely to be repeated, whereas sociology is the attempt to discover
relationships which are recurrent and universal. It follows that sociology
must in many cases turn to history for its data and that history may find
in sociology a valuable ally in the interpretation of its findings. This
paper is an attempt to study the history of a particular middle western
county with special reference to a pattern which appears to be recurrent

° Reprinted from "Divided Protestantism in a Midwest County—A Study in
the Natural History of Organized Religion" by Anton T. Boisen, *The Journal of
Religion*, Vol. 20, No. 4 (October, 1940), 359–381, by permission of The University
of Chicago Press.

The author (b. 1876) is Chaplain Emeritus, Elgin State Hospital. Onetime
Field Investigator, Country Church Work, Presbyterian Board of National Missions;
Lecturer and Research Associate, Chicago Theological Seminary. Author: *Lift Up
Your Heart: A Service Book for Use in Hospitals; Explorations of the Inner World;
Problems in Religion and Life;* and numerous papers in professional sociological, re-
ligious, and psychiatric journals.

in the development of organized religion and the forces which are operative in determining this pattern.

I

The county in question [Monroe] was selected from among a number of sample areas which I have studied because it is the one I know best. More than that, the data are unusually full and the situation revealed presents some unusually interesting features. This county is located in southern Indiana about fifty miles southwest of Indianapolis and about ninety miles northwest of Louisville. It was first opened for settlement in 1818. In 1820 it was designated as the seat of the state university—Indiana Seminary, as it was called originally.

. . . . . .

We have . . . in this early period in Monroe County three groups of churches: (1) There was, in the first place, a more or less liberal group consisting of the two Presbyterian churches and the Episcopal church. These were composed chiefly of college people and of those who wished to be identified with college people. (2) There was a very conservative group consisting of the four psalm-singing Presbyterian churches. These were characterized by great loyalty to family and clan, by their emphasis upon Old Testament morality, and by their requirement of an educated ministry. Their services were long, their sermons doctrinal and dry, and church attendance was compulsory on the part of all members of the family. Family "worship" was held every day, often morning and evening. There was among them no appeal to the emotions and no attempt to win converts. Their growth came through birth and immigration. (3) There were the churches which represented the new revivalistic movement which was sweeping the Ohio Valley. Of these the Methodists, the Disciples, the Baptists, and the Cumberland Presbyterians were represented in Monroe County. From the standpoint of our inquiry it is important to recognize that in contrast to the liberal and conservative groups this group sprang out of the spontaneous religious fervor of the common people. Instead of appealing to the desire for culture or status, instead of clinging tenaciously to the symbols of an inherited culture, these groups were attempting to meet pioneer conditions and to grapple with the moral problems of pioneer men. They brought people together in great numbers at their camp meetings, and there under the spell of vigorous singing, of stirring testimony, of exhortations by able, but often poorly educated, preachers strong emotions were often aroused. Many individuals felt themselves released from a burdening sense of sin and received the "baptism of the Spirit." Such individuals often became zealous missionaries, serving as lay leaders or being ordained as ministers to serve a group of struggling churches under the circuit-rider plan. It was through such men that Methodist, Disciples, and Baptist churches were planted throughout Monroe County, while the Presbyterians remained under the shelter of the county seat.

II

For many years the situation remained essentially unchanged. The six Presbyterian churches were, however, in time reduced to three. In 1858 the Associate and the Associate Reformed bodies merged to form the "United Presbyterian Church." The national union was marked by the characteristic "come-outer" reaction on the part of minority groups, so that the union resulted in three churches where only two had been before. Locally, however, there was agreement, as Professor Woodburn puts it, that the only differences between them were that one sang the Psalms of David and the other David's Psalms. Late in the sixties the New School and the Old School bodies succeeded in resolving their differences. In 1868 the New Side Covenanters disbanded, most of their families joining the United Presbyterian, the rest the Presbyterian Church. Here again the local action was the result of national developments, which are not without significance from the standpoint of this inquiry.

From the beginning of its existence in this country the Covenanter church had been strongly opposed to slave-holding. When in 1800 Alexander McLeod received a call from the First Reformed Presbyterian Church in New York City, he made it a condition of his acceptance that the church must be free from all slave-holding. In 1802 he and Samuel Brown Wylie were commissioned to visit the Carolinas and take counsel with their brethren there regarding the sin of slave-holding. In 1806 the church formally declared itself against slave-holding. Apparently, therefore, the opposition to slavery, which had had not a little to do with the migration from the Carolinas, was not motivated entirely by economic considerations. In any case, the Bloomington Covenanters were active in the Underground Railroad before the Civil War, and they even received Negroes into their fellowship. When war was declared, they give vigorous support to the Union side. Among the Covenanters who took a prominent part was George H. Stuart, the leading layman of the First Church in Philadelphia. He served as national president of the Christian Commission, an organization which corresponded somewhat to the Y.M.C.A. of the World War. It thus became his duty to visit other churches. This was all right so long as the war lasted, but after it was over he was admonished by the Synod regarding the sin of "occasional hearing" and especially regarding the practice of singing hymns of non-Davidic origin. When he refused to heed the Synod's admonitions, he was excluded from membership. The First Church thereupon severed its connection with the

General Synod, and the Bloomington Church, in accordance with my grandfather's advice, did likewise.

In my own early years in Bloomington at a time when the population was about five thousand and the university enrolment about five hundred we had, therefore, three different brands of Presbyterian churches. As David Starr Jordan used to put it, we had the United Presbyterians, the Reformed Presbyterians, and the Presbyterians who were neither united nor reformed. There was also a strong Methodist church, a strong Disciples church, a Baptist church, a Church of Christ (known locally as the "Sassafras Church"), a weak Episcopal and a small Catholic church. The general grouping was much the same as in the 1840's. The Presbyterian church had become mildly evangelistic in its emphasis, but this church and the Episcopal church were still made up chiefly of college people, and of those who associated with college people. The United and the Reformed Presbyterians were still very conservative in their practices, even though the former was under very able and enlightened leadership. Both of them still made exclusive use of the Psalms of David in their services of worship, while the Reformed Presbyterians still refused to allow instrumental music, and they still forbade their members to vote. The Methodists, the Disciples, and the Baptists were still dominant among the rank and file of the population, while in the county at large their sway was undisputed except for two Cumberland Presbyterian churches, a few Churches of Christ and an occasional Separate, Regular, and Primitive Baptist organization. These churches were still evangelistic in their emphasis. They were concerned with the task of "saving souls," and they held that a man must be "converted" in order to be saved. They had their annual revival meetings, and they still encouraged or tolerated emotional expression on the part of their people. Young people from the more sedate communions would frequently attend these revivals to see the fun.

Going back after many years, I find some striking changes. The town has now eighteen thousand inhabitants, and the university six thousand students. The churches also have grown. More than that, there have been some changes of type. The Methodists today worship in a large and costly building. The older people with their "Amens" have long since passed away. There is now a stately service which appeals to college people. And the old efforts to induce the conversion experience have been discontinued. What is true of the First Methodist Church is true also of the Disciples of Christ, of the First Baptist Church, and also of the fine new Methodist church on the other side of the tracks. Among all these, conversion experiences of the old type are now very rare.

But I find also a number of churches of which I had never heard in the 1890's. Among the thirty-two churches within Bloomington's city limits are three Pentecostal Assemblies of Jesus Christ, two Nazarene churches, an Assembly of God, a Wesleyan Methodist, a Free Methodist, and a Church of God. In these new churches I find somewhat the same type of service and somewhat the same message which I used to hear in the Methodist church years ago. They are interested in saving souls, and they believe that men need to be converted in order to be saved. They emphasize the reality of sin and guilt, and they proclaim deliverance through the wonder-working power of the Blood of the Lamb. Like the Methodists and Baptists of the days gone by, they have sprung from the spontaneous religious fervor of the common people, and they are propagated through the missionary zeal of those who feel that they have found the greatest of all blessings. Their membership is made up of working-class people, who have been drawn in from the surrounding countryside to man the mills and the quarries and who, since the beginning of the depression, have had tough going.

In the county at large, outside of Bloomington, there are now sixty-two churches, some of which, however, are rather feeble. Of this number fourteen are Methodist (three of these having been Methodist Protestant); ten, Baptist; two, Separate Baptist; one, regular Baptist; one, Primitive Baptist; nine, Disciples of Christ; eight, Church of Christ; while four are union chapels. The newer churches include one Nazarene, one Assembly of God, seven Pentecostal Assemblies of Jesus Christ, and four Trinity Pentecostal. Of the latter at least two are off-shoots of the Assembly of God in Bloomington.

Therefore, we still have today the same three groups of churches—the conservative churches, which persist by reason of their great resistance to change; the churches composed of college people and of those who accept the standards of college people; and the churches which spring out of the common soil of human nature. The alignment is, however, different today. The Methodists, the Disciples, and the Baptists have taken their place alongside of the Presbyterians and Episcopalians as respectable, middle-class churches, and a new group of churches has sprung up to meet the needs which formerly they had met.

III

The situation in Monroe County is by no means an average one. Its significance is rather to be found precisely in the unusually clear relief with which certain factors, which are, I think, operative in all organized religion, stand out. Let me call attention to the following considerations: (1) the coexistence throughout the one hundred and twenty years of Monroe County's history of the beginning, of the middle, and of the terminal stages of institutional religion, the types thus represented being constant as regards their general characteristics but shifting as regards the identity of the constituent bodies; (2) the presence throughout this period of a group of churches characterized by a strong clan loyalty and by a marked tendency toward splitting over relatively trivial issues; (3) the existence, especially during the early and the later years, of a considerable body of economically distressed folk, nearly all Protestants of English and Scotch-Irish descent, among whom the emotional cults have found their greatest following; and (4) the presence of an important university, which, especially in recent years, has accentuated the cultural differences and has speeded up the processes of liberalization and secularization within the larger churches.

Notice first of all that we have in this county a fine exemplification of Professor H. Richard Niebuhr's thesis regarding the life-history of organized religion. According to that thesis, the religious denomination begins usually among the underprivileged with a group of believers banded together on the basis of some vivid religious experience and the new vision which accompanies it. As time goes on, these believers' groups develop in accordance with a fairly definite pattern. They become more prosperous, and the original believers are replaced by their children. The process of institutionalization then sets in. The children accept the faith of their parents without sharing their experience. Short-cuts and protective devices are introduced. The sacraments become means of grace rather than symbols of belief. The creeds become standards of doctrine rather than confessions of faith. Even religious experience itself tends to become standardized in the form of patterns of behavior, which have to be induced by artificial devices. In general, the process is one of leveling. The prophetic forward movements are leveled down and conventionalized. The eccentric and regressive manifestations are leveled up and become respectable. This process is exemplified most strikingly in the Methodists, the Disciples, and the Baptists of Bloomington. They began under the impulse of a vital religious movement. They were believers' groups, characterized by strong emotion, insisting upon first-hand religious experience, and propagated spontaneously through the missionary zeal of their converts. They have now taken their place among the respectable. The newer cults represent the period of spontaneity and creativity. In the course of time they, likewise, will become respectable middle-class churches. And the Presbyterians? Their period of spontaneity and creativity lay in the time of John Knox three hundred years ago. They are merely a little further along in the process which characterizes any vital religious movement. In their psalm-singing offshoots we already see the terminal stages of institutional religion.

These Scotch-Irish psalm-singers, who are so unusually well represented in Bloomington, are worthy of careful consideration. In any attempt to understand them and the tragedies of loyalty presented by their much subdividing, we may begin by recognizing that a church is first of all a fellowship. It is a group banded together on the basis of a loyalty which is accepted as supreme. Doctrine and ritual are of secondary importance. These are taken over from those who represent authority and are thus functions of the social relationships, particularly to the parents and early guides. The persistence of these groups is due to that principle. If a great and beloved president of the university throughout his long period of service has remained a leader in the United Presbyterian Church in Bloomington, it is not due to any conviction on his part regarding the unique claims of the Psalms of David. So also the dean of the school of education in the university, who is equally active in the Old Side Covenanter Church, has no determining views regarding instrumental music in the church. Neither is he opposed to voting. Both these men are guided rather by considerations of loyalty. They have felt it a point of honor to be true to the church of their fathers. They have stayed with it, not because of doctrine but in spite of it.

Loyalty to family and clan is, in fact, so important in these churches that they may be said to represent tribal religion. The maintenance of group integrity in the face of changing conditions and against the onslaughts of an alien culture is with them a primary concern, and for this reason obedience and conformity to established patterns are required. The past rather than the future is the focus of attention. The German and the Scandinavian Lutherans in this country are examples. They are struggling to maintain their group identity and integrity, and in so doing they have become more conservative than their kindred in the old country. Religion of this type is especially likely to appear where the group has been subjected to pressure or to persecution. The ecclesiastical zeal of the Irish Catholics as compared with the Italians may thus be accounted for; so also the rigid attitudes of the various religious groups in Asia Minor and the legalism of the ancient Pharisees. The Scotch-Irish psalm-singers were just such a group. They had been solidified by persecution in the old country. In this country they were facing the disintegrating forces of impoverishment and disheartenment, which changed so many of their fellow-country-men into the "poor-white" or "hill-billy" type. They therefore stuck together throughout their wanderings. They clung to a faith in education. They retained a pride of race and clan.

The divisive tendencies which we find among them may be explained by the removal of external pressure and persecution and by the attempt to maintain loyalty, not through reason and love but through force and fear and arbitrary authority. The children who grow up under such conditions are likely to feel strong resentment, which sometimes takes the form of open rebellion and the disowning of the loyalty. More frequently, however, love is mingled with fear, loyalty with resentment. The individual may then accept the faith of his father, but the repressed hostility may be ready to seize upon some trivial doctrinal or ritualistic pretext in order to express itself. Divisions in the church then result, not from real issues of belief and practice but from unrecognized antagonistic social attitudes.

No consideration of these psalm-singing Presbyterians should fail to do justice to their sturdy character. They are a fine lot—strong, honest, neighborly, thrifty. Nonetheless, it must be recognized that their loyalty to race and clan is too often divorced from clear objectives. There is, in consequence, confusion as to what is important and what is unimportant in the principles emphasized and in the means employed. Therefore, their religion becomes static. There is fear of deviating even in the slightest from what is already established, and the confusion is accentuated by lurking antagonisms which are ready to find expression in church quarrels.

IV

The astonishingly rapid growth of new cults of the Holiness and Pentecostal types cannot be explained in terms of any one factor. The fact that this growth has taken place among the economically distressed factory and quarry workers and has been especially rapid since the depression is, however, significant. This is true not merely in Bloomington but in the country at large. It has also been true of other periods of economic distress. It brings to our attention the fact that the mystical experiences out of which such movements arise are most likely to occur in periods of stress and crisis. Under normal conditions the individual is busy with his customary pursuits, and his reflections upon matters philosophical and religious are generally in terms of an accepted currency of ideas. His personality may, in fact, be regarded as a reflection of the social organization and as the subjective aspect of his particular culture. His attitudes, his beliefs, his standards of value are taken over from his environment without much thought on his part. They are functions of his social relationships, particularly to those whom he admires and whose authority he accepts. In time of crisis, however, the individual finds himself face to face with the ultimate issues of life, and as his mind is stirred through strong emotion ideas come flooding in as from an outside source. These ideas he is likely to attribute to a divine or to a demonic origin. In so far as he does come to feel himself in contact with a superhuman world there will be for him a new social frame of reference. The accepted bases of judgment and reasoning no longer apply. There is a transvaluation of values—a break with the culture pattern of his particular time and race. Face to face with what he regards as ultimate reality, philosophy and theology become for such an individual no mere matters of academic concern but matters of life and death. Under such conditions meaning and emotion outstrip symbol. Instead of beginning with words and concepts according to the common practice, he is forced to seek new words to express the new ideas which come thronging in upon him. Such experiences may open the eyes to a larger universe and give insights which are new and creative. Again they may give new life and meaning to traditions and concepts which before had been stale and profitless. Frequently, they leave the individual cut loose from his moorings—perplexed, bewildered, sure only that things are not what they seem. They may thus be either constructive or destructive. They may be associated with mental disorder of the type, however, which should be recognized as an expression of nature's power to heal. They are likewise looked upon as wellsprings of religion. Even the unlettered laborer who passes triumphantly through such an experience may, like John Bunyan, emerge a poet and theologian of no mean order.

The danger of mental unbalance is at a minimum where the strain is shared by a group; it is at a maximum where the experience is a soltiary one. Studies which have been made of the effect of the economic depression upon the mental health of our people thus show that there has been no demonstrable increase in the incidence of mental disorder. The explanation is to be found in the fact that economic distress tends to increase the sense of fellowship and forces people to think together about the things that matter most. It thus tends to lessen the sense of isolation and guilt which is the primary evil in the functional types of mental illness.

The revivalism of the early nineteenth century would thus be related to the impoverishment and disheartenment of those who had been forced to seek new homes in the wilderness. Its reappearance today in this college town is to be explained in large part by the suffering and privation to which working-class families have been subjected by reason of the hard times in the stone industry. It is religion of the type which tends to appear spontaneously wherever men are grappling desperately with the issues of spiritual life and death. Such religion is rooted in the creative forces latent in struggling humanity. It is a manifestation of nature's power to heal in the face of overwhelming difficulties. Its primary concern is release from the sense of sin and guilt. It finds the solution in the acceptance of personal responsibility and emotional identification with a fellowship conceived as universal and abiding. The individual who has that experience is thereby given a role in a great world-drama. He finds a new purpose in life and goes forth with a contagious enthusiasm which communicates itself to other individuals. The group is thus formed on the basis of a shared experience, and it grows of itself through the zeal of its converts.

It is characteristic of this type of religion that it tends to break down old culture patterns and to create new social alignments. In a recent study of the Holly Roller cults I have reported the case of an intelligent, well-educated, economically well-to-do white man who received the "baptism of the Spirit" and identified himself with a Negro Holy Roller group. This is not an isolated case. Whites are not infrequently found in Negro Holy Roller meetings, and sometimes Negroes are welcomed in white groups of the Pentecostal variety. Apparently, the mystical experience means a new social identification, which tends to create new values and to break across the lines of class and caste, even lines so fixed as those which separate the Negroes from the whites. We may therefore say that the revivalism of the early part of the nineteenth century served as a solvent to many old social formations and that it was instrumental in creating a new culture suited to the pioneer conditions of the Middle West. . . .

67. HAVE WE A "NEW" RELIGION? *

PAUL HUTCHINSON

The influence that various institutions have on one another is of particular interest to sociologists. In this article, Paul Hutchinson discusses a religious point of view which he terms "The Cult of Reassurance." This approach to religion is a product of several factors, including the impersonalism of modern industry, the status-striving of middle-class Americans, secular education, and the scientific point of view. Thus, he implies that the reassurance type of religion so popular today results from the interaction of a multitude of more or less institutionalized characteristics of contemporary society. This point, if accepted, would support the idea that religion is not disappearing under the impact of science and secular education (a view once endorsed enthusiastically by many materialists); rather, it may only be changing its form in accommodation to new conditions.

The Apostle Paul, according to St. Luke, began his historic sermon on the Areopagus with a compliment: "Men of Athens, I perceive that in every way you are very religious." Visitors to these shores frequently say the same thing about Americans. Sometimes they say it with the same faint trace of irony which can be sensed in St. Paul's bow to the Athenians. D. W. Brogan, finding printed forms of grace on tables in the dining cars of the New Haven Railroad, tells his British audience that this "is only one sign among many of the degree to which religion is being pushed, 'sold' as the advertisers put it, to the American people."

There are other European observers, however, who treat the religious

* From *Life*, Vol. 38, No. 15 (April 11, 1955), 138–158.
The author (1890–1956) was managing editor of *The Christian Century*. Author of: *Storm over Asia; The Ordeal of Western Religion; The New Leviathan; From Victory to Peace.*

stirrings reported from all parts of the country with more respect. Bishop Eivind Berggrav, Norway's hero of Quisling days, assured an Oslo radio audience on his recent return from a five-month visit here that despite his prior misgiving he had found "American Christianity real, true and personal." The two things in America which impressed him most, the bishop told the Norwegians, were the American kitchen and the American church!

Regard it as you will, whether as an authentic revival of religious concern or as simply one more manifestation of the American propensity for bandwagon riding, there can be no doubt about the external facts. There is a religious boom on; almost any clergyman or rabbi can swamp you with statistics to prove it.

Charles P. Taft points out that while only one American in 10 was a church member when the first federal census was taken in 1790, the latest showed 59% holding church membership, and the Gallup poll estimates that since those figures were gathered in 1950 church membership has climbed to 79% of all adults. Mr. Taft believes this accelerated rate of growth will continue.

. . . . .

Columns could be filled with instances, bizarre or impressive, of this much-publicized "turn to religion." Once you begin to enumerate them, there seems to be no end. But just as a sample fistful, named almost at random, ponder the significance in the picture of "U.S.A. 1955" of the huge followings won by Billy Graham and Bishop Sheen, of the insertion of "under God" into the schoolchild's pledge and of "In God we trust" into the design of our postage stamps, of the monster rallies which Catholics and Protestants and Jehovah's Witnesses have proved they can assemble, of the rush by the most adventurous modernistic architects to get into the designing of churches and synagogues, of the crowding in theological seminaries and rabbinical schools, of Hollywood's belief that any film spectacle combining a biblical or semibiblical theme with sufficient exposure of the fleshpots of carnality is sure to make a mint, of recent theatrical works by T. S. Eliot and Graham Greene and Gian-Carlo Menotti which leave critics at a loss but theaters filled with brooding audiences.

Russell Lynes divides Americans into high-brows, low-brows, and middle-brows. This renewed attention to religion characterizes all three. The high-brows must at least pretend to understand the theological writings of Reinhold Niebuhr, Paul Tillich and Jacques Maritain. They applaud Harvard's new president when he turns that university's energies into the galvanizing of its divinity school. They can quote Wystan Auden's *For the Time Being, A Christmas Oratorio,* and Aldous Huxley's *The Perennial Philosophy* and acknowledge a quaint attraction in Phyllis McGinley's saints.

Among the low-brows, perennial religious interest is at present showing in so-called ecstatic sects, which specialize in faith-healing, speaking in unknown tongues, spiritualistic séances, or even practices as outlandish as snake-handling, [and] report a faster proportional growth than any other religious bodies. When the Jehovah's Witnesses converge on Yankee Stadium to proclaim their millennial tidings, they not only pack in more people than Babe Ruth ever did, but they have to hire a big swimming pool to baptize their converts. Tenement districts, especially in those parts of cities where dislocated Negroes, Puerto Ricans or West Indians have settled in large numbers, teem with all manner of "store-front" congregations—some trying to do an honest job helping these easily exploited and often nearly illiterate people, too many no better than rackets intent on sharing in the exploitation.

But perhaps the most accessible evidence of religion's appeal to our low-brow instincts is its capture of the juke box. This started a few years ago when several radio programs won national popularity with hillbilly singing of the "Grand Ole Opry" variety. Most of these songs moaned about "mother, home and heaven." Nashville, Tenn., took up the business of recording these mountaineer chants, or publishing them in sheet form, and soon was seriously competing in sales with Broadway's Tin Pan Alley. The result was what one would expect. Broadway at one end of the continent and Hollywood at the other leaped into the production of these sentimentalized religious (*Our Lady of Fatima, It Is No Secret What God Can Do*) or neoreligious (*I Believe, Count Your Blessings*) ballads. The record and sheet music sales on some of these are way up on the hit parade. As a consequence, in almost any spot with a juke box, interspersed with the frank sensualism of such traditional romantics as *Make Love to Me* or *Teach Me Tonight,* one is suddenly listening to something like the lyric which is supposed to be Jane Russell's favorite:

> Have you talked to THE MAN UPSTAIRS,
> 'Cause He wants to hear from you,
> Have you talked to THE MAN UPSTAIRS,
> He will always see you thru.
> And if trouble ever troubles you,
> Don't you run and hide,
> 'Cause if you ever need a friend,
> He'll be right there by your side.
> Just turn your eyes t'ward heaven,
> And say a simple pray'r,
> Thru clouds of lace you'll see His face
> No matter when or where.[1]

---

[1] "The Man Upstairs," by Dorinda Morgan, Harold Stanley, Garry Marmers. Copyright 1954 by Vesta Music Corporation. The sheet music carries the notation that it is to be played to "bounce tempo."

It is among us middle-brows, however, that this phenomenon of an American religious stirring is most striking. And because the middle-brows compose the most influential part of American society, the importance of this stirring is enhanced. As in the case of high-brows and low-brows, this reawakened interest in religion among the middle-brows shows itself in many forms. But it is making the deepest dent on public consciousness in what has been called "the cult of reassurance." Here is something that spills over into both high-brow and low-brow American life but it takes a peculiarly American form for the middle-brows and it derives its greatest response from them.

FROM FRUSTRATION TO REASSURANCE

What is this cult of reassurance? It is a flocking to religion, especially in middle-class circles, for a renewal of confidence and optimism at a time when these are in short supply. It is a turning to the priest for encouragement to believe that, despite everything that has happened in this dismaying century, the world is good, life is good, the human story makes sense and comes out where we want it to come out. Most of us find these things hard to believe these days. The optimistic anticipations of the Herbert Spencer period look like doleful illusions in the light of the calculated starvation of the Volga kulaks, in the light of Belsen, Hiroshima, Eniwetok. "Insecurity" and "frustration" have become key words in our contemporary vocabulary. The most talked-about philosophy of our time is existentialism which, in the thought of Jean-Paul Sartre, its most prominent living advocate, teaches that one exists but that existence has no meaning beyond bare existence.

The "cult of reassurance" now being heard from scores of American pulpits is a direct challenge to all this. It is a cult of affirmation ("positive thinking") and a rejection of all contemporary cults of denial. Naturally, it makes its greatest appeal to middle-brow Americans who are at odds with themselves and their lives. This is a huge class and it has been growing ever since Sinclair Lewis' bewildered Babbitt found himself staring into his shaving mirror and wondering what his high-geared life was all about.

The nation is full of confused persons who feel that there is something wrong, something deeply unsatisfying, about the lives they are living but would have trouble saying what it is and even more trouble in discovering what to do about it. These are the people who are not yet badly enough disturbed (or wealthy enough) to be ready for a psychoanalyst, but they are frustrated, depressed, have a feeling that they have been victimized by life and some of them are on the way to a crack-up. Already, we are told, more than half the hospital beds in this country are filled with mental cases. Doctors and clergy alike can testify that if the tension does not let up that proportion will increase.

For victims of this malady of the times—which is mainly a loss of nerve—the cult of reassurance has some undeniable benefits to offer and some therapeutic methods of very debatable worth. Its approach is two-sided: it combines admonition to relax with promise that the individual can overcome all difficulties, can achieve whatever he wants to achieve. Most of its clerical practitioners add to this he-can-who-thinks-he-can promise the pious proviso, "by the help of God." Weakness and failure are within oneself; they are unnecessary; they can be overcome by following certain simple, clear rules which, it is claimed, religion supplies, but most of which on examination turn out to be rules that any elementary knowledge of psychology and a fair amount of common sense would suggest.

This cult says that the bedeviled victim of today's pressures should discipline his thoughts to reject all pessimistic ("negative") ideas and encourage optimistic ones ("accentuate the positive," says the popular song). And then, through prayer, by reading selected texts from the Bible and "inspirational" material, observing periods of quiet reflection and exerting will power, he will relax the tension of his life and find himself filled with new energy. His personal relations with family and other associates will straighten out and he will achieve whatever he sets as his goal.

One reason why this cult makes such an appeal is that our middle-brows live in awe of the "scientist"—especially the psychological scientist. The psychologist has become our Western tribal medicine man. There is sound reason for this. Freud was no charlatan; he opened up a realm of knowledge which may terrify but is vital to our understanding of ourselves.

Most of those who have pressed forward the exploration of the unconscious which Freud pioneered no longer treat religion as the "illusion" it appeared to the great Viennese. Many of them are as ready to acknowledge the legitimacy of some religious therapy for man's inner ills as of other kinds of mental treatment. In some degree this cult of reassurance represents a balancing *rapprochement* from the side of religion, using a good deal of the jargon of psychology, with a dusting of Christian or "religious" phrases, to persuade man that he need have no sense of personal insufficiency or recognize any limits to the bounds of his achievement. And that, since our forefathers first stormed this continent's wilderness, has been a big part of the American creed.

Some have called the cult of reassurance a new religion. Is it? If by a new religion one means one without antecedents, then certainly it is not. Man has always turned to his gods for release from worry and failure. The "prudential" conception of religion is at least as old as the Book of Proverbs. The idea that if you are righteous—that is, if you follow the religious rules of the game—you will prosper was endorsed by the Pharisees and handed along by Calvin to the English Puritans, who brought it with them to this country. This is an element which bulks large in the American—especially the New England—tradition. It is not confined to those with a Protestant background. It may be seen at work today in the enormous popularity of the novenas that are spreading among Roman Catholic churches, where following the rules of devotion is supposed to dispose of every imaginable kind of personal problem, all the way from getting a job to curing disease and winning back a faithless lover.

A NEATLY PACKAGED WAY TO HAPPINESS

What we are seeing now, therefore, is rather a new development in the ancient search for a quick, neatly packaged, all-encompassing solution for man's deepest, most harassing and most persistent problem— how to be happy, how to have a satisfying life. It is a sort of alliance between one aspect of religion, the "I will fear no evil" aspect, and depth psychology to overcome modern personality disintegrations. The fact that neither ally is as yet very comfortable in the alliance does not alter the other fact that it is fast taking form. Wisely encouraged, protected against superficial exploitation, it could become one of the healthiest factors in our national life.

Ever since William James and his historic *Varieties of Religious Experience* there has been widespread recognition among ministers of the importance of psychological insight for their work in the cure of souls. But the big push toward the present development may be dated from the publication in 1946 of *Peace of Mind,* written by a young Boston rabbi, Joshua L. Liebman. There had been books on psychology-and-religion before that, but the sensational success of Rabbi Liebman's book started the stampede. *Peace of Mind* was a publishing surprise. It originated as a series of midweek lectures in which Dr. Liebman tried to disclose to his congregation the basis on which religious faith and Freudian psychology could work together to relieve modern tensions. Some enthusiastic hearers brought these lectures to the attention of Simon and Schuster. They helped the rabbi whip them into book form and 177 weeks on the best-seller list followed.

It used to be said among publishers that the sure-fire sellers were books on how to lose weight, especially if the title suggested that no cutting down on eating was involved. Since *Peace of Mind* struck oil, however, every publishing house has been hunting for the kind of book that might repeat that success. To recall just a few titles of the past seven years: *The Magic of Believing,* by Claude Bristol; *Peace of Soul,* by Bishop Sheen; *The Way to Security,* by H. C. Link; *Beyond Anxiety,* by

James A. Pike; *Man's Search for Himself*, by Rollo May; *Mind Alive*, by Harry Overstreet, and all the best sellers by Dr. Peale, whose *Guide to Confident Living* (1948) is still selling about 3,000 a week and whose *The Power of Positive Thinking* has passed the million mark. For 126 consecutive weeks it has been near or at the top of the best-seller list.

It was inevitable that a publishing success of this sort would be reflected in American pulpits. Preachers are nearly as susceptible as editors to "what the public wants." Moreover, in the harrowing world which came out of the war the clergy were becoming deeply and justifiably concerned as they discovered the psychological dislocations of their people. One consequence can be seen in the fact that, within the last decade, half the Protestant theological seminaries on the approved list have established departments of "pastoral counseling," in which young ministers are taught by psychologically trained professors to try to do what candidates for the Roman Catholic priesthood have always been trained to do in the confessional—to relieve men and women from the sense of guilt, to restore their personal confidence for living.

. . . . .

With all possible recognition for the good it may be accomplishing among those who need a restoration of hope and self-confidence, it has to be granted that this cult of reassurance is not Christianity in its classical sense or Judaism in its highest conception. It lacks—at least in most of its literature and in the popular understanding of its message—vital elements in the Christian doctrine of salvation. That doctrine has always held that man, the sinner, can only be saved by a great redemptive act on the part of God to release him from his guilt and to free him from his addiction to sin. Protestants and Catholics differ as to how man is to appropriate the benefits of God's redemptive act, but on the core of their belief in the doctrine of salvation they are at one.

. . . . .

. . . what today's cult of reassurance most lacks—and indeed disavows— is a sense of life's inevitable failures. Here is the point at which it stands in starkest contrast to the teaching of America's most searching contemporary theologian, Reinhold Niebuhr. Many say they find Niebuhr hard to understand, but there is one central idea in his writing which should be easy to grasp, for it is validated by universal experience. This is his contention that all human effort, however noble, however achieving, contains within it an element of failure. Perhaps one reason Americans say they cannot understand Niebuhr is because their minds simply will not harbor this fact that all success is dogged by failure. We Americans *must* succeed. We cannot approach life with any other expectation. But Christianity, in the most profound sense, is a religion for failures.

THE "NEW RELIGION" IN HIGH GEAR

The high priest of this cult of reassurance is—one scarcely needs tell any reader of current magazines or listener to radio and television— Norman Vincent Peale. To see this "new religion" in high gear one must study Dr. Peale, who preaches to probably the largest audience ever gathered by an American cleric.

Norman Vincent Peale is a friendly, offhand, sack-suited person whose obvious sincerity and uninhibited cordiality make him, on personal contact, easy to like. Perhaps, if he will forgive me a bit of minor negative thinking, I should put that the other way—when you meet him, it would be hard to dislike him. This, of course, is one reason for his great effectiveness. He crisscrosses the country constantly, speaking about as often outside New York as in his home pulpit, and in this jumping about he makes thousands of personal contacts. Most of these are with laymen; outside his regular preaching in his own church he speaks at far more business conventions and industrial company rallies than church gatherings. He gets along better with laymen than with clergymen; he knows it and rather prides himself on it. A year ago he was named in a list of "Twelve Best U.S. Salesmen"; he belonged there.

. . . . .

Dr. Peale's climb to public attention followed his discovery of the psychological basis of most individual disturbances. He is frequently criticized by other clergymen for not paying much attention to social and political questions. He would probably reply that an effort to deal with inner tensions provides him with a field large enough for one man's ministry. He was one of the first ministers to try to link psychology with the work of the church. He found in the respected Smiley Blanton, M.D., a psychiatrist glad to cooperate with him. Together they developed a clinic, whose medical practice Dr. Blanton directed while Dr. Peale raised most of the money either from his church or by his lecturing, which has grown into the American Foundation of Religion and Psychiatry. Its clinic, which has been on Park Avenue, is about to move into quarters about five times as large in a building adjoining the church.

. . . . .

One wonders, however, just what the clinic's psychiatrists with their top-flight medical training (Dr. Blanton was a pupil of Freud; the others on the staff all carry the highest professional credentials) think of their founder-president's preaching. For over the years Dr. Peale, as his books show, has simplified his approach to a point where almost every human problem is treated as soluble by resort to a simple technique of action that can be learned in five minutes and practiced at will. His sermons follow one pattern; he himself will say, "When you've heard one, you've heard them all." Take the topics of the first six sermons he preached this year and you have the pattern: "The Key to Self-Confidence," "How to Feel Alive and Well," "Ways to Improve Your Situation," "Wonderful Results of Faith Attitude," "Live with Joyous Vitality," "Empty Fear from Your Thoughts." His prescriptions on "how to" do these things tend increasingly to fall into a "10 rule" formula that can be—and is—printed on one side of a "How Card." Such as, for example:

HOW TO OVERCOME YOUR INFERIORITY COMPLEX

Ten Rules for Getting Self-Confidence

by NORMAN VINCENT PEALE

First: Hold in your mind a picture of yourself succeeding. Your mind will seek to actualize this image.

Second: When a negative thought comes to mind deliberately cancel it with a positive thought.

Third: Do not build up obstacles in your imagination.

Fourth: Do not be awestruck by other people or try to copy them.

Fifth: Repeat ten times a day these words, "If God be for me who can be against me."

Sixth: Get a competent counselor to help you understand the origin of your inferiority feeling which often begins in childhood. Self-knowledge leads to a cure.

Seventh: Ten times each day repeat aloud the following affirmation, "I can do all things through Christ which strengtheneth me." Conceive of yourself as receiving this strength.

Eighth: Realistically estimate your ability; then raise the estimate 10%. Do not become egotistical, but develop a wholesome self-respect.

Ninth: Through prayer attach yourself to the flow of spiritual power.

Tenth: Believe that God is with you, for nothing can defeat that partnership.

. . . . . .

Perhaps without his knowing it, Norman Vincent Peale's popularity as a preacher stems out of two things: his rejection of the dominant note of pessimism in the orthodox theology of our time and his ability to put that rejection in simple rules which are individual in their application and for which he claims the sanction of religious authority (God, Christ, Bible texts) and scientific testing (psychology, psychiatry, psychosomatic medicine). Criticism that this is a truncated theology and a psychology so oversimplified that in the long run it may do more harm than good will not deter him. He apparently has no worries at all about what his theology is, beyond a reiteration of the simple evangelical formulas of his boyhood. He can match any report of psychological harm wrought with a dozen testimonials from grateful disciples. Criticism that he harps on only one string he can shrug off. What is successful advertising but endless repetition of a single slogan? And the response to the Peale formula has been so great that—despite criticism which he knows exists and which I think distresses him, for he is a reasonably humble and sensitive man—little Peales are sprouting in clerical ranks all over the country.

THE RECKONING ON THE CREDIT SIDE

What significance for the present condition and future prospect of religion in this country has the rise of this cult of reassurance? Certainly the reckoning is not all on the debit side. Briefly, it seems to me, one can credit this cult with having done these things:

1. It has contributed much to ending a period of widespread indifference to the church and religion. So remarkable has been this change that today a crusty but perspicacious old codger like Canon Bernard Iddings Bell growls, "Religion has become a fad." One can sympathize with Canon Bell's skepticism as to the spiritual depth of the fad but the nation is better off with the faddists streaming into the churches than it would be if they were going in the other direction.

2. It has helped along the clerical discovery of the importance of man's inner conflicts, of the bearing of modern psychology on the church's responsibility for the cure of souls. This is by no means confined to Protestantism or the Jewish faith. Two of the best books in this field, for example, are by Catholic priests: *Psychoanalysis and Personality*, by a professor at the Catholic University of Louvain, Josef Nuttin, S.J., and *Psychiatry and Catholicism*, by James H. Vander Veldt, O.F.M., and Robert P. Odenwald, M.D.

3. By its very shortcomings it has promoted the development of "counseling" based on trained psychological observation as a legitimate and growing aspect of pastoral service.

4. Some people are helped. The medical profession may say that these are the only slightly depressed or disturbed who need no more than a slight ministration to their self-confidence to be set on the right track. But there are a lot of them, and if they can be helped before they fall prey to a serious neurosis, that is a service to society of no small value.

5. This cult is making a contribution to the survival of American optimism, and in today's world it is important to have some optimism somewhere outside the Communist orbit. In this respect, this cult is an offset to the pessimism of orthodox theology which, when it is overly

insistent on the futility of man's efforts to achieve the good, can do even more damage to society than does overinsistence on man's powers of attainment.

But the liability side of the ledger must be taken into account before a balance can be struck. There are certain items which must be set down there, among them:

1. Religion is always headed for a fall when an attempt is made to make it a too-simple, too-magical solution for all man's problems. The deeper the dislocation, the more tragic the condition, the less likely is any pat formula to cure it. Sometimes there is no cure, at least in this life. Job, the Bible is careful to state, was a "blameless and upright" man, but the blows life dealt him remained an insoluble mystery.

2. Reliance on a set formula for dealing with the infinite ills which distress mankind exposes religion to the consequence when the formula does not work. When the "10 easy rules" fail to accomplish all that is promised, what happens? The reaction may be a little while coming, but look out when it does.

3. The church is never more surely preparing the way for its own future discomfiture than when it succumbs to the temptation to attract a following by evading the dark facts of human failure and frustration and the ruthlessness of society. The torment in which men live is most often a consequence of that condition which Reinhold Niebuhr summed up in the title of his greatest book, *Moral Man and Immoral Society*. There, in an implacably and impersonally immoral society, is where men are caught, and in their efforts to adjust their own good intentions to the conditions of their existence they fall into despair.

How is despairing man to "serve God and find His purposes" if that, as the president of the National Council of Churches says, is the end for which religion exists? It surely will not be easy. Ask any atomic physicist who has lent his brain to opening the Pandora's box of a nuclear armament race. Ask any man in politics trying to hang on to his ideals while practicing "the art of the possible." It cannot be done in terms wholly self-concerned. It cannot seek for success recognizable by the go-getters.

The purposes of God can be perceived by finite minds only in part and darkly—"Now we see in a mirror dimly," said St. Paul—and insofar as they are perceived they are more likely to heighten the tension between the religious seeker and his environment than to smooth his road. Nevertheless, men have found and are finding, in the records of history, in the experience of the saintly, in the lofty insights of the Bible and the devotional classics, what some inner monitor certifies—though by no means infallibly—are the purposes of God. In seeking to serve those purposes they do find a sublimation of their fears, their sense of pointless striving, their sensate hungers.

The response to the "cult of reassurance" is a reminder of how universal is man's hunger for hope. But hope will not survive long if it refuses to take account of the defeats, the heartbreak and the inevitable limitations of life. This is the critical point at which the "new religion," if it is not to fade out like another Coué fad, must have what psychological insights it possesses rectified and reinforced by that most profound of all religious insights, put into words by the Teacher of Nazareth: "For whoever would save his life will lose it, but whoever loses his life for my sake and the gospel's"—in other words, in seeking to discern and serve the purposes of God—"will save it."

68. TIME ON OUR HANDS *

RUSSELL LYNES

The shorter work week and the extensive development of mechanical devices to ease the burden of our daily lives have made possible much more opportunity for leisure-time activities. Man's adjustment to this change has been given little systematic attention by sociologists. It is a subject which deserves serious attention, however, and this selection by Russell Lynes describes some of the consequences of poorly conceived use of this new-found resource of "time." He calls for intellectually challenging activities as the best means to make leisure most rewarding.

Recently I discovered among some papers that my mother had stowed away in a deserted file a clipping from a magazine of the 1920s. It was headed "Schedule for a One-Maid House." The house, it said, "has seven rooms; a living-room, dining-room, porch, kitchen, maid's room and bath, three bedrooms, and two baths." The schedule starts with:

6:45 A.M. *Wash and Dress*

and ends with:

8:00 P.M. *Plans for the evening will be adapted to the household convenience.*

Bridget, if that was her name, was busy in the intervening hours

* From Russell Lynes, "Time on Our Hands," *Harper's Magazine*, Vol. 217, No. 1298 (July, 1958), 34–39. Copyright © 1958, by Harper & Brothers. Reprinted by permission of the author.

The author (b. 1910) is Managing Editor of *Harper's Magazine*. An astute literary interpreter of sociological phenomena. Author: *Highbrow, Lowbrow, Middlebrow; Snobs; Tastemakers; A Surfeit of Honey.*

with cleaning, cooking, bed-making, baking, and polishing silver and brass. Her respite came sometime between 1:30 and 3:00 P.M. when, according to the schedule, she was to "clear table, wash dishes, go to own room to rest, bathe, and change dress." At 3:00 she was back in the kitchen, "ready to answer door, etc."

Leisure was not much of a problem for Bridget at work in a one-maid house. Her schedule covers six days (on Saturday it says: "Bake cake for Sunday") and like everyone else she had Sunday as her only day off. (She doesn't seem to have had "maid's night out" on the customary Thursday.)

The familiar picture of the maid on her day off was of a girl dressed "fit to kill" on her way to meet her friends at church. The equally familiar picture of the man of the house was father asleep in a hammock buried under the Sunday paper. Leisure in those days was merely a restorative for work. Now leisure has become work in its own right . . . and a worry to lots of earnest Americans.

Last year at the commencement exercises at New York University a clergyman said to the graduating class: "America can be undone by her misuse of leisure. Life is getting easier physically, and this makes life harder morally."

There are, of course, a great many professional and business men who wonder what all this talk about leisure is: somehow it is no problem to them—or so they think. There are also a good many women, especially young married women, who would give their heirlooms for a few minutes to themselves. They have only to wait.

But leisure is making some thoughtful people uneasy. In January the American Council of Churches met in Columbus to discuss the spare time of our increasingly urbanized populace. The Twentieth Century Fund is deep in an investigation of leisure and the University of Chicago is (with the help of Ford Foundation funds) making a study of the nature of leisure and how people use it. Corporations not only worry about the leisure of their employees; they do something about it. School-teachers and social workers and local politicians worry about it, about footloose youngsters, about long summer vacations for teen-agers, and about juvenile delinquency. City planners, safety experts, highway engineers watch the growing number of hours when families are not at work and feel they have to go somewhere. Where? To what extent is the boredom of leisure responsible for young drug addicts, for the common cold, for muggings on city streets?

Every new scientific development, whether it is aimed at saving our skins or washing our dishes, leads in one way or another to reducing still further the sweat of the public brow. The four-day week which looms on the immediate horizon (and which causes such consternation in the corporate breast) is, of course, less the product of labor's demands than of manufacturing genius. Machines not men have created the three-day weekend.

. . . . .

HOW TO KEEP THE IDLE RICH FROM COMMITTING SUICIDE

But these efforts to sponge up the ocean of the so-called leisure time which has engulfed us can only put a few drops in the bucket. The truth is that while the new leisure has come on us fairly gradually, it has found us not at all prepared. If we are to cope agreeably with it, we are going to have to change our minds about some shibboleths and even some rather basic beliefs. To do this, we need to understand what has happened to the pattern of our leisure and where it is likely to lead.

Leisure is not a new problem born of automation, but it is a new problem for a great many kinds of people who were never much concerned with it when Bridget was working her seventy- or eighty-hour week in the one-maid house. America has had a leisure class since the industrialization of our country began, and in the 1850s the art critic James Jackson Jarves complained in shocked tones of the number of scions of wealthy families who threw themselves into rivers because they were so bored that life seemed not worth living. (Mr. Jarves wanted to interest such young men in the arts as a suitable outlet for their energies and money.) These young men, whom we would call the idle rich, had on a large scale the same problem that nearly everybody in America has today on a small scale. In its simplest terms, the primary problem of leisure is how to avoid boredom.

We used to be more accomplished at being bored than we are today, or at least we seem to have taken boredom with better grace in the days of party calls and decorous parlor games. We assumed a high moral tone toward leisure, and in some respects this tone persists. "The devil finds work for idle hands," our parents said and shook their heads; and when they said, "All work and no play makes Jack a dull boy," they meant, of course, that Jack should work most of the time but not quite all of it. Primarily leisure was thought of as a way to get a man back on his feet so that after Sunday he could put in sixty or so productive hours from Monday through Saturday. Leisure for women (few women in those days had jobs) was something quite else—it was the custody of culture and good works. Women in their spare time were expected to cultivate the arts, foster the education of their children, and play the role of Lady Bountiful in the community.

It was a neat division of family functions and a tidy way of life. Father's leisure was restorative; mother's was extremely productive. But more has changed than just the roles of men and women; the whole complex machinery of leisure has changed.

Briefly the changes are these:

In the last few decades what had started about a century ago as a trickle of people from the country and small towns to the cities became a torrent. Cities filled like cisterns and overflowed into suburbs, and as we shifted from a predominantly agricultural economy to a predominantly industrial one, we changed the nature of much of our leisure from what might be called a natural one to an artificial one, from pleasures provided by nature to pleasures concocted by man. Ways of using leisure began to come in packages—in cars, in movies, in radios, and most recently in television sets, and what was once the sauce only for the city goose became the sauce for the country gander as well. City culture is now within easy reach of everyone everywhere and everyone has the same access to talent that only a few decades ago used to be reserved for the rich and the urbane.

During the time when we were changing from a rural to an urban culture, the length of the work-week fell from sixty hours or more to forty or thirty-five. Gradually the five-day week became an almost universal reality, and the four-day week is on the immediate horizon. With more leisure time, men have, quite naturally, taken on some of the household chores that only a short while ago they wouldn't have been caught dead at, and have assumed some of the cultural responsibilities which were once the domain of their wives. They have also, with time on their hands and cars at their disposal, turned again to many kinds of rural recreation . . . to fishing and hunting especially, but also to sailing and skiing. The most solitary of all sports, fishing, is also the most popular of all sports with American men.

THE CASH VALUE OF THE DEVIL'S WORK

But the greatest assault on old patterns of leisure and on the shibboleths about devil's work for idle hands, has been industry's discovery that it needs the consuming time of workers as much as it needs their producing time. In an economy geared as ours is to making life comfortable for everyone, it is essential to business that people have time to enjoy their comfort and to use up the things that make life comfortable.

A tremendous part of our production plant is committed to promoting leisure—to automobiles, to television sets, to time-saving gadgets, to sports equipment, and to hundreds of services which are unnecessary to life but which contribute to relaxed living. Our economy, in other words, is more and more involved with Time Off. Think of the industries, the purveyors of pleasure, that would collapse if we were to go back to the sixty-hour week. It looks as though we were far more likely (and not because of pressures from labor but the demands of technology and automation) to go to a twenty-eight hour week.

Urbanization, the shorter working day and week, and the changing roles of the sexes have, heaven knows, produced tremendous changes in the ways Americans live. But the premium put on the consuming time of the worker by our economic system presents us with a tidily packaged moral dilemma. When idleness is a public virtue, what becomes of the moral value of work? What are we going to substitute for the old adages on which we were brought up? What are we going to tell our children? What will happen to the economy if we go on saying that virtue is its own reward, that work is good for the soul, and that leisure is only a reward for toil? What happens to the Calvinist ethic?

This is a problem I would rather refer to a dilettante than to an economist or a clergyman or certainly to an engineer. The economist would consider it from the point of view of wealth, the clergyman of the after life, and the engineer of production. The dilettante can be counted on to look at it from the point of view of life, liberty, and especially the pursuit of happiness.

A SPECIAL KIND OF LOVER

I would like to contend in all seriousness, at this moment when there is such a cry for engineers and when our theological seminaries are bursting at the doors, that what we need is more dilettantes. Compared with good dilettantes, good engineers and good clergymen are a dime a dozen. Every newspaper account of the engineering shortage is contradicted by another story of how big corporations are hoarding engineers the way people hoarded butter during the last war. Recently, Dr. Robert J. Havighurst of the University of Chicago made it quite clear that the number of engineers and technologists being trained in our technical schools is more than adequate to our needs; the shortage, he said, is in good teachers. In the long run our civilization will be measured more accurately by our know-why than by our know-how.

It is probably because in the triumvirate of our ideals—life, liberty, and the pursuit of happiness—the last of these has always seemed to our Calvinist society rather naughty, that we have come to look down our noses at the dilettante. We have dismissed him as a trifler: we have despised him as a parasite on other people's work, the fritterer, the gadfly. But there was a time when the word dilettante was by no means the term of opprobrium it has become.

Originally *dilettante* meant a lover of the fine arts (it comes from the Latin word for delight) and it was used to distinguish the consumer from the producer. Its application spread beyond the arts in England, and in the eighteenth century the Society of the Dilettanti was a club of influential men interested not only in the arts but in the sciences and in archaeology. It meant the man of intellectual curiosity who devoted part of his time to the intelligent cultivation of the arts and sciences, to the resources of leisure and the satisfactions of the mind.

If you transplant the idea of the eighteenth-century dilettante from England to America, you discover that he was Thomas Jefferson and Benjamin Franklin—one a farmer who dabbled in architecture and introduced a new style to America, the other a printer who dabbled in natural science and flew a kite into a thunderstorm. You discover several others who got together and started a talkfest that became the Philosophical Society of Philadelphia, and others who, dabbling in the arts, somehow founded a string of distinguished museums across the nation and filled them with masterpieces, and, of course, a good many bad guesses. These men were dilettantes. There is no other word that fits them.

. . . . .

. . . What we need in our society, I contend again, is more real dilettantes, and we need to extend the meaning of the word to many delights besides the arts and sciences.

The dilettante is just a consumer. He is a man who takes the pursuit of happiness seriously, not frivolously, and he works at it. He is part sensualist, part intellectual, and part enthusiast. He is also likely to be a proselytizer for those causes in which his interests are involved, and to be rather scornful of those people who do not take their pleasure seriously and who are passive instead of active in the cultivation of them. But whatever else he may be he is not lazy. He may or may not have a job that he finds interesting, but he does not use his leisure in a miscellaneous and undirected fashion. He knows what he wants out of life and will go to a lot of trouble to get it. Primarily, in Voltaire's sense, he wants to cultivate his own garden.

THE CRANK ON QUALITY

You will find dilettantes everywhere and in every aspect of our culture. I found one a few weeks ago driving a taxi in New York. He was a man in his early sixties.

"I only drive this hack three days a week," he said. "The other four days I go fishing. I like to fish and I'm pretty good at it."

By the time he had delivered me home I knew what he fished for at what times of year, what bait he used and where and in what weather, and which were the best fishing boats and captains going out of New York harbor. I asked him what he did with all the fish he caught.

"I got a son-in-law runs a saloon," he said. "I give them to his customers."

Probably the most common and in some ways the most accomplished of American dilettantes is the baseball fan, though the national pastime is being crowded out of its position as top banana of entertainment these days by serious music. The baseball fan knows his subject with something very close to genuine scholarship. He is an expert in the minutiae of its history and understands the nuances and subtleties of its performance. He takes as much pleasure from the refinements of its details as from the outcome of any single game, and he enjoys the company of others with whom he can argue the relative virtues of performance and make comparisons with other similar situations. He demands skill on the field of a truly professional caliber, and he lets his displeasure with anything less be known in the most direct and uncompromising manner. He is, by and large, a less tolerant dilettante than the one whose interest is devoted to art, for his expert eye is less subject to changes in fashion. Unquestionably without him the standards of baseball would long since have gone to pot.

The simple fact is that the dilettante is the ideal consumer, not ideal, perhaps, from the point of view of those producers who would like their customers to accept their products with blind confidence, but ideal from the point of view of maintaining standards of quality . . . whether material or cultural. He takes his functions as a consumer seriously. He takes the trouble to know what he likes and to sort out the shoddy and the meretricious from the sound and reasonable. If he is a dilettante of music, for example, he demands the best performance from his record-player. He is unimpressed by an imitation mahogany cabinet in the Chippendale manner, but he knows that the components of his hi-fi equipment are the very best that he can afford. (He can, in fact, be credited with the very great improvement in mass-produced sound equipment; it was his interest in high-fidelity that spread the word to the general public and raised the level of public acceptance.)

We are likely to associate the dilettante only with the arts, which is one reason why he has such a bad name in America. In the rambunctious and expansive days of the nineteenth century when America was growing and fighting its way across the continent, toil was man's business; culture was left to women. So were most other refinements of life, and the arts were thought of as sissy and men who showed any interest in them as something less than virile. A man who didn't sleep through a concert or an opera was regarded with suspicion. It was only when a man retired from business that it was considered suitable for him to spend his money on art—not necessarily because he liked it or knew anything about it but because it gave him social prestige. Except in a few Eastern Seaboard cities, the arts were women's work, and there was no time and place for the dilettante.

THE ASCENT OF BABBITT

The nature of our new-found leisure is rapidly changing the old stereotypes. The businessman who doesn't make some pretense at an interest in culture, who doesn't support the local symphony and museum, who isn't on the library board or out raising money for his college is looked upon as not doing his duty, much less serving his own interests. Babbitt isn't Babbitt any more. Babbitt is by way of becoming a dilettante. A lot worse things could happen to him. In no time at all being a dilettante will not be considered un-American.

The point at which the dilettante becomes an "expert" but not a "professional" is an indistinct one. Two successful businessmen who have, in their leisure time, become naturalists of considerable reputation are an officer of J. P. Morgan & Co., R. Gordon Wasson, who has recently produced an important book of original research on mushrooms, and Boughton Cobb, a textile manufacturer who is one of the world's leading authorities on ferns. A few years ago an ancient language known to scholars as "Minoan Linear B" that had had scholars completely at sea for years was "broken" by an English architect, Michael Ventris, for whom cryptanalysis was a leisure activity. These three men became experts, not professionals, dilettantes in the best sense, not amateurs.

Obviously not many men in any generation are going to be able to extend their leisure activities to such levels of distinction. But leisure without direction, without the satisfaction of accomplishment of some sort is debilitating to anyone brought up in an atmosphere, like ours, in which the virtues of work have been so long extolled and are so deeply imbedded in our mythology. The greatest satisfaction of the dilettante is not in doing but in discovering, in discriminating, and in enjoying the fruits of his knowledge and his taste.

There will, of course, always be those who can only find satisfaction in making something, the eternal do-it-yourselfers, the cabinetmakers, and needlepointers, and gardeners, and model builders, and rug hookers. These are the amateur craftsmen who often achieve professional competence. There are also those who will find their only satisfactions apart from work in sensuous pleasures, in sports, and food and drink, and love. The dilettante finds his satisfactions primarily in the mind. He is the ideal traveler, the perfect audience, the coveted reader, and the perceptive collector.

IS HE A HIGHBROW?

But he is not by any means necessarily a highbrow. Indeed the ideal dilettante is not. He may be a professional intellectual or he may not, but he does not pose as what he isn't. His tastes and his knowledge may well run to abstruse and esoteric things, to the dances of Tibet or the jewelry of pre-Columbian Mexico, but they may just as well run to the square dance and baseball cards. The dilettante of jazz, the man who knows the names of the instrumentalists in all of the great bands of the last thirty years, is as important a dilettante as the man who knows his Mozart by Koechel numbers. It is genuine, not simulated, enthusiasm that counts. The function of the dilettante is to encourage a high degree of performance in whatever field of interest happens to be his, to be an informed, but by no means conventional, critic, and to be a watchdog. He must be both an enthusiast and irritant who will praise what measures up to his standards and needle producers into doing as well as they know how, and better. He is an incorrigible asker of hard questions. He keeps controversy in our culture alive, and if he is sometimes proved to be dead wrong, he is at least never dead on his feet. He is the want-to-know-why man and the traditional anathema of the know-how man.

Several months ago I found myself in an argument, or the beginnings of one, in a radio interview with a well-known broadcaster. "Our colleges need to produce more and better trained men," he said, and I countered with the suggestion that they needed to produce better educated men. "We need experts," he said.

"We need dilettantes," I replied, and the word so surprised him that he gingerly changed the subject to safer ground.

I would like to change my position, but only slightly. What we need are trained men with the capacity for being dilettantes. There can be no argument with the fact that an industrialized society must have a great many highly trained men and women with specialized knowledge and skills. But in this country the consumers and the producers are the same people; all of us work both sides of the economic street. We are, the great majority of us, the part-time idle rich, and no nation, so far as I know, has ever found itself in such a position before. Ours is a society in which no man's nose need be permanently to the grindstone, and where every man is a potential dilettante.

We have thought of our know-how as our most exportable commodity, and when somebody else demonstrated, moon-fashion, a superior know-how, we took it as a blow to our "national prestige." In fact our most exportable commodity has been a cultural one, a way of life that balances work and leisure for almost everyone and distributes the fruits of labor with astonishing, if not complete, evenness. Our most effective know-how has been in the production of leisure, a commodity filled with promise and booby traps. It is the engineer with his slide rule who knows how to produce leisure, but it is the dilettante who knows how to use it and make it productive.

It will be as dilettantes and consumers that we will, in the long run, determine the quality of our culture. We will determine not only the gadgets of our civilization but the fate of its arts as well. We will determine whether the pursuit of happiness has, after all, been worth it.

69. THE FUNCTION OF THE ORCHESTRA
IN COMMUNITY AND NATION *

JOHN H. MUELLER

Leisure takes a variety of institutionalized forms in any society. One of these is the symphony orchestra. In this selection J. H. Mueller shows the particular way in which certain musical arts are institutionalized in American society. His analysis demonstrates how the functional approach to social phenomena (described and used by Merton is selection 5) can often lead to insights which would be denied to those ignoring the sociocultural setting within which an activity takes place.

The symphony concert is not exclusively, nor in one sense primarily, a musical event. For, so complex and inseparable are human interests, that every social occurrence is a blended experience of varied and simultaneous motives. A concert is comparable, perhaps, to a dinner party, where the interest in food may be subordinated to business contacts, social prestige, ceremonial display, or mere convivial association. No hostess would be flattered to be assured merely that the food was nutritious, nor even that it was tastily served; for such an affair has well-accepted ramifications into many other avenues of social intercourse. A symphony concert is similarly a pluralistic event, which may supply an outlet for fashion, prestige, civic pride, heightened national consciousness, as well as musical delight. It is therefore no disparagement, but a psychological and sociological truth, that music is often secondary to nonmusical consideraions.

Since music, too, is laden with these derivative functions, which vary considerably in character and proportion from person to person, the quality and meaning of "enjoyment" of a concert displays a wide range of variation in different epochs. When, for example, we reflect on the strenuous content of our recent and contemporary symphony programs, the awe in which the masterpieces are held, the reluctance with which the audience pits its taste and judgment against that of the critic and conductor, and the frankly tentative and reserved judgments of the

* From *The American Symphony Orchestra* by John H. Mueller, published by Indiana University Press.

The author (b. 1895) is Chairman of the Department of Sociology, Indiana University. Formerly research analyst, Federal Emergency Relief Administration.

critics themselves, it is difficult for the modern patron to realize that in the classic period, often called the "golden age," music was generally considered a matter of sheer pleasure, a forthright delectation of the senses, without any pretense of satisfactions of a more edifying nature. It is quite evident from Mozart's letters that he contemplated very little beyond the pleasure of the moment and harbored no conceit about the sacredness of his scores.

. . . . .

Although much of Mozart's music is still played and enjoyed today, his guileless conception of its function has suffered eclipse, for the typical aesthetician of the romantic nineteenth century (descended, however, from eighteenth century antecedents) held in scorn the theory that music is made merely for pleasure. In fact, it need not even be beautiful. In reviewing Sibelius' Second Symphony, the late Richard Aldrich, then of the *New York Times,* expressed that notion as follows:

There is absolutely nothing in this symphony that is written to please the ear as many wish to be pleased. There is much that sounds chaotic and disordered; but it is evident to the listener who can take a larger measure of it, that it is all very definitely related, the coherent expression of a consistent idea. It is not too much to say that this Second Symphony of Sibelius is one of the strongest compositions in the symphonic form that have been heard in a considerable period.

Such a sanction for what was then cerebral cacophony would have been inconceivable to Haydn, Mozart, Beethoven, and their contemporaries. Mozart, Handel, and Bach had great difficulty in producing music in sufficient volume and at a rate to satisfy the honest appetite for novelty on the part of their audiences, while today a novelty is something the modern audience is expected to endure for the sake of possible habituation and future delight. To explain this complete reversal in the conception of the psychological function of the repertoire, in the criterion of aesthetic judgment, and in the relation between the artist and his public, one must examine the intervening period: the nineteenth century and its Romantic revolt.

The shift is largely attributable to the complete sociological metamorphosis of the audience and of the social status of the musician. During the previous century, the pre-Napoleonic era, the musician had been an employee, who performed a skilled service according to contractual obligations—analogous to the twentieth-century staff musicians in a radio or motion picture studio, allowing, of course, for the divergent requirements of the period and the much greater sense of social stratification than now prevails. His secular audience consisted primarily of the nobility, many of whom were themselves adequate performers, and who sometimes arrogated to themselves the privilege of joining the orchestra. Some even utilized their leisure moments for composing. In fact, as late as 1905 Breitkopf and Haertel published a catalogue of compositions by German royalty, including Kaiser Wilhelm—which serves to recall the piquant warning attributed to Brahms that "one should never criticize the compositions of royalty, for you never know who may have written them."

Composers were craftsmen who composed to order and who, like the architect, the portrait painter and the cook, expected their work to be appreciated forthwith. It would not have occurred to Bach, Mozart, Haydn, and the other *Kapellmeister* of the day to ignore the interest of the current generation by writing *Zukunftsmusik,* nor could they have had the temerity to expect their socially superior patrons to sit through repeated hearings of a suite or symphony on the chance that they or their descendents might possibly enjoy it at some future time. The liveried Haydn admitted that he experimented, but such experimentation was mild and inoffensive, and therefore tolerated and even enjoyed by the prince whom he was paid to serve.

By the turn of the eighteenth century, a social and political transformation had occurred with rather dramatic suddenness, as historical events go. In the history of music this consisted in the catastrophic bankruptcy, and consequent decline in power, of the musician's two richest employers: the church and the court. To gratify those who feel that they must pinpoint evolving historical events, one may suggest that it was the bombardment of Vienna in 1809, sheltering at once the aged Haydn, the middle-aged Beethoven, and the twelve-year-old Schubert, which actually and symbolically gave the *coup de grâce* to the feudal era and marked the transition from the old order to the new. The musician lost his job and became a free-lance composer and an itinerant performer, with all the risks appertaining thereto.

His audience was no longer the closed group of cultivated nobles and their leisurely satellites, before whom the composer was honored to display his accomplishments. Instead, the nineteenth century performer now served the emerging middle-class audience, the third estate, in a commercialized concert to which anyone had access who was able and willing to pay the price of admission. In this new pecuniary social order, the bourgeois audience was not sophisticated, nor well-schooled; but it was ready to be impressed by the virtuosity and the eccentricities of a Paganini, a Liszt, and a host of other virtuosi who mushroomed from that soil. Instead, therefore, of an attitude of reverence and awe on the part of the musician toward his noble audience, it was now the audience which sat in bewilderment before the musician. The artist, in fact, held his audience—his new patrons—in disdain for its crude and undeveloped aesthetic tastes. In art the customer was never right. The mass of anonymous urbanites, newly hatched under the wings of the industrial revolution, issued from office and shop, from banks and colleges, from the professions and public services. Occupied, as they were, full time in gaining a livelihood from the new competitive world, they were by no means a leisure class, they felt keenly their inadequacies in the arts, and acquired a veritable inferiority complex in their presence. They suffer from this debilitating affliction to this very day. They eagerly emulated the standards of the decaying, but still glamorous, aristocracy by cultivating and supporting the arts, and stood ready to be instructed.

Now, if the audience generated by the bourgeois social revolution thus drew away from the artist, the artist on his part also drew away from the audience. Being no longer in the immediate employ of a master whom he was being paid to serve, he developed a sense of autonomy and self-expression in standards of composition as well as in interpretation and execution. The artist even erected an ivory tower where he could commune with his aesthetic conscience and protect himself from any insinuation of being responsible to the audience.

The evolutionary development of the musical arts abetted the artist in his new independence. Orchestral instruments were being improved, orchestras were being enlarged, and composition was becoming more difficult and esoteric. Beethoven's orchestral scores looked "so black" that they literally sounded the death-knell of the amateur player-cooks who had infested the mixed ensembles during the courtly era. Music was now becoming a learned profession which a lifetime was too short to master. Art was really long, and time fleeting. Liszt and Mendelssohn contributed enormously to the enhancement of the prestige of the once lowly profession. As a consequence of these social and technical revolutions, the artistic gap between audience and musician, which had been negligible a generation or two before, was now widening; and the evident explanation was to be sought not only in musical terms, but still more significantly in terms of the social, economic, political, and technological changes unfolding during that period. It is only against such a social background that the problems of the contemporary "heavy" repertoire can be comprehended.

Synchronized with these social changes, philosophers, as is their wont and function, were drafting a system of thought designed to rationalize and buttress these overt historical trends, which were rendering music incomprehensible even to an intelligent audience. By an evolution too complex to rehearse at this point, music was elevated to the most exalted position among the arts; and in its unfettered creativeness, it approximated "pure spirit," universal and absolute Truth. Because of its mystical and supernatural characteristic, it possessed the power to exert a spiritual and ethical influence upon its auditors superior to that of any other medium. Such neo-Platonic doctrines of Hegel and Schopenhauer inevitably placed the great musician in a position of ethical leadership, conferred a certain sacrosanct validity on his "inspiration," and elevated him into the realms of near-infallibility. Music, the most exalted art, was not only a reflection of ultimate ideas and sentiments, but was actually a form of thinking in tones—an abstract, subtle, and direct communication superior to crude verbal symbols, independent of the physical actualities of the world, and therefore a "universal" language. The inspiration of the artist was thus of higher validity than the uninstructed taste of otherwise intelligent people. This was the ideology propagated by such philosophers as Schopenhauer, whose concepts dominated his disciple, Richard Wagner.

This dogma of artistic supremacy was imported to the United States from Germany in the baggage of musicians and conductors, and has set the standards for the musical repertoire to this very day. Indeed, in this country, where vertical mobility was much more rapid than in Europe, where class relations were elastic, where wealth was easier to come by, and the middle class musically unsophisticated, the musical gap was probably still wider than in the old country. Precisely because of this, the conductors assumed, and were given, greater latitude and freedom in America than in Europe. The programs in Boston and Chicago were much more radical—or "progressive"—than they ever were in London, Vienna, Leipzig, and Berlin, both in relation to the maturity of the audience and in absolute terms, as far as the latter can be measured.

. . . . .

It is not at all obvious, nor even probable, that the industrial philanthropists, who liquidated the deficits incurred by Theodore Thomas, Gericke, Mahler, and Stokowski, necessarily shared these mystical convictions with the crusading conductors whom they sponsored. Some were indeed musical and philosophical dilettantes, while many of them were downright metaphysical illiterates and calculating businessmen to whom the ethical import of the Beethoven Third probably did not make much sense. However, in the meantime, the orchestra, with its conductor and esoteric programs, had achieved a certain prestige and glamour. Like fine churches, public buildings, and parks, it soon became an element in the complete apparatus of civic life which focused not unwelcome attention upon the community, and consequently deserved support. Such "tycoon" pride was characteristically expressed by the orator of the occasion at the dedication of Orchestra Hall, December 14, 1904:

Chicago has been the most public spirited city in the world. We are proud of our rapid growth in wealth and population, but we are not satisfied with the merely industrial growth of our city—we demand something more and something better. We look through the dust and smoke of Chicago as she is, to see the fair and noble form of our city as she will be, a center of influence, intellectual and artistic as well as industrial, a school for the nation, as Pericles declared Athens was the school for Greece.

Intercity rivalry was a constant factor that stimulated audience, management, and conductors. Even the idealistic Thomas used this motif on his rebellious constituents in defense of his uncompromising stand on program construction:

The announcement of a symphony on the program was enough to keep many people from the concert. . . . When fault was found with the severity of the programs I would say: Do you wish our program to be inferior in standard to those of the Boston Orchestra? "No" was the answer . . .

That an orchestra had merit as an investment that would redound to the economic benefit of a city was a frequent theme. It was agreed, however, that a city's musical life serves as an enticement to visitors and settlers, and the tours of the orchestra are considered favorable publicity. In one instance, the orchestra was declared to be a force in "helping to sell shoes" for the greatest shoe center in the country.

There are many who are neither sensitive to the supposed ethical overtones of a symphony, nor concerned with the commercial potentialities of a fine civic orchestra, but whose private social ambitions are gratified by indulgence in such an honorific enterprise. These impulses manifest themselves in diverse ways: maintenance of boxes or other preferred locations in the auditorium; program listing as patron; socially exclusive erudition on matters artistic; all the subtle satisfactions accruing from the wide range of contact and intimacy with a fashionable concern, from the occasional ticket purchaser to the confidential relation with conductor and steering members of the board, with all its invidious prestige. The concert-hall box has now all but disappeared in the relentless democratization of audience and patrons. But it once reflected the highly prized perquisite of the social elite. The private corridor and the anteroom, which conferred a sense of aloof distinction, translated the symphony and opera into a social ritual more highly regarded than the aesthetic relaxation derived from the actual music, which, in fact, was often sacrificed.

Musical politics may run very deep, and orchestras have at times been a "football of society." With motives something less than sublime, various groups have often rallied around rival conductors, thus literally splitting the resources of the community to the detriment of higher values. On occasion, however, such competition has had its salutary moments. Witness the case of the prolonged feud between the followers of Damrosch and Thomas in New York, during which two orchestras challenged each other for supremacy. But in other less inspiring circumstances, two orchestras have been supported when nourishment was insufficient for one. That pioneer period has, in general, passed. Though factions will always exist, funds are not nowadays so plentiful as to permit the luxury of such wasteful competition.

Since 1893, when Walter Damrosch first organized them, many of the responsibilities for carrying on orchestral affairs have fallen to the ladies, whose efforts have proven indispensable to the solvency of the harassed orchestral institution. Largely for the benefit of the fashionable world, the matinee concerts (usually Friday afternoon) are maintained. Originally instituted by the New York Philharmonic as a public rehearsal which would offer bargain rates to students, musicians, or others who might wish to hear repeated performances, these matinee programs have long since graduated into more or less exclusive afternoon affairs, constituting an integral part of the winter social season. In Boston and Philadelphia, where this "Friday Spell" exerts its full potency, this particular division of the audience into two segments has been profitable, for the house is sold out. However, in other cities, for various reasons, the Friday patronage, though involving a similar principle, has for some time been hardly sufficient in volume to persuade the management that the retention of the traditional weekday matinee was practicable. History may be repeating itself, for the economic aristocracy today, analogously to the feudal aristocracy of 150 years ago, is declining in power and is relaxing its control over our artistic institutions. Musically this may mean a popularization of the repertoire and a significant alteration in the role played by the orchestra in its community relations. . . .

70. THE PUBLIC ARTS *

GILBERT SELDES

One of the significant developments in the use of leisure has been the programming of entertainment and cultural activities for mass audiences via television, radio, and films—referred to in this selection as "the public arts." Here Seldes examines briefly some of the effects of this mass programming on the content dealt with and the audiences reached. In addition, he explores the validity of the theory that the public arts can only reflect public demand.

The author (b. 1893) is a writer. Has been music critic, drama critic, and columnist for New York newspapers. Onetime Director of Television Programs, Columbia Broadcasting System. Author: *The Seven Lively Arts; Lysistrata* (a play); *The Great Audience;* also has written mysteries under pseudonym Foster Johns.

"This country, with its institutions, belongs to the people who inhabit it," said Abraham Lincoln, and as he was then facing the possible dissolution of the United States, he added, "Whenever they [the people] shall grow weary of the existing government, they can exercise their Constitutional right of amending it or their revolutionary right to dismember or overthrow it."

I am suggesting that the cultural institutions of a country also belong to its inhabitants, and, not having the courage of Lincoln's radicalism, I do not insist upon the revolutionary right of the people to destroy whatever wearies them. Moderately I propose the idea that the people have valid rights over those cultural institutions which can be properly called "the public arts." . . . I have indicated that the quality of being "public" inheres in various degrees in all the arts, that oratory and drama in ancient Greece were more public than the art of history, just as in folk arts ballads were more public than pottery, and, although the lively arts are most affected with the special public quality, the movies are more public than dancing. I now propose to bring together . . . the identifying characteristics of these public arts, knowing that to some degree the identification is shadowy, that by definition no communicative art can be totally private. I am, on the other hand, convinced that in some instances the degree of difference is so great that you can no longer compare the effect of the public and the non-public art, as if quantity—the mass of material offered or the mass of people accepting it—had resulted in a change in essence, a quality change. Also, in one single respect the public arts differ absolutely from all others. The major marks of identification are these:

The public arts are popular to the extent of being almost universally acceptable.

They tend to be more and more professionalized, less and less to be practiced privately.

They are often produced by teams rather than by individuals.

They are commissioned, the patron-sponsor-executive providing the pattern.

They are by intention ephemeral, paying well initially, but not increasing in value with the passage of time.

These are, I think, entirely self-evident.

The public arts are offered to the public as a whole, not to any segment of it.

This is, I believe, a new thing in the world, because these arts solicit the favor of the entire public (excepting the highly intellectualized fringe that turns its back on whatever is popular). This was not the case when a mural, commissioned by a ruling family, was exposed in a Renaissance church or when Shakespeare's plays were presented in the presence of "the groundlings."

Physically, the public arts have mass or velocity or both, and they tend to outstrip or displace all the other arts.

They touch large numbers of people simultaneously, and their effect is not limited to those whom they directly touch.

They interconnect and support one another, thus causing a sort of reverberation.

They are, to an extent, habit-forming, and their effect is contagious.

The social reverberation produced when millions of people follow the same entertainment or receive the same communication at one time is something different from the imitation of a royal mistress's hairdo—the diffusion is immeasurably greater, the penetration deeper. The physical reduplication of comic books and phonograph records, the velocity of radio and television, the availability of the motion-picture film, and the way the various entertainments support one another create another kind of contagion: the public mind is crammed with details about them, so that the true significance of "the mass media" becomes, not their appeal to the mass audience, but their own dimensions, the size and weight and speed and force that the mass media possess. Among these physical properties is the simple one of occupying a certain space and thus preventing any other body from occupying that space. As the public arts occupy more and more of the public mind over longer and longer periods, they are an obstacle to the extension of the other arts.

The public arts popularize the classic arts.

These classic arts they diffuse without substantial alteration, as in the broadcast of a symphony, or they adapt with respect for the original (Shakespeare, for instance), or they degrade. Whether this degradation is inevitable is a prime question. Are the public arts an illustration of "nature's tendency to degrade the organized and to destroy the meaningful"? I am not sure. In *The Human Use of Human Beings,* Dr. Norbert Wiener notes that in control and communication we always fight this entropic tendency, and he adds: "While the universe as a whole . . . tends to run down, there are local enclaves . . . in which there is a limited and temporary tendency for organization to increase. Life finds its home in some of these enclaves." I am not sure whether the parallel I observe is more than verbal. It appears to me that the degradation of the highly organized corresponds to the observed tendency of the popular arts to go steadily to lower levels of general intelligence and emotional maturity; and the enclaves would correspond to those experiments which oppose the tendency toward routine and try to bring individuality back to the mass media.

The public arts create, refuse to create, or destroy their own audiences. They are, in varying degrees, governed by public law.

The unique element: broadcasting uses a portion of the public domain.

These social factors are obviously connected with the physical items previously noted. Granted that there are no *wholly* private arts, we still perceive a difference between a poem printed on a page of a mass-circulation magazine and a song presented a dozen times a day by singers of intense popularity. There is a difference in effect between "D'ye Ken John Peel" and the singing commercial for Pepsi-Cola, which uses the same tune and whose diffusion is now so great that the original song has virtually ceased to exist. We will not understand *I Love Lucy* in the terms of Walter Pater on the Mona Lisa, nor Disney's Davy Crockett if we think he is "merely" a contemporary version of Leatherstocking.

The physical properties of the public arts give to their managers certain social powers, but the managers do not generally accept responsibility for the creation of audiences; they say they satisfy public demand. To abridge a long argument, let us say they cannot pretend, as they do, that they create audiences for Shakespeare and symphonic music but do not create an audience for crime serials. Public demand is diffused and generalized: for diversion, for escape, for excitement, for something like an emotional spree, it is not specific. The makers of entertainment satisfy demand in the ways they find most profitable— just as the processors of food satisfy a demand. It is not the only way, and it may not even be the best way. In turn, the demand must be stimulated and made specific: the public must be made to *want* split-pea soup and panel shows if the makers of these commodities are to prosper. It is, moreover, demonstrable that the producers suppress those demands which they cannot advantageously fulfill—as when programs, even popular ones, are dropped or shifted or supplied to one part of the country and not to another, to correspond to the marketing requirements of the sponsor. This power to create audiences and to manipulate demand is the least understood element in the structure of the entertainment business.

That the public arts are subject to law is well understood, but it is hard to discover a fixed principle in the shifts of opinion about censorship in the movies, pre-publication licensing of comic books, and programs for children in television. . . . The unproved but suspected link between horror books and delinquency is always available for headlines, and a quick hysterical reaction can get laws on the books which it may take years to revoke.

The last characteristic of the public arts—that they use part of the public domain—applies to the broadcasting arts only and is without complexities. The Federal government lends part of the air to a corporation—obviously it can impose conditions. If the conditions are too harsh, the broadcasters will return their franchises, as they have done recently—the requirement that they transmit programs on the UHF channels in order to hold their rights, even though receivers for these frequencies do not exist in their area, is too harsh. On the other hand, if the conditions are too easy (as in the case of broadcasting, taken as a whole), the public may be short-changed until competitors (e.g., backers of pay-TV) offer better service when a station applies for a renewal of license. The only hidden factor in this special case is that the public seems totally unaware of its legal rights—and the broadcasters are not in any hurry to enlighten them.

But the concept of the public arts to which, I am confident, we must eventually come is not drawn from this single characteristic of the entertainment-and-communications enterprises. The base of this new concept is that, by their own nature, these arts are matters of public concern, subject to public opinion; that even *outside of law* the public has sovereign rights over them, since these arts, no less than the institutions of government, belong to the people.

They belong to the people and consequently the people have certain rights and duties in respect to them. I have not put this down as one of the prime characteristics of the public arts because it seems to me highly subjective—and a matter of morality. . . . The moment we see that a transformation in the way we live is taking place, the right and the duty to direct that change becomes self-evident. This is not only an appeal to the self-interest of the intelligent, the mature, and the educated—like the appeal the Federalists made to "the rich and well-born" to support a strong Federal government when the structure of our country was shaped. There is a self-interest, obviously. But in the end I must fall back on the simple moral ground that no good citizen, no good man or woman, has the right to abandon ship while there remains a reasonable hope of steering it into safe harbor if all hands do their work. If we knew that our whole system of free education was being undermined, or the right of every citizen to vote, would any citizen have the moral right to indifference? Would any citizen have the right to remain silent if he knew that a vast power was—inadvertently or not—attempting to destroy that system?

I do not assert that either of these things is happening. I note that either or both may happen without our knowing it, that people using power, often enough unaware of the consequences of their actions, may preserve the *forms* of our educational or political system and nullify its *effects*.

I suggest that, as the fundamental values of our lives and those of our children will be affected by the revolutionary change in entertainment and communications which I have described in this book, we have an obligation to control the speed and direction of this change. Our *right* has been a thousand times established in law and custom. What we lack is the will. . . .

71. THE PAINS OF A NEW IDEA *

SHIRLEY BASCH

This chapter began with several articles which stressed the rigidity of social institutions. Such an emphasis is quite proper since institutions are, among other things, the procedures which, in any given society, are highly stable. But this fact should not be interpreted to mean that institutions never change; they do change, but not easily. Indeed, the process of institutional change can be quite "painful." As is indicated here by Shirley Basch, the proposal that medical care in the United States should be socialized has led to the expression of extreme hostility on the part of many of those who are opposed to any such change. The impassioned nature of the oratory in defense of the accustomed practices, as quoted by Basch, is understandable since the suggestion that we should have socialized medicine is, in effect, a call for fundamental changes in several of our most basic institutions including government, economics, and medical care.

Americans a century ago were fiercely divided on the question of tax supported education for all children. No punches were pulled. The opponents had ten main arguments and in flowing oratory they presented them.

History seems to be running the film over again today. Americans once more have two different opinions, this time on national health insurance. The fight is on, no punches are pulled, and once more the oratory is loud and passionate.

The strange thing is that the current arguments are exactly the same as those of a hundred years ago. And they are presented in almost exactly the same words! Then it was the public's education, today it is the public's health. That seems to be the only difference. The record speaks

* *Survey Graphic*, Vol. 84 (February, 1948), 78–79. Reprinted by permission of the publisher and the author.
At the time this selection was written, the author's husband was a physician in the United States Public Health Service.

for itself. The quotations in the column to the left, with one exception, are from the *Philadelphia National Gazette,* 1830, those at the right from recent writings and speeches.

UNIVERSAL EDUCATION

NATIONAL HEALTH INSURANCE

1. *Only Those Who Can Pay Have a Right to It*

"Literature cannot be acquired without leisure, and wealth gives leisure. . . . The 'peasant' must labor during those hours of the day, which his wealthy neighbor can give to the abstract culture of his mind; otherwise the earth would not yield enough for the subsistence of all. Languor, decay, poverty, discontent would soon be visible among all classes."

"This attitude arose, in part from the false premise that it is a function of government or philanthropy to '*give* health to the people' whereas in truth, health, like freedom and wealth, cannot be given, but must be earned. . . . The assumption that people have a 'right' to health is as false as the notion that everyone is entitled to freedom from want. Nothing could be more viciously destructive of initiative, effort and progress. Health is a privilege, not a right. . . ."—*Edward J. Stieglitz, M.D. in "A Future for Preventive Medicine." 1945*

2. *The Idea Is Foreign to Our Country*

"Some of the writers about universal public instruction and discipline seem to forget the constitution of modern society and declaim as if our communities could receive institutions . . . like those of Sparta. . . . No government, no statesman, no philanthropist can furnish what is incompatible with the very . . . being of civil society."

"In my view we need look no further for evidence that this legislation embodies proposals which find no roots in the soil of free America. . . . The system here proposed is alien to the deepest instincts of the American people."—*National Physicians Committee in "Compulsion the Key to Collectivism." 1946*

3. *It Should Be Left to Private Enterprise*

"Education generally, to be effective, must be left to the enterprise and competition of individuals, to the sagacity and liberality of parents, and to the efforts of enlightened associations."

"I believe that the whole business of teaching school should be thrown open to private enterprise and free competition, just like . . . running a shoe factory." *From Zachery Montgomery in "The School Question." 1866*

"All these activities demonstrate that an effort is being made to change radically the free system of caring for the sick as we have always known it. The broad purpose is nothing less than the shifting of responsibility from its threefold traditional base—the individual, the medical profession, and the local community—to the federal government and the states."—*From* The Nation's Business. *1940*

4. *Government Must Not Concern Itself with It*

"It is an old and sound remark that government cannot provide for the necessities of the people; that it is they who maintain the government, and not the latter the people. Education may be among their necessities; but it is one of that description which the State or National councils cannot supply except partially and in a limited degree."

"That the protection of the health of the citizen is a natural function of government is debatable. The best government is that which governs least, and all history persuades us that freedom is smothered by increasing government paternalism."—*L. S. Goin, M.D., California Medical Society, in the Twentieth Annual Debate Manual. 1946*

5. *If Public Funds Support It, Political Bureaucracy Will Be Rampant*

"In this country, nothing could prevent [public education] from becoming a political job, if a government concern."

"Shall patients and doctors retain their freedom of judgment in this matter of medical care or shall this freedom be surrendered to a federal bureaucracy?"—*H. H. Shoulders, M.D. in his 1946 presidential address to the American Medical Association*

6. *Requiring People to Pay for Its Support Is Dangerous*

"Authority—that is, the State—is to force the more eligibly situated citizens to contribute a part . . . of their means for the accommodation of the rest, and this is equivalent to the idea of an actual, compulsory partition of their substance. . . . We have no confidence in any compulsory equalizations."

"Compulsion is the key to Collectivism. If the Wagner-Murray-Dingell proposals were enacted into law they would introduce a compulsory tax to pay for a compulsory service—medical, dental, and nursing care—directly affecting the most vital and most sacred functions of each individual citizen of the United States."—*National Physicians Committee. 1946*

7. *It Is "Agrarianism"—or "Socialism"*

"The Scheme of Universal Equal Education at the expense of the State is virtually Agrarianism. It would be a compulsory application of the means of the richer for the direct use of the poorer classes."

"Such frauds like compulsory health insurance . . . anticipate the establishment of universal state medical service for everybody. That is socialism as unadulterated as if it came from the sanctified pen of Karl Marx himself."—*From* The Nation's Business. *1940*

8. *It Will Destroy Initiative and Ambition*

"One of the chief excitements to industry among the working classes is

"Ambition is destroyed in a large percentage of the population when all the hope of earning the means of educating their children respectably and liberally; that incentive would be removed, and the scheme of State and equal education be thus a premium for comparative idleness, to be taken out of the pockets of the laborious and conscientious."

the provisions of socialized medicine are put into effect. . . . The proposed bill . . . makes it possible for the government to take directly . . . earnings . . . of conscientious moral workmen . . . and give them to the lazy, shiftless, immoral individuals for sickness which they may have largely brought on themselves by riotous, immoral living."—*Edward H. Ochsner, M.D., Chicago Medical Society in 1946 Senate Committee hearings on a National Health Program*

9. *It Will Lower Standards*

"Universal Equal Education is impossible . . . unless the standard of education be greatly lowered and narrowed."

". . . any attempt to introduce compulsory health insurance in the United States . . . would inevitably result in a serious—even criminal—deterioration in the quality of medical care."—*National Physicians Committee. 1946*

10. *It Is Best to Insure It Only for the Needy*

"[State and National Governments] may endow public schools only for the indigent. . . . But to create or sustain seminaries for the tuition of all classes . . . is beyond their province and power."

"It is our recommendation that the Federal government consider some plan for aid to the states in taking care of those persons who cannot pay for it."—*Peter D. Ward, M.D., American Hospital Assn. in the Twentieth Annual Debate Manual. 1946*

And after all the smoke of the century-ago battle cleared away, we had the start of a public school system unsurpassed in the world. The dire predictions of its calamitous effect are now a shadowy memory.

72. SOCIALIZED MEDICINE,
TEN YEARS OLD *

DON COOK

Considering the "pains" involved in institutional change, as suggested by the preceding article, it would be reasonable to predict that no widely established social institution could be completely altered in a short time. Yet this is exactly what has recently happened in England. Just a few years ago, the institution of medical care in Britain—as in the United States today—was centered on the idea that health treatment should be individualized and private. The reaction to the sweeping socialization of British medical care is described here by Don Cook. And, what may be surprising to many, the great majority of Englishmen, doctors included, currently approve of the change. This suggests that the "cake of custom" may not be so hard-baked after all.

Ten years after the establishment of the British National Health Service it is difficult—in fact almost impossible—to find an opponent of "socialized medicine" left on this island. There are plenty of critics of the Health Service. There are doctors who are discouraged and bitter, and there are patients who complain loudly and frequently. There are individuals who would not dream of accepting free state medical treatment, and there are physicians who will have nothing to do with state-paid medical practice. But "opponents" who would turn back the clock ten years and return to the old medical system in this country are really non-existent.

Certainly there are none among the 49,850,000 Britons (97 per cent of the population) who are registered patients of National Health Service doctors and never pay any medical bills. Among the doctors themselves, out of a total of about 49,000 in the United Kingdom, there are still a gallant 600 or so general practitioners who ride through the valley of death relying solely on fees from private patients. But even these

* "Socialized Medicine, Ten Years Old," by Don Cook, 32–37. First published in *Harper's Magazine.* Copyright © 1959 by Harper & Brothers.

The author (b. 1920) is a foreign correspondent, Chief of the London Bureau, Press Association. Recipient of William the Silent Award for Journalism. Contributor to several popular magazines.

physicians are not exactly "opponents" of socialized medicine. In fact, their practices have probably gained from improved snob appeal.

On the tenth anniversary of the establishment of the Service, the British Medical Association *Journal* was full of praise of it from leaders of the medical profession.

"From the point of view of the 'consumer' it has been an enormous benefit and success," wrote Dr. H. Guy Dain, who was chairman of the BMA Council during the crucial negotiations between doctors and the government which preceded the take-over of private practices by the state in July of 1948. "The absence of any financial barrier between doctor and patient must make the doctor-patient relationship easier and more satisfactory."

Lord Moran, personal physician to Sir Winston Churchill for many years and one of the elder statesmen of British medicine, wrote: "If consultants were asked whether they desired to go back to the old days, I believe the overwhelming majority would prefer the conditions of today."

Iain Macleod, who was appointed Minister of Health by Sir Winston after the Conservatives came back to power, is even more sweeping and forceful about the success of socialized medicine and its soundness as political and social policy in a democracy. Now the Minister of Labor, Mr. Macleod was the son of a small-town doctor, and watched him struggle in the depression years to help poorer patients.

"I believe in the National Health Service with all my heart," he said to me. "Indeed, I believe some sort of National Health Service, whatever it may be called, will come in every country in the world. Not necessarily our model; it might not survive export. If we were starting again we might have based it more on insurance than we did. But other countries, including the United States, can and will benefit from our experiences, our successes, and our mistakes."

The National Health Service has, in fact, become a source of genuine national pride—like the Royal Navy or the Monarchy. Britons know that there may be more spectacular examples of medical skill or research or treatment in the United States or elsewhere. But in their country more of the population get better medical care than in any other major country on earth. Their pride is far from uncritical. But as the second decade of the Health Service begins, the emphasis is entirely on "How can we make it better?" Strikingly, the system itself, the structure, is almost universally judged to be sound.

FREE CARE WITHOUT RED TAPE

The Service originated in the early days of this century, when the Liberals under David Lloyd George put through the first compulsory

health-insurance act in the country. The law was amended and expanded constantly for the next forty years, as successive Liberal, Conservative, and Labor Governments endorsed and reindorsed the principle
of a state medical program. The Labor Government of 1945–51 finally
hammered out the legislation, made the basic decisions, and devised the
system of free medical care for all the people as it exists in Britain today.
The final architect was that dynamic left-wing Welshman, Aneurin
Bevan, the Labor Minister of Health of that day. Ten years later, doctors,
administrators, civil servants, and politicians of all shades of experience
and opinion agree that the structure which he established was basically
sound.

Perhaps the key to its soundness is its administrative simplicity so
far as the patient is concerned—as I discovered in abrupt personal
experience shortly after I returned to London to live three years ago.
Running to catch a double-decker bus—I slipped on the pavement and
came down heavily on my outstretched left arm. I was helped up in
considerable pain, and realized at once that this was more serious than
a bruise or sprain, although no fracture was apparent. I got into a taxi and
asked to be taken to Charing Cross Hospital not far from my London
office. I walked in and explained to a receptionist what had happened.
She asked only four questions: name, age, address, and whether or not
I was registered with a National Health Service doctor. I had no doctor
in London, but that did not matter. I was not asked my nationality, or
whether I had any kind of registration card, or whether I had paid any
contribution to a fund, or whom I worked for, or even if I had paid my
British taxes! I was simply handed a card and sent in to the emergency
ward.

After about five minutes' wait, a young intern took a quick look at
the arm and sent me upstairs to the X-ray laboratory with a form
specifying the picture he wanted. The X-ray technician was ready almost immediately, and in twenty minutes I was handed the developed
plate to take back to the emergency ward. A fracture specialist took a look
at the film and found I had a chipped elbow. It could, he said, heal up
on its own in a sling, but I should return to the regular fracture clinic
next morning. When I showed up for this second examination the pain
had become intense. The head of the clinic ordered the elbow placed in a
cast, and the pain stopped almost at once.

Two weeks later the cast was removed at the clinic and another
X-ray taken. The next week a third X-ray was taken. After each reading
the specialist assured me that although I could not yet straighten the
elbow fully, it was healing all right. Special treatment, he said, might
merely "seize" the joint rather than speed its return to normal—which,
with time, it has done. At no time was anything I might have needed for
the elbow not forthcoming. Perhaps the emergency clinic doctor should

have ordered a cast immediately instead of letting me wait until the next morning; but that was a matter of medical opinion. On the whole the care I received free could not have been simpler or better.

To an American, the most refreshing thing about my treatment was the fact that I was never asked to pay for it. I know, of course, that virtually any hospital in the United States would give a similar kind of emergency care; but the problem of money would come up sooner or later. In Britain you don't pay, no matter who you are or how complicated your problem is or how long you have to stay in the hospital. Anyone who has a heart attack or appendicitis or an automobile accident can walk (or be carried) into any hospital and receive complete care free.

"Free treatment for foreigners" has been one aspect of the National Health Service frequently criticized by Conservatives in Commons. No doubt there have been some abuses, like Frenchmen coming over from Calais to get free false teeth or eyeglasses in Dover. But the simple fact is that once having decided on "free medical care for all," it is cheaper to treat anybody and everybody than to set up a complicated screening system to make sure each patient has a "right" to Health Service care.

The French, for example, have a monstrously clumsy state health insurance scheme whereby (after endless bureaucratic forms and records and payments) you pay your own bills and then claim restitution from the state. The British pay the whole cost out of taxes, provide the Health Service free, and have managed to keep bookkeeping and administrative records at a minimum.

HOW SOCIALIZED MEDICINE WORKS

To acquire a family physician in Britain, you go to the local post office for a list of Health Service doctors practicing in the area. You may sign up with any of them, and you can change if you aren't satisfied. Likewise the doctor is free to turn you down if he feels he already has enough patients on his panel list. When he accepts you, your name goes to a central registration file maintained to see that patients are signed up with only one doctor at a time. If you should need hospitalization, surgery, or special consultations, your doctor will make the arrangements for you to receive these services just as he would in private practice.

A physician may have a maximum of 3,500 patients on his panel. The average is about 2,200. He is paid a capitation fee of 18 shillings a year (about $2.65) for each patient plus an extra 12 shillings ($1.68) for every patient from Number 501 to Number 1,500. Hospital surgeons, consultants, and specialists are paid salaries graded according to skill. There is a system of "distinction grants" for particularly qualified men. Grants or interest-free loans are also made to individual physicians or groups to get started in practice or improve their offices. All National Health Service doctors, consultants, surgeons, etc., are equally free to take private fee-paying patients along with their state-paid patients.

The average net income after expenses of general practitioners in Britain is about £2,500—or around $7,000 a year. Before the war it was less than £1,000, though taxes were much lower and the pound then worth $4 as compared to $2.80 now. By British standards, physicians are fairly well paid today. Nevertheless they are dissatisfied with the Health Service salary structure, and a Royal Commission is now investigating it.

There is no registration system for free dental care. You simply make an appointment with a National Health Service dentist of your choice. He is paid a fixed fee by the state for routine work and passes you on to a specialist for complicated dentures or oral surgery.

Utopian as it sounds, this is exactly how the Health Service works in Britain today. For the patient, of course, the ultimate test is not how smoothly the system works but how good the medical care turns out to be.

To this question there is no easy answer. There have been plenty of bad experiences—frustrations, tragedies, and tempers shortened by the problems of conforming to a state machine. But to begin with, paying a doctor a fee does not automatically make him a good doctor—any more than free medical care makes bad doctors.

THE QUALITY OF CARE

In a sense the National Health Service has created difficulties for itself by giving people the right to demand and expect medical treatment they never would have thought of buying out of their own pockets. As a result many of the criticisms of the Health Service have nothing to do with the merits of "socialized medicine *versus* private medicine." In the old days of medical charity, most people were not in a position to complain about their doctors. Today, however, in the House of Commons question hour Members of Parliament regularly belabor the Minister of Health on behalf of aggrieved citizens seeking redress of Health Service mistakes.

For example, there was the case of a middle-aged man with rheumatoid arthritis in Pembrokeshire in the extreme west of Wales. His doctor decided that hospital treatment was required and arranged for an ambulance under the Health Service to drive the patient—a stretcher case—to the nearest hospital specializing in arthritic ailments. It was two hundred miles away. But when the man arrived the hospital refused to admit him, on the ground that they only handled ambulatory cases, and that the doctor had made a mistake in sending them a bed-ridden patient. So he was driven all the way back to Pembroke and became violently ill on the way.

His MP took the matter up with the Ministry of Health. In due course, the Minister wrote that "frankly the National Health Service let the patient down and we offer our sincere apologies and sympathies. While it will not be of much comfort to him, I am sure you will wish to know that steps have been taken to prevent such a mishap in future."

This incident was typical of many—a patient desperately in need of care and a heartlessly rigid interpretation of the rules by a hospital. However, it is also a fact that ten years ago a poor Welshman far out in the Pembroke countryside would never have dreamed of hiring an ambulance to take him two hundred miles to a special hospital.

Herein is the dilemma in assessing the quality of medicine under the National Health Service: once it is accepted that a modern democratic society has a responsibility for providing free medical care for all its citizens, certain standards inevitably change. They will fall for some people but will rise for many others.

The analogy is state-supported free education (which, incidentally, nobody today calls "Socialism"). Obviously private schools can offer smaller classes, greater individual attention, less standardization, and wider curricula. Private education is open to those who want it and can afford it. But the state goes on trying to improve its own system of education—and so it is with health and medicine in Britain today.

WHAT IRKS THE DOCTOR

In trying to sort out the main lines of dissatisfaction with the National Health Service, I find that they revolve around inconveniences or frustrations rather than a basic indictment of the system or the principle. Physicians complain chiefly about "frivolous calls from patients." This was best described to me by a doctor who is one of the 600 who stayed out of the service in 1948. He still has a successful private practice in London, although he knows the problems of many of his professional colleagues who, of course, practice under National Health.

"The worst of it is what I would call the 'aggressive attitude' of patients toward the doctor," he said. "Because a patient does not have to think twice about his condition before getting on to the doctor, he is at the doctor constantly to do all sorts of things which would perfectly well work themselves out. Then if he doesn't get a prescription or something he thinks the doctor isn't looking after him properly.

"This crowds the doctor's office, and leads to very superficial examination. The leisurely and thorough examination of a patient who may genuinely be in danger has broken down under the National Health Service. Instead—because any doctor can prescribe the most expensive sort of antibiotics free under the Health Service—there is a tendency simply to have a quick look and then let the umbrella of antibiotic drugs take care of the rest, partly in order to satisfy the patient that he's being well looked after. "After a day of this sort of routine, when a doctor is bothered by frivolous night calls from patients expecting him to come running for no really good reason, his own patience and temper are ready to snap—and the whole process of medical care, and of good doctor-patient relationships breaks down."

This pretty much sums up the chief complaint of general practitioners in Britain (though it does not mean that doctors and patients are constantly snapping and snarling at each other here).

An independent analysis of doctors' grievances was made some months ago, by an American professor of economics from the Wharton School of the University of Pennsylvania, Dr. Paul F. Gemmill. He spent seven months in Britain probing the Health Service like a good old-fashioned leg-work reporter. His study of the Health Service was, he explains, "not for it, or against it, but *of* it." There was no official sponsorship of his inquiry, and as an American he might well be expected to hear all the gripes as well as the good. His method was simply to drop in unannounced at doctors' offices, and sit with the patients until all had been seen (observing waiting time as he waited), and then present himself and his questions to the physician.

He saw almost 400 doctors, and if there was no time for discussion he left a questionnaire to be returned to him in Philadelphia. He also left questionnaires with 1,500 National Health Service patients. The results, it seems fair to say, are about the most straightforward survey to date of the private opinions of doctors and patients about the Health Service.

On the question of frivolous calls, he found that 49 per cent of the doctors said they "often" had time taken up with minor ailments, 30 per cent said "occasionally," and only 21 per cent said "almost never." On the other hand, he also asked if prompt visits and early examination enabled them to catch disease early, to which 11 per cent replied "often," 60 per cent replied "occasionally," and 29 per cent "almost never." In summary, 79 per cent thought they were bothered by frivolous calls, while 71 per cent found that early visits helped to head off disease.

Paper work under the Health Service has been another doctor criticism. Dr. Gemmill found that only 39 per cent found it "burdensome" while the other 61 per cent said it was not. Both sides agreed that the National Health Service had increased certain kinds of form-filling, but that it was largely offset by no longer having to make out bills and prod patients for private fees.

As to the burden of practice, with an average of 2,200 patients each, 59 per cent of the Health Service doctors find it "reasonably easy" to give adequate care to their panel lists, 38 per cent find it "difficult," but only a minute 3 per cent said it was "impossible."

THE HOSPITAL BOTTLENECK

The patients' complaints fit mainly under the heading, "We wait, wait, wait." If fewer people went to the doctor with "frivolous calls," waiting time would be cut and doctors would have less to complain about. But there is no real answer to waiting time except more facilities, and this again is not so much a complaint *against* the National Health Service as it is a *result* of it.

Of the 1,500 patients Dr. Gemmill queried, 37 per cent said they were getting better medical care than they did before 1948, 50 per cent said it was about the same, and only 13 per cent found it worse.

The greatest problem of waiting has been in the hospitals, which is essentially a matter of government policy. In the first five years of the Health Service, all its resources went to improve existing hospital facilities, or other priority needs. In 1955, the first new hospital in England for seventeen years was completed; ten more are now being built and six are in the final planning stage. In addition thirty hospitals will be modernized and expanded in 1959–60. Thus after a very long lapse, a hospital program is now under way.

The hospital waiting-time problem has led to the rise of private health insurance which pays for special hospital beds, insuring, as it were, preferential treatment at extra charge within the National Health system. Since 1948 the number of people covered by such schemes has soared from 84,000 to 834,000.

For the doctors, a main trend of the last ten years has been into group practice—which the Ministry of Health encourages with special grants to build and equip clinics, and which, with the increasing complications of modern medicine, is regarded as the answer to the problem of the over-worked general practitioners.

There are now 13,000 physicians in group practice in Britain—or 67 per cent of those engaged in general medical work. They may include a general practitioner and colleagues specializing in heart, ear-nose-throat, or other combinations. They pool their panel lists and fees and the expense of secretarial help, and in the aggregate can probably give better collective service to their patients than they could individually.

The cost of the National Health Service is a major target of its critics. Certainly it has far exceeded the original estimates, and certainly it has risen steadily, even astronomically. Partly this was due to the general inflation in Britain. In any case, it has now leveled off and is budgeted at a lower figure this year than last. Moreover the cost has fallen each year in terms of percentage of gross national product (less than 3.5 per cent this year), and in terms of cost per head of population it is ludicrously low.

This year the Ministry of Health estimates that about £750 million will be spent—partly by the national treasury, partly by local health authorities, partly in charges to the public such as the nominal one-shilling (13-cent) service charge on prescriptions. With just over fifty million people in England, Scotland, and Wales, this works out at £15 per head—or less than $50 per person for complete medical and hospital care.

DOCTOR BILLS ARE GONE FOREVER

Perhaps the most impressive achievement of the National Health Service after ten years is in "provision of care." For example, in 1948, with private practice pulling doctors into more prosperous areas, 60 per cent of the people of Britain were living in what the Ministry of Health regarded as "under-doctored areas." Today a doctor gets the same fee whether he treats a coal miner or a bank manager, and only 18 per cent of the people now live in under-doctored areas. In this decade, the total number of doctors in the United Kingdom has increased from 36,500 to over 49,000. Even though hospital building is only starting, 30,000 hospital beds have already been added through enlargement and improvement of existing facilities.

Nobody would claim that the National Health Service alone is responsible for improved health and mortality statistics. New drugs and medical discoveries would have produced improvement no matter what the system.

Nevertheless, deaths from tuberculosis in Britain have dropped from 23,076 in 1947 to 4,784 in 1957. Notification of TB cases has fallen from 47,000 to 33,000. In the same period, infant mortality per 1,000 live births is down from 41 to 23.1, while infant mortality after four weeks of life has fallen from 22.7 to 16.5 per 1,000. Life expectancy has risen to sixty-nine years for men and seventy-four years for women.

But beyond statistics there is the conviction (Conservative Iain Macleod is one of the most convinced) that the country is simply *healthier*, that far less time is being lost from work, that energy and vitality are much improved, and that in terms of man-hours of production the Health Service has a value to the nation which can never be measured or defined. Granting that food and living conditions are much improved as against ten years ago, Mr. Macleod still believes the Health Service has played a large part.

Still another intrinsic social gain has been made by the British people. A medical tragedy can no longer become a financial disaster. In Britain the shadow of medical bills has been removed from family life forever.

For the middle classes here—with narrow budgets and little opportunity for increased incomes—this is perhaps the most significant result of the quiet social revolution which the Labor Government carried out in Britain from 1945 to 1951. The rich could afford any kind of medicine and the poor were always taken care of. The middle class, which could not plead poverty and could not stand great medical expenses, faced the worst problem when serious illness struck.

The National Health Service as it is working in Britain today affords a maximum of individual freedom to both doctors and patients. Most of the settled families of the country are signed up with the same doctor they had in the old days—only now he is paid by the state and they have no more doctor's bills. The middle class needed the Health Service most, and the middle class has profited the most. An American cannot live in Britain today and see the Health Service at work without coming to a simple realization: what has been done here by democratic processes in a free society is a great step forward and an object lesson for democracy throughout the world.

CHAPTER VIII

SOCIAL
ORGANIZATION:

Ecological

73. COMMUNITY AND ASSOCIATION *

ROBERT M. MACIVER

*Among MacIver's important works there have been three
elaborating on the nature of the modern state. This selection
clearly delineates the early analytical groundwork that was basic
to these further elaborations. When the author wrote these words,
the modern totalitarian state with its dreadful tyrannies had not
yet appeared. Yet this sociological analysis of the nature of
community and its clear-cut differentiations from the state is so
powerful a refutation of the governmental theories upon which
totalitarianism is based, that it is difficult to believe it was not
written after the fact. The confusion of thought that identifies
community as such with its instrument, the state, is here exposed,
and the results of such identification are foreseen.*

THE GENERAL RELATION OF COMMUNITY
AND ASSOCIATION

One of the greatest of the difficulties which at the present day beset
the social analyst is the confused nature of his vocabulary. Unlike the

* *Community: A Sociological Study*, 22–28. Copyright 1924, 1928 by The Macmillan Company and used with their permission.

The author (b. 1882) is Emeritus Lieber Professor of Political Philosophy and Sociology, Columbia University. Special Lecturer, Public Law and Government. Born in Stornoway, Scotland. Author: *Society: Its Structure and Changes; Social Causation; Toward Abiding Peace; The Web of Government; The Ramparts We Guard; Democracy and the Economic Challenge.*

students of most other sciences he must accept the terms of everyday life. These terms are lacking in all precision, and if the sociologist is to avoid disaster he must not hesitate to refine them to his own purposes. This is the case with the essential terms of our subject-matter, the terms society, community, association, and State. The looseness with which these terms are often used even by professed authorities is remarkable, and the results most unhappy. That must be our excuse if at the outset we insist, in spite of popular usage, on limiting each of these terms to a single and definite meaning.

Society, the most general term of all, I intend to use in a universal or generic sense to include every willed relationship of man to man. If, then, we distinguish community, association, and State from society, it must be by delimiting the former as special kinds or aspects of social fact. The essential distinction here involved, one of the utmost importance, is that between community and association.

By a community I mean any area of common life, village, or town, or district, or country, or even wider area. To deserve the name community, the area must be somehow distinguished from further areas, the common life may have some characteristic of its own such that the frontiers of the area have some meaning. All the laws of the cosmos, physical, biological, and psychological, conspire to bring it about that beings who live together shall resemble one another. Wherever men live together they develop in some kind and degree distinctive common characteristics —manners, traditions, modes of speech, and so on. These are the signs and consequences of an effective common life. It will be seen that a community may be part of a wider community, and that all community is a question of degree. For instance, the English residents in a foreign capital often live in an intimate community of their own, as well as in the wider community of the capital. It is a question of the degree and intensity of the common life. The one extreme is the whole world of men, one great but vague and incoherent common life. The other extreme is the small intense community within which the life of an ordinary individual is lived, a tiny nucleus of common life with a sometimes larger, sometimes smaller, and always varying fringe. Yet even the poorest in social relationships is a member in a chain of social contacts which stretches to the world's end. In the infinite series of social relationships which thus arise, we distinguish the nuclei of intenser common life, cities and nations and tribes, and think of them as *par excellence* communities.

An association is an organisation of social beings (or a body of social beings as *organised*) for the pursuit of some common interest or interests. It is a determinate social unity built upon common purpose. Every end which men seek is more easily attained for all when all whom it concerns unite to seek it, when all co-operate in seeking it. Thus you may have an association corresponding to every possible interest of social beings. Community bubbles into associations permanent and transient, and no student of the actual social life of the present can help being struck by the enormous number of associations of every kind, political, economic, religious, educational, scientific, artistic, literary, recreative, philanthropic, professional, which to-day more than ever before enrich communal life.

A community is a focus of social life, the common living of social beings; an association is an organisation of social life, definitely established for the pursuit of one or more common interests. An association is partial, a community is integral. The members of one association may be members of many other and distinct associations. Within a community there may exist not only numerous associations but also antagonistic associations. Men may associate for the least significant or for the most significant of purposes; the association may mean very much or very little to them, it may mean merely the excuse for a monthly dinner-party, or it may be the guardian of their dearest or highest interests— but community is something wider and freer than even the greatest associations; it is the greater common life out of which associations rise, into which associations bring order, but which associations never completely fulfil. If we reflect, we perceive at once that there is a vast difference between the living together of men which makes a village or city or country on the one hand, and the association of men in a church or trade-union—or even, as we shall see, in a State—on the other. Often state-areas do not even coincide with the areas of effective community, as, for instance, when a subject-people, incorporated in an alien State, continues to lead its own manner of life. A distinction of name is essential.

It may be well to show how infinitely associations vary in degree of permanence and significance, and the main reason of these variations, before we consider the relation to community of the most permanent and most comprehensive of all—the State.

Men may *mass* together without becoming organised. A mere aggregation is not an association. Take the case of a crowd casually collected to watch a fire. The aggregation serves no end, each individual of the crowd could watch the fire quite as well—better in fact—if the others went away. A common interest keeps them together, but it does not bind them to one another, it need bring no individual into social contact with any other. It is a physical and not a social contiguity. No association is dissolved when the fire burns out—or when the policeman moves the crowd away. But suppose the crowd had resolved to fight the fire and had organised themselves to that end. At once the aggregation would have been transformed into an association, its individuals would have fallen into social relations with one another, and the order which is attendant on social purpose would have permeated the whole. As soon as men see that any interest they share is furthered by organisation, they are preparing an association. So here an association would have come into being for an hour—and in an hour would have passed away.

Take next the case of men gathered to celebrate some occasion, say the centenary of some historical event. Here there is a purpose depending on and realised through association. The meeting-together is an essential element of the celebration. Time and place and procedure are predetermined, it is an organised association, not a casual aggregation. But the purpose may be only a trivial thing in the life of each member of the assemblage. It brings him into social contact, but a very transient and partial contact, with the rest. There is a consciousness of common interest realised in association, but it finds only a momentary expression. When the parade is over or the procession has passed, or the bonfire turned to ashes, or the dinner and the speeches are ended, the association dissolves. Because the purpose was transient, the association it created could not endure.

Consider next an association created for the achievement of some specific reform, political or religious, say for the passing of a bill or the formulation of a creed. Here a more permanent purpose animates the association, and works a deeper organisation. Each member of the association has a definite point of contact with every other. It is because each member has a certain individuality that he is a member. If he were different in a certain important way, he would not be a member. And in the association each holds a definite place, determined in part at least by his individuality. (For it is a general law of association that the deeper the purpose at work, the more complex becomes the organisation.) Yet since the purpose is specific and temporary, the association which pursues it pursues its own dissolution. When the bill is enacted or the creed formulated, in the fulfilment of its sustaining purpose the association itself dissolves. When slavery was abolished, the associations for the abolition of slavery were abolished also. Every such association dies of its success. Sometimes an association lives on when its primary purpose belongs to the past, becoming either a venerable relic, like, say, the Honourable Society of Fishmongers, or a social obstruction, like the Grand Army of the Republic.

Let us turn next to an association of a very different type, the association of marriage. The purpose on which this association rests is the deep foundation of all life, and that purpose is fulfilled not in the mere procreation of offspring and their tutelage until they attain the autonomy of manhood or womanhood. The profound purpose of the marriage-association includes the present as well as the future generations, and fulfils the lives of those who enter into it no less than it creates and develops the lives of those who issue from it. It is, therefore, a continuous and—unless perverted—permanent purpose of human life, and the association it creates is likewise continuous and permanent, strongly rooted in the heart of life.

Thus to a permanent purpose there always answers, in the nature of things, a permanent association. This appears still more clearly when we turn to such associations as Church and State. These rest on purposes more lasting than any individuals, and are thus maintained through periods of time infinitely larger than the life-periods of individuals. In so far as they are purposes necessary to the fulfilment of life, they create associations as immortal as life. And as the most enduring purposes are also those which grow and change the most, there is a continuous evolution of the greater associations.

Lastly, associations vary as much in extent as in permanence, and for the same reason. Wherever there is a character common to social beings, a common interest is implicit, an interest, that is, which can be furthered by organisation, by association. The extent of a common interest *should* measure the extent of its correspondent association. The most intimate interest is that which most directly unites just two human beings, as in the association of marriage; but at the other extreme are interests universal as mankind—the interest we call justice, for example—and the history of society is in part a history of the widening of associations (and therefore of community) as men more and more recognise how much they have in common with other men, and more and more understand that every common value is protected and furthered by association. So out of the small circles of primitive society have grown the great and ever-widening associations of the modern world.

We have been speaking of the State as simply one among other associations, but the State has obviously a very peculiar and distinctive place. Other associations are limited to the pursuit of one or at most a few interests, the State seems to have some care for nearly every interest. Other associations cannot on their own initiative enforce their decisions on recalcitrant members, the State can and does. Other associations have their members scattered over a city or district or country, the State includes within its membership, or at least within its control, all the dwellers within determined communal frontiers. It is, therefore, highly important to determine the relation of the State, first to community itself, and next to the other associations within community.

COMMUNITY AND STATE

Because the State, like community, has territorial frontiers and because it exercises control over all, or nearly all, other associations, many writers speak as if community and State were one. This seems to have been the view of Hegel and is certainly the doctrine of the neo-Hegelian writers on the State, as well as of many others to whom that epithet scarcely applies. Here is a representative statement of this doctrine from the late M. Fouillée: "Imagine," he wrote, "a great circle within which are lesser circles combining in a thousand ways to form the most varied figures without overstepping the limits that enclose them; this is an image of the great association of the State and of the particular associations that it embraces." (*La Science Sociale Contemporaine,* p. 13.)

We shall see later that this doctrine, which makes the State the limit of community and makes all other associations but elements of the State, is contradicted by the whole evolution of the modern State. For the present it will suffice to show that the doctrine, so strangely maintained in the face of history, is contrary to the present fact. Here we are not concerned with what the State ought to be and to include, but with what the State actually is and does include. So regarded, it is quite obvious that the State is neither conterminous nor synonymous with community. Every State has rigid territorial limits, but the modern world, marked off into separate States, is not partitioned into a number of isolated communities. We have already seen that community is a matter of degree, that it is a network of social interrelations, here denser, here thinner, whose ever new-woven filaments join men to men across countries and continents. The State, unlike community, is exclusive and determinate. Where one State ends, another begins; where one begins, another ends. No man can without contradiction owe allegiance to two States, any more than he can serve two masters, but he can enter into the life of as many communities as his sympathies and opportunities will allow.

Quite obviously the metaphor of Fouillée is false. Let us draw our exclusive circles and call them England, France, Germany, and so on. By hypothesis, all associations fall within these circles, and do not intersect them. Well, in which circle shall we place the international economic associations without which none of the great States could to-day exist at all? In which shall we place the numerous international unions, industrial, scientific, religious, and artistic? "Without overstepping the limits that enclose them"—that is the foundation of the neo-Hegelian doctrine of the State, and it is a foundation which is false in fact.

But, it will be answered, every association, international or intranational, is controlled by the State. Intranational associations are controlled by the separate States, international associations by agreement between States. No members of any State can enter into any association whatever unless that State permits it. Thus every other association is subordinate to the State.

We may grant the contention. At a later stage we shall see more clearly whence and why the will of the State has this pre-eminence. At that stage we shall understand more fully the distinction between community and State. Meantime we must insist that there is a false inference if we say that because the State has control over every other association, therefore all other associations are absorbed into the State, are simply parts of the State, or are completely circumscribed by its frontiers. If we hold this view, the process of conflict through which modern States have attained their present democratic forms, and in especial the long agony of strife due to the opposing claims of churches and of States, is without meaning for us.

There is an easy and direct way by which we can discover the limits of the State. The essential feature of the State is political order, the *primary* instrument of the State is political law. There has been community where no State yet existed, and even to-day we may discover, among certain Eskimo peoples, for instance, primitive forms of communal life still uncoordinated within a State. Where there is no political law, there is no State. Political law is thus the criterion of the State, and in learning the nature and limits of political law we are learning the nature and limits of the State.

Political law is in its proper nature unconditioned, formulated, and mainly negative. These characters reveal the limits of the State.

It is unconditioned. The laws of other associations bind their members, but if you don't like the laws you can leave the association—unless the *State* forbids. If you disapprove of the laws of your club or business-association or trade-union or church, you can resign. If any such association tries of its own accord to enforce its laws on you, it comes into collision with the powers of the State. It can properly do no more than deny you its special benefits and privileges. So with communal or customary law, properly so-called. If you break the customs, traditions, fashions prevalent in your community, you may expect its disapprobation. It will boycott you, refuse to enter into social relations with you, but unless you break also the law of the State, it cannot otherwise visit upon you its displeasure. But if you break a political law, you do not merely lose privileges. The State will do more than deny its benefits, it will punish. It has behind it the united force of the community, the final sanction attached to no other kind of social law. Nor can you simply resign your membership of the State to escape its law. Even if you go beyond its frontiers its claims may follow you, and within the State, even if you shut yourself up within your walls, you are subject to the laws of the State, to all the conditions it may impose either directly or by delegation of authority.

Why does the State hold this unique position? Why has it behind it the united force of the community? The force of the law is not an ultimate thing, it is always and essentially dependent upon will. The State has this power of compulsion because its members *will* that power, because they subject themselves to its law and unite their force to maintain it. To what end?

No man can wholly cut himself off from social relations while he remains in the world of men. We are forced from all sides, by every instinct and every need, into society, into relations with our fellows. Such relations must be *ordered*, or life is impossible. Mutual good demands mutual service, mutual forbearance and restraint. Thus wherever society exists there exists a system of obligations and rights. Society incessantly creates these reciprocal relations between every man and all other men. Sometimes they remain unformulated and traditional, as in a primitive community ruled by "unwritten law," but nearly always the most essential of these relationships of right and obligation are set out in clear formulæ, as political laws, and protected by a central authority endowed with communal power. Any body of men so organised that a central institution or government takes over the maintenance and development of the essential system of rights and obligations accepted among them is properly called a State. A State is thus the fundamental association for the maintenance and development of social order, and to this end its central institution is endowed with the united power of the community. It is not meant that the members of a State consciously realise why they give or permit it this final authority—if they did they would never have suffered the endless perversions of government—but only that as their political consciousness emerges, as they ask themselves why they should contribute this might to the State, the answer appears in this form. As the State develops, as its members grow in social wisdom, in the consciousness of their own needs and the possibilities of satisfying them through political order, the power of the State comes to rest more and more on its service of that end—or else there is distraction, weakness, cleavage, finally perhaps revolution.

Subjection to law is political obligation, which is only the reverse side of political right. Beyond law, beyond government, and beyond force lie the common ends, the common will of community. The end is here as always the revelation of meaning and the justification of existence. If the citizen owes obedience to government it must be in virtue of some social good which in turn determines the respect the government shall show to him. Political right and political obligation, as all right and obligation, are derived from the same source and are meaningless if separated. Already we see that the State and its government are not ultimate social phenomena but rest on what is yet deeper, communal life and will.

The special limits of the State are revealed when we consider the further characteristics of political law.

In the second place, political law is expressed in definite formulæ. A political law defines certain categories of persons as coming within its scope, and prescribes for them as precisely as possible certain forms of conduct. It is obvious, therefore, that it can apply only to general situations and can enforce only *external* fulfilments. Thus the State is at once outside large spheres of human activity. It cannot control motives save indirectly. It can enjoin actions, or rather activities, but not the spirit of their fulfilment. But large classes of action are wholly dependent on the spirit in which they are fulfilled, and many associations exist simply to foster types of ideal or spiritual values. The State *cannot* determine these associations, and it *should not* prescribe any of those actions which derive their only value from the spirit of their performance. The State can compel people to attend church, but it cannot compel them to worship, and therefore the former compulsion is folly. The State cannot create by its *fiat* a church or an artistic or literary association. It can protect and maintain and even organise such associations—to do so may be part of its function—but it cannot, if it is true to its own nature, determine and control them. Further, in its generality and externality it cannot touch (save by way of repression) that spontaneity and initiative of individual life which is the beginning of all social process and the root of all social value. There are times, pre-eminently the time of war, when cumulative force matters for the time being more than spontaneity, and the State inevitably becomes repressive. But this, like nearly all the special phenomena of war, is a throwback to the barbaric order. Certainly this repressiveness, when continued into the time of peace by the momentum of the war-habit, of necessity breeds grave social disturbance and dissension. The State must, therefore, be clearly distinguished from the community which creates it. Community is the common life of beings who are guided essentially from within, actively, spontaneously, and freely (under the conditions prescribed by the laws they make) relating themselves to one another, weaving for themselves the complex web of social unity. But the State works with an instrument which is necessarily formal, prescribing the general external conditions of social life, upholding the main system of those social obligations which may be externally fulfilled. Its instrument resembles, in Aristotle's phrase, no "leaden rule" which can adapt itself to the actual mouldings of the social structure, but an unbending rod which can measure only its general outlines.

Because it can determine only the external forms of conduct, the law of the State must be mainly (though by no means wholly) negative. It must for the most part be content (as the neo-Hegelians themselves are forced to admit, though they do not see the significance of the admission) to "hinder hindrances" to social welfare. It can prevent or punish wrong-doing rather than endorse right-doing. It can create for men the external social conditions necessary for the well-living of their lives. It can enforce these outer obligations without the fulfilment of which the inner obligations cannot be fulfilled. For this reason the sanction of political law is punishment and not reward. We reward and honour only what the theologian called "works of supererogation," not the minimal fulfilment of external law.

It is needless to say that in thus stating the limits of political activity we are not belittling the immeasurable value of that activity. The point is that the State is not equivalent to community, that the political association does not include and cannot control the whole life of men. The State is seen to be not community but a peculiarly authoritative association within it. The State is determinate, a closed organisation of social life; community is indeterminate, an ever-evolving system spreading beyond and only partially controlled within the definite framework of any State. That framework gives to the portion of community which it encloses a certain unity and definition, but neither cuts it off from a wider community of which it is essentially part nor within that portion substitutes its own external mode of action, its necessity, for the spontaneity that is the mark of all life, social and other. Social life can no longer in practice and should no longer in theory be summed up in political life. The individual should not be summed up in his citizenship, otherwise the claim of citizenship will itself become a tyranny and its essential moral value be lost. "The modern wilderness of interests" is not to be straightened out into the simple road of citizenship. For the main road of citizenship, which we must make straight as possible, though it intersects a thousand paths of social interest, cannot and should not absorb them.

These paths of social interest do not stop at the frontiers of States. The political interest is determinate and has limits, the social has none. Hence for the proper understanding of international relations it is most necessary to distinguish community and State. On the assumption of identity we can have no social unity among the nations until they are absorbed within some world-state. For each State by its very definition is a determinate and self-contained unit. In respect of the sphere of its sovereignty every State is demarcated absolutely from every other. Consequently, if political relationship were identical with social relationship, the members of one State would remain totally alien from the members of every other State. Communities would stand to one another as Spinoza and Hobbes imagined them to stand, isolated as the pre-civil individuals of their imaginations, totally irresponsible until some contract is agreed upon, even then totally irresponsible because there is no possible higher will to make agreement binding. But, of course, it is in international relations that the distinction of State and community is most clearly revealed and that the common interests of universal society most manifestly weave new unities in spite of political separation. A man may perhaps "denationalise" himself (though that is hardly the proper word) by leaving his country, but he cannot "desocialise" himself without leaving the world of men, or at least of civilised men.

Community, therefore, and not the State, is the "world the spirit has made for itself." "The spirit" does not isolate itself in States, as Hegel's argument assumes. On the contrary, the growth of civilisation means the growth of ever-widening community, the "realisation" of social interest beyond the limits of politically independent groups. Society widens and the sense of community grows. In particular, the privileged classes of the different peoples, the authors of most past wars, become more and more allied by social intercourse, by common commercial and intellectual interests. M. Tarde has pointed out how classes of men whose occupation, even if in a competitive way, brings them into constant association with one another, develop a friendlier spirit towards one another than classes not subject to this socialising influence. The same holds of peoples. It is not civilisation but intercivilisation that develops mutual sympathy between States. The highly socialised Greek cities, because each held to an ideal of autonomy and self-sufficiency, the ideal of "completely independent totality," were not intersocialised, and, accordingly, displayed the intensest hostility to one another. But the aloofness of Greek states is impossible in the modern world, which is pervaded by intersocialising influences of literature and commerce. Common ideas and common trade have formed everywhere social bonds which cut across the line of States, and have made western Europe, looked on as a whole, an effective community. Thus an educated Englishman comes to have more in common with an educated Frenchman than he has, say, with an English agricultural labourer. The alien, shut out from his State, may yet have a closer, social affinity to him than his fellow citizen. And yet the prevalent political philosophy blindly declares that "the State" is "the world the spirit has made for itself," and that "between State and State there can be no consciousness of common good." Because certain dangerously antiquated modern governments retained that philosophy, they have overwhelmed our common civilisation in the consciousness of common evil.

If we turn for a moment from fact to ideal—two things which the neo-Hegelians constantly confuse—we may admit the desirability of a wider political co-ordination of community than at present exists. This is to be achieved not by our going backwards and cutting off the bonds of relationship which make community wider in area than any single State, but by our going forward on the road of federation and making a union of States great enough to comprehend the existing intercommunity. The recognition of likeness of interests, purposes, and needs is increasing and not diminishing in the people of different nations. It is the State that is inadequate, not community that is overstepping its due bounds. The State must always, as we have seen, remain inadequate to comprehend and regulate *all* community. But it is more inadequate than need be, so long as the political relations of States are capricious and uncoordinated. At present civilised States are like masters who maintain splendid order and discipline within their workshops, and thus feel free to go out and racket in the streets.

74. THE ROLE OF THE VILLAGE
IN AMERICAN RURAL SOCIETY *

T. LYNN SMITH

Some elements of human ecology may be seen more clearly when they are examined in a relatively simple setting. This description, by T. Lynn Smith, of the American village defines it as an ecological unit which serves as the essential link between rural and urban worlds. In addition to his description of the roles played by the village as a center of trade and commerce and as the nucleus of the emerging rural community, the author analyzes other functions it performs.

INTRODUCTION

As a center of trade and commerce, the village has long played a vital rôle in American rural society. Contrary to a widespread popular belief, this function of the village continues to wax in importance. At the same time the village is also forging to the front as the social center of rural America, coming into its own as the nucleus of the emerging rural community. As the line of cleavage between the rural and urban worlds, as the point of contact between urban and rural patterns of behavior, and as a residential center for certain more dependent parts of the national population, it also performs other functions of vital importance in our general web of life. Current developments such as the increased mobility of the aged population, the expansion of the social security program, and above all the War, bid fair to increase still further the importance of the American village. The present discussion considers the village as an element in our national structure and indicates a few of the more essential functions that it performs.

Before beginning the analysis of the rôle of the village it is necessary

* *Rural Sociology*, Vol. 7, No. 1 (March, 1942), 10–21. Reprinted by permission of the author and the publisher.

The author (b. 1903) is Professor of Sociology, University of Florida. Onetime Director, Institute of Brazilian Studies, Vanderbilt University; Senior Agricultural Analyst, United States Department of State. Author: *Sociology of Rural Life; Brazil: People and Institutions; Sociology of Urban Life; Population Analysis;* editor: *Social Problems.*

to attempt some clarification of the terminology pertaining to small locality groupings. First it is essential to state precisely what is meant when the term *village* is used and to differentiate this concept from other closely related ones. This involves several considerations. There are those, such as Professor Sauer of the University of California, who would restrict the designation *village* to those small population aggregates that are composed for the most part of the homes of farmers. There is much merit to such a position. Undoubtedly throughout most of the world the use of the village pattern of arranging the population on the land has led to a situation in which agriculture is the primary occupation of the majority of persons living in the smaller population aggregates. However, such a standard would practically eliminate the term *village* from domestic application in the United States where scattered farmsteads is the prevailing mode of settlement. In the United States size must be the principal criterion utilized in the definition of the village.

At the present time, using size as the criterion, the following definition of *village* is in rather general use: a population center containing between 250 and 2,500 inhabitants, irrespective of the occupations of the residents. The upper limit coincides with present census practice in differentiating between urban and rural populations and sets villages apart from urban aggregates. The appellation *town* is proposed for centers of population varying in size from 2,500 to 10,000 inhabitants, and *city* for places with more than 10,000 residents. The lower limit is less satisfactory, but it does meet the principal objective of differentiating the village from the hamlet or the smallest aggregation of homes. It is recognized, however, that it might be better to choose 100 or some other figure as the line of demarcation between the two.

A second consideration of terminology is clarification of the difference between the terms *village* and *community*. Where nucleated settlement patterns prevail, the community consists of the village center with its cluster of residences and the lands that are tributary to it. In order to care for their crops the village population must commute regularly to their fields. The boundaries of the locality group are definite, and there is little chance for uncertainty to arise concerning village functions and community boundaries. However, in some cases, too close identification of village and community or commune results in references to villages as being constituted of several separate nuclei or hamlets. Obviously this is a misnomer; such a collection of hamlets is a community or commune rather than a village. On the other hand, in the United States where the village serves largely as a trade and service center and not as a residential center for farmers, it is only one part of the community. In this case the lands tributary to the village center are not so easily identified; there may be some confusion relative to the community attachments of many farm homes; and there remains the additional task of determining the limits of the web of life centering in the village which gives to the nucleus and the tributary farm homes the fundamental characteristics of a community. Throughout most of the United States the village is merely one part of the rural community. . . .

THE FUNCTIONS OF THE VILLAGE

1. TRADE AS THE PRIMARY FUNCTION OF THE AMERICAN VILLAGE

Most villages in the United States came into being as trade and service centers for the farm families living on the land in the surrounding territory. Today trade, manufacturing (broadly interpreted to include carpentering, bricklaying, and other skilled trades), communication and transportation, and the professions continue to constitute the *raison d'être* of most of our villages. Of the gainfully-employed male residents of United States villages, only a small portion are engaged in agricultural pursuits. In other words the primary function of the American village is to serve as a trade and service center for the farmers in the surrounding area. This is in sharp contrast with the principal function of Old World and Latin American villages which are primarily residential centers for farm families, the trading function being of secondary importance.

There are of course important differences between the villages of the nation. Many of those that are located on the fringes of cities and towns are primarily residential areas or manufacturing centers. In certain parts of the country, and particularly in the Mormon and Spanish settlements in the Rocky Mountain and southwestern parts of the country, the village pattern of settlement has been used. Just as in Europe, Asia, or Latin America, these villages are composed principally of farm homes. But most American villages are primarily trade and service centers; these should be listed as their most important functions.

2. THE VILLAGE AS THE NUCLEUS OF THE EMERGING RURAL COMMUNITY

The United States long has suffered for want of a strong, clearly defined, and well integrated rural community. Colonial America was for the most part cut to the neighborhood pattern. With minor exceptions the principal locality groupings were small in size, consisted of persons closely knit together by intimate social bonds, and were areas within which the social interaction was almost exclusively on a face-to-face basis. But despite a high degree of self-sufficiency on the part of each family, it still was necessary to go outside the group for satisfaction of many elemental needs. As settlement edged forward from the Appalachians to the Pacific, federal policies of land distribution and the scattered farmsteads type of settlement played important rôles in keeping locality groupings small, i.e., in the neighborhood stage. Until the opening of the twentieth century, closely knit neighborhoods formed the warp and woof of rural society, and for the bulk of the farm population larger areas of association were relatively unimportant. Prior to 1900 it was customary, and to a considerable extent justifiable, to speak of the American farmer as the "man without a community." With the passage of time and especially with the development of improved methods of communication and transportation, neighborhood ties have weakened, the vista of the farm family has broadened, and there is emerging in rural America a locality group that can meet most of the criteria of a real community.

These changes have meant a considerable disorganization of old structural patterns, but out of it all the village is rapidly finding its place as the center of this larger and more complex web of rural living. In addition to the economic institutions and agencies which are primary, the village is becoming of increasing importance in other social spheres. Neighborhood institutions, such as the open-country church or the one-room school, and informal recreational activities, are declining in importance or passing. On the other hand the village church is enrolling increasing proportions of farm members; centralized schools usually are located in the village center; and the movies and other forms of commercialized entertainment in the village are becoming largely dependent upon the farm population. It seems fair to say that the social functions of the village already promise to rival its economic functions.

3. THE VILLAGE AS AMERICA'S "OLD FOLKS' HOME"

Villages also perform some very highly important demographic functions for our national society. In contradistinction to the farms which are the seed bed of national population and the cities which are the consumers of population, the village is the place where a disproportionately large share of the nation's old persons live out the declining years of their lives. As Brunner and Kolb have correctly stated the village is "rural America's old folks' home." The importance of its function as an uncongested, healthful, and inexpensive abode for the aged should not be minimized. If it has played this part during years of peace, war is likely to enhance still further this rôle of the American village.

Unfortunately for those of us who are interested in rural population, the data pertaining to the demographic characteristics of the village population leave a great deal to be desired. However, enough data are available to establish the fact that the villages contain a disproportionately large share of the old people of the nation. Thus in 1930 the inhabitants of the 3,087 incorporated villages with between 1,000 and 2,500 inhabitants (the only ones for which data are available) contained only 3.9 per cent of the national population. But in these same villages resided 5.6 per cent of all persons aged 65 and over in the United States. On a relative basis, this means that the aged population was 40 per cent more important in the villages than it was in the national population. Furthermore, in almost every state in the union, the village population contained a disproportionately large share of the aged. Exceptions to this rule are to be found only in three recently settled western states (Arizona, Idaho, and Montana) in which many pioneers had not yet reached the most advanced ages. Throughout much of the nation and particularly in the northern and midwestern states, the villages contained old persons in proportions that were half again as high as the percentages in the respective states. It is not overstating the case to assert that the provision of a place of habitation for the aged members of the population is one of the more important functions of the village.

Closely allied to this demographic function is the low sex ratio of the village population and the high proportion of widowed and divorced females who reside in the small incorporated centers of the nation. It is likely that a large proportion of these widowed and divorced females have moved in from the surrounding farms.

4. THE VILLAGE AS THE ARENA OF RURAL-URBAN CONFLICT

The fact that the social and economic environment of city and country people is vastly different is widely recognized. Also rather well understood is the proposition that these differences in the man-made environment or culture of the two groups have significant influences in molding the personalities of rural and urban people. That these personality differences and the differing folkways, mores, and cultural patterns in which they have their roots lead to a constant and often severe conflict between the urban and rural parts of our society is also rather generally understood. But that the village is the arena in which this conflict occurs has seldom if ever received any detailed analysis. My immediate purpose is to illustrate the nature of this important village function.

It is because the American village serves, not as a residential center for farm families, but as a market, a trade center, and a social center for families living in the surrounding open country territory that it becomes the arena for rural-urban conflict. The stress laid upon this point is not to overlook the important fact that many rural-urban contacts result in an end highly satisfactory to both segments of society. It is merely to emphasize that the village serves as the focal point in which urban values, attitudes, and patterns of living clash head on with those from the country, and that a great deal of conflict is generated by this brusque contact. This clash of interests arises in a great many aspects of life, but it may be illustrated with a few simple examples.

Consider first one of the economic aspects. Long after the city man has become so highly specialized that he is either a laborer, a capitalist, or engaged in managerial activities, the great bulk of the farmers continue to perform all three of these economic functions. For this reason and also because he deals largely with living growing things, lives in a sparsely-populated district, and has few but intimate and enduring social contacts, the farmer has a set of attitudes towards such things as hours of work, wage rates, and prices that is considerably different from those possessed by any one class of city men. As indicated above, village banks, retail outlets, and other business firms are the media of contact between these divergent urban and rural attitudes, values, and patterns of behavior.

Thus we may cite the example of the farmer who takes his car to the village garage for a repair job. Even in the smallest crossroads center the garage is an institution that brings into the rural area the wage scales and commodity prices of Detroit and other large cities. The farmer is used to differentials: he rarely pays wage rates that are comparable to those of the city. But unless he can do the work himself, he must pay the national wage and price scales in the garage. Nothing outrages the farmer more than this situation, especially in those numerous cases in which the mechanic is the "good-for-nothing" son of a neighbor who has gone off to the village looking for an "easy job."

In the field of educational theory and practice, the village is also the scene of conflict between the traditional rural attitudes and behavior and the innovations introduced by urban trained teachers and curricula designed to meet the needs of city children. Sharp conflicts are engendered in respect to content, teaching methods, discipline, and school organization and administration. Not unusual are the cases in which the farm districts are hotbeds of discontent deeply angered with the "frills" of a school curriculum, completely horrified by the "progressive methods" of instruction, fully disgusted with "lax" school discipline, and thoroughly rebellious about actual or proposed delineation of school administration or attendance areas. Gerrymandering of school districts, which the farmer often thinks is for village advantage, and consolidations are frequently basic in all these disputes. My intention is neither to praise nor to blame either side to the disputes, merely to emphasize that the village is the place in which the clash of systems occurs.

The village is also the place in which the modernistic religious practices and beliefs of the city collide with the traditional religious attitudes and expressions of the countrymen. As has been shown by the excellent studies of Brunner and his associates, the village is increasingly becoming the focal point for rural religious activities. But in the village church the farmer comes into contact with a trained minister who has been exposed to the facts and theories of modern biological and physical science, the current contributions of the social sciences relative to social and cultural change or the social functions of the church, and perhaps to some elements of the higher criticism. The pulpit of the village church serves as the faucet through which these ideas are let loose on the countryside. Probably to the villager, and certainly to the farmer, much of the preaching of contemporary liberal or unorthodox ministers is in fundamental conflict with many traditional beliefs that are deeply imbedded in cultural and emotional foundations. Probably the conflict between "modernism" and "fundamentalism" reaches its acme in the village church.

The foregoing analysis should be sufficient to demonstrate that the village is the principal arena for the clash of rural and urban attitudes and patterns of living. Before leaving this subject, however, it should be indicated that these differences, as all others, must ultimately be resolved. Men cannot fight all the time. Some of the ways in which a *modus vivendi* are obtained are extremely interesting. *Sub rosa* the garage may fail to charge the stipulated prices or wage scales; as attested by *The Reader's Digest* survey, the vigilance of rural mores keeps exploitation at a minimum in village garages; public employees may keep longer working or office hours in the village than in the city; departures from traditional curricula or teaching methods may be less "progressive" than in the larger centers; and the minister's orthodoxy may be carefully examined before he is employed by the village church.

75. LITTLETOWN *

The Story of an American Village

WILLIAM G. MATHER, JR.

In the preceding selection T. Lynn Smith discusses the rural village as a general type. This selection by W. G. Mather, Jr., in contrast, offers a case study of one rural town in New York. After briefly reviewing the history of the community, he proceeds to depict the way of life in the village. Dismal though the picture is, it was typical of the pattern of life in many rural communities at the time this was written (1935). As the concluding paragraphs of the article imply, however, communities have a way of persisting, even though shifts in the organization of American society may distinctly change their character.

* *Harper's Magazine*, Vol. 170 (January, 1935), 199–208. Reprinted by permission of the author.

The author (b. 1901) is Professor and Head, Department of Sociology, Pennsylvania State University. Interests center in rural sociology, the church, and health, in each of which fields he has published.

The other day a farmer called on Jonas Handman to deliver a basket of apples. He knocked on the kitchen door, waited for a while, then went round to the front door and knocked there. Nobody came. Handman had said that he wanted those apples, so the farmer put the basket down on the porch and went back of the house to the barn. There he found Jonas hanging by his neck, dead.

Jonas had never been known to do any real work about Littletown; while his father was living he never had to. And when his father died he left him the store blocks downtown. Jonas seemed to get along very well on the rents up to a few years ago, and was in the pool room most of the time. There were two stores, one with a hall over it that hasn't been used for years except for a few months some time ago by the Girl Scout troop. Last year Bill and Ed Brown started a garage in the store part of that block, when the grocery which Jed Simmons had run was closed out after his funeral. The other block had been vacant for a few years, except for a rummage sale or bake-sale in it now and then. The garage did not pay much rent, and you can't charge a women's society for sales, so it seemed that things had turned out badly for Jonas. We hadn't realized they were that bad though.

The truth is, we don't miss Jonas Handman very much. He was never, so to speak, a contributing member of our community. But his suicide is the third within the past year.

Littletown is small, as its name implies, with only some fourteen hundred people. And three suicides in one year are altogether too many for that population.

Some of us are beginning to worry about what is going to happen to our town. The past thirty years have seen many changes in the world, and from the point of view of the small-town man they have not all been good in their effect. There seems to be a sinister force at work, threatening the very existence of many small towns.

Take the little hamlet a few miles from us called The Flats. Thirty years or so ago The Flats was a busy little crossroads with two cheese factories, two stores (one with a hall over it), a blacksmith shop, a shingle mill that took its power from the creek, a school, and a church. They had great times with family reunions, square dances, warm-sugar parties, and the like, and it was known as one of the best communities in our neighborhood.

To-day not a single one of those signs of business life remains. There is only the old church, empty and unused, and the school with only a handful of pupils. One out of three of the houses within two miles of the crossroads in every direction is unoccupied and falling to pieces.

No wonder that we in Littletown are becoming nervous. As the advertising posters begin to be pasted on the inside of the show windows of store after store of ours that closes, the ghost of The Flats comes over the hill and haunts us. Twenty years, forty years—and shall we also belong to the Past?

II

Littletown is a cozy village in a hollow of the beautiful, surprisingly abrupt hills of southwestern New York. The Baptist church, a few rods down Spring Street from the main corner, is at an elevation of 1400 feet above sea level, while the tops of the hills round about are 1800 and 1900 feet. The only flat land is found in the valleys, and in only small patches there; in one summer alone three men, tilling the rolling slopes, were hurt by the overturning of tractors. The land has been farmed for a century and a third but is untamed yet!

An ancient glacial lake lay to the north of Littletown long before even the foot of a Seneca Indian had disturbed the deep grass of the pastures of the deer, and the lake left behind, with its shoreline and outlet banks, a level but tortuous passage through the hills to the more gently rolling valley of the Genesee. Along this path wound the old cart road to the cities of the north in the early days of settlement in the 1790's; and when Clinton's Ditch traversed the State from east to west a canal was dug over the same gentle path to connect Rochester, with her port on Lake Ontario, to the Allegheny River. It was possible in those days to move slowly up the canal, through Littletown and across to Oleander, where one turned down the Allegheny to the Ohio, thence to the Mississippi and the Gulf. The canal is gone now, but the locks still stand, with now and then a crumbling skeleton of a gate between them; and there are men in Littletown who will tell you of unloading salt at the Port of Littletown in those days, and women who remember the Sunday School outings when heavily loaded, bunting-draped barges moved off for a day in some grove along the canal.

The Pennsylvania Railroad bought the canal and used the tow path as a base for its rails; part of the Erie main line follows the same route, and is well traveled; but the Pennsylvania is a branch line, built to serve the little towns along the old artery of travel. Such is the way of Time that it is running fewer trains each year, the rails are beginning to gather rust, and a concrete highway makes the tires whine as cars speed over the old route of the post road, the canal, and the iron horse.

It was nearly a century and a half ago that a group of men discovered the valley in which Littletown lies. It seemed a good place for a town, this little flat patch with passes through the hills to all four points of the compass, so they took up land rights. One faction wanted the village at the north end of the hollow; the other, at the south, against the hills. Each set up a store and a tavern on its chosen spot; but the liquor must have been better at the latter place, for North Littletown is now just a filling station, a house for tourists and a school.

The village grew slowly but was regarded as a coming town. A new post road from Buffalo to Pennsylvania was surveyed about 1870, and Littletown was on one of the two possible routes. The village was astir; two post roads, a canal—what more could one ask to insure prosperity? And then the road went through Oleander, a village of the same size, almost a day's journey (in reality, only sixteen miles) up the swampy valley to the west. Old timers shake their heads and date that city's rise from the changing of the road. "When I was a boy Oleander wasn't as big as we are now," they say, and sigh the sigh of men who have guessed wrong.

But the long grass was still there, and the cows were there, going about the business of the cud unmindful of the fate of village empires down below them. Within ten years after the incident of the road, the milk from more than two thousand cows was being handled in the many cheese factories tucked away in the folds of the hills, and more than three-quarters of a million pounds of rich, mild-flavored cheese were marketed through the Littletown exchange each year. Almost all of the land, even in the remotest hills, was in pasture or grain.

The little cheese factories are just about all closed now, for cheese can be made at lower cost in Wisconsin and Minnesota; but there are a few left, and a chain store and a national meat packer still maintain cheese warehouses in Littletown. The War helped to change the nature of the dairy industry, as it boosted the sale of condensed milk, and several large condensaries were established in and near our village. One of them is still operating, the milk being hauled in by trucks that rumble through when the sleepy storekeepers are sweeping out in the morning.

Milk prices are low now, and the dairymen who have to pay for long hauls of milk are finding it hard to keep going. The old days of milk-prosperity—if they could be called that—do not seem likely to come again; dairying is a serious, corner-cutting, belt-tightening business, and a good many hill pastures are growing up to brush and scrubby timber.

There was another time when Fortune gave her Mona Lisa smile to Littletown, and now and again we get a little publicity in some newspaper because of it.

It seems that away back in the early days a bowlegged man called Seneca Pete used to drive an old gray mule down from Buffalo with two empty kegs strapped on her back. A mile or so from the village is a scummy spring in a swampy hollow, that used to form a thin film of oily substance over its surface. When flint and steel were struck close to its edge, it would burn for a time. The Senecas guarded it as a treasure, dipping their blankets into it and straining out the precious oil that had oozed up from the rock below. It was thought to be good for a snakebite, good for wounds, good for general principles; and Seneca Pete would load up his mule and plod back to Buffalo, there to sell the famous "Seneca Oil" to the doctors. It was the first petroleum discovered in America.

When Drake proved the worth of drilling a shaft for oil Littletown heard the news with joy. When oil ran out of its own accord, without need of a drilled hole, how much more must there not be below the surface, waiting for the bit to free it and send it spouting up into the sun?

A well was drilled close to the edge of the old spring. The top of the casing still stands in the weeds, ragged, rusty, ashamed. But over the hills, only eight miles away, begins the rich oil field from which the world's best crude is pumped. Fortune missed us by that slight a margin.

A few years ago the men whom oil had made rich came to our town and built a monument in tribute to the spring that had led the way. We are proud of that bowlder with its bronze slab and generally motor our visitors out to see it. But we would rather have a derrick.

In the first decade of the present century, Littletown made its bid as a manufacturing center. A knife factory, a pulley works, a cheese-box factory, and a novelty concern erected buildings and began operations. Perhaps a hundred men were employed, with two dozen others in the two older mills that had been long established for the grinding of feed and flour and the sawing of lumber. An enterprising citizen with little taste put up a whole street of somber houses, all alternately alike, on the edge of town. We had our factories and our slums. We were on the way to becoming a big town.

The knife factory died first and one of the banks took it over. The novelty firm moved on. The pulley works went under two years ago. The box factory merged with the sawmill.

The buildings still stand there, sagging, empty, and the Chamber of Commerce is busy dangling bait before the eyes of small city businesses, hoping to entice them here. A year or so ago some of the younger business men became impatient and from somewhere managed to raise two thousand dollars, which they gave, together with an old barnlike structure, to a man with an idea for an airplane. The plane almost flew, at that.

Commerce, oil, manufacturing—they have all paid us but fleeting visits. They roused our hopes, they made us dream. Yet on the hillsides the sleek cows still graze, the milk trucks roll through town in the early morning, and the only mills that stood the test of time are the feed and flour mills, grinding out food for the cows. Even the sawmill is owned by the same men that own the feed mill. And it makes cheese-boxes. We have not wanted to be rural, but it seems that we cannot help it.

III

Although Littletown is small, it does not lack facilities for trade. There are three chain groceries in town, hated like poison by the proprietors of the locally owned groceries, of which there are also three. The local stores are forever urging us to keep our dollars at home, to support home industries, to remember old friends; but so far only one of them has cleaned up his place of business, painted the front an attractive color, enamelled the shelves, and removed the cat from the warm show window. He gets some of the business that the bright, neat chains get, but the other two have their troubles.

We did have two bakeries, one of them half a grocery also. The bakery has gone bankrupt; the combination hangs on. Bread trucks come in daily from Oleander with fresh rolls and bread and pastry, attractively done up in boxes or transparent paper with no flies inside, and most of our housewives prefer to buy their baked goods that way.

If you wish to buy a pair of shoes in our town, you have many opportunities. When the last census was taken, there were only two thousand eight hundred and forty-four feet in the village, but there are six places in which to buy shoes. There are two men's clothing stores, one pool room, one men's and women's clothing store, and two drygoods stores—all selling shoes. Of course, no one of them has a large assortment of either sizes or styles, but you may find what you want if you are lucky.

There are two meat markets, one run by the man who also manages the moving picture theater. But two of the chain groceries also carry meat, and so one of the markets has put in a line of bread and rolls, cakes, and canned goods. He is new to town and swears that if the competition extends to other stores he will put in dresses and cameras and a soda fountain.

There is the ever-present ice cream parlor, whose owner, in partnership with his brother, also runs an ice cream factory. They make very good ice cream, putting real cream from the local dairies into it; thus it costs more to make than do the frozen puddings turned out by the Buffalo factories, and so their business remains small. The drugstore on the opposite corner from the ice cream parlor carries the Buffalo brand.

There are two drugstores and they both sell drugs in addition to watches, alarm clocks, cameras, radios, candles, wall paper, candy, mirrors, pictures, greeting cards, toys, and what not. And there are two pool rooms, two hardware stores, two electric stores, the proprietor of one of which doubles as funeral director, three restaurants, two gift shops with jewelers' counters, two hotels, four garages.

Yes, we have the facilities for doing business. Two of everything at least, including two banks to handle the inevitable bankruptcies that come more frequently in recent years. If Prosperity ever dared walk down our main street it would be plucked raw before it had gone half a block.

We used to have business too. The farmers' teams crowded the streets, and their children the stores, and everyone was happy. They used to give you a bag of candy when you paid your bill. But business is drifting to Oleander now, with its ten-cent stores and its larger stocks of suits and dresses and furniture, only twenty-five minutes away over a good paved road that we were mighty pleased with when it was first laid down.

Sometimes we look back on the paving of that road and grin crookedly. We were proud as Punch when the job was finished. There were editorials in the paper, photographs of leading citizens, and all that. We came within an inch of having one of these celebrations with a symbolic wedding too. If our storekeepers could have seen how much of their business was going to roll over that road to Oleander, they would have worked for a symbolic funeral instead.

But they didn't see it and went right on doing business as they had done it for years before, when we had to buy from them or go without. But now, if we don't like what they have or the price that they set upon it we can try in Oleander without much trouble. A lot of small-town business men are making that same mistake; they do not seem to realize that the swamps and hills that cut their customers off from the rest of the world are being filled and levelled now, and that their business is in competition with every other store of the same line within forty miles. Even Oleander, now with nearly twenty thousand people, complains that some of its trade is going to Buffalo, seventy miles to the northeast; and Oleander has some large stores.

Of course, it is true that a man in a small town like ours cannot expect to have a large store; but sometimes I wonder if it is necessary to break up what little business we do have among so many men and make it still smaller.

One of the things that keeps business poor is the fact that there just aren't as many people to buy goods as there used to be. Our village declined 11.7 per cent in population between the last two federal censuses. As for the countryside round us, a drive over the dirt roads in any direction will show what is happening there, as house after house stands empty with its shutters banging in the wind. It does no good to call those dirt roads "side" roads; they were main roads when our village was growing and our present number of stores were founded, and the people who traded with us came over them to market.

Modern methods of agriculture have made it possible for one farmer to handle more stock and more land than several farmers could in the former days, and the surplus farmers have moved away. The poorer land is going out of cultivation, as not worth a man's time, and the better land is being tilled more cheaply and better. The population of the old canal and post road days is not needed any more. Men do not go down the meadows four and six abreast, swinging their scythes, at harvest time; one man rides round on a mower. One man sitting on a tractor turns two or three furrows at once. One man milks two cows at once while leaning against a post and watching the machine suck and blow. Farming is a business now, and the sheriff sells out the man who cannot run his farm in a business way.

I cannot sigh over the departure of the old days of hand agriculture. I was raised on a farm. I have had a double-shovel give my ribs a Dutch rub when plowing corn in the old stump field, and I am glad that men can farm now more safely for their bones and their religion. The women in farm homes too do not long for the days when the dining room was full of harvesters and the kitchen full of the fumes of hell. The new ways are better. But that does not alter the fact that they mean fewer feet to be shod, fewer legs to be overalled, fewer freckled, sun-browned misses to wear the new, soft dresses.

IV

The people that live in Littletown are nice. The Legion and the Ku Klux would accept them all. We have very few foreign families— you could count them on one hand—and still fewer colored. There are the usual number of faithful elderly spinsters waiting to join Ma and Dad, who died and left them without the job that had been husband and children to them; the usual number of widows and widowers living alone with their memories in rambling, solitary houses; the usual number of retired farmers sniffing the wind wistfully in the morning; the usual number of children playing in the yards of the smaller houses on the side streets. There are not many young people though; the population takes a running jump over the twenties, and the few that are left keep asking, "What's doing in the city? Are jobs opening up there yet?"

It makes it rather hard on the young folks in high school. They are determined not to be like Mother and Dad, but there are few in between to copy after. So they read the magazines and go to the movies and get their styles of dressing and acting from there. A little too much lipstick, talk rather coarse and loud, clothes just a bit extreme, and a faraway look of cities over the horizon when the school bell has rung for the last time, tell their story.

A year or two ago one of the men from the college of agriculture gave the young folks in our high school a questionnaire about their choice of a vocation. Only 16.5 per cent of them said they were planning to do work similar to their father's, and only 13.8 per cent were intending to stay in town. Their dreams will change of course, and disappointment will also come; but that does not change the present situation much. Our young folks do not like us and see no future for themselves with us.

On Sunday morning the bells in five steeples ring the call to worship, and the doors of five churches open for the crowds of worshippers who will not come. All of our churches have a seating capacity far in excess of their resident membership. Yet we are a fairly religious town; for a census that the churches took one year showed that over half of our population belonged to some church, and the average for the United States is less than that. The proportion is considerably smaller, however, among the country people; relatively few of them come to our churches, and they have none of their own. They say that their clothes are inferior to ours, and that we are not friendly with them. I think that their clothes are on the whole as good as ours, but they are probably right about the lack of cordiality; we have had our eyes fixed on the dream of being a big city for so long that we have forgotten the people who tend the cows that fill the milk trucks that rumble through town.

Our churches are costly affairs. In 1930 we spent, one of the ministers estimated, $17,507 for the four Protestant churches alone. Thirty years before that the records show that the cost of those same churches, with more members, was only $7,089. I do not attribute this rise to extravagance but to the upward tendency of our necessities; thirty years ago we did not feel that a college education was necessary for our ministers; but we do now, for so many of us are college-educated that we abhor scientific blunders in the pulpit. And college men cost us more than illiterate, or semi-so, ministers. The same is true of our pipe organs, our redecorated buildings, our robed choirs. Those things are part of our modern culture.

Our extravagance comes, however, in our insistence that each small church group must have those things for itself. The Methodists, with only ninety-four members, must have those things just as do the Baptists, with two and one-half times as many people over whom to spread the cost. Some people I know have actually declined to join one of our churches, not because they did not feel spiritually ready, but because they knew that they could not stand the financial pressure that is put upon its members. The gospel is far from free in our town.

Some efforts have been made toward inter-church co-operation. Union services are held on summer evenings, and even the smallest building is adequate to hold the combined audiences. The young people of three of the churches began a joint society, but the older folks of one church withdrew their young people after a few weeks, saying that they were having too good a time with the others and feared they might be "weaned away" from their own church. Two of the churches have had a joint men's class for a few years, and the men got along with one another there as well as they did in the lodges or the business men's clubs; but when talk began of union of the two churches at a time when one of them was without a minister some of the women said things that put a stop to it.

It may be after we have had a few more burials in our beautiful green cemetery on the hill that church union will come nearer, and we shall become fellow-Christians as well as fellow-Littletownians—but there are those who will term my hope sinful.

Although we are losing population, our school is becoming more crowded every year. The classrooms are full of seats. It seems that out in the country districts, as the little schools lose students until only a few are left and the cost per pupil becomes high, the schools are closed and those few children are taken in to our school by buses. Also, more young people above the age at which they are legally required to go to school are wanting to continue on through the high school; they feel the need of higher education in this day. We shall have to build a new building for them eventually, and yet we hesitate at the cost and keep putting it off. A large part of our taxpaying townsmen are retired farmers whose income is small and limited, whose children are already educated and gone, but whose influence is great.

We have a beautiful little library, built by funds which a good woman left for the purpose, and the young folks use it very well. Their parents, except for women who do a deal of novel-reading, do not use it much. We are not enthusiastic in the cultivation of our minds but are fairly satisfied to let them be as they are. One of the doctors was fuming the other day that there were eight card clubs in town but not one mother's club.

When evening settles down upon us there are several things that we can do. Generally we sit at home and listen to the radio, which is pleasant in the summer when it can be heard through an open window on the porch. If the night is fair we visit friends; and if there is something extra on at one of the lodges those of us who are not officers, who would go anyway, attend.

We have two lodges, the Odd Fellows and the Masons, the former with a large proportion of farmers in its membership. The leaders of both complain that meetings are poorly attended, not like the good old days. But the rooms are open in the afternoons, and the older men drop in to play checkers and cards and talk. The women have their Rebekahs and Eastern Star and put on bake-sales now and then.

There are, besides the Legion—which is getting a bit fat—and the Grange, a number of other organizations in town. A D.A.R. chapter that was recently formed by some lady who belonged to no other club, I think, and who wanted to join one; a chapter of Daughters of Union Veterans; a Current Topic club that should properly be called Current Gossip; the Shakespeare Club that discusses astronomy and art; any number of card clubs that are the breath of life to the two little gift shops; and in each section of town a "sunshine" club that sends flowers and gifts to the sick. The women spend a great deal of time at these various clubs; for they are, like most small-town women, forever lonesome and inquisitive about one another's affairs.

We have two business men's clubs, whose main occupation is talking about bringing "new business" to town, but none of them includes in its membership farmers, whose milk trucks bring in all the new business that ever does come.

For sport, the younger men have organized a soft-ball league that fights noisy battles in the park at twilight. The barbers have a team, the railroad men, the feed-mill men, and so on; "Lucky Tigers," "Keystones," "Barney Googles" they call them, and get real sport out of the games. Baseball loosens up the muscles that have been fighting rust on the rails or waiting behind the counters for business to come home and be forgiven, and also takes their minds off the complaining women who wait for their men folk to return at sundown and listen respectfully while they retail the gossip of the day.

v

Last year the farmers took a step that disgusted the business men. They organized a co-operative feed store in one of the empty buildings, to handle feed and flour and the like, buy seeds and fertilizer, and ship some produce as well. The business men regard it as very ungrateful of them, especially in the midst of this business depression. If they had only taken some stock in the knife factory or the airplane industry now, the farmers would have been showing real co-operation. But this event proves to them that the farmers do not understand civic needs.

One would think that the young people, even more than the women, would be very busy; for they have any number of organizations for them in the school and the churches and the Scouts and the Hi-Y. Some organization is putting on a sale of some kind, raising money for some purpose, almost all the time. But the truth is, as I have observed, that a few of them belong to nearly everything, with no time even to study, while a great many belong to nothing and do nothing except stand on the street corners and giggle.

There really is not much else for those who are not dashing off to some meeting or other to do. They can go to the movies, which cost money, or they can shoot pool, which also costs money and is not too well thought of, or they can go home. They rarely do that except to work at their lessons. What they fall back upon is the promenade. From the library they drift down one side of the street to the filling station, then cross over and back up the other side, and so on around again. Now and then they pair off and slip away down a side street where the lights are more dim.

One winter a new minister suggested opening up some of the rooms of a church and installing ping-pong tables, checkers, a piano, and the like on Friday and Saturday nights. He didn't get far with that idea. "What for?" was the attitude of his board. "We spend a lot of money on our young folks now, and then when they get through school they go off to the city and we never get it back. And besides it isn't right to use the church property that way."

So the card-tables gossip about the goings-on among the younger generation of this awful day; one of the older ministers fulminates weekly about the drinking and necking proclivities of youth, and the business men complain that the young people do not remain to marry and settle down and breed a trading population for the town. And all the while the more ambitious and worthy of the young folks are whispering impatiently among themselves, "Let's get out of here to where something's doing!"

And that probably is the very spirit that led their ancestors to come to Littletown in the first place.

We used to have, not so long ago, considerable doing in our town. Every fall we had a fair, of which we were justly proud. We had halls for exhibits, a race track, a grandstand. I can remember when I used to swallow a whole bag of popcorn without tasting it, as La Paloma won by a nose from Gelter's Pride or while I watched Zanzibar the snake eater for one dime, ten cents, the decimal part of a dollar. But the fair stopped some years ago for lack of entries, and enthusiasm, and patrons, and money; and last year we arranged to sell the old buildings that remained in order to pay off a debt we owed the printer.

The grove just south of town, a clean place of hard maples lifting round bare trunks above the grass, used to be the scene of camp meetings, chautauquas, and political rallies. Tents were pitched amid the trees, water brought from the spring, horses staked out, and the whole family settled down to enjoy religion or whatever there was, while one of the boys ran the farm between hayings. Jolly, informal, full of fist fights and love-making, of prayer and mud-slinging, summer camp meetings were the balm of sultry days. Brush grows up in the old grove now, and the cows scratch their lean necks against well-nigh obliterated hearts with arrows stuck through and letters, "H. C. and V. T." O Time, how could you?

Here it lies, the little village in the lap of the hills, about it the marks of its former happiness and hope, and before it the shadows seen only by itself and the old men who sit on the bench before the pool room on calm afternoons. They too have lived and dreamed.

And the storekeepers agitate home trade, dangle decaying buildings before decaying industries as an attraction to come to Littletown and die, and at the last do as Jonas Handman did. Just between the main highways of travel, just on the edge of the oil field, not big enough to be a city, not small enough to be a hamlet—wanting things, almost getting things, too alive to die and too dead to grow, what shall become of us?

We have the poor comfort of knowing that our lot is not solitary. There are many villages like ours to-day, facing what we face. We hear talk of the decentralization of industry, of the putting of great factories into small units scattered over many towns, but we know that salvation for us does not lie in the scheme. It may be done, but we know that it will be the villages nearer the great cities than we are that will profit. And the extent of their profit is doubtful; industry began in small towns once and left them; we had factories once, and they are gone; nor have the prodigals shed many tears of penitence as yet. Many villages like us are waiting for either factories or farmers to come back; for over one hundred thousand acres of farm land have been abandoned in our county alone, many times that in the State, and millions in the whole country.

Everywhere that this has occurred there are villages with Jonas Handmans.

Of this, I think we are certain: that the process of shrinking will go on until there are just enough farmers left outside our village to supply the milk that the market demands. And when that point is reached there will also be just enough stores left in Littletown to supply the needs of these farmers. The churches will either die or merge the one with the other until there are just enough churches to accommodate us all, villagers and farmers, in our worship. The little district schools will probably draw together in consolidation until our youth can find in the minimum number of good schools the maximum preparation for life.

These things will not happen easily. They will be accompanied by struggle and pain. But if we can see where we are going, and help one another on the way, we may be able to reduce the Jonas Handmans.

Littletown is not going to die. Littletown is going to start over again, this time with its eyes open, its goal more real. We shall gain a spiritual dividend from the re-organization of our village life, I think; for whatever we do we shall have to do together—and that is good for the soul. One with the countryside, with the old false barrier between village and farm forgotten, with the common interest of storekeeper and dairyman at last known and understood, the renascent Littletown may be a better place than before.

For life still goes on about us. Lovers marry and are given in marriage; children play in the front yards; men sweat in the fields; women peel vegetables in the kitchens; and the cows come home at evening in long patient lines, trailing down from the hill pastures.

And wherever there is life there are the needs of life, that cannot be met by any one man alone.

76. VILLAGERS IN METROPOLIS *

SVEND RIEMER

Are city planners following a mistaken lead when they attempt to revive village structures in the metropolis? Do we need to shift our thinking about the neighborhood so as to emphasize less its characteristic as an "area clearly delineated in space" and emphasize more the fact that it is "a phenomenon anchored in the mind"? These are some of the questions to which the author applies himself and in so doing shows some of the consequences of a society's becoming more urban.

I. RURAL AND URBAN SOCIAL CONTROL

While village structures vanish more and more from the urban environment, the professional city planner endeavours to keep alive or to revive in the city a social climate characterized by close internal cohesion among neighbours. The paradox ventured in the title of this article presents a goal, a desideratum rather than a fact.

Village structures are determined by a way of life (1) deeply embedded in tradition and (2) controlled by a close-knit welter of informal social relationships among the members of the group. Geographically, the village is characterized by close residential propinquity of those

* *British Journal of Sociology*, Vol. 2, No. 1 (March, 1951), 31–43. London: Routledge & Kegan Paul Ltd. Reprinted by permission of the author and the publisher.

The author (b. 1905) is Professor of Sociology, University of California, at Los Angeles. His writings have appeared in numerous professional journals. The family, housing and family living, and urban planning form his particular interests. Author: *The Modern City; Incestbrottei i Sverige.*

members of the community who—at work and play—are bound to each other by frequent social contacts.

In the large modern city of the United States, all these criteria were realized only in the flourishing immigrant neighbourhoods of the nineteenth century. Here, indeed, the village pattern of the old world was frequently transferred to urban residential sections in the new world. These immigrant neighbourhoods, however, were never successful in retaining their populations.

Successive waves of European and other nationality groups moved through the quasi-village environment of the American immigrant neighbourhood. In the process of urbanization, immigrant populations gradually lost themselves in the anonymous environment of other residential sections where they established themselves individually as members of the urban community at large without intermediate in-group loyalties. Since the cessation of large-scale immigration to the United States in 1924, these village-like immigrant communities have gradually evanesced. Some nationality groups moved to secondary settlements of higher status in a more Americanized, i.e., urbanized, environment; others lost control over their members in the younger generation who spread wide and far over the entire city.

Suburban real estate developments have attempted, at times, to provide their customers with an arrangement of construction that promised village comforts lost in the large city. With a village green and possibly a swimming-pool, a community centre or a country club in the middle of the settlement, and a protecting wall surrounding the entire area, these "guaranteed neighbourhoods" found their greatest advantage in the exclusion of others than the residential population from expensive recreational facilities. They promised protection against invasion by lower status groups. They guaranteed permanence of the family residence unendangered by the degrading influence of undesirable association.

Such village construction in the parkland of the dormitory suburb serves only the purpose of segregation without necessarily creating that overlapping and intertwining of economic and social interests in the resident group characteristic for true village structures. As a matter of fact, residential anonymity reaches its highest degree in the suburban settlement of advanced status groups. Neighbouring, in this environment, tends to be limited to the children as the only constant users of joint recreational facilities.

Rapid urban growth, of course, ensnares actual village communities in the orbit of urban extension, either at the periphery of the growing metropolis or in the midst of vast connurbations. Again, true village structures are lost as peasants and farmers turn into commuting city workers, as close economic interdependence fails to coincide with residential propinquity, and as the common interests of the residents are reduced to the private or consumption aspects of their lives.

Thus, while actual village structures are gradually being lost in the urban environment, the efforts of the planner point in the opposite direction. The planner endeavours to revive village structures in the city. He promotes a type of neighbourhood planning which by the arrangement of construction, by landscaping and by the provision of a full scope of services for purposes of everyday living, by visual separation of the area from adjacent territories and its orientation inwards towards the playground—and other recreational facilities offer the physical setting for the development of social relations typical for the village rather than the city. The reason for this anachronism lies in the attempt to stem the tide of social disorganization which—like delinquency, divorce, crime, suicide and vice—is attributed to the anonymity of urban living.

The planned neighbourhood in the city is considered a substitute for those informal means of social control assumed to keep the villager and the small town dweller in line, forcing him—through gossip, ridicule, contempt and ostracism—into the wholesome strait-jacket of provincial conformity. Two questions arise at this juncture:

1. Whether it is indeed these informal means of social control that keep the small town clean from undesirable symptoms of social disorganization, and

2. Whether the typical city dweller is susceptible to a transfer of these means of social control to the urban environment.

To both questions, our considered answer is "No."

Small town and village people are made to conform to socially approved behaviour by the inescapability of economic pressures. The overlapping of numerous economic as well as social relationships within a limited geographical area gives to even the most superficial of social contacts economic significance. Any displeasure aroused within the sphere of leisure-time activities might have economic repercussions. The people with whom financial negotiations are entertained are the same with whom the villager rubs elbows in his private life. If the minister's son steals apples, he might find that he did so in the orchard of that member of the congregation who decides about his father's reappointment. If the local grocer becomes negligent in his church attendance, a malicious whispering campaign may cost him a lot of patronage. Informal means of social control—such as gossip and spying upon each other—are certainly at work. But they could remain powerless were it not for the fact that they are backed up by economic pressures in an environment where confinement in space forces all residents either to buy from or sell to each other.

The low level of social disorganization in the non-urban environment does not necessarily reflect upon social controls in the village, the small town and the farm. Delinquents bent upon a criminal career sooner or later vanish from the small town environment and move to the city. They move because of economic pressures exerted upon them and their families. All non-conformists tend to withdraw from an environment in which their deviant behaviour is easily discovered. They move to the city where employment is not dependent upon the private conduct of the individual.

What are the chances for the transfer of these controls to the urban environment? Without proof to the contrary, we must be sceptical about their efficacy in the city. Even in the best-planned urban neighbourhood, economic pressures upon the private conduct of the individual are lacking. Whether informal social contacts by themselves will turn the trick of reducing deviant behaviour has yet to be shown. In the small town, the combination of economic with social contacts keeps the individual in line. This combination is absent from the urban neighbourhood planned for the private spheres of daily living only.

Even in leisure-time activities, the typical city dweller is not at all prone to limit himself to contacts with neighbours dwelling in close propinquity to his own home. Apart from very special situations such as recent arrival to the city with few pre-established personal or institutional contacts, or apart from special local conditions with numerous small children in families thus restricted in their movements, apart from such special situations the city dweller tends to take advantage of his unique privilege to roam far and wide in search of a select group of friends and select recreational facilities to serve his very special needs for entertainment and self-expression.

The "freedom of the city" is the freedom to choose from innumerable potential social contacts. Social contacts are not forced upon the city dweller on the basis of residential propinquity. It is doubtful that the city dweller will ever forego the privilege of association by choice. Under the circumstances, many planned neighbourhoods will never function as cohesive social units. The generous provision of park- and play-space within the confines of the planned neighbourhood may well be enjoyed as an unusual asset of the individual dwelling unit. Still, the neighbourhood and its facilities may fail to promote that experience of belonging which the planner—following the example of the village and the small town—tries to reproduce in the large city.

II. NEIGHBORING PATTERNS

To assess the city dweller's readiness to avail himself of the facilities provided in the conventional neighbourhood unit plan, we have to know about his propensity to "neighbour" under conditions of planned or unplanned urban environment. Such information is sorely lacking. Most neighbourhood planning has proceeded on the basis of foregone conclusions.

Experimental research about actual neighbourhood experiences has provided the author with two types of pertinent documentation. Family contact patterns were ascertained by way of interview in both Milwaukee and Madison, Wisconsin. In addition, students of the University of Wisconsin were induced to write about their individual neighbourhood experiences with the help of a Problem Guide. The materials so collected cover a wide range of actual neighbourhood experiences in communities of different size and families of different composition. No attempts were made to apply sampling methods that would have provided reliable conclusions. The intent of this research was truly "experimental." It was devised to produce that familiarity with a new field of investigation without which the formulation of pertinent hypotheses is impossible. The resultant conceptualization of the field of neighbourhood study appears on the following pages.

The empirical approach to our problem may concern itself with either

1. Neighbourhood consciousness, or
2. Neighbouring behaviour.

At closer scrutiny, neighbourhood consciousness reveals itself as an elusive phenomenon. Residents in a limited residential area of Milwaukee were asked what they considered "their" neighbourhood. Fifty-three out of 197 interviewees responded by pointing to an area of not more than a city block. Another 78 of the interviewees referred to an area of more than seven blocks. Obviously, these two groups did not have the same thing in mind when talking about their neighbourhood. Nearly all answers to this question were introduced with expressions of doubt such as "I don't know," "never thought about it," etc. These people were not only vague about the subject of discussion, but felt actually forced to make a choice between different types of experiences to which the term "neighbourhood" could be applied.

The neighbourhood may be considered as either a geographical or a social unit. As a geographical unit, the neighbourhood is considered a contiguous territory in which close neighbourly relations exist. As a social unit, the neighbourhood refers to social relations which may or may not pre-empt a contiguous city area. Neighbourhood consciousness as a social experience is subject to different interpretations.

WHAT DO YOU CONSIDER "YOUR" NEIGHBOURHOOD?

*(Responses from a residential environment
in the city of Milwaukee)*

One block or under	53
Two to three blocks	12
One square block	14
Three to six blocks	11
Two square blocks	13

Seven to ten blocks	20
Eleven to twenty blocks	21
Over twenty blocks	37
Whole city	2
Area outside neighbourhood	4
No neighbourhood	10

To consider the neighbourhood as a phenomenon anchored in the mind, rather than a phenomenon located in an area clearly delineated in space, a phenomenon resting in prevailing attitudes, customs and preferences, rather than a certain number of square miles of real estate, such shift in our thinking about the neighbourhood presents a departure from the customary approach. Uncritically, the neighbourhood has been discussed as a unit that combines both spatial and social characteristics. For purposes of analysis, we have to separate from each other the social and the spatial aspect of the phenomenon under observation. Only in this manner can we do justice to the practical problem that consists of placing these two aspects in best possible relationship to each other.

From the same urban environment, we receive most contradictory statements about neighbourhood experiences and neighbourhood activities prevailing in the area. The same residential area will be assessed very differently by people living at close distance from each other. More than that: neighbourhood experience is under the influence of individual dynamics. It does not change only from individual to individual but undergoes continuous changes in the individual life history. Neighbouring means something different at elementary-school age, at high-school age, at the age of family formation and in old age.

Furthermore, neighbourhood experiences may be associated by the same individual with different dimensions of social participation. Education and occupation, informal and organized leisure-time activities may lead to different clusters of social contacts which—rightly or wrongly— are referred to by the term "neighbourhood relations." These distinctions will stand out more clearly in our discussion of neighbouring behaviour.

If the existence of neighbourhood relations is to be based on overt behaviour, we must focus on behaviour that establishes social contact. We ask ourselves to what extent these social contacts remain confined to a contiguous city area. To make a "true" neighbourhood, one further condition would have to be satisfied. The neighbour—according to the history of the word—means literally near-dweller. Residential propinquity, therefore, is a necessary prerequisite to neighbourhood formation.

In the early cities of Western Civilization, residential propinquity led unavoidably to social interrelationship. In the farming environment, near-dwellers depended upon each other for help in emergency situations. City living diminished the exchange of mutual help among those living close to each other. In the city, distances were not such as to prohibit help from others than those living nearby in the large population settlement. Near-dwellers in the city were held together in the city by co-operative municipal function. Neighbourhood groups developed social cohesion by assuming collectively the responsibility for urban defence, water supply, fire protection, etc. In the course of the centuries since medieval city foundation, such responsibilities were gradually centralized and placed upon the shoulders of the urban community at large. Deprived of definite service functions, the urban neighbourhood retained only the loose bonds of informal social contacts which previously had flourished as adjuncts to decentralized urban self-government.

Even the informal social relations between neighbours in the city are withering away to-day. Many informal social relations take the city dweller far away from his family residence. The same is certainly true for formal social relations which carry the city dweller to the residential, commercial and industrial sections of town.

It is not necessary to demonstrate that the dormitory suburb is far removed from urban places of employment. It is more interesting to show that even such important functions as shopping and worship have been far removed from the range of what might properly be called a contiguous residential neighbourhood.

The extension of shopping relations beyond the confines of the residential neighbourhood is dependent upon new developments in urban food distribution. It is dependent upon improved storage facilities in the individual family home in the form of sizeable refrigerators or freeze lockers. It is dependent upon the availability of private motor-transportation. It is dependent, finally, upon the concentration of commercial food distribution in the hands of large chain-stores able to offer lower prices than the local grocery store. Weekly rather than daily shopping needs are carried beyond the confines of the individual neighbourhood. We venture to guess, however, that the volume of weekly shopping is continuously being enlarged at the cost of daily shopping. The long-term destiny of the local grocery store is easy to predict.

Worship is not necessarily confined within the residential neighbourhood. Due to prevailing heterogeneities, it takes more people than those living in easy walking distance from each other, to provide sufficient numbers for the operation of a church. Urban residential settlement is not based on denominational segregation. Consequently, church membership must reach out beyond spatial proximity to the individual church building. Those affiliated to a certain religious denomination are too sparsely settled in the urban fabric to draw desired facilities for worship close to all individual family homes.

Similar conditions prevail in other urban activities. If we consider all city contacts of the individual family, the limited importance of "neighbouring" becomes immediately apparent. The activity radius of the individual family extends over the entire city. The family picks and chooses from what the city has in store for it. In the process of choice, proximity to the family residence is obviously not the only principle of selection.

Still, family contacts are not spread at random over the entire urban fabric. They tend to cluster in characteristic patterns. . . .

.　.　.　.　.

Seen within this broader framework of family contact patterns, the urban "neighbourhood" appears as a special case within the pattern of selective contact clusters. It forms a selective contact cluster, with the added criterion of being contained in close proximity to the family residence. It becomes an empirical question, then, what contact terminals are—and under what conditions—contained close to the urban residence.

Our observations, then, reveal a phenomenon closely related to neighbouring although not identical with it: namely, the phenomenon of contact clusters established either close to the family home or close to any of the more important contact points in the city area. They are not neighbourhoods proper because this term cannot be divorced from the circumstance of "near-dwelling" or from "proximity to residential location." Different walking distance areas, not necessarily close to the family home, gain social significance for the city dweller.

Walking distance areas tend to be of either of the five following types:

1. Residential.
2. Occupational.
3. Educational.
4. Commercial.
5. Associational.

They shall be so designated according to the most frequent activity around which other contact points are clustered. In practice, an overlapping of several important activities within one and the same walking distance area will be the rule rather than the exception. The reason for the formation of such contact clusters is found in the ease of communication between one contact point and the others. It is invited also by the initiation of contacts due to chance of physical presence. The dentist close to the place of work and the ice-cream parlour close to the high school are most likely preferred to others in less accessible location. Different recreational facilities in close proximity to each other appeal to the same patronage.

In the course of the individual life cycle, the total contact pattern of the individual city dweller is subject to continuous change. Before the contact pattern reaches out to city areas far remote from the individual residence, and when they shrink again in old age, or as long as they are limited due to new arrival in the city, the "neighbourhood," i.e., the residential walking distance area, gains overwhelming importance by default. The pre-school child may be limited to contacts within the city block. The schoolchild branches out, and at high-school age, friendship and recreation and education pull the young city dweller out over a considerable section of the city. Occupational activities establish new clusters of contacts close to place of work. Shopping activities extend farther for adults and with the availability of private motor-transportation. Friendship established at work will open new contact areas for the individual city dweller in other residential areas than his own. Marriage and movements of friends and relatives and the city dweller himself furthermore extend and complicate the picture. In old age, the pattern is apt to shrink due to decreasing mobility and diminishing interests.

If the primary group is to be discovered as a socializing factor in the city environment, it will not necessarily have to be tied to the residential neighbourhood. Close and intimate contacts are established in those contact areas of the city which gain significance for the individual not only due to number of repetitive contacts and waking hours spent in this environment, but in addition due to the importance of different overlapping social contacts.

III. FROM NEIGHBORHOOD TO CITY PLANNING

Unfortunately, the endeavour to reactivate primary group relations in the large modern city has been tied to the assumption that such primary group relations are worth promoting only in the vicinity of the family home. Our thinking about social relations in the city has been dominated by the spatial dimension. A small town culture trait has thus been superimposed upon the urban environment. In the small town, the coincidence of intense social relations with proximity to the individual residence can be taken for granted. This need not be so in the city. In the city, man has gained the freedom of making social contacts with little regard to geographical distance.

The city offers opportunities to select social contacts from a large number of people and facilities gathered in the urban environment and connected by convenient and rapid means of transportation. These conditions permit the city dweller to pick and choose the social relations he wants to bother with. He does not find, like the small town dweller, the opportunities for personal and institutional contacts limited to the walking-distance area surrounding his living quarters. Social relations are not thrust upon him. He enjoys the freedom of choice.

City planning is needed in view of limitations in the urban transportation system. Transportation may be inconvenient or unduly time-consuming. For these reasons, the arrangement in space of different urban construction has to be carefully planned. Exclusive concentration upon neighbourhood planning, i.e., the planning of the walking-distance area around the individual family home, neglects those manifold opportunities which alone justify the urban way of life, which have led to city formation and which draw the farmer and the small town dweller into cityward migrations. One-sided attention to residential neighbourhood planning runs the danger of ignoring fundamental advantages that led to large population settlements in the first place. It clashes with the attitude of the typical city dweller who wants to roam within the entire urban fabric in search for occupational, educational, recreational and associational opportunities, assisted by an efficient system of transportation that releases him from the fetters of spatial confinement.

We have not yet freed ourselves, however, in thought and action, in scientific observation and planning, from domination by the spatial dimension. Preparatory to planning, urban sociology starts with the observation of "natural areas" in the urban environment and promotes the correction of minor inadequacies. The full scope of city planning invites the analysis not of urban environment as it has grown at random. It challenges the social scientist and the planner to deal with more elementary data. These data may be found in individual and family contact needs.

Such contact needs may reach out for either informal or formal personal relations. By and large, informal personal relations call for the proximity of certain residential units to each other. Formal personal relations, on the other hand, are tied to and carried out within commercial and public urban construction. For planning purposes, we have therefore to ascertain

1. The spread of family contact patterns in the city.
2. The service radius of commercial and public facilities in the city.

The purpose of functional city planning can be no other than to relate to each other family contact needs and the service areas of commercial and public facilities. They have to be related to each other in such a manner as to minimize inconvenient and time-consuming transportation.

In a well-structured urban environment services and people must be related to each other in an economical manner. Optimal conditions can be obtained by the promotion of walking-distance areas which tend to grow out of individual adjustments to the urban environment anyway. In terms of urban construction, such walking-distance areas require the clustering of commercial and public construction. Such groupings of urban construction cannot be called "neighbourhoods" because most of them will be located at longer than walking distance from the majority of family residences which they serve. These walking-distance areas have one thing in common, however, with our concern for urban neighbourhoods. They establish walking-distance areas at some maximum distance from the city residence. Here they are contained in walking distance from each other, albeit not in walking distance from the residences of most city dwellers. The city planner must concern himself with the relative desirability of different possible clusterings of commercial and public facilities in the urban environment.

The service radius of urban facilities is not entirely a matter of choice and desired convenience. If it were so, every city dweller would want to have *all* services located either next door or—if they entail nuisances—at close distance hidden by a pleasant group of trees. To provide for the satisfaction of such needs is economically impossible. To operate economically, with a profit or at reasonable cost, all urban services demand recruitment areas of different size from which to draw their clientele. The more specialized the type of service, the fewer the people who avail themselves of the service at all, and the less frequently they will make use of the service, the larger the service area will have to be.

To establish walking-distance areas in the city environment, the city planner is charged with the task of combining into a cluster of construction commercial and public facilities dependent upon service areas of equal size. A number of concentric service areas will thus be made to overlap. With increasing specialization of service, ever larger areas will be required to provide sufficient patronage. The deciding factor for the combination of some and not other services is the service radius of these facilities, which also determines the distance at which these service clusters will have to be located from each other to operate efficiently.

While a well-structured urban environment may thus be planned for, an environment that does not leave any service loopholes in the urban fabric and meets the demand for "walking-distance areas" at varying distances from the city residence, the need for informal personal relations is thereby not considered. Informal social relations call for proximity to each other of those residences the occupants of which want to associate frequently, at a minimum of inconvenience and time spent.

The scope of neighbourhood planning becomes apparent if it is realized that either of two conditions must be fulfilled to encourage the city dweller to limit his informal associations to near-dwellers. The city dweller must be either:

1. Willing to limit the majority of his leisure-time activities to association with those people who live by chance next door or in easy walking distance, i.e., he must be void of personal or activity interests that will draw him to some other location, leaving the planned neighbourhood without social function; or he must be

2. Willing to congregate within the residential neighbourhood with like-minded and like-interested people, i.e., he and his friends must stand

ready to move to put life into well-planned neighbourhood construction.

Such conditions are the exception in the modern city. It is doubtful, therefore, that even a semblance of village life will find acceptance in the modern metropolis.

77. THE STRANGEST PLACE
IN CHICAGO *

JOHN BARTLOW MARTIN

Sometimes a purely descriptive piece of writing brings to life with startling impact ideas that otherwise seem dull and mechanical, commonplace, or meaningless. In this article John Bartlow Martin performs such a feat. He never uses the social science terms "invasion," "succession," or "segregation." He does not discuss rentals, slum areas as such, city planning, race discrimination in its varied aspects. He simply describes a building in its physical aspects, its locale, the life that goes on there, and the differences between that place years ago and the time when he was writing (the building has subsequently been torn down). He makes it live for us. Invasion and succession! That's what happened here!

From the Chicago loop, where sunlight off the lakefront strikes the shining towers, State Street runs straight south, wide, busy with street-cars and heavy trucks. Quickly the buildings get shabby—little stores selling auto parts, a junkyard crammed with rusting wreckage. The city is harsh: concrete streets, brick building walls, black steel viaducts. Beyond 22nd Street the faces of the people are black. This is the South Side Negro section. Here the street is quieter, the sun is hazy and dirty and pale, the sky is a network of trolley wires. Across an expanse of new-turned earth stretches a new public housing project, with a play-yard for the children, and at 32nd Street begins the new campus of the Illinois Institute of Technology, sleek brick-and-glass buildings sur-

---

The author (b. 1915) is a journalist. Writer of real-crime articles for *Saturday Evening Post* and *Harper's*. His article "The Blast in Centralia No. 5" was a piece of masterful reporting. Author: *Call It North Country: The Story of Upper Michigan; Indiana: An Interpretation; Butcher's Dozen and Other Murders; My Life in Crime; Why Did They Kill; Break Down the Walls.*

rounded by new trees and new grass. And just beyond the Institute rises a great gray hulk of brick, four stories high, topped by an ungainly smokestack, ancient and enormous, filling half the block north of 34th Street between State and Dearborn. It is the Mecca Building.

Let us note its setting. Across State Street are a cleaning shop, a barber shop, a grocery, the Railroad Men's Social Club, McClain's Hair Goods, a Bar-B-Q, the office of H. Young the Icer, the Church of God & Saints of Christ in an old storefront. An old man pulls a handcart filled with junk across an empty lot. From a deep hole tunneled under the sidewalk emerges the head of a little Negro boy, playing. The sidewalk is cracked and broken. Nearby are rickety wooden tenements.

The Mecca Building is U-shaped. The dirt courtyard is littered with newspapers and tin cans, milk cartons and broken glass. Pigeons roost on a car on blocks. A skinny white dog huddles in a doorway. Iron fire escapes run up the building's face and ladders reach from them to the roof. There are four main entrances, two on Dearborn and two on State Street. At each is a gray stone threshold and over each is carved "The Mecca." The Mecca was constructed as an apartment building in 1891, a splendid palace, a showplace of Chicago. Today it is still an apartment building and a showplace but of a very different sort. It has become one of the most remarkable Negro slum exhibits in the world. Let us pass through the arched doorway of the Mecca; let us see what the Mecca looks like inside, see who the people in it are and how they live, whence they came and why they stay.

Inside, a powerful odor assails the visitor at once, musty, heavy, a smell compounded of urine and stale cooking and of age, not necessarily an unpleasant odor but a close powerful one, which, like that of marijuana, once smelled is never forgotten. The stone slab step is hollowed. The lower part of the walls of the vestibule once was covered with marble but now the marble has been stripped away in ragged patches, revealing naked brick and mortar. It is dark here. Ahead stretches a corridor; it is like a tunnel, it seems endless and it is indeed a block long, running all the way to the Dearborn Street entrance; down its whole length hang only five light bulbs, glowing feebly in the gloom. Tan paint is peeling from the wall, the doors of apartments open into the corridor. This is the base of the U in the U-shaped building.

The arms of the U are identical. They are great halls, each lit by a skylight four stories overhead which, because of the dirt that has accumulated on the glass through years of neglect, admits the kind of unreal light found underseas. This light slants down in great long angling shafts filled with floating dust, shifting as the sun moves across the sky, falling in fitful patches on the floor. Around the walls run three balconies guarded by ornate wrought-iron grillwork, and off these balconies open the doors to the apartments, like tiers of cells in a prison cellblock. The floor in the center of the well is of hardwood, splintered now, and beneath the balconies it is of tile, broken in many places. A janitor with a wheelbarrow is slowly patching the tile with concrete; his shovel makes a rasping, scraping sound. From somewhere in the building comes always the sound of distant human voices—women talking, a baby squalling, children screaming, men muttering, no words distinguishable. Spittle splats flatly on the tile floor, falling from a great height, spat by a man or a woman standing on an upper balcony. All day long people stand at the balconies, leaning on the wrought-iron railings with hands clasped out over them, gazing out at other people facing them across the well in silence, gazing down at the floor far below, spitting, small human figures in a vast place, two or three on each of the four floors, occasionally calling back and forth to one another but most of the time just standing silent. The building is never entirely quiet, not even very late at night, since so many people live here; but it is so vast that it seems quiet, even amid uproar.

In the center on the ground floor is a long narrow bank of mailboxes, tarnished brass, 176 of them. One has thirteen names on it, including seven different family names, indicating that thirteen adults expecting mail occupy that particular apartment. Late in the morning the postman comes, a man in blue. Three tenants wait respectfully at the side while he distributes the mail. On the balcony above, two men leaning on the railing watch him critically. "He'll never get it all done doing it one at a time," and, "He's a new man." At last he finishes, and tenants emerge from their apartments to get their mail. From a high balcony a toddler throws a chunk of broken tile; it bounces on the floor by the mailboxes. A stooped old woman wearing a black sweater and black shawl, only her hair and her eyeballs white, moves slowly and painfully in the shadows beneath the balcony, keeping close to the wall as long as possible, touching it with bony fingers, and only leaving it when she must to venture across the open floor to the mailboxes; gets her mail, then retreats along the wall to the stairs, where a man steps aside, saying kindly, "You come down to see what you got, didn't you?" and she says, in a gasping voice, "I'm going take my good time," then begins to ascend, pulling herself up by the railing, first her right foot up one step, then the left slowly after it, her body bent so low that her face almost touches the next step, stopping at the landing to rest and stare at the peeling walls with watery, half-blind eyes. Near the mailboxes three children are jumping rope, using a doubled rope, two boys swinging the two long strands in sweeping arcs while a girl rocks to and fro at one side to get into the rhythm before jumping in. Children ride battered tricycles across the floor, safe here from the traffic of the streets. On a balcony children are playing store, using a cardboard box. One of them throws a fistful of paper over the railing and it flutters down: policy slips, there must be a policy station here.

The wind blows in off Dearborn Street and a young woman neat in black enters, walking a leashed dog and humming a hymn. Somewhere a child is crying over and over, "Mummy, Mummy." In the long dark corridor a dog is nosing at garbage from an upset garbage can. From somewhere comes a clatter, perhaps of a falling garbage-can lid, and the high mad cackling laughter of an old man. A very young child standing on the third floor balcony urinates through the ornate iron grillwork and the urine falls to the ground floor far below and a woman calls to him, "Don't you do that, you got no right to do that, I'm going to tell your mother." The ice man comes wearing a leather protector on his shoulder and back, carrying a cake of ice that gleams whitely against his black face and hat. A woman calls from the third floor, "Bring fifty pounds to 304½," and he plods to the stairs.

In the shadows against a pillar marked with match-strikes leans a man, his shirt-collar buttoned but without a necktie, his hat-brim slanting low over his scarred face, a cigarette slanting from his mouth; he is just standing there watching. How many people live here? He laughs. "I don't know." Two thousand? "Oh, more than that. There's 176 apartments and some of 'em's got seven rooms and they're all full." A heavy round-faced man in a long white apron holding a ball-peen hammer approaches: "You are visiting some of the historic sites of the city? You found one all right. If it don't fall in on you while you're lookin'." How many people live here? "That," he says, "is a mystery. You'll find them sleeping in bathtubs, sleeping in the kitchen under the sink, anywhere they can sleep." Nobody, in truth, knows how many people inhabit the Mecca Building. The janitor, Jimmy Sanders, estimates 2,300; the Democratic precinct captain, William Patrick Fitzgerald, who has lived here eighteen years, estimates 1,400; the owner doesn't know. All the inhabitants except one woman are Negroes. The Mecca Building contains more people than most Chicago precincts; indeed, it constitutes a precinct in itself, the 27th Precinct of the 2nd Ward.

On the third floor an old woman stands by the railing, a towel wound round her head, a big gold ring on her finger. Watching dispassionately as children run in from school for lunch, their screams ringing piercingly through the building, she says judiciously, "That size runs to roller skates," and then, "When I first came here they used to control the children. White people hadn't been gone so long, 1917 it was. They used to have a policeman here nights, you could hear a needle drop. Now they's shooting here five times a night. Them young men and the young girls is the worst. I'd move out tonight if they'd find me a house. I moved out for a while once but I came back to have company, my daughter lives here and my granddaughter was born here," and she turns and shuffles into her flat.

In the flat, wallpaper hangs from the walls in great sheets. Clean newspapers are spread on the floor. Over the dresser are some artificial flowers, and a transparent plastic wrapper covers the bed. The sideboard, radio, and table are cluttered with family photographs. Mottoes and pictures hang on the walls, a picture of Jesus Christ and a crucifix put out by a liquor store, a plaque, "My Help cometh from the Lord," and also secular shrines: a large frame holding the pictures of Abraham Lincoln and Frederick Douglass flanked by Booker T. Washington, Paul Laurence Dunbar, W. E. B. DuBois, and other race leaders. And a framed faded campaign picture of Franklin D. Roosevelt. She calls Lincoln "Abraham." She was born in Alabama. She is bent and stooped, aged. She says, "I live here all by myself, me and my Lord," and then, as her visitor departs, she touches his arm and says gently, "Do you know anything about that man we call Jesus, do you know him personally, you ought to get in touch with him." Outside her door a teen-age boy is standing at the balcony railing, trying to spit clear across to the other side.

In the long first-floor corridor the janitor passes, Jimmy, a short squat man in a leather cap and jacket, ambling along with a Yankee drill in his hand. "I'm the maintenance man," he says. "I do a little of everything—work a little, fight a little, sleep a little, play a little." Right now he is accompanying the rent collector, a white man, a wiry Scot named John. "I go around with him," Jimmy says, shifting the stub of his dead cigar to the other corner of his mouth, "because the young fellas in the building think he's got money with him." About a year ago the young fellows robbed an insurance collector of $17. The rent collector, John, says, "I lost all my hair fighting with these people," and laughs. Actually, he has little trouble collecting rents, which are cheap. His troubles are of a different sort: he and Jimmy fight a hopeless rearguard action against decay and vandalism. "Last night they shot out the light bulbs," says Jimmy. "And the windows—in the last year I bet I put in over two hundred windows. They break 'em fast as you put 'em in." Who does it? "Outsiders, most of it. And the kids here. The kids get to playin' and throwin' at one another and first thing you know they break the glass. There's nothin' you can do about it. You can't kill one 'cause he broke the glass."

As the rent collector walks along, a woman calls from the third-floor balcony, "Hold your head up, John, John, hold your head up, I want to talk to you," but John plods on, grinning secretly. A sign by the basement stairs reads, "Put All Complaints in Mail Box." Near the State Street entrance another janitor has temporarily left his job of cementing a broken place in the floor and is stooping over at an apartment door, digging with a knife at something in the door. He gets it out: a bullet. "That's a thirty-eight," he says, turning it over in his hand, shiny and twisted. Then, to a woman who has come to the door, "They try to shoot you out last night?" She laughs. "Yeh, try to kill me. Like shootin' rabbits in a swamp down yonder." He says, "They was really shootin' here last night. Some of 'em shootin' for fun, some of 'em fightin'. That's every night around here. Couple of 'em got shot the other night." Any ever killed? "Oh, yes, one got killed summer before last up there in that corner," pointing upward. Why? "I don't know."

Down the stairs comes a man on crutches, his left leg off above the knee, his pants leg pinned up, coming down the steps, the crutch and his good leg visible first, then the man, thin, wearing white pants and a brown coat and hat; he walks diagonally past the mailboxes to the grocery, pausing to adjust his pipe.

High on the fourth west gallery, close up under the skylight, the balcony seems narrow. Two boys wrestle on it, and one falls heavily against the iron railing, which trembles but holds firm. It is four stories down to the ground floor; nobody ever heard of a child falling. An old woman is sweeping the floor. High up here at the north end a dozen young men and women are congregated, well-dressed, two of the men off to one side leaning idle on the railing and peering sullenly down, the others close together, laughing, fooling around with each other, the girls in tight white sweaters, the young men in snapbrim hats and suitcoats over sweaters.

. . . . .

When the Mecca Building was constructed it was considered one of the largest and finest apartment buildings in Chicago if not in America. It catered (almost needless to say) to a white clientele. But after 1900 the Negro migration to Chicago forced the black belt to expand, and by 1912 the Mecca Building was the home of the Negro elite—doctors, lawyers, business men.

A woman who lives there still, Mrs. Florence Clayton, arrived in 1916, and she remembers, "There were carpets on the stairs and halls. There were goldfish in the fountain. On the first floor there were lounge chairs and outdoors we had a flower garden and beautiful trees and green grass, you could go out there, oh, it was lovely. The courtyard was all fenced in and there was a lovely walk through the flowers."

The building started to deteriorate during the 1917–18 war. So did the whole neighbourhood. Booming war industries pulled thousands of Negroes to Chicago. The luckier ones abandoned the region of 35th and State to the poor and the wicked. The black-and-tans where Chicago jazz flowered were right here. Jimmy, the janitor, recalls, "There were lots of fights and cuttings. Building was full of prostitutes. I saw a man throw a prostitute over the third floor railing—from the third floor to the first floor. Didn't hurt her much. She only weighed ninety pounds, kind of light. Finally one of the pimps killed the building watchman. Did it over a woman. And she wasn't even living with him." Jimmy pushes his leather cap back off his forehead. "That about ended it, though. They got a new watchman and he was a killer. He was just a little man but he had great big eyes and he'd shoot you with either hand. He had a cemetery of his own before he died. He only killed nine people—between the basement here and that wire fence. The building got kind of decent after that—families, working people."

And then the Depression came along, and the wicked left, and almost none but the poor remained. The Depression was awful in the black belt. About 1932 the bottom fell out. One woman who lived here then recalls, "The building was partly empty. One lady told me she was sitting down on the curb and the police passed and it was cold and they asked her what was the matter and she said she'd been set out and they told her to come on in here and the first flat she'd find, sit down. They carried her to court later but they didn't make her get out, they couldn't, people had no work to do then. It was always warm and nice in here during the Depression."

The Depression accounts for the presence today of the building's only white tenant, a heavy, soft-faced, white-haired woman of sixty-six. "I'd been a housekeeper at a hotel and one of my maids, a colored girl, she was married to a white doctor and they lived here in the Mecca Building. I couldn't find a job, I just got stuck, I couldn't make it, and they took me in." Some of the Mecca inhabitants who moved in while they were on relief are now earning good money in the steel mills or on Pullman cars and one or two earn upward of $5,000 a year, but they are imprisoned here by the scarcity of dwellings for Negroes. A few of the long-time tenants remain by choice, oddly proud of the building. A few earn money by living there—they sublet rooms in their apartments for as much as $12 a week. The janitor Jimmy says, "Every day people come in, many as ten or twelve a day, lookin' for a place, they been walkin' the street, lookin' for some place to go, say, 'Janitor, if you can get me an apartment in here I'll give you $100,' but there ain't none."

There are several women's clubs in the building, such as the Old-Age Pensioners Club and the Twelve Tribes. Fitzgerald, the Democratic precinct captain, has been elected sweetheart of these. Fitzgerald, a neat, well-dressed, youngish man, has said, "If there's a weddin' I'm there, if there's a death I'm there, if there's a birth I'm there. I had a baby born in my car a while back, trying to get the mother to the hospital." Fitzgerald is a court bailiff by day. The Mecca precinct has voted Democratic since 1932. Like the other tenants, Fitzgerald worries about the children. "In summertime the police chase them off the street. One day I come home and the police had backed up a wagon ready to take a whole load to the station for standing in front of the building. I had to put a stop to it. I had three ball clubs last summer and got uniforms for 'em all."

In a vacant store on the ground floor is the Mecca Center, for children. Nobody knows how many children are being raised in the Mecca Building but most people guess five hundred, and now at 4:30 P.M. on a Thursday fifteen of the five hundred are in the Mecca Center. The Center is a big square bare room, a dais at one side, a great clutter of dusty newspapers behind a desk, a piano and a windup Victrola against one wall, a tom-tom and Indian heads in the display window. Two older boys are playing Ping-pong and at a small table two younger ones are playing checkers but the rest of the younger ones, probably from nine to twelve years old, are chasing each other around the room, snapping cap-guns at each other, and soon the checker game stops and all thirteen of the younger ones are chasing each other, climbing over tables and chairs, leaping through the air onto each others' backs, screaming wildly; the Ping-pong players, older, proceed with their game, each with an arm outstretched to fend off the littler kids, occasionally pausing to take a cut at a near one's head; a dozen chairs stacked against a wall collapse as a boy's body crashes into them. A man in a hat is standing in a corner watching, saying vaguely, "She was supposed to come and be a musical program but I ain't seen her come in."

On the wall is a program schedule allotting various hours of the week to such activities as "Teen-Age Club," "Children's Story-Telling Hour," "Parents' Club Meeting." Right now, it is "Children's Game Period." The man watching says sharply, "You—let that Victrola alone," to a boy climbing onto it in order to leap onto another boy's back. A woman arrives bustling in. "I teach music and dramatics and folk dancing. I have about sixty enrolled. From six to eight we have singing and at nine physical culture and clubs." She is taking off her gloves, as unmindful of the children as they are of her; the children are growing more serious in their play, the temper has changed, ugliness has crept in, they battle silently, not laughing or screaming, only panting hard. The man is making plans to take some of them to the circus.

In one apartment in the building a woman and her husband are raising nine children, raising them in one room. This summer afternoon she is sitting in a chair by the door of the one room, her baby on the bed, evidently asleep but looking dead it is so thin and still, and the mother is saying, "It is hot at night, at night you burn up. My husband and I sleep in the bed. The kids sleep on the cot." The nine kids. They are from nine months to fifteen years in age. The room is eight feet by eleven. In it are one bed, one davenport, one radio, one light bulb, one picture, two straight wood chairs, one wicker table (on which stand a seashell, a jar of deodorant, and a can of face powder), one calendar. Back of the bed is a closet curtained with a rag. One necktie hangs on a nail in the wall. The plaster is broken. Her husband earns $45 a week as a machine operator. They pay $6 a week for this room. They have lived in this room four years.

The mother is twenty-nine years old. When she and her husband first came to Chicago they lived in one room on Wentworth Avenue, then in three rooms on Prairie Avenue until "the lady sold the building," then in five rooms elsewhere on Prairie Avenue again "till the lady sold the building," then in four rooms elsewhere on Prairie "till the man sold the building," then here. They came here on August 6, 1946. "My husband knew the man that had this apartment so he let us have a place in it that same evening. We were out on the street." They can find no other place to live. "I looked so much that I'm just disgusted about it. They say you're a citizen of Chicago and on votin' day they're right up to your door to vote. My husband, he wrote to the Mayor of Chicago and everyone else and I don't see no results," and she rises and fumbles behind a curtain on the window ledge and finds two letters. She is young, quick-moving, pretty; her teeth flash and she wears big gold earrings and she appears about the age of her oldest daughter, fifteen, who now comes in and stands in the doorway looking reproachful. One letter is a long form letter from the Chicago Housing Authority:

"Dear Friend,

". . . The housing projects now in operation have such lengthy waiting lists that no additional applications are being taken at this time. . . ." The other is a personal letter from a Housing Authority official: "Mayor Kennelly has referred to us for reply your letter of March 2, concerning your need for adequate housing. We are very sorry."

"All this stuff's just a racket," says the mother of nine. "They ain't doing nothing about it. Makes me sick." She hitches her chair around to face the wall. "After all, my husband works and makes an honest livin' and he do support his family the best that a workin' man can. His children do get clothes, the onliest kick that they can have is that they don't have no place to live. And that's not his fault." The baby on the bed stirs a little, then lies still again.

Until 1941 the Mecca Building was owned by a New York estate. The janitor Jimmy only once saw a representative of the estate. In 1941 the estate sold the Mecca to its next-door neighbor, the Illinois Institute of Technology. The Institute bought the building for only one purpose: to tear it down. The Institute was expanding its campus in accordance with a neat plan integrated with the neat plans of numerous other agencies for clearing the South Side slums. It wanted to replace the

Mecca Building with a laboratory. But its plans ran head-on into an important need of the people who dwelt in the Mecca Building, the need for a place to live.

For nine years it has tried to evict them, taking them to court and warning them the Mecca is a firetrap. Thus far the tenants have managed to generate enough political pressure to stay. Recently, when the Institute again started eviction proceedings, State Senator C. C. Wimbish, a lawyer who has represented the tenants in court, said, "If they try to put these people out, they'll have a race riot down there on State Street and I intend to make it as tense as possible. Any roof is better than no roof."

It is quiet in the building on a summer morning, quiet as a tomb. Spit falls flatly on the ground floor, spat by a silent watcher high on the balcony, and in a dark corner recess on the topmost floor a young girl, pretty, wearing a tight white sweater, strains against a young man leaning on the wall. An old man in blue pajamas, his eyes wild and staring, his body very thin, totters along, clutching at the railing, saying in a high, cracked voice, to a visitor, "Call me a telephone number please, mister, will you call me a telephone number," but a large woman steps from a doorway and shakes her head at the visitor, making circling motions beside her temple, and moves to take the old man's arm, and seeing her he starts, as though to run, then weeps, and she leads him away. A puff of blue smoke hangs in the dead air on the second balcony where a man is leaning on the railing, smoking. A janitor collects garbage in a cart that rumbles on the broken tile like a tumbril. Everything echoes in the halls, voices are hard to comprehend, are confused with distant sounds.

A visitor twists the bell on Mrs. Griffin's apartment and she calls, "Who is it?" then unfastens the chain. Her mother is sitting by the window in the sun, as always. Mrs. Griffin says that when she got the most recent notice to vacate, she went house-hunting: "I found a place to buy at a real estate office way up on the North Side but no other colored people live right there, and I don't want to get bombed on," as indeed many Chicago Negroes have been when they tried to leave the black belt. She goes over beside her mother, who is rocking. "I think this housing situation is terrible, it's all politics, that's all. I'm not mad at the school. It's their property, we know that. I'm mad 'cause all this politics. Put 'em in office and they didn't did nothin'. They build streets and superhighways and recreation—not houses. They should turn that money loose and stop it—people has got to have some place to live. They gonna do *anything* if they don't."

She laughs, but does not sound amused: "They say they gonna place us somewhere. *Place* us! I don't wanta be placed anywhere myself. They might place me in some mudhole somewhere and I never did live in that," and she laughs again. Her mother mutters something. "I don't know what they going to do with us. After all, there's no use in pushing us around from one place to another, that's no way to live." And then, after a pause, "It's all so mean."

Her mother, rocking, has started muttering steadily; she is looking out the window, her head in its white lace cap bobbing gently up and down. What is Mrs. Griffin going to do?

"I don't know. I'll have to have a place for my mother. I couldn't tell you what I'm going to do, to save my neck." Her mother, rocking, begins to mutter louder, but her words are not intelligible, it is just a human voice, muttering, and it is impossible to tell whether in anger or in joy, it is only sound.

78. THE SUBURBAN DISLOCATION *

DAVID RIESMAN

A number of factors—automobiles, expressways, and higher per capita incomes, for example—have made it possible for more and more urbanites to live in suburbs rather than in large, central cities. This change in home location has profound implications for many aspects of the American way of life. As David Riesman indicates in this selection, people's relationships to one another are different in the suburb from those in the city. These different relationships, in turn, mean that suburbanites will have or develop attitudes toward child rearing, educational systems, politics, religious expression, and the like, that are not the same as those found among the inhabitants of central cities. What changes will occur if, with the development of wider highways, more powerful cars, helicopters, and air-foil vehicles, we move still farther from the center of our large cities? Or, what will happen to "suburban values" if urban redevelopment encourages suburbanites to begin moving back to the central city?

. . . The suburbs have become so characteristic of life "among democratic nations" that some of our most acute social observers in the post-World War II years have seen in them the shape of the egalitarian future. . . . Yet this is impression, based on a few soundings in a few

* From "The Suburban Dislocation," by David Riesman, *The Annals* of The American Academy of Political and Social Science, Vol. 314 (November, 1957), 123–146. Reprinted by permission of the publisher and of the author.
For a biographical sketch of the author see selection 26.

perhaps strategic and surely highly visible locations. We know very little about the relatively settled suburbs, especially those leapfrogged by the waves of post-World War II growth; and so far as I can see we know almost nothing about the suburbs (old or new) surrounding the smaller cities. The new developments which have altered the physical and moral landscape so strikingly may betoken a trend or a blind alley. They may fascinate us out of our contemporary fears for the loss of liberty and individuality; and intellectuals, seldom unambivalent about the suburbs —whether or not they make them their own domiciles—may generalize from them too readily to middle-class life and leisure as a whole. . . .

The city is not necessarily the seat of urbanism, and the suburban way differs from the city way only at the polarities of each and is based on variables not entirely dependent on ecology or visible from a heli-copter. Hence . . . investigations do support the common-sense observa-tion that can find suburban styles in many cities and urban ones in many suburbs; that an urban fringe is growing which is neither country nor city nor quite bedroom suburb in the older mode.

If this is so, then it means that the differences which divide Amer-icans today depend less and less on where one lives, what one does, or who one is in terms of lineage, but more and more it depends on style and social character.

. . . . .

. . . For millions of suburbanites, their post-World War II experience has been prosperous and open far beyond their depression-born expecta-tions. For them, the suburbs have been one vast supermarket, abundantly and conveniently stocked with approved yet often variegated choices. The children are less of a worry there than on city streets; the neighbors often more friendly than those city folk who "keep themselves to them-selves"; life in general is more relaxed. The confidence such people often have that things will continue to go well for them is revealed in the story told one journalist in a Southern California suburb where employ-ment depends on nearby defense plants. When he asked people what would happen to them in case of a depression or cancellation of defense contracts, they answered: "Why then the government will stockpile cars." Life on credit has worked out well for many such home owners, allow-ing them to have their children young and in circumstances far better than those in which they themselves grew up. Whatever the outsider might say about the risks blithely taken, with no allowance made for personal or social setbacks, or about the anemic quality of the relaxed life or its complacency, he would have to admit that such first-generation suburbanites have found the taste of abundance pleasant and, for the younger ones with wages rising faster than prices, not notably prob-lematic.

. . . . . .

LIFE AND WORK VALUES

. . . When, a few years ago, I studied interviews done with several hundred college seniors at twenty representative universities, asking them what they would like or expect to be doing in fifteen years, I was struck by the fact that the great majority planned to live in the suburbs. They expected to be married, and in describing their prospective spouses they hoped for what we might call station-wagon types: educated, companionable, civic-minded, and profoundly domestic. There were few who recognized some incompatability between focus on suburban life and focus on big-city ambitions (for instance, a senior who wanted to go into advertising, yet not live in or near New York). They were—with some exceptions especially among the Southerners—willing to sacrifice the heights of achievement, though not the plateaus of the luxury economy, in favor of their goals of suburban domesticity and peace. Those who hailed originally from the suburbs suffered from no disenchantment and wanted to return to them—often to the same one—while both city-bred and small-town boys also preferred the suburbs. I assume that some of the latter in an earlier day would have wanted to leave Main Street behind and make their mark in the big city, whatever lingering agrarian fears and suspicions of it they still harbored. The city today, for many, spells crime, dirt, and race tensions, more than it does culture and opportunity. While some people still escape from the small town to the city, even more people are escaping from the city to the suburbs.

The succeessful book and movie, *The Man in the Grey Flannel Suit*, dramatizes these values quite explicitly. The hero chooses unromantic suburban cosiness, with (in the movie version) a not altogether inspiring wife and progeny, in preference to a high-pressure but potentially exciting business opportunity. The head of the business is portrayed as having destroyed his family life and as virtually alienated from all human contact. Very likely, some of his junior executives would describe the company as a "mink-lined rattrap," thus explaining and justifying their withdrawal of affect from the work itself, while recognizing that they are still competitive. A recent fragmentary survey presents evidence that managers are less satisfied with their work even than unskilled workers, and it is conceivable that the middle-class occupations in general will soon be regarded as sources of funds and of periodic contacts and activity, much as the working-class occupations are now largely regarded. If work loses its centrality, then the place where it is done also comes to matter less, and the access to variety in work that the central city provides may also come to matter less. Indeed, so much is this the case already that advertising for engineers in *Scientific American* and in trade journals looks more and more like the vacation advertising in *Holiday*. Minneapolis-Honeywell offers seasons and skiing as a counter-lure to the aircraft and electronic suburbs of the Far West. In this regimen, white-collar and blue-collar move towards one another, as each group now emphasizes the consumption aspects of life.

SUBURBAN WAY OF LIFE

This life, as just indicated, is increasingly focused on the suburbs which, since World War II, have grown so in quantity as to change their quality. For, although upper-class and upper-middle-class people have lived in the suburbs of our great cities since the 1880's or earlier, the cities before World War II still retained their hegemony: They engrossed commercial, industrial, and cultural power. The city represented the division and specialization not only of labor but of attitude and opinion: By discovering like-minded people in the city, one developed a new style, a new little magazine, a new architecture. The city, that is, provided a "critical mass" which made possible new combinations—criminal and fantastic ones as well as stimulating and productive ones. Today, however, with the continual loss to the suburbs of the elite and the enterprising, the cities remain big enough for juveniles to form delinquent subcultures, but barely differentiated enough to support cultural and educational activities at a level appropriate to our abundant economy. The elite, moreover, tend to associate with like-income neighbors rather than with like-minded civic leaders, thus dispersing their potential for leadership beyond township boundaries. Ironically, these people sometimes choose to live in communities which might be almost too manageable if millions of others did not simultaneously make the same choice.

Indeed, the suburbs are no longer simply bedroom communities but increasingly absorb the energies of the men as well as the women and children. The men, that is, are not simply being good providers while still attached to the values of the industrial system: They are seekers after the good life in the suburbs on their own account. Early marriage and the rise in the birth rate are so many rivulets of individual, only barely self-conscious protest against the values inherited from industrialism and the low-birth-rate middle-class metropolis—so many decisions to prefer companionship in the present to some distant goal, and so many mortgages of the future in the benevolent shadow of the luxury economy and its escalator of slow inflation, promotion, and protection. Whereas men once identified themselves with commerce and industry—with its power, its abstractions, its achievements—and forced women to remain identified with domesticity—save for those women who broke through the barrier and became man-imitating career girls—now, as many observers have pointed out, a growing homogenization of roles is occurring.

Women take jobs to support the suburban menage periodically while men take part in its work (do-it-yourself), its civic activities (Parent-Teachers Association, and so on), and its spirit. Rather than delegating religion to their womenfolk, men go to church in increasing numbers, occasionally as in an earlier day to be respectable or to climb socially, and occasionally out of a genuine religious call, but more typically because the church, like the high school and the country club, has become a center for the family as a social and civic unit.

DECENTRALIZATION OF LEISURE

All this brings with it an increasing decentralization of leisure. Just as the suburban churches tend, within the boundaries of the "three faiths," to an amiable syncretism, ignoring doctrinal or liturgical differences, so too the other leisure activities of the suburbs tend to reduce the specialized differentiations possible in a metropolis. What I mean here can be illustrated with reference to music. A metropolis has enough music lovers to organize highly differentiated groups: Mozart lovers may split off from Bach lovers and would never encounter lovers of Wagner, while in the suburbs the music lovers—if they are to support communal activities at all—must in some measure homogenize their tastes and hence create a local market for "classical music." Indeed, they will be exposed to a good deal of community pressure to support the musical activities of their friends in return for having their own enterprises supported. The same holds, *pari passu*, for the other arts— just as it does for the differentiation of specialty stores, churches, and museums found in a large city. By the same token, the suburban activist can feel that his own contribution matters, as he would likely feel in the big city only when he is very rich, very active, or very influential. People brought up in the suburbs may not realize what they are missing, and they may relate their emotional ties entirely to their locality, not going downtown to shop or to visit friends or to go to the theatre. . . .

The suburban dweller believes, in fact, that he has the best of both worlds. In the interviews with college seniors I referred to earlier, in which such stress was placed on suburban domesticity, many students also emphasized their wish not to lose the cultural amenities they had enjoyed in college. Some of these amenities will certainly be distributed in the suburb though frequently in diluted doses: Piped in through television and radio and high-fidelity sets; the suburb may even support a theatre group and, in a few cases, amateur chamber music; the local high school will provide entertainment of a sort, as well as facilities for adult education.

However, as the radii lengthen on which people move away from the city—as they must with the crowding of the suburbs leading to the jump to the exurbs—people either learn as in California to drive great distances for dinner or confine themselves to their immediate environs: The central city as a meeting place disappears—a process which has gone further in Los Angeles and Chicago than in Boston or New York. The neighbors make up little circles based . . . largely on propinquity.

LOSS OF HUMAN DIFFERENTIATION

The decentralization of leisure in the suburbs goes further than this, however, as the home itself, rather than the neighborhood, becomes the chief gathering place for the family—either in the "family room" with its games, its TV, its informality, or outdoors around the barbecue. And while there are values in this of family closeness and "togetherness," there is also a loss of differentiation as the parents play pals to their children and the latter, while gaining a superficial precocity, lose the possibility of wider contacts. At worst, there is a tendency for family talk and activity to seek the lowest common denominator in terms of age and interest.

Some of these matters are illustrated by an interview with a housewife who had recently bought a house in one of the wealthier suburbs north of Chicago. Her husband had been transferred to Chicago from a southern city and had been encouraged by his company to buy a large house for entertaining customers. Customers, however, seldom came since the husband was on the road much of the time. The wife and three children hardly ever went downtown—they had no Chicago contacts anyway—and after making sporadic efforts to make the rounds of theater and musical activities in the suburbs and to make friends there, they found themselves more and more often staying home, eating outdoors in good weather and looking at TV in bed. Observing that "there is not much formal entertaining back and forth," the wife feared she was almost losing her conversational skills; yet she felt that her family had been pulled closer together by the shared activities, in which the husband joined on weekends, around the home. After listening to her list and discuss the friends made at church and golf, it became evident that her immediate environment just missed providing her with people close enough to her in taste and interest for intimate ties to develop.

One interview, of course, proves little, and many factors are obviously involved in choice of friends; suburban location in an older, nonhomogeneous suburb is only one of them. I recall obtaining such interviews in Kansas City, too, among people who had lived there all their lives and had potential access to wide strata in the metropolitan area. Nevertheless, there seems to me to be a tendency, though not a pronounced one, in the suburbs to lose the human differentiations which have made great cities in the past the centers of rapid intellectual and cultural advance. The suburb is like a fraternity house at a small college —or the "close propinquity" to which Tocqueville referred—in which like-mindedness reverberates upon itself as the potentially various selves within each of us do not get evoked or recognized. For people who move to the suburb to live when adult, of course, matters are different than among those who never knew another milieu. And, to be sure, creative human contact need not be face to face but can often be vicarious, through print or other mediated channels. Certainly, highly differentiated human beings have grown up in locales which gave them minimal support. Moreover, though the nonneighborly seldom seek the suburbs, a few doubtless manage to survive there. Ease of movement, in any case, permits periodic access to others, although as these others themselves scatter to the suburbs, this process becomes more difficult.

ROLE OF THE AUTOMOBILE IN SUBURBIA

Indeed, at least until each of us has his own helicopter or rocket, this pattern of life requires us to spend a great deal of time in automobiles, overcoming decentralization—but driving is itself a terribly "decentralized" activity, allowing at best for car-pool sociability, and at worst mitigated by the quiz-bits, frequent commercials, and flatulent music of AM radio. As compared with the older suburbanites who commuted by train and read the paper, did homework, or even read a book, the present and increasing tendency to travel to work by car seems aggressively vacuous and solipsistic. Whereas in preindustrial cultures and in the lower classes in industrial society, people sometimes just hang on a corner or sit vacantly, it is striking that in a society which offers many alternatives, people will consent to drive vacantly but not refreshingly—woe betide the careless or unspry pedestrian or bicyclist who gets in the way of industrial workers pouring out of the factory parking lots or white-collar workers coming home on a throughway. The human waste here is most important, but the waste of resources and land, the roadside *dreck*, the highways which eat space as railroad yards even in St. Louis or Chicago never did, are not negligible even in a huge rich country.

Where the husband goes off with the car to work—and often, in the vicious circle created by the car, there is no other way for him to travel —the wife is frequently either privatized at home or to escape isolation must take a job which will help support her own car. Whereas the rental courts of developments like Park Forest provide companionship for the stranded wives—companionship which, given the age and sex homogeneity, is sometimes oppressive—other suburbs are so built and so psychologically "unsociometric" as to limit neighboring and leave many women to the company of Mary Margaret McBride and Arthur Godfrey. Indeed, in a few instances of interviewing in the morning in new suburbs south of Chicago, I have been struck by the eagerness of the housewives to talk to somebody (and not only to a man!) who is not a salesman—once they can be weaned away from the TV which amuses them as a kind of vicarious baby sitter. It is not only the visiting intellectual who finds the lives of these women empty, their associations fragmentary. . . . The women themselves, if at all sensitive or well educated, complain of having their contacts limited to their young children and to a few other housewives in the same boat. . . . I have come to entertain the suspicion that, once started on having children, these women continue in some part out of a fear of the emptiness of life without children and of the problems they would face of relating themselves to their menfolk without the static, the noise, the pleasures, the "problems" that the presence of children provides.

The children themselves, in fact, before they get access to a car, are captives of their suburb, save for those families where the housewives surrender continuity in their own lives to chauffeur their children to lessons, doctors, and other services which could be reached via public transport in the city. In the suburban public schools, the young are captives, too, dependent on whatever art and science and general liveliness their particular school happens to have—again contrast the metropolis, with its choice of high schools, as most notably in New York.

. . . . .

SUBURBIA'S POSITIVE AND NEGATIVE ASPECTS

. . . We have the impression that the suburbanite, tied to his house as the doctor is to his practice, may actually be less likely to take off for a week end in the country than the urban dweller whose janitor can look after his apartment and even the cat. Indeed, it is the city people, freed by industrialism from long hours of grinding work, who (along, of course, with an ample supply of untied suburbanites) make up a large proportion of the outboard population of our lakes and rivers and of the thirty-five million fishermen—more than twice the number of those urban sportsmen, the bowlers. Although air-conditioning makes even the most humid and dirty city potentially habitable, people can't wait to leave town on week ends and during the summer, even though in many parts of the country it means spewing the city into the countryside and fighting with like-minded crowds for space on roads, lakes, and at motels.

. . . I believe that snobbery and imitation of the rich play a declining part in this exodus to the suburbs and that the quiet revolt against the city and industrialism plays an increasing part. I would argue that there is often less "front" in the new suburbs than in equivalent sections of a metropolis, and less pressure for a lace-curtain life concealing back-stage scrimping and meanness than there once was. . . . The whole American ethos, which once revolved about the dialectic of pure country versus wicked but exciting city, seems to me now aerated by the suburban outlook. This produces an homogenization of both city and country, but without full integration.

While on the whole the lower-middle and middle-income suburbs sponsor the relaxed life, there is one area where they impose an imperative which many city dwellers have not met, namely that of having some sort of garden—less as a cultural amenity than as a minimum contribution to civic decency: A kind of compulsory outdoor housekeeping. . . . We found in Fairlawn, a new developer's suburb, for example, that to many housewives the garden was simply one more chore. It represented neither a contrast with the asphalt jungle of the city, nor a pleasure in growing things, nor a rage for order. It was rather a tax imposed by neighborhood consciousness—the neighbors often being interpreted as more concerned and censorious than they, for the most part, were. Thus we find that many people who have moved newly to the suburbs to escape the city come without awareness of the constraints they will find—or mistakenly interpret—in the suburb. Like the appointment in Samara, they meet pressures they had thought to leave behind, though altered in form and impact.

One of these pressures, already adverted to, is the metropolis itself; its traffic, its ethnic minorities, and its tax rates tend to catch up with them. The waves of succession within the city proper do not halt at its boundaries, and many old and established suburbs are finding themselves cut in two by freeways and by the new kinds of people they bring. In this situation, some of the old kinds of people are among those tempted to become exurbanites, putting the ever-approaching city another few miles away and hoping to solve the dilemma of distance versus intimacy by a superhighway.

However, in this quandary the emphasis on superhighways—and on supercars which require them—takes on much of the lunatic quality of an arms race. As highways get bigger and better, they invite more cars, destroy what undeveloped and unschematized country (or central city) remains, and require still more highways in an unending spiral.

People have been drilled by industrialism in the values of efficiency —narrowly defined in terms of speed, performance, and a kind of streamlined look (what Jacques Barzun has referred to as "America's Romance with Practicality"). Thus even when they flee from the cities and the style of life industrialism has brought about, they cannot change the style of thought which sees the solution to ribbon developments in stretching them still further until our East and West coasts threaten to become continuous roadside slums.

What is true of the planning, or lack of it, of our road-centered culture as a whole is also true of domestic architecture. Efficiency here is less stark—and consequently often less attractive—since it must compete with traditional definitions of a suburban free-standing home. But, as many architects have pointed out, the interiors are highly modern in the sense of mechanization. Indeed, one reason why husbands have been willing to become domesticated is that they have been promoted from dishwashers to operators of dishwashers. Similarly, they use power mowers to give crew cuts to handkerchief-sized lawns and pierce their wives' and neighbors' ears with the screams of high-fidelity music. The open plan of the very newest ranch-style homes puts the TV set on a swivel in the center. Here it can be seen from all parts of the house so that urban news, fashions, gossip, and jokes can circulate in the home throughout the daily cycle of the members of the family. But all these improvements are bought at the expense of space for the individual whose bedroom in the suburban development is often smaller than in city tenements. This is especially true . . . of the newest suburban homes. These have both a family room and a living room. The latter, like the old parlor, is used only for state occasions; the family room is big enough for games, the TV, and inside barbecue, and general clutter.

. . . . .

THE AIMLESS QUALITY OF SUBURBAN LIFE

In the days of Lincoln Steffens and later, people emphasized the "shame of the cities," and in the 1920's major novelists emphasized the constraints of small-town and occasionally of small-suburban life. Today, the comparable worry, in the books dealing with the suburbs, is conformity . . . ; writers point to the uniformity of the ranch style, the ever-present television antennae, the lamp, if not the crack, in the picture window—which usually provides a view of the nearly treeless street, the cars, and someone else's picture window. Actually, uniformity and conformity are quite different matters as Georg Simmel has observed in his essay on "Fashion." The former may dictate to men only in inessentials, whereas the latter involves some psychological mechanism. And the conformity of the new suburbs is, in some important ways, far less stringent than that of the old; if it is not quite the case that "anything goes," lots of things do go which once would, if known, have brought ostracism. If one does not seek to force the new suburbanite back across the ethnic tracks he has just crossed, he is quite tolerant, even bland. If he is political at all—rather than parochially civic-minded, tending to a "garden" which includes the local schools and waterworks—he is apt to be an Eisenhower Republican, seldom informed, rarely angry, and only spasmodically partisan.

No, what is missing in suburbia, even where the quality of life has not overtly deteriorated, is not the result of claustrophobic conformity to others' sanctions. Rather, there would seem to be an aimlessness, a pervasive low-keyed unpleasure. . . . For millions of people, work no longer provides a central focus for life; and the breadwinner is no longer the chief protagonist in the family saga—just as Saturday night no longer provides a central focus for festivity. In fact, the decentralization of leisure in the suburbs is not only spatial but temporal, as evenings from Thursday through Sunday are oriented to play rather than work and are not individually accented or collectively celebrated.

At the same time, leisure has not picked up the slack—as, in earlier writings, I was too sanguine that it might. Whatever balances of work and play might have been possible for preindustrial man, postindustrial man is keyed, as I remarked earlier, to greater expectations. He has learned more "needs" and cannot in any case reconstitute the institutions industrialism destroyed. It is almost inconceivable, for example, to imagine a reconstitution of the folk arts which everywhere—in Nigeria as in New Orleans, in Damascus as in Tennessee—prove fragile in the face of mass-produced music and imagery.

. . . . .

. . . Our suburbs are an effort to build a life not based on work but instead on the family and on voluntary associations. It is surely an advance to prefer children to capital gains, and suburban *Gemütlichkeit* to urban pavements (though, as British planners discovered in building the New Towns and as writers for the *Architectural Review* have insisted, there were values concealed in the most seemingly depressed urban conglomerations which were lost in the move to the more hygienic and aseptic planned communities—much as farmers for a long time failed to realize that worms and other "varmint" were essential to a well-nourished soil). But the advances cannot be consolidated unless they are made on a broader front; otherwise, people may quickly oscillate again towards such apparent security as industrialism gave them. Faced with the mounting depreciations of the crowded suburbs and aware of their own powerlessness, they may turn to strong authority which promises to clean up the already forseeable mess. Even now, drivers in a traffic jam, frustrated by each other's presence, are not the most amiable of men. This, despite the fact that, once on the move again, it is largely the sense of moving rather than anything they actively do or enjoy which gives them pleasure and release.

TENSIONS ON THE SUBURBAN SCENE

. . . I have remarked above on the tendency for families in the new suburb of Fairlawn to assume that their neighbors, who were in fact quite tolerant, were putting pressure on them to have not merely a passable garden but a good one. Actually, the neighbor's visual sense was not that highly developed, nor their emulative sense either. They were tolerant of each other's gardens as of each other's life in general. I asked myself then what was the source of the extensive misinterpretation which led to such comments as the following by a Fairlawn housewife. She described to the interviewer an ambitious plan for a rose garden and large beds of flowers all around the house as follows:

I really hate gardening; we both do. My husband never plays golf any more and we do nothing all weekend but work in the garden. I mean work.

I recalled analogous comments made by students who were working allegedly to prepare for an exam which their intelligence told them they could not easily fail; I recalled other such comments by business and professional men who created anxieties in their work in order to give it drama and bite. I realized that, since we are not really attached to anything we are doing, we look for spurs when life no longer automatically provides them. Perhaps the housewife just quoted cannot make herself (or her spouse) work at all without picturing dire consequences for failure. Or perhaps she has in this case simply projected her own moralism or malice into her neighbors—possibly also as a part of an internal family argument with an indifferent or indolent husband. Games, the arts, conversation are all activities which have institutionalized short bursts of effort as the price both of pleasure and performance. The suburbs, however, in seeking to take the place of the city, provide insufficient comparable agendas, and housewives such as those we saw who gardened with neither pleasure nor skill still clung to the demand that neighbors and nature seemed to make.

I have lost any sanguinity that they will learn better simply by sticking it out; they may only get more bored, more destructive. Their pleasure in flowers, or in the arrangements of nature, cannot be very intense if they put up, as they seem ready enough to do, with the visual blight of so much of our suburbscape, the roads that take them there, the cars they drive in. I am not speaking of "taste," in the sense of high taste, but rather of the quality with which visual experience is assimilated. And I am certainly not speaking of the uniformity of the Levittowns as such. The row houses in Baltimore or Philadelphia are often handsome in ways which our suburbs, varied in a most studied fashion, fail to achieve. In the course of the industrial revolution and the rise of the middle classes, both elite taste and traditional taste declined. Today, despite frequent improvement in advertising and magazine layout, in interior decoration, and in corporate and public building, the sense for visual imagery of Americans remains stunted, and the children of the suburbs grow up accepting the neat, the new, the shiny, but with minimal awareness of vista, proportion, or independent critical judgment of the look of life around them. . . .

79. THE VANISHING U.S.
COUNTRYSIDE *

WILLIAM H. WHYTE, JR.

An auto ride out toward the open country from the center of any city of fifty thousand or more will demonstrate vividly, to anyone with the slightest perceptiveness, the clearly haphazard, often obviously unplanned, and frequently chaotic character of metropolitan development. This "urban sprawl" is even more visible if one examines the interlaced network of cities in the great industrial corridors of the United States. One finds, for example, an almost continuous sweep of concentrated settlement in the overlapping metropolises which stretch from Portland, Maine, to Washington, D.C. The governmental tools and devices of yesterday are no longer adequate to deal with the problems which these "multicities" create. We are already being frequently reminded of the problems of street surfacing, sewage disposal, fire and police protection, schools, and other services which are difficult and costly to maintain in the jumbled areas between our cities. Not so common is an examination of the problem scrutinized in this selection—the sheer misuse, through haphazard development, of the open spaces which make a countryside beautiful.

Take a last look. Some summer's morning drive past the golf club on the edge of town, turn off into a back road and go for a short trip through the open countryside. Look well at the meadows, the wooded draws, the stands of pine, the creeks and streams, and fix them in your

* Originally published as "A Plan to Save Vanishing U.S. Countryside," *Life*, Vol. 47, No. 7 (August 17, 1959), 88–90, 92, 94, 96, 99–100, 102. Reprinted by permission of the author.
For a biographical sketch of the author see selection 27.

memory. If the American standard of living goes up another notch, this is about the last chance you will have.

Go back toward the city five or 10 miles. Here, in what was pleasant countryside only a year ago, is the sight of what is to come. No more sweep of green—across the hills are splattered scores of random subdivisions, each laid out in the same dreary asphalt curves. Gone are the streams, brooks, woods and forests that the subdivisions' signs talked about. The streams are largely buried in concrete culverts. Where one flows briefly through a patch of weeds and tin cans it is fetid with the ooze of septic tanks.

A row of stumps marks the place where sycamores used to shade the road and if a stand of maple or walnut still exists the men with power saws will soon be at it. Here and there a farm remains, but the "For Sale" signs are up and now even the golf course is to be chopped into lots. What open space remains you can no longer see. To the eye it is all a jumble, an endless succession of driving ranges, open-air theaters, billboards, neon signs, frozen custard spas, TV aerials and pink plaster flamingos.

This is only a foretaste of the future. The mess we have made so far has been achieved with a population reaching 175 million. By 1970 there will be 35 million more Americans. Most of the housing to take care of the increase will be built on the edges of our metropolitan areas. And long before that the pattern will have been set. The new federal highway program, just now getting into gear, will visibly accelerate the exploitation of outlying areas. With each new interchange will come a speculative land rush the like of which few communities are prepared to resist. If any open spaces are to be saved they must be saved now. The options are fast expiring. At best most communities have only a year of grace.

Which is fortunate. For years planners have been warning about the economic evils of the creeping artificial blight commonly known as urban sprawl, but nobody did anything about it. Until recently most citizens assumed that there was probably no practical way to halt its progress—some have even had a sneaking feeling that it would be anti-people to try to find one. But there is no substitute for a good outrage—the kind people can see or smell. This year, thanks in part to the highway program, community after community is finally having the devil scared out of it. Never before has suburbia seethed with so many protest meetings—whether rerouting petitioners, save-our-trees groups or stop-the-rape-of-the-valley emergency committees.

In Pennsylvania several communities applied recently to the legislature for permission to start land acquisition schemes that a few years ago would have been thought wildly socialistic. In mid-New Jersey, where bulldozer drivers advancing down from New York may soon clasp hands with bulldozer drivers coming up from Philadelphia, farm groups are agitating for a green belt to keep the two cities apart. In Illinois, Rockford County has approved a plan that will ban any builder's subdivision on land bordering a river or stream.

But it is in California that the most significant experiments are under way—notably in the counties around San Francisco. This has happened partly because the area was desecrated so prodigiously so early—even loyal citizens are now openly comparing it to Los Angeles. Residents of Santa Clara County, for example, have been pioneering the concept of zoning areas exclusively for farm land. In nearby Alameda County they are considering "planned agricultural parks." In San Mateo County a running battle between the tax assessor and the golf clubs has led to the idea of exclusive recreational zoning.

Often such experimentation shows only how *not* to fight sprawl or dodge taxes, but it is no less valuable for that. In finding out what does not work, the Californians have been led to something that may work very well indeed. This June, through the initiative of Monterey County, the California legislature passed the first general "open-space bill" in the U.S. It gives the state, counties and towns the chance to make new use of an ancient legal tool: the "easement."

With an easement, instead of buying a man's property, the way land is bought for parks, the community buys only a *right* in the property. The property still belongs to the owner but he cannot sell it for subdivision. Although now almost forgotten in the eastern U.S., easements have been historically successful in protecting highway rights of way, and their constitutionality is well tested. They are only one weapon against urban sprawl—zoning and subdivision control are necessary too —but easements do what they cannot do: preserve the big spaces of natural countryside and do it right now. For communities all over the country this opens up exciting possibilities.

A good way to appreciate the potential of the easement principle is to examine the causes of urban sprawl. Many of our past difficulties in dealing with sprawl come from some very mistaken if widely held assumptions. One is that sprawl is due to too many people and not enough land. A second is that the best way to save open space is to provide more of it for each homestead. A third, following from the others, is that zoning is therefore the main antisprawl safeguard.

But a shortage of land is *not* the problem. Indeed, many communities that have become sprawling messes could have accommodated up to half again as many people and had more usable open space to boot. Most people assume that the area close to a city is "filled up." If they were to look closely they would be surprised at how much vacant space there really is—even on the city's very edge. It looks terrible, of course—

a vacant lot here, an automobile graveyard there—but if you add it all up you have quite a lot of space. The problem, simply, is that you cannot add it up. It is scattered.

There is not a shortage of land. There is a shortage of space. Ten acres have been used to do the work of one, for the pattern of suburban growth has been left almost entirely up to the speculative builder. The builder is not the villain of the piece. He is understandably interested in making money, and he can hardly be expected to double as a volunteer city planner. Where development might be best for orderly growth is generally just the place where landowners are holding out for a killing. So the builder leapfrogs, leaving behind many an unrequited cupidity, and goes out where the land is cheap.

In one year the total amount of land in an area that he and other developers finally build on may be only a fraction of the whole, but the presence of the model homes and the bulldozers has a tremendous pre-emptive effect. Because these projects have been scattered, a few casually placed developments rob the community of scores of choices that would be important to it five or 10 years from now—for parks, industrial districts, reservoirs and just plain breathing space. Already the community begins to look filled up—and the new suburbanites are only now beginning to arrive.

At about this point, if the community is a typical one, the elders get to work locking the barn door. They stiffen the zoning, setting from one to three acres as minimum lot size. In some cases this is good. Large-lot zoning does conserve the character of certain residential areas. But it also forces developers to chew up even more open spaces elsewhere to house a given number of people. Instead of several tightly knit subdivisions there will be a "scatteration" all over the landscape. The community won't be penetrated; it will be enveloped.

For the moment, however, the community leaders are very pleased with themselves. They have also tightened up regulations for builders' subdivisions, e.g., many now make a developer dedicate 3% to 4% of his subdivision to public open space. As far as the big open spaces are concerned, the elders tell the newcomer, there is nothing to worry about: "the landowners there would never dream of selling out to a developer," "too strong a feeling for tradition," "family ties," "love for the land. . . ."

But the new subdivisions have set up an inexorable chain of consequences. Being scattered, they soon prove expensive to service, and as the spring rains flush the septic tanks the high cost of decent sewage plants becomes the leading community topic. The taxes the community collects from new people turn out to be nowhere near enough to pay for the services they want, and the new people, meanwhile, are breeding a great many more new people for the schools. Up go the taxes, not only on the subdivisions but also on the open land surrounding them.

The spiral ascends. The higher assessments to pay for scatteration begin to force more land into scatteration. Farmers, who only a year ago were protesting their fealty to husbandry, begin to toy with the idea of selling out and retiring to Florida. That big landowner who "wouldn't dream of selling" begins to wonder if his neighbors might not be thinking of making a fast buck. If they do, why shouldn't he? The owner of an estate dies, and the heirs, who always seem to live somewhere else, sometimes do not even wait for the developer—they go looking for one. Here and there the omens of capitulation appear: the meadow no longer in pasture, a field of weeds, a hillside abandoned to second growth and poison ivy—140 ACRES, WILL SUBDIVIDE.

For a while the illusion of open space lingers on. There is very little within the subdivisions—if the developer did dedicate some land to the public, it is likely to be an eroded gully or a patch of swamp he couldn't do anything with. But at first the people do not mind. There are open valleys and hills around, and like parasites the subdivisions have been feeding on them.

Then one fine day residents of the Bonnie Crest Farms development look out their picture windows in horror. But they *can't* do that! The orange bulldozers are slicing into the hill, the tree killers are advancing on the woods. Fool's paradise is over.

What can be done about it? Instead of fighting a rear-guard action, the community can decide in advance what kind of pattern it wants. This does not mean one of those routinely perfect master plans, the kind that arouse little opposition because they are so abstract—and get little support for the same reason. It means forcing choices beginning right now, and for actual, specific spaces.

First there is the space *within* the subdivision. A number of communities have come to the conclusion that it is not enough simply to make the developer dedicate a portion of his land for playgrounds and parks. They are trying a new tack. They say, in effect:

"We are the ones who have to live with these subdivisions, and instead of leaving the layout up to passing developers, we are the ones who should decide the basic street pattern. In so doing we will make a deal with the developer. We won't force him to split his 100-acre tract into, say, 80 one-acre lots—which will need 20 acres of asphalt road. Instead, we'll let him group his houses into a tighter pattern that will be easier to service and will require far less road space. Sure, lot sizes will be smaller, but this will mean more usable open space. If a stream gully runs through the property, for example, it will not be chopped up into a patch of back lots that will only be a headache for the owners to keep up. Instead it will be left as a whole so that all the residents can use it. The density of the development will be the same as under the conventional pattern, but a lot more *space* will be created—and at less cost to the community, to the developer and to the residents themselves."

In the Far Northeast section of Philadelphia this pattern has been pioneered. Planner Edmund Bacon and his staff, working with 20 private builders, have started work on a community that will fit no less than 63,000 people into 2,500 acres, leaving plenty of open space within it. Compare this with the average development which has only half as many families per acre but no open space for any of them.

Even more important for a community is the problem of conserving open space *between* various developments. The most obvious step is to buy the land, and for such specific public needs as parks and reservoir sites this had better be done quickly. But for the more general task of preserving the natural countryside, there is another way which can be much more useful, not to say cheaper: the easement.

In the building of our national parkways "scenic easements" have been bought for a nominal fee from landowners of adjacent property. This cuts down land acquisition costs, it protects the parkway from billboards and it provides a natural landscape, rather than the monotonous tree-nursery green of so many parkways. Air safety easements operate on the same principle. In California, for example, authorities have been buying easement from farmers to prohibit both subdivision and tall structures around airfields (cost: about $15 an acre).

The easement device could be equally well applied to the problem of urban sprawl. The community, for example, decides that top priority should go to preserving a particular creek valley. The valley is small—about three miles long by a quarter of a mile wide—but it sets the character for an area of some 20 square miles. Mainly, residents of the area want to save it because it is beautiful, but it is also valuable for other reasons. Its soil is rich and deep and it has been well farmed. It is the heart of the watershed's drainage system: the streams that flow into it from the surrounding hills are a magnificent storm sewer network, and its flood plains act as a huge sponge to temper the flow in rainy weather and to mete it out slowly in dry. The community wants new developments too, but by saving this valley, the kind of developments it attracts will be all the better.

The community looks at the open space, in short, not as a mere buffer but as *functional* space—and functional right now. By doing so, the community also reserves for itself future choices. If at some future time, for example, it wants to buy part of the valley for a park, it has guaranteed itself that the choice will be there to make. But this is incidental. The open space is a present benefit in its own right. The watershed aspects alone of most scenic spaces are quite enough to justify the question of public purpose in any court test.

To the valley's landowners, the community officials say something like this: we know you would like to keep this land open, but we also know that you have taxes to think about, and we can't ask you to turn down a developer's bid just to make us happy. So we want to offer you something in return. We want to pay you for giving up the right to put up billboards or chop this land into a subdivision. You keep title to the land. You continue to enjoy all reasonable uses of the land. The easement "runs with the land" and applies to any future owners, but subject to that you can pass it on to your heirs or sell it to anyone you like. The cost? The usual rule of thumb is to pay the difference between what the land would fetch on the market with an easement and what it would fetch without it. In an area where developers are waving $1,000 bills around, the spread might be too high. In open country, however, it would be very little.

In such areas, indeed, it would *pay* the landowner to give an easement: he gets the protection on his flank that he wants and he gets assurance against the unfair tax assessments that often accompany poorly planned developments. In some cases, furthermore, only a part of a man's property would fall into the easement area. The remainder would be even more valuable for subsequent development.

But what about the community's tax base? An open-space program would raise it. The owner affected would pay less than he would if his land were subdivided, but because the community would then be free of the expensively scattered services that a subdivision needs, it would probably net more money. The very existence of an amenity such as a park or an open space almost always raises adjacent land values—a fact some of the biggest developers keep very much in mind when looking for sites. The postwar Illinois development of Park Forest, for example, was backed up against one of Cook County's forest preserves.

But why go to the trouble of an easement program? Why not simply zone certain areas against development? Zoning costs nothing, it does not involve a lot of haggling with individual landowners, and it is generally accepted by the public.

It is true that sound zoning is a prerequisite of good planning, but zoning cannot do the job alone. Zoning is a police power and there is a point beyond which its use can be quite unfair. It is one thing to tell a man he cannot build on a flood plain or a similarly impractical location. It is quite another thing to use the zoning power to forbid a man to build on property fit for development.

Here we come to the all-important distinction between the police power and the power of eminent domain. What does the public really want: to prevent something harmful—or to secure a benefit? The distinction may seem hazy, but a distinction there is, and it is one the courts are well aware of. In seeking to preserve open space the public really wants a benefit. Using the police power of zoning to compel an owner to provide this benefit is a shortsighted way to get out of paying for it.

Where the landowners themselves want open-space zoning, it can work for a while. Santa Clara County in California is a case in point. Several years ago, appalled at the way scattered subdivisions were wrecking the rich valley floor for agriculture, the farmers and the county planning commission pioneered the idea of "exclusive agricultural zones." They set up several zones forbidden to developers—and to the cities and towns which had been annexing farms so vigorously. For good measure, county planner Karl Belser placed several golf clubs and a private airport under the protection of exclusive agricultural zoning. "The uses," he says, with only a flicker of a smile, "are compatible with agriculture."

The farmers are glad they did the zoning—there would not be much farmland left otherwise—but they now foresee some fatal weaknesses in the scheme. As surrounding land prices have soared—to as much as $5,000 an acre—the temptation to sell out has become very strong, and it is not too hard to get a farm dezoned. To make the agricultural zones really permanent, Belser and the farmers have decided to apply the easement principle.

The most important defect of all zoning is that it gives the landowner no real protection from the tax assessor. For as growth continues there is tremendous pressure on the assessor to raise more money.

. . . . .

Harnessing the support of big landowners is only a start. The big job is to bring together the many other groups who want the same end result. Because each has somewhat different reasons for wanting it, they have failed to see each other as allies. As a matter of fact, each is likely to assume that the others are the enemy. The farmers, who couldn't care less about providing amenities for unborn generations of city people, see open space as a defense *against* the city. The city people, who are skeptical of the farmers' cropland argument, want the land saved, but with urban motives and needs in mind. Park officers, most of whom still think only of conventional land requisition, have yet to see that the bias of land-heavy gentry is better exploited than deplored. Utilities, which suffer heavily from urban sprawl, remain too ideologically muscle-bound to display any initiative. With rare exceptions, golf clubs have not even thought of it.

Education is not going to bring these groups together. A good fight may, and the best way to get one going is to start the controversial job of selecting actual open spaces. Those planners who say we need more study can go off and study. They have been saying that for 10 years. Meanwhile the assessors are not laying down their transits, the developers are not stopping their bulldozers.

And what is so difficult about selecting land? Any planner who cannot point now to at least one area worth saving should get into other work. Long-range planning is necessary, but what we need most is some *retroactive* planning: get the good land first and then, at leisure, rationalize with studies how right we were to have done it.

Let us trust our instincts. Esthetics is the driving force for action, but it is not something separate from economics. Look again at the desecration of a countryside—the buried streams, the jumble of neon signs and driving ranges, the abandoned beauty spots with those telltale signs, WILL SUBDIVIDE. Your instincts will tell you that anything that looks this terrible cannot be good economics, that it is not progress, that it is not inevitable. And that we had better get cracking.

80. THE AMERICAN WAY OF LIFE:
REGIONAL VARIATIONS *

ANONYMOUS

This selection is an antidote to the belief that mass production and mass communication have reduced all Americans to identical robots; that the exciting variations which gave our nation strength through the stimulation of contrasts and differing modes of life have disappeared. Though brief, the presentation is clear and effective in showing that diversities still exist in this country. The reader is invited to look for himself, using the insightful ideas and approaches presented here, for differences between regions, and even between cities, as he may have visited them.

. . . It will be found . . . that there is not just one American way of life. There are American *ways* of life, almost without number. For example, there are the great regional differentiations, where nature herself has conspired with American institutions to create ways of life as different from each other as those of two nations might be. It is true that these American "sub-nations" are bound together by many common ties, including the important tie of language; yet their temperamental characteristics, their customs, their values and views, their personal objectives differ so greatly that a man who is happy and effective in one might be miserable and frustrated in another.

Take the Far West. This vast area, which begins, roughly speaking,

* Reprinted from "The American Way of Life" in the February, 1951, issue of *Fortune Magazine* by Special Permission; © 1951 Time Inc.

just east of Colorado, has of course many important things in common with the rest of the U.S. Yet the ways of those people are very different from the ways of the Easterner. Nature herself has made sure of that, for the Far West is a region of majestic drama, of mountains and buttes and deserts, beside which the woods and streams of the east coast look puny. The western people, generally speaking, are more outspoken than the Easterners, more cordial, more generous of their time and money; they speak slower, and they have a way of cutting through a lot of argument to reach a quick conclusion on which they are willing to stand or fall. The Easterner is endlessly fascinated by them; but he considers them naive, unsophisticated, lacking in perspective in the ways of the world. In fact, the West is to the East as the East is to Europe.

And yet, as anyone knows who has lived out there, these generalizations misrepresent the realities. The Far West itself includes many ways of life. Take, for example, the differences between the Pacific Northwest and California. In the Pacific Northwest the great rivers rise in snow-capped mountains and wind down through gorges to the sea. The cities are incredibly young—Seattle has not yet celebrated its centenary. It is trade-union country and the standard of living is high. But happiness is pursued in the Northwest with a certain calm simplicity that is rare in America. For all the youth of his region, the Northwesterner is something of a philosopher; he expects a lot out of life, but he doesn't aim to get very rich. He attends to his business all right, but he is more interested in his mountains and his waters; he would rather pack up with his wife and kids, with about $200 worth of camping gear in the back of his car, and push off for a ten-day tour of his magnificent state parks; or go cruising in a small boat, or salmon fishing in the foaming streams of the Columbia River watershed, or skiing on the mighty slopes of Mount Rainier.

In the eyes of the Northwesterner, the Californian, therefore, is a noisy fellow. The Californian goes about in bright informal clothing of many colors and lolls on bright beaches along the shores of the bright-blue Pacific and grows oranges that shine brightly from the dark-green foliage of the orange trees. That is to say, the southern Californian does; the northern Californian is altogether different. Northern California merges with the Pacific Northwest and has its roots firmly planted in San Francisco, the westernmost metropolis of Western civilization. San Francisco has become a place where a man can find anything he wants to find, which is perhaps the best definition of metropolitanism.

But Los Angeles, which is the headquarters of the southern Californian, is not like that. Los Angeles is big and boastful and overrun with Easterners and movie actors and cultists of infinite variety. It is also the mecca of the retired couple who took the life-insurance ads seriously and have come out here to enjoy "beauty" and "leisure" and watch the sun set westwardly over the Pacific. But the Northwesterner has the feeling, as he passes the innumerable little "bungalows" that sprawl out into what was only a few decades ago a near desert, that the beauty is wasted here, that it is not appreciated as in the Northwest, that it has not been absorbed. Somehow, like the movie industry that it houses, southern California seems to be removed one step from the real, to live in a world that nature never made—or, for that matter, man. That is the big difference between southern California and the Northwest.

Then there is that other vast region of the U.S., lying between the Rocky Mountains and the Appalachians, where a river may be a thousand miles long, and where everything drains into the Mississippi. Here all lines are horizontal, life is intensely practical and "real," and the quarter sections and the fields and the towns duplicate themselves, league after league, in seemingly endless repetition. It is here in this great "valley" that the itinerant lecturer has his worst time and reaches his most pessimistic conclusions; for unless these people are studied community by community, they appear to vanish into sociological generalizations.

But actually when you come to know Kansas you find it very different from Minnesota, for example, with its high percentage of Swedes and Germans and a better-balanced economy than Kansas has ever had. Kansas, Nebraska, and the Dakotas are heavy agricultural exporters; their way of life is based upon the soil, and even their towns exist for the farmers, not the townspeople. This makes town life quite different from that of an eastern town, or even of a town in a manufacturing area of the Midwest (such as Chicago or St. Louis, for example), where the town exists, so to speak, for itself, and lives on its own exports. The Midwest farmer is fat with the world's riches—and safe from its depredations. But he is not in the least soft. On the contrary, he has time after time challenged the power of the East, which he regards with a congenital suspicion that is much more marked in the Midwest than in the Far West.

The Midwest merges into the South, and as it does the standard of living declines. The South is problem country. It grew up differently from the rest of the nation, with an economy based on big landholdings and slave labor. It still has with it the problem of the Negro; in many towns of Mississippi and Alabama the Negroes outnumber the whites, who cling to their political power by any means, fair or foul. The southern way of life differs radically from other American ways of life. The pace is slower. The extremes of poverty and riches are greater. The traditions are better preserved. The storied southern "aristocracy" is becoming something of a myth; but it has left behind it the tradition of southern cooking, which is supposed to be the best in the U.S. (though no vestige of it is to be found in the hotels and public eating places); of hospitality, which makes the New Yorker look like a boor; of flirtatious women; and of peaceful ways whose like is to be found nowhere else in the U.S.

And then there is Texas, the independent nation that became a state in 1845. Geographically Texas belongs to both the Midwest and the South, but in terms of its way of life it belongs to neither. Maybe California has outstripped Texas in population growth, but Texas has got richer faster than any comparable region of the U.S. ever has. Oil derricks, skyscrapers, flamboyant hotels, oil and gas piplines, canals, piers, and great industrial shapes have sprung like mushrooms from a landscape that the Northwesterner would consider quite drab. It is the land of the big rich; the making of wealth dominates the way of life. And yet wealth is really only a symbol for the Texan; he likes to spend it just as wildly as he makes it; he loves the "feel" of struggle, the exhilaration of victory, of "getting ahead." Everything here is on a big scale, as if the gods had lifted the curtain for a drama on Valhalla. The young folks associate in droves—one of their barbecues will be attended by a hundred or more. As an Easterner once complained, he wished that Texans could be friendly on a neighborhood basis instead of on a state basis. The ordinary Texan thinks nothing of driving two or three hundred miles just to see a "local" football game.

The Texan way of life, indeed, represents an extension into the twentieth century of certain ideas that animated all Americans up to the first world war. Here is the land of opportunity, where anybody can rise to the "top," where tomorrow is unpredictable and yesterday unnecessary. Here the intrepid individual, the risk, the adventure, the fabulous reward, have somehow come to fruition in a world largely occupied with the less romantic problems of social "security" and social "science." It is possible for the modern American to feel somewhat nostalgic about Texas, however he may smile—or cringe—at its excesses.

But in the East the way of life is crowded. In the winter the Easterner takes to the trains and planes if he wants to go anywhere; in the summer he chugs despondently along obsolete highways, breathing carbon monoxide from the car ahead, snarled in the traffic of his innumerable cities. He lives in an industrial jungle. His most awe-inspiring sights are not the works of nature but the works of man. He is caught in a maze of brick walls and steel shapes, communications lines and enormous switchboards, six-lane clover-leaf highways and railroad switchyards of such complexity that the eye cannot predict the path that a train will follow through them. The island of Manhattan consists of only twenty-two square miles of rocky land; but two million people live on it, tier above tier, with the subways and three trunkline railroads underneath them, and tunnels under the subways, and tunnels under the rivers, and eighteen bridges gripping Long Island and the mainland. And all around them are clustered miles on miles of houses, and highways extending outward to the "dormitory towns." The Westerner could not endure it.

Yet the East is exciting, too. It generates ideas—big, continental ideas that have had enormous influence in the development of America. The ideas radiate outward and merge with native ideas in the different regions, to bring forth new ventures and new shapes. Thus from the Manhattan apex there extends westward an enormous triangle, one side 900 miles to Chicago, the other 1,000 miles to St. Louis. This is the "industrial triangle," the jugular vein of Western civilization. If an enemy could knock it out, or any substantial part of it, the U.S. would be unable to fight. For it contains more than half of all the capital investment of American industry and employs more than half of the industrial workers. Yet even within the triangle the ways of life differ. The people of Pittsburgh, who live among the ruddy fires of the steel mills, are "Westerners" to the New Yorker, who works or lives several hundred feet above the earth, has two martinis for lunch, and charges the rest of the country exorbitant sums for the use of his fertile imagination. And the people of Chicago really belong to the Midwest.

Nor is the way of life in New York City the same as the way of life in Boston, the hub of another industrial complex, composed chiefly of textiles, machine tools, high skills, and industrial specialties. Perhaps New England contains more incongruities than any region. The "elite" —for here, at any rate, there are such—still cling to a great cultural tradition that reached its climax with Ralph Waldo Emerson and shed a mellow light into the twentieth century through the pen of Henry Adams. Boston still has in the Athenaeum the nation's most notable private library, whose shelves are accessible only to "proprietors"; and it also has in the Widener at Harvard the biggest university library in the world. Yet the casual visitor to New England, including the American tourist who goes there for his summer vacation, has increasing difficulty in finding vestiges of the cultural tradition; for a large part of New England is encased like one of its famous clams in a shell of modern industrialization, in all of its ugliest aspects, including a plethora of billboards and hot-dog stands, together with an ex-Governor recently released from jail.

Up in Vermont and New Hampshire you will find a stubborn folk who have never yielded to the most "advanced" versions of the industrialized life—on a number of instances they have even refused to accept federal aid. And it is commonly said that this ruggedness, for which New England was once famed, is on the wane. Yet this is not really the case, as anyone who tries to live there will soon discover.

Within its industrialized shell the New England clam still flourishes—sober, hard-working, inventive, prudent, much more reserved than the Westerner, and downright unsympathetic to the flashy airs of the California goldfish.

Which one of these ways of life does the American mean by "the American way of life"? The answer is none of them. New England is no more "American" than the Northwest, nor Denver more so than Atlanta. This diversity itself is the way of life—nations within nations.

Nor can the way of life be defined by the life of any one particular community—the late Sinclair Lewis notwithstanding. For it is at the community level that America really begins to get diverse, because American life is not regional but local. The life of one town is influenced by a newspaper editor who wrote a history of his county and is a specialist on Indian warfare; the life of another, by a doctor interested in psychology. Here is a town addicted to schottisches, another whose social life centers around a Norwegian Harmony Club, another that features Czech gymnastic festivals. Here is a town with a Chinese restaurant, over there a town with German *verein;* over there a town, redolent of frijoles, that speaks mostly Spanish. All cultures are cherished—interwoven—modified. Here there are no memories and the town is flat and everyone eats out of cans. But there the memories of the old country are strong; the housewives treasure old Finnish recipes handed down from grandmothers who never saw America; or creole dishes, or Irish remedies for the gout.

And all this is accented by the extremists, the individualists, the eccentrics: the man with a thousand canaries; the man who keeps five buffalo in Connecticut; the electrician with odd working hours who spends his mornings in the town library in blue jeans reading Shakespeare; the nudists, the vegetarians, the Indian fortunetellers, the perpetual-motion inventors; the Amish who won't wear buttons; the old lady who writes poetry in the manner of Sara Teasdale. And then there are the hobbyists—the carpenters and gardeners—the man in the Great Plains who builds model ships—the amateur painters—the man who plays the flute in the morning, and the expert on Japanese prints, and the collector of chess sets. The way of life is none of these ways of life. And as for "standardization," it is lost in a forest of human foibles.

And yet, also, the way of life is *all* of these. For there is an extraordinary unity in this diversity, a coherence that resists all eccentricities, all power concentrations even. And this unity, which is not merely national in the ordinary sense of the word, pertains to quite another level of existence, another level of values from that which manifests itself with such diversity. It has to do with ideals, with a complex of principles and beliefs, to which all American life has reference. The truth, which has thus far been difficult for the rest of the world to grasp, is that Americans live on two planes at once—the practical and the ideal. The conflicts created by this ambivalent existence, which worry other people so much that they often feel constrained to reject one plane or the other, bother the American scarcely at all. . . .

81. THE DOMINANT VALUE PROFILE OF AMERICAN CULTURE *

CORA DU BOIS

The preceding selection described regional variations in "The American Way of Life." Here, Cora Du Bois—an anthropologist trained to view a sociocultural system as a single entity—presents us with a picture of the basic elements of American life considered as a totality. It should be noted that opinions differ on how valid it is to describe a complex society in the same way that one describes the relatively simple groupings traditionally studied by anthropologists. However one feels about this issue, Du Bois has here presented a number of provocative ideas about American culture.

This paper is an attempt to synthesize and systematize the relevant insights on American values advanced by a diverse group of writers from De Tocqueville through Myrdal to the authors of the polemic or conversational pieces that have been so numerous in the last decade. It will be addressed to the dominant value system of middle-class Americans. This system is rooted in the Protestant ethic and eighteenth-century rationalism. Many of its specific values are shared with other societies, but its configuration has come to be considered peculiarly American.

. . . . .

FOUR BASIC PREMISES

For our purposes the value premises of any culture can be considered to rest upon the assumptions made concerning man's cognitive

* *American Anthropologist*, Vol. 57, No. 6, Part 1 (December, 1955), 1232–1239. Reprinted by permission of *American Anthropologist* and the author.

The author (b. 1903) is Zemurray-Stone Professor of Anthropology at Harvard and Radcliffe. Served as social science consultant, World Health Organization, and has been associated with the Department of State. Recipient of: Order of the Crown of Thailand and Santimola Peace Medal; Exceptional Civilian Service Award, United States Department of the Army. Chief interest is personality and culture. Author: *People of Alor; Social Forces in Southeast Asia; Foreign Students of Higher Education in the United States.*

view of the universe, man's relation to it, and man's relation to other men. For the American middle class it is postulated that: (1) the universe is mechanistically conceived, (2) man is its master, (3) men are equal, and (4) men are perfectible. From these four basic premises alone many of the focal and specific values, as well as the directives, of the American value system can be derived. In the context of the last three hundred years of American history these assumptions have proved valid both experimentially and integratively (i.e., in a self-reinforcing sense) for the United States as a whole and, more specifically, for the American middle class. Despite changed situations and therefore the potential loss of experiential and integrative validation, we may nevertheless expect these assumptions to persist for a considerable period of time. There may be lags in a value system as there are in other aspects of culture.

FOCAL VALUES AND THEIR DIRECTIVES

The four premises given above yield at least three major focal values: material well-being that derives from the premise that man is master of a mechanistic universe; conformity that derives from the premise of man's equality; effort-optimism that derives from the premise of man's perfectibility. . . .

The nexus of specific values and directives clustering around each of these focal values can now be considered. Simultaneously the mutual reinforcement that occurs between the basic premises and their focal values, as well as the constant effort to resolve spurious oppositions through change, can be underlined. The inner consistency of the value system here presented accounts for much of the traditional vigor of "the American way of life" in the past. However, such vigor could not have existed without the reinforcement provided by the geographic setting of the American nation and the historic forces operative in the broader setting of Western European commercial, industrial, technical, and scientific growth in which the American nation shared.

1.   EFFORT-OPTIMISM

Work is a specific value in American society. It is not so much a necessary condition of existence as a positive good. It is a specific instrumental value through which man strives to reach not only the goal of his own perfectibility but also the goal of mastering a mechanistically conceived universe. But in values Vaihinger's "law of the preponderance of the means over the ends" is frequently operative. Thus work becomes a goal in itself and in the process may acquire the quality of activity for its own sake. Thus recreation, although theoretically the antithesis of work, nevertheless in its activism shows many of the aspects of work.

"Fun" is something that most Americans work hard for and at, so that they must be warned at forty to give up tennis for golf, or hunting trips for painting. Touring, whether at home or abroad, acquires the quality of a marathon. And this in turn is closely associated with another specific value linked with the effort-optimism syndrome, the importance placed on education. However, as we shall see later, the educational effort acquires a particularly American cast when taken in conjunction with the other two focal values, material well-being and conformity. In sum, as many foreigners have observed, American life gives the impression of activism. The directives, as well as the virtues and vices, associated with this optimistic activism are numerous: "If at first you don't succeed, try, try again"; or, in the more contemporary idiom, "Let's get this show on the road." The optimistic quality that pervades the American mood is clearly conveyed by the "bigger ergo better" mentality; the "never say die"; the "up and at 'em."

Vigor, at least as motility, connotes biologic youth. The cult of youthfulness in this society is again a specific value frequently commented upon by foreign observers. This observation is borne out by the popularity of the heroes manufactured in Hollywood and in the world of sports, by the advertisements of styles and cosmetics. As the average age of the population increases, this value is already showing signs of being given new interpretations in terms of geriatrics, etc. This will be alluded to again in following paragraphs.

2.   MATERIAL WELL-BEING

If indeed effort is optimistically viewed in a material universe that man can master, then material well-being is a consistent concomitant value. Not only is it consistent within the value system, but it has been amply demonstrated in our national experience. It has been manifest in the American standard of living. The nation's geographic frontier and its natural resources, combined with an era of invention, have convinced most Americans of the validity of such a proposition. In the American scene progress and prosperity have come to have almost identical meaning. So deeply convinced are most Americans of what is generally called "prosperity" that material well-being is close to being considered a "right" due to those who have conscientiously practiced the specific value of work. The congruence of this view with the new science of geriatrics, social insurance, and the growth of investment trusts is obvious. It represents a consistent adjustment of specific values to a changing situation. However, as the situational context changes it may weaken the present linkage between effort and optimism with the resulting devaluation of both and thereby set up a new strain for consistency that may alter the present configuration of the American value system.

One of the most common stereotypes about the United States is its materialism. Viewed in the context of the value system presented here, materialism is less a value *per se* than an optimistic assertion of two value premises (mastery over material nature and the perfectibility of man) that have operated in a favorable environment. What foreign observers may call materialism, with derogatory or envious innuendos, is to the American a success that carries the moral connotation of "rightness"—of a system that proves itself or, as Americans would say with complete consistency, that "works." Within the frame of American value premises, success phrased as material well-being resolves the material-spiritual opposition and becomes a proof of right-mindedness. "Hard work pays off." The old and widely known proverb that, "Virtue is its own reward" has a particularly American slant, meaning not that virtue is in itself a reward but rather that virtue is rewarded.

If hard work is a "good thing" in a material universe and since it has been rewarded by material well-being, consistency requires that manual labor should be accorded dignity or, at least, should not be considered undignified. Furthermore, manual labor is an unambiguous manifestation of that activism alluded to earlier.

The salience of material well-being as a focal value in American life leads into many by-ways, some of which confuse and confound members of societies founded on a different value configuration. In military terms, for example, Americans are so profoundly convinced of the correctness of the material well-being formula that logistics forms our basic strategy. Personal heroism, though it may amply exist, is not assumed to be the fundamental requisite for victory, as it is in France. In American terms, victory is won by the sheet of material laid down in front of advancing infantry and by the lines of supply that must be built up to provide such a barrier between hand-to-hand combat.

In the same vein, there is little room in the American middle-class value system for the realities of physical pain, brutality, and death. Since they are nonetheless natural and undeniable, they are given a highly stylized treatment in detective fiction, newspapers, and movies that provide an acceptable discharge of tension created by the discrepancy between values and reality. Many Americans are alienated and morally repelled when they encounter the poverty and misery prevalent in certain lands. They manage to go through life untouched experientially even by those in our own population who have not succeeded—those who exist hopelessly in rural or urban slums or those who are victims of physical or psychic disasters. We have provided for the latter so effectively that they are whisked away into institutions that our national surpluses permit us to provide comparatively lavishly. Death itself has been surrounded with appurtenances of asepsis. Evelyn Waugh's *The Loved Ones* could never have been written with India as a setting. The compelling quality of this value emerges when we consider world statistics on human welfare facilities. In this respect, the United States is consistently in the lead. Yet, if we compare these statistics with the outbursts of compassion that a newspaper account of a "blue baby" will elicit, we become aware not only of the power of this focal value but also the resultant constellation that might be summarized as compulsive compassionate activism.

3. CONFORMITY

Viewed historically it seems probable that conformity is a more recent focal value in American culture than effort-optimism and material well-being. It may represent one of the valuational changes induced by the strain for consistency assumed earlier in the paper to be one of the forces that alter value systems. Over a century ago De Tocqueville saw with singular clarity the potential threat to national solidarity inherent in the values of individual liberty, on the one hand, and of the sovereignty of enfranchised masses, on the other hand. In the contemporary American value system, conformity represents an attempt to resolve this dilemma. The France of today, with a comparable dilemma, has still to find a resolution.

If the premises of perfectibility and equality are linked with the focal value labeled effort-optimism, then each middle-class American may legitimately aspire to maximal self-realization. But, if man is to master through his efforts a mechanistic universe, he must co-operate with his fellow-men, since no single man can master the universal machine. In other words, people are individuated and prized, but if they are to co-operate with their fellow-men for mastery of the universe or, in more modest terms, of the immediate physical and sociopolitical environment, too great a degree of individualization would be an impediment. Also since the American value premises—in contradistinction to much of the rest of the world—include equality, the realization of the self in such a context would not necessarily imply the development of highly personalized and idiosyncratic but rather of egalitarian traits. Self-cultivation in America has as its goal less the achievement of uniqueness and more the achivement of similarity. This is a proposition many Frenchmen, for example, find difficult to grasp. The Japanese, with their stress upon self-cultivation in order more perfectly to discharge the obligations they owe their family and society, might come closer to understanding this American formulation. . . .

The assimilation of diverse immigrant groups to middle-class American values has been one of the remarkable sociopolitical achievements of the nation and testifies to the compelling vigor of its value system. As resources and space were more fully manned, the very lack of tolerance for differences that facilitated assimilation was finally to curtail the admission to this country of those who presented such differences.

Earlier in our history self-reliance and initiative were specific values attached to the focal value of liberty. Today these specific values have a new focus. Individual self-reliance and initiative are attached to the promotion of the commonweal and to the progress of society. Conformity has replaced liberty as a focal value to which these specific traits are attached. Co-operation has been added as a specific value that has facilitated the shift-over. The present American value system manifests a highly effective integration of the individual to society.

The ramification of this nexus into the sphere of education has been alluded to already. Education is envisaged as means by which all men through effort can realize themselves. But since co-operativeness is a specific value also inserted into this equation, education comes to be envisaged as a means to make more men more effective workers and better citizens. The land-grant colleges, the vast network of public schools, and the system of free and compulsory education with its stress on education for citizenship and on technical skills have set the American educational system apart from that of many other countries. In the American context the linkage between conformity, effort-optimism, and material well-being leads inevitably to mass education with the emphasis on the common man rather than the uncommon man, to its technical and practical cast, to what seems to many observers its low standards. Simultaneously, to many Americans schooling has acquired the weight of a goal rather than a means. A college degree is a "good thing" in itself, whether or not the education entailed is prized. This concatenation does not lead one to expect perfection as a directive for performance in American life.

In a society where co-operation and good citizenship are valued and where the commonweal is served by having each man develop himself through his own efforts, a generous friendliness, openness, and relaxation of interpersonal relations are not only possible but desirable so long as the associated expanding economy furnishes the situational possibilities. Rigid class structures and protective privacies are inconsistent with the values here enumerated. Doors need not be closed to rooms; fences need not be built around properties. The tall hedges of England and the enclosing walls of France are not appropriate to the American scene, where life faces outward rather than inward. If every individual is as "good as" the next and all are good citizens—what is there to hide? The open front yards, the porches, or more recently the picture windows that leave the home open to everyone's view, the figurative and literal klieg lights under which our public figures live are all evidence of the value placed in American life on likeness and the pressure exerted for conformity. This is very different from saying that

American middle-class individuals are in fact all alike. It means merely that likeness is valued.

The American hostility to figures in authority has been frequently noted, and in this connection the almost placatory informality and familiarity of American manners that serve to play down status differences have been pointed out. The apparent contradiction between the striving for upward mobility and the distrust of those who achieve pre-eminent positions can now be seen in more balanced terms. If the argument advanced here is correct, upward mobility is valued as successful activity, but when it reaches a point where it outstrips the premise of equality and the focal value of conformity it borders on *hubris*.

In this connection then the relaxed, friendly manner of American life so frequently commented upon by foreign observers can be gauged in the broader context of an adjustment to incompatible values. The search for popularity, the desire to be liked, the wish to be considered a "good fellow," are searches for reassurance that, in striving to achieve all the ends implied by the focal value of effort-optimism, one has not exceeded the bounds set by the other focal value of conformity. That this process can operate at any level of actual achievement, from the presidency of the United States to chairmanship of an Elks Club committee, need not be stressed. It is the boss, the politician, the teacher, the "big shots" who are disvalued figures to the extent that their superordinate position implies authority. It is the movie star and the baseball hero who are valued figures since their pre-eminence connotes no authority but at the same time dramatizes the meteoric rise to fame and popularity through hard work and youthful striving.

Another aspect of American social life is thrown into relief in the effort to balance effort-optimism, material well-being, and conformity and their linked specific values. In the business and financial world, despite conservative tendencies, there has been a steady trend toward consolidation and standardization. Although the familiar and now perhaps inappropriate hue and cry is still raised about monopoly and big business, the latter, at least, serves the greater material well-being of the American mass consumer, whose values are geared to conformity. "Big business" is consonant with the American value system here portrayed so long as the owners of such enterprises are pictured as the American middle class, so long as savings are invested in the stocks and bonds of these enterprises so that the middle class shares "equally" in its successes, and so long as the authorities in such enterprises are presented as servants of the people. In these terms the American value system is served. The dangers of a too extreme individualistic power-centered authority are thus allayed, and competitive rivalry is brought under control. . . .

82. THE LOSS OF PEASANT HERITAGE IN JAPAN °

IWAO ISHINO AND JOHN D. DONOGHUE

Each culture and subculture has basic values and patterns of behavior distinguishing it from others. We commonly associate such values and behavior with types of communities or regional areas. The range of regions and community types, for which we hold images, has expanded greatly, but has not kept pace with change brought about by technological advances and other factors. Thus the images held of a given community-type sometimes persist long after extensive changes have occurred. Just as many Americans talk of rural and urban communities in terms that are no longer valid, so the authors of this selection had perceptions of the Japanese peasant village which were based on earlier acquaintance. Here they describe briefly the contemporary Japanese village and some of the changes that have occurred in recent years.

. . . Since October [we] . . . have visited nine of the thirteen villages surveyed a decade ago by a team of Japanese and American social scientists; and examined three of these nine more intensively with the aid of 15 students from the University of Tokyo. These three villages . . . exemplify respectively an isolated mountain village, a marginal coastal community, and a lowland plains village.

The authors arrived in the field with certain preconceptions and beliefs about the nature of Japanese peasantry. Some of these beliefs were implicit, but most were explicit because they have been a familiar feature of the literature of both American and Japanese scholars. The writers wish to take this opportunity to examine these preconceptions in the light of new evidence. The purpose of this paper, then, is to review these early assumptions and to summarize the authors' present views.

° Prepared for the Annual Meetings of the Central States Anthropological Society, Madison, Wisconsin, May, 1959.

Iwao Ishino (b. 1921) is Associate Professor of Anthropology and Sociology at Michigan State University. Extensive research field work in Japan and formerly Fulbright Lecturer, University of Tokyo. Author numerous articles in professional journals.

John D. Donoghue, Fulbright Research Scholar, Tohoku University. Formerly on faculty University of Texas and Notre Dame University.

OUR PRE-CONCEPTIONS

We knew that Japan was an over-populated country and poorly endowed with natural resources. The amount of arable land—only 16 percent of the total area—had reached its upper limits long ago. Further reclamation and conversion of the hillsides into arable land was deemed impossible. We also knew that a land reform program had been carried out several years before in which tenancy was drastically reduced. We had figures which told us that the average farm household operated a strip of land of only two-and-a-half acres or, more accurately, 5.9 separate strips of land totalling only 2.5 acres. We read that this rural population of 36 million represented 40 percent of the nation's population, and that it was able to produce up to 80 percent of the nation's food requirements.

Yet this 40 percent earned only 17 percent of the total national income. These figures were sufficient to suggest that the farmers of Japan were living at a standard considerably below that of the city workers and that they indeed were "peasants." What else could they do but to live frugally and to cherish the classic peasant values that hard work is a virtue in itself and that farming is not a money-making business but a way of life? How else could they maintain their self-respect if they did not maintain a closely integrated natural community which insulated itself from the impersonal, competitive, and frivolous life of the urbanite?

Such were our thoughts and impressions about Japanese peasantry before we began our studies. But this picture did not hold its shape for long. As we visited one village after another the image began to fade. The "peasant" image gave way to an image of a hard-headed commercial "farmer." The reasons for the change in image ran somewhat as follows:

ARE JAPANESE AGRICULTURALISTS "PEASANTS"?

While we did not quite expect the Japanese "peasant" to be following the same cultivation methods his great grandfather used, we thought the technical advances would be limited. We were surprised, however, at the refinements that had developed. We came to the conclusion that the Japanese farms may be small, but that it was not merely "gardening" activity.

The successful farmer must not only work with his hands, but also with his head in order to make his 2.5 acre farm produce as efficiently as it does. He works on a small margin and so he must be careful that each decision he makes is the best one. But in these days, the Japanese peasant is confronted with many kinds of decisions his grandfather never had to make. Dozens of basic innovations about farming have been placed before him in recent years. The information about them comes to him from many directions: from the farmer in the next hamlet, the local agricultural agent, the technical advisor for the cooperative, the salesman of fertilizers and farm equipment, the canning company looking for raw materials, the popular farm journal issued by the co-operatives, and his wife who might have learned about the new idea at the local Women's Club lecture meeting.

The officers in agricultural cooperatives have told us that farm families most resistant to new ideas are "holiday" farmers who work in a nearby factory or office while their women folk and children operate the farm. Perhaps these represent the small, but significant, number of farmers who are leaving the farms, after they get their sons educated and placed in a town occupation. On the other hand there are the eager farmers who actively seek technological improvements. These progressive farmers, by their example, encourage other less imaginative farmers to follow suit. They are the ones who are first to use farm machinery. Those whose role is to promote the new farm technology—like the farm extension agent and the technical advisors of the cooperatives—introduce the innovations through these action-oriented farmers.

The kinds of changes taken over by the peasants can be readily observed in the villages. The use of plastic covering to hasten the maturation of rice seedlings and to protect other kinds of crops has become a familiar part of the landscape. The characteristic odor from "night soil" fertilizers is absent even though they are still used in large quantities. The rhythmic coughing sounds of small cultivators can be heard. Technical progress can also be indicated by statistics. For instance, in five years from 1948 to 1952, the rice yields per hectare increased 64 percent.

The Japanese peasant must use his head not only for increasing his yields but also in other ways, for example in marketing. Like farmers elsewhere he is concerned with locating the best market for his crops. Except for rice, which is usually handled through the agricultural cooperatives, other commodities require personal attention and sometimes long term planning. In one of our sample villages, for example, the farmers lobbied for the construction of a highway that would lead into the city of Hiroshima. If such a road were built, this would enable them to double their income from the vegetables which they already raise, and also to raise such quality items as late season tomatoes. Where the locality has many producers of a single crop—such as silk, mandarin oranges, milk, and tea—marketing cooperatives are available. Peasants located near large cities often transport their products by their own three-wheeled trucks or contract someone to do it.

Financial problems are also matters of great concern to the Japanese peasant, particularly for obtaining farm credit. Interest rates are high and so are taxes. It is interesting to note that some farm families have incorporated themselves as a business and thereby claim tax deductions not given to farmers. Court decision on this is pending. The government has put in a crop insurance system which provides a kind of protection the farmer never had before. Farm credit, interest rates, taxes, and crop insurance are financial problems that rarely concerned the grandfather of today's peasant.

As we said before, then, the management of a two-and-a-half acre farm is a complicated business. The Japanese "peasant" is learning to adapt himself to the modern world and, incidentally, to the Great Traditions. We conclude, therefore, that the Japanese peasant is being rapidly transformed into something else: a hard-headed and hard-working commercial farmer.

But this peasant-turned-farmer is still caught in the inexorable vise between too many people on the one hand and not enough land on the other. Seen in the large perspective, however, he is not retreating to the security of his traditional ways nor escaping into the world of supernaturalism. Neither is he a revolutionist wishing to upset the existing political order. We think some of the reasons for this lie in the nature of his local community.

THE HAMLET

The face-to-face, natural community of the Japanese rural population is the hamlet. Other than the family or household there is probably no other social grouping that exerts so much influence upon the peasant's daily activities and his social outlook. Its members operate farm plots in adjoining areas, manage the communally owned pastureland and forest reserves, share the water from the same irrigation system, repair and maintain their common roads; pay their respects at the common tutelary shrine; and celebrate their annual festivals.

In this kind of tightly knit community of several dozen families, then, the Japanese farmer can and does find a certain degree of security, in spite of whatever inequities there might be between him and the city dweller. Interestingly enough, certain events have taken place in the postwar period to increase the solidarity of the hamlet. The prime motive for this was the land reform program which removed the economic dependence of the tenants upon the landlords. Social distance between the top families and those lower has decreased; overt deference patterns are diminishing; and some cases of inter-marriage between classes have been noted. Numerous members of the former tenant class have been elected to the village assembly and hold other positions of influence in the hamlet. Most of these positions were not formerly open to the tenant class. We can also say that in general the prestige of the individual has come to be based less on his family background and more on his personality and accomplishments. In this sense the hamlet has become more democratic.

Another reason for the generally healthy outlook of the Japanese farmer is that the gap in the living standards between him and his city cousin is being closed. This is not only reflected in the national statistics on income and nutrition, but can be directly observed in the villages. The range and quality of merchandise carried in the village stores are good and cannot easily be distinguished from that found in suburban shops in Tokyo. New roads have been constructed, telephone lines put in, temples renovated, and thatched roofs replaced with tile. In every village we visited, we saw hundreds of bicycles, and dozens of motorcycles, trucks, and busses. We have noted five to ten television sets in eight of the nine villages visited. The ninth village was not within the existing television telecast zone. Washing machines were becoming popular and the farmers' wives were buying ready-made work clothes at the co-operative store. They said it was cheaper to buy than to sew them at home.

SOME DIFFERENCE BETWEEN VILLAGES

The foregoing, we hope, is sufficient to suggest how the Japanese peasant is adjusting to the situation of too many people and not enough land. Scientific and technological advances have come into the peasant's way of life and as a result he is becoming less a peasant and more a commercial farmer. We see the hamlet and the favorable conditions in it, playing a vital role in helping him make this transition.

But, to look more closely at the facts, we see a basic difference among the communities in which the Japanese peasant lives—a difference which is important for understanding his adjustment to modern conditions.

Japanese rural communities have to be classified in many ways—by size, by kinship structure, by crops raised, etc. But for our purposes the most significant classification is in terms of degree of isolation from major urban centers. For convenience, let us call those which are located near the large cities or close to the major railroad lines as "hinterland" villages; while those located in remote regions such as those in the mountain areas are "isolated" communities.

With regard to these two types of villages, we note a very interesting difference. Paradoxically, the isolated villages seem to be further advanced and more progressive than hinterland communities in taking over innovations in agricultural techniques, in home improvements, in family relations (e.g., mother-in-law and daughter-in-law adjustments) and in birth control measures. The "backwardness" of these isolated villages is no longer so apparent as it was before. The reason for this, we think, is that the social solidarity is greater in the isolated communities and local pride in making it a shining example gains wider appeal. Furthermore, the capable persons and potential leaders do not leave these villages to the same extent as they do in other types. The temptations to be drawn away into the town and city are not as strong nor as real. This is to say, then, that compensating factors are operating here. The isolated villages help the Japanese peasant make a better adjustment to life by providing him with a comparatively active and progressive social environment. In the case of the peasant in the hinterland communities, his opportunities to move into the urban centers are greater and his dependence upon fellow villagers for recreation, part-time employment, and friendship is less.

These differences between village types, however, can be overstressed. We reiterate the original statement that the opportunities of the Japanese peasant to participate in the Great Tradition have increased immeasurably. His stake in the economy is larger and his status in the society is higher. The confining pressure of too many people and not enough land is still there, but what has been accomplished within this framework is remarkable. . . .

83. THE BLACKS *

PETER ABRAHAMS

This article by Peter Abrahams demonstrates that it is not the superficialities of a common race and color which unite men; men are welded into stable social organizations by value similarities. It is common social and cultural background, not biology as such, which leads men to respond alike to the same stimuli. Thus, the American Negro and the African native, living in totally different ecological and social settings, have almost nothing in common. It is significant, too, that one of the most important rallying cries in Africa today is nationalism or tribalism, not race. This fact, as Abrahams implies, is not comprehended easily by racially conscious Americans, but comprehend it we must if we are to deal effectively with the modern African.

* Reprinted by permission of the author. Copyright © by The Curtis Publishing Company. Originally published in *Holiday*, Vol. 25, No. 4, April, 1959, pp. 74–75, 118–126, passim.

The author (b. 1919) is a British journalist and novelist. Member, the Society of Authors and International P.E.N. Author: *Mine Boy; Dark Testament; Wild Conquest; Tell Freedom; Return to Goli.*

It was a hot, humid, oppressive August day in Accra, capital of the Gold Coast that was to become Ghana. The air had the stillness of death. I walked down toward the sea front. Perhaps there would be the hint of a breeze there. As I neared the sea front I was assailed by a potent stench of the sea with strong overtones of rotting fish.

The houses were drab, run-down wooden structures or made of corrugated iron, put together any way you please. The streets were wide and tarred, and each street had an open-drainage system into which young boys and old men piddled when they needed to relieve themselves. I have seen women empty chamber pots into these drains in the early morning. The fierce sun takes care of the germs, but God help you if smells made you sick.

In about eight minutes of walking, some fifteen "taxis" pulled up beside me: "Hi, massa! Taxi, massa! Me go anywhere you go cheap!" They are all private taxis with no meters and driven by strapping young men with flashing teeth. The place is full of taxi drivers willing to go anywhere and do anything cheap.

The street traders here are women. "Mammy traders," they are called. They trade in everything. They sell cigarettes, one at a time; round loaves of bread and hunks of cooked meat on which the big West African flies make sport. They love bargaining and haggling. They are a powerful economic factor in the life of the country. The more prosperous ones own their own trucks, some own fleets of trucks. These "mammy trucks" are the principal carriers of the country. They carry passengers as well as produce and go hurtling across the countryside with little regard for life or limb. Each truck has its own distinctive slogan, such as: REPENT FOR DEATH IS ROUND THE CORNER, or ENTER WITH-OUT HOPE, or THE LAST RIDE, or IF IT MUST IT WILL. My own favorite, and I traveled in this particular truck, pleaded, NOT TODAY O LORD NOT TODAY.

I passed many mammy traders, many mammy trucks, before I reached the sea front. I crossed a street, jumped over an open drain, and there was the sea. But there was no breeze, and no shade from the terrible sun. In the end I gave in to the idea of "taxi, massa, taxi" and looked about for one. But now there was no taxi in sight. Instead, I saw, suddenly, a long procession of many women and a few men. The procession swung around a corner and came into full view, twenty or thirty yards long. The women wore white flowing robes and white kerchiefs on their heads. Their faces were painted into grotesque masks made with thick streaks of black, red, white and yellow paints. The heavy thud of bare feet rose above the hum of the sea.

Then, all at once, the drums burst forth and there was no other sound about me. The marching women began to jig, then dance. As the tail of the procession passed me the drums reached a frenzy. A thin, pure note from a reed rose above the drums. The whole procession became a shivering, shaking mass. The reed note held longer than seemed human. And then, dramatically, there was silence. The thudding feet faded away out of sight and sound. There was silence and a slight racing of my heartbeat and the hum of the sea, and, of course, the overpowering fishy stench.

I thought of Richard Wright, with whom I had had breakfast that morning. This was his first visit to any part of Africa and he seemed to find it bewildering. Countee Cullen, the late American Negro poet, had speculated:

> One three centuries removed
> From the scenes his fathers loved,
> Spicy grove, cinnamon tree,
> What is Africa to me? [1]

Wright was finding the answers and finding them disconcerting. He had been astounded by the casual attitude to sex. There was, he had said, too much sex, too casually given and taken; so that it worked out as no sex, with none of the emotional involvement associated with sex in the western mind. He shook his head with a slight disgust. The open drains into which young boys and old men piddled had led him to conclude that Africans piddled rather more than other people. The sight of young men dancing together, holding hands, disturbed the puritan in him. He expressed to me that morning what he later summed up in his book on the Gold Coast: "I was black and they were black but it did not help me."

What Wright did not understand, what his whole background and training had made difficult for him to understand, was that being black did not of itself qualify one for acceptance in tribal Africa. But how could he, when there are thousands of urban-bred Africans up and down the vast continent who do not themselves understand this? The more perceptive of the urban Africans are only now beginning to comprehend, but slowly.

Being black is a small matter in tribal Africa because the attitude toward color is healthy and normal. Color does not matter. Color is an act of God that neither confers privileges nor imposes handicaps on a man. A man's skin is like the day: the day is either clear or dark. There is nothing more to it until external agencies come in and invest it with special meaning and importance.

What does matter to the tribal African, what is important, is the complex pattern of his position within his own group and his relations with the other members of the group. He is no Pan-African dreaming of a greater African glory when the white man is driven into the sea. The acute race consciousness of the American Negro, or of the black South

[1] From *Heritage*, copyright 1925 Harper & Bros. Reprinted by permission.

African at the receiving end of Apartheid, is alien to him. The important things in his life are anything but race and color—until they are forced on him. And "mother Africa" is much too vast to inspire big continental dreams in him. She is a land of huge mountains, dark jungles and vast deserts. In her rivers and in her jungles and in her grasslands lurk creatures that are the enemies of man: the leopard and the lion, the snake and crocodile. All this makes travel, by the old African methods, extremely difficult and makes for isolation between one group of people and another. The African who is in Britain is likely to be a deal better informed on what is happening all over the continent than would be his fellow African in any of the main centers of both tribal and non-tribal Africa. In terms of communications the man in the tribe lives in the Dark Ages.

Richard Wright was surprised that even educated Africans, racially conscious literate people, had not heard of him and were skeptical of a grown man earning his living by writing. They could not understand what kind of writing brought a man enough money to support a family. Wright really wanted to understand the African, but—"I found the African an oblique, a hard-to-know man."

My sympathies were all with Wright.

The heat and salty rancid fish smell had made me desperately thirsty. Across the way a mammy trader squatted beside her pile of merchandise: cooked meat, sweet potatoes—a whole host of edibles— and some bottles of opaque white liquid that could be either coconut milk or palm juice, as well as the inevitable little pile of cigarettes priced at a penny apiece. I had been warned of the risks involved in eating anything sold by the street traders. But to hell with it, I was thirsty and not exactly a stranger to African germs. I crossed the street, felt the bottles and chose the one that seemed coolest and looked the least opaque.

"How much?"

"One shilling." The carved ebony face looked at me with dead eyes.

I pulled the screwed-up newspaper stopper from the bottle, wiped its mouth and took a swig. I could not decide whether it was coconut milk or palm juice. It had been heavily watered down and sweetened. But it was wet and thirst-quenching. I drank half the bottle, firmly ignoring the little foreign bodies that floated in the liquid. Then I paid her and drank the rest. I put down the empty and began to move away.

"You African?" she asked in her harsh, cold, masculine voice.

I stopped, turned and looked at her face. It was as deadly cold and impersonal as before: not a flicker of feeling in her eyes. Like an African mask, I thought. But unlike Wright, I did not try to penetrate it. I knew the futility of trying. She would show feeling if and when she decided. Not before.

"Yes," I said, and added, "from the south. Far, far south."

She paused for so long that I began to move again.

"You like here?" Nationalism had obviously touched her.

I turned back to her. "No," I said.

"Why you don't like?"

"I don't say I don't like."

"But you don't like?"

I showed her my teeth, African-wise, which is neither smile nor grimace but a blending of the two. "*You* like Africa?" I asked.

Now it was her turn to show me her teeth. There was a flicker of feeling in her eyes, then they went dead again. She nodded. I had established my claim. Only outsiders—white people or the Richard Wrights—liked or disliked Africa.

. . . . .

My mind kept slipping back to . . . Jomo or Johnstone Kenyatta, now imprisoned in his native Kenya for leading the Mau-Mau movement. . . .

A year earlier, I had flown up to Kenya from South Africa and visited Kenyatta. I felt terribly depressed as I got off the plane. Things had grown so much uglier in the Union. The barricades were up in the ugly war of color. When I had left South Africa in the dim-and-distant past, there were isolated islands where black and white could meet in neutral territory. When I went back in 1952, the islands were submerged under the rising tide of color hatreds, and I was glad to quit that dark, unhappy land which yet compelled my love.

It was in this mood that I got off the plane. I had not seen my friend Jomo for years. Now there he was, just outside the airport terminal building, leaning on a heavy cane, bigger than I remembered him in Europe, paunchy, his face looking puffy. And behind him was a huge crowd of Africans.

. . . . .

"It's good to see you again, Johnstone." I gripped his hand.

"Jomo," he replied. The hint of ironic speculation was back in his eyes. A slightly sardonic, slightly bitter smile played on his lips.

"Welcome to Kenya, Peter," he said. Then, abruptly: "Come meet the leaders of my people. They've been waiting long."

We moved forward and the crowd gathered about us. Jomo made

a little speech in Kikuyu, then translated it for my benefit. A little old man, ancient as the hills, with huge holes in his ears, then welcomed me on behalf of the land and its people. Again Jomo translated.

After this we all bundled into the fleet of rattling old cars and set off for the Kikuyu reserve in the heart of the African bush. Kenyatta became silent and strangely remote during the journey.

We stopped at the old chief's compound, where other members of the tribe waited to welcome me. By this time the reception committee had grown to a few hundred. About me, pervading the air, was the smell of burning flesh; a young cow was being roasted in my honor. Before I entered the house a drink was handed to me. Another was handed to the old chief and a third to Kenyatta. The old man muttered a brief incantation and spilled half his drink on the earth as a libation. Jomo and I followed suit. Then the three of us downed our drinks and entered the house.

A general feasting and drinking then commenced, both inside and outside the house. I was getting a full ceremonial tribal welcome. The important dignitaries of the tribe slipped into the room in twos and threes, spoke to me through Kenyatta for a few moments and then went away, making room for others.

"Africa doesn't seem to change," Kenyatta murmured between dignitaries. There was a terrible undercurrent of bitterness behind the softly murmured words. I was startled by it and looked at his face. For a fleeting moment he looked like a trapped, caged animal.

He saw me looking at him and quickly composed his face into a slightly sardonic humorous mask. "Don't look too closely," he said.

And still the dignitaries filed in, had a drink, spoke their welcome and went out.

The ceremonial welcome reached its high point about midnight. Huge chunks of the roasted cow were brought in to us, and we gnawed at the almost raw meat between swigs of liquor. Outside, there was muted drumming. Voices were growing louder and louder.

Suddenly, in the midst of a long-winded speech by an immensely dignified Masai chief from a neighboring and friendly tribe, Kenyatta jumped up, grabbed his heavy cane and half staggered to the door.

"Come, Peter," he called.

Everybody was startled. I hesitated. He raised his cane and beckoned to me with it. I knew that this would be a dreadful breach of tribal etiquette.

"Come, man!" he snapped.

I got up, aware of the sudden silence that had descended on the huge gathering. By some strange magic everybody seemed to know that something had gone wrong.

"Jomo," I said.

"I can't stand any more," he snapped. "Come!"

I followed him to the door. I knew the discourtesy we were inflicting on the tribe. I also knew that my friend was at the breaking point. We walked through the crowd of people, got into Kenyatta's car and drove off into the night. The African moon was big and yellow, bathing the land in a soft light that almost achieved the clarity of daylight.

He took me to his home. It was a big, sprawling, empty place on the brow of a hill. Inside, it had nothing to make for comfort. There were hard wooden chairs, a few tables and only the bed in the bedroom. There were no books, none of the normal amenities of western civilization. When we arrived two women emerged from somewhere in the back and hovered about in the shadows. They brought in liquor, but I never got a clear glimpse of either of them. My friend's anguish of spirit was such that I did not want to ask questions. We sat on the veranda and drank steadily and in silence until we were both miserably, depressingly drunk.

And then Kenyatta began to speak in a low, bitter voice of his frustration and of the isolated position in which he found himself. He had no friends. There was no one in the tribe who could give him the intellectual companionship that had become so important to him in his years in Europe. The things that were important to him—consequential conversation, the drink that represented a social activity rather than the intention to get drunk, the concept of individualism, the inviolability of privacy—all these were alien to the tribesmen in whose midst he lived. So Kenyatta, the western man, was driven in on himself and was forced to assert himself in tribal terms. Only thus would the tribesmen follow him and so give him his position of power and importance as a leader.

To live without roots is to live in hell, and no man chooses voluntarily to live in hell. The people who could answer his needs as a western man had erected a barrier of color against him in spite of the fact that the taproots of their culture had become the taproots of his culture too. By denying him access to those things which complete the life of western man, they had forced him back into the tribalism from which he had so painfully freed himself over the years.

None of this was stated explicitly by either Kenyatta or myself. But it was there in his brooding bitter commentary on both the tribes and the white settlers of the land. For me, Kenyatta became that night a man who in his own life personified the terrible tragedy of Africa and the terrible secret war that rages in it. He was the victim both of tribalism and of westernism gone sick. His heart and mind and body were the battlefield of the ugly violence known as the Mau Mau revolt long before it broke out in that beautiful land. The tragedy is that he was so rarely gifted, that he could have made such a magnificent contribution in other circumstances.

What then is tribal man? Perhaps his most important single characteristic is that he is not an individual in the western sense. Psychologically and emotionally he is the present living personification of a number of forces, among the most important of which are the ancestral dead. The dead have a powerful hold on the living. They control and regulate the lives and activities of the living from the grave. They hand out the rules and codes by which the living conduct their daily affairs. If there is a drought, if there is a famine, it is a sign that the ancestors are angry because someone has broken a rule of the tribe, a law laid down by the dead. There will be no peace, no order, no prosperity in the tribe until the ancestors are appeased.

So the chief calls the whole tribe to a meeting in which the guilty ones will be "smelled out." The procedure begins with the drums—a key factor in African life. Their insistent throbs call the people to the gathering on a placid, almost momentous key at first, but working on the emotions. Everyone in the village will be present; neither man, woman nor child would think of not obeying the summons. They form a circle, with the witch doctor or medicine man and the drummers to the fore. When all the people are assembled the throbbing of the drums increases. They beat in tune to the heartbeats of the human circle.

The witch doctor is dressed in lion or leopard skin, sometimes in monkey skin. His face is painted in bold streaks of color: white, black, red. There are crisscrossing lines on his body too. He wanders about the center of the circle, almost idly at first. Every now and then he pauses and looks straight into someone's eyes and keeps on looking. For the person looked at, this is an encounter with fate. Few stare back. Their eyes slide past his face or go glazed. They fear but are not supposed to fear. They know the ancestors are just, that the innocent are never punished. To experience fear, therefore, is an acknowledgement of guilt. It is not necessary to know the nature of your guilt to be guilty. If you were not, there would be no fear in your mind.

The tempo of the drums increases. The witch doctor begins to dance, slowly at first. He begins to talk in a high-pitched nasal voice; spirits always talk through their noses. The drums and the incantations go on and on, getting faster and wilder, dominating the hearts and minds of all the circle. People begin to tremble and shiver. Some drop down in a trance and lie moaning on the ground. Everyone is possessed by the frenzy of the drums. The spirits of the ancestors are abroad.

Suddenly the drums stop. The witch doctor stands fixed for a dreadful moment that seems without end. Then he pounces. He grabs his victim and drags him or her into the center of the circle. The victim does not resist, does not protest. The ancestors are always just.

There may be one, there may be many victims. But once the victim or victims are "smelled out," the hypnotic spell of the drums is broken.

People relax. Their hearts beat normally once more. Now the ancestors will be propitiated and the living freed of the evil which beset them. Now the famine or the drought or the plague or whatever had beset the land will depart from it. And so, while the victim or victims are put to death, the rest of the tribe celebrates the passing of the great evil.

It may be that in this particular village—almost anywhere in tribal Africa—the spirits of the ancestors rest in a sacred tree. In that case the victim is taken to the tree and executed there so that the ancestors can taste his blood. Or his heart may be cut out and put at the foot of the tree. Or it may be that the spirits of the ancestors have entered the body of a snake, a very popular sacred symbol in certain areas of West Africa. In that case the living victim is taken to the snake and left there, bound, to be executed by the ancestors acting through the snake. Or it may be that the village is on the edge of a lake, especially one of the lakes of Central Africa where the spirits of the ancestors enter the body of a crocodile. In that case the victim is fed to the crocodiles. Wherever the spirits of the ancestors may be—and they are always in some living animal or plant—it is there that the victim is taken to propitiate them and so deliver the rest of the tribe from the calamity.

Another key characteristic of tribal man is that his society is exclusive and not, like western society, inclusive. The lines are drawn very clearly, very sharply. Anybody not an "insider" is an enemy, actually or potentially; is someone to distrust, someone to fear, someone to keep at bay. There is no choice, no volition about this. It is something ordained by the ancestral dead. The tribal society is therefore possibly the most exclusive society in the 20th century world. If you are not in the tribe, there is no way into it. If you are in it, there is no way out of it except death. Dissent is not recognized. To break the rules of the tribe is to court death.

Even the family, the foundation of the tribal in-group, is no simple affair. It is often a cluster of four generations. A man's family can be made up of his father, his father's first, second and third wives—there may be more—and the children of these. A man inherits the wives and children of his brothers who die before him. The wives then become his wives, the children of his brother become brothers and sisters to his own children by his own wife. Then there are the children's children. These and the old people, the grandparents, make up the immediate family, the heart of the in-group. Then there are the families related to one's family by blood ties—the families of uncles and cousins. These have the same complex structure of many wives and brothers and sisters, many of whom are inherited. A group of such blood-related families make up the clan. Clans have been known to be big enough to fill whole villages.

The blood link is generally carried through the males, though there have been rare occasions in the past when women ruled the tribes, and descent was reckoned through the female side. The senior male, the grandfather or father, is the head, and all authority over the family is vested in him. He settles all family disputes, gives or withholds land and cattle, gives or withholds consent to marriages. Even so, custom requires him to "hear" all the adult males of the family before he hands out an important decision.

. . . . .

Another and most vital factor in the life of tribal man is his attitude to life and death. Neither life nor death is ever wholly accidental. Disaster is never natural. These are brought about by the good and evil spirits all around us. The evil spirits are preoccupied with bringing disaster on the tribe, the good with protecting the tribe. To achieve their malign ends, evil spirits enter the bodies of ordinary human beings. To fight the evil spirits, good spirits enter the bodies of witch doctors. Life and death are thus out of the hands of mortal men.

The world of tribal man is so dominated by the spirits that some tribes will not eat birds because of the spirits that dwell in them; some will not eat fish; some are vegetarians; some eat meat only.

Tribal man is hemmed in, imprisoned by his ancestors. His horizons are only as wide as they permit. He is also protected by them. The rules are such that there are no orphans in the tribe, no misfits, no neurotics. And of course, the ancestral dead are hostile to change.

This, then, is the "oblique, the hard-to-know man" whom Richard Wright encountered on his first visit to Africa. He is the man who raised Nkrumah to power. He is the man whose pressures led Jomo Kenyatta to the Mau Mau and then to his lonely prison-exile in a barren and isolated spot and, probably, to banishment from Kenya in the end. He, tribal man, will have a crucial say in the future of Africa.

The ancestral dead notwithstanding, change is being imposed on him. How he reacts to the change will have a powerful bearing on tomorrow's Africa.

If the men inaugurating the new ways have the sense and the patience to preserve the finer qualities of the old ways and fuse these with the new, then we can expect something magnificently new out of Africa.

84. IMAGES OF THE UNITED STATES

AND BRITAIN HELD BY

FOREIGN-EDUCATED INDIANS *

RUTH HILL USEEM AND JOHN USEEM

*It is difficult for us to analyze our own society and culture
because we are so completely involved in it. Understanding
of a second culture frequently provides a perspective from
which we can better understand our own or a third society.
Another means of achieving this understanding is to see what other
people think of us. In this selection the Useems report some
of the perceptions which Indians, who have studied in the
United States and the United Kingdom, have of these Western
societies. The extensive international exchange of persons is
primarily designed to improve understanding of other cultures,
but those participating in these programs may return with new
ability to look at their own way of life.*

This account concerns the way a sample of Indians educated in the
United States and United Kingdom appraise American and British character and assess certain aspects of American and British life. It also includes the consequences of these attitudes for the foreign-educated
Indians and for the immediate social world in which they live.

Our information is based on the life histories of a sample of Western-
educated Indians who reside in the small towns and cities of Bombay
State, located in the central-western section of India. The cases include
persons who were trained in the West both before and after India attained its independence (1947). The majority are currently employed

* From "Images of the United States and Britain Held by Foreign-Educated
Indians," by Ruth Hill Useem and John Useem. Volume 295 of *The Annals* of The
American Academy of Political and Social Science (September, 1954), pp. 73–82.

Ruth Hill Useem (b. 1915) is a Research Consultant in Sociology and Anthropology, Michigan State University. Coauthor, with her husband, of *The Western-
Educated Man in India*.

John Useem (b. 1910) is Chairman of the Department of Sociology and Anthropology, Michigan State University. His special interests include cross-cultural relations and American culture. Contributor to: *Human Problems in Technological
Change; Cultural Patterns and Technical Change;* coauthor (with Mrs. Useem):
The Western-Educated Man in India.

in colleges and universities, the government, business and industry; a few are unemployed; and the rest are engaged full time in political affairs, as editors of newspapers, and in the social services. They stem from a variety of social classes and subcastes; most rank now as members of the middle classes in their communities.

By comparing the attitudes toward the two nations, we can discern which of the images held are common to Western countries and which are confined in particular to the United States and to the United Kingdom.

When a person looks at another society, certain factors bias what he observes. He usually makes comparisons with the individuals and patterns known to him in his own society, for the only standards he has for interpreting what he views abroad are those of his own social world. What he notices are more likely to be the contrasts than the similarities between the foreign country and his homeland. Furthermore, the social functions of human behavior within institutions may be missed and the discrete forms used as a basis for interpretation, and from fragments of the whole a model of social life imputed.

SOCIAL STRENGTHS OF THE WEST

Seen through Indian eyes, the most visible sphere of foreign life is the behavior of people in "public" situations.

To understand what they see and how they interpret it, it is necessary to give some background on "public" relations in India. Social interaction in India, outside of the family and community, tends to occur in a kind of "no man's land." It is an area of social life in which not only do contacts take place with "outsiders" who do not "count" because they are strangers, but also the contacts are with persons of whom one should be wary. The climate of opinion is analogous to that of the passengers on a New York subway. To some extent the traditional provincialism is disappearing among the middle classes in towns and cities where outsiders are in continuous juxtaposition.

The system has protective functions, for it provides security against masses of people whose identities are unknown and whose motives for establishing a personal contact in a casual meeting may be suspect. Relatives are trustworthy or, if not trustworthy, they can, at least, be held accountable for their acts; others are neither predictable nor can they always be held responsible for what they do. It is best to be cautious.

The close and heavy personal involvement with kin restricts the depth of self-involvement not only with strangers, but also with others in work relationships. On the job it is somewhat foolhardy to put too much faith in others—superiors, peers, inferiors—with whom one has no kin or communal ties. There may be only a modicum of reward for craftsmanship and extra effort, for it is commonly believed that opportunities to advance go to favored relatives rather than to the most competent, or are dispensed on the basis of seniority rather than ability. Some think that superiors grab all the credit for whatever is done by an inferior, that fellow workers have to be watched lest they manipulate to their own advantage, and that subordinates will deceive or shrug off responsibilities.

In the wider society, middle-class life moves at a less intense, frenetic pace than in the West. There are ups and downs in pace, but the average individual neither is pushed quite so hard to get things done nor is as overcommitted as the middle classes of the America we know.

ATTRACTIVE ASPECTS OF PUBLIC BEHAVIOR

To the foreign returned, the dissimilarity between foreign public life and their own way of life is conspicuous. Certain aspects seem attractive; a majority from the United Kingdom look with favor on four attributes of British character. The Indian designations for these are "personal integrity," "self-discipline," "reserved but helpful," and "thorough in whatever they do." They are applied to the manner in which the individual Englishman acts in nonfamily relationships—with strange Englishmen as well as with foreigners—on the job, in civic groups, and in public places where each man is anonymous and so thought to be free from "normal" social controls. Phrases used to portray integrity are: "solid," "reliable," "steadfast," "fair," and "people you can count on." Self-discipline appears impressive as "control over one's emotions," "strength of purpose," and "perseverance"; it is doubly so as to respect for the opinions and rights of others—including the right to privacy. On first contact, at the surface, the Britisher seems entirely formal, taciturn, if not cold, but when the ice is broken there emerges from beneath the surface layer a self that is called "goodhearted" and "hospitable." The foreign returned have much to say about the earnestness with which individuals go about their work and daily life (trying to get the most out of it), their methodical orderly nature, and the durability of the things they make.

The top four American qualities which are approved by the foreign trained overlap to a degree with the British characterization, yet they carry dissimilar referents in their concrete forms of behavior. Americans are known as individuals who are "friendly," "equalitarian," "generous," and "energetic." In any social situation, it is commonly said, the American is easy to meet, easy to mix with, and easy to get along with—the American is characterized as being pleasingly personable and informal, having a sense of humor, and enjoying life. "Everyone tried to make us feel at home." "They talk freely with anyone." "Americans at once see you as a person—I was received with open arms everywhere."

The equalitarian features of the individual that strike the eye of the foreign returned cover a wide spectrum of human relations. One man tried to put it all together in his mind's eye as "freedom—which is only in America, pure and straightforward freedom—a regard for the other fellow—that is the real American life."

Most are captivated by the opportunities for an open class system with its ample chances to climb on the basis of ability and work and with the widespread sharing of a high standard of living.

In contradistinction to the social distance in India that insulates the higher and lower classes and the economic chasm between class levels of living, they see Americans openly mixing in public places as equals and being consumers of the same products. The foreign returned remember that even working class families often had cars, that people dressed alike, and that "everyone had access to food." The American symbols of class differences are not seen or are overshadowed by the fact that all classes "have so much," just as Westerners may not see the configuration of status differences within a non-Western society, so overwhelming may be the mass poverty.

The energetic American comes into full view at work, in play, on the streets, and at home. "There is ceaseless activity. The people rush about from morning to night. They have boundless energy and work themselves to a premature death." "They go at a fast pace, everyone is busy, the tempo of life is fast—what they call progress."

SOCIAL WEAKNESSES

The one outstanding social weakness of the West, both the United Kingdom and the United States, that most of the foreign returned mentioned is that of racial discrimination. Race relations serves the foreign educated as an acid test of Western attitudes and values. Racial prejudice is a hypersensitive spot whether the Indian is the object of discrimination or only a spectator of discrimination imposed on other colored peoples. Around this issue high interest can be alerted, lurking suspicions activated, and a whole train of antipathies concerning colonialization set under way.

Less than 5 per cent of the sample studied were apathetic about the entire subject before they went and afterwards. For the majority, the foreign experience did change the conceptions of racial relations which they held. One conception which many held before going abroad but which tends to become obsolescent among the foreign returned is the simple division of mankind into two opposing camps—white Westerners and the colored peoples of the rest of the world. They are as indignant as are others in India over any signs of Western imperialism and claims of white supremacy in Asia or Africa, but they do not state the issues exclusively along racial lines nor put all the whites into one class of men.

Before, I thought that all white people were alike. I had very deep prejudices before about white skins. Now I feel that everyone is the same, that human beings are all the same.

Again:

I used to think that all Westerners were pro-British and that all were different from us. I did not have any contacts with whites before. I learned about the differences between various Europeans, and that Americans are not the same as other whites. This left a very lasting impression on my mind.

The treatment accorded Indian students in the United Kingdom is used by them as one test of the Englishman's willingness to accept them as equals and not to relegate them to the status of inferiors. In the United States the treatment of the Indian student and the treatment of the American Negro is used as a yardstick to gauge the sincerity of the American's belief in democracy. Persons who were subjected to discrimination in Britain say that they were disappointed but not surprised; persons with the same experience in America remark that they were not only disappointed but somewhat shocked.

The color bar in the United Kingdom before independence aroused resentment as being another proof of the ranking of Indians as a subject race; since independence, it is viewed as being an unfortunate flaw in British character that is offensive to a free people. The color line in the United States for the earlier generation of students was not an anxious one so far as they personally were concerned but in connection with the Negro was deemed analogous to British-Indian relations in India. The later students point to racial discrimination as an anachronism in a nation that is holding itself up to the world as the proponent of democracy.

DISCRIMINATION AGAINST INDIAN STUDENTS

Less than one-fourth of the foreign educated in either the United Kingdom or the United States had actually been the personal object of discrimination in a specific instance which they could recall; more than three-fourths had heard of Indian students who had been discriminated against. Any incident which happens to one Indian becomes known to all; stories accumulate within Indian student groups abroad and are passed on to each incoming person. If the person was the only Indian in the American or British school he was less preoccupied with the likelihood of there being discrimination against Indians—he did not have a constant stream of stories coming his way and his exceptional status often meant he was lionized as an "interesting" person.

We asked the foreign returned who were the objects of or who had observed racial discrimination while they were overseas how they felt while it was happening. The answers given add up to this proposition: For most, if the discriminatory act was directed against the self, the occurrence was not interpreted as being a threat to their own ego but as insulting to their status rights and a violation of their beliefs as to what is right.

The United Kingdom cases who experienced race discrimination say that the color bar was no worse in England than what they were used to in India before independence—and in some respects, not so bad, or that the behavior of the Englishmen was pretty much what they expected from a people with the reputation for being prejudiced and thinking of themselves as the "master race." Many add that it was not easy to distinguish between British reserve with strangers and racial prejudice, but that in most instances, once they got to know an Englishman well, they were accepted as equals. Nearly all report no discrimination in the academic community, in their intellectual relations with professors and fellow students. A number remember that their teachers took an extra amount of interest in them because they were Indians. Although away from the college they might encounter children who would yell, "Look, Mom, there is a black man," or "Look at that nigger," adults did not talk that way. The chief area of discrimination occurred in trying to get housing accommodations in which the obvious reason for rejection was race.

The American cases had more varied responses. A few took a sympathetic or neutral point of view, for example, "I knew the background of American actions and knew they were mixed up on this." "When I saw discrimination in the South, I knew these people did not know any better." "Every country has its own dirt. America has just as we do, but we are interested in America not because of its dirt but for what it can teach us." The majority grumbled, gossiped within their own Indian group, and acted opportunistically. Inside their in-group they talked wryly about the contradictions between democracy and discrimination and how strange it was for an advanced country to have racial prejudices. A minority fully identified with the Negro as being another oppressed people, sought them out as friends, were keenly offended by discrimination against this ethnic group, and now say: "American democracy is for whites." As in the case of the British educated, the American sample report with but rare exceptions that they were not discriminated against on the campus and, far more than the British educated, speak warmly of professors who took an exceptional interest in them and who went out of their way to be helpful.

OTHER REACTIONS

About other social strengths and weaknesses of the West there is no consensus. There are, however, reactions common to the British returned and others held by the American returned.

Those trained in the United Kingdom feel fairly sure that they know what the British are like but those trained in the United States are not equally sure that they know what makes Americans tick. One plausible, though untested, hypothesis is that the British culture may be more homogeneous than its American counterpart. And as a result, perhaps the Indian has a more standardized set of expectations in the United Kingdom than in the United States. It may also be that the British in their personal conduct in varying types of situations are more consistent and Americans more flexible.

Still another hypothesis can be inferred from the side comments of those who say, "The people are frank—but." The "but" refers to the observation that the English are hard to make out *before* a friendship is established; the Americans, *after* a contact is made. The Indian student is puzzled by the British because, "They want to take the initiative in deciding when to get acquainted and they resent inquisitiveness"; hence the Indian does not know where he stands until the Englishman tells him. Once the Britisher has opened up, the Indian adds, "He says what he means and means what he says."

Friendships with Americans are established more quickly, and either person is free to take the initiative. Although rarely rebuffed in starting a friendship, the Indian is not confident of the solidity of the bond: "You cannot assume that because Americans are friendly you are fully accepted. You still have to watch what you say." "Americans are free to talk but their freeness is a mannerism and we Indians often misunderstood." The American is described as smiling, polite, congenial, and careful not to offend. At first Indians impute from these cues more than they are intended to convey in American culture. Most of an Indian's friends take a span of time for each to test the other's involvement. The foreign returned are impressed by the rapidity with which strangers in America form friendships—and are upset when the attachments prove to be so temporary. It causes some to say, "Americans are friendly, but are they really sincere?" "Everyone is friendly—but it is hard to have a friend."

Eight out of ten of the foreign returned have a favorable image of the British and Americans as people, as distinguished from their political and social patterns. Those back from the United Kingdom respect the

British people (whether they like them or not) and those returned from the United States like the Americans (whether they respect them or not). Before going overseas, the students tended to be antagonistic toward the British and idealistic about the Americans; after being in the West, approximately 80 per cent revised their images—losing much of their antagonism toward the British and becoming more realistic about the Americans.

Three out of four now distinguish between the character of the foreigners in India, who are viewed most often adversely, and the character of the foreigners in their homeland, who are seen most often in a favorable light.

The Britisher at home appears to them to be a more decent person than the Britisher abroad.

There I became acquainted with Englishmen for the first time and I began to appreciate their character. I did not like them as rulers but there I found them most human.

Or:

Here in India, they are very obstinate, unbending, intolerable, aloof, arrogant, and pompous. There I met a different type—they were polite, they judged the individual as an individual and then formed an opinion, they were helpful. I am still no admirer of the British but my attitude has mellowed, and I respect them.

During the period of British rule there were few Americans in India. Beginning with the American soldiers who were stationed in India during World War II, large numbers of Americans have descended upon India. Consequently to many of the American trained, their first experiences with Americans in India came after their favorable experiences with Americans in the United States. The United Kingdom trained are surprised to find that the British in Britain are "human," the United States trained are shocked to find that Americans in India are snobbish.

It is easier to get along with Americans in America than in India. In America there is little chance to show off, for everybody has so much; here the Americans show off. Here they tend to look down on Indians. Americans here lose much of their humility—they start feeling intellectually superior. Americans here are more authoritarian than in America.

Again:

Here the Americans are clannish, they restrict themselves to their own group. Americans at home are hospitable but here they do not ask you to their house; they remain more to themselves.

And:

The foreigners in India differ from those in their own country. At first when they come they are sympathetic to Indians but in time they become anti-Indian. They forget their modesty and their notions of equality when they come here.[1]

ENIGMAS OF WESTERN SOCIETY

There are some aspects of Western society which remain enigmatic to the foreign returned.

Family life is one. It appears disorganized to some, democratic to others. The instabilities of the home, particularly in America, seem odd to most, in contrast to the stability of the Indian home. Whereas fellow feeling among coworkers is admired, the slim ties among relatives are frowned upon. Some say, "The children are taught to be independent at a young age. This is a very good thing. But a person does not know the work his father is doing, where his sisters are, and whether or not his brothers will help him. It is a curse to be old, they get little respect and they cannot maintain themselves." "There is no love in family life. I found that affection is only skin deep there." "The attachment to the family is not real. Every man and woman is interested in himself, not in parents, brothers and sisters, husbands and wives. No one gets a happy home life." Some have the opposite reaction:

There is more democracy in family life. The individual is treated on his own merits with due respect for his needs. The elders consult with the junior members and their advice or suggestions are really considered; here the elders make the decisions.

Materialism is another enigma. The preoccupation with economic gain, the identification of an individual with the work he does, the premium placed on having an ever ascending level of living draws mixed responses—hostility and envy.

The average American lacks a sense of balance between materialism on the one hand and a faith or philosophy on the other. He feels an urgent need of faith, but scientific development is far outstripping the developments in the spiritual world. He has not been able to adjust his community living with the material progress of his country. There is a general nervous condition. The interesting thing is that the people there are the first to admit all this.

Again:

They are constantly in a hurry to get done whatever they are doing and give very little thought to the meaning of what they are doing. They see only the material values in life—get more money, get more luxuries; little else matters as ends. But it is an easy life—people are not worried about tomorrow.

[1] We are concerned not with the validity of these judgments, but only with the objective presentation of a common point of view. Our own observations were that there are foreigners who do not fit the description but, as in the case of any stereotype, these are looked upon as being "different."

Others are impressed by the spirit of "always trying to make improvements in efficiency and production" and say that "spiritualism is humbug—a fact which the foreigners already know and Indians should learn." The United States is more the object of criticism for "overdoing" materialism than the United Kingdom, and the main center of attack is not on the levels of living but on the discrepancy between the economy and other phases of culture.

Each culture contains its own premises by which a member's behavior is judged—the areas in which he is supposed to exercise authority and responsibility on his own and the areas in which he is supposed to submerge himself to the group; when he can compete or must co-operate; and so forth. The stranger in a society has difficulty perceiving the premises, the behavior, and the relationship between the two, as the next three quotations show:

America is based on egotism. For example, neighbors did not once pay any attention to the problems of others. In India we talk about our neighbor's troubles and are sincerely sorry. Everyone there is busy and minds his own business.

As a group they work better than as individuals—which is conducive to social welfare. They are willing to co-operate to bring credit to the group. This is the paradox of American individualism—they want to do things in a group way, one has a sense of achievement in a group and a sense of frustration as an individual. The American mind is confused.

In America, the individual thinks that by helping the individual he is helping the community.

. . . . .

THE WISH TO BE UNDERSTOOD

The use of knowledge from one society by the members of another is animated by a demand that grows out of practical need. When India was under foreign rule, its people had to learn the ways of the British in order to deal with the governors. British authorities responsible for policy making and administration required knowledge of Indian conditions—even though most of the British people did not have to know much about Indian customs. It was not until the United States became a global power that the social facts about places like India seemed vital to the nation's leadership; at the same time, as India became a nation fashioning its own foreign policy, it has had to know more about the United States.

An American assumption is that understanding of America by Indians would enable them to recognize that American values are not inimical to India's interests and that the nation's foreign policies are idealistic in conception. An Indian assumption is that if America understood Asia and the real issues, its policies would be better. Perhaps it would not be unreasonable to observe that both parties are anxious to be understood and that currently both may be more eager to be understood than to understand.

In an increasingly interdependent world in which India is a co-ordinate rather than a subordinate power, it seems highly probable that mutual understanding will increase in the long run. It will do so in the "one world" that is coming into being, not because that would be nice but because it will be necessary. It seems appropriate to suggest in this context that the foreign educated, along with certain other segments, have the potential of acting as interpreters of the West on a face-to-face basis with a wide range of Indian groups.

85. THE VANISHING EAST °

PETER F. DRUCKER

Where once even neighboring tribes or communities were "cultural islands" having relatively little contact with each other, today entire nations and continents are involved in constant interchange. Whole cultures are modified by these interchanges even though the traits acquired are often altered in special ways to harmonize with the new setting. In this selection Drucker contends that we are witnessing a mass adoption of many elements of Western culture by Eastern nations. The East is "vanishing" but it is experiencing difficulty in incorporating these new elements in an orderly fashion into the total mode of of life.

> East is East and West is West,
> And never the twain shall meet.

So sang Kipling, laureate of empire at its high noon. Millions of people who never have heard his name know these lines. Many still accept them as folk wisdom.

It is always rash to say "never" to the future. Kipling has been

° From Peter F. Drucker, *Landmarks of Tomorrow* (New York: Harper & Brothers, 1957), pp. 230–247 passim. Copyright © 1957, 1958, 1959 by Peter F. Drucker. Reprinted by permission of Harper and Brothers.
For a biographical sketch of the author see selection 41.

dead only twenty-five years. But today "the twain have met"—in one chaotic, anarchic, explosive but common world disorder and world civilization. "East" and "West" have almost become mere geographic directions again rather than meaningful terms of politics, civilization and culture, "Commonwealth" has succeeded "Empire"; and at the Commonwealth meetings in the last ten years, the dominant figure has been Nehru, the complete East-Westerner: fiery Indian nationalist and master of English prose, high-caste, proud Brahman and agnostic Fabian Socialist, idol of the Indian villagers and fervent apostle of heavy industry.

Yet Kipling was right—though not in the way he intended to be. *His* West and *his* East have indeed not met: the nineteenth-century West of the European power system, and the mysterious East of tribal village and Peacock Throne, of peasant following the bullock behind the wooden plow, and of Confucian mandarin learning ancient texts by rote, have not met.

Both have disappeared.

Only fifty years ago the European power system was still substantially what it had been ever since the end of Europe's Religious Wars. The non-European great powers—Japan and the United States—were not accepted into full membership until World War I. For 250 years all great powers had been European; and all but Russia had already been members when the Westphalian Peace Treaties of 1648 first established the European power system.

. . . . .

One might even say that the first few years after World War II remained under the constellation of the European power system. For the traditional European countries it was a decade of weakness and power shrinkage. But the United States' military and economic hegemony during that decade filled the resulting vacuum. The situation could not last—hegemony never does. It was a delusion of Western, and especially of American, policy that it could endure or even that it should endure. But certainly in these first postwar years, during which the United States had a monopoly on atomic weapons combined with international economic predominance, the lineaments of the old Western-controlled world were still discernible.

By now they have all but disappeared. Japan's occupation of the European colonies in the Far East, Indian independence, the victory of Communism in China, the Korean War, the Suez debacle—each of these was another landslide burying the ruins of the European power system and creating a new world landscape. The final step would be European unification—both an acknowledgment of the end of the old system of

European power balance and perhaps the first major step toward a new stability and order.

. . . . .

SUCCESS OR FAILURE OF THE WEST?

The European power system died of its own success. Every one of the forces that destroyed it was of Western origin, generated by the West and propagated by it. Nationalism is West's very own *enfant terrible*. The campaign against colonialism only repeats the arguments and slogans of generations of European and American liberals. Everywhere it is being led by men trained and educated in the West, and Western in their thinking, their arguments, their principles. In the thirties it was said that only an honors degree from Oxford or Cambridge qualified an Indian to be jailed for resistance to British rule. Today this applies, with variations, to all the remaining colonial areas of the Western powers. Moscow-trained Communists are similarly the most likely leaders of resistance to the new Russian colonialism in the satellite countries. And, of course, Communism is entirely Western— a heresy, to be sure, but one that could only have grown on Western soil and out of Western heritage.

The world order that will succeed the European power system might well be anti-Western; but it will quite definitely not be un-Western. Every single one of the new countries in the world today—including those that have not yet shaken off colonial status—sees its goal in its transformation into a Western state, economy and society, and sees the means to achieve this goal in the theories, institutions, sciences, technologies and tools the West has developed.

. . . . .

Fifty years ago the borderlands of the North Atlantic had a virtual monopoly on industrial and military technology, knowledge and skills. To assume a continuation of this monopoly was perhaps not unreasonable at the time. Technology is, after all, not something by itself, but the child of values, cultural traditions and historical development, all of which were distinctly Western. Yet—beginning with Japan—industrial and military technology has proven to be far easier of acquisition by non-Western people than Western political or social beliefs and institutions. All over the world, non-Western peoples are rapidly industrializing and rapidly building Western-style armed forces. The technological monopoly of the North Atlantic countries has been broken for good.

THE FAILURE OF THE EAST

The European power system has collapsed; but at the same time, the East has vanished.

. . . . .

It is true that the West has lost its old certainty of superiority and with it its old provincialism. But it is also true—and much more important—that no viable society today can be built on non-Western foundations.

This is not speculation. It is experience. In the three oldest, most advanced and richest non-Western cultures—Japan, China and India—the attempt has been made to base a viable society on inherited, non-Western foundations—and in all three it has failed.

. . . . .

The most significant failure is probably Gandhi's in India. Unlike the Japanese and unlike Sun Yat-sen, Gandhi was not content with merging East and West. He aimed at building on the foundations of the spirit a better, purer, stronger society that could be model and inspiration to East and West alike.

Here clearly was the greatest vision, the deepest understanding. Here also was a very great man, a saint and a shrewd political leader. His impact on the people of India was probably greater than that of any other man since the Prince Buddha 2,500 years ago. Not only the educated but the masses, in the hopeless isolation of their sun-baked mud hovels, caught the vision and were moved by it. Even untouchability and landlordism, which neither force nor reason had ever been able to weaken, showed signs of melting under his moral fervor.

British rule crumpled before Gandhi. Independent India is above all his achievement. Every Indian leader today claims to be his disciple —and most actually are. Even the Indian Communists pay lip service to his greatness. Yet only ten years after his death, there is little left of his social, political or economic gospel. India today sees her salvation in rapid industrialization, in steel mills, fertilizer plants, power dams and truck transportation—rather than in the self-denying, austere anti-industrialism of Gandhi's spinning wheel. A completely Western army, rather than nonviolent resistance, is her mainstay in international affairs.

The present Indian government, though composed of Gandhi's closest associates, seems singularly unimpressed by the power of non-violent resistance such as threw the British into complete confusion. There have been many more "incidents," in which police and army were ordered to fire on demonstrators in the first ten years of Indian independence than in the last ten years of British rule. The present Indian government has given in only to violent rioting, not once—as the British so often did—to moral force. And instead of Gandhi's spiritual foundation, the present rulers base their ideas of society, economy and government on purely Western and purely secular ideas, such as, in Nehru's case, English Fabian Socialism of 1919 vintage. The only exceptions are the orthodox Hindu sectarians—but their ideal is to purge India of all innovations whether Gandhian or Western.

I am convinced of Gandhi's lasting impact—unless, indeed, independent India collapses into anarchy, civil war, totalitarianism, or before a new conquest by a foreign invader. But it is unlikely that there will ever be an attempt to realize Gandhi's society, that post-modern dream that was to be more truly a fulfillment of the basic values of the West than any Western country has ever been, and which yet was to rest on the non-Western foundations of India's own spiritual heritage. That attempt—despite its nobility and popular appeal—has failed.

Where Kipling's generation erred was in their belief that the East had such power, such deep, rock-bottom strength, that it would resist the corroding acid of Western ideas, Western institutions, Western technology and Western goods.

To the best of the West's representatives in the non-Western world this resistance was precisely its attraction. The great colonials—Gordon in China, Curzon in India, Lyautey in Morocco, Lugard in Nigeria, Lawrence in Arabia, Kipling himself—were all at odds with their own West, were strangers, rebels or misfits at home. They romanticized the East, they saw it as their mission to build it up and protect it against the West—Curzon's fantastic attempt to recreate the India of the Mogul Empire in the "Great Durbar" of 1906 was perhaps the most spectacular example, but by no means an isolated one. This explains their incredible inability to see let alone to understand, the impact and importance of the Western-trained, Westernized lawyer, teacher, journalist or politician. To the very end the Western colonial administrators persisted in the delusion that these people were "scum," that they had no influence at all on the "masses," were indeed actually repudiated by them.

In a most perceptive book written by a former colonial about European rule in the East—Philip Woodruff's *The Men Who Ruled India*—this is still a recurrent theme. Yet the book was written in 1953, six years after the "Westernized trouble makers" had forced the last Union Jack in India to be struck. A similar delusion underlies French policy in North Africa. It determines much of American policy in the Arab world and explains our worst mistakes there.

The heritage and values of non-Western society will not be lost forever. Such deep traditions of old and advanced cultures cannot remain forever powerless, inert and ineffectual. But they will again be-

come a living force only if the non-Western countries succeed in building viable societies on Western foundations: Western values and institutions; Western education, economics and technology; Western
means of mass communication and mass organization. This is the lesson
the non-Western countries themselves have learned—from Nehru in
India and Mao in China to Nasser and Bourguiba in the Arab countries
and Dr. Nkrumah in the Gold Coast.

These men do not agree among themselves on values and institutions. They mean quite different things when they say "free government." But their differences are those of Westerners, the differences
between the free West and the totalitarians; they all believe in the
strong, central, professional government of the modern West. They do
not agree on the principles of economic organization; but they all accept
industrialization and organized large-scale enterprise, economic welfare
and advancement as major goals of human society. They may not believe
in "freedom of speech" or "freedom of thought"; but they all accept and
exploit the printing press and the mass media of communication and
propaganda. And they all accept—indeed they all worship—education
in the Western sense and its product, the professional lawyer, doctor,
scientist, bureaucrat or technologist.

CAN THE WEST AND THE NEW EAST MEET?

. . . . .

The speed and ease with which Western technology—industrial
and military—is spreading throughout the non-Western world only adds
to the seriousness of the situation. Technology is not a disembodied
abstraction or a mere tool; it grows out of cultural and historical traditions and demands cultural and social foundations. Because of this,
it cannot simply be imposed on an existing culture. Any culture that
does not conform to the exacting demands of technology—whether
African tribe, Indian caste or Chinese family—will be ruthlessly destroyed. But can technology, however productive of a higher standard
of living or of a higher standard of warfare and dying, produce a culture
and a community?

Technology in the West grew out of our own cultural foundations.
The roots of the great technological changes of the last two hundred
years go back all the way to the surge of the Middle Ages (the great
cathedrals too were an "industrial revolution") and even further back
to the Rule of St. Benedict. We have had a long time to get used to
this "new growth," so that we could develop "antibodies." In the non-
Western world, however, modern technology is a "foreign body." Its

growth is explosive and much too fast to make possible the development of really effective antibodies.

This may make easier the adaptation of the non-Western world to Western political and social institutions by destroying those political and social traditions that stand in their way. It may force more thorough commitment to the basic values that underlie these institutions. But it may also uproot and weaken these non-Western countries before they can grow into cohesive societies.

In the disappearance of the East and in its Westernization the great themes of the post-modern world all come together.

Education is the cause of Westernization; but the educated society is also the great need of the new world, the shortage of educated people is its great lack, and the development of an effective model of general education its great hope.

The vision of economic development is the driving force behind Westernization. The force that, in twenty years, made trucks rather than the backs of coolies up-to-date transportation in Bangkok also changes expectations, beliefs and ways of life unchanged since time immemorial. At the same time the new danger of interracial and international class war resulting from the failure of economic development is the great threat both to the old West and the new Westernizing countries.

These countries have no choice but to imitate the political institutions of modern government; they have to become nation-states. They can only survive if their political institutions become effective. Yet these institutions are just as inadequate there for the tasks of international affairs as they are in the West, and just as endangered there by the cancerous growth of military technology and the resulting militarization of society.

. . . . .

The emergence of a common, basically Western world civilization is the greatest of our new frontiers—the greatest change and the greatest opportunity. But in whose image will it be cast?

CHAPTER IX

SOCIAL
PROCESSES

86. HOW PEOPLE INTERACT

IN CONFERENCES *

ROBERT F. BALES

*Sociologists commonly direct their attention primarily to the
study of the structure and functioning of human groups.
They usually leave the study of the performance of individuals
within small groups to social psychologists. Nevertheless, it is
useful to those interested in sociology to observe in a simple
setting the operation of the social processes, for they have
their counterparts in the behavior which may be observed
within and between larger and more complex groups and
organizations. In this selection, R. F. Bales describes some of
the significant findings which have been observed in the study
of small problem-solving groups.*

Social interaction is made up largely of the talking that people
do when they get together. Talk is an elusive object of study, in spite
of the fact that a good deal of it exists. It is also a rather sensitive
subject. Even a friend might find it hard to put up with a dissection
of the following kind: "I was just noticing how much you talk. In the
last 10 minutes I noticed that you made a total of 114 remarks, while I
made a total of 86. According to my count you have about twice as

* From *Scientific American*, Vol. 192, No. 3 (March, 1955), 31–35.
    The author (b. 1916) is Associate Professor of Social Relations, Harvard Uni-
versity. A consultant for the Rand Corporation. Special areas of interest include
small groups and small-group interaction. Author: *Interaction Process Analysis: A
Method for the Study of Small Groups.* Coauthor: *Working Papers in a Theory of
Action;* Coeditor: *Small Groups.*

many opinions as facts. Although I agreed with you 15 times and didn't disagree at all, I noticed that you stammered once and blushed twice."

I first began to develop a systematic procedure for analyzing social interaction when I became interested in trying to account for the success of Alcoholics Anonymous in helping apparently hopeless drinkers to stop drinking. Although I attended meetings and talked with many members, I did not feel free to ask all the questions I wished. Consequently I fell back on observation and began to develop crude methods for recording who did what, who spoke to whom, and how. Eventually even this quiet occupation began to appear sinister and the effort was abandoned. But by this time my fascination with the process of social interaction had developed to the point of no return. I decided that I must pursue my studies in the more favorable conditions of a laboratory.

A number of laboratories for the study of social interaction within small groups and organizations have been started in the last 10 years—in hospitals, clinics, special research centers and military installations. The studies and experiments I shall describe were conducted in one of the earliest of these laboratories, established in 1947 at Harvard University.

The laboratory consists of a large, well-lighted room for the group under study and an adjoining room for observers, who listen and watch from behind windows with one-way vision. The subjects are told at the beginning that the room has been constructed for the special purpose of studying group discussion, that a complete sound recording will be made and that there are observers behind the one-way mirrors. The purpose of the separation is not to deceive the subjects but to minimize interaction between them and the observing team.

After much research we developed a standardized task from which significant generalizations could be drawn. A group of persons (ranging from two to seven in number) is asked to discuss a complex human relations problem of the sort typically faced by an administrator. Each member of the group first reads a five-page presentation of facts about the case to be discussed, but each is left uncertain as to whether he has been given exactly the same range of facts as the others in the group. The members are not introduced to one another or coached in any way; they must develop their own organization and procedure. They are to consider the facts and report to an administrator, as if they were his staff, their joint conclusions concerning the problem and what should be done about it. They are allowed 40 minutes for the discussion. The group is observed for four such sessions.

On the other side of the one-way screen the observers systematically record every step of the interaction, not omitting such items as nods and frowns. Each observer has a small machine with a moving paper tape on which he writes in code a description of every act—an act being defined essentially as a single statement, question or gesture. Acts ordinarily occur at the rate of 15 to 20 per minute. The recorded information on each includes identification of the person speaking and the person spoken to and classification of the act according to predetermined categories. There are 12 categories, covering positive and negative reactions, questions and attempts to solve the problem by the offering of information, opinion or suggestions.

. . . On the average about half (56 per cent) of the acts during a group session fall into the categories of problem-solving attempts; the remaining 44 per cent are distributed among positive reactions, negative reactions and questions. In other words, the process tends to be two-sided, with the reactions acting as a more or less constant feed-back on the acceptability of the problem-solving attempts. The following is a typical example of the pattern of interchange:

Member 1: "I wonder if we have the same facts about the problem? [Asks for opinion.] Perhaps we should take some time in the beginning to find out." [Gives suggestion.]

Member 2: "Yes. [Agrees.] We may be able to fill in some gaps in our information. [Gives opinion.] Let's go around the table and each tell what the report said in his case." [Gives suggestion.]

This example illustrates that a speaker's first remark is likely to be a reaction, and if he continues speaking, the probability is very high that his second act will be a problem-solving attempt. . . . About 50 per cent of the time a member's first remark in a series is a reaction; if he continues, about 80 per cent of the succeeding comments are opinions or other offerings classed as attempts to solve the problem.

When we examine the reactions, we find that positive reactions commonly outnumber negative ones about two to one during a session. It is as if after every negative reaction, the members of the group feel they must make another problem-solving attempt which meets with a positive reaction "just to catch up," and net forward progress is felt to be sufficiently secure only when a repetition of the problem-solving attempt meets unopposed acceptance. It may be that members employ repetition, or near repetition, as an error-checking device to determine whether the others "really agree." Social interaction, in common with many other goal-seeking control mechanisms, seems to depend upon error and correction of error for guidance.

The process of attempting to arrive at a group decision through discussion is in many ways very like the operation of a large-scale communication and control system such as an air-defense network. I recently compared the two processes in collaboration with John Kennedy of the Systems Research Laboratory at the Rand Corporation.

In the military case there are three functions to be performed; surveillance of the air by radar, identification of planes as friendly or unknown and direction of fighters sent out to intercept unknown planes. These are something like the three problems confronting our groups in the standard interaction task: assembling the given information on the case, evaluating it and proceeding toward a solution as the goal. Now the stepwise operations involved in the air defense system may be tolerably well described as an interlocking series of seven types of information-processing operations (see chart). Here x stands for the path of a plane tracked by radar, and O represents the class of objects unknown. If no known flight plan of a friendly plane coincides with x —a fact represented by the symbol y—then x must belong to the class O. Since there is a general rule, W, that all unknown planes are to be intercepted, the conclusion is that a specific order, w, should be given to intercept x. Such a decision, involving many groups and interlocking processes, is obviously a very complicated affair, socially as well as technically. The job of the decision-making organization is essentially to build and maintain through means of communication and evaluation a sufficiently complex and commonly accepted symbolic structure to guide or control the stages of behavior of all the operating units. Effective decision making is basically a continuous process of building and maintaining a structure of cultural objects which in their totality constitute the common culture of the organization affected.

The seven types of acts, or stages, just described are very general: they apply quite as well to the interaction of five experimental subjects in the laboratory group, trying to decide in 40 minutes what the administrator in their case should do about his problem, as to the large-scale operations of an air-defense network. Not all of the elements in the process are primarily logical in character. They involve elements of perception, memory, association and perhaps inductive insight. All sorts of motivational and evaluative pressures affect the process. The steps make sense not as a formally perfect chain of logic, but rather as a set of symbol transformations which help to guide, although in an imperfect way, a process of decision-making behavior. Error checking is an integral part of this fallible process.

The reason for calling attention to the seven-step structure of the process is that it may help to explain the unequal ratios of suggestions, opinions, and information offered in the problem-solving attempts of the groups in our tests. . . . Of every seven problem-solving attempts, on the average four are opinions, two are offers of information and one is a suggestion. It seems significant that in the idealized seven-step outline of the air-defense operation two steps have the interaction form of giving information, four intermediate steps have the interaction form of giving opinion and only one step, the final one, has the form of giving a suggestion.

From the transcription of a group discussion it is often possible

1 STATES PRIMARY OBSERVATION:
  I Observe a Particular Event, x

2 MAKES TENTATIVE INDUCTION:
  This Particular Event, x, May Belong to the General Class of Objects, O

3 DEDUCES CONDITIONAL PREDICTION:
  If This Particular Event, x, Does Belong to the General Class, O, Then It Should Be Found Associated with Another Particular Event, y

4 STATES OBSERVATION OF CHECK FACT:
  I Observe the Predicted Particular Event, y

5 IDENTIFIES OBJECT AS MEMBER OF A CLASS:
  I Therefore Identify x-y as an Object Which Is a Member of the Predicted General Class of Objects, O

6 STATES MAJOR PREMISE RELATING CLASSES OF OBJECTS:
  All Members of the General Class of Objects, O, Should Be Treated by Ways of the General Class, W

7 PROPOSES SPECIFIC ACTION:
  This Particular Object, x-y, Should Therefore Be Treated in a Particular Way, w

PROCESS IN REACHING A GROUP DECISION is analogous to the operation of a large-scale communication and control system such as the air-defense network. The steps consist of observing an object or event, comparing it with several possible identifications, considering the associated facts and, once its nature is understood, taking the appropriate action.

to reconstruct complete seven-step chains leading to agreement on specific points and the final conclusion. In a general way there is even a tendency for the steps to proceed in a regular order in time. During a session the rates of giving information tend to be highest in the first third of the meeting and to decline in the next two thirds. Rates of giving opinion are usually highest in the middle portion of the meeting. Rates of giving suggestion are generally low in the early period and reach their high point in the last third. These increases may be connected mainly with social and emotional problems of the group process itself. The ratio of negative to positive reactions tends to be higher in response to suggestions than in response to factual statements. The decision point is a critical bottleneck in the process. Once the decision point has been passed, however, the rates of negative reaction usually fall off and the rates of positive reaction rise sharply. Joking and laughter, indicating solidarity and tension release, become more frequent. With the problems of the task and common values stabilized for the time being by the decision, the interaction process apparently turns to restabilizing the emotional states of the individuals and their social relations to one another.

There is a good deal of evidence that the process of social interaction, like other processes involving feedback tends to fall into oscillation as it "hunts" around a hypothetical steady state. Over a small time span the action tends to alternate every few acts between the problem-solving attempts of one person and the social-emotional reaction of some other. But this rapid oscillation is not quite rapid enough to keep all elements of the process in perfect balance. There is a drift toward inequality of participation, which in time has cumulative effects on the social relationships of the members. The reason for this drift may be seen fairly easily. When a person has completed one act, the chances are a little better than even that he will continue for another act. After each succeeding act his probability of continuing drops, but never so far as if he simply flipped a coin at each point to determine whether to continue or to yield the floor. In fact, relatively speaking, he exceeds this chance probability by a larger and larger fraction with each succeeding act.

We have already noted that when a person continues several acts in succession the probability is very high that he is giving information, opinion or suggestion—in other words, specializing in problem-solving attempts. We may also infer from the seven-step theory of problem-solving attempts that the tendency to continue for several acts in succession is probably due in part to a felt need on the part of the speaker to provide inferences and check facts which will result in the acceptance of a more advanced step in the series, with an accepted suggestion as the goal.

This tendency toward inequality of participation over the short run has cumulative side effects on the social organization of the group. The man who gets his speech in first begins to build a reputation. Success in obtaining acceptance of problem-solving attempts seems to lead the successful person to do more of the same, with the result that eventually the members come to assume a rank order by task ability. In some groups the members reach a high degree of consensus on their ranking of "who had the best ideas." (The members are interviewed by questionnaire after each meeting.) Usually the persons so ranked also did the most talking and had higher than average rates of giving suggestions and opinion.

While one person becomes a specialist in advancing ideas, another is apt to be developing a specialization on the reactive side. The men most commonly rated "best liked" typically have higher than average rates of showing tension release (mainly smiling and laughing) and showing agreement. It is not impossible for the man ranked at the top in ideas also to be best liked, but apparently it is difficult. In one set of experiments the top idea man had about an even chance of also being best liked at the end of the first meeting, but by the end of the fourth meeting his chances were only about one in 10. The best-liked man is usually second or third in the participation hierarchy.

The task specialist seems to "lock onto" the person who is most responsive to what he is saying and address more remarks to him than to the others. In turn, the best-liked man talks more and agrees more with the top-ranking idea specialist than with any other member. The idea specialist and the best-liked man often form a mutually supporting pair. However, the best-liked man may attract the idea specialist even though they are not always in agreement. Indeed, in order for a person to become established in the minds of other members as a social-emotional specialist, it is probably more important that he be representative of their reactions, both positive and negative, than that he should ardently support everything the task specialist says. Apparently, reactions that are emotionally gratifying to other members tend to be generalized by them into liking for the person who expresses the reactions.

Giving suggestions, necessary as it may be for accomplishment of the task, is more likely to arouse negative reactions than is giving information or opinion. This tends to put the task specialist in a vulnerable position. The group commonly develops a certain amount of negative feeling toward him. Not only is he likely to lose the status of being best liked, but he may lose his position as task leader unless he is sensitive to the problem and is well supported by other members. Even in a group which ends its first meeting with a high consensus on who has the best ideas, the second meeting is apt to see a challenge to his leadership, with a rise in rates of disagreement and antagonism and a precipitous drop in his popularity. But then, in a group where the original consensus was high, a peculiar thing seems to happen. Apparently as progress toward accomplishment of the task slows down, some members rally around the leader again and his popularity tends to rise. By the third meeting the rates of disagreement and antagonism go down. The task leader may not retain all the liking that was transferred to him in his time of need, but the net effect of the hunting kind of oscillation that takes place is a tendency to maintain the original rank order of task ability.

In a group that starts with a low degree of consensus on who has the best ideas, the developments usually are more dismal. There tends to be a high turnover in the top ranks throughout the four meetings, with one would-be leader replacing another. In such a group the man ranked as having the best ideas is less apt to be best liked. Furthermore an additional specialist is likely to appear—a man who talks more than anybody else but is neither best liked nor most highly respected for his task ability.

It appears probable that whether the members will agree on who has the best ideas depends to a large degree on how well they agree on basic premises or norms—what we may call the "common culture." If such consensus is not present, at least implicitly, at the beginning, it may take a long time to build. While consensus on major values does not solve all the problems of arriving at a stable social organization, probably no stable organization is possible without this control factor. If it is lacking, the interaction process becomes primarily a means for the expression of individual emotional states.

Our studies have made clear that social stability is an extremely complex achievement: it takes time and patience to arrive at a common culture extensive enough and sensitive enough to regulate strong counter motives, to promote task accomplishment, to harmonize social relationships and to rejuvenate itself whenever the conditions demand. A clear recognition of the complexity of cultural control of behavior should encourage us to believe that interminable series of meetings around the conference table, international and otherwise, are perhaps worth while after all.

87. EXPERIMENTS IN GROUP
CONFLICT °

MUZAFER SHERIF

*This selection, by Muzafer Sherif, not only explores the concept
of "conflict" but also illustrates effectively one of the methods
used by social scientists in their research. By providing a
relatively natural setting in which interaction can take place,
while at the same time establishing inconspicuous controls
over certain crucial elements or variables, Sherif has been able
to obtain evidence about the behavior of individuals and
groups in conflict situations. The reader should be cautioned,
however, against assuming that the conclusions drawn from
such experimental settings are applicable without further
retesting to all kinds of groups in all types of situations.*

Conflict between groups—whether between boys' gangs, social
classes, "races" or nations—has no simple cause, nor is mankind yet in
sight of a cure. It is often rooted deep in personal, social, economic,
religious and historical forces. Nevertheless it is possible to identify
certain general factors which have a crucial influence on the attitude
of any group toward others. Social scientists have long sought to bring
these factors to light by studying what might be called the "natural
history" of groups and group relations. Intergroup conflict and harmony
is not a subject that lends itself easily to laboratory experiments. But in
recent years there has been a beginning of attempts to investigate the
problem under controlled yet lifelike conditions, and I shall report here
the results of a program of experimental studies of groups which I
started in 1948. Among the persons working with me were Marvin B.
Sussman, Robert Huntington, O. J. Harvey, B. Jack White, William R.
Hood and Carolyn W. Sherif. The experiments were conducted in 1949,
1953 and 1954; this article gives a composite of the findings.

We wanted to conduct our study with groups of the informal type,
where group organization and attitudes would evolve naturally and

° From *Scientific American*, Vol. 195, No. 5 (November, 1956), 54–58.
The author (b. 1906) is Professor of Psychology, Director of the Institute of
Group Relations, and consulting professor, Department of Psychiatry, School of
Medicine, University of Oklahoma. Born in Turkey and educated in his native
country and the United States. Author: *The Psychology of Social Norms; An Outline
of Social Psychology; Groups in Harmony and Tension.*

spontaneously, without formal direction or external pressures. For this purpose we conceived that an isolated summer camp would make a good experimental setting, and that decision led us to choose as subjects boys about 11 or 12 years old, who would find camping natural and fascinating. Since our aim was to study the development of group relations among these boys under carefully controlled conditions, with as little interference as possible from personal neuroses, background influences or prior experiences, we selected normal boys of homogeneous background who did not know one another before they came to the camp.

They were picked by a long and thorough procedure. We interviewed each boy's family, teachers and school officials, studied his school and medical records, obtained his scores on personality tests and observed him in his classes and at play with his schoolmates. With all this information we were able to assure ourselves that the boys chosen were of like kind and background: all were healthy, socially well-adjusted, somewhat above average in intelligence, and from stable, white, Protestant, middle-class homes.

None of the boys was aware that he was part of an experiment on group relations. The investigators appeared as a regular camp staff—camp director, counselors and so on. The boys met one another for the first time in buses that took them to the camp, and so far as they knew it was a normal summer of camping. To keep the situation as lifelike as possible, we conducted all our experiments within the framework of regular camp activities and games. We set up projects which were so interesting and attractive that the boys plunged into them enthusiastically without suspecting that they might be test situations. Unobtrusively we made records of their behavior, even using "candid" cameras and microphones when feasible.

We began by observing how the boys became a coherent group. The first of our camps was conducted in the hills of northern Connecticut in the summer of 1949. When the boys arrived, they were all housed at first in one large bunkhouse. As was to be expected, they quickly formed particular friendships and chose buddies. We had deliberately put all the boys together in this expectation because we wanted to see what would happen later after the boys were separated into different groups. Our object was to reduce the factor of personal attraction in the formation of groups. In a few days we divided the boys into two groups and put them in different cabins. Before doing so, we asked each boy informally who his best friends were, and then took pains to place the "best friends" in different groups so far as possible. (The pain of separation was assuaged by allowing each group to go at once on a hike and camp-out.)

As everyone knows, a group of strangers brought together in some common activity soon acquires an informal and spontaneous kind of organization. It comes to look upon some members as leaders, divides up duties, adopts unwritten norms of behavior, develops an *esprit de corps*. Our boys followed this pattern as they shared a series of experiences. In each group the boys pooled their efforts, organized duties and divided up tasks in work and play. Different individuals assumed different responsibilities. One boy excelled in cooking. Another led in athletics. Others, though not outstanding in any one skill, could be counted on to pitch in and do their level best in anything the group attempted. One or two seemed to disrupt activities, to start teasing at the wrong moment or offer useless suggestions. A few boys consistently had good suggestions and showed ability to coordinate the efforts of others in carrying them through. Within a few days one person had proved himself more resourceful and skillful than the rest. Thus, rather quickly, a leader and lieutenants emerged. Some boys sifted toward the bottom of the heap, while others jockeyed for higher positions.

We watched these developments closely and rated the boys' relative positions in the group, not only on the basis of our own observations but also by informal sounding of the boys' opinions as to who got things started, who got things done, who could be counted on to support group activities.

As the group became an organization, the boys coined nicknames. The big, blond, hardy leader of one group was dubbed "Baby Face" by his admiring followers. A boy with a rather long head became "Lemon Head." Each group developed its own jargon, special jokes, secrets and special ways of performing tasks. One group, after killing a snake near a place where it had gone to swim, named the place "Moccasin Creek" and thereafter preferred this swimming hole to any other, though there were better ones nearby.

Wayward members who failed to do things "right" or who did not contribute their bit to the common effort found themselves receiving the "silent treatment," ridicule or even threats. Each group selected symbols and a name, and they had these put on their caps and T-shirts. The 1954 camp was conducted in Oklahoma, near a famous hideaway of Jesse James called Robber's Cave. The two groups of boys at this camp named themselves the Rattlers and the Eagles.

Our conclusions on every phase of the study were based on a variety of observations, rather than on any single method. For example, we devised a game to test the boys' evaluations of one another. Before an important baseball game, we set up a target board for the boys to throw at, on the pretense of making practice for the game more interesting. There were no marks on the front of the board for the boys to judge objectively how close the ball came to a bull's-eye, but, unknown to them, the board was wired to flashing lights behind so that an observer could see exactly where the ball hit. We found that the boys consistently overestimated the performances by the most highly regarded members of their group and underestimated the scores of those of low social standing.

The attitudes of group members were even more dramatically illustrated during a cook-out in the woods. The staff supplied the boys with unprepared food and let them cook it themselves. One boy promptly started to build a fire, asking for help in getting wood. Another attacked the raw hamburger to make patties. Others prepared a place to put buns, relishes and the like. Two mixed soft drinks from flavoring and sugar. One boy who stood around without helping was told by the others to "get to it." Shortly the fire was blazing and the cook had hamburgers sizzling. Two boys distributed them as rapidly as they became edible. Soon it was time for the watermelon. A low-ranking member of the group took a knife and started toward the melon. Some of the boys protested. The most highly regarded boy in the group took over the knife, saying, "You guys who yell the loudest get yours last."

When the two groups in the camp had developed group organization and spirit, we proceeded to the experimental studies of intergroup relations. The groups had had no previous encounters; indeed, in the 1954 camp at Robber's Cave the two groups came in separate buses and were kept apart while each acquired a group feeling.

Our working hypothesis was that when two groups have conflicting aims—i.e., when one can achieve its ends only at the expense of the other—their members will become hostile to each other even though the groups are composed of normal well-adjusted individuals. There is a corollary to this assumption which we shall consider later. To produce friction between the groups of boys we arranged a tournament of games: baseball, touch football, a tug-of-war, a treasure hunt and so on. The tournament started in a spirit of good sportsmanship. But as it progressed good feeling soon evaporated. The members of each group began to call their rivals "stinkers," "sneaks" and "cheaters." They refused to have anything more to do with individuals in the opposing group. The boys in the 1949 camp turned against buddies whom they had chosen as "best friends" when they first arrived at the camp. A large proportion of the boys in each group gave negative ratings to all the boys in the other. The rival groups made threatening posters and planned raids, collecting secret hoards of green apples for ammunition. In the Robber's Cave camp the Eagles, after a defeat in a tournament game, burned a banner left behind by the Rattlers; the next morning the Rattlers seized the Eagles' flag when they arrived on the athletic field. From that time on name-calling, scuffles and raids were the rule of the day.

Within each group, of course, solidarity increased. There were changes: one group deposed its leader because he could not "take it" in the contests with the adversary; another group overnight made something of a hero of a big boy who had previously been regarded as a bully. But morale and cooperativeness within the group became stronger. It is noteworthy that this heightening of cooperativeness and generally democratic behavior did not carry over to the group's relations with other groups.

We now turned to the other side of the problem: How can two groups in conflict be brought into harmony? We first undertook to test the theory that pleasant social contacts between members of conflicting groups will reduce friction between them. In the 1954 camp we brought the hostile Rattlers and Eagles together for social events: going to the movies, eating in the same dining room and so on. But far from reducing conflict, these situations only served as opportunities for the rival groups to berate and attack each other. In the dining-hall line they shoved each other aside, and the group that lost the contest for the head of the line shouted "Ladies first!" at the winner. They threw paper, food and vile names at each other at the tables. An Eagle bumped by a Rattler was admonished by his fellow Eagles to brush "the dirt" off his clothes.

We then returned to the corollary of our assumption about the creation of conflict. Just as competition generates friction, working in a common endeavor should promote harmony. It seemed to us, considering group relations in the everyday world, that where harmony between groups is established, the most decisive factor is the existence of "superordinate" goals which have a compelling appeal for both but which neither could achieve without the other. To test this hypothesis experimentally, we created a series of urgent, and natural, situations which challenged our boys.

One was a breakdown in the water supply. Water came to our camp in pipes from a tank about a mile away. We arranged to interrupt it and then called the boys together to inform them of the crisis. Both groups promptly volunteered to search the water line for the trouble. They worked together harmoniously, and before the end of the afternoon they had located and corrected the difficulty.

A similar opportunity offered itself when the boys requested a movie. We told them that the camp could not afford to rent one. The two groups then got together, figured out how much each group would have to contribute, chose the film by a vote and enjoyed the showing together.

One day the two groups went on an outing at a lake some distance away. A large truck was to go to town for food. But when everyone was hungry and ready to eat, it developed that the truck would not start (we had taken care of that). The boys got a rope—the same rope they had used in their acrimonious tug-of-war—and all pulled together to start the truck.

These joint efforts did not immediately dispel hostility. At first the groups returned to the old bickering and name-calling as soon as the job in hand was finished. But gradually the series of cooperative acts reduced friction and conflict. The members of the two groups began to feel more friendly to each other. For example, a Rattler whom the Eagles disliked for his sharp tongue and skill in defeating them became a "good egg." The boys stopped shoving in the meal line. They no longer called each other names, and sat together at the table. New friendships developed between individuals in the two groups.

In the end the groups were actively seeking opportunities to mingle, to entertain and "treat" each other. They decided to hold a joint camp-fire. They took turns presenting skits and songs. Members of both groups requested that they go home together on the same bus, rather than on the separate buses in which they had come. On the way the bus stopped for refreshments. One group still had five dollars which they had won as a prize in a contest. They decided to spend this sum on refreshments. On their own initiative they invited their former rivals to be their guests for malted milks.

Our interviews with the boys confirmed this change. From choosing their "best friends" almost exclusively in their own group, many of them shifted to listing boys in the other group as best friends. They were glad to have a second chance to rate boys in the other group, some of them remarking that they had changed their minds since the first rating made after the tournament. Indeed they had. The new ratings were largely favorable.

Efforts to reduce friction and prejudice between groups in our society have usually followed rather different methods. Much attention has been given to bringing members of hostile groups together socially, to communicating accurate and favorable information about one group to the other, and to bringing the leaders of groups together to enlist their influence. But as everyone knows, such measures sometimes reduce intergroup tensions and sometimes do not. Social contacts, as our experiments demonstrated, may only serve as occasions for intensifying conflict. Favorable information about a disliked group may be ignored or reinterpreted to fit sterotyped notions about the group. Leaders cannot act without regard for the prevailing temper in their own groups.

What our limited experiments have shown is that the possibilities for achieving harmony are greatly enhanced when groups are brought together to work toward common ends. Then favorable information about a disliked group is seen in a new light, and leaders are in a position to take bolder steps toward cooperation. In short, hostility gives way when groups pull together to achieve overriding goals which are real and compelling to all concerned.

88. CONFLICT IN A NEW ENGLAND COLLEGE TOWN *

VICTOR A. RAPPORT

*Many American colleges and universities with fairly large
staffs are located in relatively small communities. These staff
members often have characteristics and values that differ
from those of the townspeople. In such situations the townspeople
tend to regard the staff of the institution of higher learning as
an out-group, and vice versa. It is often but a small step
further for hostile feelings to develop. From his own experiences
V. A. Rapport describes one such "town-gown" conflict. Though
it has certain unique characteristics, it is in many respects
representative of university-community relationships everywhere.
The author concludes that under such conditions conflict is
likely to remain a permanent, institutionalized relationship,
since the cultures of the two groups are so divergent.*

A conflict situation which exists between college and town groups
is neither new nor unusual, yet the conflict manifesting itself around
Storrs, the seat of Connecticut State College, seems sufficiently individual in certain particulars, typical in others, to warrant description.
Deep-seated hates, the products of years, do not prevail since the college
itself is young. Antagonisms which have festered with time are absent.
Instead, however, is the intensity accompanying new suspicions and
dislikes, the force of pioneers who inherit no traditions of struggle but,
rather, live the struggle themselves. And the conflict, although new,
expresses ancient motivations to conflict, rallying cries of past centuries
and foreign places.

An investigation made by the author over a period of two years
provides illustrations of certain characteristics of conflict and demonstrates conflict patterns. Some doubt is cast by the facts on the accepted

* *Social Forces*, Vol. 17 (May, 1939), 527–532. Reprinted by permission of the
publisher and the author.

The author (b. 1903) is Dean, College of Liberal Arts, Wayne University.
Formerly Associate Professor of Sociology, University of Connecticut. Was a Fulbright Research Scholar in Italy, 1955–1956. Has published numerous articles in
professional journals. Coauthor, *The Recreational Uses of Land in Connecticut*. His
topics of interest include manpower planning in the field of education, criminology,
social implications of selective service.

outcomes of conflict, although there is a partial manifestation of several of these effects. The research was by personal interview with a large number of the residents of the Town of Mansfield (in which Storrs is located), and with members of the college faculty. The results do not adapt themselves to statistical interpretation; they are exclusively opinions expressed in conversation of a purposely casual nature.

Out of the statements, the following characteristics and patterns of conflict became evident: (1) the groups are highly self-conscious with respect to status and welfare; (2) organization both with and without recognized leaders is frequent, although the organizations are transitory; (3) propaganda and false reports are constant; (4) there is distinct confusion between the accepted and assigned reasons for the conflict and what appear to be the real reasons; (5) the unifying and (6) the disorganizing effects of conflict are both apparent. Finally, (7) whether the conflict will be resolved by the operation of accommodation, assimilation, or amalgamation is open to question despite indications of the existence of these processes in the present situation.

Before entering upon a description of the conflict, it would be best to clarify the peculiarities of the New England setting. Connecticut State College is located in Storrs, a village in the Town of Mansfield.

It should be remembered that the New England town is a relatively autonomous political division of the state, somewhat corresponding to the western township. Since county organization and function are relatively insignificant in New England, the town becomes a highly important grouping. Within the town are districts or villages—sometimes cities—which may or may not be separately incorporated, but which still owe a responsibility to the town. Thus, any resident of the Town of Mansfield, be he in Eagleville, Merrow or Gurleyville, is concerned with Storrs and the doings of its people, the college group.

This demarcation of the college group from the remainder of the town is indicative of the self-consciousness with respect to status and welfare. One frequently hears the former referred to as "the college" rather than as a group of individuals. Many of the townspeople make a clear distinction between themselves, who are residents of the town, and the college people who are in the same category as summer residents in a resort town. This is true despite the fact that many of the faculty have been taxpayers and property owners in the town for a score of years. Within the town group, one is "new people," according to one informant, for at least thirty years; the acceptance after that length of time does not appear to hold for those at the college. The college group, on the other hand, generally restricts its social life to colleagues and, in general, is quite ignorant of the town affairs. The self-consciousness with respect to welfare will be discussed later under organization.

Certain individuals, it should be indicated, are excluded from the conflict because of either or both of two reasons: (1) non-participation and (2) exemption. The *non-participants* are in both groups; these people do not feel antagonistic toward the other group, mix freely, and tend to merge with the *exempts,* those college people who are stamped as "regular" by the town group, and vice versa. The reasons for inclusion in the exempted group vary considerably with no characteristic pattern. In many instances, the older professors are included, though not all the older professors are exempted nor are all the exempts of the older group at the college. The exempted townspeople are frequently retired or professional men who reside in Mansfield, though not all the exempts are of this category nor is this whole group exempt. Young professors, recently arrived in Connecticut, and old farmers are accepted by the opposite groups—just why, nobody seems to know.

An illustration of the operation of the self-consciousness with respect to status is seen in Mansfield Center, another village of the Town of Mansfield, located about four miles from the college. Many residents of this community have long felt strongly about the college group. Some years ago a lone professor and his family took up residence in the village. They were not a part of it for several years and were constantly made to feel that they did not "belong." Cracks finally began to appear in the icy reception they met, and in time they found themselves accepted as satisfactory citizens. What they had done to effect this change, they were unaware. They had merely continued about their own business, greeted people pleasantly but without trying to make friends, cultivated their garden, trimmed their lawn, and lived. It is probable that the combination of all these factors was the successful formula to break down the conflict attitudes. More and more of the college families moved into Mansfield Center as Storrs became overcrowded. The village soon heard mutterings about "The college people are taking over all the fine old houses," and "A farmer can't get a place any more with the rents that these college people pay" and "The Center ain't the same with all these new people coming in." As time went by, some of the new people became exempts, others did not.

The organization of the conflicting groups is primarily for political purposes. When the townspeople believe that "the college" is coming to the town meeting (a good old New England custom) for the purpose of promulgating legislation designed to further the ends of the college group, word goes out to the back country that all are needed to fight the measure. On the other hand, the college faction is constantly cautious about being absent lest "the town" force an ordinance prejudicial to the interests of the college. That each is motivated by selfish interests which are not conducive to the greatest welfare of the town is the firm belief of the opposing groups. Leaders are self-constituted or chosen from time to time in these political controversies, but frequently the groups follow concerted action without individuals at their head. A particularly serious issue arose about ten years ago when it was proposed to replace the antiquated grammar school at Storrs with a modern building. The opposition from the town centered around the argument that the existing school had been satisfactory for a great many years and ought to be good enough now, and, further, that "the college" felt that it needed something better for its children than was provided for the remainder of the town. That the children of faculty members represented only about one-third of the school population was overlooked. The building was approved at a town meeting and erected, but the wounds of the conflict have not yet healed. It is chiefly in these political disagreements that the propaganda and false reports are most current. The latter also are frequent in personal gossip principally concerning faculty members.

The confusion between assigned reasons and real reasons is particularly interesting. Among those persons who were interrogated, few had any real justification for disliking the other group, they "just felt that way." In most instances, when pressed for a reason, the informant was forced to pause for reflection before the "reason" was forthcoming.

The "reasons" on both sides are fundamentally the same. The objections of the people of the town to the college group fall under five general headings. The college group (1) takes no interest in the town; (2) is trying to run the town for its own selfish interests; (3) is "too snooty"; (4) represents impractical and incompetent theorists; (5) is composed of non-Connecticut newcomers. The college group felt that the townspeople (1) are trying to run the town for their own selfish interests; (2) are old-fashioned, stubborn Yankee farmers; (3) lack intellectual stimulation; (4) lack broad vision.

An analysis of the assigned reasons for the antagonisms reveals that some are justified while others are merely rationalizations. The political situation, which has been discussed in part previously, has counted heavily in arousing opposition attitudes. The charge has frequently been levelled at the college group that it lived in houses rented from the college (thus not contributing to taxation), traded outside the town, and in general represented no financial gain to town funds. These facts are generally untrue. A large number of the faculty live in non-college houses, almost all have automobiles which are taxable, and even those who live in college houses contribute indirectly to the town in that Mansfield receives a special grant from the State to compensate for the tax-exempt property which the State of Connecticut holds in the town. Regardless of the general untruth of the claim, it still carries great weight in the minds of the townspeople. They resent the "non-contributing" college people coming to town meeting and voting how the town's money shall be spent. A feeling common to many of the townsfolk is that the faculty receives instructions from the administration of the college—or some unnamed group in power—and must vote accordingly.

Some years ago, "the college" was accused of taking no interest in town affairs. When a few members of the faculty interested themselves to the extent of running for office as members of the school board or for other minor offices, the tune changed to one charging an attempt to dominate town affairs. One professor who served for ten years on the school board was complimented implicitly by having a candidate placed in the field for the express purpose of opposing the professor's policies on the board. It was felt that Professor X could not be defeated for office—"the college" would elect him—but the town's leading merchant was elected to fight every proposal which the learned gentleman might make. It is interesting to note that the merchant, who was an "exempt" as far as the college was concerned, found himself agreeing with Professor X, much to the displeasure of the former's constituents.

That the college group is "snooty" is both a justified and a false accusation. While certain of the faculty hold themselves aloof from the non-college group, others are anxious to be felt a part of the town. Their isolation is often more a result of exclusion by the townspeoople than a product of their own desire. Herein is manifested a situation common to groups considered "clannish"; they are frequently so because they are not *allowed* to participate. In Mansfield, a number of the residents say that they want nothing to do with the college group, and then charge them with feeling themselves "too good to associate with plain people." An illustration of this occurred when a faculty member went into the village store one day attired in the old clothes in which he had been working in his garden. There he met one of the townspeople who was noted for his dislike of "the college." The two fell into a long conversation about a variety of things, and then the faculty member left. After his departure, the townsman asked, "Who is that fellow? He seems mighty pleasant." When told that it was Professor Y, the man felt that he had been imposed on, and continued in his opinion that the college group was "snooty."

The charge that the people at the college are theoretical and impractical is largely derived from the origin of the college as a land-grant and primarily agricultural institution. The proposals of the agricultural faculty for improvement of farming techniques are frequently met with the statement that if those men had to farm like other farmers, they couldn't get along. "As long as they've got the State to pay for all their nonsense, they can try out those damn fool notions." Or, as a variant of that theme, "Anybody could be a successful farmer if he had all the money in the world to buy equipment in the first place." With the introduction and increase of non-agricultural subjects, the attitude of the townspeople was strengthened by the strange fields and the more citified men who were brought in to teach. Now, more than ever, the rift widened.

Not only were the new faculty members urban products, in the large, but they were often from places far distant from Connecticut or even New England. Here the political conflict arose again when it was felt that persons not familiar or sympathetic with local problems were dictating (or attempting to dictate) how town affairs were to be conducted. This is not particularly strange when it is realized that many of the families have been in Mansfield for many generations, and at least five of these families ante-date the Revolution by almost a hundred years. One of the local families is directly descended from a Mayflower pioneer who left the Massachusetts Colony and settled in Mansfield. That "Westerners" (people from Ohio, Illinois, Indiana, Kansas, and Iowa) should tell them how to run *their* town was something to resent. One local resident feels that the cause of the confusion in the United States today is the adoption of all these new-fangled devices, and that all the country needs to restore equilibrium is a return to the old ways of doing things. Automobiles and telephones are foolishness, the local store should resume business on a barter basis with the farmers, and we should drive oxcarts to Norwich, twenty miles away, to do our "trading." Why we have to import strangers to teach weird subjects when there are a lot of Connecticut boys and girls available is a mystery.

The college group, on the other hand, cannot sympathize with the Connecticut tradition of proceeding slowly. Its belief that the townspeople are trying to run the town for their own selfish interests and that they are old-fashioned and stubborn arises from the reluctance of the town to accept in their entirety the proposals for radical change in school and fiscal matters. With all the experts in education and finance it is not surprising that there should exist a desire to operate a sort of laboratory here in Mansfield. The people of the town are not ready to enter whole-heartedly into such proposals. Impatient with this attitude, the college group becomes rapidly critical.

The charges that the local people lack intellectual stimulation and broad vision impress the writer as coming frequently from the fact that the townspeople "don't talk our language." This conflict situation is not limited to gown versus town; it is frequent within the college itself. We of the faculty often become so engrossed in our own fields that we are unwilling or unable to talk with someone else about his work, and his unwillingness becomes to us a sign of his narrowness. The definition of a bore as "a person who always wants to talk when I want to talk" is applicable with slight transformation in this situation.

The real reasons for the conflict are common to all conflict situations. There is a clash of mores, a conflict of interests, which cannot be resolved. The jealousy of success by either group cannot be overcome by rational argument. That there is some justification on both sides is without question, but that much of the dispute is rooted in lack of understanding, in untruths, and an unwillingness to see the opposite side is equally evident.

The unifying effect of conflict is seen in the coming together of disputing groups of the townspeople to oppose the faculty, which, in turn, disagrees about many matters of college policy but which is quite homogeneous in opinions as to town affairs. The disorganization which conflict brings is retarding the normal progress which the town would make were these two factions not present.

Accommodation and assimilation are not totally absent, although whether either process will ever be complete is doubtful. Each side accepts the presence of the other, occasional joint efforts are carried out with the usual pattern being that of the college group joining the town group; rarely does the reverse occur. Such groups as the local Red Cross, the Parent-Teachers Association, and a choral society are effecting certain joint association, but it should be noted that these are primarily groups of women. Less association of the men takes place. As has already been mentioned, exempts of both groups are universally welcome and represent well assimilated individuals. A negligible amount of intermarriage between the groups has occurred.

Discussion of this type of conflict is usually designated as "town versus gown"; the implication is that the town is the aggressor, the college the defender. Long before Simmel, Gumplowicz or Marx, men knew that "it takes two to make a fight." It is the writer's opinion that the gown versus town phase of the conflict has been neglected. The college group, it would appear, is equally responsible for the existence and preservation of the conflict situation.

Finally, the question arises as to whether, as is frequently stated regarding conflict, this situation is true only during a period of change. It may be said that the conflict is occurring while the college is growing, but the writer believes that such divergent groups will not, as has been said, complete the processes of accommodation, assimilation and amalgamation with the eventual eradication of the conflict. Each group is protected from being absorbed by the culture of the other, and, as a result, each will continue with its own culture. Evidence in support of this is seen in towns where colleges have existed for several hundred years and where the town versus gown and the gown versus town conflicts still prevail.

89. THE TOOTHPASTE TOURNAMENT *

WALTER GOODMAN

The social process of competition—the individual or intergroup struggle for a mutually desired goal—can be illustrated in many different settings. The goal may be material, like goods, money or property, or nonmaterial, like prestige or popularity. The techniques which many manufacturers use to attract and hold customers illustrates the competitive process particularly well. Walter Goodman, in this selection, contributes an amusing case study of the extremes to which some businessmen go in the competition for markets. This selection not only demonstrates "competition" but also exhibits one form of collective behavior by showing that clever advertising campaigns can sometimes convince a great many people by appealing primarily to the emotions rather than by logical and scientific evidence.

In 1859 a wholesale druggist from New York named William Henry Hall presented America with a product called Sozodont, a red liquid containing 37 percent alcohol. The nation was informed that it had been blessed with "the most convenient, efficacious and beneficial article for the teeth the world has ever seen." We've come a long way since.

While scientists in other fields have been inching their way modestly toward such attainments as hydrogen bombs and deep freezes, the dentifrice people have advanced with seven-league boots, conquering new terrain four times in the past decade. Since all toothpastes and powders are made of substantially the same three simple ingredients—soap that foams, an abrasive that scrapes and a flavorer that makes the stuff tolerable—this is no small trick. The credit for it belongs less to the men in the laboratories than to the men in the advertising agencies.

A late 19th Century ad circulated by Dr. I. W. Lyons, innovator of tooth powder in a can, stated flatly:

It is useless to say that any dentifrice will whiten the teeth or change their color one particle—anything which professes to do it is an acid.

* From *New Republic*, Vol. 135, No. 5 (July 30, 1956), 15–17.
  The author, who is Senior Editor at *Redbook Magazine*, has a B.A. in economics from Syracuse University and an M.A. in philosophy from Reading University, England. Author: *The Clowns of Commerce*, a collection of previously published magazine articles on advertising.

Fortunately for the industry, more imaginative copywriters were to take over from Dr. Lyons, as promotion-minded soap firms ("soapers" to the trade) ousted the drug companies from their positions of dentrifice leadership. The family-sized tube of soap, abrasive and flavorer which costs about 10 cents to produce (including tube), ordinarily receives about a dime's worth of advertising. Americans had been made tooth-conscious enough by 1954 to spend more than $150 million for pastes and powders, and the figure is going up all the time.

How, exactly, have the admen aroused all this enthusiasm for so grubby a chore as brushing one's teeth? Well, in the early days they could alert people to the fact that tooth-brushing was good for them (although certain African tribes are said to keep their teeth strong and shining with a vigorous tongue motion after meals, and some people in the West are still devoted to dental floss). Then there was the novelty of nationally advertised brands that tasted better than baking soda, not to mention the convenient packaging. "Comes out like a ribbon, lies flat on the brush," sang a turn-of-the-century ad for Colgate's. Between wars, the toothpaste makers discovered a great number of foul ailments which had heretofore gone neglected by the nation's medical men. Acid-mouth; pink toothbrush; germ mask; smoker's teeth; gingivitis; pyorrhea; halitosis.

As a matter of fact, pink toothbrush is a rather common phenomenon; bad breath generally starts in the stomach; and nobody's teeth are precisely white—the shades range from a pale ivory to a positive yellow. But you'd never know *that* from the ads—"You'll wonder where the yellow went when you brush your teeth with Pepsodent."

By the end of World War II, the persuasive powers of Colgate's ("It cleans your breath while it cleans your teeth") had won 40 percent of the national market. Tied for second place, with 15 percent apiece, were Lever Bros.' Pepsodent (which had coined the phrase "clinging film," destined to endure through generations of dentifrice ads) and Ipana, put out by Bristol-Myers, a drug firm.

Pepsodent is generally credited with pioneering the way into the postwar phase of toothpaste wonders with its discovery of Irium. The American Dental Association found this "special ingredient" to be sodium alkyl sulfate, a simple foaming compound. Said the ADA: "The firm has attempted to endow the word 'irium' which is applied to the soap sub-stitute used in its products with extraordinary virtues which it does not possess." Irium did, however, possess one extraordinary virtue: it rhymed with Miriam in the jingle about that poor girl's failings chorused twice each week for several seasons on the Bob Hope radio show.

Early in 1949, a new brand of tooth powder appeared on the neigh-borhood drug and supermarket counters in everybody's neighborhood, and almost immediately became one of the industry's leaders. By April,

Amm-i-dent, a powder manufactured by the Block Drug Co., had garnered almost 20 percent of the market. A $2 million advertising campaign that year helped retain much of this. "Genuine Amm-i-dent Ammoniated Toothpaste Is Here to Reduce Tooth Decay!" the ladies' magazines announced that autumn. It did this, explained Block, by virtue of the carbamide (synthetic urea) and dibasic ammonium phosphate sparkling in every tube. In 1934, it seemed a pair of Minnesota dentists had found a higher percentage of ammonia nitrogen in the saliva of people naturally immune to decay than of those subject to caries. This, they decided, was nature's way of fighting the microorganism Lactobacillus acidophilus, colonies of which swarm around every cavity. Amm-i-dent claimed that its "exclusive formula" released ammonium ions, which thereupon engaged those villainous Lactobacilli, etc., in mortal combat.

Amm-i-dent's formidable discovery presented the major firms with a dilemma. A rash of obscure ammoniated brands appeared almost at once, and the sales of the top pastes were being hurt. But to alter the chemistry of the long-established favorites was fraught with hazard. Still, who could hold out? Ipana surrendered, and soon even the front runner had added a new product to its line—Colgate's Ammoniated Tooth Powder, containing those "wonder ingredients" compounded by University of Illinois scientists—dibasic ammonium phosphate and carbamide. (The very names were enough to scare a young Lactobacillus out of a year's growth.) "Yes, Colgate's Great Dentifrice Gives *Extra Protection!*" affirmed the ads for the new ammoniated powder, while a page or two away it was reported that Colgate's good old unammoniated toothpaste "has been proved to contain all the necessary ingredients, including an effective *patented* ingredient, for effective daily dental care."

Amm-i-dent retorted peevishly that it had "more anti-decay ingredients than any other toothpaste." Un-ammoniated Listerine stood above the battle: "What about tooth decay?" It asked—and answered: "It's mainly up to *you!* If you will always brush your teeth right after eating, you will almost certainly help reduce decay in your teeth." (What an opening for the product directed at "the man who can't brush after every meal.")

Nineteen-fifty was a relatively quiet year. The Andrew Jergens Co. came up with Dentocillin, a powder containing penicillin which, in one test, reportedly reduced cavities by 55 percent. But the item somehow failed to capture the popular imagination and the latest revolution was stillborn.

Another event in 1950, however, was destined to launch one of those recurrent crazes in tooth care. The Rystan Co., a drug firm headed by a former adman named O'Neill Ryan Jr. obtained a patent on the therapeutic use of chlorophyll, the substance that makes alfalfa green. Rystan had been channeling the alfalfa extract to dentists for a decade; now it was looking toward the world at large. In the fall of 1951, Lever Bros. obtained a license from Ryan to use a water-soluble chlorophyll derivative in a commercial toothpaste. Thus was born Chlorodent, which guaranteed America a "Fresh Mouth . . . ALL DAY LONG!" The arrangement made a million dollars for Ryan and moved Lever Bros. into a second-place position where it breathed its sweet, minty breath onto Colgate's neck. . . .

After some legal preliminaries, other dentifrice manufacturers jumped onto the alfalfa wagon. In April, 1952, Amm-i-dent became Amm-i-dent Ammoniated Chlorophyll and upped its share of the national market from 10 to 14 percent. Ipana became Ipana A/C; Colgate, Kolynos and Iodent also turned green.

Commenting on the newest achievement of dental science, Dr. J. Roy Doty, secretary of the ADA's council of dental therapeutics, said:

> . . . evidence presently available does not warrant claims that dental products containing chlorophyll derivatives are useful or beneficial in preventing or curing dental decay. . . . Concerning claims for breath deodorization, the evidence as to the usefulness of products containing chlorophyll derivatives is inconclusive.

After slightly less than a year's run—about par for this course—chlorophyll was winded and the front position was taken by still another sensational additive. Experiments—at Northwestern University this time—had resulted in the discovery of two chemicals that were reputed to neutralize cavity-producing enzymes in the mouth. The Lambert Pharmaceutical Co., makers of Listerine, quickly announced that hereafter it wanted to be known as the maker of Listerine Anti-Enzyme. The trade-name developers for Colgate's burst forth joyfully: "What's new in Colgate Dental Cream that's MISSING-MISSING-MISSING in every other leading toothpaste? It's Gardol!" Lever Bros., for its part, quietly began to test-market Shield, a new paste that contained a marvelous anti-biotic.

Barely a handful of enzymes had been destroyed, however, before Proctor & Gamble, the only one of the three big soapers which had heretofore refrained from attacking man's teeth, entered the lists with Gleem. "Just *one* brushing destroys decay- and odor-causing bacteria. After one Gleem brushing, up to 90 percent of bacteria are destroyed. Only GLEEM has GL-70 to fight decay."

"*Any* toothpaste can destroy decay- and odor-causing bacteria," sneered Colgate's. "But new bacteria come back in minutes, to form acids that cause decay. Colgate's, unlike any other leading toothpaste, *keeps on* fighting tooth decay 12 hours or more."

GL-70, in case anybody is interested at this point, is a "surface-active" detergent of the variety used to brighten clothes and dishes. Proctor and Gamble has devoted an estimated $15 million to spreading the news of its contribution to America's bicuspids. Ipana, lately possessed of dibasic ammonium phosphate, carbamide and chlorophyll, now shot itself full of WD-9. "Ipana destroys decay bacteria best of all leading toothpastes." Pepsodent, for its part, added IMP (insoluble Meta-Phosphate, you know) to good old Irium.

But the latest and greatest toothpaste additive is something related to fluoride, the ingredient found in drinking water in certain areas of the country, which is thought to harden tooth enamel and thereby frustrate bacteria.

1796: Triumph Over Contagious Diseases. First inoculation by Dr. Jenner.
1848: Triumph Over Pain. Dr. Morton's discovery of ether.
1929: Triumph Over Bacterial Infections. Fleming discovers penicillin.
Now—1956—Proctor & Gamble proudly announces . . .
TRIUMPH OVER TOOTH DECAY.
Crest Toothpaste with Fluoristan strengthens tooth enamel to lock out decay from within. Crest with Fluoristan is the only toothpaste ever developed that makes possible a major reduction in tooth decay, for people of all ages. Thereby, Crest marks the turning point in man's age-old struggle against this almost universal disease.

About the time that several million households had used up their sample tubes of CREST, they received sample tubes of BRISK. The Colgate Company, late again, had bounced back with its customary verve. "Only BRISK has FLUORIDE/85 . . . HARDENS TOOTH ENAMEL, MAKES TEETH STRONGER, starts working instantly TO DEFEAT DECAY." Good old unfluorided Colgate's thereupon advertised, snidely, that kiddies under six could eat its merchandise with complete safety. Fluoride yellow seems about to join halitosis among America's major oral ailments.

(Amm-i-dent, by the way, is at present the world's first and only toothpaste containing all three of the best decay fighting ingredients known to dental science: Fluoride, Ammoniated and Anti-Enzyme SLS.2.)

Is Colgate's Fluoride/85 better than Proctor and Gamble's Fluoristan? Dr. Harold Hellenbrand, secretary of ADA, takes an impartial view:

The American Dental Association is not aware of evidence adequate to demonstrate the claimed dental caries prophylactic value of Crest. . . . Published evidence to support the usefulness of adding a fluoride in other dentifrices is even less convincing. The Association therefore believes that all fluoride dentifrices are being marketed prematurely.

In a full-page newspaper advertisement on its 150th birthday in April, the Colgate-Palmolive Co., the world's largest manufacturer of toilet goods, revealed its "infallible rules for a long happy life for a business or organization. The first is to make products that are genuinely useful to people." Continued Colgate's:

We intend to go right on trying, for another 150 years, to outdo our competitors in devising new ways to serve the desire of people everywhere to be clean, attractive, healthy. The gainer from all this will be the public—that ever-youthful, open-minded, hard-to-please, impossible-to-fool public. . . .

Happy birthday, Colgate's. You Ammoniated, Chlorophylled, Gardolled, Fluoridated Colgate's.

90. SOME SOCIOLOGICAL ASPECTS OF CONSUMERS' COOPERATION *

LEONARD C. KERCHER

Among the social processes that characterize American economic behavior, competition may seem most typical; cooperation, however, is also very important. This selection by L. W. Kercher deals with the Finnish consumers' cooperative movement in the Great Lakes region. It presents some of the distinctively sociological factors that conditioned the launching and operation of these consumer cooperatives, illustrates cooperation as an institutionalized process, and the development of a specific social movement.

Around thirty-five years ago Finnish immigrants in the Upper Lake region of the North Central states initiated a cooperative movement that has become the strongest and most unified distinctly Rochdale consumers' movement in this country. It is today a mixed rural-urban development of about 110 local distributive societies scattered mainly over northeastern Minnesota, northern Wisconsin and Upper Michigan. It has around 40,000 individual members, about 75 per cent of whom are engaged in farming. The local societies are organized into district and regional federations, the most important of which is the Central Cooperative Wholesale, a regional business and general purpose organiza-

* *Rural Sociology*, Vol. 6, No. 4 (December, 1941), 311–322. Reprinted by permission of the author and the publisher.

The author (b. 1901) is Chairman, Division of Social Science, Western Michigan University. This selection is based on doctoral dissertation, "The Finnish-Dominated Consumers' Cooperative Movement in the North Central States." This material is included in *Consumers' Cooperatives* (coauthor, Vant W. Kebker). Other books of which he is a coauthor are: *Sociological Foundations of Education* and *Twentieth Century America: Trends in Civilization*.

tion located at Superior, Wisconsin. A study of this Finnish-initiated consumers' cooperative movement brought into relief certain factors that appear to have special significance in the successful initiation, development and operation of cooperative enterprise. The more important of these factors that are more distinctly sociological in character are briefly reviewed in this article.

. . . . .

By inclination and experience immigrant Finns were mainly peasant farm workers who came to the New World in the hope of settling on small farms of their own. But generally they were poor and had to turn to whatever work there was at hand to earn the necessary funds. In the three major economic exploitations of the region they, therefore, usually played the role of common laborers; either miners or lumberjacks first, and then later, farmers. For their work in the mines and logging camps they received very moderate and uncertain wages. The low and variable incomes, as well as unfavorable working conditions, were sources of much unrest among these Finnish workers and were among the principal reasons why they took a leading part in the major labor strikes in the area.

In line with their original aspirations many Finns as soon as possible developed part-time farming activities. But, before they had accumulated adequate resources large numbers of them were forced to turn to full-time farming for a livelihood after being permanently displaced from mining or lumbering occupations. As pioneer farmers they struggled ceaselessly against unfavorable conditions of climate and soil on the one hand, and against exploitative conditions in the local markets on the other. High monopolistic prices charged by local merchants is one of the most frequently repeated reasons given by the members for starting their local consumers' cooperative.

In addition to economic handicaps these early Finns also experienced insecurity with respect to group and individual status and achievement. They unwillingly occupied the most menial of positions in the economy and found advancement extremely difficult. The language barrier, as well as other cultural or occupational differences, served to discourage genuine social relations with other groups in the community. Individual Finns found it next to impossible to achieve in relation to the whole community one of the deepest needs of personality—a sense of belonging. From the beginning they were thrown back upon their own nationality group in order to realize individual and collective goals. They have consequently evidenced a marked tendency to be clannish and to keep intact their social and cultural heritage in the New World. This social isolation and strong primary group unity made more possible the group-wise attainment of desired goals.

Virtually all of the Finnish immigrants who initiated the cooperative movement under study, came to the Upper Lake region between 1900 and 1910 as young men who had little if any direct experience with cooperation in their native country. They brought with them, however, a workingman's culture including a liberal social philosophy which had been molded by a half century of struggle on the part of Finnish-speaking lower classes to attain national unity and economic security. Various interrelated associations and institutions of this cultural heritage were transplanted and adapted here as group-wise techniques for attaining such basic satisfactions as fellowship, recognition, security, intellectual growth and recreation. These included temperance societies, workers' educational associations, trade unionism, socialism and the Finnish church. In one way or another, each of these social instruments contributed to the development of consumers' cooperation. The temperance societies and workers' associations served as propaganda agencies as well as excellent training schools in the art of democratic discussion. The socialist movement among the Finns, in particular, exerted a tremendous influence. It diffused a liberal ideology of working class welfare and urged the development of cooperatives as a phase of an aggressive labor movement. It supplied much of the early leadership in the cooperatives. Moreover, the Finnish socialist clubs, supported by the Finnish socialist press, played a major role in publicizing the Old World cooperative movement and the principles underlying it among Finnish workers in the area. This oft-repeated story of Rochdale cooperation in Finland and England acted as a potent stimulus to the development of cooperatives among these workers and also provided the basic principles underlying their organization.

The movement under study clearly had its roots in American soil in that it was an adjustment response to conditions in the Upper Lake region. On the other hand, it also had nourishing roots in the Old World since its sponsors shared and profited by the experience of cooperators abroad. In brief summary, the following factors in the total situation out of which the Finnish-initiated cooperative movement developed stand out in relief.

1. The geographical, economic and ecological situations were characterized by limited resources, a specialized, unstable economy, and a selective migration and settlement of diverse foreign-born peoples that tended to encourage social cohesion and self-sufficiency within homogeneous groups while producing social distance and conflict in intergroup relations as well as insecurity and frustration in the lives of individuals.

2. The large number of Finnish immigrants concentrated in the region were forced into unfamiliar and undesired occupations. Changes in the economy of the region increased the occupational hazards and produced as well much group and individual insecurity.

3. The social situation among Finnish immigrants made it virtually impossible earlier for individual satisfactions to be obtained except through close adherence to their own nationality group. This put a premium upon group isolation, group solidarity and the techniques of group-wise adjustment.

4. Finnish immigrants brought to America a workingman's culture that included a liberal social philosophy and a group of related associations and institutions which fostered socialism in politics, trade unionism in production and eventually consumers' cooperation in consumption.

Variable conditions in different cooperatives influence the success of the enterprises. Space is too limited here, however, to deal with these individual situations. As an alternative the author proposes to appraise the present elements of strength and of weakness in the movement as a whole.

A vital and enduring need. It is virtually a sociological axiom that a vital and enduring need for it, is a basic element of strength in any social institution. The geographical and occupational circumstances that in the past gave rise to the severe handicaps of urban and agricultural workers in the region remain, with no prospects of significant permanent improvement in the near future. It is likely, therefore, that economic need will continue to provide a strong incentive to cooperative development in the area.

The circumstances underlying the felt needs for recognition and self-realization are, however, in gradual transition. Formerly these needs were intensified by the social isolation and the inferior occupational status of the Finnish immigrant group. The Finn is now becoming more of a participating member of the community as a whole. Here in a larger social setting he will find individual sources of recognition and expression that were denied him in former days. This may reduce the feeling of need for group solidarity and for group-wise attainment of goals through cooperative effort.

Community setting. It has been in the intimate neighborly social setting of the hamlet, village or small town community that the cooperatives in this movement have, as a rule, had their firmest roots. Here occupational and other class differences are minor, and as a consequence economic wants are sufficiently commonplace and uniform to be served by a relatively simple institutional structure. Furthermore the face-to-face contacts of everyday life provide the ideal social experience for the development of common understanding and the formation of attitudes of group solidarity so essential to voluntary cooperative effort. In antithesis, the typical city situation has not proven congenial to the growth of strong cooperatives in the movement. The social groupings and the cultural standards of the city are more heterogeneous, individual interests and wants are more diversified and social contacts are more secondary and impersonal. Cooperators nurtured in such a situation are likely to feel no deep need for cooperative enterprise, nor do they form a conscious consumers' group equipped with common understanding, attitudes and habits necessary for the pursuit of long-time objectives of consumers' cooperation. Experience seems to show that if the movement is to expand into larger urban centers it must adopt the most improved merchandising methods and develop effective techniques of organizing city consumers.

In-group solidarity and democratic organization and control. An outstanding element of strength in the movement has been the unusual solidarity of the cooperative group, based largely on its social and cultural homogeneity. As noted later, the growth of a more diversified membership and the consequent weakening of the earlier cultural ties must be counteracted by a more effective educational and merchandising program.

An aspect of internal solidarity which is of growing importance concerns the harmonizing of the producer and the consumer interests of the members. The main element of strength to be observed in the situation is that through a process of democratic discussion a basis of voluntary cooperation between these two diverging interests has been evolved, whereby adjustment of prices, standardization of quality and allocation of earnings can be achieved with greater justice and satisfaction to both.

The Finns built their cooperative structure in the most orthodox Rochdale fashion—from the bottom up. By erecting their cooperatives on a foundation of local interest, local ownership and local control, Finnish cooperators strongly believed that they could obtain the understanding, the sense of responsibility and the loyalty of the membership necessary for an enduring movement. The growth of federation, both regional and district, has remained democratic and flexible. On the commercial side, and more recently on the service side as well, it is centered in the Central Cooperative Wholesale. This regional federation has coordinated the business strength of the local societies, developed expert regional leadership and forged technical and economic weapons to fight growing competition. In addition its educational department is a major factor in diffusing cooperative sentiment throughout the area and in fostering social solidarity in the movement. Nothing would seem so likely to reduce the movement to the status of local shopkeeping as the neglect or abuse of its federated regional strength.

Outside support. Its early tie-up with the Finnish liberal labor movement made the cooperative movement sectarian. To a certain extent this resulted both in internal conflict and in outside antagonisms. During the early years, the cooperative movement to the politically conservative represented radical socialist intrigue; to nationalistic elements it was a Finnish monopoly; to the religious-minded it was chiefly the work of atheists; and to the middle class consumer it was merely a common laborer's store.

The bitter factional struggle for control in the late twenties liquidated the influence of the radical socialist in the movement, strongly reaffirmed the Rochdale principles of open membership and democratic control and fostered an independent philosophy of cooperation. This transition has largely removed the sectarian barriers to expansion, and, together with the general liberal reaction which swept the country this past decade, has led to an increasing support of cooperatives by non-Finnish people and by certain elements in powerful American institutions.

The growing number of church people among the cooperatives' members and patrons, and the increasingly sympathetic attitude of many ministers in the area are indications of growing church support locally. The public schools have manifested a growing interest in the study of cooperation in all its phases. Under the pressure of public opinion legislative action has been taken in the states of Wisconsin, Minnesota and North Dakota leading to the inclusion of "Cooperation" as a definite subject in the school curriculum. During the past eight years, several officials and agencies of the federal government, from the President down, have given effective support to the cooperative idea. The governors of some states, particularly those of Wisconsin and Minnesota, have openly fostered it. What support or opposition from these sources may be forthcoming in the future is hard to judge. There is a hostile press and, of course, there are unfriendly political, religious, educational and business leaders.

Loyal and informed adherents. No institutions or movement can grow, or in the long run survive, that does not produce successive generations of loyal and informed adherents, both leaders and followers. This movement has a special problem of this nature in the transition of its controlling leadership from the older Finnish immigrant generation to the younger Finnish and non-Finnish generation. The older leaders and a large proportion of their followers have been extremely loyal and have possessed a deep understanding of cooperative principles and a religious-like determination to put them into practice. Whether or not the movement can replace these leaders and followers with others of the oncoming generations who have a sufficient amount of understanding, loyalty and determination to insure its perpetuation, is a major problem. It is, in part, a critical test of the whole educational and promotional nexus developed by the movement or allied to it.

The educational activity of the movement, designed both to develop cooperative sentiment and train personnel, has been greatly accelerated in the past four years. A variety of agencies and techniques, suited to a many-sided approach to the problem have been developed. As yet, however, only scattered and intangible evidence of the success of this educational program in meeting the problem is available.

Loyal and competent personnel. The ability to attract a loyal and competent personnel is a vital element of strength in this as in other co-operative movements. In general the movement has not lacked for loyal employees, but due to increasing competition it has a perennial need for better trained ones. The organized employee-training program, which is now primarily a responsibility of the Central Cooperative Wholesale, includes at present regional and district managers' meetings, resident employee training schools, and since 1938, circuit employee training schools for employees in service. These are functioning with considerable success.

Wage scales, hour schedules, opportunities for promotion and general economic security are normally factors that greatly influence the ordinary individual in his choice of an occupation and in the quality of his performance in it. In their religious-like zeal to further cooperation, the immigrant generation of employees tended to minimize these factors, but the younger generation is inclined to be much more strongly influenced by them. Indications are that several of the cooperatives, in order to attract and hold desirable personnel in the future, will find it necessary to make more favorable adjustments in these working conditions. Particularly, greater remuneration for responsible administrative positions seems indicated. While there is a need for the working out of well-reasoned policies of consumer-employee relationships, a strengthening element in the labor situation, if handled properly, is that the consumer-employee relationships in the movement as a whole seem favorable for progressive adjustments of all potential differences.

Ideological and philosophical foundations. An important element of strength in the movement is to be found in its deeply ingrained ideological and philosophical foundations. It is guided by sound consumers' cooperative principles, is supported by a liberal social philosophy and is rooted in realistic needs of human nature and society.

While it is true that Finnish socialist influence distorted for a time the principles of open membership and democratic control in the movement, these and other Rochdale principles have provided a reliable basis for the organization and functioning of the cooperatives from the beginning.

Although retaining the labor sympathies and strong liberal emphasis of its origin, in recent years consumers' cooperation has emerged more clearly in cooperators' minds as a transforming social movement in its own right. Although to most cooperators this philosophy is vague in its details, it nevertheless exists as a compelling general idea and as a persistent inspiration to many. It adds strength to the movement by transforming it from a mere program of collective shopkeeping to something of a social crusade.

The men and women who sponsored the Finnish-initiated cooperative movement were well acquainted with physical hardship, economic exploitation, poverty, social isolation and personal frustration. In developing cooperatives they were not hazy sentimentalists toying with an intriguing idea of a social utopia, but were hard-pressed working people who desperately sought an effective social instrument to aid them in a struggle against economic and social handicaps. The claims of individual self-realization, therefore, underlie the movement and provide it with realistic support in basic human needs and values. The pursuit of personal realization, however, has not been narrowly self-seeking or socially destructive. On the contrary, through the cooperative process the individual's interest has been best served by promoting the common good. The movement has gained strength from the realistic character and fundamental harmony of its individual and social purposes.

Conclusion. The object of the study upon which this article is based was to understand from a sociological point of view a significant adventure in consumers' cooperation in the United States. An effort was made to observe and analyze first hand the actual cooperative experiences of specific human groups in a concrete social and cultural setting. The results clearly indicate that a nexus of sociological factors conditions the genesis, development and functioning of the cooperatives in question. These factors represent several major areas of sociological interest—regional economic and ecological organization, population migration and settlement, cultural heritage and change, social aspects of personality, group organization and interaction, community structure, and institutional organization and functioning.

In general the elements of weakness in the Finnish-initiated consumers' cooperative movement in the North Central states spring from the uncertainties of its incomplete adaptation to the American community. It is still somewhat of a marginal institution with receding roots in a Finnish workingmen's culture on the one hand and with increasing social, psychological and cultural foundations in the American community on the other.

The principal elements of strength in the institution, on the other hand, lie partly in the successful adaptations that it has already made to the American scene, but even more in the sound ideological foundations and well-intrenched democratic techniques that make continued transition possible.

There is evidently a close interrelation of the main features of a specific cooperative enterprise or movement with the geographical setting, the historical background and principal socio-economic and cultural patterns of the cooperating group. For this reason conclusions and generalizations drawn from a study of one specific cooperative situation must be applied to others with understanding and insight.

91. GOSSIP IN THE SMALL TOWN *

ALBERT BLUMENTHAL

Social control—the process by which society induces conformity to group norms—is actually one of the social processes, although it is not ordinarily included with them in introductory texts. Social control can be of the informal type (for example, praise or blame) or the formal type, as by laws and codes. This selection by Albert Blumenthal well illustrates informal social control by gossip, a method which is especially effective in small towns. Says E. W. Burgess of the book from which this selection is taken, "the main characteristics of small town life stand out in clear perspective: close acquaintanceship of everyone with everyone else, the dominance of personal relations, and the subjection of the individual to continuous observation and control by the community."

One of the favorite themes of novels, stage plays, and jokes has long been the petty gossiping in small towns. Even the small-town residents themselves poke some fun at the inevitable and perennial gossiping in their midst, and are continually crying out against it and grumbling about it. For all that is so traditional about the small and isolated community is woven about the far-reaching power of gossip—of communication by word of mouth.

In Mineville, "gossip" is a term much used, especially by women and in description of them. It has two general meanings. Sometimes it includes all local news which is transmitted by word of mouth; and at other times it means only that information involving a fellow-resident which any particular resident would not want told of himself, or which people feel they must whisper stealthily lest they incur the displeasure

* *Small-Town Stuff* (Chicago: The University of Chicago Press, 1932), 128–143. Reprinted by permission of the publisher and the author.

The author (b. 1902) is Associate Professor of Sociology, Wisconsin State College, Eau Claire. *Small-Town Stuff* was a Ph.D. dissertation, University of Chicago, under the title, *A Sociological Study of a Small Town*. His interests include: criminology, juvenile delinquency, the family, and sociological theory.

of someone. Whether or not the resident wishes the word to carry a derogatory stigma is told by the intonation of his voice or by other gestures. In the following discussion it will be used in both senses under the assumption that the context will indicate to what extent a distinction is meant to be made between mere talk, and that sort of talk which anyone thinks should be whispered or not told.

WHO ARE THE GOSSIPERS?

Over the telephone a Mineville woman may quite frankly say, "I thought I would call up and see if you have heard the latest gossip." But while she is herself in the midst of spreading a scandal she is not unlikely to cast discredit upon another woman by calling her a "terrible old gossip." This illustrates the tendency of the people to make light of their own gossiping and that of their friends and to condemn it in others. For whether or not a person is rated as a gossip in the discrediting sense of the term depends not upon what he actually says but upon the attitude toward him held by the person making the rating.

Violent outbursts of anger and disgust at the "damned gossipers" are characteristic of most Minevillers when some of their own private affairs are aired in public. The part they themselves play in airing the affairs of others they seem to overlook. While it is true that most of them pretend to refrain from circulating information which will be harmful to the other fellow, all townsfolk (excepting infants and very small children) are dispensers of gossip, be it harmful or not. Those persons who might locally be known as non-gossipers are merely persons who are comparatively little interested in collecting whispered information and who, when they secure it, impart it more tactfully and considerately than the people as a whole. But even they have a few strong dislikes which cause them to show little consideration for some people.

In classifying the gossiping proclivities of the people the first criterion to suggest itself is that of sex, because from time immemorial men have jested about woman's tendency toward personal gossip. The explanation is clear. She merely talks of that about which her life is centered. She spends comparatively little time discussing the stock market, sports, politics, and impersonal problems of workaday life such as do the men. Her preoccupation is with local events—particularly those local events which have a strong tinge of the personal such as bridge parties and moral scandals. She frankly admits that when she goes calling she "talks about everybody in town." She touches at great length upon the care of babies, children, and husbands; illnesses, childbirth, cooking, clothing, and other subjects closely related to the home—always illustrating her theory in terms of Mineville personalities. Unlike her husband, she never tires of talking shop, and when she talks shop, persons

are generally involved. Also, she can gossip for an hour over the telephone at will while he works with a lone partner in a dark recess far
below the surface of the earth. In this way she may act as a gossip
collector for him during the day and detail her findings to him when he
returns from work. He may tell her what he has heard "at the mine,"
but this usually is much less than she has to tell him, and less personal.

A usual remark about those in the community who are known as
"gossips" is: "Tell Mrs. So-and-So anything as a secret if you want it
advertised all over town in a hurry." But Mineville has so many proficient gossipers that to select only those who are reputed to be gossips
and to ignore the rest would be to produce an erroneous picture. A few
typical examples will serve to bring out this point.

First we may note some factors which cause Mrs. Dunwell to be
rated as the community's leading female "gossip." Mrs. Dunwell occupies
a position of social prominence which normally places her somewhat
in the public eye aside from publicity which she might derive from her
gossiping. She is frank and quick to "jump to conclusions"; she spares
no one, not even herself, when she decides to give her opinion. This
impulsive frankness causes her to reveal passing flurries of envy and
jealousy which would remain undisclosed in the case of the ordinary
woman. Consequently, she is readily accused of having a tendency to
exaggerate and distort, and is feared and disliked by many. But there
is no doubt that were she less prominent and less frank to all persons
anywhere, she might gossip equally as much without being renowned as
a community gossip, in the derogatory sense of the term.

The leading gossips tend to be persons with unusual ability to remember "everything about everybody." One of these is Ed Slade, who is
known more as a "talker" than as a "gossip" because he is not a woman.
Another was Mrs. Drake, who was not known as a gossip mainly because
she was a recluse. Both Mr. Slade and Mrs. Drake were recognized
as vocal social historians of the community, as can be seen from the following advice given when certain inside information was sought:

MISS X: You should see Ed Slade. He can tell you anything you want to
know.

MR. X [*her father—interrupting*]: Yes, see Ed Slade. He knows all about
everything in town. I came in 1889 and he was tending bar before he worked
for me at that time. He can tell you lots and more too.

MRS. X: And he will be glad to tell you things. It's odd how some people
can remember things. There was Mrs. Drake. Whenever I wanted to know
anything I used to go over to her. She seemed to know everything about everybody and everything in town. It's too bad she died. She could have helped you.

She was not a gossip. She never told unless you asked but when you asked
she sure knew.

MR. X: Sid Marshall is quite a talker. He came here after I did but he sure
could tell you about everything since he came.

It is interesting that the men are especially prone to speak of the talkative members of their sex as "talkers" while females with the same propensities are classified as "gossips." In reply, the women contend, and perhaps not without justification, that the men are the "worst gossipers." Whatever the truth may be, Mineville has some very talkative males who are much better situated to secure and spread the news than are the women. Among these is Sid Marshall.

"Sid" is the proprietor of a tailor shop in which an almost perpetual talk-fest is in progress throughout the day and often until late at night. Man after man "drops into Sid's place" for a sociable chat and leaves such news as he has in return for a large supply from Sid and others who may have been present. Everything is discussed: from the habitual debtors of Mineville to the debtor nations of the World War; from the scandal of a Mineviller who just passed by the window to that involving presidents and kings. Religion, politics, psychology, economics, milady's styles, fishing trips, smutty stories, the weather, and the merits of one another's chewing tobacco—nothing is barred. But it would be a mistake to conceive of this visiting center as those of small towns are so often caricatured, that is, as made up of men of naïve intelligence who presume great wisdom. Their ideas and attitudes on problems of larger import are not provincialisms, but rather are the same as those had by city people, because of being derived from the same immediate sources: editors of leading periodicals, the radio, and the movies. On the other hand, on local matters the individuals force one another to keep close to facts by the ruthlessness by which they pounce upon him who errs.

There is no better place in Mineville to sense shifts in public opinion than Sid's tailor shop. For news generally is not "out" long before someone brings it to Sid's, whose position is much like that of the editor of a paper in that he tends to hear all sides of questions more rapidly than people in general. From these diverse points of view he tries to arrive at the true statement of a situation. He becomes one of the best-informed men in town on local affairs, and his shop is one of Mineville's best substitutes for a daily newspaper and scandal sheet—a function pleasant to him and in no sense to his discredit, even though he is subjected to criticism by women who imagine that they are the particular objects under discussion in his shop.

．．．．．

There are, of course, other outstanding agents of gossip and other gossiping centers on Main Street. Not only are there several business men who are very proficient gossips, but most of the business establishments have particular persons who "hang around and talk." In fact, wherever the people assemble informally a gossiping center tends to arise.

Those traditional gossip-dispensing bureaus, the barber shops, where the barber tries to talk about as many interesting things as possible to his customers, have changed somewhat since the war. One of the barbers observes:

Do you remember how there always used to be a gang of men hanging around the barber shops? I try to discourage them from hanging around my place nowadays since women and girls are an important part of my trade. Boy, how the guys used to talk in the old days! I'll bet there were more dirty jokes and more dirty remarks passed in the barber shops than anywhere in town. And how they gossiped! But things have changed. If the fellows do hang around now they have to be careful what they say in the presence of women and girls and so there isn't much to encourage them to loiter in a shop. Besides, women don't like to come into a shop if a lot of men are sitting around. There is plenty of talk now, but the subjects are different—as long as women are in the shop, at least.

Away from Main Street and from home the men do most of their gossiping in the mines and mills. Each group of workers tends to have certain members who stand out for their general talking abilities. Of forty-six men on one shift at the Salmon Mine two of these entertainers are in the limelight. To quote a fellow-workman:

Talk about gossip! On our shift we have Fred Hare and Charlie Ratner in the center of the bunch before we go down the mine and at eating time, and I'll bet there ain't a woman in town who can equal those fellows. They never run out of gossip. You ought to see how they monopolize the conversation. It seems almost impossible that they can possibly know so much. Month after month their supply of gossip holds out.

Even among children there are prominent agents of gossip. They function much as do their elders, and when they are indiscreet they are subjected to the same disrepute. Breta Gaynor (age eleven) is a good example in the grade school. She talks incessantly and keeps widely informed upon the affairs of the school children, and upon those of adults as well. At a tender age Mineville children commence to take a naïve interest in the events of community gossip because they are likely to have had some acquaintance with a large share of persons and things of which they hear adults talk. The more intelligent five-year-old kindergarten children, for instance, have already reached a stage at which they are able to impart surprising bits of information to their teacher.

Influenced by small-town conditions, as are mature residents, Mineville children have leisure time, frankness, curiosity, and close contacts with large numbers at school to facilitate their gossiping. Through the grade school and through the high school waves of gossip of all sorts surge. Indeed, the schools are the largest gossiping centers in town although townsfolk, as a rule, are not aware of the fact.

GOSSIP AND THE FORMATION OF PUBLIC OPINION

Talking of things in general appears to be the favorite indoor and outdoor sport in Mineville. This is due in part to the neighborliness and community of interest among the people, and in part to the deficiency of other leisure-time activities in which there is an element of sociability. An interesting sidelight upon the effect of a community of interest was observed by a candidate for a county office:

I'll tell you something that surprised me. Because I was never much of a mixer, I thought I would have a hard time when I ran for office. I thought I wouldn't be able to find anything to talk about to people I didn't know. It sure surprised me how easy it is to find something to talk about. We have so much in common with one another in this town, and even in the county, that we know a lot about people we've never talked to. For that reason I found that I could predict pretty well what would be an interesting topic of conversation to nearly everyone. I always knew some of their friends, where they worked, something about their children, and so forth. In a jiffy I could bridge the gap between not knowing people and becoming intimate with them. The trouble was not in finding something to talk about but rather that I had to be careful not to talk too much about intimate things for fear someone would start talk going around that the people shouldn't vote for me because I'm just an old gossiper anyhow. And then, I was pretty sure that some of the people were trying to get me to feel intimate with them so that I would confide things in them which they could use against me politically.

With such community of interest, and a general desire to tell the other fellow the latest news, it is not surprising that an exceptionally live bit of news, such as the death of a prominent citizen, attains almost complete circulation in the community in about two hours. Most of the people are likely to have the news in an hour. In a few minutes it reaches all of the business establishments on Main Street. "Too bad about Mr. So-and-So," the merchant characteristically says to his customers one by one. And wherever a group is congregated along the street the death becomes a topic of conversation. Meanwhile, with half of the people in town having telephones and by the age-old practice of "running in" to tell a neighbor, the news soon reaches those who perchance have not visited Main Street or otherwise encountered someone who might tell them. Community expectation of rapidity of circulation is attested by the fact that should such a death occur at nine o'clock in the morning and the information not reach a resident until late in the afternoon, his usual expression is, "I can't understand why I didn't hear that sooner," and others say to him, "Where have you been? Everybody knew that by noon."

For several days such a topic is likely to be focal in the community. The man, his last illness, his family, etc., are discussed and rediscussed.

A multitude of diverse bits of information and points of view have been brought into play before the subject drops out of the limelight.

Because as a social unit it is small and isolated, Mineville offers a most interesting laboratory for the study of public opinion. The participant-observer can witness the crystallizing of opinion in detail from its initial gropings to the final product in which more or less uniform attitudes and ideas in respect to a matter are characteristic over the whole community or in large factions. He will be struck with the rapid and varied shifts of opinion from one side of a question to another. He will see occasional cases when opinion becomes so fixed that there is a community-wide tendency for the people to become emotional if they are asked to consider the merits of the minority side of a matter. But he will find that such cases of callousness are usually temporary periods of high resistance, and that in the long run the "truth" is acknowledged by the people as a whole, if an item of gossip is sufficiently alive to keep it before them long enough. The people are so persistently confronted with untruths or partial truths in local rumor that they have a wholesome skepticism regarding it which naturally results in a rigorous, although often unconscious, piecing-together of evidence before a final conclusion is reached.

When news "gets out," one of the first steps of a resident is to trace it, and, as a rule, he is quite keen in tracing the origins and course of gossip because of his insight into the relations of Minevillers to one another. Resolutely he sets about to build his theory as to the channels through which an item of gossip has passed, through certain outstanding gossipers, and through a network of relatives, friends, and others who have frequent and intimate contact with one another. He knows much of the probable motives of these people and of the reliability of what they might say. In questioning the truth of a bit of news, for instance, he will say, "She got it from Mrs. Jacobs and it's a cinch Mrs. Jacobs got it from Mrs. Black and you know what a liar Mrs. Black is."

HOW GOSSIP DESTROYS PRIVACY

We have already indicated how gossip brings together odds and ends of one's private life which he reveals about himself to numerous persons over a long period of time. We have not yet discussed the factor which accounts for the feeding of most of the very intimate personal information into the streams of gossip, that is, betrayed confidences.

Everyone trusts that certain persons in possession of intimate facts of his personal life will not betray him. He would feel most wretched if he actually believed that no one is to be trusted to hold such knowledge in due respect. His father, mother, wife, brother, and several good friends he assumes will shield parts of his life from the public gaze. And while we have no evidence upon which to assert that his faith is not justified for the most part, bit by bit details of his private affairs sift out by way of betrayed confidences. This happens everywhere, but the consequences are especially serious in a small town such as Mineville where people seize with alacrity upon such information and shortly insure its perpetuation by making it a public acquisition. Husbands, for instance, little know what information of their private affairs their wives may have told "in confidence" to women friends who in turn have broadcast it to the community "in confidence." It is by means of just such a network of interlocking confidences that the "whole town" secures the most whispered of information almost as readily as it does ordinary news, despite the strong inhibitions the people have regarding "talking about" others because of being afraid that their words will "get back" to the person "talked about." Fortunately, however, most Minevillers do not seem to realize how well others know them, and so the human longing for someone in whom to confide, to whom to unburden the weight of troubles, still finds extensive expression in the town.

By way of illustration, the following phenomena attending broken confidences may be noted as commonplace in Mineville, as elsewhere:

a) There are irresponsible information purveyors—persons who must tell.

b) While people are on intimate terms they normally confide in and otherwise learn a great deal about one another. When their relations are temporarily or permanently broken, the situation is ripe for the wholesale breaking of confidences.

c) The desire to appear interesting to others often causes indiscretion to the point of violation of confidences.

d) Persons are led into disclosing confidential information in order to prove points in arguments.

e) There are "accidental slips" which are not realized as broken confidences until after they have occurred.

f) Many confidences are broken because as time passes people are likely to forget that they received the information concerned in confidence.

g) Some people care less about privacy than others and so they easily disregard what are to them the excessive requests of others for secrecy. The leading female gossip of the town, as has been indicated, secures her disrepute largely because of telling about others that which she does not care if others tell about her.

SCANDALS

Novelists have painted vivid pictures of small-town life which have captured the popular imagination and have made small-town people appear to be a peculiar species of scandal-hungry creatures. Somehow the lurid exposés featured by city daily papers have been considered to be more worthy of sophisticated people than rural gossip, and there has been a tendency to minimize the fact that city folks do a great deal of gossiping among their more intimate associates.

If Minevillers have a greater interest in scandal than urbanites, it is because of a difference in situation, not in people. It so happens that besides sensational news derived from city dailies, the residents of the town are living under conditions conducive to the ferreting-out, spreading, and perpetuation of an extensive fund of local scandal. And this news is the more interesting because it affects the status of persons with whom they are obliged to have close social relationships. Certainly it would be more interesting if one were to know that the only iceman in town has tendencies to be a paramour than it is to read in a city paper of the same proclivities on the part of some strange iceman one has never seen.

There is a fund of whispered gossip about every resident of a small town. Actually but an infinitesmal part of this is communicated directly to the person concerned, although the people say, "Everything gets back sooner or later in this town." Such news characteristically travels in channels which avoid him. It frequently buzzes among his closest friends and yet escapes him. This is particularly true of scandal. . . .

FEAR OF GOSSIP

In Mineville, individual variation in respect to fear of gossip is very wide. There is to be found the whole gamut of degrees from persons who are excessively fearsome lest their affairs become matter of gossip to those who defy, ignore, or are not well cognizant of the relentlessness with which news travels and the thorough circulation which it attains.

In the main, however, Minevillers wittingly and unwittingly are affected by a strong fear of gossip. Long experience has shown them that information tends to become distorted in passing from person to person, and so, even though the public in question is small enough that the truth is likely to become generally known in time if it is known to a few persons, the people do not wish to have their affairs thrown into the gristmill of conversation and argument through which so much news must pass before it is accurately consumed. This reluctance to be "talked about" does much to inhibit the circulation not only of reprehensible gossip but of permissible news. A warning voice is ever ready to whisper into the resident's ear, "Be careful! It will get all over town," or "What will people say?" And even in formal meetings someone may arise to say, "We'd better watch our step or the whole town will be on our necks before we adjourn."

No resident of Mineville supposes that he is not "talked about."

Even obscure townsfolk complain that they live under the spotlight of the public eye and hence must become hardened to the inevitable gossip, if they are to have peace of mind. But withal, there is so much open defiance to gossip as to suggest that many residents do not realize the harm which their acts may bring upon their reputations at present, and even twenty years in the future.

92. SOCIAL CONTROLS IN THE RACE RELATIONS PATTERN OF A SMALL NEW ENGLAND TOWN *

FRANK F. LEE

In the previous selection we have seen how gossip functions as a means of social control in a small community. In this selection Frank Lee analyzes another aspect of social control in a small-town setting. We sometimes think that in situations involving dominant and minority group relations social controls are enforced only on the minority group. The reader will note that relations in this New England town, as in other communities, involves control of the behavior of the white segment of society as well as the Negro.

What are the means of controlling and perpetuating a race relations pattern? What are the processes and techniques of social control as they operate to keep Negroes "in their place"?

It was previously pointed out that many of the obvious formal and institutionalized informal means of control have been extensively investigated in the South, in some large northern cities, and on a nation-wide basis. In the North we do not find for the most part the thinly veiled threat of violence against Negroes for getting "out of place." On the contrary, legally they have equal status, and the spoken values of the dominant white population emphasize equality. Nevertheless, Negroes do stay "in their places," and we must ask: what is "their place" and what keeps them there? This study investigates these questions in a small New England town by means of a field study.

* From *Social Forces*, Vol. 33, No. 1 (October, 1954), 36–40.

The author (b. 1920) is Assistant Professor of Sociology, University of California, Riverside. His special interest is the study of minority groups in America, especially the Negro and Mexican.

One further note should be mentioned at this time. In any situation of separation between racial, religious, or nationality groups such as exists in the United States, there is a "place" for both the dominant and the subordinate group. The white has to learn "his place" as does the Negro, and controls operate in both cases. For purposes of simplification, however, this study has stressed the maintenance of the Negro's "place."

The concept of social control generally seems inadequate, at least in regard to the interracial situation, for most authorities in this specific field seem to have neglected two important aspects. In effect, they define the white techniques for keeping the Negro "in his place," but they do not carry the concept of social control far enough. Two conceptual modifications of the theory of social control appear to be necessary. First, the theory assumes the influence of human agents but neglects the effect of such impersonal factors as different cultural and regional backgrounds, different behavior patterns, differences in living conditions and relative numbers, and so forth. Secondly, while the theory mentions the control a group exercises over its own members, it does so only in passing; the main emphasis seems to be on the controls emanating from the dominant group. The possibility of self-imposed control by the subordinate group is largely ignored. To be sure, some social psychologists have stressed the conditioning of the individual, but conditioning on a group basis has been largely overlooked.

For purposes of this study, therefore, social control consists of the pressures exerted on groups or individuals by impersonal forces as well as by others or themselves, all of which make for conformity to the established rules and social norms. It is further the sum total of techniques, mechanisms, rules, sanctions, folkways, mores, and processes whereby a community or society tries to secure the conformity of all its members to its norms and patterns.

LOCALE AND METHODOLOGY

The town where the research took place, Branford, Connecticut, is a suburban, vacation, and industrial town of just over 10,000 people, located east of New Haven. The Negro population at the time the study was made was 170 persons by the author's count, or nearly 2 percent of the total.

In obtaining data, we established areas of behavior similar to interests common to most people in a community. For example, most people are interested in their residential areas and homes, their occupations, education for their children, social relationships, religion, political and civic activities, and the use of public facilities. It is clear, of course, that while two different people may have different values, ideals, and hopes, there is a kind of least common denominator of behavior and attitudes. We therefore interviewed all informants with respect to the major activities of the community, e.g., housing, jobs and union activities, education, social and religious pursuits, politics or civic activities and the use of public facilities. In each case we tried to uncover the patterns of interracial behavior and, as this paper particularly brings out, the methods by which they are perpetuated.

Three techniques were used to obtain the necessary information: (1) open-ended interviews used in conjunction with schedules; (2) participant observation (the author's residence was in Branford during the time of the study); and (3) perusal of documented materials.

RESULTS

Our Branford findings indicate that control consists of more than pressure by the dominant white group on the subordinate Negro group. Instead, control operates primarily in terms of four separate and distinct though interrelated factors. These are the impersonal or status factors, the influence of the mores on the whites, the dynamic actions by whites against Negroes, and the attitudes and behavior (or self-imposed segregation) of the Negroes. The impersonal factors and the role of the Negro in keeping himself "in his place" were especially revealing with respect to the theory of social control. The white pressures, both on the Negro and on the white, were much as expected.

With reference to the impersonal factors, the Negroes in general are less educated and trained, less wealthy, less responsible and dependable [1] than the whites. Behind the low socio-economic status of the Negroes may be found a denial of equal opportunities in the past. But the present fact nevertheless remains that these factors to some degree tend to prohibit the Negro from participating in society to the same extent as whites. He cannot get the housing he needs and suffers more from the housing shortage; he is forced into certain types of jobs not always wholly desirable; certain social, religious, and political activities or objectives are impossible of attainment; and certain public facilities are more inaccessible to him—all these things resulting, in part at least, from his social and cultural background rather than from racist attitudes of whites.

Further, the Negro's largely non-local background (mainly south-

[1] Cf. Allison Davis, "The Motivation of the Underprivileged Worker," in William Foote Whyte (ed.), *Industry and Society* (New York: McGraw-Hill Book Co., 1946), pp. 84–106. Davis brilliantly brings out some of the cultural and socioeconomic factors which help to strengthen irresponsible behavior of any underprivileged worker. He points out that such industrial virtues as promptness and dependability are not touched upon in the socialization of the underprivileged worker because there has been no opportunity for these motives to become rewarding.

ern) results in greater suspicion and aloofness toward him, at least in this small northern town, than might otherwise be the case. His position is analogous to that of other immigrants. He faces the barriers of ethnocentrism, perhaps in a peculiarly difficult form. Because he is in fact foreign, he arouses the antagonisms which universally greet the foreigner even though he is not recognized as a cultural alien. Therefore, his unfamiliar and inept behavior is attributed to his race, and he is not regarded as eligible for the "melting pot" which is supposed to transform other "outlanders" into acceptable members of the in-group. Moreover, the fact that he does not possess the cultural "know-how," added to the knowledge that he always risks painful rebuffs, makes him hesitate to participate in community affairs, in social activities, and even to try for job opportunities which might actually be available to him.

The rapid rate of increase in the number of Negroes, while they are still only a small percentage of the total population, has also been important as far as segregation is concerned. The doubling and tripling of the Negro population from 1910 to 1920 and 1930 seem to be largely responsible for the discrimination in Branford today. On the other hand, the small number of Negroes has been a handicap to date, since the Negro vote is not large enough to be politically effective.

The second broad category involves white pressures on whites, the control of the mores over whites. The individual white appears to be uncertain in his own mind about both the mores and the actual pattern of race relations. What he thinks is the situation, or what he says is the situation, is often in conflict with his own personal feelings, or the conflict may be the result of his overestimating the situation. Examples are seen in the numerous remarks of whites to the effect that while they themselves would not mind having Negroes of their own socio-economic class move into the neighborhood, they "know" that their neighbors would object. In other words, the members of a given group act not only in terms of those mores which actually exist but also in terms of those which are thought to exist. Representing a more or less extreme form of public opinion, real or imaginary, the mores tend to keep members of the white community set apart from Negroes and to make it virtually impossible for them to participate equally with Negroes in most areas of behavior. At the same time, the mores are closely related to the rationalizations which whites customarily give for taking or not taking certain actions, and in some instances it is difficult to determine which situation actually exists.

The third and most widely known method of keeping separate "places" for both whites and Negroes consists of what we have called dynamic action by whites against Negroes. This method is customarily the final pressure applied by a dominant group and is generally employed only when other types of control have failed. In Branford these white actions run the gamut from the most flagrant to the most covert types of action. Examining the various techniques, we find they consist mostly of such subtle, informal, and ill-defined pressures as different types of refusals and excuses, ignoring, and paternalism and encouragement of segregation. In addition there are formal and institutionalized pressures aimed at preventing Negro participation, such as "blackballing" and majority vote, refusals of financial assistance by banks to Negroes seeking to buy homes, and the use by various organizations of constitutional provisions barring non-Caucasians. A contributing factor which may help explain some of these white actions is that white attitudes and behavior are marked by ignorance and lack of concern about the minority group. So these characteristics also act as types of control since they help to perpetuate the situation; they affect in one way or another all the areas of behavior although lack of white concern applies more particularly and seriously to housing.

When these white pressures are felt to be necessary for the preservation of the race relations pattern, the more informal and subtle methods of control are usually applied first. If the situation warrants it, more extreme measures are applied later. Even here, however, in the most direct and obvious of the methods of control, techniques of violence are usually not needed in order to maintain the race relations situation. The fact that such techniques have at times been used in other places (as, for example, in Cicero, Illinois, several years ago) may have the effect of deterring a subordinate group from actions which might call forth such extreme measures of control.

The final factor in the maintenance of the race relations pattern is the acceptance and support of the pattern by the Negro himself. It appears that "self-control" by a minority group may be an important factor in maintaining the status quo. The Branford Negro at least does more adjusting than does the white, and his avoidance and acceptance of the situation helps to strengthen and perpetuate the pattern. This self-control has developed out of experience and has been perpetuated by socialization. It is also based in part on what the Negro thinks the situation to be. In this he may be mistaken and hence may be reacting toward an imaginary rather than a real situation. He assumes, for example, that he cannot be employed at certain specific jobs or in certain places of work. He therefore does not apply, although there may actually be no barrier against him.

Basically, this role of "self-control" can be broken down into several parts. Most commonly it takes the form of avoidance of whites by Negroes. This occurs under several circumstances and for various reasons, such as: having been rebuffed or fear of being rebuffed, other Negroes not being present, a feeling of being unwelcome, fear of making the first move, uncertainty of reception, fear of financial retaliation, or pride. The most complete type of Negro avoidance is that of retreat or emigration. Here the individual involved leaves town either permanently or temporarily, as when he is looking for a home or for a more skilled job.

Secondly, there is acceptance by Negroes of "their place" and a wish to avoid trouble. This manifests itself in lack of aggressiveness, identification with whites and desire for paternalism, lack of interest in self-improvement, and lack of Negro organization and leadership. Habit and tradition as well as vested interest on the part of certain Negroes, consciousness of kind, and contempt for whites likewise play a part.

On an interpretative level, it may be inferred that for the Negro to stay "in his place" gives him a sense of security in that he knows what is normally expected of him and what he may legitimately expect from others. In short, he knows how to act toward those in a dominant position. In the North, however, numerous instances constantly occur where the Negro does not know what to expect. This may be exactly what some Negroes mean when they say, "Down South as long as Negroes stay 'in their place,' they are served O.K. Here you never know what will happen or how you'll be treated." They thus suggest that in some ways the South is a better place in which to live: "their place" is more clearly defined.

Parallel with the pressures the dominant group exerts on its members are the pressures the Negro group exerts on *its* members. These pressures, which strengthen group identification, are effective because in-group membership is a source of security and reward. Consciousness of kind then becomes theoretically relevant. We can see from other studies as well as our own that social barriers are not based solely on racial stigmata. As Wirth has pointed out, the in-group may be a place where the individual can relax into warm, friendly, spontaneous relations and, in a sense, let down his guard. In any case, whether or not the Negro explicitly accepts the majority group definition of his status, he may develop a conception of himself and a persistent awareness of himself as a Negro. This awareness is a social product arising from his interaction with both Negroes and whites.

Thus, in the process of adjustment to the bi-racial situation, the Negro learns to set limits to his goals. He may learn this either directly from experience at the hands of whites, or indirectly from Negroes recounting their own experiences and giving advice. He develops a set of anticipatory responses which curtail his behavior where whites are involved. He will not apply to this company, or for this job, or seek service in this public facility, for fear of suffering embarrassment or humiliation. This being the case, almost any effort on the part of a Negro to achieve positions not customarily held by Negroes in the community involves a definite, conscious, and persistent rejection of the going definitions. Not many are willing to do this. As the common saying goes, they "want advancement but not martyrdom." Consequently, even in the North and in towns like Branford, the Negro learns to avoid types of behavior and situations which he believes are potentially painful. Instead he takes the line of least resistance. The punishment which he may receive for stepping out of "his place" may consist not only of rejection by whites but also fear of this rejection. The fact that there is no clearly defined pattern of discrimination in the Branford taverns, for example, makes for insecurity and avoidance on the part of many local Negroes, while out-of-towners, not knowing any better, patronize them. As some of the Negro informants said, "When we go for a beer, all we want is to drink and have a good time." They are not interested in a crusade of reform; they do not wish trouble and embarrassment. They want to enjoy themselves, not pioneer in race relations. So this self-imposed restraint is a "built-in" form of social control.

SUMMARY AND CONCLUSIONS

Thus social control is seen to be a most complex mechanism and the theory of social control to be capable of refinement and further interpretation, as this study has suggested. Theoretically and practically speaking, some of our findings would appear to be worthy of additional study and examination as, for example, the relative parts played in social control by the four factors mentioned above. This is particularly true where the main theoretical contributions of this study are concerned, e.g., the importance of the impersonal factors and the self-imposed segregation of the Negro in the perpetuation of the race relations pattern.

In other words more than the one-to-one aspect of control from the dominant group to the subordinate group seems to be involved in this interracial situation, in the maintenance, specifically, of an established pattern of race relations. If this position is valid, we can then generalize that controls which operate directly from the dominant group to the subordinate group are actually, in most cases, only a small part of the control factors and processes in the total situation. Aside from these controls, there will be found at least three other types of control processes as mentioned above. All four of these should be considered as integral parts of the concept of social control.

93. PICTURES IN OUR HEADS *

OTTO KLINEBERG

*Several years ago Walter Lippmann made a classic analysis of
what he referred to as the stereotypes which people hold of
other persons and groups. He termed those stereotypes
"pictures in our heads" and indicated how these images, often
based on inadequate knowledge and overgeneralized ideas,
provide the basis for our behavior in relation to others. Here
Otto Klineberg examines some of the stereotypes commonly
held of several national groups. When the images of other
people are invalid they become serious barriers to understanding
and peaceful relations between nations.*

About a year ago I was in London at the invitation of British psychologists and sociologists in order to lecture on "National Stereotypes."
Throughout the preceding day, during which I was undoubtedly made
more sensitive by my preoccupation with this topic, I kept running into
examples of such stereotyped thinking.

In my hotel, I heard someone say, "Oh, she has that Scottish stub-
bornness, you know." A book review in a newspaper used the phrase,
"With true Gallic wit." At the theatre that evening, during the interval,
I caught part of a conversation in which a pretty girl said to her escort,
"I know that all Americans have a 'line'"; and in a mystery story that
I read before retiring, there was a reference to "typical German
thoroughness."

These are all instances of those "pictures in our heads" to which
Walter Lippmann gave the name of stereotypes. They are typical of the
ease with which most of us generalize about national or ethnic groups,
usually without even stopping to think where such "information" comes
from, and whether it represents the truth, the whole truth, or anything
like the truth.

There are certainly very few, if any, among us who have not succumbed to the temptation to stereotype nations. One might almost
describe the tendency as inevitable, or at least very nearly so. We *know*

* Reprinted from *UNESCO Courier*, Vol. 8, No. 4 (September, 1955), 5–9.
    The author (b. 1899) is Professor of Psychology, Columbia University. For-
merly Director of Research, "Tensions Project," UNESCO. Chief interests: race
differences, national differences, attitudes. Author: *Race Difference; Social Psychology; Tensions Affecting International Understanding*.

that Englishmen are reserved, and Irishmen pugnacious; we have heard it all our lives; besides most people agree with us. If we are asked, however, *how* we know, we would not easily find a suitable answer.

One of the earliest careful studies of this tendency was made by Katz and Braly, in 1932, in connexion with the stereotypes held by Princeton University students. The technique was simple.

Each student was given a list of traits, and a list of nationalities; from the first list he chose the five traits which he regarded as characteristic of each national or racial group.

The results showed a fair degree of unanimity, e.g. out of 100 students, 78 described the Germans as "scientifically minded," and 65 described them as "industrious"; 53 students used the adjective "artistic" for the Italians; the same percentage described the English as "sportsmanlike"; 79 agreed that the Jews were "shrewd" and 54 stated that the Turks were "cruel"; 84 regarded Negroes as "superstitious," and 75 described them as "lazy."

We may summarize the results in a slightly different manner by indicating the three or four characteristics most commonly ascribed to each nationality. These included, for the Germans: scientifically-minded, industrious, stolid; the Italians, impulsive, artistic, passionate; Negroes, superstitious, lazy, happy-go-lucky, ignorant; the Irish, pugnacious, quick-tempered, witty; the English, sportsmanlike, intelligent, conventional; the Jews, shrewd, mercenary, industrious; the Americans, industrious, intelligent, materialistic, ambitious; the Chinese, superstitious, sly, conservative; the Japanese, intelligent, industrious, progressive; the Turks, cruel, religious, treacherous.

A recent study of the stereotypes of German students at the Free University of Berlin by Sodhi and Bergius showed a similar willingness to stereotype nations and, on the whole, comparable results. Americans, for example, were described as sportsmanlike, democratic, materialistic; the Italians as warmblooded, musical, light-hearted; the Chinese as poor, inscrutable, modest; the German as conscious of duty, loving their homeland, intelligent; the English as proud of their nation, bound by traditions, sportsmanlike. There were some variations between the German and the American stereotypes, but on the whole the overlapping is considerable.

On a more extensive scale, a study conducted in 9 countries under the auspices of UNESCO in 1948 and 1949, showed that such stereotyped thinking could easily be elicited almost anywhere. In each country approximately 1,000 respondents, representing a cross-section of the population, were given a list of 12 traits, and asked to choose those which they thought were most applicable to themselves, to Americans, to Russians, and in some cases, to two or three other national groups as well. They could choose as many of the traits as they wished.

The British, for example, thought of Americans as primarily progressive, conceited, generous, peace-loving, intelligent, practical. The Americans regarded the British as intelligent, hard-working, brave, peace-loving, conceited and self-controlled. The Norwegians described the Russians as hard-working, domineering, backward, brave, cruel and practical. The full results can be found in the volume by Buchanan and Cantril, "How Nations See Each Other."

The "self-image" is also revealing. The British saw themselves as peace-loving, brave, hard-working, intelligent; the French saw themselves as intelligent, peace-loving, generous, and brave; the Americans saw themselves as peace-loving, generous, intelligent and progressive. All the groups agreed on one item: their own nation was the most peace-loving of all!

Few people realize how much the existence of stereotypes may colour our relations with other people, even to the extent of seeing them differently as a result. Psychologists have long known that our perceptions of the external world, and particularly of human beings, are determined not only by what is *out there*, but also by what is *in ourselves*. What we see is determined in part by what we expect to see. If we believe, for example, that Italians are noisy, we will have a tendency to notice those Italians who are indeed noisy; if we are in the presence of some who do not fit the stereotype, we may not even realize that they, too, are Italian. If someone points that fact out to us and says: "Look, those people are Italians, and they are not noisy," we can always dismiss them as exceptions.

Since there is no limit to the number of cases that can be so dismissed, we may continue to cling to the pictures in our heads, in spite of all the facts to the contrary. This does not always happen. Stereotypes do sometimes change in the light of new experience, and evidence for this is presented later. If we have had them for a long time, however, we surrender them with great reluctance.

A number of significant investigations have shown in a very dramatic manner how our stereotypes may determine our perceptions. Some years ago Allport and Postman, psychologists at Harvard University (Cambridge, USA) studied some of the phenomena associated with the spread of rumours, making use of a technique known as "serial reproduction," a very simple device which anyone can use with a group of friends in his own home. They showed a picture to one student, and he described to a second student what he saw in the picture. The second then told a third what the first had told him; the third told the fourth, and so on, through a series of 8 to 10 reproductions. Then a comparison was made between the final result and the original presentation.

One of the pictures used in this investigation showed a scene in a subway in which, in addition to a number of people seated, there were two men standing, one a white man, the other a Negro. The white man was dressed in working clothes, with an open razor stuck in his belt. It so happens that the stereotype of the Negro held by some people in the USA includes the notion that Negroes carry with them an open razor, of which they make ready use in an argument.

The psychologists were able to demonstrate that in half of the groups who served as subjects in these experiments, before the end of the series of reproductions had been reached, the razor had "moved" from the white man to the Negro. In some instances, the Negro was even represented as brandishing the razor violently in the face of the white man. This does not mean that half of the subjects in the experiment saw the Negro with the razor, since if only one person in the chain made this error, it would be repeated by those that followed. Interestingly enough, this did not occur when the subjects were Negroes (who rejected the stereotype), or young children (who had not yet "learned" it).

Another study conducted by Razran in New York points in the same direction. A group of college students in the USA were shown photographs of 30 girls, and asked to judge each photograph on a 5-point scale, indicating their general liking of the girl, her beauty, her intelligence, her character, her ambition, and her "entertainingness." Two months later, the same students were again shown the same photographs, but with surnames added. For some of the photographs Jewish surnames were given, such as Rabinowitz, Finkelstein, etc.; a second group received Italian names, such as Scarano, Grisolia, etc.; a third group Irish surnames, such as McGillicuddy, O'Shaughnessy, etc.; a fourth, "old American" names like Adams and Clark.

The investigator was able to demonstrate that the mere labeling of these photographs with such surnames definitely affected the manner in which the girls were perceived. The addition of Jewish and Italian names, for example, resulted in a substantial drop in general liking, and a similar drop for judgments of beauty and character. The addition of the same names resulted in a rise in the ratings for ambition, particularly marked in the case of the Jewish surnames. It seems clear that the same photographs *looked different* just because they could now be associated with the stereotype held by these students.

If a great many people agree that a particular trait is associated with a particular nation, does that make it true? There is a fairly widespread theory to the effect that "where there's smoke there's fire"; or, in other words, that the very existence of a stereotype is, to some extent at least, an argument in favour of its truth. Otherwise, the argument runs, where does the stereotype come from? How would it come into existence?

There is, however, a good deal of evidence as to the possibility that stereotypes may develop without any kernel of truth whatsoever. We all know how widespread is the notion that intelligent people have high foreheads, yet scientific investigation in this field has failed to reveal any such relationship. The stereotype of the criminal as bearing in his features the mark of his criminality is widely accepted, but it is equally without foundation; the famous British criminologist, Sir Charles Goring, was able to demonstrate that a composite photograph, representing criminals in British gaols, bore no resemblance to the accepted stereotype of the criminal.

Stereotypes frequently change. In some cases it may be argued that this corresponds to a real change in the characteristics of the people; in others, however, it seems much more likely to be due to external circumstances which have little or nothing to do with the group concerned. The Dutch sociologist, Shrieke, has, for example, made a collection of some of the descriptive phrases applied to the Chinese during the course of their residence in the state of California, U.S.A.

When the Chinese were needed in California, in order to carry on certain types of occupation, they were welcome there; during that period, newspapers and journals referred to them as among "the most worthy of our newly adopted citizens"; "the best immigrants in California"; they were spoken of as thrifty, sober, tractable, inoffensive, law-abiding. This flattering picture prevailed over a considerable period of time, but around 1860, presumably because economic competition has grown much more severe, there was a marked change in the stereotype of the Chinese. The phrases now applied to them included: "a distinct people," "unassimilable," "their presence lowered the plane of living," etc. They were spoken of as clannish, criminal, debased, servile, deceitful, and vicious.

This startling change can hardly be accounted for by any real modification of the characteristics of the Chinese population of California. The most acceptable explanation is that when it became advantageous to reduce the competition from the Chinese, the stereotype was altered in a direction which would help to justify such action. In this historical case it seems reasonable to conclude that the change in the characteristics ascribed to the Chinese throws doubt on the notion that stereotypes must necessarily contain some truth.

Another Dutch sociologist, Den Hollander, has studied the historical changes in the stereotype of the Hungarians in Europe. He points out that for centuries after the migration of Hungarians to Central Europe, they had a bad reputation, and were regarded as culturally different, and therefore inferior, to Europeans generally. During the 15th and 16th centuries, however, when they joined in the war against the Turks, they were pictured as a brave, devout, and chivalrous people.

By the second half of the 18th century their popularity had again declined, and they were described as savage, lazy, egotistical, unreliable, and tyrannous. This picture changed again a little later, when the Hungarians became romanticized and idealized. Den Hollander believes that the image followed the pattern of political interrelationships; it seems unlikely that there was sufficient transformation in the character of the people to justify the change in the national image.

One of the most amusing examples of a stereotype which has apparently developed without any kernel of truth emerges from an investigation by Schoenfeld on stereotypes associated with proper names. Here again the technique used was a simple one. The American students who served as subjects in this study were given a list of eight proper names and a list of eight adjectives; their task was to "match" or pair each name with the adjective regarded as most appropriate.

Since there were 120 students, and eight names, the results to be expected by chance alone, that is to say, if no stereotype existed, would be 120 divided by eight, or 15 for each name. The actual results showed that 63 out of the 120 judges matched Richard with "good looking"; 58 judged Herman to be "stupid"; 59 judged Rex as "athletic"; 71 associated Adrian with "artistic"; and 104 agreed that Cuthbert was "a sissy." In a similar experiment with American girls judging feminine names, 54 regarded Minnie as stupid; 60 saw Linda as sophisticated; 69 said that Mary was religious; 58 that Maisie was talkative; and 73 that Agatha was middle-aged.

Although this study was done with American students, it seems quite certain that comparable stereotypes would be found in languages other than English.

In any case, it can hardly be argued that Richard is really better looking than John, or Herman more stupid than Cuthbert. To return to ethnic stereotypes, one significant study may be cited which demonstrates the manner in which stereotypes may develop without any basis in truth. The American sociologist, La Piere, studied the attitudes of residents of California towards first and second generation Armenian immigrants in Fresno County in that State. There was almost complete agreement that these Armenians had more than their share of faults, and the general attitude toward them was relatively unfriendly.

La Piere proceeded to question non-Armenians as to the reasons for their antipathies, and he was able to classify the answers into three stereotypes. In the first place, it was stated that Armenians were treacherous, lying, deceitful. In actual fact, when measured by the criterion of business integrity, the Armenian merchants turned out to be equal and frequently superior to others. In the second place, they were alleged to be parasites, making excessive demands upon charitable organizations, free clinics, etc. Actually, such demands by them were less than half of what would be expected in terms of their proportion of the population.

Finally, it was said that they had an inferior code of morality, and they were always getting into trouble with the law. In fact, police records showed that they appeared in only 1.5% of Police Court cases, although they constituted approximately 6% of the population. La Piere concludes that all of these stereotypes have one factor in common, viz. that they are definitely false. This does not mean that stereotypes *never* contain any truth. It does mean that they *can* develop without any truth whatsoever.

There is, however, the possibility that a little truth may enter into a stereotype through the back door, so to speak. A Frenchman, with considerable experience of international meetings, once said that when he had occasion to address such a meeting he usually did so in a rather oratorical, flowery, "Latin" style. He said that otherwise his Anglo-Saxon colleagues would be disappointed! When he was with other Frenchmen, he reverted to a quieter, more matter-of-fact, "un-Latin" manner, which really suited him personally much better.

In this case, the stereotype itself determined his behavior under certain circumstances, and undoubtedly reinforced the conviction of the Anglo-Saxons that they really knew what Frenchmen were like. More rarely, the stereotype may operate in reverse. A member of a group with the reputation for frugality, may go out of his way to spend freely, and tip lavishly; if the stereotype calls for lack of punctuality, he may make it a point to arrive at his destination well before the hour specified. Since, in that case, as was indicated above, he will probably be regarded as an exception, the stereotype will still prevail.

Stereotyped thinking may be *almost* inevitable, but there is good evidence that it can at least be reduced, if not eliminated. Eighteen years after the Katz and Braly study, another psychologist (Gilbert) applied the same technique to a new generation of Princeton students. He found that there was some persistence of stereotypes, but also a very important change which he describes as "a fading effect."

There is much less agreement among the students in 1950 than in 1932; any specific trait is usually checked by a much smaller proportion of students in the later study. In 1932, for example, 84% of the students described the Negroes as lazy; in 1950 the percentage had dropped to 31. The description of Italians as artistic drops from 83 to 28.

In London, a UNESCO study conducted by H. E. O. James and Cora Tenen, showed how specific personal experiences might affect the nature and content of stereotypes. What they did was to obtain from school-children their opinions of other ethnic groups, particularly of African Negroes, and then bring them into contact with two able African women teachers who spent a few weeks in the schools.

The "before and after" picture is very striking. As an example, a child before the experience stated that "I do not like black people; it's the colour; it makes me nervous; they might be savage . . . they are different in nature to us, more savage and cruel sometimes, so you don't trust them ever." The same child after the experience said: "Miss V. and Miss W. were nice people . . . there does not seem any difference between them and us except the colour. I think that Negroes are like that— just like us, except for the colour. I like them. They are nice people."

The authors give many examples of similar changes that occurred. Stereotypes cannot always be modified so strikingly nor so fast, but the fact that they can be changed at all as a result of experience is itself encouraging.

Sometimes just growing older helps. In a study sponsored by UNESCO, Plaget and Weil report the results of a series of interviews with Swiss children of different ages. One interview with a little girl aged eight years ran as follows:

"Have you heard of foreigners?—Yes, there are Germans and French.—Are there any differences between these foreigners?—Yes, the Germans are bad, they are always making war. The French are poor and everything is dirty there. Then I have heard of Russians, but they are not at all nice.—Do you have any personal knowledge of the French, Germans, or Russians, or have you read something about them?—No.—Then how do you know?—Everyone says so."

On the other hand, a boy aged thirteen years, after having mentioned a large number of foreign countries of which he had heard, was asked, "Are there any differences between all those countries?", and his answer was, in part, "*you find all types of people everywhere.*" We are not all as "mature" as this 13-year-old boy, but perhaps we can move in that direction. Or is it possible that the Swiss are . . . ? Oh no! No stereotypes!

The understanding of national characteristics represents an important task for all of us. . . . The difficulties in the way are great: nations are made up of many different kinds of individuals, and generalizations are dangerous if they do not give adequate consideration to the range of individual variations.

An important first step will be taken if we treat "the pictures in our heads" with a strong dose of scepticism, and if we keep our minds closed to stereotypes and open only to facts. No one is denying the existence of national characteristics.

A knowledge of them can aid our understanding of people, as well as our enjoyment of the varieties of behaviour and personality that are found in different parts of the world. We need to make sure, however, that the "pictures in our heads" correspond as closely as possible to reality.

94. SOCIAL SCIENCE AND
THE DESEGREGATION PROCESS *

HERBERT BLUMER

During the present era in American history, segregation and desegregation are commonly debated by many people in an emotional vein arising from strongly held beliefs. The social scientist too, in his role as a citizen, *holds opinions and advocates action concerning segregation. As a* scientist, *however, he attempts to examine desegregation as a process through which the stratification system is modified. It is in this framework that Herbert Blumer examines the contemporary American scene.*

Segregation is continuously at work in all human societies as a natural, unguided, and unwitting process. It takes the form of a diverse and chiefly undesigned operation which sets apart groups of people inside of a larger, embracing society. This setting apart may result from practices of exclusion employed by one group against others, or by voluntary withdrawal on the part of given groups, or by the operation of natural forces which place individuals in different localities or different social spheres. The result of this undesigned process is to form disparate groups. Each group is relatively homogeneous. Each constitutes the arena for the bulk of the associations and experiences of its members. Each is limited in access to the life of other groups. Each is denied, accordingly, the special privileges granted by other groups to their members. Segregation is a primary means by which a human society develops an inner organization—an allocation of diverse elements into an articulated arrangement.

* From "Social Science and the Desegregation Process," by Herbert Blumer. *The Annals* of The American Academy of Political and Social Science, Vol. 304 (March 1956), 137–143. Reprinted by permission of the publisher and the author.

The author (b. 1900) is Professor of Sociology, University of California. Formerly editor of *The American Journal of Sociology*. Active in industrial arbitration. He is a social psychologist, with specialized interest in collective behavior. Author: *Movies and Conduct; Appraisals of Research in the Social Sciences I*. Editor: *Human Side of Social Planning*.

NATURE OF SEGREGATION

Sociologists have been concerned with two chief manifestations of this natural process of segregation. These are (1) the formation of diversified areas of residence, chiefly in large cities, and (2) the exclusion exercised by human groups in accepting members and in granting privileges. A brief consideration of these two forms of segregation will be helpful.

Ecological studies of the residential distribution of people, particularly in large cities, show a pattern of distinguishable areas. Each area tends to be distinctive in terms of the people who inhabit it, the kind of local institutions lodged in it, and the general round of life of its people. Such areas are familiar to us in the case of "black belts," "little Italies," and other ethnic areas; they are also noted in the case of slums, working-men areas, homeless-men areas, apartment-house areas, "gold coasts," and rooming-house areas.

The formation of such differentiated areas, while not unaffected by deliberate governmental policy, is primarily a natural and spontaneous process. They are the product roughly of three kinds of forces: (1) neutral forces, such as level of income and accessibility to places of work; (2) forces of attraction, such as wishing to live among people with whom one identifies oneself; and (3) forces of rejection, as when people are found unacceptable or unsuitable as residents in given areas. . . . In our modern complex world this natural process of ecological allocation has become a primary medium and cause of segregation.

The study of human group life reveals clearly another line of segregation in the form of the exclusion exercised by one group against members of other groups. Such exclusion is indigenous in human societies. Every group having a sense of identity and some kind of purpose exercises some measure of control over membership in its body and over access to the privileges which its life affords. Whether it be a family, a social club, a clique, a group of friends, a business organization, a professional society, a labor union, a church, or a self-conscious neighborhood, the group necessarily recognizes certain criteria of membership and rejects those who are deemed not to meet such criteria. Similarly, it does not grant to outsiders the particular rights and privileges open to its membership. It is only because such group exclusion is so rarely challenged that we fail to realize how basic and extensive it is in the life of human societies. If groups could not draw lines and exercise control over accessibility to their ranks and their privileges, their existence would be intrinsically doomed and group life would be chaotic. In this legitimate sense there is in play in every human society a continuous process of preserving group domains and of excluding outsiders from ingress into such domains. Quite obviously, this process of exclusion has the effect of allocating people into separate groups, of confining them to such groups, and of establishing barriers to their free participation in each other's group life.

These few remarks call attention to the fact that a twofold process of segregation is continuously at work in modern society. This process is natural, spontaneous, and inevitable. It is essential, in the form of group exclusion, to the existence of all human societies; in the form of ecological differentiation it is essential to the existence of modern, urbanized societies. One can say, rhetorically, that the process of segregation in one or the other form is accepted, employed, and condoned by all human societies.

SEGREGATION AS A SOCIAL PROBLEM

It is evident, immediately, that when we speak of segregation as a social problem, as a condition to be prevented or overcome, we are not referring to the total process of segregation. We refer instead only to special instances which have been challenged. Such challenges arise in the form of a claim to the right of being accepted into a group or sharing the privileges which the group denies through its act of exclusion. It is evident that the claim arises and has validity only through the application of the standards of a larger inclusive group, such as an embracing political society with legal rights of citizenship or a transcending moral community with a set of ethical expectations. Given lines or instances of group exclusion become suspect only when they contravene political or moral rights. . . .

Every human group may be regarded as having properly an area of private rights—chiefly in the form of deciding whom to allow to become members and to enjoy the privileges which the group life is able to provide. As suggested above, the group possession of such areas of private right is sanctioned in every society irrespective of wide differences in the nature of the rights and in the gratifications which their exercise yields. Discrimination arises when a given line of private right is defined legally or morally as a public right and the group does not accept the definition. The continuing exercise of the private right at the expense of a given group having legal or moral claims to the privileges is what constitutes segregation as a social problem. Thus segregation, as a problem, arises in the wake of the application of moral or legal definitions which stake out claims where none existed previously. . . .

In locating the problem of segregation in a clash between established group exclusion and a legal or moral claim to the privileges protected by the exclusion we can identify the lines of force affecting the outcome of the clash. On the one hand, note has to be taken of how deeply set is the practice of group exclusion and how effective is the apparatus for maintaining the practice. On the other hand, attention must be given to the authority attending the moral or legal claim and, again, to the effectiveness of the apparatus available to implement the claim. . . .

THE SEGREGATING GROUP

To understand segregation it is necessary to see its position in the life of the segregating group. Almost always the practices of exclusion or rejection which it involves have grown up naturally in the life experiences of the group. Through these life experiences the group has come to develop a social position, a sense of identity, and a conception of itself in the light of which the practice of exclusion appears natural and proper. As a natural part of the social order the practice comes to be embedded in feelings and convictions and to be justified logically by a set of reasons whose validity is self-evident. Also, the practice is usually legitimated and bulwarked by the endorsement given by institutional authorities within the group; as the spokesmen of the group their official approval places a stamp of truth and virtue on the practice. Further, as a customary practice the exclusion feeds, so to speak, on itself; its continuous routine occurrence becomes an affirmation of its validity. As each member of the group gives expression to the practice in voice and deed, he reinforces in other members the value which all of them are disposed to attach to the practice. Sustained by these various sources of strength and sanction the established practice of group exclusion tends to be a firm part of the way of life.

This general process which imparts toughness and fixity to established practices of group exclusion is usually intensified in cases of racial segregation. The reasons for this are fairly clear. The recognition of racial or physical difference sustains and intensifies the sense of social or status difference which may have happened to develop between racial groups. The observable physical difference reinforces and rivets the feeling of the dominant racial group that the subordinate racial group is alien and not of its kind. Similarly, the feeling of superiority in the dominant group derives a greater measure of natural validity by virtue of the ability to note biological differences between the two groups. Thus, the feeling of racial difference adds tenacity to the practices of exclusion.

We need to note, also, that the range of exclusions between racial groups is likely to be extensive. They meet each other not in a restricted or specialized way, as in the case of the relation of journeymen to apprentices, but over a wide area of diverse association. Where a sense of racial difference has been fused with a sense of status difference, the inevitable tendency will be to extend the practice of exclusion along the array of relations. Since each line of exclusion symbolizes to the dominant group its social position, all its established lines of exclusion hang together and sustain each other.

In a further continuation of our background remarks we wish to point out that patterns of racial exclusion may decline and wither away as naturally and unwittingly as they come into existence and grow. Any number of developments may interfere with the conditions and processes that cause and sustain such patterns. The social positions of the two racial groups may be shifted by changes in wealth, education, achievement, and prowess. The dominant group may change its conception of itself and of the subordinate group. Members of two racial groups may be forced through sheer expediency to associate in ways contrary to established lines of exclusion, as under varying conditions of complex industrial life. The dominant racial group may lose much of its identity through the mobility of its members and through their intermingling with other people who are not accustomed to draw the usual lines of exclusion; in this way practices of exclusion do not get the affirmation that comes otherwise from their regular and unquestioned repetition. The spokesmen and institutional leaders of the dominant group may come to appraise the established exclusions in new and different ways; to speak with a divided voice is to fragment the standing of the practices. Such occurrences as these may undermine in a natural and undesigned way established patterns of racial exclusion, without the benefit of organized efforts to eradicate them. The significance of a natural and unwitting disintegration of established patterns of racial exclusion is pronounced. It is doubtful if deliberate efforts to break down given forms of exclusion in a firmly established racial order can succeed without the operation of a prior or a concurrent process of their natural undermining.

DESEGREGATION

We can now consider the problem of desegregation. We are interested in considering the general problem of how practices of racial exclusion which are challenged as morally improper or illegal are eliminated through conscious policy and deliberate action. In other words we deal with desegregation not as a natural and unwitting process but as a directed effort to displace an established form of racial exclusion. In this latter form the problem of desegregation is thrown on a different plane. It is not a task of eliminating or reversing the process which led to segregation but rather of arresting or immobilizing its end operation.

To be sure, much—indeed most—of scholarly thought in current psychological and social science presumes that racial desegregation is to be achieved by the elimination or changing of the process which brings segregation into being. This process is usually given a four-step temporal sequence: (1) conditions which implant (2) attitudes of racial prejudice which (3) lead to racial discrimination which (4) results in a condition of segregation. It is thus reasoned that to eliminate segregation one has to eliminate discrimination; to eliminate discrimination one has to change the attitudes which bring it about; and, usually, to change the attitudes one has to correct the conditions that cause them.

Such a formulation is markedly unsuited to success in conscious efforts at racial desegregation. It implies, essentially, a destruction of a tightly interwoven and solid social structure. This can be appreciated by bearing in mind that a given form of racial exclusion is a customary adjustment which has evolved naturally out of given lines of historic experience; that it reflects the actual social positions occupied by the racial groups in their social order; that it expresses the fundamental conception which the dominant racial group has of itself and of the subordinate group; that it carries the virtue and the validity of authoritative endorsement; that it gains continuous affirmation through the daily reinforcement which members of the dominant group give to one another's feelings and convictions; and that it is an interlinked part of a system of racial exclusion. To try to eliminate the given practice of racial exclusion by altering the network of conditions which bring it about and sustain it is a task of formidable magnitude. To try to eliminate the practice by changing one phase or part of the network— as in the effort to inculcate attitudes of racial tolerance—is to ignore the complicated structure which sustains the phase or part. The attempt to achieve racial desegregation by a correction of the process which brings segregation about represents a highly unpromising line of action.

The alternative is to block the process from achieving its end result. This is done by controlling the decisions of the main functionaries who carry a given form of racial segregation into actual execution. It is important to recognize that in any given kind of racial segregation there are strategically placed individuals or small groups who set the policies and issue the orders without which the given practice of segregation could not be maintained. School boards, superintendents of education, real estate boards, realtors, hotel owners and managers, medical boards, hospital superintendents, and directors of recreational systems are a very few examples. All work through a system of subordinates who in carrying out orders and understood policies sustain in practice the given form of racial segregation. Thus, control of the decisions of the chief functionaries responsible for the actual operation of the practice of segregation offers a direct means of arresting or immobilizing that practice. To put the point in terms of a theory of social action we can say that it is not essential in efforts to change human conduct to alter, on the part of individuals, the feelings and attitudes behind that conduct, or, on the part of the group, the collective values, claims, and expectations which sustain the conduct. Feelings and attitudes, values and expectations, have to gain expression in conduct; the apparatus essential to such expression is, itself, vulnerable and offers pivotal points for arresting the end expression. Contemporary social and psychological science is backward in coming to see and appreciate this picture.

ROLE OF FUNCTIONARIES

To exert effective influence on the decisions of centrally placed functionaries in the operating pattern of segregation it is necessary to use the weight of transcending prestige, authority, and power. The functionaries, as members of the dominant racial group, are highly likely to share the feelings and values of that group toward the given form of exclusion, or else to respond to the expectations and pressures of that group. For them to make decisions that are opposed to the feelings and expectations of the dominant group it is necessary for them to be constrained and supported by a transcending group having prestige or power.

Basically, the outcome of the struggle to achieve racial desegregation through conscious effort depends on what influences the central functionaries have to take into account in making their decisions. If the conscious effort takes the form of an educational campaign to change the views of the members of the dominant racial group or a campaign of moral exhortation to change their feelings, the functionaries are essentially well protected. They need merely, so to speak, await the outcome of such effort; they are subjected to no special pressure to change their customary lines of decision and are not forced in juxtaposition to their own group. Parenthetically, this is another reason for the relative ineffectiveness of attempts to achieve racial desegregation through general educational and moral campaigns.

A different setting is formed if the conscious efforts at desgregation are along lines which force functionaries to take cognizance of solicitations, demands, and pressures made on them to carry out a different line of decision. Such influences, if attended by any degree of weight, have the effect, psychologically, of detaching the functionaries from their group and of leading them to weight such influences over against the views and expectations of their racial group. This is the kind of setting that is brought into being by the enactment and application of laws against segregation or by the imposition of regulations and expectations against segregation by leaders of associations and institutions in which the functionaries are in some measure incorporated. The functionaries have to take account of these demands and to form their decisions with some regard to the demands. In a genuine sense the functionary is an exposed target. This is the basic fact which structures the struggle toward deliberate racial desegregation. It also provides the opportunity for adroit advancement even where the dominant racial group is solidly opposed in feeling to a given line of desegregation.

ROLE OF ORGANIZATIONS

Recognizing the pivotal position of the decisions of functionaries, we easily see the important role of organizational pressure and support. The dominant group in a racial community, to a man, may have strong feelings of opposition to a given form of desegregation, yet be lacking in organizations to mobilize such opposition and convert it into action. Under such conditions, even though sharing the feelings of the dominant group the functionary may readily bow to the outside demands and pressures, particularly if these are backed up by weighty organizational support. Conversely, a functionary sympathetic to desegregation may be effectively deterred, not necessarily by the attitudes held by the members of the dominant racial group but by organizations among them that bespeak trouble. There is no need to spell out other possible combinations. The central point is clear. The carrying through as well as the blocking of deliberate desegregation depends on mobilizing and focusing influence and power on central functionaries. This calls, in the case of either side, for the development of organizational strength. The vehicle of procedure is strategical maneuvering, designed to marshal and utilize the potentials of power and prestige available in the given situation. Such potentials are almost certain to vary from situation to situation, thus calling for different tactical operations on local scenes.

It should be observed that in this contest, so to speak, to affect the decisions of the central functionaries, the advantage in the long run is in the hands of the side which is able to capitalize on the prestige and strength of the transcending group. Agencies seeking to achieve racial desegregation have a particularly strong strategic weapon (it is not always seen or used) in focusing on the validity of *applying* the transcending legal or moral standard. This makes it unnecessary to challenge or impugn the feelings and attitudes of the functionary toward the subordinate racial group, or to try to change such feelings and attitudes. It makes it unnecessary, further, to argue the merits or the validity of the legal or moral standard. Instead, the approach to the functionary can appropriately be made in terms of the validity and need of *applying* the standard. This provides the opportunity of shifting the contest from a question of a struggle between the racial groups to a question of obedience to the transcending legal or moral standards. Since such standards carry implicitly the dictates of obedience, one is provided with a line along which to press the case which can largely avoid the issue of racial dispute. It may be added that this line becomes the most effective basis on which to build up organizational strength in acting toward central functionaries, for it offers opportunities of enlisting a support inside the dominant racial group that would be lost on the straight issue of racial struggle.

CONCLUSIONS

A few remarks should be made, in closing, on the relation of conscious or designed racial desegregation to natural and unwitting racial desegregation. There can be no question that the former acts back on and abets the latter. Where given programs of racial desegregation succeed, they weaken the support of other established forms of segregation. They interfere with the routine, repetitive affirmation of lines of racial exclusion. Further, in allowing the members of the racial groups to associate as equals in the new situation they lay the groundwork for acting toward one another on a human and personal basis rather than on a basis of membership in racial groups. Deliberate desegregation enters, thus, into a cyclical and reciprocal relation with natural desegregation.

95. THE CHANGING STRUCTURE OF

THE DETROIT MEXICAN FAMILY

An Index of Acculturation *

NORMAN D. HUMPHREY

We live in a period of extensive human migration—sometimes voluntary, sometimes not. This mobility often exposes people to cultural patterns other than those in which they were reared. The process of modification undergone by the immigrant as he gradually discards his native cultural garb and reclothes himself in that of his adopted society is known as acculturation. Drawing upon

* *American Sociological Review*, Vol. 9, No. 6 (December, 1944), 622–626. Reprinted by permission of the publisher and the author.

The author (1911–1955) was Associate Professor of Sociology and Anthropology, Wayne State University. Visiting professor, Escuela Nor. Superior, Bogotá, Colombia, and Consultant, Instituto Nac. de Antropol. Social, auspices United States Department of State and Colombian Ministry of Education. Areas of interest: people and cultures of Middle and South America, peasants (Mexican and Colombian), American race relations, community organization. Coauthor, *Race Riot; The New Outline of the Principles of Sociology;* and *No Frontiers to Learning.*

materials with which he was intimately acquainted, the late Norman D. Humphrey, in this selection, illustrated this process.

The peasant family in Mexico often has been characterized as "patriarchal." The roles of members are rather strictly defined by the pervasive folk culture. The father occupies a position in which he exercises considerable authority over his wife and children, and some of this power is extended to his grown sons who function partly to control their sisters' activities. The concepts of acceptable family behavior are at first retained when Mexican migrants settle in Detroit. There, however, like those of other immigrants, these concepts and the behavior correlative to them undergo transformation. It is the contention of this paper that the changes in the structure of the family, under the impact of a new social and cultural environment, constitute a highly sensitized index of the process of acculturation.

The family is a *social structure*. A social structure is regarded here as a system of culturally defined status roles which form a relatively stable nexus of subordinate and superordinate selves. The significance of the social structure is the point of juncture of society and culture, and changes in the structure will index what happens in the merging of cultures. However, adjustments of social structures to changes in the total culture do not occur automatically. When there is agreement as to the definitions of status roles in a culture a social structure is stable, since duties and obligations accord with the roles which individuals must act out. New conceptions of self arise as the individual takes on new duties and obligations under the new cultural pressures. These new selves do not fit the old roles and immediately the stability of the social structure is threatened; eventually the structure changes. This is true for any structure. But since we regard the family as the one in which the self-conceptions of those who occupy roles are most intimately related to one another, we believe it will reflect most truly the changing meanings generated by the larger culture. All immigrant families obviously do not undergo simultaneous and equivalent changes. The roles portrayed, although empirically determined, will be synthesized into idealized types. Each of the several roles in the family will now be examined, at first, separately, later in combination.

The role of the father and head of the family has two major aspects: food provider, and family judge and protector.

The vicissitudes of employment, the seasonal character of work, and the long periods of unemployment, all have affected the status and role of the breadwinner, both in his own eyes and in those of other members of his family. Ill at ease when out of work, cognizant of violating a major obligation as head of the family, yet concerned with maintaining the respect from his wife and children which he considered his right, he might desert them to seek work and thus to re-establish his position. "Now I ask you," one breadwinner wrote his case worker, "for a chance to look for work in another place like I used to and as soon as I find one [a job] I will let you know as soon as possible." Refused by his case worker, he deserted, returned briefly to his family, and then left permanently for Mexico, leaving his family behind. More temporary desertions often followed flare-ups engendered by the husband's lack of employment and his accompanying loss of status in the home. This is indicated by an excerpt from a public welfare case record.

Mr. V explained to the worker that he had not deliberately deserted his family. He had gotten "mad," he said, because he wasn't working. He thought it was better to try to earn a little money on a sugar beet farm than to stay at home and do nothing.

The loss of status attendant on lack of financial support was further accentuated if the family head demanded complete subordination from his wife and grown sons. This is illustrated by Mr. P.

Mr. P admitted that on several occasions he struck his wife, but felt himself quite justified in having done so. His wife, he said, was continually accusing him of taking small sums of money which she had hidden in the house. It was beneath him, he said, to take money which did not belong to him, and when he was accused of such behavior he was enraged to the point where he struck his wife. He said that all women are fools and that he would like to be arrested so as to show the people in the United States how to treat women.

In general, however, the decline in status of the father, due to his failure to provide adequately for the family, was so gradual, both in the eyes of the wife and the children, that a lessening of respect was not accompanied by overt family conflict. The extent to which the father has continued to command respect is largely determined by the degree of assimilation of the non-patriarchal American culture by the wife and children.

A second facet of the father's role which has undergone change in Detroit is that concerned with the exercise of moral protection over the wife and female children. The protection of girls is a function the father shares with his wife, but he alone must see that no conceivable advances are made toward his mate. No man can talk to another's wife in what passes for a suspicious manner without invoking wrath on the part of her husband. This is seen in the case of Mrs. G.

Mrs. G was beaten by Mr. G because he found her talking to a former boarder in front of the G residence. She was beaten so severly that a city physician was called and he ordered her taken to Receiving Hospital where she was later released to her mother. She refused to swear out a warrant against Mr. G. Mr. G does not drink. He was reported to have become angered when his son

Harold, aged four, told "lies" about the relation between Mrs. G and the boarder, which tales he preferred to believe to those of Mrs. G.

Protection of the wife extended into the area of pregnancy and childbirth.

Mr. M refused to go to his W.P.A. job during the period immediately preceding his wife's labor, for, as he insisted, he had to "watch his wife." He did this despite the fact that his landlady volunteered to call the ambulance to take her to Herman Kiefer Hospital as soon as the child was coming.

The protective function was invoked to prevent a wife from in any way "Americanizing" herself or her home.

Mr. P complained to the worker that Mrs. P wished to Americanize their home and to disregard all of the customs of the old country that they had been used to. Mrs. P in turn said that Mr. P was so concerned with protecting herself and the girl children that he did such absurd things as to hide behind cars in the vicinity of the children's school to see if they spoke or walked home with any of the boys in their classes.

Such protection even extended to a husband quarreling with a woman who unwittingly aided in Americanizing his wife.

Mr. S called Mrs. T a bad name because Mrs. T had taken Mrs. S to a theater one afternoon. Mr. S said that he did not approve of his wife going to a show either by herself or with another woman.

Girls must be vigilantly protected from situations which would allow personal contact with men.

Joseph, a widower, and his sister Mary, a deserted woman, kept house together. Joseph brought home a friend, but the friend acted toward his sister in such a way as to displease Joseph, and he ordered the erstwhile friend from his home. Joseph said that he believed his sister better off with no friends than with "any kind of people."

Women, in general, are not in a position to oppose the exercise of these protection compulsions and are thereby bound to accept them.

The affectional role of the father toward his offspring contrasts with their unwillingness to accept his authority and protection. Mexican fathers show a genuine concern for their own children, and they easily extend this love to foster children.

When Marie's real father came and took her from Mr. O he was sincerely disappointed, for Mr. O wished always to keep the little girl.

No distinct pattern is evident in a man's treatment of his wife's illegitimate children for, while in some cases, they are readily accepted by the husband, in others they are not, and in some instances are raised by the grandparents. The duty to care for aged relatives, so strong in

Mexico, in some cases is maintained and in some cases breaks down in Detroit. When it breaks down, it is largely a consequence of the wage system in the urban environment which precludes carrying such burdens.

The role of father is given a culturally sanctioned extension in the form of the *compadre* or godparent. This role involves duties and obligations of the same general sort as does the real parental relationship. The less the assimilation of American culture, the greater the probability of the maintenance of this role.

Mexican men in Detroit generally expect their wives to behave in much the same fashion that they did in Mexico, and in order to obtain wives who will conduct themselves in traditional ways some immigrants return to Mexico to marry. Most Mexican women in Detroit have remained subordinate, home-centered creatures.

Mr. M complimented his wife by saying that he has noticed no change in her in the twenty years that she has lived in Detroit. She stays at home and "keeps the old ways." While the interview with Mr. M went on, Mrs. M sat quietly nearby with her hands folded in her lap. She spoke only when he asked her a question, answering in Spanish since she knew no English.

The woman's role is that of a homemaker, an inculcator of religious precepts, a protector of her girl children. While most women accept the restraints imposed on them by the culture of the homeland, a small proportion of Detroit Mexican women come to take advantage of the greater freedom possible here. If the wife has assimilated American culture more rapidly than has her husband, she may use her knowledge to effect a reversal, from subordination to superordination, in family roles. Regarding one wife a case record reports:

Woman is a very dominant person, quite excitable in her manner . . . very loud. . . . Mrs. A seems to be spokesman for the family.

Such transformation of roles was most possible when the wife was considerably younger than the husband, or in cases, as was true in several instances, where the wife was American-born but of Mexican derivation.

As a result of the differing degrees to which they have acquired American culture and retained Mexican culture, the members of the Mexican family have changed positions relative to one another within that unit. More abstractly, changed levels of status appear in the social structure of the family.

In general, the structure of the peon family in Detroit has changed in three ways: the status role and corresponding conception of self of the father has declined relative to that of the women and children; the wife has tended to retain her previous status role position through the greater retention of Mexican meanings and understandings, although in some instances the wife has come to occupy a position of social superordination; the status role of the children has largely reversed itself, and this is particularly true for the oldest boy, who plays an entirely new role.

The oldest child acts as mentor to later born siblings. He has paved the way. His experiences and directions in regard to Mexican and American cultural meanings and understandings serve as a framework for their later definitions. As mentor in American ways, as one who knows the rights and wrongs of American culture, the oldest child may assume parental functions. He becomes protector, orderer, and forbidder; in short, a foster parent, schooled in American ways. His ordering and forbidding, his age, may make him socially a hostile competitor, a family member exercising authority over the whole family which he could exercise only over his sister in the homeland. Young men have assumed positions either of dominance or of equality to their fathers, while in general girls have acquiesced to a subordinate, home-centered position; yet even the conformers possess more freedom for outside activities than do their mothers, and hence have somewhat higher status than their mothers.

The second generation, and particularly the boys of this generation, have been so broadly exposed to the dominant American culture that they have come to possess meanings which are at times in direct opposition to those of their parents. Thus, for a working youth to contribute his whole earnings to family support is in addition to its utility for the family, a social value (an emotionally charged meaning) to the immigrant; contrariwise, some male children, who follow American norms in this regard, do not recognize, or choose to ignore, the value elements in surrendering their pay checks. They see only a practice lacking utility for themselves and therefore to be opposed. It is clear that many things which for the parental generation were values of peasant Mexico, as for example regular church attendance or respect for the inexorable authority of the father, lie for the children in the realm of utilitarian symbols (closely empirically grounded meanings), concerning which choice may be exercised.

It is evident that the dissimilar symbols and values possessed by each member of the family is largely a consequence of differential association of family members with Americans, of unlike participation in American culture, and of the dissimilar store of meanings originally carried by these individuals. These factors have given rise to discordant conceptions of self. Conceptions of self get out of harmony with previously defined status roles. The father has tried unsuccessfully to maintain his conception of himself and of his role, particularly in the eyes of his children, whose own conceptions of themselves and definitions of their roles clash with those of their parents.

In Mexico, the status hierarchy in the family runs father, mother, son, and daughter, in that order, from high to low position. Four fairly

distinct levels are apparent, and there is a large gap between the father
on the topmost rung, and the daughter on the lowest.

In Detroit the positioning is decisively altered. The son has assumed
a position about equal with the father, and above the mother; while the
daughter has climbed at least onto the same level with the mother. Also
it appears that the possible overall range of status has been distinctly
narrowed: only two of the former four planes now accommodate all four
positions. This may be interpreted as a phenomenon of leveling out, or
democratizing within the family.

The assimilation indicated herein has been one of process, rather
than that of a completed readjustment. Reorganization on a new level
has not sufficiently advanced in the second generation to allow for the
empiric construction of emergent and stabilized status roles. Some conditions of the "typical" immigrant family can be indicated, however, and
following this some features of the second generation family may be
noted.

The immigrant family's aspirations do not as yet include the conventional middle class American ones of a better home, travel, and
education for the children. The children range in age from those in
grammar school to the oldest who has completed the tenth grade in
school, and who is now employed in an unskilled factory job. The
younger children plan to complete the twelfth grade, and then train
for a trade.

The children attend, as much as they are able, the Mexican club
dances, and together with the rest of the family go to the club picnics
in the summer months. The main occupation of the woman is housewife;
that of the man intermittent provider. The girls complain that their
parents don't want them to go out with boys, although occasionally they
disobey. The boys disregard parental restraint as much as possible.

The family somewhat irregularly attends the Catholic church, though
the children go largely to please their parents. The children speak English
among themselves, and Spanish to their parents. The children do not belong to any Mexican clubs, and although the father once belonged to
clubs, he no longer attends their regular meetings. He has accepted the
concept of individuality and recognizes the necessity of competition.
He knows that the Mexican concept, "brother helps brother," is sup-
planted in Detroit by the slogan, "every man for himself."

When the children leave home after marriage (although they may
remain at home for a time), they virtually stop speaking Spanish, and
in their own homes give up the holiday celebrations their parents enjoyed. The young husband still expects his wife to be subordinate to him,
although he allows her much more freedom than his father gave his
mother. His wife remains a quiet, "sweet" person, who is aware of the
vicissitudes of American economic life, and tries to save some of his

income for the future. Their home, however, is better furnished than that of their parents, and Mexican objects are largely absent. Their main recreational outlet is the movies, and their main goal the husband's regular employment in the "shop." In short, they have become functionally a young American working class family.

CHAPTER X

SOCIAL AND CULTURAL CHANGE

Disorganization, Planning, and Values

96. THE PROCESS OF ADJUSTMENT TO NEW INVENTIONS *

WILLIAM FIELDING OGBURN

We accept many miracles of modern scientific technology as commonplace: airplanes that span oceans and continents almost as fast as the sun; navigational aids that permit safe airplane travel regardless of local visibility; on-the-spot and up-to-the-minute reports and interpretations of significant recent events in foreign capitals around the globe by means of short-wave radio; the atom-splitting technology of nuclear physics that overnight makes necessary a re-examination of the geography of crucial natural resources. The list could be extended almost indefinitely. William F Ogburn, who made outstanding studies of cultural and social changes, was the author of the present selection. In this excerpt his

---

* Technology and International Relations (Chicago: The University of Chicago Press, 1949), 16–27. Reprinted by permission of the author and the publisher.

The author (1886–1959) was Professor Emeritus of Sociology, University of Chicago. His major interests were in sociology, social statistics, and statistical research. Ogburn held positions with the Federal Bureaus of Census and Labor Statistics, National War Labor Board, Resettlement Administration, National Resources Committee, and was Director of Research, Social Trends, President's Research Committee. He was credited with the coining of the phrase "cultural lag." Author: Social Change; American Marriage and Family Relationships; You and Machines; The Social Effects of Aviation; Technology and International Relations.

*primary concern is "with how invention and science affect
international relations," a subject of overwhelming importance.
Incidental to this discussion, the principle of multiple causation—
almost always operative in social and cultural phenomena—is also
clearly illustrated.*

The subject of international relations is often presented in terms of policies. These policies are generally seen in terms of choice, will, and action by leaders. Bismarck's policy was one of moderation as compared to that of Kaiser Wilhelm. Or Bismarck chose to wage war. Stories of alliances, of national commitments, and of diplomatic strategy are dramatic accounts of human behavior. Then, too, the explanations of international action are frequently in terms of principles. The enemy wants to enslave the world; or we wish to make it safe for democracy.

Into such an atmosphere technology appears as a strange intrusion. Against the mighty force of morals it seems incidental rather than a determining force to be reckoned with seriously. For is not an invention an instrument to do man's bidding for such ends as he chooses?

Yet few would doubt that the early acquisition of steam power by the British before other states acquired it helped them to become the leading world power of the nineteenth century and thereby made the task of British diplomacy much easier. Britain's steel mills, with their products for peace and for war, enabled her to spread much more effectively the ways of European civilization into Africa and southern and southeastern Asia. Yet we are disposed to give credit to Gladstone, or even to Queen Victoria. Another illustration is the praise we extend to Columbus for the discovery of America. Yet without the new large boats and their equipment, this continent would not have been discovered from Europe; and with such boats, if Columbus had not lived, some other adventurous navigator would have made the discovery. No one thinks of attributing the discovery of America to a boat, though.

We may say, then, that technology makes possible certain human achievements, and we may also admit that without such material aids these achievements would not be possible. But there are other ways in which invention affects human action. The purpose of this chapter is to inquire into these processes.

SOME BASIC CONCEPTIONS

We begin by pointing out a restriction of the subject. We are concerned here only with how invention and science affect international relations and not with how international relations affects science and invention. Though we recognize that international relations, to wit, war, was a factor in developing the submarine, for instance, a more proper concern under this limitation would be with how the submarine affected international relations, to wit, Germany's relations with Britain, whose ships could, without the submarine, blockade the Baltic Sea.

Furthermore, when it is found that technology affects international relations, it is not to be implied that no other factor is of any influence. Several causes often exist, of which only one is a new invention. Thus the development of heavy industry, driven with mechanical power, in the Soviet Union will increase her might as a state. But so will the growth of her population of military age, which will occur at the same time that her factory production will be increased. The problem here, however, is to trace out the processes of one factor, technology, and not to appraise the relative strength of each of the many factors involved.

Quite a problem in analysis is what to do with the factor that does not change. For instance, shall we credit Britain's increase as a power in the nineteenth century to her coal mines? But the island had coal when it was not a power, as when the Romans or the Normans occupied it. Coal only becomes useful when there are steam engines in which to burn it. The coming of the steam engine, not coal, is the variable which explains the increase of Britain as a power in the nineteenth century.

The phenomenon we seek to explain is a variable, namely, a change in Britain's position as a power. A change must be explained in terms of a change. Thus the reader is reading this page not because there is oxygen in the air but for some other reason. The necessity of the oxygen in reading is apparent, but it is useless as an explanation of why a reader is reading this page instead of attending a theater, say, or reading something else.

Returning to the illustration of coal, while it has been a constant over time in Britain and hence could not explain a change in her position, coal is not a constant between two nations. Thus, France has little coal and Germany has much; hence coal is a factor in explaining why Germany is a greater power than France. In these illustrations coal is a variable over space but not over time.

An interesting question is whether human nature should be considered a constant. Sometimes it is and sometimes it is not. Between individuals there is great variation in some traits—desire for power, for instance. But between large populations, perhaps, the percentage of the population that desires power may be about the same.

If a new invention calls forth the same response from human beings in the societies being compared which use it, we think of the new invention, a variable, as a causative factor and not human behavior, which is in this situation a constant. Thus, in all cities, automobiles have developed suburbs. Human beings in all cities want more space in which to live. The desire for more space is a constant, then, from one large city to another. Hence we do not say that the desire for space caused the suburbs. The desire for space is a variable, though, between the open country and the city. Ranchers do not desire more space in which to live and do not use the automobile for that purpose.

Inventions are made relatively suddenly and are dropped, so to speak, into a social situation. Often this social situation is the same as to basic human attitudes before the invention occurs and after the invention is adopted. So we do not say that the attitude is a factor in explaining a change following the invention, because the attitude is a constant. These social situations may vary, though, from one country to another. Thus, the appearance of contraceptives in China may not lead to the same results as did their appearance in Protestant western Europe, for attitudes on the Chinese desire for children is different, with their ancestor worship and their familial institutions. So also the effect of the airplane on international relations would be quite different in a world situation which is not warlike from what it is in a world in which a power struggle is going on.

In international relations the variables often stressed are leaders, personalities, social movements, and organizations. These are important variables in explaining particular actions and specific achievements. But because of their significance the variations of the technological factors should not be obscured. . . .

One reason technological factors are obscured is that causes appear in a sequence like the links of a chain, and the link signifying the factor of technology is often somewhat removed and not so close to the change being explained as is the leader of a movement or the head of an organization. Thus, we observed the prime minister of the United Kingdom, as World War II came to a close, repeatedly advancing the interests of France in international conferences. But back of this British policy we note the invention of the rocket carrying an explosive and the airplane, both of which have rendered water barriers to Britain less effective and have increased the value of defense in depth. Britain becomes increasingly eager for a strong and a friendly France. Thus, the inclusion of France in many postwar actions is caused first by the political leaders, but also a cause back of that is the changed nature of war occasioned by new transportation inventions. This is not to say that there were not other factors or that Britain has not wanted the support of France long before these inventions of the airplane. It is rather that the increased need of Britain for France is caused by a change in technology.

One final observation should be made on the idea of inevitability, often implied in speaking of the influence of an invention. It is as though men had no choice in the matter. Thus, we think of the invention of gunpowder as inevitably changing the course of feudalism. But, it may be argued, men had the "choice" of using the explosive to propel missiles. The Chinese did not so use it. In the past, where the effect of invention in history has already occurred, we more readily admit inevitability than we do in looking to the future, where we seem to have choice, for instance, as to what we shall do about using the atomic bomb. We are using the word "choice" as it is popularly used and shall here not go beyond this conception. It may be preferable in referring to the future to speak of "adjustment to technology" rather than to the "effect of technology."

Inevitability and choice are a dichotomy of extremes. A more realistic approach is to think in terms of degrees of a continuum rather than of two extreme categories. Hence, it is preferable to think of the influences of invention in terms of probabilities. A good way of visualizing probabilities of a relationship of two variables is in terms of a correlation table, in which the coefficient may vary from zero to one, and, when it does, there are other factors involved which if unknown may carry the idea of chance or choice. It does not appear necessary that ideas of free will complicate the analysis in the paragraphs which follow.

THE FIRST EFFECTS OF AN INVENTION

Let us start our inquiry with the fact of an invention. A new invention is made. It is here. In what ways will civilization be different because of it?

The first stage of inventional influence is in its use. It should be observed, however, that not every invention is used. Probably more than 90 per cent of them are not used. There appears to be a "choice" as to whether we shall make use of a scientific discovery or not. We did not choose to use poison gas in World War II. In other cases, where the demand is strong, continuous, and widely spread, the use is assured, as in the case of the discovery of anesthetics. All of us, except a few eccentrics, want to avoid pain.

Once a significant invention is widely used, there follow changes in the habits of the users. Steamships change the habits of sailors. So an early stage in the social effects of an invention is changes in the habits of users.

For an invention to be used, it must be produced. So, parallel with these changes due to use, there occur changes due to production. If we decide to use the atom bomb, new types of factors are set up. Using an invention makes changes due to its production inevitable, though there are some choices, as in the location of factories or in the materials to be used. The impact of an invention upon consumers and producers is generally recognized.

DERIVATIVE INFLUENCES

That the impact of inventions upon society extends beyond their influence upon consumers and producers is not generally appreciated. The influence of the long-range air bomber does not cease with its changes in the usages of warfare. It extends beyond and affects the foreign policies of states during peacetime. This influence on foreign policies is derived from its use and is therefore called a "derivative influence."

Derivative influences of science flow not only from users but also from producers. For instance, the changes in the production of explosives due to atomic fission have a derivative influence upon the relation of small states or outlying areas, with possible or actual uranium deposits, to great powers making atomic bombs. The competition for atomic bombs thus leads through the first stage of production to rivalries in the search for raw materials—a derivative effect from the production of the invention.

WHY THERE ARE DERIVATIVE EFFECTS

The reason derivative influences spread from users and producers to social institutions is the existence of interconnections between the parts of civilization. Our modern culture is put together more like a clock, with its interrelationships of parts, than it is, let us say, like a chain, where some links may be changed without greatly affecting the whole. In a total war today almost every institution, every organization, is affected, so closely interconnected are the different parts of modern civilization.

Hence, if an invention through its use changes one part of our social organization, its influence does not stop there but extends toward the other parts of our social order which are connected with it. For instance, in societies, travel is interconnected with a system of lodgings. When one travels a long distance, one must have a place to spend the night away from home. If the method of travel which depends upon time schedules and a few fixed tracks is changed by the addition of the private automobile, independent of schedules and for which there are many different highways, a change in the system of lodging is inevitable, whether it be tourist camps, motels, or guest homes. Once we decide to use private automobiles for traveling long distances, the derivative change in the hotel system follows.

Sometimes the linkages between the parts of the social order are not so strong as that between travel and inns, in which case the derivative effect is not so certain. A rather weak linkage exists, for instance, between the transportation system and resettlement—not so strong as between transportation and temporary lodgings. The addition to overseas transportation of fast and large steamships with regular schedules was accompanied by an increase in emigration from Europe to America; but such a derivative effect as migration does not appear to follow inevitably solely because of the new invention of the steamboat. For, later, this immigration was stopped while the steamboats continued to run; nor did immigration occur in transportation across the Pacific Ocean. Thus it is not at all certain that resettlement will be a derivative influence of transportation changes.

The reason resettlement is not always a derivative effect of a new transportation invention is that transportation is only one of many factors in peoples' determining to change their home. Other factors are economic opportunity, population pressure, the fluctuations of the business cycle, and political barriers. Most social phenomena, like immigration, are the products of many different variables.

CONVERGENCE

Often several of these variables which operate to produce a social change are influences from several different inventions. The influences of these inventions are said to converge to bring about a result. A good illustration is the widening differential between the small powers and the large ones since the second World War. This is one of the effects of the air bomber. Small countries with few heavy industries cannot well provide the necessary defenses in fighter planes and antiaircraft guns to stop a great power's large destructive fleet of bombers. Furthermore, the development of the airplane is achieved much better in states with a great expanse of territory, which a small state does not have. With the ability of the airbomber to hit military objectives anywhere, the resistance of a small state is greatly weakened.[1]

The invention of the armored tank has the same general effect on widening the comparative military strengths of small and large states. So also do rockets and guided projectiles, especially if there are many cities in the small state. A great power can have more scientific laboratories and greater use of mass production. There then is the convergence of the influence of many different inventions to make the great power stronger and the little power weaker. In this case the influences of these different converging inventions is additive. In convergence the contribution of any invention to a social change is a fraction.

[1] Editors' Note: This selection was published in 1949. In 1960 the author would no doubt have discussed "missiles" instead of "bombers."

SUCCESSIVE DERIVATIVES

We have shown that the effect of an invention does not stop with its uses. Nor does it stop with its first derivative influence. It proceeds to still other linked institutions. The process of successive derivative influences is much like the game of billiards when the cue ball strikes another, which in turn hits still another, and so on.

The invention of the cotton gin, for example, by removing a bottle-neck to cotton utilization, led to increased production of cotton in the southern states by an expansion of slave labor, since the world demand for cotton cloth from the mills of England was very great. There followed a struggle for new slave territory in the western states about ready to be admitted to the Union as states. This struggle for political power between the northern and southern states accentuated the issue of a high tariff versus free trade, since the South could export more cotton with free trade and since the industries of the North could grow faster under the protection of a tariff. This struggle reached a climax in the War between the States. There were, then, a succession of derivative influences following the invention of the cotton gin.

It seems absurd to imply that the invention of the cotton gin caused the war of 1860–64. But such is not the implication. The cotton gin was only one factor, large or small, in a series of successive convergences of derivative influences, such as the expanding market for textiles from British factories, the opening of new lands for settlement, the development of new factories in northern states, etc.

The proportional influence of the cotton gin becomes smaller as new influences are added in successive convergences. If an inventional influence is one in three other influences on convergence No. 1, and the influence of convergence No. 1 is one in four other influences on convergence No. 2, then the invention's influence is only one in seven on the second convergence. So the proportional influence of an invention diminishes through a succession of derivatives.

It is not customary to think of an invention like the cotton gin of the 1800's as having an influence on the tariff of the 1850's, for the invention of the gin is far removed not only in time but in successive convergences. Nevertheless, we may ask the pertinent question: "If the cotton gin had never been invented, would the tensions between the northern and southern states have reached an intensity great enough to start a conflagration of war?" The removal of an invention from society, if no substitute is provided, would show how far-reaching are its derivative influences.

RESISTANCES TO TECHNOLOGICAL INFLUENCES

Convergence is a phenomenon of social change. In a stationary society its analogue would be a pattern of linked parts of society. The family as an institution is linked to education, to production, to protection, etc. The appearance of a new invention in a system of linked material objects, institutions, and habits may modify the system, that is, the system adjusts to the invention.

These adjustments do not take place easily. Sometimes the pattern of a culture cannot assimilate a new invention. An area without coal and iron cannot assimilate the blast furnace, though it could buy the products of the Industrial Revolution. Japan could incorporate into its system the steam and steel complex, but the Australian aborigine could not. In other cases assimilation may be readily accomplished. To adopt the jet fighter plane by a country engaged in the war production of planes was not difficult.

An invention is, then, like a seed which may fall on different kinds of soil. The soils that are too sandy, too wet, too dry, or too rocky may be said to offer resistances to the growth from the seed. So there are obstacles to the adoption of inventions. A law was passed in Hungary in 1523 to prevent the use of four-wheeled coaches, since there was fear that the training of cavalry would be less effective. It should be observed that eventually the people of Hungary did use coaches.

There are also resistances to the derivative influences, as in the case of inventions of local transportation which have spread the economic city beyond the boundaries of the political city. There is great resistance to extending outward the political boundaries of an expanding city.

Similarly, the influence of various transportation, communication, and military inventions is to spread the influence of a state, which is a great center of dispersal, outward to the small border states, sometimes called a "zone of influence." But the influence of large states over the small neighboring political units is resisted. Any loss of sovereignty or change of boundary lines particularly is expected to be resisted. There are many linkages of different parts of a state with its political structure.

LAGS

This resistance, which inventions and their influences meet, means delays in time in the spread of technological effects on society. One such delay is that of straightening highways and rail tracks to permit the speeds which new engines yield. The linkage is close, but the adjustment to the new speeds lags.

Some of these lags are very long indeed. The uniting of the European states economically or politically has lagged a long time after the inventions of production and transportation have made it possible and desirable and long after the disadvantage of this lack of union is evident in comparison with large united areas like the United States and the U.S.S.R.

The long lag in yielding to the influence of technological developments has made the correlation between technological change and social change more difficult to see. An illustration is the counties in the United States. The political units were laid out in the days of horse-drawn transportation and when the technology of production was on farms fairly equably distributed. Now the administration of counties would probably be better and cheaper per capita if a state had five or ten counties instead of a hundred. If the county lines are not changed, they will become less and less functional, and the adjustments to the new technological developments will be made by grants-in-aid, new taxation procedures, and the shifting of functions to states and cities. The long delays in adjustments obscure the correlation.

THE WEIGHT OF THE TECHNOLOGICAL FACTOR

We have now traced the main steps in the process of social changes flowing from inventions and scientific discoveries. But an analysis of the process is not an assessment of the importance of technology as compared with other factors. An analysis of ideational innovations would probably have shown somewhat similar processes. Regarding the relative importance of technological forces, a few remarks in the nature of theory will be made.

THE VARIABILITY OF MODERN TECHNOLOGY

One reason we think technology is important in international relations is its great variability. There are many new and important inventions occurring every decade; facsimile transmission, radio telephone, jet propulsion, rockets, helicopters, radar, television, photography, lithoprinting, plant hormones, alloys, atomic fission, and many others. Indeed, the number of inventions tends to grow exponentially.

The significance of the variability of invention lies in the fact that we do not consider a constant as a causal factor in change. It must be a variable that explains a variation. Thus a variation from sailing ships to steamships led to changes in British foreign policy. National interest is, of course, a factor in British foreign policy, but that is a constant, which was present both before and after the appearance of the steamship, and does not explain the changes.

Another constant in international relations, at least for a time, is the desire for national security. The new inventions of war give emphasis to the policy of the Soviet Union to obtain a zone of security around it. The ideological constant is the desire for security. The new inventions lead to policies regarding particular countries.

THE VARIATION IN IDEOLOGIES

Ideologies vary, too; and, in so far as they do, they must be given weight. We have no conclusive answer as to whether in modern times as many important ideological factors vary as do important technological factors. We have recently seen the rise of fascism and communism, important ideological developments. It should not be assumed, however, that fascism and communism originated independently of technological changes. In some cases the technological factor in the origin of ideologies or their variation is clear. The safety-first movement, incorporating the social invention of workmen's compensation, was occasioned by the invention of fast-moving metal machines and vehicles. It may also be argued that the idea of the federation of the Western nations arises in part because of the variation in the transportation and military inventions. The ideology of "isolationism," so prominent in the United States, is being eliminated, by the airplane.

On the other side, ideologies cause changes in technology. The atom bomb, jet propulsion, and radar were creations of the war ideas. The influence of war on creating inventions is more the influence of demand arising from a social condition than the force of an ideology.

War is an illustration of a nontechnological factor that is not always a constant, not so much so as national interest and national security. The prospects of war vary from decade to decade and from one continent to another. Indeed, one foreign policy in which the people of the United States are deeply interested is to produce a more marked variation in this factor of war, that is, to eliminate it.

The foregoing discussion does not settle the question of the relative importance of technology but is rather an exploration of some aspects of the problem. In any case, the purpose of this paper is rather to describe the processes whereby technological change influences society.

SUMMARY

We may now summarize the processes of change instituted by the appearance of an invention in our culture. Society is different, first, because of the new habits of users and producers of the invention, assuming the invention meets a demand and is not rejected. This first step in the impact of technology upon civilization is common knowledge. But the effect of an invention is not restricted solely to its direct influence on its users and its producers. Institutions and ideologies may also make adjustments to the new habits of users and consumers. Thus an invention has a derivative influence upon social institutions indirectly through its users or producers. This derivative influence is often not recognized by casual observers because it is once removed from the invention. This observation is most commonly left unmade in the case of a chain of successive derivative influences. The phenomenon of derivative influences arises because of the intercorrelation of the parts of culture.

The derivative influence of any particular invention is often not appreciated because it is only one of many converging influences, many of which flow from other inventions, mechanical or social. In the case of successive derivative convergences of inventions, the influence of one early invention may be comparatively small.

Because of the intercorrelation of the parts of culture and the fact that many social phenomena exist because of the presence of many factors, the effects of inventions are resisted or delayed until a favorable situation develops. Sometimes the derivative influence of an invention requires for an adjustment an ideational or social invention.

All these processes may be observed in the influence of the inventions of steam and steel, aviation, and other means of transportation, the atom bomb and the mass-communications inventions, upon the ranking of powers, the federation of nations, spheres of influence, and diplomatic procedure.

97. DEATH BY DIESELIZATION

A Case Study in the Reaction to

Technological Change *

W. F. COTTRELL

The preceding selection discussed the "derivative effect," under certain conditions, of new inventions or ways of doing things.

* *American Sociological Review,* Vol. 16, No. 3 (June, 1951) 358–365. Reprinted by permission of *American Sociological Review* and the author.
The author (b. 1903) is Professor of Sociology and Political Science and Chairman of the Department of Sociology, Miami University, Oxford, Ohio. Is interested in effects of technology upon society. Author: *The Railroader; Men Cry Peace; Energy and Society.*

These derivative effects occur because the parts of a culture are interconnected. If a new development is generally considered good, we commonly assert that any derivative effects in the way of "costs" to small segments of the population are more than compensated for by the benefits to "society as a whole." We may even consider it immoral or unpatriotic for groups unfavorably affected by technological changes to call for reparations for the losses they suffer. This selection by W. F. Cottrell may help the reader not only to see sharply the widespread derivative effects of an invention but also to understand something of the position of those on whom the social "costs" of an invention fall most directly.

In the following instance it is proposed that we examine a community confronted with radical change in its basic economic institution and to trace the effects of this change throughout the social structure. From these facts it may be possible in some degree to anticipate the resultant changing attitudes and values of the people in the community, particularly as they reveal whether or not there is a demand for modification of the social structure or a shift in function from one institution to another. Some of the implications of the facts discovered may be valuable in anticipating future social change.

The community chosen for examination has been disrupted by the dieselization of the railroads. Since the railroad is among the oldest of those industries organized around steam, and since therefore the social structure of railroad communities is a product of long-continued processes of adaptation to the technology of steam, the sharp contrast between the technological requirements of the steam engine and those of the diesel should clearly reveal the changes in social structure required. Any one of a great many railroad towns might have been chosen for examination. However, many railroad towns are only partly dependent upon the railroad for their existence. In them many of the effects which take place are blurred and not easily distinguishable by the observer. Thus, the "normal" railroad town may not be the best place to see the consequences of dieselization. For this reason a one-industry town was chosen for examination.

In a sense it is an "ideal type" railroad town, and hence not complicated by other extraneous economic factors. It lies in the desert and is here given the name "Caliente" which is the Spanish adjective for "hot." Caliente was built in a break in an eighty-mile canyon traversing the desert. Its reason for existence was to service the steam locomotive. There are few resources in the area to support it on any other basis, and such as they are they would contribute more to the growth and maintenance of other little settlements in the vicinity than to that of

Caliente. So long as the steam locomotive was in use, Caliente was a necessity. With the adoption of the diesel it became obsolescent.

This stark fact was not, however, part of the expectations of the residents of Caliente. Based upon the "certainty" of the railroad's need for Caliente, men built their homes there, frequently of concrete and brick, at the cost, in many cases, of their life savings. The water system was laid in cast iron which will last for centuries. Business men erected substantial buildings which could be paid for only by profits gained through many years of business. Four churches evidence the faith of Caliente people in the future of their community. A twenty-seven bed hospital serves the town. Those who built it thought that their investment was as well warranted as the fact of birth, sickness, accident and death. They believed in education. Their school buildings represent the investment of savings guaranteed by bonds and future taxes. There is a combined park and play field which, together with a recently modernized theatre, has been serving recreational needs. All these physical structures are material evidence of the expectations, morally and legally sanctioned and financially funded, of the people of Caliente. This is a normal and rational aspect of the culture of all "solid" and "sound" communities.

Similarly normal are the social organizations. These include Rotary, Chamber of Commerce, Masons, Odd Fellows, American Legion and the Veterans of Foreign Wars. There are the usual unions, churches, and myriad little clubs to which the women belong. In short, here is the average American community with normal social life, subscribing to normal American codes. Nothing its members had been taught would indicate that the whole pattern of this normal existence depended completely upon a few elements of technology which were themselves in flux. For them the continued use of the steam engine was as "natural" a phenomenon as any other element in their physical environment. Yet suddenly their life pattern was destroyed by the announcement that the railroad was moving its division point, and with it destroying the economic basis of Caliente's existence.

Turning from this specific community for a moment, let us examine the technical changes which took place and the reasons for the change. Division points on a railroad are established by the frequency with which the rolling stock must be serviced and the operating crews changed. At the turn of the century when this particular road was built, the engines produced wet steam at low temperatures. The steel in the boilers was of comparatively low tensile strength and could not withstand the high temperatures and pressures required for the efficient use of coal and water. At intervals of roughly a hundred miles the engine had to be disconnected from the train for service. At these points the cars also were inspected and if they were found to be defective they were either removed from the train or repaired while it was standing and the new engine being coupled on. Thus the location of Caliente, as far as the railroad was concerned, was a function of boiler temperature and pressure and the resultant service requirements of the locomotive.

Following World War II, the high tensile steels developed to create superior artillery and armor were used for locomotives. As a consequence it was possible to utilize steam at higher temperatures and pressure. Speed, power, and efficiency were increased and the distance between service intervals was increased.

The "ideal distance" between freight divisions became approximately 150 to 200 miles whereas it had formerly been 100 to 150. Wherever possible, freight divisions were increased in length to that formerly used by passenger trains, and passenger divisions were lengthened from two old freight divisions to three. Thus towns located at 100 miles from a terminal became obsolescent, those at 200 became freight points only, and those at three hundred miles became passenger division points.

The increase in speed permitted the train crews to make the greater distance in the time previously required for the lesser trip, and roughly a third of the train and engine crews, car inspectors, boilermakers and machinists and other service men were dropped. The towns thus abandoned were crossed off the social record of the nation in the adjustment to these technological changes in the use of the steam locomotive. Caliente, located midway between terminals about six hundred miles apart, survived. In fact it gained, since the less frequent stops caused an increase in the service required of the maintenance crews at those points where it took place. However, the introduction of the change to diesel engines projected a very different future.

In its demands for service the diesel engine differs almost completely from a steam locomotive. It requires infrequent, highly skilled service, carried on within very close limits, in contrast to the frequent, crude adjustments required by the steam locomotive. Diesels operate at about 35 per cent efficiency, in contrast to the approximately 4 per cent efficiency of the steam locomotives in use after World War II in the United States. Hence diesels require much less frequent stops for fuel and water. These facts reduce their operating cost sufficiently to compensate for their much higher initial cost.

In spite of these reductions in operating costs the introduction of diesels ordinarily would have taken a good deal of time. The changeover would have been slowed by the high capital costs of retooling the locomotive works, the long period required to recapture the costs of existing steam locomotives, and the effective resistance of the workers. World War II altered each of these factors. The locomotive works were required to make the change in order to provide marine engines, and the costs of the change were assumed by the government. Steam engines were used up by the tremendous demand placed upon the railroads by war traffic. The costs were recaptured by shipping charges. Labor shortages were such that labor resistance was less formidable and much less acceptable to the public than it would have been in peace time. Hence the shift to diesels was greatly facilitated by the war. In consequence, every third and sometimes every second division point suddenly became technologically obsolescent.

Caliente, like all other towns in similar plight, is supposed to accept its fate in the name of "progress." The general public, as shippers and consumers of shipped goods, reaps the harvest in better, faster service and eventually perhaps in lower charges. A few of the workers in Caliente will also share the gains, as they move to other division points, through higher wages. They will share in the higher pay, though whether this will be adequate to compensate for the costs of moving no one can say. Certain it is that their pay will not be adjusted to compensate for their specific losses. They will gain only as their seniority gives them the opportunity to work. These are those who gain. What are the losses, and who bears them?

The railroad company can figure its losses at Caliente fairly accurately. It owns 39 private dwellings, a modern clubhouse with 116 single rooms, and a twelve-room hotel with dining-room and lunch-counter facilities. These now become useless, as does much of the fixed physical equipment used for servicing trains. Some of the machinery can be used elsewhere. Some part of the round-house can be used to store unused locomotives and standby equipment. The rest will be torn down to save taxes. All of these costs can be entered as capital losses on the statement which the company draws up for its stockholders and for the government. Presumably they will be recovered by the use of the more efficient engines.

What are the losses that may not be entered on the company books? The total tax assessment in Caliente was $9,946.80 for the year 1948, of which $6,103.39 represented taxes assessed on the railroad. Thus the railroad valuation was about three-fifths that of the town. This does not take into account tax-free property belonging to the churches, the schools, the hospital, or the municipality itself which included all the public utilities. Some ideas of the losses sustained by the railroad in comparison with the losses of others can be surmised by reflecting on these figures for real estate alone. The story is an old one and often repeated in the economic history of America. It represents the "loss" side of a profit and loss system of adjusting to technological change. Perhaps for sociological purposes we need an answer to the question "just who pays?"

Probably the greatest losses are suffered by the older "non-operating" employees. Seniority among these men extends only within the local shop and craft. A man with twenty-five years' seniority at Caliente has no claim on the job of a similar craftsman at another point who has only twenty-five days' seniority. Moreover, some of the skills formerly valuable are no longer needed. The boilermaker, for example, knows that jobs for his kind are disappearing and he must enter the ranks of the unskilled. The protection and status offered by the union while he was employed have become meaningless now that he is no longer needed. The cost of this is high both in loss of income and in personal demoralization.

Operating employees also pay. Their seniority extends over a division, which in this case includes three division points. The older members can move from Caliente and claim another job at another point, but in many cases they move leaving a good portion of their life savings behind. The younger men must abandon their stake in railroad employment. The loss may mean a new apprenticeship in another occupation, at a time in life when apprenticeship wages are not adequate to meet the obligations of mature men with families. A steam engine hauled 2,000 tons up the hill out of Caliente with the aid of two helpers. The four-unit diesel in command of one crew handles a train of 5,000 tons alone. Thus, to handle the same amount of tonnage required only about a fourth the man-power it formerly took. Three out of four men must start out anew at something else.

The local merchants pay. The boarded windows, half-empty shelves, and abandoned store buildings bear mute evidence of these costs. The older merchants stay, and pay; the younger ones, and those with no stake in the community will move; but the value of their property will in both cases largely be gone.

The bondholders will pay. They can't foreclose on a dead town. If the town were wiped out altogether, that which would remain for salvage would be too little to satisfy their claims. Should the town continue there is little hope that taxes adequate to carry the overhead of bonds and day-to-day expenses could be secured by taxing the diminished number of property owners or employed persons.

The church will pay. The smaller congregations cannot support services as in the past. As the church men leave, the buildings will be abandoned.

Homeowners will pay. A hundred and thirty-five men owned homes in Caliente. They must accept the available means of support or rent to those who do. In either case the income available will be far less than that on which the houses were built. The least desirable homes will stand unoccupied, their value completely lost. The others must be revalued at a figure far below that at which they were formerly held.

In a word, those pay who are, by traditional American standards, *most moral.* Those who have raised children see friendships broken and neighborhoods disintegrated. The childless more freely shake the dust of Caliente from their feet. Those who built their personalities into the structure of the community watch their work destroyed. Those too wise or too selfish to have entangled themselves in community affairs suffer no such qualms. The chain store can pull down its sign, move its equipment and charge the costs off against more profitable and better located units, and against taxes. The local owner has no such alternatives. In short, "good citizens" who assumed family and community responsibility are the greatest losers. Nomads suffer least.

The people of Caliente are asked to accept as "normal" this strange inversion of their expectations. It is assumed that they will, without protest or change in sentiment, accept the dictum of the "law of supply and demand." Certainly they must comply in part with this dictum. While their behavior in part reflects this compliance, there are also other changes perhaps equally important in their attitudes and values.

The first reaction took the form of an effort at community self-preservation. Caliente became visible to its inhabitants as a real entity, as meaningful as the individual personalities which they had hitherto been taught to see as atomistic or nomadic elements. Community survival was seen as prerequisite to many of the individual values that had been given precedence in the past. The organized community made a search for new industry, citing elements of community organization themselves as reasons why industry should move to Caliente. But the conditions that led the railroad to abandon the point made the place even less attractive to new industry than it had hitherto been. Yet the effort to keep the community a going concern persisted.

There was also a change in sentiment. In the past the glib assertion that progress spelled sacrifice could be offered when some distant group was a victim of technological change. There was no such reaction when the event struck home. The change can probably be as well revealed as in any other way by quoting from the Caliente *Herald:*

. . . [over the] years . . . [this] . . . railroad and its affiliates . . . became to this writer his ideal of a railroad empire. The [company] . . . appeared to take much more than the ordinary interest of big railroads in the development of areas adjacent to its lines, all the while doing a great deal for the communities large and small through which the lines passed.

Those were the days creative of [its] enviable reputation as one of the finest, most progressive—and most human—of American railroads, enjoying the confidence and respect of employees, investors, and communities alike!

One of the factors bringing about this confidence and respect was the consideration shown communities which otherwise would have suffered serious blows when division and other changes were effected. A notable example was . . . [a town] . . . where the shock of division change was made almost unnoticed by installation of a rolling stock reclamation point, which gave [that town] an opportunity to hold its community intact until tourist traffic and other industries could get better established—with the result that . . . [it] . . . is now on a firm foundation. And through this display of consideration for a community, the railroad gained friends—not only among the people of . . . [that town] . . . who were perhaps more vocal than others, but also among thousands of others throughout the country on whom this action made an indelible impression.

But things seem to have changed materially during the last few years, the . . . [company] . . . seems to this writer to have gone all out for glamor and the dollars which glamorous people have to spend, sadly neglecting one of the principal factors which helped to make . . . [it] . . . great: that fine consideration of communities and individuals, as well as employees, who have been happy in cooperating steadfastly with the railroad in times of stress as well as prosperity. The loyalty of these people and communities seems to count for little with the . . . [company] . . . of this day, though other "Big Business" corporations do not hesitate to expend huge sums to encourage the loyalty of community and people which old friends of . . . [the company] . . . have been happy to give voluntarily.

Ever since the . . . railroad was constructed . . . Caliente has been a key town on the railroad. It is true, the town owed its inception to the railroad, but it has paid this back in becoming one of the most attractive communities on the system. With nice homes, streets and parks, good school . . . good city government . . . Caliente offers advantages that most big corporations would be gratified to have for their employees—a homey spot where they could live their lives of contentment, happiness and security.

Caliente's strategic location, midway of some of the toughest road on the entire system has been a lifesaver for the road several times when floods have wrecked havoc on the roadbed in the canyon above and below Caliente. This has been possible through storage in Caliente of large stocks of repair material and equipment—and not overlooking manpower—which has thus become available on short notice.

. . . But [the railroad] or at least one of its big officials appearing to be almost completely divorced from policies which made this railroad great, has ordered changes which are about as inconsiderate as anything of which "Big Business" has ever been accused! Employees who have given the best years of their lives to this railroad are cut off without anything to which they can turn, many of them with homes in which they have taken much pride; while others, similarly with nice homes, are told to move elsewhere and are given runs that only a few will be able to endure from a physical standpoint, according to common opinion.

Smart big corporations the country over encourage their employees to own their own homes—and loud are their boasts when the percentage of such employees is favorable! But in contrast, a high [company] official is reported to have said only recently that "a railroad man has no business owning a home!" Quite a departure from what has appeared to be [company] tradition.

It is difficult for the Herald to believe that this official however "big" he is, speaks for the . . . [company] . . . when he enunciates a policy that, carried to the letter, would make tramps of [company] employees and their families!

No thinking person wants to stand in the way of progress, but true progress is not made when it is overshadowed by cold-blooded disregard for the loyalty of employees, their families, and the communities which have developed in the good American way through the decades of loyal service and good citizenship.

This editorial, written by a member of all the service clubs, approved by Caliente business men, and quoted with approbation by the most conservative members of the community, is significant of changing sentiment.

The people of Caliente continually profess their belief in "The American Way," but like the editor of the *Herald* they criticize decisions made solely in pursuit of profit, even though these decisions grow out of a clear-cut case of technological "progress." They feel that the company should have based its decision upon consideration for loyalty, citizenship, and community morale. They assume that the company should regard the seniority rights of workers as important considerations, and that it should consider significant the effect of permanent unemployment upon old and faithful employees. They look upon community integrity as an important community asset. Caught between the support of a "rational" system of "economic" forces and laws, and sentiments which they accept as significant values, they seek a solution to their dilemma which will at once permit them to retain their expected rewards for continued adherence to past norms and to defend the social system which they have been taught to revere but which now offers them a stone instead of bread.

IMPLICATIONS

We have shown that those in Caliente whose behavior most nearly approached the ideal taught are hardest hit by change. On the other hand, those seemingly farthest removed in conduct from that ideal are either rewarded or pay less of the costs of change than do those who follow the ideal more closely. Absentee owners, completely anonymous, and consumers who are not expected to co-operate to make the gains possible are rewarded most highly, while the local people who must co-operate to raise productivity pay dearly for having contributed.

In a society run through sacred mysteries whose rationale it is not man's privilege to criticize, such incongruities may be explained away. Such a society may even provide some "explanation" which makes them seem rational. In a secular society, supposedly defended rationally upon scientific facts, in which the pragmatic test "Does it work?" is continually applied, such discrepancy between expectation and realization is difficult to reconcile.

Defense of our traditional system of assessing the costs of technological change is made on the theory that the costs of such change are more than offset by the benefits to "society as a whole." However, it is difficult to show the people of Caliente just why *they* should pay for advances made to benefit others whom they have never known and who, in their judgment, have done nothing to justify such rewards. Any action that will permit the people of Caliente to levy the cost of change upon those who will benefit from them will be morally justifiable to the people of Caliente. Appeals to the general welfare leave them cold and the compulsions of the price system are not felt to be self-justifying "natural laws" but are regarded as being the specific consequence of specific bookkeeping decisions as to what should be included in the costs of change. They seek to change these decisions through social action. They do not consider that the "American Way" consists primarily of acceptance of the market as the final arbiter of their destiny. Rather they conceive that the system as a whole exists to render "justice," and if the consequences of the price system are such as to produce what they consider to be "injustice" they proceed to use some other institution as a means to reverse or offset the effects of the price system. Like other groups faced with the same situation, those in Caliente seize upon the means available to them. The operating employees had in their unions a device to secure what they consider to be their rights. Union practices developed over the years make it possible for the organized workers to avoid some of the costs of change which they would otherwise have had to bear. Feather-bed rules, make-work practices, restricted work weeks, train length legislation and other similar devices were designed to permit union members to continue work even when "efficiency" dictated that they be disemployed. Members of the "Big Four" in Caliente joined with their fellows in demanding not only the retention of previously existing rules, but the imposition of new ones such as that requiring the presence of a third man in the diesel cab. For other groups there was available only the appeal to the company that it establish some other facility at Caliente, or alternatively a demand that "government" do something. One such demand took the form of a request to the Interstate Commerce Commission that it require inspection of rolling stock at Caliente. This request was denied.

It rapidly became apparent to the people of Caliente that they could not gain their objectives by organized community action nor individual endeavor but there was hope that by adding their voices to those of others similarly injured there might be hope of solution. They began to look to the activities of the whole labor movement for succor. Union strategy which forced the transfer of control from the market to government mediation or to legislation and operation was widely approved on all sides. This was not confined to those only who were currently seeking rule changes but was equally approved by the great bulk of those in the community who had been hit by the change. Cries of public outrage at their demands for make-work rules were looked upon as coming from those at best ignorant, ill-informed or stupid, and at worst as being the hypocritical efforts of others to gain at the workers' expense. When the union threat of a national strike for rule changes was met by government seizure, Caliente workers like most of their compatriots across the country welcomed this shift in control, secure in their belief that if "justice" were done they could only be gainers by government intervention. These attitudes are not "class" phenomena purely nor are they merely occupational sentiments. They result from the fact that modern life, with the interdependence that it creates, particularly in one-industry communities, imposes penalties far beyond the membership of the groups presumably involved in industry. When make-work rules contributed to the livelihood of the community, the support of the churches, and the taxes which maintain the schools; when feather-bed practices determine the standard of living, the profits of the business man and the circulation of the press; when they contribute to the salary of the teacher and the preacher; they can no longer be treated as accidental, immoral, deviant or temporary. Rather they are elevated into the position of emergent morality and law. Such practices generate a morality which serves them just as the practices in turn nourish those who participate in and preserve them. They are as firmly a part of what one "has a right to expect" from industry as are parity payments to the farmer, bonuses and pensions to the veterans, assistance to the aged, tariffs to the industrialist, or the sanctity of property to those who inherit. On the other hand, all these practices conceivably help create a structure that is particularly vulnerable to changes such as that described here.

Practices which force the company to spend in Caliente part of what has been saved through technological change, or failing that, to reward those who are forced to move by increased income for the same service, are not, by the people of Caliente, considered to be unjustifiable. Confronted by a choice between the old means and resultant "injustice" which their use entails, and the acceptance of new means which they believe will secure them the "justice" they hold to be their right, they are willing to abandon (in so far as this particular area is concerned) the liberal state and the omnicompetent market in favor of something that works to provide "justice."

The study of the politics of pressure groups will show how widely the reactions of Caliente people are paralleled by those of other groups. Amongst them it is in politics that the decisions as to who will pay and who will profit are made. Through organized political force railroaders maintain the continuance of rules which operate to their benefit rather than for "the public good" or "the general welfare." Their defense of these practices is found in the argument that only so can their rights be protected against the power of other groups who hope to gain at their expense by functioning through the corporation and the market.

We should expect that where there are other groups similarly affected by technological change, there will be similar efforts to change the operation of our institutions. The case cited is not unique. Not only is it duplicated in hundreds of railroad division points but also in other towns abandoned by management for similar reasons. Changes in the location of markets or in the method of calculating transportation costs, changes in technology making necessary the use of new materials, changes due to the exhaustion of old sources of materials, changes to avoid labor costs such as the shift of the textile industry from New England to the South, changes to expedite decentralization to avoid the consequences of bombing, or those of congested living, all give rise to the question, "Who benefits, and at whose expense?"

The accounting practices of the corporation permit the entry only of those costs which have become "legitimate" claims upon the company. But the tremendous risks borne by the workers and frequently all the members of the community in an era of technological change are real phenomena. Rapid shifts in technology which destroy the "legitimate" expectations derived from past experience force the recognition of new obligations. Such recognition may be made voluntarily as management foresees the necessity, or it may be thrust upon it by political or other action. Rigidity of property concepts, the legal structure controlling directors in what they may admit to be costs, and the stereotyped nature of the "economics" used by management make rapid change within the corporation itself difficult even in a "free democratic society." Hence while management is likely to be permitted or required to initiate technological change in the interest of profits, it may and probably will be barred from compensating for the social consequences certain to arise from those changes. Management thus shuts out the rising flood of demands in its cost-accounting only to have them reappear in its tax accounts, in legal regulations or in new insistent union demands. If economics fails to provide an answer to social demands then politics will be tried.

It is clear that while traditional morality provides a means of protecting some groups from the consequences of technological change, or some method of meliorating the effects of change upon them, other large segments of the population are left unprotected. It should be equally clear that rather than a quiet acquiescence in the finality and justice of such arrangements, there is an active effort to force new devices into being which will extend protection to those hitherto expected to bear the brunt of these costs. A good proportion of these inventions increasingly call for the intervention of the state. To call such arrangements immoral, unpatriotic, socialistic or to hurl other epithets at them is not to deal effectively with them. They are as "natural" as are the "normal" reactions for which we have "rational" explanations based upon some pre-scientific generalization about human nature such as "the law of supply and demand" or "the inevitability of progress." To be dealt with effectively they will have to be understood and treated as such.

98. EXTINCTION BY THRUWAY

The Fight to Save a Town *

POLLY PRAEGER

The preceding selection describes an as yet unsuccessful attempt to avoid, or at least make amends for, the "costs" or unfavorable derivative effects of a new invention on a minority. This selection, by Polly Praeger, illustrates the successful alteration or modification of a new development so that its derivative effect on a minority is reduced. The selection also demonstrates the difficulties which may arise, even in a democracy, when citizens in a local area attempt to call up for review decisions made by centralized bureaus and commissions at the state level.

It began inconspicuously—just a brief legal notice in the newspaper announcing a public hearing to be held in the County Courthouse on January 9, 1957, in regard to the route of a federal super-highway through Broome County. But for us in Hillcrest, where surveyors had already been sighting along the quiet streets, the announcement had a note of doom.

You will probably not find Hillcrest (population approximately 3,000) on your map of upper New York State. It is an unincorporated suburb of Binghamton—and, although it is small, there is an unusually strong community spirit among its middle-class home owners. We have a progressive Board of Education and two new schools of which we are very proud—as we are of most things about Hillcrest.

* *Harper's Magazine*, Vol. 217, No. 1303 (December, 1958), 61–64, 69–71. Copyright © 1958, by Harper & Brothers. Reprinted from *Harper's Magazine* by special permission.

The author studied at Radcliffe, taught English in Hawaii. Now living in Binghamton, New York. Active in A.A.U.W. and civic affairs.

Most people were too busy with Christmas to see the legal notice, but a few of us were among the hundred or so who turned out for the hearing. I had no idea what to expect and listened with great interest to the District Engineer's technical description of the beautiful expressway that was to cost at least a million dollars a mile. Of even greater interest was the map of Broome County he displayed. Hillcrest was not even marked on it. All I could see clearly was a wide black line cutting a swath through the county.

The Engineer called for statements from organizations first. Understandably, representatives from the Chambers of Commerce, banks, unions, and auto clubs were enthusiastic about the economic advantages of a new highway that the area badly needs. But in spite of my naïveté, I felt there was a kind of "pre-sold" quality to their glowing endorsements.

There was no such quality in the statements from the Town of Fenton (in which Hillcrest is located). Robert Ford, our politically shrewd supervisor, and cautious but worried Raymond H. Moody, the town attorney, declared they could say nothing unless they knew where the route was to go in relation to Hillcrest.

Clayton Axtell, Jr., the school-board attorney—single-purposed in his causes, caustic in cross-examination—forcefully pressed the point: "This hearing is inadequate by law. Even today the route does not deal with specific localities."

But the District Engineer remained adamant: "Details cannot be given now. The route could go one way or the other."

Since Hillcrest lies between the Chenango River and the hills and is only approximately a mile long and a half mile wide, a mile could mean the difference between bisecting and by-passing.

When the District Engineer asked for individual comments, three or four men tried, without success, to get specific information on the route. . . .

Hillcresters left the hearing feeling frustrated and helpless. Every time someone asked, "What can we do?" the answer was, almost universally, "Nothing. What chance do we have against the State Department of Public Works and the U.S. Bureau of Public Roads?"

A lot of people all over America are going to feel this same bewilderment and frustration during the next few years, as the $50 billion-plus federal highway program gets under way. I don't for a minute suggest that everyone who will have his home destroyed by a super-highway should promptly object. But I do believe that citizens have the right to expect good planning from an over-all community point of view.

"The new highway program furnishes a great, if fleeting, opportunity; its new rights-of-way and interchanges will set the basic structure of the metropolitan areas of the future, and whether those areas will be livable will depend on the foresight of the communities involved as much as it will depend on the engineers," says William H. Whyte, Jr. in "Urban Sprawl" in the January 1958 *Fortune*.

"Not to act now," he continues, "is to make a decision. . . . Planners can help, so can more studies. But the citizens must not merely acquiesce; it is they who must seize the initiative. Their boldness and vision will determine the issue."

My own home, according to rumor, would not have been taken, but I felt the community would be ruined. Beyond that, I was concerned with the whole problem of sensible planning. And, for that reason, perhaps my experience—local though it is—may prove useful to others who will soon find themselves in a similar fix.

A LETTER OF PROTEST

If Clayton Axtell had not questioned the legality of the hearing, I might never have thought of taking action. Since he had, I called him up and asked if anything could be done. He said he was looking into the legal angles and was in touch with our then representative in Congress, the Honorable W. Sterling Cole.

But I was still not satisfied. I asked if he didn't think the citizens should do something—say, pass a resolution at the meeting of the Hillcrest Community Association which was about to take place.

"Sure thing. Go to it," he said.

The Hillcrest Community Association is primarily devoted to sponsoring youth programs. But my belief—from many years of working in the League of Women Voters—that citizens' efforts *can* count gave me the courage to make my suggestion: "I think the Hillcrest Community Association should write a letter of protest to John W. Johnson, Superintendent of Public Works for New York State, over the conduct of the hearing and request permission to have a statement from Hillcrest made part of the record."

That's how the fight began.

. . . . .

A lively meeting produced what we felt was a very restrained letter. . . .

The wait for the reply seemed much longer than it actually was, but the answer made us jubilant. Johnson said in part, "The official newspaper notice failed to disclose the general location of the route as is prescribed in our Department regulations. . . . The purpose of these public hearings is to permit presentation of all known factors and we would request that you file your statement as soon as possible. . . ."

Then the sentence which we read and reread: "The Department of Public Works will attempt to consider such changes in alignment as may be possible, in order to minimize destruction of property and still maintain an economical route for the project."

The State's willingness to restudy the route made us feel that it would be worth our while to do a thorough job of presenting facts in our behalf. But facts are hard to come by—especially from the Department of Public Works. Repeated visits to the District Office failed to give us the specific route.

Actually, I was the first person to see a detailed map. I happened to be in Albany for a meeting, and I could not bear to be so close to the Department of Public Works without trying to get the information we were so desperate to have. My State Senator, Warren M. Anderson, made an appointment for me. I was not able to see anyone in command, but I did see an assistant deputy engineer who was wonderfully helpful and spread a large-scale map of Hillcrest before my startled eyes. Either the point of view in Albany was different, or else I just happened to hit a psychological moment when there was a general change of heart.

For the first time, we were sure of what we were up against. The worst rumors were, in reality, the truth. You cannot superimpose a six-lane highway with four access roads and four traffic circles on an already developed community the size of ours without making mincemeat of it. A more thorough job could hardly have been done, in terms of destroying the water wells, taking a third of the new elementary-school property, some of the buildings of the Wyoming Conference Children's Home, and knocking out over a hundred new houses, the loss of which would take at least a half a million in assessed valuation from the town tax rolls. There was also an estimated loss of a million dollars in assessed valuation to the Board of Education because the area affected across the river is in our Chenango Valley Central School District.

Worst of all, the community as a community would be destroyed. All available land is already developed, and displaced people would not be able to move from one section to another. Their hardship would be great, and so would that of the people who remained—separated into little "islands" by the limited access expressway and faced with a much heavier tax burden.

We went to work to get as many facts as we could. Our committee had a session in the State's District Office in Binghamton. By now, maps were available for our inspection, and we spotted a line called "Alternate A" which obviously went outside Hillcrest, and, as we later discovered, outside the village of Port Crane as well.

"Why can't Alternate A be used?" asked Bill Morgan.

"The State never really considered that because it is too far from

Binghamton," the District Engineer explained to him. "No one would use it."

"But it is only seven miles to the Courthouse at the center of the downtown area," objected Joe Norris. "That's by a four-lane divided highway most of the way. If I could go to Syracuse by a seventy-mile-an-hour expressway, I'd drive farther than that to get on it."

"No one would use it," insisted the District Engineer.

We ourselves studied the two possibilities. We had interviews with civil-defense authorities on locations of defense highways (preferably twelve miles outside of critical target areas like Binghamton). We had interviews with bankers on increased interest rates and the difficulty of getting mortgages; with realtors on the existing housing shortage; and we held a conference with the director of the Broome County Planning Board and all manner of officials. We studied highway law, all earlier arterial plans for the area, the Planning Board's recommended land-use studies near Port Crane, construction magazines, and articles on metropolitan planning. And ceaselessly we kept Albany and the Washington Bureau of Public Roads and our legislators at all levels apprised of what we were doing. . . .

I admit engineers have their problems with our hills and narrow river valleys, and I think if they had ever told us categorically that Hillcrest was the only possible way that the road could be constructed from the engineering point of view, we would, as public-spirited citizens, have given up the fight. But the two major reasons given for the choice of the Hillcrest route were: (1) Hillcrest was closer to Binghamton by three miles, and (2) the Port Crane route had one sharper curve and hill. For these arguments, we could not see having our community ruined.

The battlefront widened. Our committee felt it would be fairer to have the entire community represented, even though most families already belonged to the Community Association. Every possible group joined with us in a large committee that included Rotary and Kiwanis, churches, the American Legion, PTA, Town Board, Board of Education, Children's Home, and garden clubs. So the Community Association Committee resigned. But the large committee promptly re-elected it to serve as a small executive committee, and we more or less officially became the Hillcrest Committee on the Penn-Can Highway.

In the meantime, we had organized a subcommittee of prominent engineers who live in Hillcrest and work for such companies as General Electric, Ansco, and Link Aviation. What had begun in self-interest as a local protest over the conduct of the hearing had become a plea for more imaginative planning. Incidentally, there was no opposition by citizens to the Port Crane route.

To bring our fellow citizens up-to-date on what we committee members were doing we held a New England style town meeting. Over five hundred residents turned out. Normally, only basketball games can produce this kind of attendance! . . .

By this time, both daily newspapers—the Binghamton *Press* and the Binghamton *Sun*—were covering the controversy in detail and publishing many letters to the editor. I received all kinds of mail. There was one anonymous clipping:

"Good Morning! Being as smart as a steel trap means knowing when to shut up."

But there was also a letter from a prominent Binghamton attorney with "congratulations to a gallant and fearless fighter" and quotations from "Gentleman Jim Corbett" which urged "Fight one more round." Most letters contained suggestions on where to place the route.

THE BATTLE IS JOINED

. . . . .

The State had agreed to restudy the route and hold an "informational" meeting (not another public hearing) at which their decision would be announced to the people of Hillcrest. There was scarcely another topic of conversation until that day arrived, and eight hundred citizens gathered to hear the outcome.

We on the committee already knew the answer. We had requested an advance meeting, and on the afternoon before, we heard the results from the consulting engineers and the Department of Public Works. That was the night we worked until 2:00 A.M. preparing a rebuttal, for we could see no evidence of a real review of alternate possibilities. No ground survey had been made of the Port Crane route, but we had all seen the surveyors busy again on the streets of Hillcrest.

The informational meeting was charged with excitement. Maps and reports were the first order of the day. Then came the climax: Hillcrest was still the recommended route—because it would be cheaper than the Port Crane route by $9,500,000!

Inevitably, most of the taxpaying audience was amazed and speechless. The consultants admitted that acquisition costs would be higher for the closely populated Hillcrest route than for the undeveloped Port Crane route. But they argued that if the expressway were built near Port Crane (with the necessary inclusion of a bridge) another $5 million six-lane bridge would still be needed at Hillcrest. They further claimed that if the highway were built three miles farther out on the Port Crane route, there would be additional costs to the road users which would amount to $4,500,000 over a twenty-year period.

Then came the people's turn. The District Engineer announced that each person might speak once and only at the time he was offered the microphone by an engineer who went up and down the aisle. No committee member would be allowed to ask questions.

I asked if, in that case, I might read a prepared statement from the committee before the questioning began. Permission was granted. I stood at the dais with my back to the State officials or I could never have done it. Our rebuttal was couched in strong words.

We denied the need of an additional bridge until the Penn-Can bridge could be tested under the resulting new traffic pattern, for the Hillcrest bridge had originally been part of a ten-year-old arterial plan. And we claimed that road users' costs were not properly costs to the taxpayers as such. We thought it only fair, if the State were going to include social costs, that it should also admit all other social and economic costs which would have to be paid by the people of Hillcrest, residents of the town, and the school district. We estimated them in dollars over the twenty-year period and found they greatly outweighed users' costs.

For the State's District Engineers the matter was ended; they were forwarding their recommendation to Albany. But what was to be our course of action? At the end of my statement I turned to the audience and said, "It is the recommendation of our committee that we continue to seek a genuine consideration of all factors. We will appreciate an expression of your opinion."

Nearly everyone in that huge group spontaneously applauded and stood up. We had our answer.

CARRYING THE FIGHT TO THE TOP

Shortly thereafter, I received an answer of another sort from the Director of Public Relations of the State Department of Public Works in Albany, in which he said: ". . . while we are in complete agreement with your right to be heard on this matter we are somewhat concerned with the lack of factual data to support statements which infer that the department does not have the knowledge, judgment, or know-how to design a highway."

(We had never questioned the design of the highway—only the location of it in terms of good planning.)

He went on, "We would be most interested to know whose judgment is used to substantiate your 'challenge the validity of the District Engineer's analysis' . . . or 'so-called users' costs are based on questionable premises.' This unsupported verbal gymnastics smacks of plain rabble rousing. . . .

"In spite of this type of abuse let us assure you that we are giving this matter a truly impartial study. Our final determination will be based on sound engineering and economical judgment taking into account those legitimate local objections which are offered in a spirit of good will and without malice."

Swallowing our resentment at the charge of rabble rousing, the committee wrote a reply in which our sources were given for every point. But on second thought we never sent it! We decided instead to secure the services of an impartial expert to assess the validity of our position.

Since the issue was not the engineering feasibility of one route over the other but the social and economic costs to the area, we felt that we needed not an engineer but a community planning expert. One of the professors at Harpur, the State's liberal-arts college in nearby Endicott, was Dr. Seymour Z. Mann, who had been active in community and county planning in our general area. We approached him, but he refused to accept unless he was free to draw his own conclusions. To this we agreed.

On Dr. Mann's visit to the District Engineer, he was asked, "How can you deal with these emotional people who run to their elected representatives in Albany and Washington?"

"If people feel strongly about a problem that requires political action, then citizens should use all legitimate means at their disposal," Dr. Mann replied. "It is part of the representative process. This is what I teach my students in political science."

Aside from Dr. Mann, elected representatives now seemed our only hope. Congressman W. Sterling Cole, who had earlier blasted the public hearing as a "Star Chamber procedure," assured us that the position of the community would be given thoughtful consideration by the federal Bureau of Public Roads. Senators Javits and Ives looked into the matter. A petition with over a thousand signatures, telegrams, and letters appealed to Governor Harriman. His office wrote that the Governor was concerned and had been in touch with the State Department of Public Works.

State Senator Warren M. Anderson, after attending a meeting of the Hillcrest Committee on the Penn-Can Highway, decided that our objections were valid and promised to arrange a meeting between some of the committee and Superintendent Johnson in Albany. After considerable pressure from the Senator, Mr. Johnson agreed but only on condition that the Senator be present, that there be no more than three committee members—and that under no circumstances Mrs. Praeger be one of them.

. . . . .

Dr. Mann's excellent analysis—which upheld our position—was first presented at this meeting. One of the many interesting points he made was that "citizens who participate in the activities that lead up to the public decisions which affect their individual persons or communities will have less reason and less desire to obstruct improvements for the public good even against their own short-run interests."

After the Albany conference in May, Superintendent Johnson ordered the full review we wanted, and the citizens' committee rested its case.

CITIZENS VS. SUPER-HIGHWAYS

From January 9 to October 20 is a long time when you are waiting to know the fate of your home or community. But on that day came the eventful words, "Hillcrest 'By-passed,' " and the headlines announcing a totally new concept for two major routes. We read for the first time of a proposed common route for several miles through Binghamton and Johnson City for both the Penn-Can and Route 17 (the East-West state highway). This confluence was to make the area a transportation crossroads and bring great economic prosperity.

The Binghamton *Press* did an outstanding job and devoted many pages to delineating every aspect of the proposed routes. Quite a change from the original legal notice!

Whether the new route is the best possible one is another story— one which I have not studied. At least this time, many community leaders have been consulted. Mayor Burns of Binghamton has given his approval. The Broome County Planning Board, which played no part in the location of the first route, has worked with the engineers and endorsed the new routes as the best possible use of city land. Highly publicized hearings have been held, both Albany and Washington have approved the new routes, and the design contracts have been let.

We Hillcresters will never know how much our stand had to do with the new plan. Our recommended alternate was not chosen, but it is impossible to contrast the new plan with ours because it is concerned with two highways, not one. It seems evident, however, that the original plan failed to consider the relationship of Route 17 to the Penn-Can, although they have been concurrent problems. In fairness, I must say that the District Engineer was new here and it has been said that he inherited the former plan. Perhaps the more thorough study called for by the citizens of Hillcrest gave him an opportunity to develop his own more comprehensive plan. In any case there is evidence that the State is realizing, belatedly, the need for improved road-building public relations.

Governor Harriman at the eighteenth annual convention of the New York State Association of Highway Engineers called for a better job of public relations on the part of engineers: "We ought to recognize that in government the public is always right." The State Department of Public Works has itself recognized that there is more to the new super-highway program than merely designing good highways.

Better public relations is a step in the right direction, it seems to me. If we expect to build 41,000 miles of interstate highways within the next fifteen years, it is obvious that there will be a tremendous number of persons affected. If the officials responsible for the program do a constant educational job, citizens and super-highways need not be incompatible.

Unfortunately, many bureaucrats are not yet convinced that the home-owning citizen has an important stake in this vast new program. They apparently feel that public hearings and consultation with citizens' groups merely delay "progress," and that we must keep moving at all costs—even if costs include citizens' rights and vital community considerations.

Our experience has convinced me that Congress was wise in providing citizens with the opportunity to be heard on a program that deeply affects so many lives.

It is understandable that many a highway official, beset by a multitude of problems and harassment on all sides, will regard the old approach to highway building with nostalgia. But if the new program is to do its job for community as well as for the transcontinental road user, citizen and highway engineer must work together.

The new program, as John T. Howard, associate professor of city planning at MIT, has pointed out, forces highway engineers to make decisions that have repercussions far outside their field—the highways to be built during the next twenty years "will have more effect upon all form and pattern of growth, and therefore upon the character and structure of our metropolitan areas, than all of the metropolitan planning done by city planners between 1945 and now." And he added, "Just as wars are too important to be left to generals, so the building of the new super-highways is too important to leave just to engineers."

. . . . .

A network of super-highways across the face of America will be an empty achievement if it kills democratic processes and ignores long-range community planning. There is good evidence that the best in American life has always been achieved through co-operation between citizens and government.

99. STEEL AXES FOR
STONE AGE AUSTRALIANS *

LAURISTON SHARP

*Perhaps exaggerating somewhat "to make a point," Lauriston Sharp
illustrates in this selection how the introduction of a single new
element into a closely integrated society can undermine the society
and may even, in extreme cases, lead to the disappearance of
the entire group. One writer has referred to this particular article
as the story of "The Steel Axe That Destroyed a Tribe." It is
important to note that a similar story could hardly be written
about a complex and less integrated society such as ours. But
problems that are only quantitatively (not qualitatively) different
from those faced by the Yir Yoront do appear in every society
that undergoes change.*

THE PROBLEM

Like other Australian aboriginals, the Yir Yoront group at the mouth
of the Coleman River on the west coast of tropical Cape York Peninsula
originally had no knowledge of metals. Technologically their culture
was of the old stone age or paleolithic type; they supported themselves
by hunting and fishing, obtaining vegetable foods and needed materials
from the bush by simple gathering techniques. Their only domesticated
animal was the dog, and they had no domesticated plants of any kind.
Unlike some other aboriginal groups, however, the Yir Yoront did have
polished stone axes hafted in short handles, and these implements were
most important in their economy.

Toward the end of the nineteenth century metal tools and other
European artifacts began to filter into the Yir Yoront territory. The
flow increased with the gradual expansion of the white frontier outward
from southern and eastern Queensland. Of all the items of western
technology thus made available, none was more acceptable, none

* From Edward H. Spicer, ed., *Human Problems in Technological Change* (New
York: Russell Sage Foundation, 1952), Case 5, pp. 69–90.

The author (b. 1907) is Professor of Anthropology and Director, Studies in
Culture and Applied Sciences, at Cornell University. Chief interests center in the
study of Oceania and Southeast Asia. Author: *Siamese Rice Village* and numerous
articles in scientific journals.

more highly valued by aboriginals of all conditions than the hatchet or short-handled steel axe. . . .

RELEVANT FACTORS

If we concentrate our attention on Yir Yoront behavior centering about the original stone axe, rather than on the axe—the thing—we should get some conception of the role this implement played in aboriginal culture. This conception, in turn, should permit us to foresee with considerable accuracy some of the results of the displacement of stone axes by steel axes acquired directly or indirectly from Europeans by the Yir Yoront.

The production of a stone axe required a number of simple skills. With the idea of the axe in its various details well in mind, the adult men—and only the adult men—could set about producing it, a task not considered appropriate for women or children. . . .

The use of the stone axe as a piece of capital equipment for the production of other goods indicates its very great importance in the subsistence economy of the aboriginal. Anyone—man, woman, or child— could use the axe; indeed, it was used more by women, for theirs was the onerous, daily task of obtaining sufficient wood to keep the campfire of each family burning all day for cooking or other purposes and all night against mosquitoes and cold (in July, winter temperature might drop below forty degrees). In a normal lifetime any woman would use the axe to cut or knock down literally tons of firewood. Men and women, and sometimes children, needed the axe to make other tools, or weapons, or a variety of material equipment required by the aboriginal in his daily life. . . .

While the stone axe helped relate men and women and often children to nature in technological behavior, in the transformation of natural into cultural equipment, it also was prominent in that aspect of behavior which may be called conduct, primarily directed toward persons. Yir Yoront men were dependent upon interpersonal relations for their stone axe heads, since the flat, geologically recent alluvial country over which they range, provides no stone from which axe heads can be made. The stone they used comes from known quarries four hundred miles to the south. It reached the Yir Yoront through long lines of male trading partners, some of these chains terminating with the Yir Yoront men, while others extended on farther north to other groups, having utilized Yir Yoront men as links. Almost every older adult man had one or more regular trading partners, some to the north and some to the south. His partner or partners in the south he provided with surplus spears, and particularly fighting spears tipped with the barbed spines of sting ray which snap into vicious fragments when they penetrate human flesh. For a dozen spears, some of which he may have obtained from a partner to the north, he would receive from a southern partner one stone axe head. . . . Thus trading relations, which may extend the individual's personal relationships out beyond the boundaries of his own group, are associated with two of the most important items in a man's equipment, spears and axes, whether the latter are of stone or steel. Finally, most of the exchanges between partners take place during the dry season at times when the great aboriginal fiestas occur, which center about initiation rites or other totemic ceremonials that attract hundreds and are the occasion for much exciting activity besides trading.

Returning to the Yir Yoront, we find that not only was it adult men alone who obtained axe heads and produced finished axes, but it was adult males who retained the axes, keeping them with other parts of their equipment in camp, or carrying them at the back slipped through a human hair belt when traveling. Thus, every woman or child who wanted to use an axe—and this might be frequently during the day—must get one from some man, use it promptly, and return it to the man in good condition. While a man might speak of "my axe," a woman or child could not; for them it was always "your axe," addressing a male, or "his axe."

This necessary and constant borrowing of axes from older men by women and children was done according to regular patterns of kinship behavior. A woman on good terms with her husband would expect to use his axe unless he were using it; a husband on good terms with his wives would let any one of them use his axe without question. If a woman was unmarried or her husband was absent, she would go first to her older brother or to her father for an axe. Only in extraordinary circumstances would she seek a stone axe from a mother's brother or certain other male kin with whom she had to be most circumspect. A girl, a boy, or a young man would look to a father or an older brother to provide an axe for her or his use, but would never approach a mother's brother, who would be at the same time a potential father-in-law, with such a request. Older men, too, would follow similar rules if they had to borrow an axe.

It will be noted that these social relationships in which the stone axe had a place are all pair relationships and that the use of the axe helped define and maintain the character of the relationships and the roles of the two individual participants. Every active relationship among the Yir Yoront involved a definite and accepted status of superordination or subordination. A person could have no dealings with any other on exactly equal terms. Women and children were dependent on, or subordinate to, older males in every action in which the axe entered. Among the men, the younger was dependent on the older or on certain kinds of kin. The nearest approach to equality was between brothers, although the older was always superordinate to the younger. Since the exchange of goods in a trading relationship involved a mutual reciprocity, trading partners were usually a kind of brother to each other or stood in a brotherly type of relationship, although one was always classified as older than the other and would have some advantage in case of dispute. It can be seen that repeated and widespread conduct centering on the axe helped to generalize and standardize throughout the society these sex, age, and kinship roles, both in their normal benevolent and in exceptional malevolent aspects, and helped to build up expectancies regarding the conduct of others defined as having a particular status.

The status of any individual Yir Yoront was determined not only by sex, age, and extended kin relationships, but also by membership in one of two dozen patrilineal totemic clans into which the entire community was divided. A person's names, rights in particular areas of land, and, in the case of a man, his roles in the totemic ceremonies (from which women are excluded) were all a function of belonging to one clan rather than another. Each clan had literally hundreds of totems, one or two of which gave the clan its name, and from any of which the personal names of clan members were derived. These totems included not only natural species or phenomena like the sun, stars, and daybreak, but also cultural "species": imagined ghosts, rainbow serpents, heroic ancestors; such eternal cultural verities as fires, spears, huts; and such human activities, conditions, or attributes as eating, vomiting, swimming, fighting, babies and corpses, milk and blood, lips and loins. While individual members of such totemic classes or species might disappear or be destroyed, the class itself was obviously ever present and indestructible. The totems therefore lent permanence and stability to the clans, to the groupings of human individuals who generation after generation were each associated with one set of totems that distinguished one clan from another.

Among the many totems of the Sunlit Cloud Iguana clan, and important among them, was the stone axe. The names of many members of this clan referred to the axe itself, or to activities like trading or wild honey gathering in which the axe played a vital part, or to the clan's mythical ancestors with whom the axe was prominently associated. When it was necessary to represent the stone axe in totemic ceremonies, it was only men of this clan who exhibited it or pantomimed its use. In secular life the axe could be made by any man and used by all; but in the sacred realm of the totems it belonged exclusively to the Sunlit Cloud Iguana people.

Supporting those aspects of cultural behavior which we have called

technology and conduct is a third area of culture, including ideas, sentiments, and values. These are most difficult to deal with, for they are
latent and covert or even unconscious and must be deduced from overt
actions and language or other communicating behavior. In this aspect
of the culture lies the "meaning" of the stone axe, its significance to the
Yir Yoront and to their cultural way of life. The ideal conception of the
axe, the knowledge of how to produce it (apart from the purely muscular
habits used in its production) are part of the Yir Yoront adult masculine
role, just as ideas regarding its technical use are included in the feminine
role. These technical ideas constitute a kind of "science" regarding the
axe which may be more important in relation to behavioral change than
are the neurophysiological patterns drilled into the body by years of
practice. Similarly there are normative ideas regarding the part played
by the axe in conduct which constitute a kind of "morality" of the axe,
and which again may be more important then the overt habits of social
interaction in determining the role of the axe in social relationships.
More than ideas regarding technology, ideas regarding conduct are likely
to be closely associated, or "charged," with sentiment or value. Ideas
and sentiments help guide and inform overt behavior; in turn, overt
behavior helps support and validate ideas and sentiments. . . .

Important for an understanding of the Yir Yoront culture is a system
of ideas, which may be called their totemic ideology. A fundamental
belief of the aboriginal divided time into two great epochs, a distant and
sacred period at the beginning of the world, when the earth was peopled
by mildly marvelous ancestral beings or culture heroes who in a special
sense are the forebears of the clans; and a second period, when the old
was succeeded by a new order that includes the present. Originally there
was no anticipation of another era supplanting the present; the future
would simply be an eternal continuation and reproduction of the present,
which itself had remained unchanged since the epochal revolution of
ancestral times.

The mythical sacred world of the ancestors with which time began
turns out on investigation to be a detailed reproduction of the present
aboriginal world of nature, man, and culture altered by phantasy. In
short, the idea system expressed in the mythology regarding the ancestral
epoch was directly derived from Yir Yoront behavior patterns—normal
and abnormal, actual and ideal, conscious and unconscious. The important thing to note, however, is that the native believed it was just the
other way around, that the present world, as a natural and cultural environment, was and should be simply a detailed reproduction of the
world of the ancestors. He believed that the entire universe "is now as
it was in the beginning" when it was established and left by the ancestors.
The ordinary cultural life of the ancestors became the daily life of the

Yir Yoront camps, and the extraordinary life of the ancestors remained extant in the recurring symbolic pantomimes and paraphernalia found only in the most sacred atmosphere of the totemic rites.

.   .   .   .   .

ANALYSIS

The introduction of the steel axe indiscriminately and in large numbers into the Yir Yoront technology was only one of many changes occurring at the same time. It is therefore impossible to factor out all the results of this single innovation alone. Nevertheless, a number of specific effects of the change from stone axes to steel axes may be noted; and the steel axe may be used as an epitome of the European goods and implements received by the aboriginals in increasing quantity and of their general influence on the native culture. The use of the steel axe to illustrate such influences would seem to be justified, for it was one of the first European artifacts to be adopted for regular use by the Yir Yoront; and the axe, whether of stone or steel, was clearly one of the most important items of cultural equipment they possessed.

The shift from stone to steel axes provided no major technological difficulties. While the aboriginals themselves could not manufacture steel axe heads, a steady supply from outside continued; and broken wooden axe handles could easily be replaced from bush timbers with aboriginal tools. Among the Yir Yoront the new axe never acquired all the uses it had on mission or cattle stations (carpentry work, pounding tent pegs, use as a hammer, and so on); and indeed, it was used for little more than the stone axe had been, so that it had no practical effect in improving the native standard of living. It did some jobs better, and could be used longer without breakage; and these factors were sufficient to make it of value to the native. But the assumption of the white man (based in part on a realization that a shift from steel to stone axe in his case would be a definite regression) that his axe was much more efficient, that its use would save time, and that it therefore represented technical "progress" toward goals which he had set for the native was hardly borne out in aboriginal practice. Any leisure time the Yir Yoront might gain by using steel axes or other western tools was invested, not in "improving the conditions of life," and certainly not in developing aesthetic activities, but in sleep, an art they had thoroughly mastered.

Having acquired an axe head through regular trading partners of whom he knew what to expect, a man wanting a stone axe was then dependent solely upon a known and an adequate nature and upon his own skills or easily acquired techniques. A man wanting a steel axe, however, was in no such self-reliant position. While he might acquire one through trade, he now had the new alternative of dispensing with technological behavior in relation with a predictable nature and conduct in relation with a predictable trading partner and of turning instead to conduct alone in relation with a highly erratic missionary. If he attended one of the mission festivals when steel axes were handed out as gifts, he might receive one simply by chance or if he had happened somehow to impress the mission staff that he was one of the "better" bush aboriginals (their definition of "better" being quite different from that of his bush fellows). Or he might—but again almost by pure chance—be given some brief job in connection with the mission which would enable him to earn a steel axe. In either case, for older men a preference for the steel axe helped create a situation of dependence in place of a situation of self-reliance and a behavior shift from situations in technology or conduct which were well structured or defined to situations in conduct alone which were ill defined. It was particularly the older ones among the men, whose earlier experience or knowledge of the white man's harshness in any event made them suspicious, who would avoid having any relations with the mission at all, and who thus excluded themselves from acquiring steel axes directly from that source.

The steel axe was the root of psychological stress among the Yir Yoront even more significantly in other aspects of social relations. This was the result of new factors which the missionary considered all to the good: the simple numerical increase in axes per capita as a result of mission distribution; and distribution from the mission directly to younger men, women, and even children. By winning the favor of the mission staff, a woman might be given a steel axe. This was clearly intended to be hers. The situation was quite different from that involved in borrowing an axe from a male relative, with the result that a woman called such an axe "my" steel axe, a possessive form she never used for a stone axe. (Lexically, the steel axe was differentiated from the stone by an adjectival suffix signifying "metal" the element "axe" remaining identical.) Furthermore, young men or even boys might also obtain steel axes directly from the mission. A result was that older men no longer had a complete monopoly of all the axes in the bush community. Indeed, an old man might have only a stone axe, while his wives and sons had steel axes which they considered their own and which he might even desire to borrow. All this led to a revolutionary confusion of sex, age, and kinship roles, with a major gain in independence and loss of subordination on the part of those able now to acquire steel axes when they had been unable to possess stone axes before.

The trading partner relationship was also affected by the new situation. A Yir Yoront might have a trading partner, in a tribe to the south whom he defined as a younger brother, and on whom as an older brother he would therefore have an edge. But if the partner were in contact with the mission or had other easier access to steel axes, his subordination to his bush colleague was obviously decreased. Indeed, under the new dispensation he might prefer to give his axe to a bush "sweetheart" in return for favors or otherwise dispose of it outside regular trade channels, since many steel axes were so distributed between natives in new ways. Among other things, this took some of the excitement away from the fiesta-like tribal gatherings centering around initiations during the dry season. These had traditionally been the climactic annual occasions for exchanges between trading partners, when a man might seek to acquire a whole year's supply of stone axe heads. Now he might find himself prostituting his wife to almost total strangers in return for steel axes or other white men's goods. With trading partnerships weakened, there was less reason to attend the fiestas, and less fun for those who did. A decline in one of the important social activities which had symbolized these great gatherings created a lessening of interest in the other social aspects of these events.

Not only did an increase in steel axes and their distribution to women change the character of the relations between individual and individual, the paired relationships that have been noted, but a new type of relationship, hitherto practically unknown among the Yir Yoront, was created in their axe-acquiring conduct with whites. In the aboriginal society there were almost no occasions outside the immediate family when one individual would initiate action to several other people at once. For in any average group, while a person in accordance with the kinship system might be superordinate to several people to whom he could suggest or command action, at the same time he was also subordinate to several others, in relation with whom such behavior would be tabu. There was thus no over-all chieftainship or authoritarian leadership of any kind. Such complicated operations as grass-burning, animal drives, or totemic ceremonies could be carried out smoothly because each person knew his roles both in technology and conduct.

On both mission and cattle stations, however, the whites imposed upon the aboriginals their conception of leadership roles, with one person in a controlling relationship with a subordinate group. Aboriginals called together to receive gifts, including axes, at a mission Christmas party found themselves facing one or two whites who sought to control their behavior for the occasion, who disregarded the age, sex, and kinship variables among them of which they were so conscious, and who considered them all at one subordinate level. Or the white might impose similar patterns on a working party. (But if he placed an aboriginal in charge of a mixed group of post hole diggers, for example, half of the group, those subordinate to the "boss," would work while the other half, who were superordinate to him, would sleep.) The steel axe, together, of course, with other European goods, came to symbolize for the aboriginal this new and uncomfortable form of social organization, the leader-group relationship.

The most disturbing effects of the steel axe, operating in conjunction with other elements also being introduced from the white man's several subcultures, developed in the realm of traditional ideas, sentiments, and values. These were undermined at a rapidly mounting rate, without new conceptions being defined to replace them. The result was a mental and moral void which foreshadowed the collapse and destruction of all Yir Yoront culture, if not, indeed, the extinction of the biological group itself.

From what has been said it should be clear how changes in overt behavior, in technology and conduct, weakened the values inherent in a reliance on nature, in androcentrism or the prestige of masculinity, in age prestige, and in the various kinship relations. A scene was set in which a wife or young son, his initiation perhaps not even yet completed, need no longer bow to the husband or father, who was left confused and insecure as he asked to borrow a steel axe from them. For the woman and boy the steel axe helped establish a new degree of freedom which was accepted readily as an escape from the unconscious stress of the old patterns, but which left them also confused and insecure. Ownership became less well defined, so that stealing and trespass were introduced into technology and conduct. Some of the excitement surrounding the great ceremonies evaporated, so that the only fiestas the people had became less festive, less interesting. Indeed, life itself became less interesting, although this did not lead the Yir Yoront to invent suicide, a concept foreign to them.

The whole process may be most specifically illustrated in terms of the totemic system, and this will also illustrate the significant role which a system of ideas, in this case a totemic ideology, may play in the breakdown of a culture.

In the first place, under pre-European aboriginal conditions in which the native culture has become adjusted to a relatively stable environment in which there can occur few, if any, unheard of or catastrophic crises, it is clear that the totemic system must serve very effectively to inhibit radical cultural changes. The closed system of totemic ideas, explaining and categorizing a well-known universe as it was fixed at the beginning of time, presents a considerable obstacle to the adoption of new or the dropping of old culture traits. The obstacle is not insurmountable and the system allows for the minor variations which occur about the norms of daily life, but the inception of major changes cannot easily take place.

Among the bush Yir Yoront the only means of water transport is a light wood log, to which they cling in their constant swimming of rivers, salt creeks, and tidal inlets. These natives know that forty-five miles north of them are tribes who have a bark canoe. They know these northern tribes can thus fish from midstream or out at sea, instead of clinging to the river banks and beaches, and can cross coastal waters infested with crocodiles, sharks, sting rays, and Portuguese-men-of-war without the recurring mortality, pain, or anxiety to which they themselves are constantly subjected. They know they lack any magic to do for them what the canoe could do. They know the materials of which the canoe is made are present in their own environment. But they also know, as they say, that their own mythical ancestors lacked the canoe, and therefore they lack it, while they assume that the canoe was part of the ancestral universe of the northern tribes. For them, then, the adoption of the canoe would not be simply a matter of learning a number of new behavioral skills for its manufacture and use. The adoption would require at the same time a much more difficult procedure, the acceptance by the entire society of a myth, either locally developed or borrowed, which would explain the presence of the canoe, associate it with some one or more of the several hundred mythical ancestors (and how decide which?), and thus establish it as an accepted totem of one of the clans ready to be used by the whole community. The Yir Yoront have not made this adjustment, and in this case we can only say that ideas have for the time being at least won out over very real pressures for technological change. In the elaborateness and explicitness of the totemic ideologies we seem to have one explanation for the notorious stability of Australian cultures under aboriginal conditions, an explanation which gives due weight to the importance of ideas in determining human behavior.

At a later stage of the contact situation, as has been indicated, phenomena unaccounted for by the totemic ideological system begin to appear with regularity and frequency and remain within the range of native experience. Accordingly, they cannot be ignored (as the "Battle of the Mitchell River" was apparently ignored), and an attempt is made to assimilate them and account for them along the lines of principles inherent in the ideology. The bush Yir Yoront of the mid-1930's represent this stage of the acculturation process. Still trying to maintain their aboriginal definition of the situation, they accept European artifacts and behavior patterns, but fit them into their totemic system, assigning them as totems to various clans on a par with original totems. There is an attempt to have the myth-making process keep up with these cultural changes so that the idea system can continue to support the rest of the culture. But analysis of overt behavior, of dreams, and of some of the new myths indicates that this arrangement is not entirely satisfactory; that the native clings to his totemic system with intellectual loyalty, lacking any substitute ideology; but that associated sentiments and values are weakened. His attitudes toward his own and toward European culture are found to be highly ambivalent.

All ghosts are totems of the Head-to-the-East Corpse clan. They are thought of as white, and are, of course, closely associated with death. The white man, too, is white and was closely associated with death, so that he and all things pertaining to him are naturally assigned to the Corpse clan as totems. The steel axe, as a totem, was thus associated with the Corpse clan. But it is an "axe," and is clearly linked with the stone axe, which is a totem of the Sunlit Cloud Iguana clan. Moreover, the steel axe, like most European goods, has no distinctive origin myth, nor are mythical ancestors associated with it. Can anyone, sitting of an afternoon in the shade of a ti tree, create a myth to resolve this confusion? No one has, and the horrid suspicion arises that perhaps the origin myths are wrong, which took into account so little of this vast new universe of the white man. The steel axe, shifting hopelessly between one clan and the other, is not only replacing the stone axe physically, but is hacking at the supports of the entire cultural system.

The aboriginals to the south of the Yir Yoront have clearly passed beyond this stage. They are engulfed by European culture, in this area by either the mission or cattle station subcultures, or for some natives a baffling, paradoxical combination of both incongruent varieties. The totemic ideology can no longer support the inrushing mass of foreign culture traits and the myth-making process in its native form breaks down completely. Both intellectually and emotionally a saturation point is reached, so that the myriad new traits which can neither be ignored nor any longer assimilated simply force the aboriginal to abandon his totemic system. With the collapse of this system of ideas, which is so closely related with so many other aspects of the native culture, there follows an appallingly sudden and complete cultural disintegration and a demoralization of the individual such as has seldom been recorded for areas other than Australia. Without the support of a system of ideas well devised to provide cultural stability in a stable environment but admittedly too rigid for the new realities pressing in from outside, native behavior and native sentiments and values are simply dead. Apathy reigns. The aboriginal has passed beyond the reach of any outsider who might wish to do him well or ill. . . .

100. AN EXPERIMENT IN
APPLIED SOCIAL SCIENCE *

JOHN AND MARY COLLIER

> *The previous selection demonstrated that planned technological*
> *change may have serious unanticipated consequences. This selection*
> *is a description of social changes that have had a beneficial effect*
> *on the social fabric. Although the use of social science knowledge*
> *does not guarantee successful and nondisruptive change, there is*
> *much evidence that wise application of such knowledge will help*
> *to avoid many pitfalls in social engineering. The Colliers illustrate*
> *how this knowledge has been effectively used in a community*
> *in South America.*

In a beautiful mountain valley in the high Andes of Peru, inhabited by some 380 families of Indians, an eventful social experiment has been under way during the past five years. It is an experiment in "applied anthropology" [or "applied social science"]. Under the guidance of scientists a "backward" population has been stirred to break away from the hopeless traditions of centuries and raise itself to a more abundant life. The way in which this has been accomplished makes the experiment significant for millions of people in the underdeveloped areas of the world.

In the decade since World War II the U.S. has found itself assuming, partly from necessity and partly as a matter of wise long-range policy, responsibility for aid to peoples all around the globe—in the Pacific, in Asia, in Europe, in Africa, in South America. This experience has made plain that aid raises problems which reach beyond money and technology. There is the problem of persuading a backward people to accept not only technological innovations but also the economic and social changes made necessary by these innovations. Even more im-

---

* From "An Experiment in Applied Anthropology," *Scientific American*, Vol. 196, No. 1 (January, 1957), 37–44; see for the impressive photographic evidence included.

John Collier (b. 1913) and his wife, Mary (b. 1919), work together both in writing and documentary photography. He teaches photography, and also a course in cultural change, at the California School of Fine Arts in San Francisco. They have lived among the Indians of Ecuador, the Acadians of Nova Scotia, and the Navajo. Authors of *The Awakening Valley* and magazine articles; they have in preparation a documentary, *Photography for Anthropology*, under a grant from the Guggenheim Foundation.

portant, there is the problem of giving help without making them dependent. Benevolence all too often defeats its basic purpose by destroying a people's self-reliance.

It was these considerations that prompted a group of social scientists to undertake their experiment in applied anthropology in the Peruvian valley. Their aim was to learn how an impoverished population might be stimulated to lift its standard of living by its own efforts and within the framework of its own culture. The scientists undertook to acquire a thorough understanding of the people's customs and tradition and then to assist the community as "participating interventionists."

The originator of the project was Allan R. Holmberg of Cornell University, an anthropologist who had studied Indian groups in Peru for the Smithsonian Institution and later in association with the University of San Marcos. Holmberg enlisted his Peruvian colleagues and students in a search for a laboratory in which to study how a backward group would respond to the introduction of modern technological change. On a field trip with his students Holmberg found an ideal community for such a program. It was an ancient estate, called Hacienda Vicos, on the upper slopes of a long, narrow valley paralleling Peru's highest mountain range, the Cordillera Blanca. The hacienda was in decay, its lands eroded, its more than 2,000 Indians living in hunger and disease. Holmberg conceived the bold idea of renting the hacienda and operating it in the conventional way, but under a scientific group instead of the usual private patron. With a grant of funds from the Carnegie Corporation of New York, the Cornell department of sociology and anthropology rented the hacienda from the Peruvian Government and launched a five-year experiment, known as the Cornell-Peru Project, in cooperation with Peruvian scientists and government agencies.

Hacienda Vicos is an estate of some 35,000 acres at an altitude of from 9,000 to 12,000 feet in a valley called the Callejón de Huaylas. Its history goes back to the Spanish Conquest. Legend says that nearly 400 years ago its then owner, a very wealthy Spanish woman, on her deathbed gave the hacienda, complete with its Indians, to a hospital in Lima. Whether or not this story is true, Hacienda Vicos has been in public custody since the early 17th century, first under Spanish authorities and later under the Peruvian national government. For hundreds of years the estate, with its lands and peonage system intact, has passed from one lessee to another, recently by public auction to the highest bidder.

The hacienda system, established by the Spanish conquerors, is maintained by rigid traditions which even the patron is often powerless to change radically. The Indians who live on a hacienda are its serfs, and the owner or lessee is their lord—their benefactor and exploiter. One member of each serf household must work for the hacienda three days a week without pay. In return the Indians are allowed to farm a few acres of land, drink water from the streams, gather faggots for their fires and graze their animals in allotted pastures. They turn to the patron for assistance and advice in times of trouble and leave every important decision in his hands. Within the hacienda they attend chapel, bury their dead, celebrate their fiestas and remain bound for generation after generation.

The Cornell-Peru staff's decision to operate the hacienda under the traditional rules was the core of their anthropological approach. They wished to avoid disrupting the community or creating confusion and anxiety. Their purpose was to acquire a full understanding of the Indians and their problems in the customary pattern of their lives, to persuade them to improve their farming methods, to plow back the higher returns into a better life for the community and eventually to lead the Indians to a free and self-reliant life. The change would develop from the bottom up, not be imposed from the top.

Peru is a land of the Indian. Its leaders have long been aware that the country is held back by the traditional prejudices and fetters of its Indian masses, and they therefore welcomed the anthropologists' project, hoping, with the scientists, that it would be a practical demonstration of wide benefit. The Cornell-Peru experiment received enthusiastic cooperation from the country's universities, scientists, educators and authorities in agriculture and public health.

At Vicos the anthropologists found a clear epitome of Peru's problems. Its Indians were almost completely illiterate: only 2 per cent could read and write, and most spoke only the Indian language Quechua. Hunger was their chronic condition, and drinking almost their only recreation. Epidemics brought death to nearly every home. They were little better than slaves, despised by their neighbors. Between the hacienda Indians and the *mestizos* (mixed Spanish-Indian breeds) of surrounding communities there was strong hostility. *Mestizos* look down on Indians, considering them biologically inferior; the Indians are submissive but fear and distrust the *mestizos*. Nevertheless, the Project scientists has to hire *mestizos* for skilled work on the hacienda, and they took advantage of the necessity to study the relationship between the groups. They were confident that cooperation would eventually improve the relationship. The Project even kept on the administrator who had been in charge of the hacienda for several years under the former lessee.

The first task was to increase the food crop. Most of the Vicosinos were living at a level of bare subsistence. A blight had hit the potato fields in the two preceding years, and the corn crop also had failed. Food was so scarce and costly that the Indians were eating the seed grain, digging up seed potatoes as soon as they were planted, selling their cattle to buy food and stealing as much of the hacienda crop as they could.

The Project staff had an agricultural survey made and took steps to rebuild the potato culture. It obtained blight-resistant potato seed, fertilizer and insecticides from agricultural experiment stations, and then offered them to the Indians at cost.

Few came to buy. Days passed and the Indians paid no attention to the announcement. Recognizing that most of the Indians could not pay for the seed even if they had wanted to, the Project then worked out a credit plan. It proposed to advance the seed, fertilizer and insecticide on a crop-sharing arrangement—half of the crop to the hacienda, half to the farmer.

This plan was first presented to a meeting of the *mayorales,* the Indian leaders of the community who served as foremen in directing the work of the other peons. The *mayorales* listened, and shook their heads. They declared the plan would never work. But it became plain that the leaders were hostile to the proposal because vested interests were at stake. They feared that improvement of the prospects of the other peons would undermine their own favored position.

Notwithstanding this discouraging opposition by the leaders, the Project staff decided to offer the plan directly to the community as a whole. At the peons' weekly meeting (the *mando*) for assignment of the week's work, the scientists described their proposal. It evoked excited discussion among the peons. They appeared to approve it at first, but after one of the *mayorales* spoke against it, the approval seemed to cool. Only nine of the 125 peons present came forward to sign up for the plan at the end of the meeting. Later 22 more did so privately. But a majority of the community hung back, and active opposition grew. Rumors, perhaps initiated by landowners and *mestizos* in the area, spread among the distrustful and suspicious peons. Why had the *gringos* come to the valley? What were their reasons for offering help to the Indians? The *mestizos* whispered that the fair-appearing scheme surely hid some plan to cheat and exploit the peons. One rumor went so far as to suggest that the Americans had come to Vicos to fatten the Indians on potatoes and then boil down their bodies for oil for American machinery! The credulity that accepted such lurid tales was fed by the Indians' fear of change— of what the unknown might bring.

Mario Vásquez and other Peruvian scientists in the Project worked hard to allay the Indians' fears. Vásquez visited scores of Indians in their homes and in the fields and signed up nine more peons to participate in the program. But of the total of 40 who agreed to take part, only 17 actually took the seed and entered into the farming project when the planting season began. Most of these were the poorest of the poor; against the disapproval of their wives in some instances they decided to take the chance to save themselves from starvation and improve their position.

The participating Indians were required to carry out to the letter instructions from Peruvian Government agricultural specialists. They had to disinfect the seed potatoes and the land, to plant the seed at 18-inch intervals in rows three feet apart, to apply guano as fertilizer, to spray insecticides at set times and to remove blossoms from the plants. They were instructed in techniques of cultivation, irrigation and so on.

Besides supervising every step of the cultivation—the fumigating, the planting, the harvesting—the Project staff also kept a careful watch on the farmers' working relations and social behavior. By doing so, they were able to forestall small frictions and points of resistance that often defeat a whole program. For example, at one point the staff employed a young, intelligent Vicosino as a supervisor. Their close observation at once disclosed that this was a mistake. Taking orders from a young member of their own group hurt the vanity of the older Indians; they preferred to be directed by outsiders. This delicate pride was illustrated by another incident. A peon whose plots had somehow been overlooked during a routine inspection of the participating fields turned up at the hacienda highly agitated. He complained: "If you don't pay as much attention to my field as you do to the others, people will think it is because my field isn't being cultivated correctly and that you are displeased!" Incidents such as these demonstrated how important it is to enlist the perceptions and skills of social science (applied anthropology) in any aid program among a proud and sensitive people.

Throughout this first season the other Vicosinos felt sorry for the 17 Indians who had been foolish enough to be taken in by the Project. They would surely lose everything, and have thrown away their season's labor. But at harvest time the nonparticipants were taken aback. The 17 participants harvested more than double the usual crop of potatoes. Each of them divided his crop into two piles, one to be taken by the Project, the other to be kept by himself. The Project staff then invited the farmer to take his choice of the piles. The Indians were deeply impressed. This was something foreign to their experience: the *gringos* did not cheat; they kept their word!

The following season 87 Indians, including one of the *mayorales* who had opposed the program, took advantage of the seed. Even some of the *mestizos* asked to be included in the experiment. By the third year 135 Indians took part, and they accounted for nearly 80 per cent of the total potato crop raised on Hacienda Vicos. In that year some of the Indians bought the seed and other materials on credit, instead of sharecropping. All but one of the borrowers paid his debt in full at harvest time. Consequently the sharecropping system was dropped entirely in 1955. The Indians proved in that season that they were sufficiently skilled in the new farming techniques to take the full risk and responsibility of buying the seed and to realize a yield adequate to support themselves at a higher level than they had known.

Economic reforms sowed their own seeds of social reform. For example, the hacienda Indians had constantly stolen cattle from one another and fought over the ownership of animals. The Project staff suggested that they brand their cattle. The Indian leaders showed no enthusiasm for this, but when one of them observed bitterly that the wealthiest had built their herds by rustling, the owner of the largest herd began to brand his cattle to prove his innocence. The other Indian families followed his example, and cattle rustling stopped.

Along with the rehabilitation of their agriculture, the Indians also began to rehabilitate the collapsing ruins of the hacienda. Under the direction of skilled craftsmen they rebuilt their crumbling dwellings, erected storage buildings for the crops and soon were able to turn to the construction of a school.

Although school attendance is theoretically compulsory in Peru, fewer than 5 per cent of the eligible children in Vicos were enrolled, and these came only sporadically. As Vásquez observed, even these few Vicosino families treated schooling like their forced labor for the patron: so long as one child of a household was in school, it didn't matter whether the child who sat on the school bench on Monday was the same child who had sat there Friday. School was kept in an open porch, where a woman instructor tried to teach about eight children of assorted ages something of reading, writing, and arithmetic in Spanish, a language almost totally foreign to most of the Quechua-speaking Vicosinos.

Soon after the Project began in 1951, the Indians were invited to a meeting to discuss the possibility of a new school. They agreed to provide all the labor, and the Project offered to buy needed materials. Plans were drawn for a modern schoolhouse, and ground was broken in May, 1952. The Indians made thousands of adobes (clay bricks), quarried great piles of rock for the foundations and felled tall eucalyptus trees to make the doors, window frames and roof beams. The only materials that had to be purchased were glass for the windows, lime for the plaster, cement for the floor and tiles for the roof. Although much of the building project was at first quite beyond the Indians' limited skills, the work was accomplished, under the direction of the contractor and a few *mestizo* craftsmen. In 1953 the first unit of six classrooms was opened, and the following year saw the completion of a second unit with three more classrooms, a spacious auditorium, a dining room and kitchen for the hot-lunch program. Later living quarters for teachers were built.

The Peruvian educational authorities, who operate the school, have staffed it with eight teachers, and more than 200 children are now enrolled. Most of these are boys, who receive vocational instruction, including carpentry and agriculture. A small group of girls attends a technically separate primary school in the same building.

This beautiful school has become a symbol. It has given new confidence to the community, for the building is notably finer than any other rural school of the region. And it has inspired the Indians with the pride of achievement. Visitors have come even from Lima to see the modern school the Vicosinos have built with their own hands.

Hacienda Vicos has seen a third major improvement—its first health program. With the cooperation of the Cornell-Peru Project, the regional Peruvian public health agency has set up a clinic which serves not only the hacienda but also the neighboring *mestizo* town of Marcará. Twice a week a truck, supplied by the United Nations International Children's Emergency Fund, arrives at Vicos with a doctor and nurses and public health specialists. Though their program is chiefly concerned with child and maternal welfare, the clinic at Vicos gives attention to all, dispensing medicine and advice on the full range of ailments from itches to tuberculosis. The doctors visit critically ill patients in their homes, though this sometimes means an hour's ride on horseback on the rocky mountain trails. The clinic gives a thorough physical examination to all the children attending the school. It keeps careful medical records which supply an invaluable body of data for studying the health of Peruvian Indians. The clinic is gradually educating the Indians to combat their ailments with modern medicine rather than with native religious methods or magic. . . .

Along with the basic projects—food, education, health—there have been special programs, one of which deserves particular mention. All young Peruvian men who have not served in the army are required to attend military drill every Sunday for a two-year period. This had been a hateful service for the Vicosinos and a further exploitation of their status, for the politicos of the town where they drilled, five miles from the hacienda, had merely used the pretense of the Sunday drill to make the Indians do community work. The Cornell-Peru Project arranged for the young men to be drilled right at the hacienda, not only conforming to the national law, but providing an exercise in working together and fostering pride in their own group, which they had sadly lacked. The Project also used the Sunday gathering to provide classes in Spanish, reading, writing, and arithmetic. Two years ago the Indians of Vicos, marching in sandals with wooden guns and wooden bayonets, won a citation at the annual military review of their province.

Foremost among all the purposes of the Project has been a calculated endeavor to develop the Indians' self-reliance and change their own image of themselves—an image of serfs destined to poverty and endless unrewarding work. The Project ended tyrannical exploitation of the Indians, not only by the hacienda but also by outside employers. The peons no longer are sent out to work without pay in mines or factories. No longer do neighboring communities come to the hacienda to conscript crews for construction of bridges and public buildings. The weekly meetings of the *mayorales* and of the peons have been turned into discussion sessions at which both the foremen and the peons can air their grievances and take part in decisions. The goal of the entire program is to enable the Vicosinos themselves to continue their progress toward a higher level of living when the Project staff withdraws from the community.

Beyond all this, the Project's broader concern has been to develop a body of scientific experience which will serve to establish equations for work in other underdeveloped areas—in Peru itself and in the world at large. In the Vicos research U.S. scientists have teamed up with scientists of Peru. Indeed, a great part of the detailed research has been carried out by Holmberg's Peruvian student and assistant Mario Vásquez. He lived with an Indian family on the hacienda and was largely responsible for dispelling distrust and enlisting the Indians' cooperation. As a research project the Vicos experiment has also attracted dozens of other students from the University of San Marcos and from Cornell and other universities.

Perhaps the biggest single lesson the Project has demonstrated is that, by working within the existing structure of a society, with sufficient understanding of both its limitations and its potentialities, it is possible to accomplish basic social changes without a staggering budget or swarms of personnel. The anthropologists at Hacienda Vicos have shown that in the field of social reform, understanding may be a far more important tool than money or power.

101. DESCENT TO ANOMY *

ROBERT M. MACIVER

To most of us our social ties, the values by which we live, and our sense of "belonging" are so much a part of us that we have little conception of their deep significance to us and to our society. Hence, we are inclined to take social cohesion for granted. But this social cohesion through which the unity of our personalities is secured and maintained always rests in delicate balance. In a complex society, even under the most favorable conditions, there are individuals who fall into anomy (now usually spelled anomie) —a condition where the sense of "belonging" to the group is lost

* *The Ramparts We Guard*, 84–92. Copyright 1950 by The Macmillan Company and used with their permission.
For a biographical sketch of the author see selection 73.

and the norms or values of society are ignored or rejected. In times of crisis such as these, "whole groups are exposed to the malady." In this selection, MacIver describes the anomic person, and shows how the presence of anomy is evidenced in a modern society.

Let us look next at *anomy*, the other malady of democratic man that becomes most virulent in times of crisis and turbulent change, the breakdown of the individual's sense of attachment to society, to all society. Anomy is not simply lawlessness. A gangster or a pirate or a mere law-evading rogue is not as such, indeed is not likely to be, anomic. He has his own code of law against law and is under strong sanctions to obey it. He need not be the victim of that inner detachment, of that cleavage between the real self and the projected self, of that total rejection of indoctrinated values that characterizes the anomic person. Anomy signifies the state of mind of one who has been pulled up from his moral roots, who has no longer any standards but only disconnected urges, who has no longer any sense of continuity, of folk, of obligation. The anomic man has become spiritually sterile, responsive only to himself, responsible to no one. He derides the values of other men. His only faith is the philosophy of denial. He lives on the thin line of sensation between no future and no past.

In any times particular individuals may fall into anomy. It happens when sensitive temperaments suffer without respite a succession of shocks that disrupt their faith. And not a few men have temporary moods that resemble anomy, periods when the spirit of denial rules them, after they have experienced some grave bafflement. But there are times of profound disturbance when whole groups are exposed to the malady. The soldiers in Mailer's novel, *The Naked and the Dead,* talk the language of anomy. They have been torn in youth from their environments, their careers, their dreams, their hopes, to face laborious tedium and the ugliest forms of death. They have been bereft of the sustaining ways of their culture. They are thrust back on the immediate needs and demands of each perilous hour. The present offers nothing but sensations; there are periods of boredom and drudgery, and then they are alone with nature and sudden death. So they use the language of sensation—there is nothing else to express. It means little but there is nothing else to mean. The livid, gory, sexy words they utter soon convey precisely nothing, nothing but the denudation they feel. For them, however, for those who survive, there is a return to nearly all the things they have lost. For most of them anomy wears away in their restoration to their society. But there are others, the hopelessly displaced, the totally uprooted, the permanently insecure, those who need the support of authority and have lost it without hope of recovery, the over-sophisticated who find that the challenges of life cannot be met by sophistication—among such people anomy takes full command.

Anomy is a state of mind in which the individual's sense of social cohesion—the mainspring of his morale—is broken or fatally weakened. In this detachment of the anomic person from social obligation his whole personality is injured. He has lost the *dynamic unity* of personality. The anomic fall into various types, though we do not have so far the psychological researches necessary for the adequate classification of these types. We can, however, broadly distinguish the following.

First, there are those who, having lost altogether, or in great measure, any system of values that might give purpose or direction to their lives, having lost the compass that points their course into the future, abandon themselves to the present, but a present emptied of significance. They resort, in other words, to a sophisticated cynicism, by aid of which they rationalize their loss. They live by the hour, seeking immediate gratification on whatever level it is available. They tend to be sensationalists and materialists. It is their defense against the ghosts of perished values.

Second, there are those who, having lost their ethical goals, having no longer any intrinsic and socialized values to which they can harness their drive to action, transfer this drive to extrinsic values instead, to the pursuit of means instead of to the pursuit of ends beyond them, and particularly to the pursuit of power, so far as that lies within their reach. It has been claimed that there is a "strain toward anomy" in modern capitalistic society, with its emphasis on competitive success measured by the purely extrinsic standard of money-making. There can be little doubt that engrossment in the competitive struggle, especially when it is carried on under the aegis of the "soul-less body-less" corporation, diverts men from the search for intrinsic satisfactions and erodes their recognition of the common interests of their society, the inclusive more abiding interests that bind men in the responsible fellowship of their community. At the same time, the experience of the past two generations suggests that it requires the violence of change, the deeper perturbations that disorient and displace men from their former ways, their former goals, their former faiths, to bring anomy to its full being, and in particular this second type of anomy. Those who exhibit it tend to be domineering, sadistic, ruthless, irascible, vain, inherently destructive. Unlike the first type, they live for a future, they have objectives that bind today to the further tomorrow, but these objectives are self-centered, ego-glorifying, bereft of social obligation. Often they profess adherence to some intrinsic faith or value, but primarily because that profession enhances their private designs. They are then like Machiavelli's prince, who must appear to be religious and high-minded if he is to retain his prestige and power. Moreover, they make the creeds of other men the instruments of their own aggrandisement, the utilitarian myths of their authority. On another level they are racketeers, buccaneers of industry or finance, unprincipled exploiters of whatever position, privilege, or power they acquire. All men or nearly all men cherish their private interest and frequently enough they allow it to overcome their public obligation. But they are restrained within certain limits set by loyalties of one kind or another, and when they transgress they are conscious of dereliction. But the truly anomic man has no limit short of necessity and no conscience that is more than expediency.

Third, we may distinguish a type of anomy that is characterized above all by a fundamental and tragic insecurity, something that cuts deeper than the anxieties and dreads that beset other men. It is the insecurity of the hopelessly disoriented. They have lost the ground on which they stood, the ground of their former values. Usually it happens when they have lost also their former environment, their former connections, their social place, their economic support. In the profoundest sense they are "displaced persons." The displacement, however, may not be physical. There is, for example, the social alienation of those who feel themselves rejected and become the victims of a persecution complex. This is perhaps the bitterest of all forms of anomy. There is a crushing sense of indignity, of exclusion, of injustice, of defeat, arousing feelings of intense hate, counter-aggressiveness, total revulsion from things as they are, sometimes accompanied by unquiet introspection and self-torture.

This cursory review is intended to suggest types, not to classify them. In any event there is a considerable overlapping of attributes between our types. We should also remember that many people approach the full bent of anomy in various degrees. As we have already suggested, the conditions of our civilization create some predisposition to it and when our kind of civilization is racked by abrupt and violent change anomy grows rampant. Anomy is a disease of the civilized, not of the simpler peoples. As Durkheim pointed out, one index of anomy is the number of suicides, and suicide is much more frequent among the civilized.

It is noteworthy that modern doctrines of violent social change are initiated by those who have at least a tendency to anomy. Let us take for example the case of Karl Marx. He was from his early youth subjected to some of the conditions that breed anomy. His family belonged to the rabbinical elite in Germany. While he was still an infant his father, to the general surprise, announced his conversion to the Protestant Evangelical Church. This was the cause of a bitter dispute between his father and his mother. In the end, when Karl was six years old, his father had his way, and Karl, along with the six other children of the family, was baptized into the new faith. We know from modern studies how deeply disturbing it is to the mind of a child to have his first indoctrinations shattered by a "culture clash" on the hearth. The secret churning of the young boy's mind was the first preparation of the revolutionist-to-be, greatly heightening that sense of aloofness and disorientation that is the lot of many a Jewish boy in a society that stupidly clings to its hoary prejudices. The first obvious effect on Karl Marx was his loathing of all religions.

He grew into an impetuous, irascible, opinionated, and still idealistic youth. Then his ambitions suffered a series of reverses and frustrations. At this stage he fell in with the "communist rabbi," Moses Hess. He was ripe for the new gospel. He embraced it avidly, inclining at first toward the French socialists but soon repudiating and scorning them to assert his own truly scientific brand. It was the culmination of a process that began in the disorientation of childhood. Marx had become completely alienated from the society in which he lived, not its economic order particularly but its whole being and all the culture it nourished. In the background of his mind there flickered visions of an ideal society. But his love of the ideal was pale and distant compared with his hatred of the actual. He turned early to dreams of power, of lonely mastery. He was at enmity with the world. He denounced with incredible bitterness his own best friends the moment they ventured to question in any way his authority.

A man may condemn the society in which he lives without being himself anomic. But only if he is sustained by the engrossing vision of a better society, only if he is working to hasten the coming of some "new Jerusalem," only if he lives in fellowship with some brotherhood of the faithful who share his vision, only, in the last resort, if he is already, prophetically, a member of the society for which he yearns. There are those who believe the main inspiration of Marx was just some such redemption of mankind, that he was filled with the vision of a world in which men would be liberated from exploitation and injustice, from the gross oppression of every form of power. To the present writer that seems a mistaken interpretation. In the voluminous writings of Marx there are only one or two most fleeting references to "the good society." There is no evidence that he really cared for his fellowmen. He never uses kindly language except for those who looked upon him as their infallible leader. He hated those of his own party who showed any independence of thought. He was venomous toward all whom he could not dominate.

Marx focused his sharp intelligence on the worst sore of the society he hated. A new industrial system had been growing up. It was being exploited with callous disregard for the welfare of the workers. In the "dark Satanic mills," as the poet Blake called them, men, women, and young children labored endlessly long days, under the worst conditions, for subsistence wages or less. There were riots and threats of revolution. The French Revolution had shown how a class system could be overthrown. Here Marx found his opportunity. With immense vigor and remarkable propagandistic skill he proclaimed the inevitable victory of the proletariat. Marx had never mixed with any proletarians. He was himself a bourgeois. He never showed any interest in proletarians as human beings—only as a class. As he himself said, he found in the proletariat the "material weapon of philosophy," of his philosophy, of his revenge on society, of his triumph. He was the wrathful divider. The "bourgeoisie" became the fixed objective of his hate, the source of all evil. He identified it with the society that had rejected him. It was anathema. He devoted his being to its destruction.

The presence of anomy in modern society is evidenced by the spread of violently divisive doctrines, doctrines of all-or-nothing, doctrines that loudly preach a reactionary or a revolutionary authoritarianism, doctrines that appeal to men not as human beings but as de-individualized masses in motion. The anomic and near-anomic persons of the second and third types are particularly prone to such doctrines. For they offer a congenial release from anomy, a drastic remedy for its bitterness and frustration, a refuge from its insecurity, a means of reconciling its destructive tendencies with its secret need for social reintegration.

All these doctrines are enemies of democracy. They reject its tolerance, its acceptance of difference, its respect for the individual, its faith in the healing processes of free opinion. The anomic man has lost the balance of social health, mostly through no fault of his own. In his alienation he seeks a quick and false prescription. The anomic who cannot be masters are often ready to be slaves. They cry out for the superman to save them, for some equivalent of a Providence, a God, the ineluctable authority who will end their alienation by saying, "I command you to follow," making his command ring with the magic of a lost obligation.

What then can democracy do to meet these two perils that threaten it in this age of violent change—group anarchy and individual anomy? We remarked in passing that we should not blame the anomic for their plight; they are suffering from a disease incident to our civilization. The remark may seem at best a truism—of what other social ailment might not the same be said? But it was said to call attention to the proper ways in which democracy can safeguard itself against these dangers. When we seek to heal a social ailment—or a physical one— we should always treat it as a disease and not as a sin. Unfortunately we often proceed on the latter assumption, as we have been doing, for example, in our "denazification" policies, with mostly unhappy consequences. To protect democracy against anomy or against group anarchy we must endeavor to get at and to remove their causes.

In the first place we should realise that all our efforts to protect democracy against these and other dangers are wholly futile unless we can protect it first against the catastrophe of war. For war has now become so immeasurably ruinous that the shaken and impoverished survivors would be driven to desperate measures that might be fatal to the very existence of democracy. Therefore while we still possess the inestimable spiritual heritage of democracy we must assure it against the very possibility of war, showing an alertness and a forethought that in the past two generations the democratic world most deplorably failed to show.

To achieve this end democracy must be strong in its quality as democracy, not only in its arms. The spiritual weakness of democracy is the strength of its enemies. In some respects we still make only a pretence at democracy. Ask the Mexican-Americans within our borders, whom we do not permit to sit at the same table with our noble Nordics. Ask the Negroes, whom we segregate as pariahs, so that we may not be contaminated by the social presence of a lower caste. Ask the Jewish people, who cannot live in the same hotels, sometimes cannot even be treated in the same hospitals as their democracy-loving fellow-Americans. Ask the Eastern Europeans, who are still frequently treated as second-class citizens, especially if their names have a Slavic sound. Ask the Chinese among us, the Japanese, the Filipinos, the Hindus—and remember that by our treatment of these people we are betraying our democracy before the greater part of the human race; remember also that the Orient is now stirring to new political life and that its decision between democracy and dictatorship will profoundly affect our future and the future of all mankind. Ask these questions, remember these things, and you must see that *our* failure to be true to *our* democracy is in the last resort the main reason why democracy is in danger.

The diseases of group anarchy and of personal anomy are peculiarly incident to modern democracies. The unfree systems are authoritarian; by authority and by sheer compulsion they suppress such manifestations. Democracy places responsibility in the individual and in the group— it asks their free allegiance, their free cooperation. But it must on that account assure its citizens the conditions in which they can exercise their freedom. It must guard them from haunting economic insecurity or their civic freedom becomes a mockery. It must guard them against the rank prejudice that cuts them off from the equal partnership of democratic society. Otherwise democracy will breed the seeds of its own destruction.

Lastly, it must make its own meaning, its own philosophy, its own spirit, positive and vital. It cannot rest in the outworn liberalism that never rose above the negative of non-intervention. No vague negative faith can meet men's needs in this age where dogmatic authoritarian creeds deride the democratic ideal, and promise men, however falsely, a greater security and a greater reward. Democracy must become self-conscious of its own worth. Here we reach a theme that needs our most earnest attention.

102. WHY AMERICANS FEEL INSECURE *

ARNOLD W. GREEN

We Americans frequently pride ourselves on the flexibility and social change which characterize our society. But we pay a price for this fluid setting and rapid change in our patterns of living, for we need at least a few consistent and dependable social and physical anchorages to which we can attach ourselves. If we are constantly faced with new or ambiguous situations we may become uncertain as to how to act and thus develop feelings of insecurity. It is because it is often but a short step from feelings of insecurity to neurosis to complete mental breakdown that social scientists need to study seriously the nature and origins of insecurity. In this selection, by A. W. Green, are portrayed some of the factors which produce insecurity in Americans. To counterbalance the rather strong charges implied here against our way of life, it should be pointed out that societies which are extremely rigid, inflexible, and stratified may err in the direction of defining appropriate behavior so completely as to produce their own special form of frustration.

Historically, from the ancient Hebrews, Greeks, and Romans, through the Middle Ages, and down to recent decades, a basic family tradition has been preserved in the West: the patriarchal, rural-familistic system. Within that system, the person lived out his life, rooted to the land and to a way of life that encompassed all his activities. Unquestioned duties and obligations were enforced, but there was financial and emotional security, intimate emotional ties, and close identification with one's fellows.

The division of labor was familial, all working together toward a common goal of family maintenance and perpetuation. The family

* Reprinted from *Commentary*, Vol. 6, No. 1 (July, 1948), 18–28. Copyright American Jewish Committee.

The author (b. 1914) is a writer of monographs, articles, and textbooks in sociology. Formerly Professor of Sociology, Pennsylvania State University. Author: *Henry Charles Carey: Nineteenth-Century Sociologist; Sociology;* and numerous other works in sociology.

circle and the local community comprised a complete and virtually isolated social world. Economic life, recreation, education, religious observances, were all a matter of intimate association among a small group of life-long relatives and friends. While the pressures to conformity were overwhelming, the individual nevertheless controlled his fate in ways denied to modern man.

He, in his family, owned or had equity in his own land and tools of production. He was not swept hither and thither by the vagaries of a market economy. Many of the important economic and political issues were local ones, and he could directly affect their development. In this isolated world, social action did not ramify out in unanticipated ways to produce incalculable results. There was an obvious and close relationship between social cause and effect, reward and punishment. As one moved from childhood into adolescence, courtship, and marriage, and the assumption of adult responsibilities, the blueprint for behavior was stable, consistent, unquestioned. Finally, the individual possessed a single status in all of the intimate groups of which he was an important part.

Over against this description—made extreme for the sake of contrast—of the traditional family, another can be placed: the modern, secular, individualized conjugal unit, composed of a restricted unit of husband, wife, and one or two offspring, living in an urban apartment. It finds itself in an impersonal world, in which personal relationships are scattered, partial, specialized. The old familial functions are no longer home-centered: the husband works away from home, among strangers; the children are educated outside the home by hired specialists; religious observances have waned; and each member of the family goes his own way in seeking recreation, which is today highly specialized for each age group.

Rights and duties are no longer rigidly defined. The demands of shifting and specialized groups with which the individual is associated in home, office, social and professional contacts, require specialized conformities, and not the total personality, but different parts of it, are involved. Emotional security has diminished. The roles assigned the person at different stages in his life history within the family are inconsistent and contradictory; similarly, one's status ebbs and flows as one moves rapidly from one association to another, one career situation to another. Under the impact of the competing needs and value of the various individuals in the unit, the family's solidarity is destroyed, leaving in its wake dissatisfaction, frustration, and intra-familial conflict.

. . . . .

What does this mean psychologically? Since the family is no longer empowered to make plans and decisions and direct its own operations to anywhere near the extent that once was possible, the *individuals* who make it up are pushed and pulled by forces of which they are only dimly aware, and which they can neither control nor stop. A new technological development, a bank failure in Austria, an unidentifiable bureaucrat's decision, the rise to power of a fanatic across the Atlantic, any and all of these may blast and ruin. And all the individual citizen can do is read about it. The concrete world of reality in which he, his family, his associates operated becomes less real than the "paper world" which informs him what "they" are doing, what "they" are planning, what decisions "they" have made, what new scientific discoveries "they" have blessed him with.

Can the laborer find out whether his union leaders are taking him out on strike only to secure a higher wage for him, as they may claim, instead of political advantage for themselves? Can the citizen actually find out what is going on in one of the federal agencies, or the stockholder how the affairs of "his" corporations are being administered? How much control does the voter have over either of the two political machines he has the political right to help into office? As bureaucracy extends, power and responsibility become more and more hidden, with greater possibilities of setting off forces that will ramify out to change, disrupt, control, and manipulate individual lives. The average American scorns the average German's plea that he had no responsibility for the concentration camps, but the average American knows that *he* had nothing to do with the development of the atomic bomb. And, indeed, he did not.

The individual finds himself in a world in which personal and business ethics increasingly go by the board as personal long-range planning becomes more difficult, and life-long residence in one location is no longer the pattern. It is a world of insecurity and uncertainty, blaring headlines and sudden shocks, in which the accumulation of experience is insufficient preparation for the next, unforeseen stimulus. And meanwhile a tremendous discharge of nervous energy runs into a hundred deviant channels. Bitterness, despondency, dependency spread like a pall, along with the belief that all is chance. We are still oriented, in terms of thought pattern and emotional pattern, to the slow, stable rhythms of family life on the farm. But the structure that created this basic ideology of living is gone.

. . . . . .

We have already spoken of the confusion of statuses in the new way of life. At one time, status, taken over from the family, was relatively fixed and definitive. Today, the person interacts within a plethora of groups, and will be accorded a *different* status as he steps from one to another: the moral religious adolescent may be praised at home and vilified in school; the liberal may be appreciated by his college professor and scoffed at later by his business associates. Under the dispensation of modern success-striving, social approbation and a sense of security must be constantly reaffirmed, and this pressure is aggravated by the fact that one is really not in control of one's economic fortunes, the chief determinant of status. Thus it happens that anxiety and conviction of personal failure are endemic in our society.

. . . . . .

The psychological pressures thus created impinge directly upon the life of the family, since they divert energy, time, and talent away from the home. And the new economic order, with its demands for rationality, its dividing-up of the personality, its schooling of impulses, combined with the constant threat of sheer job-insecurity as well as ultimate failure, places a tremendous emotional overload on the modern family. Within it love-relationships must compensate for all the shocks, frustrations, and damming up of impulse that success-striving demands.

The function of "love" in modern society is peculiarly complex. With the partial disintegration of the rural-familistic system, the actual day-by-day involvement of personal relations—both in work and play—disappeared, and the improvisation and demonstration of a total *emotional* involvement became doubly important as an ideal. The emphasis on such emotional involvement was stepped up as codes of proper conduct with various kinds of persons became increasingly vague. When the behavior of husband and wife, for example, became more and more a matter to be settled in each marriage, rather than by reference to convention, the answer of the culture was to jazz up the tempo of romantic love.

The concept of romantic love rests on a myth. Two young persons arrive at an indeterminate age, meet, and a mysterious cosmic process informs each that this is the "one." They marry, and live happily ever after, constantly fulfilling in every act their *unique* relationship. Marriage becomes, then, not so much an institutional arrangement as a device by which each can secure his or her *individual* desire for personal happiness. Sadly enough, the very fact of basing marriage on romance operates to create a well-nigh universal frustration of the prized sentiment.

In the first place, romantic love is a highly stylized drama that demands some modicum of natural physical endowment and fitting surroundings. But the majority of men are not handsome, the majority of women are not beautiful, and the majority of both are poor. Frustration is inevitable.

Second, success and love, particularly for that segment of the population known as the "middle class," work at cross-purposes. Marriage is still the woman's chief career. The middle-class girl hopes to marry not only a man but a bank balance, so that she may combine the two major goals of her career in a single activity—courtship. But when a man is striving toward success, early marriage seriously interferes with his career. In the rural-familistic system a man's wife was a necessary adjunct to his economic activity; today, a wife is an unproductive luxury that an ambitious young man cannot afford. He needs time, energy, and his available funds for education and to get started in his individual career, a career that is no longer integrated with family life. Thus, at the very time when the culture demands the intensive idealization of courtship, the stage is set for a battle of the sexes, often involving sexual exploitation, in a context of what Dr. Willard Waller has called "pluralistic ignorance of each other's motives," where pre-marital relations are no longer supervised closely by family and community.

Third, the romantic concept of love in marriage must carry a tremendous overload of emotion engendered through success-striving. With marriage less "practical," there tends to arise a constant questioning of the extent to which one is receiving the expected emotional service: a ceaseless seeking-out of the other's motivations, with the feeling of betrayal if the other does not conform to expectations. . . .

Fourth, while romantic love appears to be needed in modern society in order to get people married, serving as an emotional drive that smashes past individualistic considerations of success, it cannot be depended upon to keep a marriage together through the years. The family remains, in however truncated a form, an *institution* with a certain minimum of obligations that must be met in a certain way regardless of the present emotional tone of relations between husband and wife. The tragedy of love, as Somerset Maugham has so honestly observed, is that it does not last. Marriage, as sexual-emotional interaction, in time inevitably seeks a lower level of habitual expression, and the aging mate no longer fulfills the romantic ideal. Sociologists in the field of marriage and the family have been somewhat dishonest in this regard, writing confidently of "another kind of love" which replaces the erotic euphoria of the honeymoon. Perhaps there is such a love, but it most certainly is not the kind of love that moderns have been specifically conditioned to expect in their marriage—an effortless, timeless ecstasy. And so we have the phenomenon of "romantic divorce"—if this other person no longer fits the romantic ideal, I will retain my ideal intact, and seek another love-object. That the same failure will only be repeated with another partner is not considered, and so, in 1946, there was one divorce for every three marriages.

It is questionable whether the new freedom in marriage has appreciably raised the general level of happiness. In most cultures, and in our own historical perspective, people have not married for individual happiness or the development of their personalities, but to form a necessary basic economic unit, and the necessity of maintaining it was as unquestioned as it was unquestionable.

Interestingly enough, various schools of psychotherapy have recently been soft-pedalling the neo-Freudian injunction to allow children to develop their egos without restriction, in favor of pointing out the valuable psychological security that can derive from a child's knowledge of absolute limits to "freedom." A similar formulation has yet to be devised for the child's parents. Paradoxically, "freedom" for the individual has value, or even meaning, only in terms of some indeterminate authoritarian framework. The divorce rate does not begin to measure the amount of dissatisfaction, the wistful longing for escape, that is generated by the mere knowledge that the back door of divorce is swinging wider. (No advocacy of restricting divorce legislation is implied here. To do so would be to mistake effect for cause.) It may be that the Victorian, with all his "repressions," had the better of the argument. His marriage and family were buttressed by a no-nonsense set of community, family, and religious exactions. He was not at the same time forced to uphold an institution and impelled to "develop his own personality," i.e., fulfill individualistic cravings at the expense of that institutional structure.

Mental health or emotional stability (the term used is not a critical matter, being imprecise in any case) in a sociological framework, depends upon a continuity of conditioning and group-expectation: either personal roles, goals, and self-conceptions remain fairly uniform throughout the life-history, or undergo a series of easy transpositions. The typical modern family, which contains the majority of the population and embodies the dominant social trends, rips that continuity to shreds.

Let us consider what happens in such a family—let us say, a family of the Protestant, urban, college-educated, lower-middle income group. (The training of children born to parents who can thus be characterized is so consistent as to permit prediction, in a certain range.)

The father's primary goal is success; yet he cannot use his *child* to this end. The child, far from being an economic asset as he was under rural-familistic conditions, has become a serious liability: the sheer dollar-outlay for medical care, diets, lengthening schooling, etc., represents a diversion of energy as well as funds at the very time when the father's career is in its early, and crucial, stages. This is made more painful by the feeling that the child will in all probability never contribute to his father's support.

The child also interferes with pleasures. Modern recreation is no longer designed for family-wide participation: rather, whether in the form of movies, sports events, plays, golf, bridge, tennis, dinner parties, it is designed for individual or couple participation.

And what is the role of so-called scientific child care in this complex? The child must not be spanked, parents must be patient, the child's ego development must not be curbed. The assumption of much of the literature on child rearing seems to be that the parents have a combined culinary, nursing, and psychiatric function, and nothing more. But note that in a commercial, industrial, specialized job-world, cooks, nurses, and psychiatrists are paid for what they do.

In other words, the father's duties and obligations constantly increase, while his rights diminish. An ambivalence toward his child emerges, which is more or less widespread, though very rarely admitted, even to confidants.

The child's mother also feels somewhat ambivalent toward him. Nutured on the romantic concept of love, possessing a success-drive only slightly less intensive than her husband's, having embarked upon a career of her own prior to marriage, or at least dallied in fantasy with the idea of a career, she is left ill-fitted for the drudgery of housecleaning, child care, and the preparation of meals. The freedom that modern household conveniences have brought her has been commonly misinterpreted as well as exaggerated. While the housewife in the past had more work to do, that work was part of a well-integrated system of household and community activities. The modern housewife, with more leisure time, still must work at a number of household tasks for which she has not been trained, for which she has no respect, and which are isolated from her social activities.

Having little to do, in or out of the home, she is her child's constant companion. So-called scientific child care enforces a ubiquitous supervision and diffused worrying over the child's health, diet, and ego development; this is complicated by the expenditure of much energy aimed at forcing early walking, toilet-training, talking, because in an intensively competitive milieu the parents are constantly comparing their own child's development with that of the neighbor's children.

Under constant supervision, with limited play area in a house touching other homes on all sides, or in an apartment, and lacking companions, the child's physiological expansiveness, fed by his boredom, persists in getting him into trouble. Similar behavior was not so likely to occur in the rural-familistic household, and even when it did, it did not constitute so much of a crisis.

Already the parents have made "love" of supreme importance in their relation to their child, theirs for him and his for them, partly because of the love complex of our time, and partly as a compensation for the many sacrifices they have made for the child, long debated before and after its arrival. The child, in turn, comes to need love desperately, precisely because he has been conditioned to need it. Now, the more ambivalent the parents are towards the child, the more seriously is the "trouble" he causes them interpreted. He should not act in such a way because of the sacrifices they have made on his behalf, and the least he can do is show his gratitude by "loving" them in turn, i.e., keeping out of "trouble." When the trouble inevitably occurs, the most effective punishment imaginable is the threat to withdraw love from him. To the extent that the child's personality has been absorbed and blanketed by lack of companionship other than with his parents, he will be thrown into a panic, and will develop guilt feelings to help keep him from getting into further trouble.

But obedience and propitiation are not enough. The modern child, particularly the boy, having tried to escape from anxiety and guilt by blind obedience and "love" for his parents, finds he cannot stabilize his relationships with others on that basis. His play group, which may be denied him until he has reached school age, makes him feel a certain shame and inadequacy in approaching its members with his accustomed techniques. He also discovers that he is involved in competition with others—as an individual with his contemporaries, and as a representative of his family unit with other families. Before he has developed a real self-awareness he becomes part of a process of invidious comparison with other families.

But effective competition demands a certain degree of independence, firmness of purpose, perhaps aggressiveness. His earliest conditioning was toward obedience, dependence, and love, and he is still expected to exhibit these virtues within the home, but he must "do things" outside the home. In the case of the boy, the father, as the representative of the outside male world, makes this demand uncompromisingly—this, incidentally, may be one of the unsuspected sources of the so-called Oedipus complex. In any event, contradictory demands are made on the child, and an integration of the conflicting roles is virtually impossible. Thus is laid the basis for so many self-blocking drives in modern society, and the widespread feeling of frustration and inadequacy.

In the earlier years, the girl's training tends to be not so traumatic as the boy's. Girls are still for the most part being prepared for marriage as an ultimate goal. Girls are not subjected to so much familial pressure to assume early roles of independent, aggressive action. For both sexes, however, but perhaps especially in the case of the boy, adolescence is a period of "storm and stress," not so much because of the biological changes taking place at that period, but rather because the parents received their basic life-orientation as children in a milieu that was radically different from the one the modern adolescent encounters outside the home. Thus the parents attempt to impose on the child a life-organization that is out of gear with the adolescent's outside experience. Also, the period of dependence upon parents is steadily lengthening.

The adolescent of either sex must defer sexual satisfaction and the assumption of responsible adult activities until long after the period when he is biologically and intellectually (if not emotionally) mature. This is complicated by the fact that the culture has not worked out guides for the gradual relinquishment of parental authority over children, so that a conflict tends to arise: the parents attempting to lengthen the period of parental authority, the adolescent attempting to cut it short. Since the job world has no place for the adolescent, the age at marriage is on the average increasing,[1] he must fight out the battle on minor personal issues, such as when he must get home from the dance, the use of the family automobile, the right to "express" himself. Postponement of adult roles slows the process of emotional maturity, and represents malpreparation for marriage.

The girl's childhood may not be beset by so many contradictory familial demands as the boy's, but as she grows older, the inchoate values of "female emancipation" involve her. Perhaps she won't get married. There is always the possibility of a career. In any event, she also has been caught up in the new values of individualism and success and is no longer willing to accept the subordinate role in marriage that once was unchallenged. If marriage can be used to secure a high standard of living, she "succeeds," otherwise she may be assailed by doubts. The writer has traced, in case records taken over a period of years in a university psychological clinic, the educated woman's reluctance to accept *any* marriage as a way out.

A new role is emerging for the woman in marriage, the role of equal partner, which is more acceptable to her than the traditional housewife-and-mother role. Yet, despite the growing tendency to regard marriage not as an institutional complex but as an opportunity to get something for herself, to fulfill the romantic ideal, to develop her own personality, there remains a widespread reluctance to renounce the protection and security of the older role. At the same time the bearing of children, and the domestic service performed for the husband, are unacceptable. And her husband hardly simplifies her problem. He was raised in a home which had its chronological setting two decades ago, but centuries ago in terms of social change. His recollection of his own father's role is strikingly patriarchal compared to his wife's expectations of him. He is not ready to forego the rights accruing to the patriarch though

---

[1] Editors' Note: The author's statement concerning the average age at marriage is in error, but this does not deny the major theme.

he may be perfectly willing that his wife work, assume equal responsibility in making decisions, manage family finances. And so the stage is set for a conflict of expectations.

. . . . .

It is questionable that moral exhortation will change this whole picture. Family stability in the modern world (as Lewis M. Terman thoroughly demonstrated in his *Psychological Factors in Marital Happiness,* 1939), as well as individual adjustment within it, are dependent upon the preservation of older patterns, since no new bases for the family have taken their place. At the same time, the socio-economic structure which was the underpinning of the older values has been too greatly modified to support an effective demand that a generation of vipers cease chasing its strange new gods. We may well have to reconcile ourselves to the fact that we will have to live, for some time to come, in a society increasingly made up of persons subjected to the process we have described. . . .

103. NAGASAKI'S MAGIC MOUNTAIN *

NORMAN COUSINS

Is war the most pressing social problem of our time? Many would assert that it is because of the nature of modern weapons. According to the available military and scientific information, an "annihilation" raid on any country is now possible with existing hydrogen bombs and ballistic missiles. A single such raid on America would mean immediate death for up to thirty million people and almost complete destruction of all our major production, communication, distribution, government, and health care centers. Thus, it seems reasonable to predict, the secondary results of the annihilation raid would be mass anarchy and chaos. It is harsh facts such as these that Norman Cousins tries to convey to us, indirectly, in his discussion of Nagasaki. The implication would seem to be this: If international tensions are not soon resolved, then "Nagasaki" (but usually without a magic mountain) will be the name of all of our towns. If, in contemplating the potential holocaust, we decide to strike first, most of us would also die—from a lingering radiation illness, since the entire atmosphere would be poisoned by any

* From *Saturday Review,* Vol. 36, No. 2 (January 9, 1954), 22–24.
For a biographical sketch of the author see selection 35.

*raid strong enough to keep "the enemy" from retaliating. The
belief that fear of such dangers will prevent war, or, at the very
least, encourage belligerents to refrain from using atomic
weapons, is unverifiable. Localized conflicts can involve the
major powers. Once such a conflict begins, the belligerents
cannot be expected to "wait and see" if an opponent is going to
use the hydrogen bomb (or, perhaps, the cobalt bomb combined
with deadly bacteria); if they wait, it may be too late to marshal
any resistance at all. Try to keep these points in mind, however
unpleasant they may be, when you read about the Nagasaki
raid—a raid which, though it resulted in more than a hundred
thousand casualties, was as nothing compared with what could be
done with a few of the many nuclear weapons now being
stockpiled.*

Fumiko Narahara is a seamstress in Nagasaki. When the bomb fell
eight years ago she had just turned fifteen. She is alive today because of
Nagasaki's magic mountain. And so are at least seventy-five thousand of
her fellow citizens who happened to be on the right side of the mountain
on August 9, 1945.

It isn't much of a mountain. More precisely, it is a ridge, a high
and uneven lump of land jutting into the heart of the city. The ridge
falls away quickly where it approaches the sea. A road skirts the shore
and connects a network of streets on both sides of the mountain. The
far or Urakami side of the mountain is where most of the heavy industry used to be located. It is also a densely populated area. For the people
of Nagasaki today all life is reckoned according to the side of the mountain you were on when the bomb fell. The bomb fell low enough for
the mountain to contain the radioactive ball of fire to the Urakami
valley. If you were on the right side of the mountain you felt the shock
—but you lived.

On the morning of August 9, 1945, Fumiko Narahara was at the
home of her aunt on the right side of the mountain. The aunt had been
ill and Fumiko's mother had sent the girl to care for her. Fumiko's
mother was unable to come because she was employed. Fumiko's father
worked at the iron smelting plant on the wrong side of the mountain,
where the Narahara home was also located.

At two minutes past eleven the explosion occurred. The aunt's
home shook at the impact and the windows were smashed. But the house
itself remained erect; it was not touched by the ball of fire that mushroomed through the Urakami valley, consuming seventy thousand lives
and severely burning fifty thousand others. When Fumiko rushed outside her aunt's home she saw that the houses nearby were all right; but
beyond the mountain the city was a vast furnace. The Narahara home

was inside the furnace. So was the weaver's shop where her mother worked. So was the foundry where her father worked.

Fumiko was one of many thousands of survivors who experienced the agonizing wait of endless days on the fringe of the furnace until the fires died down. When, finally, she was able to go around the mountain she took the road skirting the shore and passed the foundry, now a charred skeleton. But the road ended at about that point. Beyond that were no streets, no landmarks, no homes. There was not even a city. There were only acres of smoking black rubble. Except for a vague idea where her home had been Fumiko had no way of identifying the site. The bodies of her mother, father, and two smaller brothers were not recovered from any of the ruins.

For the first few years after the bomb Fumiko lived with a deep sense of guilt for having survived. She says now that whenever she took the shore road to Urakami in the early days she hated herself for not having been in Urakami with the others. This feeling was not hers alone. There were many who had homes on the far side of the mountain but who were outside the valley on the day of the bomb, leaving their wives or husbands or children behind. Like Fumiko, they felt cut off from their real selves, unable to understand why they should have been spared. But with the passing of the years the guilt feeling has tended to lose its heaviness, returning only now and then when something special happens, like a medical examination by doctors assigned to study the effects of the bombing, or a propaganda movie put out by people who are trying to stir up passions against America.

Fumiko says she no longer hates the mountain for having spared her. She no longer cringes when she hears people refer to the mountain as a blessing. For she knows the good the magic mountain has done for Nagasaki. Unlike Hiroshima, which suffered almost total devastation within one mile of the center of the bomb and severe fire damage beyond that, Nagasaki's death toll and damage was largely confined to one section of the city. Consequently, in the emergency period after the bomb the city could mobilize some of its own medical and hospital facilities from the undamaged part that remained. And, though the bomb was a more powerful type than the one that fell on Hiroshima, there were fewer casualties, thanks not only to the magic mountain but to the early care of many of the victims.

Today the Urakami valley of Nagasaki has been almost completely rebuilt. Some of the scars remain. The old iron and steel works is still in its charred skeletal state. And on the beginning of the ridge, only a few hundred yards from the center of the explosion, is the empty shell of the Church of Urakami, once the largest Catholic cathedral in the Orient, with a capacity of almost 9,000. A temporary church has been built alongside the old one; there is the hope that someday soon the means may be forthcoming to put up a new cathedral every bit as magnificent as the old.

At what is believed to be the center of the explosion a memorial park has been laid out, with a high tower in the center and appropriate exhibits at various spots, such as a crumpled steel girder or slate that had melted and fused again. A small museum facing the tower contains some notable mementoes of the bombing, such as a grandfather's clock that was stopped by the bomb at exactly two minutes past eleven. The clock was in a home at the end of the valley some six miles from the center of the explosion. The city plans to erect a large cultural center around a mammoth statue dedicated to the peace, on the present site of the memorial. This, too, awaits necessary funds.

. . . . .

There are still some inner scars. As more and more is known about the period immediately preceding the end of the war the feeling has grown that the bomb may not have been as essential to ending the war as at first was widely believed. The memoirs of Secretary Stimson, Secretary Forrestal, and General Eisenhower have thrown a new light on the decision to drop the bomb. On August 9, three days after the Hiroshima bomb, there was no doubt about the fact that Japan would surrender. The only doubt concerned the circumstances of the surrender. America wanted no discussion about terms or anything else. We wanted absolute surrender and we wanted it within a matter of hours, and the bomb of Nagasaki was designed to achieve just that, which it did.

But today, as we prod Japan to become a mighty military nation again, there are people in Nagasaki who cannot convince themselves that seventy thousand of their number died because there was a good reason for it, or because there was no other way. At a college not very far from the new memorial park a young instructor put it to me succinctly during a small open forum following my talk.

"History now knows," he said, "that Japan asked for peace terms even before Hiroshima was bombed. And history knows that Japan was certainly ready to surrender after Hiroshima. But the Americans were afraid perhaps that Japan would not want to give up as much as you wanted her to give up in defeat. So you used the atomic bomb for the second time on Nagasaki and you got what you wanted. You said that what you wanted was a Japan which would completely destroy its military machine and the spirit of militarism and nationalism which built it. We agreed. You tore down our armaments plants, and you dumped all our munitions and weapons into the sea, and you put our military leaders in jail, and you wrote new textbooks for us in which you denounced militarism and war, and you helped us to write a new Constitution in which we said we would never arm or fight again.

"But now you are telling us that it was all a big mistake. You tell us that it was a mistake to get rid of the military machine, a mistake to say all those terrible things about our militarists and nationalists, a mistake to have written that clause in our Constitution against war and the means of war.

"Very well. If we are to believe you now what are we to think of the bombing of Nagasaki and the seventy thousand who died here? If the reason for your bombing of Nagasaki was to get Japan to agree to do the very things you now say was a mistake, then you can only mean that you acknowledge that the bombing of Nagasaki was a mistake, too. And a mistake such as this is not something that passes easily. We are talking now about an atomic explosion over a living city and about what happened to the people who are inside it. Some people say that one way to die is as bad as another, and that death by atomic bomb is no worse than death by any other means. But what about the people who were not quite killed? We had many thousands of them, people with atomic disease who died very slowly over a long period of time. We had thousands of children with new kinds of scars and burns that have not yet been treated adequately—even now, eight years after the bomb. Should I say to them that your policy about Japan has now changed, that the bomb wasn't really necessary after all, and that therefore there is no real reason for their burns?

"I am no Communist, although there are many Communists who hate America and are doing everything possible to make you look ridiculous because you don't seem to know what you want in the world or where you're going. I don't side with the Communists, because where they say they are going is all wrong, and it will be a bad thing for Japan if we become a totalitarian nation again, whether Communist or militarist. But it is true that you can't expect people to follow America when you make so many big mistakes. How do we know that what you are telling us now will not turn out to be another mistake that you will admit a few years from now after even more damage is done?

"When you go back to America I wish you would tell the American people that it's not what the Communists are saying about you that is what is really hurting you. The main thing that is hurting you is that you never sit still long enough to think deeply before you do something. You change from day to day, and no one on the outside ever really knows who speaks for your country. We know that at heart you are all right but we aren't sure you know enough about the people outside America whom you expect to follow you. You have so much power and so little purpose. We'd like to follow you but it's not easy when you make so many strange turns and when you seem to be more afraid of yourself than of the power you identify as your enemy.

"You have probably visited the office of the Atomic Bomb Casualty

Commission in Nagasaki, where American doctors examine Japanese who survived the explosion. They are wonderful men, these doctors, and they have made many friends among the Japanese people, for they have done things as individuals which their official jobs try to discourage them from doing. I am talking about the fact that these doctors are not officially able to do anything but examine the people here. They are not allowed to treat the Japanese they examine, by American law. But as individuals they have done a great deal to help us and we are grateful to the United States for sending them.

"But what puzzles many Japanese every time we pass the ABCC is this: now that America knows all the terrible things that happen to people during an atomic explosion, what new ideas do you have to do away with atomic explosions altogether—on us, on you, or on anyone else?"

104. ENCOUNTERS BETWEEN CIVILIZATIONS *

ARNOLD J. TOYNBEE

*A certain professor of sociology sometimes takes his classes
on an airplane ride over the city so they may see the general
ecological pattern of the city. From such a vantage point one
gets a special perspective. Details become smaller and often
obscured, but relationships between larger elements stand out.
In this article, historian Arnold Toynbee takes us up above
the confining horizon of our own time and culture and reveals
to us a great panorama of societal interaction. We see civilizations
growing, blending, and dying. We see our own culture as it is
related to this larger pattern. Some aspects of our civilization
take on greater significance while others shrink in proportion.
Ethnocentric attitudes and interpretations seem less reasonable.
Cultural variability, diffusion, and borrowing become
more meaningful concepts.*

* *Harper's Magazine*, Vol. 194 (April, 1947), 289–294. Reprinted by permission of the author.

The author (b. 1889) is a British historian and economist. He is Professor Emeritus of History, University of London. Onetime Director of Studies, Royal Institute of International Affairs; Editor, British Commonwealth Relations; lectured in the United States. Author: *A Journey to China; Study of History* (10 vols.); *Civilization on Trial; A Survey of International Affairs; War and Civilization; The World and the West; An Historian's Approach to Religion.*

What will be singled out as the salient event of our time by future historians, centuries hence, looking back on the first half of the twentieth century and trying to see its activities and experiences in that just proportion which the time-perspective sometimes reveals? Not, I fancy, any of those sensational or tragic or catastrophic political and economic events which occupy the headlines of our newspapers and the foregrounds of our minds; not wars, revolutions, massacres, deportations, famines, gluts, slumps, or booms, but something of which we are only half-conscious, and out of which it would be difficult to make a headline. The things that make good headlines attract our attention because they are on the surface of the stream of life, and they distract our attention from the slower, impalpable, imponderable movements that work below the surface and penetrate to the depths. But of course it is really these deeper, slower movements that, in the end, make history, and it is they that stand out huge in retrospect, when the sensational passing events have dwindled, in perspective, to their true proportions.

Mental perspective, like optical perspective, comes into focus only when the observer has put a certain distance between himself and his object. When, for example, you are traveling by air from Salt Lake City to Denver, the nearest view of the Rockies is not the best one. While you are actually over the mountains, you see nothing but a maze of peaks, ridges, gullies, and crags. It is not until you have left the mountains behind you and are looking back at them as you fly over the plains that they rise up before you in their magnificent order, range behind range. It is only then that you have a vision of the Rockies themselves.

With this vision in my mind, I believe that future historians will be able to see our age in better proportion than we can. What are they likely to say about it?

Future historians will say, I think, that the great event of the twentieth century was the impact of the Western Civilization upon all the other living societies of the world of that day. They will say of this impact that it was so powerful and so pervasive that it turned the lives of all its victims upside down and inside out—affecting the behavior, outlook, feelings, and beliefs of individual men, women, and children in an intimate way, touching chords in human souls that are not touched by mere external material forces—however ponderous and terrifying This will be said, I feel sure, by historians looking back on our times even from as short a time hence as A.D. 2047.

What will the historians of A.D. 3047 say? If we had been living a century ago, I should have had to apologize for the fantastic conceit of pretending to speculate about anything that might be said or done at so immensely remote a date. Eleven hundred years was a very long time for people who believed that the world had been created in 4004 B.C.

But I need not apologize today; for, since our great-grandfathers' time, there has been so great a revolution in our time scale that, if I were to try to plot out to scale, on one of these pages, a chart of the history of this planet since its birth, I should not be able to make so short a period as eleven hundred years visible to the naked eye.

The historians of A.D. 3047, then, may have something far more interesting than those of A.D. 2047 to say, because they, by their time, may know much more of the story of which we, today, are perhaps in a rather early chapter. The historians of A.D. 3047 will, I believe, be chiefly interested in the tremendous countereffects which, by that time, the victims will have produced in the life of the aggressor. By A.D. 3047, our Western Civilization, as we and our Western predecessors have known it, say, for the last twelve or thirteen hundred years, since its emergence out of the Dark Ages, may have been transformed, almost out of all recognition, by a counterradiation of influences from the foreign worlds which we, in our day, are in the act of engulfing in ours—influences from Orthodox Christendom, from Islam, from Hinduism, from the Far East.

By A.D. 4047 the distinction—which looms large today—between the Western Civilization, as an aggressor, and the other civilizations, as its victims, will probably seem unimportant. When radiation has been followed by counterradiation of influences, what will stand out will be a single great experience, common to the whole of mankind: the experience of having one's parochial social heritage battered to bits by collision with the parochial heritages of other civilizations, and then finding a new life—a new common life—springing up out of the wreckage. The historians of A.D. 4047 will say that the impact of the Western Civilization on its contemporaries, in the second half of the second millennium of the Christian Era, was the epoch-making event of that age because it was the first step toward the unification of mankind into one single society. By their time, the unity of mankind will perhaps have come to seem one of the fundamental conditions of human life—just part of the order of nature—and it may need quite an effort of imagination on their part to recall the parochial outlook of the pioneers of civilization during the first six thousand years or so of its existence. Those Athenians, whose capital city was no more than a day's walk from the farthest frontiers of their country, and those American contemporaries—or virtual contemporaries—of theirs, whose country you could fly across from sea to sea in sixteen hours—how could they behave (as we know they did behave) as if their own little country were the universe?

And the historians of A.D. 5047? The historians of A.D. 5047 will say, I fancy, that the importance of this social unification of mankind was not to be found in the field of technics and economics, and not in the field of war and politics, but in the field of religion.

II

Why do I venture on these prophecies about how the history of our own time will appear to people looking back at it several thousand years hence? Because we have about six thousand years of past history to judge by, since the first emergence of human societies of the species we call "civilizations."

Six thousand years is an almost infinitesimally short time compared to the age of the human race, of mammals, of life on earth, of the planetary system round our sun, of the sun itself, and of the star-cluster of which our sun is a not particularly conspicuous member. Still, for our present purpose, these last six thousand years—brief though they are—do provide us with other examples of the phenomenon we are studying—examples of encounters between different civilizations. In relation to some of these cases, we ourselves, in our day, are already enjoying the advantage—which the historians living in A.D. 3047 or 4047 are going to have in looking back at us—of knowing the whole story. It is with some of these past encounters in mind that I have been speculating on how our own encounter with our own contemporaries is likely to turn out.

Take the history of one of our predecessors, the Græco-Roman civilization, and consider how this looks to us in the fairly distant perspective in which we are now able to see it:

As a result of the conquests of Alexander the Great and of the Romans, the Græco-Roman civilization radiated over most of the old world—into India, into the British Isles, and even as far as China and Scandinavia. The only civilizations of that day which remained untouched by its influence were those of Mexico and Peru, so that its expansion was not incomparable to our own in extent and vigor. When we look back on the history of the Græco-Roman World during the last four centuries B.C., it is this great movement of expansion and penetration that stands out now. The wars, revolutions, and economic crises that ruffled the surface of Græco-Roman history during those centuries, and occupied so much of the attention of the men and women who were struggling to live through them, do not mean much to us now compared with that great tide of Greek cultural influence invading Asia Minor, Syria, Egypt, Babylonia, Persia, India, China.

But why does the Græco-Roman impact on these other civilizations matter to us now? Because of the counterattack of these other civilizations on the Græco-Roman World.

This counterattack was partly delivered in the same style as the original Græco-Roman attack: that is, by force of arms. But we are not much interested today in the forlorn hope of Jewish armed resistence to Greek and Roman imperialism in Palestine; or in the successful counterattack of the Parthians and their Persian successors under the Sassanian Dynasty east of the Euphrates; or in the sensational victories of the early Muslim Arabs, who in the seventh century of the Christian era liberated the Middle East from Græco-Roman rule in as short a number of years as it had taken Alexander the Great to conquer it a thousand years earlier.

But there was another counterattack, a non-violent one, a spiritual one, which attacked and conquered, not fortresses and provinces, but hearts and minds. This attack was delivered by the missionaries of new religions which had arisen in the worlds which the Græco-Roman civilization had attacked by force and submerged. The prince of these missionaries was Saint Paul, who, starting from Antioch, made the audacious march on Macedonia, Greece, and Rome which King Antiochus the Great had once attempted unsuccessfully. These religions were different in kind from the native religion of the Græco-Roman World. The gods of Græco-Roman paganism had been rooted in the soil of particular communities; they had been parochial and political: Athene Polias, Fortuna Praenestina, Dea Roma. The gods of the new religions that were making this non-violent counterattack on Greek and Roman hearts and minds had risen above their original local origins. They had become universal gods, with a message of salvation for all mankind, Jew and Gentile, Scythian and Greek. Or, to put this great historical event in religious terms, one might say that the One True God had taken this opportunity of the opening of men's minds through the collision and collapse of their old local traditions; He had taken advantage of this excruciating experience in order to illuminate these momentarily open minds with a fuller and truer vision of His nature and purpose than they had been capable of receiving before.

Take the two words "Jesus Christ," which are so very important for us, and which, we may venture to prophesy, will still be important for mankind two or three thousands years hence. These very words are witnesses to the encounter between a Græco-Roman civilization and a Syrian civilization out of which Christianity came to birth. "Jesus" is the third person singular of a Semitic verb; "Christ" is the passive participle of a Greek verb. The double name testifies that Christianity was born into this world from a marriage between those two cultures.

Consider the four higher religions, with a world-wide mission, which exist in the world today: Christianity, Islam, Hinduism, and the Mahayana form of Buddhism which prevails in the Far East. All four are, historically, products of the encounter between the Græco-Roman civilization and its contemporaries. Christianity and Islam arose as alternative responses of the Syrian World to Græco-Roman penetration: Christianity a non-violent response, Islam a violent one. Mahayanian Buddhism and Hinduism are the gentle and the violent responses of the Hindu World to the same Græco-Roman challenge.

Looking back on Græco-Roman history today, about thirteen hundred years after the date when the Græco-Roman civilization became extinct, we can see that, in this perspective, the most important thing in the history of the Græco-Roman World is its meeting with other civilizations; and these encounters are important, not for their immediate political and economic consequences, but for their long-term religious consequences. This Græco-Roman illustration, of which we know the whole story, also gives us some idea of the time-span of encounters between civilizations. The Græco-Roman World's impact upon other contemporary civilizations, which corresponds to the modern Western World's impact on its own contemporaries since the turn of the fifteenth and sixteenth centuries, started with the conquests of Alexander the Great in the fourth century B.C.; and the Middle Eastern World was still translating the classical works of Greek philosophy and science some five or six centuries after the liberation of the Middle East from Græco-Roman rule by the early Muslim Arabs in the seventh century of the Christian era. From the fourth century B.C. to the thirteenth century of the Christian era, it took the best part of sixteen hundred years for the encounter between the Græco-Roman civilization and its contemporaries to work itself out.

Now measure against that span of sixteen hundred years the duration, to date, of the encounter between our modern Western Civilization and its contemporaries. One may say that this encounter began with the Ottoman attack on the homelands of the Western Civilization and with the great Western voyages of discovery at the turn of the fifteenth and sixteenth centuries of our era. That makes only four-and-a-half centuries to the present.

Let us assume, if you like, that people's hearts and minds move rather faster nowadays (though I know of no evidence that the unconscious part of the human psyche ever greatly varies its pace)—even so, it looks as if we were still only in an early chapter of the story of our encounter with the civilizations of Mexico and Peru and Orthodox Christendom and Islam and the Hindu World and the Far East. We are just beginning to see some of the effects of our action on them, but we have hardly begun to see the effects—which will certainly be tremendous—of their coming counteraction upon us.

It is only in our generation that we have seen one of the first moves in this counteroffensive, and we have found it very disturbing; whether we have liked it or not, we have felt it to be momentous. I mean, of course, the move made by the offshoot of Orthodox Christendom in Russia. It is momentous and disturbing not because of the material power behind it. The Russians . . . have already shown (and this is the point) the power to convert Western souls to a non-Western "ideology."

The Russians have taken up a Western secular social philosophy, Marxism; you might equally well call Marxism a Christian heresy, a leaf torn out of the book of Christianity and treated as if it were the whole gospel. The Russians have taken up this Western heretical religion, transformed it into something of their own, and are now shooting it back at us. This is the first shot in the anti-Western counteroffensive; but this Russian counterdischarge in the form of Communism may come to seem a small affair when the probably far more potent civilizations of India and China respond in their turn to our Western challenge. In the long run India and China seem likely to produce much deeper effects on our Western life than Russia can ever hope to produce with her Communism. But even the comparatively feeble native civilization of Mexico is beginning to react. The revolution through which Mexico has been passing since A.D. 1910 may be interpreted as a first move to shake off the top-dressing of Western Civilization which we imposed on Mexico in the sixteenth century; and what is happening today in Mexico may happen tomorrow in the seats of the native civilization of South America: in Peru, Bolivia, Ecuador, and Colombia.

III

Before leaving off, I must say a word about one question which I have begged up to this point, and that is: what do we mean by a "civilization"? Clearly, we do mean something, for even before we have tried to define what our meaning is, this classification of human societies —the Western Civilization, the Islamic, the Far Eastern, the Hindu, and so on—does seem to make sense. These names do call up distinct pictures in our minds in terms of religion, architecture, painting, manners, and customs. Still, it is better to try to get closer to what we mean by a term which we have already been working so hard. I believe I do know what I mean by a civilization; at least, I am sure I know how I have arrived at my own idea of it.

I mean, by a civilization, the smallest unit of historical study at which one arrives when one tries to understand the history of one's own country: the United States, say, or the United Kingdom. If you were to try to understand the history of the United States by itself, it would be unintelligible: you could not understand the part played in American life by federal government, representative government, democracy, industrialism, monogamy, Christianity, unless you looked beyond the bounds of the United States—out beyond her frontiers to Western

Europe and the other overseas countries founded by West Europeans, and back beyond her local origins to the history of Western Europe in centuries before Columbus or Cabot had crossed the Atlantic. But, to make American history and institutions intelligible for practical purposes, you need not look beyond Western Europe into Eastern Europe or the Islamic World, nor behind the origins of our Western European civilization to the decline and fall of the Græco-Roman civilization. These limits of time and space give us the intelligible unit of social life of which the United States or Great Britain or France or Holland is a part: call it Western Christendom, Western Civilization, Western Society, the Western World. Similarly, if you start from Greece or Serbia or Russia, and try to understand their histories, you arrive at an Orthodox Christendom or Byzantine World. If you start from Morocco or Afghanistan, and try to understand their histories, you arrive at an Islamic World. Start from Bengal or Mysore or Rajputana, and you find a Hindu World. Start from China or Japan and you find a Far Eastern World.

While the state of which we happen to be citizens makes more concrete and more imperious claims on our allegiance, especially in the present age, the civilization of which we are members really counts for more in our lives. And this civilization of which we are members includes—at most stages in its history—the citizens of other states besides our own. It is older than our own state: the Western Civilization is about thirteen hundred years old, whereas the Kingdom of England is only one thousand years old, the United Kingdom of England and Scotland less than two hundred and fifty, the United States not more than one hundred and fifty. States are apt to have short lives and sudden deaths: the Western Civilization of which you and I are members may be alive centuries after the United Kingdom and the United States have disappeared from the political map of the world like their late contemporaries, the Republic of Venice and the Dual Monarchy of Austria-Hungary. This is one of the reasons why I have been asking you to look at history in terms of civilizations, and not in terms of states, and to think of states as rather subordinate and ephemeral political phenomena in the lives of the civilizations in whose bosoms they appear and disappear.

105. ILYA EHRENBURG'S AMERICA *

Translations of Six Articles Published in Izvestia

ILYA EHRENBURG

*Our journalists give us as much information as they can gather
about life in Russia. Here is some information about us given to the
Russian people by Ilya Ehrenburg, recently characterized as "the
foremost Soviet journalist." It is enlightening to see ourselves
and our institutions through the eyes of someone from a different
social milieu, especially from a social system so much at variance
with ours that its proponents show positive hostility to much that we
value. We may wince at the ridicule and resent the distortions that
at times amount to misrepresentation more monstrous than out-and-
out lies. But though the picture as a whole is out of focus, to the
extent that some of these unpleasant statements have a basis in
fact, we cannot do otherwise than acknowledge the criticisms as
valid.*

In my time I have traveled a good deal and have been all over
Europe. I sometimes thought I had lost the ability to be amazed. Upon
arriving in America I realized that there was much of which I had no
conception. Everything here is different—the cities, the trees, and the
customs. The summer here is very hot, but the heat is not European;
the air is damp, as in a hothouse. The olives here are larger than plums
and devoid of taste. People gesticulate more often with their legs than
with their arms, and in the theaters spectators who wish to show approval
whistle deafeningly.

Modernity cannot be understood without understanding America.
Hundreds of odes and pamphlets have been dedicated to her; she can
be exalted or ridiculed with ease. But this is not merely a peculiar
country, but also a diverse one, difficult to understand. It is hard to set
forth vivid, often contradictory, impressions in brief notes. Behind the

* Ilya Ehrenburg, *Harper's Magazine*, Vol. 193 (December, 1946), 562–576.
Reprinted by permission of the publisher.

The author (b. 1891) is a Russian novelist, poet, short-story writer; war corre-
spondent, U.S.S.R.; broadcasts from Moscow Radio. His books include *Out of Chaos;
Moscow Does Not Believe in Tears; The Love of Jeanne Ney; Russia at War; A
Street in Moscow; The Fall of Paris* (received Stalin Prize); *The Storm; The Ninth
Wave; The Thaw.*

complexity of technology there is sometimes concealed spiritual simplicity, and behind this simplicity—unexpected complexity.

I rate American literature very highly. It is not easy now to find writers in Western Europe equal to Hemingway, Faulkner, Steinbeck, or Caldwell. I might venture to add two or three more names. Right behind them is a vacuum—stories in illustrated weeklies which are so cheap and stupid that even the most unexacting readers in Europe would recoil from them. There is no intermediate literature here, just as there are no four- or five-story houses. The skyscrapers of New York are justified by geography: this is a huge city built on small islands. But in any provincial city one may see several skyscrapers surrounded by thousands of single-story houses.

At the railway station in Atlanta I was amazed by the automatic checking booths which have replaced the cloakroom. You insert a coin, receive a key, and can lock up your luggage yourself. I was about to say to my American companion, "You know how to make human existence easier," but before I could speak I noticed a dark, noisome room marked "For non-Whites" in which Negroes and mulattoes were dozing. In the state of Mississippi I saw the home of a plantation owner. It had a refrigerator, a washing machine, a marvelous radio, and wonderful ventilators. The planter calmly explained to me that black-skinned people aren't people at all. Neither the radio nor the ventilators had any reflection on the mental development of this slave-owner.

I stayed in several university towns. In America a great deal is done to elevate knowledge to its proper height. I saw superb libraries and laboratories: I saw scientists surrounded with attention. But in Tennessee professors told me they were not allowed the right to expound the theory of evolution in the schools: the law forbids any departure from the biblical myth of Adam and Eve.

In all American cities there are "lions'" clubs: I was fortunate enough to attend a luncheon at such a club in one town. Respectable business men assembled there, each one wearing a tag indicating the place and nature of his business; luncheons are closely associated with business. Before those present at the luncheon began to eat their compotes and mayonnaise and ham with raisins, the chairman banged the table with a wooden hammer and exclaimed: "Greetings, lions!" The middle-aged business men at once rose and chorused: "Woo-woo-woo-woo." I quailed, but they explained that they were imitating the lion's roar.

Naturally, the sound-imitations of dealers in suspenders are an innocent affair. There are worse ideas. A parade of the Ku Klux Klan recently took place in Georgia. The members of this supposedly secret society donned fools' hoods and took an oath of loyalty to the local fascist *führer,* whom they call the "Grand Dragon." They then swore to hang several Negroes and kill several freethinkers.

Everyone knows that in America money is surrounded with respect. Apart from many hundreds of registered churches and sects there is still another cult—the dollar. An art critic, after introducing a young artist to me, reeled off his surname and then, enunciating precisely, said, "Three thousand dollars." A master of ceremonies at a cabaret announced that eminent visitors were present: an actress, a senator, and a business man "who has tripled his capital turnover since the war." I attended many dinner meetings with a program much like this one: first, everybody quickly chews the chicken, then orators give lengthy speeches; then a female singer renders a sentimental ballad; and finally a pastor takes a collection for charity. He recites the names of the liberal donors: "Mr. Smith gave five hundred dollars." Everyone applauds and Mr. Smith rises and bows.

It is not well known that, along with brisk business men, there are also many naïve day-dreamers and noble idealists in America. I met a prominent inventor who renounced a fortune, fearing that the machine he invented would deprive hundreds of thousands of workers of their bread. I spoke to provincial Utopians who go without food and sleep, devoting their money and energy to the fantastic project of creating a "world government." In one town I found a circle of eccentrics who were convinced that they could render the atomic bomb harmless with the aid of Esperanto. Everywhere there are societies to protect the rights of Negroes. Every year innocent Negroes are condemned and put to death in the electric chair, and every year the best people in America protest against racial barbarism. Yes, the cult of the dollar does exist in America, but in America there are also people who deny themselves a pair of shoes and tickets to the cinema in order to send gifts to Yugoslav children.

There is much that is childish in Americans. They are not artificial; they are frank, curious, and noisy. The oldest part of America is called New England. Everything in America is new; everything is young. In New Orleans, however, houses built in the seventeenth and eighteenth centuries have been preserved in the French Quarter. Such houses are legion in Europe and are ignored by even the most painstaking tourists. But the "Old Quarter" of New Orleans is like Pompeii—a real center of pilgrimage. There is either an antique shop or a stylized tavern in almost every house. I was in New Orleans on a very sultry day (the tropics are not far off), and a fire was burning in the grate of one house —to re-create the atmosphere of a bygone epoch. Perspiring Americans were sitting by the fire drinking iced water; they wanted to spend several minutes in an *old* house. One must remember the age of the country to understand Americans.

People here like to wander about. If they are sitting in a room, they jump up from time to time and change seats; they move readily from city to city and from state to state. They regard a person who lives in the place where he was born as a rarity.

There is nothing more the reverse of the British character and customs than the character and customs of the average American. The Englishman is polite and phlegmatic; he loves to live out his life in the home of his grandfather; he orders his suit of first-quality material, expecting to wear it, if not until he dies, at least until the next elections. The American likes only new clothes. Hardly has he furnished his apartment than he is looking for another. He never has a suit made to order; why should he? In any shop he can find a cheap, well-made suit; can wear it a little and then throw it out. He will buy a shirt that is not worth washing. He respects old stones, but loves flashy new ties— and noise.

The history of the United States is indeed a new history. I might say, incidentally, that history studied by school children appears to vary in different states: in the North the Southerners are called "defenders of slavery," and in the South the Northerners are called "oppressors." Vexed issues here frequently hide the feeling of history. For the average American nearly a whole epoch passes between the morning and evening papers; he doesn't always remember in the evening exactly what disturbed him in the morning. One lady told me: "Don't read this novel. It's not a new one; it came out two years ago."

. . . . .

Anti-Soviet ideologists like to depict our country as a sort of barracks in which everyone is deprived of individuality. The Soviet reader will be amused by the surprise of some American editors who, on seeing us three visitors, said in amazement: "Why, they don't look much like one another."

As a matter of fact, I don't know of any country which has achieved such perfection in standardization as the United States. I was in dozens of American cities which were impossible to distinguish from each other. Every city has its Main Street—the principal street—with fashion shops, a cinema, and lighted signs advertising cigarettes or Coca-Cola. Not a single American can distinguish Main Street in one town from Main Street in one of a hundred others from a photograph. . . .

Trousers, percolators, and armchairs are standardized, too. I do not say this reproachfully, for Americans have succeeded in raising the material level of life, thanks to mass production. I think we can learn something from the Americans: how to turn out shoes or saucepans quickly and well. However, almost all luxury articles in America are imported and a salesman who wishes to explain why this or that is expensive says, "But this is *imported.*"

There is a certain depression in such uniformity: the same houses, the same furniture, the same crockery; men in identical suits, women in identical dresses. But still I do not agree with the European aesthetes who have ridiculed the standardization in America. Perhaps all the suits are alike; on the other hand, they are accessible to all.

Much more deplorable is a certain spiritual standardization. Americans are fond of speaking about their liberty; but their views, tastes, emotions, and consequent behavior are regulated from outside. The cinema, for instance, lays down the standard for beauty, and the papers supply all the details of the "ideally shaped" woman. This is the standard of desire. All American women are guided by these references in their efforts to resemble some film star, while men fall in love according to the same references without noticing it. There are no books with average circulation. Even the most remarkable book will not be circulated in more than several thousand copies unless it has been pronounced worth reading by some "book club," in which case it will be published in hundreds of thousands of copies. Since the average American does not like to choose, he entrusts the right to choose to his "club." The press and cinema de-personalize the ideas of people who stroll along thousands of Main Streets in the evening. This forms the key to the sense of depression which is linked with leisure in America.

Americans know very well how to earn money, but they have not yet learned to spend it. I do not mean that they are mean; they spend money swiftly and energetically—but without originality. They work with much greater talent than they amuse themselves. I would say that the gayest times in America are when townspeople meet nature; on the seashore, for instance, youth is full of *joie-de-vivre*. But in the cinema one is struck by their drowsiness and torpor, the rare laughter in response to the most humorous, or apparently humorous, situations.

There are many drunks, despite the fact that the sale of strong drink is restricted in one way or another in the majority of states. There are "dry" states, those in which whiskey is rationed, those in which liquor sales cannot be made on Sunday, and those in which one may drink sitting but not standing.

Automoblies in America are wonderful and numerous, and the average American loves a car. . . . I understand the love of Americans for cars. But I do not understand why some of them turn their car into a home. There are restaurants which one is not allowed to enter; dinner is brought out on a tray and people eat in their cars. There are cinemas outside towns where people can draw up their cars in the yard in front of the screen and watch the films without getting out. Finally, it is sufficient to take a walk through Central Park, New York, in the evening to see yet another purpose of the automobile: it replaces the nuptial bed for lovers. Such habits make life somewhat mournful, not because people wear fashionable jackets, but because underneath these fashionable jackets there are at times fashionable feelings. . . .

In a relatively short time the Americans have created an astonishing technology. I saw how swiftly they build skyscrapers, how well and with what precision they produce automobiles in Detroit, and how many inventions they possess which ease the daily life of man. How can one not praise American roads, with their cheap and comfortable roadhouses for motorists who decide to spend a night on the road? Some Americans, glancing at the factories, the excellent bridges of New York, the automatic restaurants, and the electric razors, are prepared to believe that the whole of human culture is concentrated in America. One journalist in Jackson said to me: "Rome is a dirty and ugly city; there is nothing to look at in it—not a single skyscraper or a good drug store. After Rome, Jackson seemed to me more like a capital." How is one to explain to such a man that the ancient basilicas and palaces of the Renaissance are worth the skyscrapers of Jackson, or that, besides drug stores where cigars, fountain pens, chewing gum, and even sausages may be bought, there also exist the mosaics of Byzantium and the frescoes of Raphael?

The Americans are inadequately acquainted with the rest of the world. They do not know the history and geography of the Old World. One group of school children was not able to name to me a single city in the Soviet Union. Their political level is just as low. People know the intimate side of the lives of different senators, but in many states the word "Socialist" (let alone "Communist") is considered offensive. American papers frequently write that the existence of two parties is a guarantee of genuine democracy. One might note that no one is capable of explaining where the ideological demarcation line runs between the two parties, and in what way the Northern Republicans differ from the Southern Democrats.

Some Europeans have ridiculed America for her cult of technology. Now the same Europeans look to their ridiculed cousins with servility in the hope of obtaining from them an old car or an out-dated suit. There is nothing to laugh at here and nothing to flatter. American development has proceeded along a different path from the ways of old Europe. France started almost from the Gothic cathedral and the troubadours. America started with automobiles, drug store feeding houses, and gold fever. She swiftly reached a high level of material culture, but her spiritual culture is only awakening. Knowing the intelligence, liveliness, and energy of the Americans, we have the right to say that the spiritual culture of this great people will be great and independent.

Certain changes have taken place in the political consciousness of the average American; he is gradually moving away from the abyss. Roosevelt was surrounded by people who were honest thinkers, capable of realizing the trend of history. Even if these people have now been removed (or have removed themselves), there is still a trace of the late President's activity. I observed a beginning of independent thought, genuine solidarity, and a consciousness of their national mission among many workers. The era in which they were led only by demagogues and adventurers is coming to an end. We see the contributions made to the world by American scientists. The American writers are not renegades or salon aesthetes; they are people connected with the nation, even though the reading masses don't read them. In contrast to French writers, American writers seem to me organic, like huge trees with tenacious roots. The American cinema has already created genuine, universal humor; apart from the genius Chaplin, I will name the Brothers Marx. The cinema has also created the multiplicity of Disney, real poetry capable of stirring a man devoid of all lyricism. Finally, there is beauty —uneasy, but indisputable—in the architecture of New York.

The American intelligentsia has been born. It is still weak and lacks self-confidence; it hides from the illuminated advertisements, from the deafening juke-boxes in the bars, from ecclesiastical sermons with references to business firms, and advertisements with quotations from the Bible. It hides itself in a melancholy which I will call Chekhovian, sometimes in cynicism and sometimes in Utopianism. But among the intelligentsia more and more bold people are appearing. They understand that salvation does not lie in flight or repulsion or solitude. The spiritual world of the average American must be raised to the level of the technology which surrounds him from the maternity home to the crematorium.

. . . . .

It would seem that in this country of diverse races united by patriotism, national equality would prevail. However, America, which never knew feudalism, has established a *racial* hierarchy. The aristocracy are the English, Scotch, and Irish. After them come the Scandinavians and Germans, then the French and Slavs; much lower are the Italians, even lower still the Jews and Chinese; lower still the Puerto Ricans, and finally, at the bottom of the scale, the Negroes.

In the war against Hitlerism America played a prominent part; yet racialism here has a legal standing. When I entered America I had to fill out a questionnaire which contained the question: "Race—White or Colored?" If a person has a "colored" great-grandfather he is designated as "colored" and is subject to various restrictions. We were the guests of the government, and I was often amused by the thought of the reaction the representatives of the State Department might have had if Pushkin had come to America. I met a lawyer in Nashville who spent a long time trying to persuade me that there are "inferior and superior races." He reiterated the theories of Rosenberg and other ideologists of the Third Reich. Then he showed me the portrait of his brother who was killed on the Rhine; he was proud of his brother, who had perished in the struggle against racialists.

Anti-Semitism is an ordinary phenomenon to most Americans; it seems quite natural to them that some institutions accept only Aryans and that certain hotels do not admit Jews. On the West Coast the Chinese are the pariahs. There are organizations in which Italians are not accepted as members. The fate of the Negroes is especially tragic. There are twelve million of them in the United States, and it may be said that one out of every ten Americans is deprived of all human rights.

Natives of New York like to emphasize the liberalism of the North— "*Our* grandfathers fought against slavery." In any Southern town, on the other hand, you may see a monument to the soldiers of the Southern Army. This is a monument to the vanquished, because in the war which shook America the Southerners were defeated. However, it seemed to me more than once that these were monuments, not to the vanquished, but to the victors; since the South not only preserved the principles of slavery but was able, in some degree, to inject them into the North. Certainly equal rights among the races exist *theoretically* in New York. A Negro may not be ejected from a restaurant because he is a Negro, but not a single well-ordered American restaurant will admit a Negro. If it occurs to him to persist, he is told that the empty tables are reserved. A Negro cannot rent a room anywhere except in a Negro "ghetto." He may work in the most different sort of quarters, but he is obliged to live in Harlem, a Negro city within a city—dirty and impoverished, unhappy but still gay. New Yorkers amuse themselves in the cabarets in Harlem. The Negroes are the best dancers and musicians in America; they are gifted with a high sense of rhythm and are not as inherently mechanical as other Americans. In the center of New York there are theaters where Negro troupes perform excellently and are willingly applauded by the whites. But if a Negro wants to have a snack in a restaurant near the theater in which he is playing, he is calmly evicted.

Real estate speculators have a favorite trick; they buy a house in a good residential district and settle a Negro in it. The quarter then becomes taboo immediately, and all the whites depart. The speculator then buys the neighboring houses for a song, moves out the single Negro, and the section again becomes respectable—and the houses rise in price.

Still, in order to understand the place of the Negro in America, it is essential to see the South. When we were asked which part of America we wanted to see, my fellow-travelers chose California and Chicago. I wanted to see the Southern states. Remembering stories I had read —the novels of Steinbeck and Faulkner—I wanted to find out if reality resembled literature. Thus, after the skyscrapers of New York I saw Uncle Tom's Cabin, and I can say that this cabin has changed little.

In all the Southern states there is a "segregation of the races" law. Negroes are not forbidden to use railroads, but they must travel in special cars (always over-crowded). In streetcars, seats are set aside for Negroes in the rear. A car frequently leaves almost empty while Negroes stand and wait for the next one, as the seats for them are occupied. Negroes may not attend meetings of whites, they dare not enter a church where white people are praying, and of course they must not even dream of entering theaters or cinemas for whites.

The Constitution of the United States guarantees that all citizens, male and female, have the right to take part in elections. However, the Negroes in the Southern states do not possess the right to vote. In the state of Alabama there are three million inhabitants, of whom 1,100,000 are Negroes. Among the voters of the state are 496,000 whites and 4,000 Negroes. In Birmingham, Alabama, there are 130,000 Negroes who have reached the age of twenty-one, but the total number of Negro voters is only 1,400. How do the Southern states get around the federal Constitution? There are several ways: one, the poll tax; another, examinations. The qualified voter must know and "be able to interpret" the Constitution. Clearly the examiners can cut out many Negroes. Finally, if the Negroes pay their poll tax, pass the examination, and go to the voting places, the guardians of slavery frighten away the unwanted voters with sturdy clubs. Obviously they do indeed know how to "interpret" the Constitution in the Southern states! In the state of Mississippi, Negroes form half of the population; half the inhabitants of the state are deprived of the right to vote. All this is done cynically and is well-known to all Americans both in the North and the South.

. . . . . .

Not a few Negroes have been in Europe; many fought for America against racialist Germany. They saw that in Paris or Rome no one looked at them as though they were plagued, and they returned home with even greater bitterness. The South is on the eve of a decisive event: either the owners will yield, or the Negroes—yesterday's men of the front line— will open the struggle for equality.

I am convinced that in the end racialism will be overthrown in America; but it must be understood that this disease has penetrated deeply into the mind of the average American. I did not meet a single white in the South who was not contaminated with racialism. One of the most fervent opponents of the slaveowners admitted to me in a frank and intimate conversation: "Yes, I defend the Negroes, but just the same, for me these are not people. I was playing yesterday with our Negro maid's child and found myself thinking that I was playing, not with a child, but with a nice puppy." Racialism has infected even the persecuted; I met Negro anti-Semites and Jews convinced of the superiority of whites over blacks. . . .

The famous journalist, Walter Lippmann, said that in my article on America I was criticizing what was easy to criticize—racial intolerance; Americans themselves know about this vice and are happy to be able to criticize their own vices. Lippmann says that when we Soviet people are capable of appreciating the merits of America and criticizing our own faults, then he, Lippmann, will agree to accept us as "real people." Yes, I know that the best people are ashamed of their attitude toward the Negro. But in my opinion doctors are good, not because they treat, but because they heal. It is no easier for Negroes because Lippmann recognizes Senator Bilbo as an evil and writes articles in New York, while Bilbo and others like him are oppressing Negroes in Mississippi. As for ourselves, we have never denied the merits of America, nor have ever hidden from ourselves or others our own faults. In America, for instance, there are wonderful telephones; from New York it is easier to speak by telephone to San Francisco than from Moscow to Tula. In America there are good passenger planes which fly from city to city every hour day and night. Perhaps Lippmann will say that I am limiting myself to praising technology. No, I have already written that I like American literature. I think we can learn much from American writers, American architects, and even (despite the shattering cheapness of the average production) from American cinema producers. We know our own faults—we criticize our own bureaucracy, our rudeness, and at times our technical backwardness—but we do not criticize just to criticize, but to improve. We have no slaveowners, and it is not a question of whether Lippmann recognizes us as a people, but of whether we recognize racialists and slaveowners as people. I believe in the great future of America, and I am convinced that the American nation will soon be healed of its most bitter and shameful ailment.

.   .   .   .

When American friends asked me what should be done to improve our mutual relations, I replied: "Set up a single standard." The reader must not think that I am proposing that the Americans introduce the metric system; I have no wish to interfere in their affairs. If they like having water freeze at 32 degrees Fahrenheit, that is their business. But a single standard should be set up in evaluating behavior. Too frequently I saw two standards here: one for the virtuous Anglo-Saxons and another for the dishonorable "Reds." If the Americans consider Iceland their base, it is called a "guarantee of security for the entire world"; but if the Soviet Union does not wish to have states which neighbor upon it become bases for an attack upon Russia, this is "Red imperialism."

When the Americans are engaged in manufacturing atom bombs, this is an innocent game like football; but when Red Army men play football in the suburbs of Moscow, this is "preparation for conquering the world."

The American people are kind-hearted and industrious; they do not want war. At present the country is rich, particularly as compared with a Europe ravaged by war. In Detroit the automobile plants are working at top speed and still cannot satisfy all the would-be customers. People "sign up" for refrigerators, vacuum cleaners, and radios. America did not feel the iron boot of war; inconveniences which are trifling to a European seem to be great deprivations here. You will hear amusing complaints here: "There is little butter . . . poultry or mutton instead of beefsteak . . . the line for nylon stockings . . . it is hard to get white shirts, only colored ones." Here and there strikes are breaking out; the workers are seeking an increase in wages to match the rising cost of living. Demobilized servicemen have returned. The country reminds one of a housewarming or of the beginning of the school year. The people are thinking with pleasure about tomorrow, which will certainly be better than today. They have long since forgotten yesterday, and they are little concerned with the day after tomorrow. If occasionally someone stops to think that suddenly a depression and unemployment may be upon him, he at once drives away these gloomy thoughts. These are people who do not want to look into the future. Many of them have more than once lived through the transitions from wealth to poverty and from poverty to wealth. They have adopted a peculiar fatalism and take things in their stride. They do not want a depression and they do not want war. Newspaper articles about a "Third World War" make them justly indignant. But such articles, talks, and sermons repeated too often are designed to accustom the average American to the idea that a Third World War is inevitable.

. . . . . .

I left many sincere friends in America—not only personal friends, but friends of the Soviet people, friends of thought and conscience. Americans are fond of directness. I stated frankly what I liked and did not like in America. Only the sick and impotent should have their feelings spared. Americans have a super-abundance of youth and health. Besides, they now have many European flatterers, eager for loans, trousers, and canned goods. And the Americans themselves love to judge—to judge and condemn. I know that they will receive my words as the words of a friend. This great people has great strength and great will. Its history must be worthy of it.

106. IGNORANCE IS STRENGTH *

GEORGE ORWELL

Lightened in part though it is by the inevitable boy-meets-girl theme, the novel 1984 from which this selection is taken is a deadly serious, satirical exposition of life in the totalitarian society of the future. Its author, George Orwell, develops to their ostensibly logical limits the institutions that characterize all modern authoritarian cultures. By the device of a book within a book he presents, in this selection, the core of the theory of his 1984 society. The central problem in the theory seems to be this: Modern science, mass production, and technology offer the possibility of practically eliminating the great class differences in material and mental well-being that, up to now, have always characterized the major societies of the world. Under these conditions, how can a hierarchical society, with all the tangible and intangible differential benefits this implies, be indefinitely maintained by the "ruling class"?

Throughout recorded time, and probably since the end of the Neolithic Age, there have been three kinds of people in the world, the High, the Middle, and the Low. They have been subdivided in many ways, they have borne countless different names, and their relative numbers, as well as their attitude toward one another, have varied from age to age; but the essential structure of society has never altered. Even after enormous upheavals and seemingly irrevocable changes, the same pattern has always reasserted itself, just as a gyroscope will always return to equilibrium, however far it is pushed one way or the other. . . .

The aims of these groups are entirely irreconcilable. The aim of the High is to remain where they are. The aim of the Middle is to change places with the High. The aim of the Low, when they have an aim— for it is an abiding characteristic of the Low that they are too much crushed by drudgery to be more than intermittently conscious of any-

* *Nineteen Eighty-Four* by George Orwell, 202–218. Copyright, 1949 by Harcourt, Brace and Company, Inc.

George Orwell was the pseudonym of Eric Blair (1903–1951), a British writer born in Motihari, Bengal, of Anglo-Indian parents. After being badly wounded in Spain, he settled down in England to write. His books include *Down and Out in Paris and London; Burmese Days; The Lion and the Unicorn; Animal Farm; Shooting an Elephant; Critical Essays.*

thing outside their daily lives—is to abolish all distinctions and create a society in which all men shall be equal. Thus throughout history a struggle which is the same in its main outlines recurs over and over again. For long periods the High seem to be securely in power, but sooner or later there always comes a moment when they lose either their belief in themselves, or their capacity to govern efficiently, or both. They are then overthrown by the Middle, who enlist the Low on their side by pretending to them that they are fighting for liberty and justice. As soon as they have reached their objective, the Middle thrust the Low back into their old position of servitude, and themselves become the High. Presently a new Middle group splits off from one of the other groups, or from both of them, and the struggle begins over again. Of the three groups, only the Low are never even temporarily successful in achieving their aims. It would be an exaggeration to say that throughout history there had been no progress of a material kind. Even today, in a period of decline, the average human being is physically better off than he was a few centuries ago. But no advance in wealth, no softening of manners, no reform or revolution has ever brought human equality a millimeter nearer. From the point of view of the Low, no historic change has ever meant much more than a change in the name of their masters.

By the late nineteenth century the recurrences of this pattern had become obvious to many observers. There then arose schools of thinkers who interpreted history as a cyclical process and claimed to show that inequality was the unalterable law of human life. This doctrine, of course, had always had its adherents, but in the manner in which it was now put forward there was a significant change. In the past the need for a hierarchical form of society had been the doctrine specifically of the High. It had been preached by kings and aristocrats and by the priests, lawyers, and the like who were parasitical upon them, and it had generally been softened by promises of compensation in an imaginary world beyond the grave. The Middle, so long as it was struggling for power, had always made use of such terms as freedom, justice, and fraternity. Now, however, the concept of human brotherhood began to be assailed by people who were not yet in positions of command, but merely hoped to be so before long. In the past the Middle had made revolutions under the banner of equality, and then had established a fresh tyranny as soon as the old one was overthrown. The new Middle groups in effect proclaimed their tyranny beforehand. Socialism, a theory which appeared in the early nineteenth century and was the last link in a chain of thought stretching back to the slave rebellions of antiquity, was still deeply infected by the Utopianism of past ages. But in each variant of Socialism that appeared from about 1900 onwards the aim of establishing liberty and equality was more and more openly abandoned. The new movements which appeared in the middle years of the century, Ingsoc in Oceania, Neo-Bolshevism in Eurasia, Death-worship, as it is commonly called, in Eastasia, had the conscious aim of perpetuating *un*freedom and *in*equality. These new movements, of course, grew out of the old ones and tended to keep their names and pay lip-service to their ideology. But the purpose of all of them was to arrest progress and freeze history at a chosen moment. The familiar pendulum swing was to happen once more, and then stop. As usual, the High were to be turned out by the Middle, who would then become the High; but this time, by conscious strategy, the High would be able to maintain their position permanently.

The new doctrines arose partly because of the accumulation of historical knowledge, and the growth of the historical sense, which had hardly existed before the nineteenth century. The cyclical movement of history was now intelligible, or appeared to be so; and if it was intelligible, then it was alterable. But the principal, underlying cause was that, as early as the beginning of the twentieth century, human equality had become technically possible. It was still true that men were not equal in their native talents and that functions had to be specialized in ways that favored some individuals against others; but there was no longer any real need for class distinctions or for large differences of wealth. In earlier ages, class distinctions had been not only inevitable but desirable. Inequality was the price of civilization. With the development of machine production, however, the case was altered. Even if it was still necessary for human beings to do different kinds of work, it was no longer necessary for them to live at different social or economic levels. Therefore, from the point of view of the new groups who were on the point of seizing power, human equality was no longer an ideal to be striven after, but a danger to be averted. In more primitive ages, when a just and peaceful society was in fact not possible, it had been fairly easy to believe in it. The idea of an earthly paradise in which men should live together in a state of brotherhood, without laws and without brute labor, had haunted the human imagination for thousands of years. And this vision had had a certain hold even on the groups who actually profited by each historic change. The heirs of the French, English, and American revolutions had partly believed in their own phrases about the rights of man, freedom of speech, equality before the law, and the like, and had even allowed their conduct to be influenced by them to some extent. But by the fourth decade of the twentieth century all the main currents of political thought were authoritarian. The earthly paradise had been discredited at exactly the moment when it became realizable. Every new political theory, by whatever name it called itself, led back to hierarchy and regimentation. And in the general hardening of outlook that set in round about 1930, practices which had been long abandoned, in some cases for hundreds of years—imprisonment without trial, the use of war prisoners as slaves, public executions, torture to extract confessions, the use of hostages and the deportation of whole populations—not only became common again, but were tolerated and even defended by people who considered themselves enlightened and progressive.

It was only after a decade of national wars, civil wars, revolutions and counterrevolutions in all parts of the world that Ingsoc and its rivals emerged as fully worked-out political theories. But they had been fore-shadowed by the various systems, generally called totalitarian, which had appeared earlier in the century, and the main outlines of the world which would emerge from the prevailing chaos had long been obvious. What kind of people would control this world had been equally obvious. The new aristocracy was made up for the most part of bureaucrats, scientists, technicians, trade-union organizers, publicity experts, sociologists, teachers, journalists, and professional politicians. These people, whose origins lay in the salaried middle class and the upper grades of the working class, had been shaped and brought together by the barren world of monopoly industry and centralized government. As compared with their opposite numbers in past ages, they were less avaricious, less tempted by luxury, hungrier for pure power, and, above all, more con-scious of what they were doing and more intent on crushing opposition. This last difference was cardinal. By comparison with that existing today, all the tyrannies of the past were half-hearted and inefficient. The ruling groups were always infected to some extent by liberal ideas, and were content to leave loose ends everywhere, to regard only the overt act, and to be uninterested in what their subjects were thinking. Even the Catholic Church of the Middle Ages was tolerant by modern standards. Part of the reason for this was that in the past no govern-ment had the power to keep its citizens under constant surveillance. The invention of print, however, made it easier to manipulate public opinion, and the film and the radio carried the process further. With the development of television, and the technical advance which made it possible to receive and transmit simultaneously on the same instrument, private life came to an end. Every citizen, or at least every citizen im-portant enough to be worth watching, could be kept for twenty-four hours a day under the eyes of the police and in the sound of official propaganda, with all other channels of communication closed. The possibility of enforcing not only complete obedience to the will of the State, but complete uniformity of opinion on all subjects, now existed for the first time.

After the revolutionary period of the Fifties and Sixties, society re-grouped itself, as always, into High, Middle, and Low. But the new High group, unlike all its forerunners, did not act upon instinct but knew what was needed to safeguard its position. It had long been realized that the only secure basis for oligarchy is collectivism. Wealth and privilege are most easily defended when they are possessed jointly. The so-called "abolition of private property" which took place in the middle years of the century meant, in effect, the concentration of property in far fewer hands than before; but with this difference, that the new owners were a group instead of a mass of individuals. Individually, no member of the Party owns anything, except petty personal belongings. Collectively, the Party owns everything in Oceania, because it controls everything and disposes of the products as it thinks fit. In the years following the Revolution it was able to step into this commanding position almost unopposed, because the whole process was represented as an act of collectivization. It had always been assumed that if the capitalist class were expropriated, Socialism must follow; and unquestionably the capitalists had been expropriated. Factories, mines, land, houses, transport—everything had been taken away from them; and since these things were no longer private property, it followed that they must be public property. Ingsoc, which grew out of the earlier Socialist movement and inherited its phraseology, has in fact carried out the main item in the Socialist program, with the result, foreseen and intended beforehand, that economic inequality has been made permanent.

But the problems of perpetuating a hierarchical society go deeper than this. There are only four ways in which a ruling group can fall from power. Either it is conquered from without, or it governs so inefficiently that the masses are stirred to revolt, or it allows a strong and discontented Middle Group to come into being, or it loses its own self-confidence and willingness to govern. These causes do not operate singly, and as a rule all four of them are present in some degree. A ruling class which could guard against all of them would remain in power permanently. Ultimately the determining factor is the mental attitude of the ruling class itself.

After the middle of the present century, the first danger had in reality disappeared. Each of the three powers which now divide the world is in fact unconquerable, and could only become conquerable through slow demographic changes which a government with wide powers can easily avert. The second danger, also, is only a theoretical one. The masses never revolt of their own accord, and they never revolt merely because they are oppressed. Indeed, so long as they are not permitted to have standards of comparison they never even become aware that they are oppressed. The recurrent economic crises of past times were totally unnecessary and are not now permitted to happen, but other and equally large dislocations can and do happen without having political results, because there is no way in which discontent can become articulate. As for the problem of overproduction, which has been latent in our society since the development of machine technique, it is solved by the device of continuous warfare, which is also useful in keying up public morale to the necessary pitch. From the point of view of our present rulers, therefore, the only genuine dangers are the splitting-off of a new group of able, underemployed, power-hungry people, and the growth of liberalism and skepticism in their own ranks. The problem, that is to say, is educational. It is a problem of continuously molding the consciousness both of the directing group and of the larger executive group that lies immediately below it. The consciousness of the masses needs only to be influenced in a negative way.

Given this background, one could infer, if one did not know it already, the general structure of Oceanic society. At the apex of the pyramid comes Big Brother. Big Brother is infallible and all-powerful. Every success, every achievement, every victory, every scientific discovery, all knowledge, all wisdom, all happiness, all virtue, are held to issue directly from his leadership and inspiration. Nobody has ever seen Big Brother. He is a face on the hoardings, a voice on the telescreen. We may be reasonably sure that he will never die, and there is already considerable uncertainty as to when he was born. Big Brother is the guise in which the Party chooses to exhibit itself to the world. His function is to act as a focusing point for love, fear, and reverence, emotions which are more easily felt toward an individual than toward an organization. Below Big Brother comes the Inner Party, its numbers limited to six million, or something less than two per cent of the population of Oceania. Below the Inner Party comes the Outer Party, which, if the Inner Party is described as the brain of the State, may be justly likened to the hands. Below that come the dumb masses whom we habitually refer to as "the proles," numbering perhaps eighty-five per cent of the population. In the terms of our earlier classification, the proles are the Low, for the slave populations of the equatorial lands, who pass constantly from conqueror to conqueror, are not a permanent or necessary part of the structure.

In principle, membership in these three groups is not hereditary. The child of Inner Party parents is in theory not born into the Inner Party. Admission to either branch of the Party is by examination, taken at the age of sixteen. Nor is there any racial discrimination, or any marked domination of one province by another. Jews, Negroes, South Americans of pure Indian blood are to be found in the highest ranks of the Party, and the administrators of any area are always drawn from the inhabitants of that area. In no part of Oceania do the inhabitants have the feeling that they are a colonial population ruled from a distant capital. Oceania has no capital, and its titular head is a person whose whereabouts nobody knows. Except that English is its chief lingua franca and Newspeak its official language, it is not centralized in any way. Its rulers are not held together by blood ties but by adherence to a common doctrine. It is true that our society is stratified, and very rigidly stratified, on what at first sight appear to be hereditary lines. There is far less to-and-fro movement between the different groups than happened under capitalism or even in the pre-industrial ages. Between the two branches of the Party there is a certain amount of interchange, but only so much as will ensure that weaklings are excluded from the Inner Party and that ambitious members of the Outer Party are made harmless by allowing them to rise. Proletarians, in practice, are not allowed to graduate into the Party. The most gifted among them, who might possibly become nuclei of discontent, are simply marked down by the Thought Police and eliminated. But this state of affairs is not necessarily permanent, nor is it a matter of principle. The Party is not a class in the old sense of the word. It does not aim at transmitting power to its own children, as such; and if there were no other way of keeping the ablest people at the top, it would be perfectly prepared to recruit an entire new generation from the ranks of the proletariat. In the crucial years, the fact that the Party was not a hereditary body did a great deal to neutralize opposition. The older kind of Socialist, who had been trained to fight against something called "class privilege," assumed that what is not hereditary cannot be permanent. He did not see that the continuity of an oligarchy need not be physical, nor did he pause to reflect that hereditary aristocracies have always been short-lived, whereas adoptive organizations such as the Catholic Church have sometimes lasted for hundreds or thousands of years. The essence of oligarchical rule is not father-to-son inheritance, but the persistence of a certain world-view and a certain way of life, imposed by the dead upon the living. A ruling group is a ruling group so long as it can nominate its successors. The Party is not concerned with perpetuating its blood but with perpetuating itself. *Who* wields power is not important, provided that the hierarchical structure remains always the same.

All the beliefs, habits, tastes, emotions, mental attitudes that characterize our time are really designed to sustain the mystique of the Party and prevent the true nature of present-day society from being perceived. Physical rebellion, or any preliminary move toward rebellion, is at present not possible. From the proletarians nothing is to be feared. Left to themselves, they will continue from generation to generation and from century to century, working, breeding, and dying, not only without any impulse to rebel, but without the power of grasping that the world could be other than it is. They could only become dangerous if the advance of industrial technique made it necessary to educate them more highly; but, since military and commercial rivalry are no longer important, the level of popular education is actually declining. What opinions the masses hold, or do not hold, is looked on as a matter of indifference. They can be granted intellectual liberty because they have no intellect. In a Party member, on the other hand, not even the smallest deviation of opinion on the most unimportant subject can be tolerated.

A Party member lives from birth to death under the eye of the Thought Police. Even when he is alone he can never be sure that he is alone. Wherever he may be, asleep or awake, working or resting, in his bath or in bed, he can be inspected without warning and without knowing that he is being inspected. Nothing that he does is indifferent. His friendships, his relaxations, his behavior toward his wife and children, the expression of his face when he is alone, the words he mutters in sleep, even the characteristic movements of his body, are all jealously scrutinized. Not only any actual misdemeanor, but any eccentricity, however small, any change of habits, any nervous mannerism that could possibly be the symptom of an inner struggle, is certain to be detected. He has no freedom of choice in any direction whatever. On the other hand, his actions are not regulated by law or by any clearly formulated code of behavior. In Oceania there is no law. Thoughts and actions which, when detected, mean certain death are not formally forbidden, and the endless purges, arrests, tortures, imprisonments, and vaporizations are not inflicted as punishment for crimes which have actually been committed, but are merely the wiping-out of persons who might perhaps commit a crime at some time in the future. A Party member is required to have not only the right opinions, but the right instincts. Many of the beliefs and attitudes demanded of him are never plainly stated, and could not be stated without laying bare the contradictions inherent in Ingsoc. If he is a person naturally orthodox (in Newspeak, a *goodthinker*), he will in all circumstances know, without taking thought, what is the true belief or the desirable emotion. But in any case an elaborate mental training, undergone in childhood and grouping itself round the Newspeak words *crimestop, blackwhite,* and *doublethink,* makes him unwilling and unable to think too deeply on any subject whatever.

A Party member is expected to have no private emotions and no respites from enthusiasm. He is supposed to live in a continuous frenzy of hatred of foreign enemies and internal traitors, triumph over victories, and self-abasement before the power and wisdom of the Party. The discontents produced by his bare, unsatisfying life are deliberately turned outwards and dissipated by such devices as the Two Minutes Hate, and the speculations which might possibly induce a skeptical or rebellious attitude are killed in advance by his early acquired inner discipline. The first and simplest stage in the discipline, which can be taught even to young children, is called, in Newspeak, *crimestop. Crimestop* means the faculty of stopping short, as though by instinct, at the threshold of any dangerous thought. It includes the power of not grasping analogies, of failing to perceive logical errors, of misunderstanding the simplest arguments if they are inimical to Ingsoc, and of being bored or repelled by any train of thought which is capable of leading in a heretical direction. *Crimestop*, in short, means protective stupidity. But stupidity is not enough. On the contrary, orthodoxy in the full sense demands a control over one's own mental processes as complete as that of a contortionist over his body. Oceanic society rests ultimately on the belief that Big Brother is omnipotent and that the Party is infallible. But since in reality Big Brother is not omnipotent and the Party is not infallible, there is need for an unwearying, moment-to-moment flexibility in the treatment of facts. The key word here is *blackwhite*. Like so many Newspeak words, this word has two mutually contradictory meanings. Applied to an opponent, it means the habit of impudently claiming that black is white, in contradiction of the plain facts. Applied to a Party member, it means a loyal willingness to say that black is white when Party discipline demands this. But it means also the ability to *believe* that black is white, and more, to *know* that black is white, and to forget that one has ever believed the contrary. This demands a continuous alteration of the past, made possible by the system of thought which really embraces all the rest, and which is known in Newspeak as *doublethink*.

The alteration of the past is necessary for two reasons, one of which is subsidiary and, so to speak, precautionary. The subsidiary reason is that the Party member, like the proletarian, tolerates present-day conditions partly because he has no standards of comparison. He must be cut off from the past, just as he must be cut off from foreign countries, because it is necessary for him to believe that he is better off than his ancestors and that the average level of material comfort is constantly rising. But by far the more important reason for the readjustment of the past is the need to safeguard the infallibility of the Party. It is not merely that speeches, statistics, and records of every kind must be constantly brought up to date in order to show that the predictions of the Party were in all cases right. It is also that no change of doctrine or in political alignment can ever be admitted. For to change one's mind, or even one's policy, is a confession of weakness. If, for example, Eurasia or Eastasia (whichever it may be) is the enemy today, then that country must always have been the enemy. And if the facts say otherwise, then the facts must be altered. Thus history is continuously rewritten. This day-to-day falsification of the past, carried out by the Ministry of Truth, is as necessary to the stability of the regime as the work of repression and espionage carried out by the Ministry of Love.

The mutability of the past is the central tenet of Ingsoc. Past events, it is argued, have no objective existence, but survive only in written records and in human memories. The past is whatever the records and the memories agree upon. And since the Party is in full control of all records, and in equally full control of the minds of its members, it follows that the past is whatever the Party chooses to make it. It also follows that though the past is alterable, it never has been altered in any specific instance. For when it has been recreated in whatever shape is needed at the moment, then this new version *is* the past, and no different past can ever have existed. This holds good even when, as often happens, the same event has to be altered out of recognition several times in the course of a year. At all times the Party is in possession of absolute truth, and clearly the absolute can never have been different from what it is now. It will be seen that the control of the past depends above all on the training of memory. To make sure that all written records agree with the orthodoxy of the moment is merely a mechanical act. But it is also necessary to *remember* that events happened in the desired manner. And if it is necessary to rearrange one's memories or to tamper with written records, then it is necessary to *forget* that one has done so. The trick of doing this can be learned like any other mental technique. It *is* learned by the majority of Party members, and certainly by all who are intelligent as well as orthodox. In Oldspeak it is called, quite frankly, "reality control." In Newspeak it is called *doublethink*, although *doublethink* comprises much else as well.

Doublethink means the power of holding two contradictory beliefs in one's mind simultaneously, and accepting both of them. The Party intellectual knows in which direction his memories must be altered; he therefore knows that he is playing tricks with reality; but by the exercise of *doublethink* he also satisfies himself that reality is not violated. The process has to be conscious, or it would not be carried out with sufficient precision, but it also has to be unconscious, or it would bring with it a feeling of falsity and hence of guilt. *Doublethink* lies at the very heart of Ingsoc, since the essential act of the Party is to use conscious deception while retaining the firmness of purpose that goes with complete honesty. To tell deliberate lies while genuinely believing in them, to forget any fact that has become inconvenient, and then, when it becomes necessary again, to draw it back from oblivion for just so long as it is needed, to deny the existence of objective reality and all the while to take account of the reality which one denies—all this is indispensably necessary. Even in using the word *doublethink* it is necessary to exercise *doublethink*. For by using the word one admits that one is tampering with reality; by a fresh act of *doublethink* one erases this knowledge; and so on indefinitely, with the lie always one leap ahead of the truth. Ultimately it is by means of *doublethink* that the Party has been able—and may, for all we know, continue to be able for thousands of years—to arrest the course of history.

All past oligarchies have fallen from power either because they ossified or because they grew soft. Either they became stupid and arrogant, failed to adjust themselves to changing circumstances, and were overthrown, or they became liberal and cowardly, made concessions when they should have used force, and once again were overthrown. They fell, that is to say, either through consciousness or through unconsciousness. It is the achievement of the Party to have produced a system of thought in which both conditions can exist simultaneously. And upon no other intellectual basis could the dominion of the Party be made permanent. If one is to rule, and to continue ruling, one must be able to dislocate the sense of reality. For the secret of rulership is to combine a belief in one's own infallibility with the power to learn from past mistakes.

It need hardly be said that the subtlest practitioners of *doublethink* are those who invented *doublethink* and know that it is a vast system of mental cheating. In our society, those who have the best knowledge of what is happening are also those who are furthest from seeing the world as it is. In general, the greater the understanding, the greater the delusion: the more intelligent, the less sane. One clear illustration of this is the fact that war hysteria increases in intensity as one rises in the social scale. Those whose attitude toward the war is most nearly rational are the subject peoples of the disputed territories. To these people the war is simply a continuous calamity which sweeps to and fro over their bodies like a tidal wave. Which side is winning is a matter of complete indifference to them. They are aware that a change of overlordship means simply that they will be doing the same work as before for new masters who treat them in the same manner as the old ones. The slightly more favored workers whom we call "the proles" are only intermittently conscious of the war. When it is necessary they can be prodded into frenzies of fear and hatred, but when left to themselves they are capable of forgetting for long periods that the war is happening. It is in the ranks of the Party, and above all of the Inner Party, that the true war enthusiasm is found. World-conquest is believed in most firmly by those who know it to be impossible. This peculiar linking-together of opposites—knowledge with ignorance, cynicism with fanaticism—is one of the chief distinguishing marks of Oceanic society. The official ideology abounds with contradictions even where there is no practical reason for them. Thus, the Party rejects and vilifies every principle for which the Socialist movement originally stood, and it chooses to do this in the name of Socialism. It preaches a contempt for the working class unexampled for centuries past, and it dresses its members in a uniform which was at one time peculiar to manual workers and was adopted for that reason. It systematically undermines the solidarity of the family, and it calls its leader by a name which is a direct appeal to the sentiments of family loyalty. Even the names of the four Ministries by which we are governed exhibit a sort of impudence in their deliberate reversal of the facts. The Ministry of Peace concerns itself with war, the Ministry of Truth with lies, the Ministry of Love with torture, and the Ministry of Plenty with starvation. These contradictions are not accidental, nor do they result from ordinary hypocrisy: they are deliberate exercises in *doublethink*. For it is only by reconciling contradictions that power can be retained indefinitely. In no other way could the ancient cycle be broken. If human equality is be forever averted—if the High, as we have called them, are to keep their places permanently—then the prevailing mental condition must be controlled insanity.

But there is one question which until this moment we have almost ignored: It is: *why* should human equality be averted? Supposing that the mechanics of the process have been rightly described, what is the motive for this huge, accurately planned effort to freeze history at a particular moment of time?

Here we reach the central secret. As we have seen, the mystique of the Party, and above all of the Inner Party, depends upon *doublethink*. But deeper than this lies the original motive, the never-questioned instinct that first led to the seizure of power and brought *doublethink*, the Thought Police, continuous warfare, and all the other necessary paraphernalia into existence afterwards. This motive really consists. . . .

107. THE TRAGIC PARADOX
OF OUR AGE *

JAWAHARLAL NEHRU

It is, perhaps, fitting that the final selection in this book should be written, not by a sociologist but by the great political and intellectual leader of India, Jawaharlal Nehru, who for years was second only to Ghandi in influence throughout his nation. It is fitting because it is the voice of a significant world leader challenging us, as social scientists and citizens concerned with human behavior, not to lose sight of the great issues of the world and not to permit our attention to be monopolized by the details and minutiae of the situation immediately around

* From *The New York Times Magazine* (September 7, 1958), 13, 110–111.
    The author (b. 1889) has been Prime Minister of India since 1947. Education in India, England, and the United States. Author: *Autobiography; Eighteen Months in India; Glimpses of World History; Discovery of India.*

us. In this selection Nehru spells out the nature of some of these great issues and indicates the scope of the challenge facing mankind.

I rather envy those who have got fixed ideas and therefore need not take the trouble to look deeper into the problems of today.

Whether it is from the point of view of some religion, or ideology, they are not troubled with the mental conflicts which are always the accompaniment of great ages of transition. And yet, even though it may be more comfortable to have fixed ideas and be complacent, surely that is not to be commended, and that can only lead to stagnation and decay. The basic fact of today is the tremendous pace of change in human life. In my own life I have seen amazing changes, and I am sure that, in the course of the life of the next generation, these changes will be even greater, if humanity is not overwhelmed and annihilated by an atomic war.

Nothing is so remarkable as the progressive conquest or understanding of the physical world by the mind of man today, and this process is continuing at a terrific pace. Man need no longer be a victim of external circumstances, at any rate to a very large extent. While there has been this conquest of external conditions, there is at the same time the strange spectacle of a lack of moral fiber and of self-control in man as a whole.

Conquering the physical world, he fails to conquer himself.

That is the tragic paradox of this atomic and sputnik age. The fact that nuclear tests continue, even though it is well recognized that they are very harmful in the present and in the future; the fact that all kinds of weapons of mass destruction are being produced and piled up, even though it is universally recognized that their use may well exterminate the human race, brings out this paradox with startling clarity.

Science is advancing far beyond the comprehension of a very great part of the human race, and posing problems which most of us are incapable of understanding, much less of solving. Hence the inner conflict and tumult of our times. On the one side there is this great and overpowering progress in science and technology and of their manifold consequences; on the other a certain exhaustion of civilization itself.

Religion comes into conflict with rationalism. The disciplines of religion and social usage fade away without giving place to other disciplines, moral or spiritual. Religion, as practiced, either deals with matters rather unrelated to our normal lives, and thus adopts an ivory-tower attitude, or is allied to certain social usages which do not fit in with the present age. Rationalism, on the other hand, with all its virtues, somehow appears to deal with the surface of things, without uncovering the inner core. Science itself has arrived at a stage where vast new possibilities and mysteries loom ahead. Matter and energy and spirit seem to overlap.

In ancient days life was simpler and more in contact with nature. Now it becomes more and more complex and more and more hurried, without time for reflection or even for questioning. Scientific developments have produced an enormous surplus of power and energy which are often used for the wrong purposes.

The old question still faces us as it has faced humanity for ages past: What is the meaning of life? The old days of faith do not appear to be adequate in a changing world; living should be a continuous adjustment to these changes and happenings. It is the lack of this adjustment that creates conflicts.

The old civilizations, with the many virtues that they possess, have obviously proved inadequate. The new Western civilization, with all its triumphs and achievements and also with its atomic bombs also appears inadequate and, therefore, the feeling grows that there is something wrong with our civilization. Indeed, essentially our problems are those of civilization itself.

Religion gave a certain moral and spiritual discipline; it also tried to perpetuate superstition and social usages. Indeed, those superstitions and social usages enmeshed and overwhelmed the real spirit of religion. Disillusionment followed.

Communism comes in the wake of this disillusionment and offers some kind of faith and some kind of discipline. To some extent it fills a vacuum. It succeeds, in some measure, by giving a content to man's life. But in spite of its apparent success, it fails, partly because of its rigidity but even more so because it ignores certain essential needs of human nature.

There is much talk in communism of the contradictions of capitalist society, and there is truth in that analysis. But we see the growing contradictions within the rigid framework of communism itself. Its suppression of individual freedom brings about powerful reactions. Its contempt for what might be called the moral and spiritual side of life not only ignores something that is basic in man but also deprives human behavior of standards and values. Its unfortunate association with violence encourages a certain evil tendency in human beings.

I have the greatest admiration for many of the achievements of the Soviet Union. Among these great achievements is the value attached to the child and the common man. Their systems of education and health are probably the best in the world. But it is said, and rightly, that there is suppression of individual freedom there. And yet the spread of education in all its forms is itself a tremendous liberating force which ultimately will not tolerate that suppression of freedom. This again is another contradiction. Unfortunately, communism became too closely associated with the necessity for violence and thus the idea which it placed before the world became a tainted one. Means distorted ends. We see here the powerful influence of wrong means and methods.

Communism charges the capitalist structure of society with being based on violence and class conflict. I think this is essentially correct, though that capitalist structure itself has undergone, and is continually undergoing, a change because of democratic, and other, struggles and inequality. The question is how to get rid of this and have a classless society with equal opportunities for all. Can this be achieved through methods of violence, or can it be possible to bring about those changes through peaceful methods?

Communism has definitely allied itself to the approach of violence, even if it does not indulge normally in physical violence. Its language is of violence, its thought is violent and it does not seek to change by persuasion or peaceful, democratic pressures, but by coercion and, indeed, by destruction and extermination. Fascism has all these evil aspects of violence and extermination in their grossest forms and, at the same time, has no acceptable ideal.

This is completely opposed to the peaceful approach which Gandhi taught us. Communists, as well as anti-Communists, both seem to imagine that a principle can be stoutly defended only by the language of violence, and by condemning those who do not accept it. For both of them there are no shades; there is only black and white. That is the old approach of the bigoted aspects of some religions.

It is not the approach of tolerance, of feeling that perhaps others might have some share of the truths also. Speaking for myself, I find this approach wholly unscientific, unreasonable and uncivilized, whether it is applied in the realm of religion or economic theory or anything else. I prefer the old pagan approach of tolerance, apart from its religious aspects. But whatever we may think about it, we have arrived at a stage in the modern world where an attempt at forcible imposition of ideas on any large section of people is bound ultimately to fail. In present circumstances, this will lead to war and tremendous destruction. There will be no victory, only defeat for everyone.

. . . . .

We talk of the welfare state and of democracy and socialism. They are good concepts but they hardly convey a clear and unambiguous meaning. This was the argument, and then the question arose as to what our ultimate objective should be. Democracy and socialism are means to an end, not the end itself. We talk of the good of society. Is this something apart from, and transcending, the good of the individuals composing it? If the individual is ignored and sacrificed for what is considered the good of the society, is that the right objective to have?

It was agreed that the individual should not be so sacrificed and, indeed, that real social progress will come only when an opportunity is given to the individual to develop, provided the individual is not a selected group but comprises the whole community. The touchstone, therefore should be how far any political or social theory enables the individual to rise above his petty self and thus think in terms of the good of all.

The law of life should not be the competition of acquisitiveness but cooperation, the good of each contributing to the good of all. In such a society, the emphasis will be on duties, not on rights; the rights will follow the performance of the duties. We have to give a new direction to education and evolve a new type of humanity.

. . . .

In a sense, every country, Socialist or Communist, accepts the ideal of the welfare state. Capitalism, in a few countries at least, has achieved this common welfare to a very large extent, though it has far from solved its own problems and there is a basic lack of something vital. Democracy allied to capitalism has undoubtedly toned down many of its evils and, in fact, it is different now from what it was a generation or two ago.

In industrially advanced countries there has been a continuous and steady upward trend of economic development. Even the terrible losses of world wars have not prevented this trend in so far as these highly developed countries are concerned. Further, this economic development has spread, though in varying degrees, to all classes. This does not apply to countries which are not industrially developed. Indeed, in those countries, the struggle for development is very difficult and sometimes, in spite of efforts, economic inequalities not only remain but tend to become worse.

Normally speaking, it may be said that the forces of a capitalist society, if left unchecked, tend to make the rich richer and the poor poorer, and thus increase the gap between them. This applies to countries as well as groups or regions or classes within the countries. Various democratic processes interfere with these normal trends. Capitalism itself has therefore developed some socialistic features even though its major aspects remain. Socialism, of course, deliberately wants to interfere with the normal processes, and this not only adds to the productive forces but lessens inequalities. But what is socialism? It is difficult to give a precise answer, and there are innumerable definitions of it. Some people probably think of socialism vaguely just as something which does good and which aims at equality. That does not take us very far.

Socialism is basically a different approach from that of capitalism, though I think it is true that the wide gap between them tends to lessen because many of the ideas of socialism are gradually incorporated even in the capitalist structure. Socialism is, after all, not only a way of life but a certain scientific approach to social and economic problems. If socialism is introduced in a backward and underdeveloped country, it does not suddenly make it any less backward. In fact, we have a backward and poverty-stricken socialism. Unfortunately, many of the political aspects of communism have tended to distort our vision of socialism. Also the technique of struggle evolved by communism has given violence a predominant part.

Socialism should, therefore, be considered apart from these political elements or the inevitability of violence. It tells us that the general character of social, political and intellectual life in a society is governed by its productive resources. As those productive resources change and develop so the life and thinking of the community changes.

Imperialism, or colonialism, suppressed, and suppresses, the progressive social forces. Inevitably, it aligns itself with certain privileged groups or classes because it is interested in preserving the social and economic *status quo*. Even after a country has become independent, it may continue to be economically dependent on other countries. This kind of thing is euphemistically called having close cultural and economic ties.

We discuss sometimes the self-sufficiency of the village. This should not be mixed up with the idea of decentralization, though it may be a part of it. While decentralization is, I think, desirable to the largest possible extent, if it leads to old and rather primitive methods of production, then it simply means that we do not utilize modern methods which have brought great material advance to some countries of the West. That is, we remain poor and, what is more, tend to become poorer because of the pressure of an increasing population.

I do not see any way out of our vicious circle of poverty except by utilizing the new sources of power which science has placed at our disposal. Being poor, we have no surplus to invest; we sink lower and lower.

We have to break through this barrier by profiting by new sources of power and modern techniques. But, in doing so, we should not forget the basic human element and the fact that our objective is individual improvement and lessening of inequalities; and we must not forget the ethical and spiritual aspects of life which are ultimately the basis of culture and civilization and which have given some meaning to life.

It has to be remembered that it is not by some magic adoption of the Socialist or capitalist method that poverty suddenly leads to riches. The only way is through hard work and increasing the productivity of the nation, and organizing an equitable distribution of its products.

It is a lengthy and difficult process. In a poorly developed country, the capitalist method offers no chance. It is only through a planned approach on Socialist lines that steady progress can be attained, though even that will take time. As this process continues, the texture of our life and thinking gradually changes.

Planning is essential for this because, otherwise, we waste our resources, which are very limited. Planning does not mean a mere collection of projects or schemes but a thought-out approach of how to strengthen the base and pace of progress so that the community advances on all fronts. In India we have a terrible problem of extreme poverty in certain large regions, apart from the general poverty of the country. We have always a difficult choice before us: whether to concentrate on production by itself in selected and favorable areas, thus for the moment rather ignoring poor areas, or try to develop the backward areas at the same time, so as to lessen the inequalities between regions. A balance has to be struck and an integrated national plan evolved.

That national plan need not—and, indeed, should not—have rigidity. It need not be based on any dogma; but should rather take the existing facts into consideration. It may—and, I think, in present-day India it should—encourage private enterprise in many fields, though even that private enterprise must necessarily fit in with the national plan and have such controls as are considered necessary.

Land reforms have a peculiar significance because without them, more especially in a highly congested country like India, there can be no radical improvement in productivity in agriculture. But the main object of land reforms is a deeper one. They are meant to break up the old class structure of a society that is stagnant.

We want social security, but we have to recognize that social security comes only when a certain stage of development has been reached. Otherwise, we shall have neither social security nor any development.

It is clear that, in the final analysis, it is the quality of the human beings that counts. It is man that builds up the wealth of a nation, as well as its cultural progress. Hence, education and health are of high importance so as to produce that quality in human beings. We have to suffer here, also, from lack of resources, but still we have always to remember that it is right education and good health that will give the foundation for economic as well as cultural and spiritual progress.

A national plan has this as both a short-term objective and a long-term one. The long-term objective gives a true perspective. Without it, short-term planning is of little avail and will lead us into blind alleys. Planning will thus always be perspective planning, and hard, in view of the physical achievements for which we strive. In other words, it has to be physical planning, though it is obviously limited and conditioned by financial resources and economic conditions.

The problems that India faces are, to some extent, common to other countries, but much more so; there are new problems for which we have not got parallels or historical precedents elsewhere. What has happened in the past in the industrially advanced countries has little bearing on us today. As a matter of fact, the countries that are advanced today were economically better off than India today, in terms of per capita income, before their industrialization began.

Western economics, therefore, though helpful, has little bearing on our present-day problems. So also has Marxist economics, which is in many ways out of date, even though it throws considerable light on economic processes. We have thus to do our own thinking, profiting by the example of others, but essentially trying to find a path for ourselves suited to our own conditions.

In considering these economic aspects of our problems, we have always to remember the basic approach of peaceful means; and perhaps we might also keep in view the old pedantic ideal of the life force which is the inner base of everything that exists.

SOCIOLOGISTS
AT WORK

A. CAREERS IN SOCIOLOGY °

MYRON F. LEWIS

*The editors of this book recognize that most students who
take a course in introductory sociology are not planning
to become sociology "majors." Nevertheless, we believe that
sociology will increasingly be recognized as providing a focus
for a preprofessional or a liberal arts education. Moreover,
even today sociology is being chosen as a major field of study
by increasing numbers of undergraduates at many institutions.
With these thoughts in mind we have sought in this final
section to give information about some of the many vocations
that these students may later enter. A number of the vocations
are discussed in a general sense in this selection by M. F. Lewis.*

The practice of sociology as a profession is a distinctively American
development. While its roots are as old in history as speculations about
the nature of human society, it is only during the last thirty years that
the idea of a social technology based on theory and tested by empirical
investigation has become acceptable. The field is still a small one—
there are today less than 5000 sociologists—and is at present especially
short of persons trained to act as practicing professionals. Indeed, there
is reason to think that some of the important social conflicts of our

° *School and College Placement*, Vol. 12, No. 1 (October, 1951), 48–53. Reprinted by permission of the Association of School and College Placement and the
author.

The author (b. 1913) is Research Director for Wells Organization, and President, Church Finance Company, Inc. Formerly economist with the United States
government and Professor of Sociology at Loyola University in Louisiana. Major
interests are sociology of the church and educational sociology.

time remain unresolved because of the absence of competent social technologists.

Sociology is one of the social sciences, closely related academically to anthropology, education, psychology and social administration. It is not easy to draw clearcut boundaries which divide sociology from the other behavior sciences. If it is assumed that it is worthwhile to study and investigate the nature of personality, culture, and society, one may then conveniently identify sociology with the study of society, psychology with the study of personality and anthropology with the study of culture. In actual fact it is becoming increasingly difficult to distinguish among the three, for they are in process of merging into a unified science of social relations to which each contributes essentially complementary theory and finding.

More specifically, sociology is the study of situations in which human beings are in relationship with one another. It analyzes the forms of group organization of which a vast number are found in any modern society: communities, families, clubs, fraternal orders, labor unions, business associations, professions, etc. Sociology seeks to explain social institutions, standards, cultures, and the forces that operate in social change such as leadership and invention. In combination with psychology, sociology becomes social psychology, which is concerned with the mental processes and reactions of men in groups or masses. This part of sociology especially has contributed to the treatment of problems of human behavior under stress, as in time of war, defense mobilization or inter-group conflict of any kind.

The study of American society and its culture is carried on at all school levels, beginning with the elementary social studies of the grammar school. The social studies are often developed in the high schools in terms of social problems and the inadequacy of social institutions. In the first half of a college course, many students are required to take introductory courses in social science as a part of the program of general education, and these courses often include subject matter from anthropology and sociology. It is usually not until the senior college level that a student encounters sociology as a distinct discipline or major course of study. Most American colleges and universities have the resources for a major in sociology, either as an independent department or as a part of a social science major.

WHY STUDENTS MAJOR IN SOCIOLOGY

Students select a major in sociology at the undergraduate level for one of three reasons. Probably the most important is the selection of this field as an area of undergraduate concentration for the sake of a general liberal arts education on the same basis as other students major in biology or literature. In such cases students feel that study of the structure, functions and changes in modern society contributes meaningfully to their standing as educated individuals.

Many other students choose an undergraduate major in sociology as preprofessional training. The majority of persons accepted into graduate schools of social work have had prior training in sociology, and the relationship between sociology and social work is about the same as that between biology and medicine. Sociology courses, with or without a major in the subject, can also be an important part of preprofessional training for careers in law, business, industrial relations, personnel work and public administration. The idea is to provide the student with some basic ideas about human society and human relations. The more complex our culture becomes, the more necessary it is to obtain adequate background training for any sort of managerial or administrative work. To some extent the skills basic to organization and administration are obtained through formal instruction in sociology, psychology and the other social sciences.

The third group of students who select an undergraduate major in sociology consists of those who wish to plan for careers as professional social scientists. For these the bachelor's degree program, allowing for about 36 semester hours in the field, is necessarily only an introduction to further university study. Only in very few cases, and these more rarely than formerly, can the bachelor's program of studies be used as a basis for a professional career in the social sciences. The period of university (graduate) study is required not only to master the discipline but also to provide maturity necessary to a scientist working with behaving human beings. Accordingly, the prospective sociologist should plan to spend four years in advanced study and to obtain the doctorate. The minimum professional preparation is four semesters of full-time graduate work and the master's degree.

SELECTING THE UNIVERSITY

One of the chief decisions facing the graduate student is the choice of a university at which to pursue his studies. Approximately half of the 100 or more American universities which offer the doctorate provide higher training in sociology, but of these some ten or twelve institutions train about 90 per cent of the active professionals in this field. One of the best ways for a student to judge the merit of a given institution is to determine how many graduate students it had in a given year and how many doctorates were granted in that same year. It is rarely wise to attend any university where the ratio of students to degrees granted is higher than ten to one; a better ratio would be five to one. Graduate students are a valuable asset to a large university, especially after they have successfully completed their first year of advanced study. They are frequently assigned to work as instructors, readers and research assistants. The majority of advanced students in sociology, particularly those in the last two years of graduate work, may expect to obtain part-time professional duties which will serve to finance in part the lengthy period of advanced study.

The areas of specialization within a university sociology curriculum vary considerably from one institution to another. Often the first graduate year will consist of a group of basic courses, several of which may be required of all students. The entire four-year study program must necessarily have several objectives and sometimes these are not entirely compatible. Instruction must be organized so as to continue to provide information on a level much more advanced than in the undergraduate course. The student must be provided with instruction in research methods and techniques to prepare him for his doctoral research study. The curriculum must also take into account the fact that many sociologists make permanent careers in teaching, and most of them teach at the college level at one time or another, while relatively few earn a living as research investigators alone. Finally, an increasing number of sociologists enter some form of professional practice, although not ordinarily of a type involving the person-to-person relationship which characterizes the physician and his patient.

Training in research, which some universities announce as the sole function of their graduate schools, is often not the best way to prepare for careers in social technology. While some universities have modified their doctoral study programs to permit preparation for other types of careers, the majority have not yet done so. This may account in part for the scarcity of competent social administrators, and the reluctance of some sociologists to forego teaching for careers as practitioners and technologists.

During his last two years of graduate study each student is required to master general and theoretical sociology and methods of research, but to some extent the choice of other areas of study is his own. He may elect industrial relations, social psychology, correctional administration, demography, marriage and family counseling, communications research, public opinion management, group dynamics or other specialties. He is guided in his choice not only by his own interests and preference, but by the resources of the department in which he is working.

In every doctoral program the student must undertake an extensive research project, usually in the area in which he intends to specialize. Ordinarily he cannot complete such a study by the use of library facilities alone. This means that the young sociologist is faced with the problem of acquiring funds, time, contacts, and field-work facilities in order to bring his dissertation to a successful conclusion. While some universities plan the administration of the student's research program, others refuse to assist in any way with part of the degree requirements. Every effort should be made to determine departmental policy in this matter well in advance since it can make an appreciable difference in the cost of and time required to complete the degree. The student needs to have, if possible, a definite commitment regarding what he may expect from the faculty and department in this respect.

In June, 1950, the Social Science Research Council published a directory of 281 organizations conducting or financing research in the social sciences in 104 colleges and universities. While only a fraction of these conducted research in sociology, it is probably wise for the prospective graduate student to consider no university not listed in this directory. In general the large private universities have a better record for training sociologists than do the publicly supported institutions, many of which must of necessity concentrate their facilities on undergraduates.

The young sociologist who has obtained the doctorate or its equivalent possesses certain skills, knowledge and information not available to anyone who has not completed the same training. It is customary to point out that he is trained to conduct certain types of research, but since little basic sociological research is carried on in the world of work outside the academic environment, it is possibly more accurate to say that the trained sociologist is able to comprehend, analyze and interpret certain kinds of situations and the data relating thereto, and to solve or assist in solving certain kinds of problems. In every case the data and problems are those of human beings in action situations, either past, present or planned or anticipated in the future. There is literally no limit to the vast variety of social situations which may be so studied and interpreted, and over which controls may be established on the basis of the knowledge obtained. Sociologists at work today have analyzed a great variety of these social situations and their patterns of inter-personal relations. The range and scope of social analysis extends from international warfare to the interaction of a seven-year-old youngster with his playmates. The focus of such analysis is not the occurrences themselves in their unique or particular characteristics, but rather the regular patterns of behavior repeatedly found in the series of events under observation. This broad scope of interest which the trained sociologist has means that his professional preparation is adaptable to a variety of specific jobs.

HOW SOCIOLOGISTS ARE EMPLOYED

Actually very few individuals are at work today under the job title of sociologist, although their number is larger than ten or even five years ago. By far the largest number of the members of the profession are college teachers and some teach sociology and other social sciences in high schools. By and large, those who carry on basic theoretical research in sociology are also members of university teaching staffs. It should not be supposed, however, that these academic sociologists have no other professional activities. From time to time a sociology professor will be found acting as a consultant to a city or state planning board, serving as advisor to a citizens' housing commission, taking part as a professional on a mayor's committee for intergroup relations, serving on a board of probation and parole or helping to solve the problem of juvenile delinquency in a given locality.

More and more frequently the sociologist is leaving his teaching job and going to work as a staff professional for public and private institutions and agencies. Sometimes he finds employment with a business organization, perhaps in the field of labor relations or personnel administration or as an industrial research specialist. Market analysis, public opinion polling, radio research and other fact-finding services have sociologists as staff members and occasionally as directors of research. Utilization of sociologists and other social scientists in connection with the management of men is on the increase. Such work depends for its future expansion upon a recognition of the need for facts about social situations as the bases for making policy and for solving all sorts of social-conflict problems. Inter-racial, industrial, labor, personnel and even familial relations, if productive of conflict and social disorganization, can be diagnosed and treated by the sociologist working as a professional practitioner.

The results which can be achieved along these lines were amply demonstrated during World War II. In a time of national crisis answers to problems in human relations must be obtained, especially when these exist within the armed forces, in civilian morale or in defense plants producing goods for war. If a race riot breaks out in a war plant, a team of social science experts is likely to be consulted in order to avert future outbreaks of social tension. The work performed may be called social research or social administration. In any case, expert diagnosis and some form of skilled therapy will be called for. If excessive absenteeism exists in another plant, the cure will require an analysis of the action-patterns of the workers. Sociologists took part in propaganda analysis, in psychological warfare campaigns, in the selection of personnel, in intelligence work, in area studies and in the many attitude and opinion surveys conducted as evaluations or checks on the efficiency of both civilian and military operations. In all of these important wartime projects sociologists worked alongside other behavior scientists —psychiatrists, anthropologists, educationists and psychologists.

Not only during the war years, but since the early 1930's, there has been a growing recognition that sociology and the allied social sciences could contribute to policy formation and to the conduct of public administration in government at the national level. In the beginning, during the depression years, sociology furnished some of the criteria which served as bench-marks of national welfare. Very gradually, and especially during the last decade, individual sociologists have begun to find employment in the federal service and to make a contribution in specific jobs as trained scientists. All students of sociology and those planning to make careers in the field as professional workers should read the pamphlet published in 1950 by the Russell Sage Foundation, "Effective Use of Social Science Research in the Federal Service." The purpose of the publication is to describe what the social scientist can do as well as to promote the greater utilization of social research within the government service.

GOVERNMENT OPPORTUNITIES

There are at present four "series" or classes of positions defined by the U.S. Civil Service Commission which contain positions for which sociologists may qualify by means of the regularly scheduled examinations. These are the social science series, the social administration series, the intelligence research series and the military intelligence research series. For each of the last three of these several different examinations were kept open during 1950 and 1951 in order to recruit qualified personnel for defense mobilization work in Washington. Examinations opened for new workers (entry federal jobs) were junior management assistant, junior professional assistant, and junior social science analyst.

Two units of government—the Population Division of the Census Bureau and the Division of Farm Population of the Bureau of Agricultural Economics—have for some years employed a few sociologists, although under other job titles. Several other agencies each have a few professionals, often selected as much for their knowledge of an allied field (economics, statistics, housing, demography, etc.) as for their professional competence as sociologists.

Leading sociologists are occasionally asked to provide specialist consultant services to government agencies and to supervise operating research projects on a temporary basis. Although there are no federal jobs bearing the job title of sociologist, a rather large number of individuals numbering perhaps several thousands are performing successful and responsible work in the federal service because of prior training in sociology which fitted them for these careers. In some cases the formal education in sociology is used rather specifically; in other cases it has served these workers as a background for technical or administrative work. Occasionally the trained sociologist has been able to create his own professional job and in doing so to improve some aspect of government operations.

The whole field of government work is still very much open for sociologists who can pay especial attention to its needs and requirements. In the summer of 1951 there were less than 50 persons with the doctorate in sociology at work in Washington. The government's needs for trained social scientists has increased as a result of the Korean conflict and sociologists with the doctor's degree were locating positions without difficulty.

The long-run outlook for social scientists in government service is expected to be excellent. While there is little prospect that the federal government will undertake any work in sociology as such, the nation's need for trained social technologists in many areas of operating research and administrative work will increase. Whether sociologists or other social scientists obtain these positions will depend in part on whether the traditional graduate sociology curriculum is modified so as to train competent social technologists at the highest level.

The American Sociological Society is the national professional organization for sociologists. It publishes the official *American Sociological Review*, provides employment information, and holds an annual meeting of its members. Several regional societies affiliated with the national group hold meetings somewhat more frequently and each makes provision for student memberships. This year the American Sociological Society began publication of a series of bulletins, the first of which was issued in April and reports on employment opportunities in the federal service, describes civil service procedures relevant to making application for such positions, and discusses salaries paid in government work at the time the bulletin was issued. The Society has about 2500 members, most of whom are engaged in teaching. Many sociologists not in academic work do not as yet belong to the Society. Membership classes are student, associate and active.[1] The requirements are set by the members themselves, and the minimum amount of graduate training specified for active membership is, in effect, the official definition of the professional sociologist. The executive secretary of the American Sociological Society maintains permanent headquarters at the Washington Square Campus of New York University.

---

[1] Editors' Note: Since this article was written, the name of the organization has been changed to the American Sociological Association, its membership has more than doubled, and the category of "Fellow" has been added to the classes of membership.

B. SOCIOLOGISTS INVADE
THE PLANT *

ANONYMOUS

Undergraduates frequently ask: "What kind of work will a sociology major lead to?" In the preceding article we have seen that most professional sociologists are working in higher educational institutions. Increasingly in the last few years, however, they have demonstrated their usefulness in various other fields. This article describes some of the activities of sociologists in the business world.

The sociologists snooping through the factory . . . listening to gossip, watching how the workers behave at work, at lunch, and in coffee breaks, eying the finished product for its consumer appeal—represent a newly developed breed.

They have turned their back on the "social problems" of crime and broken homes that were their original domain. Now they are part of a fast-growing field of industrial sociology—and they are invading the business world because business has invited them in through the front door.

LAST IN

But the invitation has been long in coming. One by one, the other academic disciplines which school administrators like to call "social studies" have scraped out a place for themselves in the business community. First to come were the full-fledged economists, with doctorates in their hands. It has been estimated that 30 years ago fewer than 100 economists graced the corporate payrolls. Today there are thousands.

After World War II, fresh from wide-ranging experience in the armed forces, came the psychologists. With their background in personality rating, they offered advice on personnel selection. Their delvings into sensory perception gave them a background for advising on product and package design. Their studies of the inner broodings of the human

* Reprinted from the March 21, 1959 issue of *Business Week* by special permission. Copyrighted © 1959 by the McGraw-Hill Publishing Company, Inc.

mind provided new tools for ad-men, put such terms as "motivational research" into common use.

Now come the sociologists (and their first cousins, the social psychologists and the anthropologists), scouting along somewhat the same paths, but with a different set of field glasses and charting equipment. And businessmen, far from discouraging their ardor, are handing out money to them and turning them loose to find answers to numerous business problems.

1. WHAT DO THEY DO?

But what do the sociologists have to offer that business can't get from the economists or the psychologists? The sociologists' specialty is the study, not of man as an individual, but of the way he behaves in groups, and the forms and functions of the groups themselves. And their particular contribution to business is just that—their knowledge of how groups act and how they differ from one another.

Economists, for example, chart the buying power of consumer groups, and similar matters; sociologists delve into their value patterns— the things that make various consumer types, urban or rural, upper or lower bracket, white or blue collar, responsive or hostile to certain products or appeals. Pajama makers, for example, learned something about styling from a study by the Bureau of Applied Social Research; they found that the kind of virile styling that sold high-priced outfits in men's stores didn't go over well in middle-priced lines, where women do the buying in department stores. Sociologists can come up with some similar answers regarding behavior of workers in specific groups.

In these probings, the sociologists tread a bit on the toes of market researchers on one side and psychologists on the other. But businessmen find the sociologists have a special contribution to make, too.

HOW MANY AND HOW MUCH

No one is willing to guess just how many of the 6,000-plus sociologists in the U.S. today are regular corporate employees:

The American Sociological Society, in fact, has just launched a study to find the answer. In 1950, 5% of its members worked for industry. Since then, the society is sure, the percentage "has been growing greatly—but we don't know just how much."

Nor will anyone estimate how much business spends on such social research, on its own and through grants to universities, beyond the guess that the total "runs into millions." But here's one indicator: In six years of collecting funds for sociological research, the Foundation for Research on Human Behavior has rounded up $226,000 from 27 companies, ranging from Detroit Edison Co. through Aluminum Co. of America to Federated Department Stores, Inc. And these 27 have promised regular annual gifts.

WHAT FOR?

Sometimes businessmen have turned to the sociologists in desperation, or as a last resort when nobody else could come up with the right answer.

A dictation machine maker, for example, wanted to find out why it was having a tough time breaking into big companies. Social researchers turned up this answer: Secretaries feared the machines would turn them into little more than pool typists, with no direct contact with the boss; and the boss felt that dictating to his own secretary was a symbol of status.

Usually, though, the sociologizing is more in the nature of a forward look to see how things can be improved. In some corporate circles it has become a fashion, and there the sociologists can carve out their own projects. Most of the work contracted out to universities is more general in application, not aimed at finding some specific cure.

SALES AIDS

One of the earliest sociological research units organized to deal with business problems was the Bureau of Applied Social Research set up at Columbia University in 1937 by Dr. Paul Lazarsfeld. In the 1940s, it did research largely for advertising media, picking out the influential groups in communities and showing how the pattern of influence changed with the idea or product involved. The media gladly underwrote the research, grabbed at it to persuade the potential advertiser that theirs was the best channel for his product story.

Lately the advertiser himself has just jumped in. Two Iowa State College sociologists charted the pattern of adoption for new farm products—the kind of people most receptive to innovation and those who would wait longest, where they got their information, how long they were likely to wait. Eli Lilly & Co. used this to map a campaign for a new beef cattle hormone feed additive. It made no special appeal to the self-starters who go looking for new products at experimental stations, directed its first farm magazine campaign at the middle-of-the-roaders, delayed until a year later its local farm paper campaign aimed at the bulk of the prospects. Use each year has come within 2% of predicted sales.

On similar lines, Monsanto Chemical Co. is working with university researchers to see how consumers who sent in a coupon for a free sample of a new product compare with a cross-section of all potential users.

PERSONNEL

The social researchers have put employees as well as consumers under their microscopes. Companies sending employees overseas have called in anthropologists to brief them on local customs and traditions—to avoid such missteps as chucking an Iranian baby under the chin and thus, according to superstition, putting an evil eye on him.[1]

At home, Esso Standard Oil Co. runs training sessions, based on National Training Laboratories techniques, to teach supervisors about group dynamics. Men are brought together—say, at the Gulf Hills dude ranch in Mississippi—but with little advance briefing on what it's all about. As they begin to interact, choose leaders, decide what to do, the training leader points out how the group has made decisions and various members have influenced it. The idea is to make more effective group members—important in this committee-run company.

In other companies, sociologists have looked at internal communications, tracing how a rumor spreads through a plant, for instance; or tried to determine the corporate climate that best fosters creativity, or to "type" company stockholders so management can reach them more effectively.

Sometimes the sociologists' contribution is something more obvious —like telling the company that employee group discussions of a supervisor's shortcomings would be more honest if the supervisor wasn't present.

ANSWERS

At times the sociologists retreat behind a scientific façade and give the company a "we just report the findings, you must interpret them yourself" routine. But frequently businessmen do get a specific answer about what to do—the pajama makers, for example, got and accepted a suggestion to make colors "bright but not too loud." The worried dictation machine maker got one, too—to set up, with much pomp, a "training institute" for girls getting dictation machines—but turned it down.

II. TWO-WAY STREET

With sociology getting a business reputation, tomorrow's businessmen themselves are likely to come to their jobs with more training in

[1] *Business Week* January 9, 1956, p. 75.

the subject. The schools of business are getting on the band wagon, putting more social studies into their curricula.

The University of Pennsylvania's Wharton School of Finance & Commerce has long had a required course in "society as a system of interdependent human relationships."

Columbia University's Graduate School of Business, a revamped program being introduced next fall, will have a required course dubbed "Human Behavior in Organizations," aimed at enabling a manager to assess the effects on group behavior of proposed changes in organization or technology.

The University of Chicago's School of Business now includes "behavior science" as one of the four "basic disciplines" for each student.

The Ford Foundation has given money to business schools at five state universities for work in social sciences, and makes funds available for business school faculty members to take time off to study these fields.

RESERVE ACTION

Social researchers, too, are becoming more interested in business. The American Sociological Society currently lists 115 research projects going on in industrial sociology—up from 84 four years ago. Its September meeting will probably have twice as many papers on the subject as there were only five years ago.

The Ford Foundation has financed work on such business problems as the effect of a new man in a top job, or the relationship between a big corporation and the cities where it has plants. Another $125,000 has been set aside to help graduate students' research on business organization.

C.   SOCIOLOGIZING SOCIETY *

PAUL PICKREL

The editors of this readings book recognize, as sociologists,
that it is altogether too easy to make theories about human
behavior sound like proven laws, and narrowly tested conclusions

---

* From Paul Pickrel, "Images of Society" and "Desociologizing Society," *Harper's Magazine*, Vol. 218, No. 1309, 90–91. (June 1959). Copyright © 1959 by Harper & Brothers. Reprinted by permission of the author.

The author (b. 1917) is lecturer in English at Yale University and Chief Book Critic, *Harper's Magazine*.

seem like generalizations applying to everyone. And even
though one tries to be extremely cautious in what is asserted,
citizens not trained in sociology may extend the conclusions
drawn far beyond what was ever intended. The result is that
some people not only become excessively self-conscious about
their "sociological" behavior but may even begin *behaving*
the way (they believe) sociologists say they behave. In this
brief selection, Paul Pickrel exposes us to the thinking to
which he was stimulated by a sociology book which he was
asked to review. He not only reviews the book, which examines
critically the responsibilities of sociologists, but precedes it with
a few searching comments of his own about sociologists and
society.

Perhaps no attitude is more characteristic of the present than the
feeling of being at the same time both a participant in life and an observer of it. Nobody thinks it strange when we introduce observations
of less than cosmic significance with some such phrase as "in our society" or "in our culture," as if a part of us were about to take flight to
Mars and give the world the benefit of our backward glances. And
when the grandeur of sociological generalization momentarily eludes
us we can always call on "the future historian" who will take over the
task of looking at the present occasion from the outside and of doing
justice to its grandeur or infamy. "The future historian," incidentally,
is going to be one of the most overworked of men—so overworked that
he will never get around to the vast job we are cutting out for him.

Since we have all become observers of society and of ourselves
in society, we have all become in some sense sociologists. In *The Organization Man* William H. Whyte, Jr. expresses some surprise that
the people he interviewed to get material for his book had so much
awareness of their own sociological situation; he was unprepared for
the extent to which people—or at least the younger, urban, white-
collar, college-educated members of the population—have become so-
ciologized.

This may be a dangerous thing, because sociology can go wrong;
perhaps, given the complexity of its material, it always has to go wrong;
and when it does the result is a good deal worse than when a natural
science goes wrong. Geology can be wrong for a few thousand years
without doing anyone any harm whatever—except for a few searchers
after the philosopher's stone—simply because rocks do not read textbooks of geology, and they continue to be whatever they are no matter
what nonsense gets written down about them. But human beings do
read books of sociology, and they may take what they read seriously
enough so that they tend to become the monsters they read about. There

is a serious question whether a book like Whyte's (or other works of popular sociology published in recent years) does not tend to create or intensify the very conditions it deplores. If you tell enough people often enough with enough graphs to "prove" it that they are inter-changeable parts in a big impersonal machine, some of them are going to believe it. Yet there may have been some woman in that housing development Whyte describes who could tell her husband from the man next door.

The only way you can beat a sociologist at his own game is by never quite believing what he tells you about yourself. There is an apposite passage in *The Organization Man* (fortunately Whyte's book is quite good enough to withstand any little belated punching around I may give it). It seems that Whyte spent some hours interviewing a lady while her husband was at work, and the neighbors talked about it. Therefore Whyte solemnly concluded that this was a community in which there was great pressure on the individual to "conform," or, in older sociological terminology, that the neighbors were nosy. But sup-pose the neighbors hadn't talked? Then Whyte would have concluded that this was an alienated society in which no one cared about what anyone else did, in which the individual was isolated, there was no sense of community, etc., etc. The sociologist wins either way, but his very commitment to social investigation blinds him to the real point—namely, that there is hope for the human race as long as its members continue to suppose that a man and a woman who spend a few hours together might be up to something more interesting and even more rewarding than sociological research.

David Riesman somewhere has an observation to the effect that any attempt to describe society will result in a group of metaphors. I think he is right, and I think that sociologists who write for the public at large need to remember that there are a good many literal-minded readers around.

All this is by way of preface to—and perhaps apology for—a few words about C. Wright Mills's new book, *The Sociological Imagination*. . . . In a way, this is a specialized, even a technical work, for it is a professional sociologist's talk with other professional sociologists about how to think and write about society. But any fairly intelligent reader can follow the argument, and anyone who is trying to think about the world he lives in will find it worth the trouble. (It is odd but I believe true that, of all the fields of study in a modern university, sociology and education are the least respected, yet the best writers in these fields have a public outside the universities that the best writers in more reputable fields very rarely have. This in itself is testimony to the extent to which we have all become sociologists.)

Mills's thesis is very simple: he believes that society exists and is worth taking seriously. Or, to put it another way, he believes that sociologists ought to be responsible people. Stated in that way, nothing could be more obvious; yet what Mills has to say is by no means trivial, for he is combating major tendencies in contemporary attempts to portray society. He thinks that sociologists should be boldly pushing forward to try to understand and interpret and criticize society but they are in fact pusillanimously taking shelter in two safe but insignificant shelters, which he labels with the hard words "psychologism" and "scientism."

By "psychologism" Mills means the habit of thought which, in effect denying that society exists, sees all discontent in the individual mind. An extreme example (mine, not Mills's) would be to tell a man who is worried about the possibility of society's destroying itself in war that he really is not afraid of thermonuclear weapons but of his own capacity for violence instead. Mills is not in the least against psychology; in fact he believes that the social sciences (a term he deplores as much as anybody) must be concerned with the intersection of individual psychology and the world out there; he is only against those who say that the world out there doesn't exist.

A much larger part of Mills's book is devoted to what he calls "scientism," which for him is represented by two rather different kinds of people. The first are those he calls the "grand theorists," speculators who get drunk on the cheap muscatel of sociological verbiage and spin out the obvious in incomprehensible illiteracy (an example—again mine, not Mills's—"there is a tendency, with advancement in terms of real or chronometric time, as distinguished from psychological or experiential time, for the individual members of society to undergo a variety of psychosomatic alterations which we may for the purposes of our present schematization classify loosely under the rubric of 'aging' "; i.e., people grow old). Mills's account of the grand theorists is both telling and amusing, but he is a little unfair in singling out one man as his victim. I say this in part because I have read some of his victim's work with pleasure and enlightenment and in part because there are a good many other candidates for the position.

Mills is even more devastating when he gets to the other group of devotees of "scientism"—the pollsters and samplers. He sees them as triflers, for the most part as semi-educated technicians who do not take society seriously and who therefore cannot investigate it responsibly.

The Sociological Imagination may well be the best book Mills has written. . . . His strength, apart from his qualifications of intellectual vigor and wide reading, lies in the strength of his feelings, but . . . his feelings do not always move with the subject; he is sometimes too anxious to scare himself or the reader, he has more emotion than he knows what to do with. But in *The Sociological Imagination* the feeling behind the book—the passionate commitment to society—informs and drives the argument to its conclusion. At the end most readers will be convinced that the author has said what he thinks and feels about a subject of great importance to himself and of no negligible importance to us.

D. SOCIAL WORK AS A PROFESSION *

ANONYMOUS

In many colleges the undergraduate sociology curriculum is strongly oriented toward preparation for careers in social work. This common emphasis underscores the fact that almost all graduate schools of social work consider sociology a particularly appropriate preprofessional undergraduate major. In some, undergraduate training in social work is provided by the sociology department. Thus, one may conclude that sociological knowledge has been found to be especially useful to the professional social worker as he tries to deal successfully with a great variety of groups and personality types. Social-work utilization of sociological and other social (and psychological) knowledge is described in this selection.

PERSONAL REQUIREMENTS AND REWARDS

The selection of a vocation is a matter of individual preference and choice—no more important choice is made in a lifetime. Because it is so important it is essential to know beforehand what one should have to give to the job to make it a good job. What are the personal qualifications that make for success in social work? And what has the job to give to the individual? What are the financial and other rewards that ensue? If there is reciprocity, then both sides know satisfaction and a person may find a profession of which he can be genuinely a part, and to which he responds from "an inner summons."

There are two things that one gives to a job—one's innate qualities and capacities and one's acquired knowledge and skills. Anyone interested in entering a school of social work for professional education should ask himself what he will bring with him in terms of native ability. A keen, flexible mind and common sense are important. With these qualities should be combined a sense of humor and a sense of responsibility. An interest in people, a faith that human beings have

* Reprinted with permission from "Social Work as a Profession," revised edition 1947, published by the American Association of Social Workers.

within themselves the power to change—these are indispensable. Dealing with people who may not be behaving normally or desirably requires patience, tolerance, adaptability, resourcefulness, and sound judgment. It means too, that the social worker himself must be mentally and emotionally well balanced, in good health with a zest for living.

In the realm of the acquired, that which is basic to all kinds of social work is an understanding of the world in which one lives. Economics, sociology, political science, biology, history, psychology, literature—these are the raw materials of which that understanding is formed. The rest of acquired learning that should be brought to the job is the special knowledge and technical skill that is learned in professional schools. Some of it is basic to all kinds of social work, some of it is peculiar to specialized jobs. All of it is the body of known truth that is the nucleus of social work as a profession.

But what about the rewards of social work—its contribution to the lives of those who are dedicated to it?

Social work is not a profession to be selected by those who are ambitious for large financial returns. Nevertheless, the salaries compare favorably with those in teaching and public health nursing; their trend is upward, particularly in the public services; and for those with professional education, a reasonable standard of living is assured.

. . . . .

But it is not the economic advantages, such as they are, that should be the determining factor in leading a person to choose social work as a profession. There are others that will appeal still more strongly to young people of intelligence, vigor, and some insight into the social problems that now beset our modern world. Social work offers an opportunity of rendering a service to the community that is clearly constructive. It is a profession that is still comparatively undeveloped, with much pioneering and working on social frontiers to be done. It gives to those who become proficient in it a broad understanding of the stream of human life about them. It offers rich rewards in warm human associations for those who "like people" and can associate freely and happily with their fellowmen in all walks of life. It is not an easy profession, one to be entered into casually as a means of making a living. But for those who are concerned with a way of life as well as with a vocation it can be challenging and vital in the extreme and can offer great satisfaction in experience and in accomplishment.

EMPLOYMENT OPPORTUNITIES IN SOCIAL WORK

Since social work deals with a wide range of human needs, social workers are employed in many different types of programs and agencies.

Sometimes these are primarily social work agencies, such as county or state public welfare departments or private family and child welfare societies. Sometimes they are other types—schools, hospitals, or courts —to which social workers are attached as specialists. Since ninety per cent of social work is public, many of the opportunities lie with governmental agencies.

Expansion of the public social services has been so rapid that schools of social work have been able to supply only a portion of their personnel needs. Furthermore, the personnel required is increasing because the public social services are still expanding, and new ones are constantly being added. They include all governmental social services, whether local, state, or federal. And since they cover all the major fields of social work, they employ all types of workers—family and child welfare workers, medical and psychiatric workers, as well as those trained in group work, community organizations, and social research. All grades of maturity and experience are needed, from the beginning case worker to the widely experienced executive and administrator. The challenge and opportunity are great, not only because trained leadership in program-planning and skillful practice may influence the whole development of public welfare, but because many of the programs are new and policies are still in the making.

The greatest number of social workers is probably employed by county or state welfare departments in the administration of public assistance. But other programs, too, use thousands of workers—child welfare, recreation, and the newer programs like social insurance and housing.

There is increasing recognition of the importance of the quality of service in these far-flung programs that reach from our most congested cities to our most remote rural counties. It is recognized, for instance, that the giving of financial relief is not a mechanical process but a service demanding knowledge, judgment, and skill in understanding the needs of each applicant as a person, and in helping him to deal with the social difficulties that are associated with his economic distress. The social worker who understands the complex psychological problems involved in sickness and dependency can do much to prevent more serious incapacity. Treatment of each applicant as an individual shifts the emphasis from palliative service toward a more vigorous goal, aiming at the greatest possible degree of rehabilitation to active, social life.

In recognition of these truths, the public services for the most part require that those who work in them demonstrate their competence in civil service examinations. Furthermore, training for social work is regarded as an essential for the public assistance and child welfare programs and as having a potential contribution for other programs like the employment services and unemployment insurance.

In reviewing the major social work fields, it becomes evident that for the most part they fall into—Social Case Work, Social Group Work, Community Organization, and Social Research. Social Case Work involves direct service to individuals and families. Social Group Work deals primarily with persons in their group relationships and Community Organization is the method of furthering inter-group relationships toward social ends.

SOCIAL CASE WORK

Some of the areas in which social case workers are most frequently found are family social work, child welfare, medical social work, and psychiatric social work.

Family social work is one of the oldest and most basic types of service. Here the social worker gives assistance in relation to situations where family friction, broken homes, economic distress, personality maladjustments, and similar difficulties are affecting individuals within a family group or the family as a whole. The aim is to build up the strengths of individual personality and family life. Family social work is of special importance because it is here that most of the fundamental case work processes were first defined and that present practice has reached a high level of skilled performance.

Child welfare deals with problems similar to those in family welfare work but focuses upon the needs of the child. Many children live in families that lack the economic security, healthful environment, and affection that every child needs. When the deficiencies are so great that remedial work cannot be done, effort is made to supply a substitute through a foster-home or institutional plan of living. Many agencies and institutions, public and private, have been established for the care and protection of children who are dependent, neglected, delinquent, physically handicapped, and mentally defective, and for children whose physical and moral welfare is endangered by conditions in the home or in the community. Under the leadership of the United States Children's Bureau a child welfare program has in recent years been successfully established to meet the needs of children in rural areas throughout the country. Often the problem is first manifested when the child develops some type of behavior that creates difficulty in the home, the school, or the community. Social workers prepared to deal with these particularly complex problems are employed on the staffs of child guidance clinics, schools, and juvenile courts. School social work, in particular, is a field of interest to social case workers who wish an opportunity to help individual children make creative use of their school experience. It involves counseling with children who are having difficulty in school and with their parents and teachers. Whatever its type, however, child welfare work has strong appeal. The need of the child is great, and it is in childhood that the best preventive work can be done.

Medical social work is practiced under the auspices of a hospital or program of medical care. Medical social workers collaborate with doctors and nurses in meeting social problems related to illness and medical care. Through their efforts, the doctor is helped toward a better understanding of the patient's needs while the patient and his family are aided to solve the difficulties that stand in the way of successful medical treatment and a return to normal living. The medical social worker may be a member of the hospital staff or attached to an agency with a health program covering a whole county or state. Rapid developments in scientific medicine and public health have made medical social work a stimulating field. Before the war there was already a shortage of qualified workers because of the spread of medical social work from the hospital into broader community programs. Now the demands of military medical institutions have increased that shortage.

Psychiatric social work resembles medical social work in that it is always practiced in association with another profession—in this instance, that of psychiatry. Both medical and psychiatric social workers work so closely and continuously with physicians, psychiatrists, nurses, dietitians, psychologists, occupational therapists, and others, that they must be particularly successful at teamwork. While medical social work deals primarily with problems of physical illness, psychiatric social work is concerned with mental illness and defects and the more serious emotional difficulties. From its earliest beginnings in the last war, psychiatric social work has been making a continuous contribution to the rest of social work through a deepening of the understanding of personality and of methods of working with emotionally disturbed persons. Psychiatric social workers have therefore been employed not only in the characteristic environment of the child guidance clinic and mental hospital but also in all types of social case work. War needs now create a special demand for their services in military institutions.

Such, then, are some of the kinds of case work that social workers do. It is impossible to describe them all. Mention should be made, however, of positions of this sort associated with courts and other agencies set up to deal with problems of delinquency. In the formal court setting, the social worker may be a probation officer; in the less formal setting of a children's agency or child guidance clinic he may work with pre-delinquent children. It is a challenging area that is not as yet clearly organized, and those interested in pioneer work will feel its appeal. It is a good field for men since boys and young men predominate among delinquents.

SOCIAL GROUP WORK

Social group work deals primarily with persons in their group relationships. Its greatest development has been in recreational and informal educational activities where the trained social worker functions chiefly as a supervisor of volunteer and paid leaders of groups.[1] Through the use of group work methods, these activities become a potent means for making democratic principles meaningful in daily life. Social workers who have had professional preparation in group work find positions in such organizations as social settlements, community centers, churches, camps, housing projects, and a wide variety of projects sponsored by both public and private agencies and receiving both local and national support. Group workers are employed by the federal government in about sixteen different federal departments or bureaus. They are employed by state and local governments in supervisory positions related to recreational and educational work in parks, playgrounds, and indoor activities. They are also employed by such well-known private organizations as the Boy and Girl Scouts, Y.M.C.A., Y.W.C.A., and Jewish centers. Agencies serving special sections of the population, like foreign-born groups, farm groups, and industrial-worker groups, likewise need workers with this training. New programs that have developed in response to war needs, such as the recreational activities of the United Service Organizations, also need them. In addition, they are wanted by the Red Cross in its extensive recreational programs in Army and Navy hospitals and in mobile field units that go overseas with the armed forces. Both men and women are in demand for group work posts, and promotion is rapid for the well-qualified.

COMMUNITY ORGANIZATION

Some types of social work programs have to do with larger aggregations than those commonly known as "groups"—several groups for instance, or a whole community. The social worker who works with these inter-group processes works in the field of community organization. Its method is the furthering of inter-group relationships toward social ends. While all social workers are naturally to some degree working

[1] Ed. note: In recent years there has been increasing use of the group medium and the group work method in the treatment of socially and emotionally maladjusted children and adults. This is seen as complementary to the individual method of treating such problems.

in this area, it is essential that some should be especially trained for it. Such agencies as councils of social agencies, coordinating councils, and councils of defense, have community organization as their primary function. By bringing together representatives of all kinds of agencies, the social worker helps organize for the purpose of welfare planning and of coordination of efforts within a given neighborhood or community. For mature, experienced persons, this is a fascinating and remunerative field.

SOCIAL RESEARCH

Another type of social work, in addition to case work, group work, and community organizations, also deserves mention. That is social research—which offers positions to those who have obtained education and experience in both social work practice and statistical and research methods. While all social workers are continually in touch with social data, it is the primary function of research personnel to bring together facts for purposes of social planning. All types of social agencies, public and private, engage in research. Sometimes this is undertaken as a special survey or study project for the analysis of community needs or for the evaluation of an agency program. Sometimes there is a permanent research department, continually engaged in carrying on various types of investigation. In still other instances, there are social agencies whose primary activity is research. Many social research positions are to be found in national and federal agencies, universities, councils of social agencies, and similar organizations. For the person who combines interest in scientific methods with the wish to keep in touch with vital human problems, social research is stimulating work.

SOCIAL ADMINISTRATION

Still another angle from which the field of social work must be approached in order to appreciate its many opportunities is that of the various grades of responsibility assigned to the personnel within any social agency or program. Education in a school of social work prepares a younger worker to begin usually in giving direct service to persons with one or another kind of need. As the worker becomes more experienced, additional responsibilities are assigned to him. These may be supervision of other workers, teaching, consultant service, or administration. For the latter, because of the complexity of the problems involved in operating an agency or program, special education and experience are needed; and while only the most highly qualified and capable persons may expect to function as administrators, all social workers need to understand the principles of administration and may have opportunity to participate in program-planning and administrative activities.

Whatever the setting within which they work, however, social workers have the same basic purposes and methods. On the one hand, they endeavor to develop the community's resources and programs toward a healthier, more satisfying, and more meaningful way of life for all persons, with a special emphasis upon underprivileged sections of the population. On the other hand, they work directly with individuals and groups in relation to their particular needs and problems, helping them to make more effective use of their own capacities and the community's resources.

Their purpose is to serve both the individual and the community. It is an inspiring task whichever field, whichever agency is chosen. . . .

GENERAL EDUCATION

The best foundation for social work is completion of an undergraduate course of study in liberal arts with a group major in the social sciences. Since the social worker is concerned with the whole range and complex of social, economic, and psychological factors which affect the welfare and happiness of individuals, groups, and communities, whatever contributes to the growth of understanding and the broadening and deepening of sympathies is pertinent. Thus, any study of art, literature, science, social science, and philosophy is germane. Some courses relating to the field of social work may also be given at the college level, but experience in schools of social work and in social agencies during the past two decades shows that they should be general and nontechnical.

Most of the member schools of the American Association of Schools of Social Work require that applicants for admission show that they have completed a certain amount of study in the social sciences. Some schools also require that a minimum amount of work in the biological sciences has been completed. Economics, political science, psychology, and sociology, including social anthropology, are usually considered the pre-professional subjects most closely related to the social service curriculum. While it is desirable that the student know something about each of these, no one has been designated as more important than the other.

This policy with reference to the social sciences is supported by the membership requirements of the American Association of Social Workers, which specify, in addition to certain minimum professional education, that the applicant must have completed fifteen semester hours of social and biological sciences for junior membership, and twenty semester hours of social and biological sciences for full membership. Sociology, economics, political science, psychology, and anthropology may be offered to meet these social science requirements although certain other courses are acceptable substitutes.

INDEX

M